An Index
to Book Reviews
in the Humanities

Volume 31
1990

Phillip Thomson
Williamston, Michigan

This volume of the Index contains data collected up to 31 December 1990.

This is an index to book reviews in humanities periodicals. Beginning with volume 12 of the Index (dated 1971), the former policy of selectively indexing reviews of books in certain subject categories only was dropped in favor of a policy of indexing all reviews in the periodicals indexed, with the one exception of children's books – the reviews of which will not be indexed.

The form of the entries used is as follows:

Author. Title.
Reviewer. Identifying Legend.

The author's name used is the name that appears on the title-page of the book being reviewed, as well as we are able to determine, even though this name is known to be a pseudonym. The title only is shown; subtitles are included only where they are necessary to identify a book in a series. The identifying legend consists of the periodical, each of which has a code number, and the date and page number of the periodical where the review is to be found. PMLA abbreviations are also shown (when a periodical has such an abbreviation, but such abbreviations are limited to four letters) immediately following the code number of the periodical To learn the name of the periodical in which the review appears, it is necessary to refer the code number to the numeri-cally arranged list of periodicals beginning on page iii. This list also shows the volume and number of the periodical issues indexed in this volume.

Reviews are indexed as they appear and no attempt is made to hold the title until all the reviews are published. For this reason it is necessary to refer to previous and subsequent volumes of this Index to be sure that the complete roster of reviews of any title is seen. As an aid to the user, an asterisk (*) has been added immediately following any title that was also indexed in Volume 30 (1989) of this Index.

Authors with hyphenated surnames are indexed under the name before the hyphen, and the name following the hyphen is not cross-indexed. Authors with more than one surname, but where the names are not hyphenated, are indexed under the first of the names and the last name is cross-indexed. When alphabetizing surnames containing umlauts, the umlauts are ignored. Editors are always shown in the author-title entry, and they are cross-indexed (except where the editor's surname is the same as that of the author). Translators are shown only when they are necessary to identify the book being reviewed (as in the classics), and they are not cross-indexed unless the book being reviewed has no author or editor. Certain reference works and anonymous works that are known primarily by their title are indexed under that title and their editors are cross-indexed.

A list of abbreviations used is shown on page ii.

ABBREVIATIONS

Anon . . . . Anonymous
Apr . . . . . April
Aug . . . . . August
Bk . . . . . . Book
Comp(s) . . Compiler(s)
Cont . . . . Continued
Dec . . . . . December
Ed(s) . . . . Editor(s) [or] Edition(s)
Fasc . . . . Fascicule
Feb . . . . . February
Jan . . . . . January
Jul . . . . . July
Jun . . . . . June
Mar . . . . . March
No . . . . . Number
Nov . . . . . November
Oct . . . . . October
Prev . . . . Previous volume of this Index
Pt . . . . . . Part
Rev . . . . . Revised
Sep . . . . September
Ser . . . . . Series
Supp . . . . Supplement
Trans . . . . Translator(s)
Vol . . . . . Volume
* . . . . . . This title was also shown in
              the volume of this Index
              immediately preceding this
              one

The periodicals in which the reviews appear are identified in this Index by a number. To supplement this number, and to promote ready identification, PMLA abbreviations are also given following this number. Every attempt will be made to index those issues shown here as "missing" in a later volume of this Index.

The following is a list of the periodicals indexed in volume 31:

2(AfrA) – African Arts. Los Angeles.
  Nov88 thru Aug89 (Vol 22 complete)
4 – Agenda. London.
  Spring89 thru Winter89/Spring90 (Vol 27 No 1 thru 3, Vol 27 No 4 & 28 No 1)
16 – American Art Journal. New York.
  Vol 21 complete [no reviews indexed]
18 – American Film. New York.
  Oct88 thru Sep89 (Vol 14 complete) [no reviews indexed]
24 – American Journal of Philology. Baltimore.
  Spring89 thru Winter89 (Vol 110 complete)
26(ALR) – American Literary Realism, 1870-1910. Jefferson.
  Fall89 thru Spring90 (Vol 22 complete)
27(AL) – American Literature. Durham.
  Mar89 thru Dec89 (Vol 61 complete)
29(APR) – The American Poetry Review. Philadelphia
  Jan/Feb89 thru Nov/Dec89 (Vol 18 complete)
30 – American Poetry. Jefferson.
  Fall89 thru Spring90 (Vol 7 complete)
31(ASch) – American Scholar. Washington.
  Winter89 thru Autumn89 (Vol 58 complete)
34 – American Theatre. New York.
  Apr89 thru Mar90 (Vol 6 complete)
35(AS) – American Speech. Tuscaloosa.
  Spring89 thru Winter89 (Vol 64 complete)
36 – The Americas Review. Houston.
  Spring89 thru Fall-Winter89 (Vol 17 complete)
37 – The Américas. Washington.
  Vol 41 No 1 & 2 [no reviews indexed]
38 – Anglia. Tübingen.
  Band 107 complete
39 – Apollo. London.
  Jan89 thru Dec89 (Vols 129 & 130 complete)
40 – AEB: Analytical and Enumerative Bibliography. De Kalb.
  Vol 3 No 1 & 2
41 – Ancient Philosophy. Pittsburgh.
  Spring89 & Fall89 (Vol 9 complete)
42(AR) – Antioch Review. Yellow Springs.
  Winter89 thru Fall89 (Vol 47 complete)
43 – Architectura. München.
  Band 19 complete
44 – Architectural History. London.
  Vol 32 [no reviews indexed]
45 – Architectural Record. New York.
  Jan89 thru Dec89 (Vol 177 complete)
46 – Architectural Review. London.
  Jan89 thru Dec89 (Vols 185 & 186 complete)

47 – Architecture. Washington.
  Jan89 thru Dec89 (Vol 78 complete)
48 – Archivo Español de Arte. Madrid.
  Jan-Mar89 thru Oct-Dec89 (Vol 62 complete)
49 – Ariel. Calgary.
  Jan89 thru Oct89 (Vol 20 complete)
50(ArQ) – Arizona Quarterly. Tucson.
  Spring89 thru Winter89 (Vol 45 complete) [note that both Vol 44 No 4 & Vol 45 No 4 are dated Winter89]
52 – Arcadia. Berlin.
  Band 24 complete
53(AGP) – Archiv für Geschichte der Philosophie. Berlin.
  Band 71 complete
54 – Art Bulletin. New York.
  Mar89 thru Dec89 (Vol 71 complete)
55 – ArtNews. New York.
  Jan89 thru Dec89 (Vol 88 complete)
57 – Artibus Asiae. Ascona.
  Vol 49 No 3/4 [no reviews indexed]
59 – Art History. Oxford.
  Mar89 thru Dec89 (Vol 12 complete)
60 – Arts of Asia. Hong Kong.
  Jan-Feb89 thru Nov-Dec89 (Vol 19 complete)
61 – The Atlantic. Boston.
  Jan90 thru Dec90 (Vols 265 & 266 complete)
62 – Artforum. New York.
  Sep89 thru Summer90 (Vol 28 complete)
63 – Australasian Journal of Philosophy. Bundoora
  Mar89 thru Dec89 (Vol 67 complete)
64(Arv) – ARV: Scandinavian Yearbook of Folklore. Uppsala.
  Vol 44
70 – ANQ (ex-American Notes and Queries). Lexington.
  Jan89 thru Oct89 (Vol 2 complete)
71(ALS) – Australian Literary Studies. St. Lucia.
  May89 & Oct89 (Vol 14 No 1 & 2)
72 – Archiv für das Studium der neueren Sprachen und Literaturen. Berlin.
  Band 226 Heft 1
77 – Biography. Honolulu.
  Winter89 thru Fall89 (Vol 12 complete)
78(BC) – Book Collector. London.
  Spring89 thru Winter89 (Vol 38 complete)
81 – Boundary 2. Binghamton.
  Winter/Spring88 (Vol 16 No 2/3) [no reviews indexed]
82 – Brontë Society Transactions. Keighley.
  Vol 19 No 7 & 8
83 – The British Journal for Eighteenth-Century Studies. Oxford.
  Spring89 & Autumn89 (Vol 12 complete)
84 – The British Journal for the Philosophy of Science. Oxford.
  Mar89, Sep & Dec89 (Vol 40 No 1, 3 & 4) [issue dated Jun89 missing]
85(SBHC) – Studies in Browning & His Circle. Waco.
  Vol 16
86(BHS) – Bulletin of Hispanic Studies. Liverpool.
  Jan89 thru Oct89 (Vol 66 complete)

87(BB) – Bulletin of Bibliography. West-
port.
Mar89 thru Dec89 (Vol 46 complete)
88 – Blake, An Illustrated Quarterly.
Rochester.
Spring89 thru Spring90 (Vol 23 complete)
89(BJA) – The British Journal of Aesthetics. Oxford.
Winter89 thru Autumn89 (Vol 29 complete)
90 – Burlington Magazine. London.
Jan89 thru Dec89 (Vol 131 complete)
91 – The Black Perspective in Music.
Cambria Heights.
Vol 17
92(BH) – Bulletin Hispanique. Bordeaux.
Jan–Jun88 & Jul–Dec88 (Vol 90 complete)
95(CLAJ) – CLA Journal. Atlanta.
Sep89 thru Jun90 (Vol 33 complete)
97(CQ) – The Cambridge Quarterly. Cambridge.
Vol 17 No 4 & Vol 18 complete
98 – Critique. Paris.
Jan–Feb89 thru Dec89 (Vol 45 complete)
102(CanL) – Canadian Literature. Vancouver.
Winter88 thru Autumn–Winter89 (No
119 thru 122/123)
103 – Canadian Philosophical Reviews
/Revue Canadienne de Comptes rendus en
Philosophie. Edmonton.
Jan90 thru Dec90 (Vol 10 complete)
104(CASS) – Canadian–American Slavic
Studies/Revue canadienne–américaine
d'études slaves. Irvine.
Spring–Winter88 & Spring89 (Vol 22 No
1/4, Vol 23 No 1)
105 – Canadian Poetry. London, Ontario.
Spring/Summer89 & Fall/Winter89 (No
24 & 25)
106 – The Canadian Review of American
Studies. London, Ontario.
Summer89 thru Winter89 (Vol 20 No 1
thru 3)
107(CRCL) – Canadian Review of Comparative Literature/Revue Canadienne de Littérature Comparée. South Edmonton.
Sep/Dec88 (Vol 15 No 3/4) [no reviews
indexed]
108 – Canadian Theatre Review. Downsview.
Spring89 thru Winter89 (No 58–61)
110 – Carolina Quarterly. Chapel Hill.
Fall89 thru Spring90 (Vol 42 complete)
111 – Cauda Pavonis. Pullman.
Spring90 & Fall90 (Vol 9 complete)
115 – The Centennial Review. East Lansing.
Winter89 thru Fall89 (Vol 33 complete)
116 – Chinese Literature: Essays, Articles,
Reviews. Madison.
Jul88 & Dec89 (Vols 10 & 11)
121(CJ) – Classical Journal. Greenville.
Oct–Nov89 thru Apr–May90 (Vol 85
complete)
122 – Classical Philology. Chicago.
Jan89 thru Oct89 (Vol 84 complete)
123 – Classical Review. Oxford.
Vol 39 complete

124 – Classical World. Pittsburgh.
Sep/Oct89 thru Jul/Aug90 (Vol 83 complete)
125 – Clio. Ft. Wayne.
Fall88 thru Summer89 (Vol 18 complete)
126(CCC) – College Composition and Communication. Urbana.
Feb89 thru Dec89 (Vol 40 complete)
127 – Art Journal. New York.
Spring89 thru Winter89 (Vol 48 complete)
128(CE) – College English. Urbana.
Jan89 thru Nov89 (Vol 51 No 1 thru 7)
130 – Comparative Drama. Kalamazoo.
Spring89 thru Winter89/90 (Vol 23
complete)
131(CL) – Comparative Literature. Eugene.
Winter89 thru Fall89 (Vol 41 complete)
133 – Colloquia Germanica. Bern.
Band 22 complete
136 – Conradiana. Lubbock.
Spring89 thru Autumn89 (Vol 21 complete)
137 – Contemporary Verse 2. Winnipeg.
Spring89 thru Winter90 (Vol 12 complete)
139 – American Craft. New York.
Feb/Mar89 thru Dec89/Jan90 (Vol 49
complete)
140(CH) – Crítica Hispánica. Pittsburgh.
Vol 11
141 – Criticism. Detroit.
Winter89 thru Fall89 (Vol 31 complete)
142 – Philosophy & Social Criticism.
Chestnut Hill.
Vol 15 complete
143 – Current Musicology. New York.
No 44
144 – Critical Review. Chicago.
Winter–Spring90 & Summer90 (Vol 4 No
1/2 & 3)
146 – Crazyhorse. Little Rock.
Spring89 & Winter89 (No 36 & 37)
147 – Critical Texts. New York.
Vol 6 complete
148 – Critical Quarterly. Manchester.
Winter86, Winter88 & Spring89 thru
Winter89 (Vol 28 No 4, Vol 30 No 4,
Vol 31 complete)
149(CLS) – Comparative Literature Studies.
University Park.
Vol 26 complete
150(DR) – Dalhousie Review. Halifax.
Winter88/89 & Spring89 (Vol 68 No 4,
Vol 69 No 1)
151 – Dancemagazine. New York.
Jan89 thru Dec89 (Vol 63 complete)
152(UDQ) – The Denver Quarterly. Denver.
Summer89 thru Spring90 (Vol 24 complete)
153 – Diacritics. Baltimore.
Spring 89 thru Fall–Winter89 (Vol 19
complete)
154 – Dialogue. Waterloo.
Vol 28 complete
155 – The Dickensian. London.
Spring89 thru Autumn89 (Vol 85 complete)
156(ShJW) – Deutsche Shakespeare–Gesellschaft West Jahrbuch. Bochum.
Jahrbuch 1989

157 – Drama/The Quarterly Theatre Review. London.
No 171 & 173 [No 172 missing]
158 – Dickens Quarterly. Louisville.
Mar89 thru Dec89 (Vol 6 complete)
159 – Diachronica. Hildesheim.
Vol 6 complete
160 – Diálogos. Río Piedras.
Jan89 & Jul89 (Vol 24 complete)
162(TDR) – The Drama Review. Cambridge.
Spring89 thru Winter89 (Vol 33 complete)
165(EAL) – Early American Literature. Chapel Hill.
Vol 25 complete
166 – Eighteenth-Century Fiction. Hamilton.
Oct89 thru Jul90 (Vol 2 complete)
167 – Erkenntnis. Dordrecht.
Mar89 thru Sep89 (Vols 30 & 31 complete)
168(ECW) – Essays on Canadian Writing. Toronto.
Spring89 thru Fall89 (No 37-39)
172(Edda) – Edda. Oslo.
1989/1 thru 1989/4 (Vol 89 complete)
173(ECS) – Eighteenth-Century Studies. Northfield.
Fall89 thru Summer90 (Vol 23 complete) [Summer89 issue missing]
174(Eire) – Eire-Ireland. St. Paul.
Fall88, Spring89 thru Winter89 (Vol 23 No 3, Vol 24 complete)
176 – English. Oxford.
Spring89 thru Autumn89 (Vol 38 complete)
177(ELT) – English Literature in Transition. Greensboro.
Vol 32 complete
178 – English Studies in Canada. Edmonton.
Mar89 thru Dec89 (Vol 15 complete)
179(ES) – English Studies. Lisse.
Feb89 thru Dec89 (Vol 70 complete)
183(ESQ) – ESQ: A Journal of the American Renaissance. Pullman.
Vol 04 complete, Vol 35 No 1 & 2
184(EIC) – Essays in Criticism. Oxford.
Jan89 thru Oct89 (Vol 39 complete)
185 – Ethics. Chicago.
Oct89 thru Jul90 (Vol 100 complete)
187 – Ethnomusicology. Bloomington.
Winter89 thru Fall89 (Vol 33 complete)
188(ECr) – L'Esprit Créateur. Baton Rouge.
Spring89 thru Winter89 (Vol 29 complete)
189(EA) – Etudes Anglaises. Paris.
Jan-Mar89 thru Oct-Dec89 (Vol 42 complete)
191(ELN) – English Language Notes. Boulder.
Sep89 thru Jun90 (Vol 27 complete)
192(EP) – Les Études Philosophiques. Paris.
Jan-Mar89 thru Jul-Dec89
193(ELit) – Études Littéraires. Québec.
Spring89 & Autumn89 (Vol 22 No 1 & 2) [no reviews indexed]
196 – Fabula. Berlin.
Band 30 complete
198 – The Fiddlehead. Fredericton.
Spring89 thru Winter89 (No 159 thru 162)

199 – Field. Oberlin.
Spring89 & Fall89 (No 40 & 41)
201 – Fifteenth-Century Studies. Detroit.
Vol 15
203 – Folklore. London.
Vol 100 complete
204(FdL) – Forum der Letteren. Leiden.
Mar89 thru Dec89 (Vol 30 complete)
207(FR) – French Review. Champaign.
Oct89 thru May90 (Vol 63 complete)
208(FS) – French Studies. London.
Jan89 thru Oct89 (Vol 43 complete)
209(FM) – Le Français Moderne. Paris.
Oct89 (Vol 57 No 3/4) [Oct88 & Apr89 issues missing]
210(FrF) – French Forum. Lexington.
Jan89 thru Sep89 (Vol 14 complete)
215(GL) – General Linguistics. University Park.
Vol 29 complete
219(GaR) – Georgia Review. Athens.
Spring89 thru Winter89 (Vol 43 complete)
221(GQ) – German Quarterly. Cherry Hill.
Winter89 thru Fall89 (Vol 62 complete)
222(GR) – Germanic Review. Washington.
Winter89 thru Fall89 (Vol 64 complete)
223 – Genre. Norman.
Spring89 thru Fall89 (Vol 22 No 1-3)
224(GRM) – Germanisch-Romanische Monatsschrift. Heidelberg.
Band 39 complete
228(GSLI) – Giornale storico della letteratura italiana. Torino.
Vol 166 complete
229 – Gnomon. München.
Band 61 complete
234 – The Hemingway Review. Ada.
Fall89 & Spring90 (Vol 9 complete)
235 – Hermathena. Dublin.
Winter88 thru Winter89 (No 145-147)
236 – The Hiram Poetry Review. Hiram.
Spring-Summer89 & Winter90 (No 46 & 47)
238 – Hispania. University.
Mar89 thru Dec89 (Vol 72 complete)
239 – Hispanic Linguistics. Pittsburgh.
Fall89 (Vol 3 No 1/2) [Vol 2 No 2 missing]
240(HR) – Hispanic Review. Philadelphia.
Winter89 thru Autumn89 (Vol 57 complete)
241 – Hispanófila. Chapel Hill.
Jan89 thru Sep89 (No 95-97)
242 – History of European Ideas. Oxford.
Vol 10 No 1-6
244(HJAS) – Harvard Journal of Asiatic Studies. Cambridge.
Jun89 & Dec89 (Vol 49 complete)
249(HudR) – Hudson Review. New York.
Spring89 thru Winter89 (Vol 42 complete)
250(HLQ) – The Huntington Library Quarterly. San Marino.
Winter89 thru Autumn89 (Vol 52 complete)
254 – Hypatia. Bloomington.
Spring89 thru Fall89 (Vol 4 complete)
257(IRAL) – IRAL: International Review of Applied Linguistics in Language Teaching. Heidelberg.
Feb89 thru Nov89 (Vol 27 complete)

258 – International Philosophical Quarterly.
New York and Namur.
Mar89 thru Dec89 (Vol 29 complete)
259(IIJ) – Indo-Iranian Journal. Dordrecht.
Jan89 thru Oct89 (Vol 32 complete)
260(IF) – Indogermanische Forschungen.
Berlin.
Band 94
262 – Inquiry. Oslo.
Mar89 thru Dec89 (Vol 32 complete)
263(RIB) – Revista Interamericana de Bib-
liografía/Inter–American Review of Bibli-
ography. Washington.
Vol 39 No 1, 2 & 4 [Vol 39 No 3 miss-
ing]
268(IFR) – The International Fiction
Review. Fredericton.
Summer89 thru Summer90 (Vol 16 No 2,
Vol 17 complete)
269(IJAL) – International Journal of
American Linguistics. Chicago.
Jan89 thru Oct89 (Vol 55 complete)
271 – The Iowa Review. Iowa City.
Winter89 thru Fall89 (Vol 19 complete)
272(IUR) – Irish University Review. Dublin.
Spring89 (Vol 19 No 1)
275(IQ) – Italian Quarterly. New Brunswick.
Spring–Summer88 (Vol 29 No 112/113)
[no reviews indexed] [Issues No 118–
111 missing]
276 – Italica. Madison.
Spring89 thru Winter89 (Vol 66 complete)
278(IS) – Italian Studies. London.
Vol 43 & Vol 44
279 – International Journal of Slavic Linguistics and Poetics. Columbus.
Vol 35/36 & Vol 37
284 – The Henry James Review. Baltimore.
Winter89 thru Fall89 (Vol 10 complete)
285(JapQ) – Japan Quarterly. Tokyo.
Jan–Mar89 thru Oct–Dec89 (Vol 36
complete)
287 – Jewish Frontier. New York.
Jan–Feb89 thru Nov–Dec89 (Vol 56
complete)
289 – The Journal of Aesthetic Education.
Champaign–Urbana.
Spring89 thru Winter89 (Vol 23 com-
plete)
290(JAAC) – Journal of Aesthetics & Art
Criticism. Greenvale.
Winter89 thru Fall89 (Vol 47 complete)
291 – Journal of Applied Philosophy.
Abingdon.
Vol 6 complete
292(JAF) – Journal of American Folklore.
Washington.
Jan–Mar89 thru Oct–Dec89 (Vol 102
complete)
293(JASt) – Journal of Asian Studies. Ann
Arbor.
Feb89 thru Nov89 (Vol 48 complete)
294 – Journal of Arabic Literature.
Leiden.
Mar89 & Sep89 (Vol 20 complete)
295(JML) – Journal of Modern Literature.
Philadelphia.
Summer88 thru Spring89 (Vol 15 com-
plete)

297(JL) – Journal of Linguistics. Cambridge.
Mar89 & Sep89 (Vol 25 complete)
298 – Journal of Canadian Studies/Revue
d'études canadiennes. Peterborough.
Spring89 thru Winter89/90 (Vol 24
complete)
300 – Journal of English Linguistics.
Whitewater.
Apr88 & Oct88 (Vol 21 complete)
301(JEGP) – Journal of English and Ger-
manic Philology. Champaign.
Jan89 thru Oct89 (Vol 88 complete)
303(JoHS) – Journal of Hellenic Studies.
London.
Vol 109
304(JHP) – Journal of Hispanic Philology.
Tallahassee.
Winter89 thru Winter90 (Vol 13 No 2 &
3, Vol 14 No 1 & 2)
305(JIL) – The Journal of Irish Literature.
Newark.
Jan89 thru Sep89 (Vol 18 complete)
307 – Journal of Literary Semantics.
Heidelberg.
Apr89 thru Dec89 (Vol 18 complete)
308 – Journal of Music Theory. New
Haven.
Spring 89 & Fall89 (Vol 33 complete)
309 – Journal of Musicological Research.
London.
Vol 9 complete
310 – The Journal of Musicology. Berke-
ley.
Winter89 thru Fall89 (Vol 7 complete)
311(JP) – Journal of Philosophy. New
York.
Jan89 thru Dec89 (Vol 86 complete)
313 – Journal of Roman Studies. London.
Vol 79
316 – Journal of Symbolic Logic. Pasa-
dena.
Mar89 thru Dec89 (Vol 54 complete)
317 – Journal of the American Musicological Society. Philadelphia.
Spring89 thru Fall89 (Vol 42 complete)
318(JAOS) – Journal of the American Oriental Society. New Haven.
Jan–Mar88 thru Oct–Dec88 (Vol 108
complete)
319 – Journal of the History of Philosophy.
St. Louis.
Jan90 thru Oct90 (Vol 28 complete)
320(CJL) – Canadian Journal of Linguistics.
Ottawa.
Mar89 thru Dec89 (Vol 34 complete)
321 – The Journal of Value Inquiry. Dordrecht.
Mar89 thru Dec89 (Vol 23 complete)
322(JHI) – Journal of the History of Ideas.
Philadelphia.
Jan–Mar89 thru Oct–Dec89 (Vol 50 complete)
323 – JBSP: Journal of the British Society
for Phenomenology. Manchester.
Jan89 thru Oct89 (Vol 20 complete)
324 – RSA Journal. London.
Dec89 thru Oct90 (Vol 138 No 5401–
5411)
329(JJQ) – James Joyce Quarterly. Tulsa.
Fall89 thru Summer90 (Vol 27 complete)

340(KSJ) – Keats-Shelley Journal. New
York.
Vol 38
341 – Konsthistorisk Tidskrift. Stockholm.
Vol 58 complete
342 – Kant-Studien. Berlin.
Band 80 complete
344 – The Kenyon Review. Gambier.
Winter90 thru Fall90 (Vol 12 complete)
345(KRQ) – Romance Quarterly. Lexington.
Feb89 thru Nov89 (Vol 36 complete)
346(KJ) – The Kipling Journal. London.
Mar89 thru Dec89 (Vol 63 complete)
348(L&S) – Language and Speech. London.
Jan-Mar89 thru Oct-Dec89 (Vol 32
complete)
350 – Language. Baltimore.
Mar90 thru Dec90 (Vol 66 complete)
351(LL) – Language Learning. Ann Arbor.
Mar89 thru Dec89 (Vol 39 complete)
352(LATR) – Latin American Theatre Review. Lawrence.
Fall89 & Spring90 (Vol 23 complete)
353 – Linguistics. Amsterdam.
Vol 27 complete
354 – The Library. Oxford.
Mar89 thru Dec89 (Vol 11 complete)
355(LSoc) – Language in Society New
York.
Mar89 thru Dec89 (Vol 18 complete)
356(LR) – Les Lettres Romanes Louvain.
Feb-May89 thru Nov89 (Vol 43 complete)
357 – Legacy. Amherst.
Spring90 & Fall90 (Vol 7 complete)
358 – Liber. Paris.
Feb90 & Jun90 (Vol 2 No 1 & 2)
359 – Linguistics and Philosophy. Dordrecht.
Feb89 thru Aug89 (Vol 12 No 1-4)
[Nov88 issue missing]
961 Lingua. Amsterdam.
Jan89 thru Dec89 (Vols 77-79 complete)
363(LitR) – The Literary Review. Madison.
Fall89, Spring90 & Summer90 (Vol 33
No 1, 3 & 4) [Winter90 issue missing]
364 – London Magazine. London.
Apr/May89 thru Feb/Mar90 (Vol 29
complete)
365 – Literary Research. College Park.
Spring/Summer88 & Fall88 (Vol 13 No
2/3 & 4)
367(L&P) – Literature and Psychology.
Providence.
Vol 35 complete
376 – Malahat Review. Victoria.
Mar89 thru Dec89 (No 86-89)
377 – Manuscripta. St. Louis.
Mar89 thru Nov89 (Vol 33 complete)
379(MedR) – Medioevo romanzo. Bologna.
Apr89 thru Dec89 (Vol 14 complete)
380 – Master Drawings. New York.
Spring89 thru Winter89 (Vol 27 complete)
381 – Meanjin Quarterly. Parkville.
Autumn89 thru Summer89 (Vol 48 complete)
382(MAE) – Medium Aevum. Oxford.
1989/1 & 1989/2 (Vol 58 complete)
385(MQR) – Michigan Quarterly Review. Ann
Arbor.
Winter90 thru Fall90 (Vol 29 complete)

389(MQ) – The Midwest Quarterly.
Pittsburg.
Autumn89 thru Summer90 (Vol 31 complete)
390 – Midstream. New York.
Jan89 thru Dec89 (Vol 35 complete)
391 – Milton Quarterly. Athens.
Mar89 thru Dec89 (Vol 23 complete)
392 – The Mississippi Quarterly. Mississippi State.
Winter88/89 thru Fall89 (Vol 42 complete)
393(Mind) – Mind. Oxford.
Jul88 & Jan89 thru Oct89 (Vol 97 No
387 & Vol 98 Complete)
394 – Mnemosyne. Leiden.
Vol 42 complete
395(MFS) – Modern Fiction Studies. West
Lafayette.
Spring89 thru Winter89 (Vol 35 complete)
397(MD) – Modern Drama. Toronto.
Mar89 thru Dec89 (Vol 32 complete)
399(MLJ) – Modern Language Journal.
Madison.
Spring89 thru Winter89 (Vol 73 complete)
400(MLN) – MLN [Modern Language Notes].
Baltimore.
Jan89 thru Dec89 (Vol 104 complete)
401(MLQ) – Modern Language Quarterly.
Seattle.
Dec87 thru Sep88 (Vol 48 No 4 & Vol
49 No 1-3)
402(MLR) – Modern Language Review. London.
Jan90 thru Oct90 (Vol 85 complete)
403(MLS) – Modern Language Studies. Middlebury.
Winter89 thru Fall89 (Vol 19 complete)
405(MP) – Modern Philology. Chicago.
Aug89 thru May90 (Vol 87 complete)
406 – Monatshefte. Madison.
Spring89 thru Winter89 (Vol 81 complete)
407(MN) – Monumenta Nipponica. Tokyo.
Spring89 thru Winter89 (Vol 44 complete)
410(M&L) – Music & Letters. Oxford.
Feb89 thru Nov89 (Vol 70 complete)
411 – Music Analysis. Oxford.
Mar/Jul89 & Oct89 (Vol 8 complete)
412 – Music Review. Cambridge.
Nov88, Feb89 & May90 (Vol 48 No 4,
Vol 50 No 1 & 2)
413 – Music Perception. Berkeley.
Fall89 thru Summer90 (Vol 7 complete)
414(MusQ) – Musical Quarterly. New York.
Vol 74 complete
415 – The Musical Times. London.
Jan89 thru Dec89 (Vol 130 complete)
416 – Musiktheorie. Laaber.
Band 4 complete
417 – Die Musikforschung. Kassel.
Jan-Mar89 thru Oct-Dec89 (Band 42
complete)
424 – Names. New York.
Mar89 thru Dec89 (Vol 37 complete)
432(NEQ) – New England Quarterly. Boston.
Mar89 thru Dec89 (Vol 62 complete)

434 – New England Review and Bread Loaf
Quarterly. Middlebury.
  Autumn89 thru Summer90 (Vol 12 complete)
438 – The New Scholasticism. Washington.
  Winter89 thru Autumn89 (Vol 63 complete)
439(NM) – Neuphilologische Mitteilungen.
Helsinki.
  1989/1 thru 1989/3&4 (Vol 90 complete)
440 – New York Folklore. Newfield.
  Winter–Spring89 (Vol 15 No 1/2)
441 – New York Times Book Review. New
York.
  7Jan90 thru 30Dec90 (Vol 95 complete)
442(NY) – New Yorker. New York.
  1Jan90 thru 31Dec90 (Vol 65 No 46–
  52, Vol 66 No 1–46) [Vol 66 begins
  with issue dated 19Feb90]
445(NCF) – Nineteenth-Century Literature.
Berkeley.
  Jun89 thru Mar90 (Vol 44 complete)
446(NCFS) – Nineteenth-Century French
Studies. Fredonia.
  Fall–Winter89/90 & Spring–Summer90
  (Vol 18 complete)
447(N&Q) – Notes & Queries. Oxford.
  Mar89 thru Dec89 (Vol 36 complete)
448 – Northwest Review. Eugene.
  Vol 27 complete
449 – Noûs. Bloomington.
  Mar89 thru Dec89 (Vol 23 complete)
450(NRF) – La Nouvelle Revue Française.
Paris.
  Jan89 thru Dec89 (Vols 73 & 74 com-
  plete)
451 – 19th Century Music. Berkeley.
  Summer89 thru Spring90 (Vol 13 complete)
452(NJL) – Nordic Journal of Linguistics.
Oslo.
  Vol 12 complete
453(NYRB) – The New York Review of
Books. New York.
  18Jan90 thru 20Dec90 (Vol 36 No
  21/22, Vol 37 No 1–20)
454 – Novel. Providence.
  Fall89 thru Spring90 (Vol 23 complete)
455 – The North American Review. Cedar
Falls.
  Mar89 thru Dec89 (Vol 274 complete)
456(NDQ) – North Dakota Quarterly. Grand
Forks.
  Winter89 thru Fall89 (Vol 57 complete)
459 – Obsidian II. Raleigh.
  Spring89 thru Winter89 (Vol 4 complete)
460(OhR) – The Ohio Review. Athens.
  No 44
462(OL) – Orbis Litterarum. Copenhagen.
  Vol 44 complete
463 – Oriental Art. Richmond.
  Spring89 thru Winter89/90 (Vol 35
  complete)
464 – Orbis. Louvain.
  Vol 33 fasc 1/2
465 – The Opera Quarterly. Chapel Hill.
  Spring90 & Summer90 (Vol 7 No 1 & 2)
468 – Paideuma. Orono.
  Spring & Fall89 and Winter89 (Vol 18
  complete)

470 – Papers of the Bibliographical Society
of Canada/Cahiers de la Société
bibliographique du Canada. Toronto.
  Vol 27
472 – Parnassus: Poetry in Review. New
York.
  Vol 16 No 1
473(PR) – Partisan Review. Boston.
  Vol 56 complete
475 – Papers on French Seventeenth Century Literature. Seattle & Tübingen.
  Vol 16 complete
477(PLL) – Papers on Language and Literature. Edwardsville.
  Summer88, Fall88 & Winter89 thru
  Fall89 (Vol 24 No 3 & 4, Vol 25 complete)
478(P&L) – Philosophy and Literature.
Baltimore.
  Apr89 & Oct89 (Vol 13 complete)
479(PhQ) – The Philosophical Quarterly.
Oxford.
  Apr87 & Jan89 thru Oct89 (Vol 37 No
  147 & Vol 39 complete)
480(P&R) – Philosophy & Rhetoric. University Park.
  Vol 22 complete
481(PQ) – Philological Quarterly. Iowa
City.
  Winter89 thru Fall89 (Vol 68 complete)
482(PhR) – Philosophical Review. Ithaca.
  Jan89 thru Oct89 (Vol 98 complete)
483 – Philosophy. Cambridge.
  Jan89 thru Oct89 (Vol 64 complete)
484(PPR) – Philosophy & Phenomenological
Research. Providence.
  Sep89, Mar90 & Jun90 (Vol 50 No 1, 3
  & 4) [Dec89 issue missing]
485(PE&W) – Philosophy East & West.
Honolulu.
  Jan89 thru Oct89 (Vol 39 complete)
486 – Philosophy of Science. East Lansing.
  Mar89 thru Dec89 (Vol 56 complete)
487 – Phoenix. Toronto.
  Spring89 thru Winter89 (Vol 43 complete)
488 – Philosophy of the Social Sciences.
Waterloo.
  Mar89 thru Sep89 (Vol 19, No 1–3)
489(PJGG) – Philosophisches Jahrbuch.
Freiburg.
  Band 96 complete
491 – Poetry. Chicago.
  Apr89 thru Mar90 (Vols 154 & 155
  complete)
493 – Poetry Review. London.
  Spring89 thru Winter89/90 (Vol 79
  complete)
494 – Poetics Today. Durham.
  Spring89 thru Winter89 (Vol 10 complete)
495(PoeS) – Poe Studies. Pullman.
  Dec88 thru Dec89 (Vol 21, No 2 & Vol
  22 complete)
496 – Poet Lore. Bethesda.
  Spring89, Fall89 & Winter89/90 (Vol 84
  No, 1, 3 & 4) [Summer89 issue missing]
497(PolR) – Polish Review. New York.
  Vol 34 complete
498 – Popular Music and Society. Bowling
Green.
  Spring89 thru Winter89 (Vol 13 complete)

500 – Post Script. Jacksonville.
Summer89 thru Summer90 (Vol 8 No 3
& Vol 9 complete)
502(PrS) – Prairie Schooner. Lincoln.
Spring89 thru Winter89 (Vol 63 complete)
505 – Progressive Architecture. Cleveland.
Jan89 thru Dec89 (Vol 70 complete)
506(PSt) – Prose Studies. London.
May87, May89 thru Dec89 (Vol 10 No 1
& Vol 12 complete)
507 – Print. New York.
Jan/Feb89 thru Nov/Dec89 (Vol 43
complete)
508 – Prooftexts. Baltimore.
Jan89 thru Sep89 (Vol 9 complete)
509 – Philosophy & Public Affairs. Princeton.
Winter89 thru Fall89 (Vol 18 complete)
510 – The Piano Quarterly. Wilmington.
Winter88/89 thru Fall89 (Vol 37 complete)
511 – Plays and Players. London.
Jan89 & Mar89 thru Oct89 (No 423 &
425-432) [issues dated Nov88, Dec88 &
Feb89 missing]
513 – Perspectives of New Music. Seattle.
Winter89 & Summer89 (Vol 27 complete)
517(PBSA) – Papers of the Bibliographical
Society of America. Brooklyn.
Mar89 thru Sep89 (Vol 83 No 1-3)
518 – Philosophical Books. Oxford.
Jan89 thru Oct89 (Vol 30 complete)
519(PhS) – Philosophical Studies.
Dordrecht.
Jan89 thru Jul89 (Vol 55 & Vol 56
complete) [no reviews indexed]
520 – Phronesis. Assen.
Vol 34 complete
521 – Philosophical Investigations. Oxford.
Jan89 thru Oct89 (Vol 12 complete)
526 – Quarry. Kingston.
Winter89 thru Fall89 (Vol 38 complete)
529(QQ) – Queen's Quarterly. Kingston.
Spring89 thru Winter89 (Vol 96 complete)
600 Recherches sur Diderot et sur
l'"Encyclopédie." Paris.
Apr89 & Oct89 (No 6 & 7)
531 – Revue de Synthèse. Paris.
Jan-Mar89 & Jul-Dec89 (Vol 110 No 1
& 3/4) [Jan-Mar88 thru Oct-Dec88 &
Apr-Jun89 issues missing]
532(RCF) – The Review of Contemporary
Fiction. Elmwood Park.
Spring89 thru Fall89 (Vol 9 complete)
533 – Raritan. New Brunswick.
Summer89 thru Winter90 (Vol 9 No 1-
3)
535(RHL) – Revue d'Histoire Littéraire de
la France. Vineuil.
Jan-Feb89 thru Nov-Dec89 (Vol 89
complete)
537 – Revue de Musicologie. Paris.
Vol 75 complete
538(RAL) – Research in African Literatures.
Austin.
Spring89 thru Winter89 (Vol 20 complete)
539 – Renaissance & Reformation/Renais-
sance et Réforme. Toronto.
Vol 13 No 3 & 4, Vol 14 No 1

540(RIPh) – Revue Internationale de Philosophie. Wetteren.
Vol 42 fasc 4 thru Vol 43 fasc 2
541(RES) – Review of English Studies.
Oxford.
Feb89 thru Nov89 (Vol 40 complete)
542 – Revue Philosophique de la France et
de l'Étranger. Paris.
Oct-Dec89 (Vol 179 No 4) [Jan-Mar89
thru Jul-Sep89 issues missing]
543 – Review of Metaphysics. Washington.
Sep89 thru Jun90 (Vol 43 complete)
544 – Rhetorica. Berkeley.
Winter89 thru Autumn89 (Vol 7 complete)
545(RPh) – Romance Philology. Berkeley.
Aug89 thru May90 (Vol 43 complete)
546(RR) – Romanic Review. New York.
Jan89 thru Nov89 (Vol 80 complete)
547(RF) – Romanische Forschungen.
Frankfurt am Main.
Band 101 complete
548 – Revista Española de Lingüística.
Madrid.
Jan-Jun89 & Jul-Dec89 (Vol 19 complete)
549(RLC) – Revue de Littérature Comparée.
Paris.
Jan-Mar89 thru Oct-Dec89 (Vol 63
complete)
550(RusR) – Russian Review. Cambridge.
Jan89 thru Oct89 (Vol 48 complete)
551(RenQ) – Renaissance Quarterly. New
York.
Spring89 thru Winter89 (Vol 42 complete)
552(REH) – Revista de estudios hispánicos.
Poughkeepsie.
Jan89 thru Oct89 (Vol 23 complete)
554 – Romania. Paris.
Vol 108 No 2/3 & 4
555 – Revue de Philologie. Paris.
Vol 62 complete
556 – Russell. Hamilton.
Summer89 & Winter89/90 (Vol 9 com-
plete)
557 – Renaissance Studies. Oxford.
Mar89 thru Dec89 (Vol 6 complete)
558(RLJ) – Russian Language Journal. East
Lansing.
Winter89 & Spring-Fall89 (Vol 43 complete)
559 – Russian Linguistics. Dordrecht.
Vol 13 complete
560 – Salmagundi. Saratoga Springs.
Winter89 (No 81)
561(SFS) – Science Fiction Studies.
Montréal.
Mar89 thru Nov89 (Vol 16 complete)
562(Scan) – Scandinavica. Norwich.
May89 & Nov89 (Vol 28 complete)
563(SS) – Scandinavian Studies. Eugene.
Winter89 thru Autumn89 (Vol 61 com-
plete)
564 – Seminar. Downsview.
Feb89 thru Nov89 (Vol 25 complete)
565 – Stand Magazine. Newcastle upon
Tyne.
Winter88/89 thru Autumn89 (Vol 30
complete)
566 – The Scriblerian. Philadelphia.
Spring89, Autumn89 & Spring90 (Vol 21
No 2 & Vol 22 complete)

567 – Semiotica. Berlin.
Vol 73 thru Vol 77 complete
568(SCN) – Seventeenth-Century News.
University Park.
Spring–Summer89 & Fall–Winter89 (Vol
47 complete)
569(SR) – Sewanee Review. Sewanee.
Winter89 thru Fall89 (Vol 97 complete)
570(SQ) – Shakespeare Quarterly. Washington.
Spring89 thru Winter89 (Vol 40 complete)
571(ScLJ) – Scottish Literary Journal.
Aberdeen.
May89 thru Winter89 (Vol 16 complete
& supps 30 & 31)
572 – Shaw: The Annual of Bernard Shaw
Studies. University Park.
Vol 9 [no reviews indexed]
573(SSF) – Studies in Short Fiction. New-
berry.
Summer88 thru Summer89 (Vol 25 No 3
& 4, Vol 26 No 1–3)
574(SEEJ) – Slavic & East European Journal. Tucson.
Spring89 thru Winter89 (Vol 33 complete)
575(SEER) – Slavonic and East European
Review. London.
Jan89 thru Oct89 (Vol 67 complete)
576 – Journal of the Society of Architectural Historians. Philadelphia.
Mar89 thru Dec89 (Vol 48 complete)
577(SHR) – Southern Humanities Review.
Auburn.
Winter89 thru Fall89 (Vol 23 complete)
578 – Southern Literary Journal. Chapel
Hill.
Spring90 & Fall90 (Vol 22 No 2 & Vol
23 No 1)
579(SAQ) – South Atlantic Quarterly. Dur-
ham.
Winter89 thru Fall89 (Vol 88 complete)
[no reviews indexed]
580(SCR) – The South Carolina Review.
Clemson.
Fall89 thru Fall90 (Vol 22 complete &
Vol 23 No 1)
581 – Southerly. Sydney.
Mar89 thru Dec89 (Vol 49 complete)
582(SFQ) – Southern Folklore. Lexington.
Vol 46 No 1 & 2 [Vol 45 missing]
585(SoQ) – The Southern Quarterly.
Hattiesburg.
Summer89 thru Summer90 (Vol 27 No 4
& Vol 28 complete)
587(SAF) – Studies in American Fiction.
Boston.
Spring89 & Autumn89 (Vol 17 complete)
589 – Speculum. Cambridge.
Jan89 thru Oct89 (Vol 64 complete)
590 – Studies in the Humanities. Indiana.
Dec89 & Jun90 (Vol 16 No 2 & Vol 17
No 1)
591(SIR) – Studies in Romanticism. Boston.
Spring89 thru Winter89 (Vol 28 com-
plete)
593 – Symposium. Washington.
Spring89 thru Winter89/90 (Vol 43
complete)
594 – Studies in the Novel. Denton.
Spring89 thru Winter89 (Vol 21 complete)

595(ScS) – Scottish Studies. Edinburgh.
Vol 29
596(SL) – Studia Linguistica. Stockholm.
Vol 42 complete
597(SN) – Studia Neophilologica. Stockholm.
Vol 61 complete
598(SoR) – The Southern Review. Baton
Rouge.
Winter90 thru Autumn90 (Vol 26 complete)
599 – Style. De Kalb.
Winter89 thru Fall90 (Vol 23 No 4 &
Vol 24 No 1–3)
600 – Simiolus. Utrecht.
Vol 19 complete
601(SuF) – Sinn und Form. Berlin.
Jan–Feb89 thru Nov–Dec89 (Vol 41
complete)
602 – Sprachkunst. Vienna.
Band 20 complete
603 – Studies in Language. Amsterdam.
Vol 13 complete
604 – Spenser Newsletter. Chapel Hill.
Fall87 & Winter89 thru Fall89 (Vol 18
No 3 & Vol 20 complete)
605(SC) – Stendhal Club. Grenoble.
15Oct89 thru 15Jul90 (Vol 32 complete)
606 – Synthese. Dordrecht.
Jan89 thru Dec89 (Vols 78–81 complete)
607 – Tempo. London.
Mar89 thru Dec89 (No 168–171)
609 – Theater. New Haven.
Fall89 (Vol 20 No 3) [no reviews
indexed]
610 – Theatre Research International.
Oxford.
Spring89 thru Autumn89 (Vol 14 complete)
611(TN) – Theatre Notebook. London.
Vol 43 complete
612(ThS) – Theatre Survey. Bloomington.
Nov88 (Vol 29 No 2)
615(TJ) – Theatre Journal. Baltimore.
Mar89 thru Dec89 (Vol 41 complete)
616 – Thalia. Ottawa.
Vol 10 No 2
617(TLS) – Times Literary Supplement.
London.
5–11Jan90 thru 21–27Dec90 (No 4527–
4577)
618 – Trivia. North Amherst.
Spring89 & Fall89 (No 14 & 15)
619 – Transactions of the Charles S. Peirce
Society. Buffalo.
Winter89 thru Fall89 (Vol 25 complete)
620(TSWL) – Tulsa Studies in Women's Literature. Tulsa.
Spring89 (Vol 8 No 1)
627(UTQ) – University of Toronto Quarterly. Toronto.
Fall89 thru Summer90 (Vol 59 complete)
628(UWR) – University of Windsor Review.
Windsor.
Vol 22 No 1
635(VPR) – Victorian Periodicals Review.
Edwardsville.
Spring89 thru Winter89 (Vol 22 complete)
636(VP) – Victorian Poetry. Morgantown.
Spring89 thru Autumn–Winter89 (Vol 27
complete)

637(VS) – Victorian Studies. Bloomington.
Autumn89 thru Summer90 (Vol 33 complete)
639(VQR) – Virginia Quarterly Review. Charlottesville.
Winter89 thru Autumn89 (Vol 65 complete)
640 – Vivarum. Leiden.
May89 & Nov89 (Vol 27 complete)
646(WWR) – Walt Whitman Quarterly Review. Iowa City.
Summer89 thru Spring90 (Vol 7 complete)
647 – Wascana Review. Regina.
Spring89 & Fall89 (Vol 24 complete)
648(WCR) – West Coast Review. Burnaby.
Vol 23 No 2-4
649(WAL) – Western American Literature. Logan.
May89 thru Feb90 (Vol 24 complete)
650(WF) – Western Folklore. Glendale.
Jan89 thru Oct89 (Vol 48 complete)
651(WHR) – Western Humanities Review. Salt Lake City.
Spring89 thru Winter89 (Vol 43 complete) [no reviews indexed]
654(WB) – Weimarer Beiträge. Berlin.
1/1989 thru 10/1989 & 12/1989 (Vol 35 No 1-10 & Vol 35 No 12) [issue dated 11/1989 missing]
656(WMQ) – William & Mary Quarterly. Williamsburg.
Jan89 thru Oct89 (Vol 46 complete)
658 – Winterthur Portfolio. Chicago.
Spring89 thru Winter89 (Vol 24 complete)
659(ConL) – Contemporary Literature. Madison.
Spring90 thru Winter90 (Vol 31 complete)
660(Word) – Word. New York.
Apr-Aug89 (Vol 40 No 1/2) [no reviews indexed]
661(WC) – The Wordsworth Circle. Philadelphia.
Winter89 thru Autumn89 (Vol 20 complete)
662 – Woman's Art Journal. Knoxville.
Spring/Summer89 & Fall89/Winter90 (Vol 10 complete)
675(YER) – Yeats Eliot Review. Little Rock.
Winter-Spring89 thru Fall90 (Vol 10 complete)
676(YR) – Yale Review. New Haven.
Spring89 thru Winter90 (Vol 78 No 3 & 4, Vol 79 No 1 & 2)
677(YES) – The Yearbook of English Studies. London.
Vol 20
678(YCGL) – Yearbook of Comparative & General Literature. Bloomington.
No 36
679 – Zeitschrift für allgemeine Wissenschaftstheorie. Stuttgart.
Band 20 complete
680(ZDP) – Zeitschrift für deutsche Philologie. Berlin.
Band 108 complete
682(ZPSK) – Zeitschrift für Phonetik, Sprachwissenschaft und Kommunikationsforschung. Berlin.
Band 42 complete

683 – Zeitschrift für Kunstgeschichte. München.
Band 52 complete
684(ZDA) – Zeitschrift für deutsches Altertum und deutsche Literatur [Anzeiger section]. Stuttgart.
Band 188 complete
685(ZDL) – Zeitschrift für Dialektologie und Linguistik. Stuttgart.
1/1989 thru 3/1989 (Vol 56 complete)
687 – Zeitschrift für Philosophische Forschung. Meisenheim/Glan.
Jan-Mar89 thru Oct-Dec89 (Vol 43 complete)
688(ZSP) – Zeitschrift für slavische Philologie. Heidelberg.
Band 49 complete
703 – Sulfur. Ypsilanti.
Spring88, Spring89 & Fall89 (No 22, 24 & 25)
704(SFR) – Stanford French Review. Saratoga.
Spring89 & Fall-Winter89 (Vol 13 complete)
705 – The Wallace Stevens Journal. Potsdam.
Spring89 & Fall89 (Vol 13 complete)
706 – Studia Leibnitiana. Stuttgart.
Band 21 complete
707 – Sight and Sound. London.
Winter88/89 thru Autumn89 (Vol 58 complete)
708 – Studi Linguistici Italiani. Rome.
Vol 13 fasc 1 & Vol 14 fasc 1
709 – Studies in Art Education. Reston.
Fall89 thru Winter91 (Vol 31 complete, Vol 32 No 1 & 2)
710 – Studies in Second Language Acquisition. New York.
Mar89 thru Dec89 (Vol 11 complete)
711(RHM) – Revista Hispánica Moderna. New York.
Jun89 & Dec89 (Vol 42 complete)

Each year we are unable (for one reason or another) to index the reviews appearing in all of the periodicals scanned. The following is a list of the periodicals whose reviews were not included in this volume of the Index. Every attempt will be made to index these reviews in the next volume of the Index.

99 – Canadian Forum. Toronto.
112 – Celtica. Dublin.
134(CP) – Concerning Poetry. Bellingham.
138 – Conjunctions. New York.
161(DUJ) – Durham University Journal. Durham.
181 – Epoch. Ithaca.
182 – Enclitic. Los Angeles.
202(FMod) – Filología Moderna. Madrid.
205(ForL) – Forum Linguisticum. Lake Bluff.
206(FoLi) – Folia Linguistica. Berlin.
296(JCF) – Journal of Canadian Fiction. Montreal.
299 – Journal of Beckett Studies. San Francisco.
302 – Journal of Oriental Studies. Hong Kong.

314 – Journal of South Asian Literature.
  East Lansing.
326 – Journal of the William Morris Society. London.
339 – The Keats-Shelley Review. Hesling-
  ton.
343 – Komparatistische Hefte. Bayreuth.
349 – Language and Style. Flushing.
366 – Literature and History. London.
396(ModA) – Modern Age. Bryn Mawr.
466 – Oxford Studies in Ancient Philosophy. Oxford.
476 – Journal of Arts Management and
  Law. Washington.
490 – Poetica. Amsterdam.
534(RALS) – Resources for American Literary Study. College Park.
536(Rev) – Review. Charlottesville.
553(RLiR) – Revue de Linguistique Romane.
  Strasbourg.
588(SSL) – Studies in Scottish Literature.
  Columbia.
592 – Studio International. London.
608 – TESOL Quarterly. Washington.
702 – Shakespeare Studies. New York.

Aakhus, P. The Voyage of Mael Duin's Cur-
ragh.
  K. Weber, 441:28Jan90-22
Aarseth, A. Romantikken som konstruksjon.*
  H-P. Naumann, 562(Scan):May89-87
Aarts, J. & W. Meijs, eds. Corpus Linguistics.
  G. Bourquin, 189(EA):Apr-Jun89-205
Abbate, C. & R. Parker, eds. Analyzing
Opera.
  P. Griffiths, 617(TLS):20-26Jul90-778
Abbey, E. Hayduke Lives.
  M. Pellecchia, 441:4Feb90-18
Abbot, I. Avoiding the Gods.
  T. Nairn, 571(ScLJ):Spring89-54
Abbott, K. Downstream from "Trout Fishing
in America."
  S. Moore, 532(RCF):Fall89-228
  F. Salas, 649(WAL):Nov89-287
Abbott, L.K. Dreams of Distant Lives.*
  W. Cummins, 573(SSF):Summer89-360
Abbott, P. Seeking Many Inventions.
  R.A. Rutherdale, 106:Summer89-89
Abbott, P. States of Perfect Freedom.
  R.F. Sayre, 481(PQ):Fall89-530
Abbs, P., ed. Living Powers.*
  A. Simpson, 289:Summer89-124
Abdul-Jabbar, K., with M. McCarthy. Kareem.
  G. Plimpton, 441:25Mar90-9
Abel, D. The Moral Picturesque.
  J.L. Idol, 573(SSF):Winter89-107
Abel, D.C. Freud On Instinct and Morality.
  J. Clapp, 103:Jul90-259
Abel, E. The Shattered Bloc.
  T. Swick, 441:29Apr90-16
Abel, G. Nietzsche.
  M. Haar, 192(EP):Apr-Jun89-265
Abel, L. Important Nonsense.
  S.P., 295(JML):Fall88/Winter89-222
Abel, R., ed. French Film Theory and Criti-
cism 1907-1939.
  A. Neill & A. Ridley, 103:Sep90-345
  D. Polan, 500:Fall89/Winter90-125
Abelson, E.S. When Ladies Go A-Thieving.
  J. Katz, 441:18Feb90-13
Abelson, R. Lawless Mind.
  C. Williams, 103:Feb90-45
Abernathy, F.E., ed. Tales from the Big
Thicket.
  E.L. Montenyohl, 582(SFQ):Vol46No2-199
Abinun, M. Les Lumières de Sarajevo.
  L. Kovacs, 450(NRF):Apr89-103
Ableman, P. I Hear Voices.
  J. Domini, 441:25Nov90-18
Ablin, D.A. & M. Hood, eds. The Cambodian
Agony.
  B. Kiernan, 293(JASt):Aug89-668
Abold, V. & R. Bratfisch. Blues Heute.
  A.J.M. Prévos, 91:Vol17-185
Abondolo, D.M. Hungarian Inflectional Mor-
phology.
  S. Matthews, 350:Mar90-183
Abragam, A. De la physique avant toute
chose.
  J. Merleau-Ponty, 531:Jul-Dec89-551
Abraham, G., ed. The New Oxford History of
Music. (Vol 9)
  J. Warrack, 617(TLS):30Nov-6Dec90-
1295
Abraham, N. & M. Torok. The Wolf Man's
Magic Word.*
  L. Stern, 473(PR):Vol56No1-161
Abraham, R. Alexander Kerensky.*
  H. Shukman, 575(SEER):Jan89-145

Abraham, W. & R. Árhammar, eds. Linguistik
in Deutschland.*
  K.H. Schmidt, 685(ZDL):2/1989-196
Abrahams, R.D., ed. African Folktales. Afro-
American Folktales.
  W.F.H. Nicolaisen, 292(JAF):Oct-Dec89-
476
Abrahams, W., ed. Prize Stories 1988: The O.
Henry Awards.
  T.E. Holt, 219(GaR):Spring89-189
Abrahams, W., ed. Prize Stories 1990: The O.
Henry Awards.
  A. Brumer, 441:12Aug90-16
Abrams, M.H. Doing Things with Texts.
  R.M. Adams, 453(NYRB):1Mar90-38
  G.G. Harpham, 617(TLS):17-23Aug90-872
Abrams, M.H. & J. Ackerman. Theories of
Criticism.
  S. Sim, 148:Winter86-114
Abramson, G., ed. The Blackwell Companion
to Jewish Culture.
  H. Maccoby, 617(TLS):3-9Aug90-828
Abse, D., ed. The Hutchinson Book of Post-
War British Poets.
  T. Dooley, 617(TLS):6-12Jul90-734
Abse, D. Remembrance of Crimes Past.
  M. Walters, 617(TLS):2-8Nov90-1184
Abu-Laban, B. & B.G. Rule, eds. The Human
Sciences.
  R.S. Harris, 627(UTQ):Fall89-230
Aburish, S.K. Children of Bethany.
  I. Dushnaq, 441:11Feb90-35
Accardo, P. Diagnosis and Detection.
  E. Lauterbach, 395(MFS):Summer89-346
Achebe, C. Hopes and Impediments.*
  G.D. Killam, 538(RAL):Fall89-508
Acheson, J.M. The Lobster Gangs of Maine.
  N.R. Lipfert, 432(NEQ):Mar89-127
Acholonu, C.O. Western and Indigenous Tra-
ditions in Modern Igbo Literature.
  C. Maduka, 538(RAL):Spring89-116
Achugar, H. Las Mariposas Tropicales.
  R. Yamal, 403(MLS):Fall89-118
Acker, K. Empire of the Senseless.
  639(VQR):Autumn89-130
Acker, K. In Memoriam to Identity.
  P. Baker, 617(TLS):26Oct-1Nov90-1146
  S. Schiff, 441:22Jul90-11
Acker, K. Young Lust.*
  M. Horovitz, 493:Autumn89-56
Acker, R. & M. Burkhard, eds. Blick auf die
Schweiz.*
  H.A. Arnold, 221(GQ):Summer89-441
  H. Bänziger, 133:Band22Heft3/4-382
  R. Kieser, 406:Winter89-491
Ackerley, J.R. My Sister and Myself. (F.
King, ed)
  617(TLS):19-25Oct90-1137
Ackerman, D. A Natural History of the
Senses.
  A. Broyard, 441:29Jul90-8
  442(NY):17Sep90-109
Ackerman, D. Reverse Thunder.
  K.A. Myers, 385(MQR):Summer90-453
Ackerman, J.S. The Villa.
  M. Filler, 441:2Dec90-22
  W. Rybczynski, 453(NYRB):20Dec90-24
  J. Summerson, 617(TLS):6-12Jul90-730
Ackerman, K.D. The Gold Ring.
  639(VQR):Spring89-66

Ackerman, R. J.G. Frazer.*
  B. Feldman, 31(ASch):Spring89-305
  J.P. Holoka, 124:Jul-Aug90-527
  I.C. Jarvie, 488:Sep89-345
  M. Manganaro, 77:Spring89-160
  C.R. Phillips 3d, 24:Winter89-636
  R.A. Segal, 598(SoR):Spring90-470
  P.J. Wilson, 242:Vol10No2-248
Ackerman, S.E. & R.L.M. Lee. Heaven in
  Transition.
  J. Nagata, 293(JASt):Feb89-213
Ackermann, I., ed. Frauen in Afrika.
  A. Adams, 538(RAL):Fall89-570
Ackermann, R.J. Wittgenstein's City.
  B-M. Schiller, 319:Apr90-310
Ackrill, J.L. - see Aristotle
Ackroyd, P. Chatterton.*
  P. Lewis, 565:Summer89-66
Ackroyd, P. Dickens.
  S. Gill, 617(TLS):31Aug-6Sep90-911
Ackroyd, P. The Diversions of Purley.
  J.D. McClatchy, 491:Apr89-29
Ackroyd, P. First Light.*
  P. Lewis, 364:Jun/Jul89-124
  P. Lewis, 565:Summer89-66
Acorn, M. I Shout Love and Other Poems. (J.
  Deahl, ed)
  M.H. Keefer, 102(CanL):Winter88-136
"Acta Classica Universitatis Scientiarum
  Debreceniensis." (Vol 19)
  J-C. Richard, 555:Vol62Fasc1-191
"Actas de Congreso internacional de estudios
  sobre Rosalía de Castro e o seu tempo."*
  J. Palley, 240(HR):Spring89-248
"Actas del Simposio Filosofia y Ciencia en el
  Renacimiento."
  A. Guy, 542:Oct-Dec89-597
"Actes de premières Assises de la traduction
  littéraire." "Actes des deuxièmes Assises
  de la traduction littéraire." "Actes des
  troisièmes Assises de la traduction littér-
  aire."
  Y. Chevrel, 549(RLC):Apr-Jun89-259
"Actes du Ve Colloque International sur le
  Moyen Français, Milan, 6-8 mai 1985."
  M.J. Freeman, 382(MAE):1989/1-172
Acton, P.N. Invasion of Privacy.
  K.M. McCarthy, 395(MFS):Summer89-293
Aczel, P. Non-Well-Founded Sets.
  M. Boffa, 316:Sep89-1111
Aczel, T. The Hunt.
  P. Sherwood, 617(TLS):7-13Dec90-1327
Adair, R.K. The Physics of Baseball.
  S.L. Glashow, 441:1Apr90-16
Adam, W. Poetische und Kritische Wälder.
  M. Morton, 221(GQ):Fall89-511
Adamczyk, A.J. Black Dance.
  R. Johnson, 151:Nov89-92
Adamczyk, R. Die realitätsbezogene Kon-
  struktion des Entwicklungsromans bei
  Gottfried Keller.
  M. Swales, 402(MLR):Jan90-262
Adamov, A. Le Professeur Taranne [together
  with] Arrabal, F. Pique-nique en cam-
  pagne. (P. Norrish, ed)
  M. Sorrell, 402(MLR):Oct90-988
Adams, A. Angels of Soho.
  E. Bartlett, 493:Spring89-64
Adams, A. & others, eds. The Changing Face
  of Arthurian Romance.*
  P.J.C. Field, 382(MAE):1989/2-313

Adams, A., J. Adams & T. Jefferson. The
  Adams-Jefferson Letters. (L.J. Cappon, ed)
  P.J. Degategno, 365:Fall88-223
"Ansel Adams: Letters and Images 1916-
  1984."* (M.S. Alinder & A.G. Stillman, eds)
  M. Esterow, 55:Apr89-129
Adams, D. The Long Dark Tea-Time of the
  Soul.*
  639(VQR):Summer89-93
Adams, D.J. Diderot: Dialogue and Debate.*
  I.L. Greenberg, 345(KRQ):May89-226
Adams, D.Q. Tocharian Historical Phonology
  and Morphology.
  D.A. Ringe, Jr., 350:Jun90-400
Adams, E. Chelsea Porcelain.
  R. Hildyard, 39:Jan89-66
Adams, E.B., with D.C. Haberman, eds. Ber-
  nard Shaw. (Vol 2)
  C.A. Berst, 177(ELT):Vol32No1-71
  B.F. Dukore, 610:Autumn89-302
Adams, G. Cage Eleven.
  P. Hillyard, 617(TLS):31Aug-6Sep90-924
Adams, G.G. The Purchase of Order.
  M. Whitt, 152(UDQ):Fall89-103
Adams, H. The Academic Tribes. (2nd ed)
  R.W. Lewis, 456(NDQ):Winter89-246
Adams, H. Thomas Hart Benton.
  P-L. Adams, 61:Feb90-108
  P-L. Adams, 61:Aug90-92
Adams, H. The Letters of Henry Adams,
  1858-1891. (J.C. Levenson & others, eds)
  P. Lagayette, 189(EA):Apr-Jun89-182
Adams, H. The Letters of Henry Adams,
  1892-1918. (J.C. Levenson & others, eds)
  E.N. Harbert, 432(NEQ):Sep89-443
  H. Kaplan, 27(AL):Oct89-458
  P. Lagayette, 189(EA):Apr-Jun89-182
  T. Wortham, 445(NCF):Jun89-122
Adams, J.C. Sir Charles God Damn.
  L. Ricou, 102(CanL):Summer89-143
Adams, J.R. The Big Fix.*
  J.K. Galbraith, 453(NYRB):18Jan90-15
Adams, J.R.R. The Printed Word and the Com-
  mon Man.
  S. Davies, 83:Autumn89-207
Adams, M.M. William Ockham.*
  W.J. Courtenay, 589:Jul89-641
Adams, R. A Book of British Music Festivals.
  R. Finnegan, 187:Fall89-530
Adams, R. The Day Gone By.
  P. Reading, 617(TLS):11-17May90-488
Adams, R., ed. Teaching Shakespeare.
  G. Schmitz, 156(ShJW):Jahrbuch1989-332
Adams, S. The World of the Impressionists.
  M.V., 324:Apr90-376
Adams, S. & D. Ross, Jr. Revising Mytholo-
  gies.
  R. Sattelmeyer, 27(AL):Dec89-689
Adamson, H.D. Variation Theory and Second
  Language Acquisition.
  R. Coppieters, 350:Mar90-163
Adamson, I. Bangor Light of the World.
  R. Fréchet, 189(EA):Jan-Mar89-114
Adamson, J. Bugs Bunny.
  R. Scheier, 441:8Jul90-17
Adamson, J. "Troilus and Cressida."*
  S. Billington, 610:Spring89-87
  L. Normand, 447(N&Q):Sep89-380
  J. Rees, 541(RES):Nov89-554
  K. Tetzeli von Rosador, 156(ShJW):Jahr-
  buch1989-357
Adamson, J. - see Greene, G.

Adamson, N. Feminist Organizing for Change.
K. Dubinsky, 529(QQ):Autumn89-775
Adamy, B. – see Pfitzner, H.
Adamzik, K. Probleme der Negation im Deut-
schen.
E. Koller, 685(ZDL):2/1989-212
Adcock, F., ed. The Faber Book of 20th Cen-
tury Women's Poetry.*
H. Buck, 4:Summer89-78
Addas, C. Ibn'Arabi ou la quête du Souffre
Rouge.
O. Merzoug, 98:Nov89-911
Addiss, S. Tall Mountains and Flowing
Waters.*
E. Horton, 293(JASt):May89-380
Adelaide, D., ed. A Bright and Fiery Troop.
S. Sheridan, 71(ALS):May89-118
Adelson, A. & R. Lapides, with M. Web, eds.
Lódź Ghetto.*
D. Pryce-Jones, 617(TLS):20-26Apr90-
423
W. Reich, 441:6May90-41
Adembri, B. & others. La Ceramica degli
Etruschi. (M. Martelli, ed)
N. Spivey, 313:Vol79-177
Adeney, B.T. Just War, Political Realism, and
Faith.
I.C., 185:Oct89-221
Aderhold, W., W. Dürr & W. Litschauer, eds.
Franz Schubert: Jahre der Krise 1818-1823.
W. Seidel, 417:Oct-Dec89-366
Adey, L. Class and Idol in the English Hymn.*
N. Temperley, 637(VS):Spring90-494
Adler, I., B. Bayer & H. Dehleifer, ods. Yuval
(Vol 5)
P. Laki, 187:Winter89-151
Adler, J. "Eine fast magische Anziehungs-
kraft."
M.K. Flavell, 402(MLR):Jan90-247
W.J. Lillyman, 301(JEGP):Oct89-585
Adler, K. & T. Garb. Berthe Morisot.
N.M. Mathews, 662:Spring/Summer89-46
Adler, K. & T. Garb – see Morisot, B.
Adler, R., with L. Davis. "You Gotta Have
Heart."
D. Kaufman, 441:26Aug90-15
Adler, T.P. Mirror on the Stage.*
R.N.C., 295(JML):Fall88/Winter89-261
Admoni, W. Die Tagebücher der Dichter in
sprachlicher Sicht.
L. Hermodsson, 597(SN):Vol61No2-237
Admoni, W.G. Die Entwicklung des Satzbaus
der deutschen Literatursprache im 19. und
20. Jahrhundert.
H. Ebert, 680(ZDP):Band108Heft3 470
Adolf, H. – see Spitzer, L.
Adolphs, D.W. Literarischer Erfahrungshoriz-
ont.
S.R. Cerf, 133:Band22Heft2-187
Adorno, T.W. Alban Berg.
J-L. Jacob, 450(NRF):Oct89-117
Adorno, T.W. The Jargon of Authenticity.*
(French title: Jargon de l'authenticité.)
R. Rochlitz, 98:Apr89-277
Adriani, G. Toulouse-Lautrec.
R. Kendall, 39:May89-366
Adshead, S.A.M. China in World History.
E.L. Farmer, 293(JASt):Aug89-583
Aelfric. Fifty-six Aelfric Fragments.* (E.
Fausbøll, ed)
D.N. Dumville, 72:Band226Heft1-132
H. Gneuss, 38:Band107Heft1/2-159
A.L. Meaney, 179(ES):Feb89-78

Aeschbach, M. – see Lefèvre, A.
Aeschimann, W. La Pensé e d'Edgar Quinet,
étude sur la formation de ses idées avec
écrits de jeunesse et documents inédits.
O.A. Haac, 446(NCFS):Fall-Winter89/90-
285
Aeschimann, W. & J. Tucoo-Chala – see Qui-
net, E.
Aeschylus. Choephori.* (A.F. Garvie, ed)
J. Dillon, 235:Summer89-63
M. Griffith, 122:Oct89-335
M. McCall, 303(JoHS):Vol109-214
Agamben, G. Idée de la prose.
P. Pachet, 450(NRF):Jun89-106
Aganbegian, A. The Economic Challenge of
Perestroika.
L. Turgeon, 550(RusR):Jul89-328
Aganbegyan, A., ed. Perestroika 1989.*
639(VQR):Summer89-95
Agar, E., with A. Lambirth. A Look at My
Life.*
F. Spalding, 90:Nov89-791
Agassi, J. The Gentle Art of Philosophical
Polemics.
A.J. Dale, 103:Mar90-89
"The Age of Correggio and the Carracci."*
C. Lloyd, 278(IS):Vol44-168
Agee, J. Bend This Heart.*
P. Metcalf, 532(RCF):Fall89-211
Agee, J. Pretend We've Never Met.
P. Glasser, 455:Sep89-69
P. Metcalf, 532(RCF):Fall89-211
Agee, J., R. Blakely & S. Welch, eds. Stiller's
Pond
J.B. Gidmark, 456(NDQ):Winter89-218
Agnew, J-C. The Market and the Theater in
Anglo-American Thought, 1550-1750.
R.D. Abrahams, 292(JAF):Apr-Jun89-202
Agnew, J-C. Worlds Apart.*
L. Engle, 670(SQ):Fall89-372
Agnon, S.Y. Shira.*
D. Aberbach, 617(TLS):20-26Apr90-428
G. Amran, 453(NYRD):29Mar90-14
Agoos, J. Above the Land.*
J. Parini, 473(PR):Vol56No3-510
Agosín, M. Brujas y algo mas/Witches and
Other Things.
N.G. Díaz, 30.3pring09 118
Agosin, M., ed. Landscapes of a New Land.
S.A. Lee, 441:29Apr90-19
Agosin, M. Pablo Neruda.
C. Perriam, 86(BHS):Jul89-315
Agosin, M. Women of Smoke.*
J. Shreve, 238:Sep89-568
Agovi, K.E. Novels of Social Change.
C. Sarvan, 538(RAL):Fall89-543
Aguilar Piñal, F. Un escritor ilustrado.
D.T. Gies, 240(HR):Spring89-243
I.L. McClelland, 86(BHS):Oct89-382
de Aguirre, J.M. – see under Martínez de
Aguirre, J.
Agulhon, M. Histoire vagabonde.*
J-Y. Grenier, 531:Jul-Dec89-540
Ahearn, E.J. Marx and Modern Fiction.
S. Petrey, 446(NCFS):Fall-Winter89/90-
289
S. Sprenger, 400(MLN):Sep89-971
Ahenakew, F. Cree Language Structures.
R. Darnell, 355(LSoc):Dec89-602
Ahenakew, F., ed & trans. Kiskinahamawâ-
kan-âcimowinisa/Student Stories. (2nd ed)
B.D. Joseph, 350:Sep90-619

Ahl, F. Metaformations.*
 A. Moss, 131(CL):Spring89-188
Ahlberger, C. Vävarfolket.
 A. Gustavsson, 64(Arv):Vol44-199
Ahluwalia, I.J. Industrial Growth in India.
 A. Bhargava, 293(JASt):May89-413
Ahmed, A.S. Discovering Islam.
 T.P. Wright, Jr., 293(JASt):Feb89-114
Ahmed, A.S. Pakistan Society.
 S. Baruah, 293(JASt):Aug89-641
Ahmed, I. The Concept of an Islamic State.
 R.D. Long, 293(JASt):Feb89-193
Ahmed, S.U. Dacca.
 H. Spodek, 293(JASt):May89-414
Ahrends, G. & H.U. Seeber, eds. Englische
 und amerikanische Naturdichtung im 20.
 Jahrhundert.
 G. Schmitz, 38:Band107Heft3/4-530
Ahroni, R. Yemenite Jewry.
 Y.K. Stillman, 318(JAOS):Apr-Jun88-311
Aigner-Foresti, L. Zeugnisse etruskischer
 Kultur im Nordwesten Italiens und in Süd-
 frankreich.
 M. Cristofani, 229:Band61Heft7-648
Aiken, S.H. & others, eds. Changing Our
 Minds.
 S. Groves, 50(ArQ):Autumn89-98
Ainaud i de Lasarte, J. & others. Els vitralls
 de la catedral de Girona.
 M.P. Lillich, 589:Oct89-917
Ainsa, F. Identidad cultural de Iberoamérica
 en su narrativa.*
 P. Standish, 86(BHS):Jul89-312
Airaksinen, T. Ethics of Coercion and
 Authority.
 R.Y., 185:Jan90-449
Aird, C. The Body Politic.
 P. Craig, 617(TLS):1-7Jun90-593
Aisenberg, N., ed. We Animals.
 J.E. Becker, 363(LitR):Spring90-395
Aisenberg, N. & M. Harrington. Women of
 Academe.
 M.G. Lewis, 529(QQ):Spring89-117
Aissen, J. Tzotzil Clause Structure.
 M. Dryer, 320(CJL):Dec89-458
Aitchison, J. The Golden Harvester.*
 H. Hewitt, 571(ScLJ):Spring89-13
Aitchison, J. Words in the Mind.*
 T. Berg, 361:Dec89-342
Aitken, J.L. Masques of Morality.*
 L. Moore, 529(QQ):Spring89-170
Aizlewood, R. Verse Form and Meaning in the
 Poetry of Vladimir Maiakovskii.
 B.P. Scherr, 402(MLR):Oct90-1045
Ajzenstat, J. The Political Thought of Lord
 Durham.
 B. Irvine, 529(QQ):Winter89-988
Akashi Motojirō. Rakka Ryūsui. (O.K. Fält &
 A. Kujala, eds)
 J.J. Stephan, 407(MN):Autumn89-363
Akenson, D.H. Small Differences.
 D. Bowen, 529(QQ):Autumn89-728
Akerholt, M-B. Patrick White.
 M. Yong, 402(MLR):Apr90-429
Akers, E. Knocking on the Earth.
 L. Upton, 152(UDQ):Summer89-124
Akhmatova, A. The Complete Poems of Anna
 Akhmatova. (R. Reeder, ed)
 J. Bayley, 441:13May90-9
Akins, E. Little Woman.
 S. Dundon, 441:7Oct90-40

Akkerman, E. & others. Designing a Comput-
 erized Lexicon.
 G. Bourquin, 189(EA):Apr-Jun89-205
Akkerman, E., P. Masereeuw & W. Meijs. De-
 signing a Computerized Lexicon for Lin-
 guistic Purposes.
 G. Bourquin, 189(EA):Apr-Jun89-205
Akkerman, E., K. Voogt-van Zutphen & W.
 Meijs. A Computerized Lexicon for Word-
 Level Tagging.
 G. Bourquin, 189(EA):Apr-Jun89-205
Akst, D. Wonder Boy.
 J.B. Ciulla, 441:25Feb90-20
Aksu-Koç, A. The Acquisition of Aspect and
 Modality.
 E.V. Clark, 361:Nov89-262
Aksyonov, V. Say Cheese!*
 S. Laird, 617(TLS):30Mar-5Apr90-338
"Akutagawa and Dazai: Instances of Literary
 Adaptation." (J. O'Brien, trans)
 D. Fahy, 293(JASt):Aug89-623
 M.N. Wilson, 407(MN):Autumn89-352
Alain. Mythes et fables.
 J-M. Le Lannou, 192(EP):Jul-Dec89-531
Alain-Fournier. Colombe Blanchet. (G.
 Manca, ed)
 R. Gibson, 617(TLS):16-22Nov90-1231
Aland, K. & B. The Text of The New Testa-
 ment.
 J. Herington, 124:Mar-Apr90-360
Alanen, A.R. & J.A. Eden. Main Street Ready-
 Made.
 M.C. Sies, 576:Mar89-97
Alapuro, R. & others, eds. Small States in
 Comparative Perspective.
 R.A. Bevan, 563(SS):Autumn89-428
Alas, L. The Moral Tales. (K.A. Stackhouse,
 ed)
 S. Miller, 238:Dec89-980
Alatis, J.E., ed. Language Teaching, Testing,
 and Technology.
 R.W. Cole, 350:Dec90-858
Alazraki, J. Borges and the Kabbalah and
 Other Essays on His Fiction and Poetry.
 E. Aizenberg, 478(P&L):Oct89-400
 E. Fishburn, 402(MLR):Jul90-773
 D.T. Jaen, 263(RIB):Vol39No2-202
 L. Olsen, 395(MFS):Summer89-314
de Alba, J.G.M. - see under Moreno de Alba,
 J.G.
Alba, R.D. Ethnic Identity.
 A. Hacker, 453(NYRB):22Nov90-19
Albanese, C.L. Nature Religion in America.
 G.S. Wood, 617(TLS):27Jul-2Aug90-794
Alberti, J. Beyond Suffrage.
 A. Summers, 617(TLS):1-7Jun90-592
Alberti, L.B. Dinner Pieces.* (D. Marsh,
 trans)
 D. Knox, 551(RenQ):Summer89-300
Alberti, L.B. On the Art of Building in Ten
 Books.* (J. Rykwert, N. Leach & R. Taver-
 nor, eds & trans)
 D. Cruickshank, 46:Nov89-12
Albertoni, E.A. Mosca and the Theory of
 Elitism.
 639(VQR):Winter89-31
Albertus Magnus. Alberti Magni opera omnia.
 (Vol 4, Pt 1) (P. Hossfeld, ed)
 J. Brams, 53(AGP):Band71Heft3-344
Albertus Magnus. Physica. (Bks 1-4) (P.
 Hossfeld, ed)
 J.M.M.H. Thijssen, 640:Nov89-159

Albinski, N.B. Women's Utopias in British and American Fiction.
   L. Yelin, 637(VS):Spring90–507
Alblas, J.B.H. Johannes Boekholt (1656–1693).
   T. Bögels, 179(ES):Jun89–272
   N.H. Keeble, 447(N&Q):Mar89–108
   S. Roach, 354:Jun89–163
Albore Livadie, C. Tremblements de terre, éruptions volcaniques et vie des hommes dans la Campanie antique.
   H.M. Hine, 123:Vol39No1–157
Albrecht, D. Designing Dreams.
   A. Blanc, 47:Dec89–119
Albrecht, G.A. Das sinfonische Werk Hans Pfitzners.
   R. Stephan, 417:Jan–Mar89–97
Albrecht, W. – see Nicolai, F.
Albright, D. Stravinsky.
   R. Holloway, 617(TLS):26Oct–1Nov90–1154
Albright, D. – see Yeats, W.B.
Albritton, R. A Japanese Reconstruction of Marxist Theory.
   L. Nowak, 488:Mar89–81
Alcock, J. Sonoran Desert Summer.
   D. Quammen, 441:8Apr90–18
Alcott, L.M. The Journals of Louisa May Alcott. (J. Myerson & D. Shealy, with M.B. Stern, eds)
   D. Manuel, 441:14Jan90–31
Alcott, L.M. The Selected Letters of Louisa May Alcott. (J. Myerson & D. Shealy, with M.B. Stern, eds)
   L.A. Carlson, 27(AL):Dec89–699
Alcover, J.V. – see under Vidal Alcover, J.
Alderson, J.C., K.J. Krahnke & C.W. Stansfield, eds. Reviews of English Language Proficiency Tests.
   D. Douglas, 710:Sep89–358
Aldiss, B. Bury My Heart at W.H. Smith's.
   V. Cunningham, 617(TLS):24–30Aug90–901
Aldiss, B. Forgotten Life.*
   42(AR):Summer89–374
Aldiss, B.W. A Romance of the Equator.
   G. Jonas, 441:16Jul90–13
Aldiss, B.W. – see Kavan, A.
Aldridge, A.O. The Reemergence of World Literature.*
   A.C. Yu, 678(YCGL):No36–166
Alegretto, M. Blood Stone.
   639(VQR):Winter89–21
Aleixandre, V. Vicente Aleixandre, Epistolario. (J.L. Cano, ed)
   J.C. Wilcox, 240(HR):Winter89–122
Aleixandre, V. Pasión de la tierra. (G. Morelli, ed)
   G. Connell, 86(BHS):Oct89–384
Aleixandre, V. Shadow of Paradise.*
   S. Jiménez–Fajardo, 238:May89–318
Alenius, M. Brev til eftertiden.
   A. Heitmann, 562(Scan):Nov89–201
Alenius, M. & P. Zeeberg, eds. Litteratur og laerdom.
   G.C. Schoolfield, 562(Scan):May89–82
Aler, J. & J. Enklaar, eds. Zur Wende des Jahrhunderts.
   M. Lauster, 402(MLR):Jan90–263
   M. Winkler, 221(GQ):Spring89–284
Aleshkovsky, Y. The Hand.
   A.W. Bouis, 441:6May90–28
   D. Ugrešić, 617(TLS):12–18Oct90–1088

Aleshkovsky, Y. Kangaroo.
   D. Ugrešić, 617(TLS):12–18Oct90–1088
Alexander, C. One Dry Season.
   T. Cahill, 441:10Jun90–48
   C. Moorehead, 617(TLS):26Jan–1Feb90–97
   442(NY):19Mar90–110
Alexander, C. – see Brontë, C.
Alexander, E. The Jewish Idea and Its Enemies.
   A.H. Rosenfeld, 390:Feb/Mar89–60
Alexander, E. The Venus Hottentot.
   D.J. Austin, 441:30Sep90–20
Alexander, I.W. French Literature and the Philosophy of Consciousness.
   E. Morot–Sir, 535(RHL):Mar–Apr89–338
Alexander, J.J.G., T.J. Brown & J. Gibbs – see Wormald, F.
Alexander, J.H. Reading Wordsworth.*
   E.D. Mackerness, 447(N&Q):Jun89–247
Alexander, L. Six Months Off.
   S. Pickering, 569(SR):Spring89–297
Alexander, M.A. & others. Thuburbo Majus, 1.
   R.E. Kolarik, 589:Jul89–643
Alexander, P. Ideas, Qualities and Corpuscles.*
   R. Specht, 53(AGP):Band71Heft2–248
Alexander, P.F. William Plomer.*
   A. Ross, 364:Jun/Jul89–115
Alexander, R.D. The Biology of Moral Systems.*
   A. Oldenquist, 393(Mind):Jul89–461
Alexander, R.J., ed. Biographical Dictionary of Latin American and Caribbean Political Leaders.
   R.A. Camp, 263(RIB):Vol39No1–69
Alexander, S. The Triple Myth.
   J.S. Conway, 104(CASS):Spring89–92
Alexander, S. When She Was Bad.
   W. Wasserstein, 441:8Apr90–13
Alexander, W. Vertical Rainbow Climber.
   S. Foster, 448:Vol27No3–156
Alexander of Aphrodisias. The "De Anima" of Alexander of Aphrodisias. (A.P. Fotinis, ed & trans)
   A. Silverman, 41:Fall89–354
Alexiadis, M.A. E Ellēnikē kai diethneis epistēmonikō onomatóthesia tēz laographiaz.
   C. Stewart, 292(JAF):Oct–Dec89–510
Alfageme, I.R. – see under Rodríguez Alfageme, I.
Alfau, F. Chromos.
   P–L. Adams, 61:May90–133
   J. Brenkman, 441:13May90–25
   442(NY):10Dec90–158
Alfau, F. Locos: A Comedy of Gestures.*
   A.L. Six, 617(TLS):26Jan–1Feb90–86
Alféri, P. Guillaume d'Ockham, le Singulier.
   O. Boulnois, 98:Oct89–734
Alföldy, G. Die römische Gesellschaft.* Römische Heeresgeschichte.*
   J.J. Wilkes, 313:Vol79–225
Alfonsi, F. Alberto Moravia in Italia.
   A. Terrizzi, 276:Summer89–206
Saint Alfonso. S. Alfonso Maria de' Liguori, "Brevi avvertimenti di grammatica e aritmetica." (R. Librandi, ed)
   E.F. Tuttle, 545(RPh):May90–607
Alfonso X el Sabio. Obras de Alfonso X el Sabio (Selección). (F.J. Díez de Revenga, ed)
   J.T. Snow, 240(HR):Winter89–78

Alford, J. & K. Hunt, eds. Europe in the Western Alliance.
 C. Kennedy, 575(SEER):Oct89-646
Alford, J.A., ed. A Companion to "Piers Plowman."
 D.C. Fowler, 405(MP):May90-391
 P. Hardman, 402(MLR):Oct90-908
 S.S. Hussey, 447(N&Q):Dec89-492
Alford, J.A. & D.P. Seniff, eds. Literature and Law in the Middle Ages.
 F.R.P. Akehurst, 207(FR):Mar90-702
Alford, J.A. & M.T. Tavormina – see "The Yearbook of Langland Studies"
Algren, N. Never Come Morning. The Neon Wilderness. The Man with the Golden Arm. A Walk on the Wild Side.
 T.R. Edwards, 453(NYRB):28Jun90-22
Ali, T. Redemption.
 P. Kincaid, 617(TLS):9-15Nov90-1214
Alighieri, D. – see under Dante Alighieri
Alinder, M.S. & A.G. Stillman – see "Ansel Adams: Letters and Images 1916-1984"
Aline, Countess of Romanones. The Spy Went Dancing.
 J. Kaufman, 441:4Mar90-25
Alkalay-Gut, K. Alone in the Dawn.
 E. Butscher, 219(GaR):Fall89-620
 S.K. Harris, 26(ALR):Winter90-80
Alkon, P.K. The Origins of Futuristic Fiction.*
 A.B. Evans, 561(SFS):Mar89-94
 J. Huntington, 405(MP):Nov89-181
 L. Leibacher-Ouvrard, 210(FrF):May89-253
 P. Parrinder, 173(ECS):Winter89/90-226
 J.R. Pfeiffer, 149(CLS):Vol26No4-371
Allaby, M. A Guide to Gaia.
 M. Oppenheimer, 441:6May90-29
Allan, J. & C. Roberts, eds. Syria and Iran.
 R. Hillenbrand, 59:Mar89-109
Allan, K. Linguistic Meaning.
 B. Peeters, 320(CJL):Mar89-119
Allard, Y. Le Roman historique.
 A. Walsh, 627(UTQ):Fall89-186
Allbeury, T. Deep Purple.
 N. Callendar, 441:15Apr90-19
Allégret, M. Carnets du Congo.* (C. Rabel-Jullien, ed)
 A. Goulet, 535(RHL):Mar-Apr89-323
Allen, C.V. Illusions.
 T. Goldie, 102(CanL):Winter88-128
Allen, E. Straight Through the Night.*
 639(VQR):Summer89-94
Allen, G.W. & R. Asselineau. St. John de Crèvecoeur.*
 B. Chevignard, 189(EA):Apr-Jun89-229
Allen, J. & others. From Text to Speech.
 G. Olaszy, 353:Vol27No6-1160
Allen, J. & I.M. Young, eds. The Thinking Muse.
 R.T., 185:Apr90-696
Allen, M. Baseball.
 F.E. Halpert, 441:22Apr90-25
Allen, M. Charles Dickens' Childhood.
 W. Burgan, 637(VS):Spring90-501
Allen, M. & J.H. Fisher. The Essential Chaucer.
 C.C. Morse, 447(N&Q):Dec89-489
 R.A. Peck, 589:Apr89-380
Allen, P. The Concept of Woman.
 L. Damico, 254:Spring89-172

Allen, P. 3d. Proof of Moral Obligation in Twentieth-Century Philosophy.
 M.T., 185:Apr90-691
Allen, P.W. Building Domestic Liberty.*
 K. MacIntosh, 46:Mar89-14
Allen, R., ed. Modern Arabic Literature.*
 E.S., 295(JML):Fall88/Winter89-192
 S.A. Simawe, 271:Winter89-156
Allen, R.C., ed. Channels of Discourse.*
 T. Goldie, 102(CanL):Winter88-128
Allén, S., B. Loman & B. Sigurd. Svenska Akademien och svenska språket.
 J.E. Cathey, 563(SS):Winter89-83
Allen, W.R., ed. Conversations with Kurt Vonnegut.
 E. Carroll, 395(MFS):Winter89-761
Allen, W.R. Walker Percy.*
 J.H. Justus, 27(AL):Mar89-127
Allert, B. Die Metapher und ihre Krise.*
 M.R. Higonnet, 221(GQ):Fall89-534
 W. Koepke, 564:May89-175
 D.F. Mahoney, 406:Spring89-126
Allesch, C.G. Geschichte der psychologischen Aesthetik.
 H. Bruen, 289:Summer89-121
Alletzhauser, A. The House of Nomura.
 K. van Wolferen, 617(TLS):31Aug-6Sep90-926
Allibone, J. Anthony Salvin.*
 M. Brooks, 637(VS):Autumn89-193
 J. Frew, 576:Dec89-400
Allières, J. La Formation de la langue française. (2nd ed)
 K. Klingebiel, 207(FR):Dec89-418
Allingham, M. The Return of Mr. Campion.
 T.J. Binyon, 617(TLS):5-11Jan90-18
Allman, J. Curve Away from Stillness.
 K.E. Duffin, 472:Vol16No1-41
Allman, T.D. Miami.
 J.N. Stull, 106:Fall89-265
Allman, W.F. Apprentices of Wonder.
 J. Gliedman, 441:8Apr90-21
Allmand, C. The Hundred Years War.
 H. Kaminsky, 589:Oct89-920
Allott, M., ed. Matthew Arnold: A Centennial Review.
 J.J. Savory, 637(VS):Spring90-509
Allott, M., ed. Matthew Arnold 1988.
 G.B. Tennyson, 445(NCF):Sep89-254
Allott, T. – see Boursault, E.
Alloula, M. The Colonial Harem.
 A.E. Coombes & S. Edwards, 59:Dec89-510
Allport, A. & others, eds. Language Perception and Production.
 C. Futter, 320(CJL):Dec89-462
"Alltag – Lebensweise – Kultur."
 H. Hanke, 654(WB):8/1989-1396
Allworth, E., ed. Central Asia.
 F. Halliday, 617(TLS):22-28Jun90-661
Allwright, D. Observation in the Language Classroom.
 J.S. Falk, 350:Mar90-183
Almeida, O.T. – see under Teotónio Almeida, O.
Alméras, P. Les Idées de Céline.
 K. Anderson, 210(FrF):Jan89-110
Almog, S. Nationalism and Antisemitism in Modern Europe 1815-1945.
 R.S. Wistrich, 617(TLS):23-29Nov90-1261
Almond, B. Moral Concerns.*
 T.J. Donaldson, 518:Jan89-44

Almond, B. & B. Wilson, eds. Values.
　C.W. Gowans, 518:Oct89-232
　D.J., 185:Oct89-203
Almond, P.C. The British Discovery of Bud-
　dhism.
　S.T. Dean, 637(VS):Winter90-362
Almquist, S. Gengångarförestållningar i
　svensk folktro i genreanalytisk synpunkt.
　J. Lindow, 563(SS):Autumn89-410
Almqvist, B., S. Ó Catháin & P. Ó Héalaí, eds.
　The Heroic Process.
　P. Aalto, 196:Band30Heft3/4-301
Alofsin, A., ed. Frank Lloyd Wright: An Index
　to the Taliesin Correspondence.
　P.J. Meehan, 47:Dec89-124
　J. Quinan, 576:Sep89-300
Alonso, C.J. The Spanish American Regional
　Novel.
　G. Martin, 617(TLS):7-13Sep90-957
Alonso, D.O. - see under Ocón Alonso, D.
Alonso-Núñez, J.M. Die politische und soz-
　iale Ideologie des Geschichtsschreibers
　Florus.
　L. de Blois, 394:Vol42fasc3/4-564
Alonzo, A-M. Écoute, Sultane.
　B. Godard, 102(CanL):Winter88-123
Alòs, L.F. - see under Ferrer i Alòs, L.
Alpern, S. Freda Kirchwey.
　E.I. Perry, 106:Fall89-223
Alpers, S. The Art of Describing.
　M. Bal, 567:Vol76No3/4-283
Alpers, S. Rembrandt's Enterprise.*
　M. Bal, 567:Vol76No3/4-283
　I.M. Nash, 59:Jun89-388
　P.C. Sutton, 90:Jun89-428
Alperson, P., ed. What is Music?
　F. Berenson, 89(BJA):Autumn89-371
　M. Krausz, 103:Feb90-47
　H. Niblock, 290(JAAC):Summer89-292
Alpert, H. The Life and Times of "Porgy and
　Bess."
　R. Siegel, 441:18Nov90-29
　442(NY):24Dec90-100
van Alphen, E. Bij wijze van lezen.
　R. Wolfs, 204(FdL):Dec89-313
Alston, R.C. A Bibliography of the English
　Language from the Invention of Printing to
　the Year 1800. (Vol 12, Pt 2)
　B. Richardson, 354:Mar89-73
Alston, W.P. Divine Nature and Divine Lan-
　guage.
　J. Newman, 103:Aug90-301
Altemöller, E-M. Fragespiele für den Unter-
　richt zur Förderung der spontanen münd-
　lichen Ausdrucksfähigkeit.
　R. Ambacher, 399(MLJ):Summer89-230
Altena, I.Q.V. - see under van Regteren
　Altena, I.Q.
Altenberg, B. Prosodic Patterns in Spoken
　English.
　M. Shapley, 350:Jun90-409
Altenburg, D. & R. Kleinertz - see Liszt, F.
Alter, J. Elmer Kelton and West Texas.
　B.J. Frye, 649(WAL):Nov89-289
Alter, J. Mattie.
　J.W. Lee, 649(WAL):Feb90-395
Alter, R. The Art of Biblical Narrative. The
　Art of Biblical Poetry.
　D.L. Jeffrey, 627(UTQ):Summer90-569
Alter, R. Motives for Fiction.
　K. Sutherland, 148:Winter86-105

Alter, R. The Pleasures of Reading in an
　Ideological Age.*
　H. Meynell, 289:Winter89-109
　S. Pinsker, 219(GaR):Winter89-818
　R. Schoolcraft 3d, 400(MLN):Dec89-1228
　566:Spring90-217
Alter, R. & F. Kermode, eds. The Literary
　Guide to the Bible.*
　D.C. Fowler, 401(MLQ):Dec87-378
　S. Helmling, 569(SR):Summer89-462
　R.E. Hosmer, Jr., 403(MLS):Spring89-87
　D.L. Jeffrey, 627(UTQ):Summer90-569
Alter, S. Renuka.*
　J. Mellors, 364:Jun/Jul89-133
Althaus, H. Zwischen alter und neuer besitz-
　ender Klasse.
　W. Asholt, 72:Band226Heft1-210
Althen G. American Ways.
　P.B. Nimmons, 399(MLJ):Autumn89-353
Alther, L. Bedrock.
　T. Cochran, 441:3Jun90-23
　D. Montrose, 617(TLS):17-23Aug90-868
Altick, R.D. Deadly Encounters.
　M. Distad, 635(VPR):Spring89-35
Altick, R.D. Paintings from Books.*
　G.J. Worth, 158:Jun89-76
Altick, R.D. Writers, Readers, and Occasions.*
　639(VQR):Autumn89-120
Altman, R. The Video Connection.
　P.K. Mosele, 207(FR):Feb90-587
Altolaguirre, M. Obras completas, I. (J. Val-
　ondor, od)
　J.M. Naharro-Calderon, 552(REH):Oct89-
　141
Altwegg, J., ed. Die Heidegger Kontroverse.
　P. Trotignon, 542:Oct-Dec89-605
Alvar, C. & A. Gómez Moreno. La poesía lírica
　medieval.*
　J. Weiss, 86(BHS):Oct89-374
Alvar, M., ed. El lenguaje político.
　E. Anglada Arboix, 548:Jul-Dec89-469
Alvar, M. El mundo novelesco de Miguel
　Delibes.*
　B. de la Fuente, 547(RF):Band101Heft
　2/3-385
　L. Hickey, 86(BHS):Jul89-299
Alvarez, R.A., Jr. Familia.
　R. Ocasio, 106:Fall89-284
Alvarez-Altman, G. & F.M. Burelbach, eds.
　Names in Literature.
　C. Millward, 424:Jun89-183
Alvarez Barrientos, J. & A. Cea Gutiérrez,
　eds. Actas das jornadas sobre el teatro
　popular en España.
　C. Stern, 240(HR):Autumn89-493
Alvarez García, L. Poétique du direct télé-
　visuel.
　M. Rector, 567:Vol75No1/2-131
Álvarez Lopera, J. De Cean a Cossío.
　J.M. Cabañas Bravo, 48:Apr-Jun89-232
"Amadís de Gaula." (A. Rosenblat, ed)
　F. Pierce, 86(BHS):Jan89-201
Amann, K. Der Anschluss österreichischer
　Schriftsteller an das Dritte Reich.
　H.F. Pfanner, 221(GQ):Fall89-547
Amanuddin, S. Creativity and Reception.
　N. Iyer, 395(MFS):Winter89-878
Amaral, P.V. - see Sellars, W.
Amberg, L. Kirche, Liturgie und Frömmigkeit
　im Schaffen von N.V. Gogol'.
　R-D. Keil, 688(ZSP):Band49Heft1-173

7

Ambrière, F. Le Siècle des Valmore.*
  M. Danahy, 446(NCFS):Spring–Summer90–
  590
Ambrose, J. Willa Cather.
  C. Petty–Schmitt, 649(WAL):Feb90–374
Amedick, R. Frühkaiserzeitliche Bildhauer-
  stile.
  D. Boschung, 229:Band61Heft3–279
"American Folk Paintings."
  658:Spring89–111
"American Reference Books Annual." (Vol 20)
  (B. Wynar, ed)
  M.L. Goold, 87(BB):Dec89–258
"America's Aging."
  M.C. Comerio, 47:Jul89–37
Ames, A. Five Houses.
  D. Kesler, 45:Sep89–55
Amichai, Y. Selected Poetry of Yehuda Ami-
  chai.* (C. Bloch & S. Mitchell, eds & trans)
  S. O'Brien, 493:Summer89–44
Amidon, S. Splitting the Atom.
  P. Kincaid, 617(TLS):1–7Jun90–585
Amigues, S. – see Theophrastus
Amis, K. Kingsley Amis in Life and Letters.
  (D. Salwak, ed) The Amis Collection.
  P. Kemp, 617(TLS):5–11Oct90–1061
Amis, K. The Folks That Live on the Hill.
  W.H. Pritchard, 441:1Jul90–5
  L. Sage, 617(TLS):30Mar–5Apr90–339
Amis, M. London Fields.*
  J. Mellors, 364:Dec89/Jan90–126
  B. Pesetsky, 441:4Mar90–1
Ammon, U., N. Dittmar & K.J. Mattheier, eds.
  Sociolinguistics/Soziolinguistik. (Vol 1)
  D. Hymes, 355(LSoc):Jun89–257
Ammon, U., K.J. Mattheier & P.H. Nelde – see
  "sociolinguistica"
Amor, A.C. William Holman Hunt.
  E. Claridge, 364:Dec89/Jan90–117
Amorós, A. – see Gala, A.
Amorós, A. & others. Letras Españolas 1976–
  1986.
  L. Hickey, 86(BHS):Oct89–388
  G. Navajas, 240(HR):Autumn89–530
  R.C. Spires, 238:May89–305
Amory, C. The Cat and the Curmudgeon.
  J.E. Butler, 441:9Dec90–25
Amos, A.C. & others. Dictionary of Old Eng-
  lish: C.
  A.S.G. Edwards, 402(MLR):Jul90–679
Amprimoz, A. Bouquet de signes.
  K.W. Meadwell, 102(CanL):Autumn–
  Winter89–157
Amprimoz, A.L. A l'ombre de Rimbaud.*
  L. Forestier, 535(RHL):Jan–Feb89–133
Amprimoz, A.L. Hard Confessions.
  V. Hollinger, 102(CanL):Summer89–177
Amusson, S.D. An Ordered Society.
  P. Divinsky, 529(QQ):Autumn89–765
Anacker, S. – see Vasubandhu
Analis, D.T. Terre d'errance.
  P. Dubrunquez, 450(NRF):Jul–Aug89–188
"Ancient Tales in Modern Japan." (F.H.
  Mayer, trans)
  R.H. Minear, 318(JAOS):Jan–Mar88–146
Ancillotti, A. Elogio del variabile.
  R. Antilla, 350:Sep90–619
Andersen, C. Citizen Jane.
  H. Dudar, 441:10Jun90–20
Andersen, F.E. & J. Weinstock, eds. The Nor-
  dic Mind.
  J.S. Veisland, 563(SS):Autumn89–424

Andersen, F.G. & others, eds. Popular Drama
  in Northern Europe in the Later Middle
  Ages.
  H. Bergner, 72:Band226Heft1–173
Andersen, H., ed. Sandhi Phenomena in the
  Languages of Europe.*
  D.C. Walker, 297(JL):Sep89–539
Andersen, J.P. Agent provocateur.
  H.M. Ordower, 563(SS):Spring/Summer89–
  286
Andersen, R. Arranging Deck Chairs on the
  Titanic.
  D. Shea, 577(SHR):Summer89–267
Anderson, A. Some Native Herbal Remedies.
  A.R. Taylor, 269(IJAL):Jul89–359
Anderson, A.A. – see Lorca, F.G.
Anderson, B. I Think We Should Go Into the
  Jungle.
  F. Adcock, 617(TLS):2–8Feb90–123
Anderson, B. The Wine Atlas of Italy and
  Traveller's Guide to the Vineyards.
  J. Rosselli, 617(TLS):21–27Dec90–1373
Anderson, C., ed. Literary Nonfiction.
  P. Walmsley, 506(PSt):Dec89–285
Anderson, C. Style as Argument.*
  S.P., 295(JML):Fall88/Winter89–222
Anderson, C. – see Jacob, V.
Anderson, D.G., Jr. On Elevating the Com-
  monplace.
  C. Perriam, 86(BHS):Jul89–315
Anderson, D.K., Jr., ed. "Concord in Discord."
  M. Garrett, 541(RES):Nov89–561
  M.L. Kessel, 568(SCN):Spring–Summer89–
  19
  P.S. Spinrad, 130:Summer89–191
Anderson, D.R. Creativity and the Philosophy
  of C.S. Peirce.
  T.L.S. Sprigge, 89(BJA):Winter89–88
Anderson, E. Streetwise.
  T. Jacoby, 441:9Dec90–14
Anderson, E.N. The Food of China.
  E.J. Croll, 617(TLS):7–13Sep90–952
  L.M. Li, 293(JASt):May89–346
Anderson, F.J. A Treasury of Flowers.
  L. Yang, 441:2Dec90–21
Anderson, G. Ancient Fiction.
  M. Laplace, 487:Summer89–179
Anderson, G. Philostratus.*
  L. de Lannoy, 394:Vol42fasc1/2–205
Anderson, J. Ballet and Modern Dance.
  J. Adshead, 289:Summer89–117
Anderson, J. Stories from the Warm
  Zone/Sydney Stories.
  D. Durrant, 364:Jun/Jul89–130
Anderson, J. Taking Shelter.
  T. Glyde, 617(TLS):14–20Sep90–980
  J. Wilcox, 441:11Mar90–12
Anderson, J. Zero Time.
  N. Callendar, 441:18Nov90–41
Anderson, J. & J. Durand, eds. Explorations
  in Dependency Phonology.*
  K. Arnason, 353:Vol27No2–319
Anderson, J.D. The Education of Blacks in
  the South, 1860–1935.
  639(VQR):Spring89–44
Anderson, J.E., ed & trans. Two Literary
  Riddles in the Exeter Book.*
  H. Sauer, 38:Band107Heft3/4–517
Anderson, J.M. & C.J. Ewen. Principles of
  Dependency Phonology.
  K. Arnason, 353:Vol27No2–319
  L. Kálmán, 603:Vol13No2–477

Anderson, L.R. Bennett, Wells, and Conrad.
B.G. Caraher, 637(VS):Spring90-527
G.A. Hudson, 594:Fall89-339
W.J. Scheick, 136:Spring89-63
B. Teets, 177(ELT):Vol32No3-326
639(VQR):Winter89-14
Anderson, M. Cold Comfort.
M. Scates, 502(PrS):Spring89-118
Anderson, M. - see Bachmann, I.
Anderson, M.J. The American Census.
639(VQR):Winter89-10
Anderson, N.F. Woman Against Women in Victorian England.*
N. Auerbach, 620(TSWL):Spring89-131
D. Worzala, 635(VPR):Summer89-83
Anderson, N.G. - see Warren, L.
Anderson, P.M. A Structural Atlas of the English Dialects.
M. Görlach, 685(ZDL):2/1989-204
Anderson, R.B. Dostoevsky.*
R.F. Miller, 104(CASS):Spring-Winter88-496
Anderson, R.J., J.A. Hughes & W.W. Sharrock. Philosophy and the Human Sciences.
L.A.D., 185:Oct89-208
Anderson, R.R., U. Goebel & O. Reichmann, eds. Frühneuhochdeutsches Wörterbuch.* (Vol 1, Pts 1 & 2)
H. Schmidt, 682(ZPSK):Band42Heft2-250
Anderson, S. Sherwood Anderson's Love Letters to Eleanor Copenhaver Anderson. (C.E. Modlin, ed)
G. Johnson, 441:25Feb90-25
Anderson, S. Letters to Bab.* (W.A. Sutton, ed)
42(AR):Fall89-505
Anderson, S., with D. Ewald. Sparky!
M. Lichtenstein, 441:15Apr90-15
Anderson, S.C. Grass and Grimmelshausen.*
H. Joldersma, 564:Nov89-369
Anderson, W. Cecil Collins.*
A. Summerfield, 39:Aug89-139
Anderson, W.S. & M.P. Frederick - see Ovid
Anderson, W.T. - see Wilder, L.I. & R.W. Lane
Andersson, T.M. A Preface to the "Nibelungenlied."*
C.L. Gottzmann, 301(JEGP):Jan90-61
E.R. Haymes, 589:Jan89-111
H. Kratz, 133:Band22Heft3/4-304
H. Mayer, 564:Nov89-344
"Tadao Ando: The Yale Studio & Current Works."
D. London, 45:Oct89-71
Andocides. Andokides, "On the Mysteries." (D.M. MacDowell, ed)
M. Nouhaud, 555:Vol62Fasc2-350
de Andrade, E. Memory of Another River.
J. Meek, 456(NDQ):Winter89-227
Andrae, O. Dreeundartig Mullsbülten.
K. Kehr, 685(ZDL):3/1989-392
André, S. Gobineau et la féminité.
M. Biddiss, 208(FS):Oct89-477
Andreae, B. Plimius und der Laokoon.
R.R.R. Smith, 313:Vol79-213
Andreae, B. & B. Conticello. Skylla und Charybdis.
N. Hannestad, 229:Band61Heft7-655
Andreau, J. La vie financière dans le monde romain.
A. Bürge, 229:Band61Heft4-318
A.M. Burnett, 123:Vol39No2-323
D. Nightingale, 313:Vol79-176

Andreesen, W. & F. Heidtmann. Wie finde ich slawistische Literatur.
M. Stuart, 104(CASS):Spring-Winter88-477
Andreoli-de-Villers, J-P. Le Premier manifeste du futurisme. (F.T. Marinetti, ed)
K.W. Meadwell, 102(CanL):Autumn-Winter89-157
Andreotti, G. Gli USA visti da vicino.
J.L. Harper, 617(TLS):25-31May90-546
Andrès, B.J. La Trouble-Fête.
D. Essar, 102(CanL):Spring89-191
Andreski, S. Syphilis, Puritanism and Witch Hunts.
M. Holub, 617(TLS):5-11Oct90-1051
Andrew, C. & O. Gordievsky. KGB.
J. Bamford, 441:18Nov90-9
A. Knight, 617(TLS):7-13Dec90-1309
Andrew, J. Women in Russian Literature, 1780-1863.
S. Sandler, 402(MLR):Jan90-270
M.F. Zirin, 550(RusR):Oct89-422
639(VQR):Winter89-15
Andrews, E. The Poetry of Seamus Heaney.*
T.F. Merrill, 305(JIL):Sep89-59
639(VQR):Spring89-64
Andrews, J.F., ed. William Shakespeare.*
A.F. Kinney, 250(HLQ):Spring89-310
Andrews, K. & J. Jacobs. Punishing the Poor.
F. Cairncross, 617(TLS):9-15Mar90-251
Andrews, M. The Search for the Picturesque.*
609(VQR):Autumn89-138
Andrews, W. The Surrealist Parade.
R. Durgin, 441:1Jul90-8
442(NY):1Oct90-111
Andrews, W.G. Poetry's Voice, Society's Song.
J.S. Meisami, 318(JAOS):Jan-Mar88-170
Andrews, W.L. To Tell a Free Story.*
J. Sekora, 173(ECS):Fall89-107
Andrews, W.T., ed. Sisters of the Spirit.
M. Fabre, 189(EA):Apr-Jun89-234
Andreyev, C. Vlasov and the Russian Liberation Movement.*
A. Dallin, 104(CASS):Spring89-88
Andreyev, L. Photographs by a Russian Writer. (British title: Leonid Andreyev: Photographs.)
C.R. Pierpont, 442(NY):17Dec90-124
A. Ross, 364:Aug/Sep89-137
Andreyev, L. Visions.* (O.A. Carlisle, ed)
G. Woodcock, 569(SR):Spring89-308
Andriessen, L. & E. Schönberger. The Apollonian Clockwork.
P. Griffiths, 617(TLS):30Mar-5Apr90-353
Andriopoulos, D.Z. The Concept of Causality in Presocratic Philosophy.
P. Mitsis, 242:Vol10No4-490
Andrle, V. Workers in Stalin's Russia.
H. Kuromiya, 550(RusR):Jul89-351
A. McAuley, 575(SEER):Oct89-642
Andronov, M.S. & B.P. Mallik, with S. Banerjee, eds. Linguistics - A Soviet Approach.
M. Gatzlaff, 682(ZPSK):Band42Heft6-864
Anesko, M. "Friction with the Market."*
A.W., 70:Oct89-160
Ang, I. Watching Dallas.
T. Goldie, 102(CanL):Winter88-128
Ang, L. - see under Li Ang
Angelini, A., ed. Il Nuovo Corriere (1945-1956).
R. Pickering-Iazzi, 276:Winter89-451

Angelomatis–Tsougarakis, H. The Eve of the Greek Revival.
C.M. Woodhouse, 617(TLS):2–8Nov90–1188
Angelou, A.D. – see Nicholas of Methone
Angels Santa i Banyeres, M., ed. Stendhal.*
D–H. Pageaux, 535(RHL):Nov–Dec89–1060
Angermeyer, J. My Father's Island.
C. Moorehead, 617(TLS):24–30Aug90–905
Angier, C. Jean Rhys.*
H. Mantel, 617(TLS):23–29Nov90–1257
Angioni, G. & A. Sanna, eds. Sardegna.
S. Gruber, 576:Dec89–404
"The Anglo–Saxon Chronicle."* (Vol 3) (J.M. Bately, ed)
M. Griffith, 382(MAE):1989/1–142
L. Kornexl, 72:Band226Heft1–142
D.G. Scragg, 38:Band107Heft1/2–146
Anikst, M., ed. Soviet Commercial Design of the Twenties. (C. Cooke, ed)
V. Margolin, 574(SEEJ):Summer89–318
dos Anjos, C. Diary of a Civil Servant.
K.H. Brower, 238:May89–317
Ankarloo, B. & G. Henningsen, eds. Early Modern European Witchcraft.
L. Martines, 617(TLS):7–13Dec90–1328
"Ankündigung eines Symposions zum Thema 'Klassik im europäischen Vergleich'."
52:Band24Heft1–106
"Annales Benjamin Constant, 6."
C.P. Courtney, 208(FS):Jan89–93
"Annales Benjamin Constant, 7."
C.P. Courtney, 208(FS):Jan89–93
M. Paganini, 446(NCFS):Fall–Winter89/90–236
"Annales Benjamin Constant 8–9." (E. Hofmann & A–L. Delacrétaz, eds)
D. Wood, 402(MLR):Oct90–967
Annan, N. Our Age.
P. Addison, 617(TLS):2–8Nov90–1169
Annas, J. – see "Oxford Studies in Ancient Philosophy"
Annas, J. & J. Barnes. The Modes of Scepticism.*
A. Bühler, 53(AGP):Band71Heft1–81
Annas, J. & R. Grimm – see "Oxford Studies in Ancient Philosophy"
Annas, P.J. A Disturbance in Mirrors.
S. Lurie, 27(AL):Oct89–492
Saint Anselm. A New Interpretative Translation of St. Anselm's "Monologion" and "Proslogion." (J. Hopkins, ed & trans)
T.A. Losoncy, 589:Jul89–716
Anselment, R.A. Loyalist Resolve.
V. Kahn, 551(RenQ):Autumn89–598
Anselmi, S. & G. Volpe, eds. Marche.
S. Gruber, 576:Dec89–403
Ansermet, E. Les Fondements de la Musique dans la Conscience Humaine.* (rev by J–C. Piguet)
M. Musgrave, 89(BJA):Winter89–86
Antalovsky, T. Der russische Frauenroman (1890–1917).
S. McLaughlin, 575(SEER):Apr89–276
Anthonioz, M., ed. L'album "Verve."*
L.E. Nesbitt, 55:Feb89–91
Antin, P. Himalayan Odyssey.
C. Thubron, 441:2Dec90–20
Antle, M. Théâtre et Poésie surréalistes.*
J.G. Miller, 210(FrF):Sep89–375
Antoine, G. Paul Claudel ou l'enfer du génie.
P. Larthomas, 209(FM):Oct89–258

Antokoletz, E. Béla Bartók.
P.A. Autexier, 537:Vol75No1–119
M. Gillies, 410(M&L):Aug89–428
Antolini, B.M. & A. Bini. Editori e librai musicali a Roma nella prima metà dell'ottocento.
H. Lenneberg, 309:Vol9No4–303
Antonioli, M., G. Ginex & A. Panaccione, eds. Per cent'anni della festa del lavoro.
E. Hobsbawm, 358:Jun90–10
Antor, H. The Bloomsbury Group.
R. Omasreiter, 38:Band107Heft1/2–252
Anttila, R. Historical and Comparative Linguistics. (2nd ed)
V. Bubeník, 159:Vol6No1–123
C. van Kerckvoorde, 350:Sep90–620
Antunes, A.L. – see Lobo Antunes, A.
Anwar, R. The Tragedy of Afghanistan.
639(VQR):Spring89–61
Anyi, W. – see under Wang Anyi
Anzaldúa, G. Borderlands/La Frontera.
L. Nelson, 618:Spring89–90
A. Ramírez, 36:Fall–Winter89–185
Aoki, H. & D.E. Walker, Jr. Nez Perce Oral Narratives.
D. Hymes, 350:Dec90–858
Aoki, M. Information, Incentives, and Bargaining in the Japanese Economy.
M. Smitka, 293(JASt):Nov89–849
Apfel, E. Die Lehre vom Organum, Diskant, Kontrapunkt und von der Komposition bis zum 1480.
A. Traub, 416:Band4Heft2–178
Apollinaire, G. Correspondance avec son frère et sa mère. (G. Boudar & M. Décaudin, eds)
M. Davies, 208(FS):Apr89–230
Apollonius. Apollonio Rodio, "Le Argonautiche."* (G. Paduano, trans; G. Paduano & M. Fusillo, eds)
D.M. Schenkeveld, 394:Vol42fasc1/2–198
Appel, A. & P. Muysken. Language Contact and Bilingualism.*
Y. Bader, 257(IRAL):May89–164
P. Mühlhäusler, 361:Nov89–247
S. Romaine, 353:Vol27No3–579
Appelfeld, A. For Every Sin.*
A. Balaban, 390:Aug/Sep89–57
Appelfeld, A. The Healer.
B. Cheyette, 617(TLS):2–8Nov90–1182
L. Segal, 441:23Sep90–11
Appelfeld, A. The Immortal Bartfuss.*
W. Phillips, 473(PR):Vol56No1–143
Appia, A. Essays, Scenarios, and Designs. (R.C. Beacham, ed)
P. Carnegy, 617(TLS):14–20Dec90–1352
Appian. Appian von Alexandria: "Römische Geschichte." (Pt 1) (O. Veh, trans; K. Brodersen, ed)
C.B.R. Pelling, 123:Vol39No2–202
Appignanesi, L. & S. Maitland, eds. The Rushdie File.
E. Mortimer, 441:22Jul90–3
Applegate, S. Skookum.
M. Strelow, 448:Vol27No2–145
G. Venn, 649(WAL):May89–85
639(VQR):Autumn89–128
Appleyard, B. The Pleasures of Peace.*
H. Lomas, 364:Aug/Sep89–119
M. Pawley, 46:Oct89–12
Aptekar, L. Street Children of Cali.
C. Moorehead, 617(TLS):16–22Mar90–297

Apter, T. Altered Loves.
  C. Tavris, 441:1Jul90-9
Apter-Gabriel, R., ed. Tradition and Revolution.
  C. Lodder, 90:Mar89-231
Aquila, R. That Old Time Rock and Roll.
  B.L. Cooper, 498:Winter89-89
Aquila, R.E. Matter in Mind.
  D.P. Dryer, 103:Mar90-91
  P. Kitcher, 543:Jun90-851
Aquilon, P., J. Chupeau & F. Weil, eds.
  L'Intelligence du passé.
  D. Bourel, 531:Jul-Dec89-551
  P. Dandrey, 475:Vol16No31-594
Aquilon, P., H-J. Martin & F.D. Desrousilles,
  eds. Le Livre dans l'Europe de la Renaissance.
  E.L. Eisenstein, 551(RenQ):Autumn89-540
Aquin, H. Writing Quebec. (A. Purdy, ed)
  J.M. Paterson, 529(QQ):Autumn89-749
Arabena Williams, H. Ensayos de exégesis
  literaria.
  C.M. Boyle, 86(BHS):Jan89-100
Arac, J. Critical Genealogies.*
  P.B. Armstrong, 290(JAAC):Winter89-83
  H. Bertens, 402(MLR):Jan90-137
Arac, J., ed. Postmodernism and Politics.*
  M. Conroy, 577(SHR):Winter89-71
Arac, J., W. Godzich & W. Martin, eds. The
  Yale Critics.
  S. Sim, 148:Winter86-114
Aragonés, J.E. Veinte años del teatro
  español (1960-1980).
  D. Gagen, 86(BHS):Jul89-300
  H.R.M., 295(JML):Fall88/Winter89-192
Arapura, J.G. Gnosis and the Question of
  Thought in Vedānta.
  M. Comans, 259(IIJ):Oct89-313
  A. Unterman, 323:May89-191
Arasaratnam, S. Merchants, Companies, and
  Commerce on the Coromandel Coast, 1650-
  1740.
  A. Das Gupta, 293(JASt):May89-415
Arasse, D. The Guillotine and the Terror.
  (French title: La Guillotine et l'imaginaire
  de la Terreur.)
  J.R. Censer, 322(JHI):Oct-Dec89-652
  G. Lewis, 617(TLS):26Jan-1Feb90-93
Arbeitman, Y.L., ed. FUCUS.
  B.M. Sietsema, 350:Jun90-409
Arbib, M.A. & M.B. Hesse. The Construction of
  Reality.
  E. Baer, 567:Vol73No1/2-137
Arce, J. Funus imperatorum.
  L. Schumacher, 229:Band61Heft6-523
Archer, R. The Pervasive Image.*
  L. Badia, 545(RPh):Aug89-220
Archi, A., ed. The Circulation of Goods in
  Non-Palatial Context in the Ancient Near
  East.
  N. Yoffee, 318(JAOS):Oct-Dec88-660
Arcipreste de Hita – see under Ruiz, J.
Ardagh, J. Germany and the Germans.*
  A. Williams, 402(MLR):Oct90-1036
Ardagh, J. Writers' France.
  T. Swick, 441:10Jun90-49
Arden, H.M. The Romance of the Rose.*
  L.C. Brook, 208(FS):Jul89-318
Ardener, E. The Voice of Prophecy and Other
  Essays. (M. Chapman, ed)
  R. Just, 617(TLS):7-13Sep90-951

Ardizzone, M.L. Ezra Pound e la scienza.
  G. Singh, 4:Summer89-24
Ardouin, P. Devises et emblèmes d'amour
  dans la "Délie" de Maurice Scève.
  F. Lecercle, 535(RHL):Jul-Aug89-704
Arduini, M.L. Non fabula sed res.
  B. Newman, 589:Jan89-113
Arellano, I. Jocinto Alonso Maluenda y su
  poesía jocosa.
  L.S. Lerner, 240(HR):Autumn89-521
Arellano, I. Poesía satirico burlesca de Que-
  vedo.
  A.M. Snell, 400(MLN):Mar89-501
Arenal, E. & S. Schlau. Untold Sisters.
  A. Weber, 304(JHP):Winter90-190
Arend, E. "Bibliothèque" – Geistiger Raum
  eines Jahrhunderts.
  G. Breuer, 72:Band226Heft1-204
Arends, J. Syntactic Developments in Sranan.
  J.W. de Vries, 204(FdL):Sep89-239
Arends, J.F.M. Die Einheit der Polis.
  R.F. Stalley, 123:Vol39No2-254
Arendt, H. La tradition cachée.
  D. Lories, 192(EP):Jan-Mar89-91
Arens, A. Das Phänomen Simenon.
  U. Schulz-Buschhaus, 547(RF):Band101
  Heft1-136
Arens, A. Untersuchungen zu Jean Bodels
  Mirakel "Le Jeu de Saint Nicolas."
  T.D. Hemming, 208(FS):Jul89-317
Arentzen, J. & U. Ruberg, eds. Die Ritteridee
  in der deutschen Literatur des Mittelalters.
  A. Classen, 221(GQ):Spring89-252
Aretino, P. The Marescalco. (L.G. Ebreuohl &
  J.D. Campbell, trans)
  D. Shemek, 276:Spring89-50
Argersinger, J.E. Toward a New Deal in Bal-
  timore.
  G. Burbank, 106:Fall89-237
de Arguijo, J. Obra completa de don Juan de
  Arguijo (1567-1622). (S.B. Vranich, ed)
  A. Carreño, 240(HR):Winter89-92
Argyros, A. Crimes of Narration.
  J.T. Booker, 207(FR):Oct89-174
Aria, B. Misha.
  R. Johnson, 151:Nov89-92
"Ariadne's Thread."* (S. Bassnett & P. Ku-
  hiwczak, trans)
  D. O'Driscoll, 493:Summer89-47
Arias, A. After the Bombs.
  A. Whitehouse, 441:25Nov90-18
Arias, R., ed. Tres églogas sacramentales
  inéditas.
  C.P. Thompson, 402(MLR):Apr90-473
Aricò, D. Il Tesauro in Europa.
  J. Tribby, 400(MLN):Dec89-1213
Ariel, Y. K'ung-ts'ung-tzu.
  L. Kohn, 293(JASt):Nov89-815
Aristophanes. Aristophanes' "Lysistrata."
  (J. Henderson, trans)
  J.C. Gilbert, 124:Jan-Feb90-253
Aristophanes. As mulheres no Parlamento.
  (M. de Fátima Sousa e Silva, ed & trans)
  R.G. Ussher, 123:Vol39No2-384
Aristophanes. Lysistrata.* (J. Henderson,
  ed)
  R.G. Ussher, 24:Fall89-502
Aristophanes of Byzantium. Aristophanis
  Byzantii Fragmenta.* (W.J. Slater, ed)
  A.R. Dyck, 122:Jul89-256

Aristotle. Aristotle's "Poetics" I, with the "Tractatus Coislinianus," a Hypothetical Reconstruction of "Poetics" II, the Fragments of the "On Poets." (R. Janko, ed & trans)
  W.G. Arnott, 123:Vol39No2-195
Aristotle. L'Homme de génie et la mélancolie. (C. Lazam, trans)
  P. Pachet, 450(NRF):Jan89-88
Aristotle. A New Aristotle Reader.* (J.L. Ackrill, ed)
  D.W. Hamlyn, 483:Apr89-261
Aristotle. The Poetics of Aristotle. (S. Halliwell, ed & trans)
  L. Golden, 124:Sep-Oct89-66
van Arkel, A. & others. Möðruvallabók.
  H. Fix, 684(ZDA):Band118Heft4-156
Armani, A.S. Maurice Scève nelle "Vies des poëtes françois" di Guillaume Colletet.
  F. Lecercle, 475:Vol16No30-263
  G.H. Tucker, 208(FS):Jul89-320
Armani, E.P. - see under Parma Armani, E.
de Armas, F.A. The Return of Astraea.*
  D.W. Bleznick, 149(CLS):Vol26No1-74
  C. Bradford, 568(SCN):Fall-Winter89-50
Armistead, S.G. & J.H. Silverman. Folk Literature of the Sephardic Jews.* (Vol 2, Pt 1)
  R. Haboucha, 292(JAF):Apr-Jun89-216
Armistead, S.G. & J.H. Silverman. Judeo-Spanish Ballads from Oral Tradition. (Vol 1)
  J.H. Mauleón-Berlowitz, 545(RPh):Nov89-343
Armitage, S. Human Geography.
  I. McMillan, 493:Winter89/90-65
Armitage, S. The Walking Horses.
  I. McMillan, 493:Winter89/90-65
Armitage, S. Zoom!
  L. Norfolk, 617(TLS):5-11Jan90-19
Armstrong, A. Farmworkers in England and Wales.
  P. Perry, 637(VS):Summer90-672
Armstrong, A.H. - see "Plotinus"
Armstrong, D.M. A Combinatorial Theory of Possibility.
  T. Williamson, 617(TLS):16-22Nov90-1241
Armstrong, D.M. Universals.
  R. Teichmann, 103:Jul90-261
Armstrong, E. Robert Estienne, Royal Printer.
  M. Rothstein, 345(KRQ):Feb89-107
Armstrong, J.C.W. Champlain.*
  A. Purdy, 102(CanL):Autumn-Winter89-153
Armstrong, N. Desire and Domestic Fiction.*
  J. Rothschild, 577(SHR):Summer89-296
  J.G. Turner, 173(ECS):Fall89-99
  P. Yaeger, 454:Winter90-203
Armstrong, N. & L. Tennenhouse, eds. The Ideology of Conduct.*
  R.B.D., 295(JML):Fall88/Winter89-182
Arnberg, L. Raising Children Bilingually.
  O. Garcia, 399(MLJ):Summer89-209
Arndt, M. & M. Walter - see "Jahrbuch für Opernforschung"
Arnold, E. Marilyn Monroe.
  P. Rist, 106:Summer89-111
Arnold, G. One Woman's War.
  G. Drolet, 102(CanL):Summer89-166
Arnold, H.L., ed. Peter Rühmkorf.
  W. Hoffmeister, 221(GQ):Fall89-561

Arnold, J. Queen Elizabeth's Wardrobe Unlocked.
  L. von Wilckens, 683:Band52Heft3-431
Arnold, M. - see March, J.
Arnold, P.E. Making the Managerial Presidency.
  J. Braeman, 106:Summer89-41
Arnold, W., W. Dittrich & B. Zeller, eds. Die Erforschung der Buch- und Bibliotheksgeschichte in Deutschland, Paul Raabe zum 60. Geburtstag gewidmet.
  D. Paisey, 354:Mar89-67
Arnold-Forster, F. Florence Arnold-Forster's Irish Journal. (T.W. Moody & R.A.J. Hawkins, with M. Moody, eds)
  C. Ó Gráda, 272(IUR):Spring89-184
Arntzen, H., ed. Komödiensprache.
  W.E. Yates, 301(JEGP):Oct89-602
Aron, P., ed. Charles Plisnier.
  J. Decock, 207(FR):Oct89-173
Aron, R. History, Truth, Liberty.* (F. Draus, ed)
  W.H. Dray, 449:Apr89-277
Aronne-Amestoy, L. Utopía, paraíso e historia.
  S. Boldy, 86(BHS):Jan89-108
Aronowitz, S. Science as Power.*
  S. Fuller, 543:Sep89-145
  A. Lopes, 147:Vol6No2-85
Aronsen, L. & M. Kitchen. The Origins of the Cold War in Comparative Perspective.
  J. Richter, 550(RusR):Jul89-342
Aronson, G. Israel, Palestinians and the Intifada.
  A. Hertzberg, 453(NYRB):25Oct90-41
  I. Rabinovich, 617(TLS):21-27Sep90-996
Aronson, H.I. Georgian.
  S.P. Cowe, 318(JAOS):Apr-Jun88-322
Aronson, N. Madame de Rambouillet ou la magicienne de la chambre bleue.
  M-O. Sweetser, 475:Vol16No31-577
Aronson, R. Sartre's Second Critique.*
  D.B., 295(JML):Fall88/Winter89-403
  H. Gordon, 323:May89-183
Aronson, R. "Stay Out of Politics."
  D. Papineau, 617(TLS):29Jun-5Jul90-686
Arpolenko, G.P. & others. Slovar' staroslavjanskogo jazyka vostočnoslavjanskoj redakcii XI-XIIIvv. Prospekt.
  G. Hüttl-Folter, 559:Vol13No3-325
Arrabal, F. The Tower Struck by Lightning.
  639(VQR):Winter89-20
Arrabal, F. - see under Adamov, A.
Arrathoon, L.A., ed & trans. The Lady of Vergi.
  N.V. Durling, 589:Apr89-381
de Arredondo, G. Vida rimada de Fernán González. (M. Vaquero, ed)
  B. Powell, 402(MLR):Jan90-223
Arrigoni, O.O. Robert Musil: "Die Versuchung der stillen Veronika."
  J. Hösle, 52:Band24Heft2-224
Arrington, R.L. Rationalism, Realism, and Relativism.
  O.A. Johnson, 103:Jun90-217
  R. Paden, 543:Jun90-852
Arrowsmith, J. The Reformation.
  M.L. Kessel, 568(SCN):Spring-Summer89-19
"Art et mythologie: Figures tshokwe."
  D.J. Crowley, 2(AfrA):May89-23
"The Art of Paolo Veronese, 1528-1588."
  H. Coutts, 380:Autumn89-229

Arter, D. The Nordic Parliaments.
  E.S. Einhorn, 563(SS):Winter89-106
Arthur, R.G. Medieval Sign Theory and "Sir
  Gawain and the Green Knight."*
  R.A. Peck, 589:Jul89-647
  S.H.A. Shepherd, 447(N&Q):Dec89-494
  E. Wilson, 541(RES):May89-247
Arumaa, P. Urslavische Grammatik. (Vol 3)
  H. Birnbaum, 279:Vol37-179
Arvastson, G. Maskinmänniskan.
  A. Gustavsson, 64(Arv):Vol44-201
Arya, P.U. Yoga-sūtras of Patañjali with the
  Exposition of Vyāsa. (Vol 1)
  J.W. de Jong, 259(IIJ):Jul89-248
Asals, F. Flannery O'Connor.
  F. Crews, 453(NYRB):26Apr90-49
Asante, M.K. The Afrocentric Idea.
  M. Dixon, 441:7Jan90-35
Ascher, A. The Revolution of 1905.*
  S.J. Seregny, 550(RusR):Apr89-192
Ascher, A., ed. Studying Russian and Soviet
  History.
  L. Hughes, 575(SEER):Oct89-641
Ascoli, A.R. Ariosto's Bitter Harmony.*
  J.E. Everson, 278(IS):Vol44-164
  C.S. Lonergan, 402(MLR):Jan90-208
  P.D. Wiggins, 276:Winter89-444
Ash, S.V. Middle Tennessee Society Trans-
  formed, 1860-1870.
  639(VQR):Spring89-45
Ash, T.G. The Magic Lantern.
  J.T. Gross, 441:22Jul90-29
Ash, T.G. The Uses of Adversity.
  G.F. Kennan, 460(NYRB):1Mar90-8
  G.M. Tamás, 617(TLS):10-16Aug90-843
Ash, T.G. We the People.
  G.M. Tamás, 617(TLS):10-16Aug90-843
Ashbee, A., ed. Records of English Court
  Music.* (Vol 2)
  I. Cholij, 410(M&L):Feb89-95
Ashbery, J. April Galleons.*
  D. McDuff, 565:Spring89-76
  S. Romer, 97(CQ):Vol18No3-310
  K.A. Weisman, 529(QQ):Spring89-156
Ashbery, J., ed. The Best American Poetry
  1988.*
  639(VQR):Spring89-65
Ashbery, J. Reported Sightings. (D. Bergman,
  ed)
  R. Wollheim, 617(TLS):25-31May90-553
Ashbery, J. 3 Plays.
  S. Romer, 97(CQ):Vol18No3-310
Ashcraft, R. Revolutionary Politics and
  Locke's "Two Treatises of Government."*
  G.J. Schochet, 322(JHI):Jul-Sep89-491
Asher-Greve, J.M. Frauen in altsumerischer
  Zeit.
  T. Meltzer, 318(JAOS):Jan-Mar88-158
Asheri, D. - see Herodotus
Ashley, M. Charles I and Oliver Cromwell.
  W.P. Williams, 568(SCN):Spring-
  Summer89-20
Ashliman, D.L. A Guide to Folktales in the
  English Language Based on the Aarne-
  Thompson Classification System.*
  E.W. Baughman, 292(JAF):Jan-Mar89-102
Ashton, D. Fragonard in the Universe of
  Painting.*
  E. Shanes, 39:Mar89-219
Ashton, S.R. In Search of Détente.
  A. Milward, 617(TLS):26Jan-1Feb90-81
Ashworth, E.J. - see Bricot, T.

Asimov, I. & R. Silverberg. Nightfall.
  G. Jonas, 441:9Dec90-32
Aske, M. Keats and Hellenism.
  A. Bewell, 591(SIR):Summer89-310
  J. Stillinger, 131(CL):Spring89-198
Askedal, J.O., C. Fabricius-Hansen & K.E.
  Schöndorf, eds. Gedenkschrift für Ingerid
  Dal.
  H. Tiefenbach, 685(ZDL):2/1989-186
Askew, P. Caravaggio's "Death of the Virgin."
  C. Dempsey, 617(TLS):7-13Dec90-1322
Aslan, O. Roger Blin and Twentieth Century
  Playwrights.
  D. Bradby, 402(MLR):Jul90-750
  S.E. Gontarski, 397(MD):Dec89-593
Aslet, C. The American Country House.
  M. Filler, 617(TLS):12-18Oct90-1091
  W. Rybczynski, 453(NYRB):20Dec90-24
Aspden, B. Blind Man's Meal.
  S. Pugh, 493:Summer89-60
"Aspects of Language: Studies in Honour of
  Mario Alinei."
  B. García-Hernández, 548:Jul-Dec89-467
Aspetsberger, F. Der Historismus und seine
  Folgen.
  P. Görlich, 654(WB):7/1989-1226
Assad, M.L. La Fiction et la mort dans
  l'oeuvre de Stéphane Mallarmé.*
  D.M. Betz, 207(FR):Oct89-168
  N.M. Huckle, 446(NCFS):Fall-
  Winter89/90-268
Assefa, H. & P. Wahrhaftig. The Move Crisis
  in Philadelphia.
  B. Dantos, 441:09Apr90-09
Assouline, P. An Artful Life.
  H. Kramer, 441:2Sep90-8
Assoun, P-L. Freud et Wittgenstein.
  J-P. Cometti, 540(RIPh):Vol43fasc2-311
  P. Engel, 542:Oct-Dec89-621
Astafjew, V. Der traurige Detektiv.
  A. Hiersche, 654(WB):3/1989-485
Astin, A.E. & others, eds. The Cambridge
  Ancient History. (2nd ed) (Vol 8)
  J.A. North, 617(TLS):15-21Jun90-649
Astley, N. Darwin Survivor.*
  J. May, 493:Autumn89-51
Astley, N., ed. Poetry with an Edge.*
  M. Holland, 493:Spring89-59
Astley, T. Hunting the Wild Pineapple.
  H. Wolitzer, 441:23Dec90-6
Astley, T. Reaching Tin River.
  U. Perrin, 441:22Apr90-13
Aston, M. England's Iconoclasts.* (Vol 1)
  N. Llewellyn, 90:Sep89-653
Aswell, E.C. & E. Nowell. In the Shadow of
  the Giant: Thomas Wolfe.* (M.A. Doll and C.
  Stites, eds)
  L. Field, 395(MFS):Summer89-287
Atasoy, N. & J. Raby. Iznik. (Y. Petsopoulos,
  ed)
  V. Porter, 617(TLS):30Mar-5Apr90-352
Atchity, K., R. Hogart & D. Price, eds. Critical
  Essays on Homer.
  J.D. Smart, 123:Vol39No1-1
Athanassoglou-Kallmyer, N. French Images
  from the Greek War of Independence 1821-
  1830.
  E. Shanes, 39:Dec89-435
Atholl, D. & M. Cherkinian. That Girl and
  Phil.
  M. Corey, 441:23Dec90-13
Atkin, M. The Subtlest Battle.
  F. Halliday, 617(TLS):22-28Jun90-661

Atkins, B.T. & others – see "Collins–Robert French–English, English–French Dictionary/Robert–Collins dictionnaire français-anglais, anglais–français"
Atkins, G.D. Quests of Difference.*
  H. Erskine–Hill, 566:Autumn89–55
Atkins, G.D. & L. Morrow, eds. Contemporary Literary Theory.
  J.R. Bennett, 599:Spring90–126
  B. Robbins, 395(MFS):Winter89–856
  L. Sage, 617(TLS):18–24May90–523
Atkins, J. Sex in Literature. (Vol 4)
  P–G. Boucé, 566:Spring90–218
Atkinson, A. Camden.
  F.B. Smith, 617(TLS):9–15Mar90–261
Atkinson, M., D. Kilby & I. Roca. Foundations of General Linguistics. (2nd ed)
  J.L. Malone, 350:Sep90–573
Atlan, H. A tort et à raison.
  M. Espinoza, 160:Jan89–218
Atlas, A.W. Music at the Aragonese Court of Naples.
  T. Carter, 278(IS):Vol43–147
"An Atlas of Venice." (E. Salzano, ed)
  D.J.R. Bruckner, 441:23Sep90–20
Attal, J–P. Grammaire et usage de l'anglais.
  J.D. Gallagher, 189(EA):Oct–Dec89–456
  G. Price, 402(MLR):Jan90–137
Attali, J. Noise.
  J. Erickson, 615(TJ):Mar89–118
  R.M. Radano, 187:Winter89–161
Attallah, N. Singular Encounters.
  A. Foster, 617(TLS):9–15Nov90–1204
Attebery, L.W., ed. Idaho Folklife.
  T. Carter, 292(JAF):Apr–Jun89–245
Atterbury, P., ed. The Parian Phenomenon.
  R. Reilly, 324:Jul90–568
Attfield, R. A Theory of Value and Obligation.*
  L.E. Johnson, 63:Mar89–111
"Atti del VI Congresso internazionale di studi sulla Sicilia antica." (Vol 1)
  P. Flobert, 555:Vol62Fasc1–191
Attridge, D. Peculiar Language.*
  C. Baldick, 301(JEGP):Oct89–531
  L. Milesi, 395(MFS):Summer89–323
Attridge, D., G. Bennington & R. Young, eds. Post-Structuralism and the Question of History.*
  S. Moulthrop, 677(YES):Vol20–221
Attridge, D. & D. Ferrer, eds. Post-Structuralist Joyce.*
  U. Schneider, 38:Band107Heft1/2–253
Attuel, J. L'affirmation de l'individu dans la société du début du XIXe siècle.
  V.D.L., 605(SC):15Oct89–79
Atwan, R. & V. Vinokurov, eds. Openings.
  B.W. Bloch, 441:22Jul90–21
Atwood, M. Cat's Eye.*
  G. Krist, 249(HudR):Winter89–664
  C. Overall, 529(QQ):Summer89–478
  42(AR):Summer89–374
Atwood, M. The Handmaid's Tale.
  P. Lewis, 565:Winter88/89–77
Atwood, M. Interlunar.*
  S. Pugh, 493:Autumn89–60
Atwood, W.G. Fryderyk Chopin.*
  J. Methuen–Campbell, 415:Jan89–27
"Au Royaume du Signe."
  M. Adams, 2(AfrA):Feb89–19
Aubenque, P., ed. Études sur Parménide.
  G. Kerferd, 520:Vol34No2–227
  H. Schmitz, 229:Band61Heft3–193

Aubert, J., ed. Joyce avec Lacan.*
  S.B., 295(JML):Fall88/Winter89–357
Aubrac, L. – see Tuquoi, J–P.
Aubrey, P. Mr. Secretary Thurloe.
  J. Miller, 617(TLS):14–20Dec90–1356
Auchard, J. Silence in Henry James.*
  S. Nalbantian, 284:Winter89–74
Auchincloss, L. Fellow Passengers.*
  B. Morton, 617(TLS):24–30Aug90–902
Auchincloss, L., ed. The Hone & Strong Diaries of Old Manhattan.
  P–L. Adams, 61:Jan90–100
  442(NY):5Mar90–107
Auchincloss, L. The Lady of Situations.
  L.G. Sexton, 441:8Jul90–11
Auchincloss, L. The Vanderbilt Era.*
  639(VQR):Autumn89–138
Audard, C., J–P. Dupuy & R. Sève, eds. Individu et justice social.
  J. Pestieau, 154:Vol28No3–473
Auden, W.H. & C. Isherwood. Plays and Other Dramatic Writings by W.H. Auden 1928–1938.* (E. Mendelson, ed)
  E. Callan, 130:Fall89–284
  L. McDiarmid, 676(YR):Autumn89–136
  J. Whitehead, 184(EIC):Jul89–263
Audi, R. & W.J. Wainwright, eds. Rationality, Religious Belief, and Moral Commitment.
  W.H. Austin, 449:Jun89–383
Audretsch, J. & K. Mainzer, eds. Philosophie und Physik der Raum–Zeit.
  M. Stöckler, 679:Band20Heft2–373
"Audubon's Birds of America." (rev)
  G. Plimpton, 441:2Dec90–45
von Aue, H. – see under Hartmann von Aue
Auel, J.M. The Plains of Passage.
  D.M. Delince, 441:18Nov90–29
Auer, P. & A. di Luzio, eds. Variation and Convergence.
  C. Silva–Corvalan, 350:Sep90–621
Auerbach, N. Ellen Terry.*
  S. Watt, 637(VS):Autumn89–206
Auger, M–L. La Collection de Bourgogne (MSS 1–74) à la Bibliothèque Nationale.
  C.B. Bouchard, 589:Jul89–650
Saint Augustine. Oeuvres de Saint Augustin.* (Vol 4, Pt 1) (J. Doignon, ed & trans)
  G.J.M. Bartelink, 394:Vol42fasc1/2–230
Saint Augustine. Tractates on the Gospel of John 1–10. (J.W. Rettig, trans)
  A.M. Devine, 124:Jul–Aug90–539
Saint Augustine. La vie heureuse.* (J. Doignon, ed & trans)
  J–C. Fredouille, 555:Vol62Fasc1–167
Auld, L.E. The Lyric Art of Pierre Perrin, Founder of French Opera.
  J.R. Anthony, 317:Summer89–410
Aullón de Haro, P. Los géneros ensayísticos en el siglo XX.
  B. Jordan, 86(BHS):Oct89–384
von Aulock, H. Münzen und Städte Phrygiens.
  H–D. Schultz, 229:Band61Heft1–37
Ault, D. Narrative Unbound.
  P. Mann, 88:Fall89–80
Aumont, J. Montage Eisenstein.*
  T.C., 295(JML):Fall88/Winter89–266
  V. Kepley, Jr., 550(RusR):Oct89–450
Aumont, J. & M. Marie. L'Analyse des films.
  R.J. Nelson, 207(FR):Dec89–400
Aune, B. Metaphysics: The Elements.*
  J.E. Malpas, 63:Mar89–100

Aune, D.E. The New Testament in its Literary Environment.*
  A.J.M. Wedderburn, 123:Vol39No2-388
Aung San Suu Kyi. Burma and India.
  P. Carey, 617(TLS):6-12Jul90-717
Auping, M., ed. Abstract Expressionism.
  W. Jeffett, 39:Jul89-65
Aurelius, M. - see under Marcus Aurelius
"Aurora." (Vol 45) (W. Frühwald & others, eds)
  T.C. Fox, 133:Band22Heft1-65
"Aurora." (Vol 46) (W. Frühwald & others, eds)
  R. Hoermann, 301(JEGP):Oct89-589
Austen, J. Jane Austen's Manuscript Letters in Facsimile. (J. Modert, ed)
  J. Bender, 617(TLS):10-16Aug90-854
Austen-Leigh, J. Stephanie at War.
  G. Drolet, 102(CanL):Autumn-Winter89-188
Austen-Leigh, W. & R.A. Jane Austen. (rev by D. Le Faye)
  J. Bender, 617(TLS):10-16Aug90-854
Auster, P. Ground Work.
  J. Loose, 617(TLS):27Apr-3May90-443
Auster, P. Moon Palace.*
  42(AR):Spring89-249
Auster, P. The Music of Chance.
  M.S. Bell, 441:4Nov90-15
Auster, P., ed. The Random House Book of Twentieth Century French Poetry.
  L. Sail, 403:Spring89-94
Austin, A. The Poetry of the Period.
  W.H. Scheuerle, 635(VPR):Summer89-85
Austin, C.N., ed. Cross-Cultural Reentry.
  J.A. Baughin, 399(MLJ):Spring89-75
Austin, D. The Portable City. The Lost Tribe.
  D. Dowling, 102(CanL):Autumn-Winter89-185
Austin, D.F., ed. Philosophical Analysis.
  P. Smith, 103:Nov90-437
Austin, L. Poetic Principles and Practice.*
  N. Bracher, 345(KRQ):May89-234
  G. Cesbron, 356(LR):Feb-May89-119
  A. Fongaro, 535(RHL):Jan-Feb89-145
Austin, M. Cactus Thorn.*
  R.G. Ballard, 649(WAL):Aug89-175
Austin, M. Stories from the Country of Lost Borders.* (M. Pyrse, ed)
  F.W. Kaye, 502(PrS):Spring89-117
Austin, M. Western Trails.* (M. Graulich, ed)
  F.W. Kaye, 26(ALR):Winter90-82
Austin, P., ed. Complex Sentence Constructions in Australian Languages.
  B. Alpher, 350:Jun90-356
Austin, S. Parmenides.*
  J.W. Forrester, 449:Sep89-551
  M. Kerkhoff, 160:Jan89-161
Autrand, M. Le Dramaturge et ses personnages dans "Le Soulier de satin" de Paul Claudel.
  M. Longstaffe, 208(FS):Jul89-349
Autrand, M. Le Soulier de satin.
  G. Antoine, 535(RHL):Jul-Aug89-744
Auwärter, M. Sprachgebrauch in Abhängigkeit von Merkmalen der Sprecher und der Sprechsituation.
  T.L. Markey, 355(LSoc):Mar89-87
van der Auwera, J. Language and Logic.
  T.E. Zimmermann, 353:Vol27No5-957

van der Auwera, J. & L. Goossens, eds. Ins and Outs of the Predication.*
  B.J. Hoff, 204(FdL):Sep89-224
Auzas, P-M. - see Mérimée, P.
Avalle-Arce, J.B., ed. "La Galatea" de Cervantes - cuatrocientos años después.*
  F. Díaz-Jimeno, 552(REH):Jan89-131
Avalle-Arce, J.B. Lecturas.
  S.G. Dahlgren, 403(MLS):Summer89-93
Avalle-Arce, J.B. - see de Cervantes Saavedra, M.
Avanesova, R.I., ed. Russkie narodnye govory.
  M. Comtet, 559:Vol13No1-73
Aveline, C. Moi par un autre. Le point du jour.
  F. George, 98:Oct89-811
Avery, C. & D. Finn. Giambologna.*
  M.W. Gibbons, 551(RenQ):Winter89-861
  D. Shawe-Taylor, 557:Mar89-61
Avetta, L., ed. Roma - Via Imperiale.*
  T.P. Wiseman, 313:Vol79-212
Avezzù, G. - see Lysias
Avigad, N. Hebrew Bullae from the Time of Jeremiah.
  G.A. Rendsburg, 318(JAOS):Oct-Dec88-663
Avis, G., ed. The Making of the Soviet Citizen.
  J.J. Tomiak, 575(SEER):Apr89-326
Avis, P. Gore.
  D. Hewlett, 235:Summer89-78
Avishur, Y., ed & trans. Women's Folk Songs in Judaeo-Arabic from Jews in Iraq.
  Y.K. Stillman, 292(JAF):Apr-Jun89-218
Avramides, A. Meaning and Mind.*
  R. Elugardo, 103:Nov90-439
Avrich, P. Anarchist Portraits.
  M. Confino, 550(RusR):Oct89-403
Avril, F. & P. Stirnemann. Manuscrits enluminés d'origine insulaire VIIe-XXe siècle.
  M. Michael, 90:Oct89-709
Avtokratova, M.I. & V.I. Buganov. Sokrovishchnitsa dokumentov proshlogo.
  J.T. Alexander, 550(RusR):Jan89-114
Awad, L., ed & trans. The Literature of Ideas in Egypt.* (Pt 1)
  F.X. Paz, 318(JAOS):Oct-Dec88-672
Awkward, M. Inspiriting Influences.
  E. Kraft, 95(CLAJ):Mar90-342
  L. Wagner-Martin, 659(ConL):Fall90-392
Axel-Nilsson, G. Thesaurus Cathedralis Lundensis.
  M. Lindgren, 341:Vol58No3-141
Axelrod, P. & J.G. Reid, eds. Youth, University and Canadian Society.
  E.Z. Friedenberg, 160(DR):Winter88/89-528
Axelson, B. Kleine Schriften zur lateinischen Philologie. (A. Önnerfors & C. Schaar, eds)
  E.J. Kenney, 123:Vol39No2-369
Axinn, S. A Moral Military.
  A.E.H., 185:Jul90-922
Ayala, F. Usurpers.
  P. Zatlin, 238:Dec89-981
de Ayala, P.L. - see under López de Ayala, P.
Ayer, A.J. Thomas Paine.*
  M. Philp, 83:Autumn89-215
  W. Randel, 27(AL):Oct89-473
  D.A. Wilson, 656(WMQ):Oct89-826
Ayerbe-Chaux, R., ed. Textos y concordancias de la obra completa de Juan Manuel.
  B. Taylor, 304(JHP):Winter89-151

15

Ayerbe-Chaux, R. – see Manuel, J.
Ayling, R., ed. O'Casey: the Dublin Trilogy.*
  S.B., 148:Winter86-125
Ayres, P. – see Jonson, B.
Ayres-Bennett, W. Vaugelas and the Devel-
  opment of the French Language.
  J. Fox, 402(MLR):Jan90-183
  P. Rickard, 208(FS):Jan89-86
Azéma, J-P. 1940: L'Année terrible.
  T. Judt, 617(TLS):28Sep-4Oct90-1018
Azzolina, D.S. Tale Type and Motif-Indexes.
  H.J. Uther, 292(JAF):Oct-Dec89-479

Bâ, A.H. L'interprete Briccone.
  B. Hickey, 538(RAL):Fall89-522
Ba, O.A. Guinée Camp Boiro.
  S. Gasster, 207(FR):Mar90-739
Baader, R. Dames de Lettres.*
  J. Grimm, 547(RF):Band101Heft1-118
Babbage, C. The Works of Charles Babbage.*
  (M. Campbell-Kelly & others, eds)
  S. Alderson, 324:Dec89-63
Babine, A. A Russian Civil War Diary. (D.J.
  Raleigh, ed)
  639(VQR):Spring89-55
Bacarisse, P. The Necessary Dream.
  J.A. Duncan, 402(MLR):Oct90-1009
Bach, E. Informal Lectures on Formal Seman-
  tics.
  M.J. Cresswell, 350:Jun90-392
Bach, F.T. Constantin Brancusi, Metamor-
  phosen Plastischer Form.
  E. Shanes, 39:Jun89-439
Bach, K. Thought and Reference.*
  C.A. Brewster, 350:Sep90-622
  D. Freedman, 393(Mind):Jan89-167
  C. Hookway, 518:Apr89-97
  F. Recanati, 192(EP):Apr-Jun89-274
Bachelard, G. Fragments d'une Poétique du
  Feu.* (S. Bachelard, ed)
  M. Mansuy, 98:May89-344
"Gaston Bachelard: L'Homme du poème et du
  théorème."
  G. Cesbron, 356(LR):Feb-May89-127
Bachelin, C. Complainte cimmérienne.
  J. Bens, 450(NRF):Jul-Aug89-187
Bacheller, F.I. Start Writing.
  B.W. Robinett, 399(MLJ):Summer89-214
Bachmann, I. In the Storm of Roses.* (M.
  Anderson, ed & trans)
  P. Filkins, 473(PR):Vol56No2-320
Bachmann, I. The Thirtieth Year.*
  D.P. Deneau, 573(SSF):Summer88-326
  P. Filkins, 473(PR):Vol56No2-320
Bachmann, I. Three Paths to the Lake.
  K. Washburn, 441:18Feb90-36
  442(NY):5Mar90-106
Bachmann, R., W. Hettsche & J. Neuendorff-
  Fürstenau – see Jolles, C. & W. Müller-
  Seidel
Back, D.M. Rig pa ṅo sprod gcer mthoṅ raṅ
  grol.
  J.W. de Jong, 259(IIJ):Jul89-230
Bäcker, J., ed & trans. Märchen aus der
  Mandschurei.
  M. Flitsch, 196:Band30Heft3/4-303
Backman, M. – see McKeon, R.
Backscheider, P.R. Daniel Defoe.*
  M. Bignami, 677(YES):Vol20-271
  P.C. Brückmann, 173(ECS):Fall89-78
  P. Earle, 166:Apr90-261
      [continued]

[continuing]
  M.E. Novak, 617(TLS):4-10May90-469
  P. Rogers, 441:14Jan90-11
Bacon, F. Novum Organum. (M. Malherbe &
  J-M. Pousseur, eds & trans)
  F. Vert, 192(EP):Apr-Jun89-251
Bacque, J. Other Losses.
  M. Howard, 617(TLS):14-20Sep90-965
Bácskai, V., ed. Bürgertum und bürgerliche
  Entwicklung in Mittel- und Osteuropa.
  G.E. Munro, 575(SEER):Jul89-486
Badanes, J. The Final Opus of Leon Solomon.*
  N. Schwerner, 42(AR):Summer89-367
Badawi, M.M. Early Arabic Drama. Modern
  Arabic Drama in Egypt.
  N. Tomiche, 610:Summer89-211
Badawi, M.M. Modern Arabic Literature and
  the West.
  F.X. Paz, 318(JAOS):Oct-Dec88-673
Baden, J.A. & D. Leal, eds. The Yellowstone
  Primer.
  M. Olson, 441:13May90-12
Badinter, E., ed. Qu'est-ce-qu'une femme?*
  C. Slawy-Sutton, 207(FR):Apr90-913
Badinter, E. – see d'Epinay, L.
Badiou, A. L'être et l'événement.
  G.L., 185:Jul90-915
Baeck-Schilders, H. Emile Wambach (1854-
  1924) et het Antwerpse Muziekleven.
  G. Moens-Haenen, 417:Jul-Sep89-286
de Baecque, A., L.M. Vovelle & W. Schmale.
  L'An I des droits de l'homme.
  J. Starobinski, 453(NYRB):12Apr90-47
Baetens, J. Aux frontières du récit.
  M. Praeger, 210(FrF):Jan89-116
Baetjer, K. & J.G. Links. Canaletto.
  M. Rutenberg, 453(NYRB):15Mar90-42
Baffoni-Licata, M.L. La poesia di Vittorio
  Sereni.
  L. Re, 276:Summer89-207
Bagley, R.W. Shang Ritual Bronzes in the
  Arthur M. Sackler Collections.*
  E. Childs-Johnson, 54:Mar89-149
Baglow, J. Hugh MacDiarmid.*
  R. Crawford, 541(RES):Nov89-591
  N.H. MacKenzie, 529(QQ):Spring89-140
  C. Pullen, 178:Jun89-240
Bagnall, R.S. & others. Consuls of the Later
  Roman Empire.
  R.W. Burgess, 487:Summer89-143
  J. Harries & M. Whitby, 123:Vol39No1-90
  A. Lippold, 229:Band61Heft4-325
  J.R. Martindale, 313:Vol79-254
  R.D. Weigel, 124:Nov-Dec89-121
Bagni, P. Benedetto Gennari e La Bottega del
  Guercino.
  D. Miller, 90:Jan89-40
Bahr, E., ed. Geschichte der deutschen Liter-
  atur. (Vol 1)
  W. McConnell, 221(GQ):Spring89-249
  J. Strelka, 133:Band22Heft3/4-296
Bahr, E., ed. Geschichte der deutschen Liter-
  atur. (Vols 2 & 3)
  J. Strelka, 133:Band22Heft3/4-296
Bahry, D. Outside Moscow.
  A.J. Motyl, 550(RusR):Oct89-435
Baida, P. Poor Richard's Legacy.
  J. Taylor, 441:8Jul90-12
Bailey, A. The Outer Banks.*
  G. Oldham, 42(AR):Fall89-497
Bailey, B.L. From Front Porch to Back Seat.*
  L.A. Erenberg, 658:Winter89-295

Bailey, C.J. Catalogue of the Collection of Drawings in the Ashmolean Museum.* (Vol 5)
  C. McCorquodale, 39:Feb89-138
Bailey, D. Bring Me Your Passion.*
  F. Sweet, 102(CanL):Autumn-Winter89-249
Bailey, D.R.S. - see under Shackleton Bailey, D.R.
"Lee Bailey's Southern Food & Plantation Houses."
  R. Flaste, 441:10Jun90-12
Bailey, M. Young Vincent.
  A.S. Byatt, 617(TLS):29Jun-5Jul90-683
Bailey, P. An Immaculate Mistake.
  P.N. Furbank, 617(TLS):30Nov-6Dec90-1280
Bailin, S. Achieving Extraordinary Ends.
  D. Swanger, 289:Winter89-118
Bailly, C.R. Shaiva Devotional Songs of Kashmir.
  J.W. de Jong, 259(IIJ):Jul89-204
Baily, J. Music of Afghanistan.
  C. Capwell, 293(JASt):Nov89-896
Bailyn, B. Faces of Revolution.
  F. McDonald, 441:9Sep90-10
  442(NY):8Oct90-117
Bailyn, B. The Peopling of British North America.*
  A. Murdoch, 83:Spring89-89
Bailyn, B., with B. De Wolfe. Voyagers to the West.*
  A. Murdoch, 83:Spring89-89
Baine, R.M., with M.R. Baine. The Scattered Portions.*
  D. Fuller, 83:Spring89-109
  T.A. Hoagwood, 88:Summer89-39
Bair, D. Simone de Beauvoir.
  M. Gallant, 617(TLS):14-20Sep90-963
  D. Johnson, 441:15Apr90-1
  S.R. Suleiman, 61:Jun90-113
Baird, J.W. To Die for Germany.
  R. Overy, 617(TLS):29Jun-5Jul90-699
Bajard, J-P. & C. Sibieude. Les Affaires en français.
  E. Doss-Quinby, 207(FR):Feb90-588
  P.A. Gaeng, 399(MLJ):Summer89-220
Bak, J.M., ed. Coronations.
  S. Price, 617(TLS):9-15Nov90-1212
Baker, A.J. Australian Realism.
  R. McLaughlin, 63:Mar89-93
Baker, C. Aspects of Bilingualism in Wales.
  N.H. Hornberger, 355(LSoc):Sep89-389
Baker, C. Key Issues in Bilingualism and Bilingual Education.
  J. Thomas, 399(MLJ):Autumn89-350
Baker, D.L. Narcissus and the Lover.*
  R.D. Cottrell, 551(RenQ):Winter89-876
  F. Lecercle, 535(RHL):Jul-Aug89-703
Baker, G. Wittgenstein, Frege, and the Vienna Circle.*
  P. Engel, 542:Oct-Dec89-622
Baker, G.B. & others. Sources in the Law Library of McGill University for a Reconstruction of the Legal Culture of Quebec, 1760-1890.
  D. Howes, 470:Vol27-125
Baker, H.A., Jr. Modernism and the Harlem Renaissance.*
  R.K. Barksdale, 301(JEGP):Apr89-267
  M.A. Reid, 141:Spring89-204
Baker, J. Arguing for Equality.
  R. Young, 63:Mar89-113

Baker, K., ed. Unauthorized Versions.
  P. Kemp, 617(TLS):14-20Sep90-971
Baker, K.M. Condorcet.
  E. Brian, 531:Jul-Dec89-539
Baker, K.M., ed. The French Revolution and the Creation of Modern Political Culture. (Vol 1)
  N. Hampson, 208(FS):Jul89-333
Baker, K.M. Inventing the French Revolution.
  J.R. Censer, 322(JHI):Oct-Dec89-652
Baker, K.M., ed. The Old Regime and the French Revolution.
  J. Black, 83:Spring89-79
Baker, L.R. Saving Belief.
  A. Avramides, 154:Vol28No4-693
  H. Lehman, 103:Jun90-219
  G. Madell, 262:Mar89-107
Baker, M.J. & J-P. Cauvin. Panaché Littéraire. (2nd ed)
  G.A. Perla, 207(FR):May90-1091
Baker, N. The Mezzanine.*
  S. Moore, 532(RCF):Summer89-249
Baker, N. Room Temperature.
  P-L. Adams, 61:Jul90-105
  W. Lesser, 441:15Apr90-17
  L. Norfolk, 617(TLS):27Apr-3May90-456
Baker, P., comp. International Guide to African Studies Research/Etudes Africaines: Guide International de Recherches. (2nd ed)
  N.J. Schmidt, 538(RAL):Spring89-160
Baker, P.R. Stanny.
  B. Gill, 442(NY):29Jan90-90
  I.F. Nesbitt, 441:20May90-21
Baker, P.S. & others - see Boswell, J.
Baker, S. Finding Signs.
  C. Goodrich, 441:29Jul90-21
Baker-Smith, D. & C.C. Barfoot, eds. Between Dream and Nature.
  G. Bonifas, 189(EA):Oct-Dec89-445
Bakhtin, M.M. Speech Genres and Other Late Essays.* (C. Emerson & M. Holquist, eds)
  A.S., 295(JML):Fall88/Winter89-223
Bakker, B.H. - see Zola, E.
Bakker, P. Autonomous Languages.
  G. Bartelt, 710:Sep89-358
Bal, M. Lethal Love.
  R. Chow, 567:Vol75No3/4-335
Balaban, O. Subject and Consciousness.
  A. Kerby, 103:Oct90-891
Balakian, A., ed. Proceedings of the Xth Congress of the International Comparative Literature Association/Actes du Xe Congrès de l'Association Internationale de Littérature Comparée. (Vols 1-3)
  I. Navarrete, 678(YCGL):No36-156
Balakian, P. Reply from Wilderness Island.
  B. Howard, 491:Sep89-349
Balakian, P. Theodore Roethke's Far Fields.
  S. Pinsker, 363(LitR):Spring90-400
Balan, J. & Y. Klynovy, eds. Yarmarok.
  Y. Slavutych, 627(UTQ):Fall89-219
Balandier, G. Le Désordre - Eloge du Mouvement.
  H. Cronel, 450(NRF):Apr89-107
Balard, M. - see "Notai genovesi in Oltre-mare"
Balard, M., A.E. Laiou & C. Otten-Froux. Les italiens à Byzance.
  J.W. Barker, 589:Apr89-382
Balayé, S. & L. Omacini - see Madame de Staël

Balbert, P. & P.L. Marcus, eds. D.H. Law-
rence.*
    42(AR):Fall89-505
Balcer, J.M. Herodotus & Bisitun.*
    M. Menu, 555:Vol62Fasc2-338
Balcerzan, E. Poezja polska w latach 1939-
1945. (Pt 2)
    S. Barańczak, 497(PolR):Vol34No2-188
Balcou, J., ed. La mer au siècle des Encyclo-
pédies.*
    L. Perol, 535(RHL):Mar-Apr89-289
Baldauf, K. Untersuchungen zum Relativsatz
in der Luthersprache.
    F. Simmler, 685(ZDL):2/1989-238
Balderston, D. & others. Ficción y política.
    K. Kohut, 547(RF):Band101Heft2/3-391
Baldi, G. "I promessi sposi."
    R.S. Dombroski, 400(MLN):Jan89-251
Baldick, C. The Concise Oxford Dictionary of
Literary Terms.
    L. Mackinnon, 617(TLS):14-20Sep90-971
Baldick, C. In Frankenstein's Shadow.*
    P. Arnaud, 189(EA):Oct-Dec89-479
    P.A. Cantor, 301(JEGP):Jul89-440
    W.B. Hutchings, 661(WC):Autumn89-212
    A.K. Mellor, 405(MP):Nov89-193
    639(VQR):Winter89-14
Baldwin, B., ed. An Anthology of Byzantine
Poetry.
    K. Snipes, 123:Vol39No1-133
Baldwin, B., ed. An Anthology of Later Latin
Literature.
    R.P.H. Green, 123:Vol39No1-142
Baldwin, D.R. V.S. Pritchett.
    D.A. Hughes, 573(SSF):Summer88-329
Baldwin, W. Beware the Cat.* (W.A. Ringler,
Jr. & M. Flachmann, eds)
    A.F. Kinney, 405(MP):May90-396
Baldwin of Ford. Spiritual Tractates. (D.N.
Bell, trans)
    J.R. Sommerfeldt, 589:Apr89-384
Bales, R. - see Proust, M.
Balestrini, N. L'editore. The Unseen.
    G. Reid, 617(TLS):5-11Oct90-1074
Balfour, I. Northrop Frye.
    A.C. Hamilton, 529(QQ):Summer89-500
    T. Willard, 627(UTQ):Fall89-165
Balke, G., ed. Hong Kong Voices.
    I. Buruma, 453(NYRB):12Apr90-41
Ball, A.M. Russia's Last Capitalists.
    J. Aves, 575(SEER):Jul89-479
    N. Weissman, 550(RusR):Apr89-214
    639(VQR):Winter89-8
Ball, B. Appalachian Patterns.
    G. Johnson, 219(GaR):Summer89-406
Ball, C. & H. Eggins, eds. Higher Education in
the 1990s.
    J.D.E. Beynon, 324:Jun90-503
Ball, D. Victorian Publishers' Bindings.
    S. Allen, 517(PBSA):Jun89-240
Ball, M.J., ed. The Use of Welsh.*
    R.S. Burton, 710:Dec89-479
Ball, N. Security and Economy in the Third
World.
    R.J. Latham, 293(JASt):May89-333
Ball, W.M. Intermittent Diplomat. (A. Rix, ed)
    R.A. Moore, 293(JASt):May89-400
Ballabriga, A. Le soleil et le Tartare.*
    D. Arnould, 555:Vol62Fasc1-137
Ballanche, P.S. L'Homme sans nom. (A. Kett-
ler, ed)
    C. Nesci, 446(NCFS):Spring-Summer90-
561

Ballard, J.G. Running Wild.*
    P. Lewis, 565:Summer89-66
Ballard, J.G. War Fever.
    M.J. Harrison, 617(TLS):23-29Nov90-
1271
Ballard, W.L. The History and Development of
Tonal Systems and Tone Alternations in
South China.
    L. Sagart, 350:Sep90-614
Ballerini, L. & C. Traub. Italy Observed in
Photography and Literature.
    C. Stevens, 507:Sep/Oct89-175
Ballester, G.T. - see under Torrente Balles-
ter, G.
Bally, C. Unveröffentliche Schriften. (W.
Hellmann, ed)
    R. Posner, 402(MLR):Jul90-739
Balmelle, C. Recueil général des mosaïques de
la Gaule. (Vol 4, Pt 2)
    K.M.D. Dunbabin, 123:Vol39No1-120
Balslev-Clausen, P., ed. Songs from Denmark.
    H.C. Andersen, 562(Scan):May89-113
Baltin, M.R. & A.S. Kroch, eds. Alternative
Conceptions of Phrase Structure.
    T. Wasow, 350:Dec90-817
de Balzac, H. Gillette or the Unknown Mas-
terpiece. (A. Rudolf, trans)
    M. James, 364:Apr/May89-125
    P. Lewis, 565:Summer89-66
de Balzac, Madame H. Lettres inédites à
Champfleury, 1851-1854. (L.A. Uffenbeck
& E. Fudakowska, eds)
    B.J. Metha, 446(NCFS):Spring-Summer90-
555
"Balzac et la Révolution française."
    M.J. Call, 446(NCFS):Spring-Summer90-
563
Balzer, B. Heinrich Böll.
    G. Beckers, 221(GQ):Fall89-552
Balzer, B. & others. Die deutschsprachige
Literatur in der Bundesrepublik Deutsch-
land.
    V.R. Petersen, 221(GQ):Fall89-548
Bamforth, S. & others. Prosateurs Latins en
France au XVIe Siècle.
    M.C. Smith, 551(RenQ):Summer89-337
Bammesberger, A. English Linguistics.
    J.A.C. Greppin, 617(TLS):2-8Feb90-113
    H. Penzl, 350:Sep90-623
Banac, I. With Stalin against Tito.*
    639(VQR):Summer89-97
Banac, I. & F.E. Sysyn, eds. Concepts of Na-
tionhood in Early Modern Eastern Europe.
    L. Hughes, 242:Vol10No1-122
Banc, C. & A. Dundes. First Prize: Fifteen
Years!
    M. Belgrader, 196:Band30Heft1/2-111
Bancheri, S. & others. Lettura e Conver-
sazione.*
    R. Bellino-Giordano, 276:Winter89-446
Bancquart, M-C. - see France, A.
Bandak, H. Syndefaldet - taenkning og
eksistens.
    Ø. Rottem, 172(Edda):1989/4-364
Banerjee, J., ed. The Music of Bengal.
    C. Capwell, 187:Fall89-541
Banes, S. - see Souritz, E.
Banfield, S. Sensibility and English Song.
    J. Michon, 189(EA):Apr-Jun89-227
Bang, M.L. Johan Christian Dahl.
    A. Wilton, 90:Oct89-719
Bangerter, L.A. German Writing Since 1945.
    J. Ryan, 221(GQ):Fall89-549

18

Banks, D.J. From Class to Culture.
    A. Sweeney, 293(JASt):Nov89-923
Banks, I. Canal Dreams.
    J. Mellors, 364:Oct/Nov89-133
Banks, I. The Player of Games.
    T. Bacciarelli, 571(ScLJ):Winter89-56
Banks, J.T. - see Woolf, V.
Banks, R. Affliction.*
    J. Loose, 617(TLS):26Oct-1Nov90-1146
    C. Rooke, 376:Sep89-113
Banks, R., ed. Costing the Earth.
    J. Elkington, 324:Jan90-142
Banks, R. Family Life. (rev)
    B.K. Horvath, 532(RCF):Spring89-273
Bann, S. The True Vine.
    S. Gardner, 617(TLS):10-16Aug90-850
Bannerman, R.L. Norman Corwin and Radio.
    D. Belgrad, 106:Fall89-231
Baño, J.S. - see under Servera Baño, J.
Banon, D. La lecture infinie.
    C. Chalier, 192(EP):Jan-Mar89-93
Bansard, R. & others. Les romans de la table
  ronde.
    S. Woodward, 589:Jul89-651
Banta, M. Imaging American Women.*
    M. Bell, 27(AL):Oct89-470
    P. Currah, 529(QQ):Summer89-568
    S.L. Mizruchi, 432(NEQ):Mar89-105
Banta, M. & C.M. Hinsley. From Site to Sight.
    A.E. Coombes & S. Edwards, 59:Dec89-
    510
Banta, M. & O.A. Silverman - see Joyce, J.
Banti, G. On the Morphology of Vedic Gen-
  der-Distinguishing Pronominals.
    S.W. Jamison, 259(IIJ):Oct89-290
Banton, M. Racial Theories.
    J. Dwyer, 242:Vol10No2-246
Banville, J. The Book of Evidence.*
    E. Abeel, 441:15Apr90-11
    J. Bayley, 453(NYRB):17May90-6
    442(NY):7May90-108
Banville, J. Mefisto.
    A. Boaz, 441:25Feb90-24
Banyeres, M.A.S. - see under Angels Santa i
  Banyeres, M.
Bänziger, H. Frisch und Dürrenmatt.
    E.M. Click, 221(GQ):Summer90-433
    W. Paulsen, 564:Nov89-367
Bar-Yosef, H. Metaforot usmalim beyetsiratro
  shel U.N. Gnessin.
    A. Balaban, 508:May89-177
Barak, A. Judicial Discretion.
    M.T., 185:Jan90-457
Barańczak, S. Breathing under Water and
  other East European Essays.
    L. Weschler, 617(TLS):2-8Nov90-1173
Barańczak, S. A Fugitive from Utopia.*
    B. Czaykowski, 104(CASS):Spring-Win-
    ter88-446
    D. McDuff, 565:Spring89-76
Barańczak, S. Przed i po.
    M.G. Levine, 497(PolR):Vol34No4-376
Baranskaya, N. A Week Like Any Other.
    J. Daynard, 441:27May90-16
    P. Lewis, 565:Autumn89-72
Barany, G. The Anglo-Russian Entente Cor-
  diale of 1697-1698.
    N.E. Saul, 550(RusR):Jan89-85
Barasch, M. Giotto and the Language of Ges-
  ture.*
    J.M. Massing, 551(RenQ):Spring89-115
    A.F. Moskowitz, 589:Jul89-652
    E. Shanes, 39:Mar89-220

Baratto, M. La letteratura teatrale del Set-
  tecento in Italia.* (G. Da Pozzo, F. Fido &
  M. Santagata, eds)
    B. Guthmüller, 72:Band226Heft1-221
Barber, B. The Conquest of Politics.*
    R. Marlin, 529(QQ):Autumn89-763
    R.B. Schultz, 185:Apr90-673
Barber, C. The Theme of Honour's Tongue.
    E. Cuvelier, 189(EA):Apr-Jun89-212
Barber, C.L. Creating Elizabethan Tragedy.*
  (R.P. Wheeler, ed)
    R. Martin, 529(QQ):Autumn89-710
Barber, C.L. & R.P. Wheeler. The Whole Jour-
  ney.*
    C.T. Neely, 551(RenQ):Summer89-351
    W. Kerrigan, 301(JEGP):Apr89-231
    R.W.F. Martin, 541(RES):Aug89-414
Barber, J. & J. Barratt. South Africa's For-
  eign Policy.
    L. Thompson, 617(TLS):1-7Jun90-579
Barber, L. & J. Tonkin-Covell. Freyberg.
    B.H. Reid, 617(TLS):2-8Feb90-120
Barber, P. The School of Love.
    H. Mittelmark, 441:23Sep90-48
Barber, R.L. - see under Lloréns Barber, R.
Barber, R.L.N. The Cyclades in the Bronze
  Age.*
    E. Schofield, 303(JoHS):Vol109-258
Barbera, J. & W. McBrien. Stevie.
    F. Breslin, 405(MP):Nov90-000
    P.T.S., 295(JML):Fall88/Winter89-409
Barbey d'Aurevilly, J. "L'Ensorcelée," "Les
  Diaboliques."
    J-M. Ballbé, 535(RHL):Nov-Dec89-1067
    T. Unwin, 208(FS):Jul89-342
"Barbey d'Aurevilly, 12."* "Barbey d'Aure-
  villy, 13." (P. Berthier, ed of both)
    J-L. Pire, 356(LR):Nov89-330
Barbieri, P. Acustica, Accordatura e Temper-
  amento nell'Illuminismo Veneto.
    B. Billeter, 416:Band4Heft2-171
Barbour, B. - see Stewart, W.D.
"Barbour's Bruce." (Vol 1) (M.P. McDiarmid &
  J.A.C. Stevenson, eds)
    K. Bitterling, 38:Band107Heft1/2-203
de la Barca, P.C. - see under Calderón de la
  Barca, P.
Barchatova, Y. & others. A Portrait of Tsar-
  ist Russia.
    L. Hughes, 617(TLS):14-20Dec90-1354
Barchilon, J. & C. Velay-Vallantin - see Per-
  rault, C.
Barclay, B. Winter of the White Wolf.
    B. Powell, 647:Fall89-74
Bardèche, M. Léon Bloy.
    J-C. Polet, 356(LR):Nov89-336
Bardet, J.P. & others. Histoire de la Popula-
  tion Française. (Vol 2)
    A. Otten, 42(AR):Summer89-364
Bardhan, P. The Political Economy of Devel-
  opment in India.
    A. Gupta, 293(JASt):Nov89-787
Bareau, M. & others, eds. Les Contes de Per-
  rault.
    H.T. Barnwell, 208(FS):Jan89-84
"Rubén Bareiro Saguier; Co-Textes, No. 14."
    S. Bacarisse, 86(BHS):Oct89-397
Barel, Y. La Quête du sens.
    F. de Polignac, 531:Jul-Dec89-499
Barella Vigal, J. Las "Noches de invierno" de
  Antonio de Eslava.
    G.A. Davies, 86(BHS):Jul89-279
Barella Vigal, J. - see de Eslava, A.

Barentsen, A.A., B.M. Groen & R. Sprenger, eds. Dutch Studies in South Slavic and Balkan Linguistics.*
R. Alexander, 574(SEEJ):Winter89–611
V.M. Du Feu, 575(SEER):Apr89–264
Barentsen, A.A., B.M. Groen & R. Sprenger – see Schaeken, J.
Bargainnier, E.F., ed. Comic Crime.
E. Lauterbach, 395(MFS):Summer89–346
Barge, L. God, the Quest, the Hero.
P.H. Solomon, 395(MFS):Winter89–815
Bariolla, O. Keyboard Compositions. (C.W. Young, ed)
A. Silbiger, 317:Spring89–172
Bark, D.L. & D.R. Gress. A History of West Germany.
G.A. Craig, 453(NYRB):18Jan90–28
P. Pulzer, 617(TLS):2–8Feb90–109
Barkalow, C., with A. Raab. In the Men's House.
A. Banks, 441:4Nov90–28
Barkan, L. The Gods Made Flesh.*
R.J. Du Rocher, 604:Fall87–56
C. Martindale, 131(CL):Spring89–177
M.U. Sowell, 589:Jul89–655
R.H. Terpening, 276:Autumn89–340
Barker, A.M. The Mother Syndrome in the Russian Folk Imagination.*
G. Cox, 104(CASS):Spring–Winter88–486
Barker, C. The Great and Secret Show.
K. Tucker, 441:11Feb90–11
Barker, F. & others, eds. Literature, Politics and Theory.*
M.G. Cooke, 677(YES):Vol20–215
Barker, J.R.V. The Tournament in England, 1100–1400.
G.S. Burgess, 208(FS):Apr89–198
M. Vale, 382(MAE):1989/1–146
Barker, N. – see "The York Gospels"
Barkus, M. Illustrated History.
G. Gessert, 448:Vol27No3–130
Barley, N. The Coast.
R. Brain, 617(TLS):22–28Jun90–674
Barley, N. Foreheads of the Dead.
M. Anderson, 2(AfrA):May89–18
Barlow, H., C. Blakemore & M. Weston–Smith, eds. Images and Understanding.
D. Papineau, 617(TLS):9–15Nov90–1213
Barlow, M. Working with Computers.
K.M. Pederson, 399(MLJ):Spring89–75
Barlow, M. & C.A. Ferguson, eds. Agreement in Natural Language.
U. Shlonsky, 350:Dec90–820
Barlow, W. "Looking Up At Down."
B.L. Cooper, 498:Winter89–91
Barlow, W.P., Jr. – see Taylor, A.
Bärmann, M. & E.C. Lutz. Ritter Johannes Brunwart von Auggen.
H. Heinen, 406:Fall89–383
Barmé, G. & J. Minford, eds. Seeds of Fire.*
D. Davin, 617(TLS):23–29Mar90–304
A. Denman, 42(AR):Spring89–245
Barnard, F.M. Self–Direction and Political Legitimacy.*
H.B. Nisbet, 402(MLR):Jul90–788
Barnard, J. John Keats.*
A. Bewell, 677(YES):Vol20–292
V. Newey, 541(RES):May89–278
L. Waldoff, 340(KSJ):Vol38–170
Barnard, M.E. The Myth of Apollo and Daphne from Ovid to Quevedo.*
L.S. Lerner, 240(HR):Summer89–383
[continued]

[continuing]
L. Nelson, Jr., 551(RenQ):Summer89–330
M. Turón, 552(REH):Jan89–134
Barnard, R. At Death's Door.
639(VQR):Spring89–57
Barnard, R. A City of Strangers.
J. Rubins, 441:14Oct90–38
Barnard, R. Death of a Salesperson.
M. Stasio, 441:7Jan90–29
Barner, W. & others. Lessing. (5th ed)
F.J. Lamport, 402(MLR):Jan90–244
R.E. Schade, 301(JEGP):Jul89–379
Barnes, A. On Interpretation.
S. Davies, 478(P&L):Apr89–216
M. Hancher, 103:Mar90–93
Barnes, C. Boris Pasternak. (Vol 1)
D. Bethea, 441:2Sep90–12
H. Gifford, 453(NYRB):31May90–26
G. Josipovici, 617(TLS):9–15Feb90–135
Barnes, D. Ryder.
P. West, 472:Vol16No1–157
Barnes, G.L. Protohistoric Yamato.
J.E. Kidder, Jr., 407(MN):Winter89–524
Barnes, J. A History of the World in 10 1/2 Chapters.*
P. Lewis, 364:Jun/Jul89–124
P. Lewis, 565:Summer89–66
Barnes, J. Irish Industrial Schools, 1868–1908.
S.M. Parkes, 235:Winter89–94
Barnes, J. Staring at the Sun.*
P. Lewis, 565:Summer89–66
Barnes, L. Coyote.
M. Stasio, 441:16Dec90–33
Barnes, R.B. Prophecy and Gnosis.
R. Kolb, 551(RenQ):Autumn89–560
Barnet, R.J. The Rockets' Red Glare.
A. Tonelson, 441:4Feb90–34
Barnett, A. The Body and Its Dangers.
M. Wolitzer, 441:15Jul90–17
Barnett, A. The Resting Bell.
R. Caddel, 493:Summer89–35
Barnett, P. Is the New Testament History?
A.M. Devine, 124:Nov–Dec89–119
Barnette, D. & L.J., eds. Studies in Eighteenth–Century Spanish Literature and Romanticism in Honor of John Clarkson Dowling.*
P. Deacon, 402(MLR):Jan90–228
N. Glendinning, 86(BHS):Jul89–284
Barnhart, D.K. The Barnhart Dictionary Companion Index (1982–1985).*
J. Algeo, 35(AS):Fall89–256
Barnlund, D.C. Communicative Styles of Japanese and Americans.
Yoshida Ritsuko, 285(JapQ):Apr–Jun89–218
Barnouw, D. Weimar Intellectuals and the Threat of Modernity.
A. Bohm, 529(QQ):Autumn89–722
W. Paulsen, 133:Band22Heft3/4–370
Barnouw, D. & G. van der Stroom – see Frank, A.
Barny, R. Rousseau dans la Révolution.*
T. Scanlan, 207(FR):Oct89–163
Baro, J. Glosario completo de "Los Milagros de Nuestra Señora" de Gonzalo de Berceo.*
S.N. Dworkin, 240(HR):Winter89–76
Barocchi, P., K.L. Bramanti & R. Ristori, eds. Il Carteggio Indiretto di Michelangelo I.
G. Bull, 557:Sep89–320
E.H. Ramsden, 90:Mar89–227

20

Barolsky, P. Walter Pater's Renaissance.*
B. Richards, 506(PSt):May89-102
D.C. Wixon, 125:Winter89-201
Baron, D.E. Declining Grammar and Other
Essays on the English Vocabulary.
J. Sivell, 350:Dec90-859
Baron, D.E. Grammar and Gender.*
S. McConnell-Ginet, 301(JEGP):Apr89-
211
Baron, S.W. The Contemporary Relevance of
History.
N. Rosenstreich, 390:Apr89-60
Barone, M. Our Country.
G. Hodgson, 441:29Apr90-14
Baroni, D. & A. D'Auria. Kolo Moser.
P.V., 90:Feb89-162
Barooshian, V.D. The Art of Liberation.
J. Milner, 575(SEER):Jan89-119
Barr, M.S. Alien to Femininity.
N. Easterbrook, 295(JML):Fall88/
Winter89-240
Barr, N.V. We Called It Macaroni.
R. Flaste, 441:2Dec90-14
Barr, W. - see Persius
Barratt, A. Between Two Worlds.*
R.B., 295(JML):Fall88/Winter89-297
E.C. Haber, 574(SEEJ):Spring89-134
Barreca, R., ed. Last Laughs.*
J. Berman, 659(OonL):Summer90-251
Barroca, R., ed. Sex and Death in Victorian
Literature.
C. Lennox-Boyd, 617(TLS):23-29Mar90-
311
Barrel, Y. La quête du sens.
F. Wolff, 192(EP):Apr-Jun89-270
Barrell, R.A. Bolingbroke and France.
H.T. Dickinson, 402(MLR):Oct90-956
B.S. Hammond, 566:Spring90-222
Barrera-Vidal, A., H. Kleineidam & M. Rau-
pach, eds. Französische Sprachlehre und
"bon usage."
D. Nehls, 257(IRAL):Nov89-358
Barrero Pérez, O. La novela existencial
española de posguerra.*
B. Jordan, 86(BHS):Oct89-387
R.D. Pope, 552(REH):May89-135
G. Roberts, 240(HR):Winter89-124
G. Thomas, 402(MLR):Apr90-484
Barret-Ducrocq, F. L'Amour sous Victoria.
F. Duroux, 98:Dec89-999
M. Rapoport, 358:Feb90-8
Barrett, A.A. Caligula.
B. Knox, 61:Apr90-98
H. Lloyd-Jones, 453(NYRB):6Dec90-49
Barrett, H. The Sophists.
G.B. Kerferd, 123:Vol39No1-143
Barrett, W. Death of the Soul.*
B.H. Dowden, 449:Apr89-259
Barrett, W.L.S. Brunei and Nusantara.
L. de Guise, 60:Mar-Apr89-173
Barricelli, G.P. Giacomo Leopardi.*
O.M. Casale, 276:Summer89-209
Barrick, M.E., ed. German-American Folk-
lore.*
J.M. Coggeshall, 292(JAF):Apr-Jun89-
241
Barrientos, J.A. & A. Cea Gutiérez, A. - see
under Alvarez Barrientos, J. & A. Cea
Gutiérrez
Barrientos, J.J. Borges y la imaginación.
M. Shaul, 238:Sep89-556
Barrier, N.G. India and America.
M.L.P. Patterson, 293(JASt):May89-426

Barron, C.M. & C. Harper-Bill, eds. The
Church in Pre-Reformation Society.
L.V. Gerulaitis, 201:Vol15-323
Barron, W.R.J. English Medieval Romance.*
F. Alexander, 541(RES):Feb89-110
R. Field, 175:Autumn89-251
C. Gauvin, 189(EA):Oct-Dec89-463
S.S. Hussey, 677(YES):Vol20-238
D. Mehl, 72:Band226Heft1-157
Barron, W.R.J. & S.C. Weinberg, eds & trans.
Lazamon's Arthur.
M. Fries, 617(TLS):24-30Aug90-904
Barros, J. Trygve Lie and the Cold War.
M. Howard, 617(TLS):29Jun-5Jul90-686
Barrow, S. Private Moments.
H. Rubin, 441:4Feb90-19
Barry, B. Democracy, Power and Justice.
J. Lively, 617(TLS):5-11Jan90-7
Barry, D. Dave Barry Turns 40.
C. Sommers, 441:1Jul90-15
Barry, J.M. The Ambition and the Power.*
N. Lemann, 453(NYRB):17May90-18
442(NY):1Jan90-84
Barry, K. Language, Music and the Sign.*
R. Bourke, 89(BJA):Spring89-188
C.S. Brown, 131(CL):Fall89-399
R. Ginsberg, 242:Vol10No3-377
N. Roe, 447(N&Q):Mar89-115
Barry, P. The Rise and Fall of Alan Bond.
R. Fleming, 617(TLS):00Nov-6Dec90-1286
Daroby, J. - see Plautus
Barshay, A.E. State and Intellectual in Impe-
rial Japan.*
J.V. Koschmann, 298(JASt):Nov89-861
Barstow, P. The English Country House Party.
J. Ure, 617(TLS):11-17May90-506
Bart, A.R. - see under Rossebastiano Bart, A.
Bart, P. Fade Out.
A. Latham, 441:24Jun90-11
Bartel, H. Frankreich und die Sowjetunion
1938-1940.
R.K. Debo, 550(RusR):Jan89-105
Bartenieff, I., with D. Lewis. Body Movement.
E.D. Chapple, 567:Vol76No3/4-365
Barth, F. Cosmologies in the Making.
F. Reynolds, 292(JAF):Jul-Sep89-362
Barth, J.R. Coleridge and the Power of Love.
A. Taylor, 661(WC):Autumn89-177
Barth, R.S. Improving Schools from Within.
P. Lopate, 441:1Jul90-16
Barthelemy, A.G. Black Face, Maligned Race.*
A.C. Carver, 469:Summer89-107
Barthelme, D. The King.
J. Parini, 441:27May90-8
442(NY):9Jul90-92
Barthelme, F. Natural Selection.
A. Hempel, 441:19Aug90-13
Barthes, R. Criticism and Truth. (K.P. Kneu-
neman, ed & trans)
D.T.O., 295(JML):Fall88/Winter89-223
478(P&L):Apr89-224
Barthes, R. A Lover's Discourse.
J.T. Bagwell, 153:Spring89-97
Barthes, R. Michelet.
A. Demaitre, 242:Vol10No4-481
Barthes, R. The Rustle of Language.
S. Mills, 506(PSt):May89-90
Barthes, R. Writer Sollers.
P. Bonila, 295(JML):Fall88/Winter89-409
Bartholomae, D. & A. Petrosky. Facts, Arti-
facts and Counterfacts.
N.R. Comley, 128(CE):Feb89-192

Bartholomé, M., B. Combettes & M. Francard, eds. Pragmatique et enseignement du français.
    A. Beyrer, 682(ZPSK):Band42Heft5-693
Bartholomeuz, R.J. Too Many Crayfish Not Enough Brains.
    G. Turcotte, 581:Jun89-270
Bartholomew, J.R. The Formation of Science in Japan.
    D. Kevles, 617(TLS):6-12Apr90-371
Bartle, B.K. Computer Software in Music and Music Education.
    P. Manning, 410(M&L):Feb89-137
Bartlett, E.A. - see Grimké, S.
Bartlett, L. William Everson.
    D.A. Carpenter, 649(WAL):May89-78
    A. Charters, 27(AL):May89-322
Bartlett, L. Kenneth Rexroth.
    C. White, 649(WAL):Aug89-163
Bartlett, L. Nathaniel Tarn.
    R.J. Bertholf, 470:Vol27-139
Bartlett, M.D., ed. The New Native American Novel.
    L.M. Hasselstrom, 649(WAL):May89-74
Bartlett, N. Who Was That Man?
    J. Davidson, 381:Summer89-785
Bartlett, R. Trial by Fire and Water.
    S.D. White, 589:Apr89-385
Bartlett, R.P., A.G. Cross & K. Rasmussen, eds. Russia and the World of the Eighteenth Century.
    K.J. McKenna, 574(SEEJ):Fall89-447
Bartlett, T. & others. Irish Studies.
    E. Walshe, 272(IUR):Spring89-186
Bartley, N.V., ed. The Evolution of Southern Culture.
    C. Morris, 106:Fall89-282
    639(VQR):Winter89-9
Bartók, B. Black Pocket Book, Shetches 1907-1922. (L. Somfai, ed)
    P.A. Autexier, 537:Vol75No1-118
Bartoloni, G. & others. Le urne a capanna rinvenute in Italia.
    D. Briquel, 555:Vol62Fasc2-378
Barton, A. The Names of Comedy.
    R.M. Adams, 453(NYRB):6Dec90-67
Barton, H.A. Scandinavia in the Revolutionary Era, 1760-1815.
    C. Gold, 563(SS):Spring/Summer89-272
Barton, J. West of Darkness.
    M.T. Lane, 198:Spring89-104
Bartoněk, A. Prehistorie a protohistorie řeckých dialektů.
    J.T. Hooker, 123:Vol39No1-147
Bartoszewski, W.T. The Convent at Auschwitz.
    P. Hebblethwaite, 617(TLS):21-27Dec90-1379
Bartsch, R. & T. Vennemann. Grundzüge der Sprachtheorie.
    R. Emons, 38:Band107Heft3/4-452
Bartsch, U. Alan Ayckbourns Dramenfiguren.
    H.W. Drescher, 38:Band107Heft1/2-273
Baruch, E.H., A.F. D'Amado, Jr. & J. Seager, eds. Embryos, Ethics, and Women's Rights.
    A.B., 185:Jul90-925
    H.B. Holmes, 254:Fall89-150
Baruch, E.H. & L.J. Serrano. Women Analyze Women.*
    K. Ford, 617(TLS):12-18Jan90-46
Barwise, J. The Situation in Logic.
    A. Urquhart, 103:Mar90-96

Barwise, J. & J. Etchemendy. The Liar.
    A. Gupta, 486:Dec89-697
    B. Hale, 479(PhQ):Jan89-118
    W.D. Hart, 393(Mind):Jul89-451
de Bary, W.T. East Asian Civilizations.*
    J. Ching, 485(PE&W):Jul89-361
de Bary, W.T. The Message of the Mind in Neo-Confucianism.
    T.A. Wilson, 293(JASt):Nov89-824
Barzun, J. A Word or Two Before You Go.* Jacques Barzun on Writing, Editing, and Publishing.
    D. Dutton, 478(P&L):Apr89-226
Bas, J. & G. Iwanaga. Manual de Términos Literarios.
    R. Ruiz, 399(MLJ):Spring89-106
Basanta, A. - see de Quevedo, F.
Basie, C., with A. Murray. Good Morning Blues.
    U. Mazurowicz, 417:Apr-Jun89-188
Basker, J.G. Tobias Smollett.*
    B. Gassman, 405(MP):Feb90-311
    M. Golden, 301(JEGP):Jul89-425
    P. Sabor, 566:Spring89-164
    R.D. Spector, 477(PLL):Spring89-225
Baskerville, P., ed. The Bank of Upper Canada.*
    S.C. Dow, 529(QQ):Spring89-137
Bass, A.L.T. Plain Southern Eating. (J.K. Crellin, ed)
    639(VQR):Winter89-29
Bass, R. The Watch.*
    P. Glasser, 455:Sep89-69
    C. Merrill, 434:Winter89-208
    J. Saari, 42(AR):Fall89-499
    639(VQR):Autumn89-131
Bass, T.A. Camping with the Prince and Other Tales of Science in Africa.
    T. Eprile, 441:29Jul90-8
Bass, T.A. The Newtonian Casino.
    P. Seabright, 617(TLS):14-20Dec90-1339
Bassani, E. & W. Fagg. Africa and the Renaissance.
    F. Willett, 90:Dec89-856
Bassnett, S. Sylvia Plath.*
    N. Corcoran, 677(YES):Vol20-348
Bassnett, S. & P. Kuhiwczak - see "Ariadne's Thread"
Basso, A., ed. Dizionario enciclopedico universale della musica e dei musicisti: Le Biografie.
    F. Lesure, 537:Vol75No2-288
Basso, E.B. A Musical View of the Universe.
    C.E. Robertson, 187:Fall89-104
Bassola, P. Wortstellung im Ofner Stadtrecht.
    K-P. Wegera, 680(ZDP):Band108Heft1-138
Bassuk, D.E. Incarnation in Hinduism and Christianity.
    H.W. French, 293(JASt):May89-416
Bastein, F.H., ed. Kanada heute.*
    E-M. Kröller, 72:Band226Heft1-236
Bastianoni, C. & G. Catoni. Impressum Senis.
    D.E. Rhodes, 354:Mar89-60
Bastianutti, D.L. - see de Vega Carpio, L.
Bastid, M. Educational Reform in Early Twentieth-Century China.
    A.B. Linden, 293(JASt):Nov89-816
Bastien, J-L., P. McDuff & others. La Nouvelle Compagnie théâtrale.
    L.E. Doucette, 627(UTQ):Fall89-188
Bastien, J.W. Healers of the Andes.
    D.Y. Arnold, 650(WF):Jan89-80

Bastien, P. Le Monnayage de l'Atelier de Lyon du Règne de Jovien à la Mort de Jovin (363-413).
  R. Bland, 313:Vol79-266
Bastin, B. Red River Blues.*
  S.C. Tracy, 582(SFQ):Vol46No1-90
Baswell, C. & W. Sharpe, eds. The Passing of Arthur.
  R.J. Schrader, 637(VS):Spring90-492
Bataille, G. Inner Experience.
  A.B., 185:Oct89-208
  A. Brown, 208(FS):Oct89-491
Batchelor, J. "Lord Jim."
  R.G. Hampson, 402(MLR):Jan90-159
  A. Hunter, 447(N&Q):Jun89-257
  D.R. Schwarz, 395(MFS):Summer89-318
  J.H. Stape, 177(ELT):Vol32No3-332
Batchelor, J.C. Gordon Liddy is My Muse By Tommy "Tip" Paine.
  J. Rubins, 441:1Apr90-25
Bate, J. Shakespeare and the English Romantic Imagination.*
  V. Newey, 541(RES):Feb89-129
  E.H. Schor, 570(SQ):Spring90-121
Bate, J. Shakespearean Constitutions.
  A. Barton, 453(NYRB):1Feb90-15
  A. Kirsch, 617(TLS):20-26Apr90-421
Bate, J. - see Lamb, C.
Bately, J.M. - see "The Anglo-Saxon Chronicle"
Bates, C.H. see Jacquot de La Guerre, E-C.
Bates, D. A Bibliography of Domesday Book.
  W.E. Kapelle, 589:Jul89-600
Bates, H.E. A Party for the Girls.
  B. Hooper, 573(SSF):Fall88-491
Bates, M.J. - see Stevens, W.
Bath, A. Pere Calders, ideari i ficció.
  D. George, 86(BHS):Jul89-305
Bätschmann, O. Nicolas Poussin.
  D. Carrier, 617(TLS):7-13Dec90-1322
Battail, J-F. - see Lindroth, S.
Battersby, C. Gender and Genius.
  L. Hudson, 617(TLS):9-15Mar90-243
Battesti-Pelegrin, J. Lope de Stúñiga.
  N.G. Round, 86(BHS):Apr89-169
Battesti-Pelegrin, J. - see under de Stúñiga, L.
Battestin, M.C. - see Fielding, H.
Battestin, M.C., with R.R. Battestin. Henry Fielding.*
  D. Jarrett, 453(NYRB):22Nov90-40
Battiferri, L. Ricercari. (G.C. Butler, ed)
  A. Silbiger, 317:Spring89-172
Battle, L. The Past is Another Country.
  M. Binchy, 441:19Aug90-12
"The Battle of Kosovo." (J. Matthias & V. Vučković, trans)
  D. McDuff, 565:Spring89-76
  J.S. Miletich, 402(MLR):Apr90-542
Battler, L. The Polar Bear Express.
  F. Sweet, 102(CanL):Autumn-Winter89-249
Bauchau, H. L'Ecriture et la circonstance.
  M-F. Resnard, 356(LR):Aug89-228
Bauckham, R. Moltmann.
  A.D. Falconer, 235:Summer89-80
Baudelaire, C. Baudelaire; The Poems in Prose and La Fanfarlo. (F. Scarfe, trans) Baudelaire, Intimate Journals. (C. Isherwood, trans)
  L. Sail, 493:Autumn89-54

Baudelaire, C. The Parisian Prowler. The Poems in Prose, with "La Fanfarlo."
  P. Keegan, 617(TLS):30Nov-6Dec90-1294
Baudoin, E.M., & others. Reader's Choice. (2nd ed)
  C.F. McCreary, 399(MLJ):Summer89-215
Baudouin, J. Karl Popper.
  J. Largeault, 542:Oct-Dec89-606
Baudot, G. - see de Motolinía, T.
Baudrillard, J. Selected Writings. (M. Poster, ed)
  S. Helmling, 344:Winter90-204
  I. Whitehouse, 402(MLR):Oct90-989
Bauer, B. Jesuitische "ars rhetorica" im Zeitalter der Glaubenskämpfe.
  W. Neuber, 680(ZDP):Band108Heft4-615
Bauer, D.M. Feminist Dialogics.
  P.S. Berggren, 27(AL):May89-295
  P. Hitchcock, 147:Vol6No3-84
  P.J. Rabinowitz, 454:Spring90-314
  E.B. Thompson, 395(MFS):Summer89-393
Bauer, G. Einführung in die Diachrone Sprachwissenschaft.
  W. Elmer, 179(ES):Apr89-190
Bauer, G. Gefangenschaft und Lebenslust.
  J.C. Pettey & P.M. Lützeler, 406:Winter89-508
Bauer, K.J. A Maritime History of the United States.
  E.W. Sloan, 432(NEQ):Mar89-137
Bauer, M. & R. Düsterberg. Oskar Panizza.
  T. Schneider, 602:Band20Heft2-326
  T. Schneider, 680(ZDP):Band108Heft4-601
Bauer, N. The Opening Eye.
  G. Creese, 102(CanL):Spring89-217
Bauer, R., with M. de Graat & J. Wertheimer, eds. Das Shakespeare-Bild in Europa zwischen Aufklärung und Romantik.
  R. Paulin, 402(MLR):Apr90-502
Bauer, R., with M. de Graat & J. Wertheimer, eds. Der theatralische Neoklassizismus um 1800.
  M. Carlson, 678(YCGL):No36-177
  J. Voisine, 549(RLC):Jul-Sep89-415
Baum, A.T. Komsomol Participation in Soviet First Five Year Plan
  L. Viola, 550(RusR):Jan89-103
Baum, L.F. The Classical Wizard: Magus Mirabilis in Oz. (C.J. Hinke & G. Van Buren, trans)
  H.E. Moritz, 399(MLJ):Winter89-496
Baum, M. Deduktion und Beweis in Kants Transzendentalphilosophie.*
  B. Rang, 342:Band80Heft3-214
Baum, M. Die Entstehung der Hegelschen Dialektik.*
  E. Angehrn, 687:Oct-Dec89-702
Baum, R. Hochsprache, Literatursprache, Schriftsprache.
  T. Schippan, 682(ZPSK):Band42Heft5-662
Bauman, M. Milton's Arianism.
  T.N. Corns, 447(N&Q):Jun89-240
Bauman, R. Story, Performance, and Event.*
  K.H. Basso, 355(LSoc):Mar89-91
  W.O. Hendricks, 567:Vol73No3/4-305
Bauman, T. W.A. Mozart: "Die Entführung aus dem Serail."*
  A. Steptoe, 410(M&L):Feb89-104
Bauman, T. North German Opera in the Age of Goethe.*
  H. Watanabe-O'Kelly, 83:Autumn89-246

Bauman, Z. Modernity and the Holocaust.*
  D. Cesarani, 617(TLS):20-26Apr90-423
Baumann, U. & H.P. Heinrich. Thomas Morus -
  Humanistiche Schriften.
  R.J. Schoeck, 551(RenQ):Winter89-854
Baumbach, J. Separate Hours.
  S.G. Kellman, 441:15Jul90-10
Bäumer, A. Gustav Klimt Women.
  M.L. Wagener, 662:Spring/Summer89-53
Bäumer, K. "Bettine, Psyche, Mignon."*
  J.F. Hyde, Jr., 406:Winter89-476
Baumgarten, A.G. Esthétique.
  P. Somville, 542:Oct-Dec89-634
Baumgartner, F.J. Henry II: King of France,
  1547-1559.
  B. Diefendorf, 551(RenQ):Summer89-318
Baumgold, D. Hobbes's Political Theory.
  S.A. Lloyd, 185:Jan90-421
  M.L. Morgan, 319:Oct90-619
  T. Sorell, 518:Apr89-86
Bausch, R. The Fireman's Wife.
  B. Pesetsky, 441:19Aug90-9
Bauschinger, S. & A. Reh, eds. Hermann
  Hesse.*
  A. Otten, 564:Feb89-70
Bausinger, S. & A. Reh, eds. Hermann Hesse.
  A. Hsia, 301(JEGP):Jul89-386
Bautier, R.H. & others. Histoire de la Popula-
  tion Française. (Vol 1)
  A. Otten, 42(AR):Summer89-364
Bawcutt, P. & F. Riddy, eds. Longer Scottish
  Poems.* (Vol 1)
  A.A. MacDonald, 179(ES):Apr89-175
  S. Mapstone, 541(RES):Aug89-442
Bawer, B. Diminishing Fictions.
  T. Wilhelmus, 249(HudR):Summer89-345
Baxter, C. First Light.*
  G. Davenport, 569(SR):Summer89-468
Baxter, C. A Relative Stranger.
  W. Ferguson, 441:21Oct90-18
Bayard, T.O. & S-G. Young, eds. Economic
  Relations Between the United States and
  Korea.
  J.T. Bennett, 293(JASt):Nov89-885
Bayertz, K. GenEthik.
  A. Sobolewski, 679:Band20Heft2-376
Bayless, S. God's Coach.
  R. Blount, Jr., 441:5Aug90-5
Bayley, I. - see Porter, K.A.
Bayley, J. The Short Story.*
  C. Hanson, 677(YES):Vol20-312
  A.H. Petry, 573(SSF):Winter89-106
  M. Rohrberger, 395(MFS):Winter89-875
Bayley, P.C. An A.B.C. of Shakespeare.
  G. Schmitz, 156(ShJW):Jahrbuch1989-332
Bayley, S., P. Garner & D. Sudjic. Twentieth
  Century Style and Design.
  S.J., 90:Feb89-162
Bayly, S. Saints, Goddesses and Kings.
  B. Metcalf, 617(TLS):6-12Jul90-718
Bazerman, C. Shaping Written Knowledge.
  R.W. Dasenbrock, 126(CCC):Oct89-354
  C.R. Miller, 544:Winter89-101
Beacham, R.C. Adolphe Appia.*
  M-L. Bablet, 610:Spring89-96
  J. Fisher, 615(TJ):May89-258
Beacham, R.C. - see Appia, A.
Beake, F. The Fisher Queen.
  D. McDuff, 565:Spring89-76
Beal, P., comp. Index of English Literary
  Manuscripts. (Vol 2, Pt 1)
  I. Jack, 541(RES):Aug89-417

Beales, D. Joseph II.* (Vol 1)
  I. de Madariaga, 83:Spring89-91
Beall, T.S. Josephus' Description of the Ess-
  enes Illustrated by the Dead Sea Scrolls.
  S.J.D. Cohen, 124:Jul-Aug90-525
Beamon, S.P. & S. Roaf. The Ice-Houses of
  Britain.
  E. David, 617(TLS):21-27Dec90-1373
Bean, J.M.W., ed. The Political Culture of
  Modern Britain.
  J.O. Baylen, 635(VPR):Spring89-37
Bear, G. Queen of Angels.
  G. Jonas, 441:2Sep90-18
Beard, G. The National Trust Book of the
  English House Interior.
  D. Cruickshank, 617(TLS):6-12Jul90-730
Beard, M. & M.H. Crawford. Rome in the Late
  Republic.
  L. de Blois, 394:Vol42fasc1/2-248
Beard, M. & J. North, eds. Pagan Priests.
  S. Price, 617(TLS):11-17May90-508
Beard, R. & B. Szymanek, comps. Bibliography
  of Morphology 1960-1985.*
  G. Gazdar, 353:Vol27No5-969
Beardsell, P.R. Quiroga: "Cuentos de amor de
  locura y de muerte."*
  M.S. Peden, 240(HR):Winter89-127
  P. Swanson, 86(BHS):Jan89-102
Beardsley, D. Country on Ice.
  D. Moffat, 102(CanL):Autumn-Winter89-
  226
Beardsmore, H.B. Bilingualism.* (2nd ed)
  G. González, 710:Mar89-92
  J. John, 257(IRAL):Feb89-69
Beardy, L. Pisiskiwak kâ-pîkiskwêcik/Talk-
  ing Animals. (H.C. Wolfart, ed & trans)
  B.D. Joseph, 350:Sep90-619
Bearzot, C. Focione tra storia e trasfigur-
  azione ideale.
  G. Dobesch, 229:Band61Heft6-514
Beasley, D. How to Use a Research Library.
  J.L. Harner, 365:Fall88-225
Beasley, J. Journal of an Era.
  M. Wilding, 71(ALS):Oct89-264
Beasley, J.C. & O.M. Brack - see Smollett, T.
Beaton, M.C. Death of a Hussy.
  M. Stasio, 441:30Dec90-26
Beattie, A. Picturing Will.
  T.C. Boyle, 441:7Jan90-1
  A. Hulbert, 453(NYRB):31May90-33
Beatty, B. & V. Newey, eds. Byron and the
  Limits of Fiction.
  M.G.H. Pittock, 447(N&Q):Dec89-521
Beauchamp, D.E. The Health of the Republic.
  B.A.B., 185:Oct89-229
Beauchamp, E.R. & R. Rubinger, comps. Edu-
  cation in Japan.
  M.I. White, 407(MN):Autumn89-385
Beauchamp, T. & N. Bowie, eds. Ethical The-
  ory and Business.
  K. Hanly, 103:Jan90-1
Beauchemin, Y. Juliette Pomerleau.
  M. Naudin, 207(FR):May90-1096
Beaufret, J. De l'existentialisme à Heideg-
  ger.
  P. David, 192(EP):Apr-Jun89-269
Beaujeu, J. - see Cicero
Beaulieu, G. Sortie d'elle(s) mutante.
  D.W. Russell, 102(CanL):Autumn-
  Winter89-247
Beaulieu, V-L. Steven Le Hereault.
  J. Harrison, 102(CanL):Spring89-193

Beauman, S. Dark Angel.
  E. Stumpf, 441:12Aug90-16
de Beaumarchais, P.A.C. Oeuvres. (P. Lar-
  thomas, with J. Larthomas, eds)
  R. Arveiller, 209(FM):Oct89-260
Beaumont, A. - see Busoni, F.
Beaumont, B. - see Huysmans, J-K.
Beaumont, F. & J. Fletcher. The Maid's Trag-
  edy. (T.W. Craik, ed)
  G. McMullan, 447(N&Q):Sep89-389
Beaumont, K. Jarry: "Ubu Roi."
  D. Bradby, 402(MLR):Jan90-197
de Beauregard, O.C. - see under Costa de
  Beauregard, O.
Beaussant, P. Vous avez dit "Baroque"?
  J-C. Vuillemin, 207(FR):Dec89-363
de Beauvoir, S. Lettres à Sartre. (Vols 1 &
  2) Journal de guerre, septembre 1939-jan-
  vier 1941.
  M. Gallant, 617(TLS):14-20Sep90-963
Beauvois, D., ed. Les Confins de l'Ancienne
  Pologne.*
  M. Raeff, 497(PolR):Vol34No2-173
Beaver, H. "Huckleberry Finn."
  G.C. Carrington, Jr., 599:Spring90-150
Beavis, I.C. Insects and Other Invertebrates
  in Classical Antiquity.*
  E.K. Borthwick, 123:Vol39No2-362
  L. Gil, 229:Band61Heft7-620
Debbington, D.W. Evangelicalism in Modern
  Britain.*
  D. Bowen, 637(VS):Spring90-505
Beccarelli-Saad, T. Les Passantes.
  B. Belyea, 102(CanL):Winter88-109
Becher, B. & H. Blast Furnaces.
  A. Grundberg, 441:2Dec90-71
Becher, B. & H. Water Towers.
  K. Shirley, 42(AR):Spring89-244
Bechert, H. Die Lebenzeit des Buddha.
  C. Vogel, 259(IIJ):Jan89-49
Bechert, H., ed. Zur Schulzugehörigkeit von
  Werken der Hīnayāna-Literatur.* (Pt 1)
  W. Thomas, 260(IF):Band94-336
Beck, B.E.F. & others, eds. Folktales of In-
  dia.*
  K-H. Golzio, 196:Band30Heft3/4-304
  F.J. Korom, 318(JAOS):Jan-Mar88-191
  L.D. Shinn, 293(JASt):Nov89-897
  D. Shulman, 292(JAF):Jul-Sep89-345
Beck, F.A.G. Bibliography of Greek Education
  and Related Topics.*
  P. Louis, 555:Vol62Fasc1-148
Beck, H., ed. Heldensage und Heldendichtung
  im Germanischen.
  D.H. Green, 402(MLR):Jan90-237
Beck, H., ed. Parliament House Canberra.*
  P. Drew, 47:Jan89-34
Beck, H.H.H. The Elusive "I" in the Novel.*
  A. Zweig, 131(CL):Summer89-294
  566:Spring90-204
Beck, J., ed. Théâtre et propagande aux
  débuts de la Réforme.*
  A.E. Knight, 589:Apr89-388
Beck, L.W., with others - see Kant, I.
Becker, H. & G. - see Meyerbeer, G.
Becker, H., H-J. Dahms & C. Wegeler, eds. Die
  Universität Göttingen unter dem National-
  sozialismus.
  C.J. Classen, 229:Band61Heft1-73
Becker, J. Jakob the Liar.
  S.S. Prawer, 617(TLS):3-9Aug90-829
Becker, J. Pattern and Loom.*
  V. Wilson, 463:Summer89-110

Becker, J. & A.H. Feinstein, eds. Karawitan.*
  (Vol 2)
  L. Rowell, 318(JAOS):Oct-Dec88-642
Becker, J. & A.H. Feinstein, eds. Karawitan.
  (Vol 3)
  E. Heins, 293(JASt):Nov89-924
  N. Sorrell, 410(M&L):Nov89-525
Becker-Bertau, F., ed. Die Inschriften von
  Klaudiu Polis.*
  A.G. Woodhead, 303(JoHS):Vol109-243
Becker-Cantarino, B. Der lange Weg zur Mün-
  digkeit.
  M. Maurer, 224(GRM):Band39Heft2-234
Becker-Cantarino, B., ed. Satire in der Frü-
  hen Neuzeit.*
  W. Beutin, 400(MLN):Apr89-746
  J.B. Dallett, 564:Nov89-345
  G.R. Hoyt, 133:Band22Heft1-57
Becker-Cantarino, B. - see Hoyers, A.O.
Beckett, J. & D. Cherry, eds. The Edwardian
  Era.
  K. Adler, 59:Mar89-118
Beckett, J.V. A History of Laxton.
  W. Minchinton, 617(TLS):5-11Jan90-20
Beckett, M. A Literary Woman.
  P. Craig, 617(TLS):4-10May90-480
Beckett, S. As the Story Was Told.
  G. Craig, 617(TLS):20-26Jul90-782
Beckett, S. La Quête spirituelle chez Henri
  Bosco.
  A.P. Colombat, 207(FR)-May90-1071
  A.M. David, 402(MLR):Jul90-745
  A.M Smith, 529(QQ):Autumn89-748
Beckett, W. Contemporary Women Artists.
  A. Summerfield, 324:Jan90-144
Beckman, M.E. Stress and Non-Stress Accent.
  D.R. Ladd, 297(JL):Mar89-269
Becksmann, R. Deutsche Glasmalerei des Mit-
  telalters.
  U. Ballay, 39.Oct89-287
Beckson, K. Arthur Symons.*
  F. Austin, 179(ES):Feb89-95
  A. Brown, 637(VS):Autumn89-202
  J. Genet, 189(EA):Apr-Jun89-223
Beckson, K. & J.M. Munro - see Symons, A.
Beckwith, J. & D.R. Cooper, eds. Hello Out
  There!
  R. Crawford, 627(UTQ):Fall89-245
  H.J. McLean, 415:Sep89-548
Beckwith, J. & F.A. Hall, eds. Musical
  Canada.
  R. Crawford, 627(UTQ):Fall89-245
  R. Elliott, 529(QQ):Spring89-110
Becom, J. Mediterranean Color.
  P-L. Adams, 61:Dec90-133
Becquart, P. & H. Vanhulst, eds. Musique des
  Pays-Bas anciens.
  G. Dixon, 410(M&L):Nov89-526
Beddoe, D. Back to Home and Duty.
  E. Roberts, 617(TLS):2-8Mar90-218
Bedford, S. As It Was.
  D. Murphy, 617(TLS):26Oct-1Nov90-1144
Bedford, S. Jigsaw.*
  42(AR):Summer89-373
Bedford, W. Happiland.
  M. Illis, 617(TLS):16-22Feb90-181
Bedient, C. He Do the Police in Different
  Voices.*
  B. Bergonzi, 677(YES):Vol20-331
  R. Crawford, 541(RES):Aug89-435
Bedouelle, G. & P. Le Gal. Le "Divorce" du Roi
  Henry VIII.
  D. Loades, 551(RenQ):Autumn89-566

25

Bee, O.J. – see under Ooi Jin Bee
Beebe, L.M., ed. Issues in Second Language Acquisition.
   K. McCormick, 351(LL):Sep89–447
Beeby, D. & W. Kaplan – see Watkins, J.
Beecher, D.A. & M. Ciavolella – see Ferrand, J.
Beecher, J. Charles Fourier.*
   C. Crossley, 208(FS):Jul89–338
Beegel, S.F. Hemingway's Craft of Omission.*
   P.R.J., 295(JML):Fall88/Winter89–346
Beegel, S.F. Hemingway's Neglected Short Fiction.
   A. De Fazio 3d, 234:Spring90–178
Beehler, M. T.S. Eliot, Wallace Stevens, and the Discourses of Difference.*
   R.W.B., 295(JML):Fall88/Winter89–211
   R. Crawford, 541(RES):May89–293
Beekes, R.S.P. Vergelijkende taalwetenschap.
   J.A.C. Greppin, 617(TLS):19–25Oct90–1119
Beer, G. Arguing with the Past.
   J. Bayley, 617(TLS):19–25Jan90–67
Beer, G. George Eliot.
   K. Sutherland, 148:Winter86–105
Beer, M. Romanzi di cavalleria.*
   D. Javitch, 276:Winter89–447
   D. Quint, 557:Mar89–57
   M. Slawinski, 402(MLR):Jul90–752
   E. Speciale, 551(RenQ):Winter89–874
Beer, P. Collected Poems.*
   D. Houston, 493:Summer89–51
Beerbohm, M. Rossetti and His Circle.
   I. Grushow, 177(ELT):Vol32No1–91
Beers, H.P. French and Spanish Records of Louisiana.
   P.E. Hoffman, 585(SoQ):Summer90–128
Beers, J.M., ed. A Commentary on the Cistercian Hymnal/Explanatio super hymnos quibus utitur ordo Cisterciensis.*
   R.W. Pfaff, 589:Jul89–657
Beesley, S.W., ed. Vietnam.
   M. Westbrook, 456(NDQ):Winter89–242
Begiebing, R.J. Toward a New Synthesis.
   J.M. Lennon, 395(MFS):Winter89–876
Begnal, M.H. Dreamscheme.*
   P. Van Caspel, 395(MFS):Summer89–328
Begni Redona, P.V., with G.A. dell'Acqua & G. Vezzoli. Alessandro Bonvicino, Il Moretto da Brescia.
   A. Bayer, 90:Dec89–855
Begum, H. Moore's Ethics.
   N. Griffin, 556:Summer89–80
Behan, B. An Giall [and] The Hostage.* (R. Wall, ed & trans)
   N. Grene, 235:Winter88–82
Béhar, H. Les Cultures de Jarry.
   K. Beaumont, 402(MLR):Oct90–975
Behar, P. Silesia Tragica. (Vol 1)
   R.T. Llewellyn, 402(MLR):Jul90–786
Behbehani, H. The Soviet Union and Arab Nationalism, 1917–1966.
   F. Halliday, 575(SEER):Oct89–644
Behler, E., ed. The Philosophy of German Idealism.
   H. Reiss, 133:Band22Heft1–63
Behler, E. & J. Hörisch, eds. Die Aktualität der Frühromantik.
   N. Lohse, 680(ZDP):Band108Heft4–625
Behme, H., ed. Angewandte Sprechwissenschaft.
   C.M. Heilmann, 685(ZDL):3/1989–381

Behn, A. The Luckey Chance. (J.A. Coakley, ed)
   566:Spring89–194
Behn, R. Paper Bird.*
   B. Howard, 491:May89–111
Behr, K., ed. Weimarer Republik.
   E. Schürer, 133:Band22Heft3/4–372
Behr, S. Women Expressionists.
   A. Summerfield, 324:Jan90–144
Behre, M. "Des dunkeln Lichtes voll."
   E.E. George, 406:Summer89–258
Behrendt, P. & H. Pontoppidan. Det ideale hjem.
   A.P. Weiner, 563(SS):Spring/Summer89–277
Behrendt, S.C. Shelley and His Audiences.
   A. Leighton, 617(TLS):30Mar–5Apr90–354
Behrens-Abouseif, D. Islamic Architecture in Cairo.
   R. Irwin, 617(TLS):18–24May90–530
Bei Dao. The August Sleepwalker.*
   C. Byron, 493:Autumn89–211
   J.D. Spence, 441:12Aug90–6
Bei Dao. Waves.* (B.S. McDougall, ed)
   J.D. Spence, 441:12Aug90–6
Beicken, P. Ingeborg Bachmann.
   E. Boa, 402(MLR):Jan90–264
   K. Remmler, 221(GQ):Fall89–558
Beig, M. Lost Weddings.
   U. Hegi, 441:29Jul90–26
Beik, J. Hausa Theatre in Niger.
   G. Furniss, 538(RAL):Fall89–553
Beile, W. & A. Deutsch einfach 1.
   R. Ambacher, 399(MLJ):Autumn89–367
Beilharz, P. Trotsky, Trotskyism and the Transition to Socialism.*
   R.B. Day, 242:Vol10No2–261
Beilin, E.V. Redeeming Eve.*
   R.A. Houlbrooke, 677(YES):Vol20–245
Beinfeld, S. & S.J. Stang – see Ford, F.M.
Beiser, F.C. The Fate of Reason.*
   K. Ameriks, 482(PhR):Jul89–398
   W. Goetschel, 221(GQ):Spring89–235
   E.M. Knodt, 478(P&L):Oct89–422
Beissel, H. Poems New and Selected.
   M.H. Keefer, 102(CanL):Winter88–136
Beisser, A.R. A Graceful Passage.
   C.L. Sulzberger, 441:18Mar90–28
Béja, J-P. – see Liu Binyan
Beja, M., ed. Critical Essays on Virginia Woolf.
   J. Marcus, 620(TSWL):Spring89–101
Beja, M. & others, eds. James Joyce.*
   P. Parrinder, 677(YES):Vol20–329
Beja, M. & S. Benstock, eds. Coping with Joyce.
   B. Cheyette, 617(TLS):5–11Jan90–17
   J. Whittier-Ferguson, 329(JJQ):Fall89–143
Bek, A. Die Ernennung.
   C. Ebert, 654(WB):7/1989–1162
Bekker, H. Gottfried von Strassburg's "Tristan."
   A. Classen, 597(SN):Vol61No1–127
   T. Kerth, 301(JEGP):Apr89–284
   J.F. Poag, 221(GQ):Spring89–251
Belamri, R. Proverbes et dictons algériens.
   H. Bouraoui, 538(RAL):Summer89–277
Belamri, R. Regard blessé.
   C. Mackey, 207(FR):Dec89–402
Bélanger, R. – see Saint Gregory I
Belasco, W.J. Appetite for Change.
   L. Shapiro, 441:24Jun90–23

Belaval, Y. Digressions sur la rhétorique.
  J. Taylor, 532(RCF):Spring89−261
Belaval, Y. & D. Bourel, eds. Le Siècle des
  Lumières et la Bible.
  R.G. Bonnel, 531:Jan−Mar89−159
Belcher, M. Bird Imagery in the Lyric Poetry
  of Tristan L'Hermite.*
  P. Bouysse, 535(RHL):Nov−Dec89−1054
Belcher, M. A.W.N. Pugin.*
  L. Lambourne, 78(BC):Summer89−269
de' Beldomandi, P. − see under Prosdocimo de'
  Beldomandi
Belenky, M.R. & others. Women's Ways of
  Knowing.
  M.G. Lewis, 529(QQ):Spring89−117
Belford, B. Violet.
  M. Hodgson, 441:21Oct90−16
  M. Seymour, 617(TLS):23−29Nov90−1258
Belfrage, B. − see Berkeley, G.
Belfrage, C. The American Inquisition 1945−
  1960.
  H. Brogan, 617(TLS):29Jun−5Jul90−708
Belfrage, S. Living with War.
  C. Bedient, 472:Vol16No1−195
Bell, A.O. − see Woolf, V.
Bell, B.W. The Afro−American Novel and Its
  Tradition.*
  T.D., 295(JML):Fall88/Winter89−193
  E.L. Steeves, 395(MFS):Summer89−310
Bell, C. The Pérez Family.
  R. Plunket, 441:19Aug90−5
Bell, D., D. Johnson & P. Morris, eds. A Bio−
  grapical Dictionary of French Political
  Leaders since 1870.
  P. McCarthy, 617(TLS):9−15Nov90−1205
Bell, D.F. Models of Power.*
  C. Bertrand−Jennings, 210(FrF):May89−
  246
Bell, J. & M. Watson. Irish Farming.
  P. Perry, 637(VS):Summer90−672
Bell, J.M. & S. Mendus, eds. Philosophy and
  Medical Welfare.
  M. Adam, 542:Oct−Dec89−627
  B.B., 185:Jul90−923
Bell, L.A. Sartre's Ethics of Authenticity.
  D.D., 185:Jul90−916
Bell, M. Martin Bell: Complete Poems. (P.
  Porter, ed)
  F. Grubb, 364:Apr/May89−126
  G. Szirtes, 493:Spring89−66
Bell, M. The Development of American
  Romance.
  G. Dekker, 183(ESQ):Vol35No1−69
Bell, M. New and Selected Poems.*
  G. Kuzma, 502(PrS):Summer89−129
  L. Levis, 29(APR):Jan/Feb89−16
Bell, M., Jr. Major Butler's Legacy.
  D.A. Pyron, 639(VQR):Winter89−146
Bell, M.S. Barking Man.
  R. De Marinis, 441:8Apr90−11
Bell, Q. Bad Art.
  H. Fromm, 219(GaR):Fall89−611
  M. James, 364:Jun/Jul89−137
Bell, R. Radio Poems.
  W.N. Herbert, 571(ScLJ):Winter89−40
Bell, R.E. Place Names in Classical Mythol−
  ogy: Greece.
  W.R. Biers, 124:Mar−Apr90−365
Bell, S.M. Sarraute: "Portrait d'un inconnu"
  and "Vous les entendez?"
  V. Minogue, 402(MLR):Oct90−978

Bell, V.M. The Achievement of Cormac McCar−
  thy.
  L.A. Lawson, 569(SR):Fall89−cx
  A. Shepherd, 392:Spring89−200
  639(VQR):Spring89−50
Bell−Villada, G.H., A. Giménez & G. Pistorius,
  eds. From Dante to García Márquez.
  U. Schulz−Buschhaus, 547(RF):Band101
  Heft2/3−293
  J.J. Smoot, 238:Dec89−964
Bellamy, C. Administering Central−Local
  Relations 1871−1919.
  M. Pugh, 637(VS):Autumn89−208
Bellamy, J.D. Suzi Sinzinnati.
  R.P. Brickner, 441:28Jan90−22
Bellamy, M. A Darling of the Twenties.
  D. Kaufman, 441:25Nov90−19
Bellamy, R. Modern Italian Social Theory.*
  P. Allum, 278(IS):Vol44−181
Bellamy, R., ed. Victorian Liberalism.
  R. Pinker, 617(TLS):16−22Nov90−1224
Bellamy, R. − see Bobbio, N.
Bellefroid, J. Le Festin de Kronos.
  H. Carn, 460(NRF):Sep89−97
Bellenger, Y. Montaigne.*
  K. Cameron, 208(FS):Jan89−81
Bellenger, Y. & D. Quéruel, eds. Thibaut de
  Champagne.
  R. Cormier, 207(FR):Dec89−368
  G. Zaganelli, 547(RF):Band101Heft2/3−
  322
Beller, M. Le Metamorfosi di Mignon
  W. Ross, 52:Band24Heft1−87
  I.H. Solbrig, 133:Band22Heft3/4−320
Beller, S. Vienna and the Jews 1867−1938.*
  R. Morgan, 617(TLS):9−15Mar90−263
Bellestri, J. Basic Sicilian−English Dictio−
  nary.
  A. Vàrvaro, 545(RPh):Feb90−456
Bellet, R. Jules Vallès. (new ed)
  W. Redfern, 402(MLR):Apr90−452
Belletto, R. Eclipse.
  L. Simon, 441:4Feb90−12
Belletto, R. La Machine.
  P. Burton−Page, 617(TLS):30Nov−
  6Dec90−1289
Bellincioni, M.S. − see under Scarpat Bellin−
  cioni, M.
Bellini, M. & others. Emilio Ambasz.
  J.S.R., 45:Oct89−71
Bellos, D. Honoré de Balzac: "Old Goriot."*
  C. Nesci, 210(FrF):May89−238
Bellosi, L., ed. Simone Martini.
  J, Gardner, 90:Jul89−487
Bellow, S. A Theft.*
  W.H. Pritchard, 249(HudR):Autumn89−490
  S. Pinsker, 390:Jun/Jul89−62
Bellush, J. & D. Netzer, eds. Urban Politics,
  New York Style.
  R. Cohn, 441:7Oct90−41
de Belmont, L.A.L. − see under Leo de Bel−
  mont, L.A.
Belmont, N. Paroles païennes.
  B. Lane, 292(JAF):Jul−Sep89−364
Belmonte Serrano, J. − see Sáez, A.
Beloff, J. The Relentless Question.
  M. Gardner, 617(TLS):3−9Aug90−832
Belting, H. Bild und Kult.
  J.M. Massing, 617(TLS):3−9Aug90−826
Belting, H. The End of the History of Art?*
  M. Bell, 529(QQ):Summer89−473
  I. Gaskell, 89(BJA):Spring89−182

Bely, A. Selected Essays of Andrey Bely. (S. Cassedy, ed & trans)
S.J. Rabinowitz, 104(CASS):Spring-Winter88-479

Bement, P. – see Jonson, B.

Ben, T. Conflicts of Interest.
C. Townshend, 617(TLS):2-8Nov90-1168

Benabou, M. Remus, le mur et la mort.
M. Detienne, 98:Apr89-211

Benardete, J.A. Metaphysics.*
R.E. Aquila, 543:Sep89-146
D.E. Bradshaw, 103:Dec90-481

Benardete, S. Socrates' Second Sailing.
S. Corbett, 103:Dec90-483
R.A. Hornsby, 124:Mar-Apr90-374

Benati, D., ed. Il tempo di Nicolò III.
C.B. Strehlke, 90:Aug89-563

Bencard, M., with G.A. Markova. Christian IV's Royal Plate and his Relations with Russia.
C.S., 90:May89-365

Bencheikh, J.E. Les Mille et Une Nuits ou la Parole prisonnière.
H. Cronel, 450(NRF):Oct89-121
E.J. MacArthur, 166:Apr90-257

Bencivenga, E. Kant's Copernican Revolution.*
H. Robinson, 319:Jul90-458

Bender, B. Sea-Brothers.
V. Brehm, 481(PQ):Summer89-383
V. Hyles, 594:Winter89-444
J.W. Tuttleton, 395(MFS):Winter89-743

Bender, J. Imagining the Penitentiary.*
J.P. Carson, 481(PQ):Spring89-275
J.A. Dussinger, 301(JEGP):Jan89-104
T. Erwin, 290(JAAC):Fall89-385
B. Harlow, 454:Winter90-209
J. McVeagh, 566:Spring90-206
A. Morvan, 189(EA):Jul-Sep89-344
M.E. Novak, 677(YES):Vol20-276
P. Sabor, 529(QQ):Spring89-174

Bender, K-H., with H. Kleber, eds. Les Epopées de Croisade.
G.J. Brault, 589:Oct89-921
S.B. Rinne, 345(KRQ):Nov89-488
D.A. Trotter, 382(MAE):1989/1-162
C-A. Van Coolput, 356(LR):Feb-May89-109

Benderson, B. Pretending To Say No.
J. Howard, 441:5Aug90-18

Bendixson, T. Transport in the Nineties.
S. Joseph, 324:Feb90-223

Béné, C., A. Godin & S. Dresden – see Erasmus

Benedetti, J. Stanislavski.*
G. McVay, 511:Apr89-46
L. Senelick, 610:Autumn89-296
B. Whitrow, 364:Apr/May89-144

di Benedetto, V. Sofocle.
M. Heath, 123:Vol39No2-382

Benedict, H. A World Like This.
B. Kent, 441:8Apr90-29

Benedikt, M. For an Architecture of Reality.
R. Kimball, 45:May89-81

Benes, P., ed. The Farm.
S. McMurry, 658:Summer/Autumn89-189

Benes, P., ed. Itinerancy in New England and New York.
J.R. Garrison, 658:Spring89-76

Benestad, F. & D. Schjelderup-Ebbe. Edward Grieg.* (new ed)
J.H., 412:Feb89-68
R. Layton, 415:May89-282

Benezra, N. Ed Paschke.
R. Lippincott, 441:2Sep90-17

Bengtson, H. Die hellenistische Weltkultur.
A. Kuhrt, 123:Vol39No2-286

Bengtson, H. History of Greece from the Beginnings to the Byzantine Era. (E.F. Bloedow, ed & trans)
E. Will, 555:Vol62Fasc2-315

Benhabib, S. Critique, Norm and Utopia.*
E.L. Jurist, 311(JP):Apr89-203

Benhabib, S. & D. Cornell, eds. Feminism as Critique.*
V. Kahn, 153:Summer89-21
D.M. Rosen, 103:Jan90-3

Bénichou, P. Les Mages romantiques.*
J-L. Diaz, 535(RHL):Jul-Aug89-689

Benitez, E.E. Forms in Plato's "Philebus."
S. Scolnicov, 103:Aug90-303

Benítez Rojo, A. The Magic Dog. (F. Janney, ed)
J. Polk, 441:26Aug90-23

Benítez Rojo, A. Sea of Lentils.
F. Luciani, 441:16Dec90-28

Benjamin, A. – see Lyotard, J-F.

Benjamin, A.E., G.N. Cantor & J.R.R. Christie, eds. The Figural and the Literal.*
A. Morvan, 189(EA):Jul-Sep89-341

Benjamin, W. Lumières pour enfants. (R. Tiedeman, ed)
S. Brussell, 450(NRF):Jul-Aug89-192

Benjamin, W. & G. Scholem. The Correspondence of Walter Benjamin and Gershom Scholem: 1932-40.
G. Steiner, 442(NY):22Jan90-133

Ben Jelloun, T. The Sacred Night.* (French title: La Nuit sacrée.)
R. Buss, 617(TLS):15-21Jun90-654

Benn, G. Prosa I, Prosa 2. (I. Benn & G. Schuster, eds)
H. Hartung, 358:Feb90-7

Benn, S.I. A Theory of Freedom.*
P. Gilbert, 518:Oct89-226

Bennassar, B. & L. Les Chrétiens d'Allah.
R. Irwin, 617(TLS):9-15Feb90-151

Bennett, A. The Death of the Organization Man.
M.A. Elliott, 441:18Mar90-21

Bennett, A. Letters of Arnold Bennett.* (Vol 4) (J. Hepburn, ed)
J. Lucas, 677(YES):Vol20-320

Bennett, B. Goethe's Theory of Poetry.*
J.F. Hyde, Jr., 406:Winter89-476

Bennett, B. Hugo von Hofmannsthal.*
639(VQR):Spring89-46

Bennett, B. Modern Drama and German Classicism.*
K.F. Hilliard, 83:Spring89-123

Bennett, B.T. – see Shelley, M.W.

Bennett, D. Emily Davies and the Liberation of Women 1830-1921.
B. Harrison, 617(TLS):16-22Mar90-296

Bennett, D.H. The Party of Fear.*
W. McCuaig, 529(QQ):Winter89-962

Bennett, H.S. English Books and Readers.
617(TLS):24-30Aug90-905

Bennett, J.A.W. Middle English Literature.* (D. Gray, ed)
A.E. Hartung, 589:Oct89-922
D. Mehl, 38:Band107Heft1/2-176
G. Schmitz, 72:Band226Heft1-147

Bennett, J.F. Events and Their Names.*
L.B. McHenry, 543:Sep89-148

Bennett, J.G. My Father's Geisha.
M. Gingher, 441:24Jun90-15
Bennett, J.R. A Bibliography of Stylistics and Related Criticism, 1967-1983.
D. Burton, 599:Spring90-153
Bennett, J.S. Reviving Liberty.*
J.H. Sims, 568(SCN):Fall-Winter89-33
Bennett, M. Artists of the Pre-Raphaelite Circle: The First Generation.
V. Surtees, 90:Nov89-788
Bennett, M.J. Lambert Simnel and the Battle of Stoke.*
L. Attreed, 589:Jan89-117
Bennett, P. An Endangered Happiness.
S. Mackay, 617(TLS):17-23Aug90-868
Bennett, P. Rough and Rowdy Ways.
E.P. Sewell, 649(WAL):Aug89-179
Bennett, S.M. Thomas Stothard.*
G.E. Bentley, Jr., 88:Spring90-205
D.B. Brown, 90:Nov89-786
Bennington, G. Lyotard.
I. Whitehouse, 402(MLR):Oct90-989
Bennington, G. Sententiousness and the Novel.*
M.E. Vialet, 345(KRQ):Feb89-110
Bennis, H. & T. Hoekstra. Generatieve Grammatica.
A. Foolen, 204(FdL):Dec89-309
Benny, J. & J. Sunday Nights at Seven.
P. Keepnews, 441:11Nov90-61
Benoit, F. & P. Chaveau. Acceptation Globale.
T. Goldie, 102(CanL):Winter88-128
Benoit, P., P. Le Brigand & D. Truchot. Films de pub.
A.J.M. Prévos, 207(FR):Feb90-602
Bensaïd, D. & A. Krivine. Mai si! 1968-1988.
A.J.M. Prévos, 207(FR):Mar90-756
Benseler, D.P., W.F.W. Lohnes & V. Nollendorfs, eds. Teaching German in America.
R. Brod, 399(MLJ):Summer89-231
Benski, S. Missing Pieces.
J. Bayley, 453(NYRB):19Jul90-23
E. Hanson, 441:2Sep90-16
Bensmaia, R. The Barthes Effect.*
A.J. Sabatini, 295(JML):Fall88/Winter89-283
Benson, C.D. Chaucer's Drama of Style.*
R.F. Green, 589:Jul89-658
Benson, E. & L.W. Connoly. English-Canadian Theatre.*
R.G. Lawrence, 611(TN):Vol43No1-36
Benson, J., comp. Uncle Joe's Record Guide: Eric Clapton, Jimi Hendrix, and The Who. Uncle Joe's Record Guide: Hard Rock, The First Two Generations.
B.L. Cooper, 498:Fall89-104
Benson, J.J. Looking for Steinbeck's Ghost.
R.W. Lewis, 456(NDQ):Summer89-264
J.R. Millichap, 395(MFS):Winter89-753
N.E. Zane, 27(AL):Dec89-707
Benson, L.D. - see Chaucer, G.
Benson, M., ed. From Pittsburgh to the Rocky Mountains.
D. Engel, 649(WAL):Aug89-161
Benson, M., E. Benson & R. Ilson, comps. The BBI Combinatory Dictionary of English.
A.S. Kaye & K. McDaniel, 361:Apr89-375
T.M. Paikeday, 35(AS):Winter89-354
Benson, P. The Other Occupant.
M. Casserley, 617(TLS):11-17May90-496

Benson, T.O. Raoul Hausmann and Berlin Dada.*
L.A. Lensing, 564:Feb89-65
E.S., 295(JML):Fall88/Winter89-182
Benstock, B., ed. Critical Essays on James Joyce's "Ulysses."
B. Cheyette, 617(TLS):5-11Jan90-17
C. Ford, 329(JJQ):Summer90-878
Benstock, B., ed. James Joyce: The Augmented Ninth.
B. Cheyette, 617(TLS):5-11Jan90-17
M. Ellmann, 329(JJQ):Fall89-139
C. Shloss, 395(MFS):Autumn89-617
Benstock, S., ed. Feminist Issues in Literary Scholarship.*
A.S.L., 295(JML):Fall88/Winter89-183
Benstock, S., ed. The Private Self.*
42(AR):Summer89-370
Bensussan, G. Questions juives.
P. Trotignon, 542:Oct-Dec89-641
Bent, I., with W. Drabkin. Analysis.*
M. Musgrave, 411:Mar/Jul89-177
van Bentham, J. A Manual of Intensional Logic. (2nd ed)
R.A. Bull, 316:Dec89-1489
Bentley, D.M.R. - see Cary, T.
Bentley, D.M.R. - see Crawford, I.V.
Bentley, D.M.R. - see Lampman, A.
Bentley, D.M.R. - see Mackay, J.
Bentley, D.M.R., with C.R. Steele - see Kidd, A.
Bentley, G.E., Jr. Blake Records Supplement.*
L.M. Findlay, 447(N&Q):Dec89-520
Bentley, J.H. Politics and Culture in Renaissance Naples.
C.L. Stinger, 551(RenQ):Winter89-830
Bentley, N., M. Slater & N. Burgis. The Dickens Index.*
A.S. Watts, 155:Summer89-118
Benton, J. Naomi Mitchison.
M. Beard, 617(TLS):19-25Oct90-1116
Bentsen, C. Maasai Days.*
E. Gillies, 617(TLS):26Jan-1Feb90-97
Benussi, C. & G. Lughi. Il romanzo d'esordio tra immaginario e mercato.
R. Zaiser, 547(RF):Band101Heft2/3-361
Benware, W.A. Phonetics and Phonology of Modern German.*
M. Bonner, 685(ZDL):2/1989-193
Benya, R., comp. Children and Languages.* (K. Muller, ed)
M. Met, 238:May89-312
Benziman, U. Sharon.
A. Margalit, 453(NYRB):26Apr90-38
"Beowulf." (R.P.M. Lehmann, trans)
J.M. Hill, 496:Spring89-50
Bepler, J. Ferdinand Albrecht, Duke of Braunschweig-Lüneberg (1636-1687).
A.J. Harper, 402(MLR):Jan90-241
Berberova, N. Three Novels.
L. Chamberlain, 617(TLS):20-26Jul90-781
Bercé, F. & B. Foucart. Viollet-le-Duc.
W.W. Clark, 127:Winter89-356
de Berceo, G. El Libro de los "Milagros de Nuestra Señora."* (J. Montoya Martínez, ed)
D. Devoto, 92(BH):Jul-Dec88-429
Berchez Gómez, J. Arquitectura y academicismo en el siglo XVIII valenciano.
A. Ubeda de los Cobos, 48:Oct-Dec89-477

Bereiter, C. & M. Scardamalia. The Psychology of Written Composition.
A. Cumming, 399(MLJ):Spring89–74
Berend, I.T. The Crisis Zone of Europe.*
A.C. Janos, 104(CASS):Spring89–126
Berenson, B. & I.S. Gardner, with M. Berenson. The Letters of Bernard Berenson and Isabella Stewart Gardner 1887–1924, with Correspondence by Mary Berenson.* (R.V. Hadley, ed)
D. Garstang, 39:Feb89–135
Berenson, B. & C. Marghieri. A Matter of Passion. (D. Biocca, ed)
J. Rosselli, 617(TLS):9–15Feb90–139
Beresford, A. The Sele of the Morning.
W.S. Milne, 4:Summer89–44
Beresford, G. Goltho. (J. Geddes, ed)
K. Biddick, 589:Jul89–660
Beresford-Howe, C. Prospero's Daughter.
C. Rooke, 376:Mar89–124
Berg, A. & A. Schoenberg. Berg-Schoenberg Correspondence, Selected Letters.* (J. Brand, C. Hailey & D. Harris, eds)
P. Banks, 415:Feb89–84
Berg, A.S. Goldwyn.*
S.G. Kellman, 390:Dec89–32
Berg, H.W. Das Erbe der Grossmoguln.
A. Bharati, 293(JASt):Aug89–643
Berg, S.C. Le Sacre du Printemps.
R. Johnson, 151:Nov89–92
Berg, T. Die Abbildung des Sprachproduktionsprozesses in einem Aktivationsflussmodell.
H-G. Bosshardt, 348(L&S):Apr–Jun89–179
Bergan, R. & R. Karney. Bloomsbury Foreign Film Guide.
N. Roddick, 707:Winter88/89–69
Berge, K.L. Skolestilen som genre.
F.H. Mortensen, 172(Edda):1989/1–85
Berger, B. The Telling Distance.
J. Alcock, 441:2Sep90–13
Berger, B.M., ed. Authors of Their Own Lives.
P. Thomas, 441:19Aug90–22
Berger, E. Der Parthenon in Basel.*
R. Brilliant, 576:Mar89–80
Berger, E., ed. Parthenon-Kongress Basel.*
R. Brilliant, 576:Mar89–80
Berger, H., Jr. Revisionary Plan.
E.J. Bellamy, 604:Winter89–2
639(VQR):Spring89–49
Berger, H., Jr., ed. Second World and Green World.
J. Dillon, 402(MLR):Oct90–898
Berger, J. Lilac and Flag.
R. Boyers, 441:19Aug90–20
Berger, K. Musica ficta.
C. Berger, 417:Oct–Dec89–372
G. Durosoir, 537:Vol75No1–105
J. Herlinger, 317:Fall89–640
D. Leech-Wilkinson, 415:Apr89–213
P.N. Schubert, 143:No44–99
Berger, M. Labyrinths.
L.E. Nesbitt, 441:16Sep90–23
Berger, M.R. Sprachkontakt in der Bretagne.
J. Le Dû, 547(RF):Band101Heft4–465
Berger, P. Big Time.
C. Salzberg, 441:18Nov90–28
Berger, P. The Goddess Obscured.*
J. Chiti, 662:Spring/Summer89–50
Berger, P. Libro y lectura en la Valencia del Renacimiento.
J-L. Marfany, 86(BHS):Oct89–390

Berger, S., F. Slocum & R. Foley. Topps Baseball Cards.
D. Thornburgh, 441:2Dec90–44
Berger, T. Changing the Past.*
J. Clute, 617(TLS):27Apr–3May90–456
Berger, T. Orrie's Story.
T.M. Disch, 441:7Oct90–12
Bergeron, D.M. & G.U. de Sousa, eds. Shakespeare.
J.J. Yoch, Jr., 570(SQ):Spring89–113
Berges, D. Hellenistische Rundaltäre Kleinasiens.
H. Lauter-Bufe, 229:Band61Heft4–376
Berghahn, K.L. Schiller.*
T. Kontje, 222(GR):Spring89–85
Berghaus, G. Die Quellen zu Andreas Gryphius' Trauerspiel "Carolus Stuardus."
G. Hillen, 133:Band22Heft1–59
Berglund-Nilsson, B., ed. Correspondance littéraire secrète, 1 janvier–22 juin 1776.
J. Lough, 208(FS):Jan89–91
D. Williams, 402(MLR):Oct90–965
Bergman, D. – see Ashbery, J.
Bergman, I. The Magic Lantern.* (French title: Laterna Magica.)
D. Flower, 249(HudR):Summer89–330
G. Weales, 219(GaR):Summer89–417
Bergmann, J.R. Klatsch.
M. Faust, 685(ZDL):2/1989–267
Bergmann, M.S. The Anatomy of Loving.
G.S. Reed, 473(PR):Vol56No3–515
Bergmann, P. Nietzsche, "the Last Antipolitical German."*
A. Del Caro, 221(GQ):Winter89–131
F.R. Love, 406:Summer89–268
Bergmann, R., with E.P. Diedrichs & C. Treutwein. Katalog der deutschsprachigen geistlichen Spiele und Marienklagen des Mittelalters.
E. Simon, 589:Jan89–118
B. Thoran, 680(ZDP):Band108Heft1–123
Bergmann, R., H. Tiefenbach & L. Voetz, with others, eds. Althochdeutsch.
J.M. Jeep, 350:Sep90–624
Bergreen, L. As Thousands Cheer.
G. Lees, 441:1Jul90–1
E.S. Turner, 617(TLS):31Aug–6Sep90–918
Bergström, I. Grammatical Correctness and Communicative Ability.*
L. Kuure, 710:Sep89–342
Bering, D. Der Name als Stigma.*
S.L. Gilman, 406:Summer89–248
W.F.H. Nicolaisen, 424:Mar89–97
Berio, T.P. – see under Pecker Berio, T.
Bériou, N. – see Ranulphe de la Houblonnière.
Berjonneau, G. & J-L. Sonnery, eds. Rediscovered Masterpieces of African Art.
L.T. Wells, Jr., 2(AfrA):Nov88–29
Berke, D. & D. Hanemann, eds. Alte Musik als ästhetische Gegenwart.
W. Rathert, 417:Jul–Sep89–272
Berke, J.H. The Tyranny of Malice.
639(VQR):Summer89–103
Berkeley, G. George Berkeley's Manuscript Introduction.* (B. Belfrage, ed & trans)
H.M. Bracken, 319:Jul90–455
Berkenbusch, G. Sprachpolitik und Sprachbewusstsein in Barcelona am Anfang dieses Jahrhunderts.
H. Hina, 547(RF):Band101Heft2/3–304
Berki, J. Tales of Janos Berki. (V. Görög, ed)
S. Douglas, 203:Vol100No2–259
Berkove, L.I. – see De Quille, D.

Berkovitz, J.R. The Shaping of Jewish Identi-
ty in Nineteenth-Century France.
R.S. Wistrich, 617(TLS):23-29Nov90-1261
Berkowitz, B.D. American Security.
A.J.T., 185:Oct89-224
Berkson, W. & J. Wettersten. Learning from
Error.
B.T. Wilkins, 606:Mar89-357
Berkvens-Stevelinck, C. Catalogue des man-
uscrits de la collection Prosper Marchand.
Prosper Marchand.
D. McKitterick, 78(BC):Autumn89-301
Berlin, I. The Crooked Timber of Humanity.
(H. Hardy, ed)
J. Dunn, 617(TLS):5-11Oct90-1053
"Berlin Antikenmuseum: Kaiser Augustus und
die Verlorene Republik."
R.R.R. Smith, 313:Vol79-213
Berliner, J.S. Soviet Industry from Stalin to
Gorbachev.
J.R. Millar, 550(RusR):Apr89-226
Berman, A. From the New Criticism to Decon-
struction.*
H. Bertens, 402(MLR):Jul90-675
Berman, A. Rebels on Eighth Street.
R. Robinson, 441:15Apr90-16
442(NY):23Apr90-116
Berman, D. A History of Atheism in Britain:
From Hobbes to Russell.
A. Flew, 518:Apr89-126
M. Tyacke, 242.Vol10No4 407
Berman, I.V. - see "The Talmud"
Berman, W.C. William Fulbright and the Viet-
nam War.*
G.S. Smith, 529(QQ):Winter89-986
Bermingham, A. Landscape and Ideology.*
D. Robinson, 90:Jun89-431
E. Shanes, 39:Mar89-220
Bernabé, A. Poetae Epici Graeci. (Pt 1)
M. Davies, 123:Vol39No1-4
Bernal, M. Black Athena.* (Vol 1)
J. Donelan, 147:Vol6No3-98
M.A. Malamud, 141:Summer89-317
Bernard, A. Blackbird Bye Bye.*
A. Corn, 491:Jan90-283
Bernard, A. Pirate Jenny.
B. Kent, 441:17Jun90-16
Bernard, J.W. The Music of Edgard Varèse.
J.C., 412:Nov88-313
S. Trezise, 411:Oct89-337
Bernard, W. Rezeptivität und Spontaneität
der Wahrnehmung bei Aristoteles.
H. Schmitz, 489(PJGG):Band96Heft2-394
Bernardo, A.S. - see Petrarch
Bernasconi, R. - see Gadamer, H-G.
Bernau, G. Candle in the Wind.
F.J. Prial, 441:21Oct90-24
Bernauer, J. & D. Rasmussen, eds. The Final
Foucault.
D. Latané, 147:Vol6No1-39
L. McWhorter, 103:Sep90-352
Bernd, C.A., ed. Grillparzer's "Der arme
Spielmann."*
A. Classen, 597(SN):Vol61No2-245
R.C. Holub, 221(GQ):Spring89-278
Berner, C. - see Schleiermacher, F.D.E.
Bernet, C. Le Vocabulaire des tragédies de
Jean Racine.*
J. Kirkness, 208(FS):Jan89-85
Bernet, C. & P. Rézeau. Dictionnaire du fran-
çais parlé.
D. Coward, 617(TLS):27Apr-3May90-451

Bernet Kempers, A.J. The Kettledrums of
Southeast Asia.
K.M. Hood, 187:Spring/Summer89-330
Bernhard, T. Maîtres anciens, comédie.
C. Thomas, 98:Mar89-128
Bernhard, T. Wittgenstein's Nephew.*
639(VQR):Summer89-92
Bernheimer, C. Figure of Ill Repute.
J.F. McMillan, 617(TLS):7-13Dec90-1317
Bernier, O. Words of Fire, Deeds of Blood.*
J.P. Gilroy, 207(FR):May90-1112
Bernier, O. - see Duchesse D'Ambrantès
Bernier, R. Aux sources de la biologie. (Vol
2)
D. Asselin, 154:Vol28No4-689
Bernini, C., T. Sprecher & H. Wysling, eds.
Internationales Thomas-Mann-Kolloquium
1986 in Lübeck.
R.S. Lucas, 402(MLR):Apr90-525
Bernofsky, S. - see Walser, R.
Bernos, M., ed. Sexualité et religions.
F. Merllié, 542:Oct-Dec89-641
Berns, G.N. Greek Antiquity in Schiller's
"Wallenstein."*
A. Schmitt, 52:Band24Heft1-90
Bernstein, A. Grounded.
W. Stockton, 441:26Aug90-11
Bernstein, C. Loyalties.*
H. Brogan, 617(TLS):9-15Mar90-255
L. Quart, 390:Jun/Jul89-63
Bernstein, G.L. & H. Fukui, eds. Japan and
the World.*
J.M. Maki, 293(JASt):May89-383
Bernstein, H. & others, eds. The Food Ques-
tion.
F. Judd, 324:Sep90-710
Bernstein, I. A Caring Society.
J. Braeman, 106:Summer89-41
Bernstein, I. The New York City Draft Riots.
J.M. McPherson, 453(NYRB):12Apr90-33
R. Wechsler, 441:7Jan90-20
Bernstein, J.A. Nietzsche's Moral Philoso-
phy.*
K.D. Jolley, 319:Jul90-463
Bernstein, R. Fragile Glory.
D. Bair, 441:7Oct90-13
Bernstein, R.J., ed. Habermas and Modernity.
J. Zuñiga, 449:Apr89-072
Béroalde De Verville. Le Moyen de parvenir.
(I. Zinguer, ed)
M.J. Giordano, 207(FR):Oct89-158
Beroul. Tristran and Yseut. (G.R. Mermier,
ed)
S. Gregory, 208(FS):Jul89-316
Berresford Ellis, P. & S. Mac a'Ghobhainn.
The Scottish Insurrection of 1820.
617(TLS):29Jun-5Jul90-708
Berrio, G.D. - see under Díez Berrio, G.
Berrong, R.M. Rabelais and Bakhtin.*
R.C. La Charité, 210(FrF):Sep89-352
E. Ragland-Sullivan, 345(KRQ):Feb89-
104
Berrouët-Oriol, R. Lettres urbaines.
J.P. Gilroy, 102(CanL):Spring89-187
Berruto, G. Sociolinguistica del l'italiano
contemporaneo.
M. Palermo, 708:Vol14Fasc2-278
Berry, C. Human Nature.
S.M., 185:Jan90-441
Berry, C. Vocal Chamber Duets.
A.F.L.T., 412:May89-146

Berry, H. Shakespeare's Playhouses.*
  S.P. Cerasano, 570(SQ):Fall89-366
  R.L. Knutson, 551(RenQ):Spring89-135
  J. Orrell, 402(MLR):Jul90-689
Berry, R. A Pope Chronology.
  V. Carretta, 566:Spring89-181
  K. Combe, 447(N&Q):Dec89-513
Berry, R. Shakespeare and Social Class.
  S.G. Putt, 570(SQ):Fall89-359
Berry, S. A Stranger in Tibet.
  J.H. Crook, 617(TLS):5-11Oct90-1081
Berry, W. Home Economics.*
  J.T. Barbarese, 219(GaR):Spring89-208
  B. Christophersen, 502(PrS):Winter89-131
Berry, W. Remembering.*
  J. Kilgo, 569(SR):Spring89-lvi
  639(VQR):Spring89-56
Berry, W. What Are People For?
  H. Bevington, 441:15Apr90-12
  B. McKibben, 453(NYRB):14Jun90-30
Berryman, J. Collected Poems 1937-1971.*
  (C. Thornbury, ed)
  M. Hofmann, 617(TLS):6-12Apr90-363
  B. Leithauser, 442(NY):30Apr90-110
Berryman, J. The Dream Songs.
  M. Hofmann, 617(TLS):6-12Apr90-363
Berryman, J. We Dream of Honour. (R.J.
  Kelly, ed)
  K. Davis, 27(AL):Mar89-141
  M. Hofmann, 617(TLS):6-12Apr90-363
Bersani, L. The Culture of Redemption.
  J. Sturrock, 441:19Aug90-23
Berschin, W. Biographie und Epochenstil im
  lateinischen Mittelalter. (Vol 2)
  G.J.M. Bartelink, 640:May89-83
Bersianik, L. & others. La Théorie, un dim-
  anche.
  A-M. Picard, 627(UTQ):Fall89-206
Bertaud, M. "L'Astrée" et "Polexandre."*
  E. Woodrough, 402(MLR):Jan90-182
Bertelà, M. Stendhal et l'Autre.
  L. Czyba, 535(RHL):Mar-Apr89-302
Bertelsmeier-Kierst, C. "Griseldis" in
  Deutschland.
  J.L. Flood, 402(MLR):Jul90-784
Bertelson, D. Snowflakes and Snowdrifts.
  G. McCann, 488:Mar89-133
Bertens, H. & T. D'haen. Het postmodernisme
  in de literatuur.
  E. van Alphen, 204(FdL):Sep89-234
Berthelot, J-M. - see Durkheim, E.
Berthet, F. Daimler s'en va.
  N. Ekstein, 207(FR):May90-1097
Berthier, B. La Dame-du-bord-de-l'eau.
  S. Naquin, 293(JASt):Nov89-817
Berthier, P. "L'Ensorcelée," "Les Diaboliques"
  de Barbey d'Aurevilly.
  G. Mead, 446(NCFS):Fall-Winter89/90-
  253
  A. Toumayan, 210(FrF):Jan89-107
Berthier, P., ed. Relire "Les Mémoires d'un
  touriste" (1838-1988).
  G. De Wulf, 356(LR):Aug89-215
  W.A. Guentner, 446(NCFS):Fall-
  Winter89/90-242
  P. Petitier, 535(RHL):Mar-Apr89-301
Berthier, P. Stendhal et Chateaubriand.*
  J.T. Day, 207(FR):Mar90-716
  R. Pearson, 208(FS):Jan89-94
  E.J. Talbot, 210(FrF):May89-241
Berthier, P. Stendhal et la Sainte Famille.
  G. De Wulf, 356(LR):Feb-May89-116

Berthier, P. Le Théâtre au XIXe siècle.
  J-M. Thomasseau, 535(RHL):Mar-Apr89-
  314
Berthier, P. - see "Barbey d'Aurevilly"
Berthier, P. & K. Ringger, eds. Littérature et
  opéra.
  A. Laster, 535(RHL):Mar-Apr89-336
  R. Lloyd, 208(FS):Jan89-113
Berthoff, W. Hart Crane.
  L. Woodman, 27(AL):Dec89-719
Berthold-Bond, D. Hegel's Grand Synthesis.
  125:Summer89-424
Bertière, S. - see Cardinal de Retz
Bertin, C. Marie Bonaparte.
  J.P. Plottel, 77:Winter89-73
Bertin, M., ed. The Play and Its Critic.*
  G. Armstrong, 610:Summer89-214
Bertini, G. La Galleria del Duca di Parma -
  Storia di una collezione.
  G. Perini, 90:Aug89-566
Bertola, A.D. Viaggio sul Reno e ne' suoi
  contorni. (M. & A. Stäuble, eds)
  S. Buccini, 276:Autumn89-343
Bertoncini, E.Z. Kiswahili kwa furaha. (Pt 1)
  S. Brauner, 682(ZPSK):Band42Heft6-872
Bertoni, A. - see Marinetti, F.T.
Bertrand, C. Fiction-nuit.
  B. Godard, 102(CanL):Winter88-123
Bertrand, M. Langue romanesque et parole
  scripturale.
  J. Pierrot, 535(RHL):Mar-Apr89-346
Bertrand de Muñoz, M. La guerra civil españ-
  ola en la novela. (Vol 3)
  M. Lentzen, 547(RF):Band101Heft2/3-383
Bertrand-Jennings, C. Espaces romanesques:
  Zola.*
  C. Becker, 535(RHL):Jul-Aug89-739
  S. Capitanio, 208(FS):Jan89-345
  G. Regn, 547(RF):Band101Heft4-486
  P.H. Solomon, 345(KRQ):Aug89-383
  P. Walker, 210(FrF):Jan89-108
Bérubé, A. Coming Out Under Fire.
  D.K. Goodwin, 441:8Apr90-9
  442(NY):2Jul90-74
de Berval, R., ed. Présence du Bouddhisme.*
  J.W. de Jong, 259(IIJ):Jul89-232
Berwick, D. Amazon.
  S. Mills, 617(TLS):7-13Dec90-1315
Besch, W. & others, eds. Dialektologie.
  D. Hymes, 355(LSoc):Jun89-259
Besch, W., O. Reichmann & S. Sonderegger,
  eds. Sprachgeschichte.* (Vols 1 & 2)
  W. Fleischer, 682(ZPSK):Band42Heft2-260
"Le Bescherelle 2."
  W. Greenberg, 399(MLJ):Winter89-503
Besharov, D.J. Recognizing Child Abuse.
  M. Sandmaier, 441:9Sep90-34
Beskow, B. Ny himmel, ny jord.
  L. Karlsson, 341:Vol58No2-92
Besner, N.K. The Light of Imagination.*
  L.D. Clement, 627(UTQ):Fall89-159
  S.R. Dorscht, 49:Jul89-92
  B. Powell, 647:Spring89-77
Besnier, J-M. & J-P. Thomas, eds. Chron-
  iques des idées d'aujourd'hui.
  P. Livet, 192(EP):Jul-Dec89-535
Besques, S. Musée du Louvre: Catalogue rai-
  sonné de figurines et reliefs en terre-cuite
  grecs, étrusques et romains. (Vol 4, Pt 1)
  D. Graepler, 229:Band61Heft8-752

Bessai, D. & D. Kerr, eds. NeWest Plays by Women.*
  M. Day, 102(CanL):Summer89-138
  529(QQ):Summer89-570
Bessière, J., ed. Modernités de Jules Verne.
  K. Berri, 561(SFS):Nov89-369
Besson, L. Le Grand Bleu.
  J. Decock, 207(FR):Dec89-394
Best, G., ed. The Permanent Revolution.*
  J.P. Gilroy, 207(FR):May90-1112
Best, T.W., ed. Cancer; Edmund Stubbe: Fraus Honesta.
  G. Eatough, 123:Vol39No1-129
  R. Green, 447(N&Q):Dec89-498
Besterman, T. - see de Voltaire, F.M.A.
Besters-Dilger, J. Zur Negation im Russischen und Polnischen.
  J.A. Dunn, 575(SEER):Oct89-603
Beston, H. Herbs and the Earth.
  L. Yang, 441:2Dec90-21
Bestor, T.C. Neighborhood Tokyo.
  W. Edwards, 407(MN):Autumn89-372
  C.S. Littleton, 293(JASt):Nov89-852
Bestul, T.H., ed. A Durham Book of Devotions.
  G.R. Evans, 589:Jul89-661
Betancourt, P.P. The History of Minoan Pottery.*
  W-D. Niemeier, 229:Band61Heft8-720
Betancourt, R.F. - see under Fornet Betancourt, R.
Bethea, D.M. The Shape of Apocalypse in Modern Russian Fiction.
  P.R. Hart, 574(SEEJ):Winter89-622
  T.G. Marullo, 395(MFS):Winter89-836
  C. Whitcomb, 593:Winter89/90-304
Bettelheim, B. Freud's Vienna and Other Essays.
  W.J. McGrath, 441:21Jan90-22
Bettelheim, B. Recollections and Reflections.
  A. Clare, 617(TLS):30Mar-5Apr90-340
Betten, A. Grundzüge der Prosasyntax.
  M.R. Barnes, 133:Band22Heft0/4-383
  K. Kelnäslö, 439(NM):1989/0&4-005
  E. Meineke, 685(ZDL):1/1989-94
Betterton, R., ed. Looking On.
  P. Mathews, 662:Fall89/Winter90-44
Betthausen, P. & others, eds. The Romantic Spirit.
  K. Andrews, 90:Oct89-718
Bettinotti, J. & others. La corrida de l'amour.
  T. Goldie, 102(CanL):Winter88-128
Bettoni, C., ed. Altro Polo: Italian Abroad.
  F.J. Bosco, 355(LSoc):Sep89-395
  M. Danesi, 276:Summer89-212
  H.W. Haller, 276:Summer89-214
Betts, J.H., J.T. Hooker & J.R. Green. Studies in Honour of T.B.L. Webster. (Vol 2)
  J. Boardman, 123:Vol39No2-424
Beuchot, M. Esayos marginales sobre Aristóteles.
  P. Louis, 555:Vol62Fasc1-147
Beuchot, M. La filosofía del lenguaje en la Edad Media.
  C. Rojas Osorio, 160:Jan89-221
Beum, R. Celebrations.
  R. Scheele, 569(SR):Winter89-xvii
Bevan, D., ed. Literary Gastronomy.
  A. Armstrong, 395(MFS):Winter89-863
  B. Fink, 207(FR):Oct89-152
  U. Schulz-Buschhaus, 602:Band20Heft2-332
Bevan, D. - see Langlois, W.
Bevegni, C. - see Manuel II Palaeologus

Beveridge, J. The Domesticity of Giraffes.
  V. Newsom, 581:Mar89-118
Beverley, J. Del Lazarillo al sandinismo.
  E. Rhodes, 304(JHP):Winter89-169
Bevington, D. Action Is Eloquence.
  J.A. Bryant, Jr., 569(SR):Summer89-445
Bevington, D. & others - see Shakespeare, W.
Bevis, R.W. English Drama.*
  J. Conaghan, 541(RES):Aug89-445
  D. Wykes, 447(N&Q):Dec89-508
Bevis, W.W. Mind of Winter.
  R.R. Labbe, 705:Fall89-229
  639(VQR):Autumn89-120
Bew, P. Conflict and Conciliation in Ireland 1890-1910.*
  J.D. Fair, 637(VS):Spring90-516
Bewell, A. Wordsworth and the Enlightenment.*
  D. Perkins, 445(NCF):Mar90-543
Beyen, R. Bibliographie de Michel de Ghelderode.*
  J. Decock, 207(FR):Dec89-381
Beyer, M. Das Staunen in Shakespeares Dramen.
  E. Auberlen, 156(ShJW):Jahrbuch1989-377
Beyer, T.R., Jr. - see Lourié, V.
Beyer, T.R., Jr., G. Kratz & Z. Werner. Russian Berlin.
  T. Pachmuss, 574(SEEJ):Fall89-457
  G.S. Smith, 575(SEER):Jul89-442
Beyer, V., C. Wild-Block & F. Zschokke. Les Vitraux de la Cathédrale Notre-Dame de Strasbourg.*
  M.H. Caviness, 90:Jan89-38
Beylie, C. Marcel Pagnol ou le cinéma en liberté.
  J.J. Michalczyk, 207(FR):Oct89-194
de Beynac, J.C. & M. Magnien - see under Cubelier de Beynac, J. & M. Magnien
Beyrer, A., K. Bochmann & S. Bronsert. Grammatik der rumänischen Sprache der Gegenwart.
  J. Erfurt & A. Turculeţ, 682(ZPSK):Band42Heft1-108
Beyssade, J-M. & M. - see Descartes, R.
Bozantakos, N.P. Ho archaios Hellenikos mithos
  A.G. Geddes, 123:Vol39No1-101
Bezeczky, T. Roman Amphorae from the Amber Route in Western Pannonia.
  S. Martin-Kilcher, 229:Band61Heft7-650
Bhabha, H.K., ed. Nation and Narration.
  B. Cheyette, 617(TLS):14-20Sep90-979
Bhabra, H.S. Gestures.
  T. Goldie, 102(CanL):Winter88-128
Bhalla, A. Latin American Writers.
  P. Swanson, 86(BHS):Jan89-111
Bhaskar, R. Reclaiming Reality.
  E. James, 617(TLS):2-8Mar90-227
Bhatia, T.K. A History of the Hindi Grammatical Tradition.*
  M.C. Shapiro, 293(JASt):Aug89-644
Bhaṭṭa, N. The Bridge to the Three Holy Cities. (R. Salomon, ed & trans)
  P.E. Muller-Ortega, 318(JAOS):Jan-Mar88-184
  S. Pollock, 293(JASt):May89-429
Bhattacharyya, D.P. "Pāgalāmi."
  L.A. Rhodes, 293(JASt):Feb89-194
Bialer, S. & M. Mandelbaum. The Global Rivals.
  A. Milward, 617(TLS):26Jan-1Feb90-81

Białostocki, J. The Message of Images.
  J.M. Massing, 90:Jun89-436
Bian Xiaoxuan. Liu Yuxi congkao.
  W.H.N., 116:Dec89-169
Bianchi, U. Problemi di storia delle religioni.
  J-C. Richard, 555:Vol62Fasc1-171
Bianciardi, F. & C. Porta. Keyboard Composi-
  tions. (B. Billeter, ed)
  A. Silbiger, 317:Spring89-172
Bianco, D. Heat Wave.
  B.L. Cooper, 498:Summer89-111
Bianconi, L. Music in the Seventeenth Cen-
  tury.
  W. Braun, 417:Oct-Dec89-377
  G.J. Buelow, 410(M&L):Feb89-91
  E.T. Harris, 309:Vol9No2/3-212
Bianconi, L. & G. Pestelli, eds. Storia dell'-
  opera italiana. (Vol 5)
  M. Ambrose, 410(M&L):Nov89-531
Biardeau, M. Hinduism.
  R.S. Khare, 617(TLS):21-27Sep90-1008
de Biasi, P-M. - see Flaubert, G.
Biba, O. - see Griesinger, G.A.
Bibby, R.W. Fragmented Gods.
  M. van Die, 529(QQ):Spring89-208
Biber, D. Variation Across Speech and Writ-
  ing.
  A.H. Jucker, 297(JL):Sep89-480
von Biberach, R. - see under Rudolf von Bib-
  erach
de Bibiena, J.G. La Poupée.*
  V. Mylne, 208(FS):Jan89-89
"Biblia Pauperum."* (A. Henry, ed)
  R. Ellis, 382(MAE):1989/1-133
Bibolet, J-C., ed. Le "Mystère de la Passion"
  de Troyes.*
  H. Arden, 589:Apr89-390
  J. Enders, 207(FR):Mar90-704
Bickel, G.A.C. Jean Genet.*
  M. Autrand, 535(RHL):Nov-Dec89-1083
  M.A.F. Witt, 210(FrF):Sep89-364
Bickerman, E.J. The Jews in the Greek Age.*
  A. Tripolitis, 124:Jan-Feb90-256
Bickerton, D. Language & Species.
  R. Wright, 441:23Dec90-11
Bickham, J.M. Dropshot.
  N. Callendar, 441:11Mar90-33
Bickley, R.B., Jr. Joel Chandler Harris.*
  E.L. Montenyohl, 582(SFQ):Vol46No2-199
Bicknell, P. The Picturesque Scenery of the
  Lake District 1752-1855.
  J. Wordsworth, 617(TLS):21-27Dec90-
  1386
Bideaux, M. - see Cartier, J.
Bidney, M. Blake and Goethe.
  C. Gallant, 661(WC):Autumn89-216
  J. Mee, 447(N&Q):Dec89-521
Bielefeldt, C. Dōgen's Manuals of Zen Medita-
  tion.
  H. Dumoulin, 407(MN):Autumn89-377
  J.R. McRae, 293(JASt):Nov89-853
Bieler, M. Still wie die Nacht.
  P. Graves, 617(TLS):6-12Apr90-366
Bieman, E. Plato Baptized.
  M.F. Dixon, 627(UTQ):Fall89-118
  J.A. Quitslund, 604:Spring/Summer89-25
Bienek, H. Earth and Fire.*
  G. Kearns, 249(HudR):Summer89-342
  42(AR):Summer89-375
Bier, C., ed. Woven from the Soul, Spun from
  the Heart.*
  L. de Guise, 60:Jan-Feb89-146

Bier, L. Sarvistan.
  H. Crane, 576:Dec89-389
Bierbrauer, V.M. Invillino-Ibligo in Friaul.
  (Vols 1 & 2)
  T. Ulbert, 229:Band61Heft3-281
Bierds, L. The Stillness, the Dancing.
  D. Allen, 249(HudR):Summer89-324
  D. Walker, 199:Spring89-86
  C. Wright, 434:Winter89-193
  639(VQR):Summer89-98
Bierhorst, J. Die Mythologie der Indianer
  Nord-Amerikas.
  C.F. Feest, 196:Band30Heft3/4-306
Bierman, J. Dark Safari.
  P-L. Adams, 61:Nov90-172
  T. Jeal, 441:11Nov90-23
Bietenholz, P.G. - see Erasmus
Bietenholz, P.G. & T.B. Deutscher, eds. Con-
  temporaries of Erasmus.
  J. Kraye, 447(N&Q):Jun89-228
Bigelow, C., P.H. Duensing & L. Gentry, eds.
  Fine Print on Type.
  517(PBSA):Jun89-252
Bigelow, J. The Reality of Numbers.
  D. Lewis, 63:Dec89-487
  S. Pollard, 543:Jun90-854
Bigler, N. & R. Schläpfer, with R. Börlin - see
  Hotzenköcherle, R.
Bignami, M. - see Conrad, J.
Bigsby, C.W.E., ed. Plays by Susan Glaspell.
  G. Bas, 189(EA):Oct-Dec89-499
Bihl, L. & K. Epting. Bibliographie franzö-
  sischer Übersetzungen aus dem Deutschen
  1487-1944.
  Y. Chevrel, 549(RLC):Apr-Jun89-259
Bikai, P.M. - see under Maynor Bikai, P.
Biles, J.I., ed. British Novelists Since 1900.
  W. Blazek, 295(JML):Fall88/Winter89-241
Biles, J.I., ed. British Novelists Since 1960.
  J. Batchelor, 541(RES):Aug89-433
Biles, R. Memphis in the Great Depression.
  J. Braeman, 106:Summer89-41
Biles, R.E., ed. Inter-American Relations.
  J. Finan, 263(RIB):Vol39No2-203
Bilimoria, P. & P. Fenner, eds. Religions and
  Comparative Thought.
  K.N. Tiwari, 63:Sep89-354
Bilinski, B. La fortuna di Virgilio in Polonia.
  A. Novara, 555:Vol62Fasc2-369
Bill, V.T. Chekhov.*
  G. Pahomov, 104(CASS):Spring-Winter88-
  451
  G. Woodcock, 569(SR):Spring89-308
Billeter, B. - see Bianciardi, F. & C. Porta
Billeter, J-F. L'Art chinois de l'écriture.
  F. Jullien, 98:Aug-Sep89-672
Billings-Yun, M. Decision Against War.
  J. Prados, 293(JASt):Nov89-926
Billingsley, P. Bandits in Republican China.*
  H.R. Chauncey, 293(JASt):Aug89-584
Billington, M. Peggy Ashcroft.*
  H. Hobson, 157:No173-38
  M. Seldes, 441:17Jun90-9
Billington, M. Stoppard, the Playwright.*
  R.F.S., 295(JML):Fall88/Winter89-411
Billington, R. Living Philosophy.
  G.J.F., 185:Oct89-204
  E. Pybus, 518:Apr89-109
Billington, R. Loving Attitudes.
  639(VQR):Winter89-21
Billows, R.A. Antigonos the One-Eyed and
  the Creation of the Hellenistic State.
  S. Hornblower, 617(TLS):15-21Jun90-648

34

Billy, T., ed. Critical Essays on Joseph Conrad.*
   R.C. Murfin, 136:Spring89-66
Bilmes, J. Discourse and Behavior.
   W.A. Corsaro, 355(LSoc):Mar89-94
Binchy, M. Circle of Friends.
   S. Isaacs, 441:30Dec90-8
Binder, A. & others, eds. Slavica Ludomiro Durovic Sexagenario Dedicata.
   H. Birnbaum, 279:Vol35/36-375
Binder, G., ed. Saeculum Augustum I.*
   E. Gabba, 229:Band61Heft6-568
Binder, H., ed. Franz Kafka und die Prager Deutsche Literatur.
   A. Reiter, 402(MLR):Oct90-1026
Binder, W. & others - see Naumann, B.
Binding, P. Kingfisher Weather.
   L. Doughty, 617(TLS):16-22Feb90-181
Bingen, N. Le Maître italien (1510-1660).
   M. Marietti, 547(RF):Band101Heft4-468
Binyan, L. - see under Liu Binyan
Biocca, D. - see Berenson, B. & C. Marghieri
Bioy Casares, A. The Adventures of a Photographer in La Plata.*
   J. Updike, 442(NY):5Feb90-116
Bioy Casares, A. The Diary of the War of the Pig.
   E. Echevarría, 268(IFR):Summer90-138
Birch, D. Language, Literature and Critical Practice.
   J.R. Bennett, 599:Spring90-119
   J.J. Weber, 307:Dec89-230
Birch, D. Ruskin's Mythe.
   S. Emerson, 184(EIC):Oct89-332
   E.D. Mackerness, 447(N&Q):Dec89-530
   P. Mallett, 402(MLR):Jul90-704
   P.L. Sawyer, 637(VS):Summer90-664
Birch, D. & M. O'Toole, eds. Functions of Style.
   J.R. Bennett, 599:Spring90-119
Birckbichler, D.W., ed. Proficiency, Policy, and Professionalism in Foreign Language Education.
   W. Anthony, 399(MLJ):Autumn89-347
Bird, C. Woodpecker Point and Other Stories.*
   T. Clyde, 617(TLS):14-20Sep90-980
   P. Wolfe, 573(SSF):Spring89-203
Bird, G. William James.*
   C. Hookway, 482(PhR):Oct89-547
Birdsell, S. The Missing Child.
   C. Rooke, 376:Dec89-119
Birdsong, D. & J-P. Montreuil, eds. Advances in Romance Linguistics.
   F. Nuessel, 361:May89-99
Birenbaum, H. Myth and Mind.
   W. Donlan, 124:Sep-Oct89-58
Birgegard, U. - see Sparwenfeld, J.G.
Birke, L., S. Himmelweit & G. Vines. Tomorrow's Child.
   R. Cullen, 617(TLS):7-13Sep90-943
Birkeland, B. & B.N. Kvalsvik. Folkemål og Danning.*
   P. Trudgill, 562(Scan):May89-110
Birkett, J. The Sins of the Fathers.*
   C. Ploye, 446(NCFS):Spring-Summer90-548
Birkfellner, G., ed. "Po povody knigi" Teutscher, Und Reussischer, Dictionarium.
   A.B. Straxov & O.B. Straxova, 559:Vol13 No1-33
Birkfollner, G., ed. Sprache und Literatur Altrusslands.
   T. Henninger, 575(SEER):Jul89-498

Birkin, K., ed. Richard Strauss: "Arabella."
   M. Tanner, 617(TLS):15-21Jun90-642
Birkmann, T. Präteritopräsentia.*
   B. Meineke, 685(ZDL):1/1989-85
Birks, T. Lucie Rie.*
   W. MacKenzie, 139:Oct/Nov89-20
Birley, A.R. Septimius Severus. (rev)
   H.W. Benario, 124:Jan-Feb90-253
Birley, A.R. - see Syme, R.
Birley, E. The Roman Army.
   L. Keppie, 123:Vol39No2-324
   J.J. Wilkes, 313:Vol79-225
Birnbaum, M.D. Humanists in a Shattered World.
   G.F. Cushing, 575(SEER):Jan89-138
Birnbaum, N. The Radical Renewal.
   T.M.R., 185:Apr90-697
   F. Siegel, 473(PR):Vol56No4-665
Birnbaum, P. Un Mythe politique.
   P-F. Moreau, 531:Jul-Dec89-542
Birrell, A., ed & trans. New Songs from a Jade Terrace.
   M.M-L. Chu, 116:Jul88-175
Birx, H.J. Human Evolution.
   C.G. Holland, 529(QQ):Autumn89-773
Bisanz, H. Peter Altenberg.
   L.A. Lensing, 221(GQ):Summer89-396
Bischoff, C. & others, eds. Frauen Kunst Geschichte.
   S.L. Cocalis, 406:Summer89-230
Bishop, A. Gentleman Rider.*
   J. Mellors, 364:Apr/May89-136
Bishop, A. & Y.A. Bennett - see Brittain, V.
Bishop, D. & K. Mogford, eds. Language Development in Exceptional Circumstances.
   S. Goldin-Meadow, 348(L&S):Jul-Sep89-285
Bishop, G. When the Master Relents.
   V.C. Fowler, 177(ELT):Vol32No3-372
Bishop, I. The Narrative Art of the "Canterbury Tales."
   C. Batt, 175:Spring89-69
   H. Cooper, 447(N&Q):Sep89-370
   A. Wawn, 402(MLR):Oct90-910
Bishop, J. Joyce's Book of the Dark.*
   B. Benstock, 177(ELT):Vol32No2-264
   M.P. Gillespie, 177(PLL):Fall88-450
   M.J. O'Shea, 403(MLS):Spring89-78
Bishop, J.E. & M. Waldholz. Genome.
   N. Angier, 441:12Aug90-8
Bishop, L. The Poetry of Alfred de Musset.
   C. Crossley, 208(FS):Jul89-344
Bishop, M. Michel Deguy.
   B.L. Knapp, 207(FR):May90-1076
Bishop, P. The Myth of Shangri-La.
   J.H. Crook, 617(TLS):5-11Oct90-1081
   J. Mirsky, 453(NYRB):20Dec90-63
Bishop, P. Sand Against the Tide.
   N. Callendar, 441:7Oct90-39
Bishop, R. African Literature, African Critics.
   B.M. Ibitokun, 395(MFS):Summer89-391
Bisnow, M. In the Shadow of the Dome.
   J. Gillenkirk, 441:8Jul90-17
   442(NY):16Jul90-87
Bissell, C. Ernest Buckler Remembered.
   A.R. Young, 150(DR):Spring89-133
Bissinger, H.G. Friday Night Lights.
   M. Swindle, 441:7Oct90-20
Bisson, T. Voyage to the Red Planet.
   G. Jonas, 441:2Sep90-18
Bisson, T.N. The Medieval Crown of Aragon.*
   K.T. Utterback, 589:Jul89-661

Bissoondath, N. A Casual Brutality.*
   B. Holmes, 198:Winter89-109
   J. Panabaker, 529(QQ):Winter89-956
Bissoondath, N. On the Eve of Uncertain Tomorrows.
   F. Kanga, 617(TLS):23-29Nov90-1271
Bisztray, G. Hungarian-Canadian Literature.*
   N.F. Dreisziger, 298:Summer89-153
Bitekhtina, G. & others. Russian: Stage One. (4th ed)
   R.F. Druien, 399(MLJ):Winter89-526
Bittner, J.W. Approaches to the Fiction of Ursula K. Le Guin.
   J.K.G., 295(JML):Fall88/Winter89-371
Biville, F. Graphie et prononciation des mots grecs en latin (BIG).
   P. Flobert, 555:Vol62Fasc2-356
Bizzocchi, R. Chiesa e potere nella Toscana del Quattrocento.
   D.S. Peterson, 551(RenQ):Summer89-293
Bjørhovde, G. Rebellious Structures.*
   T. Cosslett, 447(N&Q):Dec89-551
   A. Sadrin, 189(EA):Jul-Sep89-350
   R. Sherry, 172(Edda):1989/4-362
   J. Simons, 541(RES):Nov89-583
Bjork, D.W. William James.
   G. Cotkin, 619:Spring89-207
Björk, L. Psychological Vision and Social Criticism in the Novels of Thomas Hardy.
   P. Widdowson, 637(VS):Winter90-368
Bjork, R.E. The Old English Verse Saints' Lives.*
   J. Price, 38:Band107Heft1/2-161
Bjørkelo, A. Prelude to the Mahdiyya.
   M.W. Daly, 617(TLS):18-24May90-532
Björkvall, G., ed. Les deux tropaires d'Apt, mss. 17 et 18.* [shown in prev under title Corpus troporum V.]
   P. Jeffery, 589:Jan89-120
Bjørnson, B. Bjørnstjerne Bjørnsons Briefwechsel mit Deutschen.* (Pts 1 & 2) (A. Keel, ed)
   H.S. Naess, 301(JEGP):Jan89-55
   B. Sandberg, 172(Edda):1989/1-90
Bjornson, R., ed. Faces of African Independence.
   C. Zimra, 207(FR):Feb90-539
Black, C. & M. Horsnell. Counterfeiter.
   S. Shapiro, 441:18Mar90-21
Black, G. The Good Neighbor.*
   639(VQR):Summer89-96
Black, J. The Collapse of the Anglo-French Alliance, 1727-1731.*
   P.D.G. Thomas, 83:Autumn89-217
   G.M. Townend, 566:Autumn89-85
Black, J. Eighteenth Century Europe 1700-1789.
   W. Doyle, 617(TLS):27Jul-2Aug90-806
Black, J. The English Press in the Eighteenth-Century.*
   J.A. Downie, 677(YES):Vol20-275
   M. Kelsall, 541(RES):May89-273
Black, J., ed. The Origins of War in Early Modern Europe.
   M. Hughes, 83:Spring89-88
   H.L. Snyder, 173(ECS):Fall89-114
Black, J. You Can't Win.*
   D. Blaise, 532(RCF):Spring89-262
Black, J. & P. Woodfine, eds. The British Navy and the Use of Naval Power in the Eighteenth Century.
   P. Luff, 566:Spring90-221

Black, M. Perplexities.
   M. Ring, 103:Nov90-442
Blackburn, B.J. Music for Treviso Cathedral in the Late Sixteenth Century.
   T. Carter, 309:Vol9No1-60
   M. Pozzobon, 417:Oct-Dec89-379
Blackburn, J. Charles Waterton, 1782-1865.*
   E. Dennis, 324:Jan90-146
   J. Wilson, 364:Apr/May89-159
Blackburn, R.J. The Vampire of Reason.
   H. Kearney, 617(TLS):12-18Oct90-1092
Blackburn, T. The Adjacent Kingdom.* (J. MacVean, ed)
   F. Grubb, 364:Dec89/Jan90-98
Blackhall, S. The Nor'East Neuk. A Nippick o' Nor' East Tales.
   C. Gow, 571(ScLJ):Winter89-53
Blackmur, R.P. Selected Essays of R.P. Blackmur. (D. Donoghue, ed)
   J.A. Bryant, Jr., 569(SR):Winter89-153
Blackwell, L. & L. Bullivant. International Interiors 2.
   T. Crosby, 324:Oct90-793
Blackwell, M.J. Persona.*
   G. Bisztray, 562(Scan):May89-107
"The Blackwell Biographical Dictionary of British Political Life in the Twentieth Century." (K. Robbins, ed)
   P. Johnson, 617(TLS):15-21Jun90-634
Blackwill, R.D. & F.S. Larrabee, eds. Conventional Arms Control and East-West Security.
   G. Duffy, 441:28Jan90-30
Blackwood, E. The Structure of Recognizable Diatonic Tunings.*
   M. Lindley & R. Turner-Smith, 410(M&L):May89-238
   W. Voigt, 417:Jan-Mar89-99
Blaim, A. Failed Dynamics.
   G. Bystydzieńska, 566:Spring90-207
Blain, W.E. Passion Play.
   M. Stasio, 441:20May90-53
Blainey, A. Immortal Boy.
   S. Monod, 158:Mar89-26
Blais, M. L'autre Thomas d'Aquin.
   D. Simpson, 103:Nov90-443
Blaise, C. & B. Murkherjee. The Sorrow and the Terror.
   G. Drolet, 102(CanL):Summer89-166
Lord Blake & C.S. Nicholls, eds. The Dictionary of National Biography: 1981-1985.
   R. Foster, 617(TLS):27Apr-3May90-450
Blake, G. No Other Choice.
   R. Cecil, 617(TLS):9-15Nov90-1204
Blake, N.F. Traditional English Grammar and Beyond.
   F.R. Palmer, 677(YES):Vol20-208
Blake, W. Äktenskapet mellan Himmel och Helvete. (F. Isaksson, trans)
   M.D. Paley & G. Tottie, 88:Spring90-209
Blake, W. The Essential Blake. (S. Kunitz, ed)
   P. Mariani, 434:Spring90-313
Blake, W. "The Four Zoas" by William Blake. (C.T. Magno & D.V. Erdman, eds)
   W.H. Stevenson, 184(EIC):Apr89-161
Blake, W. An Island in the Moon.* (M. Phillips, ed)
   P.L. Caracciolo, 354:Jun89-172
   R.N. Essick, 250(HLQ):Winter89-139
   K.E. Smith, 83:Autumn89-231
   J. Wordsworth, 541(RES):Nov89-571

Blake, W. Oeuvres IV. (J. Blondel, ed & trans)
  M. Bidney, 88:Fall89-79
Blake, W. The Oxford Authors: William Blake.* (M. Mason, ed)
  L.M. Findlay, 447(N&Q):Dec89-519
  B. Wilkie, 402(MLR):Apr90-418
Blakely, A. Russia and the Negro.
  J. Vaillant, 550(RusR):Oct89-428
Blakemore, C. & S. Greenfield, eds. Mind-waves.
  D. Mitchell, 518:Jan89-40
Blakemore, S. Burke and the Fall of Language.
  M. Kelsall, 402(MLR):Oct90-926
  J.C. McKusick, 591(SIR):Fall89-511
Blakey, G.T. Hard Times and New Deal in Kentucky 1929-1939.
  J. Braeman, 106:Summer89-41
Blamires, A. "The Canterbury Tales."*
  J.W. Nicholls, 677(YES):Vol20-234
Blancart-Cassou, J. Le Rire de Michel de Ghelderode.
  J-Y. Guérin, 535(RHL):Jul-Aug89-750
Blanchard, J., ed. La "Moralité à cincq personnages" du manuscrit B.N. fr. 25467.*
  K. Schoell, 547(RF):Band101Heft2/3-318
Blanchard, M.E. In Search of the City.*
  J. Martínez-Tolentino, 345(KRQ):Feb89-112
Blanchard, P. The Life of Emily Carr.*
  M.J. Dwyer, 662:Fall89/Winter90-38
  E-J. Orford, 102(CanL):Spring89-233
Blanche-Benveniste, C., A. Chervel & M. Gross, eds. Grammaire et histoire de la grammaire.
  W.J. Ashby, 207(FR):Feb90-594
Blanche-Benveniste, C. & C. Jeanjean. Le Français parlé.*
  B. Tranel, 207(FR):Oct89-180
Blanchot, M. Thomas the Obscure.*
  I. Malin, 532(RCF):Summer89-241
Blanchot, M. The Unavowable Community.
  42(AR):Fall89-503
Blandiana, A. The Hour of Sand.
  L. Chamberlain, 617(TLS):19-25Jan90-59
Blandin, A. Afrique de l'ouest.
  E.W. Herbert, 2(AfrA):Aug89-83
Blandy, D. & K.G. Congdon, eds. Art in a Democracy.
  C.K. Dewhurst, 292(JAF):Jul-Sep89-368
  D.K. Holt, 709:Winter91-117
Blangenois, B. Des jeux parmi les arbres.
  R. Jacquelin, 450(NRF):Feb89-143
Blank, G.K. Wordsworth's Influence on Shelley.
  S.C. Behrendt, 661(WC):Autumn89-186
  K.R. Johnston, 445(NCF):Jun89-93
  M.A. Quinn, 340(KSJ):Vol38-178
Blank, H. Goethe und Manzoni - Weimar und Mailand.
  K. Heitmann, 72:Band226Heft1-223
  I. Klein, 52:Band24Heft3-314
Blankenburg, W., ed. Heinrich Schütz in seiner Zeit.
  W. Braun, 416:Band4Heft1-91
Blankert, A., J.M. Montias & G. Aillaud. Vermeer.
  C. Brown, 39:Nov89-360
Blaser, R. & R. Dunham, eds. Art and Reality.
  T. Goldie, 102(CanL):Winter88-128

Blaser, W. The Temple and Teahouse in Japan.
  G. Vorreiter, 46:Feb89-10
Blasing, M.K. American Poetry.*
  M. Fisher, 577(SHR):Winter89-87
  L. Goldstein, 271:Fall89-159
Blasing, R. The Double House of Life.
  S. Radhuber, 363(LitR):Spring90-401
Blatchly, J. The Town Library of Ipswich, Provided for the Use of the Town Preachers in 1599.
  D. McKitterick, 78(BC):Autumn89-301
  J. Morrill, 617(TLS):5-11Jan90-20
Blaugrund, A. Paris 1889.
  R. Siegel, 441:11Feb90-18
Bleicken, J. Die athenische Demokratie.
  M.H. Hansen, 122:Apr89-137
Bleser, C. - see Hammond, J.H.
Blessington, F.C. "Paradise Lost."
  M.A. Mikolajczak, 568(SCN):Spring-Summer89-7
Blew, M.C. Runaway.
  K. Mathieson, 441:25Nov90-18
Blewett, M.H. The Last Generation.
  R.B. Smith, 441:23Sep90-49
Blezzard, J. Borrowings in English Church Music, 1550-1950.
  W. Mellers, 617(TLS):21-27Dec90-1378
Blier, S.P. The Anatomy of Architecture.
  L. Prussin, 2(AfrA):Nov88-16
Blight, J.G. & D.A. Welch. On the Brink.*
  639(VQR):Autumn89-134
Blinken, A.J. Ally versus Ally.
  A.P. Allison, 550(RusR):Oct89-438
Bliss, L. Francis Beaumont.
  E.C. Bartels, 551(RenQ):Spring89-142
  R.G. Barlow, 568(SCN):Spring-Summer89-17
Bliss, M. Northern Enterprise.
  M. McInnis, 529(QQ):Spring89-138
Blitzer, W. Territory of Lies.*
  D. Stone, 287:Nov-Dec89-32
Bloch, C. & S. Mitchell - see Amichai, Y.
Bloch, E. The Principle of Hope.
  R. Boyne, 323:Oct89-292
Bloch, E. The Utopian Function of Art and Literature.*
  N. Finkelstein, 153:Summer89-54
  E. Goodheart, 473(PR):Vol56No4-661
  J.E. MacKinnon, 89(BJA):Spring89-185
Bloch, H. Monte Cassino in the Middle Ages.
  F. Newton, 589:Jul89-663
Bloch, J. Recueil d'articles de Jules Bloch (1906-1955).* (C. Caillat, ed)
  P. Flobert, 555:Vol62Fasc1-189
Bloch, M.J. La Bande de Möbius.
  G.E. Reed, 207(FR):Feb90-574
Bloch, R. & C. Guittard - see Livy
Block, A.B. Outfoxed.
  M.B. Grover, 441:25Mar90-23
Block, J. Motherhood as Metamorphosis.
  E. Hegeman, 441:9Sep90-33
Block, J.F. Eva Watson-Schütze.
  J. Loughery, 662:Fall89/Winter90-48
Block, L. A Ticket to the Boneyard.
  M. Stasio, 441:9Sep90-39
Blodgett, E.D. & R.A. Swanson - see "The Love Songs of the Carmina Burana"
Bloedow, E.F. - see Bengtson, H.
de Blois, L. The Roman Army and Politics in the First Century B.C.
  J.F. Lazenby, 123:Vol39No1-150

Blok, A., G. Steen & L. Wesseling, eds. De historische roman.
 A. Rigney, 204(FdL):Sep89-226
Blok, J. & P. Mason, eds. Sexual Asymmetry.
 G. Clark, 123:Vol39No1-103
Blom, E., ed. The New Everyman Dicitonary of Music. (rev by D. Cummings)
 A. Jacobs, 410(M&L):May89-236
 W. Mellers, 415:Jan89-26
Blomberg, G. "Liten och gammal – duger ingenting till."
 H. Eppstein, 417:Apr–Jun89-190
Blomberg, N.J. Navajo Textiles.
 M.E. Rodee, 2(AfrA):Feb89-27
Blomhert, B. The Harmoniemusik of "Die Entführung aus dem Serail."
 R. Hellyer, 410(M&L):May89-260
Blondel, J. – see Blake, W.
Blondiaux, I. Une Écriture psychotique.
 D. O'Connell, 207(FR):May90-1072
Bloom, A. The Closing of the American Mind.*
 B.H. Gelfant, 434:Autumn89-93
 S. Hook, 31(ASch):Winter89-123
 D. Howard, 142:Vol15No1-95
 J. Seaton, 580(SCR):Spring90-149
Bloom, A. Giants and Dwarfs.
 W. Steiner, 441:4Nov90-14
Bloom, C. The "Occult" Experience and the New Criticism.
 P. Bonila, 295(JML):Fall88/Winter89-183
Bloom, H., ed. The Art of the Critic. (Vol 7) The Chelsea House Library of Literary Criticism. (Vol 9)
 D.R. Schwarz, 177(ELT):Vol32No3-391
Bloom, H., ed. James Dickey.
 R.J. Calhoun, 392:Winter88/89-83
Bloom, H., ed. John Dryden.
 J.D. Canfield, 566:Spring89-177
Bloom, H., ed. Thomas Hardy's "The Return of the Native."
 W.E. Davis, 177(ELT):Vol32No1-106
Bloom, H., ed. Nathaniel Hawthorne.
 S.R. Portch, 573(SSF):Winter89-105
Bloom, H., ed. Victor Hugo.
 J.A. Frey, 188(ECr):Winter89-107
Bloom, H., ed. James Joyce. James Joyce's "Ulysses." James Joyce's "Dubliners." James Joyce's "A Portrait of the Artist as a Young Man."
 B. Benstock, 177(ELT):Vol32No3-378
Bloom, H., ed. John Milton.
 R.J. Du Rocher, 577(SHR):Winter89-84
Bloom, H., ed. Flannery O'Connor.
 S. Felton, 573(SSF):Fall88-484
Bloom, H. The Poetics of Influence.* (J. Hollander, ed)
 S. Helmling, 344:Summer90-154
Bloom, H., ed. Thomas Pynchon.* Thomas Pynchon's "Gravity's Rainbow."
 B. Duyfhuizen, 454:Fall89-75
Bloom, H. Ruin the Sacred Truths.*
 S. Helmling, 344:Summer90-154
 V. Nemoianu, 400(MLN):Dec89-1176
 I. Stavans, 287:Jul–Aug89-29
Bloom, H., ed. George Bernard Shaw. George Bernard Shaw's "Man and Superman."
 E.B. Adams, 177(ELT):Vol32No2-252
Bloom, H., ed. George Bernard Shaw's "Pygmalion." George Bernard Shaw's "Major Barbara."
 G.A. Hudson, 177(ELT):Vol32No4-515

Bloom, H., ed. George Bernard Shaw's "Saint Joan."
 B. Henderson, 177(ELT):Vol32No2-248
Bloom, H., ed. Tobias Smollett.
 566:Spring89-180
Bloom, H., ed. Laurence Sterne's "Tristram Shandy."
 566:Autumn89-72
Bloom, H., ed. Jonathan Swift's "Gulliver's Travels."
 566:Spring89-178
Bloom, H., ed. John Millington Synge's "The Playboy of the Western World."
 A. Ganz, 177(ELT):Vol32No4-511
Bloom, H., ed. Eudora Welty.
 E. Current-Garcia, 573(SSF):Summer88-332
Bloom, H., ed. Oscar Wilde's "The Importance of Being Earnest."
 K. Powell, 177(ELT):Vol32No3-338
Bloom, H., ed. Virginia Woolf.*
 J. Marcus, 620(TSWL):Spring89-101
Bloom, H., ed. Richard Wright.
 A.W. France, 223:Spring89-98
Bloom, H. – see "The Book of J"
Bloom, I. – see Lo Ch'in-shun
Bloom, J.D. The Stock of Available Reality.
 J.A. Bryant, Jr., 569(SR):Winter89-153
Bloomfield, L. A Leonard Bloomfield Anthology.* (abridged) (C.F. Hockett, ed)
 D.H., 355(LSoc):Mar89-143
 F.W. Householder, 361:Sep89-80
Bloomfield, M.W. & C.W. Dunn. The Role of the Poet in Early Societies.
 P. Ryan, 617(TLS):24-30Aug90-904
Blount, R., Jr. First Hubby.
 C. Buckley, 441:10Jun90-7
 442(NY):1Oct90-111
Bluestone, N.H. Women and the Ideal Society.
 M. Deslauriers, 488:Jun89-211
 S. Shute, 319:Apr90-283
 N. Smits, 124:Jan–Feb90-246
Blum, C. Rousseau and the Republic of Virtue.*
 J.R. Censer, 322(JHI):Oct–Dec89-652
 J. Starobinski, 453(NYRB):12Apr90-47
Blum, H. Out There.
 J.A. Adam, 441:9Sep90-7
Blum, P.Z. – see Crosby, S.M.
Blumberg, S.A. & L.G. Panos. Edward Teller.
 R. Rhodes, 441:11Feb90-3
Blume, H. – see von Feuchtersleben, E.
Blümel, W., ed. Die Inschriften von Mylasa. (Vol 1)
 A.G. Woodhead, 303(JoHS):Vol109-243
Blumenberg, H. The Genesis of the Copernican World.*
 W.G. Regier, 400(MLN):Apr89-752
Blumenfeld-Kosinski, R. Not of Woman Born.
 M. Beard, 617(TLS):20-26Jul90-784
Blumenthal, J. Bruce Rogers.
 517(PBSA):Sep89-407
Blumenthal, S. Pledging Allegiance.
 A. Brinkley, 441:14Oct90-1
 442(NY):19Nov90-156
Blumenthal, U-R. The Investiture Controversy.
 J.M. Powell, 377:Mar89-54
Blunt, C.E., B.H.I.H. Stewart & C.S.S. Lyon. Coinage in Tenth-Century England.
 R. McKitterick, 617(TLS):18-24May90-538

Blust, R.A. Austronesian Root Theory.
T. Kaufman, 350:Sep90-625

Bly, P.A., ed. Galdós y la historia.
S. Finkenthal, 593:Summer89-138
J. Lowe, 402(MLR):Jul90-767

Bly, R. American Poetry.
D. Anderson, 441:30Sep90-29

Bly, R. Iron John.
M. Csikszentmihalyi, 441:9Dec90-15

Blyth, A., ed. Song on Record 2.
G. Hall, 415:Jul89-416

Boak, D. Sartre: "Les Mots."
D.A. MacLeay, 207(FR):Dec89-385
M. Scriven, 208(FS):Oct89-493
P. Thody, 402(MLR):Apr90-460

Boardman, B.M. Between Heaven and Charing
Cross.
J. North, 447(N&Q):Dec89-531
42(AR):Summer89-372
639(VQR):Summer89-89

Boardman, J., ed. The Cambridge Ancient
History: Plates to Volume IV.
P. MacKendrick, 124:Mar-Apr90-361

Boardman, J. & others, eds. The Cambridge
Ancient History.* (2nd ed) (Vol 4)
P. MacKendrick, 124:Jan-Feb90-237

Boardman, J., J. Griffin & O. Murray, eds.
Greece and the Hellenistic World.
J. Dillon, 235:Winter89-78

Boardman, J., J. Griffin & O. Murray, eds. The
Roman World.
A. Smith, 235:Winter89-80

Boatwright, M.T. Hadrian and the City of
Rome.*
R. Brilliant, 122:Oct89-358
J. De Laine, 313:Vol79-218
A. Frazer, 576:Mar89-82

Boban, V. & J. Pheby — see "The Oxford-
Duden Pictorical Serbo-Croat & English
Dictionary"

Bobbio, N. Democracy and Dictatorship.
J. Lively, 617(TLS):5-11Jan90 7

Bobbio, N. The Future of Democracy. (R.
Bellamy, ed)
M.B. Turits, 577(SHR):Spring89-175

Bobes, M.D. Semiología de la obra dramática.
E. Bergmann, 240(HR):Autumn89-600

Bobin, C. La Part manquante.
R. Blin, 450(NRF):Dec89-120

Bobrick, B. Ivan the Terrible.
P. Longworth, 617(TLS):12-18Oct90-1090

Bobrinskoy, T. & I. Gsovskaya. How to Pro-
nounce Russian Correctly.
J.E. Bernhardt, 399(MLJ):Spring89-95

Boccaccio, G. Amorosa Visione.* (R. Hollander, T. Hampton & M. Frankel, trans)
S. Huot, 276:Spring89-42

Boccaccio, G. The Decameron. (G.H. McWil-
liam, ed & trans) The Decameron. (M. Musa
& P. Bondanella, trans) Decameron: The
John Payne Translation. (rev by C.S. Sin-
gleton)
C. Kleinhenz, 678(YCGL):No36-104

Boccaccio, G. Eclogues. (J.L. Smarr, ed &
trans)
J.B. Dillon, 276:Spring89-44
G.H. McWilliam, 278(IS):Vol44-154

Boccaccio, G. Il Filostrato. (V. Pernicone, ed;
R.P. ap Roberts & A.B. Seldis, trans)
C.D. Benson, 589:Jan89-125
D. Wallace, 276:Spring89-48

Bocchi, F., ed. Emilia-Romagna.
S. Gruber, 576:Dec89-403

Bocharov, G. Russian Roulette.
J. Kifner, 441:4Nov90-26

Bochmann, K. Regional- und Nationalitäten-
sprachen in Frankreich, Italien und Spanien.
K. Heger, 685(ZDL):3/1989-346

Bock, H. & T.W. Gaehtgens, eds. Holländische
Genremalerei im 17. Jahrhundert.
P. Hecht, 90:Sep89-655

Bockstoce, J. — see Maguire, R.

Bodden, M-C., ed & trans. The Old English
"Finding of the True Cross."*
R.P. McGerr, 179(ES):Apr89-173
D.G. Scragg, 541(RES):Feb89-106

Boddy, J. Wombs and Allen Spirits.
I.M. Lewis, 617(TLS):1-7Jun90-590
T. Luhrmann, 441:25Mar90-33

Bode, C. Ästhetik der Ambiguität.
J.H. Petersen, 52:Band24Heft2-199

Bode, C. Mencken.
D. Fowler, 70:Oct89-156

Bodelot, C. L'Interrogation indirecte en
Latin.
J.N. Adams, 123:Vol39No2-405
M. Baratin, 555:Vol62Fasc2-358

Boden, A. F.W. Harvey.*
P. Dickinson, 364:Jun/Jul89-119

Bodenheimer, R. The Politics of Story in Vic-
torian Social Fiction.*
R. Ivy, 677(YES):Vol20-297
K.B. Stockton, 637(VS):Autumn89-177

Bodett, T. The Big Garage on Clear Shot.
B. Franzen, 441:21Oct90-25

Bodin, J. Exposé du droit universel. (H-M.
Rampelberg, ed)
M. Ducos, 555:Vol62Fasc1-188
R. Sève, 192(EP):Jul-Dec89-531

Bodin, T. — see Sand, G.

den Boeft, J., D. den Hengst & H.C. Teitler.
Philological and Historical Commentary on
Ammianus Marcellinus XX.
J.M. Alonso-Núñez, 123:Vol39No2-397
J. Szidat, 229:Band61Heft8-677

Boeker, P.H. Lost Illusions.
R.G. Hellman, 441:29Apr90-30

Boër, S.E. & W.G. Lycan. Knowing Who.*
G.A. Rovane, 482(PhR):Jul89-392

Boesche, R. The Strange Liberalism of Alexis
de Tocqueville.*
H.C. Clark, 242:Vol10No1-110

Boese, H. — see Proclus

Boethius. Boethian Number Theory. (M. Masi,
ed & trans)
A.C. Bowen, 41:Spring89-137

Boethius. In Ciceronis Topica. (E. Stump, ed
& trans)
S. Bobzien, 313:Vol79-263
S. Ebbesen, 319:Oct90-607
R.P. Sonkowsky, 124:Nov-Dec89-129

Boethius of Dacia. On the Supreme Good, On
the Eternity of the World, On Dreams.*
(J.F. Wippel, trans)
A.J. Celano, 319:Apr90-286

Boffey, J. Manuscripts of English Courtly
Love Lyrics in the Later Middle Ages.*
A.S.G. Edwards, 589:Jan89-125

Bogard, T. Contour in Time.
639(VQR):Winter89-12

Bogard, T. — see O'Neill, E.

Bogard, T. & J.R. Bryer — see O'Neill, E.

Bogdan, C. & E. Preda. Spheres of Influence.
J.A. Koumoulides, 242:Vol10No6-747

Bogdanor, V., ed. Constitutions in Democratic Politics.
    S.L., 185:Jan90-458
Boggs, S.T., with K. Watson-Gegeo & G. McMillen. Speaking, Relating, and Learning.
    C. Emihovich, 355(LSoc):Dec89-587
Boguraev, B. & T. Briscoe, eds. Computational Lexicography for Natural Language Processing.
    T.A. Waldspurger, 350:Sep90-626
van Boheemen, C. The Novel as Family Romance.*
    S.B., 295(JML):Fall88/Winter89-252
    E.D. Ermarth, 166:Jul90-362
    J. Rothschild, 577(SHR):Summer89-296
Böhler, D., T. Nordenstam & G. Skirbekk, eds. Die pragmatische Wende.
    P. Bachmaier, 679:Band20Heft1-148
Bohlke, L.B. - see Cather, W.
"Gottfried Böhm." (S. Raev, ed)
    P.B. Jones, 46:Jan89-14
Böhme, G. Philosophieren mit Kant.
    D. Ginev, 679:Band20Heft1-153
    S. Majetschak, 342:Band80Heft2-222
Böhme, G. & N. Stehr, eds. The Knowledge Society.
    D.A. Hollinger, 385(MQR):Winter90-123
Böhme, J. Arnold Mendelssohn und seine Klavier- und Kammermusik.
    A. Werner-Jensen, 416:Band4Heft3-273
Böhme, R. Aeschylus und seine Epigonen.
    P. Demont, 555:Vol62Fasc2-342
Bohnaker, W. The Hollow Doll.
    S. Chira, 441:6May90-23
Bohrer, K.H. Nach der Natur.
    J.P. Stern, 617(TLS):26Jan-1Feb90-83
Bohringer, R. C'est beau une ville la nuit.
    R.A. Hartzell, 207(FR):Mar90-740
Boime, A. The Art of Exclusion.
    R. Dorment, 453(NYRB):27Sep90-54
Boime, A. A Social History of Modern Art.* (Vol 1)
    E. Shanes, 39:Dec89-435
du Bois, P. Sowing the Body.
    R. Rousselle, 124:Nov-Dec89-118
Boissel, T. Sophie de Grouchy marquise de Condorcet 1764-1822.
    V.D.L., 605(SC):15Oct89-80
Boissiere, R. Meditations with The Hopi.
    P.K. Kett, 649(WAL):Aug89-161
de Boissieu, J-L. & A-M. Caragnon. Commentaires stylistiques.
    G. Cesbron, 356(LR):Feb-May89-102
    G. Molinié, 535(RHL):Mar-Apr89-348
Boisvert, R.D. Dewey's Metaphysics.
    J.J. Stuhr, 619:Summer89-361
Boitani, P., ed. The European Tragedy of Troilus.
    S. Lerer, 617(TLS):24-30Aug90-904
Boitani, P. The Tragic and the Sublime in Medieval Literature.
    S. Lerer, 617(TLS):24-30Aug90-904
Boitani, P. & J. Mann, eds. The Cambridge Chaucer Companion.*
    E.D. Kennedy, 38:Band107Heft3/4-523
    J.W. Nicholls, 677(YES):Vol20-234
    J. Norton-Smith, 447(N&Q):Mar89-80
    P.G. Ruggiers, 589:Apr89-391
Boivin, A., ed. Le Conte fantastique québécois au XIXe siècle.
    M.E. Ross, 627(UTQ):Fall89-181

Bok, D. Universities and the Future of America.
    N.S. Dye, 441:23Sep90-45
Böker, U., H. Breuer & R. Breuer. Die Klassiker der englischen Literatur.
    W. Weiss, 72:Band226Heft1-136
Bokobza, S. Contribution à la titrologie romanesque.*
    K. Ringger, 535(RHL):Jan-Feb89-120
Bol, P.C., comp. Bildwerke aus Stein und aus Stuck von archaischer Zeit bis zur Spätantike.
    H. Lauter-Bufe, 229:Band61Heft7-642
Bol, P.C., with E. Kotera, comps. Bildwerke aus Terrakotta aus mykenischer bis römischer Zeit.
    H. Lauter-Bufe, 229:Band61Heft7-642
Bol, P.C. & T. Weber, comps. Bildwerke aus Bronze und Bein aus minoischer bis byzantinischer Zeit.
    H. Lauter-Bufe, 229:Band61Heft7-642
Boland, E. Selected Poems.*
    S. Kantaris, 493:Autumn89-42
    S. Knight, 364:Oct/Nov89-115
Bolcom, W. - see Rochberg, G.
Bold, A., ed. W.H. Auden.
    P. Hobsbaum, 677(YES):Vol20-339
Bold, A. MacDiarmid.*
    P. Crotty, 571(ScLJ):Spring89-16
Bold, A., ed. The Quest for le Carré.
    D. Monaghan, 395(MFS):Winter89-823
Bold, A. Muriel Spark.
    M. Del Sapio, 677(YES):Vol20-342
Bold, C. Selling the Wild West.*
    J. Tavernier-Courbin, 178:Jun89-237
Bold, J. John Webb.
    A. Gomme, 617(TLS):2-8Feb90-128
Boldrini, S. Fedro e Perotti.
    M.C. Davies, 313:Vol79-264
Bolger, D. The Journey Home.
    D. Montrose, 617(TLS):6-12Jul90-731
Bolick, C. Changing Course.
    C.N.S., 185:Jan90-463
Bolinger, D.L. Intonation and Its Parts.*
    M.R. Key, 35(AS):Summer89-168
Bolinger, D.L. Intonation and Its Uses.
    D.R. Ladd, 350:Dec90-806
Böll, H. Women in a River Landscape.* The Casualty.
    P. Lewis, 565:Summer89-66
Boll, M.M. National Security Planning.
    639(VQR):Autumn89-132
de Bolla, P. Harold Bloom.
    O.M. Meidner, 89(BJA):Autumn89-386
Bolon, C.R., R.S. Nelson & L. Seidel, eds. The Nature of Frank Lloyd Wright.
    H. Gottfried, 47:Feb89-38
    P.B. Jones, 46:Oct89-12
Bolster, R., ed. Le Destin extraordinaire du baron de Trenck.
    R. Waller, 83:Spring89-116
Bolt, T. Out of the Woods.
    A. Corn, 491:Jan90-285
Bolton, H.P. Dickens Dramatized.*
    P. Schlicke, 611(TN):Vol43No1-44
Bomba, A. Chansons de Geste und französisches Nationalbewusstsein im Mittelalter.
    T.D. Hemming, 208(FS):Oct89-453
Bombal, M.L. New Islands and Other Stories.
    J. Shreve, 238:Sep89-568

de Bombelles, M. Marc de Bombelles: Journal de voyage en Grand Bretagne et en Irelande 1784. (J. Gury, ed)
  D.G.C. Allan, 324:Sep90-716
Bon, F. Décor ciment.
  Y. Leclerc, 98:Apr89-247
  J. Taylor, 532(RCF):Fall89-218
Bon, F. Sortie d'usine. Limite. Le crime de Buzon.
  Y. Leclerc, 98:Apr89-247
Bonaccorso, R. Sean O'Faolain's Irish Vision.*
  C.A. Buckley, 447(N&Q):Mar89-128
Bonacina, G. Storia universale e filosofia del diritto.
  P. Trotignon, 542:Oct-Dec89-600
Bond, D.F. - see "The Spectator"
Bond, D.F. - see "The Tatler"
Bond, E. Poems 1978-1985.
  L. Sail, 565:Summer89-75
Bond, E. Restoration.
  P. Holland, 611(TN):Vol43No2-84
Bonds, D.S. Language and the Self in D.H. Lawrence.*
  D.T.O., 295(JML):Fall88/Winter89-368
Bonelli, G. Il mondo poetico di Pindaro.
  D.E. Gerber, 124:Sep-Oct89-57
  S. Instone, 303(JoHS):Vol109-213
Bonenfant, R. & L. Jacob. Les Trains d'exils.
  D. Essar, 102(CanL):Spring89-191
Bonfiglio, T.P. Achim von Arnim's "Novellensammlung 1812."
  H.M.K. Riley, 133:Band22Heft3/4-338
Bonfiglio Dosio, G., ed. "Ragioni antique spettanti all'arte del mare et fabriche de vasselli."
  A. Sattin, 708:Vol14Fasc2-268
Bonghi Jovino, M., ed. Gli Etruschi di Tarquinia.
  T. Rasmussen, 123:Vol39No1-117
Böning, H. Ulrich Bräker.
  G. Bersier, 406:Fall89-389
  G. Braungart, 224(GRM):Band39Heft2-245
  J.T. Malloy, 221(GQ):Winter89-108
Bonino, G.D., A. Lezza & P. Scialò - see Viviani, R.
Bonk, F. Marcel Duchamp.
  T. Phillips, 617(TLS):16-22Mar90-281
Bonn, T.L. Heavy Traffic and High Culture.
  S.C. Enniss, 219(GaR):Winter89-825
Bonnafé, A. Poésie, Nature et Sacré.* (Vol 1)
  P. Demont, 555:Vol62Fasc2-340
Bonnefis, P. - see de Maupassant, G.
Bonnefoy, Y. The Act and the Place of Poetry. (J.T. Naughton, ed)
  E. Grosholz, 249(HudR):Winter89-667
Bonnefoy, Y. Une Autre époque de l'écriture.
  D. Combe, 98:Dec89-955
  D. Leuwers, 450(NRF):Jan89-85
  J. Taylor, 532(RCF):Summer89-250
Bonnefoy, Y. Là où retombe la flèche.
  D. Leuwers, 450(NRF):Jan89-85
  J. Taylor, 532(RCF):Summer89-250
Bonner, A. Averting the Apocalypse.
  M. Ispahani, 441:21Oct90-25
Bonner, A. - see Llull, R.
Bonner, J. Wang Kuo-wei.*
  S.S-J. Hou, 116:Dec89-163
Bonner, T., Jr., ed. The Kate Chopin Companion.
  L. Wagner-Martin, 392:Spring89-193
Bonner, W.N. The Natural History of Seals.
  T. Halliday, 617(TLS):30Nov-6Dec90-1299

Bonnerot, O.H. La Perse dans la littérature et la pensée française au XVIIIe siècle.
  P. Kra, 166:Apr90-259
  L. Versini, 535(RHL):Nov-Dec89-1056
Bonnet, A-M. Rodenegg und Schmalkalden.
  A. Masser, 684(ZDA):Band118Heft2-91
Bonnet, C. Melqart.
  W. Huss, 229:Band61Heft2-142
Bonnet, M., ed. L'affaire Barrès.
  M-A. Graff, 535(RHL):Mar-Apr89-322
Bonnet, M., with others - see Breton, A.
Bonneville, H. - see de Salinas, J.
Bonnie, F. Wide Load.
  M.A. Jarman, 376:Mar89-124
  T.J. Palmer, 102(CanL):Spring89-208
Bonnier, A.C. Kyrkorna berättar.
  A. Nisbeth, 341:Vol58No1-26
Bonniffet, P. Un ballet démasqué.
  G. Durosoir, 537:Vol75No1-108
Bonvesin de la Riva. Volgari scelti. (R. Stefanini, ed)
  F. Bruni, 379(MedR):Aug89-290
Booij, G. & J. van Marle - see "Yearbook of Morphology"
"The Book of J." (D. Rosenberg, trans; H. Bloom, interpreter)
  J. Barton, 453(NYRB):22Nov90-3
  F. Kermode, 441:23Sep90-1
"The Book of Saints." (6th ed)
  G. Irvine, 617(TLS):9-15Mar90-260
Bookchin, M. Remaking Society.
  M. Oppenheimer, 441:25Nov90-13
Boomgaarden, D.R. Musical Thought in Britain and Germany during the Early Eighteenth Century.
  G.J. Buelow, 410(M&L):Feb89-96
  G. Lenz, 417:Jul-Sep89-281
Boone, J.A. Tradition Counter Tradition.*
  L.K. Barnett, 677(YES):Vol20-299
  E. Béranger, 189(EA):Oct-Dec89-451
  M. Melaver, 494:Fall89-639
Boorman, S.C. Human Conflict in Shakespeare.*
  J.W. Saunders, 541(RES):Nov89-555
  P. Thomson, 610:Summer89-189
Boose, L.E. & B.S. Flowers, eds. Daughters and Fathers.*
  L. Yelin, 637(VS):Spring90-507
Boosen, M. Etruskische Meeresmischwesen.*
  A. Hus, 555:Vol62Fasc1-178
Booth, M. Dreaming of Samarkand.
  B. Allen, 441:1Jul90-14
Booth, M. The Triads.
  M. Swallow, 617(TLS):7-13Sep90-952
Booth, P. Malibu.
  J. Cohen, 441:12Aug90-17
Booth, S. "King Lear," "Macbeth," Indefinition, and Tragedy.
  J.A. Bryant, Jr., 569(SR):Summer89-445
Booth, W.C. The Company We Keep.*
  B. Bawer, 31(ASch):Autumn89-610
  S. Connor, 402(MLR):Oct90-891
  V. Nemoianu, 400(MLN):Dec89-1178
  S. Pinsker, 219(GaR):Summer89-395
  E. Rothstein, 166:Jan90-180
  T. Siebers, 478(P&L):Oct89-375
  P.M. Spacks, 454:Spring90-328
  S.M. Sperry, 395(MFS):Winter89-845
Booth, W.C. The Vocation of a Teacher.*
  S. Pinsker, 219(GaR):Summer89-395
Borbein, V., J. Laubépin & M-L. Parizet. Le français actif: Approches I.^
  J.W. Cross, 399(MLJ):Winter89-504

Borchardt, E. Mythische Stukturen im Werk
Heinrich von Kleists.*
  R.E. Helbling, 406:Winter89-496
Borchmeyer, D. & V. Žmegač, eds. Moderne
Literatur in Grundbegriffen.
  M.W. Rectanus, 221(GQ):Spring89-242
Borck, J.S. - see "The Eighteenth Century"
Bord, A. Pascal et Jean de la Croix.*
  J. Lafond, 475:Vol16No31-580
  J.M. Pinto, 92(BH):Jul-Dec88-455
  L. Thirouin, 535(RHL):Mar-Apr89-276
Bordelois, I., H. Contreras & K. Zagona, eds.
Generative Studies in Spanish Syntax.
  F. Martineau, 320(CJL):Jun89-202
"Paul-Emile Borduas: Ecrits I." (A-G. Bour-
assa, J. Fisette & G. Lapointe, eds)
  L.S. Carney, 627(UTQ):Fall89-236
Bordwell, D. Ozu and the Poetics of Cinema.*
  D. Desser, 293(JASt):May89-383
  K. McDonald, 407(MN):Summer89-239
Borella, L. Plaidoyer pour Arnauld.
  R. Parish, 208(FS):Oct89-465
Borer, H., ed. Syntax and Semantics. (Vol 19:
The Syntax of Pronominal Clitics.)
  M-L. Rivero, 320(CJL):Jun89-214
Boretzky, N., W. Enninger & T. Stolz, eds.
Beiträge zum 4. Essener Kolloquium über
"Sprachkontakt, Sprachwandel, Sprach-
wechsel, Sprachtod."
  M. Perl, 682(ZPSK):Band42Heft6-866
Borgeaud, P. The Cult of Pan in Ancient
Greece.*
  M.R. Christ, 124:Jul-Aug90-546
Börger, E. Berechenbarkeit, Komplexität,
Logik. (2nd ed) (D. Rödding, ed)
  D. Siefkes, 316:Dec89-1490
Borgomano, L. & A. Nysenholc. André Del-
vaux.
  J. Van Baelen, 207(FR):Apr90-920
Boris, E. Art and Labor.
  M.A. Stankiewicz, 289:Fall89-122
Bork, R.H. The Tempting of America.*
  L. Sager, 453(NYRB):25Oct90-23
Borland, M. Wilde's Devoted Friend.
  T.D. Smith, 617(TLS):13-19Apr90-402
von Bormann, A., ed. Sehnsuchtsangst.
  J. Koppensteiner, 221(GQ):Summer89-440
de Borneil, G. - see under Giraut de Borneil
Bornstein, G. Poetic Remaking.
  I.F.A. Bell, 447(N&Q):Dec89-547
  J. Korg, 85(SBHC):Vol16-143
Bornstein, G. & H. Witemeyer - see Yeats, W.B.
Borodine, L. Gologor [suivi de] les Règles du
jeu.
  J. Blot, 450(NRF):Oct89-116
Borofsky, R. Making History.
  R. Price, 292(JAF):Jan-Mar89-116
Börsch-Supan, H. Die Deutsche Malerei von
Anton Graff bis Hans von Marées, 1760-
1870.
  K. Andrews, 90:Oct89-718
Borsi, F. The Monumental Era.
  D.P. Doordan, 576:Mar89-88
Borsody, S., ed. The Hungarians.
  M. Rady, 575(SEER):Oct89-640
  G.M. Tamás, 617(TLS):10-16Aug90-843
Borson, R. Intent, or Weight of the World.
  M. Cookshaw, 376:Sep89-122
  K. Irie, 526:Spring89-91
  D. Thirlwall, 137:Spring89-62
Borthwick, P. Between Clouds and Caves.
  I. McMillan, 493:Winter89/90-65

Børtnes, J. Visions of Glory.
  P-A. Bodin, 172(Edda):1989/2-174
  S. Franklin, 402(MLR):Jan90-269
  G. Lenhoff, 567:Vol75No3/4-353
Boruah, B.H. Fiction and Emotion.*
  R.C. Solomon, 543:Mar90-620
Boruch, M. Descendant.
  P. Booth, 219(GaR):Spring89-161
  639(VQR):Autumn89-137
Böschenstein, B. & J. Le Rider, eds. Hölderlin
vu de France.
  N. Gabriel, 52:Band24Heft1-98
Boschetti, A. The Intellectual Enterprise.
  L.D. Kritzman, 188(ECr):Winter89-97
  G. Prince, 478(P&L):Apr89-181
Boschma, N. & others. Lesen, na und?
  J.F. Lalande 2d, 399(MLJ):Summer89-234
Boschung, D. Antike Grabaltäre aus den Nek-
ropolen Roms.
  G. Davies, 313:Vol79-220
  F. Sinn-Henninger, 229:Band61Heft3-240
Bosco, R.A. - see Wigglesworth, M.
Bose, T. - see Colbeck, N.
Bosewitz, R. Waifdom in the Soviet Union.
  E. Elsey, 575(SEER):Oct89-649
  W. Goldman, 550(RusR):Jul89-335
Bosher, J.F. The French Revolution.
  G. Lewis, 617(TLS):26Jan-1Feb90-93
Bosinelli, R.M., P. Pugliatti & R. Zacchi, eds.
Myriadminded Man.*
  B.M., 494:Fall89-640
Boskin, J. Sambo.
  D. Royot, 189(EA):Oct-Dec89-495
Boskovits, M. Gemäldegalerie Berlin: Frühe
italienische Malerei. (E. Schleier, ed)
  U. Ballay, 39:Sep89-211
  J. Gardner, 683:Band52Heft3-433
Bosman, P., with A. Hall-Martin. Elephants
of Africa.
  Y.A. Andrews, 441:7Oct90-40
Bosque, I. & M. Pérez Fernández. Diccionario
inverso de la lengua española.
  A. Valladares Reguero, 548:Jul-Dec89-
476
Bossaglia, R., ed. Manzù.
  J. Hale, 90:Sep89-661
Bosshardt, H-G., ed. Perspektiven auf
Sprachen.*
  K. Goede, 682(ZPSK):Band42Heft5-694
Bossy, M-A., ed & trans. Medieval Debate
Poetry.
  N. Wilkins, 208(FS):Jan89-77
  J.M. Ziolkowski, 589:Oct89-925
Bost, J-P. & others. Belo IV: Les monnaies.
  H.J. Hildebrandt, 229:Band61Heft3-266
Bostock, D. Plato's "Phaedo."
  C.C. Meinwald, 482(PhR):Jan89-127
  R.W. Sharples, 303(JoHS):Vol109-224
Bostock, D. Plato's "Theaetetus."*
  E.E. Benitez, 543:Dec89-385
  J.E. Tiles, 518:Oct89-209
Bostock, W.W. Francophonie.*
  B. Brown, 207(FR):May90-1079
Boston, R. Osbert.*
  A. Ross, 364:Oct/Nov89-138
Boswell, J. Boswell: The English Experiment
1785-1789.* (I.S. Lustig & F.A. Pottle, eds)
  P. Clayton, 447(N&Q):Mar89-115
Boswell, J. Boswell: The Great Biographer,
1789-1795. (M.K. Danziger & F. Brady, eds)
  D. Jarrett, 453(NYRB):26Apr90-11

Boswell, J. The Correspondence of James Boswell with David Garrick, Edmund Burke and Edmond Malone. (P.S. Baker & others, eds)
T. Crawford, 571(ScLJ):Spring89-3
P. Martin, 481(PQ):Winter89-125
Bosworth, A.B. Conquest and Empire.
A.R. Burn, 123:Vol39No2-290
Bosworth, A.B. From Arrian to Alexander.
N.G.L. Hammond, 123:Vol39No1-21
P.A. Stadter, 24:Summer89-376
W. Will, 229:Band61Heft6-554
Bosworth, B.P. & A.M. Rivlin, eds. The Swedish Economy.
T.S. Nesslein, 563(SS):Autumn89-433
Botez, M-H. & others. Romania.
N. Malcolm, 617(TLS):19-25Jan90-57
Botha, R.P. Form and Meaning in Word Formation.
L. Bauer, 353:Vol27No6-1137
von Bothmer, D. Greek Vase Painting.
D.W.J. Gill, 39:Apr89-293
Botkin, D.B. Discordant Harmonies.
J.W. Kirchner, 441:29Apr90-43
Bottari, P. Ricerche saussuriane.
J.E. Joseph, 353:Vol27No2-341
Botterweck, G.J. & H. Ringgren, eds. Theological Dictionary of the Old Testament.
J.I. Ades, 477(PLL):Spring89-220
Bottigheimer, R.B., ed. Fairy Tales and Society.*
S. Neumann, 196:Band30Heft3/4-308
Bottigheimer, R.B. Grimms' Bad Girls and Bold Boys.*
R. Bendix, 292(JAF):Jan-Mar89-95
J.M. McGlathery, 301(JEGP):Jan89-77
Bottoms, D. Easter Weekend.
D. O'Brien, 441:25Feb90-34
Botwinick, A. Skepticism and Political Participation.
P. Gottfried, 543:Mar90-621
Bouchard, C.B. Sword, Miter, and Cloister.
G. Koziol, 589:Jan89-127
Bouchard, L.D. Tragic Method and Tragic Theology.
P.D. Murphy, 590:Dec89-122
Boucher, D. Lettres d'Italie.
V. Raoul, 102(CanL):Autumn-Winter89-243
Boucher, D. The Social and Political Thought of R.G. Collingwood.
S. Blackburn, 617(TLS):6-12Apr90-370
Boucher, D. Texts in Context.
P. Flaherty, 488:Jun89-225
Boucher, D. - see Collingwood, R.G.
Boudar, G. & M. Décaudin - see Apollinaire, G.
Boudon, F. & J. Blécon. Philibert Delorme et le château royal de Saint-Léger-en-Yvelines.
H. Ballon, 576:Dec89-391
Bouet, P. & others. Cyprien, Traités.
P. Monat, 555:Vol62Fasc1-169
Boulez, P. Jalons (pour une décennie).
M-O. Dupin, 358:Feb90-8
Boulez, P. Orientations. (J-J. Nattiez, ed)
S. Blaustein, 513:Winter89-273
617(TLS):29Jun-5Jul90-708
Boulnois, O., ed. Jean Duns Scot.
K. Hedwig, 489(PJGG):Band96Heft2-417
Boulnois, O. - see Scotus, J.D.
Boulton, J. Neighbourhood and Society.
M. Ingram, 242:Vol10No2-262

Bouraoui, H., ed. Robert Champigny.
C. Shorley, 208(FS):Jul89-365
Bouraoui, H. Reflet pluriel.
K.W. Meadwell, 102(CanL):Autumn-Winter89-157
Bourassa, A-G. Surréalisme et littérature québécoise.
S. Grace, 102(CanL):Summer89-147
Bourassa, A-G., J. Fisette & G. Lapointe - see "Paul-Emile Borduas: Ecrits I"
Bourassa, A-G. & G. Lapointe. Refus global et ses environs.
L.S. Carney, 627(UTQ):Fall89-234
de Bourbon Busset, J. Confession de Don Juan.
D. O'Connell, 207(FR):Apr90-887
Bourdieu, P. Distinction.*
P. Burke, 242:Vol10No1-98
Bourdieu, P. Homo Academicus.
T.M.R., 185:Apr90-697
Bourdieu, P. Sozialer Sinn.
I. Dölling, 654(WB):3/1989-513
Bourgeois, B. - see Hegel, G.W.F.
Bourgeois, G. Le Baccalauréat n'aura pas lieu.
A.J.M. Prévos, 207(FR):May90-1119
Bourgeois, J-L. & C. Pelos. Spectacular Vernacular.
S. MacNeille, 441:30Sep90-29
Bourget, E. & J-L. Lubitsch, ou la Satire Romanesque
M. Lefanu, 189(EA):Apr-Jun89-007
Bourget, J-L. Hollywood, Années 30.
M. Lefanu, 189(EA):Apr-Jun89-237
Bourjaily, V. Old Soldier.
H.F. Mosher, 441:28Oct90-15
Bourne, J.M. Britain and the Great War, 1914-1918.
D. French, 617(TLS):5-11Jan90-6
Bourne, R. The Red King's Rebellion.
J. Axtell, 441:15Jul90-14
Bournique, G. La Philosophie de Josiah Royce.
F.M. Oppenheim, 619:Fall89-557
Bourriau, J. Pharaohs and Mortals.
K.P. Foster, 124:Nov-Dec89-121
Boursault, E. Les Fables d'Esope. (T. Allott, ed)
H.G. Hall, 208(FS):Oct89-467
G. Mombello, 535(RHL):Nov-Dec89-1055
D. Shaw, 402(MLR):Jul90-732
Bouson, J.B. The Empathic Reader.
M. Magalaner, 395(MFS):Winter89-849
Boutelle, S.H. Julia Morgan, Architect.
J. Bamberger, 139:Aug/Sep89-20
L.M. Roth, 576:Sep89-297
S. Woodbridge, 505:Jan89-135
G. Wright, 617(TLS):6-12Apr90-379
Bouwsma, W.J. John Calvin.
S. Selinger, 551(RenQ):Summer89-313
Bouysse, P. Essai sur la jeunesse d'un moraliste.*
L. Godard de Donville, 535(RHL):Mar-Apr89-279
E.D. James, 208(FS):Apr89-207
W.C. Marceau, 207(FR):May90-1061
L. Thirouin, 547(RF):Band101Heft2/3-341
Bouza, A.V. The Police Mystique.
R.G. Powers, 441:6May90-7
Bové, P.A. Destructive Poetics.
K. Ziarek, 153:Fall-Winter89-114
Bové, P.A. Intellectuals in Power.*
D.A. Hollinger, 385(MQR):Winter90-123

Bovey, J. The Silent Meteor.
   S. Pickering, 569(SR):Summer89-lxxxiv
Bowden, B. Chaucer Aloud.
   A.T. Gaylord, 589:Jul89-670
   E. Green, 184(EIC):Apr89-156
   C.C. Morse, 447(N&Q):Mar89-81
Bowden, C. Mezcal.
   D. Kirkpatrick, 649(WAL):May89-96
Bowe, N.G. The Life and Works of Harry
   Clarke.
   R. Dorment, 617(TLS):13-19Apr90-401
Bowen, A., ed. The Story of Lucretia.
   L. Ascher, 124:Nov-Dec89-128
Bowen, G. - see Eluard, P.
Bowen, G. & R. Marken. 1919.
   M. Mason, 102(CanL):Autumn-Winter89-
   218
Bowen, J. Fighting Back.
   V. Fitzpatrick, 364:Jun/Jul89-140
Bowen, R. Innocence Is Not Enough.*
   R. Dingman, 407(MN):Autumn89-365
Bower, W. "Scotichronicon" in Latin and Eng-
   lish. (Vol 2) (J. & W. MacQueen, eds)
   G.W.S. Barrow, 617(TLS):20-26Apr90-415
Bower, W. Scotichronicon. (Vol 8) (D.E.R.
   Watt, ed & trans)
   V. Chandler, 589:Oct89-926
Bowering, A. Figures Cut in Sacred Ground.*
   J. Kertzer, 102(CanL):Autumn-Winter89-
   172
   L. Lamont-Stewart, 102(CanL):Autumn-
   Winter89-174
   P. Monk, 627(UTQ):Fall89-154
Bowering, G. Caprice.*
   D. Barbour, 102(CanL):Winter88-103
Bowering, G. Delayed Mercy and Other
   Poems.*
   M.T. Lane, 168(ECW):Fall89-90
   P. O'Brien, 102(CanL):Autumn-Winter89-
   236
Bowering, G. Selected Poems: Particular
   Accidents.
   F. Stewart, 168(ECW):Summer89-56
Bowering, M. Anyone Can See I Love You.
   L. Wevers, 102(CanL):Autumn-Winter89-
   260
Bowering, M. Grandfather was a Soldier.
   M. Mason, 102(CanL):Autumn-Winter89-
   218
Bowering, M. To All Appearances a Lady.
   E. Hower, 441:12Aug90-71
Bowers, F. - see "Dictionary of Literary Biog-
   raphy"
Bowers, J.E. A Sense of Place.*
   R. Gish, 456(NDQ):Spring89-182
Bowers, J.M. The Crisis of Will in "Piers
   Plowman."*
   A. Middleton, 589:Jan89-130
Bowers, N. James Dickey.
   R.J. Calhoun, 392:Winter88/89-83
Bowersock, G.W. Hellenism in Late Antiquity.
   C. Kelly, 441:23Sep90-43
Bowie, A. Aesthetics and Subjectivity.
   M. Tanner, 617(TLS):26Oct-1Nov90-1156
Bowie, M. Freud, Proust and Lacan.*
   P. Brady, 478(P&L):Oct89-391
   A. Lavers, 402(MLR):Jan90-133
   V.K. Ramazani, 188(ECr):Spring89-104
   D. Wood, 242:Vol10No1-85
Bowie, N.E., ed. Equal Opportunity.*
   J. Iwanicki, 103:May90-175
   R. Young, 63:Sep89-369

Bowker, G., ed. Malcolm Lowry: "Under the
   Volcano."
   C. Ackerley, 102(CanL):Autumn-
   Winter89-167
   M.P.L., 295(JML):Fall88/Winter89-375
Bowlby, J. Charles Darwin.
   M. Ridley, 617(TLS):6-12Jul90-719
Bowlby, R. Virginia Woolf.*
   R. Rooksby, 447(N&Q):Dec89-540
Bowler, M. Destiny of Dreams.
   K. Weber, 441:11Nov90-60
Bowles, G. Louise Bogan's Aesthetic of Limi-
   tation.*
   C.K. Doreski, 577(SHR):Summer89-290
   N. Sweet, 295(JML):Fall88/Winter89-291
Bowles, P. Their Heads Are Green and Their
   Hands are Blue.* (British title: Their
   Heads Are Green.)
   617(TLS):9-15Mar90-266
Bowles, P. Two Years Beside the Strait.
   M. Dillon, 617(TLS):7-13Sep90-938
Bowles, P. Without Stopping.
   S. Gray, 364:Feb/Mar90-141
Bowles, S. & H. Gintis. La Démocratie post-
   libérale.
   J-Y. Grenier, 531:Jul-Dec89-543
Bowlt, J.E., ed. Russian Art of the Avant-
   Garde.
   C. Lodder, 90:Sep89-648
Bowlt, J.E., ed. Russian/Soviet Theme Issue:
   The Journal of Decorative and Propaganda
   Arts.
   L. Hecht, 574(SEEJ):Spring89-138
Bowlt, J.E. - see Lavrentiev, A.
Bowman, F.P. Le Christ des barricades, 1789-
   1848.
   K. Beaumont, 208(FS):Jul89-337
   R.T. Denommé, 210(FrF):May89-236
   P.J. Siegel, 446(NCFS):Fall-Winter89/90-
   298
Bowman, F.P. - see Grégoire, H-B.
Bown, M.C. Contemporary Russian Art.*
   M.A. Svede, 441:21Jan90-36
Bowring, R. Murasaki Shikibu: "The Tale of
   Genji."
   L. Miyake, 407(MN):Autumn89-349
Boyce, J.K. Agrarian Impasse in Bengal.
   S. Bose, 293(JASt):Aug89-645
Boyd, B. Vladimir Nabokov: The Russian
   Years.
   S. Davydov, 441:14Oct90-3
   J. Grayson, 617(TLS):16-22Nov90-1227
   G. Steiner, 442(NY):10Dec90-153
Boyd, B. Nabokov's "Ada."*
   C. Ross, 395(MFS):Summer89-295
Boyd, B. - see Chaucer, G.
Boyd, M. Bach.
   A.F.L.T., 412:May89-146
Boyd, S. Language Survival.
   S. Gal, 355(LSoc):Sep89-399
Boyd, S.J. The Novels of William Golding.
   R. Stevenson, 402(MLR):Jul90-709
Boyd, W. Brazzaville Beach.
   R. Brain, 617(TLS):14-20Sep90-970
Boyd, W. The New Confessions.*
   G. Davenport, 569(SR):Summer89-468
Boydell, B. A Dublin Musical Calendar 1700-
   1760.
   H. White, 272(IUR):Spring89-177
Boydston, J., M. Kelley & A. Margolis, eds.
   The Limits of Sisterhood.
   M-M. Byerman, 26(ALR):Winter90-76
   W. Mitchinson, 106:Fall89-276

Boydston, J.A. - see Dewey, J.
Boyer, E.L. College.
G. Graff, 473(PR):Vol56No2-291
Boyer, R. Gone to Earth.
M. Stasio, 441:30Sep90-32
Boyer, R. & others. L'épopée. (J. Victorio,
with J-C. Payen, eds)
A.V., 379(MedR):Dec89-469
Boyer, Y., P. Lellouche & J. Roper, eds. Fran-
co-British Defence Cooperation.
T. Scanlan, 207(FR):Apr90-919
Boyers, R. After the Avant-Garde.
H. Bertens, 402(MLR):Jan90-137
Boyers, R. Atrocity and Amnesia.
W.R. Katz, 242:Vol10No1-100
Boylan, A.M. Sunday School.
J.D. Hedrick, 432(NEQ):Dec89-610
Boylan, C. Black Baby.*
442(NY):29Jan90-95
Boylan, C. Concerning Virgins.
P. Craig, 617(TLS):19-25Jan90-66
D. Durrant, 364:Feb/Mar90-133
Boylan, H., comp. Checklist and Historical
Directory of Prince Edward Island Newspa-
pers, 1787-1986.
E.L. Swanick, 470:Vol27-124
Boylan, H. A Dictionary of Irish Biography.
(2nd ed)
J.B. Davenport, 174(Éire):Winter89-131
Boylan, J. Remind Me to Murder You Later.
P.J. Bailey, 455:Dec89-61
P. La Salle, 573(33F):Spring90-001
639(VQR):Spring89-59
Boylan, P., D. Rissel & J.A. Lett, Jr. ¡En
Directo!
D. McAlpine, 399(MLJ):Summer89-236
Boyle, A.J., ed. The Imperial Muse.
S.A. Rackley, 124:Mar-Apr90-369
Boyle, A.J. - see Seneca
Boyle, T. Black Swine in the Sewers of Hamp-
stead.
D. Grylls, 617(TLS):2-8Feb90-125
Boyle, T.C. East is East.
P-L. Adams, 61:Oct90-135
G. Godwin, 441:9Sep90-13
Boyle, T.C. If the River Was Whiskey.*
J.D. Bellamy, 455:Dec89-59
Boyt, R. Sexual Intercourse.*
J. Mellors, 364:Aug/Sep89-130
K. Olson, 441:25Nov90-20
Bozal, V. Mímesis.
A. Savile, 89(BJA):Spring89-181
Bozeman, T.D. To Live Ancient Lives.*
S. Bush, Jr., 165(EAL):Vol25No1-78
J. Gatta, 568(SCN):Spring-Summer89-14
Bracciolini, P. Lettere. (Vols 2 & 3) (H.
Harth, ed)
D. Marsh, 551(RenQ):Autumn89-552
Bracco, V., ed. Inscriptiones Italiae. (Vol 1,
Regio 1, fasc 1)
H. Solin, 229:Band61Heft8-708
Brack, O.M., Jr. - see "Studies in Eighteenth-
Century Culture"
Brackenbury, A. Christmas Roses and Other
Poems.*
S. Kantaris, 493:Spring89-62
S. Knight, 364:Apr/May89-129
Bradbury, M. The Modern World.
639(VQR):Spring89-52
Bradbury, M. No, Not Bloomsbury.*
J.V. Knapp, 395(MFS):Summer89-345
Bradbury, M. Unsent Letters.*
E.C.J., 395(MFS):Summer89-385

Bradbury, R. A Graveyard for Lunatics.
T. Nolan, 441:2Sep90-24
Bradby, D. & D. Williams. Directors' Theatre.
L. Kruger, 615(TJ):Oct89-414
Bradfield, S. Dream of the Wolf.
S.G. Kellman, 441:25Nov90-33
Bradford, D.E. The Fundamental Ideas.
J.K. Swindler, 449:Jun89-404
Bradford, M.E. - see Lytle, A.
Bradford, S. The Reluctant King.* (British
title: Georve VI.)
D. Cannadine, 442(NY):13Aug90-91
W.F. Kimball, 441:17Jun90-24
Bradley, A. Ruskin and Italy.
J. Clubbe, 637(VS):Winter90-353
Bradley, C.J. & J.B. Coover, eds. Richard S.
Hill - Tributes from Friends.
L. Coral, 309:Vol9No1-45
Bradley, F.H. Ethical Studies. (2nd ed)
F. Schoeman, 637(VS):Spring90-523
Bradley, J.E. The Best There Ever Was.
B. Kent, 441:18Nov90-36
Bradley, J.E. Popular Politics and the Ameri-
can Revolution in England.*
H.T. Dickinson, 83:Autumn89-221
Bradley, J.L. & I. Ousby - see Ruskin, J. &
C.E. Norton
Bradley, J.W. Evolution of the Onondaga Iro-
quois.
J. Ferling, 432(NEQ):Mar89-124
Bradshaw, G. Shakespeare's Scepticism.*
B. Engler, 179(ES):Oct89-466
T. Mason, 97(CQ):Vol18No4-428
L. Normand, 447(N&Q):Dec90-000
Bradstock, M. & L. Wakeling, eds. Words from
the Same Heart.
D. Saravanamuttu, 581:Mar89-124
Bradstreet, A. & E. Taylor. Early New Eng-
land Meditative Poetry. (C.E. Hambrick-
Stowe, ed)
S. Arch, 165(EAL):Vol25No2-220
Brady, A.P. Pompilia.
A. Falk, 637(VS):Winter90-328
Brady, F. Citizen Welles.*
P. French, 617(TLS):15-21Jun90-630
Brady, F.N. Ethical Managing
K. Hanly, 103:Mar90-98
Braestrup, K. Onion.
R. Short, 441:22Apr90-24
Bragantini, R. Il riso sotto il velame.
J.R. Snyder, 402(MLR):Jan90-211
Bragg, M. Rich.
H. Hobson, 157:No171-50
Bragg, M. A Time to Dance.
J. O'Grady, 617(TLS):15-21Jun90-653
Bragger, J.D. & D.B. Rice. Allons-y!* (2nd
ed)
M. Donaldson-Evans, 399(MLJ):
Autumn89-356
Brague, R. Aristote et la question du monde.
D.R. Lachterman, 543:Dec89-387
Braham, R.L., ed. The Tragedy of Hungarian
Jewry.
C. Patrias, 104(CASS):Spring89-124
Braine, D. The Reality of Time and the Exis-
tence of God.*
P. Helm, 518:Jul89-185
H. Meynell, 483:Jan89-119
Braine, D. & H. Lesser, eds. Ethics, Technol-
ogy and Medicine.
V. Bergum, 103:Oct90-394
J. Harris, 291:Vol6No2-240

Braithwaite, J. & P. Pettit. Not Just Deserts.
R. Hood, 617(TLS):7–13Sep90–944
Bralczyk, J. O języku polskiej propagandy
politycznej lat siedemdziesiątych.
G. Stone, 575(SEER):Apr89–265
Brambilla, A., ed. Un'amicizia petrarchesca –
Carteggio Nolhac–Novati.
G. Lucchini, 379(MedR):Dec89–478
Brami, J. Les Troubles de l'invention.
J.P. McNab, 210(FrF):Sep89–363
Branagh, K. Beginning.*
P–L. Adams, 61:Sep90–123
Branca, V., ed. Esopo toscano dei frati e dei
mercanti trecenteschi.
R. Librandi, 379(MedR):Aug89–291
M. Marti, 228(GSLI):Vol166fasc536–606
Branch, E.M., M.B. Frank & K.M. Sanderson –
see Twain, M.
Branch, T. Parting the Waters.*
G.R., 185:Apr90–707
Brand, J., C. Hailey & D. Harris – see Berg, A.
& A. Schoenberg
Brand, M. & R.M. Harnish, eds. The Represen-
tation of Knowledge and Belief.
R. Carston, 361:Jul89–233
Brandell, G. Strindberg – ett författarliv.
M. Robinson, 562(Scan):May89–94
Brandenburg, S. & M. Gutiérrez–Denhoff, eds.
Beethoven und Böhmen.
W. Kinderman, 415:Nov89–680
Brandenburg, S. & H. Loos, eds. Beiträge zu
Beethovens Kammermusik.
B. Cooper, 410(M&L):Feb89–107
W. Rathert, 417:Jul–Sep89–273
Brandes, G. Georg Brandes: Selected Letters.
(W.G. Jones, ed & trans)
M. Meyer, 617(TLS):29Jun–5Jul90–703
Brandon, P. & B. Short. The South East from
AD 1000.
G.E. Mingay, 617(TLS):14–20Dec90–1356
Brandon, R. The New Women and the Old Men.
P–L. Adams, 61:Jul90–104
S. Harries, 617(TLS):16–22Mar90–296
Brandt, A.M. No Magic Bullet. (2nd ed)
G.S. Smith, 529(QQ):Summer89–244
Brandt, D. questions i asked my mother.
R.E. Conway, 102(CanL):Autumn–
Winter89–278
Brandt, G. Volksmassen – sprachliche Kom-
munikation.
B.J. Koekkoek, 350:Sep90–627
Brandt, J. Argumentative Struktur in Sene-
cas Tragödien.
K. Heldmann, 229:Band61Heft6–548
Brandt, N. The Town That Started the Civil
War.
S.W. Sears, 441:20May90–22
Brandt, P. Becoming the Butlers.
B.F. Williamson, 441:11Nov90–61
Brandys, K. Paris, New York 1982–1984.
639(VQR):Spring89–54
Brandys, K. Rondo.*
J. Bayley, 453(NYRB):19Jul90–23
442(NY):1Jan90–84
Brang, P., ed. Schweizerische Beiträge zum X.
Internationalen Slavistenkongress in Sofia,
September 1988.
W. Busch, 688(ZSP):Band49Heft2–391
Branham, R.B. Unruly Eloquence.
J. Romm, 124:Jan–Feb90–242
Branick, V.P. Wonder in a Technical World.*
D.E. Cody, 438:Autumn89–517

Brantlinger, P., ed. Energy and Entropy.
F. McConnell, 637(VS):Spring90–496
Brantlinger, P. Rule of Darkness.*
P. Bose, 538(RAL):Fall89–582
C.D. Eby, 445(NCF):Jun89–114
P. Faulkner, 402(MLR):Apr90–418
R. Gagnier, 405(MP):Feb90–316
P. Stansky, 177(ELT):Vol32No1–75
639(VQR):Winter89–15
Bras, G. Hegel et l'art.
P. Somville, 542:Oct–Dec89–601
Brass, P.R. The New Cambridge History of
India. (Vol 4, Pt 1)
G. Hawthorn, 617(TLS):19–25Oct90–1120
Brass, P.R. & F. Robinson, eds. Indian
National Congress and Indian Society,
1885–1985.
G. Prakash, 293(JASt):Nov89–917
Brasseur, P. Ma Vie en vrac.
E.B. Turk, 207(FR):Dec89–399
Braswell, B.K. A Commentary on the Fourth
Pythian Ode of Pindar.
D.E. Gerber, 123:Vol39No2–181
Braswell, L., comp. The Index of Middle Eng-
lish Prose, Handlist IV.
N.F. Blake, 179(ES):Oct89–453
V. Gillespie, 382(MAE):1989/1–149
H. Gneuss, 38:Band107Heft1/2–169
O.S. Pickering, 72:Band226Heft1–153
Bratcher, J.W. 3d & E. Szoka, eds. 3 Contem-
porary Brazilian Plays.
J.I. Bissett, 352(LATR):Fall89–157
Brater, E. Beyond Minimalism.*
D.B., 295(JML):Fall88/Winter89–285
L. Oppenheim, 615(TJ):Mar89–119
Brater, E., ed. Feminine Focus.
T.S. Zinman, 34:Feb90–36
Brathwaite, E.K. X/Self.*
L. Breiner, 473(PR):Vol56No2–316
Bratton, J.S. – see Shakespeare, W.
Bratman, M.E. Intention, Plans, and Practical
Reason.*
F. Adams, 185:Oct89–198
M. Zimmerman, 484(PPR):Sep89–189
Braude, A. Radical Spirits.
M. Rugoff, 441:14Jan90–19
Braude, S.E., ed. The Limits of Influence.*
P. Grim, 449:Mar89–126
Braudel, F. The Identity of France.* (Vol 1)
639(VQR):Summer89–79
Brault, J. Death–Watch.*
T.J. Palmer, 102(CanL):Spring89–208
Brault, J. Poèmes I.
K.W. Meadwell, 102(CanL):Autumn–
Winter89–157
Brault, J–R. Bibliographie des Éditions Fides
(1937–1987).
J. Michon, 470:Vol27–122
Braun, J. & K. Brambats, eds. Selected Writ-
ings on Latvian Music.
M.M. Lutz, 187:Winter89–163
Braun, M. How to Write Western Novels.
M.T. Marsden, 649(WAL):Aug89–172
Braun, M. – see Huch, R.
Braun, V. Unvollendete Geschichte. (A. Hol-
lis, ed)
I. Wallace, 402(MLR):Jul90–812
Braunbehrens, V. Mozart in Vienna: 1781–
1791.
P–L. Adams, 61:Jun90–121
N. Kenyon, 617(TLS):16–22Nov90–1238
E. Leinsdorf, 441:25Feb90–7

Braund, D., ed. The Administration of the
Roman Empire 241 BC – AD 193.
M. Hammond, 124:Mar–Apr90–377
Braund, S.H. Beyond Anger.
L. Ascher, 124:Jan–Feb90–245
N. Rudd, 123:Vol39No2–218
Braune, W. Althochdeutsche Grammatik.
(14th ed) (H. Eggers, comp)
K. Gärtner, 685(ZDL):3/1989–349
H. Penzl, 301(JEGP):Jan89–58
Braunfels, W. Urban Design in Western
Europe.*
D. Bass, 46:Nov89–12
Braunlich, P.C. Haunted by Home.
J.H. Maguire, 649(WAL):Aug89–180
Braunmuller, A.R. & J.C. Bulman, eds. Comedy
from Shakespeare to Sheridan.
A.F. Kinney, 250(HLQ):Autumn89–509
Braunstein, J–F. Broussais et le matérial-
isme.
A. Pichot, 192(EP):Jul–Dec89–533
Braverman, K. Squandering the Blue.
S. Ferguson, 441:16Dec90–18
Braxton, J.M. & A.N. McLaughlin, eds. Wild
Women in the Whirlwind.
E.J. Sundquist, 441:25Feb90–11
Bray, L. César–Pierre Richelet (1626–1698).*
J. Cornette, 531:Jul–Dec89–507
M. Glatigny, 475:Vol16No30–267
Braybrooke, D. Meeting Needs.*
A.F.H., 185:Apr90–090
H. Laycock, 529(QQ):Summer89–523
S. Sayers, 518.Jul89–179
Braybrooke, D. Philosophy of Social Science.*
D.M. Levin, 482(PhR):Oct89–588
W.W. Miller, 518:Jan89–58
Braybrooke, M. Time To Meet.
A. Race, 617(TLS):14–20Dec90–1342
Brazell, K., ed. Twelve Plays of the Noh and
Kyogen Theaters.
R. Teele, 407(MN):Winter89–509
Breazeale, D. – see Fichte, J.G.
Brecht, B. Letters, 1913–1956. (J. Willett,
ed)
M. Hofmann, 617(TLS):5–11Oct90–1063
G. Steiner, 442(NY):10Sep90–119
Brecht, B. Poems and Songs from the Plays.
(J. Willett, ed & trans)
M. Hofmann, 617(TLS):5–11Oct90–1063
Brecht, R.D. & J.S. Levine, eds. Case in Slav-
ic.
O.T. Yokoyama, 574(SEEJ):Spring89–144
"The Brecht Yearbook."* (Vol 12) (J. Fuegi,
G. Bahr & J. Willett, eds)
S.L. Cocalis, 406:Summer89–231
Brédif, J. Toiles de Jouy.
B. Nevill, 617(TLS):30Mar–5Apr90–352
Brednich, R.W., ed. Enzyklopädie des Märch-
ens. (Vol 5, issues 4 & 5)
E. Ettlinger, 203:Vol100No2–257
Brednich, R.W., ed. Grundriss der Volkskunde.
H. Gerndt, 196:Band30Heft3/4–310
Breebaart, A.B. Clio and Antiquity.
J.M. Alonso–Núñez, 123:Vol39No2–411
Breig, W., with others – see "Schütz Jahrbuch
7/8"
Breitman, R. & A.M. Kraut. American Refugee
Policy and European Jewry, 1933–1945.
M.I. Urofsky, 390:Feb/Mar89–61
Bremer, J.M., A.M. van Erp Taalman Kip & S.R.
Slings. Some Recently Found Greek Poems.
M. Davies, 229:Band61Heft2–97
M.L. West, 123:Vol39No1–9

Bremer, J.M., I.J.F. de Jong & J. Kalff, eds.
Homer: Beyond Oral Poetry.
J.B. Hainsworth, 123:Vol39No2–173
Bremmer, J.N. & N.M. Horsfall. Roman Myth
and Mythography.
T.P. Wiseman, 313:Vol79–129
Bremmer, R.H., Jr., ed. The Five Wyttes.
A. Barratt, 179(ES):Oct89–452
A. Crépin, 189(EA):Jul–Sep89–338
V.M. O'Mara, 72:Band226Heft1–171
H.L. Spencer, 382(MAE):1989/1–157
Brenkman, J. Culture and Domination.*
A. Richardson, 147:Vol6No1–65
Brenna, D. The Book of Mamie.
H. Middleton, 441:7Jan90–12
Brennan, A. Conditions of Identity.
W.R. Carter, 393(Mind):Apr89–315
G. Forbes, 479(PhQ):Jul89–368
E.J. Lowe, 518:Apr89–103
Brennan, A. Shakespeare's Dramatic Struc-
tures.
A.F. Kinney, 481(PQ):Fall89–443
S.J. Phillips, 447(N&Q):Jun89–233
Brennan, A. Thinking about Nature.
R. Attfield, 291:Vol6No2–237
E.T., 185:Apr90–714
Brennan, J.F. Enlightened Despotism in Rus-
sia.*
J. Le Donne, 550(RusR):Apr89–200
Brennan, K. Here on Earth.
D. Allen, 249(HudR):Summer89–327
Brennan, M. Wordsworth, Turner, and Roman-
tic Landscape.
D.Q. Smith, 661(WC):Autumn89–184
Brennan, M.G. Literary Patronage in the
English Renaissance.
J. Gouws, 447(N&Q):Dec89–499
V. Houliston, 97(CQ):Vol18No3–327
Brennan, R.P. Levitating Trains and Kami-
kaze Genes.
B. Sharp, 441:8Apr90–20
Brennan, T., ed. Between Feminism and Psy-
choanalysis.
K. Ford, 617(TLS):12–18Jan90–46
Brennan, T. Public Drinking and Popular
Culture in Eighteenth Century Paris.
E. Weber, 31(ASch):Spring89–312
Brennan, T. Salman Rushdie and the Third
World.
A. Gurnah, 617(TLS):2–8Mar90–221
Brennels, D.L. & F.R. Myers, eds. Dangerous
Words.
D. Hymes, 355(LSoc):Jun89–261
Brenner, A., ed. Chafetz Graphics.
K. Kadish, 42(AR):Fall89–494
Brenner, M. House of Dreams.
R. Mason, 639(VQR):Winter89–165
Brenner, R., with G.A. Brenner. Gambling and
Speculation.
P. Seabright, 617(TLS):14–20Dec90–1339
Brenner, S. Dancers & the Dance.
C. Innes, 441:9Sep90–27
Brennert, A. Her Pilgrim Soul.
G. Jonas, 441:9Dec90–32
Brenni, V.J., comp. The Art and History of
Book Printing. Book Printing in Britain and
America.
517(PBSA):Mar89–109
"Brennpunkt Düsseldorf 1962–1987."
I. Rogoff, 59:Jun89–240
Brentano, C. Erzählungen: Prosa IV. (G.
Kluge, ed)
H.M.K. Riley, 133.Band22Heft3/4–339

Brentano, F. Philosophical Investigations on Space, Time and the Continuum.* (S. Körner & R. Chisholm, eds)
    B. Terrell, 518:Apr89–89
Brentano, F. Über Ernst Machs "Erkenntnis und Irrtum." (R.M. Chisholm & J.C. Marek, eds)
    R. George, 103:Jun90–222
Breslauer, B.H. Count Heinrich IV zu Castell.
    N. Barker, 78(BC):Summer89–266
Breslauer, B.H. & R. Folter. Bibliography. 517(PBSA):Mar89–113
Breslauer, B.H. & E.W.G. Greib. Martin Breslauer, Catalogue 109.
    N. Barker, 78(BC):Summer89–266
Breslin, P. The Psycho-Political Muse.*
    A. Golding, 27(AL):Mar89–143
    L. Goldstein, 271:Fall89–159
    M. Halliday, 191(ELN):Dec89–77
    P. Lapp, 529(QQ):Autumn89–744
Breton, A. Mad Love.*
    A.S.L., 295(JML):Fall88/Winter89–295
    I. Malin, 532(RCF):Spring89–262
Breton, A. Oeuvres complètes. (Vol 1) (M. Bonnet, with others, eds)
    E. Adamowicz, 208(FS):Oct89–488
Breton, M., ed. Hot and Cool.
    W. Balliett, 442(NY):18Jun90–93
Bretone, M. Storia del Diritto romano.
    O.F. Robinson, 313:Vol79–192
de la Bretonne, R. – see under Rétif de la Bretonne
Brett, B. Evolution in Every Direction.
    D.A. Precosky, 102(CanL):Summer89–193
Brett, G. Through Our Own Eyes.
    P. Dufrene, 709:Summer90–253
Brett, S. Pargeter's Package.
    P. Craig, 617(TLS):21–27Dec90–1382
Brettell, R. & others. Exposition Gauguin.
    E. Darragon, 98:Apr89–228
Brettell, R.R. Pissarro and Pontoise.
    J. Russell, 441:2Dec90–9
Breuer, R. Tragische Handlungsstrukturen.
    D.R. Midgley, 89(BJA):Summer89–276
Breuer, W.B. Geronimo!
    P. Dye, 441:18Feb90–21
Brewer, A.M., ed. Dictionaries, Encyclopedias, and other Word-Related Books. (4th ed)
    K.B. Harder, 424:Sep89–294
Brewer, D. An Introduction to Chaucer.*
    C.J. Watkin, 148:Winter86–96
Brewer, D., ed. Studies in Medieval English Romances.
    P. Hardman, 402(MLR):Jul90–686
    M. McCarthy, 447(N&Q):Dec89–491
    D. Mehl, 72:Band226Heft1–159
    J. Simpson, 203:Vol100No2–256
Brewer, J. The Sinews of Power.*
    L. Stone, 453(NYRB):15Mar90–50
Brewster, E. Entertaining Angels.
    D. Precosky, 198:Summer89–116
Brewster, E. Visitations.*
    M. Junyk, 529(QQ):Spring89–159
Brewster, J. & others. Four Fife Poets.
    W.N. Herbert, 571(ScLJ):Spring89–43
Brian, D. The True Gen.*
    R.W. Lewis, 456(NDQ):Summer89–266
Brians, P. Nuclear Holocausts.*
    A.H. McIntire, Jr., 561(SFS):Mar89–110
Briant, P. Etat et pasteurs au Moyen-Orient ancien.
    E. Kettenhofen, 229:Band61Heft1–32

Bricot, T. Tractatus insolubilium. (E.J. Ashworth, ed)
    E.D. Sylla, 589:Apr89–392
Bridger, S. Women in the Soviet Countryside.
    J. Pallot, 575(SEER):Jan89–158
Bridges, C.W., with T.A. Lopez & R.F. Lunsford, eds. Training the New Teacher of College Composition.
    D. George, 128(CE):Apr89–418
Bridgman, J. The End of the Holocaust.
    H. Maccoby, 617(TLS):14–20Sep90–966
Bridgman, R. Traveling in Mark Twain.*
    B.M., 494:Fall89–641
    L.C. Mitchell, 301(JEGP):Jan89–142
Brienza, S.D. Samuel Beckett's New Worlds.*
    D.B., 295(JML):Fall88/Winter89–285
Briganti, G., A. Chastel & R. Zapperi. Gli Amori degli Dei.
    G. Perini, 90:Jan89–39
Brigden, S. London and the Reformation.
    B. Bradshaw, 617(TLS):27Jul–2Aug90–806
Briggs, A. Victorian Things.
    D. Cannadine, 453(NYRB):15Feb90–25
    P. Greenhalgh, 39:Dec89–433
    R.H. Super, 637(VS):Summer90–651
    639(VQR):Autumn89–115
Briggs, C.L. Learning How to Ask.*
    R. Blutner, 682(ZPSK):Band42Heft1–135
Briggs, J. A Woman of Passion.
    S. Rahn, 177(ELT):Vol32No4–475
Briggs, W.W. & W.M. Calder 3d, eds. Classical Scholarship.
    J.H.C. Leach, 617(TLS):27Apr–3May90–440
Briggs, W.W., Jr. – see Gildersleeve, B.L.
Briggs, W.W., Jr. & H.W. Benario, eds. Basil Lanneau Gildersleeve.
    C.R. Phillips 3d, 24:Winter89–636
Bright, D.F. The Miniature Epic in Vandal Africa.
    A. Gérard, 538(RAL):Spring89–124
    J.P. Holoka, 124:Nov–Dec89–119
    J. Parsons, 313:Vol79–261
Brill, S. & others. Trial by Jury.
    A. Boyer, 441:22Jul90–20
Brilliant, R. Visual Narratives.
    R. Adam, 555:Vol62Fasc1–176
Brimelow, P. The Patriot Game.*
    D.E. Smith, 298:Summer89–146
Brin, D. Earth.
    G. Jonas, 441:8Jul90–22
von den Brincken, A–D. Kartographische Quellen.
    G. Kish, 589:Oct89–1047
Brind'Amour, P. Le Calendrier romain.
    G.J. Tiene, 124:Jan–Feb90–236
Bringmann, K. Die Agrarreform des Tiberius Gracchus.
    A.J.L. van Hooff, 394:Vol42fasc1/2–247
Brink, A. Die Nilpferdpeitsche.
    K. Wendt–Riedel, 654(WB):1/1989–126
Brink, C.O. English Classical Scholarship.*
    W.M. Calder 3d, 394:Vol42fasc1/2–256
Brink, D.O. Moral Realism and the Foundations of Ethics.
    J. Dancy, 617(TLS):23–29Mar90–326
    J.B. Killoran, 543:Mar90–622
Brinke, H. & A. Lutz. Chinese Cloisonné.
    M. Medley, 463:Winter89/90–228
Brinker–Gabler, G., ed. Deutsche Literatur von Frauen. (Vol 2)
    E. Boa, 402(MLR):Jul90–803

Brinkman, J.A. Prelude to Empire.
  B.T. Arnold, 318(JAOS):Oct–Dec88–661
Brinkmann, S.C. Die deutschsprachige Pas-
  tourelle.
  V. Mertens, 680(ZDP):Band108Heft3–412
Brinkmeyer, R.H., Jr. The Art and Vision of
  Flannery O'Connor.
  F. Crews, 453(NYRB):26Apr90–49
  A.F. Kinney, 585(SoQ):Summer90–123
Brinton, L.J. The Development of English
  Aspectual Systems.
  W.N. Francis, 350:Jun90–410
Briosi, S. & H. Hillenaar, eds. Vitalité et
  contradictions de l'avant-garde.
  A. de Jong, 204(FdL):Mar89–75
Bristol, M.D. Carnival and Theater.*
  R.D. Abrahams, 292(JAF):Apr–Jun89–202
  F.E. Manning, 162(TDR):Spring89–19
Bristow, J., ed. The Victorian Poet.
  B. Richards, 447(N&Q):Jun89–249
Britchky, S. The Restaurants of New York
  1989.
  639(VQR):Summer89–101
Brittain, V. Diary 1939–1945. (A. Bishop &
  Y.A. Bennett, eds)
  A. Chisholm, 617(TLS):2–8Mar90–218
Britten, B. My Brother Benjamin.
  P. Evans, 415:Sep89–544
Britton, C. Claude Simon.*
  M. Melaver, 494:Fall89–652
  A.C. Pugh, 208(FS):Jul89–360
Britton, D. Lady Chatterley
  R. Booth, 175:Spring89–87
  J. Meyers, 639(VQR):Summer89–555
  M. Storch, 402(MLR):Apr90–425
  K. Widmer, 395(MFS):Summer89–332
  J. Worthen, 447(N&Q):Dec89–544
Brixhe, C. & R. Hodot. L'Asie Mineure du nord
  au sud.
  G. Neumann, 229:Band61Heft5–431
Broad, C.D. – see McTaggart, J.M.E.
Broadie, A. Notion and Object.
  T.B. Noone, 543:Dec89–390
Brochier, J-J. Alain Robbe-Grillet.
  C.J. Murphy, 207(FR):Oct89–193
Brochu, A. La Visée critique.
  N.B. Bishop, 627(UTQ):Fall89–209
Brock, D. If I Never Get Back.
  A. Solomon, 441:11Mar90–18
Brock, E. Five Ways to Kill a Man.
  J. Le Saux, 617(TLS):17–23Aug90–871
Brock, S. – see Hawkesworth, W.
Brock, S.P. & S.A. Harvey, eds & trans. Holy
  Women of the Syrian Orient.
  G.P. Corrington, 124:Jan–Feb90–255
Brock-Broido, L. A Hunger.*
  D. Allen, 249(HudR):Summer89–325
  B. Costello, 473(PR):Vol56No4–671
Brockbank, P. On Shakespeare.
  A. Kirsch, 617(TLS):20–26Apr90–421
Brockbank, P., ed. Players of Shakespeare.
  C.J. Carlisle, 612(ThS):Nov88–213
Brockhoff, V. Götter, Dämonen, Menschen.
  W. Röllig, 196:Band30Heft1/2–112
Brockington, J.L. Vier Pole expressionis-
  tischer Prosa.*
  M. Winkler, 133:Band22Heft3/4–363
Brockliss, L.W.B. French Higher Education in
  the Seventeenth and Eighteenth Centuries.
  E.D. James, 208(FS):Jan89–115
  H.M. Scott, 83:Spring89–92
Brockman, J., ed. Speculations.
  J. Kinoshita, 441:9Sep90–27

Brockman, W.S. Music.
  J. Wagstaff, 410(M&L):Aug89–394
Brod, M. & F. Kafka. Max Brod, Franz Kafka:
  Eine Freundschaft. (M. Pasley & H. Rod-
  lauer, eds)
  M. Anderson, 221(GQ):Summer89–402
Brodersen, K. – see Appian
Brodeur, P. Currents of Death.
  W.J. Broad, 441:8Apr90–21
Brodey, V., ed. Las coplas de Mingo Revulgo.*
  B. Tate, 86(BHS):Apr89–172
Brodhead, R.H. The School of Hawthorne.*
  A.H. Petry, 577(SHR):Winter89–88
Brodkey, H. Stories in an Almost Classical
  Mode.
  G. Johnson, 219(GaR):Winter89–784
  I. Malin, 532(RCF):Spring89–241
  E. Rothstein, 453(NYRB):15Feb90–36
Brodman, J.W. Ransoming Captives in Cru-
  sader Spain.*
  D.W. Lomax, 86(BHS):Apr89–167
"Brodovitch."
  C. Pittel, 441:7Jan90–18
Brodsky, C.J. The Imposition of Form.*
  C.E. Brown, 478(P&L):Oct89–396
  W. Goetschel, 221(GQ):Spring89–235
  A. Rigney, 204(FdL):Dec89–316
Brodsky, J. To Urania.*
  639(VQR):Winter89–27
Brodsky, P.P. Rainer Maria Rilke.*
  B.L. Bradley, 221(GQ):Fall89–535
Brody, B. Life and Death Decision Making
  R.S. Downie, 518:Oct89–234
Brody, E. Paris: the Musical Kaleidoscope
  1870–1925.
  R.L. Smith, 410(M&L):May89–276
  J. Wauck, 31(ASch):Winter89–151
Brody, J.E. Jane Brody's Good Food Gourmet.
  I. Tracy, 441:2Dec90–73
Brodzki, B. & C. Schenck, eds. Life/Lines.
  L. Simon, 385(MQR):Winter90–133
  H.D. Wong, 77:Fall89–336
Broe, M.L. & A. Ingram, eds. Women's Writing
  in Exile.
  K. Ford, 617(TLS):29Jun–5Jul90–702
Broehl, W.G., Jr. Crisis of the Raj.
  M.H. Fisher, 293(JASt):Feb89–195
Broer, W., & D. Kopp, eds. Dietrich Christian
  Grabbe (1801–1836).
  W. Paulsen, 221(GQ):Winter89–124
Brogan, O. & D.J. Smith. Ghirza.
  D.J. Mattingly, 313:Vol79–233
Brogan, T.V.F. Verseform.
  B.P. Scherr, 574(SEEJ):Winter89–632
Droich, U. & M. Pfister, eds. Intertextualität.
  H. Grabes, 38:Band107Heft1/2–275
Broide [Brojde], A.M. A.V. Družinin – Žizn' i
  tvorčestvo.
  C.N. Lee, 574(SEEJ):Spring89–122
  M. Raeff, 104(CASS):Spring–Winter88–515
  D. Richards & E. Terrar, 550(RusR):
  Jan89–95
Broido, V. Lenin and the Mensheviks.*
  J.D. Basil, 104(CASS):Spring89–127
  A. Liebich, 550(RusR):Jan89–67
Brolin, B.C. The Battle of St. Barts.
  J.M. Fitch, 47:Nov89–37
Brombert, V. The Hidden Reader.*
  D. Knight, 402(MLR):Oct90–969
  D. La Capra, 401(MLQ):Sep88–295
  H. Levin, 131(CL):Winter89–107
  J. Parini, 249(HudR):Spring89–171
  S. Petrey, 207(FR):Feb90–547

Bromfield, L. Louis Bromfield at Malabar. (C.E. Little, ed)
639(VQR):Summer89-103

Bromke, A. The Meaning and Uses of Polish History.
S.A. Blejwas, 104(CASS):Spring89-90

Bromley, A.C. Midwinter Transport.
E. Falco, 502(PrS):Summer89-135

Bromwich, D. A Choice of Inheritance.
H. Beaver, 441:4Feb90-22
J. Mullan, 617(TLS):12-18Jan90-43

Bromwich, D., ed. Romantic Critical Essays.
E.D. Mackerness, 447(N&Q):Jun89-245

Broner, K. New York face à son patrimoine.
M. Pearson, 576:Mar89-95

Bronfen, E. Der literarische Raum.
K. Marti, 38:Band107Heft1/2-268

Bronner, E. Battle for Justice.*
L. Sager, 453(NYRB):25Oct90-23

Bronner, E.B. & D. Fraser - see Penn, W.

Bronner, S.J. American Folklore Studies.*
W.F. Nicolaisen, 440:Winter-Spring89-139

Bronson, B.H. & J.M. O'Meara - see Johnson, S.

Bronson, F. The Billboard Book of Number One Hits. (rev)
R.S. Denisoff, 498:Fall89-96

Brontë, A. Agnes Grey. (H. Marsden & R. Inglesfield, eds)
D. Hewitt, 447(N&Q):Dec89-524
M. Seaward, 82:Vol19No7-322

Brontë, B. Brother in the Shadow. (R.J. Duckett, ed)
E. Flintoff, 82:Vol19No7-320

Brontë, C. An Edition of the Early Writings of Charlotte Brontë.* (Vol 1) (C. Alexander, ed)
H. Glen, 402(MLR):Jan90-154
K.M. Hewitt, 447(N&Q):Jun89-250
P. Thomson, 541(RES):May89-283

Brontë, C. Jane Eyre. (2nd ed) (R.J. Dunn, ed)
M. Smith, 82:Vol19No7-321

Brontë, C. The Professor.* (M. Smith & H. Rosengarten, eds)
K.M. Hewitt, 447(N&Q):Jun89-250
M. Seaward, 82:Vol19No7-322
P. Thomson, 541(RES):Aug89-431
A. Welsh, 405(MP):Nov89-198

Brontë, C. Villette. (H. Rosengarten & M. Smith, eds)
M. Seaward, 82:Vol19No7-322

Bronzino, A. Rime in burla. (F. Petrucci Nardelli, ed)
C. Plazzotta, 90:Oct89-715

Brook, B.S., ed. The Ringmacher Catalogue (1773).
R. Andrewes, 415:Dec89-746

Brook, P. The Shifting Point.*
E. Brater, 130:Summer89-184

Brooke, C. & R. Highfield, with W. Swaan. Oxford and Cambridge.*
M.H. Port, 447(N&Q):Dec89-562

Brooke, C.K., ed. Tapping Potential.
M. Morgan & M. Foster, 355(LSoc):Dec89-605

Brooke, C.N.L. The Church and the Welsh Border in the Central Middle Ages.
S.J. Ridyard, 250(HLQ):Spring89-305

Brooke, C.N.L. The Medieval Idea of Marriage.
M. Keen, 453(NYRB):22Nov90-37

Brooke, M. The Manx Shearwater.
R.W. Ashford, 617(TLS):24-30Aug90-894

Brooke, P. Ulster Presbyterianism.
L. Carruthers, 272(IUR):Spring89-193

Brooke-Rose, C. Verbivore.
M. Walters, 617(TLS):20-26Jul90-782

Brooker, J.S. Approaches to Teaching Eliot's Poetry and Plays.
G. Kerley, 675(YER):Fall90-104

Brookes, C. A Public Nuisance.
R.P. Knowles, 108:Winter89-80

Brookfield, A. Alice Alone.*
J. Dunford, 441:7Jan90-19

Brookfield, S.D. Developing Critical Thinkers.
N.R. Comley, 128(CE):Oct89-623

Brookner, A. Brief Lives.
L. Duguid, 617(TLS):24-30Aug90-889

Brookner, A. Jacques-Louis David.
A. Strugnell, 83:Spring89-124

Brookner, A. Latecomers.*
639(VQR):Autumn89-129

Brookner, A. The Misalliance.* (British title: A Misalliance.)
B.K. Horvath, 532(RCF):Spring89-272

Brookner, A. Lewis Percy.*
P. Lopate, 441:11Mar90-10
442(NY):23Apr90-115

Brooks, C. On the Prejudices, Predilections, and Firm Beliefs of William Faulkner.*
C.S. Brown, 569(SR):Fall89-556
I. Jackson, 447(N&Q):Dec89-524
P. Knights, 402(MLR):Oct90-936
L. Wagner-Martin, 573(SSF):Summer88-336
J.G. Watson, 395(MFS):Summer89-281

Brooks, H.F. & others, eds. Du Romantisme au surnaturalisme.
R.T. Cargo, 345(KRQ):May89-231

Brooks, H.F. & R. Selden - see Oldham, J.

Brooks, J. When Russia Learned to Read.
V. Ripp, 131(CL):Summer89-299

Brooks, M.W. John Ruskin and Victorian Architecture.*
C. Jones, 506(PSt):Sep89-197

Brooks, S. You May Plow Here. (T. Simonsen, ed)
C. Mitchell, 582(SFQ):Vol46No2-194

Brooks, S. & A.G. Gagnon. Social Scientists and Politics in Canada.
N. Ward, 529(QQ):Winter89-990

Brooks, W. Bibliographie critique du théâtre de Quinault.
P. Tomlinson, 475:Vol16No30-271

Broome, P. André Frénaud.
D. Briolet, 535(RHL):Jan-Feb89-149

Brophy, C. The Liberation of Margaret McCabe.
R.W. Lewis, 456(NDQ):Winter89-245

Brophy, E.B. Samuel Richardson.*
A. Gibson, 566:Spring89-163
K. Sutherland, 541(RES):Nov89-566

Brophy, J.D. & E. Grennan, eds. New Irish Writing.
R. Bonaccorso, 174(Éire):Summer89-150

Brophy, R.J. - see Jeffers, R.

Brosche, G., ed. Huldigung der Tonsetzer Wiens an Elisabeth Kaiserin von Österreich (Wien 1854).
H-J. Bracht, 417:Oct-Dec89-392

Brosman, C.S. Art as Testimony.
R.J. Golsan, 210(FrF):Jan89-120

Brossard, N. Le Désert mauve.
　　D. Brautman, 207(FR):Mar90-741
　　L.H. Forsyth, 102(CanL):Autumn-
　　　Winter89-190
Brossard, N. Lovhers.
　　L.H. Forsyth, 102(CanL):Autumn-
　　　Winter89-190
Brostrøm, T. Fantasi og dokument.
　　B. Baldwin, 563(SS):Winter89-99
Brostrøm, T. Folkeeventyrets moderne gen-
　　brug eller Hvad forfatteren gør.
　　T. Lundell, 563(SS):Autumn89-415
Broszinsky-Schwabe, E. Zwischen Magie und
　　moderner Technik.
　　R. Arnold, 654(WB):4/1989-695
Brothers, A.J. - see Terence
Broude, N. The Macchiaioli.*
　　C. McCorquodale, 39:Jul89-66
Broudy, H.S. The Uses of Schooling.
　　R.R., 185:Oct89-229
Broughton, T.A. The Jesse Tree.
　　W. Cummins, 573(SSF):Winter89-100
Broughton, T.R.S. The Magistrates of the
　　Roman Republic.* (Vol 3)
　　E. Champlin, 122:Jan89-51
　　R. Rilinger, 229:Band61Heft2-173
Broun, E. Albert Pinkham Ryder.
　　D.M. Lubin, 617(TLS):25-31May90-553
　　M. Nixon, 441:27May90-15
　　J. Updike, 453(NYRB):8Nov90-17
Brouwer, A. & T.L. Wright. Working in Holly-
　　wood.
　　K. Turan, 441:15Jul90-15
Brouwer, D. & D. de Haan, eds. Women's Lan-
　　guage, Socialization and Self-Image.
　　K. Geissler, 710:Dec89-485
Brouwers, J. Sunken Red.*
　　R. Todd, 617(TLS):13-19Apr90-404
Brovkin, V.N. The Mensheviks After Octo-
　　ber.*
　　S.F. Jones, 575(SEER):Jul89-477
　　A. Liebich, 550(RusR):Jan89-67
　　F.S. Zuckerman, 242:Vol10No5-614
Brower, D.R. For Earth's Sake.
　　R.B. Swain, 441:20May90-11
Brower, S. Design in Familiar Places.
　　W. Rybczynski, 17:Mar90-57
Brown, A., ed. Political Leadership in the
　　Soviet Union.
　　O. Figes, 617(TLS):10-16Aug90-844
Brown, A.C. Geordies.
　　R. Pybus, 565:Winter88/89-67
Brown, B. Lone Tree.
　　C. Salzberg, 441:21Jan90-21
Brown, C.S. Music and Literature.*
　　R. Cox, 577(SHR):Spring89-180
Brown, D. Hammerheads.
　　N. Callendar, 441:19Aug90-17
Brown, D. Let Me Entertain You.
　　G. Johnson, 441:22Apr90-25
Brown, D., ed. Newman.
　　B. Martin, 617(TLS):7-13Dec90-1330
Brown, D.A. Andrea Solario.
　　J. Anderson, 90:Dec89-854
Brown, D.E. Hierarchy, History, and Human
　　Nature.
　　A. Kumar, 293(JASt):Aug89-573
Brown, D.E. & J.A. Murray, eds. The Last
　　Grizzly and Other Southwestern Bear Sto-
　　ries.
　　R.F. Gish, 456(NDQ):Winter89-221
Brown, G. The Information Game.
　　M.B. Williams, 103:Aug90-306

Brown, G.H. Bede the Venerable.
　　M. Clayton, 541(RES):May89-307
Brown, G.M. The Masked Fisherman and Other
　　Stories.*
　　A. Lumsden, 571(ScLJ):Winter89-51
Brown, G.M. The Wreck of the Archangel.
　　G. Maxwell, 617(TLS):11-17May90-495
Brown, G.M. - see Muir, E.
Brown, H.I. Observation and Objectivity.*
　　F. Dretske, 486:Sep89-544
　　J. Forge, 63:Sep89-358
Brown, H.I. Rationality.*
　　B.W. Kobes, 185:Apr90-672
Brown, I.G. Building for Books.
　　A. Bell, 78(BC):Winter89-445
　　H.G. Slade, 617(TLS):2-8Mar90-232
Brown, I.G. - see Scott, W.
Brown, J. Agriculture in England.
　　P. Perry, 637(VS):Summer90-672
Brown, J. The Art and Architecture of
　　English Gardens.
　　C.L. Ridgway, 617(TLS):2-8Feb90-128
Brown, J. Zero Mostel.*
　　M. Bloom, 34:Oct89-82
Brown, J. Secrets from the Back Room.
　　C. Alborg, 240(HR):Autumn89-533
Brown, J.A., with J. Gaines. Joyce Ann
　　Brown.
　　K. De Witt, 441:14Oct90-40
Brown, J.C. Immodest Acts.
　　A. Brown, 278(IS):Vol43-142
Brown, J.D. Understanding Research in Sec-
　　ond Language Learning.*
　　R.G. Kern, 207(FR):Feb90-591
　　R. Smith, 238:Dec89-978
　　W.F. Smith, 399(MLJ):Winter89-483
Brown, J.K. Goethe's "Faust."*
　　J.F. Hyde, Jr., 406:Winter89-476
Brown, J.L. Secrets from the Back Room.*
　　K.M. Glenn, 238:May89-306
Brown, J.M. Gandhi.
　　R. Nayar, 617(TLS):8-14Jun90-603
Brown, K.D. Social History of the Noncon-
　　formist Ministry in England and Wales,
　　1800-1930.
　　D. Bowen, 637(VS):Spring90-505
Brown, L. Big Bad Love.
　　B. Allen, 441:23Sep90-21
Brown, L. Conversation and Practical Morali-
　　ty.
　　H.R., 185:Oct89-230
Brown, L. Dirty Work.*
　　T. McLaurin, 110:Winter90-94
Brown, L. Facing the Music.
　　J. Klinkowitz, 455:Mar89-69
　　42(AR):Winter89-115
Brown, M.H. The Search for Eve.
　　N. Angier, 441:8Apr90-16
Brown, M.H., with M. Mazo - see L'vov, N. & I.
　　Prach
Brown, M.N. - see Savile, G.
Brown, P. The Body and Society.*
　　S. Rudikoff, 249(HudR):Summer89-307
Brown, P., ed. Sibton Abbey Cartularies and
　　Charters. (Vols 1 & 2)
　　J.H. Lynch, 589:Jan89-134
Brown, P. & E.D. Higgs. The Index of Middle
　　English Prose. (Handlist V)
　　E.G. Stanley, 447(N&Q):Dec89-489
Brown, P. & S.C. Levinson. Politeness.*
　　R. Blutner, 682(ZPSK):Band42Heft1-135
Brown, P. & E.J. Mikkelsen. No Safe Place.
　　A.H. Malcolm, 441:30Sep90-33

Brown, P.F. — see under Fortini Brown, P.
Brown, P.R., G.R. Crampton & F.C. Robinson, eds. Modes of Interpretation in Old English Literature.*
    J. Hill, 38:Band107Heft3/4–512
    M.A.L. Locherbie–Cameron, 382(MAE): 1989/1–139
Brown, R. Analyzing Love.*
    M. Budd, 479(PhQ):Jul89–364
    C.B. McCullagh, 63:Jun89–248
Brown, R. James Joyce and Sexuality.*
    U. Schneider, 38:Band107Heft1/2–253
Brown, R. The Terrible Girls.
    S. Roe, 617(TLS):14–20Dec90–1359
Brown, R.D. Knowledge is Power.
    R.B. Winans, 165(EAL):Vol25No3–318
Brown, R.D. Lucretius on Love and Sex.*
    J. Godwin, 313:Vol79–199
Brown, R.E. Chester's Last Stand.*
    M.G. Porter, 649(WAL):Nov89–280
Brown, R.H. Society as Text.
    T.W. Crusius, 480(P&R):Vol22No2–149
Brown, R.M. The Ceramics of South–East Asia. (2nd ed)
    H.L. Lefferts, Jr. & L.A. Cort, 293(JASt):Nov89–927
    J. Shaw, 60:Nov–Dec89–163
Brown, R.M. Wish You Were Here.
    M. Stasio, 441:16Dec90–33
Brown, S., ed. Caribbean New Wave.
    D. Dabydeen, 617(TLS):14–20Sep90–979
Brown, S. Lugard's Bridge.
    S. Carnell, 617(TLS):16–22Feb90–179
Brown, S., M. Morris & G. Rohlehr, eds. Voice Print.
    G. Foden, 617(TLS):2–8Mar90–236
Brown, S.A. The Bayeux Tapestry.
    B.B. Klier, 207(FR):May90–1110
Brown, S.A. Collected Poems.
    J. Campbell, 617(TLS):27Jul–2Aug90–793
Brown, S.A. The Genius of Japanese Carpentry.
    B.A. Coats, 407(MN):Winter89–521
Brown–Guillory, E. Their Place on the Stage.
    W.L. Fletcher, 612(ThS):Nov88–233
Browne, A. The Eighteenth–Century Feminist Mind.
    K.M. Rogers, 566:Spring89–172
Browne, C. Abraham.
    L. Inbar, 102(CanL):Summer89–180
Brownell, M.R. Samuel Johnson's Attitude to the Arts.
    R. Paulson, 173(ECS):Spring90–358
Brownell, W. & R.N. Billings. So Close to Greatness.*
    R. Roazen, 31(ASch):Winter89–135
Browning, E.B. Selected Poems. (M. Forster, ed)
    A. Falk, 637(VS):Winter90–328
Browning, E.B. & M.R. Mitford. Women of Letters. (M.B. Raymond & M.R. Sullivan, eds)
    C.H. MacKay, 85(SBHC):Vol16–151
Browning, P. Yosemite Place Names.
    B. Julyan, 424:Sep89–290
Browning, R. The Poetical Works of Robert Browning. (Vol 3) (I. Jack & R. Fowler, eds)
    J. Korg, 85(SBHC):Vol16–140
    639(VQR):Winter89–29
Browning, R. & E. Barrett. The Courtship Correspondence, 1845–1846.* (D. Karlin, ed)
    K.M. McKay, 402(MLR):Jul90–702

Browning, R. & E.B. The Brownings' Correspondence.* (Vol 4) (P. Kelley & R. Hudson, eds)
    P. Drew, 677(YES):Vol20–301
Browning, R. & E.B. The Brownings' Correspondence. (Vols 6 & 7) (P. Kelley & R. Hudson, eds)
    S. Raitt, 617(TLS):4–10May90–470
"Browning Institute Studies."* (Vol 14) (A.A. Munich, ed)
    D. Birch, 541(RES):Nov89–579
    R.T. Van Arsdel, 85(SBHC):Vol16–135
"Browning Institute Studies."* (Vol 15) (A.A. Munich & J. Maynard, eds)
    R.T. Van Arsdel, 85(SBHC):Vol16–135
Brownjohn, A. The Way You Tell Them.
    M. Wormald, 617(TLS):19–25Jan90–66
Brownlee, M.S. The Status of the Reading Subject in the "Libro de buen amor."*
    B.B. Thompson, 589:Apr89–393
Brownlow, K. Behind the Mask of Innocence.
    M. Kammen, 441:16Dec90–20
Broyles, M. Beethoven.
    B. Cooper, 410(M&L):Nov89–551
    W. Drabkin, 415:Feb89–86
    R. Hatten, 309:Vol9No4–306
Bruccoli, M.J. The Fortunes of Mitchell Kennerley, Bookman.*
    517(PBSA):Mar89–128
Bruce, D.D., Jr. Black American Writing from the Nadir.
    K. Byerman, 395(MFS):Winter89–768
Bruchac, J. Near the Mountains.
    L.D. Moore, 456(NDQ):Spring89–197
Bruche–Schulz, G. Russische Sprachwissenschaft.
    J. Udolph, 685(ZDL):3/1989–388
Bruchet, J. Voyage à Villers. A mon avis.
    L.K. Martin, 399(MLJ):Autumn89–357
Bruchey, S. Enterprise.
    R.D. Bartel, 441:29Apr90–28
    A. Francis, 617(TLS):19–25Oct90–1136
Brucker, G. Giovanni and Lusanna.*
    A. Brown, 278(IS):Vol43–142
Brückner, A. Die slavischen Ansiedelungen in der Altmark und im Magdeburgischen.
    J. Udolph, 685(ZDL):2/1989–268
Bruckner, D.J.R. Frederic Goudy.
    J. Updike, 441:16Dec90–10
Brückner, T. Die erste französische Aeneis.*
    P–Y. Badel, 554:Vol108No2/3–400
    G. Demerson, 549(RLC):Apr–Jun89–277
    A. Gier, 547(RF):Band101Heft1–114
    C. Smith, 402(MLR):Oct90–951
Bruhn, H., R. Oerter & H. Roesing, eds. Musikpsychologie.
    H. Petsche, 413:Fall89–69
Brulé, G. — see under Gace Brulé
Brulotte, G. Double Exposure.
    E. Thompson, 198:Spring89–120
Brulotte, G. L'Emprise.
    G.R. Montbertrand, 207(FR):May90–1098
Brümann, I.M. Apollinaire und die deutsche Avantgarde.
    S. Buck, 224(GRM):Band39Heft4–483
Brumbaugh, R.S. Platonic Studies of Greek Philosophy.
    B. Hendley, 543:Dec89–391
Brumberg, A., ed. Chronicle of a Revolution.
    O. Figes, 617(TLS):5–11Oct90–1056
    R. Richter, 441:26Aug90–15
Brumberg, J.J. Fasting Girls.*
    M. Bala, 529(QQ):Autumn89–751

Brumble, H.D. 3d. American Indian Autobiography.
    H.D. Wong, 27(AL):Dec89-686
Bruna, M.J.S. - see under Soto Bruna, M.J.
Brundage, A. England's "Prussian Minister."
    C. Hamlin, 637(VS):Winter90-340
Brundage, J.A. Law, Sex and Christian Society in Medieval Europe.*
    R.C. Figueira, 589:Jul89-674
    P. Fouracre, 242:Vol10No4-495
    M. Keen, 453(NYRB):22Nov90-37
Brunel, P. - see Rimbaud, A.
Brunel, P. & others, eds. L'Esprit nouveau dans tous ses états.
    P. Broome, 208(FS):Jul89-354
Bruner, J. Actual Minds, Possible Worlds.*
    D. Arnstine, 289:Winter89-112
    J.J. Maier, 478(P&L):Apr89-210
    S. Schroeder, 438:Winter89-115
Brunet, E. Le Vocabulaire de Victor Hugo.
    R.J. Steiner, 207(FR):Mar90-725
Brunet, E. Le Vocabulaire de Zola.
    P. Ouvrard, 356(LR):Aug89-221
Bruni, L. The Humanism of Leonardo Bruni.*
    C. Trinkaus, 551(RenQ):Spring89-94
Bruni, S. I lastroni a scala.*
    D. Briquel, 555:Vol62Fasc1-178
Bruno, G. Le Banquet des Cendres. (Y. Hersant, ed & trans)
    M-A. Lescourret, 98:Apr89-300
Bruns, G.L. Heidegger's Estrangements.
    N. Lukacher, 153:Fall-Winter89-128
Bruns, G.L. Modern Poetry and the Idea of Language.
    K. Ziarek, 153:Fall-Winter89-114
Brunsdale, M. Sigrid Undset.
    J.A. Luscher, 395(MFS):Winter89-843
Brunt, P.A. The Fall of the Roman Republic and Related Essays.
    J.A. North, 313:Vol79-151
Brusse, C.B. Sacred Vocal Duets.
    A.F.L.T., 412:May89-146
Brustein, R. Who Needs Theatre.
    A. Strachan, 511:May89-46
    J.E. Tammany, 615(TJ):Oct89-434
Brutian, G.A. & I.S. Narskij, with others, eds. Filosofskie problemy argumentatsii.
    T. Nemeth, 480(P&R):Vol22No3-212
Bruton, J.W. - see Cibber, C.
Bruun, P.M. Die spätrömische Münze als Gegenstand der Thesaurierung.
    P. Bastien, 229:Band61Heft6-569
Bruyère, C. Sherwood Anderson.
    J. Templeton, 189(EA):Apr-Jun89-234
Bruyn, J. & others. Rembrandt Research Project, A Corpus of Rembrandt Paintings. (Vol 1)
    L.J. Slatkes, 54:Mar89-139
Bryan, F.R. Beyond the Model T.
    N. Adams, 617(TLS):30Nov-6Dec90-1286
Bryant, H.B. Robert Graves.
    K. Quinlan, 580(SCR):Fall89-144
Bryant, J., ed. A Companion to Melville Studies.*
    D. Knickerbocker, 27(AL):May89-283
Bryant, J.A., Jr. Shakespeare and the Uses of Comedy.*
    H. Castrop, 156(ShJW):Jahrbuch1989-360
    R. Knowles, 677(YES):Vol20-251
Bryant, L.M. The King and the City in the Parisian Royal Entry Ceremony.
    R.A. Jackson, 589:Jul89-678

Bryce, T.R. The Lycians in Literary and Epigraphic Sources.*
    C. Le Roy, 123:Vol39No1-98
Brydon, D. Christina Stead.
    J. Dolphin, 178:Dec89-506
Bryer, A.A.M. & D.C. Winfield. The Byzantine Monuments and Topography of the Pontos.*
    S. Hill, 303(JoHS):Vol109-276
Bryson, B. The Mother Tongue.
    B. Hochberg, 441:5Aug90-8
Bryson, N., ed. Calligram.*
    M. Bull, 90:Jun89-435
    D. Carrier, 290(JAAC):Summer89-286
    J.F. Codell, 207(FR):Dec89-386
    P. Florence, 208(FS):Jul89-369
    C. Wilde, 89(BJA):Autumn89-374
Bryson, N. Looking at the Overlooked.
    L. Gowing, 617(TLS):20-26Jul90-772
Bryson, N. Vision and Painting. Word and Image. Tradition and Desire.
    M. Bal, 567:Vol76No3/4-283
Bubenheimer, U. Thomas Müntzer.
    A. Hamilton, 617(TLS):14-20Sep90-983
Bublitz, W. Supportive Fellow-Speakers and Cooperative Conversations.
    J. Coates, 350:Jun90-379
Bubnova, T. F. Delicado puesto en diálogo.
    B.M. Damiani, 238:Sep89-541
Buch, H.C. Haïti Chérie.
    J.J. White, 617(TLS):5-11Oct90-1073
Buchan, J. The Four Adventures of Richard Hannay.
    J.R. Cox, 177(ELT):Vol32No4-496
Buchanan, D. The Corpse Had a Familiar Face.
    J.N. Stull, 106:Fall89-265
Buchanan, E. Nobody Lives Forever.
    M. Stasio, 441:18Mar90-33
Buchanan, R.A. The Engineers.
    D.H. Porter, 637(VS):Summer90-666
Bücher, J. Bonn-Beueler Sprachschatz.
    R. Damme, 685(ZDL):3/1989-377
Buchheim, T. Die Sophistik als Avantgarde normalen Lebens.
    C.J. Classen, 229:Band61Heft6-547
Buchholz, O. & W. Fiedler. Albanische Grammatik.
    R. Lötzsch, 682(ZPSK):Band42Heft3-397
Büchler, E. & E. Dirkschnieder - see Pasierbsky, F.
Büchler-Hauschild, G. Erzählte Arbeit.
    J.A. Kruse, 680(ZDP):Band108Heft2-298
    L. Tatlock, 221(GQ):Spring89-280
Buchmann-Moller, F. You Just Fight for Your Life.
    T. Teachout, 441:11Mar90-14
Buci-Glucksmann, C. & others. Imaginaires de l'autre.
    L. Tremaine, 538(RAL):Summer89-294
Buck, A. & M. Bircher, eds. Respublica Guelpherbytana.*
    G.R. Hoyt, 221(GQ):Spring89-253
    M. Lentzen, 547(RF):Band101Heft1-98
Buck-Morss, S. The Dialectics of Seeing.
    H. Muschamp, 62:Apr90-17
Buckaway, C. Blue Windows.
    B. Rendall, 647:Fall89-79
Buckle, R., with J. Taras. George Balanchine.*
    D. McMahon, 31(ASch):Winter89-154

Buckley, C. Blossoms and Bones.
C.H. Daughaday, 649(WAL):Aug89-191
R.B. Shaw, 491:Aug89-287
L. Upton, 152(UDQ):Summer89-124
Buckley, C. Potters and Paintresses.
A. Britton, 324:Sep90-715
Buckley, J. Statute of Limitations.
A. Gelb, 441:26Aug90-14
Buckley, M., ed. Soviet Social Scientists Talking.
J.S. Pedersen, 242:Vol10No6-745
Buckley, M. & M. Anderson, eds. Women, Equality and Europe.
J.S. Pedersen, 242:Vol10No6-745
Buckley, M.J. At the Origins of Modern Atheism.
J.E. Force, 322(JHI):Jan-Mar89-153
Buckley, T. & A. Gottlieb, eds. Blood Magic.
B. Vorpagel, 292(JAF):Oct-Dec89-491
Buckley, W.F., Jr. Gratitude.
T.C. Sorensen, 441:28Oct90-1
Buckley, W.K. Critical Essays on Louis-Ferdinand Céline.
T.C. Spear, 207(FR):Dec89-383
Bucknall, B.J., ed. Critical Essays on Marcel Proust.
E. Hughes, 208(FS):Apr89-229
Bucknell, R.S. & M. Stuart-Fox. The Twilight Language.*
P.J. Griffiths, 259(IIJ):Apr89-165
L. Nordstrom, 485(PE&W):Jan89-104
Buday, G. The Venetian.
M. Bowering, 102(CanL):Autumn-Winter89-181
Budd, L.J. & E. Cady, eds. On Mark Twain.*
J.W. Gargano, 573(SSF):Summer88-331
A. Hook, 447(N&Q):Jun89-271
Budd, M. Wittgenstein's Philosophy of Psychology.
R.J. Fogelin, 617(TLS):19-25Jan90-73
"The Buddhist I Ching." (T. Cleary, trans)
K. Smith, 318(JAOS):Apr-Jun88-350
Budge, I. & H. Keman. Parties and Democracy.
D. Leonard, 617(TLS):7-13Sep90-942
Budick, E.M. Fiction and Historical Consciousness.
G. Dekker, 183(ESQ):Vol35No1-69
J.W. Tuttleton, 395(MFS):Winter89-743
Budnick, R., comp. Hawaiian Street Names.
T.J. Gasque, 424:Dec89-386
Budziszewski, J. The Nearest Coast of Darkness.
J.C.C., 185:Jul90-909
Buell, J. A Lot to Make Up For.
W. Smith, 441:15Jul90-18
Buell, L. New England Literary Culture.
L. Kelly, 402(MLR):Jul90-713
Buero Vallejo, A. Las Meninas.
M.A. Compitello, 238:Sep89-569
D. Gagen, 86(BHS):Oct89-389
Buero Vallejo, A. Today's a Holiday. (J.A. Dunlop & others, eds & trans)
M.A. Compitello, 238:Sep89-569
D. Gagen, 86(BHS):Oct89-389
Bufalino, G. Blind Argus (Or The Fables of The Memory).
I. Thomson, 364:Oct/Nov89-128
Bufalino, G. Night's Lies.
P. Hainsworth, 617(TLS):12-18Oct90-1088
Bufalino, G. The Plague Sower.
42(AR):Spring89-248

Bugnet, G. Nipsya.
P. Collet, 627(UTQ):Fall89-205
Buhle, P. C.L.R. James.
K. Worcester, 147:Vol6No3-75
Buhlmann, R. & A. Fearns. Handbuch des Fachsprachenunterrichts.
A. Galt, 399(MLJ):Autumn89-366
Buhr, M. & S. Dietzsch – see Kant, I.
Buin, Y. Thelonious Monk.
J. Laurans, 450(NRF):Mar89-96
A.J.M.P., 91:Vol17-189
Buisine, A. Laideurs de Sartre.*
F. Thumerel, 535(RHL):Sep-Oct89-945
van Buitenen, J.A.B. Studies in Indian Literature and Philosophy. (L. Rocher, ed)
R.P. Goldman, 293(JASt):Nov89-914
Buitenhuis, P. The Great War of Words.*
B.C., 295(JML):Fall88/Winter89-241
J. Ferns, 102(CanL):Spring89-173
K. Neilson, 529(QQ):Summer89-496
J.H. Stape, 189(EA):Oct-Dec89-487
Bujić, B., ed. Music in European Thought 1851-1912.*
L. Botstein, 451:Fall89-168
R. Hollinrake, 410(M&L):Aug89-423
P. Kivy, 309:Vol9No1-43
Bujnicki, T. & W. Wyskiel, eds. Pisarz na obczyźnie.
R. Grol-Prokopczyk, 497(PolR):Vol34No1-84
Bukowski, C. Hollywood.*
M.A. Jarman, 376:Dec89-120
Bukowski, C. Septuagenarian Stew.
L.E. Nesbitt, 441:25Nov90-19
J. Smith, 617(TLS):7-13Sep90-956
Bulaxov, M.G., M.A. Žovtobrjux & V.I. Koduxov. Vostočnoslavjanskie jazyki.
J.A. Van Campen, 574(SEEJ):Spring89-147
Bulgin, K. The Making of an Artist.
K.M. Grossman, 446(NCFS):Spring-Summer90-529
Bulhan, H.A. Frantz Fanon and the Psychology of Oppression.
N. Gibson, 147:Vol6No2-92
Bull, G. – see della Valle, P.
Bull, T., E.H. Jahr & G. Wiggen, eds. Mål og medvit.
C.A. Creider, 350:Mar90-184
Bullen, J.B., ed. Post-Impressionists in England.
N.V. Halliday, 39:Dec89-433
B. Kennedy, 89(BJA):Summer89-286
S. Watney, 90:Jan89-45
Bullen, J.B., ed. The Sun is God.
R. Fraser, 402(MLR):Oct90-901
P.L. Sawyer, 637(VS):Summer90-664
Bullivant, K., ed. The Modern German Novel.*
S. Mandel, 395(MFS):Summer89-351
R.M.P., 295(JML):Fall88/Winter89-194
Bullivant, K. Realism Today.*
M. Eifler, 221(GQ):Summer89-427
Bullock, A. Domenico Tordi e il carteggio colonnese Biblioteca Nazionale di Firenze.*
R. Catani, 278(IS):Vol43-174
Bullock, M. Dark Water.
G. Harding-Russell, 102(CanL):Summer89-175
Bullough, V. & B. Women and Prostitution.
L.S., 185:Apr90-710

Bulman, J.C. & H.R. Coursen, eds. Shakespeare on Television.
T.L. Berger, 570(SQ):Summer89–237
M. Wiggins, 447(N&Q):Dec89–505
Bulmer, M., J. Lewis & D. Piachaud, eds. The Goals of Social Policy.
F. Cairncross, 617(TLS):9–15Mar90–251
Bulmer-Thomas, V. Studies in the Economics of Central America.
J.B. Nugent, 263(RIB):Vol39No2–203
Bulsterbaum, A. H.L. Mencken.
P.Z. Du Bois, 87(BB):Dec89–257
D. Fowler, 70:Oct89–156
Bulte, I. Het laatste woord heeft het eerste.
W. Smulders, 204(FdL):Dec89–296
Bulteau, M. Le Club des longues moustaches.
C. Chaufour-Verheyen, 450(NRF):Apr89–105
Bulyginoj, T.V. & A.E. Kibrika, eds. Novoe v zarubežnoj lingvistike. (Vol 15)
N.M. Salnikow, 559:Vol13No2–182
Bumiller, E. May You Be the Mother of a Hundred Sons.
S. Suleri, 441:24Jun90–17
Bumke, J. Höfische Kultur.*
W. Störmer, 680(ZDP):Band108Heft3–438
Bunbongkarn, S. The Military in Thai Politics, 1981–86.
H. Crouch, 293(JASt):Aug89–669
Buning, M. T.F. Powys.
F. Schenkel, 38:Band107Heft1/2–266
Bünker, B.C. Lei nit lafn onfongen.
K. Kehr, 685(ZDL):3/1989–392
Bunt, G.H.V., ed. One Hundred Years of English Studies in Dutch Universities.
G. Bourcier, 189(EA):Oct–Dec89–444
Bunt, G.H.V., ed. William of Palerne an Alliterative Romance.
F.G. Stanley, 447(N&Q):Jun89–220
Buñuel, L. Los olvidados.
P.W. Evans, 86(BHS):Jul89–299
Bunyan, J. The Miscellaneous Works of John Bunyan.* (Vol 9) (J.S. McGee, ed)
M. Hardman, 677(YES):Vol20–268
Buonaventura, W. Serpent of the Nile.
G. Levitas, 441:11Feb90–20
Buonocore, M. Le Iscrizioni Latine e Greche
H. Freis, 229:Band61Heft7–637
Burac, R. – see Péguy, C.
Burbat, W. Die Harmonik des Jazz.
B. Riede, 416:Band4Heft2–184
Burbick, J. Thoreau's Alternative History.*
A.S. Lang, 27(AL):May89–291
Burchfield, R., ed. Studies in Lexicography.*
V. McDavid, 405(MP):Feb90–331
F.C. Robinson, 677(YES):Vol20–209
M. Stokes, 541(RES):Nov89–540
A.R. Tellier, 189(EA):Apr–Jun89–201
Burchfield, R.W. – see "The Compact Edition of the Oxford English Dictionary"
Burchfield, R.W. – see "A Supplement to the Oxford English Dictionary"
Burckhardt, J. The Altarpiece in Renaissance Italy.* (P. Humfrey, ed & trans)
D. Norman, 59:Sep89–366
Burden, M. & I. Cholij, eds. A Handbook for Studies in 18th-Century English Music.
H.D. Johnstone, 410(M&L):Feb89–98
Burdick, T. & C. Mitchell. Blue Thunder.
J. Katzenbach, 441:25Nov90–26
Bürger, C. & P., eds. Alltag, Allegorie und Avantgarde.
I. Hoesterey, 221(GQ):Fall89–505

Bürger, P. Prosa der Moderne.
R. Rochlitz, 98:May89–366
Burgess, A. Any Old Iron.*
J. Mellors, 364:Jun/Jul89–133
42(AR):Spring89–249
Burgess, A. The Devil's Mode.*
P-L. Adams, 61:Jan90–100
Burgess, A. You've Had Your Time.
J. Sutherland, 617(TLS):26Oct–1Nov90–1143
Burgess, G.S. The Lais of Marie de France.*
P. Clifford, 382(MAE):1989/1–166
E.J. Mickel, Jr., 210(FrF):Jan89–89
Bürgin, H. & H.O. Mayer. Die Briefe Thomas Manns. (Vols 4 & 5)
H. Lehnert, 462(OL):Vol44No3–267
Burgin, V., J. Donald & C. Kaplan, eds. Formations of Fantasy.*
V. Hollinger, 102(CanL):Summer89–177
Burgler, R.A. The Eyes of the Pineapple.
P. Carey, 617(TLS):2–8Nov90–1172
Burgos, F., ed. Los ochenta mundos de Cortázar.*
I. Stavans, 238:Mar89–154
Burgos, J., P. Caizergues & others. Apollinaire en 1918.
M. Davies, 402(MLR):Jul90–741
Burian, P., ed. Directions in Euripidean Criticism.*
M.A. Harder, 394:Vol42fasc1/2–170
Burian, P. – see Else, G.F.
Burk, K. Morgan Grenfell 1838–1988.
R. Davenport-Hines, 617(TLS):5–11Jan90–9
Burk, R.F. The Corporate State and the Broker State.
A. Brinkley, 617(TLS):13–19Jul90–756
J.M. Burns, 441:15Apr90–10
Burkard, M. Fictions from the Self.*
F. Chappell, 219(GaR):Summer89–385
Burke, E. The Political Philosophy of Edmund Burke. (I. Hampsher-Monk, ed)
M. Fitzpatrick, 83:Autumn89–217
Burke, E. Writings and Speeches. (Vol 8) (L.G. Mitchell, ed)
J. Dunn, 617(TLS):29Jun–5Jul90–691
Burke, J.L. A Morning for Flamingos.
M. Stasio, 441:4Nov90–30
Burke, K. & M. Cowley. The Selected Correspondence of Kenneth Burke and Malcolm Cowley, 1915–1981.* (P. Jay, ed)
H. Bak, 598(SoR):Winter90–226
E. Butscher, 219(GaR):Summer89–419
D.W. Faulkner, 569(SR):Summer89–482
T. Poland, 27(AL):Oct89–505
639(VQR):Spring89–55
Burke, P. Atomic Candy.
V. Clapham, 617(TLS):6–12Apr90–376
Burke, P. The Historical Anthropology of Early Modern Italy.
A. Brown, 90:Mar89–228
A.D. Wright, 278(IS):Vol43–151
Burke, P. The Italian Renaissance.
A. Brown, 90:Mar89–228
Burkert, W. Ancient Mystery Cults.*
F.E. Brenk, 229:Band61Heft4–289
B.C. Dietrich, 123:Vol39No1–58
B.M. Metzger, 24:Winter89–658
Burkhard, M. & J. Clausen – see "Women in German Yearbook"
Burkhardt, F., C. Eveno & B. Podrecca, eds. Jože Plečnik, Architect, 1872–1957.
S. Pepper, 617(TLS):27Jul–2Aug90–802

Burkhardt, F. & S. Smith – see Darwin, C.
Burkhardt, F.H., F. Bowers & I.K. Skrupske-
lis – see James, W.
Burkhart, C. The Pleasure of Miss Pym.
S.A.S., 295(JML):Fall88/Winter89–397
Burkman, T.W., ed. The Occupation of Japan:
Arts and Culture.
G.K. Goodman, 407(MN):Autumn89–370
B. Stronach, 293(JASt):Aug89–609
Burleigh, M. Germany Turns Eastwards.
A. Glees, 617(TLS):13–19Apr90–392
P. Schöttler, 358:Jun90–6
Burlingham, C. & J. Cuno. French Caricature
and the French Revolution, 1789–1799.
R. Wrigley, 59:Dec89–520
Burman, E. – see "Logan Pearsall Smith: An
Anthology"
Burmeister, B. Anders oder Vom Aufenthalt
in der Fremde.
D. Schlenstedt, 654(WB):4/1989–637
Burmeister, H–P., F. Boldt & G. Mészáros, eds.
Mitteleuropa.
G.M. Tamás, 617(TLS):10–16Aug90–843
Burmeister, L.L. Research, Realpolitik, and
Development in Korea.
C.W. Sorensen, 293(JASt):May89–409
Burn, L. The Meidias Painter.
K. Huber, 229:Band61Heft7–609
E. Moignard, 123:Vol39No2–338
Burnard, B. Women of Influence.
C. Rooke, 376:Mar89–125
Burne–Jones, E. Letters to Katie from
Edward Burne–Jones.
C. Newall, 39:Oct89–288
Burnet, J.R., with H. Palmer. Coming Canadi-
ans.
N.F. Dreisziger, 529(QQ):Autumn89–731
Burney, F. Cecilia, or Memoirs of an Heiress.*
(P. Sabor & M.A. Doody, eds)
E. Brophy, 166:Oct89–80
Burnham, D. A Law Unto Itself.
A. Hacker, 441:11Feb90–1
Burnham, J.C. Paths into American Culture.
R.M. Crunden, 106:Fall89–279
Burns, C. The Condition of Ice.
S. Altinel, 617(TLS):11–17May90–496
Burns, C. The Flint Bed.*
J. Mellors, 364:Jun/Jul89–133
Burns, C. Hardboiled Defective.
G. Gessert, 448:Vol27No1–124
Burns, E. Character and Being on the Pre-
modern Stage.
K. Worth, 617(TLS):27Jul–2Aug90–801
Burns, E. Restoration Comedy.*
J. Ogden, 83:Autumn89–230
A. Snider, 173(ECS):Spring90–340
Burns, E. – see Stein, G. & C. Van Vechten
Burns, J. A Celebration of the Light.
M. McCulloch, 571(ScLJ):Spring89–11
Burns, J. Out of the Past.*
D. McDuff, 565:Spring89–76
Burns, J. Poems for Tribune.
E. Bartlett, 493:Spring89–64
Burns, J.P. Political Participation in Rural
China.
L.R. Sullivan, 293(JASt):Feb89–125
Burns, M.A.T. & J.F. O'Connor. The Classics
in American Schools.
M. Cleary, 121(CJ):Apr–May90–364
Burns, P. Fatal Success. (H. Richardson, ed)
R. Clifton, 617(TLS):2–8Feb90–120

Burns, R.I., ed. The Worlds of Alfonso the
Learned and James the Conqueror.
J.T. Snow, 86(BHS):Jul89–273
Burns, S. Pastoral Inventions.
A.L. Miller, 658:Winter89–280
Burns, W. Enfin Céline vint.
E.F. Gray, 395(MFS):Winter89–833
Burnshaw, S., T. Carmi & E. Spicehandler, eds.
The Modern Hebrew Poem Itself.
J. Lewis, 390:Dec89–58
Burnside, J. The Hoop.*
R. Crawford, 571(ScLJ):Spring89–47
S. O'Brien, 493:Autumn89–63
Burow, J. Corpus Vasorum Antiquorum.*
(Deutschland, Band 54)
B.A. Sparkes, 303(JoHS):Vol109–269
Burrough, B. & J. Helyar. Barbarians at the
Gate.
M. Massing, 617(TLS):10–16Aug90–846
P. O'Toole, 441:21Jan90–7
M.M. Thomas, 453(NYRB):29Mar90–3
Burroughs, W. Interzone.* (J. Grauerholz, ed)
A. Ansen, 532(RCF):Fall89–210
Burroughs, W.S. The Adding Machine.
617(TLS):24–30Aug90–905
Burrow, J.A. The Ages of Man.*
D.G. Calder, 401(MLQ):Dec87–386
H. Tristram, 38:Band107Heft1/2–183
Burrows, A. & I. Schumacher. Portraits of the
Insane.
O. Reynolds, 617(TLS):26Oct–1Nov90–
1158
Burrows, J.F. Computation into Criticism.*
T.K. Bender, 301(JEGP):Jan89–111
D. Le Faye, 541(RES):Aug89–429
J. Wiltshire, 97(CQ):Vol17No4–369
Burrus, V. Chastity as Autonomy.
G. Anderson, 123:Vol39No2–410
Bursk, C. Places of Comfort, Places of Jus-
tice.
P. Harris, 639(VQR):Spring89–240
Burstein, D. Yen!
Kobayashi Kaoru, 285(JapQ):Apr–Jun89–
214
Burt, E.C. Ethnoart.
D.J. Crowley, 2(AfrA):Aug89–84
Burt, J. Robert Penn Warren and American
Idealism.*
C. Brooks, 569(SR):Fall89–586
R.B. Heilman, 301(JEGP):Jul89–459
K. Quinlan, 392:Spring89–197
K. Vanderbilt, 401(MLQ):Mar88–87
J. Walker, 402(MLR):Jul90–716
Burt, J. The Way Down.*
F. Chappell, 219(GaR):Summer89–385
Burt, S., L. Code & L. Dorney, eds. Changing
Patterns.
K. Dubinsky, 529(QQ):Autumn89–775
Burton, D.G. The Legend of Bernardo del Car-
pio from Chronicle to Drama.
A.J. Cardenas, 304(JHP):Autumn89–99
Burton, R. The Anatomy of Melancholy. (Vol
1) (T.C. Faulkner, N.K. Kiessling & R.L.
Blair, eds)
H.R. Woudhuysen, 617(TLS):5–11Jan90–
16
Burton, R.D.E. Baudelaire in 1859.
P. Collier, 402(MLR):Jul90–735
A.S. Rosenthal, 446(NCFS):Fall–
Winter89/90–261
Burton, T.L. & J., eds. Lexicographical and
Linguistic Studies.
G. Kennedy, 596(SL):Vol42No2–173

Buruma, I. God's Dust.*
  J. Haylock, 364:Feb/Mar90-130
Burunat, S., J. Burunat & E.D. Starčević. El
  español y su sintaxis.*
  D.N. Flemming, 399(MLJ):Spring89-105
  J. Shreve, 238:May89-315
Burwick, F. The Haunted Eye.*
  B. Allert, 221(GQ):Spring89-274
Burwick, F. & P. Douglass - see Nathan, I. &
  Lord Byron
Busch, F. Harry and Catherine.
  R. Carlson, 441:11Mar90-11
Busch, H. - see Verdi, G.
Busch, R.L. Humor in the Major Novels of F.M.
  Dostoevsky.*
  R. Anderson, 574(SEEJ):Spring89-124
  R. Freeborn, 575(SEER):Jan89-123
  G. Rosenshield, 104(CASS):Spring-Win-
  ter88-443
Busch, T.W. The Power of Consciousness and
  the Force of Circumstances in Sartre's Phi-
  losophy.
  R. Goldthorpe, 617(TLS):14-20Dec90-
  1347
  G.J. Stack, 543:Jun90-855
Busch, W. Wilhelm Busch: "Max and Moritz" in
  English Dialects and Creoles.* (M. Görlach,
  ed)
  H. Hargreaves, 541(RES):May89-306
  E.W. Schneider, 35(AS):Winter89-362
  W. Viereck, 685(ZDL):1/1989-123
Busch, W. Hans Jakob Christoffel von Grim-
  melshausen.
  W.G. Marigold, 221(GQ):Fall89-520
Buscombe, E., ed. The BFI Companion to the
  Western.
  P. Biskind, 441:13May90-14
  R. Maltby, 707:Spring89-137
Bush, B. Millie's Book.
  Garfield, 441:16Sep90-9
Bush, D. The Genre of Silence.
  W.D. Ehrhart, 639(VQR):Winter89-176
Bush, M. A Place of Light.
  D. Leavitt, 441:21Jan90-14
Bushart, B. Hans Holbein der Ältere.
  J.R., 90:Jan89-47
  J.R., 90:Jun89-437
Bushnaq, I., ed & trans. Arab Folktales.
  W.F.H. Nicolaisen, 292(JAF):Oct-Dec89-
  476
Bushnell, R.W. Prophesying Tragedy.
  639(VQR):Winter89-14
Busi, A. The Standard Life of a Temporary
  Pantyhose Salesman.*
  42(AR):Winter89-116
Busoni, F. Ferruccio Busoni: Selected Let-
  ters.* (A. Beaumont, ed & trans)
  E. Morris, 442(NY):8Jan90-96
Buss, R. The French through their Films.
  C.P. James, 207(FR):Dec89-398
  P. Kenez, 242:Vol10No3-380
  K.A. Reader, 208(FS):Apr89-239
Busse, W. Altenglische Literatur und ihre
  Geschichte.
  A. Fischer, 72:Band226Heft1-139
  J.C. Pope, 589:Jan89-135
  U. Schaefer, 38:Band107Heft1/2-152
  E.G. Stanley, 447(N&Q):Jun89-216
Busset, J.D. - see under de Bourbon Busset, J.
de Bussy, C. - see Spitzmüller, A
de Bussy-Rabutin, R. Correspondance avec le
  Père Bouhours. (C. Rouben, ed)
  M. Gérard, 535(RHL):Mar-Apr89-280

Butchvarov, P. Skepticism in Ethics.*
  S.G. Clarke, 185:Jul90-890
Buthelezi, M.G. South Africa.
  M. Clough, 441:16Dec90-24
Buthlay, K. - see MacDiarmid, H.
Butler, G.C. - see Battiferri, L.
Butler, J. Awash in a Sea of Faith.
  J. Lewis, 441:1Apr90-33
  D. Martin, 617(TLS):21-27Sep90-1003
Butler, J. Gender Trouble.
  C. Card, 103:Sep90-356
  L. Hudson, 617(TLS):1-7Jun90-588
Butler, J.H. The Iskra Incident.
  N. Callendar, 441:16Sep90-26
Butler, M. Jane Austen and the War of Ideas.*
  R. Gard, 447(N&Q):Jun89-248
Butlin, M. & E. Joll. The Paintings of J.M.W.
  Turner. (rev)
  A. Staley, 90:Nov89-777
"Butlletí de la Biblioteca de Catalunya, Volum
  desè: 1982-1984."
  G. Reaney, 410(M&L):Nov89-524
Butor, M. Avant-Goût II.
  J. Kolbert, 207(FR):Oct89-201
Butrica, J.L. The Manuscript Tradition of
  Propertius.*
  J. den Boeft, 394:Vol42fasc3/4-558
  P. Fedeli, 313:Vol79-208
  A. La Penna, 229:Band61Heft2-118
Butscher, E. Conrad Aiken.* (Vol 1)
  C.S. Brown, 569(SR):Summer89-lxxxii
  S.E. Olson, 42(AR):Winter89-103
  T.R. Spivey, 27(AL):Oct89-485
  639(VQR):Autumn89-120
Butt, J. & C. Benjamin. A New Reference
  Grammar of Modern Spanish.*
  R.M. Barasch, 399(MLJ):Summer89-237
  J. Freeland, 402(MLR):Jul90-758
Buttenwieser, A.L. Manhattan Waterbound.
  B. Benepe, 576:Mar89-94
Butter, P.H. - see Muir, E.
Butterick, G. - see Olson, C. & R. Creeley
Butterick, G.F. - see Olson, C.
Butters, R.R. The Death of Black English.
  W. Wolfram, 350:Mar90-121
Buttigieg, J.A., ed. Criticism without Bound-
  aries.*
  B. Newman, 177(ELT):Vol32No3-387
Buttigieg, J.A. "A Portrait of the Artist" in
  Different Perspective.*
  S.B., 295(JML):Fall88/Winter89-358
  J.C.C. Mays, 541(RES):Nov89-587
Button, J., ed. The Green Fuse.
  Lord Bridges, 324:Aug90-639
Buttress, F.A., ed. World Guide to Abbrevia-
  tions of Organizations.
  K.B. Harder, 424:Sep89-294
Butts, L. The Novels of John Gardner.
  R.A. Morace, 395(MFS):Summer89-304
  S. Strehle, 27(AL):Mar89-130
Butts, R.E. Kant and the Double Government
  Methodology.
  R. Meerbote, 449:Apr89-266
Butts, R.E., ed. Kant's Philosophy of Physical
  Science.*
  V. Mudroch, 342:Band80Heft4-477
van Buuren, M.B. Filosofie van de algemene
  literatuurwetenschap.
  J. van Luxemburg, 204(FdL):Mar89-71
Buxarin, V.I. Kommunikativnyj sintaksis v
  prepodavanii russkogo jazyka kak inos-
  trannogo.
  J. Radecker, 682(ZPSK):Band42Heft5-666

Buxbaum, M.H. Benjamin Franklin.
    O. Seavey, 365:Fall88-219
Buxton, J. Sir Philip Sidney and the English
    Renaissance. (3rd ed)
    J.E. Van Domelen, 568(SCN):Fall-
    Winter89-52
Buyck, P. & K. Humbeeck, eds. De/Construc-
    tie, kleine diergaerde voor kinderen van
    nu.
    O. Heynders, 204(FdL):Sep89-231
de Buys, W. & A. Harris. River of Traps.
    B. Kingsolver, 441:23Sep90-33
Buzzoni, M. Paul Ricoeur.
    P. Trotignon, 542:Oct-Dec89-609
Byatt, A.S. Possession.
    R. Jenkyns, 617(TLS):2-8Mar90-213
    J. Parini, 441:21Oct90-9
    J. Thurman, 442(NY):19Nov90-151
Byer, K.S. The Girl in the Midst of the Har-
    vest.
    C.A. Russell, 502(PrS):Winter89-129
Byers, T.B. What I Cannot Say.
    J. Duemer, 705:Fall89-232
Bygrave, S. Coleridge and the Self.
    C.J. Rzepka, 591(SIR):Winter89-656
Bykov, V. Sign of Misfortune.
    I. Zabytko, 441:24Jun90-20
Bynum, C.W. Holy Feast and Holy Fast.*
    R. Copeland, 589:Jan89-143
Bynum, W.F. & R. Porter, eds. William Hunter
    and the Eighteenth-Century Medical World.
    V. Smith, 83:Spring89-81
Byrkit, J.W. - see Lummis, C.
Byrne, A. Bedford Square.
    J.M. Crook, 617(TLS):14-20Sep90-982
Byrne, F. Grammatical Relations in a Radical
    Creole.*
    T. Stolz, 353:Vol27No3-562
Byrne, P.W. "Les Liaisons dangereuses."
    D.A. Coward, 166:Apr90-271
Byrne, R.W. & A. Whiten, eds. Machiavellian
    Intelligence.
    J-M. Gabaude, 542:Oct-Dec89-627
Lord Byron. The Complete Poetical Works.*
    (Vol 5) (J.J. McGann, ed)
    T. Tessier, 189(EA):Apr-Jun89-217
Lord Byron. The Essential Byron. (P. Mul-
    doon, ed)
    P. Mariani, 434:Spring90-313
Lord Byron. Lettres et journaux intimes.
    (J-P. Richard & P. Bensimon, trans)
    T. Tessier, 189(EA):Apr-Jun89-216
Lord Byron. The Manuscripts of the Younger
    Romantics: Lord Byron. (Vols 3 & 4) (A.
    Levine & J.J. McGann, eds)
    T.L. Ashton, 340(KSJ):Vol38-197
Lord Byron. The Oxford Authors: Byron.*
    (J.J. McGann, ed)
    T. Tessier, 189(EA):Apr-Jun89-218

Caballero, A.A. & H.A. Schifini. The English-
    Spanish Real Estate Dictionary/Diccionario
    Español-Inglés de Bienes Raíces.
    D.E. Rivas, 399(MLJ):Winter89-532
Cabanes, P. Les Illyriens de Bardylis à Gent-
    hios (IVe-IIe siècles avant J-C.).
    N.G.L. Hammond, 123:Vol39No2-294
Cabanes, P., ed. L'Illyrie méridionale et
    l'Epire dans l'antiquité.
    N.G.L. Hammond, 123:Vol39No2-294

Cabani, M.C. Le forme del cantare epico-
    cavalleresco.
    M. Praloran, 228(GSLI):Vol166fasc536-
    611
Cabré, M.T. & G. Rigau. Lexicologia i semàn-
    tica.
    M.W. Wheeler, 86(BHS):Jul89-302
Cachia, P. Popular Narrative Ballads of Mod-
    ern Egypt.
    M. Al-Rashid, 677(YES):Vol20-365
Cachin, F. Gauguin.
    E. Darragon, 98:Apr89-228
Cadell, P. & A. Matheson, eds. For the
    Encouragement of Learning.
    H.G. Slade, 617(TLS):2-8Mar90-232
Cadrin-Rossignol, Y. Félix-Antoine Savard.
    T. Lavoie, 627(UTQ):Fall89-203
Cadwalader, G. Castaways.
    R. Parker, 432(NEQ):Mar89-146
Cady, D.L. From Warism to Pacifism.
    K.W.K., 185:Apr90-717
Caesar. C. Iulii Caesaris "commentarii rerum
    gestarum."* (Vol 1: Bellum Gallicum.) (W.
    Hering, ed)
    J.G.F. Powell, 123:Vol39No2-392
Caesar. Caesar's War in Alexandria: Bellum
    Civile III 102-112 & Bellum Alexandrinum
    1-33. (G. Townend, ed)
    J.S. Ruebel, 124:Jul-Aug90-543
Caesarius of Arles. Césaire d'Arles, "Sermons
    au peuple." (Vol 3) (M-J. Delage, ed &
    trans)
    G.J.M. Bartelink, 394:Vol42fasc1/2-232
    P. Flobert, 555:Vol62Fasc2-373
Caffey, D.L. - see La Farge, O.
Cafritz, R.C., L. Gowing & D. Rosand. Places
    of Delight.
    A. Wilton, 90:Oct89-721
Cage, J. I-VI.
    P. Griffiths, 617(TLS):25-31May90-552
    J. Rockwell, 441:13May90-10
Çağman, F. & Z. Tanindi. The Topkapı Saray
    Museum: The Albums and Illustrated Manu-
    scripts. (J.M. Rogers, ed & trans)
    R. Hillenbrand, 59:Mar89-109
    J. Raby, 90:May89-360
Cahalan, J.M. The Irish Novel.*
    M. Throne, 594:Winter89-446
"Cahier No. 10 du Centre culturel Arthur
    Rimbaud."
    M-J. Whitaker, 535(RHL):Jan-Feb89-132
"Cahiers de l'Herne, 1987."
    H. Behar, 535(RHL):Jan-Feb89-158
"Cahiers de Linguistique Française 9."
    M. Wieland, 710:Dec89-480
"Cahiers d'Onomastique Arabe." "Cahiers
    d'Onomastique Arabe, 1981." "Cahiers
    d'Onomastique Arabe, 1982-1984." (J.
    Sublet, ed)
    T. Walz, 318(JAOS):Jan-Mar88-172
"Cahiers François Mauriac, 14." (M-F. Caner-
    ot, ed)
    G. Cesbron, 535(RHL):Jul-Aug89-748
"Cahiers Saint-John Perse. 8-9."
    H. Levillain, 535(RHL):Jan-Feb89-150
"Cahiers V.L. Saulnier." (No. 3)
    M-M. de la Garanderie, 535(RHL):Jan-
    Feb89-85
"Cahiers Stendhal." (No 2)
    V.D.L., 605(SC):15Jul90-408
Cahm, C. Kropotkin and the Rise of Revolu-
    tionary Anarchism, 1872-1886.
    D. Miller, 617(TLS):23-29Mar90-306

Cahm, E., ed. Teaching French Civilisation in Britain, The United States and Australia.
T. Scanlan, 207(FR):Apr90–911
Cahn, H.A. & others. Griechische Münzen aus Grossgriechenland und Sizilien.
A. Cutroni Tusa, 229:Band61Heft6–553
Caiger–Smith, A. Lustre Pottery.*
R. Hillenbrand, 59:Mar89–109
Caillat, C. – see Bloch, J.
Cailler, B. Conquérants de la nuit nue.
H. Wylie, 538(RAL):Fall89–566
Cain, W.E. The Crisis in Criticism.
J. Seaton, 580(SCR):Spring90–149
Cain, W.E. F.O. Matthiessen and the Politics of Criticism.
N. Baym, 432(NEQ):Sep89–466
P.A. Bové, 659(ConL):Fall90–373
T. Poland, 27(AL):Dec89–714
Caine, M. Acting in Film.
A. Barra, 441:27May90–14
Cairns, D. Berlioz.* (Vol 1)
I. Keys, 415:Sep89–541
Cairns, D. & S. Richards. Writing Ireland.
A. Guillaume, 189(EA):Jan–Mar89–115
E. Walshe, 272(IUR):Spring89–186
Cairns, E.A. – see Gildon, C.
Cairns, E.M., comp. Catalogue of the Collection of Children's Books 1617–1939 in the Library of the University of Reading.
C. Hurst, 78(BC):Summer89–261
Caistor, N., ed. The Faber Book of Contemporary Latin American Short Stories.*
J. Wilson, 364:Dec89/Jan90–143
Calaferte I. Memento mori
J. Taylor, 532(RCF).Summer89–238
Calame, C. Alcman.
C.J. Ruijgh, 394:Vol42fasc1/2–163
Calame, C., ed. Métamorphoses du mythe en Grèce antique.
D. Arnould, 555:Vol62Fasc2–329
Calder, A. T.S. Eliot.
R. Crawford, 541(RES)·May89–293
P.R.J., 295(JML):Fall88/Winter89–318
Calder, R. Willie.*
L.E. Beattie, 441:25Mar90–23
G. Vidal, 453(NYRB):1Feb90–39
J. Whitehead, 364:Jun/Jul89–113
442(NY):19Mar90–109
Calder, W.M. 3d & others, eds. Friedrich Gottlieb Welcker.
C.R. Phillips 3d, 24:Winter89–636
Calderón de la Barca, P. El castillo de Lindabridis.* (V.B. Torres, ed)
T.S. Soufas, 240(HR):Autumn89–520
Calderón de la Barca, P. La estatua de Prometeo. (M.R. Greer, with L.K. Stein, eds)
H.W. Sulivan, 240(HR):Winter89–101
J.E. Varey, 86(BHS):Jul89–281
Calderwood, J.L. If It Were Done.*
J.L. Sanderson, 551(RenQ):Spring89–138
J. Singh, 570(SQ):Summer89–232
Calderwood, J.L. Shakespeare and the Denial of Death.*
J.A. Bryant, Jr., 569(SR):Summer89–445
P. Honan, 447(N&Q):Sep89–382
A. Kirsch, 570(SQ):Fall89–348
Caldwell, J.T. Come Dungeons Dark.
M. McGrath, 571(ScLJ):Spring89–40
Calero Vaquera, M.L. Historia de la gramática española (1847–1920).
A. Moreno Ayora, 548:Jan–Jun89–185
Caley, M. Dancing in the Lone Star Diner.
I. McMillan, 493:Winter89/90–65

Calhoon, R.M. Evangelicals and Conservatives in the Early South, 1740–1861.*
639(VQR):Autumn89–115
Calhoun, T.O., L. Heyworth & A. Pritchard – see Cowley, A.
Calì, A. La Narration et le sens.
P. Berthier, 535(RHL):Jan–Feb89–134
Calin, W. In Defense of French Poetry.*
P. Bouysse, 535(RHL):Nov–Dec89–1084
Calinescu, M. Five Faces of Modernity. (2nd ed)
S. Connor, 402(MLR):Jan90–134
I. Hoesterey, 221(GQ):Fall89–505
Calinescu, M. & D. Fokkema, eds. Exploring Postmodernism.
S. Connor, 402(MLR):Oct90–904
I. Hoesterey, 221(GQ):Fall89–505
B. Robbins, 395(MFS):Summer89–372
Calisher, H. Age.
C. Rooke, 376:Jun89–125
Call, M.J. Back to the Garden.*
D.G. Charlton, 402(MLR):Oct90–968
B. Seaton, 446(NCFS):Spring–Summer90–526
Callaghan, M. A Wild Old Man on the Road.
K. McNeilly, 529(QQ):Autumn89–717
Callahan, D. Dangerous Capabilities.
J.S. Nye, Jr., 441:9Sep90–22
Callahan, D. Setting Limits.
N.K. Bell, 254:Summer89–169
D.W. Brock, 509:Summer89–297
L.R. Churchill, 185:Oct89–169
Callahan, D. What Kind of Life.*
442(NY):5Mar90–106
Callahan, J.C. Ethical Issues in Professional Life.
K.L., 185:Oct89–218
Callahan, J.S. In the African–American Grain.
W. Hall, 402(MLR):Jan90–173
N. Harris, 395(MFS):Summer89–307
Callahan, N. Carl Sandburg *
R. Gray, 447(N&Q):Jun89–276
Callander, M.B. Willa Cather and the Fairy Tale.
M. Doane, 649(WAL):Aug89–186
Callejo, A. & M.T. Pajares. Fábula de Polyfemo y Galatea y las Soledades.
M.J. Woods, 86(BHS):Jul89–283
Callen, M. Surviving AIDS.
J. Laurence, 441:9Dec90–18
Callicott, J.B. In Defense of the Land Ethic.
J–M. Gabaude, 542:Oct–Dec89–642
H.R., 185:Apr90–714
Callicott, J.B. & R.T. Ames, eds. Nature in Asian Traditions of Thought.
R.C.P., 185:Jul90–920
Callimachus. Hymns, Epigrams, Select Fragments.* (S. Lombardo & D. Rayor, eds & trans)
R.F. Thomas, 124:Sep–Oct89–74
Callipolitis–Feytmans, D. Corpus Vasorum Antiquorum. (Grèce, Vol 3, Pt 3)
M.B. Moore, 229:Band61Heft5–457
B.A. Sparkes, 303(JoHS):Vol109–270
Callot, E. Les étapes de la biologie.*
A. Pichot, 192(EP):Jul–Dec89–534
Callow, S. Charles Laughton.
J. Harvey, 453(NYRB):15Feb90–43
Calloway, S. Twentieth–Century Decoration.*
C. McCorquodale, 39:Nov89–359
Calore, A. La rimozione del giuramento.
K. Hackl, 229:Band61Heft8–746

Calvé, P. & A. Mollica. Le Français langue
seconde.
R.M. Terry, 399(MLJ):Spring89-85
Calvet de Maglahães, T. Signe ou Symbole.
Un, Deux, Trois.
A. De Tienne & C.J.W. Kloesel,
619:Summer89-341
Calvet-Sebasti, M-A. & P-L. Gatier – see
Firmus de Césarée
Calvi, G. Histories of a Plague Year.
P. Burke, 617(TLS):19-25Jan90-70
Calvino, I. Six Memos for the Next Millen-
nium.*
M.B. Cloud, 532(RCF):Spring89-245
C.R. Frisch, 400(MLN):Jan89-259
42(AR):Winter89-112
Calvino, I. La strada di San Giovanni.
L. Sage, 617(TLS):5-11Oct90-1060
Calvo, R. & others. Doce a las doce (teatro
breve).
M.S. Gann, 352(LATR):Spring90-180
Camarasa, A.V. – see under Viudas Camarasa,
A.
Camarero, M. Comprensión y expresión.
T.L. Ballman, 238:Dec89-975
Cambiano, G., ed. Storiografia e dossografia
nella filosofia antica.*
C. Viano, 192(EP):Jul-Dec89-558
Cambria, E.F. – see under Fernández Cambria,
E.
Cameron, A. The Annie Poems.
M. Junyk, 529(QQ):Spring89-159
Cameron, A. Stubby Amberchuk & the Holy
Grail.
M. Body, 102(CanL):Autumn-Winter89-
179
Cameron, A. & others – see "Dictionary of Old
English"
Cameron, B. John Metcalf.
M. Darling, 168(ECW):Spring89-172
Cameron, D., ed. The Free Trade Papers.
M. Bradfield, 298:Spring89-146
Cameron, J.S. Mag.
S. Roe, 617(TLS):9-15Feb90-149
Cameron, K. Concordance des Oeuvres poét-
iques de Joachim du Bellay.
Y. Bellenger, 535(RHL):Sep-Oct89-923
D.G. Coleman, 402(MLR):Jul90-726
J.C. Nash, 207(FR):Dec89-369
G.H. Tucker, 208(FS):Apr89-201
Cameron, K.M. Into Africa.
D.L. Manzolillo, 617(TLS):10-16Aug90-
857
Cameron, P. Leap Year.
E. Pall, 441:25Feb90-10
Cameron, R. A Concise Economic History of
the World.
F. Spooner, 617(TLS):2-8Mar90-228
Cameron, S. Thinking in Henry James.*
D.M. Fogel, 598(SoR):Summer90-697
Camisa, E. The Fratelli Camisa Cookery Book.
J. Keates, 617(TLS):27Jul-2Aug90-809
de la Campa, H. Diccionario inverso del
español.
A. Valladares Reguero, 548:Jul-Dec89-
476
B.L. Velleman, 238:May89-313
Campana, D. Canti orfici. (F. Ceragioli, ed)
M. King, 276:Summer89-244
Campbell, A. The Frigate Bird.
F. Baveystock, 617(TLS):2-8Feb90-122
Campbell, A.T. To Square with Genesis.
P. Henley, 617(TLS):6-12Apr90-369

Campbell, B.M. Sweet Summer.*
A. Solanke, 617(TLS):26Oct-1Nov90-
1148
Campbell, C. The Romantic Ethic and the
Spirit of Modern Consumerism.
E. Boa, 89(BJA):Winter89-95
Campbell, D. That Was Business, This Is Per-
sonal.
L. Taylor, 617(TLS):4-10May90-478
Campbell, D.T. Methodology and Epistemology
for Social Science.
R.H. Potvin, 543:Mar90-624
Campbell, J., ed. The Experience of World War
2.
H. Strachan, 617(TLS):17-23Aug90-865
Campbell, J., with B. Moyers. The Power of
Myth. (B.S. Flowers, ed)
R.A. Segal, 598(SoR):Spring90-470
Campbell, J.A. & W.W. Lamar. The Venomous
Reptiles of Latin America.
M. O'Shea, 617(TLS):29Jun-5Jul90-707
Campbell, K. What He Really Wants Is a Dog.
K. Bucknell, 617(TLS):9-15Feb90-148
Campbell, L. Renaissance Portraits.
R. Brilliant, 441:5Aug90-22
Campbell, M. Not Being Miriam.
I. Indyk, 581:Mar89-127
Campbell, M. Studies in the Third Book of
Apollonius Rhodius' "Argonautica."
D.M. Schenkeveld, 394:Vol42fasc1/2-198
Campbell, M.B. The Witness and the Other
World.
J. Knapp, 551(RenQ):Winter89-851
Campbell, R. The Gift Horse's Mouth.
M. Stasio, 441:30Dec90-26
Campbell, R. Juice.*
I. Sinclair, 617(TLS):24-30Aug90-903
639(VQR):Autumn89-131
Campbell, R. & D. Collinson. Ending Lives.*
M.B.M., 185:Apr90-713
Campbell, S.E. The Enemy Opposite.
A. Munton, 402(MLR):Jul90-707
B.K. Scott, 395(MFS):Summer89-336
G.W., 102(CanL):Summer89-197
Campbell, T. The Earliest Printed Maps
1472-1500.
M. Pastoureau, 78(BC):Autumn89-414
N.J.W. Thrower, 589:Jul89-680
Campbell, T. Justice.*
R.W. Hoag, 518:Oct89-247
Campbell, T.P. & C. Davidson, eds. The
Fleury Playbook.*
J. Stevens, 447(N&Q):Mar89-90
Campbell-Kelly, M. & others – see Babbage,
C.
Campins, A.S. – see under Serrà Campins, A.
Campion, T. The Essential Campion. (C.
Simic, ed)
P. Mariani, 434:Spring90-313
Camus, R. L'Élégie de Chamalières.
J. Baetens, 98:Nov89-909
Canac-Marquis, N. Le Syndrome de Cézanne.
L.E. Doucette, 108:Spring89-84
Canady, H.P. Gentlemen of the Bar.
W.S. Price, Jr., 656(WMQ):Jan89-189
Canavaggio, J. Cervantes.*
F. Luciani, 441:25Mar90-24
Candau de Cevallos, M.D. Historia de la len-
gua española.
G.D. Greenia, 545(RPh):Nov89-320
Candelaria, N. The Day the Cisco Kid Shot
John Wayne.
P. de la Fuente, 649(WAL):May89-68

Cañedo, J. & I. Arellano, eds. Edición y ano-
tación de textos del Siglo de Oro.
E.H. Friedman, 238:Mar89–143
Canellada, M.J. & J.K. Madsen. Pronunciación
del español.
J.R. Lodares, 548:Jan–Jun89–187
B.L. Velleman, 238:Sep89–564
Canerot, M–F. – see "Cahiers François Maur-
iac"
Canetti, V. Die gelbe Strasse.
S. Beller, 617(TLS):5–11Oct90–1062
Canfield, J.D. & J.P. Hunter, eds. Rhetorics of
Order/Ordering of Rhetorics in English
Neoclassical Literature.
C.T. Probyn, 166:Jul90–347
Canfora, L. Tucidide.
H.D. Westlake, 123:Vol39No2–387
Canfora, L. The Vanished Library.
H. Lloyd–Jones, 453(NYRB):14Jun90–27
P. Parsons, 617(TLS):9–15Mar90–249
Canguilhem, G. Ideology and Rationality in
the History of the Life Sciences.
K.A. Long, 125:Summer89–407
Cannadine, D. The Decline and Fall of the
British Aristocracy.
N. Annan, 453(NYRB):6Dec90–29
R. Blake, 441:4Nov90–13
C. Russell, 617(TLS):19–25Oct90–1123
442(NY):10Dec90–159
Cannon, G. Historical Change and English
Word–Formation.*
L. Bauer, 35(AS):Fall89–252
Cano, J.L. – see Aleixandre, V.
Canobbio, A. Vasi chiusi
A. Caesar, 617(TLS):5–11Oct90–1074
Cantalupo, J. & T.C. Renner. Body Mike.
M. Gallagher, 441:28Jan90–23
Cantarella, E. The Role and Status of Women
in Greek and Roman Antiquity.
S. Dixon, 487:Spring89–84
Cantarino, V. Civilización y cultura de
España.
A. Amell, 238:Mar89–161
Cantelli Domenicis, M. & J.J. Reynolds.
Repase y escriba.
T.A. Lathrop, 238:Dec89–976
Cantora, M.J.R. – see under Redono Cantora,
M.J.
Canto, M. L'intrigue philosophique.*
C. Gill, 303(JoHS):Vol109–223
Cao Xueqin & Gao E. The Story of Stone.
(Vol 5)
E. Widmer, 318(JAOS):Oct–Dec88–650
Capaldi, N. Hume's Place in Moral Philosophy.
J. Gray, 617(TLS):22–28Jun90–672
Capasso, M. & others. Momenti della storia
degli studi classici fra Ottocento e Nove-
cento.
N. Horsfall, 123:Vol39No2–427
Capasso, M. & T. Dorandi – see Cavallo, G.
Capdevielle, J. & R. Mouriau. Mai 68.
A.J.M. Prévos, 207(FR):Mar90–756
Capdevielle, J–P. & P–E. Knabe, eds. Les
écrivains français et l'opéra.
K. Ringger, 535(RHL):Jan–Feb89–169
Cape, T. The Cambridge Theorem.
G. Jacobs, 617(TLS):11–17May90–496
Capek, K. Nine Fairy Tales by Karel Capek.
P–L. Adams, 61:Sep90–123
L. Belfer, 441:15Jul90–18
M. Warner, 617(TLS):28Sep–4Oct90–1036

Capek, K. Toward the Radical Center. (P.
Kussi, ed) War with the Newts. Three
Novels.
H. Kovaly, 441:25Mar90–18
Čapek, K. Univerzitní studie. (M. Pohorský,
ed)
R.B. Pynsent, 575(SEER):Apr89–284
Capel Margarito, M. Orfebrería religiosa de
Granada. (Vol 2)
A. López–Yarto Elizalde, 48:Jan–Mar89–
105
Capelle, T. Kultur– und Kunstgeschichte der
Wikinger.
T. Krömmelbein, 684(ZDA):Band118Heft3–
107
zur Capellen, J.M. – see under Meyer zur
Capellen, J.
Caplan, D. Neurolinguistics and Linguistic
Aphasiology.*
M.P. Lorch, 361:May89–90
L.K. Obler, 350:Jun90–383
Caplan, H.H. The Classified Dictionary of
Artists' Signatures, Symbols and Mono-
grams.
J. Stourton, 39:Apr89–291
Caplan, J. Framed Narratives.*
S. Gearhart, 131(CL):Spring89–192
D. Marshall, 173(ECS):Fall89–90
M.F. O'Meara, 400(MLN):Sep89–968
Caplan, L. Class and Culture in Urban India.
J. Cox, 293(JASt):May89–418
Caplan, L. An Open Adoption.
P. Theroux, 441:8Jul90–7
Caplan, P., ed. The Cultural Construction of
Sexuality.*
A–J. Morey, 577(SHR):Summer89–273
Caplan, U. & M.W. Steinberg – see Klein, A.M.
Caponegro, M. The Star Cafe & Other Stories.
P. Finn, 441:16Sep90–22
Caponigro, P. Seasons.
H. Martin, 507:May/Jun89–156
Capovilla, G. La formazione letteraria del
Pascoli a Bologna. (Vol 1)
E. Favretti, 228(GSLI):Vol166fasc505–
470
Capps, B. Sam Chance. The White Man's
Road. The Brothers of Uterica.
L. Rodenberger, 649(WAL):Nov89–262
Capretz, P.J. & others. French in Action.
A. Shewmake, 207(FR):May90–1092
Caput, J–P. L'Académie française.
A. Viala, 535(RHL):Jan–Feb89–164
Caputo, J.D. Radical Hermeneutics.*
V.B. Leitch, 478(P&L):Apr89–151
C.O. Schrag, 323:Jan89–86
Caputo–Mayr, M.L. & J.M. Herz. Franz Kafka.*
J. Hibberd, 133:Band22Heft2–180
N. Oellers, 680(ZDP):Band108Heft4–633
Caracciolo, P.L., ed. The "Arabian Nights" in
English Literature.
N.V. Workman, 637(VS):Spring90–521
Caraman, P. Ignatius Loyola.
P. Hebblethwaite, 617(TLS):2–8Nov90–
1185
Caramel, L. & A. Longatti. Antonio Sant'-
Elia.*
R. Padovan, 46:Jun89–12
Carby, H.V. Reconstructing Womanhood.*
E.C.R., 295(JML):Fall88/Winter89–194
E.L. Steeves, 395(MFS):Summer89–310

Cárdenas, A.J., ed. The Text and Concordance of Biblioteca Nacional Manuscript RES. 270–271.
G. West, 304(JHP):Autumn89–97
Cardew, M. Michael Cardew. (S. Cardew, ed)
D. Hamilton, 324:Jan90–143
Cardinal, R. Breton: "Nadja."*
S. Levy, 402(MLR):Apr90–458
Cardinal, R. The Landscape Vision of Paul Nash.
M. James, 617(TLS):12–18Oct90–1102
Cardini, F. Europe 1492.
S. Coates, 441:18Mar90–20
Cardona, G.R. Dizionario di linguistica.
V. Della Valle, 708:Vol14Fasc2–265
Cardoni, E., ed. Blatant Artifice 2/3.
S. Moore, 532(RCF):Spring89–264
Carducci, G. Prime Odi Barbare. (P. van Heck, ed) Odi Barbare. (G.A. Papini, ed)
A. Brambilla, 228(GSLI):Vol166fasc536–569
Cardullo, B., ed. Before his Eyes.
G. Armstrong, 610:Summer89–214
Carens, J.F., ed. Critical Essays on Evelyn Waugh.
A. Blayac, 189(EA):Oct–Dec89–488
Carey, B. Undressing the Dark.*
J. McCombs, 102(CanL):Spring89–202
Carey, G. Anita Loos.
639(VQR):Summer89–89
Carey, J. John Donne.
617(TLS):29Jun–5Jul90–708
Carey, J.W., ed. Media, Myths, and Narratives.
B. Zelizer, 292(JAF):Oct–Dec89–493
Carey, P. Oscar and Lucinda.*
M. Harris, 581:Mar89–109
Carey, R. Baja Journey.
R. Bass, 649(WAL):Nov89–272
Cargill, C., ed. A TESOL Professional Anthology.
A. Bollati, 399(MLJ):Winter89–484
Carkeet, D. The Full Catastrophe.
M. Chernoff, 441:18Feb90–12
Carles, P., A. Clergeat & J-L. Comolli. Dictionnaire du jazz.
A.J.M.P., 91:Vol17–189
Carley, L. – see Delius, F. & others
Carlisle, O.A. – see Andreyev, L.
de Carlo, A. Yucatan.
P-L. Adams, 61:Apr90–108
Carlsen, P. The Player-Piano Music of Conlon Nancarrow.
P. Rapoport, 607:Mar89–40
Carlshamre, S. Language and Time.
J. Llewelyn, 323:Jan89–89
Carlson, B.F. & P. Flett, comps. Spokane Dictionary.
I.G. Doak, 350:Jun90–410
Carlson, E.W., ed. Critical Essays on Edgar Allan Poe.*
H. Justin, 189(EA):Jul–Sep89–360
Carlson, J., ed. Banned in Ireland.
D. Donoghue, 617(TLS):7–13Dec90–1324
Carlson, S. Women of Grace.*
C.M. Mazer, 610:Summer89–203
Carlsson, S. Studies on Middle English Local Bynames in East Anglia.
O. Arngart, 179(ES):Dec89–587
Carlyle, T. & J.W. The Collected Letters of Thomas and Jane Welsh Carlyle.* (Vols 10–12) (C.R. Sanders & others, eds)
G.B. Tennyson, 506(PSt):May87–115

Carlyle, T. & J.W. The Collected Letters of Thomas and Jane Welsh Carlyle.* (Vols 13–15) (C.D. Ryals & K.J. Fielding, eds)
R.L. Brett, 541(RES):Nov89–577
Carnero, G. – see Martínez Colomer, V.
Carney, G.O., ed. The Sounds of People and Places.
A. Kaye, 187:Winter89–164
Carnochan, W.B. Gibbon's Solitude.*
M. Brownley, 481(PQ):Winter89–122
G. Davenport, 31(ASch):Summer89–468
Caro, R.A. The Years of Lyndon Johnson: Means of Ascent.
E.R. May, 617(TLS):28Sep–4Oct90–1024
R. Steel, 441:11Mar90–1
G. Wills, 453(NYRB):26Apr90–7
Caroli, F. Fede Galizia.
L. Gowing, 617(TLS):20–26Jul90–772
Carosso, V.P. The Morgans.*
L. Schweikart, 106:Summer89–143
Carpanetto, D. & G. Ricuperati. Italy in the Age of Reason 1685–1789.
M.S. Miller, 173(ECS):Fall89–118
D. Thompson, 278(IS):Vol44–171
Carpelan, B. Axel.*
R. Layton, 415:Jul89–413
Carpelan, B. Room Without Walls.*
L. Sail, 565:Summer89–75
Carpenter, C.A. Modern Drama Scholarship and Criticism 1966–1980.*
B.F. Dukore, 397(MD):Dec89–587
Carpenter, D. From a Distant Place.*
D.M. Fine, 649(WAL):Aug89–187
Carpenter, D. God's Bedfellows.
A. Weiss, 102(CanL):Autumn–Winter89–259
Carpenter, D.A. The Minority of Henry III.
J. Catto, 617(TLS):20–26Jul90–773
Carpenter, H. The Brideshead Generation.*
P-L. Adams, 61:Feb90–108
D. Cannadine, 441:7Jan90–11
Carpenter, H. Geniuses Together.*
J.G. Kennedy, 27(AL):Mar89–114
H.R. Lottman, 473(PR):Vol56No3–504
Carpenter, H. A Serious Character.*
C. Tomlinson, 249(HudR):Summer89–191
J. Whalen-Bridge, 27(AL):Oct89–484
Carpenter, H. – see Tolkien, J.R.R.
Carpenter, L. – see Fletcher, J.G.
Carpenter, L. & L. Rudolph – see Fletcher, J.G.
Carpenter, T.H. Dionysian Imagery in Archaic Greek Art.
K.W. Arafat, 235:Summer89–69
Carpentier, A. The Chase.*
J. Sturrock, 617(TLS):30Mar–5Apr90–339
Carpentier, A. Concierto Barroco.
D. Zalacaín, 238:Dec89–983
Carpentier, A. The Harp and the Shadow.
I. Stavans, 441:3Jun90–18
G. Wills, 453(NYRB):22Nov90–6
Carpentier, G. Tous couchés.
J.W. Cross, 207(FR):Mar90–742
Carpi, U., ed. Carducci poeta.
A. Brambilla, 228(GSLI):Vol166fasc536–569
Carpio, L.D. – see under de Vega Carpio, L.
Carr, A.W. Byzantine Illumination, 1150–1250.
H. Maguire, 589:Oct89–927
Carr, D. Interpreting Husserl.*
R. Holmes, 154:Vol28No3–517

Carr, D. Time, Narrative, and History.*
  T. Postlewait, 615(TJ):Dec89-557
Carr, H., ed. From My Guy to Sci-Fi.
  K. Ford, 617(TLS):29Jun-5Jul90-702
Carr, P. Sonahchi.
  B.A. St. Andrews, 219(GaR):Summer89-424
Carr, R. Woman's Own.
  A.Z. Leventhal, 441:5Aug90-18
Carr, V.S. Understanding Carson McCullers.
  L.E. Harding, 585(SoQ):Summer90-126
"Les Carrache et les décors profanes."
  D. Posner, 54:Sep89-523
Carradice, P., ed. The Unsaid Goodnight.
  C. Hurford, 617(TLS):21-27Dec90-1383
Carrasco, E.G. - see under Gil y Carrasco, E.
Carré, O., ed. Islam and the State in the World Today.
  S. Baruah, 293(JASt):Aug89-641
Carreira, A. Descrições oitocentistas das Ilhas de Cabo Verde.
  P.E.H. Hair, 86(BHS):Oct89-394
Carreira, A. - see Roiz Lucas de Senna, M.
Carrell, P.L., J. Devine & D.E. Eskey, eds. Interactive Approaches to Second Language Reading.
  M. Haynes, 710:Dec89-468
  R.G. Kern, 207(FR):Dec89-413
  J.F. Lee, 399(MLJ):Summer89-201
Carreño, A. - see de Góngora, L.
Carrère, E. The Mustache.*
  I. Malin, 532(RCF):Spring89-256
Carri, J.J. Contribution of the Bhaṭṭa Dhārkura Midru to Vedic Exegesis.
  C.Z. Minkowski, 259(IIJ):Apr89-144
Carrier, D. Artwriting.*
  G. Bennington, 89(BJA):Autumn89-375
  H. Pardee, 127:Summer89-194
Carrier, R. Heartbreaks Along the Road.
  J. Lennox, 102(CanL):Autumn-Winter89-209
Carrière, J-C. The Mahabharata.
  E. Brater, 130:Summer89-184
Carroll, J. A Child Across the Sky.
  C. Greenland, 617(TLS):23Feb-1Mar90-202
Carroll, J. Wallace Stevens' Supreme Fiction.*
  W.E. Cain, 301(JEGP):Jan89-151
Carroll, L. Annie Chambers.
  L.B. Osborne, 441:29Jul90-20
Carroll, N. Mystifying Movies.
  A. Neill & A. Ridley, 103:Sep90-345
  A. Sesonske, 290(JAAC):Summer89-284
  T. Whittock, 89(BJA):Autumn89-379
Carroll, N. Philosophical Problems of Classical Film Theory.
  E.W. Cameron, 290(JAAC):Winter89-85
  A. Neill & A. Ridley, 103:Sep90-345
Carruth, H. Tell me Again How the White Heron Rises and Flies Across the Nacreous River at Twilight Toward the Distant Islands.
  D. Weiss, 598(SoR):Spring90-466
Carson, C. Belfast Confetti.
  N. Corcoran, 617(TLS):2-8Nov90-1184
Carson, C. The Irish for No.
  J. Drexel, 434:Winter89-179
Carson, C. The New Estate and Other Poems.
  B. O'Donoghue, 493:Summer89-62
Carson, J. Céline's Imaginative Space.*
  C. Krance, 210(FrF):Jan89-112

Carson, N. A Companion to Henslowe's Diary.*
  A.F. Kinney, 130:Summer89-181
  L. Potter, 611(TN):Vol43No2-85
  W.P. Williams, 447(N&Q):Jun89-231
Carson, R. Mount St. Helens.
  P-L. Adams, 61:Sep90-122
Carstairs, A. Allomorphy in Inflexion.
  J.T. Jensen, 297(JL):Mar89-235
  J. Klausenburger, 320(CJL):Mar89-45
Carstens, S.A., ed. Cultural Identity in Northern Peninsular Malaysia.
  J. Nagata, 293(JASt):Nov89-929
Cartelle, E.M. - see under Montero Cartelle, E.
Carter, A.H. 3d. Italo Calvino.*
  F. Cromphout, 561(SFS):Jul89-236
Carter, D. The Final Frontier.
  J. Tabbi, 532(RCF):Spring89-274
Carter, E. & M.W. Stolper. Elam.
  D. Fleming, 318(JAOS):Jul-Sep88-514
Carter, E.D., Jr. Julio Cortázar.
  S. Boldy, 86(BHS):Jan89-112
Carter, H.B. Sir Joseph Banks (1743-1828).
  M.A.E. Nickson, 354:Jun89-170
Carter, J.J. & J.H. Pittock, eds. Aberdeen and the Enlightenment.
  M. Fitzpatrick, 83:Spring89-99
  F.W. Freeman, 571(ScLJ):Spring89-1
Carter, M.L., ed. "Dracula."
  G. Hirsch, 637(VS):Spring90-522
Carter, R. The Pleasure Within.
  R.L. Buckland, 573(SSF):Summer89-367
Carter, R. Vocabulary.
  C. Myers, 126(CCC):May90-010
  T. Piotrowski, 257(IRAL):Aug89-253
  P. Scholfield, 307:Apr89-79
Carter, R. & M. McCarthy. Vocabulary and Language Teaching.
  T. Piotrowski, 257(IRAL):Aug89-253
Carter, R. & P. Simpson, eds. Language, Discourse and Literature.
  H. Bonheim, 402(MLR):Jul90-668
  C. Calvo, 307:Dec89-220
Carter, S.D. The Road to Komatsubara.*
  K. Brazell, 293(JASt):May89-384
Carter, T., ed. W.A. Mozart: "Le nozze di Figaro."*
  A. Steptoe, 410(M&L):Feb89-104
Carter, T. & P. Goss. Utah's Historic Architecture, 1847-1940.
  S.A. Chambers, Jr., 576:Sep89-299
  658:Spring89-110
Cartier, J. Relations. (M. Bideaux, ed)
  C.R.P. May, 208(FS):Jan89-114
Cartledge, P. Agesilaos and the Crisis of Sparta.*
  J.G. De Voto, 122:Oct89-346
  J.F. Lazenby, 123:Vol39No2-283
Cartledge, P. & A. Spawforth. Hellenistic and Roman Sparta.
  M. Crawford, 617(TLS):31Aug-6Sep90-928
Cartledge, P.A. & F.D. Harvey, eds. Crux.
  K.H. Kinzl, 123:Vol39No2-303
Carton, E. The Rhetoric of American Romance.*
  G. Dekker, 183(ESQ):Vol35No1-69
Cartwright, J. Look At It This Way.
  G. Sutton, 617(TLS):19-25Oct90-1132
Caruso, E., Jr. & A. Farkas. Enrico Caruso.
  P. Constantine, 441:30Sep90-29
Carver, C.M. American Regional Dialects.
  M. Görlach, 685(ZDL):2/1989-206

Carver, R., ed. Ariel at Bay.
    L. Duguid, 617(TLS):12–18Oct90–1104
Carver, R. A New Path to the Waterfall.*
    F. Chappell, 344:Summer90–168
    G. Ewart, 364:Dec89/Jan90–99
Carver, R. Where I'm Calling From.*
    G. Johnson, 219(GaR):Winter89–784
    W. Kittredge, 649(WAL):May89–63
    G. Krist, 249(HudR):Spring89–125
Carver, T. Friedrich Engels.
    G.S. Jones, 617(TLS):10–16Aug90–853
Cary, J. Mister Johnson.
    T.C. Holyoke, 42(AR):Fall89–501
Cary, T. Abram's Plains. (D.M.R. Bentley, ed)
    C. Ballstadt, 470:Vol27–119
    W.J. Keith, 168(ECW):Spring89–83
    D. Latham, 102(CanL):Autumn–Winter89–
    141
Casadei, A. La strategia delle varianti.
    E. Bigi, 228(GSLI):Vol166fasc535–447
Casado, H. Señores, mercaderes y campesinos.
    B. Leroy, 92(BH):Jul–Dec88–453
Casares, A.B. – see under Bioy Casares, A.
Casati, M.D. & M. Pavarani – see under Di
    Gregorio Casati, M. & M. Pavarani
Cascardi, A.J. The Limits of Illusion.
    R. Moore, 345(KRQ):May89–245
Cascardi, A.J., ed. Literature and the Ques-
    tion of Philosophy.*
    R. Eldridge, 540(RIPh):Vol43fasc1–160
    P. Lamarque, 89(BJA):Winter89–82
    R. Seamon, 103:Jul90–264
Case, S–E. Feminism and Theatre.
    L. Hart, 615(TJ):May89–261
    R.C. Lamont, 397(MD):Mar89–159
Case, T.E. – see de Vega Carpio, L.
Caserta, E.G. Croce and Marxism.
    M.A. Finocchiaro, 276:Winter89–449
Casertano, G., ed. Democrito dall' atomo alla
    città.
    J.F. Procopé, 303(JoHS):Vol109–238
Casertano, G. I Filosofi e il Potere nella Soc-
    ieta et nella Cultura antiche.
    P. Louis, 555:Vol62Fasc2–347
Casey, B. Dance Across Texas.
    V.R. Brown, 582(SFQ):Vol46No2–187
Casey, D.J. & L.M., eds. Stories by Contempo-
    rary Irish Women.
    C.D. Thompson, 441:23Sep90–48
Casey, E.S. Remembering.*
    N.E. Wetherick, 323:May89–179
Casey, E.S. & D.V. Morano, eds. The Life of
    the Transcendental Ego.
    W.F. Vallicella, 449:Jun89–386
Casey, J. Pagan Virtue.
    G. Strawson, 617(TLS):12–18Oct90–1093
Casey, W. The Secret War Against Hitler.
    A. Glees, 617(TLS):13–19Apr90–392
Casillo, R. The Genealogy of Demons.*
    J. Berman, 390:May89–61
    B. Fogelman, 27(AL):May89–308
    L.S. Rainey, 301(JEGP):Oct89–559
Caskey, M.E., with others. Keos. (Vol 2, Pt 1)
    W. Schiering, 229:Band61Heft4–339
de Caso, J. David d'Angers.
    S.G. Lindsay, 54:Sep89–525
    N. Penny, 90:Sep89–657
Cass, C. Grand Illusions.
    C. McCorquodale, 39:Sep89–211
Cassady, C. Off the Road.
    S. Shapiro, 441:2Sep90–16
Cassedy, S. – see Bely, A.

Cassel, J. The Secret Plague.
    G.S. Smith, 529(QQ):Summer89–244
Cassian, N. Call Yourself Alive?*
    D. O'Driscoll, 493:Summer89–47
Casson, L., ed & trans. The Periplus Maris
    Erythraei.
    S.E. Sidebotham, 124:Jan–Feb90–236
    C.R. Whittaker, 617(TLS):26Jan–1Feb90–
    95
Castaldo, J.B. Vida ilustrada de San Caye-
    tano. (P.G. Llompart, ed)
    W. Rincón García, 48:Jan–Mar89–100
Castan, C. Conflicts of Love.
    A. Corkhill, 71(ALS):Oct89–271
Castañeda, O.S. Cunuman.
    I. Stavans, 36:Summer89–120
Castedo, E. Paradise.
    P–L. Adams, 61:Mar90–116
    L.B. de Jenkins, 441:1Apr90–8
Castein, H. & A. Stillmark, eds. Deutsche
    Romantik und das 20. Jahrhundert.
    N. Saul, 402(MLR):Jan90–251
Castellanos, I. & J. Inclán, eds. En torno a
    Lydia Cabrera.
    I. Alvarez–Borland, 238:Mar89–153
Castelvecchi, A. – see Trissino, G.G.
Castelvetro, G. The Fruit, Herbs and Vegeta-
    bles of Italy.
    J. Keates, 617(TLS):27Jul–2Aug90–809
Casteras, S.P. Images of Victorian Woman-
    hood in English Art.*
    A. Faxon, 635(VPR):Spring89–41
    M. Pointon, 59:Mar89–115
Casteras, S.P. & R. Parkinson, eds. Richard
    Redgrave 1804–1888.
    D.N. Mancoff, 637(VS):Autumn89–196
Casti, G.B. Gli animali parlanti. (L. Pedroia,
    ed)
    E. Bonora, 228(GSLI):Vol166fasc535–460
Casti, J.L. Paradigms Lost.
    42(AR):Fall89–504
Castillo, A. My Father Was a Toltec.
    S. Foster, 448:Vol27No3–160
Castle, B. Sylvia and Christabel Pankhurst.
    J. Damousi, 637(VS):Autumn89–210
Castle, T. Masquerade and Civilization.*
    M. Irwin, 541(RES):May89–269
Castleden, R. The Knossos Labyrinth.
    J.T. Hooker, 617(TLS):9–15Mar90–249
Castoriadis, C. The Imaginary Institution of
    Society.
    P.J.S., 185:Oct89–211
de Castris, P.L. Arte di Corte nella Napoli
    Angioina.
    J. Gardner, 90:Aug89–562
de Castro, F.J.D. – see under Díaz de Castro,
    F.J.
de Castro, G. Las mocedades del Cid. (C.
    Faliu–Lacourt, ed)
    A.R. Lauer, 240(HR):Summer89–389
Castro Lee, C. & C.C. Soufas, eds. En torno al
    hombre y a los monstruos.
    G.S. Forrest, 238:Mar89–147
    M.E.W. Jones, 86(BHS):Jul89–301
Castronovo, D. The English Gentleman.*
    E.R. August, 635(VPR):Spring89–43
    D.K. Jeffrey, 125:Winter89–212
    J.H. Wiener, 177(ELT):Vol32No1–84
Catalá, R. Para una lectura americana del
    barroco mexicano.
    G. Sabat–Rivers, 238:Dec89–966
Catalá, V. Soledad.
    J. Martí–Olivella, 240(HR):Autumn89–537

Catalán, D., with others. Catálogo general del Romancero.
    M.E. Barrick, 545(RPh):Nov89-347
Catalano, J.S. A Commentary on Jean-Paul Sartre's Critique of Dialectical Reason.* (Vol 1)
    D.B., 295(JML):Fall88/Winter89-404
Catalli, F. Tarquinia, Museo Archaeologico Nazionale: Le Monete.
    A.M. Burnett, 313:Vol79-265
"Catalogue de la collection de Canadiana Louis Melzack."
    J.E. Hare, 470:Vol27-130
"Catalogue of Manuscripts in the Houghton Library, Harvard University."
    J.P. Hudson, 354:Jun89-166
Catano, J.V. Language, History, Style.
    T.C. Frazer, 350:Mar90-185
Cathcart, A. The Missionary.
    G. Telfer, 571(ScLJ):Spring89-50
Cather, W. Willa Cather in Person.* (L.B. Bohlke, ed)
    M.A. Peterman, 106:Fall89-211
    P. Reilly, 447(N&Q):Mar89-133
    D. Stineback, 106:Fall89-219
Catledge, O.E. Cabbagetown.
    L. Jasud, 585(SoQ):Fall89-69
Catlin, A. & D. Swift. Textiles as Texts.
    M. Roseman, 293(JASt):Nov89-940
Catterall, P. - see "Contemporary Britain"
Catullus. The Poems of Catullus. (G. Lee, trans) The Poems of Catullus. (C. Martin, trans)
    R. Jenkyns, 617(TLS):15-21Jun90-648
Catz, R.D. - see under Mendes Pinto, F.
Caufield, C. Oscuridad divina. 34th Street and Other Poems (1982-1984).
    L. Hernández, 36:Fall-Winter89-187
Causley, C. A field of vision
    S. Knight, 364:Apr/May89-129
    W. Magee, 493:Spring89-50
Caute, D. The Fellow Travellers. (rev)
    P. Hollander, 473(PR):Vol56No4-664
Cavaccio, G. Sudori musicali (1626). (I.E. Kreider, ed)
    A. Silbiger, 317:Spring90-172
Cavafy, C.P. The Greek Poems. Collected Poems.
    H. Gifford, 617(TLS):24-30Aug90-887
Cavaglion, A. Felice Momigliano (1866-1924).
    P. Treves, 228(GSLI):Vol166fasc534-307
Cavalcanti, G. The Poetry of Guido Caval-canti.* (L. Nelson, Jr., ed & trans)
    J.H. Levin, 589:Apr89-443
Cavalli-Björkman, G., ed. Bacchanals by Titian and Rubens.
    M.R. Lagerlöf, 341:Vol58No1-29
Cavalli-Björkman, G. Dutch and Flemish Paintings I.
    I.G., 90:Jun89-437
Cavalli-Björkman, G., ed. Netherlandish Mannerism.
    A. Grosjean, 341:Vol58No1-30
Cavallo, A.S. Textiles: Isabella Stewart Gardner Museum.
    M.S., 90:May89-366
Cavallo, G. Libri Scritture Scribi a Ercolano.* (M. Capasso & T. Dorandi, eds)
    P.J. Parsons, 123:Vol39No1-358
Cavallo, G., ed. Le strade del testo.
    M. Winterbottom, 123:Vol39No1-160

Cavallo, G. & H. Maehler. Greek Bookhands of the Early Byzantine Period A.D. 300-800.*
    N.G. Wilson, 123:Vol39No1-127
Cavallo, S. La poética de José Hierro.*
    W.D. Barnette, 240(HR):Autumn89-529
    D. Harris, 86(BHS):Oct89-386
Cave, N. And the Ass Saw the Angel.
    M. Mifflin, 441:30Sep90-28
Cave, R.A. New British Drama in Performance on the London Stage, 1970-1985.
    G. Giesekam, 615(TJ):Oct89-413
    E. Kraft, 397(MD):Dec89-592
Cave, R.A., ed. The Romantic Theatre.*
    M. Hays, 591(SIR):Winter89-665
Cave, R.A. "The White Devil" and "The Duch-ess of Malfi."
    M. Wiggins, 447(N&Q):Sep89-386
Cave, T. Recognitions.*
    C.P. Brand, 557:Sep89-343
    C. Burrow, 175:Summer89-162
    D.F. Connon, 402(MLR):Jul90-672
    P. France, 208(FS):Apr89-235
    S. Rendall, 131(CL):Fall89-378
Cavell, S. Disowning Knowledge in Six Plays of Shakespeare.*
    P. Honan, 447(N&Q):Mar89-101
    G. Monsarrat, 189(EA):Oct-Dec89-467
    R.A. Sharpe, 518:Apr89-119
Cavell, S. In Quest of the Ordinary.*
    C. Dove, 400(MLN):Dec89-1181
    B. Krajewski, 543:Dec89-393
    N. Yousef, 147:Vol6No3-30
Cavell, S. Themes Out of School.
    478(P&L).Apr89-223
Cavell, S. This New Yet Unapproachable America.
    C. Dove, 400(MLN):Dec89-1181
    G. Henderson, 627(UTQ):Spring90-442
Caven, B. Dionysius I
    S. Hornblower, 617(TLS):15-21Jun90-648
Cavillac, C. L'Espagne dans la trilogie "pica-resque" de Lesage.*
    D-H. Pageaux, 549(RLC):Jan-Mar89-119
Cawelti, J.G. & B.A. Rosenberg. The Spy Story.*
    J. Hunter, 639(VQR):Winter89-161
    R.P. Moses, 295(JML):Fall88/Winter89-242
    G. Smith, 677(YES):Vol20-213
Caws, I. The Ragman Totts.
    M. Wormald, 617(TLS):1-7Jun90-584
Caws, M.A. Edmond Jabès.
    S. Hand, 402(MLR):Jul90-750
Caws, M.A. Women of Bloomsbury.
    S. Raitt, 617(TLS):14-20Dec90-1346
Caws, P., ed. The Causes of Quarrel.
    M.H. Lessnoff, 103:Oct90-396
Cazelles, B. & R. Girard, eds. D'une passion l'autre, mélanges offerts à A. Juilland.
    G. Brée, 535(RHL):Nov-Dec89-1080
Céard, J. & J-C. Margolin, eds. Rabelais et son demi-millénaire.
    F. Gray, 551(RenQ):Summer89-346
    K.M. Hall, 402(MLR):Jul90-727
Céard, J. & J-C. Margolin, eds. Voyager à la Renaissance.
    F. Moureau, 535(RHL):Nov-Dec89-1052
de Ceballos, A.R.G. - see under Rodríguez G. de Ceballos, A.
Cèbe, J-P. - see Varro
Cebrián, J.L. The Press and Main Street.
    D. Gilmour, 617(TLS):1-7Jun90-578

Cebrián García, J. La fábula de Marte y Venus de Juan de la Cueva.
R.M. Price, 86(BHS):Apr89-173
Ceccarelli, L. L'allitterazione a vocale interposta variabile in Virgilio.*
J. Soubiran, 555:Vol62Fasc1-165
Cecchetti, D. L'evoluzione del latino umanistico in Francia.*
B. Löfstedt, 545(RPh):Nov89-329
Cecchetti, D. Il primo Umanesimo francese.
A. Buck, 547(RF):Band101Heft2/3-324
Cecchin, G. Americani sul Grappa.
L. Palanca, 456(NDQ):Summer89-254
Cecil, H. & M. Clever Hearts.
A. Ross, 617(TLS):20-26Jul90-770
Cecil, R. A Divided Life.*
639(VQR):Autumn89-124
Cela, C.J. Journey to the Alcarria.
X. Fielding, 617(TLS):12-18Oct90-1108
Cela-Conde, C.J. On Genes, Gods and Tyrants.
M.R., 185:Jan90-443
Celan, P. Poems of Paul Celan.* (rev) (M. Hamburger, ed & trans)
J.M. Cameron, 453(NYRB):18Jan90-3
E. Morgan, 493:Summer89-24
Celeyrette-Pietri, N. & J. Robinson-Valéry – see Valéry, P.
Cellard, J. Ah! ça ira, ça ira ... ces mots que nous devons à la Révolution.
A.J.M. Prévos, 207(FR):Mar90-724
Celsus. Celso, "il discorso vero." (G. Lanata, trans)
A. Meredith, 123:Vol39No1-135
Cendrars, B. Confessions of Dan Yack.
P. Reading, 617(TLS):26Jan-1Feb90-86
Cenkner, W. A Tradition of Teachers.*
E.B. Findly, 318(JAOS):Jan-Mar88-182
"Census of India 1981: Households and Household Population by Language Mainly Spoken in the Household."
T.A. Waldspurger, 350:Sep90-628
Ceragioli, F. – see Campana, D.
Cerdà Massó, R. & others. Diccionario de lingüística.
R. Wright, 86(BHS):Jan89-199
Cerezo, M.D. El obsceno pájaro de la noche.
H.D. Oberhelman, 238:Dec89-969
Cerf, C. & M. Albee, eds. Small Fires.
D. Gurevich, 441:18Nov90-46
Cerquiglini, B. Éloge de la variante.
A.V., 379(MedR):Dec89-474
Cervantes, J.R. & A.V. Walls. Spanish and English Dictionary.
J.J. Rodriguez-Florido, 399(MLJ):Summer89-238
de Cervantes Saavedra, M. Don Quixote de la Mancha.* (T. Smollett, trans)
E.C. Riley, 86(BHS):Apr89-176
de Cervantes Saavedra, M. La Galatea. (J.B. Avalle-Arce, ed)
P.N. Dunn, 240(HR):Summer89-380
Cervigni, D.S. Dante's Poetry of Dreams.
M. Trovato, 276:Autumn89-349
Cesarani, D., ed. The Making of Modern Anglo-Jewry.
B. Wasserstein, 617(TLS):20-26Apr90-426
de Cevallos, M.D.C. – see under Candau de Cevallos, M.D.
Cevasco, G.A. The Sitwells.
M.G.H. Pittock, 677(YES):Vol20-337

"Cézanne: the Early Years 1859-1872."
R.D. Reck, 207(FR):Dec89-388
Chace, J. What We Had.
S. Kenney, 441:17Jun90-6
Chadwick, H. Enfleshings.
R. Cardinal, 617(TLS):12-18Jan90-38
Chadwick, M., D. Long & M. Nissanke. Soviet Oil Exports.
D. Wilson, 575(SEER):Apr89-321
Chadwick, O. Britain and the Vatican during the Second World War.
P. Furlong, 278(IS):Vol43-185
Chadwick, O. Michael Ramsey.
D. Nineham, 617(TLS):16-22Mar90-272
Chadwick, R.F., ed. Ethics, Reproduction and Genetic Control.*
D.J. Shaw, 518:Jan89-45
Chadwick, W. Women, Art and Society.
A. Britton, 324:Sep90-715
C. Darwent, 617(TLS):1-7Jun90-574
Chafets, Z. Devil's Night.
L. Green, 441:11Nov90-9
Chaffee-Sorace, D. Góngora's Poetic Textual Tradition.
D. Garrison, 304(JHP):Autumn89-109
Chahin, M. The Kingdom of Armenia.
T. Braun, 123:Vol39No2-308
Chai, J.C.H. & C-K. Leung, eds. China's Economic Reforms.
J.T.H. Tsao, 293(JASt):May89-348
Chai, L. The Romantic Foundations of the American Renaissance.*
P. Douglass, 677(YES):Vol20-315
M. Jehlen, 301(JEGP):Jul89-457
de Chaisemartin, N. Les Sculptures romaines de Sousse et des Sites Environnants.
R.M. Harrison, 313:Vol79-236
Chaitin, G.J. Algorithmic Information Theory.
P. Gacs, 316:Jun89-624
Chalk, F. & K. Jonassohn. The History and Sociology of Genocide.
P. Carey, 617(TLS):2-8Nov90-1172
Chalkia, I. Lieux et espace dans la tragédie d'Euripide.
E.M. Craik, 303(JoHS):Vol109-230
Chall, J.S., V.A. Jacobs & L.E. Baldwin. The Reading Crisis.
B.E. Cullinan, 441:1Jul90-17
Challinor, R. A Radical Lawyer in Victorian England.
D.J.V. Jones, 617(TLS):6-12Jul90-719
Cham, M.B. & C. Andrade-Watkins, eds. Blackframes.
R. Bell-Metereau, 538(RAL):Fall89-551
Chamay, J. & J-L. Maier. Lysippe et son influence.
F. Ghedini, 229:Band61Heft2-180
Chamberlain, J.T. Latin Antecedents of French Causative "Faire."
J. Ambrose, 207(FR):Mar90-726
Chamberlain, L. In the Communist Mirror.
N. Malcolm, 617(TLS):4-10May90-465
Chamberlain, L. – see Marinetti, F.T.
Chamberland, P. The Courage of Poetry.
S. Simon, 168(ECW):Fall89-104
Chambers, C. The Story of Unity Theatre.*
J. Peter, 441:28Jan90-28
Chambers, F.M. Old Provençal Versification.
G.R. Mermier, 207(FR):Apr90-867
Chambers, G. The Last Man Standing.
A. Clyde, 441:29Apr90-38
Chambers, H., ed. Causley at 70.
W. Magee, 493:Spring89-50

Chambers, H., ed. Peterloo Preview I.*
  D. Kennedy, 493:Summer89-54
Chambers, I. Popular Culture.
  T. Goldie, 102(CanL):Winter88-128
Chambers, R. A Course of Lectures on the
  English Law Delivered at the University of
  Oxford 1767-1773 by Sir Robert Chambers.*
  (T.M. Curley, ed)
  S. Soupel, 189(EA):Apr-Jun89-241
Chambers, R. Mélancolie et Opposition.*
  L. Frappier-Mazur, 210(FrF):May89-248
Chambon, J-P., ed. Französisches Etymol-
  ogisches Wörterbuch. (Vol 25, fasc 149)
  R. Arveiller, 209(FM):Oct89-271
de Chambrun, R. Mes combats pour Pierre
  Laval.
  T. Judt, 617(TLS):28Sep-4Oct90-1018
Champagne, G. - see Evanturel, E.
Champeaux, J. Fortuna.
  G. Radke, 229:Band61Heft1-27
Champlin, T.S. Reflexive Paradoxes.
  H.W. Noonan, 483:Oct89-568
Chan, M. & J. Kassler - see North, R.
Chan, W-T. Chu Hsi.
  S-H. Liu, 485(PE&W):Apr89-211
Chan, W-T. - see Ch'en Ch'un
Chan, W-T. - see "Neo-Confucian Terms
  Explained"
Chancellor, J. Peril and Promise.
  C. Dean, 441:17Jun90-16
  P. Kennedy, 453(NYRB):28Jun90-31
Chandler, A.D., Jr. Scale and Scope.
  R. Heilbroner, 453(NYRB):11Oct90-48
  J. Hughes, 441:6May90-26
  A. Silberston, 617(TLS):19-25Oct90-1135
Chandler, R. & R.B. Parker. Poodle Springs.*
  P. Spenser, 617(TLS):24-30Aug90-903
Chandra, S., ed. The Indian Ocean.
  J.F. Richards, 293(JASt):Aug89-651
Chandra, V. Imperialism, Resistance, and
  Reform in Late Nineteenth-Century Korea.
  M. Robinson, 293(JASt):Aug89-634
Chandrasekhar, S. Truth and Beauty.
  J. Holt, 31(ASch):Summer89-474
Chaney, E. The Grand Tour and the Great
  Rebellion.*
  R. Flannagan, 301:May90-70
Chang, D.W-W. China Under Deng Xiaoping.*
  M.M. Pearson, 293(JASt):Nov89-818
Chang, G.H. Friends and Enemies.
  J.C. Thomson, Jr., 441:29Jul90-25
Chang, H. Chinese Intellectuals in Crisis.*
  D.H. Bays, 318(JAOS):Oct-Dec88-646
Chang, K.C., ed. Studies of Shang Archaeol-
  ogy.*
  V.C. Kane, 293(JASt):Feb89-126
Chang-Rodriguez, E. & R.G. Hellman, eds.
  APRA and the Democratic Challenge in
  Peru.
  T.M. Davies, Jr., 263(RIB):Vol39No2-204
Chang-Rodríguez, R. La apropiación del
  signo.
  R.J. Morris, 238:Sep89-554
Chang-Rodríguez, R. & M.E. Filer. Voces de
  Hispanoamérica.
  J.B. McInnis, 399(MLJ):Autumn89-385
Chant, C. The Encyclopedia of Codenames in
  World War II.
  L.R.N. Ashley, 424:Jun89-191
Chanteur, J. De la Guerre à la paix.
  M. Cranston, 617(TLS):6-12Apr90-377
Chao Tzang Yanghwe. The Shan of Burma.
  N. Tannenbaum, 293(JASt):Aug89-671

Chaplin, A.H. GK: 150 Years of the General
  Catalogue of Printed Books in the British
  Museum.
  C.Y. Ferdinand, 447(N&Q):Jun89-212
Chapman, F.C. Grandmother's House.
  S. Pickering, 569(SR):Spring89-297
Chapman, G. Mosan Art.
  P.M. de Winter, 589:Oct89-930
Chapman, G. The Plays of George Chapman:
  The Tragedies with "Sir Gyles Goose-
  cappe."* (A. Holaday, with G.B. Evans &
  T.L. Berger, eds)
  P. Bement, 541(RES):May89-254
  J. Jowett, 447(N&Q):Mar89-102
Chapman, M., ed. The Drum Decade.
  M. Jaggi, 617(TLS):7-13Dec90-1326
Chapman, M. - see Ardener, E.
Chapman, P. The French Revolution as Seen
  by Madame Tussaud.
  G. Lewis, 617(TLS):26Jan-1Feb90-93
Chappell, F. First and Last Words.
  W.H. Green, 580(SCR):Spring90-142
Chappell, V. & W. Doney, eds. Twenty-five
  Years of Descartes Scholarship, 1960-1984.
  D.A. Cress, 319:Jul90-449
Chapuis, N. - see Qian Zhongshu
Char, R. Eloge d'une soupçonnée.*
  E. Soos, 207(FR):Feb90-574
Charach, R. The Big Life Painting.
  M. Jones, 102(CanL):Summer89-186
Charef, M. Tea in the Harem.
  I. Hill, 617(TLS):13-19Apr90-404
Charents, E. Land of Fire. (D. Der Hovanes-
  sian & M. Margossian, eds & trans) Across
  Two Worlds. (J. Antreassian & M. Margos-
  sian, trans)
  P. Balakian, 29(APR):Jan/Feb89-27
Charle, C. Naissance des "intellectuels",
  1880-1900.
  P. Brooks, 617(TLS):5-11Oct90-1075
Charmé, S.L. Meaning and Myth in the Study
  of Lives.
  P.S. Morris, 323:Oct89-295
Charney, M., ed. "Bad" Shakespeare.*
  A. Leggatt, 570(SQ):Fall89-352
Charney, M. Hamlet's Fictions.
  P. Milton, 447(N&Q):Sep89-392
  A. Leggatt, 551(RenQ):Winter89-886
Chartier, M. & R., eds. Histoire de l'édition
  française. (Vols 3 & 4)
  78(BC):Summer89-153
Charyn, J. The Good Policeman.
  M. Stasio, 441:5Aug90-29
Chase, G. America's Music.* (3rd ed)
  E. Southern, 91:Vol17-191
  J. Tick, 187:Spring/Summer89-325
Chase, J. The Evening Wolves.*
  W. Brandmark, 617(TLS):27Apr-3May90-
  456
Châteaureynaud, G-O. Le jardin dans l'île.
  J. Taylor, 532(RCF):Fall89-214
  J. Taylor, 617(TLS):7-13Sep90-955
Châteaureynaud, G-O. Les Messagers.
  J. Taylor, 617(TLS):7-13Sep90-955
Châtellier, L. The Europe of the Devout.
  A. Hamilton, 617(TLS):29Jun-5Jul90-690
Chatenet, M. Le château de Madrid au bois de
  Boulogne.*
  H. Ballon, 576:Dec89-391
Chatfield, H. Poetry and Love.
  D.B. Hopes, 236:Spring-Summer89-50

67

Chatterjee, R. Aspect and Meaning in Slavic and Indic.
A.R. Wedel, 350:Dec90-860
Chatterji, J.C. Kashmir Shaivaism.
P.E. Muller-Ortega, 318(JAOS):Oct-Dec88-642
Chatterji, S.A. The Indian Women's Search for an Identity.
D. Nag, 293(JASt):Nov89-898
Chattopadhyaya, D. History of Science and Technology in Ancient India - the Beginnings.
L. Rocher, 293(JASt):Nov89-899
Chatwin, B. Utz.*
C. Rooke, 376:Jun89-125
Chaucer, G. The Canterbury Tales.* (D. Wright, ed & trans)
W. Sauer, 38:Band107Heft1/2-190
Chaucer, G. The Legend of Good Women. (A. McMillan, trans)
M.C.E. Shaner, 589:Jul89-681
Chaucer, G. The Physician's Tale.* (H.S. Corsa, ed)
L.Y. Baird-Lange, 589:Oct89-931
J.D. Burnley, 541(RES):Aug89-401
H.C., 382(MAE):1989/1-152
Chaucer, G. The Prioress's Tale.* (B. Boyd, ed)
N.F. Blake, 179(ES):Jun89-271
F.H. Ridley, 589:Jul89-682
Chaucer, G. The Riverside Chaucer.* (3rd ed) (L.D. Benson, ed)
R.P. McGerr, 301(JEGP):Apr89-221
A. Wawn, 402(MLR):Oct89-910
Chaucer, G. Troilus and Criseyde. (R.A. Shoaf, ed)
D. Mehl, 72:Band226Heft1-233
Chaudenson, R. 1989.
A. Valdman, 207(FR):Apr90-906
Chaudhuri, N.C. The Autobiography of an Unknown Indian.
442(NY):5Mar90-107
Chaunu, P. La Liberté.
T. Lecoq, 531:Jan-Mar89-167
Chauveau, J-P., ed. Anthologie de la poésie française du XVIIe siècle.*
F. Nepote-Desmarres, 535(RHL):Jan-Feb89-105
Chauviré, C. Ludwig Wittgenstein.
V. Descombes, 98:Oct89-723
Chauvot, A. Procope de Gaza, Priscien de Césarée, Panégyriques de l'Empereur Anastase Ier.
P. Coyne, 313:Vol79-262
Chavy, P. Traducteurs d'autrefois.
Y. Chevrel, 549(RLC):Apr-Jun89-259
Chawaf, C. Rédemption.
M.F. Nagem, 207(FR):Mar90-743
Chazan, R. European Jewry and the First Crusade.
I.G. Marcus, 589:Jul89-685
Checa, J. Gracián y la imaginación arquitectónica.*
J. Cammarata, 403(MLS):Winter89-89
A. Torres-Alcalá, 552(REH):Jan89-132
Chee, C.H. & O. ul Haq - see Rajaratnam, S.
Cheek, M. Parlor Games.
N. Sonenberg, 441:18Mar90-21
Cheepen, C. The Predictability of Informal Conversation.
S.A. Thompson, 350:Sep90-629

Cheever, J. The Letters of John Cheever.* (B. Cheever, ed)
J.J. Benson, 27(AL):Oct89-465
R. McPhillips, 569(SR):Spring89-293
Chehak, S.T. Harmony.
R.F. Moss, 441:9Dec90-29
Chekhov, A. The Tales of Chekhov. (Vol 13) (C. Garnett, trans) The Unknown Chekhov. (A. Yarmolinsky, trans)
G. Woodcock, 569(SR):Spring89-308
Cheles, L. The Studiolo of Urbino.*
M. Rogers, 278(IS):Vol44-166
Chelotti, M. & others. Le epigrafi romane di Canosa, I.
M.H. Crawford, 123:Vol39No2-353
Ch'en Ch'un. Neo-Confucian Terms Explained (The Pei-hsi tzu-i).* (W-T. Chan, ed & trans)
R.L. Taylor, 318(JAOS):Jul-Sep88-509
Chen Kaige & T. Rayns. King of the Children and The New Chinese Cinema.
N. Tisdall, 364:Oct/Nov89-141
Chen, Y. Images and Ideas in Chinese Classical Prose.
J.M. Hargett, 293(JASt):May89-349
Chen, Y-S. Realism and Allegory in the Early Fiction of Mao Tun.*
T.E. Barlow, 318(JAOS):Jul-Sep88-513
Chênerie, M-L. Le chevalier errant dans les romans arthuriens en vers des douzième et treizième siècles.*
B. Guidot, 547(RF):Band101Heft2/3-319
Chénetier, M. Au-delà du soupçon.
A. Bleikasten, 395(MFS):Winter89-767
Chenevière, A. Russian Furniture; the Golden Age 1780-1840.*
S. Jervis, 90:Oct89-719
Cheney, D.L. & R.M. Seyfarth. How Monkeys See the World.
P.C. Lee, 617(TLS):30Nov-6Dec90-1299
Cheng, C-Y., ed. Sun Yat-sen's Doctrine in the Modern World.
M. Gasster, 293(JASt):Nov89-820
Cheng, F. Souffle-Esprit.
J. Giès, 98:Aug-Sep89-711
Cheng, P.P., ed. Marxism and Capitalism in the People's Republic of China.
J.A. Rapp, 293(JASt):Nov89-821
Chénier, M-J. Jean Calas.* (M. Cook, ed)
S. Davies, 83:Spring89-117
S. Jean-Bérard, 535(RHL):Mar-Apr89-298
Chénieux-Gendron, J. Surrealism.
A. Moszynska, 617(TLS):29Jun-5Jul90-684
Chénieux-Gendron, J. & M-C. Dumas, eds. L'Objet au défi.
M. Sheringham, 208(FS):Oct89-489
Chenu, J. - see Peirce, C.S.
Cherchi, L. La Grammaire anglaise au fil des textes.
J. Lavédrine, 189(EA):Apr-Jun89-199
Cherkasova, N.V. Formirovanie i razvitie advokatury v Rossii: 60-80 gody XIX v.
W.E. Pomeranz, 575(SEER):Jul89-497
Cherniak, C. Minimal Rationality.
S.P. Stich, 486:Mar89-171
Cherniss, M.D. Boethian Apocalypse.*
K. Kerby-Fulton, 677(YES):Vol20-232
E.C. Quinn, 589:Jul89-688
H. White, 382(MAE):1989/1-151

Chernow, R. The House of Morgan.
  J.E. Garten, 441:18Mar90-9
  D.M. Kennedy, 61:Apr90-103
  M. Massing, 617(TLS):10-16Aug90-846
Chernyshevsky, N. What Is to Be Done?
  639(VQR):Autumn89-120
Cheron, F.I. Nemetskii plen i sovetskoe
  osvobozhdenie [together with] Lugin, I.A.
  Polglotka svobody.
  J.A. Armstrong, 550(RusR):Jan89-107
Cherpillod, A. Dictionnaire étymologique des
  noms géographiques.
  A. Room, 424:Mar89-94
Cherrington, D., ed. Candidly Yours ... John
  Cherrington.
  J.M. Stratton, 324:Apr90-372
Cherry, F. Dancing with Strings.
  F. Adcock, 617(TLS):2-8Feb90-123
Cherry, K. My Life and Dr. Joyce Brothers.
  D. Finkle, 441:27May90-14
Chertok, H. We Are All So Close.
  A. Balaban, 390:Nov89-59
Cheselka, P. The Poetry and Poetics of Jorge
  Luis Borges.
  J. King, 86(BHS):Oct89-396
du Chesnay, C-F.G. - see under Guillemay du
  Chesnay, C-F.
Chessman, H.S. The Public is Invited to
  Dance.*
  R. Dubnick, 400(MLN):Dec89-1217
  M.J. Hoffman, 395(MFS):Winter89-746
Chester, G. & S. Nielson, eds. In Other Words.
  G. Creese, 102(CanL):Spring89-217
Chesters, G. Baudelaire and the Poetics of
  Craft.*
  R. Chambers, 210(FrF):May89-245
  C. Scott, 208(FS):Jan89-98
  D. Wood, 242:Vol10No1-85
Chesterton, G.K. The Collected Works of G.K.
  Chesterton. (Vol 15) (A.S. Dale, ed)
  R. Brookhiser, 61:Dec90-127
Chestnut, J.L., Jr. & J. Cass. Black in Selma.
  D. McWhorter, 441:26Aug90-13
Cheung, Y-W. Missionary Medicine in China.
  K. Minden, 293(JASt):May89-350
Cheuse, A. The Light Possessed.
  K. Reed, 441:7Oct90-33
Cheuse, A. The Tennessee Waltz.
  S. Lowell, 441:20May90-20
Chevalier, D., P. Chevalier & P-F. Bertrand.
  Les Tapisseries D'Aubusson et de Felletin.
  (S. Thierry, ed)
  B. Scott, 39:Sep89-210
Chevallier, R. Voyages et déplacements dans
  l'empire romain.
  G. Radke, 229:Band61Heft6-560
Chevassu, F. Faire un film.
  R.J. Nelson, 207(FR):May90-1082
Chevrel, Y., ed. Le Naturalisme en question.*
  L.R. Furst, 678(YCGL):No36-179
  U. Schulz-Buschhaus, 52:Band24Heft2-
  221
Chew, A. Stoicism in Renaissance English
  Literature.
  639(VQR):Autumn89-122
Cheymol, M. Miguel Angel Asturias dans le
  Paris des Années Folles.
  G. Martin, 86(BHS):Jan89-103
Chialant, M.T. & C. Pagetti. La Città e il
  Teatro.
  R.M. Colombo, 402(MLR):Jul90-703

Chiarelli, A. I codici di musica della raccolta
  estense.
  C. Gianturco, 410(M&L):May89-257
Chiarello, C., ed. Right Hemisphere Contribu-
  tions to Lexical Semantics.
  S. Bentin, 348(L&S):Jan-Mar89-69
Chiarini, P., ed. Bausteine zu einem neuen
  Goethe.*
  H.J. Schueler, 564:Nov89-356
Chiarini, P. & H.D. Zimmermann, eds. "Immer
  dicht von dem Sturze..."
  M. Harman, 221(GQ):Summer89-406
Chiba, M. Legal Pluralism.
  T.L. Bryant, 293(JASt):Nov89-798
Chibka, R. A Slight Lapse.
  B. Allen, 441:25Mar90-22
Child, L.M. - see Jacobs, H.A.
Childers, M. Things Undone.
  M. Kirby, 441:2Sep90-16
Childress, M. Tender.
  K. Tucker, 441:23Sep90-12
Childs, V. Lady Hester Stanhope.
  A.W. Masters, 617(TLS):6-12Jul90-718
Childs, W.R. Trucking and the Public Inter-
  est.
  J. Braeman, 106:Summer89-41
Chiles, F. Octavio Paz.*
  C. Cosgrove, 86(BHS):Jul89-314
Chilton, B.D. The Isaiah Targum.
  B.L. Visotzky, 508:Jan89-93
Chilton, P. Orwellian Language and the Me-
  dia.
  E.D. Kuhn, 350:Jun90-411
Chilvers, I. & H. Osborne, with D. Farr - see
  "The Oxford Dictionary of Art"
Chin, F. The Chinaman Pacific and Frisco
  R.R. Co.*
  E. Lesser, 434:Autumn89-98
Chin, T. - see under Tsai Chin
Ch'in-shun, L. - see under Lo Ch'in-shun
Ching, F. Ancestors.
  J. Meskill, 293(JASt):Feb89-128
Ching, J. Probing China's Soul.
  B.D. Sanders, 441:5Aug90-19
Ching, J., with C-Y. Fang & others - see
  Huang Tsung-hsi
Chinn, G. They Worked All Their Lives
  N. Lo Patin, 637(VS):Spring90-500
Chinoy, H.K. & L.W. Jenkins, eds. Women in
  American Theatre. (rev)
  N.C. Barnes, 610:Autumn89-308
  K. Laughlin, 397(MD):Mar89-163
Chinweizu, ed. Voices from Twentieth-Cen-
  tury Africa.*
  K. Ramchand, 49:Jul89-84
Chion, M. La voix au cinéma. Le son au
  cinéma. La toile trouée.
  J. Baetens, 567:Vol74No3/4-353
Chippindale, P. & C. Horrie. Stick It Up Your
  Punter!
  C. Hitchens, 617(TLS):30Nov-6Dec90-
  1285
Chirot, D., ed. The Origins of Backwardness
  in Eastern Europe.
  P. Longworth, 617(TLS):23-29Mar90-306
Chisholm, R.M. Brentano and Intrinsic Value.*
  J.C. Klagge, 482(PhR):Jul89-390
Chisholm, R.M. On Metaphysics.
  J.F.X. Knasas, 543:Jun90-856
Chisholm, R.M. & J.C. Marek - see Brentano,
  F.
Chitham, E. A Life of Emily Brontë.*
  J. Ferns, 541(RES):Nov89-580

Chittick, W.C. – see Tabātabā'i, S.M.H.
Chitty, S. That Singular Person Called Lear.*
639(VQR):Summer89–90
Chiuni, G., ed. Umbria.
S. Gruber, 576:Dec89–403
Chiyo, U. – see under Uno Chiyo
Chloupek, J. & J. Nekvapil, eds. Reader in
Czech Sociolinguistics.
E. Hajičová, 603:Vol13No2–523
J. Hronek, 361:Apr89–377
J. Scharnhorst, 682(ZPSK):Band42Heft3–
399
Cho, O–K. Traditional Korean Theater.
C. Choi, 293(JASt):May89–410
Choat, P. Agents of Influence.
J. Fallows, 453(NYRB):8Nov90–33
Choate, P. Agents of Influence.
J.E. Garten, 441:7Oct90–9
Chocheyras, J. & G.A. Runnalls, eds. La Vie
de Marie Magdaleine par personnages.*
J. Fox, 208(FS):Jan89–76
Chodorow, N.J. Feminism and Psychoanalytic
Theory.
K. Ford, 617(TLS):12–18Jan90–46
S. Schneiderman, 441:21Jan90–12
Ch'oe Soja. Tongsŏ munhwa koryusa yŏn'gu.
J–H.K. Haboush, 293(JASt):Feb89–130
Ch'oe, Y–H. The Civil Examinations and the
Social Structure in the Early Yi Dynasty
Korea: 1392–1600.
F. Kawashima, 293(JASt):Feb89–187
"Choisir la poésie."
C. May, 102(CanL):Spring89–200
Chomarat, J., ed. Prosateurs latins en France
au XVIe siècle.
J. O'Brien, 557:Jun89–221
Chomsky, N. Knowledge of Language.*
E.P. Stabler, Jr., 486:Sep89–533
Chomsky, N. Language and Problems of
Knowledge.
D.W. Hamlyn, 402(MLR):Oct90–889
E.P. Stabler, Jr., 486:Sep89–533
Chomsky, N. La Nouvelle Syntaxe.* (A. Rou-
veret, ed)
A. Azoulay-Vicente, 207(FR):Dec89–419
Chŏngju, S. – see under Sŏ Chŏngju
Chou, C–P. Yüan Hung-tao and the Kung-an
School.
A. Barr, 116:Jul88–188
J. Chaves, 293(JASt):Feb89–131
Chou Fa-kao. Papers in Chinese Linguistics
and Epigraphy.
G.L. Mattos, 318(JAOS):Apr–Jun88–341
Chrétien de Troyes. Guillaume d'Angleterre.*
(A.J. Holden, ed)
S. Gregory, 402(MLR):Oct90–946
Chrétien de Troyes. Yvain. (B. Raffel, trans)
C. Corley, 208(FS):Oct89–454
W.W. Kibler, 545(RPh):May90–623
S. White, 589:Jan89–147
Christen, H. Der Gebrauch von Mundart und
Hochsprache in der Fernsehwerbung.
J. Macha, 685(ZDL):3/1989–374
Christen, H. Sprachliche Variation in der
deutschsprachigen Schweiz.
P. Auer, 685(ZDL):1/1989–104
Christensen, A.P & others – see under Papa-
nicolaou Christensen, A. & others
Christensen, D.E. Hegelian/Whiteheadian
Perspectives.*
G.R. Lucas, Jr., 543:Dec89–394

Christensen, J. Practicing Enlightenment.*
A. Louch, 478(P&L):Apr89–163
A. Morvan, 189(EA):Jan–Mar89–104
J.V. Price, 83:Spring89–104
Christensen, J. & J. From Arnold Schoen-
berg's Literary Legacy.*
J. Dunsby, 410(M&L):Aug89–428
Christian, D., W. Wolfram & N. Dube. Varia-
tion and Change in Geographically Isolated
Communities.
W.N. Francis, 350:Sep90–630
Christiano, K.J. Religious Diversity and
Social Change.
R.D. Cross, 432(NEQ):Jun89–309
Christiansen, E. The Roman Coins of Alexan-
dria.
A.M. Burnett, 123:Vol39No2–349
Christiansen, K., L.B. Kanter & C.B. Strehlke.
Painting in Renaissance Siena: 1420–1500.
M. Mallory & G. Moran, 127:Winter89–353
Christiansen, R. Romantic Affinities.*
N. Miller, 42(AR):Winter89–105
Christianson, C.P. Memorials of the Book
Trade in Medieval London.*
A.I. Doyle, 354:Jun89–155
Christianson, G.E. Fox at the Wood's Edge.
P. Shipman, 441:19Aug90–11
Christie, J. & S. Shuttleworth, eds. Nature
Transfigured.
J.A.V. Chapple, 617(TLS):27Apr–3May90–
452
Christie, J.D. – see Knight, G.W.
Christin, A–M. – see Fromentin, E.
Christine de Pizan. Le livre de la cité des
dames.
C.M. Reno, 589:Jul89–690
Christman, M.C.S. The First Federal Congress,
1789–1791.
J.A. Moore, Jr., 173(ECS):Spring90–353
Christmann, H.H., F–R. Hausmann & M. Brie-
gel, eds. Deutsche und Österreichische
Romanisten als Verfolgte des Nationalsozi-
alismus.
J. Jurt, 358:Feb90–7
Christmas, L. Chopping Down the Cherry
Trees.
F. Cairncross, 617(TLS):9–15Mar90–251
Christol, M. Essai sur l'évolution des car-
rières sénatoriales dans la 2e moitié du IIIe
s. ap. J–C.
J. Nicols, 122:Apr89–170
Christoph, E–M. Studien zur Semantik der
Eigennamen.
W.F.H. Nicolaisen, 424:Mar89–106
Christopher, N. Desperate Characters.
A. Brumer, 441:11Feb90–16
R.B. Shaw, 491:Aug89–283
639(VQR):Winter89–26
Chrystos. Not Vanishing.
J. Gomez, 618:Spring89–82
A. Lerner, 649(WAL):Nov89–266
Chudacoff, H.P. How Old Are You?
R.H. Binstock, 441:18Feb90–36
Chukhontsev, O. Vetrom i peplom.
G.S. Smith, 617(TLS):20–26Apr90–429
Chukovskaya, L. To the Memory of Childhood.
C.R. Pierpont, 442(NY):17Dec90–124
J. Russell, 453(NYRB):15Feb90–12
Ch'un, C. – see under Ch'en Ch'un
Chung, H–K. Interest Representation in So-
viet Policymaking.
A.P. Allison, 550(RusR):Oct89–438
J.C. Moses, 104(CASS):Spring89–99

Chung, N.K. & Nguyen Duc Nghinh – see under
Ngo Kim Chung & Nguyen Duc Nghinh
Churchill, W.S. Savrola.
S. Collini, 617(TLS):17–23Aug90–867
Churchill, W.S. The Story of the Malakand
Field Force. The Boer War. My African
Journey.
N. Bliven, 442(NY):26Mar90–94
Churchland, P.M. A Neurocomputational Per-
spective.
J. Foss, 103:Oct90–399
B. Hannan, 617(TLS):24–30Aug90–892
Churchward, L.G. Soviet Socialism.
S. White, 575(SEER):Jul89–487
Chuvin, P. A Chronicle of the Last Pagans.
C. Kelly, 617(TLS):8–14Jun90–621
Chwastek, S. Pikareske Persönlichkeitsent-
wicklung im spanischen Schelmenroman.
F. Baasner, 72:Band226Heft1–213
A. San Miguel, 547(RF):Band101Heft4–
499
Ciabattari, M. Dreams of an Imaginary New
Yorker Named Rizzoli.
L. Tillman, 441:27May90–5
Ciafardone, R. La "Critica della ragion pura"
nell'Aetas Kantiana.
S. Carboncini, 706:Band21Heft2–213
Ciardi, J. Echos.
D. Wakoski, 219(GaR):Winter89–804
Cibber, C. The Double Gallant. (J.W. Bruton,
ed)
566:Autumn89–78
Cicero. Cato Maior de Senectute. (J.G.F.
Powell, ed)
A.E. Douglas, 313:Vol79–198
E. Fantham, 124:Nov–Dec89–123
N. Horsfall, 123:Vol39No2–227
Cicero. M. Tullius Cicero, Scripta quae man-
serunt omnia. (fasc 22: Oratio pro P.
Sestio.) (T. Maslowski, ed)
K. Wellesley, 123:Vol39No1–36
Cicero. Cicéron, Correspondance. (Vol 9) (J.
Beaujeu, ed & trans)
D.R. Shackleton Bailey, 229:Band61
Heft4–354
Cicero. De Legibus I. (N. Rudd & T. Wiede-
mann, eds)
J.G.F. Powell, 123:Vol39No2–225
Cicero. Philippics.* (D.R. Shackleton Bailey,
ed & trans)
A. Vassileiou, 555:Vol62Fasc2–364
Cicero. Verrines.* (Vol 2, Pt 1) (T.N. Mitch-
ell, ed & trans)
A. Smith, 235:Winter88–64
Cicurel, F., E. Pedoya & R. Porquier. Commu-
niquer en français.
L.K. Martin, 399(MLJ):Autumn89–357
Cienkowska-Schmidt, A. Sehnsucht nach dem
Heiligen Land.
L. Thompson, 562(Scan):Nov89–211
Ciesielski, Z. Od Fredry do Różewicza.
R. Kejzlar, 562(Scan):Nov89–198
Ciocchetti, M., ed. Milano Sera (1945–1954).
R. Pickering-Iazzi, 276:Winter89–451
Ciochon, R., J. Olsen & J. James. Other Ori-
gins.
J.N. Wilford, 441:14Oct90–11
Cipriani, G. Sallustio e l'immaginario.
G.M. Paul, 123:Vol39No2–233
de Ciria, E.C. & J.M. Díaz de Guereñu – see
under Cordero de Ciria, E. & J.M. Díaz de
Guereñu

Citati, P. Kafka.
L. Klepp, 441:4Mar90–24
G. Steiner, 442(NY):28May90–107
Citroen, K.A. Haarlemse Zilversmeden en Hun
Merken.
A. Grimwade, 39:Nov89–359
Citron, M.J. – see Hensel, F.
Citron, P. Giono 1895–1970.
W. Redfern, 617(TLS):21–27Sep90–1006
Citron, P. – see Mallarmé, S.
"Città italiane del '500 tra Riforma e Contro-
riforma."
S. Cohn, Jr., 551(RenQ):Autumn89–557
Citti, P. Contre la décadence.
D. Millet-Gérard, 549(RLC):Jul–Sep89–
420
Citti, V. & others. An Index to the "Antho-
logia Graeca," "Anthologia Palatina" and
"Planudea." (fasc 2)
P.A. Hansen, 123:Vol39No2–386
"City Souvenir."
G. Gessert, 448:Vol27No3–126
Clabburn, P. The National Trust Book of Fur-
nishing Textiles.*
C. McCorquodale, 39:Jun89–442
Clahsen, H. Normale und gestörte Kinder-
sprache.
J. Tesak, 350:Dec90–861
Claiborne, C. The New York Times Cook Book.
(rev)
E. Tait, 441:10Jun90–12
Claiborne, R. Loose Cannons and Red Her-
rings.
40(AH)/Winter90–113
Clampitt, A. Westward.
D. Kirby, 441:23Dec90–16
Clampitt, A. – see Donne, J.
Clandfield, D. Canadian Film.
S. Feldman, 627(UTQ):Fall89–250
de Claramonte, A. "El burlador de Sevilla."*
(A. Rodríguez López-Vázquez, ed)
J.M. Ruano de la Haza, 402(MLR):Apr90–
471
de Claramonte, A. La infelice Dorotea. (C.
Ganelin, ed)
H. Cazorla, 238:Sep89–542
F.A. De Armas, 140(CH):Vol11No1&2–115
J.A. Drinkwater, 402(MLR):Jul90–764
R.L. Fiore, 304(JHP):Winter89–167
Clare, J. John Clare and the Bounds of Cir-
cumstance.*
E. Robinson, 591(SIR):Winter89–660
Clare, J. Selected Letters. (M. Storey, ed)
617(TLS):23Feb–1Mar90–204
Clarenbach, K.F. & E.L. Kamarck, eds. The
Green Stubborn Bud.
E. Lauter, 662:Spring/Summer89–45
Lord Clarendon. Two Dialogues.
J. Egan, 568(SCN):Spring–Summer89–12
Clark, A., ed. Anthologie Mitterrand.
J. Howorth, 208(FS):Jul89–371
Clark, A. Microcognition.
A. Smith, 617(TLS):9–15Mar90–259
Clark, C. The Vulgar Rabelais.
G. Jondorf, 208(FS):Oct89–458
Clark, C.E., J.S. Leamon & K. Bowden, eds.
Maine in the Early Republic.
G.E. Kershaw, 656(WMQ):Oct89–832
I.M.G. Quimby, 658:Winter89–269
Clark, E.A. Ascetic Piety and Women's Faith.
G. Clark, 313:Vol79–259
Clark, F. The Pseudo-Gregorian Dialogues.
C. Straw, 589:Apr89–397

Clark, G. The Eccentric Teapot.
139:Dec89/Jan90–24
Clark, H.N.B. Francis W. Edmonds.
S. Burns, 658:Winter89–276
S. Webster, 127:Spring89–99
Clark, I. Waging War.
J.W.C., 185:Apr90–716
D.A. Hoekema, 518:Jul89–180
Clark, J. The Victory of Geraldine Gull.
P. Lougheed, 198:Winter89–120
C. Rooke, 376:Jun89–126
Clark, J.P.H. & C. Taylor – see Hilton, W.
Clark, K. & M. Holquist. Mikhail Bakhtin.*
R.D. Abrahams, 292(JAF):Apr–Jun89–202
F. Stockholder, 104(CASS):Spring–Winter88–502
Clark, L.D. A Charge of Angels.
R.B. Melendez, 649(WAL):Feb90–396
Clark, L.D. – see Lawrence, D.H.
Clark, M. Dos Passos's Early Fiction, 1912–1938.*
P.R.J., 295(JML):Fall88/Winter89–315
Clark, M. Jacques Lacan.
W. Ver Eecke, 543:Jun90–857
Clark, N. Melozzo da Forli. (A. Lillie & D. Brown, with others, eds)
C. Hope, 617(TLS):1–7Jun90–574
Clark, P. Chinese Cinema.
C. Mackerras, 293(JASt):May89–352
Clark, P.P. Literary France.*
F.W.J. Hemmings, 208(FS):Apr89–239
C.L. Lloyd, 345(KRQ):Nov89–492
Clark, R.W. Lenin.*
639(VQR):Summer89–88
Clark, S.L., ed. C.P.E. Bach Studies.
B. Harrison, 410(M&L):Nov89–537
K. Komlos, 415:Nov89–679
Clark, S.R.L. Civil Peace and Sacred Order.
J.M. Cameron, 617(TLS):16–22Mar90–295
Clark, T.J. The Painting of Modern Life.
P.H. Salus, 567:Vol75No3/4–357
Clark, W.W. Courtauld Institute Illustration Archives: Laon Cathedral Architecture. (Vol 2)
N.C., 90:Feb89–161
Clarke, A.C. Astounding Days.
M.G. Butler, 441:6May90–22
Clarke, A.C. & G. Benford. Beyond the Fall of Night.
G. Jonas, 441:8Jul90–22
Clarke, D.M. Occult Powers and Hypotheses.*
E. van Leeuwen, 543:Mar90–625
Clarke, D.S., Jr. Principles of Semiotic.
B.A. Beatie, 350:Mar90–186
H. Bredin, 89(BJA):Spring89–186
H. Laycock, 529(QQ):Summer89–524
Clarke, D.S., Jr. Rational Acceptance and Purpose.
C. Misak, 103:Feb90–52
Clarke, E. & R. Bencini. The Gardens of Tuscany.
L. Yang, 441:2Dec90–21
Clarke, E. & L.S. Jacyna. Nineteenth-Century Origins of Neuroscientific Concepts.
A. Scull, 637(VS):Spring90–503
Clarke, G., ed. The American City.
J. Hurt, 402(MLR):Oct90–937
Clarke, G. Capote.
42(AR):Winter89–107
Clarke, G. T.S. Eliot.
A.P. Frank, 675(YER):Spring90–84

Clarke, H. Vergil's "Aeneid" and Fourth ("Messianic") "Eclogue" in the Dryden Translation.
A. Sherbo, 566:Spring90–211
Clarke, M. Healing Song.
P. Lougheed, 198:Winter89–120
Clarke, M. & C. Crisp. Ballerina.
M. McQuade, 151:Sep89–56
Clarke, P. Pen Portraits.
S. Sheridan, 71(ALS):May89–118
Clarke, S.G. & E. Simpson, eds. Anti-Theory in Ethics and Moral Conservatism.
D.M., 185:Jul90–907
Clarke, T. Equator.*
S. Pickering, 569(SR):Spring89–297
Clarke, W.M. The Secret Life of Wilkie Collins.
S. Mitchell, 637(VS):Winter90–344
Clarke, W.N. The Universe as Journey. (G.A. McCool, ed)
P. Madigan, 543:Sep89–149
Clarysse, W. & G. Van der Veken, with S.P. Vleeming. The Eponymous Priests of Ptolemaic Egypt.
H. Heinen, 229:Band61Heft6–557
Clasen, W.C–W. & G. Lehnert–Rodiek, eds. Zei(t)räume.
R. Borgmeier, 52:Band24Heft1–103
Classe, O. – see Pradon, J.
Classen, A. Zur Rezeption norditalienischer Kultur des Trecento im Werk Oswalds von Wolkenstein (1376/77–1445).*
F. Delbono, 684(ZDA):Band118Heft4–173
Classen, C.J. Recht–Rhetorik–Politik.
D.H. Berry, 313:Vol79–198
Claude, J. – see Gide, A. & J. Copeau
Claudel, P. Oeuvres complètes. (Vol 29)
D. Millet-Gérard, 535(RHL):Mar–Apr89–324
Claus, H. The Sorrow of Belgium.
S. Ruta, 441:1Jul90–6
R. Todd, 617(TLS):29Jun–5Jul90–704
Clausen, M.L. Frantz Jourdain and the Samaritaine.
A. Willis, 576:Mar89–86
Clausen, W. Virgil's "Aeneid" and the Tradition of Hellenistic Poetry.*
K. Galinsky, 24:Spring89–171
P.R. Hardie, 122:Oct89–354
S.J. Harrison, 313:Vol79–204
Clausing, G. & L. Rings. Deutsch natürlich!
J.L. Cox, 399(MLJ):Winter89–513
Claussen, P.C. Magistri doctissimi Romani.
D.F. Glass, 589:Apr89–399
Clavaud, R. – see Demosthenes
Clay, D. Lucretius and Epicurus.
P.H. Schrijvers, 394:Vol42fasc1/2–218
Clay, M. & K. Lehrer, eds. Knowledge and Skepticism.
P.K. Moser, 103:Nov90–447
Clayton, J. Romantic Vision and the Novel.*
J. Loesberg, 340(KSJ):Vol38–188
K. Shabetai, 141:Summer89–304
G. Smith, 677(YES):Vol20–213
Clayton, L. Ranch Rodeos in West Texas.
K.W. Davis, 649(WAL):May89–90
Cleary, A.S.E. The Ending of Roman Britain.
P. Salway, 617(TLS):23–29Mar90–329
Cleary, J. Babylon South.
M. Stasio, 441:7Jan90–29
Cleary, J.J., ed. Proceedings of the Boston Area Colloquium in Ancient Philosophy.* (Vol 1)
D.K. Glidden, 449:Dec89–711

Cleary, J.J., ed. Proceedings of the Boston Area Colloquium in Ancient Philosophy.* (Vol 3)
 A. Smith, 235:Winter88-74
Cleary, J.J. & D.C. Shartin, eds. Proceedings of the Boston Area Colloquium in Ancient Philosophy. (Vol 4)
 M. Deslauriers, 103:Feb90-54
 B. Inwood, 235:Winter89-75
Cleary, T. - see "The Buddhist I Ching"
Cleary, T. - see "The Taoist I Ching"
Clein, W. Concepts of Chivalry in "Sir Gawain and the Green Knight."
 I. Bishop, 447(N&Q):Dec89-493
 E. Wilson, 541(RES):May89-247
Clemen, W. Shakespeare's Soliloquies.
 J. Rees, 447(N&Q):Mar89-99
 K. Smidt, 179(ES):Apr89-179
 U. Suerbaum, 156(ShJW):Jahrbuch1989-374
 D.K. Weiser, 541(RES):Nov89-556
Clément, C. Opera, or the Undoing of Women.*
 S.C. Cook, 414(MusQ):Vol74No3-445
 A. Koek, 511:Jun89-46
 J.K. Law, 465:Summer90-137
 42(AR):Summer89-370
Clément, M. Nekuia ou le chant des morts.
 P. Haeck, 102(CanL):Spring89-204
Clements, P. Baudelaire and the English Tradition.*
 R.P. Poggenburg, 535(RHL):Jan-Feb89-143
Cleminson, R., comp. The Anno Pomilington Catalogue.
 C. Roberts, 402(MLR):Jan90-266
Clemo, J. Selected Poems.
 J. Greening, 493:Spring89-55
Clemoes, P. & others, eds. Anglo-Saxon England.* (Vol 14)
 J. Hill, 38:Band107Heft1/2-136
Clendinen, D., ed. The Prevailing South.
 E.C. Lynskey, 585(SoQ):Spring90-116
Clewlow, C. Keeping the Faith.
 F. Wilson, 441:11Mar90-19
Clibbon, E.B., ed. The Best of British Corporate Identity and Design.
 P. Gorb, 324:Jan90-140
Cliff, M. Bodies of Water.
 L. Doughty, 617(TLS):23Feb-1Mar90-203
 D. Durrant, 364:Feb/Mar90-133
 E. Nunez-Harrell, 441:23Sep90-22
Clifford, C. & T. Pilkington, eds. Range Wars.
 C.M. Wright, 649(WAL):Nov89-281
Clifford, J. Maurice Leenhardt.
 D. Merllié, 542:Oct.-Dec89-592
Clifford, J. The Predicament of Culture.*
 D. Halle, 658:Winter89-299
 G. Lienhardt, 617(TLS):19-25Jan90-68
 K. McGill, 292(JAF):Oct-Dec89-485
Clifford, S. The Red-Haired Woman.
 J.F. Clarity, 441:8Jul90-16
Clifton, L. Good Woman.*
 D. Plant, 502(PrS):Spring89-115
Clive, J. Not by Fact Alone.
 J.W. Burrow, 617(TLS):2-8Feb90-125
 G. Himmelfarb, 441:11Mar90-16
Clodfelter, M. The Limits of Air Power.*
 J. Mirsky, 453(NYRB):16Aug90-29
Clough, A.H. The Oxford Diaries of Arthur Hugh Clough. (A. Kenny, ed)
 N. Shrimpton, 617(TLS):31Aug-6Sep90-912

Cloughly, C.P., J.G.L. Burnby & M.P. Earles - see Pereira, J.
Cloutier, G. Entrée en matière(s).
 N.B. Bishop, 627(UTQ):Fall89-211
Clowes, E.W. Maksim Gorky.*
 G. McVay, 575(SEER):Jul89-455
Clowes, E.W. The Revolution of Moral Consciousness.
 T.G. Marullo, 395(MFS):Winter89-836
 S.J. Rabinowitz, 104(CASS):Spring-Winter88-463
Clunas, C. Chinese Furniture.
 S. Markbreiter, 60:Jul-Aug89-134
 M. Medley, 463:Autumn89-172
Cmiel, K. Democratic Eloquence.
 H. Rawson, 441:26Aug90-10
Coakley, J.A. - see Behn, A.
Coales, J., ed. The Earliest English Brasses.*
 J.E. Powell, 39:Apr89-292
Coarelli, F. I santuari del Lazio in età repubblicana.
 J. Scheid, 313:Vol79-180
 T.P. Wiseman, 229:Band61Heft3-278
Cobb, R. The People's Armies.*
 A.J. Hayter, 83:Autumn89-205
Cobb, R. & C. Jones, eds. Voices of the French Revolution.*
 J.P. Gilroy, 207(FR).Apr90-916
Cobban, A.B. The Medieval English Universities.*
 D. Leader, 551(RenQ):Winter89-826
Cobo-Borda, J.G., ed. José Asunción Silva.
 L.M. Umphrey, 263(RIB):Vol39No1-70
Cocker, M. Richard Meinertzhagen.*
 J. Wilson, 364:Jun/Jul89-143
Cocks, R.C.J. Sir Henry Maine.*
 A. Horstman, 637(VS):Summer90-660
Cocteau, J. Souvenir Portraits.
 442(NY):3Sep90-108
Coddou, M. Para leer a Isabel Allende.
 D.L. Heyck, 238:Dec89-971
Code, L. Epistemic Responsibility.*
 E. Fricker, 393(Mind):Jul89-457
 A. Gallois, 63:Jun89-256
Codignola, L. The Coldest Harbour of the Land.
 J.G. Reid, 656(WMQ):Jan89-174
Codoñer Merino, C. Evolución del concepto de historiografía en Roma.*
 J.M. Alonso-Núñez, 229:Band61Heft1-69
Codrescu, A. American Poetry Since 1970: Up Late.
 R. McDowell, 249(HudR):Winter89-600
 W. Marsh, 466(NDQ):Spring89-194
Coe, J. The Dwarves of Death.
 M. Casserley, 617(TLS):27Jul-2Aug90-804
Coetzee, F. For Party or Country.
 A. Sykes, 617(TLS):2-8Nov90-1170
Coetzee, J.M. Age of Iron.
 G. Annan, 453(NYRB):8Nov90-8
 P. Reading, 617(TLS):28Sep-4Oct90-1037
 L. Thornton, 441:23Sep90-7
Coetzee, J.M. White Writing.*
 S. Gray, 538(RAL):Summer89-304
 R. Smith, 529(QQ):Autumn89-739
Coffey, M. Great Plains Patchwork.
 F. Handman, 441:25Mar90-23
Cogan, T.J., ed & trans. The Tale of the Soga Brothers.*
 M.H. Childs, 293(JASt):Feb89-154
 L. Kominz, 244(HJAS):Jun89-244

Coger, G.M.K., comp. Index of Subjects, Prov-
erbs, and Themes in the Writings of Wole
Soyinka.
  J. Gibbs, 538(RAL):Fall89-512
Coghill, N. The Collected Papers of Nevill
Coghill.* (D. Gray, ed)
  H. Cooper, 447(N&Q):Jun89-226
Cogny, P. - see Huysmans, J-K.
Cohan, S. & L.M. Shires. Telling Stories.
  U. Margolin, 599:Summer90-330
  J.A. Varsava, 268(IFR):Summer90-136
Cohen, A.A. Artists & Enemies.*
  S. Pinsker, 287:Jan-Feb89-31
Cohen, B-F. Elie Wiesel.
  J. Kolbert, 207(FR):Apr90-885
Cohen, C.B., ed. Casebook on the Termination
of Life-sustaining Treatment and the Care
of the Dying.
  L.L.H., 185:Oct89-228
Cohen, D. Being a Man.
  R. Porter, 617(TLS):1-7Jun90-589
Cohen, D. Shakespearean Motives.
  A. Leggatt, 570(SQ):Spring89-102
Cohen, F.G. The Poetry of Christian Hofmann
von Hofmannswaldau.*
  A. Classen, 597(SN):Vol61No2-244
Cohen, G. & J. O'Connor, eds. Fighting
Toxics.
  N. Wade, 441:22Apr90-1
Cohen, G.A. History, Labour, and Freedom.*
  W.H. Shaw, 262:Dec89-437
Cohen, G.L. Pursuit of Linguistic Insight.
  R. Anttila, 350:Jun90-412
Cohen, H. & T.P. Coffin, eds. The Folklore of
American Holidays.
  S. Samuelson, 292(JAF):Apr-Jun89-244
Cohen, I.B. Benjamin Franklin's Science.
  E. Wright, 441:30Sep90-15
Cohen, I.B. The Newtonian Revolution.
  D. Fallon, 568(SCN):Fall-Winter89-56
Cohen, J. Max Lakeman and the Beautiful
Stranger.
  M-A.T. Smith, 441:13May90-24
Cohen, J.L. The New Chinese Painting: 1949-
1986.
  E.J. Laing, 293(JASt):Feb89-133
Cohen, J.S. Cowtown Moderne.
  S. Gutterman, 45:Sep89-59
  R. Striner, 658:Winter89-297
Cohen, L.J. The Dialogue of Reason.
  E. Eells, 482(PhR):Jan89-118
  G. Helman, 480(P&R):Vol22No1-78
Cohen, M. Engaging English Art.*
  M.C. Brennan, 577(SHR):Summer89-288
  H. Sussman, 566:Spring89-189
Cohen, M. Living on Water.*
  K. McNeilly, 529(QQ):Autumn89-717
Cohen, M. Nadine.*
  J. Lennox, 168(ECW):Spring89-127
Cohen, M.A. Poet and Painter.*
  R.S. Kennedy, 295(JML):Fall88/Winter89-
  310
Cohen, M.G. Women's Work, Markets, and Eco-
nomic Development in Nineteenth-Century
Ontario.
  S. Tillotson, 529(QQ):Summer89-559
Cohen, M.N. Health and the Rise of Civiliza-
tion.
  A. Wear, 617(TLS):23Feb-1Mar90-191
Cohen, M.N. & A. Gandolfo, eds. Lewis Carroll
and the House of Macmillan.*
  G.J. Worth, 635(VPR):Spring89-42

Cohen, M.P. The History of the Sierra Club
1892-1970.
  A. Ronald, 649(WAL):Aug89-157
Cohen, R. Diary of a Flying Man.
  E. Weiner, 441:25Feb90-25
Cohen, R., ed. New Literary History Interna-
tional Bibliography of Literary Theory and
Criticism (1984-1985).
  D.B. Downing, 40(AEB):Vol3No2-78
  R.E. Hegel, 116:Jul88-198
Cohen, R. The Organ Builder.
  42(AR):Winter89-115
Cohen, R.S., R.M. Martin & M. Westphal, eds.
Studies in the Philosophy of J.N. Findlay.
  J. Prabhu, 485(PE&W):Jan89-96
Cohen, R.S. & T. Schnelle, eds. Cognition and
Fact.
  D.Z., 185:Jan90-454
Cohen, S. Dodgers!
  R. Siegel, 441:1Apr90-18
Cohen, S. & N. Taub, eds. Reproductive Laws
for the 1990s.
  N.D., 185:Apr90-713
  H.B. Holmes, 254:Fall89-150
Cohen, S.B., ed. Jewish Wry.
  M.D.O., 295(JML):Fall88/Winter89-194
Cohen, S.F. & K. vanden Heuvel. Voices of
Glasnost.*
  D. Lieven, 617(TLS):15-21Jun90-632
Cohen, S.P., ed. The Security of South Asia.
  S.D. Muni, 293(JASt):May89-419
Cohen, T. Remaking Japan.* (H. Passin, ed)
  P.K. Frost, 293(JASt):Feb89-155
Cohen, W. Drama of a Nation.
  E.H. Friedman, 149(CLS):Vol26No4-362
Cohen de Herrera, A. Puerta del cielo. (K.
Krabbenhoft, ed)
  L. López-Baralt, 240(HR):Spring89-235
  T. Oelman, 86(BHS):Jul89-282
  R.H. Popkin, 319:Apr90-293
Cohler, A.M. Montesquieu's Comparative Pol-
itics and the Spirit of American Constitu-
tionalism.*
  J. Black, 173(ECS):Spring90-343
Cohn, B.S. An Anthropologist Among the His-
torians and Other Essays.
  F.F. Conlon, 293(JASt):Aug89-647
Cohn, D.J., ed & trans. Vignettes from the
Chinese.
  R.E. Hegel, 116:Jul88-199
Cohn, J. Romance and the Erotics of Prop-
erty.*
  S. Felton, 27(AL):Mar89-148
Cohn, R., ed. Beckett: "Waiting for Godot."
  J. Kalb, 397(MD):Dec89-588
  J. Pilling, 447(N&Q):Mar89-127
  J. Rudlin, 402(MLR):Jan90-202
Cohn, R. From "Desire" to "Godot."*
  R.N.C., 295(JML):Fall88/Winter89-261
Cohn, R.G. Mallarmé's Prose Poems.*
  P. Dayan, 208(FS):Apr89-223
Cohn, S.K., Jr. Death and Property in Siena,
1205-1800.*
  T. Astarita, 551(RenQ):Winter89-833
Coiro, A.B. Robert Herrick's "Hesperides" and
the Epigram Book Tradition.
  M.G. Brennan, 447(N&Q):Dec89-507
  M.T. Crane, 551(RenQ):Summer89-363
  C.J. Summers, 191(ELN):Mar90-80
Coker, C. NATO, the Warsaw Pact and Africa.
  M. Chorośnicki, 497(PolR):Vol34No3-268
Colacello, B. Holy Terror.
  P. Taylor, 441:26Aug90-6

Colapietro, V.M. Peirce's Approach to the Self.
H. Joswick, 619:Fall89–549
Colbeck, N., comp. A Bookman's Catalogue.* (T. Bose, ed)
I. Fletcher, 177(ELT):Vol32No2–223
517(PBSA):Mar89–110
Colby, W., with J. McCarger. Lost Victory.*
J. Mirsky, 453(NYRB):16Aug90–29
Coldewey, J.C. & B.F. Copenhaver, eds. Thomas Watson: Antigone; William Alabaster: Roxana; Peter Mease: Adrastus Parentans Sive Vindicta.
G. Eatough, 123:Vol39No1–129
R. Green, 447(N&Q):Dec89–498
Cole, D. & B. Lockner – see Dawson, G.M.
Cole, D.B. & J.J. McDonough – see French, B.B.
Cole, H. Malcolm Arnold.
M. Anderson, 607:Dec89–42
W. Sutton, 415:Dec89–748
Cole, J.R.I. Roots of North Indian Shi'ism in Iran and Iraq.
M.H. Fisher, 293(JASt):Nov89–901
Cole, R.C. Irish Booksellers and English Writers 1740–1800.*
A. O'Day, 517(PBSA):Jun89–244
Colegate, I. Deceits of Time.*
639(VQR):Summer89–93
Coleman, D. Coleridge and "The Friend" (1809–1810).
M. Lofobure, 661(WC):Autumn89–179
639(VQR):Autumn89–122
Coleman, D.G. & G. Jondorf, eds. Words of Power.
C. Robinson, 208(FS):Jul89–364
Coleman, F.X.J. Neither Angel nor Beast.*
D. Fouke, 449:Mar89–115
Coleman, J.D. Pleiku.
639(VQR):Spring89–62
Coleman, J.E., with K. Abramovitz. Excavations at Pylos in Elis.*
V. Mitsopoulos-Leon, 229:Band61Heft3–275
Coleman, K.M. – see Statius
Coleman, P. Gay Christians.
A. Macgregor, 617(TLS):9–15Mar90–260
Coleman, S.S. & M.J. Preston. A KWIC Concordance to John Cleland's "Memoirs of a Woman of Pleasure."
A. Hammond, 166:Oct89–86
Coleman, V. The Last Exquisite.
H. Carpenter, 617(TLS):21–27Dec90–1368
Coleman, W. Heavy Daughter Blues.
S. Foster, 448:Vol27No3–157
Coleman, W. A War of Eyes and Other Stories.
G. Locklin, 573(SSF):Spring89–200
Coleridge, S.T. Carnets. (P. Leyris, trans)
S. Rappaport, 450(NRF):Apr89–109
Coleridge, S.T. Coleridge's "Dejection."* (S.M. Parrish, ed)
E. Birdsall, 40(AEB):Vol3No1–26
G. Dekker, 661(WC):Autumn89–175
M. Everest, 402(MLR):Jan90–150
Coleridge, S.T. The Collected Works of Samuel Taylor Coleridge.* (Vol 5: Lectures 1808–1819: On Literature.) (R.A. Foakes, ed)
J. Engell, 405(MP):Feb90–313
J.R.D. Jackson, 661(WC):Autumn89–173
J.R. Watson, 506(PSt):Sep89–195
Coleridge, S.T. Selected Letters.* (H.J. Jackson, ed)
D. Degrois, 189(EA):Jul–Sep89–348

Coles, B. & J. People of the Wetlands.
F. Pryor, 617(TLS):19–25Jan90–72
Coles, D. K. in Love.
C. Levenson, 529(QQ):Summer89–531
Coles, R. The Call of Stories.*
E.L. Galligan, 569(SR):Fall89–cxxiii
S. Pinsker, 219(GaR):Summer89–395
Coles, R. The Red Wheelbarrow.
E.L. Galligan, 569(SR):Fall89–cxxiii
639(VQR):Spring89–46
Coles, R. The Spiritual Life of Children.
M. Gordon, 441:25Nov90–1
Coles, R. Time of Surrender.*
E.L. Galligan, 569(SR):Fall89–cxxiii
Coles, R.A., H. Maehler & P.J. Parsons, eds. The Oxyrhynchus Papyri. (Vol 54)
W. Luppe, 123:Vol39No1–124
Coles, W.E., Jr. The Plural I – and After. Seeing Through Writing.
K. Flachmann, 126(CCC):Oct89–357
Coletti, T. Naming the Rose.
B.M., 494:Winter89–851
M. Viegnes, 395(MFS):Summer89–362
Coley, W.B. – see Fielding, H.
Colin, A.D., ed. Argumentum e Silentio.
K. Weissenberger, 133:Band22Heft3/4–361
Colish, M. The Stoic Tradition from Antiquity to the Early Middle Ages.
B. Inwood, 41:Fall89–337
Coll, A.M. – see under Martín y Coll, A.
Collcutt, M., M. Jansen & I. Kumakura. Cultural Atlas of Japan.
M. Cooper, 407(MN):Autumn89–389
Coller, B., J.E. Gedo & D. Kuspit. The Artist's Mother.
B. Collins, Jr., 662:Spring/Summer89–41
Collet, A. Stendhal et Milan.*
K.G. McWatters, 535(RHL):Nov–Dec89–1063
L.R. Wilkinson, 546(RR):Mar89–325
Collett, B. Italian Benedictine Scholars and the Reformation.
D.S. Chambers, 278(IS):Vol43–141
Collette, J-Y. Perspectives.
J. Le Blanc, 102(CanL):Autumn–Winter89–268
Colley, L. Lewis Namier.*
K. Thomas, 453(NYRB):14Jun90–46
Collie, J. & S. Slater. Literature in the Language Classroom.
L.K. Penrod, 399(MLJ):Autumn89–342
Collie, M. Henry Maudsley.
D. Leigh, 78(BC):Winter89–549
Collier, D.G. The Invisible Women of Washington.
L. Wevers, 102(CanL):Spring89–181
Collier, J.L. Duke Ellington.
R.S. Clark, 249(HudR):Spring89–101
R. Handler, 639(VQR):Spring89–270
Collier, J.L. The Reception of Jazz in America.
L. Gushee, 187:Spring/Summer89–352
Collier, M. The Clasp and Other Poems.
J. Parini, 473(PR):Vol56No3–510
Collier, P. Proust and Venice.
G. Josipovici, 617(TLS):26Jan–1Feb90–84
Collin, F. Theory and Understanding.
P. Pettit, 482(PhR):Apr89–266
Collingwood, R.G. Essays in Political Philosophy. (D. Boucher, ed)
S. Blackburn, 617(TLS):6–12Apr90–370

Collini, S. Arnold.*
  S. Monod, 402(MLR):Jan90–156
  J.J. Savory, 637(VS):Spring90–509
  H.W, 636(VP):Summer89–220
Collini, S. – see Mill, J.S.
Collins, B. The Apple that Astonished Paris.*
  D. Allen, 249(HudR):Summer89–326
Collins, C. Sachiko's Wedding.
  J. Loose, 617(TLS):14–20Dec90–1360
Collins, D. The Story of Kodak.
  A. Grundberg, 441:2Dec90–71
Collins, G. & R. Sandell. Women, Art and Ed-
ucation.
  L. Petrovich-Mwaniki, 709:Fall89–62
Collins, H.M. Changing Order.*
  C. Bazerman, 488:Mar89–115
Collins, J. Lady Boss.
  J. Gerston, 441:30Sep90–37
Collins, J. E.T. Mensah.
  B. King, 538(RAL):Summer89–281
Collins, J. Winifred Nicholson.
  R.K. Tarbell, 662:Fall89/Winter90–52
Collins, J. Uncommon Cultures.
  B. Rotman, 617(TLS):6–12Apr90–379
Collins, L. Studies in Characterization in the
"Iliad."
  L.E. Doherty, 124:Mar–Apr90–372
  M.M. Willcock, 123:Vol39No2–380
Collins, M. Mission to Mars.
  R. Bazell, 441:9Dec90–11
Collins, M.S. Pío Baroja's "Memorias de un
hombre de acción" and the Ironic Mode.
  J. Alberich, 86(BHS):Jul89–294
  C.A. Longhurst, 402(MLR):Jul90–769
Collins, P., ed. Thinking about South Africa.
  L. Thompson, 617(TLS):1–7Jun90–579
Collins, R. The Arab Conquest of Spain.
  P. Linehan, 617(TLS):2–8Feb90–126
Collins, R. Satellite TV in Western Europe.
  J. Thompson, 324:Aug90–642
Collins, R.G. E.J. Pratt.
  S.E. Billingham, 529(QQ):Autumn89–735
  J.M. Kertzer, 105:Spring/Summer89–86
"Collins COBUILD English Language Dictio-
nary."* (J. Sinclair, ed-in-chief)
  F.G.A.M. Aarts, 179(ES):Jun89–282
"Collins–Robert French–English, English–
French Dictionary/Robert–Collins diction-
naire français–anglais, anglais–français.*
(2nd ed) (B.T. Atkins & others, comps)
  W. Ayres-Bennett, 208(FS):Apr89–240
  C. Corcoran, 207(FR):Feb90–593
"Collins Spanish–English English–Spanish
Dictionary/Collins Diccionario Español–
Inglés Inglés–Español." (2nd ed) (C. Smith,
with M. Bermejo Marcos, E. Chang-Rodríguez
& others, eds)
  J. Butt, 402(MLR):Oct90–997
Collis, H. 101 American English Idioms.
  S. Plann, 399(MLJ):Autumn89–354
Collis, M. The Grand Peregrination.
  J.S. Cummins, 617(TLS):9–15Mar90–262
Collomb, M. La Littérature art deco.*
  P.A.M., 295(JML):Fall88/Winter89–175
"Colloque Paul Valéry."
  A. Chevrel-Giorgi, 549(RLC):Jul–Sep89–
  425
Collot, M. L'Horizon fabuleux.
  G. Cesbron, 356(LR):Nov89–318
  A. Rothwell, 208(FS):Oct89–484

Collot, M. & J-C. Mathieu, eds. Espace et
poésie.
  G. Cesbron, 356(LR):Feb–May89–103
  A. Rothwell, 208(FS):Jul89–355
Colls, R. The Pitmen of the Northern Coal-
field.*
  A. Howkins, 637(VS):Summer90–657
Colls, R. & P. Dodd, eds. Englishness.*
  A. Jumeau, 189(EA):Apr–Jun89–226
Colombani, R. L'Affaire Weidmann.
  R. Cobb, 617(TLS):9–15Feb90–139
Colomer, V.M. – see under Martínez Colomer,
V.
Colquhoun, A. Modernity and the Classical
Tradition.
  J.S. Curl, 324:Feb90–222
  A. Saint, 617(TLS):2–8Feb90–128
Colton, J. & S. Bruchey, eds. Technology, the
Economy, and Society.
  J.L. Meikle, 106:Fall89–275
Coluccia, R. – see Ferraiolo
Colum, P. Selected Poems of Padraic Colum.
(S. Sternlicht, ed)
  B. Dolan, 305(JIL):Jan89–60
Colville, G.M.M. Beyond and Beneath the Man-
tle.
  J.M. Krafft, 395(MFS):Winter89–774
Colvin, H. The Canterbury Quadrangle, St.
John's College.
  D. Howarth, 90:Jun89–430
  P.B. Jones, 46:Mar89–14
Colwell, D.J. Bibliographie des études sur G.
Flaubert (1921–1959). Bibliographie des
études sur G. Flaubert (1960–1982).
  B.F. Bart, 207(FR):Mar90–717
  D. Knight, 402(MLR):Oct90–972
  L.M. Porter, 446(NCFS):Fall–Winter89/90–
  279
Colwin, L. Goodbye Without Leaving.
  J. Olshan, 441:13May90–12
  442(NY):18Jun90–96
de Combarieu du Grès, M. & J. Subrenat – see
Gréban, A.
Combe, T. Theater of Fine Devices.
  O. Reynolds, 617(TLS):15–21Jun90–651
Comberiati, C.P. Late Renaissance Music at
the Habsburg Court.
  H. Leuchtmann, 410(M&L):Feb89–84
Combs, D.W. Early Gravestone Art in Georgia
and South Carolina.*
  S.A. Grider, 582(SFQ):Vol46No1–87
Combs–Schilling, M.E. Sacred Performances.
  R. Jamous, 617(TLS):27Jul–2Aug90–807
Comeau, P.T. Diehards and Innovators.
  B.T. Cooper, 446(NCFS):Fall–
  Winter89/90–246
Comer, J. Combat Crew.
  S. James, 569(SR):Spring89–xlix
Comini, A. The Changing Image of Beethoven.
  M. Solomon, 309:Vol9No2/3–196
Commoner, B. Making Peace with the Planet.
  S.J. Gould, 441:22Apr90–15
Comninel, G.D. Rethinking the French Revo-
lution.
  T.R. Judt, 242:Vol10No6–732
  S. Petrey, 188(ECr):Summer89–92
Comoli Mandracci, V., ed. Piemonte.
  S. Gruber, 576:Dec89–403
"The Compact Edition of the Oxford English
Dictionary."* (Vol 3) (R.W. Burchfield, ed)
  L. Lipka, 38:Band107Heft1/2–126
Compagnon, A. Proust entre deux siècles.*
  F.C. St. Aubyn, 207(FR):Feb90–552

Compagnon, A. – see Proust, M.
Comrie, B., ed. The World's Major Languages.*
　D.E. Ager, 402(MLR):Jan90-124
　T.G. Griffith, 278(IS):Vol44-146
Comtet, M., ed. IVe Colloque de linguistique
　russe.
　M. Kirkwood, 575(SEER):Apr89-263
Conacher, D.J. Aeschylus' "Oresteia."*
　A.F. Garvie, 303(JoHS):Vol109-215
　W.C. Scott, 24:Winter89-663
　M.J. Smethurst, 121(CJ):Feb-Mar90-260
　W.G. Thalmann, 487:Summer89-169
Conacher, D.J. – see Euripides
Conacher, J.B. Britain and the Crimea, 1855-
　56.*
　B. Bond, 637(VS):Autumn89-191
Conaway, J. Napa.
　R. Flaste, 441:21Oct90-14
Conca, F. – see Nilus
Conche. M. L'aléatoire.
　A. Comte-Sponville, 98:Dec89-997
　J. Largeault, 542:Oct-Dec89-647
Conche, M. Montaigne et la philosophie.*
　W.J.A. Bots, 535(RHL):Nov-Dec89-1049
Conche, M. – see Epicurus
Conche, M. – see Heraclitus
Concheff, B.J. Bibliography of Old Catalan
　Texts.
　L. Badia, 545(RPh):Nov89-351
Concolato, M.G.P. – see Lupton, T.
Condat, J-B., ed. Nombre d'or et Musique/
　Goldener Schnitt und Musik/Golden Section
　and Music.
　P.A. Autexier, 537:Vol76No1-102
Condell, D. & J. Liddiard. Working for Victo-
　ry?
　J. Chiti, 662:Spring/Summer89-50
Condon, R. Emperor of America.
　R. Blount, Jr., 441:11Feb90-14
Marquis de Condorcet. Moyens d'apprendre à
　compter sûrement et avec facilité. (C.
　Coutel, N. Picard & G. Schubring, eds)
　E. Brian, 531:Jul-Dec89-140
Condren, C. George Lawson's "Politica" and
　the English Revolution.
　J. Miller, 617(TLS):24-30Aug90-898
Cone, E.T., J. Frank & E. Kooley, eds. The
　Legacy of R.P. Blackmur.
　J.A. Bryant, Jr., 569(SR):Winter89-153
Conermann, K., ed. Fruchtbringende Gesell-
　schaft.*
　K.F. Otto, Jr., 301(JEGP):Jul89-375
Confucius. Les Entretiens de Confucius.* (P.
　Ryckmans, ed & trans)
　M. Détrie, 549(RLC):Jul-Sep89-387
Conkin, P.K. Gone with the Ivy.
　L. Lyday, 580(SCR):Fall90-173
Conkin, P.K. The Southern Agrarians.*
　T. Bonner, Jr., 585(SoQ):Winter90-70
　M.E. Bradford, 569(SR):Fall89-cii
　L. Lyday, 580(SCR):Fall90-173
　T.A. Underwood, 27(AL):Mar89-115
Conley, R.J. "The Witch of Goingsnake" and
　Other Stories.
　R.L. Buckland, 573(SSF):Winter89-99
　J. Rice, 649(WAL):Aug89-170
Conlon, D.J., ed. "Simon de Puille," chanson
　de geste.*
　W.G. van Emden, 208(FS):Jan89-73
　E.A. Heinemann, 589:Apr89-401
　D.A. Trotter, 382(MAE):1989/1-164
Conlon, G. Proved Innocent.
　P. Hillyard, 617(TLS):31Aug-6Sep90-924

Conlon, P.M. Le Siècle des Lumières. (Vol 5)
　P. Jansen, 535(RHL):Jul-Aug89-715
Conn, J., comp. Robert Burton and "The
　Anatomy of Melancholy."
　N.K. Kiessling, 365:Spring/Summer88-153
Conn, P. Literature in America.*
　S. Fender, 617(TLS):25-31May90-550
Conn, S. In the Kibble Palace.*
　R. Pybus, 565:Winter88/89-67
Connah, G. African Civilizations.
　C.R. De Corse, 2(AfrA):May89-24
Connah, R. Writing Architecture.
　J.M. Richards, 617(TLS):22-28Jun90-671
　W. Rybczynski, 441:23Sep90-54
Connelly, B. Arabic Folk Epic and Identity.
　P. Heath, 318(JAOS):Apr-Jun88-315
Connelly, J.B. Votive Sculpture of Hellenistic
　Cyprus.
　A. Weis, 124:Jan-Feb90-240
Connolly, C. Shade Those Laurels. (conclud-
　ed by P. Levi)
　J. Melmoth, 617(TLS):7-13Dec90-1325
Connolly, J.W. & S.I. Ketchian, eds. Studies in
　Russian Literature in Honor of Vsevolod
　Setchkarev.*
　M. Pavlovszky, 574(SEEJ):Winter89-609
Connolly, W.E. Appearance and Reality in
　Politics. Politics and Ambiguity. Political
　Theory and Modernity.
　R. Boesche, 242:Vol10No6-721
Connon, D.F. Innovation and Renewal.
　J. Chouillet, 530:Oct89-151
Connor, P. Horace's Lyric Poetry.
　H.P. Syndikus, 680:Band61Heft6-438
　D. West, 313:Vol79-207
　C.R. Wohlers, 124:Nov-Dec89-125
　A.J. Woodman, 123:Vol39No2-208
Connor, S. Samuel Beckett.
　P. Davies, 402(MLR):Jan90-170
　A. King, 395(MFS):Winter89-812
Connor, W.D. Socialism's Dilemmas.
　639(VQR):Winter89-25
Conolly, L.W., ed. Canadian Drama and the
　Critics.*
　S. Grace, 102(CanL):Spring89-156
Conquest, R. The Great Terror.
　N. Davies, 441:13May90-20
　J. Keep, 617(TLS):5-11Oct90-1056
Conquest, R. Inside Stalin's Secret Police.
　J.A. Getty, 104(CASS):Spring89-119
Conquest, R. Stalin and the Kirov Murder.*
　J.A. Getty, 550(RusR):Jul89-348
　639(VQR):Summer89-80
Conquest, R. Tyrants and Typewriters.
　J. Keep, 617(TLS):5-11Oct90-1056
Conrad, B. Hemingway's Spain.
　A. De Fazio 3d, 234:Spring90-179
Conrad, D. – see Fontana, D.
Conrad, J. Chance. (M. Ray, ed)
　S. Monod, 189(EA):Apr-Jun89-224
Conrad, J. The Collected Letters of Joseph
　Conrad. (Vol 3) (F.R. Karl & L. Davies, eds)
　J. Halperin, 395(MFS):Winter89-786
　R.G. Hampson, 402(MLR):Jan90-159
　J. Meyers, 627(UTQ):Winter89/90-359
　R. Stevens, 177(ELT):Vol32No1-98
Conrad, J. Joseph Conrad: Author's Notes.
　(M. Bignami, ed)
　D. Hewitt, 541(RES):Nov89-602
Conrad, J. Heart of Darkness. (R. Kimbrough,
　ed)
　D. Hewitt, 447(N&Q):Jun89-273

Conrad, P. Down Home.
　C. Pybus, 381:Summer89-797
Conrad, P. The Everyman History of English Literature.*
　F.J.M. Blom, 179(ES):Feb89-74
Conrad, P. A Song of Love and Death.*
　M. Hall, 415:Jan89-28
Conrad, P. Where I Fell to Earth.
　F. MacCarthy, 617(TLS):2-8Mar90-217
　D. Sacks, 441:22Jul90-33
Conrad, R., ed. Lexikon sprachwissenschaftlicher Termini.
　W. Braun, 682(ZPSK):Band42Heft4-539
　M. Bujňáková, 682(ZPSK):Band42Heft4-
Conran, T. Blodeuwedd.
　D. McDuff, 565:Spring89-76
Conroy, J. Belfast Diary.*
　C. Bedient, 472:Vol16No1-195
Conroy, P.V., Jr. Intimate, Intrusive and Triumphant.
　D. Coward, 402(MLR):Jan90-190
　S. Davies, 208(FS):Oct89-470
　W.F. Edmiston, 210(FrF):Jan89-100
　P.H. Meyer, 207(FR):Mar90-711
　V. Mylne, 535(RHL):Mar-Apr89-295
Constable, J. - see Richards, I.A.
Constable, W.G. Canaletto. (rev by J.G. Links)
　M. Rutenberg, 453(NYRB):15Mar90-42
Constant, B. Political Writings.* (B. Fontana, ed & trans)
　M.A. Wegimont, 446(NCFS):Spring-Summer90-570
Constant, C. The Palladio Guide.
　C. McCorquodale, 39:Feb89-139
Constantine, D. Hölderlin.
　R. Harrison, 402(MLR):Jul90-793
Constantine, D. Madder.*
　L. Sail, 565:Summer89-75
Constantine, D., ed. The Poetry Book Society Anthology 1988-1989.
　M. Holland, 493:Spring89-59
Constantine, K.C. Sunshine Enemies.
　M. Stasio, 441:3Jun90-32
Conte, G.B. The Rhetoric of Imitation.* (C. Segal, ed & trans)
　W.S. Anderson, 131(CL):Winter89-100
　D.C. Feeney, 313:Vol79-206
Conte-Helm, M. Japan and the North East of England, From 1862 to the Present Day.
　G.R. Marks, 324:Jan90-139
"Contemporary Britain." (1990) (P. Catterall, ed)
　J. Vincent, 617(TLS):21-27Sep90-994
Contini-Morava, E. Discourse Pragmatics and Semantic Categorization.
　T.C. Schadeberg, 350:Sep90-584
de Contreras, A. The Adventures of Captain Alonso de Contreras. (P. Dallas, ed & trans)
　J.H. Elliott, 453(NYRB):1Mar90-26
de Conty, E. - see under Evrart de Conty
Converse, J.M. Survey Research in the United States: Roots & Emergence, 1890-1960.
　D.A. Hollinger, 385(MQR):Winter90-123
Conway, D. A Farewell to Marx.
　A. Haworth, 291:Vol6No1-111
Conway, G.R. & E.B. Barbier. After the Green Revolution.
　F. Judd, 324:Sep90-710
Conyngham, J. The Arrowing of the Cane.
　M.E. Ross, 441:11Feb90-18

Coogan, T.P. Michael Collins.
　P. Johnson, 617(TLS):7-13Dec90-1307
Cook, A. Figural Choice in Poetry and Art.*
　B. Thibault, 207(FR):Apr90-866
Cook, B. Paper Chase.
　N. Callendar, 441:15Apr90-19
Cook, B.F. Greek Inscriptions.*
　R.J. Iorillo, 124:Sep-Oct89-68
　A.G. Woodhead, 303(JoHS):Vol109-242
Cook, E. Poetry, Word-Play, and Word-War in Wallace Stevens.*
　I.F.A. Bell, 402(MLR):Jul90-715
　J.V. Brogan, 191(ELN):Jun90-83
　G. MacLeod, 27(AL):Oct89-490
Cook, E. Seeing Through Words.*
　J. Altieri, 301(JEGP):Jan89-94
　D. Higgins, 568(SCN):Spring-Summer89-11
　C. Malcolmson, 677(YES):Vol20-260
Cook, J. Directors' Theatre.
　G. Gordon, 511:May89-45
Cook, M. - see Chénier, M-J.
Cook, M.L. & S.T. Miller. Mystery, Detective, and Espionage Fiction.
　P. Wolfe, 573(SSF):Fall88-486
Cook, N. Angel, Archangel.
　N. Callendar, 441:18Nov90-41
Cook, N. A Guide to Musical Analysis.*
　M. Musgrave, 411:Mar/Jul89-177
Cook, R. Harmful Intent.
　L. Lee, 441:11Feb90-15
Cook, R. Vital Signs.
　J. Queenan, 441:16Dec90-12
Cook, R.F. The Sense of the "Chanson de Roland."
　R. Noël, 207(FR):Dec89-366
Cook, T.H. Night Secrets.
　M. Stasio, 441:24Jun90-22
Cook-Gumperz, J., W.A. Corsaro & J. Streeck, eds. Children's Worlds and Children's Language.
　C. Futter, 320(CJL):Dec89-464
　S. Romaine, 355(LSoc):Mar89-141
Cook-Lynn, E. The Power of Horses.
　G. McFall, 441:12Aug90-16
Cooke, C. Architectural Drawings of the Russian Avant-Garde.
　M. Kempton, 453(NYRB):16Aug90-21
Cooke, C. - see Anikst, M.
Cooke, C. - see Gozak, A. & A. Leonidov
Cooke, D. Gustav Mahler. (2nd ed)
　A.F.L.T., 412:May89-146
Cooke, J.B. South of the Border.*
　A. Putnam, 649(WAL):Nov89-277
Cooke, K. A Modern Girl's Guide to Everything.
　M. Hardie, 616:Vol10No2-55
Cooke, R. Velimir Khlebnikov.*
　R. Aizlewood, 575(SEER):Oct89-614
　P. Schmidt, 574(SEEJ):Summer89-308
　R.W. Vroon, 104(CASS):Spring-Winter88-429
Cooley, D. Perishable Light.
　G. Harding-Russell, 526:Winter89-99
Cooley, D. The Vernacular Muse.*
　M. Macaulay, 102(CanL):Spring89-162
Cooley, P. The Van Gogh Notebook.
　639(VQR):Winter89-26
Coones, P. Euroclydon.
　N. Purcell, 123:Vol39No2-422
Coonts, S. Under Siege.
　N. Callendar, 441:18Nov90-41

Coontz, S. The Social Origins of Private Life.*
    Y.H., 185:Apr90-698
Cooper, A.M. Doubt and Identity in Romantic Poetry.
    G. Crossan, 447(N&Q):Sep89-401
    F. Garber, 340(KSJ):Vol38-173
    C.J. Rzepka, 661(WC):Autumn89-197
    S.J. Wolfson, 405(MP):May90-413
Cooper, C. - see "Race Relations Survey, 1988-9"
Cooper, D. Road to the Isles.
    C. Moorehead, 617(TLS):24-30Aug90-905
Cooper, D.E. Existentialism.
    A. Hannay, 617(TLS):30Nov-6Dec90-1297
Cooper, H. Elizabeth Barrett Browning.
    T.J. Collins, 445(NCF):Mar90-560
    A. Falk, 637(VS):Winter90-328
    C.H. MacKay, 85(SBHC):Vol16-151
Cooper, H.M., A.A. Munich & S.M. Squier, eds. Arms and the Woman.
    M. Lefkowitz, 617(TLS):1-7Jun90-591
Cooper, J. Us.
    J. O'Grady, 617(TLS):8-14Jun90-616
Cooper, J. Victorian and Edwardian Furniture and Interiors.*
    A.M.M.R., 90:May89-366
Cooper, J.C. Family.
    R. Hoffman, 441:30Dec90-12
Cooper, J.M., Jr. Pivotal Decades.
    H. Brogan, 441:22Apr90-28
Cooper, J.X. T.S. Eliot and the Politics of Voice.
    D.O., 295(JML):Fall88/Winter89-319
Cooper, M. Judgements of Value.* (D. Cooper, ed)
    B. Nelson, 465:Summer90-145
    P. Stadlen, 410(M&L):Nov89-559
Cooper, R.R. The Last to Go.*
    W.H. Pritchard, 249(HudR):Autumn89-484
Cooper, S. The Politics of Ernest Hemingway.
    P.R.J., 295(JML):Fall88/Winter89-347
Cooper, W. From Early Life.
    V. Cunningham, 617(TLS):3-9Aug90-821
Cooper, W.F. Claude McKay.*
    C.T. Donohue, 295(JML):Fall88/Winter89-377
Cooper, W.J., Jr. & T.E. Terrill. The American South.
    A.F. Hill, 441:30Dec90-15
Cooper-Wiele, J.K. The Totalizing Act.
    J.P. Miller, 543:Mar90-627
Cooreman, A.M. Transitivity and Discourse Continuity in Chamorro Narratives.
    N. Desnier, 353.Vol27No1-170
    T.E. Payne, 350:Sep90-631
Coover, J., comp. Antiquarian Catalogues of Musical Interest.
    A.H. King, 78(BC):Winter89-561
Copernicus, N. Complete Works.* (Vol 3: Minor Works.) (P. Czartoryski, ed)
    W.R. Laird, 551(RenQ):Spring89-107
Copland, A. & V. Perlis. Copland: Since 1943.
    L. Kuhn, 441:18Feb90-27
Copley, A. C. Rajagopalachari.
    P. Price, 293(JASt):May89-421
Copley, S. - see Fielding, H.
Copoloff-Mechanic, S. Pilgrim's Progress.
    B. Pell, 627(UTQ):Fall89-157
    529(QQ):Winter89-1002
Coppa, F.J., ed-in-chief. Dictionary of Modern Italian History.*
    D. Thompson, 278(IS):Vol43-165

Coppe, A. Selected Writings. (A. Hopton, ed)
    N. Smith, 447(N&Q):Jun89-241
"Les Coq-à-l'âne."
    E. Maakaroun, 98:Oct89-785
Corbatta, J. Mito personal y mitos colectivos en las novelas de Manuel Puig.
    L. Kerr, 238:Dec89-972
Corbeil, J-C. & M-V. Lee. The Facts on File English/Chinese Visual Dictionary.
    T. Light, 399(MLJ):Autumn89-352
Corbett, M. Byron and Tragedy.
    C. Burroughs, 615(TJ):May89-251
    J. Clubbe, 445(NCF):Sep89-233
    A. Nicholson, 340(KSJ):Vol38-168
Corbin, A. Le Village des cannibales.
    P. Higonnet, 617(TLS):28Sep-4Oct90-1028
Corbin, A. Women for Hire.
    J.F. McMillan, 617(TLS):7-13Dec90-1317
Corbin, G.A. Native Arts of North America, Africa, and the South Pacific.
    F.T. Smith, 2(AfrA):Nov88-93
Corcoran, J. Bitter Harvest.
    K. Flynn, 441:12Aug90-15
Corcoran, N. Seamus Heaney.*
    W. Bedford, 4:Spring89-79
Cordero, N-L. - see Parmenides
Cordero de Ciria, E. & J.M. Díaz de Guereñu - see Larrea, J.
Cording, R. Life-List.
    C. Wright, 434:Winter89-193
Corelli, A. Historisch-kritische Gesamtausgabe der musikalischen Werke. (Vol 2) (J. Stenzl, ed)
    W. Kolneder, 417:Jan-Mar89-102
Coreth, E., W.N. Neidl & G. Pfligersdorffer, eds. Christliche Philosophie im katholischen Denken des 19. und 20. Jahrhunderts. (Vol 1)
    J-F. Courtine, 192(EP):Apr-Jun89-275
Corey, E. Bachelor Bess. (P.L. Gerber, ed)
    C. Harnack, 441:9Dec90-7
Corfis, I.A., ed. Historia de la linda Melosina.*
    P.E. Grieve, 240(HR):Summer89-366
    D. Hook, 86(BHS):Apr89-169
Corfis, I.A. - see de San Pedro, D.
Corfis, I.A. - see Solalinde, A.G.
Cork, R. David Bomberg.
    J. Meyers, 364:Apr/May89-119
Corley, C.F.V. The Second Continuation of the Old French "Perceval."*
    D.D.R. Owen, 208(FS):Oct89-455
Corman, R., with J. Jerome. How I Made a Hundred Movies in Hollywood and Never Lost a Dime.
    B. Gewen, 441:12Aug90-16
Cormier, R., ed & trans. Three Ovidian Tales of Love.*
    N.V. Durling, 589:Jan89-148
Corn, A. The West Door.*
    F. Chappell, 219(GaR):Summer89-385
Corn, J.J., ed. Imagining Tomorrow.*
    C.W. Graham, 47:Mar89-53
Corneille, P. Le Cid.* (V.J. Cheng, trans)
    A. Limoges-Miller, 568(SCN):Spring-Summer89-21
    H. Phillips, 208(FS):Jul89-325
Cornelisen, A. Where It All Began.
    F. Randall, 441:18Feb90-29
    442(NY):7May90-110

Cornelissen, G. Das Niederländische im preussischen Gelderland und seine Ablösung durch das Deutsche.
  W. Sanders, 680(ZDP):Band108Heft1-147
Cornford, S. - see Young, E.
Corngold, S. The Fate of the Self.
  M. Anderson, 222(GR):Spring89-89
  T. Bahti, 131(CL):Fall89-403
  M.T. Jones, 221(GQ):Spring89-272
  J.H. Smith, 153:Summer89-80
Corngold, S. Franz Kafka.*
  R. Heinemann, 395(MFS):Winter89-826
  M.I. Spariosu, 400(MLN):Dec89-1221
Corns, T.N., ed. The Literature of Controversy.
  B.S. Hammond, 677(YES):Vol20-266
  D. Womersley, 447(N&Q):Mar89-107
Cornwell, B. Crackdown.
  N. Callendar, 441:7Oct90-39
Cornwell, J. A Thief in the Night.*
  L. Harris, 442(NY):5Mar90-101
Cornwell, N. Pasternak's Novel.*
  Z. Gimpelevich-Schwartzman, 104(CASS):Spring-Winter88-525
Cornwell, N. - see Odoyevsky, V.F.
Cornwell, P.D. Postmortem.
  M. Stasio, 441:7Jan90-29
Corpi, L. Delia's Song.
  L. Torres, 649(WAL):Nov89-278
Corral, C.G-C. - see under Gutiérrez-Cortines Corral, C.
Correas de Zapata, C., ed. Short Stories by Latin American Women.
  A. Whitehouse, 441:27May90-16
Corredor, E.L. György Lukács and the Literary Pretext.
  B. Lang, 478(P&L):Apr89-176
Corrigan, J. The Hidden Balance.*
  J. Knight, 165(EAL):Vol25No1-86
Corrigan, T., ed. The Films of Werner Herzog.*
  K.Z. Moore, 295(JML):Fall88/Winter89-350
Corrington, R.S. The Community of Interpreters.
  F.M. Oppenheim, 619:Winter89-57
Corrington, R.S., C. Hausman & T.M. Seebohm, eds. Pragmatism Considers Phenomenology.
  E. Walther, 619:Spring89-203
Corsa, H.S. - see Chaucer, G.
Corsi, P. Science and Religion.*
  C. Blanckaert, 531:Jan-Mar89-165
  R. Yeo, 637(VS):Winter90-333
Corsi, S. Il "modus digressivus" nella "Divina Comedia."
  S. Botterill, 547(RF):Band101Heft4-493
Corsten, S. & R.W. Fuchs, eds. Der Buchdruck im 15. Jahrhundert. (Pt 1)
  J.E. Walsh, 354:Sep89-276
Corta, P.D. - see under de Jérica y Corta, P.
Cortazzi, H. The Japanese Achievement.
  M. Conte-Helm, 324:Jun90-504
Cortazzi, H. & G. Webb - see Kipling, R.
Cosenza, M.E. - see Petrarch
Coseriu, E. Formen und Funktionen.
  L. Seppänen, 685(ZDL):1/1989-69
Cosgrove, D. & S. Daniels, eds. The Iconography of Landscape.
  A. Carlson, 290(JAAC):Spring89-196
Cosi, D.M. Casta Mater Idaea.
  J. Bouffartigue, 555:Vol62Fasc2-376
  A.J.L. van Hooff, 394:Vol42fasc1/2-212

Coskran, K. The High Price of Everything.
  M. Phillips, 456(NDQ):Spring89-206
Cossa, R. Teatro 2.
  O. Pellettieri, 352(LATR):Spring90-176
Cosslett, T. Woman to Woman.*
  R. Ivy, 402(MLR):Jan90-155
  P.J. Rabinowitz, 454:Spring90-314
  A. Sisson, 177(ELT):Vol32No2-233
da Costa, A.G. & others - see under Gomes da Costa, A. & others
Costa de Beauregard, O. Time, the Physical Magnitude.
  R. Batterman, 486:Dec89-710
da Costa Fontes, M., ed. Romanceiro da Província de Trás-os-Montes.*
  M. Guterres, 86(BHS):Jan89-205
  C. Slater, 292(JAF):Oct-Dec89-500
Costello, M.A., T.R. Leinbach & R. Ulack. Mobility and Employment in Urban Southeast Asia.
  A.E. Booth, 293(JASt):Aug89-672
"Cöthener Bach-Hefte 4."
  A. Dürr, 417:Apr-Jun89-171
Cotnoir, L. L'Audace des mains.
  B. Godard, 102(CanL):Winter88-123
Cotsell, M. The Companion to "Our Mutual Friend."*
  L. Černy, 38:Band107Heft1/2-241
Cotsell, M. Barbara Pym.*
  L.L. Doan, 395(MFS):Winter89-820
Cott, N.F. The Grounding of Modern Feminism.*
  P. Currah, 529(QQ):Summer89-568
  L. Shrage, 185:Oct89-189
Cotta, I. - see Rubens, P.P.
Cotte, R.J.V. Musique et Symbolisme.
  P.A. Autexier, 537:Vol75No1-103
Cotten, L. The Elvis Catalog.
  B.L. Cooper, 498:Fall89-97
Cotten, L. Shake, Rattle, and Roll. (Vol 1)
  B.L. Cooper, 498:Fall89-98
Cotter, J.S., Jr. Complete Poems. (J.R. Payne, ed)
  J. Mason, 578:Fall90-104
Cottingham, J. Descartes.*
  L. Alanen, 311(JP):Jan89-44
Cottingham, J. The Rationalists.*
  R. Imlay, 103:Jan90-6
Cottle, B. The Language of Literature, English Grammar in Action.
  E.G. Stanley, 447(N&Q):Mar89-84
Cotton, E.G. & J.M. Sharp. Spanish in the Americas.*
  D.N. Flemming, 399(MLJ):Summer89-239
  J.M. Lipski, 239:Fall89-271
Cottret, B. & M-M. Martinet. Partis et factions dans l'Angleterre du premier XVIIIe siècle.
  M. Hearn, 189(EA):Oct-Dec89-474
Coughlin, E.V., ed. Ten Unedited Works by Ramón de la Cruz.
  J.H.R. Polt, 238:Sep89-544
Coughlin, E.V. & J.O. Valencia - see Godínez, F.
Couliano, I.P. Eros and Magic in the Renaissance.*
  R. Boenig, 568(SCN):Fall-Winter89-53
  L. Helms, 615(TJ):Oct89-416
  E. Peters, 292(JAF):Jul-Sep89-359
Coulmas, F., ed. Direct and Indirect Speech.
  S. Thomas, 355(LSoc):Mar89-97

Coulombe, M., M. Jean & others, eds. Le Dic-
tionnaire du cinéma québécois.
D. Clandfield, 627(UTQ):Fall89-253
Couloubaritsis, L. Mythe et philosophie chez
Parménide.*
J. Frère, 192(EP):Jan-Mar89-94
M. Kerkhoff, 160:Jan89-161
Coulston, J.C. & E.J. Phillips. Corpus of
Sculpture of the Roman World: Great Brit-
ain; Hadrian's Wall West of the North Tyne,
and Carlisle.
M.A.R. Colledge, 123:Vol39No2-416
Count, E.W. The Hundred Percent Squad.
M. Stasio, 441:26Aug90-26
Couper-Kuhlen, E. An Introduction to Eng-
lish Prosody.*
J.L.G. Baart, 353:Vol27No5-939
Coupland, N., ed. Styles of Discourse.*
A.H. Jucker, 355(LSoc):Jun89-290
Courcelle, P. Lecteurs païens et lecteurs
chrétiens de l'Énéide. (Vol 1)
B. Schneider, 229:Band61Heft3-253
Courcelle, P. & J. Lecteurs païens et lecteurs
chrétiens de l'Énéide. (Vol 2)
B. Schneider, 229:Band61Heft3-253
Couric, E. The Trial Lawyers.
639(VQR):Spring89-59
Courlander, H. The Bordeaux Narrative.
N.S. Charles, 441:7Oct90-40
Courter, G. Flowers in the Blood.
J. Kaye, 441:7Oct90-41
Courtney, R. Dictionary of Developmental
Drama.
H.B. Redfern, 89(BJA):Winter89-79
Courtney-Clarke, M. African Canvas.
C.R. Stimpson, 441:2Sep90-9
Courtois, J-C. & others. Les objets des
niveaux stratifiés d'Enkomi.
F.G. Maier, 303(JoHS):Vol109-259
Courtois, J-C., J. Lagarce & E. Lagarce. En-
komi et le bronze récent à Chypre.
V. Hankey, 303(JoHS):Vol109-260
H. Matthäus, 229:Band01Heft3-273
Coustillas, P. & P. Bridgwater, eds. George
Gissing at Work.
H-P. Breuer, 395(MFS):Winter89-792
J. Korg, 637(VS):Summer90-674
M.S. Vogeler, 177(ELT):Vol32No1-88
Coutel, C., N. Picard & G. Schubring – see
Marquis de Condorcet
Couto, M. Graham Greene.
H-P. Breuer, 395(MFS):Summer89-337
J.M. Davis, 594:Winter89-448
A. Gibson, 175:Autumn89-273
R. Sharrock, 125:Winter89-193
Couton, G. Richelieu et le théâtre.
P. Dandrey, 475:Vol16No30-275
D. Lopez, 535(RHL):Jan-Feb89-98
Couture, C. Solo Boys & Girls.
A.J.M. Prévos, 207(FR):Dec89-392
Covington, V. Bird of Paradise.
R. Weinreich, 441:8Jul90-16
Covino, W.A. The Art of Wondering.
J. Schilb, 126(CCC):May89-233
Cowan, P. The Hills of Apollo Bay.
R. Jolly, 581:Dec89-667
Cowan, W., M.A. Foster & K. Koerner, eds.
New Perspectives in Language, Culture and
Personality.
R. Macmillan, 488:Jun89-201
R.H. Robins, 361:Apr89-380

Coward, H.G., ed. Modern Indian Responses to
Religious Pluralism.
A. Parpola, 293(JASt):Nov89-902
Cowart, D. History and the Contemporary
Novel.
R.F. Kiernan, 27(AL):Dec89-713
Cowart, J. & others. Matisse in Morocco.
N. Bryson, 617(TLS):13-19Jul90-749
Cowart, J., J. Hamilton & S. Greenough. Geor-
gia O'Keeffe, Art and Letters.*
J. Loughery, 662:Fall89/Winter90-40
Cowdery, L.T. The Nouvelle of Henry James
in Theory and Practice.*
C. Wegelin, 284:Fall89-221
Cowgill, A., Lord Brimelow & C. Booker. The
Repatriations from Austria in 1945.
R. Knight, 617(TLS):19-25Oct90-1126
Cowie, L.W. The French Revolution.
J. Black, 83:Spring89-80
Cowie, P. Coppola.
A. Barker, 707:Spring89-138
Cowley, A. The Collected Works of Abraham
Cowley. (Vol 1) (T.O. Calhoun, L. Heyworth
& A. Pritchard, eds)
A. Rudrum, 617(TLS):7-13Sep90-953
Cowley, A. A Critical Edition of Abraham
Cowley's "Davideis."
R. Flannagan, 391:Mar89-40
Cowling, M. Religion and Public Doctrine in
Modern England.* (Vol 2) [entry in prev
was Vols 1 & 2)
K. Willis, 656:Winter89/90-184
Cox, C., comp. A Pocket Dictionary of Con-
temporary France/Petit lexique de la
France contemporaine.
M. Offord, 208(FS):Apr89-242
Cox, E. Thanksgiving.
G. Kolata, 441:8Apr90-25
Cox, J.D. Shakespeare and the Dramaturgy of
Power.*
P. Erickson, 551(RenQ):Winter89-883
Cox, J.M. Recovering Literature's Lost
Ground.
W.B. Clark, 569(SR):Fall89-cxii
639(VQR):Summer89-90
Cox, J.N. In the Shadows of Romance.*
J.K. Brown, 340(KSJ):Vol38-195
C. Crossley, 208(FS):Jan89-92
Cox, P. The Australian Functional Tradition.
J.M. Richards, 46:Feb89-8
Cox, R. The World's Best Tennis Vacations.
T. Swick, 441:10Jun90-49
Coxon, A.H. – see Parmenides
Coyle, B. The Kneeling Bus.
P. Cytrynbaum, 441:18Feb90-21
442(NY):7May90-108
Coyle, B. A Thought to be Rehearsed.
S.J. Adams, 106:Summer89-134
Coyle, H. Bright Star.
N. Callendar, 441:17Jun90-19
Cozzo, A. Kerdos.
M.J. Edwards, 123:Vol39No2-408
Crabbe, G. George Crabbe: The Complete Po-
etical Works. (N. Dalrymple-Champneys &
A. Pollard, eds)
G. Edwards, 184(EIC):Jan89-84
P. New, 541(RES):Feb89-127
Crace, J. The Gift of Stones.*
G. Krist, 249(HudR):Winter89-660
Crackel, T.J. Mr. Jefferson's Army.
P.D. Nelson, 656(WMQ):Jan89-204

Cracraft, J. The Petrine Revolution in Rus-
sian Architecture.*
  G. Walton, 576:Dec89-398
Cracraft, J., ed. The Soviet Union Today.
(2nd ed)
  S. Welch, 575(SEER):Oct89-655
Craddock, J.R. The Legislative Works of Al-
fonso X, el Sabio.
  J.E. Keller, 86(BHS):Apr89-167
Craddock, P.B. Edward Gibbon: A Reference
Guide.
  M. Baridon, 189(EA):Jan-Mar89-103
Craddock, P.B. Edward Gibbon: Luminous His-
torian, 1772-1794.*
  639(VQR):Summer89-89
Craft, R. Small Craft Advisories.
  P. Brinson, 324:Mar90-297
  M. Tanner, 617(TLS):6-12Apr90-366
Crahay, R. D'Érasme à Campanella.
  F. Bierlaire, 539:Vol13No3-339
Craig, A. Foreign Bodies.
  R. Kaveney, 617(TLS):24-30Aug90-889
Craig, E. The Mind of God and the Works of
Man.*
  R. Harrison, 518:Jan89-27
Craig, E.G. Black Figures. (L.M. Newman, ed)
  R.C. Beacham, 617(TLS):12-18Jan90-33
Craig, G. & M. McGowan, eds. Moy qui me voy.
  M. Sheringham, 617(TLS):16-22Feb90-
178
Craig, G.A. The Triumph of Liberalism.*
  M. John, 617(TLS):3-9Aug90-816
Craig, P., ed. The Oxford Book of English
Detective Stories.
  D. Trotter, 617(TLS):30Nov-6Dec90-1288
Craig, R.T. & K. Tracy, eds. Conversational
Coherence.
  D. Carbaugh, 355(LSoc):Mar89-103
Craig, T., ed & trans. Musui's Story.*
  42(AR):Winter89-108
Craig, T. Racial Attitudes in English-
Canadian Fiction, 1905-1980.
  T. Goldie, 49:Jul89-95
  K.P. Stich, 102(CanL):Spring89-168
  M.E. Turner, 168(ECW):Fall89-156
Craik, R. & J. St. Clair. The Advocates'
Library.
  A. Bell, 78(BC):Winter89-445
Craik, T.W. - see Beaumont, F. & J. Fletcher
Craik, T.W. & R.J. - see Donne, J.
Cramb, R.A. & R.H.W. Reece, eds. Development
in Sarawak.
  C. Bailey, 293(JASt):May89-432
Cramer, K. & others, eds. Theorie der Subjek-
tivität.
  U. Unnerstall, 687:Apr-Jun89-387
Crane, D. The Transformation of the Avant-
Garde.
  R. Francis, 90:Aug89-567
Crane, G. Calypso.
  W. Moskalew, 124:Jul-Aug90-529
  M.M. Willcock, 123:Vol39No2-380
Crane, J.K. The Yoknapatawpha Chronicle of
Gavin Stevens.
  B. Kawin, 27(AL):May89-313
  V. Strandberg, 395(MFS):Summer89-283
Crane, S. The Correspondence of Stephen
Crane.* (S. Wertheim & P. Sorrentino, eds)
  E.H. Cady, 27(AL):Oct89-457
  B. Lee, 402(MLR):Oct90-935
  T. Wortham, 445(NCF):Jun89-121

Crane, S.D. Insular Romance.*
  J.F., 382(MAE):1989/2-321
  A.J. Holden, 554:Vol108No2/3-391
Cranford, B. The Rattlesnake Master.
  M. Kirby, 441:11Feb90-19
Cranna, J. Visitors.
  F. Baveystock, 617(TLS):2-8Feb90-122
Cranston, M. Philosophers and Pamphleteers.*
  A. Strugnell, 83:Spring89-100
Crapsey, A. The Complete Poems and Col-
lected Letters of Adelaide Crapsey. (S.S.
Smith, ed)
  L.R. Pratt, 502(PrS):Winter89-115
Craven, W. Colonial American Portraiture.*
  M.M. Lovell, 658:Spring89-69
Cravens, G. The Gates of Paradise.
  B. Christophersen, 441:23Dec90-12
Craw, W. & W. Kidd, eds. French Writers and
Politics, 1936-1944.
  J. Flower, 208(FS):Oct89-500
Crawford, C. The Beginnings of Nietzsche's
Theory of Language.
  G.J. Stack, 543:Sep89-151
Crawford, F.D. British Poets of the Great War.
  P.E. Firchow, 177(ELT):Vol32No1-78
Crawford, I.V. Malcolm's Katie.* (D.M.R.
Bentley, ed)
  C. Ballstadt, 470:Vol27-119
Crawford, J.M. Cocopa Dictionary.
  D. Hymes, 350:Sep90-632
Crawford, M., ed. Sources for Ancient His-
tory.
  F.G. Maier, 229:Band61Heft6-550
Crawford, M.H. Coinage and Money under the
Roman Republic.
  T.V. Buttrey, 122:Jan89-68
Crawford, R. The Savage and the City in the
Work of T.S. Eliot.*
  B. Bergonzi, 402(MLR):Jan90-168
  R. Bush, 405(MP):Aug89-104
  W. Harmon, 301(JEGP):Oct89-565
  F. McCombie, 447(N&Q):Jun89-263
Crawford, R. A Scottish Assembly.
  M. Walters, 617(TLS):1-7Jun90-584
Crawford, S. Mayordomo.*
  C. Merrill, 434:Winter89-208
Crawford, S.G. Log of the S.S. "The Mrs.
Unguentine."
  S. Moore, 532(RCF):Fall89-226
Crawford, T., D. Hewitt & A. Law, eds. Longer
Scottish Poems.* (Vol 2)
  A.A. MacDonald, 179(ES):Apr89-175
  S. Mapstone, 541(RES):Aug89-442
  G.R. Roy, 566:Autumn89-76
Cray, E. General of the Army George C. Mar-
shall.
  N. Bliven, 442(NY):6Aug90-97
  R.F. Weigley, 441:17Jun90-14
Cray, R.E., Jr. Paupers and Poor Relief in New
York City and Its Rural Environs, 1700-
1830.
  B.G. Smith, 656(WMQ):Apr89-392
Creasy, V.C. & V.A. Dearing. Microcomputers
and Literary Scholarship.
  517(PBSA):Jun89-243
Crecelius, K.J. Family Romances.
  E. McCormack, 208(FS):Jul89-341
"CREDO." (7 introductory vols)
  E.M. Craik, 123:Vol39No2-402
Creech, J. Diderot.*
  P.H. Meyer, 207(FR):Dec89-374
Creed, J.L. - see Lactantius

Creedy, J., ed. Foundations of Economic Thought.
C. Johnson, 617(TLS):10–16Aug90–846
Creel, B.L. "Don Quijote."
E.H. Friedman, 304(JHP):Winter89–162
Creel, M.W. "A Peculiar People."
P.D. Morgan, 656(WMQ):Oct89–812
Creigh, G. & J. Belfield, eds. The Cobler of Caunterburie and Tarltons Newes out of Purgatorie.
N. Rhodes, 447(N&Q):Mar89–93
Crellin, J.K. – see Bass, A.L.T.
Crémieux–Brilhac, J–L. Les Français de l'an 40.
T. Judt, 617(TLS):28Sep–4Oct90–1018
Crespo, R., B.D. Smith & H. Schultink, eds. Aspects of Language. (Vol 2)
L. Lipka, 38:Band107Heft1/2–99
Cressy, D. Bonfires and Bells.
C. Haigh, 617(TLS):2–8Feb90–126
Le comte de Creutz. Lettres inédites de Paris 1766–1770.* (M. Molander, ed) Un ambassadeur à la cour de France.* (G. Mary, ed)
J. Lough, 208(FS):Jul89–332
Crewe, J. Hidden Designs.*
D. Bevington, 405(MP):Feb90–295
T. Hyde, 677(YES):Vol20–244
P. Stallybrass, 551(RenQ):Spring89–130
L. Tennenhouse, 301(JEGP):Apr89–228
Crews, H. Body.
F. Weldon, 441:9Sep90–14
Criado, D.L. – see under López Criado, F.
Crichton, M. Jurassic Park.
G. Jennings, 441:11Nov00–14
Crick, B. Political Thoughts and Polemics.
J. Vincent, 617(TLS):20–26Jul90–768
Crick, B. Socialism.
D.L., 185:Jul90–911
Crickillon, J. Le Tueur birman.
J. Decock, 207(FR):Feb90–575
Crimp, D., with A. Rolston. AIDS Demo Graphics.
S. Heller, 441:5Aug90–3
Crisp, C.G. Eric Rohmer.
E. Benson, 207(FR):Feb90–565
Crispell, K.R. & C.F. Gomez. Hidden Illness in the White House.*
639(VQR):Summer89–94
Crispolti, E. Storia e critica del Futurismo.
M. Lentzen, 72:Band226Heft1–228
Cristiani, M. – see Scoto, G.
Critchfield, R. An American Looks at Britain.
A. Burgess, 61:Jul90–100
C.R. Whitney, 441:15Jul90–25
Critchfield, R. Among the British.
J. Vincent, 617(TLS):21–27Sep90–994
Critchfield, R. & W. Koepke, eds. Eighteenth-Century German Authors and their Aesthetic Theories.
R.E. Norton, 221(GQ):Spring89–260
Crittenden, B. Parents, the State and the Right to Educate.
J.B., 185:Apr90–709
Crociata, M. Umanesimo e teologia in Agostino Steuco.
J. Jolivet, 542:Oct–Dec89–594
Crofts, D.W. Reluctant Confederates.
639(VQR):Autumn89–117
Crofts, W. Coercion or Persuasion?
B. Appleyard, 617(TLS):9–15Feb90–142
Croissant, J. Etudes de philosophie ancienne.
J. Frère, 192(EP):Jan–Mar89–95

de la Croix, H. & R.G. Tansey – see Gardner, H.
Croizier, R. Art and Revolution in Modern China.
J.D. Spence, 293(JASt):May89–353
Crombie, W. Free Verse and Prose Style.*
K. Millard, 447(N&Q):Jun89–283
Cromley, E.C. Alone Together.
442(NY):18Jun90–97
Crone, P. Meccan Trade and the Rise of Islam.
F.S. Paxton, 293(JASt):Aug89–574
Cronin, A. The End of the Modern World.
W. Scammell, 617(TLS):18–24May90–522
Cronin, R. Imagining India.
C.A. Bayly, 617(TLS):7–13Dec90–1313
Cronk, D. – see Richardson, J.
Crook, J.M. The Dilemma of Style.*
J. Rykwert, 505:Sep89–183
J. Wilton–Ely, 39:Feb89–137
Cropp, M. & G. Fick. Resolutions and Chronology in Euripides.*
E.M. Craik, 123:Vol39No2–183
Crosby, A.W. America's Forgotten Pandemic.
A.M. Brandt, 617(TLS):26Oct–1Nov90–1158
Crosby, D.A. The Specter of the Absurd.*
G.J. Stack, 319:Oct90–627
Crosby, S.M. The Royal Abbey of Saint-Denis.* (P.Z. Blum, ed)
S. Murray, 90:Feb89–153
Crosby, V. The Fast Death Factor.
M. Stasio, 441:06Nov90–22
Croskey, R.M. Muscovite Diplomatic Practice in the Reign of Ivan III.
L. Hughes, 575(SEER):Jul89–470
Crosland, S. Ruling Passions.
V. Weissman, 441:1Jul90–14
Cross, A. The Players Come Again.
A. Fraser, 441:14Oct90–36
Cross, C., D. Loades & J.J. Scarisbrick, eds. Law and Government Under the Tudors.
S.A. Burrell, 551(RenQ):Summer89–324
Cross, D. Col.umns.
G. Gessert, 448:Vol27No1–128
Cross, J.E., ed. Cambridge, Pembroke College MS. 25.
H. Gneuss, 38:Band107Heft1/2–157
J. Stevenson, 382(MAE):1989/1–141
Cross, T., ed. The Lost Voices of World War I.*
B. Bergonzi, 402(MLR):Oct90–903
"Cross Currents." (Vol 6) (L. Matejka, ed)
M.D. Birnbaum, 279:Vol35/36–358
Crossley, C. & I. Small, eds. The French Revolution and British Culture.
J. Dunn, 617(TLS):29Jun–5Jul90–691
Crossley, R, – see Stapledon, O. & A. Miller
Crossley–Holland, K. The Painting Room.*
J. May, 493:Autumn89–51
Crosta, S., R.A. Miller & G.N. Onyeoziri, eds. Perspectives théoriques sur les littératures africaines et caribéennes/Theoretical Perspectives on African and Caribbean Literatures.
P.N. Uwajeh, 538(RAL):Spring89–139
Crouch, H. The Army and Politics in Indonesia. (rev)
U. Sundhaussen, 293(JASt):Nov89–930
Crouch, S. Notes of a Hanging Judge.
D. English, 441:11Mar90–9
Crouzet, M. Le Héros Fourbe chez Stendhal.*
C.W. Thompson, 402(MLR):Oct90–969

Crouzet, M. Stendhal ou Monsieur Moi-même.
J. Ducruet, 605(SC):15Jul90-407
Crouzet, M. - see Mérimée, P.
Crow Dog, M. & R. Erdoes. Lakota Woman.
P-L. Adams, 61:May90-133
P. Guthrie, 441:1Jul90-15
Crowe, M.J. The Extraterritorial Life Debate
1750-1900.*
D. Knight, 83:Spring89-102
Crowley, T. An Introduction to Historical
Linguistics.
B.D. Joseph, 350:Sep90-633
Crowther, P. - see Perelman, S.J.
Crozier, L. Angels of Flesh, Angels of
Silence.*
J. Camlot, 526:Spring89-96
Crucefix, M. Beneath Tremendous Rain.
T. Gooderham, 617(TLS):16-22Nov90-
1248
Cruden, S. Scottish Medieval Churches.*
J.P. McAleer, 576:Mar89-84
M. Thurlby, 589:Apr89-402
Cruickshank, D. & N. Burton. Life in the
Georgian City.
K. Downes, 617(TLS):11-17May90-506
M. Filler, 441:2Dec90-22
Cruickshanks, E. & J. Black, eds. The Jaco-
bite Challenge.
G.M. Townend, 566:Autumn89-84
Cruise, D. & A. Griffiths. Lords of the Line.
G.W., 102(CanL):Autumn-Winter89-302
Cruise, E.J. English Grammar for Students of
Russian.*
C.E. Townsend, 558(RLJ):Spring-Fall89-
280
Crummey, R.O. The Formation of Muscovy,
1304-1613.*
N.S. Kollmann, 550(RusR):Jan89-83
"La Crusca nella tradizione letteraria e lin-
guistica italiana."
A. Scaglione, 545(RPh):May90-627
Cruz, A.J. Imitación y transformación.*
J. Gornall, 402(MLR):Oct90-1001
M.P. Manero Sorolla, 547(RF):Band101
Heft2/3-366
Cruz, F.F. John Dewey's Theory of Commu-
nity.
P.T.M., 185:Jan90-455
Cruz, J.G. Lo neofantástico en Julio Cortázar.
W.L. Siemens, 238:Dec89-969
de la Cruz, J.I. - see under Inés de la Cruz, J.
Cruz, V.H., ed. Obra dramática de Manuel
Galich. (Vol 1)
P. Bravo-Elizondo, 352(LATR):Spring90-
174
Cruz García de Enterría, M., ed. Romancero
viejo.
R. Wright, 86(BHS):Jan89-200
de Cruz-Sáenz, M.S., ed. Romancero tradicio-
nal de Costa Rica.*
D.P. Seniff & D.M. Wright, 545(RPh):
Nov89-348
Cruz Seoane, M. Historia del periodismo en
España. (Vol 2)
A. Sinclair, 86(BHS):Jul89-286
Crystal, D. The Cambridge Encyclopedia of
Language.*
J. Ard, 710:Sep89-339
Crystal, D. The English Language.
W.N. Francis, 350:Dec90-861
Csapodi, C. & K. Caspodi-Gárdonyi. Biblio-
theca Corviniana: 1490-1990.
H.R. Trevor-Roper, 453(NYRB):19Jul90-8

Csikszentmihalyi, M. Flow.
C. Tavris, 441:18Mar90-7
Cuarón, B.G. - see under Garza Cuarón, B.
Cubbs, J., ed. Hmong Art.
S. Peterson, 292(JAF):Jul-Sep89-373
Cubelier de Beynac, J. & M. Magnien, eds.
Acta Scaligeriana.*
M. Pozzi, 228(GSLI):Vol166fasc534-287
Cuddihy, M. A Walled Garden.
W. Harmon, 472:Vol16No1-136
Cude, W. The Ph.D. Trap.*
P.J.M. Robertson, 529(QQ):Autumn89-680
Cudjoe, S.R. V.S. Naipaul.
H.S. Mann, 395(MFS):Summer89-389
Ćuk, R. Srbija i Venecija u XIII i XIV veku.
B. Krekić, 589:Jul89-691
Culhane, J. The American Circus.
A. Aronson, 441:22Apr90-25
Culioli, A. & others. Particules et connec-
teurs.
P. Laurendeau, 320(CJL):Mar89-114
Cullen, P. & T.P. Roche, Jr. - see "Spenser
Studies"
Cullen, R. Soviet Sources.
N. Callendar, 441:17Jun90-19
Culler, J. Framing the Sign.
R.M. Adams, 453(NYRB):1Mar90-38
W.E. Cain, 478(P&L):Oct89-393
J. Saville, 400(MLN):Dec89-1183
Culler, J. Ferdinand de Saussure.* (rev)
J.E. Joseph, 353:Vol27No2-341
"La cultura classica a Napoli nell'Ottocento."
P. Treves, 228(GSLI):Vol166fasc533-137
Cummer, W.W. & E. Schofield, with S. Andreou.
Keos. (Vol 3)
S. Hiller, 229:Band61Heft8-724
Cumming, M. A Disimprisoned Epic.
P. Brantlinger, 445(NCF):Dec89-410
M. Kelsall, 402(MLR):Oct90-926
R. Tarr, 637(VS):Winter90-331
Cummings, D. - see Blom, E.
Cummings, D.M. & D.K. McIntire - see "Inter-
national Who's Who in Music and Musicians'
Directory"
Cummings, J. & E. Volkman. Goombata.
M. Chambers, 441:8Apr90-12
Cummings, S. Mark Twain and Science.*
S.K. Harris, 27(AL):Oct89-480
R.B. Hauck, 395(MFS):Winter89-739
J.Y. Lee, 26(ALR):Winter90-85
P.C. Wermuth, 432(NEQ):Dec89-625
Cummins, J.G. - see López de Ayala, P.
Cummins, R. Meaning and Mental Representa-
tion.*
S.P. Stich, 103:May90-177
Cunliffe, B. The City of Bath.*
W.B. Hutchings, 568(SCN):Spring-
Summer89-21
Cunliffe, B.W. Greeks, Romans and Barbari-
ans.
G. Woolf, 313:Vol79-236
Cunningham, F. Democratic Theory and So-
cialism.
D. Schweickart, 185:Apr90-678
Cunningham, I.C. - see Herodas
Cunningham, L.G. - see under Guerra Cun-
ningham, L.
Cunningham, M. A Home at the End of the
World.
J.R. Kornblatt, 441:11Nov90-12

Cunningham, V. British Writers of the Thirties.*
　　R.S. Baker, 659(ConL):Spring90-97
　　M. Donald, 184(EIC):Apr89-169
　　F. McCombie, 447(N&Q):Jun89-259
　　A. Robinson, 541(RES):Nov89-584
　　F. Warner, 594:Spring89-96
Cuno, J., ed. French Caricature and the French Revolution, 1789-1799.*
　　L. Lambourne, 39:Jul89-66
Cupaiuolo, G. Bibliografia Terenziana (1470-1983).
　　Y-F. Riou, 555:Vol62Fasc1-163
Curioni, S.B. Per sconfiggere l'oblio.
　　E. Agnesi, 228(GSLI):Vol166fasc533-134
Curl, J.S. Victorian Architecture.
　　D. Linstrum, 324:Aug90-645
Curland, D. España Viva.
　　D. McAlpine, 238:Dec89-977
Curley, E. Behind the Geometrical Method.*
　　483:Jul89-426
Curley, T.M. - see Chambers, R.
Curnow, A. Look Back Harder. (P. Simpson, ed)
　　R.F. Anderson, 49:Apr89-86
　　P. Quartermaine, 447(N&Q):Jun89-278
Curnow, A. Selected Poems, 1940-1989.
　　G. Foden, 617(TLS):14-20Sep90-978
Curran, J.M. Hibernan Green on the Silver Screen.
　　D. Clark, 174(Éire):Summer89-145
Curran, S. Poetic Form and British Romanticism.*
　　A.F. Janowitz, 591(GIR) Spring90-140
Curran, W. Big Sticks.
　　D. Nasaw, 441:1Apr90-18
Currey, C.B. Edward Lansdale.*
　　L. Fish, 440:Winter-Spring89-145
Currey, R. The Wars of Heaven.
　　J. Davis, 441:8Apr90-27
"A Curriculum of Inclusion."
　　A. Hacker, 453(NYRB):22Nov90-19
Curry, G. Charles Dickens and Annie Fields.
　　W. Burgan, 637(VS):Spring90-501
　　J. Meckier, 158:Sep89-123
Curry, N. Ships in Bottles.
　　J. May, 493:Autumn89-51
　　S. O'Brien, 364(Feb/Mar90-111
Curtis, A. Sweelinck's Keyboard Music.
　　M. Desmet, 537:Vol75No1-111
Curtis, A. & J. Whitehead, eds. W. Somerset Maugham: The Critical Heritage.
　　G. Rowell, 610:Spring89-100
Curtis, G.L. The Japanese Way of Politics.*
　　K.E. Calder, 293(JASt):May89-386
Curtis, G.M. 3d & J.J. Thompson, Jr. - see Weaver, R.M.
Curtis, J. Between Flops.
　　G. O'Brien, 453(NYRB):20Dec90-6
Curtis, J., ed. Bronzeworking Centres of Western Asia c. 1000-539 B.C.
　　J. Boardman, 123:Vol39No2-411
Curtis, J.A.E. Bulgakov's Last Decade.*
　　R.B., 295(JML):Fall88/Winter89-298
Curtis, M.E., ed. The Nature of Vocabulary Acquisition.
　　Masonori Kimura, 351(LL):Jun89-277
Curtis, S. Sports Extra.
　　D. Kennedy, 493:Autumn89-48
Curtis, T. The Last Candles.
　　S. Carnell, 617(TLS):16-22Feb90-179
　　P. Gross, 493:Autumn89-65

Curtis, W.J.R. Balkrishna Doshi.
　　R. Saksena, 47:Sep89-47
　　M. Wortman, 45:Oct89-69
Cusatelli, G., ed. Viaggi e viaggiatori del settecento in Emilia e in Romagna.
　　N. Jonard, 535(RHL):Jan-Feb89-160
Cushman, K. - see Lawrence, D.H.
Cussler, C. Dragon.
　　N. Callendar, 441:17Jun90-19
The Marquis de Custine. Empire of the Czar.
　　V. Erofeev, 453(NYRB):14Jun90-23
Cutler, A., ed. Slips of the Tongue and Language Production.
　　C. Moss, 685(ZDL):1/1989-114
Cynkin, T.M. Soviet and American Signalling in the Polish Crisis.
　　M. Light, 575(SEER):Jul89-496
Czarnecka, E. & A. Fiut. Conversations with Czeslaw Milosz.*
　　Y. Wawrzycka, 295(JML):Fall88/Winter89-384
　　W.W. Werner, 577(SHR):Fall89-384
Czartoryski, P. - see Copernicus, N.
Czerwinski, E.J. Contemporary Polish Theater and Drama (1956-1984).
　　Z. Folejewski, 130:Winter89/90-381
　　M. Kobialka, 574(SEEJ):Winter89-633
Czerwinski, E.J., ed & trans. Slavic and East European Arts.
　　C.A. Moser, 574(SEEJ):Spring89-141

Dabit, E. Journal intime 1928-1936.* Ville Lumière. (P-E. Robert, ed of both)
　　L. Kovacs, 450(NRF):Nov89-118
Dabney, V.B. Once There was a Farm...
　　P. Hampl, 441:1Apr90-20
Dachy, M. Journal du mouvement Dada.
　　J.A. Vloemans, 358:Feb90-8
Daemmrich, H.S. & I. Themes and Motifs in Western Literature.* (German title: Themen und Motiv in der Literatur.)
　　F. Bassan, 446(NCFS):Spring-Summer90-554
　　C. Dolmetsch, 221(GQ):Winter89-101
　　M. Palencia-Roth, 301(JEGP):Oct89-605
　　W. Paulson, 406:Winter89-487
Dagen, P. Le Jugement dernier.
　　R. Kopp, 207(FR):May90-1099
Dagens, B. Entre Alampur Et Srisailam.
　　J.F. Mosteller, 318(JAOS):Jan-Mar88-189
Daggett, K.P. Fifty Years of Fortitude.
　　M.S. Creighton, 432(NEQ):Jun89-301
D'Agostino, A. Soviet Succession Struggles. Kremlinology and the Russian Question from Lenin to Gorbachev.
　　M. Merritt, 575(SEER):Jul89-493
d'Agostino, F. Chomsky's System of Ideas.*
　　B. Rundle, 521:Jul89-250
Dagron, G. & H. Mihǎescu - see Nicephorus Phocas
D'Aguiar, F. Airy Hall.*
　　P. Gross, 493:Autumn89-65
"Johan Christian Dahl, Caspar David Friederichs Malerfreund."
　　A. Wilton, 90:Oct89-719
Dahl, M.K. Political Violence in Drama.*
　　D.I. Rabey, 610:Autumn89-312
Dahl, N.O. Practical Reason, Aristotle, and Weakness of the Will.
　　T. Scaltsas, 41:Fall89-326
Dahl, R. Ah, Sweet Mystery of Life.
　　P-L. Adams, 61:May90-133

Dahl, R.A. Democracy and its Critics.*
  J. Lively, 617(TLS):5–11Jan90–7
Dahl, T.S. Women's Law.
  S. Anderson, 563(SS):Spring/Summer89–287
Dahlberg, C. The Literature of Unlikeness.
  K. Kerby-Fulton, 402(MLR):Jul90–683
Dahlhaus, C. Nineteenth-Century Music.*
  G. Martin, 465:Summer90–129
Dahlhaus, C. Schoenberg and the New Music.*
  E. Haimo, 308:Spring89–210
  A. Ridley, 89(BJA):Spring89–189
  A. Whittall, 415:May89–285
Dahlmann, D. Land und Freiheit.
  M.S. Shatz, 550(RusR):Apr89–181
Dahlmann, H. Zu Fragmenten römischer Dichter. (Vol 3)
  D.R. Shackleton Bailey, 229:Band61 Heft5–440
Dahmen, W. & others, eds. Latein und Romanisch.
  D.A. Trotter, 402(MLR):Jul90–667
Dahrendorf, R. Reflections on the Revolution in Europe.
  H.S. Hughes, 441:21Oct90–15
Daichman, G.S. Wayward Nuns in Medieval Literature.*
  W.W. Kibler, 345(KRQ):Nov89–485
Daigle, J.O. A Dictionary of the Cajun Language.
  B. Brown, 355(LSoc):Sep89–402
Dailey, J. Masquerade.
  J. Kaye, 441:13May90–24
Daitch, S. The Colorist.
  K. Lynch, 441:13May90–24
Daiyun, Y. – see under Yue Daiyun
Daiyun, Y. & C. Wakeman – see under Yue Daiyun & C. Wakeman
The Dalai Lama. Freedom in Exile. My Tibet.
  J. Mirsky, 453(NYRB):20Dec90–53
  R.G. Weakland, 441:30Sep90–3
Dalakoura, V. The Game of the End.
  J. Taylor, 532(RCF):Spring89–252
Dalby, R., ed. Victorian Ghost Stories by Eminent Women Authors.
  42(AR):Summer89–372
Daldry, G. Charles Dickens and the Form of the Novel.*
  T.J. Cribb, 541(RES):May89–281
Dale, A.S. – see Chesterton, G.K.
Dale, P.N. The Myth of Japanese Uniqueness.*
  V.C. Gessel, 318(JAOS):Oct–Dec88–654
Dales, R.C. & E.B. King – see Grosseteste, R.
Daleski, H.M. The Forked Flame.
  R.G. Walker, 177(ELT):Vol32No1–113
d'Alessandro, D.A. & A. Ziino, eds. La Musica a Napoli durante il Seicento.
  D. Brandenburg, 417:Apr–Jun89–172
Daley, R. A Faint Cold Fear.
  R.S. Nathan, 441:14Oct90–44
Dalglish, C. Refugees from Vietnam.
  B. Harrell-Bond & S. Elliott, 617(TLS):13–19Jul90–744
Dalio, M. Mes années folles.
  M-N. Little, 207(FR):Oct89–196
Dallapiazza, M. Die Boccaccio-Handschriften in den deutschsprachigen Ländern.
  G. Breuer, 547(RF):Band101Heft2/3–356
Dallapiccola, L. Dallapiccola on Opera.* (Vol 1) (R. Shackelford, ed & trans)
  J.C.G. Waterhouse, 410(M&L):Aug89–438
Dallas, P. – see de Contreras, A.

Dallas, S. Buster Midnight's Cafe.
  T. Sandlin, 441:3Jun90–39
Dällenbach, L. Claude Simon.
  R. Sarkonak, 400(MLN):Sep89–939
Dallmayr, F.R. Polis and Praxis.
  K. Ziarek, 400(MLN):Dec89–1186
Dallmayr, F.R. Twilight of Subjectivity.
  J.H. Smith, 153:Summer89–80
Dally, A. A Doctor's Story.
  J.F. Watkins, 617(TLS):20–26Apr90–412
Dally, P. Elizabeth Barrett Browning.
  K. Millard, 617(TLS):30Mar–5Apr90–354
Dalrymple, W. In Xanadu.*
  J. Haylock, 364:Feb/Mar90–130
Dalrymple-Champneys, N. & A. Pollard – see Crabbe, G.
Dalton, D. Playing the Viola.
  R. Stowell, 415:Oct89–615
Daly, M.W., ed. Modernization in the Sudan.
  P.M. Holt, 318(JAOS):Jan–Mar88–168
Daly, P.M., ed. The English Emblem and the Continental Tradition.*
  C.W.R.D. Moseley, 402(MLR):Jan90–145
Daly, P.M., with L.T. Duer & A. Raspa, eds. The English Emblem Tradition.* (Vol 1)
  C.W.R.D. Moseley, 402(MLR):Apr90–407
Damascius. Traité des premiers principes.* (Vol 1) (L.G. Westerink, ed; J. Combès, trans)
  L. Siorvanes, 123:Vol39No1–139
di Damasco, N. Vita di Augusto. (B. Scardigli, with P. Delbianco, eds & trans)
  G. Dobesch, 229:Band61Heft1–45
D'Amato, B. Hardball.
  M. Stasio, 441:4Mar90–35
Damblemont, A. Le français pour la profession.*
  P.A. Gaeng, 399(MLJ):Winter89–505
Duchesse D'Ambrantès. At the Court of Napoleon. (O. Bernier, ed)
  P-L. Adams, 61:Jan90–101
D'Ambrosio, V-M. Eliot Possessed.
  J.F. Hooker, 675(YER):Fall90–102
Damiani, B. Moralidad y Didactismo en el Siglo de Oro (1492–1615).
  F.A. de Armas, 238:Dec89–956
Damiani, B.M. Renaissance and Golden Age Essays in Honor of D.W. McPheeters.
  D.P. Seniff, 345(KRQ):May89–241
D'Amico, J.F. Theory and Practice in Renaissance Textual Criticism.
  A.F. Kinney, 568(SCN):Fall-Winter89–40
  L.V.R., 568(SCN):Fall-Winter89–69
Damigeron. De Virtutibus Lapidum. (J. Radcliffe, ed)
  W.D. Hearell, 111:Fall90–9
Damm, S. – see Lenz, J.M.R.
Damrosch, D. The Narrative Covenant.*
  D. Norton, 478(P&L):Oct89–424
Damrosch, L., Jr. The Imaginative World of Alexander Pope.*
  B.S. Hammond, 83:Autumn89–237
  N.C. Jaffe, 301(JEGP):Jul89–422
  D.L. Patey, 639(VQR):Summer89–563
  J. Sitter, 173(ECS):Fall89–81
  D.H. White, 405(MP):Nov89–188
  T. Woodman, 677(YES):Vol20–274
Damrosch, L., Jr., ed. Modern Essays on Eighteenth-Century Literature.*
  C.R. Kropf, 566:Spring89–176
  D.W. Lindsay, 506(PSt):May89–101
  A. Varney, 447(N&Q):Dec89–517

Dan, L.O. Iz arkhiva L.O. Dan. (B. Sapir, ed)
  A. Liebich, 550(RusR):Jan89-67
Dana, J.T. Monterrey is Ours! (R.H. Ferrell,
  ed)
  P-L. Adams, 61:Apr90-109
Dance, D.C. Long Gone.
  S. Hobbs, 203:Vol100No1-124
  J.W. Roberts, 292(JAF):Apr-Jun89-231
Danchin, L. Jean Dubuffet, peintre-philos-
  ophe.*
  J-M. Le Lannou, 542:Oct-Dec89-634
Danchin, P., ed. The Prologues and Epilogues
  of the Restoration 1660-1700.* (Pt 1)
  I. Simon, 541(RES):Feb89-122
Danchin, P., ed. The Prologues and Epilogues
  of the Restoration 1660-1700.* (Pt 2)
  R.D. Hume, 612(ThS):Nov88-229
  I. Simon, 541(RES):Feb89-122
Danchin, P., ed. The Prologues and Epilogues
  of the Restoration 1660-1700.* (Pt 3)
  R.D. Hume, 612(ThS):Nov88-229
  S. Rosenfeld, 611(TN):Vol43No1-35
  I. Simon, 541(RES):Feb89-122
Danchin, P., ed. The Prologues and Epilogues
  of the Restoration 1660-1700. (Pt 4)
  R.D. Hume, 612(ThS):Nov88-229
  S. Rosenfeld, 611(TN):Vol43No2-90
  I. Simon, 541(RES):Feb89-122
Dancy, J. Introduction to Contemporary
  Epistemology.
  A. Boyer, 542:Oct-Dec89-649
Dancy, J., ed. Perceptual Knowledge.
  M. Espinoza, 542:Oct-Dec89-647
  D.L.C. MacLachlan, 103:Mar90-101
Dancy, J., J.M.E. Moravcsik & C.C.W. Taylor,
  eds. Human Agency.
  P. Noordhof, 185:Jan90-417
  D. Novitz, 103:Jan90-9
Dandurand, A. Voilà c'est moi.
  V. Raoul, 102(CanL):Autumn-Winter89-
  243
Dane, J.A. Parody.
  C. Robinson, 447(N&Q):Dec89-516
  566:Spring90-202
Danek, G. Studien zur Dolonie.
  M.M. Willcock, 123:Vol39No2-178
Daneman, M., ed. Reading Research. (Vol 6)
  L.B. Feldman, 348(L&S):Oct-Dec89-381
Danesi, M. Loanwords and Phonological
  Methodology.
  T.D. Cravens, 276:Summer89-216
Danesi, M. Manuale di Tecniche per la Didat-
  tica delle Lingue Moderne.
  ʹA. Moneti, 276:Winter89-453
Danesi, M. Teaching a Heritage Language to
  Dialect-Speaking Students.
  T.D. Cravens, 276:Winter89-455
Danezis, G. Spaneas.
  B. Baldwin, 589:Jan89-149
Danforth, L.M. Firewalking and Religious
  Healing.
  R. Just, 358:Feb90-16
Dang, W. - see under Wang Dang
Daniel, A. Diderot világa.
  O. Penke, 530:Apr89-161
Daniel, H. Liars.
  T. Thwaites, 71(ALS):Oct89-266
Daniel, J. Common Ground.
  O. Siporin, 649(WAL):Nov89-265
Daniel, J. & Y. Afanassiev. Cette grande
  lueur à l'est.
  N. Clive, 617(TLS):10-16Aug90-844

Daniel, M. Unbridled.
  M. Stasio, 441:4Feb90-26
Daniel, R.W., M. Gronewald & H.J. Thissen.
  Griechische und demotische Papyri der Uni-
  versitätsbibliothek Freiburg. (Vol 4)
  R. Coles, 123:Vol39No1-122
Daniele, A. - see de' Dottori, C.
Daniele, A. & L. Renzi, eds. Ugo Angelo Can-
  ello e gli inizi della filologia romanza in
  Italia.
  S.N. Rosenberg, 276:Winter89-457
Daniels, C.B., J.B. Freeman & G.W. Charlwood
  Toward an Ontology of Number, Mind and
  Sign.
  F. Orilia, 449:Dec89-699
  L. Wetzel, 316:Sep89-1102
Daniels, D.G. Always a Sister.
  E.O. Perry, 441:14Jan90-31
Daniëls, G. Folk Jewelry of the World.
  139:Dec89/Jan90-24
Daniels, K. The Niobe Poems.
  639(VQR):Autumn89-137
Daniels, N. Am I My Parents' Keeper?*
  D.W. Brock, 509:Summer89-297
  L.R. Churchill, 185:Oct89-169
Daniels, N. Just Health Care.*
  A. Donchin, 449:Dec89-697
Daniels, N. Thomas Reid's "Inquiry."
  E.H. Madden, 543:Dec89-396
  D.D. Todd, 154:Vol28No4-671
Daniels, R.V. Is Russia Reformable?
  A. Dallin, 550(RusR):Jul89-330
Daniels, V.K., B.H. Bennett & H. McQueen.
  Windows Onto Worlds.
  B. Matthews, 71(ALS):May89-135
Danielson, J.D., with E.K. Gambarini - see
  Quiroga, H.
Daninos, G. Comprendre "Tribaliques" d'Henri
  Lopès.
  A. Adams, 538(RAL):Summer89-292
Dann, O. & J. Dinwiddy, eds. Nationalism in
  the Age of the French Revolution.*
  M. Hughes, 83:Autumn89-220
Dannemark, F. L'Hiver ailleurs suivi de Sans
  nouvelles du paradis.
  S. Rava, 207(FR):Apr90-888
Dannen, F. Hit Men
  R. Christgau, 441:12Aug90-11
Danon, R. Work in the English Novel.*
  K. Sutherland, 148:Winter86-105
Dante Alighieri. Inferno. (T. Phillips, trans)
  A. Woods, 97(CQ):Vol18No1-98
Danto, A. & others. Art/Artifact.
  P. Stevens, Jr., 2(AfrA):Nov88-10
Danto, A.C. Encounters & Reflections.
  M. Vaizey, 441:5Aug90-9
Danto, A.C. The Philosophical Disenfran-
  chisement of Art.*
  G. Sircello, 482(PhR):Apr89-268
Danuser, H., ed. Gattungen der Musik und
  ihre Klassiker.
  P. Jost, 416:Band4Heft1-88
Danuser, H. Gustav Mahler: "Das Lied von der
  Erde."
  I. Werck, 537:Vol75No1-118
Danuser, H. & others, eds. Das musikalische
  Kunstwerk.
  D. Kämper, 416:Band4Heft2-179
Danuser, H., D. Kämper & P. Terse, eds.
  Amerikanische Musik seit Charles Ives.
  P. Gradenwitz, 417:Jan-Mar89-81

Dany, M. & C. Noé. Le Français des employ-
és – services–commerce–industrie.
   J.C. Bednar, 207(FR):Apr90–900
Danylewycz, M. Taking the Veil.*
   V. Raoul, 102(CanL):Autumn–Winter89–
   241
   J. Stoddart, 529(QQ):Summer89–565
Danys, M. DP.
   A. Tamasauskas, 529(QQ):Winter89–968
Danzinger, M.K. & F. Brady – see Boswell, J.
Danziger, N. Danziger's Travels beyond For-
bidden Frontiers.
   S. Pickering, 569(SR):Spring89–297
Dao, B. – see under Bei Dao
Da Pozzo, G., F. Fido & M. Santagata – see
Baratto, M.
Daraki, M. Dionysos.
   E. Kearns, 303(JoHS):Vol109–239
d'Arbeloff, N. Small Packages (The Augustine
Adventures).
   G. Gessert, 448:Vol27No1–130
Darbo–Peschanski, C. Le discours du partic-
ulier.
   M. Menu, 555:Vol62Fasc1–142
   M. Narcy, 192(EP):Apr–Jun89–246
Darby, W. Necessary American Fictions.*
   P.R.J., 295(JML):Fall88/Winter89–243
Darcey, J.M., ed. The Language Teacher.
   C.K. Knop, 399(MLJ):Winter89–485
Dardis, T. The Thirsty Muse.*
   J. McInerney, 617(TLS):27Jul–2Aug90–
   792
Dargan, A. & S. Zeitlin. City Play.
   K. Ray, 441:9Dec90–14
   442(NY):22Oct90–143
Daria, I. The Fashion Cycle.
   S. Menkes, 441:25Nov90–21
d'Arles, C. – see under Césaire d'Arles
Darley, G. Octavia Hill.
   H. Hobhouse, 324:Jul90–565
Darling, M., ed. Perspectives on Mordecai
Richler.
   I.S. MacLaren, 102(CanL):Spring89–196
Darnell, R. Edward Sapir.
   R. Handler, 617(TLS):24–30Aug90–891
Darnton, R. The Kiss of Lamourette.
   P–L. Adams, 61:Feb90–109
   442(NY):1Jan90–84
Darnton, R. Mesmerism and the End of the
Enlightenment.
   M. Cranston, 242:Vol10No1–102
Darnton, R. & D. Roche, eds. Revolution in
Print.*
   J.R. Censer, 322(JHI):Oct–Dec89–652
   639(VQR):Autumn89–117
Darragh, J., ed. A New Brooklyn Museum.
   S. Gutterman, 45:Feb89–67
   P.L. Pinnell, 658:Spring89–105
Darst, D.H. Diego Hurtado de Mendoza.
   N.C. Davis, 552(REH):May89–138
   C.D. Martínez, 238:Mar89–141
   I.P. Rothberg, 240(HR):Winter89–89
Darst, D.H. Sendas literarias: España.
   J.B. McInnis, 399(MLJ):Spring89–99
Darwin, C. The Correspondence of Charles
Darwin. (Vol 6) (F. Burkhardt & S. Smith,
eds)
   R. Porter, 617(TLS):14–20Dec90–1343
Dary, D. Kanzana, 1854–1900.
   517(PBSA):Mar89–115
Das, G.K. & G. Salgado, eds. The Spirit of D.H.
Lawrence.
   J. Voelker, 395(MFS):Summer89–334

Das, R.P. – see Hillebrandt, A.
Dascal, M. Leibniz: Language, Signs and
Thought.*
   M.A. Kulstad, 484(PPR):Jun90–849
Das Gupta, A. & M.N. Pearson, eds. India and
the Indian Ocean, 1500–1800.
   J.F. Richards, 293(JAst):Aug89–651
Da Silva, Z.S. A Concept Approach to Span-
ish. (4th ed)
   C.M. Cherry, 399(MLJ):Summer89–239
Dassmann, E. & others, eds. Reallexikon für
Antike und Christentum. (Pts 97–104)
   H.D. Betz, 229:Band61Heft7–617
Daston, L. Classical Probability in the
Enlightenment.*
   J. Barnouw, 173(ECS):Winter89/90–200
Data, I.F. & A. Colturato – see under Fragalà
Data, I. & A. Colturato
Datlow, E., ed. Alien Sex.
   G. Jonas, 441:8Jul90–22
Daub, M. Canadian Economic Forecasting.
   R.L. Mansell, 529(QQ):Summer89–475
d'Aubigné, T.A. Histoire Universelle. (Vol 4)
(A. Thierry, ed)
   J. Brunel, 535(RHL):Sep–Oct89–928
   K. Cameron, 208(FS):Jul89–322
ibn Daud, A. The Exalted Faith. (N.M. Sam-
uelson, trans; G. Weiss, ed)
   A.L. Ivry, 589:Jul89–721
Daudet, A. Sappho.
   J.D. Fife, 446(NCFS):Spring–Summer90–
   584
Dauenhauer, B.P. The Politics of Hope.*
   R. Boyne, 323:Oct89–292
Dauphiné, J. Ésotérisme et littérature.
   C. de Grève, 535(RHL):Mar–Apr89–348
d'Aurevilly, J.B. – see under Barbey d'Aure-
villy, J.
Daurio, B. If Summer Had a Knife.*
   F. Manley, 102(CanL):Autumn–Winter89–
   216
Dauster, F. The Double Strand.*
   B.B.A., 295(JML):Fall88/Winter89–195
Daux, G. & E. Hansen. Fouilles et Delphes.
(Vol 2)
   R.A. Tomlinson, 303(JoHS):Vol109–260
Davenport, G. The Drummer of the Eleventh
North Devonshire Fusiliers.
   R. Burgin, 441:21Oct90–24
Davenport, W.A. Chaucer.
   C. Batt, 175:Spring89–69
   D. Pitard, 382(MAE):1989/2–326
Davenport–Hines, R. Sex, Death and Punish-
ment.
   R. Porter, 617(TLS):30Mar–5Apr90–341
Davenport–Hines, R.P.T. & G. Jones, eds.
British Business in Asia since 1860.
   N.R. Clifford, 293(JAst):Nov89–799
Daverio Rocchi, G. Frontiera e confini nella
Grecia antica.
   R. Osborne, 123:Vol39No2–407
Davey, F. The Abbotsford Guide to India.
   K. Garebian, 168(ECW):Spring89–169
Davey, F. Reading Canadian Reading.
   S. Scobie, 376:Mar89–130
Daviau, D.G., ed. Major Figures of Contempo-
rary Austrian Literature.*
   L.J. King, 406:Spring89–116
David, A.R. The Egyptian Kingdoms.
   A.R. Schulman, 124:Mar–Apr90–360
David, C–P. Debating Counterforce.
   M.N. Kramer, 550(RusR):Oct89–441
David, L. – see under Jacob, M.

Davidson, A. In the Wake of the Exxon Val-
dez.
P. Moser, 441:27May90-6
Davidson, C. Race and Class in Texas Poli-
tics.
M. Oreskes, 441:16Dec90-23
Davidson, C. Visualizing the Moral Life.
R.W. Vince, 612(ThS):Nov88-228
Davidson, C.N. Revolution and the Word.*
J.A.L. Lemay, 656(WMQ):Apr89-415
C.J. Singley, 454:Winter90-199
Davidson, H.R.E. Myths and Symbols in Pagan
Europe.
J.E. Doan, 292(JAF):Jul-Sep89-358
Davidson, J. & J. Rugge. Great Heart.
639(VQR):Winter89-31
Davidson, J.H.C.S., ed. Laī Sū' Thai.
C. Court, 293(JASt):Feb89-214
Davidson, M. Convictions of the Heart.
W.R. Scott, 456(NDQ):Winter89-234
Davidson, M. The Greek Interpreter.
S. Rae, 617(TLS):9-15Mar90-257
Davidson, M., ed. Picture Collections: Mexico.
M.J. Grothey, 263(RIB):Vol39No1-70
Davidson, P. The Poetic Imagination of Vya-
cheslav Ivanov.
D. Rayfield, 617(TLS):23Feb-1Mar90-201
J. West, 402(MLR):Oct90-1043
Davidson, R.V. Did We Think Victory Great?
J. Beecherj, 446(NCFS):Spring-
Summer90-585
Davie, D. Czesław Miłosz and the Insufficien-
cy of Lyric.*
B. Bal-Kamiński, 104(CASS):Spring-Win-
ter88-523
A. Livingstone, 575(SEER):Apr89-290
Y. Wawrzycka, 295(JML):Fall88/Winter89-
386
Davie, D. To Scorch or Freeze.*
D. Houston, 493:Summer89-51
Davie, D. Under Briggflatts.*
H. Lomas, 364:Dec89/Jan90-94
E. Longley, 493:Winter89/90-22
Davies, A. Dirty Faxes.
J. O'Grady, 617(TLS):9-15Nov90-1214
Davies, A. Filming Shakespeare's Plays.
G. Gottlieb, 570(SQ):Winter89-513
Davies, A. Infected Christianity.
I. Hexham, 627(UTQ):Fall89-226
Davies, A. Other Theatres.*
P. Hollindale, 541(RES):Feb89-140
S. Lacey, 677(YES):Vol20-360
Davies, C. Rosalía de Castro no seu tempo.
D.L. Shaw, 402(MLR):Jan90-229
Davies, C. High Tech Architecture.
H. Aldersey-Williams, 45:May89-83
J. Winter, 46:Feb89-8
Davies, D. William Gerhardie.
J. Symons, 617(TLS):13-19Apr90-387
Davies, E. The English Imperative.
L.J. Brinton, 320(CJL):Mar89-85
Davies, G. Mallarmé et la "couche suffisante
d'intelligibilité."
M.L. Assad, 446(NCFS):Fall-Winter89/90-
270
B. Marchal, 535(RHL):Nov-Dec89-1069
E. Souffrin-Le Breton, 208(FS):Jan89-
101
Davies, H. Sartre and "Les Temps Modernes."*
L.S. Kramer, 242:Vol10No1-107
L.D. Kritzman, 188(ECr):Winter89-97
P.A.M., 295(JML):Fall88/Winter89-404

Davies, H.S. Wordsworth and the Worth of
Words.* (J. Kerrigan & J. Wordsworth, eds)
A. Bewell, 677(YES):Vol20-292
Davies, M. The Early Italian Schools before
1400. (rev by D. Gordon)
H.B.J. Maginnis, 90:Jul89-490
Davies, P. Dollarville.*
R. Kaveney, 617(TLS):9-15Mar90-258
Davies, P. The Penguin Guide to the Monu-
ments of India. (Vol 2)
G.H.R. Tillotson, 617(TLS):10-16Aug90-
856
Davies, P.J. Mozart in Person.
W.A. Frosch, 414(MusQ):Vol74No1-170
N. Kenyon, 617(TLS):16-22Nov90-1238
Davies, P.V. & A.J. Kennedy, eds. Rewards
and Punishments in the Arthurian Romanc-
es and Lyric Poetry of Medieval France.
K. Busby, 382(MAE):1989/1-167
S. Gaunt, 541(RES):Aug89-400
R. Pensom, 402(MLR):Jan90-175
Davies, R., ed. Leonid Andreyev.*
C. Reid, 617(TLS):16-22Mar90-290
Davies, R. The Lyre of Orpheus.*
M.J. Friedman, 268(IFR):Winter90-55
W.J. Keith, 298:Spring89-140
P. Monk, 150(DR):Winter88/89-524
G. Oldham, 42(AR):Spring89-246
W.H. Pritchard, 249(HudR):Autumn89-491
639(VQR):Spring89-59
Davies, R. The Rebel Angels.
W.J. Keith, 298:Spring89-140
Davies, R. Ronald Searle.
A. Ross, 617(TLS):2-8Nov90-1176
Davies, R. What's Bred in the Bone.
W.J. Keith, 298:Spring89-140
M. Peterman, 168(ECW):Fall89-29
Davies, S. The Feminine Reclaimed.*
D. McColley, 70:Jul89-110
Davies, S. Laclos: "Les Liaisons danger-
euses."
R.C. Rosbottom, 402(MLR):Jan90-189
Davies, S. Primavera.
R. Clare, 617(TLS):1-7Jun90-586
Davin, D., ed. The Dragon's Head. The Kill-
ing Bottle.
G. Das, 108(FA):Oct-Dec89-490
Davis, C. Dog Horse Rat.
B. Probst, 441:1Jul90-14
Davis, C. Michel Tournier.
E.F. Gray, 395(MFS):Winter89-833
K.D. Levy, 207(FR):Apr90-881
M. Worton, 208(FS):Oct89-496
Davis, D. Devices and Desires.*
P. Gross, 493:Autumn89-65
S. O'Brien, 364:Feb/Mar90-111
Davis, D.B. Revolutions.
G.S. Wood, 453(NYRB):27Sep90-32
Davis, E. Challenging Colonialism.
J. Beinin, 318(JAOS):Jan-Mar88-167
Davis, F. Outcats.
J. Berry, 441:17Jun90-17
Davis, G.V. & M. Senior. South Africa.
R.N. Choonoo, 538(RAL):Fall89-548
Davis, J.H., Jr. The Happy Island.
R. Runte, 207(FR):Oct89-162
R. Waller, 83:Spring89-114
Davis, J.M., ed. Conversations with Robert-
son Davies.
L.E. Beattie, 441:15Apr90-14
P. Monk, 150(DR):Spring89-139
Davis, K. Labrador.*
42(AR):Winter89-116

Davis, K.C. Don't Know Much About History.
J.M. Cornelius, 441:30Sep90-42
Davis, K.F. George N. Barnard.
A. Grundberg, 441:2Dec90-71
Davis, L. Break It Down.
B. Haviland, 473(PR):Vol56No1-151
Davis, L. Sexuality and Textuality in Henry
James.
S.B. Daugherty, 395(MFS):Winter89-729
Davis, L.J. Resisting Novels.*
T. Craig, 102(CanL):Summer89-154
D. Elam, 454:Winter90-212
B. Foley, 49:Oct89-189
D.T.O., 295(JML):Fall88/Winter89-243
Davis, M. Ancient Tragedy and the Origins of
Modern Science.
N.D.S., 185:Oct89-217
Davis, M., with Q. Troupe. Miles.*
F. Davis, 61:Jan90-96
M. Wood, 617(TLS):2-8Mar90-215
Davis, M.P. Mexican Voices/American Dreams.
S. Coates, 441:16Dec90-19
Davis, N.Z. Fiction in the Archives.*
R.B. Bottigheimer, 196:Band30Heft1/2-
115
R.C. Trexler, 551(RenQ):Spring89-124
Davis, O. Drawing from That Well.
C. Hurford, 617(TLS):21-27Dec90-1383
Davis, P. Being a Boy.
R.G. Benson, 569(SR):Spring89-lvii
Davis, P. & M. Rinvolucri. Dictation.
H.J. Siskin, 399(MLJ):Winter89-486
Davis, R. Kendrew of York and his Chapbooks
for Children.
J. Barr, 354:Sep89-285
517(PBSA):Jun89-254
Davis, R.C. & L. Finke. Literary Criticism and
Theory.
L. Sage, 617(TLS):18-24May90-523
Davis, R.C. & R. Schleifer, ed. Contemporary
Literary Criticism. (2nd ed)
J.R. Bennett, 677(YES):Vol20-218
Davis, R.M. & others. A Bibliography of
Evelyn Waugh.
J. Meyers, 87(BB):Jun89-141
Davis, S. & R. Haley, eds. The Penguin Book
of Contemporary New Zealand Short Stories.
F. Baveystock, 617(TLS):2-8Feb90-122
Davis, S.C. The World of Patience Gromes.
42(AR):Winter89-107
Davis, S.G. Parades and Power.
R.H. Saltzman, 292(JAF):Jul-Sep89-365
Davis, S.M. Apartheid's Rebels.
G.M. Fredrickson, 453(NYRB):27Sep90-20
Davis, W. Passage of Darkness.
E. Bourguignon, 292(JAF):Oct-Dec89-495
Davis, W.C. - see Jackman, J.S.
Davison, P. "Othello."
M. Neill, 402(MLR):Jul90-692
d'Avray, D.L. The Preaching of the Friars.*
S.G. De Maris, 589:Jan89-151
Dawe, R.D. - see Sophocles
Dawidowicz, L.S. From That Place and Time.*
639(VQR):Autumn89-128
Dawisha, K. Eastern Europe, Gorbachev and
Reform.
V.V. Kusin, 575(SEER):Oct89-652
Dawkins, R. The Extended Phenotype.
S. Rose, 617(TLS):23Feb-1Mar90-204
Dawson, C. November 1948.
H. Pakula, 441:29Jul90-22

Dawson, C. Prophets of Past Time.*
J. Halperin, 77:Fall89-328
N. Page, 177(ELT):Vol32No4-485
J. Pilling, 402(MLR):Apr90-422
639(VQR):Winter89-18
Dawson, F.G. The First Latin American Debt
Crisis.
J. Lynch, 617(TLS):19-25Oct90-1136
Dawson, G.M. The Journals of George M. Daw-
son. (D. Cole & B. Lockner, eds)
G.W., 102(CanL):Autumn-Winter89-287
Dawson, J. Kindred Crimes.
M. Stasio, 441:9Sep90-39
Day, D. A Cold Killing.
N. Callendar, 441:22Jul90-22
Day, F. Arthur Koestler.
P.G. Reeve, 580(SCR):Fall89-140
Day, G. From Fiction to the Novel.*
M. Irwin, 541(RES):May89-269
M. Kirkham, 83:Autumn89-226
J.T. Parnell, 566:Spring90-205
Day, J. God's Conflict with the Dragon and
the Sea.
S.B. Parker, 318(JAOS):Jan-Mar88-152
Day, J. Mrs. Snow and the Colonel.
P. Craig, 617(TLS):24-30Aug90-889
Day, R. Larkin.*
R. Crawford, 541(RES):Nov89-593
A. Haberer, 189(EA):Jul-Sep89-355
Day, R.A. - see Smollett, T.
Day, W.G. - see Pepys, S.
Dayan, J. Fables of Mind.*
R. Regan, 301(JEGP):Jan89-135
Dazai, O. Crackling Mountain and Other
Stories.
F. Tuohy, 617(TLS):16-22Nov90-1233
Deahl, J., ed. The Northern Red Oak.
M.H. Keefer, 102(CanL):Winter88-136
Deahl, J. - see Acorn, M.
Deák, I. Beyond Nationalism.
S. Beller, 617(TLS):2-8Nov90-1174
R.J.W. Evans, 453(NYRB):16Aug90-47
Dean, C. Arthur of England.*
H. Cooper, 447(N&Q):Mar89-89
P.J.C. Field, 541(RES):Nov89-544
Dean, J. Meeting Gorbachev's Challenge.
G. Duffy, 441:28Jan90-30
Dean, W. & J.M. Knapp. Handel's Operas
1704-1726.*
R. Elliott, 529(QQ):Spring89-188
De Andrea, W.L. Atropos.
N. Callendar, 441:15Apr90-19
Deane, S. The French Revolution and
Enlightenment in England, 1789-1832.
J. Black, 173(ECS):Spring90-343
M. Kelsall, 402(MLR):Apr90-415
A.K. Mellor, 591(SIR):Fall89-509
K. Tetzeli von Rosador, 445(NCF):Sep89-
225
J. Voisine, 549(RLC):Oct-Dec89-593
639(VQR):Spring89-44
Deaver, P.F. Silent Retreats.*
J.L. Halio, 573(SSF):Fall88-499
De Benedetti, C. & C. Chatfield. An American
Ordeal.
S.M. Evans, 441:17Jun90-18
Debenham, W. Laughter on Record.
B.L. Cooper, 498:Summer89-120
De Boel, G. Goal Accusative and Object
Accusative in Homer.
A.C. Moorhouse, 123:Vol39No2-403
Debon, C. - see Queneau, R.

90

Debord, G. La société du spectacle.
   L. Jenny, 98:Oct89-765
Debray, R. A demain de Gaulle.
   T. Judt, 617(TLS):28Sep-4Oct90-1018
Debray-Genette, R. Métamorphoses du récit.
   M.P. Ginsburg, 446(NCFS):Fall-
      Winter89/90-257
Debray-Genette, R. & J. Neefs, eds. Romans
   d'archives.*
   R. Mahieu, 535(RHL):Mar-Apr89-313
"Debrett's Peerage and Baronetage, 1990."
   (C. Kidd & D. Williamson, eds)
   H. Trevor-Roper, 617(TLS):27Apr-
      3May90-449
Debreuille, J-Y., ed. Lire Tardieu.
   W. Scott, 402(MLR):Oct90-979
Debus, F., M.W. Hellmann & H.D. Schlosser,
   eds. Sprachliche Normen und Normierungs-
   folgen in der DDR.
   H. Poethe, 682(ZPSK):Band42Heft4-527
De Busscher, G., ed. American Literature in
   Belgium.
   R. Asselineau, 189(EA):Oct-Dec89-500
Debussy, C. Préludes: Livre I, Livre II. (R.
   Howat, with C. Helffer, eds) Oeuvres pour
   deux pianos. (N. Lee, ed)
   D. Grayson, 451:Spring90-243
"Début et fin des Lumières en Hongrie, en
   Europe centrale et en Europe orientale."
   D-H. Pageaux, 549(RLC):Jan-Mar89-121
"Décadence et Apocalypse."
   D. Millet Gérard, 549(RLC):Jul-Sep89-
      422
Dechert, H.W. & M. Raupach, eds. Psycholin
   guistic Models of Production.
   D. Wolff, 710:Dec89-460
Decke-Cornill, A. Vernichtung und Selbstbe-
   hauptung.
   B. Allert, 406:Summer89-262
Declerck, R. Studies on Copular Sentences,
   Clefts and Pseudo-Clefts.
   A.C. Harris, 350:Dec90-862
Decleve, H. - see Patočka, J.
Decreus, F. De structurele analyse van
   poëzie.
   P. Swiggers, 567:Vol75No3/4-345
Décsy, G. A Select Catalog of Language Uni-
   versals.A
   B. Comrie, 159:Vol6No1-137
Décsy, G. Statistical Report on the Languages
   of the World as of 1985.
   S. Levin, 215(GL):Vol29No3-209
Décsy, G. The Uralic Protolanguage.
   L. Campbell, 350:Dec90-863
Decter, J., with others. Nicholas Roerich.
   C. Reid, 617(TLS):16-22Mar90-290
Dédéyan, C. Diderot et la pensée anglaise.
   A.G. Raymond, 535(RHL):Jan-Feb89-116
Dédéyan, C. Montesquieu ou l'alibi persan.*
   L. Versini, 535(RHL):Sep-Oct89-933
Dedner, B., ed. Georg Büchner, "Leonce und
   Lena."
   T.M. Holmes, 402(MLR):Jan90-255
   G.P. Knapp, 564:Sep89-269
Dedora, B. White Light.
   D.A. Precosky, 102(CanL):Summer89-193
Dee, J. The Lover of History.
   A. Solomon, 441:4Nov90-24
   442(NY):10Dec90-158
"John Dee's Library Catalogue." (J. Roberts &
   A.G. Watson, eds)
   T.A. Birrell, 617(TLS):21-27Dec90-1386

Dees, A., with others. Atlas des formes lin-
   guistiques des textes littéraires de l'ancien
   français.*
   M.R. Harris, 589:Apr89-405
Defant, C. Kammermusik und Stylus phantas-
   ticus.
   W. Werbeck, 417:Jan-Mar89-87
Defaux, G. Marot, Rabelais, Montaigne.*
   W.J. Beck, 207(FR):Oct89-155
   M. Heath, 208(FS):Jan89-78
   F. Lestringant, 535(RHL):Jul-Aug89-705
De Ferrari, G. A Cloud on Sand.
   J. Baumel, 441:24Jun90-21
De Forest, O. & D. Chanoff. Slow Burn.
   R. Manning, 441:22Apr90-12
   J. Mirsky, 453(NYRB):16Aug90-29
Deforge, B. Eschyle, poète cosmique.*
   P. Demont, 555:Vol62Fasc2-342
Degand, L. Abstraction - Figuration.
   A. Moeglin-Delcroix, 98:Nov89-819
De Gennaro, A.A. The Reader's Companion to
   Dante's "Divine Comedy."
   C. Slade, 276:Summer89-219
Degrada, F., ed. Andrea Gabrieli e il suo
   tempo.
   A.F. Carver, 410(M&L):Feb89-87
De Grand, A. In Stalin's Shadow.
   F.H. Adler, 42(AR):Winter89-101
De Gruson, G. - see Sinclair, U.
De Haven, T. Sunburn Lake.
   D. Flower, 249(HudR):Spring89-135
Dehoux, V. Chants à penser gbaya (Centra-
   frique).
   F.A. Noss, 538(RAL):Summer89-273
Deighton, L. Spy Sinker.
   K. Jeffery, 617(TLS):30Nov-6Dec90-1300
   M. Kondracke, 441:2Sep90-6
Deininger, J. - see Weber, M.
De Jean, J. Fictions of Sappho 1546-1937.
   T. Moi, 617(TLS):31Aug-6Sep90-913
Déjeux, J. Mohammed Dib.
   L. Tremaine, 538(RAL):Spring89-127
Déjeux, J. Le sentiment religieux dans la
   littérature maghrébine de langue française.
   A. Lippert, 538(RAL):Spring89-122
Dekker, G. The American Historical
   Romance.*
   J-L. Bourget, 189(EA):Apr-Jun89-231
   T. D'haen, 179(ES):Apr89-186
   D.H. Hirsch, 401(MLQ):Jun88-173
   L.J. Reynolds, 594:Spring89-98
Delage, C. Le Moine partisan.
   W. Greenberg, 207(FR):Feb90-576
Delage, M-J. - see Caesarius of Arles
Delaney, J.G.P. Charles Ricketts.
   M. Morgan, 617(TLS):22-28Jun90-660
De-la-Noy, M. Michael Ramsey.
   D. Nineham, 617(TLS):16-22Mar90-272
Delaporte, A. L'idée d'égalité en France au
   XVIIIe siècle.
   T.E. Kaiser, 242:Vol10No1-111
Delay, C. Les Ouragans sont lents.
   N. Naudin, 207(FR):Dec89-403
Delay, F. & J. Roubaud. Partition Rouge.
   C-P. Pérez, 450(NRF):Mar89-78
   P-Y. Petillon, 98:Apr89-239
Delbanco, A. The Puritan Ordeal.*
   P.F. Gura, 432(NEQ):Dec89-617
   F. Shuffelton, 165(EAL):Vol25No2-200
   639(VQR):Autumn89-118
Delbanco, N. The Writers' Trade.
   N. Mairs, 441:18Mar90-12

Delbecque, N. Problèmes et méthodes de l'étude de la variation syntaxique.*
   B.R. Lavandera, 361:Aug89-360
Delbée, A. & G. Forestier – see Racine, J.
Del Chiaro, M.A. & W.R. Biers, eds. Corinthiaca.
   G.P. Schaus, 487:Autumn89-260
Delcroix, M. & F. Hallyn, eds. Méthodes du texte.*
   R. Zaiser, 547(RF):Band101Heft1-103
Deledalle, G. Charles S. Peirce, Phénoménologue et sémioticien.*
   G. Bouchard, 619:Winter89-61
Deledda, G. Cosima.
   M. Aste, 276:Spring89-49
Deleuze, G. Bergsonism.
   P. Kidder, 543:Sep89-152
Deleuze, G. Foucault. (S. Hand, ed & trans)
   G.J. Stack, 543:Mar90-629
Deleuze, G. & F. Guattari. A Thousand Plateaus.
   C.J. Stivale, 207(FR):Mar90-701
De Ley, H. Le Jeu classique.
   R.W. Tobin, 208(FS):Oct89-464
D'Elia, G. & C. Williams. La nuova letteratura inglese.
   M.T. Chialant, 677(YES):Vol20-352
Delibes, M. Die heiligen Narren.
   M. Walter, 654(WB):12/1989-2033
Delibes, M. 377A, Madera de héroe.
   D.K. Herzberger, 238:May89-306
Delicado, F. Portrait of Lozana.*
   J.V. Ricapito, 238:Mar89-162
Delière, J. & R. Lafayette. Connaître la France. (2nd ed)
   A.G. Suozzo, Jr., 207(FR):Mar90-733
De Lillo, D. Libra.*
   W.E. Cain, 385(MQR):Spring90-275
   J. Tabbi, 532(RCF):Spring89-244
   42(AR):Winter89-116
De Lio, T. Circumscribing the Open Universe.
   S. Blaustein, 513:Winter89-280
   H. Sabbe, 513:Winter89-312
De Lio, T., ed. Contiguous Lines.
   S. Blaustein, 513:Winter89-280
Delisle, R. Le mercanaire de LG2.
   A.M. Miraglia, 102(CanL):Winter88-139
Delius, F. & others. Delius: A Life in Letters 1909-1934. (L. Carley, ed)
   R. Anderson, 415:Jan89-23
Delivorrias, A., ed. Greece and the Sea.
   S.E. Sidebotham, 123:Vol39No1-155
Délivoyatzis, S. La dialectique du phénomène (Sur Merleau-Ponty).
   P. Doïkos, 192(EP):Jan-Mar89-97
Della Casa, G. Galateo.
   D. Shemek, 276:Spring89-50
Della Vida, G.L. & M.G. Amadasi Guzzo. Iscrizioni puniche della Tripolitania (1927-1967).
   W. Huss, 229:Band61Heft4-300
Delmas, C. Mythologie et mythe dans le théâtre français (1650-1676).*
   B. Guthmüller, 72:Band226Heft1-201
   V. Kapp, 475:Vol16No30-279
Delmay, B. I personaggi della "Divina Commedia."
   R. Stillers, 72:Band226Heft1-218
Delon, M. L'Idée d'énergie au tournant des Lumières (1770-1820).
   D.P. Kinloch, 208(FS):Jul89-335
   R. Mortier, 535(RHL):Mar-Apr89-295
   R. Niklaus, 402(MLR):Jul90-733

Delon, M. – see Mirbeau, O.
Delon, M. – see Restif de La Bretonne
Delon, M. – see Sénac de Meilhan, G.
De Long, D.G. Bruce Goff.*
   J. Cook, 505:Mar89-129
   E. McCoy, 47:Jan89-33
De L'orme, P. Traités d'architecture. (J-M. Pérouse de Montclos, ed)
   H. Ballon, 576:Dec89-391
Delorme, R.L., comp. Latin America, 1983-1987.
   M.H. Sable, 263(RIB):Vol39No2-205
De Luca, I. Tre poeti traduttori.
   E. Favretti, 228(GSLI):Vol166fasc535-466
Delumeau, J. Sin and Fear.
   W. Doniger, 441:23Sep90-27
De Lupis, I.D. The Law of War.
   I.C., 185:Oct89-221
Del Vecchio, J.M. For the Sake of All Living Things.
   D. Murray, 441:18Feb90-24
Delvigo, M.L. Testo virgiliano e tradizione indiretta.
   S.J. Harrison, 313:Vol79-204
   H.D. Jocelyn, 123:Vol39No1-27
De Lynn, J. Don Juan in the Village.
   B. Harris, 441:21Oct90-15
Delz, J. – see Silius
Demadre, A. Essais sur Thomas Nashe.
   E. Cuvelier, 189(EA):Oct-Dec89-466
De Maegd-Soëp, C. Chekhov and Women.*
   S.M. Carnicke, 550(RusR):Jan89-101
   B. Heldt, 279:Vol35/36-373
   K.D. Kramer, 574(SEEJ):Winter89-624
   G. McVay, 575(SEER):Jul89-454
   N. Rosen, 104(CASS):Spring-Winter88-427
Demaine, H. & R.E. Malong, eds. Decentralization.
   C. Henderson, 293(JASt):Nov89-800
De Mallie, R.J. & D.R. Parks, eds. Sioux Indian Religion.
   A. Hultkrantz, 292(JAF):Jan-Mar89-120
Deman, A. & M-T. Raepsaet-Charlier. Les inscriptions latines de Belgique (ILB).
   W. Kuhoff, 229:Band61Heft2-174
Demaray, J.G. Dante and the Book of the Cosmos.
   P. Armour, 382(MAE):1989/1-179
De Maria, L. La nascita dell'avanguardia.
   M. Lentzen, 72:Band226Heft1-228
De Maria, R., Jr. Johnson's Dictionary and the Language of Learning.*
   M.G.H. Pitock, 83:Spring89-111
De Marinis, R. The Coming Triumph of the Free World.
   J. Klinkowitz, 455:Mar89-69
   G. Krist, 249(HudR):Spring89-130
   639(VQR):Winter89-22
Demastes, W.W. Beyond Naturalism.*
   T. Pyzik, 27(AL):Oct89-502
Dembo, J. – see Littell, N.M.
Dembo, L.S. The Monological Jew.
   L. Field, 395(MFS):Summer89-288
   S.E. Marovitz, 27(AL):Oct89-504
Dembowski, P.F. – see Froissart, J.
De Mente, B. Discovering Cultural Japan.
   Y-H. Tohsaku, 399(MLJ):Autumn89-376
De Mente, B. Japanese Etiquette and Ethics in Business. (5th ed)
   J.L. Huffman, 399(MLJ):Spring89-95

De Mente, B. Korean in Plain English.
  J.J. Ree, 399(MLJ):Autumn89–377
De Meritt, L.C. New Subjectivity and Prose
  Forms of Alienation.
  T.F. Barry, 221(GQ):Summer89–436
  C. Bedwell, 395(MFS):Winter89–829
  G.M. Stoffel, 133:Band22Heft3/4–377
Demetz, H. The Journey from Prague Street.
  B.F. Williamson, 441:1Jul90–15
D'Emilio, J. & E. Freedman. Intimate Matters.
  G.S. Smith, 529(QQ):Summer89–244
De Mille, N. The Gold Coast.
  J. Kaufman, 441:27May90–14
Demirović, H. – see Whitman, W.
De Molen, R.L. The Spirituality of Erasmus of
  Rotterdam.
  M. Heath, 557:Jun89–220
  A.M. O'Donnell, 551(RenQ):Summer89–308
Demonet-Launay, M.L. Histoire de la littéra-
  ture française sous la direction de Daniel
  Couty.
  E. Armstrong, 208(FS):Jul89–323
Demonte, V. & M. Fernandez Lagunilla, eds.
  Sintaxis de las lenguas románicas.
  R.J. Blake, 350:Dec90–864
Démoris, R. Lectures de ...
  D.J. Culpin, 535(RHL):Jan–Feb89–140
Demosthenes. Démosthène: Lettres et Frag-
  ments. (R. Clavaud, ed & trans)
  G.O. Rowe, 124:Nov–Dec89–117
De Mott, B. The Imperial Middle.
  B. Ehrenreich, 441:14Oct90–9
De Mott, R. – see Steinbeck, J.
Dempster, D. Willing Home.
  P. Stevens, 150(DR):Spring89–150
Demus, O. The Mosaics of San Marco in
  Venice.
  D. Mouriki, 54:Mar89–132
Dendle, B.J. Galdós: The Early Historical
  Novels.*
  D.F. Urey, 86(BHS):Jul89–289
Dendle, B.J., ed. Galdós y Murcia.
  P.A. Bly, 402(MLR):Jan90–231
  R.B. Klein, 238:Mar89–145
  G. Paolini, 552(REH):May89–142
Denoef, A.L. Traherne in Dialogue.
  639(VQR):Spring89–65
Denes, G., C. Semenza & P. Bisiacchi, eds.
  Perspectives on Cognitive Neuropsychology.
  R.B. Katz, 348(L&S):Oct–Dec89–387
Denham, R.D. Northrop Frye.*
  R.M. Baine, 88:Fall89–88
  G. Forst, 102(CanL):Autumn–Winter89–
  189
  L. Laakso, 470:Vol27–110
  T. Willard, 627(UTQ):Fall89–165
  J.F. Woodruff, 405(MP):Feb90–324
Denis, J. Treatise on Harpsichord Tuning by
  Jean Denis.* (V.J. Panetta, ed & trans)
  S. Pollens, 415:Apr89–213
Denisoff, R.S. Inside MTV.
  G. Plasketes, 498:Winter89–92
Denitch, B. The End of the Cold War.
  L.V. Sigal, 441:29Jul90–24
Denkler, H. Neues über Wilhelm Raabe.*
  J.L. Sammons, 221(GQ):Spring89–281
Denley, P., ed. History of Universities. (Vol
  6)
  E. Dubois, 242:Vol10No1–105
Dennerline, J. Qian Mu and the World of Sev-
  en Mansions.*
  P.A. Cohen, 293(JASt):Aug89–585

Dennett, D.C. Elbow Room.* (German title:
  Ellenbogenfreiheit.)
  M. Thornton, 486:Sep89–543
Dennett, D.C. The Intentional Stance.*
  S.J. Brison, 518:Jul89–169
  P. Engel, 98:Nov89–864
  R.A. Sharpe, 262:Jun89–233
  S.P. Stich, 185:Jul90–891
  E.N. Zalta, 543:Dec89–397
Denning, M. Cover Stories.*
  R.P. Moses, 295(JML):Fall88/Winter89–
  242
Dennis, M. Court and Garden.
  R. Middleton, 90:Feb89–157
Dennis, M. German Democratic Republic.
  M. McCauley, 575(SEER):Apr89–322
Dennis, N., ed. Ramón Gómez de la Serna.
  R. Gardiol, 238:Dec89–963
Denooz, J. Aristote, "Poetica."
  P. Louis, 555:Vol62Fasc2–345
Dent, B. Blue Guide Hungary.
  G. Szirtes, 617(TLS):27Apr–3May90–440
De Paepe, C. – see Lorca, F.G.
De Paolo, C. Coleridge's Philosophy of Social
  Reform.
  A. Young, 125:Summer89–417
De Petris, C., ed. Joyce Studies in Italy 2.
  C. del Greco Lobner, 329(JJQ):Fall89–164
d'Epinay, L. Les Contre-Confessions. (E.
  Badinter, ed)
  C. Slawy-Sutton, 207(FR):Apr90–913
d'Epinay, L. Lettres à mon fils, essais sur
  l'éducation, et Morceaux choisis, corres-
  pondance et extraits. (R.P. Weinreb, ed)
  J.F. Jones, Jr., 173(ECS):Spring90–365
Deprez, K., ed. Sociolinguistics in the Low
  Countries.
  L. Kremer, 685(ZDL):1/1989–124
De Quille, D. Dives and Lazarus.* (L.I.
  Berkove, ed)
  J.Y. Lee, 26(ALR):Winter90–91
De Quille, D. The Fighting Horse of the Stan-
  islaus. (L.I. Berkove, ed)
  T. Hillerman, 441:23Sep90–33
Der Hovanessian, D. & M. Margossian – see
  Charents, E.
Deriabin, P. & T.H. Bagley. The KGB.
  A. Knight, 617(TLS):7–13Dec90–1309
Derian, J-C. America's Struggle for Leader-
  ship in Technology.
  W. Leontief, 441:24Jun90–31
De Ridder, P. Inventaris van het oud Archief
  der Kapittelkerk van Sint-Michiel en Sint-
  Goedele te Brussel.
  L.R. Baratz, 415:Dec89–744
Derolez, A. Codicologie des manuscrits en
  écriture humanistique sur parchemin.
  J.F. Preston, 589:Jan89–153
De Rooij, J., ed. Variatie en norm in de stan-
  daardtaal.
  C. van Bree, 204(FdL):Sep89–220
Derr, M. Some Kind of Paradise.
  J. Tallmadge, 441:7Jan90–22
Derrida, J. The Archeology of the Frivolous.
  M. Hobson, 208(FS):Jul89–329
Derrida, J. Glas.*
  K. Hart, 63:Jun89–243
Derrida, J. Memoires for Paul de Man.
  R. Selden, 677(YES):Vol20–223
Derrida, J. Of Spirit.* (French title: De
  l'esprit.)
  R. Burch, 103:Oct90–403
  J. Sallis, 153:Fall–Winter89–25

Derrida, J. The Truth in Painting.*
 M. Bull, 90:Jun89-435
 P. Crowther, 89(BJA):Summer89-271
 D.T.O., 295(JML):Fall88/Winter89-224
 D. Worrall, 88:Fall89-89
Derry, J.W. Politics in the Age of Fox, Pitt
 and Liverpool.
 F. O'Gorman, 617(TLS):21-27Sep90-1004
Dertouzos, M.L., R.M. Solow & R.K. Lester.
 Made in America.*
 R.B. Reich, 617(TLS):31Aug-6Sep90-925
Desai, A. Baumgartner's Bombay.*
 42(AR):Summer89-373
Desai, B. The Memory of Elephants.
 B. Finkelstein, 441:29Jul90-20
Desai, N. & M. Krishnaraj. Women and Society
 in India.
 M. Maskiell, 293(JASt):Aug89-648
De Salvo, L. Virginia Woolf.*
 Q. Bell, 453(NYRB):15Mar90-3
 A. Pratt, 268(IFR):Summer89-146
 S.H. Sweeney, 363(LitR):Spring90-394
De Salvo, L. & M.A. Leaska - see Sackville-
 West, V.
Desautels, D. Un livre de Kafka à la main
 [suivi de] la Blessure.
 P. Haeck, 102(CanL):Spring89-204
Desbiens, P. Les Cascadeurs de l'amour.
 D. Williams, 102(CanL):Autumn-
 Winter89-263
Descartes, R. Correspondance avec Elisabeth
 et autres lettres. (J-M. & M. Beyssade,
 eds)
 J-P. Cavaillé, 542:Oct-Dec89-598
Descartes, R. & M. Schoock. La Querelle
 d'Utrecht. (T. Verbeek, ed & trans)
 P. Guenancia, 98:Nov89-904
Deschodt, E. Le Royaume d'Arles.
 C.A. Baker, 207(FR):Oct89-202
Descombes, V. Objects of All Sorts.
 N. Parker, 323:May89-184
Descombes, V. Proust.*
 J-C. Dumoncel, 98:May89-352
 P. Somville, 542:Oct-Dec89-635
Descotes, M. Le cas Boileau.
 A.G. Wood, 475:Vol16No30-282
De Silva, Z.S. Beginning Spanish.* (6th ed)
 T.R. Arrington, 238:Sep89-565
Desjardins, A. Aline Desjardins s'entretient
 avec François Truffaut.
 A. Thiher, 207(FR):Feb90-568
Des Landes, C. Michel Garneau écrivain pub-
 lic.
 L.H. Forsyth, 627(UTQ):Fall89-192
Desmond, A. The Politics of Evolution.
 J. Secord, 617(TLS):13-19Jul90-751
Desmond, J.F. Risen Sons.*
 M. Kowalewski, 585(SoQ):Summer89-112
 L. Lawson, 578:Fall90-107
Desmond, R. A Celebration of Flowers.
 M. Lambourne, 39:Dec89-432
Desmond, W. Art and the Absolute.*
 E. von der Luft, 125:Summer89-409
Despland, M. The Education of Desire.
 J.B. Allis, 41:Spring89-121
Des Pres, T. Praises and Dispraises.*
 C. Bedient, 472:Vol16No1-195
Dessen, A.C. Shakespeare and the Late Moral
 Plays.*
 M. Lomax, 677(YES):Vol20-252
Desser, D. Eros Plus Massacre.
 J.L. Anderson, 293(JASt):Feb89-157
 K. McDonald, 407(MN):Summer89-239

Detienne, M. The Creation of Mythology.*
 (French title: L'invention de la mythol-
 ogie.)
 A.W.H. Adkins, 41:Spring89-109
Detienne, M., ed. Les Savoirs de l'écriture en
 Grèce ancienne.
 C.G. Thomas, 123:Vol39No2-242
Detlefsen, M. Hilbert's Program.*
 D.D. Auerbach, 316:Jun89-620
Detmer, D. Freedom as a Value.
 L.A.B., 185:Apr90-699
 125:Summer89-427
Deuchar, S. Sporting Art in Eighteenth-Cen-
 tury England.*
 D.H. Solkin, 90:Nov89-783
 639(VQR):Spring89-67
Deutsch, G.N. Iconographie de l'illustration
 de Flavius Josèphe au temps de Jean Fou-
 quet.
 A.H. van Buren, 589:Jul89-695
"Deutsche Literatur: Ein Jahresüberblick
 1981-1987." (V. Hage & others, eds)
 P.M. Lützeler, 221(GQ):Summer89-443
De Venney, D.P. Early American Choral
 Music.
 R. Andrewes, 415:Dec89-746
Deverell, W. Platinum Blues.
 M. Stasio, 441:30Sep90-32
De Verville, B. - see under Béroalde De Ver-
 ville
Devet, R.M. Mrs. Houdini.
 M. Cookshaw, 376:Dec89-124
Deville, P. Longue vue.
 G.W. Fetzer, 207(FR):Feb90-578
Devine, A.M. & L.D. Stephens. Language and
 Metre.
 C.J. Ruijgh, 394:Vol42fasc1/2-139
Devine, J., P.L. Carrell & D.E. Eskey, eds.
 Research in Reading in English as a Second
 Language.
 M.A. Barnett, 710:Sep89-351
Devinney, M.K. The Legends of Gertrud von
 Le Fort.
 M.C. Ives, 402(MLR):Oct90-1034
Devitt, M. & K. Sterelny. Language and Real-
 ity.*
 J. Bigelow, 63:Mar89-95
 Q. Cassam, 393(Mind):Apr89-313
 D.H., 355(LSoc):Jun89-304
Devlin, D. Collected Poems. (J.C.C. Mays, ed)
 B. O'Donoghue, 617(TLS):17-23Aug90-
 871
Devlin, D. Mask and Scene.
 J. Wilders, 617(TLS):5-11Jan90-14
Devlin, D.D. The Novels and Journals of
 Fanny Burney.*
 M. Scheuermann, 594:Spring89-100
Devlin, J. The Superstitious Mind.
 S.P. Conner, 446(NCFS):Spring-
 Summer90-576
Devlin, P. Dora.
 P. Craig, 617(TLS):21-27Sep90-999
Devon, G. Bad Desire.
 W.H. Banks, Jr., 441:14Oct90-48
Devriès, A. & F. Lesure. Dictionnaire des
 éditeurs de musique français. (Vol 2)
 H. Lenneberg, 309:Vol9No4-303
Dewarrat, M-C. Carême.
 Y. Jenny, 207(FR):Oct89-203
Dewdney, C. Permugenesis. The Radiant In-
 ventory.
 C. Messenger, 102(CanL):Autumn-
 Winter89-282

Dewey, J. John Dewey: The Later Works, 1925-1953.* (Vols 9, 10 & 12) (J.A. Boydston, ed)
  R.D. Boisvert, 258:Mar89-91
Dewey, J. The Later Works, 1925-1953. (Vol 11) (J.A. Boydston, ed)
  R.H. Evans, 619:Winter89-65
Dewey, J. The Later Works, 1925-1953. (Vols 13 & 14) (J.A. Boydston, ed)
  E.G. Mesthene, 619:Winter89-69
Dewey, P.E. British Agriculture in the First World War.
  W. Minchinton, 617(TLS):5-11Jan90-20
Dews, P. Logics of Disintegration.*
  T. Docherty, 541(RES):Nov89-598
Dexter, C. The Wench is Dead.
  M. Stasio, 441:20May90-53
Deyermond, A. El "Cantar de Mio Cid" y la épica medieval española.*
  D.G. Pattison, 402(MLR):Apr90-466
Dezon-Jones, E. - see de Gournay, M.
D'haen, T. & H. Bertens, eds. Postmodern Fiction in Europe and the Americas.
  C.K. Columbus, 395(MFS):Winter89-858
  S. Connor, 402(MLR):Oct90-904
  U. Schulz-Buschhaus, 602:Band20Heft2-327
Dhammapala, G., R. Gombrich & K.R. Norman, eds. Buddhist Studies in Honor of Hammalava Saddhātissa.
  S.B. Goodman, 318(JAOS):Apr-Jun88-329
d'Hausay, O., ed. Liturgie et espace liturgique.
  A. Bordeaux, 189(EA):Oct-Dec89-442
d'Holbach, P.T. Die Gesamte Erhaltene Korrespondanz.* (H. Sauter & E. Loos, eds)
  J-L. Lecercle, 535(RHL):Jan-Feb89-113
  H-J. Lope, 547(RF):Band101Heft4-478
Dhondy, F. Bombay Duck.
  N. Berry, 617(TLS):1-7Jun90-585
D'Hulst, L. L'évolution de la poésie en France (1780-1830).
  G. Robb, 535(RHL):Jul-Aug89-727
Diamond, M.J. Crossings.
  M. De Koven, 473(PR):Vol56No1-157
Diamonstein, B. The Landmarks of New York.
  D. Waterman, 55:May09-112
Di Antonio, R.E. Brazilian Fiction.
  L. Helena, 268(IFR):Summer90-141
  M.N. Silverman, 263(RIB):Vol39No2-206
"Diario de los Literatos de España [1737-1741]."
  R.P. Sebold, 240(HR):Summer89-391
Dias, P. & M. Hayhoe. Developing Response to Poetry.
  R.L. Houghton, 97(CQ):Vol18No2-219
Díaz, J. Romances, canciones y cuentos de Castilla y León. (3rd ed)
  E. Martinell Gifre, 548:Jul-Dec89-485
Díaz, N.G. - see under Gray Díaz, N.
Díaz-Bernardo, E.G. - see under Gutiérrez Díaz-Bernardo, E.
Díaz de Castro, F.J. La poesía de Jorge Guillén.
  A.P. Debicki, 240(HR):Winter89-120
Díaz Jimeno, F. Hado y fortuna en la España del siglo XVI.
  A. Hermenegildo, 240(HR):Summer89-376
  T. O'Reilly, 402(MLR):Apr90-469
  S. Paun de García, 552(REH):Oct89-130
Díaz Martín, L.V. Los oficiales de Pedro I de Castilla. (2nd ed)
  R.A. MacDonald, 589:Oct89-933

Díaz-Modesto Martín, J. Adivinanzas de Castilla y León. (2nd ed) Trabalenguas de Castilla y León. (2nd ed)
  E. Martinell Gifre, 548:Jul-Dec89-485
Díaz-Peterson, R. Las novelas de Unamuno.
  P.L. Ullman, 403(MLS):Summer89-87
Díaz y Díaz, M.C. Libros y librerías en la Rioja altomedieval.
  C.B. Faulhaber, 589:Jul89-698
Dibdin, M. The Tryst.
  C. McWilliam, 441:11Mar90-21
Di Benedetto, A. Vittorio Alfieri.*
  E. Kanduth, 547(RF):Band101Heft2/3-359
"Diccionario General Ilustrado de la Lengua Española." [VOX87]
  D. Mighetto, 548:Jan-Jun89-191
Dicke, G. & K. Grubmüller. Die Fabeln des Mittelalters und der frühen Neuzeit.
  I. Tomkowiak, 196:Band30Heft1/2-116
Dickens, B. Royboys.
  M. Gilman, 616:Vol10No2-56
Dickens, C. A December Vision. (N. Philip & V. Neuburg, eds)
  M. Andrews, 635(VPR):Summer89-88
Dickens, C. Dickens' Working Notes for His Novels. (H. Stone, ed)
  J.J. Brattin, 158:Mar89-17
  W. Burgan, 637(VS):Spring90-501
  L. Hartveit, 179(ES):Feb89-93
  D. Hewitt, 447(N&Q):Jun89-252
  S. Monod, 189(EA):Apr-Jun89-221
Dickens, C. Hard Times. (T. Eagleton, ed)
  S. Monod, 189(EA):Apr-Jun89-222
Dickens, C. The Letters of Charles Dickens.* (Vol 6) (G. Storey, K. Tillotson & N. Burgis, eds)
  R. Mason, 447(N&Q):Dec89-525
  639(VQR):Autumn89-124
Dickens, C. Selected Letters of Charles Dickens. (D. Paroissien, ed)
  J.J. Brattin, 158:Mar89-17
Dickens, C. The Speeches of Charles Dickens.* (K.J. Fielding, ed)
  T.N.C., 506(PSt):Sep89-200
  S. Monod, 637(VS):Spring90-513
Dickens, C., C. Fruttero & F. Lucentini. La verità sul caso D.
  M. D'Amico, 617(TLS):2-8Mar90-231
"Dickens Studies Annual."* (Vol 15) (M. Timko, F. Kaplan & E. Guiliano, eds)
  T.J. Cribb, 541(RES):May89-281
"Dickens Studies Annual." (Vols 16 & 17) (M. Timko, F. Kaplan & E. Guiliano, eds)
  J.M. Warner, 158:Dec89-167
Dickenson, D. George Sand.*
  K.H. Francis, 402(MLR):Jan90-193
  E. McCormack, 208(FS):Jul89-341
  D.A. Powell, 207(FR):Oct89-165
Dickey, C. Expats.
  J.A.C. Greppin, 617(TLS):7-13Sep90-938
  S. Mackey, 441:24Jun90-14
  442(NY):3Sep90-108
Dickey, L. Hegel.
  T.C. Hopton, 83:Spring89-103
  R.C. Solomon, 242:Vol10No2-251
Dickinson, C. With or Without.
  P. Marx, 573(SSF):Fall88-495
Dickinson, D.C. Dictionary of American Book Collectors.
  517(PBSA):Mar89-127

Dickinson, L. Self-instruction in Language Learning.
  Y. Bader, 257(IRAL):May89-162
  E.K. Horwitz, 710:Mar89-104
Dickinson, P. The Music of Lennox Berkeley.*
  E. Forbes, 324:Jul90-570
Dickinson, P. A Sun Dog.
  E. Bartlett, 493:Spring89-64
Dickson, D., ed. The Gorgeous Mask.
  P. Borsay, 83:Autumn89-211
  D. Hayton, 235:Summer89-90
Dickson, D. New Foundations.
  J. Hill, 235:Summer89-86
  P.D.G. Thomas, 83:Spring89-96
Dickson, D.R. The Fountain of Living Waters.
  D.T. Benet, 301(JEGP):Jul89-414
  E.B. Gilman, 551(RenQ):Autumn89-587
  E. Mackenzie, 447(N&Q):Sep89-392
  G.A. Stringer, 568(SCN):Spring-Summer89-12
  G. Watson, 677(YES):Vol20-258
Dickson, J. The Hospital for Wounded Angels.
  J. Cobley, 376:Jun89-133
"Dictionary of Canadian Biography."* (Vol 6) (F.G. Halpenny, general ed)
  M.L. MacDonald, 102(CanL):Autumn-Winter89-215
"Dictionary of Canadian Biography." (Vol 7) (F.G. Halpenny & J. Hamelin, general eds)
  529(QQ):Autumn89-781
"Dictionary of Canadian Biography."* (Vol 8) (F.G. Halpenny, general ed)
  P.M. St. Pierre, 102(CanL):Autumn-Winter89-238
"Dictionary of Literary Biography." (Vol 56) (J. Hardin, ed)
  H.J. Schmidt, 221(GQ):Winter89-131
"Dictionary of Literary Biography."* (Vol 58) (F. Bowers, ed)
  W.P. Williams, 447(N&Q):Jun89-236
"Dictionary of Literary Biography." (Vol 66, Pts 1 & 2) (J. Hardin, ed)
  H.J. Schmidt, 221(GQ):Winter89-132
"Dictionary of Literary Biography." (Vol 69) (W.D. Elfe & J. Hardin, eds)
  H.J. Schmidt, 221(GQ):Winter89-132
"Dictionary of Old English: Preface and List of Texts and Index of Editions."* "Dictionary of Old English."* (fasc D) (A. Cameron & others, eds of both)
  D. Donoghue, 589:Jan89-155
  M. Korhammer, 38:Band107Heft1/2-127
"Dictionnaire de l'Amérique française." (C. Dufresne & others, eds)
  L.E. Doucette, 627(UTQ):Fall89-175
"Dictionnaire des oeuvres littéraires du Québec." (Vol 5) (M. Lemire, ed)
  B-Z. Shek, 627(UTQ):Fall89-172
"Dictionnaire des usages socio-politiques."
  J.R. Censer, 322(JHI):Oct-Dec89-652
"Dictionnaire du français plus." (C. Poirier, ed-in-chief)
  S. Pellerin, 320(CJL):Dec89-490
  T.R. Wooldridge, 627(UTQ):Fall89-176
"Dictionnaire International des Termes Litté-raires."* (fasc 1-5)
  B.F. Scholz, 678(YCGL):No36-152
"Diderot Studies." (Vol 23) (O. Fellows & D.G. Carr, eds)
  P.H. Meyer, 546(RR):Mar89-327
  R. Niklaus, 402(MLR):Oct90-962
  R. Rey, 530:Apr89-164

Didier, B. Écrire la Révolution 1789-1799.
  M.R. Morris, 207(FR):Feb90-535
Didier, B. La Voix de Marianne.*
  V. Mylne, 208(FS):Apr89-211
Didier, B. - see Sand, G.
Didier, B. & J. Neefs, eds. Diderot.
  D.J. Adams, 208(FS):Jul89-328
  S. Lecointre, 535(RHL):Mar-Apr89-287
Didier, B. & J. Neefs, eds. Hugo, de l'écrit au livre.
  P.W.M. Cogman, 208(FS):Jul89-339
  C. Gely, 535(RHL):Jul-Aug89-732
  S. Metzidakis, 446(NCFS):Fall-Winter89/90-247
Didier, H. - see Xavier, F.
Didinger, R. & others. The Super Bowl.
  R. Strauss, 441:7Oct90-21
Didion, J. Miami.*
  J.N. Stull, 106:Fall89-265
Diebner, S. Reperti Funerari in Umbria a Sinistra del Tevere I sec.A.C.-I sec.D.C.*
  T. Clay, 313:Vol79-231
Diebold, J. The Innovators.
  P. Gorb, 324:Sep90-711
  G. Winslow, 441:4Feb90-19
Diederichs, U., ed. Die Helden von Thule.
  U. Strerath-Bolz, 196:Band30Heft1/2-119
Diefendorf, J.M., ed. Rebuilding Europe's Bombed Cities.
  J. Rykwert, 617(TLS):11-17May90-502
Diehl, M. Me & You.
  E. Benedict, 441:11Feb90-28
Diehl, W. 27.
  B. Hochberg, 441:13May90-24
Dienes, L. Soviet Asia.
  R. North, 104(CASS):Spring89-83
Dienhart, J.M. The Mayan Languages.
  L. Campbell, 350:Dec90-865
Diény, J-P. Le Symbolisme du dragon dans la Chine antique.
  M. Détrie, 549(RLC):Jul-Sep89-387
Dierick, A.P. German Expressionist Prose.
  N.H. Donahue, 222(GR):Fall89-182
  S. Grace, 102(CanL):Spring89-156
  M. Winkler, 133:Band22Heft3/4-363
Dieth, E. Schwyzertütschi Dialäktschrift. (2nd ed) (C. Schmid-Cadalbert, ed)
  A. Lötscher, 685(ZDL):2/1989-250
Diethart, J.M. & K.A. Worp, eds. Notarunterschriften im byzantinischen Ägypten (Byz. Not.).
  E. Wipszycka, 229:Band61Heft6-559
Dietiker, S.R. En Bonne Forme. (4th ed)
  K.E. Kintz, 399(MLJ):Spring89-85
Dietrich, B.C. Tradition in Greek Religion.*
  C. Sourvinou-Inwood, 123:Vol39No1-51
Dietrich, R.F. British Drama 1890 to 1950.
  J. Wilders, 617(TLS):5-11Jan90-14
Dieudonné, J. Pour l'honneur de l'esprit humain.
  M. Espinoza, 160:Jan89-214
Díez Berrio, G. Los refranes en la sabiduría popular. (2nd ed) Dichos populares castellanos.
  E. Martinell Gifre, 548:Jul-Dec89-485
Díez de Revenga, F.J. Panorama crítico de la generación del 27.*
  J. Issorel, 92(BH):Jul-Dec88-457
  J. Palley, 240(HR):Summer89-394
Díez de Revenga, F.J. Poesía de senectud.
  S.J. Poeta, 552(REH):Oct89-144
Díez de Revenga, F.J. - see Alfonso X el Sabio

Díez de Revenga, F.J. – see Polo de Medina, J.
Díez de Revenga, F.J. & M. de Paco, eds.
Estudios sobre Vicente Medina.
  B.J. Dendle, 240(HR):Winter89–117
Diffey, T.J. Tolstoy's "What is Art?"*
  J.M. Armstrong, 242:Vol10No3–374
Diffley, P.B. Paolo Beni.
  P.F. Grendler, 551(RenQ):Spring89–92
  T.G. Griffith, 402(MLR):Jan90–210
  B. Richardson, 278(IS):Vol44–167
Di Franco, R.A. & J.J. Labrador Herraiz, eds.
Cancionero de poesías varias.
  T.J. Dadson, 304(JHP):Winter90–189
Di Franco, R.A., J.J. Labrador Herraiz & C.A.
Zorita, eds. Cancioneros Reales.
  C. Gariano, 238:May89–298
Di Franco, R.A., J.J. Labrador Herraiz & C.A.
Zorita – see Morán de la Estrella, F.
Diggers, S.G. & R.J. Dunn, with S. Gordon.
The Manuscripts of Flannery O'Connor at
Georgia College.
  V. Macys, 517(PBSA):Sep89–401
Di Gregorio Casati, M. & M. Pavarani, eds.
Ernani ieri e oggi.
  E. Hudson, 410(M&L):Aug89–420
Di Gregorio Casati, M. & M. Pavarani, eds.
Nuove prospettive nella ricerca verdiana.
  D.R.B. Kimbell, 410(M&L):Feb89–118
van Dijk, T.A., ed. Discourse and Communi-
cation.
  D. Payno, 360:Mar90–175
Dijkhuis, W. An Achillean Glossary.
  W. van Peer, 204(FdL):Mar89–70
Dijkstra, B. Defoe and Economics.*
  M.E. Novak, 405(MP):Aug89–89
  S. Peterson, 166:Jan90–157
Dijkstra, B. Idols of Perversity.*
  L.K. Worley, 133:Band22Heft3/4–348
Dillard, R.H.W. Understanding George Gar-
rett.*
  L. Lawson, 578:Fall90–107
  S. Wright, 569(SR):Spring89–liv
Dille, G.F. Antonio Enríquez Gómez.*
  M.S. Arrington, Jr., 552(REH):Oct89–132
Dillier, J. Landsgmeindsgred.
  K. Kehr, 685(ZDL):3/1989–392
Dillon, G.H. The Falklands, Politics and War.
  F. Crawley, 617(TLS):11–17May90–492
Dillon, J.M. – see Proclus
Dillon, M. After Egypt.
  H. Herrera, 441:17Jun90–23
Dilthey, W. Oeuvres 3. (S. Mesure, ed &
trans)
  R. Rochlitz, 98:Nov89–839
Dilthey, W. Selected Works. (Vol 1) (R.A.
Makkreel & F. Rodi, eds & trans)
  A. Giddens, 617(TLS):2–8Feb90–111
Dilworth, S. The Long White.*
  S. McAulay, 573(SSF):Summer89–358
Dilworth, T. The Shape of Meaning in the
Poetry of David Jones.*
  K.H. Staudt, 659(ConL):Winter90–570
Dima, N. Journey to Freedom.
  D. Deletant, 617(TLS):19–25Jan90–57
Di Maggio, D., with B. Gilbert. Real Grass,
Real Heroes.
  A. Krakowski, 441:5Aug90–19
"The Di Maggio Albums."
  A. Rust, Jr., 441:1Apr90–19
Dimler, G.R. Friedrich Spee von Langenfeld.
(Pt 2)
  J. Hardin, 133:Band22Heft2–156

Dimock, W–C. Empire for Liberty.
  B. Hume, 125:Winter89–219
Ding, Y. – see under Ya Ding
Dinges, J. Our Man in Panama.
  M. Massing, 453(NYRB):17May90–43
  T. Powers, 441:18Feb90–1
Dinhofer, S.M. The Art of Baseball.
  A.E. Johnson, 441:1Apr90–19
Dinnage, R. The Ruffian on the Stair.
  L. Hudson, 617(TLS):27Apr–3May90–438
D'Introno, F., J. Guitart & J. Zamora. Funda-
mentos de lingüística hispánica.
  J. Lipski, 350:Mar90–187
Dinzelbacher, P. & H–D. Mück, eds. Volks-
kultur des europäischen Spätmittelalters.*
  A. Classen, 597(SN):Vol61No1–125
Dio, C. Cassius Dio: The Roman History. (I.
Scott–Kilvert, trans)
  J.E. Phillips, 124:Sep–Oct89–55
Dion, R. Histoire de la vigne et du vin en
France.
  A. Forrest, 617(TLS):2–8Nov90–1186
Dionigi, I. Lucrezio.
  C.D.N. Costa, 123:Vol39No2–389
Dionisotti, A.C., A. Grafton & J. Kraye, eds.
The Uses of Greek and Latin.
  H. Lloyd–Jones, 123:Vol39No2–374
Diouf, M. Comprendre "Véhi–Ciosane" et "Le
Mandat" d'Ousmane sembène.
  J.A. Peters, 538(RAL):Fall89–524
Di Pietro, R.J. Strategic Interaction.*
  B. Van Patten, 710:Mar89–117
Dipple, E. The Unresolvable Plot.
  D. Erdinast–Vulcan, 447(N&Q):Dec89–553
d'Ippolito, F. Giuristi e sapienti in Roma ar-
caica.*
  M. Ducos, 555:Vol62Fasc1–172
Dirven, R. & V. Fried. eds. Functionalism in
Linguistics.*
  J. Fife, 307:Apr89–75
  E.A. Moravcsik, 710:Dec89–485
Dirven, R. & G. Radden, eds. Fillmore's Case
Grammar.
  A. Kakouriotis, 257(IRAL):Nov89–355
Di Scanno, T. – see Michelet, J.
Di Sciullo, A–M. & E. Williams. On the Defi-
nition of Word.
  R. Beard, 361:Jan89–81
  A. Carstairs, 297(JL):Mar89–225
"Disegni e dipinti Leonardeschi dalle colle-
zioni milanesi."
  D.A. Brown, 90:Jul89–491
Di Silvestro, R.L. Audubon Perspectives.
  M. Nichols, 441:15Jul90–19
Diski, J. Then Again.
  J. O'Grady, 617(TLS):18–24May90–535
Dissanayake, E. What is Art For?
  A. Alland, 290(JAAC):Fall89–392
Dissanayake, W., ed. Cinema and Cultural
Identity.
  D. Desser, 293(JASt):May89–334
Di Stefano, G., ed. De Villon à Villon.
  W. Pöckl, 547(RF):Band101Heft4–473
Distel, A. Impressionism.
  J. Shulevitz, 441:12Aug90–17
Dittmar, J., ed. Dokumentationsprobleme
heutiger Volksmusikforschung.
  H. Braun, 417:Apr–Jun89–176
Diuk, N. & A. Karatnycky. The Hidden
Nations.
  P–L. Adams, 61:Dec90–131
Diuzhev, I. Novizna traditsii.
  K. Parthé, 550(RusR):Apr89–222

"Otto Dix, Dessins de guerre 1915-1917."
   M. Rogister, 402(MLR):Apr90-522
Dixon, B.L. Diderot, Philosopher of Energy.
   R. Rey, 530:Apr89-156
Dixon, P. - see Farquhar, G.
Dixon, R.M.W. A Grammar of Boumaa Fijian.
   D.L. Everett, 350:Jun90-413
Dixon, R.M.W., ed. Studies in Ergativity.
   M. Alekseev, 361:Sep89-74
   B. Comrie, 353:Vol27No2-364
Dixon, S. All Gone.
   S. Erickson, 441:1Jul90-18
Dixon, S. Garbage.*
   J.P. Zanes, 580(SCR):Fall89-122
Dixon, S. The Play and Other Stories.*
   G. Monteiro, 573(SSF):Spring89-199
   J.P. Zanes, 580(SCR):Fall89-122
Dixon, S. The Roman Mother.
   L. Bonfante, 124:Nov-Dec89-127
   J.F. Gardner, 123:Vol39No1-105
   J.E. Phillips, 121(CJ):Feb-Mar90-264
Dixon, W., with D. Snowden. I Am the Blues.
   C.J. May, 617(TLS):2-8Feb90-129
Diz, M.A. Patronio y Lucanor.
   D. Seidenspinner-Núñez, 545(RPh):
   Feb90-492
Djebar, A. Fantasia.
   I. Hill, 617(TLS):13-19Apr90-404
Djelassi, M.S. - see Rosidor
Djerassi, C. Cantor's Dilemma.*
   P. Kincaid, 617(TLS):22-28Jun90-674
Djobadze, W., with others. Archeological
   Investigations in the Region West of
   Antioch-on-the-Orontes.
   J. Rosser, 589:Oct89-934
Djwa, S. The Politics of the Imagination.*
   A. Purdy, 102(CanL):Summer89-126
   B. Trehearne, 105:Fall/Winter89-79
Dmitriev, L.A. - see Romodanovskaja, E.K.
Doane, J. & D. Hodges. Nostalgia and Sexual
   Difference.*
   K.Z. Moore, 295(JML):Fall88/Winter89-
   184
   E. Wright & D. Chisholm, 541(RES):
   May89-305
Doane, M. Six Miles to Roadside Business.
   J.K. Peters, 441:9Dec90-24
Doane, M.A. The Desire to Desire.*
   T.C., 295(JML):Fall88/Winter89-267
Dobbins, J.C. Jōdo Shinshū.
   A. Bloom, 407(MN):Autumn89-380
Dobie, K. In Hospital.
   J. McGonigal, 571(ScLJ):Winter89-61
Dobrian, W.A. Poesía española.
   P.L. Ullman, 140(CH):Vol11No1&2-117
Dobrinsky, J. The Artist in Conrad's Fiction.
   J. Feaster, 395(MFS):Winter89-789
Dobson, J. Dickinson and the Strategies of
   Reticence.
   E. Emerson, 357:Spring90-67
Dobyns, S. Body Traffic.
   D. Kirby, 441:23Dec90-16
Dobyns, S. The House on Alexandrine.
   J. Clute, 617(TLS):21-27Dec90-1381
Dobyns, S. Saratoga Hexameter.
   442(NY):17Sep90-110
Dobyns, S. The Two Deaths of Señora Puccini.
   G. Davenport, 569(SR):Summer89-468
Docherty, T. After Theory.
   G.G. Harpham, 617(TLS):17-23Aug90-872
Dochery, T. On Modern Authority.*
   J.V. Price, 541(RES):Aug89-443
Dockray, K. - see Heath, R.

Doctorow, E.L. Billy Bathgate.*
   M. Elliott, 364:Dec89/Jan90-130
   S. Pinsker, 287:Jul-Aug89-31
   L. Quart, 390:May89-63
"Documenta 8."
   I. Rogoff, 59:Jun89-240
Dod, E. Die Vernünftigkeit der Imagination in
   Aufklärung und Romantik.*
   R. Simon, 52:Band24Heft1-95
Dodd, P., ed. Modern Selves.*
   H.P. Abbott, 677(YES):Vol20-353
Dodd, S. Hell-Bent Men and Their Cities.
   J. Agee, 441:28Jan90-11
Dodd, S. Mamaw.
   D. Hecker, 649(WAL):Aug89-176
Dodd, V.A. George Eliot.
   J.S. Clarke, 617(TLS):28Sep-4Oct90-1043
Doder, D. & L. Branson. Gorbachev.
   M.D. Shulman, 441:17Jun90-5
   442(NY):17Sep90-109
Dodge, J. Stone Junction.
   M. Slung, 441:4Feb90-13
Dodille, N. Le Texte autobiographique de
   Barbey d'Aurevilly.
   T. Unwin, 208(FS):Jul89-342
Dodsworth, M. Hamlet Closely Observed.
   J.A. Bryant, Jr., 569(SR):Summer89-445
Doerfer, G., ed & trans. Sibirische Märchen.
   (Vol 2)
   E. Ettlinger, 203:Vol100No1-123
Doff, A. Teach English.
   M.E. Call, 399(MLJ):Autumn89-343
   S.M. Gass, 710:Sep89-360
Doflein, E. Gestalt und Stil in der Musik. (H.
   Oberer, ed)
   A. Wittek, 687:Jul-Sep89-570
Dog, M.C. & R. Erdoes - see under Crow Dog,
   M. & R. Erdoes
Dogaer, G. Flemish Miniature Painting in the
   15th and 16th Centuries.*
   J. Backhouse, 39:Dec89-428
Dogo, M. Lingua e nazionalità in Macedonia.
   C.W. Bracewell, 575(SEER):Jan89-143
Dohaney, M.T. The Corrigan Women.
   L. Hunter, 102(CanL):Autumn-Winter89-
   198
   R.E. Jones, 198:Summer89-122
Döhl, R. Das Neue Hörspiel.
   M.E. Cory, 221(GQ):Fall89-550
Dohrn, V. Die Literaturfabrik.
   S. Spieker, 575(SEER):Oct89-615
Doig, I. Ride With Me, Mariah Montana.
   S.O. Warner, 441:30Sep90-28
Doignon, J. - see Saint Augustine
Dolan, J. The Feminist Spectator as Critic.
   L. Hart, 397(MD):Mar89-161
   H. Keyssar, 615(TJ):Oct89-431
   S.E. Marlowe, 456(NDQ):Spring89-192
   P.D. Murphy, 590:Dec89-122
D'Olesa, F. Art nova de trobar. (J. Vidal
   Alcover, ed)
   J-L. Marfany, 86(BHS):Apr89-206
Dolezal, F. Forgotten But Important Lexicog-
   raphers.*
   A.W. Stanforth, 685(ZDL):1/1989-122
Doleželová-Velingerová, M., ed. Selective
   Guide to Chinese Literature, 1900-1949.
   (Vol 1)
   P.F. Williams, 116:Jul88-194
d'Olivet, A.F. - see under Fabre d'Olivet, A.
Doll, M.A. Beckett and Myth.
   M.J. Friedman, 395(MFS):Summer89-341

Doll, M.A. & C. Stites – see Aswell, E.C. & E. Nowell

Dollenmayer, D.B. The Berlin Novels of Alfred Döblin.
   C. Bedwell, 395(MFS):Winter89–829
   P. Milbouer, 221(GQ):Fall89–540

Dollenmayer, D.B. & T.S. Hansen. Neue Horizonte. (2nd ed)
   M.E. Wildner-Bassett, 399(MLJ): Autumn89–367

Dollimore, J. & A. Sinfield, eds. Political Shakespeare.
   D. Ellis, 97(CQ):Vol18No1–86

Domanick, J. Faking it in America.
   D. Cole, 441:11Mar90–19

Dombrowski, D.A. Hartshorne and the Metaphysics of Animal Rights.
   R.G.F., 185:Oct89–215

Domenach, J–L. & Hua Chang-Ming. Le mariage en Chine.
   F. Botton, 293(JASt):May89–355
   C. Salmon, 98:Aug–Sep89–710

Doménech, R., ed. "El castigo sin venganza" y el teatro de Lope de Vega.
   M. McKendrick, 86(BHS):Oct89–380
   J.M. Ruano de la Haza, 240(HR):Spring89–237

Domenicis, M.C. & J.J. Reynolds – see under Cantelli Domenicis, M. & J.J. Reynolds

Domenig, M. Entwurf eines dedizierten Datenbanksoyotoms für Lexika
   D. Reimann, 682(ZPSK):Band42Heft3–403

Domínguez, F.A. Love and Remembrance.
   D.H. Darst, 238:Sep89–540

Domínguez de Paz, E.M. La obra dramática de Juan de la Hoz y Mota.
   V. Arizpe, 240(HR):Spring89–238

Domínguez Rey, A. El signo poético.
   C. Newton, 552(REH):Jan89–139

Domínguez Roche, J. La Pola.
   F. González Cajiao, 352(LATR):Spring90–163

Dommen, A.J. Laos.
   C.F. Keyes, 293(JASt):Feb89–216

Dompierre, L. John Lyman 1886–1967.
   L. Jessup, 627(UTQ):Fall89–242

Donagan, A. Choice.*
   B. Aune, 484(PPR):Jun90–845
   J. Bishop, 63:Sep89–375
   J. Hornsby, 262:Mar89–95

Donagan, A. Spinoza.*
   P.J. Bagley, 543:Dec89–400

Donaghy, H.J. Graham Greene. (2nd ed)
   P. Bonila, 295(JML):Fall88/Winter89–341

Donaghy, M. Shibboleth.*
   G. Maxwell, 493:Spring89–52

Donaghy, P.J. & M.T. Newton. Spain.
   J. Harrison, 86(BHS):Oct89–388

Donahue, H.C. The Battle to Control Broadcast News.
   J.C.M., 185:Jul90–920

Donaldson, F. – see Wodehouse, P.G.

Donaldson, M.L. Children's Explanations.
   K.S. Ebeling, 710:Mar89–100
   C. Futter, 320(CJL):Mar89–102

Donaldson, S. John Cheever.*
   J.J. Benson, 27(AL):Oct89–465
   J.W. Crowley, 432(NEQ):Jun89–297
   R. McPhillips, 569(SR):Spring89–293
   L.M. Waldeland, 395(MFS):Summer89–301
   639(VQR):Winter89–16

Donaldson, S., ed. Conversations with John Cheever.
   R. McPhillips, 569(SR):Spring89–293

Donaldson, W. The Jacobite Song.
   M.G.H. Pittock, 571(ScLJ):Spring89–5

Donaldson-Evans, M. A Woman's Revenge.*
   R. Lethbridge, 535(RHL):Jan–Feb89–127

Donbaz, V. & A.K. Grayson. Royal Inscriptions on Clay Cones from Ashur now in Istanbul.
   K. Deller, 318(JAOS):Jul–Sep88–516

Doney, W., ed. Eternal Truth and the Cartesian Circle.
   D.A. Cress, 319:Jul90–449

Donhauser, K. Der Imperativ im Deutschen.
   U. Engel, 680(ZDP):Band108Heft1–149
   B. Haftka, 682(ZPSK):Band42Heft5–667
   A. Lötscher, 685(ZDL):2/1989–211

Dönhoff, M. Before the Storm. Weit ist der Weg nach Osten. Foe into Friend. Preussen – Mass und Masslosigkeit.
   G.A. Craig, 453(NYRB):6Dec90–3

Donleavy, J.P. A Singular Country.
   C. Thubron, 441:2Dec90–72
   442(NY):16Jul90–87

Donne, J. The Essential Donne. (A. Clampitt, ed)
   P. Mariani, 434:Spring90–313

Donne, J. Selected Poetry and Prose.* (T.W. & R.J. Craik, eds)
   M.L.K. Lally, 568(SCN):Spring–Summer89–13

Donnell, D. The Natural History of Water.
   D. O'Rourke, 102(CanL):Spring89–206

Donnelly, J. Charlie Donnelly.
   G. Dawe, 272(IUR):Spring89–172

Donnelly, J. Universal Human Rights in Theory and Practice.
   A.J.M. Milne, 103:Dec90–487

Donner, P., ed. Idols and Myths in Music.
   E. Tolbert, 187:Winter89–156

Donnert, E. Russia in the Age of Enlightenment.
   L. Hughes, 675(SEER):Jan89–140

Donoghue, D. Reading America.*
   S. Birkerts, 473(PR):Vol56No3–495
   G. Core, 639(VQR):Winter89–166

Donoghue, D. Style in Old English Poetry.
   R.P. Creed, 191(ELN):Jun90–73
   A.S.G. Edwards, 402(MLR):Apr90–400
   A.A. MacDonald, 603:Vol13No2–525
   B. Mitchell, 589:Apr89–407
   R.L. Thomson, 215(GL):Vol29No1–68

Donoghue, D. Warrenpoint.
   J. Banville, 453(NYRB):25Oct90–48
   W.H. Pritchard, 441:14Oct90–13
   442(NY):10Dec90–160

Donoghue, D. – see Blackmur, R.P.

Donohue, A.A. XOANA and the Origins of Greek Sculpture.
   C.L. Cheal, 124:Nov–Dec89–125

Donovan, J. After the Fall.
   M. Littenberg, 357:Spring90–65

Donovan, J., ed. Feminist Literary Criticism. (2nd ed)
   W. Baker, 599:Summer90–338

Donovan, J. New England Local Color Literature.
   A. Romines, 26(ALR):Fall89–89

Donskov, A. Essays on L.N. Tolstoj's Dramatic Art.
   L. Senelick, 550(RusR):Jan89–99

van Donzel, E.J. – see al-Ḥaymī, H.A.

Doob, P.R. The Idea of the Labyrinth from Classical Antiquity through the Middle Ages.
  A. Fowler, 617(TLS):31Aug-6Sep90-920
Doody, M.A. Frances Burney.*
  J.F. Bartolomeo, 594:Winter89-450
  J. Epstein, 173(ECS):Fall89-95
  M.A. Schofield, 166:Jan90-163
  P.M. Spacks, 445(NCF):Dec89-405
Doody, M.A. & P. Sabor, eds. Samuel Richardson.
  R.A. Erickson, 166:Apr90-266
Dooley, D. The Volcano Inside.
  D. Allen, 249(HudR):Summer89-323
Dor, J. L'a-scientificité de la psychanalyse.
  A. Reix, 542:Oct-Dec89-628
Doran, P.F. Andrew Mitchell and Anglo-Prussian Diplomatic Relations during the Seven Years War.
  H.M. Scott, 83:Spring89-94
Dore, C. Theism.
  M. MacBeath, 479(PhQ):Jan89-131
Doreski, W. The Years of Our Friendship.
  J.E. Brown, 580(SCR):Fall90-158
Dorf, F. A Reasonable Madness.
  M. Stasio, 441:28Oct90-41
Dorfman, A. Hard Rain.
  R. Burgin, 441:16Dec90-22
Dorfman, A. Mascara.
  639(VQR):Spring89-58
Dorfman, A. My House is on Fire.*
  P-L. Adams, 61:Feb90-108
Dorian, N.C., ed. Investigating Obsolescence.
  R. Hudson, 350:Dec90-831
Dörig, J. Les trésors d'orfèvrerie thrace.
  L.A. Schneider, 229:Band61Heft5-458
Dorman, P. The Monuments of Senenmut.
  W.H. Peck, 124:Mar-Apr90-376
Dorpalen, A. German History in Marxist Perspective.
  W. Schmidt, 125:Winter89-189
Dörrie, H. Der Platonismus in der Antike.* (Vol 1) (A. Dörrie, ed)
  P. Louis, 555:Vol62Fasc2-345
  L.P. Schrenk, 543:Dec89-401
Dorris, M. The Broken Cord.*
  P. Lomas, 617(TLS):24-30Aug90-893
Dorris, M. Yellow Raft in Blue Water.*
  R.D. Narveson, 502(PrS):Fall89-126
Dorsch, T.S., ed. Charmed Lives.
  G. Bas, 189(EA):Oct-Dec89-490
Dorsch, T.S. - see Shakespeare, W.
Dorsett, L.W. - see Lewis, C.S.
Dorsinville, M. Solidarités.
  G. Lang, 538(RAL):Fall89-526
D'Orta, M. Io speriamo che me la cavo.
  C. Moorehead, 617(TLS):5-11Oct90-1080
Dosio, G.B. - see under Bonfiglio Dosio, G.
Dostoevsky, F. The Brothers Karamazov. (R. Pevear & L. Volokhonsky, trans)
  A. Navrozov, 441:11Nov90-62
Dostoevsky, F. Fyodor Dostoevsky: Complete Letters.* (Vol 1) (D. Lowe & R. Meyer, eds & trans)
  R.F. Christian, 575(SEER):Apr89-271
Dostoevsky, F. Fyodor Dostoevsky: Complete Letters.* (Vol 2) (D.A. Lowe, ed & trans)
  L. Knapp, 617(TLS):23Feb-1Mar90-201
Dostoevsky, F. The Village of Stepanchikovo and Its Inhabitants.
  G. Woodcock, 569(SR):Spring89-308

Dostoevsky, F. Winter Notes on Summer Impressions.
  A.R. Durkin, 395(MFS):Winter89-839
Dosuna, J.M. - see under Méndez Dosuna, J.
Dotoli, G. Littérature et société en France au XVIIe siècle.
  T. Allott, 402(MLR):Jan90-181
  J. Lough, 475:Vol16No30-285
  M.M. McGowan, 208(FS):Oct89-463
  J.A. Schmidt, 207(FR):Mar90-709
Dotoli, G. Lo Scrittore totale.
  N. Blumenkranz-Onimus, 535(RHL):Jan-Feb89-141
Dotter, F. & M., comps. Der Inn und seine Zuflüsse.
  T. Steiner, 685(ZDL):3/1989-385
Dotti, U. Vita di Petrarca.
  D. Cecchetti, 228(GSLI):Vol166fasc533-128
Dotto, L. Losing Sleep.
  D. Sobel, 441:26Aug90-7
de' Dottori, C. L'asino.* (A. Daniele, ed)
  M.L. Doglio, 228(GSLI):Vol166fasc535-454
Doty, C.S., ed. The First Franco-Americans.
  Y. Frenette, 298:Fall89-140
Doty, W.G. Mythography.*
  R.A. Segal, 292(JAF):Jan-Mar89-110
Doubiago, S. The Book of Seeing With One's Own Eyes.
  E. Lesser, 434:Autumn89-98
Doucette, L.E. Theatre in French Canada.
  D. Salter, 49:Apr89-80
Douchet, J. L'Art d'aimer.
  F.A. Worth, 207(FR):May90-1083
Dougan, C. & S. Weiss. The American Experience in Vietnam.
  639(VQR):Winter89-23
Dougherty, D. Valle-Inclán y la segunda república.*
  A. Sinclair, 86(BHS):Jul89-293
  P.C. Smith, 345(KRQ):Nov89-497
Doughtie, E. English Renaissance Song.*
  C. Monson, 570(SQ):Spring89-123
  J. Stevens, 557:Mar89-64
Doughtie, E., ed. Liber Lilliati.*
  J. Michon, 189(EA):Jul-Sep89-365
Douglas, C. - see Khlebnikov, V.
Douglas, C.N. Good Night, Mr. Holmes.
  M. Stasio, 441:16Dec90-33
Douglas, E. Can't Quit You, Baby.
  W. Brandmark, 617(TLS):20-26Jul90-782
Douglas, K. Dance with the Devil.
  R.S. Nathan, 441:10Jun90-16
Douglas, M. How Institutions Think.
  R. Sheffy, 494:Winter89-847
Douglas, S.J. Inventing American Broadcasting, 1899-1922.*
  D. Belgrad, 106:Fall89-231
Douglass, P. Bergson, Eliot, and American Literature.*
  C. Daufenbach, 52:Band24Heft3-327
  J.F. Desmond, 478(P&L):Apr89-173
  K.E. Roby, 149(CLS):Vol26No1-85
Douin, J-L. Tavernier.
  H.A. Garrity, 207(FR):Oct89-200
Dove, M. The Perfect Age of Man's Life.*
  F. Wallis, 589:Oct89-936
Dove, M.R., ed. The Real and Imagined Role of Culture in Development.
  J.R. Bowen, 293(JASt):Nov89-932
Dove, R. Grace Notes.
  S. Burris, 598(SoR):Spring90-456

Dover, K.J. Greek and the Greeks.*
    M.L. West, 447(N&Q):Mar89-88
Dover, K.J. The Greeks and their Legacy.*
    H. Lloyd-Jones, 123:Vol39No2-370
Dovey, K., L. Laughton & J-A. Durandt, eds.
    Working in South Africa.
    C.B. Davies, 128(CE):Jan89-88
Dovey, T. The Novels of J.M. Coetzee: Lacan-
    ian Allegories.
    D. Attwell, 538(RAL):Fall89-515
Dovlatov, S. The Suitcase.
    P-L. Adams, 61:Jun90-120
    K. Karbo, 441:2Sep90-10
Dowden, S.D. Sympathy for the Abyss.*
    W. Hoffmeister, 301(JEGP):Jan89-84
    C. Koelb, 406:Spring89-135
Dowling, D. Fictions of Nuclear Disaster.
    A.H. McIntire, Jr., 561(SFS):Mar89-110
Dowling, L. Language and Decadence in the
    Victorian Fin de Siècle.*
    B. Richards, 541(RES):May89-284
Downes, D., ed. Crime and the City.
    A. Coleman, 617(TLS):11-17May90-505
Downes, D.A. Ruskin's Landscape of Beati-
    tude.
    J. Loesberg, 506(PSt):May87-119
Downes, J. Roscius Anglicanus. (J. Milhouse
    & R.D. Hume, eds)
    D. Hughes, 402(MLR):Oct90-919
    J.P. Vander Motten, 179(ES):Feb89-91
Downes, K. Sir John Vanburgh.*
    F. McCormick, 566:Spring90-183
Downie, G. An X-Ray of Longing.*
    R.J. Merrett, 102(CanL):Autumn-
    Winter89-223
Downs, D.A. The New Politics of Pornography.
    F.E. Zimring, 441:28Jan90-18
Doyé, P. Typologie der Testaufgaben für den
    Unterricht Deutsch als Fremdsprache.
    C.J. James, 399(MLJ):Autumn89-369
Doyle, A.I., ed. The Vernon Manuscript.*
    M. Görlach, 38:Band107Heft3/4-520
Doyle, C. Richard Aldington.
    P. Parker, 617(TLS):16-22Feb90-162
    C. Zilboorg, 659(ConL):Summer90-227
Doyle, D.W. An Accurate Watch.
    N. Callendar, 441:17Jun90-10
Doyle, J. The Sixth Day.
    D. Hopes, 236:Winter90-56
Doyle, R. The Snapper.
    S. Leslie, 617(TLS):21-27Dec90-1381
Doyon, P. Le Bout du monde.
    J-A. Elder, 102(CanL):Autumn-
    Winter89-159
Doz, A. La Logique de Hegel et les Problemes
    traditionnelles de l'Ontologie.
    C. Butler, 125:Summer89-426
Drabble, M. A Natural Curiosity.*
    J. Mellors, 364:Dec89/Jan90-126
    N.F. Stovel, 268(IFR):Winter90-62
Drabble, M., ed. The Oxford Companion to
    English Literature.
    F.J.M. Blom, 179(ES):Feb89-74
Drabble, M. & J. Stringer, eds. The Concise
    Oxford Companion to English Literature.*
    F.J.M. Blom, 179(ES):Feb89-74
Drach, A. "Z.Z." das ist die Zwischenzeit.
    I. Brunskill, 617(TLS):3-9Aug90-829
Draghi, G.B. Harpsichord Music. (R. Klako-
    wich, ed)
    A. Silbiger, 317:Spring89-172
Draghici, S. - see Swift, J.

Dragić Kijuk, P.R., ed. Mediaeval and Renais-
    sance Serbian Poetry.
    C. Hawkesworth, 575(SEER):Jan89-115
Drainie, B. Living the Part.
    K. Garebian, 529(QQ):Winter89-951
    V. Tovell, 108:Fall89-86
Drakakis, J., ed. Alternative Shakespeares.*
    D. Ellis, 97(CQ):Vol18No1-86
    A.F. Kinney, 481(PQ):Fall89-443
Drake, D.B. & D.L. Finello. An Analytical and
    Bibliographical Guide to Criticism on "Don
    Quijote" (1790-1893).
    J. Checa, 240(HR):Autumn89-516
Drake, R. Survivors and Others.*
    S. McAulay, 573(SSF):Summer88-324
Drake, S.E. Wilson Harris and the Modern
    Tradition.
    H. Maes-Jelinek, 538(RAL):Spring89-134
Draper, M. H.G. Wells.
    D.Y. Hughes, 561(SFS):Mar89-103
    J. Huntington, 177(ELT):Vol32No3-323
    P. Parrinder, 447(N&Q):Sep89-411
Draper, R. Rolling Stone Magazine.
    C. Kaiser, 441:17Jun90-7
Draper, R.P., ed. Thomas Hardy: Three Pasto-
    ral Novels.
    M. Thorpe, 179(ES):Jun89-279
Draper, T. A Present of Things Past.
    P. Berman, 441:28Jan90-9
    G.A. Craig, 453(NYRB):15Mar90-46
Draus, F. - see Aron, R.
Dravecky, D., with T. Stafford. Comeback.
    M.E. Ross, 441:1Apr90-19
Drawert, K. Zweite Inventur.
    J. Engler, 654(WB):6/1989-1022
Dray, W.H. On History and Philosophers of
    History.
    R. Martin, 103:Sep90-359
Dreher, D.E. Domination & Defiance.*
    J.A. Bryant, Jr., 569(SR):Summer89-445
    A.F. Kinney, 481(PQ):Fall89-443
Dreiser, T. Theodore Dreiser: Journalism.
    (Vol 1) (T.D. Nostwich, ed)
    R.J. Reising, 395(MFS):Summer89-275
Dreiser, T. & H.L. Mencken. Dreiser-Mencken
    Letters.* (T.P. Riggio, ed)
    Yoshinobu Hakutani, 587(SAF):
    Autumn89-249
Dresch, P. Tribes, Government and History in
    Yemen.
    S.C. Caton, 617(TLS):18-24May90-532
Dresler-Brumme, C. Nietzsches Philosophie in
    Musils Roman "Der Mann ohne Eigenschaft-
    en."*
    D.C. Riechel, 221(GQ):Summer89-407
Dressler, W.U., ed. Leitmotifs in Natural Mor-
    phology.
    A. Carstairs, 297(JL):Mar89-266
    P.H. Salus, 567:Vol74No1/2-145
Dressler, W.U. Morphonology.*
    J. Lenerz, 260(IF):Band94-328
Dressler, W.U. & others, eds. Phonologica
    1984.*
    G. Hudson, 710:Sep89-357
Dretske, F. Explaining Behavior.*
    M.E. Bratman, 484(PPR):Jun90-795
    R.G. Millikan, 484(PPR):Jun90-807
    R. Smook, 518:Oct89-228
    D.W. Stampe, 484(PPR):Jun90-787
    S.P. Stich, 484(PPR):Jun90-801
    R. Tuomela, 484(PPR):Jun90-813
Drew, B. Nelson Algren.*
    T.R. Edwards, 453(NYRB):28Jun90-22

Drew, D. Kurt Weill.*
　　I. Kemp, 410(M&L):Feb89–131
　　W. Mann, 607:Mar89–39
Drew, E. Blue Taxis.
　　C. Spindel, 441:25Feb90–21
Drew, J. India and the Romantic Imagina-
tion.*
　　M. Green, 293(JASt):Feb89–197
　　M.M. Mahood, 541(RES):Feb89–139
　　P. Mudford, 402(MLR):Jan90–135
　　D. Nagarajan, 529(QQ):Summer89–492
Drewal, H.J. & J. Pemberton 3d, with R. Abio-
dun. Yoruba.
　　P. Verger, 617(TLS):12–18Oct90–1102
Drewes, G.W.J. & L.F. Brakel – see Hamzah
Fansuri
Drews, R. The Coming of the Greeks.
　　G.P. Verbrugghe, 124:Jul–Aug90–527
　　639(VQR):Spring89–44
Drexler, H. Politische Grundbegriffe der
Römer.
　　J. Hellegouarc'h, 229:Band61Heft8–740
Dreyer, C., ed. Das Kāṭhaka–Gṛhya–Sūtra mit
Vivaraṇa des Adityadarśana. (Pt 1, Vol 1)
　　K.G. Zysk, 318(JAOS):Oct–Dec88–639
Dreyer, J.T., ed. China Defense and Foreign
Policy.
　　S.J. Hood, 293(JASt):Nov89–825
Dreyfus, L. Bach's Continuo Groups.*
　　J.A. Brokaw 2d, 309:Vol9No2/3–157
Drèze, J. & A. Sen. Hunger and Public Action.
　　A. de Waal, 617(TLS):13–19Jul90–743
Driggers, S.G. & R.J. Dunn, with S. Gordon.
The Manuscripts of Flannery O'Connor at
Georgia College.
　　A.F. Kinney, 585(SoQ):Spring90–126
Drinkwater, J.F. The Gallic Empire.*
　　J. Harries, 123:Vol39No1–89
Driscoll, K. William Carlos Williams and the
Maternal Muse.
　　T.H. Crawford, 27(AL):Dec89–720
Driver, E. & A. Droisen, eds. Child Sexual
Abuse.
　　C. Moorehead, 617(TLS):16–22Mar90–297
Droit, R–P. L'oubli de l'Inde.
　　C. Rosset, 98:May89–393
Dronke, P. Dante and Medieval Latin Tradi-
tions.*
　　J.T. Schnapp, 276:Winter89–460
Dronke, P., ed. A History of Twelfth–Century
Western Philosophy.*
　　S. MacDonald, 543:Sep89–154
　　A.R. Perreiah, 242:Vol10No5–621
Dronke, P. The Medieval Poet and his World.
　　J. Usher, 278(IS):Vol43–130
Dronke, P. Women Writers of the Middle Ages.
　　R. Copeland, 545(RPh):Aug89–224
von Droste–Hülshoff, A. Historisch–kritische
Ausgabe. (Vol 13, Pt 2) (A. Kansteiner, ed)
　　J. Guthrie, 402(MLR):Jan90–260
Drotner, K. English Children and their Maga-
zines, 1751–1945.*
　　C. Nelson, 637(VS):Winter90–341
　　639(VQR):Summer89–80
Drucker, P.F. Managing the Non–Profit Orga-
nization.
　　P. Baida, 441:28Oct90–21
Drummond, P. & R. Paterson, eds. Television
& its Audience.
　　D. Docherty, 707:Winter88/89–68
Drury, A. Toward What Bright Glory?
　　D. Murray, 441:8Jul90–16

Drury, J., ed. Critics of the Bible, 1724–
1873.
　　B. Horne, 617(TLS):6–12Jul90–737
Drury, S.B. The Political Ideas of Leo
Strauss.
　　L.H. Craig, 103:Mar90–104
Dryden, E.A. The Form of American Romance.
　　G. Dekker, 183(ESQ):Vol35No1–69
　　G. Dekker, 445(NCF):Dec89–388
　　G. Scharnhorst, 594:Fall89–341
　　J.W. Tuttleton, 395(MFS):Winter89–743
Dryden, J. The Works of John Dryden. (Vols
5 & 6) (W. Frost & V.A. Dearing, eds)
　　S. Archer, 568(SCN):Fall–Winter89–42
　　D. Hopkins, 566:Autumn89–52
　　W.M. Porter, 405(MP):Nov89–179
　　A. Sherbo, 481(PQ):Winter89–115
Dryden, J. & T. Shadwell. The Literary Con-
troversy and Mac Flecknoe (1668–1678).
　　J. Freehafer, 566:Autumn89–69
Drysdale, D., with B. Verdi. Once a Bum,
Always a Dodger.
　　J.F. Clarity, 441:1Apr90–18
Dryzek, J.S. Rational Ecology.
　　M. Sagoff, 185:Oct89–192
"Du visible à l'invisible: pour Max Milner."
　　M. Jarrety, 450(NRF):Jun89–113
Duara, P. Culture, Power, and the State.
　　J.W. Esherick, 293(JASt):Aug89–587
Dubé, P.H. & A. Bibliographie de la critique
sur François–René de Chateaubriand,
1801–1986.
　　F. Bassan, 446(NCFS):Spring–Summer90–
553
　　D. Bourel, 531:Jul–Dec89–549
Duberman, M.B. Paul Robeson.*
　　J. Daraja, 42(AR):Fall89–495
Dubie, N. Groom Falconer.
　　F. Chappell, 344:Summer90–168
　　A. Hudgins, 249(HudR):Winter89–679
　　D. Wojahn, 219(GaR):Fall89–589
Dubin, F. & E. Olshtain. Course Design.
　　W.D. Baker, 238:Mar89–158
　　L. Book, 399(MLJ):Spring89–76
Dubinsky, R. Stormy Applause.*
　　A. George, 617(TLS):23–29Mar90–322
Dubois, R–D. Being at Home with Claude.
　　E.F. Nardocchio, 102(CanL):Spring89–189
Dubovsky, A. Chabad: In Shul.
　　G. Gessert, 448:Vol27No1–123
Dubrow, H. Captive Victors.*
　　A.F. Kinney, 481(PQ):Fall89–443
Dubrow, H. & R. Strier, eds. The Historical
Renaissance.
　　M.J. Haddad, 570(SQ):Winter89–514
　　L. Martines, 551(RenQ):Autumn89–572
Dubuffet, J. Asphyxiating Culture and Other
Writings.*
　　M. Ward, 55:Oct89–132
Dubuisson, M. Le Latin de Polybe.
　　J–L. Ferrary, 313:Vol79–188
Dubus, A. Selected Stories.
　　F. Baveystock, 617(TLS):6–12Apr90–376
　　G. Johnson, 219(GaR):Winter89–784
　　W.H. Pritchard, 249(HudR):Autumn89–491
Duby, G., ed. A History of Private Life.* (Vol
2)
　　J.A. Brundage, 589:Oct89–939
Duby, G. The Legend of Bouvines.
　　M. Vale, 617(TLS):26Oct–1Nov90–1157
Ducasse, F. La Double Vie de Léonce et Léo-
nil.
　　N. Bishop, 102(CanL):Winter88–113

Ducharme, R. Ha! Ha!
 P. Coleman, 168(ECW):Spring89-146
Duchêne, R. Madame de La Fayette, la
 romancière aux cent bras.*
 N. Boursier, 166:Jan90-155
 R. Parish, 208(FS):Jan89-86
Duchêne, R. La Fontaine.
 R. Mettam, 617(TLS):12-18Oct90-1107
Duchet, M., ed. L'Amérique de Théodore de
 Bry.
 M-C. Gomez-Géraud, 535(RHL):Mar-
 Apr89-272
 R.A. Mentzer, Jr., 207(FR):Feb90-596
Duckett, R.J. - see Brontë, B.
Duckworth, C. & H. Le Grand - see "Studies in
 the Eighteenth Century"
Ducos, M. Les Romains et la Loi.*
 A.D.E. Lewis, 313:Vol79-193
Dudek, L. In Defence of Art.
 W.J. Keith, 627(UTQ):Fall89-152
 J. Kertzer, 102(CanL):Autumn-Winter89-
 172
Dudman, H. Street People.
 E.D. Lawson, 424:Dec89-384
Duerr, H.P. Dreamtime.
 N. Davey, 323:May89-197
Dufallo, R. Trackings.
 P. Constantine, 441:14Jan90-31
Lord Dufferin. Letters from High Latitudes.
 C. Moorehead, 617(TLS):24-30Aug90-905
Duffy, C. Frederick the Great.
 J.E.O. Screen, 575(SEER):Apr89-300
Duffy, C. The Military Experience in the Age
 of Reason.
 J. Black, 83:Spring89-94
Duffy, C.A., ed. Home and Away.
 M. Holland, 493:Spring89-59
Duffy, C.A. The Other Country.
 R. Padel, 617(TLS):11-17May90-495
Duffy, C.A. Selling Manhattan.*
 L. Sail, 565:Summer89-75
Duffy, D. Sounding the Iceberg.*
 G. Noonan, 102(CanL):Autumn-Winter89-
 233
Duffy, M., ed. The English Satirical Print
 1660-1832.
 P. Rogers, 83:Autumn89-243
Duffy, M. Soldiers, Sugar and Seapower.
 J. Black, 83:Spring89-87
Dufour, G., ed. El clero afrancesado. Tres
 figuras del clero afrancesado.
 R. Andioc, 240(HR):Spring89-245
Dufournet, J., ed. Ami et Amile.
 S. Kay, 382(MAE):1989/1-165
Dufournet, J., ed. Approches du Lancelot en
 prose.
 C-A. Van Coolput, 356(LR):Feb-May89-
 113
Dufournet, J., ed. La Farce de Maître Pierre
 Pathelin.
 J. Beck, 545(RPh):Nov89-331
Dufournet, J., ed. Relire le "Roman d'Enéas."
 W.W. Kibler, 201:Vol15-327
Dufournet, J. & M. Rousse. Sur La "Farce de
 Maître Pierre Pathelin."*
 J. Beck, 545(RPh):Nov89-331
Dufrenne, M. In the Presence of the Sensu-
 ous.* (M.S. Roberts & D. Gallagher, eds &
 trans)
 D. Pollard, 89(BJA):Spring89-177
Dufresne, C. & others - see "Dictionnaire de
 l'Amérique française"
Duganov, R. - see Khlebnikov, V.

Duganov, R. & S. Lesnevskii - see Khlebni-
 kov, V.
Dugas, G. Bibliographie de la littérature
 "marociane" des français, 1875-1983.
 E. Sellin, 538(RAL):Fall89-562
Duggan, J.J. The "Cantar de mio Cid."
 R. Fletcher, 617(TLS):13-19Apr90-400
 T. Montgomery, 304(JHP):Autumn89-94
Dukakis, K., with J. Scovell. Now You Know.
 F. Butterfield, 441:16Sep90-14
Dulac, G. Editer Diderot.
 N. Sclippa, 207(FR):Dec89-375
 A. Thomson, 530:Oct89-154
Dulière, C., ed. Victor Horta Mémoires.
 S. Levine, 576:Sep89-287
van Dülmen, R. Kultur und Alltag in der Frü-
 hen Neuzeit. (Vol 1)
 S.C. Ogilvie, 617(TLS):17-23Aug90-879
Dumas, A. Sur Gérard de Nerval.
 R. Sieburth, 617(TLS):17-23Aug90-869
Dumas, A. Une aventure d'amour. (C. Schopp,
 ed)
 F. Bassan, 446(NCFS):Spring-Summer90-
 528
Dumas, D. Nos façons de parler.*
 B. Rochet, 320(CJL):Jun89-217
Dumas, M-C., ed. "Moi qui suis Robert Des-
 nos."
 H. Behar, 535(RHL):Jan-Feb89-158
Dumas, R. Études sur Théodore Aubanel, le
 poète ligoté et Avignon au XIXe siècle.
 P. Martel, 535(RHL):Sep-Oct89-935
Dümling, A. & P. Girth, eds. Entartete Musik.
 J.B. Robinson, 415:Mar89-159
Dummett, A. & A. Nicol. Subjects, Citizens,
 Aliens and Others.
 D. Pannick, 617(TLS):3-9Aug90-830
Dummett, M. Ursprünge der Analytischen
 Philosophie.
 H.J. Glock, 393(Mind):Oct89-646
Dumont, L. A South Indian Subcaste.
 G.G. Raheja, 293(JASt):Feb89-198
 G.G. Raheja, 293(JASt):Aug89-649
Dumouchel, P., ed. Violence and Truth.
 R.M., 185:Jul90-919
Dumoulin, B. Analyse génétique de la "Méta-
 physique" d'Aristote.
 L-A. Dorion, 154:Vol28No3-520
Dunant, G. L'Impudeur.
 M-T. Noiset, 207(FR):Mar90-744
Dunaway, D.K. Huxley in Hollywood.*
 D. Bradshaw, 617(TLS):16-22Feb90-162
 R. Craft, 453(NYRB):31May90-32
Dunbar, L. The Common Interest
 R. Coles, 639(VQR):Autumn89-764
Duncan, D.D. Picasso and Jacqueline.
 42(AR):Winter89-109
Duncan, H. Kate Rice Prospector.
 G. Whitlock, 102(CanL):Summer89-168
Duncan, M., ed. Section Lines.
 R. Dyck, 649(WAL):May89-76
Dundes, A. Cracking Jokes.
 L.E. Mintz, 292(JAF):Apr-Jun89-235
Dundes, A., ed. The Flood Myth.
 H.V. Bender, 124:Jul-Aug90-526
Dundes, A. Parsing through Customs.
 J.A. Arlow, 292(JAF):Jan-Mar89-105
Dundes, A. & C.R. Pagter. When You're Up to
 Your Ass in Alligators.
 M.O. Jones, 292(JAF):Apr-Jun89-233
Dunkley, J. Gambling.*
 A-M. Anthonioz, 535(RHL):Jan-Feb89-
 109

Dunkling, L. A Dictionary of Days.
  A. Room, 424:Jun89-195
Dunlap, D.W. On Broadway.
  T. Hiss, 441:2Dec90-11
Dunlop, J.A. & others - see Buero Vallejo, A.
Dunmore, H. The Raw Garden.*
  S. Pugh, 493:Spring89-47
Dunn, D. Cades Cove.
  T.D. Clark, 585(SoQ):Summer89-122
  M.A. Williams, 658:Spring89-91
  639(VQR):Winter89-10
Dunn, D. Under the Influence.
  J.C. Hall, 571(ScLJ):Spring89-33
Dunn, J. A Very Close Conspiracy.
  S. Raitt, 617(TLS):14-20Dec90-1346
Dunn, R.J. - see Brontë, C.
Dunn, R.S. & M.M., eds. The World of William
  Penn.
  S.V. James, 656(WMQ):Jan89-165
Dunn, R.S. & M.M., with others - see Penn, W.
Dunn, S. Between Angels.
  A. Corn, 491:Jan90-289
  S. Dobyns, 441:28Jan90-26
  D. Wojahn, 219(GaR):Fall89-589
  639(VQR):Autumn89-136
Dunne, D. An Inconvenient Woman.
  J. Robinson, 441:10Jun90-14
Dunne, J.G. Crooning.
  M. Dowd, 441:5Aug90-7
Dunne, J.G. Harp.*
  D. Rifkind, 617(TLS):11-17May90-488
  42(AR):Fall89-503
Dunnigan, J.F. & A.A. Nofi. Dirty Little
  Secrets.
  J. Glenn, 441:23Dec90-13
Dunsby, J. & A. Whittall. Music Analysis in
  Theory and Practice.*
  M.D. Green, 309:Vol9No2/3-174
  M. Musgrave, 411:Mar/Jul89-177
  A. Pople, 410(M&L):Feb89-76
  P.C. van den Toorn, 308:Spring89-165
Dunstan, J., ed. Soviet Education Under
  Scrutiny.
  J.J. Tomiak, 575(SEER):Jan89-160
Dunthorne, H. The Maritime Powers 1721-
  1740.
  M. Hughes, 83:Autumn89-213
Duparc, F.J. Landscape in Perspective.
  G. Keyes, 380:Summer89-163
Dupin, J. Chansons troglodytes.
  G.W. Fetzer, 207(FR):Apr90-889
  L. Ray, 450(NRF):Dec89-117
Dupré, L. Chambres.
  A. Moorhead, 207(FR):Feb90-579
  M. Naudin, 102(CanL):Spring89-218
Duquesne, T. - see "Sappho of Lesbos: The
  Poems"
Durán, D.T. - see under Troncoso Durán, D.
Durán, F.F. - see under Florit Durán, F.
Duran, R., J. Ortiz Cofer & G. Pérez Firmat.
  Triple Crown.
  L.M. Umpierre, 36:Fall-Winter89-191
Durand, J-L. Sacrifice et labour en Grèce
  ancienne.
  A. Burnett, 122:Apr89-149
Durand, P. Moteur! Coupez!
  R.J. Nelson, 207(FR):Feb90-570
Durante, S. & D. Fabris, eds. Girolamo Fres-
  cobaldi nel IV centenario della nascita.
  R. Jackson, 410(M&L):Feb89-89
Duras, M. Practicalities.
  G. Josipovici, 617(TLS):9-15Mar90-248
  J. Marcus, 441:20May90-30

Duras, M. & X. Gauthier. Woman to Woman.*
  R.B.D., 295(JML):Fall88/Winter89-212
Durbach, R. Kipling's South Africa.
  A. Parry, 346(KJ):Mar89-25
Durband, A. - see Shakespeare, W.
Durbè, D. Fattori e la scuola di Castiglion-
  cello.
  J. Sillevis, 90:Apr89-299
Durbin, M. Lima Beans and City Chicken.
  R.E. Morsberger, 649(WAL):Aug89-185
Durcan, P. Daddy, Daddy.
  G. Foden, 617(TLS):23-29Nov90-1273
Durcan, P. Jesus and Angela.
  B. O'Donoghue, 493:Summer89-62
Durian-Ress, S., ed. Fächer, Kunst und Mode
  aus fünf Jahrhunderten.
  L. von Wilckens, 683:Band52Heft1-136
Durieux, M. Un Héros malgré lui.
  M. Lacombe, 102(CanL):Autumn-
  Winter89-203
Durix, J-P. The Writer Written.
  K. Goodwin, 538(RAL):Spring89-109
  C. Kaplan, 395(MFS):Spring89-181
  E.S., 295(JML):Fall88/Winter89-196
Durkheim, E. Les règles de la méthode socio-
  logique. (J-M. Berthelot, ed)
  D. Merllié, 542:Oct-Dec89-642
Durman, K. Lost Illusions.
  R.C. Hall, 550(RusR):Apr89-199
  D.W. Spring, 575(SEER):Oct89-633
Durman, K. The Time of the Thunderer.
  D. MacKenzie, 550(RusR):Oct89-419
Du Rocher, R.J. Milton and the Renaissance
  Ovid.
  D. McColley, 70:Jul89-110
Duroisin, P. Montherlant et l'Antiquité.
  P. Danger, 535(RHL):Sep-Oct89-943
Duroselle, J-B. Clemenceau.
  E. Weber, 242:Vol10No6-743
Ďurovič, L., ed. Child Language in Diaspora.
  B. Sljivic-Simsic, 279:Vol35/36-347
Durrell, L. An Irish Faustus.
  J. Saunders, 565:Autumn89-76
Durrell, L. & H. Miller. The Durrell-Miller
  Letters, 1935-80. (I. MacNiven, ed)
  J. Haegert, 395(MFS):Winter89-808
Durschmied, E. Don't Shoot the Yanqui.
  V. Mallet, 617(TLS):1-7Jun90-578
Dusinberre, J. Alice to the Lighthouse.
  H.R.M., 295(JML):Fall88/Winter89-225
Düsing, K. Die Teleologie in Kants Weltbe-
  griff. (2nd ed)
  R.M., 342:Band80Heft4-498
Dussel, E. Philosophy of Liberation.
  M.J. Kerlin, 438:Winter89-104
Düsterberg, R. "Die gedrukte Freiheit."
  T. Schneider, 602:Band20Heft2-326
  T. Schneider, 680(ZDP):Band108Heft4-
  631
Dutertre, E. Scudéry dramaturge.
  C. Abraham, 207(FR):Oct89-159
  W. Brooks, 402(MLR):Jul90-730
  G.J. Mallinson, 208(FS):Oct89-464
  M-O. Sweetser, 475:Vol16No31-582
  H. Wolff, 209(FM):Oct89-260
Dutfield, M. A Marriage of Inconvenience.
  A. Tetteh-Lartey, 617(TLS):1-7Jun90-
  579
Duthie, E.L. The Brontës and Nature.*
  G.A. Hudson, 594:Spring89-100

Dutschke, C.W., with others. Guide to Medieval and Renaissance Manuscripts in the Huntington Library.*
  A.S.G. Edwards, 517(PBSA):Sep89-385
  P.E. Webber, 377:Jul89-145
Dutschke, C.W. & R.H. Rouse, with M. Ferrari. Medieval and Renaissance Manuscripts in the Claremont Libraries.*
  A.S.G. Edwards, 517(PBSA):Sep89-385
Dutschke, D. Census of Petrarch Manuscripts in the United States.
  C. Kleinhenz, 276:Autumn89-352
Duval, Y-M. - see Saint Jerome
de Duve, T. Au nom de l'art.
  F. Dupuy-Sullivan, 207(FR):Apr90-890
Duyker, E. Tribal Guerrillas.
  C.V. Hill, 293(JASt):Nov89-904
Dworkin, A. Mercy.
  Z. Heller, 617(TLS):5-11Oct90-1072
Dworkin, G. The Theory and Practice of Autonomy.*
  B. Mayo, 483:Oct89-571
Dworkin, R. A Matter of Principle.*
  D. Jabbari, 242:Vol10No6-729
Dwyer, E. Homes for the Mad.
  C.K. Warsh, 529(QQ):Summer89-487
Dwyer, J. John Masefield.
  W. Blazek, 295(JML):Fall88/Winter89-380
  D.E. Stanford, 569(SR):Winter89-vi
Dwyer, J. Virtuous Discourse.*
  J.D. Brims, 83:Autumn89-203
  L. Hartveit, 179(ES):Jun89-270
Dwyer, T.R. Strained Relations.
  L.E. Gelfand, 272(IUR):Spring89-190
Dyal, S. Preserving Traditional Arts.
  M. Herndon, 187:Winter89-182
Dybek, S. The Coast of Chicago.
  K. Weber, 441:20May90-30
Dyck, E., ed. Saskatchewan Writing.
  K. Jirgens, 102(CanL):Spring89-216
Dyck, I., ed. Citizen of the World.
  M. Philp, 83:Autumn89-215
Dyer, J. Ancient Britain.
  R. Bradley, 617(TLS):2-8Nov90-1187
"Dykeversions: Lesbian Short Fiction."
  R. Buchanan, 102(CanL):Summer89-182
Dymke, S. & J. Harvey. Sometime Other Than Now.
  I. McMillan, 493:Winter89/90-65
Dyson, A. & J. Harris, eds. Experiments on Embryos.
  S. Lee, 617(TLS):27Apr-3May90-438
Dyson, R.W. - see Giles of Rome
Dzielska, M. Apollonius of Tyana in Legend and History.
  E.L. Bowie, 313:Vol79-252
Dziemidok, B. & P. McCormick, eds. On the Aesthetics of Roman Ingarden.
  L. Stern, 103:Jun90-225
Dziewanowski, M.K. War at any Price.
  B.H. Reid, 242:Vol10No6-734

Eagleton, M., ed. Feminist Literary Theory.*
  E.D. Harvey, 106:Summer89-132
Eagleton, T. Against the Grain.
  R. Strickland, 494:Fall89-635
Eagleton, T. The Ideology of the Aesthetic. The Significance of Theory.
  S. Gardner, 617(TLS):30Mar-5Apr90-337
Eagleton, T. Literary Theory.*
  H. Buckingham, 565:Winter88/89-45
  F. Stockholder, 104(CASS):Spring-Winter88-502
Eagleton, T. Marxism and Literary Criticism.
  J.R. Bennett, 599:Spring90-119
Eagleton, T. Myths of Power.* (2nd ed)
  A. Pollard, 82:Vol19No8-378
Eagleton, T. Saints and Scholars.*
  E. Cobley, 376:Sep89-114
Eagleton, T. William Shakespeare.*
  D. Ellis, 97(CQ):Vol18No1-86
  K. Tetzeli von Rosador, 156(ShJW):Jahrbuch1989-351
Eagleton, T. - see Dickens, C.
Eakin, P.J. Fictions in Autobiography.*
  J. Pilling, 402(MLR):Apr90-422
Eakin, P.J. - see Lejeune, P.
Eales, J. Puritans and Roundheads.
  J.P. Kenyon, 617(TLS):21-27Sep90-1004
Earhart, H.B. Gedatsu-kai and Religion in Contemporary Japan.
  R.F. Young, 407(MN):Winter89-514
Earle, T.F. The Muse Reborn.*
  M.J. Freeman, 557:Sep89-327
  T.R. Hart, 402(MLR):Jul90-776
Early, G. Tuxedo Junction.
  442(NY):21May90-96
Earman, J. A Primer on Determinism.*
  M. Wilson, 486:Sep89-502
Eason, A. In that Country
  I. McMillan, 493:Winter89/90-65
Easson, A. - see Gaskell, E.
East, C., ed. The New Writers of the South.*
  E.C. Lynskey, 577(SHR):Spring89-190
Easterman, D. Brotherhood of the Tomb.
  N. Callendar, 441:19Aug90-17
Easthope, A. Poetry and Phantasy.*
  E. Longley, 493:Summer89-15
Easton, C. Jacqueline du Pré.
  R. Anderson, 415:Oct89-610
  P. Constantino, 441:17Jun90-17
Easton, E.W. The Intimate Interiors of Edouard Vuillard.
  J.A. Shulevitz, 441:25Feb90-24
  J. Updike, 453(NYRB):28Jun90-6
Eaton, C.E. New and Selected Poems, 1942-1987.*
  H. Chatfield, 236:Winter90-58
Eaton, K.B. The Theater of Meyerhold and Brecht.
  A. Tatlow, 133:Band22Heft1-85
Eaton, V. Self-Portrait of Someone Else.
  S. Shapiro, 441:14Jan90-30
Ebbinghaus, J. Gesammelte Schriften. (H. Oberer & G. Geismann, eds)
  W. Steinbeck, 342:Band80Heft4-496
Eber, I., ed. Confucianism.
  R.L. Taylor, 318(JAOS):Oct-Dec88-652
Eberhard, W. A Dictionary of Chinese Symbols.* (German title: Lexikon chinesischer Symbole.)
  J. Bäcker, 196:Band30Heft1/2-121
Eberhardt, I. Ecrits sur le sable.
  T. Spear, 207(FR):Apr90-891
Eberhardt, O. Verkleidung und Verwechslung in der erzählenden Dichtung Eichendorffs.
  W. Paulsen, 406:Fall89-397
Ebersole, A.V. - see de Quevedo, F.
Ebert-Schifferer, S. & others. Guido Reni und Europa.
  D.S. Pepper, 380:Autumn89-234

Eberts, J. & T. Ilott. My Indecision is Final.
P. Bart, 441:28Oct90-27
F. Raphael, 617(TLS):13-19Jul90-760
Ebin, L.A. Illuminator Makar Vates.
D.J. Parkinson, 571(ScLJ):Winter89-4
Ebrey, P.B. & J.L. Watson, eds. Kinship Orga-
nization in Late Imperial China, 1000-
1940.
T.A. Telford, 318(JAOS):Apr-Jun88-352
Eby, C.D. The Road to Armageddon.*
K. Beckson, 177(ELT):Vol32No2-211
Eccles, J.C. Evolution of the Brain.
P. Kitcher, 441:4Feb90-20
S. Rose, 617(TLS):20-26Apr90-412
Eccles, M. Requiem for a Dove.
P. Craig, 617(TLS):24-30Aug90-889
Echevarría, R.G. - see under González Eche-
varría, R.
Echikson, W. Lighting the Night.
A. Husarska, 441:30Sep90-34
"Echtzeit."
G. Gessert, 448:Vol27No3-126
Eck, W. & H. Wolff, eds. Heer und Integra-
tionspolitik.
B. Campbell, 313:Vol79-227
L. Keppie, 123:Vol39No1-153
Ecker, H-P. Poetisierung als Kritik.
J. Knowlton, 221(GQ):Summer89-432
N.A. Lauckner, 133:Band22Heft3/4-373
B. Schöning, 196:Band30Heft1/2-122
Eckstein, A.M. Senate and General.*
U. Hackl, 229:Band61Heft3-264
Eco, U. The Aesthetics of Thomas Aquinas.
D. Barbiero, 147:Vol6No2-103
B.M., 494:Winter89-851
R.E. Wood, 543:Jun90-859
Eco, U. Art and Beauty in the Middle Ages.*
R.E. Wood, 543:Jun90-859
Eco, U. Foucault's Pendulum.* (Italian title:
Il pendolo di Foucault.)
J. Updike, 442(NY):5Feb90-117
Eco, U. Le Signe.
B.M., 494:Winter89-851
Eco, U., V.V. Ivanov & M. Rector. Carnival!
F.E. Manning, 162(TDR):Spring89-19
École, J. & others - see Wolff, C.
Eddison, S. A Patchwork Garden.
A. Lacy, 441:10Jun90-13
Edel, L. - see James, H.
Edel, L. & L.H. Powers - see James, H.
Edel, L. & A.R. Tintner, eds. The Library of
Henry James.*
G. Caramello, 395(MFS):Summer89-267
Edelberg, C.D. Jonathan Odell.*
D.F. Havens, 656(WMQ):Apr89-412
Edelman, G.M. The Remembered Present.
S. Sutherland, 441:14Jan90-18
Edelman, L. Transmemberment of Song.*
S.A.S., 295(JML):Fall88/Winter89-309
Edelman, M. The Ghetto Fights.
A. Brumberg, 617(TLS):14-20Dec90-1342
Edelsky, C. Writing in a Bilingual Program.*
S.M. Sotillo, 355(LSoc):Dec89-609
Edelson, M. Psychoanalysis.*
E. Erwin, 103:Apr90-132
Eden, K. Poetic and Legal Fiction in the Ar-
istotelian Tradition.*
P. Rollinson, 131(CL):Winter89-104
Eden, M.G. Energy and Individuality in the
Art of Anna Huntington, Sculptor, and Amy
Beach, Composer.
D. Nicholls, 410(M&L):Feb89-121

Edgar, D. The Second Time as Farce.
T. Dunn, 511:Mar89-44
D.I. Rabey, 610:Autumn89-311
Edgecombe, R.S. Vision and Style in Patrick
White.
P. Wolfe, 395(MFS):Winter89-873
Edgerton, C. The Floatplane Notebooks.
T. Rash, 580(SCR):Spring90-131
639(VQR):Winter89-18
Edgerton, G.R., ed. Film and the Arts in Sym-
biosis.
W.D. Romanowski, 498:Fall89-100
"Editio." (Vol 1) (W. Woesler, ed)
P.M. Mitchell, 301(JEGP):Apr89-283
"Le edizioni italiane del XVI secolo." (Vol 1)
J.E. Everson, 557:Sep89-333
Edlund, I.E.M. The Gods and the Place.
F.R.S. Ridgway, 123:Vol39No2-414
Edmiston, W.F. Diderot and the Family.*
S. Kupsch-Losereit, 72:Band226Heft1-
206
Edmond, L. Hot October.
F. Adcock, 617(TLS):2-8Feb90-123
Edmond, M. Rare Sir William Davenant.
A. Capelle, 189(EA):Jul-Sep89-366
D. Hughes, 541(RES):May89-265
A.H. Scouten, 677(YES):Vol20-265
J.P. Vander Motten, 179(ES):Jun89-274
Edmond, R. Affairs of the Hearth.
T.J. Collins, 637(VS):Summer90-677
R. Rooksby, 175:Spring89-83
Edmonds, W.D. Jacobinism and the Revolt of
Lyon 1789-1793.
G. Lewis, 617(TLS):14-20Dec90-1355
Edmondson, W. Spoken Discourse.
L. Hemphill, 355(LSoc):Mar89-142
Edmunds, L. Cleon, "Knights," and Aristoph-
anes' Politics.*
R.G. Ussher, 24:Fall89-502
Edric, R. In the Days of the American
Museum.
R. Kaveney, 617(TLS):6-12Apr90-375
Edström, V. Selma Lagerlöfs litterära profil.
I. Scobbie, 562(Scan):May89-96
Edwards, A.S.G. & D. Pearsall, eds. Middle
English Prose.
H. Gneuss, 38:Band107Heft1/2-169
Edwards, D.L. Christian England. (Vol 2)
566:Autumn89-84
Edwards, D.L. Tradition and Truth.
A. Race, 617(TLS):9-15Mar90-260
Edwards, J., ed. Linguistic Minorities, Poli-
cies, and Pluralism.
N.H. Hornberger, 355(LSoc):Sep89-389
Edwards, J.C. The Authority of Language.
D.E. Cooper, 617(TLS):23-29Nov90-1269
Edwards, L.M., with J.S. Ramirez & T.A. Bur-
gard. Domestic Bliss.*
S. Webster, 127:Spring89-99
Edwards, M. Poetry and Possibility.*
M. Alexander, 4:Summer89-66
Edwards, M.W. Homer, Poet of the "Iliad."*
W.C. Scott, 24:Summer89-339
Edwards, P., ed. Last Voyages.
T.N.C., 506(Pst):Sep89-199
Edwards, P. Shakespeare.*
J.A. Bryant, Jr., 570(SQ):Spring89-116
A.F. Kinney, 481(PQ):Fall89-443
K. Tetzeli von Rosador, 166(ShJW):Jahr-
buch1989-351
Edwards, P. - see Lewis, W.

Edwards, P.D. Idyllic Realism from Mary Russell Mitford to Hardy.
　N. Page, 445(NCF):Mar90-571
Edwards, R. - see Guinizelli, G.
Edwards, R.D. The School of English Murder.
　P. Craig, 617(TLS):1-7Jun90-593
Edwards, W. Modern Japan through its Weddings.
　L.L. Cornell, 293(JASt):Nov89-855
　D.W. Plath, 407(MN):Autumn89-387
Edwards, W.F. & W.A. Wallace - see Galileo
Egan, D. A Song for My Father.
　W. Scammell, 617(TLS):18-24May90-522
Egan, D.R. & M.A. Russian Autocrats from Ivan the Great to the Fall of the Romanov Dynasty.
　R. Scrivens, 575(SEER):Apr89-297
Egan, P. Fathers of Invention.
　J. Saunders, 565:Autumn89-77
Egan, S.C. A Latterday Confucian.
　P. West, 116:Dec89-157
Egan, T. The Good Rain.
　S. Boxer, 441:29Jul90-17
　442(NY):16Jul90-86
Egelius, M. Ralph Erskine, Architect.
　U. Grønvold, 46:Aug89-14
Egert, G. Die sprachliche Stellung des Katalanischen auf Grund seiner Lautentwicklung.
　J. Lüdtke, 86(BHS):Apr89-205
Eggebrecht, A., ed. Albanien: Schätze aus dem Land der Skipetaren.
　M. Meyer, 229:Band61Heft8-731
Eggeling, W. Die Prosa sowjetischer Kinderzeitschriften (1919-1925).
　J.J. Tomiak, 575(SEER):Oct89-620
Eggers, H. - see Braune, W.
Eggum, A. Munch and Photography.
　M. Vaizey, 324:Jul90-569
Egido, A. Bosquejo para una historia del teatro en Aragón hasta finales del siglo XVIII.
　E. Florensa García, 240(HR):Autumn89-406
Egleton, C. In the Red.
　N. Callendar, 441:16Sep90-26
Egnal, M. A Mighty Empire.*
　E. Countryman, 656(WMQ):Oct89-819
　L. Handlin, 432(NEQ):Dec89-626
　R.R. Menard, 106:Fall89-271
Egremont, M. Secret Lives.
　P-L. Adams, 61:Aug90-92
Ehle, J. Trail of Tears.
　R.E. Morsberger, 649(WAL):Aug89-177
Ehlers, G. Alttürkische Handschriften. (Pt 2)
　J.W. de Jong, 259(IIJ):Jul89-251
Ehlich, K. Interjektionen.*
　U. Engel, 685(ZDL):3/1989-354
Ehni, R-N. Le Voyage en Belgique.
　J-M. Le Sidaner, 450(NRF):Feb89-148
Ehrard, J. & M-C. Chemin, eds. La Légende de la Révolution.
　C. Jones, 402(MLR):Oct90-966
Ehrenburg, I. The Life of the Automobile.
　442(NY):28May90-110
Ehrenpreis, I. Poetries of America.
　L. Menand, 617(TLS):5-11Jan90-4
　639(VQR):Summer89-87
Ehrenreich, B. Fear of Falling.*
　J. Fallows, 453(NYRB):1Mar90-14
Ehrenreich, B. The Worst Years of Our Lives.
　H.J. Geiger, 441:20May90-9

Ehrhart, M.J. The Judgment of the Trojan Prince Paris in Medieval Literature.
　R. Blumenfeld-Kosinski, 589:Apr89-409
　S. Justice, 301(JEGP):Jul89-391
　J.B. Trapp, 447(N&Q):Jun89-214
　K. Varty, 382(MAE):1989/1-138
Ehrismann, O. "Nibelungenlied."*
　C.M. Sperberg-McQueen, 301(JEGP):Jul89-363
Ehrlich, C. Harmonious Alliance.*
　S. Frith, 415:Nov89-683
　P. Waller, 410(M&L):Nov89-565
Ehrlich, H.J. Campus Ethnoviolence and the Policy Options.
　A. Hacker, 453(NYRB):22Nov90-19
Ehrlich, P.R. & A.H. The Population Explosion.
　F.D. Bean, 441:1Apr90-27
Eichberger, D. Bildkonzeption und Weltdeutung im New Yorker Diptychon des Jan van Eyck.
　C.R., 90:Jun89-436
von Eichendorff, J. Werke. (Vol 5) (K-D. Krabiel, ed)
　J. Purver, 402(MLR):Apr90-511
Eichler, S. & others. Tall al-Ḥamīdīya 1.
　M.C. Astour, 318(JAOS):Apr-Jun88-304
Eickmans, H. Gerard van der Schueren.
　F. Claes, 685(ZDL):2/1989-226
Eidelberg, P. Beyond the Secular Mind.
　M.D. Yaffe, 103:Jan90-11
Eigeldinger, F.S., ed. Table de concordances rythmiques et syntaxiques des "Illuminations" d'Arthur Rimbaud.*
　M-J. Whitaker, 535(RHL):Jan-Feb89-133
Eigeldinger, J-J. Chopin.* (R. Howat, ed)
　J. Kallberg, 317:Spring89-189
Eigeldinger, M. Mythologie et intertextualité.*
　Y-A. Favre, 535(RHL):Jul-Aug89-728
　J. Ferguson, 208(FS):Jan89-112
"The Eighteenth Century: A Current Bibliography." (n.s., Vols 8 & 9) (J.S. Borck, ed)
　P.J. Korshin, 566:Autumn89-67
Figler, H. Monologische Redeformen bei Valerius Flaccus.
　M.J. Dewar, 123:Vol39No1-34
Eigner, E.M. The Dickens Pantomime.*
　N. Auerbach, 158:Sep89-118
　S. Monod, 637(VS):Spring90-513
　P. Schlicke, 445(NCF):Dec89-414
Eikelmann, M. Denkformen im Minnesang.
　H. Bekker, 301(JEGP):Jul89-366
Einberg, E. & J. Egerton. The Age of Hogarth.
　O. Millar, 90:Nov89-782
Einstein, A. The Collected Papers of Albert Einstein. (Vol 2 & Supp) (J. Stachel, ed)
　I. Stewart, 617(TLS):8-14Jun90-615
Eiseman, C.J. & B.S. Ridgway. The Porticello Shipwreck.
　J.F. Lazenby, 303(JoHS):Vol109-257
Eisenberg, D. Cervantes.
　L. Lipson, 402(MLR):Apr90-470
Eisenberg, D. A Study of "Don Quixote."*
　C.B. Johnson, 240(HR):Winter89-95
Eisenberg, D. - see Percy, T. & J. Bowle
Eisenbichler, K. & O.Z. Pugliese, eds. Ficino and Renaissance Neoplatonism.*
　A. Ansani, 276:Autumn89-354
Eisenhauer, R.G. Mythology of Souls.
　M.R. Higonnet, 221(GQ):Fall89-534
Eisenman, P. Houses of Cards.*
　P. Tabor, 46:Jan89-12

Eisenstein, S. Nonindifferent Nature.*
  F. Beardow, 402(MLR):Jan90-271
Eisler, C. The Genius of Jacopo Bellini.
  L. Gowing, 441:4Mar90-28
  C. Hope, 453(NYRB):19Jul90-28
  M. Kemp, 617(TLS):3-9Aug90-826
Eisler, C. Paintings in the Hermitage.
  J. Russell, 441:2Dec90-9
Eisler, D. Rumours of Glory.
  D.E. Smith, 298:Summer89-146
Eisler, K.I. Shark Tank.
  T. Goldstein, 441:25Mar90-7
Ejdel'man, N. Putkin.
  L. O'Bell, 574(SEEJ):Summer89-303
Ekirch, A.R. Bound for America.
  J. Horn, 656(WMQ):Jan89-180
  A. Morvan, 189(EA):Oct-Dec89-477
  A. Murdoch, 83:Autumn89-201
Eklund, G. A Thunder on Neptune.
  G. Jonas, 441:11Feb90-29
Eksteins, M. Rites of Spring.*
  M. Howard, 617(TLS):9-15Feb90-138
  R. Johnson, 151:Nov89-92
  C. Lock, 627(UTQ):Spring90-433
Ekstrom, M. The Day I Began My Studies in
  Philosophy.
  M. Giles, 441:4Mar90-30
Elbaz, R. The Changing Nature of the Self.*
  A.O.J. Cockshut, 447(N&Q):Jun89-284
Elbert, S. A Hunger for Home.*
  A.H. Petry, 577(SHR):Fall89-380
Eldredge, N. Life Pulse.
  S. Rose, 617(TLS):23Feb-1Mar90-204
Eldridge, M. The Woman at the Window.
  D. Ellison, 581:Dec89-672
  C. See, 441:29Apr90-26
Eldridge, R. On Moral Personhood.
  B. Harrison, 617(TLS):18-24May90-524
Elegant, R. Pacific Destiny.
  B. Slavin, 441:22Apr90-34
  S. Winchester, 617(TLS):1-7Jun90-577
Elfe, W.D. & J. Hardin - see "Dictionary of
  Literary Biography"
Elgar, E. Edward Elgar: The Windflower Let-
  ters.* (J.N. Moore, ed)
  R. Anderson, 415:Dec89-747
Eliade, M. Autobiography.* (Vol 2)
  S. Cain, 390:Nov89-27
  639(VQR):Spring89-55
Eliade, M. Youth without Youth and other
  Novellas.* Journal I. Journal II. Journal
  III. Jourval IV.
  G. Steiner, 617(TLS):28Sep-4Oct90-1015
Elie, N. La Gourou.
  A.M. Miraglia, 102(CanL):Winter88-139
Eliot, G. Collected Poems. (L. Jenkins, ed)
  G. Beer, 617(TLS):3-9Aug90-819
Eliot, T.S. The Letters of T.S. Eliot.* (Vol 1)
  (V. Eliot, ed)
  W. Bedford, 4:Summer89-70
  K. Blackwell, 556:Winter89/90-187
  R. Bush, 365:Spring/Summer88-159
  G. Kerley, 675(YER):Spring90-82
  J. Longenbach, 250(HLQ):Summer89-421
  J. Meyers, 627(UTQ):Winter89/90-359
  W.H. Pritchard, 249(HudR):Spring89-141
  S. Schwartz, 432(NEQ):Sep89-445
  M. Scofield, 175:Autumn89-267
  R. Spoo, 27(AL):Oct89-463
Elizur, J. & S. Minuchin. Institutionalizing
  Madness.
  P.L. Wachtel, 441:25Feb90-26
Elkaïm-Sartre, A. - see Sartre, J-P.

Elkann, A. Misguided Lives.
  T. Le Clair, 441:28Jan90-35
Elkhadem, S. Canadian Adventures of the
  Flying Egyptian.
  A.F. Cassis, 268(IFR):Summer90-142
Elkhadem, S. The Plague/Al-Ta'un.
  J. Werner-King, 268(IFR):Summer89-154
Elkin, J.L. & G.W. Merkx, eds. The Jewish
  Presence in Latin America.
  I. Stavans, 390:Jan89-60
Elkin, R. Pricking Out.
  E. Bartlett, 493:Spring89-64
Elkins, A. Icy Clutches.
  M. Stasio, 441:9Sep90-39
Elkon, J. Umfaan's Heroes.
  K.A. Appiah, 441:30Sep90-30
Elliot, A. My Country.
  M. Walters, 617(TLS):23-29Mar90-327
Elliott, A.G. Roads to Paradise.
  E.D. Hunt, 313:Vol79-260
  D. Robertson, 545(RPh):Aug89-209
  M. Whitby, 123:Vol39No1-43
Elliott, E. & others, eds. Columbia Literary
  History of the United States.*
  C.N. Davidson, 115:Winter89-89
  A. Hook, 447(N&Q):Jun89-268
  J.W. Rathbun, 26(ALR):Fall89-87
Elliott, J. Necessary Rites.
  J. O'Grady, 617(TLS):19-25Oct90-1132
Elliott, J.H. Spain and its World, 1500-1700.*
  639(VQR):Autumn89-115
Elliott, M. Shakespeare's Invention of
  Othello.
  V.M. Vaughan, 570(SQ):Fall89-363
  639(VQR):Spring89-49
Elliott, S.L. Fairyland.
  C. Bram, 441:20May90-30
Ellis, A., ed. Ethics and International Rela-
  tions.*
  J. Thompson, 63:Mar89-120
Ellis, A.T. The Inn at the Edge of the World.
  C.A. Duffy, 617(TLS):21-27Sep90-999
Ellis, B.E. The Rules of Attraction.*
  S. Pinsker, 577(SHR):Spring89-194
Ellis, C.G. Oriental Carpets in the Philadel-
  phia Museum of Art.*
  R. Pinner, 90:Jan89-45
Ellis, D. & H. Mills. D.H. Lawrence's Non-Fic-
  tion.
  M. Kalnins, 402(MLR):Jan90-166
  J. Meyers, 177(ELT):Vol32No2-259
  K. Widmer, 395(MFS):Summer89-332
Ellis, D.G. & W.A. Donahue, eds. Contempo-
  rary Issues in Language and Discourse
  Processes.
  B.K. Barnes, 399(MLJ):Summer89-202
  A. Pomerantz, 355(LSoc):Mar89-109
Ellis, J. Brute Force.
  B.E. Trainor, 441:4Nov90-18
Ellis, J. & J. Donohue, eds. English Drama of
  the Nineteenth Century.
  L. James, 611(TN):Vol43No2-93
  W.J. Meserve, 610:Summer89-199
Ellis, J.M. Against Deconstruction.*
  D. Dutton, 478(P&L):Oct89-430
  D. Fowler, 223:Spring89-97
  I.E. Harvey, 599:Spring90-113
Ellis, P.B. & S. Mac a'Ghobhainn - see under
  Berresford Ellis, P. & S. Mac a'Ghobhainn
Ellis, R., ed. The Liber Celestis of St. Bridget
  of Sweden.
  M-J. Arn, 179(ES):Oct89-450

Ellis, R. Peter Weiss in Exile.
    J.E. Michaels, 406:Spring89-138
    R.J. Rundell, 615(TJ):May89-267
Ellis, R.H., comp. Catalogue of Seals in the
Public Record Office: Monastic Seals 1.
    B.B. Rezak, 589:Jan89-158
Ellis, W.M. Alcibiades.*
    P.J. Rhodes, 235:Winter89-81
Ellison, E. The Picture Makers.
    W.L. Taitte, 441:14Oct90-16
Ellison, E. & J.B. Hill, eds. Our Mutual Room.
    J. Eis, 502(PrS):Winter89-119
Ellmann, M. The Poetics of Impersonality.*
    B. Bergonzi, 402(MLR):Jan90-168
    R. Bush, 403(MLS):Summer89-83
    M. Dickie, 301(JEGP):Oct89-563
    M-A. Gillies, 49:Jul89-90
    J. Mellard, 599:Summer90-302
    42(AR):Winter89-113
Ellmann, R. a long the riverrun.*
    639(VQR):Autumn89-118
Ellmann, R. Oscar Wilde.*
    J. Davidson, 381:Summer89-785
    M.D. Denny, 615(TJ):May89-264
    W. Harmon, 569(SR):Winter89-148
Ellmann, R. & R. O'Clair, eds. The Norton
Anthology of Modern Poetry. (2nd ed)
    B. Galvin, 569(SR):Winter89-xvi
Ellrodt, R. & B. Brugière, eds. Age d'Or et
Apocalypse.
    M. Lévy, 189(EA):Oct-Dec89-447
Ellroy, J. L.A. Confidential.
    M. Stasio, 441:15Jul90-26
Ellsberg, M.R. Created to Praise.*
    P.J. McCarthy, 301(JEGP):Jan89-124
Ellsworth, R.H. Later Chinese Painting and
Calligraphy 1800-1950.*
    O. Impey, 39:Oct89-285
Elmer, P. The Library of Dr. John Webster.
    T.A. Birrell, 354:Mar89-71
    D. McKitterick, 78(BC):Autumn89-301
Elon, A. Jerusalem.*
    W. Blitzer, 390:Nov89-58
Eloy Martínez, T. The Perón Novel.
    639(VQR):Winter89-20
Elphinstone, M. A Sparrow's Flight.
    J. Clute, 617(TLS):23Feb-1Mar90-202
Elsaesser, T. New German Cinema.
    J. Petley, 707:Summer89-213
Else, G.F. Plato and Aristotle on Poetry.* (P.
Burian, ed)
    S. Halliwell, 303(JoHS):Vol109-232
Elster, C.H. There is No Zoo in Zoology and
Other Beastly Mispronunciations.
    W.A.K., 300:Oct88-223
Elster, J. Making Sense of Marx.
    G.M. Horowitz, 488:Jun89-232
Elster, J. Solomonic Judgements. Nuts and
Bolts for the Social Sciences. The Cement
of Society.
    D. Miller, 617(TLS):25-31May90-563
Elster, J. & A. Hylland, eds. Foundations of
Social Choice Theory.*
    P.J. Hammond, 185:Oct89-190
Elster, J. & K.O. Moene, eds. Alternatives to
Capitalism.
    B.B., 185:Jul90-911
Elton, W.R. King Lear and the Gods.
    M. Elliott, 447(N&Q):Dec89-501
Eluard, P. Selected Poems. (G. Bowen, ed &
trans)
    M. Davies, 402(MLR):Apr90-457
Elvers, R. - see Mendelssohn, F.

Emboden, W.A. The Visual Art of Jean
Cocteau.
    J. Shulevitz, 441:1Jul90-15
van Emden, W., ed. Vivien de Monbranc.
    L.S. Crist, 589:Jan89-229
    J-P. Martin, 356(LR):Aug89-213
Emecheta, B. The Family.
    R. McKnight, 441:29Apr90-30
Emecheta, B. Gwendolen.
    T. Dooley, 617(TLS):20-26Apr90-430
Emerson, C. Boris Godunov.*
    H. Robinson, 550(RusR):Jan89-115
Emerson, C. & M. Holquist - see Bakhtin, M.M.
Emerson, E.W. Help Wanted: Orphans Pre-
ferred.
    M. Stasio, 441:18Mar90-33
Emerson, J.A. Catalog of Pre-1900 Vocal
Manuscripts in the Music Library, Univer-
sity of California at Berkeley.
    O. Neighbour, 410(M&L):Aug89-395
Emerson, R.W. The Collected Works of Ralph
Waldo Emerson. (Vol 4) (W.E. Williams &
D.E. Wilson, eds)
    639(VQR):Winter89-12
Emerson, S. Fire Child.
    C. Fein, 441:25Feb90-24
Emerson, S. & B. Duffy. The Fall of Pan Am
103.
    M. Wines, 441:29Apr90-12
Emilsson, E.K. Plotinus on Sense-Perception.
    J. Dillon, 123:Vol39No2-265
    D.W. Hamlyn, 479(PhQ):Jan89-122
    D.K.W. Modrak, 520:Vol34No1-111
Emlen, R.P. Shaker Village Views.*
    C. Van West, 658:Summer/Autumn89-192
Emmerick, R.E. & P.O. Skjaervø. Studies in
the Vocabulary of Khotanese, II.
    N. Sims-Williams, 259(IIJ):Jan89-47
Emmerig, T. Wolfgang Joseph Emmerig (1772-
1839).
    R. Münster, 417:Oct-Dec89-382
Emmet, D. The Effectiveness of Causes.
    T. Kapitan, 449:Apr89-276
Emmet, H.L. Fruit Tramps.
    J.M. Gutman, 441:13May90-11
Emmrich, C., ed. Literatur und Medienkünste
für junge Leute.
    I. Dreher, 654(WB):7/1989-1223
Emond, M., ed. Anthologie de la nouvelle et
du conte fantastique québécois au XXe
siècle.
    M.E. Ross, 627(UTQ):Fall89-181
Empereur, J-Y. & Y. Garlan, eds. Recherches
sur les amphores grecques.
    V. Stürmer, 229:Band61Hoft1-71
Empson, W. Argufying.* (J. Haffenden, ed)
    P. Bonila, 295(JML):Fall88/Winter89-225
    W.H. Pritchard, 31(ASch):Autumn89-592
Empson, W. Essays on Shakespeare.* (D.B.
Pirie, ed)
    P.C. McGuire, 615(TJ):Mar89-114
Empson, W. Faustus and the Censor. (J.H.
Jones, ed)
    R. Gill, 541(RES):Nov89-551
    J. Jowett, 447(N&Q):Mar89-94
Empson, W. The Royal Beasts and Other
Works.* (J. Haffenden, ed)
    W.H. Pritchard, 31(ASch):Autumn89-592
Emshwiller, C. Carmen Dog.
    C. Innes, 441:29Apr90-38
Emshwiller, C. Verging on the Pertinent.
    D. Stead, 441:18Mar90-20

Encrevé, P. La liaison avec et sans enchaîn-
ement.
    J. Casagrande, 207(FR):Dec89-417
    M. Kilani-Schoch, 209(FM):Oct89-250
    A. Rialland, 350:Mar90-134
"Encyclopaedia Iranica." (Vol 1) (E. Yarsha-
ter, ed)
    R.N. Frye, 318(JAOS):Jan-Mar88-169
Endelman, T.M. Radical Assimilation in Eng-
lish Jewish History, 1656-1945.
    R.S. Wistrich, 617(TLS):23-29Nov90-1261
Endicott-West, E. Mongolian Rule in China.
    J-S. Tao, 293(JASt):Nov89-827
Endō, S. Foreign Studies.*
    R. Billington, 441:6May90-34
    J. Haylock, 364:Feb/Mar90-137
Endō, S. Scandal.*
    639(VQR):Spring89-58
Endrei, W. & L. Zoknay. Fun and Games in
Old Europe.
    B. Sutton-Smith, 292(JAF):Oct-Dec89-
    503
Endresen, R.T. Fonetikk.
    C.A. Creider, 350:Mar90-188
Engel, H. Die Stellung des Musikers im Arab-
isch-Islamischen Raum.
    P.V. Bohlman, 309:Vol9No2/3-202
Engel, J. Rod Serling.
    E. Stein, 441:18Mar90-21
Engel, U. Deutsche Grammatik.*
    K.B. Lindgren, 439(NM):1989/2-217
Engelberg, E. The Vast Design. (2nd ed)
    G.J. De La Vars, 177(ELT):Vol32No4-527
Engelberg, K.K. The Making of the Shelley
Myth.
    K. Everest, 402(MLR):Jan90-150
Engelhardt, H.T., Jr. The Foundations of
Bioethics.*
    K. Hartmann, 323:May89-166
    C. Overall, 254:Summer89-179
Engelhardt, T. The Foundations of Bioethics.
    G. Gillett, 291:Vol6No1-114
Engelhardt, U. Die klassische Tradition der
Qi-Übungen.
    L. Kohn, 318(JAOS):Jul-Sep88-465
Engell, J. Forming the Critical Mind.
    D.L. Patey, 173(ECS):Winter89/90-205
Engell, J., ed. Johnson and his Age.
    P. Rogers, 506(PSt):May87-111
Engell, J. & D. Perkins, eds. Teaching Litera-
ture.
    P. Brantlinger, 141:Fall89-333
    42(AR):Winter89-113
Engelmann, L. Tears Before the Rain.
    J. Mirsky, 453(NYRB):16Aug90-29
Engelstad, I. & others. Norsk kvinnelittera-
turhistorie. (Vol 1)
    J. Garton, 172(Edda):1989/1-84
Engleberg, K.K. The Making of the Shelley
Myth.
    E. James, 78(BC):Spring89-124
Englefield, R. Critique of Pure Verbiage.
(G.A. Wells & D.R. Oppenheimer, eds)
    J. Bell, 617(TLS):7-13Dec90-1316
Engler, B. & G. Kreis, eds. Das Festspiel.
    R. Jackson, 611(TN):Vol43No2-92
Englert, W.G. Epicurus on the Swerve and
Voluntary Action.*
    J.S. Purinton, 319:Jan90-123
    J.E. Rexine, 124:Sep-Oct89-62
English, E.D. Enterprise and Liability in
Sienese Banking, 1230-1350.
    L.D. Snyder, 589:Oct89-941

English, T.J. The Westies.
    D.H. Bain, 441:8Apr90-12
    442(NY):21May90-96
Enklaar, J. & H. Ester, eds. Albert Vigoleis
Thelen.
    H. Wagener, 133:Band22Heft2-191
Enkvist, I. Las técnicas narrativas de Vargas
Llosa.
    M.A. Lewis, 238:Mar89-156
Enlart, C. Gothic Art and the Renaissance.
(D. Hunt, ed & trans)
    H. Loyn, 39:Apr89-291
Ennen, E. The Medieval Woman.
    L. Roper, 617(TLS):7-13Dec90-1328
Enninger, W., ed. Studies on the Languages
and the Verbal Behavior of the Pennsylva-
nia Germans I.*
    G.J. Humpa, 221(GQ):Fall89-515
Ennius. The "Annals" of Quintus Ennius.*
(O. Skutsch, ed)
    S. Jackson, 235:Summer89-73
Enos, R.L. The Literate Mode of Cicero's
Legal Rhetoric.
    J.T. Gage, 126(CCC):May89-230
Enquist, P.O. Fra regnormenes liv. (3rd ed)
    P. Vinten-Johansen, 563(SS):Winter89-73
Enright, D.J. The Alluring Problem.*
    D. Dowling, 102(CanL):Winter88-118
Enright, D.J. Selected Poems 1990.
    M. Walters, 617(TLS):9-15Mar90-248
Enríquez Gómez, A. Loa sacramental de los
siete planetas. (C.H. Rose & T. Oelman,
eds)
    T.R.A. Mason, 402(MLR):Apr90-474
von Ense, K.A.V. - see under Varnhagen von
Ense, K.A.
Enskat, R. Wahrheit und Entdeckung.
    R. Ferber, 687:Oct-Dec89-709
Ensoli, S. L'Heróon di Dexileos nel Ceramico
di Atene.
    R.H.W. Stichel, 229:Band61Heft2-157
de Enterría, M.C.G. - see under Cruz García
de Enterría, M.
Enzensberger, H.M. Europe, Europe!* (Ger-
man title: Ach Europe!)
    H.C., 450(NRF):Mar89-86
Enzensberger, H.M. Political Crumbs.
    I. Brunskill, 617(TLS):16-22Nov90-1226
Enzensberger, H.M. The Sinking of the
Titanic.
    S. O'Brien, 493:Summer89-44
Eörsi, I. Emlékezés a régi szép idökre.
    G. Szirtes, 617(TLS):23Feb-1Mar90-195
Epicurus. Épicure: Lettres et Maximes. (M.
Conche, ed & trans)
    S. Jackson, 235:Summer89-64
Epperly, E.R. Anthony Trollope's Notes on
the Old Drama.
    G. Butte, 637(VS):Winter90-347
Eppsteiner, F., ed. The Path of Compassion.
(2nd ed)
    V. Urubshurow, 293(JASt):Nov89-802
Epstein, D.F. Personal Enmity in Roman Poli-
tics 218-43 B.C.*
    R.P. Hock, 124:Jan-Feb90-249
    K-J. Hölkeskamp, 313:Vol79-189
Epstein, J. Once More Around the Block.*
    H.B., 295(JML):Fall88/Winter89-226
Epstein, J. Partial Payments.*
    G. Core, 249(HudR):Winter89-692
    639(VQR):Summer89-102
Epstein, L. Pinto and Sons.
    J. Crowley, 441:4Nov90-3

Epstein, W.H. Recognizing Biography.*
  P. Alkon, 301(JEGP):Jul89-449
  M. Jones, 31(ASch):Summer89-459
  N. Page, 506(PSt):Dec89-307
  A. Pailler, 189(EA):Oct-Dec89-443
  J. Pilling, 402(MLR):Apr90-422
Erasmus. Collected Works of Erasmus.* (Vol
  7) (P.G. Bietenholz, ed)
  J. Kraye, 447(N&Q):Jun89-228
Erasmus. Collected Works of Erasmus.* (Vol
  8) (P.G. Bietenholz, ed)
  L.V.R., 568(SCN):Fall-Winter89-67
Erasmus. Collected Works of Erasmus.* (Vols
  27 & 28) (A.H.T. Levi, ed)
  M. Brunyate, 447(N&Q):Mar89-91
Erasmus. Collected Works of Erasmus. (Vol
  49) (E. Rummel, ed & trans)
  L.V.R., 568(SCN):Fall-Winter89-72
Erasmus. Collected Works of Erasmus. (Vol
  66) (J.W. O'Malley, ed)
  L.V.R., 568(SCN):Fall-Winter89-68
Erasmus. Novum Instrumentum. (H. Holeczek,
  ed)
  J.H. Bentley, 539:Vol13No3-341
Erasmus. Opera Omnia. (Vol 2, Pt 4 cd by F.
  Heinimann & E. Kienzle; Vol 5, Pt 2 ed by C.
  Béné, A. Godin & S. Dresden; Vol 5, Pt 3 ed
  by A.G. Weiler, R. Stupperich & C.S.M. Rad-
  emaker)
  E. Rummel, 551(RenQ):Summer89-304
Erasmus. Opera omnia. (Vol 4, Pt 2) (F.
  Heinimann & E. Kienzle, eds)
  R. Kassel, 229:Band01Heft2-130
Erbse, H. Studien zum Prolog der euripi-
  deischen Tragödien.
  M.A. Harder, 394:Vol42fasc1/2-173
Erbse, H. Untersuchungen zur Funktion der
  Götter im homerischen Epos.
  B.C. Dietrich, 303(JoHS):Vol109-208
Erdinast-Vulcan, D. Graham Greene's Child-
  less Fathers.*
  A. Gibson, 175:Autumn89-273
Erdman, D.V. Commerce des Lumières.*
  J.K. Chandler, 591(SIR):Fall89-493
  A.S. Gourlay, 481(PQ):Winter89-127
  P. Marshall, 677(YES):Vol20-286
von Erdmann-Pandžić, E. "Poema bez geroja"
  von Anna A. Achmatova.
  I. Masing-Delic, 550(RusR):Apr89-220
  W. Rosslyn, 575(SEER):Jul89-458
Erdoes, R. & A. Ortiz, eds. American Indian
  Myths and Legends.
  W.F.H. Nicolaisen, 292(JAF):Oct-Dec89-
  476
Erdrich, L. Tracks.
  D. Flower, 249(HudR):Spring89-136
  S. Shane, 649(WAL):May89-66
  42(AR):Winter89-116
  639(VQR):Spring89-57
Eremina, V.I., ed. Russkij fol'klor.
  M. Lunk, 574(SEEJ):Summer89-329
Erhard, N. First in Its Class.
  529(QQ):Spring89-212
Erickson, B., ed. Call to Action.
  N. Wade, 441:22Apr90-17
Erickson, R.A. Mother Midnight.*
  J. Richetti, 166:Oct89-83
Ericsson, C.H. Navis oneraria.
  H.T. Wallinga, 394:Vol42fasc1/2-238
Eriksen, T.B. Nietzsche og det moderne.
  P. Buvik, 172(Edda):1989/4-366

Erkkila, B. Whitman the Political Poet.
  T. Gunn, 617(TLS):5-11Jan90-3
  H.J. Levine, 27(AL):Dec89-696
  M.W. Thomas, 646(WWR):Summer89-28
Erlande-Brandenburg, A. La Cathédrale.
  A. Saint, 617(TLS):9-15Mar90-265
Erler, A. & E. Kaufmann, with R. Schmidt-
  Wiegand, eds. Handwörterbuch zur Deut-
  schen Rechtsgeschichte.*
  K. Hyldgaard-Jensen, 680(ZDP):Band108
  Heft3-474
Erlmann, V. Music and the Islamic Reform in
  the Early Sokoto Empire.
  J. Kuckertz, 417:Jan-Mar89-100
Ermann, K. Goethes Shakespeare-Bild.
  J. Osborne, 549(RLC):Jul-Sep89-414
Ermen, R. Musik als Einfall.
  R. Stephan, 417:Jan-Mar89-97
Ernaux, A. La Place.* (P.M. Wetherill, ed)
  L. Day, 402(MLR):Apr90-465
Ernst, C.W. Words of Ecstasy in Sufism.
  J. Renard, 318(JAOS):Oct-Dec88-668
Ernst, G. Gesprochenes Französisch zu Be-
  ginn des 17. Jahrhunderts.*
  R. de Gorog, 545(RPh):Feb90-431
Ernst, R. Dictionnaire général de la tech-
  nique industrielle, tenant compte des tech-
  niques et procédés les plus modernes. (Vol
  4) Wörterbuch der industriellen Technik,
  unter weitgehender Berücksichtigung neu-
  zeitlicher Techniken und Verfahren. (Vol
  4) (4th ed)
  C. Schmitt, 72:Band226Heft1-181
Eroms, H.W. Funktionale Satzperspektive.
  J. Lenerz, 353:Vol27No1-162
Errington, J. The Lion, the Eagle, and Upper
  Canada.*
  N. Christie, 529(QQ):Spring89-168
Errington, M. Geschichte Makedoniens.*
  A.B. Bosworth, 122:Apr89-160
Erwitt, E. Personal Exposures.*
  H. Martin, 507:May/Jun89-156
Erzgräber, W. & P. Goetsch, eds. Mündliches
  Erzählen im Alltag, fingiertes mündliches
  Erzählen in der Literatur.
  P. Morf, 196:Band30Heft3/4-312
Escarpanter, J.A. & J.A. Madrigal - see
  Felipe, C.
Eschbach, A. & W.A. Koch, eds. A Plea for
  Cultural Semiotics.
  E. Baer, 567:Vol73No3/4-339
Eschbach-Szabo, V. Temporalität im Japan-
  ischen.
  H. Silberstein, 682(ZPSK):Band42Heft2-
  264
Escobedo, H., ed. Mexican Monuments.
  M. Torgovnik, 62:Oct89-23
Escott, C. Clyde McPhatter.
  B.L. Cooper, 498:Summer89-113
Eshleman, C. Antiphonal Swing.
  D. Anderson, 441:26Aug90-15
Eskin, S.G. Simenon.*
  D.J. Bond, 345(KRQ):May89-236
  J. Fabre, 535(RIIL):Nov-Dec89-1077
de Eslava, A. Noches de invierno. (J. Barella
  Vigal, ed)
  G.A. Davies, 86(BHS):Jul89-279
Esler, G. Loyalties.
  K. Jeffery, 617(TLS):30Nov-6Dec90-1300
Espejo-Saavedra, R. Nuevo acercamiento a la
  poesía de Salvador Rueda.*
  G. Hambrook, 86(BHS):Apr89-186

Esposito, P. Il racconto della strage.
  R. Mayer, 123:Vol39No2-392
Esser, J., with A. Polomski. Comparing Read-
  ing and Speaking Intonation.
  G. Bruce, 348(L&S):Jan-Mar89-81
Essick, R.N. William Blake and the Language
  of Adam.
  R.F. Gleckner, 661(WC):Autumn89-219
Essick, R.N. The Works of William Blake in
  the Huntington Collections.
  P. Malekin, 541(RES):Nov89-573
Esslin, M. The Field of Drama.*
  E. Brater, 130:Summer89-184
  B.M. Hobgood, 289:Winter89-116
Essop, A. Hajji Musa and the Hindu Fire-
  Walker.*
  42(AR):Winter89-114
"Establecimientos Tradicionales Madrileños."
  W. Rincón García, 48:Jan-Mar89-104
Ester, H. & G. van Gemert, eds. Annäherun-
  gen.
  M. Shafi, 133:Band22Heft3/4-379
Esterházy, P. Trois anges me surveillent.
  L. Kovacs, 450(NRF):Sep89-112
Estes, D.C. - see Thorpe, T.B.
Estévez, M.V. - see under Vázquez Estévez,
  M.
Estleman, L.D. The Best Western Stories of
  Loren D. Estleman. (B. Pronzini and M.H.
  Greenburg, eds)
  J. Loose, 617(TLS):10-16Aug90-855
  M.T. Marsden, 649(WAL):Feb90-393
Estleman, L.D. Sweet Women Lie.
  M. Stasio, 441:20May90-53
Estleman, L.D. Whiskey River.
  W. Walker, 441:14Oct90-50
Estorick, M. What Are Friends For.
  B. Cheyette, 617(TLS):27Jul-2Aug90-804
Estrada, F.L. - see under López Estrada, F.
de la Estrella, F.M. - see under Morán de la
  Estrella, F.
Estudillo, J.M. Sketches of California in the
  1860s. (M. Schlichtmann, ed)
  M. Margolin, 649(WAL):May89-79
Etherege, G. The Man of Mode. (S. Trussler,
  ed)
  P. Holland, 611(TN):Vol43No2-84
Ethier-Blais, J. Le désert blanc.
  M. Benson, 102(CanL):Autumn-Winter89-
  154
Etiemble. L'Europe chinois I.
  M. Détrie, 549(RLC):Jul-Sep89-387
Etiemble, R. Ouverture/s/ sur un compara-
  tisme planétaire.
  E.E. Fitz, 149(CLS):Vol26No3-285
Etienne, G. Rural Development in Asia.
  R. Barker, 293(JASt):Feb89-115
Étienvre, J-P. Figures du jeu.*
  G. Carnero, 240(HR):Winter89-73
  P. Heugas, 92(BH):Jul-Dec88-448
Etter, D. Electric Avenue. Midlanders.
  M. Vinz, 456(NDQ):Summer89-255
Etty, R. Hovendens Violets.
  D. Kennedy, 493:Autumn89-48
"Études Jean-Jacques Rousseau." (No. 1 & 2)
  M-H. Cotoni, 535(RHL):Nov-Dec89-1059
"Études rabelaisiennes, 18."
  B. Teuber, 547(RF):Band101Heft4-474
"Études Rabelaisiennes, 22."
  K.M. Hall, 402(MLR):Jul90-727

Etulain, R.W. Ernest Haycox.
  C. White, 649(WAL):Aug89-163
Euben, J.P., ed. Greek Tragedy and Political
  Theory.
  N.D. Smith, 185:Oct89-187
Eunomius. Eunomius, The Extant Works.
  (R.P. Vaggione, ed & trans)
  R. Williams, 313:Vol79-257
Euripides. Alcestis. (D.J. Conacher, ed &
  trans)
  P. Riemer, 229:Band61Heft7-621
Euripides. Euripide: "Ifigenia in Tauride"
  [and] "Ifigenia in Aulide." (F. Ferrari, ed &
  trans)
  J. Ferguson, 123:Vol39No2-382
Euripides. Euripides' "Kresphontes" and
  "Archelaos."* (A. Harder, ed)
  W. Luppe, 394:Vol42fasc1/2-175
Euripides. Hippolytus. (G. & S. Lawall,
  trans)
  E.M. Thury, 124:Nov-Dec89-114
Euripides. Orestes.* (M.L. West, ed & trans)
  S.G. Daitz, 124:Nov-Dec89-112
  P.G. Mason, 303(JoHS):Vol109-220
Euripides. Orestes.* (C.W. Willink, ed)
  C. Collard, 123:Vol39No1-13
  J.C. Kamerbeek, 394:Vol42fasc3/4-531
  P.G. Mason, 303(JoHS):Vol109-220
Evangeliou, C. Aristotle's "Categories" and
  Porphyry.
  L.P. Schrenk, 543:Sep89-157
Evangelista, M. Innovation and the Arms
  Race.
  R. Malcolmson, 529(QQ):Autumn89-758
Evangelista, S. Carlos Bulosan and His
  Poetry.
  S. Foster, 448:Vol27No3-158
Evans, A. The God of Ecstasy.
  R. Seaford, 123:Vol39No1-145
Evans, A.B. Jules Verne Rediscovered.
  K. Berri, 561(SFS):Nov89-369
Evans, C. Cometary Phases.
  S. Carnell, 617(TLS):16-22Feb90-179
Evans, D.A.H., ed. Hávamál.
  R. McTurk, 562(Scan):May89-79
Evans, D.A.H. - see Faulkes, A.
Evans, D.S. Medieval Religious Literature.*
  D.N. Klausner, 589:Apr89-412
Evans, G. Collected Papers.*
  T. Baldwin, 479(PhQ):Apr87-209
  J. Campbell, 311(JP):Mar89-156
  S. Soames, 311(JP):Mar89-141
Evans, G. Lesage: "Crispin rival de son
  maître" [and] "Turcaret."
  H. Klüppelholz, 356(LR):Nov89-327
  G.E. Rodmell, 402(MLR):Jan90-187
Evans, G.B., ed. Elizabethan-Jacobean
  Drama.
  K. Sturgess, 611(TN):Vol43No1-43
Evans, J., P. Reed & P. Wilson, comps. A Brit-
  ten Source Book.*
  P. Evans, 415:Sep89-544
  P. Howard, 410(M&L):Feb89-133
Evans, J.C. The Metaphysics of Transcen-
  dental Subjectivity.
  D. Sturma, 489(PJGG):Band96Heft2-423
Evans, J.D. & A. Helbo, eds. Semiotics and
  International Scholarship.
  R.J. Parmentier, 567:Vol74No1/2-109
Evans, M. Jane Austen and the State.
  E. Gillooly, 147:Vol6No1-87
  M. Kirkham, 83:Autumn89-226
  [continued]

[continuing]

D. Le Faye, 541(RES):Aug89-429
J. Wiltshire, 97(CQ):Vol17No4-369
Evans, M. Claude Simon and the Transgressions of Modern Art.
R.R. Brock, 594:Fall89-342
J.H. Duffy, 208(FS):Oct89-495
C. Gaudin, 210(FrF):Jan89-119
E.F. Gray, 395(MFS):Winter89-833
M-A. Hutton, 402(MLR):Oct90-981
Evans, M., H. McQueen & I. Wedde, eds. The Penguin Book of Contemporary New Zealand Poetry.
L. Norfolk, 617(TLS):2-8Feb90-122
Evans, M.N. Masks of Tradition.
H.R.M., 295(JML):Fall88/Winter89-196
Evans, P.A. - see Mullen, E.J. & D.H. Darst
Evans, P.M. John Fairbank and the American Understanding of Modern China.
M.H. Hunt, 293(JASt):May89-356
Evans, R. The Ultimate Test.
A.L. Le Quesne, 617(TLS):26Oct-1Nov90-1159
Evans, R.J. In Hitler's Shadow.*
A.J. Nicholls, 617(TLS):2-8Feb90-110
Evanturel, E. L'Oeuvre poétique d'Eudore Evanturel. (G. Champagne, ed)
D.M. Hayne, 627(UTQ):Fall89-198
Everaert, M. & others, eds. Morphology and Modularity.
R. Lieber, 350:Jun90-367
Everett, D. Young Hamlet.
A. Barton, 453(NYRB):1Feb90-15
A. Kirsch, 617(TLS):20-26Apr90-431
Everett, P. Zulus.
E. Stumpf, 441:30Dec90-14
Everman, W.D. Who Says This?
J.M. Davis, 594:Spring89-102
W. Martin, 395(MFS):Summer89-374
Everson, S., ed. Epistemology.
M. Schofield, 617(TLS):27Jul-2Aug90-805
Everson, W. The Excesses of God.
R. Kern, 27(AL):May89-323
P.D. Murphy, 649(WAL):May89-82
L. Wagner-Martin, 115:Spring89-187
639(VQR):Summer89-100
Evison, V.I. Dover: The Buckland Anglo-Saxon Cemetery.
B.K. Young, 589:Apr89-414
Evrart de Conty. L'harmonie des sphères. (R. Hyatte & M. Ponchard-Hyatte, eds)
L. Braswell-Means, 589:Apr89-416
Ewald, F. L'Etat-providence.
P. Livet, 192(EP):Jul-Dec89-507
Ewart, G. Penultimate Poems.*
M. Horovitz, 493:Autumn89-56
S. O'Brien, 364:Feb/Mar90-111
Ewen, S. All Consuming Images.
T. Druckrey, 147:Vol6No1-81
Ewens, G. Luambo Franco and 30 Years of O.K. Jazz, 1956-86.
B. King, 538(RAL):Summer89-281
Ewers, H-H., ed. Zauberei im Herbste.
M. Grätz, 196:Band30Heft3/4-316
Ewig, E. Die Merowinger und das Frankenreich.
L. Buisson, 547(RF):Band101Heft2/3-353
Ewin, R.E. Liberty, Community and Justice.*
J. Burnheim, 63:Sep89-366
Ewing, K.D. & C.A. Gearty. Freedom under Thatcher.
J. Lively, 617(TLS):15-21Jun90-633

Exley, F. Last Notes from Home.*
D. Montrose, 617(TLS):31Aug-6Sep90-917
639(VQR):Spring89-57
Eyer, P. Perlokutionen.*
E. Luge, 257(IRAL):Feb89-73
Eynat-Confino, I. Beyond the Mask.
J. Fisher, 610:Summer89-209
Eysenck, H. Rebel With a Cause.
A. Clare, 617(TLS):30Mar-5Apr90-340
Ezekiel, N. & M. Mukherjee, eds. Another India.
M. Couto, 617(TLS):14-20Sep90-980
Ezell, M.J.M. The Patriarch's Wife.
R. Janes, 566:Autumn89-81

Fa-kao, C. - see under Chou Fa-kao
Faas, E. Retreat into the Mind.
T.J. Collins, 637(VS):Summer90-677
Faas, E. Shakespeare's Poetics.
H.F. Plett, 156(ShJW):Jahrbuch1989-366
Fabb, N. & others, eds. The Linguistics of Writing.*
J. Paccaud, 189(EA):Oct-Dec89-453
Fabel, R.F.A. The Economy of British West Florida, 1763-1783.
J.J. Te Paske, 656(WMQ):Jul89-615
Fabiani, J-L. Les Philosophes de la république.
R. Good, 242:Vol10No4-492
"Fables from Old French: Aesop's Beast and Bumpkins." (N.R. Shapiro, trans)
R. Edson, 472:Vol16No1-87
Fabre, F. The Abbé Tigrane.
W.W. Thomas, 446(NCFS):Spring-Summer90-582
Fabre, J.P. - see under Palau i Fabre, J.
Fabre, S. Douche écossaise.
E.B. Turk, 207(FR):Dec89-399
Fabre d'Olivet, A. La langue d'oc rétablie - Grammaire.* (G. Kremnitz, ed)
C. Torreilles, 209(FM):Oct89-262
Facer, G.S., ed. Erasmus and His Times.
J.E. Phillips, 124:Jan-Feb90-251
Faegri, K. Dikteren og hans blomster.
A. Aarseth, 172(Edda):1989/2-173
Faerch, C. & G. Kasper. Introspection in Second Language Research.*
M-A. Reiss, 399(MLJ):Spring89-77
Faessler, S. A Basket of Apples and Other Stories.
R. Donovan, 198:Spring89-116
A. Van Wart, 102(CanL):Spring89-170
Faeta, F., ed. Calabria.
S. Gruber, 576:Dec89-403
Fagan, C. Nora by the Sea.
L. Drew, 198:Autumn89-118
Fahey, D. Metamorphoses.
W. Tonetto, 581:Jun89-263
Fahy, C. Saggi di bibliografia testuale.
B. Richardson, 278(IS):Vol44-163
Faietti, M. & K. Oberhuber. Bologna e l'umanesimo 1490-1510.
M. Bury, 90:Dec89-853
Fainlight, H. Selected Poems.
K. Jebb, 493:Summer89-31
Fainlight, R. The Knot.
V. Rounding, 617(TLS):27Jul-2Aug90-803
Fairbairn, S. & G., eds. Psychology, Ethics and Change.*
A. Maclean, 291:Vol6No1-117

Fairbank, J.K. & A. Feuerwerker, eds. The
Cambridge History of China.* (Vol 13, Pt 2)
J.W. Esherick, 318(JAOS):Apr–Jun88–344
Fairbanks, C. Prairie Women.*
K.S. Langlois, 250(HLQ):Summer89–433
Fairburn, M. The Ideal Society and its
Enemies.
R. Shannon, 617(TLS):2–8Feb90–121
"The Fairest Flower."
A. Scaglione, 545(RPh):May90–627
Fairley, J. Racing in Art.
J. Reid, 617(TLS):26Oct–1Nov90–1159
Falassi, A. Time Out of Time.
F.E. Manning, 162(TDR):Spring89–20
Falck, C. Myth, Truth and Literature.*
E. Longley, 493:Summer89–15
Falco, E. Plato at Scratch Daniel's.
B. Christophersen, 441:23Sep90–48
Faldbakken, K. The Honeymoon.
N. Ingwersen, 563(SS):Spring/Summer89–
298
Faldbakken, K. The Sleeping Prince.*
A.J. Sabatini, 441:11Feb90–18
Faliu-Lacourt, C. – see de Castro, G.
Falk, Q. Anthony Hopkins.
A. Rattansi, 511:Jul89–47
Falk, W.D. Ought, Reasons, and Morality.
R.B. Brandt, 449:Jun89–401
S.L. Darwall, 311(JP):Apr89–208
Falkenburg, B. Die Form der Materie.
G. di Giovanni, 342:Band80Heft2–226
Falkenburg, R.L. Joachim Patinir.
E. Buijsen, 600:Vol19No3–209
Falkner, D. Nine Sides of the Diamond.
R. Barber, 441:1Apr90–12
Fallaci, O. Insciallah.
D. Davis, 617(TLS):28Sep–4Oct90–1039
Fallaize, E. Étienne Carjat and "Le Boule-
vard" (1861–1863).
R. Hobbs, 402(MLR):Jan90–194
G. Robb, 535(RHL):Jul–Aug89–735
Fallaize, E. The Novels of Simone de Beau-
voir.
J. Fletcher, 268(IFR):Winter90–49
T. Keefe, 402(MLR):Oct90–979
E. Marks, 210(FrF):Sep89–368
Faller, L.B. Turned to Account.*
J. Bender, 566:Spring89–184
Fallon, M. Working Hot.
M. Hardie, 581:Dec89–654
Fallon, P. Collected Poems.
D. Johnston, 617(TLS):23–29Nov90–1273
Fallon, P. The News and Weather.
B. O'Donoghue, 493:Summer89–62
Fält, O.K. & A. Kujala – see Akashi Motojirō
Faludy, G. Notes from the Rainforest.
A. Pritchard, 627(UTQ):Fall89–170
Famiglietti, R.C. Royal Intrigue.
D.M. Bessen, 589:Apr89–419
Fancy, M. & I. Cohen, eds. The Crake Lec-
tures of 1984.
T.G. Elliott, 487:Spring89–93
Fandel, J. Five A.M. & Other Times.
R. Scheele, 569(SR):Winter89–xvii
Fanning, C., ed. The Exiles of Erin.
R.E. Rhodes, 177(ELT):Vol32No1–110
Fanning, D. The Breath of the Symphonist.
E. Roseberry, 410(M&L):May89–281
R. Walker, 411:Oct89–342
Fanning, S. A Bishop and His World before
the Gregorian Reform.
U–R. Blumenthal, 377:Jul89–148
Fansuri, H. – see under Hamzah Fansuri

Fanthorpe, U.A. A Watching Brief.*
L. Sail, 565:Summer89–75
Fantini, A.E. Language Acquisition of a Bi-
lingual Child.
N.H. Hornberger, 355(LSoc):Sep89–389
al–Fārābī. Al Farabi's "Commentary" and
"Short Treatise" on Aristotle's "De Inter-
pretatione."* (F.W. Zimmermann, ed &
trans)
J.E. Montgomery, 123:Vol39No1–143
Faraggiana di Sarzana, C. – see Proclus
Faragher, J.M. & F. Howe, eds. Women and
Higher Education in American History.
J. McNew, 639(VQR):Autumn89–742
Farah, C. Literature & Landscape.
S. Trimble, 649(WAL):Nov89–269
Farge, A. Le goût de l'archive.
P. Roger, 98:Dec89–931
Farías, V. Heidegger and Nazism.* (French
title: Heidegger et le nazisme.) (J. Margolis
& T. Rockmore, eds)
P. Lacoue–Labarthe,153:Fall–Winter89–
38
Faris, W.B. Labyrinths of Language.
C.K. Columbus, 395(MFS):Winter89–858
R.B. Kershner, 219(GaR):Fall89–602
Farkas, A., ed. Lawrence Tibbett.
W. Albright, 465:Spring90–190
Farley, F.H. & R.W. Neperud, eds. The Found-
ations of Aesthetics, Art and Art Educa-
tion.
A. Simpson, 709:Winter91–120
Farmer, B. A Body of Water. Place of Birth.
T. Glyde, 617(TLS):14–20Sep90–980
Farmer, D., L. Vasey & J. Worthen – see Law-
rence, D.H.
Farmer, M.N., ed. Consensus and Dissent.
S. Stotsky, 128(CE):Nov89–750
Farmer, P. Away From Home.
F. Handman, 441:15Jul90–18
Faro, L.J. – see Jiménez Faro, L.
Fárová, A. Josef Sudek, Poet of Prague.
442(NY):21May90–96
Farquhar, G. The Constant Couple. (S.
Trussler, ed)
P. Holland, 611(TN):Vol43No2–84
Farquhar, G. The Recruiting Officer.* (P.
Dixon, ed)
R.W.F. Kroll, 83:Autumn89–214
Farquhar, G. The Works of George Farquhar.
(S.S. Kenny, ed)
R.D. Hume, 481(PQ):Summer89–378
D.J. Womersley, 447(N&Q):Dec89–510
Farrar, C. The Origins of Democratic Think-
ing.
H. Yunis, 124:Jan–Feb90–244
Farrell, D., comp. The Stinehour Press.
J. Dreyfus, 517(PBSA):Sep89–397
Farrell, K. Play, Death, and Heroism in
Shakespeare.
C.H. Kullman, 580(SCR):Fall90–177
Farrell, S., with T. Bentley. Holding On to
the Air.
J. Acocella, 453(NYRB):11Oct90–29
W. Clemons, 441:16Sep90–3
A. Croce, 442(NY):15Oct90–124
Farrer, C.R., ed. Women and Folklore.
J. Ice, 440:Winter–Spring89–121
Farris, D. Evensong.
G. Gessert, 448:Vol27No2–124
Farwick, P. Deutsche Volksliedlandschaften.
A.K. Schaller–Wenzlitschke,
187:Winter89–178

Fasel, C. Herder und das klassische Weimar.
  H.B. Nisbet, 402(MLR):Jul90-788
Fasold, R. Sociolinguistics of Language.
  T. Shippey, 617(TLS):19-25Oct90-1117
Fasold, R. The Sociolinguistics of Society.
  A. Bell, 355(LSoc):Jun89-262
Fasold, R.W. & D. Schiffrin, eds. Language
  Change and Variation.
  D. Stein, 159:Vol6No2-271
Fast, H. Being Red.
  M. Isserman, 441:4Nov90-14
Fathers, M. & A. Higgins. Tiananmen.*
  J. Mirsky, 453(NYRB):1Feb90-21
de Fátima Sousa e Silva, M. - see Aristo-
  phanes
Fåtu, M. & M. Muşat, eds. Horthyist-Fascist
  Terror in Northwestern Romania.
  M. Rady, 575(SEER):Oct89-663
Faulhaber, C.B. Libros y bibliotecas en la
  España medieval.*
  R. Hitchcock, 304(JHP):Autumn89-89
Faulhaber, U. & others, eds. Exile and En-
  lightenment.*
  E. Glass, 221(GQ):Summer89-419
Faulkes, A., comp. Hávamál. (D.A.H. Evans,
  ed)
  R. McTurk, 562(Scan):May89-79
Faulkes, A. - see "Snorri Sturluson's Edda:
  Prologue and Gylfaginning"
Faulkner, P., ed. A Modernist Reader.*
  J. Osborne, 506(PSt):May87-121
Faulkner, T C., N.K. Kiessling & R.L. Blair -
  see Burton, R.
Faulkner, W. The Sound and the Fury. (D.
  Minter, ed)
  D. Hewitt, 447(N&Q):Jun89-273
Faulks, S. The Girl at the Lion d'Or.*
  M. Elliott, 364:Dec89/Jan90-130
Faunce, S. & L. Nochlin. Courbet Reconsid-
  ered.*
  639(VQR):Spring89-67
Fauquet, J-M., ed. Musiques, Signes, Images.
  R. Nichols, 415:Aug89-479
  H. Vanhulst, 537:Vol75No2-285
Fauré, C. Les Déclarations de droits de
  l'homme et du citoyen.
  J. Starobinski, 453(NYRB):12Apr90-47
Fauré, G. Gabriel Fauré. A Life in Letters.*
  (B. Jones, ed & trans)
  R.L. Smith, 415:Sep89-543
Fausbøll, E. - see Aelfric
Fausing, B. Drømmebilleder.
  Ø. Rottem, 172(Edda):1989/3-282
Faust, D.G. The Creation of Confederate
  Nationalism.
  M. Kreyling, 392:Spring89-183
  C.V. Woodward, 453(NYRB):15Mar90-39
  639(VQR):Summer89-80
Fava Guzzetta, L. & others. L'età romantica e
  il romanzo storico in Italia.
  J. Smith, 402(MLR):Jul90-755
Favier, J. The World of Chartres.
  M. Filler, 441:2Dec90-22
Favre, Y-A., ed. Victor Segalen.
  M. Détrie, 549(RLC):Jul-Sep89-387
Fawcett, B. Cambodia.*
  N. Zacharin, 102(CanL):Winter88-106
  639(VQR):Summer89-93
Faxon, A.C. Dante Gabriel Rossetti.
  P-L. Adams, 61:Jan90-101
  K. Flint, 617(TLS):19-25Oct90-1134
Fay, B., E.O. Golub & R.T. Vann - see Mink,
  L.O.

Feal, C. En nombre de Don Juan.
  J.F. Gaines, 475:Vol16No30-287
Feal, R.G. - see under Geisdorfer Feal, R.
Feather, J. A History of British Publishing.
  J.A. Wiseman, 470:Vol27-132
Feather, J. The Provincial Book Trade in
  Eighteenth-Century England.*
  O.M. Brack, Jr., 566:Autumn89-79
Featherstone, K. & D.K. Katsoudas, eds. Po-
  litical Change in Greece Before and After
  the Colonels.
  D. Hunt, 303(JoHS):Vol109-279
Fecher, C.A. - see Mencken, H.L.
Fedeli, P. Properzio, Il libro terzo delle
  elegie.*
  J. den Boeft, 394:Vol42fasc3/4-558
  A. Ramírez de Verger, 24:Spring89-180
Fedeli, P. - see Propertius
Federspiel, J. Geographie der Lust.
  A. Vivis, 617(TLS):12-18Jan90-41
Fedorov, A. Innokentij Annenskij.
  W. Busch, 688(ZSP):Band49Heft1-190
Fee, M., ed. Canadian Poetry in Selected
  English-Language Anthologies.
  G. Ripley, 470:Vol27-100
Feferman, S. & others - see Gödel, K.
Feher, F. The Frozen Revolution.
  T.E. Kaiser, 173(ECS):Spring90-348
Fehr, K. Jeremias Gotthelf.*
  R. Godwin-Jones, 301(JEGP):Jul89-381
  R.D. Hacken, 406:Spring89-130
Feibleman, P. Lilly.*
  D. Miller, 569(SR):Spring89-283
  S. Rusowski, 585(SoQ):Winter90-62
Feilchenfeld, K. Deutsche Exilliteratur
  1933-1945.
  E. Schürer, 222(GR):Fall89-185
Feilchenfeldt, K. - see Varnhagen von Ense,
  K.A.
Fein, P.L-M. Women of Sensibility or Reason.
  O.B. Cragg, 166:Oct89-70
  S. Davies, 83:Autumn89-240
  M. Hall, 208(FS):Jan89-90
Feinberg, J. Harm to Self.*
  J.M. Fischer, 482(PhR):Jan89-129
Feinberg, J. Harmless Wrongdoing.
  R.J. Arneson, 185:Jan90-368
  M. Clark, 518:Oct89-251
Feinberg, J. The Moral Limits of the Criminal
  Law.* (Vol 2) [entry in prev was of Vols 1
  & 2]
  G. Dworkin, 482(PhR):Apr89-239
  J. Gray, 617(TLS):12-18Jan90-31
Feinberg, J. The Moral Limits of the Criminal
  Law. (Vols 3 & 4)
  J. Gray, 617(TLS):12-18Jan90-31
Feinberg, R.E. & R. Ffrench-Davis, eds.
  Development and External Debt in Latin
  America.
  T.H. Cohn, 106:Fall89-255
Feinstein, C.H. & S. Pollard, eds. Studies in
  Capital Formation in the United Kingdom
  1750-1920.
  W. Ashworth, 637(VS):Spring90-526
Feinstein, E. All You Need.*
  J. Mellors, 364:Dec89/Jan90-126
Feinstein, E. City Music.
  R. Padel, 617(TLS):16-22Nov90-1248
Feinstein, E. Mother's Girl.*
  D. Constantine, 493:Spring89-61
Feinstein, J. Forever's Team.
  H. Elliott, 441:7Jan90-12

Feintuch, B., ed. The Conservation of Culture.
  S.J. Bronner, 658:Spring89-103
  D.J. Dyen, 187:Fall89-546
Feirstein, F., ed. Expansive Poetry.
  D. Kellogg, 30:Winter90-86
Fekete, J., ed. Life After Postmodernism.*
  M.H. Keefer, 102(CanL):Spring89-225
Feldbusch, E. Geschriebene Sprache.*
  U. Knoop, 684(ZDA):Band118Heft1-31
Feldman, E. Looking for Love.
  C. Cohen, 441:21Jan90-31
Feldman, P.R. & D. Scott-Kilvert - see Shelley, M.
Feldschuh, J., with D. Weber. Safe Blood.
  R. Bazell, 441:14Oct90-15
Feldstein, R. & J. Roof, eds. Feminism and Psychoanalysis.
  K. Ford, 617(TLS):12-18Jan90-46
Felger, R.S. & M.B. Moser. People of the Desert and Sea.
  P. Nabokov, 456(NDQ):Spring89-198
Felice, D. Jean-Jacques Rousseau in Italia.
  V. Santi, 549(RLC):Jan-Mar89-118
  F.A. Spear, 207(FR):Dec89-377
Felipe, C. Teatro.* (J.A. Escarpanter & J.A. Madrigal, eds)
  V.B. Levine, 238:May89-312
Felix, J. Les Pavages du désert.
  C.F. Coates, 207(FR):Oct89-204
Felkay, N. Balzac et ses éditeurs, 1822-1837.
  F. Bassan, 446(NCFS):Fall-Winter89/90-240
Fell, A. The Crystal Owl.
  S. Pugh, 493:Spring89-47
Feller, B., with B. Gilbert. Now Pitching Bob Feller.
  P. Constantine, 441:1Apr90-19
Fellman, M. Inside War.*
  J.M. McPherson, 453(NYRB):12Apr90-33
Fellows, O. & D.G. Carr - see "Diderot Studies"
Fellows, R.A. Sir Reginald Blomfield.
  N. Jackson, 576:Sep89-289
Felman, S. Jacques Lacan and the Adventure of Insight.*
  S.B., 295(JML):Fall88/Winter89-226
  G.D. Chaitin, 567:Vol75No1/2-139
  M.N. Evans, 188(ECr):Spring89-97
  P.L. Rudnytsky, 242:Vol10No1-118
Felmingham, M. The Illustrated Gift Book 1880-1930.*
  R. McLean, 78(BC):Spring89-122
  C. Newall, 39:Aug89-137
Felmy, S. Märchen und Sagen aus Hunza.*
  B. Hoffmann, 196:Band30Heft1/2-130
Felsing, R.H. - see Price, E.J.
Felski, R. Beyond Feminist Aesthetics.
  C. Korsmeyer, 103:Dec90-489
  H. Vendler, 453(NYRB):31May90-19
Feltes, N.N. Modes of Production of Victorian Novels.*
  M. Berg, 529(QQ):Spring89-181
  L.G. Zatlin, 158:Mar89-24
"The Female Soldier."
  M. Scheuermann, 566:Spring90-213
Fénelon, F.D.D. Correspondance.* (Vols 8 & 9) (J. Orcibal, with J. Le Brun & I. Noye, eds)
  J.L. Goré, 535(RHL):Mar-Apr89-283

Fenik, B. Homer and the "Nibelungenlied."*
  E. Cook, 303(JoHS):Vol109-209
  A.G. Martin, 131(CL):Summer89-286
Fenlon, I., ed. The Renaissance.
  D. Fallows, 617(TLS):20-26Jul90-778
Fenlon, J., N. Figgis & C. Marshall, eds. New Perspectives.
  M. Wynne, 235:Winter88-78
Fenton, J. All the Wrong Places.* Manila Envelope.*
  W. Scammell, 493:Autumn89-4
Fenton, J.Y. Transplanting Religious Traditions.
  A.W. Helweg, 293(JASt):Nov89-905
Fenton, W.N. The False Faces of the Iroquois.*
  E. Tooker, 292(JAF):Apr-Jun89-250
Fenwick, G. Contributors Index to The Dictionary of National Biography 1885-1901.
  T. Russell-Cobb, 324:Mar90-302
Fenyő, M.D. Literature and Political Change.
  R.L. Aczel, 575(SEER):Apr89-279
Fenyvesi, C. When the World Was Whole.
  J. Kisseloff, 441:14Oct90-9
Fenz, W. Koloman Moser - Graphik, Kunstgewerbe, Malerei.
  V.J. Behal, 683:Band52Heft2-294
Ferg, A., ed. Western Apache Material Culture.
  C. Taylor, 2(AfrA):Feb89-28
Ferguson, A.B. The Chivalric Tradition in Renaissance England.
  C.M. Meale, 589:Oct89-942
Ferguson, J. Catullus.
  D.T. Benediktson, 124:Nov-Dec89-132
Ferguson, J. Euripides, "Medea & Electra."
  E.M. Craik, 123:Vol39No1-132
Ferguson, M.W., M. Quilligan & N.J. Vickers, eds. Rewriting the Renaissance.*
  J.H. Anderson, 604:Fall87-59
Ferguson, N. Putting Out.
  M.E. Ross, 441:26Aug90-14
Ferguson, R. The Unbalanced Mind.*
  J.A. Winn, 301(JEGP):Jan89-102
Ferguson, T. The Kinkajou.
  M. Kenyon, 376:Jun89-126
Ferguson, W.C. Pica Roman Type in Elizabethan England.
  D. McKitterick, 617(TLS):2-8Mar90-232
Ferlan, F. Le Thème d'Ondine dans la littérature et l'opéra allemands au XIXème siècle.
  J. Rissmann, 196:Band30Heft3/4-318
Ferlinghetti, L. European Poems and Transitions.
  M. Horovitz, 493:Autumn89-56
Ferlinghetti, L. Wild Dreams of a New Beginning.
  M. Horovitz, 493:Autumn89-56
  D. Wakoski, 219(GaR):Winter89-804
Fernandes, S.L.D. Foundations of Objective Knowledge.*
  G.G. Brittan, Jr., 486:Sep89-537
Fernández, A.R. & I. Arellano - see Vélez de Guevara, L.
Fernández, M. El discurso narrativo en la obra de María Luisa Bombal.
  M. Grünfeld, 552(REH):May89-143
  E.M. Martínez, 238:Dec89-968
  V. Soto, 711(RHM):Dec89-191
Fernández, M.J. - see under Jos Fernández, M.

Fernández, T. La poesía hispanoamericana en el siglo XX.
C. Perriam, 86(BHS):Oct89-395
Fernández, X.A. - see Tirso de Molina
Fernández-Armesto, F. The Spanish Armada.*
A.W. Lovett, 86(BHS):Jul89-278
Fernández Cambria, E. Teatro español del siglo XX para la infancia y la juventud (desde Benavente hasta Alonso de Santos).
H. Cazorla, 238:Mar89-146
Fernández Madrid, J. Atala y Guatimoc.
F. González Cajiao, 352(LATR):Spring90-163
Fernández Martínez, C. La Categoría verbal "modo" en Plauto.
V. Bonmatí Sánchez, 548:Jul-Dec89-457
Fernández-Morera, D. & G. Bleiberg - see de León, L.
Fernández Sánchez, J. Historia de la bibliografía en España.
R. Pageard, 92(BH):Jul-Dec88-458
Fernández Valverde, J., ed. Roderici Ximenii de Rada Historia de rebus Hispanie siue Historia Gothica.
B. Löfstedt, 229:Band61Heft4-296
Fernández-Vázquez, A.A. - see Keller, J.E.
Fernando Múgica, L. Tradición y revolución.
M. Adam, 542:Oct-Dec89-602
Ferns, J. Lytton Strachey.
M.A. Griffith, 402(MLR):Oct90-930
G. Merle, 189(EA):Jul-Sep89-304
H. Thomas, 539(QQ):Summer89-508
Ferraiolo. Cronaca.* (R. Coluccia, ed)
N De Blasi, 379(MedH):Apr89-146
Ferrand, J. A Treatise on Lovesickness. (D.A. Beecher & M. Ciavolella, eds & trans)
R. Davenport-Hines, 617(TLS):18-24May90-525
Ferrand, M. Le Suffixe -"nja" en russe moderne.
R.J. Lagerberg, 575(SEER):Apr89-262
Ferrari, F. - see Euripides
Ferrari, G.R.F. Listening to the Cicadas.*
G.B. Kerferd, 303(JoHS)·Vol109-226
M.L. Morgan, 319:Jan90-121
Ferraro, B. & P. Hussey, with J. O'Reilly. No Turning Back.
E. Kennedy, 441:23Sep90-1
Ferrars, E. Smoke Without Fire.
P. Craig, 617(TLS):17-23Aug90-867
Ferrater Mora, J. El juego de la verdad.
H. Young, 238:May89-307
Ferraton, Y. Cinquante ans de vie musicale à Lyon.
M. Noiray, 537:Vol75No1-120
Ferré, F. & C. Mitcham, eds. Research in Philosophy and Technology. (Vol 9)
L. Hickman, 103:Apr90-136
Ferreira, M.J. Scepticism and Reasonable Doubt.*
J. Broackes, 393(Mind):Jul88-490
Ferreira, V. Pour toujours.
J-M. le Sidaner, 450(NRF):Sep89-111
Ferrell, R.H. - see Dana, J.T.
Ferrer, A-L. La patrie imaginaire.
J-L. Marfany, 86(BHS):Jul89-306
J.M. Sobrer, 240(HR):Winter89-103
Ferrer i Alòs, L. Pagesos, rabassaires i industrials a la Catalunya central (Segles XVIII-XIX).
J-L. Marfany, 86(BHS):Oct89-392

Ferretti, A. Renaissance en Paganie.
M. Benson, 102(CanL):Autumn-Winter89-154
Ferrier, C., ed. Gender, Politics and Fiction.
D.A. Wright, 131(CL):Summer89-300
Ferrigno, R. The Horse Latitudes.
M. Stasio, 441:8Apr90-26
442(NY):23Apr90-115
Ferrill, A. The Fall of the Roman Empire.
H. Castritius, 229:Band61Heft7-596
Ferro, V. El dret públic català.
J-L. Marfany, 86(BHS):Jul89-308
Ferron, M. Un singulier amour.
J-A. Elder, 102(CanL):Autumn-Winter89-159
Ferry, A. The Art of Naming.
J. Goldberg, 570(SQ):Fall89-374
Ferry, L. Philosophie politique. (Vols 1-3)
L.K. Sosoe, 687:Jul-Sep89-548
Ferster, J. Chaucer on Interpretation.*
C.J. Watkin, 148:Winter86-96
Feshbach, O. A Vanitas Self-Portrait Book.
G. Gessert, 448:Vol27No2-120
Fetherling, D., ed. Documents in Canadian Art.
S. Grace, 102(CanL):Summer89-147
Fetherling, D., ed. Documents in Canadian Film.
S. Feldman, 627(UTQ):Fall89-250
Fetscher, I. Die Wirksamkeit der Träume.
K.L. Schultz, 406:Spring89-110
Fetzer, J.H., ed. Principles of Philosophical Reasoning.*
W.G. Lycan, 449:Mar89-101
von Feuchtersleben, E. Sämtliche Werke und Briefe. (Vol 1, Pts 1 & 2) (H. Blume, ed)
W.E. Yates, 402(MLR):Apr90-514
Feuchtmair, B. "Und Kunst geknebelt von der groben Macht."
D. Redepenning, 417:Jul-Sep89-285
Feuchtwang, S., A. Hussain & T. Pairault, eds. Transforming China's Economy in the Eighties.
W-J. Hsieh, 293(JASt):Aug89-588
Feuillot, J. Introduction à l'analyse morphosyntaxique.
M. Harris, 402(MLR):Apr90-404
Fewster, C. Traditionality and Genre in Middle English Romance.
R. Field, 175:Autumn89-251
P. Hardman, 402(MLR):Jul90-686
A.C. Spearing, 541(RES):Nov89-546
Feyerabend, P. Farewell to Reason.*
R.A. Sharpe, 89(BJA):Winter89-92
H. Siegel, 262:Sep89-343
Feynman, R.P. What Do You Care What Other People Think?
T.C. Holyoke, 42(AR):Spring89-242
Ffinch, M. G.K. Chesterton.*
J.C. Pennell, 635(VPR):Spring89-44
Fforde, M. Conservatism and Collectivism 1886-1914.
A. Sykes, 617(TLS):2-8Nov90-1170
Fichte, J. The Vocation of Man.
R. Cristi, 154:Vol28No2-344
Fichte, J.G. Early Philosophical Writings.* (D. Breazeale, ed & trans)
F. Neuhouser, 319:Oct90-624
Fichte, J.G. Essai d'une critique de toute révélation. (J-C. Goddard, ed & trans)
M. Elie, 192(EP):Apr-Jun89-256

Fichte, J.O., ed. Chaucer's Frame Tales.*
  H. Cooper, 541(RES):Feb89-114
  P. Hardman, 677(YES):Vol20-236
  M. Lehnert, 72:Band226Heft1-165
Fichtner, P.S. Protestantism and Primogeni-
  ture in Early Modern Germany.
  B. Scribner, 617(TLS):9-15Feb90-151
Ficola, D., ed. Musica sacra in Sicilia tra
  rinascimento e barocco.
  G. Dixon, 410(M&L):May89-253
Ficowski, J. - see Schulz, B.
Fiddian, R.W. & P.W. Evans. Challenges to
  Authority.
  A.E. Lee, 402(MLR):Jul90-771
Fido, M. The Crimes, Detection and Death of
  Jack the Ripper.
  L. James, 637(VS):Autumn89-201
Fido, M. Murder Guide to London.
  T. Swick, 441:10Jun90-49
Fiedeler, D., ed. The Pythagorean Sourcebook
  and Library. (K.S. Guthrie, trans)
  J.A. Novak, 103:Jan90-24
Fiedler, J., ed. Photography at the Bauhaus.
  A. Grundberg, 441:2Dec90-71
Fiedler, L.M. & M. Lang, eds. Grete Wiesen-
  thal.
  S. Bogosavljević, 602:Band20Heft1-146
Field, J.V. Kepler's Geometrical Cosmology.*
  R.W. Burch, 568(SCN):Fall-Winter89-55
  B.T. Moran, 551(RenQ):Spring89-112
  R. Torretti, 160:Jan89-209
Field, L. Thomas Wolfe and His Editors.*
  F.W. Shelton, 27(AL):Mar89-122
  J. Stillinger, 301(JEGP):Jan89-146
  S. Stutman, 295(JML):Fall88/Winter89-
  422
Fielding, H. Joseph Andrews. (S. Copley, ed)
  J. McLaverty, 447(N&Q):Mar89-110
  S. Soupel, 189(EA):Jul-Sep89-366
  K. Sutherland, 541(RES):Nov89-566
Fielding, H. Joseph Andrews with Shamela
  and Related Writings. (H. Goldberg, ed)
  J. McLaverty, 447(N&Q):Mar89-110
  K. Sutherland, 541(RES):Nov89-566
Fielding, H. "The Covent-Garden Journal"
  and "A Plan of the Universal Register-
  Office."* (B.A. Goldgar, ed)
  J. Black, 447(N&Q):Sep89-399
  T. Lockwood, 402(MLR):Oct90-922
  S. Varey, 166:Jul90-352
  639(VQR):Summer89-82
Fielding H. "An Enquiry into the Causes of
  the Late Increase of Robbers" and Related
  Writings.* (M.R. Zirker, ed)
  T. Lockwood, 405(MP):May90-410
  P. Rogers, 447(N&Q):Dec89-519
  S. Varey, 166:Jul90-352
  639(VQR):Spring89-50
Fielding, H. New Essays by Henry Fielding.
  (M.C. Battestin, ed)
  D. Jarrett, 453(NYRB):22Nov90-40
Fielding, H. The True Patriot and Related
  Writings.* (W.B. Coley, ed)
  K. Sutherland, 541(RES):Nov89-566
Fielding, J. Good Intentions.
  D. Hofmann, 441:28Jan90-23
Fielding, K.J. - see Dickens, C.
Fielding, X. One Man in His Time.
  R. Owen, 617(TLS):2-8Nov90-1176
Fields, A. Henri Rivière.
  J. Anzalone, 446(NCFS):Fall-
  Winter89/90-277

Fields, W. What the River Knows.
  L.A. Schreiber, 441:7Oct90-9
Fiennes, R. Living Dangerously.
  639(VQR):Summer89-91
Fife, A.E. Exploring Western Americana. (A.
  Fife, ed)
  D.H. Stanley, 649(WAL):Feb90-379
Fifield, C. Max Bruch.*
  P. Banks, 410(M&L):May89-268
Figes, E. The Seven Ages.
  R. Buckeye, 532(RCF):Spring89-257
  G. Davenport, 569(SR):Summer89-468
Figes, E. The Tree of Knowledge.
  P.J. Kleeb, 617(TLS):19-25Oct90-1131
Figes, O. Peasant Russia, Civil War.
  R. Pipes, 617(TLS):23-29Mar90-305
Figueras, J.F. - see under Forradellas Fig-
  ueras, J.
"Figures et images de la condition humaine
  dans la littérature française du dix-
  neuvième siècle."
  L. Le Guillou, 535(RHL):Jan-Feb89-137
Filewod, A. Collective Encounters.*
  H. Jones, 178:Jun89-244
  R.P. Knowles, 102(CanL):Autumn-
  Winter89-206
Filipczak, Z.Z. Picturing Art in Antwerp,
  1550-1700.
  M. Russell, 39:Feb89-134
  J. Wood, 90:Oct89-715
"Filologia e forme letterarie, Studi offerti a
  Francesco Della Corte."
  P. Flobert, 555:Vol62Fasc2-385
Finch, R. Exporting Danger.
  D.G. Haglund, 529(QQ):Summer89-517
Findley, T. Stones.
  D. Murray, 198:Summer89-111
  S.O. Warner, 441:29Apr90-38
Fine, A. The Shaky Game.*
  R.W. Miller, 482(PhR):Apr89-215
  F. Rohrlich, 167:May89-409
Fine, A. Taking the Devil's Advice.
  L. Doughty, 617(TLS):22-28Jun90-674
Fine, J., ed. Second Language Discourse.*
  R. Scarcella, 710:Sep89-344
Fine, J.V.A., Jr. The Late Medieval Balkans.
  J.M. Bak, 104(CASS):Spring89-112
Fine, S. Violence in the Model City.
  J. Barnard, 385(MQR):Spring90-288
Finegan, E. & N. Besnier. Language.
  J.L. Malone, 350:Sep90-573
Finger, A. Basic Skills.
  M. Hallissy, 573(SSF):Winter89-98
Finger, A.G. & G.A. Barnes. Let's Laugh
  Together.
  J. Kaplan-Weinger, 399(MLJ):Winter89-
  499
Fink, C. Marc Bloch.*
  N.Z. Davis, 453(NYRB):26Apr90-27
Fink, H. & J. Jackson, eds. All the Bright
  Company.*
  J.T. Goodwin, 102(CanL):Spring89-213
  A. Wagner, 168(ECW):Fall89-113
Fink, K.J. & M.L. Baeumer, eds. Goethe as a
  Critic of Literature.
  J.F. Hyde, Jr., 406:Winter89-476
Fink, M. - see Smith, J.
Finke, L.A. & M.B. Shichtman, eds. Medieval
  Texts and Contemporary Readers.
  R.M. Jordan, 301(JEGP):Apr89-219
  M.J. Schenck, 481(PQ):Fall89-524
  J. Summit, 141:Fall89-471

Finkelstein, N. The Utopian Moment in Contemporary American Poetry.
  D. Porter, 27(AL):Mar89-146
Finlay, M. Western Writing Implements in the Age of the Quill Pen.
  J.I. Whalley, 617(TLS):20-26Jul90-786
Finler, J.W. The Hollywood Story.
  T. Pulleine, 707:Winter88/89-67
Finley, M.I. Sur l'histoire ancienne.
  J-P. Guinle, 450(NRF):Feb89-151
  É. Will, 555:Vol62Fasc2-319
Finn, L.M., ed & trans. The Kulacūḍāmaṇi Tantra and The Vāmakeśvara Tantra with the Jayaratha Commentary.
  T. Goudriaan, 318(JAOS):Oct-Dec88-640
Finnemann, N.O. Traek af naturbegrebets historie.
  J.L. Greenway, 563(SS):Autumn89-417
Finneran, R.J. Editing Yeats's Poems.
  H. Kenner, 441:27May90-10
  J. McGann, 617(TLS):11-17May90-493
Finneran, R.J. - see Yeats, W.B.
Finney, E.J. Winterchill.
  K. Ahearn, 649(WAL):Feb90-390
  42(AR):Spring89-249
Finnimore, B. Houses from the Factory.
  B. Russell, 46:Oct89-12
Finnis, J., J.M. Boyle, Jr. & G. Grisez. Nuclear Deterrence, Morality and Realism.*
  R. Hittinger, 258:Jun89-229
  T.L.S. Sprigge, 518:Jan89-47
Finocchiaro, M.A. Gramsci and the History of Dialectical Thought.
  J.V.F., 185:Apr90-700
  P. Guietti, 543:Sep89-157
Finotti, F. Sistema letterario e diffusione del decadentismo nell'Italia di fine '800.
  J. Smith, 402(MLR):Oct90-996
Firbank, R. The Flower beneath the Foot.
  S. Moore, 532(RCF):Spring89-246
Firchow, P.E. The Death of the German Cousin.*
  B. Bjorklund, 406:Winter89-504
Firda, R.A. Erich Maria Remarque.
  M. Travers, 402(MLR):Oct90-1031
Firmat, G.P. - see under Pérez Firmat, G.
Firmus de Césarée. Lettres. (M A. Calvet Sebasti & P-L. Gatier, eds & trans)
  É. des Places, 555:Vol62Fasc2-354
Firor, J. The Changing Atmosphere.
  M.W. Browne, 441:25Nov90-12
Fischer, B. "Gehen" von Thomas Bernhard.*
  K. Weissenberger, 133:Band22Heft1-89
Fischer, B. "Kabale und Liebe."
  K.A. Wurst, 221(GQ):Winter89-119
Fischer, C. Italian Drawings in the J.F. Willumsen Collection.
  J.B. Shaw, 90:Jul89-493
Fischer, D.H. Albion's Seed.
  P. Clark, 617(TLS):29Jun-5Jul90-698
  E.S. Morgan, 453(NYRB):1Feb90-18
Fischer, E. & W. Haefs, eds. Hirnwelten funkeln.
  A.D. White, 680(ZDP):Band108Heft4-630
Fischer, G. Enemy Aliens.
  P. Panayi, 617(TLS):18-24May90-536
Fischer, G. & V. Dietrich. No Future?? - Nein Danke!!
  K.P. Murti, 399(MLJ):Autumn89-370
Fischer, H. Wörterbuch der unteren Sieg.
  O. Reichmann, 685(ZDL):2/1989-228

Fischer, J.M., ed. God, Foreknowledge, and Freedom.
  L. Zagzebski, 103:Aug90-309
Fischer, J.M. & others, eds. Erkundungen.
  M. Morton, 221(GQ):Spring89-243
Fischer, L., ed. Literatur in der Bundesrepublik Deutschland bis 1967.*
  K. Pezold, 654(WB):1/1989-145
Fischer, M. Stanley Cavell and Literary Skepticism.
  T. Gould, 103:Jan90-13
  G. Henderson, 627(UTQ):Spring90-442
Fischer, M.E. Nicolae Ceaușescu.
  N. Malcolm, 617(TLS):19-25Jan90-57
Fischer, R.A. Tippecanoe and Trinkets Too.
  H. Holzer, 658:Spring89-92
  639(VQR):Winter89-24
Fischer, V., ed. Design Now.
  C. Frayling, 617(TLS):16-22Mar90-292
Fischer, V.F. Tres hombres de teatro.
  C.M. Boyle, 86(BHS):Jul89-316
Fischer, W.B. The Empire Strikes Out.
  J. Hienger, 133:Band22Heft2-194
Fischerova, S. The Tremor of Racehorses.
  M. Parker, 617(TLS):27Jul-2Aug90-803
Fish, S. Doing What Comes Naturally.*
  F. Donoghue, 400(MLN):Dec89-1189
  G.G. Harpham, 617(TLS):9-15Mar90-247
  483:Oct89-573
Fishburn, K. Doris Lessing.
  A. Malak, 268(IFR):Summer89-144
Fisher, A. The Logic of Real Arguments.
  D. Collinson, 518:Oct89-219
  P. Mott, 479(PhQ):Jul89-370
Fisher, A.B. Wall Street Women.
  M.S. Forbes, Jr., 441:4Feb90-13
Fisher, B.F. 4th. The Gothic's Gothic.
  S.E. Marovitz, 87(BB):Sep89-205
  D. Richter, 402(MLR):Jul90-698
  D.A. Ringe, 365:Spring/Summer88-156
Fisher, C. Immrama.
  S. Pugh, 493:Summer89-60
Fisher, C. Surrender the Pink.
  E. Lipman, 441:9Sep90-9
Fisher, C.G. La Cosmogonie d'Hélène Cixous.
  G. Cesbron, 356(LR):Feb-May89-130
  A.D. Ranwez, 207(FR):May90-1078
  M. Whitford, 208(FS):Apr89-232
Fisher, D.E. Fire & Ice.
  R. Kanigel, 441:4Mar90-3
Fisher, J. Listen to Dancing.
  I. McMillan, 493:Winter89/90-65
Fisher, L. Constitutional Dialogues.*
  G.R., 185:Jan90-458
Fisher, M., ed. Letters to an Editor.
  W. Scammell, 617(TLS):16-22Mar90-276
Fisher, M.F.K. Serve It Forth.*
  42(AR):Summer89-370
Fisher, M.H. A Clash of Cultures.
  T.R. Metcalf, 293(JASt):May89-422
Fisher, R. Poems 1955-1987.*
  J. Mole, 493:Summer89-27
Fisher, S. In the Patient's Best Interests.*
  E. Dorsch, 254:Summer89-188
Fisher, W.R. Human Communication as Narration.
  M.J. Hyde, 480(P&R):Vol22No1-71
  W.F. Woods, 126(CCC):May89-236
Fishman, J.A. & others, eds. The Fergusonian Impact.*
  D. Hymes, 355(LSoc):Jun89-267

Fishman, J.A. & others. The Rise and Fall of
the Ethnic Revival.*
   N.H. Hornberger, 355(LSoc):Sep89-405
Fishman, R. Bourgeois Utopias.*
   P. Goodman, 47:Aug89-32
   M.C. Sies, 576:Mar89-97
Fishman, W.J. East End 1888.
   R.B. Henkle, 637(VS):Winter90-363
Fishwick, D. The Imperial Cult in the Latin
West.* (Vol 1)
   P. Gros, 229:Band61Heft5-466
   J.H.W.G. Liebeschuetz, 123:Vol39No2-321
   C.R. Phillips 3d, 124:Jan-Feb90-235
   E. Smadja, 313:Vol79-239
Fisiak, J., ed. A Bibliography of Writings for
the History of the English Language. (2nd
ed)
   F. Chevillet, 189(EA):Oct-Dec89-460
   J.R.J. North, 603:Vol13No2-518
Fisiak, J., ed. Papers and Studies in Con-
trastive Linguistics. (Vol 22)
   L. Selinker, 350:Mar90-188
Fisk, E.J. A Cape Cod Journal.
   T. Foote, 441:28Oct90-7
Fisk, R. Pity the Nation.
   A. Hourani, 617(TLS):2-8Mar90-219
   D. Lamb, 441:16Dec90-14
Fiske, R. English Theatre Music in the Eigh-
teenth Century. (2nd ed)
   566:Spring90-225
Fister, P., with F.K. Yamamoto. Japanese
Women Artists, 1600-1900.
   B. Klein, 407(MN):Spring89-128
   C. Wheelwright, 293(JASt):Nov89-857
Fitch, B.T. Beckett and Babel.
   J. Pilling, 402(MLR):Jul90-682
Fitch, J.G. Seneca's Anapaests.
   R. Mayer, 123:Vol39No2-391
Fitch, J.G. - see Seneca
Fitch, N.R. Literary Cafés of Paris.
   234:Fall89-102
Fitzgerald, E. That Place in Minnesota.
   A. Cooper, 441:12Aug90-17
Fitzgerald, G., ed. Annals of the Metropolitan
Opera.
   J.B. Steane, 617(TLS):7-13Dec90-1331
Fitzgerald, M.J. Rope-Dancer. Concertina.
   W. Kelley, 473(PR):Vol56No4-683
Fitzgerald, M.W. The Union League Movement
in the Deep South.
   M. Rothstein, 585(SoQ):Summer90-129
Fitzgerald, P. The Gate of Angels.
   J.K.L. Walker, 617(TLS):24-30Aug90-889
Fitzgerald, P. Innocence.
   M.B. Cloud, 532(RCF):Spring89-255
Fitzgerald, P. Charlotte Mew and Her
Friends.*
   J.T. Owens, 177(ELT):Vol32No2-229
Fitzgerald, S. - see O'Connor, F.
Fitz Lyon, A. Maria Malibran.
   C. Hatch, 465:Spring90-185
Fitzpatrick, F.J. Ethics in Nursing Practice.
   J. Harris, 291:Vol6No2-240
Fitzsimmons, M.P. The Parisian Order of Bar-
risters and the French Revolution.
   N. Hampson, 83:Spring89-79
Fiva, T. Possessor Chains in Norwegian.*
   C.A. Creider, 350:Mar90-189
Fjeldså, J. & N. Krabbe. The Birds of the High
Andes.
   M. Kelsey, 617(TLS):12-18Oct90-1109
Flach, F., with R.F. Hartman. Rickie.
   A. Whitehouse, 441:11Mar90-19

Flacks, R. Making History.*
   639(VQR):Winter89-25
Fladt, E. Die Musikauffassung des Johannes
de Grocheo im Kontext der hochmittelalter-
lichen Aristoteles-Rezeption.
   M. Haas, 417:Jul-Sep89-282
Flaherty, D.H. Protecting Privacy in Surveil-
lance Societies.
   J.B. Rule, 441:4Mar90-34
Flanagan, T. The Tenants of Time.
   P. Stevens, 529(QQ):Autumn89-720
Flanders, J. Timepiece.*
   B. Howard, 491:May89-105
Flaschka, H. Goethes "Werther."
   F. Amrine, 221(GQ):Winter89-110
Flaubert, G. Carnets de travail.* (P-M. de
Biasi, ed)
   G. Falconer, 446(NCFS):Spring-
    Summer90-534
   C. Gothot-Mersch, 535(RHL):Jan-Feb89-
    125
   A. Tooke, 208(FS):Apr89-221
Flaubert, G. Trois Contes. (P.M. Wetherill,
ed)
   R.B. Leal, 402(MLR):Oct90-974
Flaubert, G. & M. du Camp. Par les champs et
par les grèves. (A.J. Tooke, ed)
   R. Stanley, 446(NCFS):Spring-Summer90-
    536
   P.M. Wetherill, 402(MLR):Apr90-450
Flaubert, G. & I. Turgenev. Gustave Flaubert
- Ivan Tourguéniev: Correspondance. (A.
Zviguilsky, ed)
   P. Brang, 688(ZSP):Band49Heft2-444
Flavell, M.K. George Grosz.*
   E. Clegg, 39:Aug89-137
Flax, J. Thinking Fragments.
   D. Gunn, 617(TLS):21-27Dec90-1372
Flay, J.C. Hegel's Quest for Certainty.
   C-A. Scheier, 53(AGP):Band71Heft1-102
Fleck, R.F. Earthen Wayfarer.
   D.C. Gessaman, 649(WAL):Aug89-191
Flecknoe, R. The Prose Characters of Richard
Flecknoe. (F. Mayer, ed)
   P. Hammond, 566:Spring89-190
Fleetwood, M., with S. Davis. Fleetwood.
   R. Waddell, 441:18Nov90-29
Flegel, W. Das einzige Leben.
   R. Neubert, 654(WB):6/1989-1033
Fleischer, C.H. Bureaucrat and Intellectual in
the Ottoman Empire.
   S. Soucek, 318(JAOS):Oct-Dec88-670
Fleischer, W. & others. Wortschatz der deut-
schen Sprache in der DDR.
   E. Fischer, 682(ZPSK):Band42Heft4-552
Fleischer, W., R. Grosse & G. Lerchner, eds.
Beiträge zur Erforschung der deutschen
Sprache.
   T. Schippan, 682(ZPSK):Band42Heft5-664
Fleischhauer, C. & B.W. Brannan, eds. Docu-
menting America, 1935-1943.*
   639(VQR):Summer89-104
Fleischhauer, I. Die Deutschen im Zarenreich.
Das Dritte Reich und die Deutschen in der
Sowjetunion.
   M. McCauley, 575(SEER):Apr89-303
Fleishman, L. Boris Pasternak.
   D. Bethea, 441:2Sep90-12
   H. Gifford, 453(NYRB):31May90-26
   H. Gifford, 617(TLS):25-31May90-560
Fleishman, L. & others - see "Stanford Slavic
Studies"

Fleissner, R.F. Ascending the Prufrockian
Stair.
  D.J. Childs, 184(EIC):Oct89-348
  A. Dorn, 95(CLAJ):Sep89-94
  K. Smidt, 179(ES):Dec89-592
  42(AR):Summer89-370
Fleissner, R.F. A Rose by Another Name.
  G. Monteiro, 95(CLAJ):Jun90-448
Fleitmann, S. Walter Charleton (1620-1707),
"Virtuoso."
  B. Nugel, 566:Autumn89-73
Fleming, J. & H. Honour. The Penguin Dictio-
nary of Decorative Arts. (new ed)
  L. Taylor, 441:13May90-16
Fleming, P.L. Upper Canadian Imprints, 1801-
1841.
  J. Egles, 354:Sep89-282
  D.B. Kotin, 470:Vol27-126
  J. Roseneder, 517(PBSA):Sep89-399
Fletcher, B. A History of Architecture. (J.
Musgrove, ed)
  90:Feb89-160
Fletcher, D.J., E. Jacobs & N. Masson - see de
Voltaire, F.M.A.
Fletcher, H.G. 3d. New Aldine Studies.*
  R. Mortimer, 551(RenQ):Winter89-838
Fletcher, I. Aubrey Beardsley.
  A. Brown, 637(VS):Autumn89-202
Fletcher, I. W.B. Yeats and his Contemporar-
ies.*
  A. Robinson, 541(RES):Nov89-585
  R. Taylor, 402(MLR):Jan90-160
Fletcher, I. - see Gray, J.
Fletcher, J.C. Arkansas.
  W.B. Gatewood, Jr., 389(MQ):Winter90-
  280
Fletcher, J.G. The Autobiography of John
Gould Fletcher. (L. Carpenter, ed)
  T.D. Young, 585(SoQ):Summer89-116
Fletcher, J.G. Selected Poems of John Gould
Fletcher.* (L. Carpenter & L. Rudolph, eds)
  639(VQR):Spring89-64
Fletcher, K.K. The Paris Conservatoire and
the Contest Solos for Bassoon.*
  E. Blakeman, 410(M&L):May89-273
Fletcher, L., ed. Modernismo.*
  V.P. Dean-Thacker, 345(KRQ):Nov89-498
Fletcher, R. The Quest for El Cid.*
  P-L. Adams, 61:May90-133
  I. Gibson, 441:8Apr90-35
Fletcher, S. Maude Royden.
  M. Webster, 617(TLS):13-19Apr90-390
Fletcher, W. Creative People.
  J. Pilditch, 324:Aug90-643
Flett, U. Revisiting Empty Houses.
  L.B. Osborne, 441:28Jan90-22
"Fleur en Fiole d'Or (Jin Ping Mei cihua)."
  (A. Lévy, trans)
  A.H. Plaks, 318(JAOS):Jan-Mar88-142
Flew, A. Equality in Liberty and Justice.
  P.J., 185:Apr90-693
Flew, A. The Logic of Mortality.
  J.M., 185:Apr90-695
Flew, A. Thinking About Social Thinking.*
  R. Fellows, 479(PhQ):Apr87-221
Flew, A. & G. Vesey. Agency and Necessity.*
  M.S., 185:Oct89-207
Flier, M.S. & S. Karlinsky, eds. Language,
Literature, Linguistics.
  G. Schaarschmidt, 104(CASS):Spring-Win-
  ter88-413
  D. Shepherd, 575(SEER):Jan89-128
  D.W. & J.N. Roney, 574(SEEJ):Fall89-445

Flinn, D.M. What They Did For Love.*
  M.B. Siegel, 34:Mar90-34
Flint, H. In Full Possession.
  D. Jersild, 441:18Feb90-20
Flint, K. Dickens.*
  L. Davis, 637(VS):Autumn89-180
  S. Shatto, 677(YES):Vol20-304
Flint, K., ed. The Victorian Novelist.
  N. Bradbury, 541(RES):Aug89-425
Flocon, A. & A. Barre. Curvlinear Perspec-
tive.
  C. Korsmeyer, 290(JAAC):Spring89-190
Floeck, W., ed. Tendenzen des Gegenwarts-
theaters. Zeitgenössisches Theater in
Deutschland und Frankreich/Théâtre con-
temporain en Allemagne et en France.
  G. von Rauner, 224(GRM):Band39Heft3-
  359
Flood, C.B. Hitler.*
  A. Glees, 617(TLS):13-19Apr90-392
Florescu, R.R. & R.T. McNally. Dracula, Prince
of Many Faces.
  K. Ramsland, 441:15Apr90-15
Florit Durán, F. Tirso de Molina ante la co-
media nueva.
  A.A. Heathcote, 86(BHS):Apr89-182
Florit Durán, F. - see Tirso de Molina
Flory, S. The Archaic Smile of Herodotus.*
  J.M. Bigwood, 487:Summer89-172
  C.W. Fornara, 303(JoHS):Vol109-217
  M. Menu, 555:Vol62Fasc2-336
Flory, W.S. The American Ezra Pound.*
  V. Li, 150(DR):Spring89-145
  L. Mackinnon, 617(TLS):12-18Jan90-43
Floss, R. Dezemberlicht.
  G. Lindner, 654(WB):12/1989-2027
Flower, J.E. - see Mauriac, F. & J. Rivière
Flowers, B.S. - see Campbell, J., with B.
Moyers
Flury-Lemberg, M. Textile Conservation and
Research.
  C. Blair, 39:Jun89-434
Flynn, E.A. & P.P. Schweickart, eds. Gender
and Reading.^
  P.L. Caughie, 477(PLL):Summer88-317
Flynn, G. Luis Coloma.
  D.T. Gies, 552(REH):Jan80-137
  H. Gold, 240(HR):Winter89-107
  N.M. Valis, 238:May89-302
  J. Whiston, 402(MLR):Apr90-479
Flynn, S. A Parameter-Setting Model of L2
Acquisition.*
  M.A. Alvarez, 548:Jan-Jun89-189
Flynn, T.R. Sartre and Marxist Existential-
ism.
  J. Pappin 3d, 438:Summer89-371
Flythe, S., Jr. Lent: The Slow Fast.
  J. Freeman, 441:17Jun90-6
Foakes, R.A. - see Coleridge, S.T.
Foakes, R.A. - see Tourneur, C.
Focher, F. Cattaneo storico e filosofo della
storia.
  A. Cavaglion, 228(GSLI):Vol166fasc533-
  146
Foden, F. The Examiner.
  J. Tomlinson, 324:Jun90-502
Fogel, J. - see Ono Kazuko
Fogel, R.W. Without Consent or Contract.*
  D. Macleod, 617(TLS):9-15Nov90-1211
Fogel, S. The Postmodern University.
  M.H. Keefer, 102(CanL):Spring89-225

Fogelin, R.J. Hume's Skepticism in "The Treatise of Human Nature."*
  I.M. Fowlie, 479(PhQ):Jan89-124
Fogelman, B. Shapes of Power.
  C.D.K. Yee, 27(AL):May89-306
Fogelson, R.M. America's Armories.
  N. Adams, 617(TLS):27Jul-2Aug90-802
Fohrmann, J. & W. Vosskamp, eds. Von der gelehrten zur disziplinären Gemeinschaft.
  P. Boden, 654(WB):10/1989-1750
Fokkema, D. & H. Bertens, eds. Approaching Postmodernism.*
  I. Hoesterey, 221(GQ):Fall89-505
Fokkema, D. & E. Ibsch. Modernist Conjectures.
  S. Connor, 402(MLR):Oct90-904
  A. Fleishman, 177(ELT):Vol32No4-487
  B.M., 494:Fall89-642
  P. Meisel, 395(MFS):Winter89-852
Fokkema, D. & E. Ibsch. Theories of Literature in the Twentieth Century.*
  M. Calinescu, 149(CLS):Vol26No2-185
Fokker, A.D. Corpus Microtonale. (R. Rasch, ed)
  A. Barbera, 308:Fall89-393
Fol, M. Jean de Boschère ou le chemin du retour.
  J. Anzalone, 207(FR):Feb90-551
  J. Onimus, 535(RHL):Nov-Dec89-1079
Foley, J., ed. New Englishes.
  R.H. Southerland, 350:Dec90-866
Foley, J.M., ed. Comparative Research on Oral Traditions.*
  R. Finnegan, 292(JAF):Jul-Sep89-349
Foley, J.M., ed. Oral-Formulaic Theory and Research.
  C. Hawkesworth, 575(SEER):Apr89-331
Foley, J.M., ed. Oral Tradition: A Festschrift for Walter J. Ong.
  D.F. Reynolds, 292(JAF):Jan-Mar89-114
Foley, J.M., ed. Oral Tradition in Literature.
  M. Harney, 545(RPh):Nov89-359
  F.J. Oinas, 104(CASS):Spring-Winter88-498
Foley, J.M. The Theory of Oral Composition.
  R. Beaton, 303(JoHS):Vol109-278
  D.E. Bynum, 104(CASS):Spring-Winter88-455
  E.C. Hawkesworth, 575(SEER):Oct89-604
  J. Opland, 292(JAF):Oct-Dec89-489
Foley, R. The Theory of Epistemic Rationality.*
  W.P. Alston, 484(PPR):Sep89-135
  R. Feldman, 484(PPR):Sep89-149
  E. Fricker, 393(Mind):Jul89-457
  M. Swain, 484(PPR):Sep89-159
Foley, W.A. The Papuan Languages of New Guinea.*
  G.P. Reesink, 603:Vol13No1-206
Folgarait, L. So Far From Heaven.*
  J. Hutton, 54:Jun89-319
Folguera, J.M.M. - see under Morales Folguera, J.M.
"La Folie d'Artois."
  B. Scott, 39:Aug89-137
von Folsach, K. Fra Nyklassicisme til Historicisme.
  I. Sjöström, 341:Vol58No4-180
Folter, S. Private Libraries of Musicians and Musicologists.
  H. Lenneberg, 309:Vol9No2/3-227

Foltinek, H. Charles Dickens und der Zwang des Systems.
  R. Böhm, 224(GRM):Band39Heft2-251
Folz, R. les saints rois du moyen âge en occident (VIe-XIIIe siècles).
  A.W. Lewis, 589:Apr89-421
Foner, E. Reconstruction.
  E.L. Ayers, 639(VQR):Autumn89-735
Fong, G.S. Wu Wenying and the Art of Southern Song Ci Poetry.*
  R.H. Smitheram, 318(JAOS):Jul-Sep88-512
Fongaro, A. Apollinaire poète.
  W.F. Motte, Jr., 207(FR):Apr90-880
Fonseca, R. Bufo & Spallanzani.
  R. Di Antonio, 268(IFR):Summer90-137
Fontaine, J. Culture et spiritualité en Espagne du IVe et VIIe siècles.
  D.W. Lomax, 86(BHS):Jan89-199
Fontaine, P.F.M. The Light and the Dark. (Vols 2 & 3)
  R.W. Jordan, 123:Vol39No2-268
Fontán, A. - see Livy
Fontán, A. & A. Moure Casas. Antología del Latín Medieval.
  R. Wright, 86(BHS):Jul89-271
Fontana, B. - see Constant, B.
Fontana, D. Del mondo tenuto nei transportare l'obelisco vaticano. (D. Conrad, ed)
  L. Beckmann, 43:Band19Heft2-210
Fontenrose, J. Didyma.
  C.A. Faraone, 124:Jul-Aug90-530
  C. Morgan, 235:Summer89-64
  R. Parker, 123:Vol39No2-270
Fontes, M.D. - see under da Costa Fontes, M.
Fontinell, E. Self, God, and Immortality.
  J.P. Moreland, 258:Dec89-480
Foon, D. Skin & Liars.
  S. Gibson, 108:Fall89-88
Foote, H. Selected One-Act Plays of Horton Foote. (G.C. Wood, ed)
  J.H. Maguire, 649(WAL):Feb90-372
Forbath, P. The Last Hero.
  639(VQR):Spring89-57
Forbes, B. A Spy at Twilight.
  N. Callendar, 441:19Aug90-17
Forbes, D. Public & Confidential.
  M. Wormald, 617(TLS):22-28Jun90-673
Forbes, G. The Metaphysics of Modality.*
  M.A. Brown, 484(PPR):Mar90-615
Forbes, J. The Stunned Mullet.
  R. Crawford, 493:Autumn89-23
Forbes, L. A Table in Tuscany.
  J. Keates, 617(TLS):27Jul-2Aug90-809
Forbes, M., with J. Bloch. What Happened to Their Kids?
  D. Leimbach, 441:22Apr90-25
Forbes-Watt, D. - see von Hassell, F.
Forcione, A.K., H. Lindenberger & M. Sutherland - see Spitzer, L.
Ford, B., ed. The Cambridge Guide to the Arts in Britain.* (Vols 1 & 2)
  R. Wibberley, 410(M&L):Nov89-519
Ford, B., ed. The New Pelican Guide to English Literature.* (Vol 9)
  S. Hutchinson, 447(N&Q):Sep89-412
Ford, F.M. A History of Our Own Times.* (S. Beinfeld & S.J. Stang, eds)
  M. Dooley, 4:Winter89/Spring90-156
  K. Rentz, 177(ELT):Vol32No4-478
Ford, P. & G. Jondorf, eds. Ronsard in Cambridge.*
  T. Cave, 208(FS):Jan89-80

Ford, R. Wildlife.
  S. Ballantyne, 441:17Jun90-3
  F. Baveystock, 617(TLS):10-16Aug90-
    841
  D. Johnson, 453(NYRB):22Nov90-16
"Före Picasso."
  J. Povey, 2(AfrA):May89-32
Foreman, L. Bax, a Composer and his Times.
    (2nd ed)
  M. Kennedy, 415:Feb89-89
Forest, J-D. Les Pratiques funéraires en
  Mésopotamie du cinquième millénaire au
  début du troisième.
  S. Dunham, 318(JAOS):Oct-Dec88-655
Forester, T. & P. Morrison. Computer Ethics.
  B. Sharp, 441:7Oct90-41
Forestier, G. Esthétique de l'identité dans le
  théâtre français (1550-1680).
  D.A. Watts, 402(MLR):Apr90-442
des Forêts, L-R. Poèmes de Samuel Wood.
  S. Piron, 98:May89-396
  R. Rabaté, 450(NRF):Nov89-113
Forgacs, D. Italian Culture in the Industrial
  Era, 1880-1980.
  C. Duggan, 617(TLS):3-9Aug90-816
Forgacs, D., ed. Rethinking Italian Fascism.
  C.E.J. Griffiths, 278(IS):Vol43-180
Forkner, B. & P.J. Samway, eds. A Modern
  Southern Reader.
  J.P. Kaetz, 577(SHR):Winter89-91
Formaini, H. Men.
  R. Porter, 617(TLS):1-7Jun90-589
Forman, A. & D.A. Sloane. Required Vocabu-
  lary and Workbook to Accompany "Making
  Progress in Russian: A Second Year Course."
  K.L. Nalibow, 574(SEEJ):Summer89-327
Forman, B.M. American Seating Furniture
  1630-1730.*
  S. Jervis, 90:Jan89-43
Forman, F. The Metaphysics of Liberty.*
  G.L., 185:Jul90-913
Formicola, C. - see Grattius
"Forms and Forces."
  A.A. Johnson, 2(AfrA):Nov88-97
Fornaro, M. Scuole di psicoanalisi.
  J-M. Gabaude, 542:Oct-Dec89-629
Fornet Betancourt, R. Comentario a la Feno-
  menología del espíritu.
  C. Cordura, 160:Jul89-245
Forradellas Figueras, J. Cartapacio poético
  del Colegio de Cuenca.
  T.J. Dadson, 86(BHS):Apr89-171
  W. Ferguson, 240(HR):Spring89-241
Forrer, M. Hokusai.*
  T.T. Clark, 290(JASt).Nov89-859
Forrest, A. Conscripts and Deserters.
  W. Scott, 617(TLS):25-31May90-561
Forrest, P. The Dynamics of Belief.*
  B. Ellis, 393(Mind):Apr89-317
Forrester, A. Frontiers.
  E.U. Irving, 399(MLJ):Summer89-219
Forrester, J. The Seductions of Psychoanaly-
  sis.
  D. Gunn, 617(TLS):21-27Dec90-1372
Forrester, J.W. Why You Should.
  J. Morreall, 103:Jan90-16
  W. Tolhurst, 185:Jul90-888
Forry, S.E. Hideous Progenies.
  C. Baldick, 617(TLS):27Jul-2Aug90-801
Forsch, G.J. Casanova und seine Leser.
  W. Ross, 52:Band24Heft1-84
Forsell, M. Heirloom Herbs.
  L. Yang, 441:2Dec90-21

Forster, M. Lady's Maid.
  B. Hardy, 617(TLS):20-26Jul90-781
Forster, M. - see Browning, E.B.
Forster, M.H. & J. Ortega, eds. De la crónica
  a la nueva narrativa mexicana.*
  S. Menton, 240(HR):Winter89-126
Forster, M.N. Hegel and Skepticism.
  R. Hanna, 543:Mar90-630
  M. Inwood, 617(TLS):19-25Jan90-73
    125:Summer89-422
Forsyth, M. Buildings for Music.
  B. Coeyman, 576:Sep89-292
Forsyth, N. The Old Enemy.*
  P. Brown, 589:Jul89-699
  H.A. Kelly, 292(JAF):Jan-Mar89-107
  B.M., 494:Winter89-853
Forsyth, N. Satan and the Combat Myth.
  G.R. Evans, 541(RES):Nov89-594
Forti-Lewis, A. Italia autobiografica.
  M. Viano, 276:Winter89-463
Fortini, P. Le giornate delle novelle dei
  novizi. (A. Mauriello, ed)
  M. Pozzi, 228(GSLI):Vol166fasc536-617
Fortini Brown, P. Venetian Narrative Paint-
  ing in the Age of Carpaccio.
  J. Fletcher, 90:Sep89-651
Fortis, A. Viaggio in Dalmazia. (E. Viani, ed)
  Ž. Muljačić, 688(ZSP):Band49Heft1-216
"La Fortuna di Virgilio."
  P. Flobert, 555:Vol62Fasc2-368
Forys, M. Antonio Buero Vallejo and Alfonso
  Sastre.
  R.L. Nicholas, 240(HR):Summer89-401
Fosburg, V.C. Place Names in Alabama.
  R.M. Rennick, 424:Mar89-103
Foss, C. & D. Winfield. Byzantine Fortifica-
  tions.
  R. Ousterhout, 576:Jun89-182
Fossey, J.M. The Ancient Topography of
  Eastern Phokis.*
  T.E. Gregory, 487:Winter89-381
Fossier, F. Steinlen's Cats.
  P-L. Adams, 61:Jun90-120
Fossier, F., F. Heilbrun & P. Neagu. Henri
  Rivère, Graveur et Photographie.
  J. Anzalone, 446(NCFS):Fall-
    Winter89/90-277
Foster, D.A. Confession and Complicity in
  Narrative.
  T. Docherty, 541(RES):May89-300
  P.M. Weinstein, 301(JEGP):Apr89-215
Foster, D.W. Elegy by W.S.
  R. Proudfoot, 617(TLS):8-14Jun90-619
Foster, D.W., ed. Handbook of Latin American
  Literature.*
  M.P.L., 295(JML):Fall88/Winter89-197
Foster, D.W. Social Realism in the Argentine
  Narrative.*
  P. Hulme, 86(BHS):Jan89-104
Foster, F.S. - see Harper, F.E.W.
Foster, H. Recodings.*
  D. Elam, 454:Winter90-212
Foster, H.W. The Coquette.
  D. Seed, 83:Spring89-110
Foster, J. A.J. Ayer.
  A.L. Brueckner, 482(PhR):Jan89-97
  R. Fellows, 323:Oct89-305
Foster, J. & H. Robinson, eds. Essays on
  Berkeley.*
  K. Ameriks, 449:Apr89-263
  D. Berlioz, 192(EP):Apr-Jun89-255
  P. Dubois, 242:Vol10No5-603
  T.L.S. Sprigge, 479(PhQ):Apr87-218

Foster, J.W. Fictions of the Irish Literary Revival.*
  Z.B., 295(JML):Fall88/Winter89-197
Foster, K. Petrarch.
  C. Trinkaus, 589:Apr89-423
Foster, P., T. Brighton & P. Garland. An Arundel Tomb.
  R. Crawford, 541(RES):Nov89-593
Foster, R.F. Modern Ireland 1600-1972.*
  J.P. Rossi, 174(Éire):Winter89-129
Foster, T.C. Form and Society in Modern Literature.
  S.V. Donaldson, 27(AL):May89-316
Foster, T.C. Seamus Heaney.
  S. Deane, 617(TLS):16-22Mar90-275
Fothergill-Payne, L. Seneca and Celestina.
  639(VQR):Summer89-87
Fotheringham, R. - see Rudd, S.
Fotia, C. & A. Coccuzzo - see Orlando, L.
Fotinis, A.P. - see Alexander of Aphrodisias
Foucart, C., ed. Actualité de Jouhandeau.
  J-C. Gateau, 535(RHL):Nov-Dec89-1082
Foucault, M. Death and the Labyrinth.
  D.T.O., 295(JML):Fall88/Winter89-226
Foucault, M. Politics, Philosophy, Culture.
  (L.D. Kritzman, ed)
  J.M.B., 185:Jul90-907
  D. Latané, 147:Vol6No1-39
  B. McDonald, 400(MLN):Sep89-945
  L. McWhorter, 103:Sep90-352
Foucault, M. & M. Blanchot. Foucault/Blanchot.
  D. Latané, 147:Vol6No1-39
Fouché, C. Clés pour une chronique.*
  G. Pilotte, 207(FR):Oct89-172
  M. Rieuneau, 535(RHL):Mar-Apr89-332
Fouché, P. - see Proust, M. & G. Gallimard
Foulkes, R., ed. Shakespeare and the Victorian Stage.*
  J. McDonald, 570(SQ):Summer89-235
"Four New Comedies."
  R.P. Knowles, 102(CanL):Autumn-Winter89-207
Fourny, J-F. Introduction à la lecture de Georges Bataille.
  M-C. Lala, 208(FS):Oct89-490
Fowble, E.M. Two Centuries of Prints in America, 1680-1880.
  B.F. Reilly, 658:Summer/Autumn89-184
Fowden, G. The Egyptian Hermes.*
  D.T. Runia, 394:Vol42fasc3/4-566
Fowke, E. Canadian Folklore.
  B. McKendry, 529(QQ):Winter89-961
Fowler, A. A History of English Literature.*
  D.J.G., 604:Spring/Summer89-28
  M.J. Haddad, 568(SCN):Spring-Summer89-5
  J. Pafford, 447(N&Q):Sep89-374
Fowler, C. The Logic of U.S. Nuclear Weapons Policy.
  P.A.W., 185:Oct89-223
Fowler, D. & A.J. Abadie, eds. Faulkner and Race.*
  V. Strandberg, 395(MFS):Summer89-283
Fowler, D. & A.J. Abadie, eds. Faulkner and the Craft of Fiction.
  K.J. Phillips, 268(IFR):Winter90-60
Fowler, D. & A.J. Abadie, eds. Faulkner and Women.*
  T. Hammond, 223:Summer89-205

Fowler, E. The Rhetoric of Confession.
  I. Hijiya-Kirschnereit, 407(MN):Autumn 89-337
  Irie Takanori, 285(JapQ):Jan-Mar89-96
  M.N. Layoun, 293(JASt):Feb89-158
  M. Marcus, 395(MFS):Summer89-397
Fowler, M. Below the Peacock Fan.
  C. Hoyser, 637(VS):Summer90-655
  B.F. MacDonald, 102(CanL):Spring89-185
Fowler, R., ed. A Dictionary of Modern Critical Terms.
  S.R. Yarbrough, 568(SCN):Spring-Summer89-24
Fowler, R. Linguistic Criticism.
  J.R. Bennett, 599:Spring90-119
  H. Tristram, 38:Band107Heft1/2-95
Fowler, R.L. The Nature of Early Greek Lyric.*
  C. Leach, 447(N&Q):Sep89-362
Fox, B.A. Discourse Structure and Anaphora.
  M. Ariel, 297(JL):Sep89-493
  F. Chevillet, 189(EA):Jul-Sep89-335
  F. Cornish, 361:Nov89-229
Fox, C. Graphic Journalism in England During the 1830s and 1840s.
  D. McKitterick, 78(BC):Summer89-262
Fox, C., ed. Psychology and Literature in the Eighteenth Century.*
  A. Ingram, 402(MLR):Apr90-414
Fox, D. Kings in Calderón.
  A.R. Lauer, 238:Mar89-143
Fox, D. - see Henryson, R.
Fox, J.J., ed. To Speak in Pairs.
  J. Sherzer, 292(JAF):Jan-Mar89-112
Fox, L., ed & trans. The Jew's Harp.
  M. McLean, 410(M&L):Nov89-549
Fox, P. The God of Nightmares.
  J. McCorkle, 441:8Jul90-18
  442(NY):2Jul90-73
Fox, R. The Search for Society.
  A. Kuper, 617(TLS):22-28Jun90-665
Fox, R.E. Conscientious Sorcerers.*
  P.A. Muckley, 295(JML):Fall88/Winter89-198
Fox, T.C. Louise von François and "Die letzte Reckenburgerin."
  T.A. Bennett, 221(GQ):Winter89-127
Fox-Genovese, E. Within the Plantation Household.*
  J.V. Hawks, 585(SoQ):Winter90-74
Foz, B. Vida de Pedro Saputo. (F. & D. Ynduráin, ed)
  A.H. Clarke, 86(BHS):Apr89-184
Fracastoro, G. Lehrgedicht über die Syphilis. (G. Wöhrle, ed & trans)
  L.V.R., 568(SCN):Fall-Winter89-71
Fradejas Rueda, J.M. - see Moamín
Fradette, B. L'Ecrit-Vent.
  J.I. Donohue, Jr., 102(CanL):Spring89-235
Fradkin, P.L. Fallout.*
  42(AR):Summer89-369
Fragalà Data, I. & A. Colturato. Biblioteca nazionale universitaria di Torino. (Vol 1)
  M. Talbot, 410(M&L):Aug89-396
Fragonard, M-M. La pensée religieuse d'Agrippa d'Aubigné et son expression.
  K. Csűris, 539:Vol13No4-409
Fraisse, S. Péguy et la terre.
  F. Gerbod, 535(RHL):Nov-Dec89-1073
Fraisse, S. - see Weil, S.

Fraistat, N., ed. Poems in Their Place.* [shown in prev under Fraisat, N.] S.A.S., 295(JML):Fall88/Winter89-255

Fraleigh, S.H. Dance and the Lived Body. A. Daly, 615(TJ):Oct89-421 S.B. Fowler, 290(JAAC):Winter89-89

Frame, P. & others. The Harmony Illustrated Encyclopedia of Rock. (6th ed) B.L. Cooper, 498:Winter89-89

Frame, R. Bluette. C. Hawtree, 617(TLS):6-12Jul90-731

Frampton, K., ed. The Architecture of Hiromi Fujii. M. Treib, 576:Sep89-304

France, A. Oeuvres. (Vol 2) (M-C. Bancquart, ed) A. Vandegans, 535(RHL):Mar-Apr89-319

France, P. Rousseau: "Confessions." J. Still, 402(MLR):Jan90-188 D. Williams, 83:Autumn89-241

Francès, R. The Perception of Music. L.L. Cuddy, 413:Fall89-70

Franceschetti, A., ed. Letteratura italiana e arti figurative. Z.G. Barański, 402(MLR):Oct90-991

Francis, D. Longshot. P-L. Adams, 61:Nov90-173 T. Cahill, 441:14Oct90-45 P. Craig, 617(TLS):30Nov-6Dec90-1300

Francis, R. The Land Where Lost Things Go by Olive Watson. M. Sanderson, 617(TLS):21-27Sep90-999

Franco, E. Perception, Knowledge and Disbelief. J.W. de Jong, 259(IIJ):Jul89-209 K.H. Potter, 485(PE&W):Apr89-216

Franco, N. Le pistole volgari. (F. Romana de' Angelis, ed) Novo libro di lettere scritte da i più rari auttori e professori della lingua volgare italiana. (G. Moro, ed) M. Pozzi, 228(GSLI):Vol166fasc535-451

Franco, P. The Political Philosophy of Michael Oakeshott. J. Waldron, 617(TLS):6-12Jul90-715

François, G., with G. Falleur. Précieuses et autres indociles aspects du féminisme dans la littérature du XVIIe siècle. E.T. Dubois, 535(RHL):Jul-Aug89-711 I. Maclean, 208(FS):Apr89-211 M.E. Vialet, 475:Vol16No31-585

Frank, A. The Diary of Anne Frank.* (D. Barnouw & G. van der Stroom, eds) G. Motola, 390:Dec89-55 R.S. Wistrich, 617(TLS):13-19Apr90-393

Frank, F.S. The First Gothics.* R. Beecham, 541(RES):Aug89-423

Frank, F.W. & P.A. Treichler, with others. Language, Gender, and Professional Writing. E. Battistella, 350:Mar90-190

Frank, J. Dostoevsky: The Stir of Liberation, 1860-1865.* A. Gleason, 550(RusR):Jan89-96

Frank, K. A Chainless Soul. G. Levine, 441:11Nov90-13

Frank, L.A., with P. Huyghe. The Big Splash. D. Overbye, 441:11Nov90-61

Frank, M. Das individuelle Allgemeine. Was ist Neostrukturalismus? Die Unhintergehbarkeit von Individualität. J.H. Smith, 153:Summer89-80

Frank, R. & H. Sayre, eds. The Line in Postmodern Poetry. J. Mellard, 599:Summer90-302

Frankel, F.R. India's Political Economy, 1947-1977. A. Gupta, 293(JASt):Nov89-787

Frankfurt, H.G. The Importance of What We Care About.* C.F. Cranor, 185:Jul90-886

Franklin, B. The Papers of Benjamin Franklin. (Vol 27) (C.A. Lopez & others, eds) 639(VQR):Autumn89-124

Franklin, B. Writings.* (J.A.L. Lemay, ed) D. Royot, 189(EA):Apr-Jun89-230

Franklin, D.O., ed. Bach Studies.* D. Hush, 414(MusQ):Vol74No3-451

Franklin, H.B. War Stars.* K. Hume, 27(AL):Oct89-469

Franklin, J.H. Race and History. D.G. Faust, 441:3Jun90-13

Franklin, U. Exiles and Ironists. B.L. Knapp, 446(NCFS):Fall-Winter89/90-271

Frantz, D.O. Festum Voluptatis. J. Tassoni, 590:Dec89-121

Frantz, S.K. Contemporary Glass. P. Hunter-Stiebel, 139:Dec89/Jan90-20

Frantzen, A.J. King Alfred.* D. Donoghue, 589:Apr89-425

Franz, M. Die Darstellung von Faschismus und Antifaschismus in den Romanen von Anna Seghers 1933-1949. E-M. Siegel & S. Schulz, 654(WB):4/1989-679

Franz, T.R. The Word in the World. T. Mermall, 238:Mar89-146

Franz, U. Deng Xiaoping.* R. Terrill, 293(JASt):Nov89-828

Franzbach, M. Die Hinwendung Spaniens zu Europa. W.L. Bernecker, 547(RF):Band101Heft2/3-374

Fraser, A. The Cavalier Case. P. Craig, 617(TLS):29Jun-5Jul90-709

Fraser, D.M. The Collected Works. (Vol 1) M. Cohen, 526:Spring89-85

Fraser, G. Interweaving Patterns in the Works of Joseph Conrad. I.V., 295(JML):Fall88/Winter89-307 J. Verleun & J. de Vries, 177(DLT), Vol32No1-101

Fraser, J. Private View. O. Stuart, 151:Jan89-66

Fraser, P.M. & E. Matthews, eds. A Lexicon of Greek Personal Names. (Vol 1) J-L. Perpillou, 555:Vol62Fasc2-326 C. Tuplin, 123:Vol39No2-300

Fraser, R. Charlotte Brontë. M. Smith, 82:Vol19No8-376

Fraser, R. Young Shakespeare.* J.A. Bryant, Jr., 569(SR):Spring89-xxxii R.Y. Turner, 551(RenQ):Summer89-354 639(VQR):Spring89-52

Fraser, T.P. The French Essay.* É. Morot-Sir, 535(RHL):Mar-Apr89-339

Fraser-Lu, S. Handwoven Textiles of South-East Asia.* P.M. Coudoux, 293(JASt):Aug89-673

Frassica, P., G. Pacchiano & C. Springer, eds. Immagini del Novecento italiano. R.R. Pietanza, 276:Summer89-220

Frawley, W. Text and Epistemology. N.S. Baron, 567:Vol74No3/4-337

Frayn, M. The Trick of It.* J. Grossman, 441:18Mar90-7

Frazier, A. Behind the Scenes.
J.M. Cahalan, 590:Jun90–77
Frazier, I. Great Plains.*
P.N. Limerick, 617(TLS):27Jul–2Aug90–794
Freccero, J. Dante.* (R. Jacoff, ed)
Z.G. Barański, 278(IS):Vol43–134
P. Hainsworth, 447(N&Q):Jun89–215
J. Kleiner, 478(P&L):Oct89–412
Fréchet, G. Barbey d'Aurevilly, 1808–1889.
J–C. Polet, 356(LR):Nov89–335
Fréchette, L. L'Ecran Brisé.
M. Lacombe, 102(CanL):Autumn–Winter89–203
Fredborg, K.M. – see Thierry of Chartres
Freddoso, A.J. – see de Molina, L.
Frede, M. & G. Patzig, eds & trans. Aristoteles, "Metaphysik Z."
M.L. Gill, 319:Oct90–602
F. Inciarte, 489(PJGG):Band96Heft2–382
Fredericksen, B. & C. Dowd – see Mundler, O.
Fredericksen, B.B., ed. The Index of Paintings Sold in the British Isles during the Nineteenth Century. (Vol 1)
F. Russell, 90:Feb89–160
Frederiksen, I. & H. Rømer, eds. Kvinder, mentalitet, arbejde.
C. Gold, 563(SS):Spring/Summer89–289
Fredriksen, P. From Jesus to Christ.*
M. Dimaio, Jr., 124:Mar–Apr90–366
"Free Speech Yearbook." (Vol 26) (S.A. Smith, ed)
42(AR):Spring89–248
Freed, B. & E. Knutson. Contextes.
J.P. Kaplan, 207(FR):Mar90–736
Freedberg, D. The Power of Images.*
E.H. Gombrich, 453(NYRB):15Feb90–6
Freeden, M., ed. Reappraising J.A. Hobson.
R. Pinker, 617(TLS):16–22Nov90–1224
Freedle, R.O. & R.P. Duran, eds. Cognitive and Linguistic Analyses of Test Performance.
K.A. Mullen, 399(MLJ):Summer89–202
Freedman, J. Drawing Heat.
P. Rist, 106:Summer89–111
Freedman, L. & V. Gamba-Stonehouse. Signals of War.
E. Crawley, 617(TLS):11–17May90–492
Freedman, S.G. Small Victories.
L. Harris, 442(NY):24Sep90–113
I. Howe, 441:20May90–3
Freedman, S.W. Response to Student Writing.
P.R. Meyer, 126(CCC):Feb89–102
Freehling, W.W. The Road to Disunion. (Vol 1)
R.V. Remini, 441:30Sep90–22
442(NY):17Sep90–109
Freeling, N. Sand Castles.
M. Stasio, 441:18Feb90–23
Freeling, N. Those in Peril.
S. Altinel, 617(TLS):19–25Oct90–1132
Freeman, E. & others, eds. Myth and its Making in the French Theatre.
D.F. Connon, 402(MLR):Apr90–435
K. Gore, 208(FS):Oct89–499
Q.M. Hope, 207(FR):May90–1058
R.S. Mall, 446(NCFS):Spring–Summer90–579
D. Maskell, 447(N&Q):Dec89–509
Freeman, J. The Chinchilla Farm.*
D. Johnson, 453(NYRB):15Mar90–28

Freeman, J.B. In Transit.
A. Brinkley, 453(NYRB):28Jun90–16
S. Poger, 174(Éire):Winter89–136
Freeman, J.M. Hearts of Sorrow.
W.W. Larsen, 441:28Jan90–25
J. Mirsky, 453(NYRB):16Aug90–29
D. Rieff, 617(TLS):25–31May90–543
Freeman, M. – see Storni, A.
Freeman, M.J. – see Jodelle, E.
Freeman, M.J. – see de Larivey, P.
Freeman, S. Mutton and Oysters.*
C. Hawtree, 364:Feb/Mar90–143
Freeman, T. Hans Henny Jahnn.*
W. Paulsen, 406:Fall89–402
Freemantle, B. O'Farrell's Law.
N. Callendar, 441:25Feb90–35
Freese, R. & R. McKenzie. Commutator Theory for Congruence Modular Varieties.
M. Valeriote, 316:Sep89–1114
Freidel, F. Franklin D. Roosevelt.
M. Kazin, 441:4Mar90–29
Freidin, G. A Coat of Many Colors.*
C.R. Isenberg, 550(RusR):Jan89–111
Freixas, M.A.G. – see under González Freixas, M.A.
Frel, J., A. Houghton & M. True, eds. Ancient Portraits in the J. Paul Getty Museum. (Vol 1)
H.R. Goette, 229:Band61Heft1–51
Fremlin, C. Listening in the Dark.
P. Craig, 617(TLS):23–29Nov90–1272
French, A. All Cretans are Liars.*
L. Sail, 565:Summer89–75
French, B.B. Witness to the Young Republic.* (D.B. Cole & J.J. McDonough, eds)
F. Allen, 441:11Feb90–28
French, D. Ishbel and the Empire.
D.B. Mack, 529(QQ):Autumn89–701
French, D. Salt-Water Moon.
R. Nunn, 108:Fall89–89
French, K.M. Insights into Tagalog.
B.L. Pritchett, 350:Mar90–191
French, L.A. & K. Nelson. Young Children's Knowledge of Relational Terms.
K. Meng, 682(ZPSK):Band42Heft1–110
French, T. & D. O'Connor. York Minster, a Catalogue of Medieval Glass. (fasc 1)
M. Michael, 90:Nov89–781
French, W. J.D. Salinger Revisited.
W. De Martino, 573(SSF):Winter89–103
Frenk, M. Corpus de la Antigua Lírica Popular Hispánica (siglos XV a XVII).*
S.G. Armistead, 240(HR):Autumn89–503
F.A. Domínguez, 241:May89–97
Frenzel, E. Stoffe der Weltliteratur. (7th ed)
K. Horn, 196:Band30Heft3/4–319
Fresco, M.F. Filosofie en kunst.
W. Poelstra, 204(PdL):Dec89–318
Fresco, M.F., R.J.A. Van Dijk & H.W.P. Vijgeboom, eds. Heideggers These vom Ende der Philosophie.
P. Trotignon, 542:Oct–Dec89–610
"Fresh Oceans."
C. Gow, 571(ScLJ):Winter89–53
Frettlöh, R. Die Revisionen der Lutherbibel in wortgeschichtlicher Sicht.
J. West, 402(MLR):Apr90–498
Freud, S. Freud on Women. (E. Young-Bruehl, ed)
C. Harman, 617(TLS):12–18Oct90–1097

Freudenstein, R. & C.V. James, eds. Confidence through Competence in Modern Language Learning.*
  G.A. Jarvis & A.M. Salomone, 710:Sep89-340
Freudenthal, G. - see Metzger, H.
Freund, E. The Return of the Reader.*
  E.C.R., 295(JML):Fall88/Winter89-227
  S. Vice, 447(N&Q):Mar89-136
Freund, F. & B. Sundqvist. Tysk grammatik.
  K.B. Lindgren, 439(NM):1989/2-215
Freund, N.C. Nonviolent National Defense.
  P.A.W., 185:Oct89-222
Freund, V. Hans Pfitzners Eichendorff-Lieder.
  R. Stephan, 417:Jan-Mar89-97
Freund, W. Theodor Storm.
  R.D. Hacken, 406:Fall89-397
  M.T. Peischl, 221(GQ):Winter89-129
Frey, C.H. Experiencing Shakespeare.
  R.A. Cave, 402(MLR):Oct90-912
  R. Hapgood, 570(SQ):Summer89-228
  M. Wiggins, 447(N&Q):Dec89-505
Frey, J.A. "Les Contemplations" of Victor Hugo.*
  P.W.M. Cogman, 208(FS):Jul89-339
Friar, K. & K. Myrsiades - see Ritsos, Y.
Frick, J. & C. Ward, eds. Directory of Historic American Theatres.
  G.C. Izenour, 610:Autumn89-298
Frick, N.A. Image in the Mind.*
  J.T. Goodwin, 102(CanL):Summer89-133
Fricke, W. The Court-Martial of Jesus.
  A. Burgess, 61:Aug90-89
Fricker, H-P. Die musikkritischen Schriften Robert Schumanns.
  J.A. Deaville, 309:Vol9No2/3-179
Friday, L. & R. Laskey, eds. The Fragile Environment.
  E. Goldsmith, 324:Dec89-67
Friebertshäuser, H., ed. Lexikographie der Dialekte.
  W. Diercks, 685(ZDL):2/1989-220
Fried, I., Z. Kanyó & J. Pál, eds. Comparative Literary Studies.
  R. Bauer, 549(RLC):Jul-Sep89-400
Fried, M. Absorption and Theatricality
  M. Bal, 567:Vol76No3/4-283
Fried, M. Realism, Writing, Disfiguration.*
  M. Bal, 567:Vol76No3/4-283
  A. Wallach, 127:Spring89-95
Fried, P. Mutual Trespasses.
  J. Meek, 456(NDQ):Winter89-227
Fried, R.M. Nightmare in Red.
  A. Boyer, 441:4Feb90-19
Friedberg, A.L. The Weary Titan.*
  W. Ashworth, 637(VS):Spring90-526
Friedberg, M. & H. Isham, eds. Soviet Society under Gorbachev.
  B.A. Chotiner, 550(RusR):Jul89-321
  R. Walker, 575(SEER):Jan89-163
Frieden, B.J. & L.B. Sagalyn. Downtown, Inc.
  H. Muschamp, 62:Apr90-18
  E.A. Schwartz, 441:17Jun90-25
Frieden, K. Freud's Dream of Interpretation.
  D. Aberbach, 617(TLS):6-12Jul90-724
Friedenreich, K., R. Gill & C.B. Kuriyama, eds. A Poet and a Filthy Play-maker.
  S. Shepherd, 402(MLR):Jan90-140
Friedgut, T.H. Iuzovka and Revolution. (Vol 1)
  O. Figes, 617(TLS):12-18Jan90-29

Friedl, B., ed. On to Victory.
  M-M. Byerman, 26(ALR):Winter90-76
  K. Worth, 447(N&Q):Sep89-409
Friedl, G. Verhüllte Wahrheit und entfesselte Phantasie.
  J. Golz, 406:Summer89-255
Friedl, H. Beginn der Errichtung eines Denkmals.
  M. Swales, 402(MLR):Jan90-261
Friedlander, J. Vilna on the Seine.
  G. Josipovici, 617(TLS):9-15Nov90-1205
Friedman, A. Agnelli.* (British title: Agnelli and the Network of Italian Power.)
  T. Goldwasser, 441:25Feb90-25
Friedman, A.T. House and Household in Elizabethan England.*
  J.M. Robinson, 46:Dec89-14
Friedman, A.W., ed. Critical Essays on Lawrence Durrell.*
  M.P.L., 295(JML):Fall88/Winter89-317
Friedman, A.W., C. Rossman & D. Scherzer, eds. Beckett Translating/Translating Beckett.
  J. Fletcher, 208(FS):Jul89-360
  J. Kalb, 397(MD):Dec89-588
  M.P.L., 295(JML):Fall88/Winter89-286
  J. Pilling, 677(YES):Vol20-338
  R. Pountney, 447(N&Q):Jun89-265
  T.C. Ware, 174(Eire):Fall88-158
Friedman, B. Day of Reckoning.
  639(VQR):Spring89-60
Friedman, B.R. Fabricating History.
  R. Jann, 637(VS):Spring90-511
  V. Newey, 402(MLR):Oct90-923
  M. Rossington, 175:Autumn89-261
  K. Tetzeli von Rosador, 445(NCF):Sep89-225
  A.M. Urdank, 591(SIR):Fall89-506
Friedman, D. Florentine New Towns.
  J. Loeffler, 47:Nov89-160
Friedman, E.G. & M. Fuchs, eds. Breaking the Sequence *
  S.S. Friedman, 395(MFS):Winter89-864
  E. Kafalenos, 268(IFR):Summer89-142
  J. Kuehl, 532(RCF):Summer89-252
  P.D. Murphy, 590:Jun90-83
Friedman, E.H. The Antiheroine's Voice.*
  T.E. Lewis, 240(HR):Summer89-378
Friedman, I. - see Schiff, Z. & E. Ya'ari
Friedman, J. Blasphemy, Immorality, and Anarchy.*
  J. Morrill, 541(RES):May89-263
Friedman, J., ed. Regnum, Religio et Ratio.
  R.B. Barnes, 551(RenQ):Summer89-310
Friedman, J.B. Creation in Space. (Vol 1)
  R. Geddes & J. Dill, 505:Nov89-115
Friedman, L. Meetings with Remarkable Women.
  R.B. Pilgrim, 485(PE&W):Jan89-106
Friedman, L.J. Menninger.
  A. Cooper, 441:24Jun90-20
  442(NY):16Jul90-87
Friedman, M. & P. Freshman, eds. Graphic Design in America.
  J. Drucker, 62:Mar90-25
Friedman, M.L. The Emperor's Kites.*
  P.T.S., 295(JML):Fall88/Winter89-292
  D.L. Shaw, 86(BHS):Jan89-106
Friedman, P. Reasonable Doubt.
  L. Wolfe, 441:22Apr90-32
Friedman, R.E. Who Wrote the Bible?
  S. Helmling, 569(SR):Summer89-462

Friedman, R.I. The False Prophet.
  A. Hertzberg, 453(NYRB):25Oct90-41
  R. Leiter, 441:13May90-18
  P. Seale, 617(TLS):24-30Aug90-890
Friedman, T.L. From Beirut to Jerusalem.*
  W. Blitzer, 390:Oct89-58
  R. Owen, 617(TLS):29Jun-5Jul90-687
Friedman, Y., ed. Islam in Asia. (Vol 1)
  E. Naby, 318(JAOS):Jan-Mar88-173
Friedmann, F.G. Hannah Arendt.
  D. Barnouw, 221(GQ):Summer89-422
Friedrich, O. Glenn Gould.*
  R.J. Silverman, 510:Summer89-56
  42(AR):Fall89-502
Friedrich, O. The Grave of Alice B. Toklas
  and Other Reports from the Past.
  42(AR):Fall89-502
Friedwald, W. Jazz Singing.
  T. Piazza, 441:19Aug90-12
Friend, T. The Blue-Eyed Enemy.
  A. Reid, 293(JASt):Aug89-674
Friesen, A. Thomas Muentzer, a Destroyer of
  the Godless.
  A. Hamilton, 617(TLS):14-20Sep90-983
Friesen, V.C. The Windmill Turning.
  M.G. Shelton, 529(QQ):Summer89-513
Friis-Jensen, K. Saxo Grammaticus as Latin
  Poet.
  F. Amory, 589:Jul89-701
  A. Önnerfors, 229:Band61Heft6-507
"Elizabeth Frink: Sculpture."*
  W. Jeffett, 39:Jul89-65
Frink, H. Animal Symbolism in Hofmanns-
  thal's Works.
  D.C. Van Handle, 221(GQ):Summer89-395
Frisbie, C.J., ed. Explorations in Ethnomusi-
  cology.*
  A. Seeger, 292(JAF):Jul-Sep89-354
Frisch, M. Homo faber. (K. Müller-Salget, ed)
  A.D. White, 680(ZDP):Band108Heft2-304
Frisch, T.G. Gothic Art, 1140-c 1450.
  C. Lord, 589:Jan89-162
Frisch, W., ed. Schubert.*
  R. Kramer, 410(M&L):Feb89-111
  R.V., 412:Nov88-310
Fritsch-Bournazel, R. Confronting the Ger-
  man Question.
  M. Fulbrook, 242:Vol10No5-628
Fritz, A.D. Thought and Vision.*
  D. Bergman, 27(AL):Mar89-139
Fritze, K., E. Müller-Mertens & J. Schild-
  hauer, eds. Der Ost- und Nordseeraum.
  D. Stellmacher, 685(ZDL):2/1989-220
Frobose, M. Practicamos más español.
  M. Roe, 399(MLJ):Summer89-241
Frobose, M. Recits divertissants.*
  F.I. Andrus, 399(MLJ):Autumn89-360
Froissart, J. "Le Paradis d'Amour; L'Orloge
  amoureuse" de Jean Froissart.* (P.F. Dem-
  bowski, ed)
  G.T. Diller, 207(FR):Oct89-154
"From Gatekeeper to Gateway."
  A. Hacker, 453(NYRB):22Nov90-19
Fromentin, E. Dominique. (A-M. Christin, ed)
  B. Wright, 208(FS):Oct89-478
Fromkin, D. A Peace to End all Peace.*
  B. Wasserstein, 617(TLS):30Mar-5Apr90-
  343
Frontisi-Ducroux, F. La cithare d'Achille.
  H.P. Foley, 122:Jul89-252

Frösén, J. with others. Papyri Helsingienses,
  I.
  W. Clarysse, 303(JoHS):Vol109-246
  D.J. Thompson, 123:Vol39No1-159
Frost, K.B. Exits and Entrances in Menander.
  W.G. Arnott, 123:Vol39No2-385
  N.J. Lowe, 303(JoHS):Vol109-229
  J.M. Walton, 610:Spring89-86
Frost, O.W. - see Steller, G.W.
Frost, W. John Dryden.
  J.D. Canfield, 173(ECS):Spring90-370
  K. Combe, 447(N&Q):Dec89-513
  C.H. Hinnant, 566:Spring89-171
  C. Koralek, 184(EIC):Jul89-242
  G. Parfitt, 402(MLR):Oct90-917
Frost, W. & V.A. Dearing - see Dryden, J.
Frow, J. Marxism and Literary History.*
  M. Bullock, 125:Fall88-82
  K. Hirschkop, 494:Fall89-623
  M. Janiak, 290(JAAC):Summer89-296
Fruehwald, S. Authenticity Problems in
  Joseph Haydn's Early Instrumental Works.
  A.P. Brown, 309:Vol9No2/3-170
  D. McCaldin, 415:Feb89-90
Frühling, P. Swedish Development Aid in
  Perspective.
  B.L. Hanson, 563(SS):Spring/Summer89-
  282
Frühmorgen-Voss, H. & N.H. Ott. Katalog der
  deutschsprachigen illustrierten Handsch-
  riften des Mittelalters. (Vol 1, Pts 1 & 2)
  M.E. Kalinke, 301(JEGP):Jul89-373
  P. Kern, 680(ZDP):Band108Heft1-131
  J.A. Rushing, Jr., 589:Oct89-945
Frühwald, W. & others - see "Aurora"
Frutiger, A. Signs and Symbols.
  G. Mackie, 324:Jun90-505
Fry, C.M. Sartre and Hegel.
  P. Trotignon, 542:Oct-Dec89-611
Fry, J., N. Nzegwu & J-C. Muller. Heroic Fig-
  ures.
  R. Hoffman, 2(AfrA):Feb89-22
Fryckstedt, M.C. Geraldine Jewsbury's "Ath-
  enaeum" Reviews.*
  N.H. Platz, 38:Band107Heft1/2-239
Fryde, E.B. William de la Pole.
  R.W. Kaeuper, 589:Jul89-706
Frye, N. Anatomy of Criticism.
  617(TLS):19-25Oct90-1137
Frye, N. Northrop Frye on Education. Some
  Reflections on Life and Habit.
  T. Willard, 627(UTQ):Fall89-164
Frye, N. Northrop Frye on Shakespeare.* (R.
  Sandler, ed)
  K. Tetzeli von Rosador, 156(ShJW):Jahr-
  buch1989-351
Frye, R.M. The Renaissance "Hamlet."
  J.A. Bryant, Jr., 569(SR):Summer89-445
Frye, R.N. The History of Ancient Iran.
  J.R. Russell, 318(JAOS):Apr-Jun88-324
Fryer, J. Felicitous Space.*
  E.P. Stengel, 27(AL):Mar89-117
Fryer, S.B. Fitzgerald's New Women.
  L. Miller, 587(SAF):Autumn89-253
  R. Wexelblatt, 27(AL):May89-305
Fryer, T.B. & H.J. Faria. Talking Business in
  Spanish.
  D.E. Rivas, 399(MLJ):Winter89-532
Frykenberg, R.E., ed. Delhi Through the
  Ages.
  N. Kumar, 293(JASt):May89-423

Fu Xuancong. Tang caizi zhuan jiaojian. (Vol 1)
  W.H.N., 116:Dec89-169
Fuchs, E. Israeli Mythogynies.*
  H.W.N., 295(JML):Fall88/Winter89-198
Fuchs, G. Ils resteront.
  M-C.W. Koop, 207(FR):Oct89-185
Fuchs, I. Die Herausforderung des Nihilismus.
  A. McMillin, 575(SEER):Apr89-272
Fuchs, L.H. The American Kaleidoscope.
  A. Hacker, 453(NYRB):22Nov90-19
Fucini, J.J. & S. Working for the Japanese.
  G. Tyler, 441:12Aug90-7
Fuegi, J. Bertolt Brecht.*
  K-H. Schoeps, 301(JEGP):Oct89-600
Fuegi, J., G. Bahr & J. Willett - see "The Brecht Yearbook"
Fuentes, C. Aura.* (P. Standish, ed)
  S. Boldy, 86(BHS):Jan89-112
Fuentes, C. Constancia.
  D. Donoghue, 441:8Apr90-15
  A. González, 268(IFR):Summer90-148
Fuentes, J.L. - see under Lomba Fuentes, J.
Fuentes, N. Ernest Hemingway Rediscovered.*
  W.J. Stuckey, 395(MFS):Winter89-747
Fuerch, M.A., ed. The Text and Concordance of Biblioteca Nacional Manuscript 4987: Tratado Jurídico.
  L.P. Harvey, 86(BHS):Apr89-168
Fühmann, F. Unter den Paranyas. (I. Prignitz, ed)
  I. Engler, 601(SuF):Mar-Apr90-427
Fuhring, P. Design into Art.
  J.S. Ackerman, 617(TLS):9-15Feb90-152
Fuhrman, C.J. Publicity Stunt!
  J. Gerston, 441:29Apr90-35
Fukuda, J.K. Japanese-Style Management Transferred.
  F.C. Deyo, 293(JASt):Aug89-610
Fukuoka Masayuki. Nihon no seiji fūdo Niigata Sanku ni miru Nihon seiji no genkei.
  G.D. Allinson, 293(JASt):May89-324
Fulcher, J.F. The Nation's Image.*
  S. Huebner, 410(M&L):Feb89-114
Fulford, R. Best Seat in the House.
  B. Trotter, 529(QQ):Autumn89-700
Fülleborn, U. & M. Engel, eds. Das neuzeitliche Ich in der Literatur des 18. und 20. Jahrhunderts.*
  J.H. Petersen, 52:Band24Heft2-199
  W. Tschacher, 221(GQ):Fall89-531
Fuller, D. Blake's Heroic Argument.
  P.H. Butter, 677(YES):Vol20-288
  J. Mee, 447(N&Q):Jun89-244
  K.E. Smith, 83:Autumn89-231
Fuller, J. The Burning Boys.*
  J. Mellors, 364:Jun/Jul89-133
Fuller, J., ed. The Chatto Book of Love Poetry.
  A.S. Byatt, 617(TLS):31Aug-6Sep90-913
Fuller, M. The Letters of Margaret Fuller.* (Vol 5) (R.N. Hudspeth, ed) [entry in prev was of Vols 1-5]
  T. Wortham, 445(NCF):Jun89-122
Fuller, P. Images of God.
  617(TLS):19-25Oct90-1137
Fuller, P. Left High and Dry.
  J. Campbell, 617(TLS):12-18Oct90-1094
Fuller, P. Theoria.*
  D. Barrie, 39:Jan89-64
Fuller, R. Available for Dreams.*
  D. Houston, 493:Summer89-51
  S. O'Brien, 364:Jun/Jul89-91

Fuller, S. Philosophy of Science and its Discontents.
  A. Juarrero Roqué, 543:Jun90-863
  M. Malone, 103:Oct90-407
Fuller, S., ed. The Poetry of War, 1914-1989.
  G. Ewart, 617(TLS):6-12Jul90-734
Fuller, S. Social Epistemology.
  R. D'Amico, 103:Sep90-362
Fuller, T. - see Oakeshott, M.
Fumento, M. The Myth of Heterosexual AIDS.
  D. Shaw, 441:7Jan90-7
Funderburk, D.B. Pinstripes and Reds.
  D. Deletant, 617(TLS):19-25Jan90-57
Funigiello, P.J. American-Soviet Trade in the Cold War.
  639(VQR):Winter89-25
Funkenstein, A. Theology and the Scientific Imagination from the Middle Ages to the Seventeenth Century.*
  J.D. North, 589:Jan89-163
Funto, F. - see Wittgenstein, L.
Furbank, P.N. & W.R. Owens. The Canonization of Daniel Defoe.*
  H. Amory, 78(BC):Autumn89-410
  F. Bastian, 566:Spring89-166
  F.H. Ellis, 541(RES):Aug89-419
  M. Golden, 301(JEGP):Jul89-425
  A. Varney, 447(N&Q):Dec89-514
Furet, F. La Gauche et la Révolution Française au milieu du XIXe siècle.
  K.S. Vincent, 242:Vol10No1-77
Furet, F. & M. Ozouf, eds. A Critical Dictionary of the French Revolution.* (French title: Dictionnaire critique de la révolution française.)
  J.R. Censer, 322(JHI):Oct-Dec89-652
  G. Lewis, 617(TLS):26Jan-1Feb90-93
  C.C. O'Brien, 453(NYRB):15Feb90-46
  J. Starobinski, 453(NYRB):12Apr90-47
Furler, B. Augen-Schein.*
  H-J. Lehnert, 654(WB):7/1989-1219
Furley, D.J. The Greek Cosmologists.* (Vol 1)
  D.W. Graham, 123:Vol39No2-249
  É. des Places, 555:Vol62Fasc1-137
Furniss, G. & P.J. Jaggar, eds. Studies in Hausa Language and Linguistics.
  I.R. Dihoff, 399(MLJ):Winter89-519
  B. Heine, 353:Vol27No2-370
Fürnkäs, J. Surrealismus als Erkenntnis.
  K. Hughes, 221(GQ):Fall89-542
Furstenberg, G. & N. Schott-Desrosiers. En Direct.
  S. Denbow, 399(MLJ):Autumn89-359
Furth, M. Substance, Form and Psyche.
  T. Scaltsas, 518:Apr89-82
Furtwängler, W. Wilhelm Furtwängler: Notebooks 1924-54.* (M. Tanner, ed)
  R. Holloway, 607:Dec89-43
Fusillo, M. Il tempo delle Argonautiche.
  D.M. Schenkeveld, 394:Vol42fasc1/2-198
Füssel, S. & H.J. Kreutzer, eds. Historia von D. Johann Fausten.
  F. Baron, 221(GQ):Fall89-522
  J.L. Flood, 402(MLR):Apr90-500
Fussell, B. Home Plates.
  R. Flaste, 441:10Jun90-12
Fussell, P. Killing in Verse and Prose and Other Essays.
  R. Monk, 617(TLS):16-22Nov90-1230
Fussell, P., ed. The Norton Book of Travel.*
  P. Dailey, 31(ASch):Spring89-300

Fussell, P. Wartime.*
 J. Marwil, 385(MQR):Summer90-431
 E. Reichek, 62:Jan90-23
Fyfield, F. Not that Kind of Place.
 M. Stasio, 441:3Jun90-32
Fynsk, C. Heidegger.*
 S. Watson, 153:Fall-Winter89-49

"GISTI: Le Nouveau Guide juridique des
 étrangers en France." "GISTI: Le Guide des
 jeunes étranger en France." "GISTI: Le
 Guide des étrangers face à l'administra-
 tion."
 A.J.M. Prévos, 207(FR):Oct89-189
Gabbay, D. & F. Guenthner, eds. Handbook of
 Philosophical Logic. (Vol 1)
 K. Bruce, 316:Sep89-1090
 J.N. Crossley, 316:Sep89-1094
 M. Davies, 316:Dec89-1483
 H.B. Enderton, 316:Sep89-1089
 G. Kreisel, 316:Sep89-1092
Gabbay, D. & F. Guenthner, eds. Handbook of
 Philosophical Logic. (Vol 2)
 C.B. Cross, 316:Dec89-1477
 S.T. Kuhn, 316:Dec89-1472
 D. Makinson, 316:Dec89-1481
 A. Visser, 316:Dec89-1479
 L.D. Zuck, 316:Dec89-1480
Gabbay, D. & F. Guenthner, eds. Handbook of
 Philosophical Logic. (Vol 4)
 J. van Benthem, 350:Jun90-396
Gabel, G.U. Immanuel Kant. (2nd ed)
 R.M., 342:Band80Heft4-487
Gabel, J.B. & C.B. Wheeler. The Bible as Lit-
 erature.
 D.L. Jeffrey, 627(UTQ):Summer90-569
Gabler, N. An Empire of Their Own.*
 S.G. Kellman, 390:Dec89-31
 N. Roddick, 707:Autumn89-283
Gabor, A. The Man Who Discovered Quality.
 M.J. Feuer, 441:28Oct90-24
Gabriel, A.L. The University of Paris and Its
 Hungarian Students and Masters during the
 Reign of Louis XII and François Ier.
 W.J. Courtenay, 589:Apr89-427
Gabriel, H.P. & R. Wool. The Inner Child.
 L. Bernstein, 441:9Sep90-34
Gabriele, J.P., ed. Genio y virtuosismo de
 Valle-Inclán.
 W.J. Smither, 238:May89-303
Gabrieli, V. & G. Melchiori – see Munday, A. &
 others
Gace Brulé. The Lyrics and Melodies of Gace
 Brulé.* (S.N. Rosenberg & S. Danon, eds &
 trans)
 D.H. Nelson, 545(RPh):Nov89-338
Gadamer, H-G. The Idea of the Good in Pla-
 tonic-Aristotelian Philosophy.* (P.C.
 Smith, ed & trans)
 N.P. White, 449:Apr89-254
Gadamer, H-G. The Relevance of the Beauti-
 ful and Other Essays.* (R. Bernasconi, ed)
 E. Schaper, 323:Jan89-91
Gaddis, W. Carpenter's Gothic. (French title:
 Gothique charpentier.)
 P-Y. Petillon, 98:Mar89-133
Gadet, F. Saussure.
 J.E. Joseph, 353:Vol27No2-341
Gaehtgens, B. Adriaen van der Werff, 1659-
 1722.
 H-J. Raupp, 683:Band52Heft3-437
 [continued]

[continuing]
 M. Royalton-Kisch, 90:Jan89-41
 M. Russell, 39:Apr89-291
Gaeng, P.A. Le Monde de l'entreprise fran-
 çaise.
 M. Elton, 207(FR):May90-1089
Gagarin, M. Early Greek Law.
 J.F. Oates, 124:Mar-Apr90-366
 N. Robertson, 487:Autumn89-262
 E. Ruschenbusch, 122:Oct89-342
 R.W. Wallace & R. Westbrook,
  24:Summer89-362
Gage, J. J.M.W. Turner.*
 A. Staley, 90:Nov89-777
Gage, N. A Place For Us.*
 E. Meleagrou, 617(TLS):20-26Apr90-416
Gage, R.P. Order and Design.
 S.B. Daugherty, 395(MFS):Winter89-729
 B.J. Eckstein, 27(AL):Dec89-693
 A.R. Tintner, 26(ALR):Winter90-86
Gaggi, S. Modern/Postmodern.
 W.V. Spanos, 659(ConL):Spring90-108
Gaggin, J. Hemingway and Nineteenth-Cen-
 tury Aestheticism.
 I.V., 295(JML):Fall88/Winter89-347
Gagnon, F-M. Paul-Emile Borduas.
 G. Moray, 627(UTQ):Fall89-237
Gagnon, J.C. Dans l'attente d'une aube.
 C. May, 102(CanL):Spring89-200
Gagnon, M. L'Infante immémoriale.
 B. Godard, 102(CanL):Winter88-123
Gahlinger-Beaune, R. The Canadian Artists'
 Survival Manual.
 529(QQ):Summer89-572
Gaide, F. Les substantifs masculins latins en
 ... (i)ō, ... (i)ōnis.
 E.B. Holtsmark, 350:Jun90-414
Gailey, A. Ireland and the Death of Kindness.
 J.D. Fair, 637(VS):Spring90-516
Gaiman, N. & T. Pratchett. Good Omens.
 J. Queenan, 441:7Oct90-27
Gaines, J.F. Pierre du Ryer and his Trage-
 dies.
 W.O. Goode, 210(FrF):May89-231
 D. Maskell, 208(FS):Apr89-206
Gaite, C.M. – see under Martín Gaite, C.
Gaius. The "Institutes" of Gaius. (W.M. Gor-
 don & O.F. Robinson, trans)
 D. Ingsley, 313:Vol79-266
 R. Seager, 123:Vol39No2-274
Gala, A. Los buenos días perdidos. (A.
 Amorós, ed)
 J. Lyon, 402(MLR):Jul90-772
 M.V. Morales, 711(RHM):Dec89-194
Galand, P. – see Politien, A.
Galántai, E. & J. Kristó – see de Thurocz, J.
Galanti, M. En Mouvement.* (2nd ed)
 A. Caprio, 399(MLJ):Spring89-87
Galarneau, C. & M. Lemire, eds. Livre et lec-
 ture au Québec (1800-1850).
 D.M. Hayne, 470:Vol27-98
Galbraith, J.K. A Tenured Professor.
 P-L. Adams, 61:Mar90-115
 L. Auchincloss, 453(NYRB):26Apr90-21
 B. Ehrenreich, 441:11Feb90-9
 442(NY):5Mar90-106
Galdós, B.P. – see under Pérez Galdós, B.
Galdos, J.S. – see under Sagasta Galdos, J.
Gale, P. The Cat Sanctuary.
 R. Kaveney, 617(TLS):7-13Dec90-1325
Gale, P. Little Bits of Baby.*
 R. Nicholls, 441:9Sep90-26

Gale, S.H. S.J. Perelman.
 S.P., 295(JML):Fall88/Winter89-391
Gale, S.H., ed. Harold Pinter.*
 S.H. Merritt, 397(MD):Sep89-459
Gálffy, M. & G. Márton. Székely nyelvföld-
 rajzi szótár.
 T. Kesztyüs, 685(ZDL):1/1989-126
Galgiani, P. Basic Meaning in Four Parts.
 G. Gessert, 448:Vol27No1-130
Galileo. Tractatio de Praecognitionibus et
 Praecognitis and Tractatio de Demonstra-
 tione. (W.F. Edwards & W.A. Wallace, eds)
 E. de Jong, 543:Sep89-161
Galili, Z. The Menshevik Leaders in the Rus-
 sian Revolution.
 O. Figes, 617(TLS):4-10May90-466
Galitz, R. Literarische Basisöffentlichkeit als
 politische Kraft.
 P. Currie, 83:Spring89-121
Galkin, E.W. A History of Orchestral Con-
 ducting in Theory and Practice.*
 N. Del Mar, 415:Oct89-612
 P. Heyworth, 617(TLS):26Jan-1Feb90-92
Gall, L. Bismarck, The White Revolutionary.
 (Vols 1 & 2)
 G.A. Craig, 453(NYRB):28Jun90-25
Gall, L. Bürgertum in Deutschland.
 C. Charle, 358:Jun90-8
 G.A. Craig, 453(NYRB):28Jun90-25
 J. Whaley, 617(TLS):16-22Feb90-177
Gallagher, C. & T. Laqueur, eds. The Making
 of the Modern Body.*
 A.C. Vila, 400(MLN):Sep89-927
Gallagher, T. Amplitudo.
 S. Gorham, 456(NDQ):Summer89-248
 L. Gregerson, 491:Dec89-231
 E. Nobles, 146:Spring89-129
 L. Runciman, 649(WAL):May89-85
Gallagher, T. The Lover of Horses and Other
 Stories.*
 D. Durrant, 364:Apr/May89-154
Galland, C. Longing for Darkness.
 C. Zaleski, 441:30Sep90-3
Gallant, C. Shelley's Ambivalence.
 A. Leighton, 617(TLS):30Mar-5Apr90-354
Gallant, M. In Transit.*
 T.L. Cottrell, 529(QQ):Winter89-957
 G. Mangan, 617(TLS):13-19Apr90-403
Gallas, J. Practical Anarchy.*
 S. O'Brien, 493:Autumn89-63
Galley, E. & A. Estermann, eds. Heinrich
 Heines Werk im Urteil seiner Zeitgenossen.
 (Vol 3)
 E. Feistner, 72:Band226Heft1-123
Gallicchio, M.S. The Cold War Begins in Asia.*
 Nakatsuji Keiji, 285(JapQ):Apr-Jun89-
 211
Gallie, R.D. Thomas Reid and "The Way of
 Ideas."
 J.W. Manns, 543:Jun90-864
Gallier, J.H. Logic for Computer Science.
 F. Pfenning, 316:Mar89-288
Gallo, I. Greek and Latin Papyrology.*
 P. Cauderlier, 555:Vol62Fasc2-380
Gallop, D. - see Parmenides
Gallop, J. Thinking Through the Body.
 M. Dorenkamp, 456(NDQ):Spring89-179
 E.C. Goldsmith, 207(FR):Mar90-723
Gallotta, B. Germanico.
 B.M. Levick, 229:Band61Heft3-268
Galloway, J. The Trick is to Keep Breathing.
 K. Jamie, 617(TLS):4-10May90-480

Galluzzi, P., ed. Leonardo da Vinci, Engineer
 and Architect.
 S. Pepper, 576:Jun89-188
Galperin, W.H. Revision and Authority in
 Wordsworth.
 D. Perkins, 445(NCF):Mar90-543
Galván, D.V. La ficción reciente de Elena
 Garro 1979-1983.
 R. Geisdorfer Feal, 238:Dec89-970
Gálvez, M. La novela hispanoamericana con-
 temporánea.
 R.W. Fiddian, 86(BHS):Jan89-105
Gálvez Lira, G. María Luisa Bombal.
 V.B. Levine, 238:Dec89-967
Galvin, J. Elements.*
 S.E. Gunter, 649(WAL):May89-95
 C. Merrill, 434:Winter89-208
Galvin, M. Wild Card.
 D. Chorlton, 496:Winter89/90-43
Gambee, R. Wall Street Christmas.
 M.S. Forbes, Jr., 441:2Dec90-45
Gamble, P. & P. Symes. Focus on Jazz.
 A. Shipton, 415:Aug89-479
Gamkrelidze, T.V. & V.V. Ivanov. Indojev-
 ropejskij jazyk i indojevropejcy.*
 K.M. Hayward, 361:May89-37
Gane, M., ed. Towards a Critique of Foucault.
 M. Rosello, 345(KRQ):Feb89-114
Ganelin, C. - see de Claramonte, A.
Ganesan, I. The Journey.
 M. Dery, 441:9Sep90-26
 442(NY):17Sep90-108
Gans, E. "Madame Bovary."
 M. Donaldson-Evans, 207(FR):Mar90-718
Gansemans, J. & others. Zentralafrika.
 V.K. Agawu, 410(M&L):Feb89-74
Gänzl, K. & A. Lamb. Gänzl's Book of the
 Musical Theatre.
 N. Douglas, 410(M&L):Aug89-425
 E. Levi, 415:Jul89-414
Garafola, L. Diaghilev's Ballets Russes.*
 R. Orledge, 617(TLS):28Sep-4Oct90-1035
 C.R. Pierpont, 442(NY):20Aug90-82
Garavaglia, R. & A. Sinigaglia - see Mila, M.
Garavini, F. & L. Lazzorini, eds. Macaronee
 Provenzali.
 L. Löfstedt, 545(RPh):May90-620
Garb, T. Women Impressionists.
 N.M. Mathews, 662:Spring/Summer89-46
Garber, F. Self, Text, and Romantic Irony.
 F.L. Beaty, 340(KSJ):Vol38-165
 M. Kelsall, 445(NCF):Mar90-548
Garber, M., ed. Cannibals, Witches, and Di-
 vorce.
 A.F. Kinney, 481(PQ):Fall89-443
Garber, M. Shakespeare's Ghost Writers.
 P. Edwards, 677(YES):Vol20-253
 M. de Grazia, 570(SQ):Fall89-345
 D.R.C. Marsh, 447(N&Q):Jun89-235
Garboli, C. Falbalas.
 G. Dego, 617(TLS):31Aug-6Sep90-914
Garbrecht, G., comp. Historische Talsperren.
 U. Buske, 229:Band61Heft7-641
Garcia, A. Thomas Hobbes.
 J-L. Dumas, 192(EP):Jul-Dec89-538
Garcia, A.M. - see under Muñoz Garcia, A.
Garcia, E.E. & R.V. Padilla, eds. Advances in
 Bilingual Education Research.*
 N.H. Hornberger, 355(LSoc):Sep89-389
Garcia, J., R. Kilpatrick & M. Richards, eds.
 The Politics of Maternity Care.
 R. Cullen, 617(TLS):18-24May90-525
García, J.C. - see under Cebrián García, J.

García, L.A. – see under Alvarez García, L.
García, L.G. Handscrub.
   K. Ray, 441:25Feb90–24
García, M.T. Mexican Americans.
   R.A. Anaya, 441:4Mar90–20
   D. Rieff, 617(TLS):25–31May90–543
García–Castañeda, S. – see de Saavedra, A.
García Lorenzo, L. – see de Vega Carpio, L.
García–Luengos, G.V. – see under Vega
   García–Luengos, G.
García Márquez, G. Collected Novellas.
   R.M. Adams, 453(NYRB):11Oct90–17
García Márquez, G. The General in His Laby-
   rinth.* (Spanish title: El general en su
   laberinto.)
   P–L. Adams, 61:Oct90–137
   R.M. Adams, 453(NYRB):11Oct90–17
   M. Atwood, 441:16Sep90–1
García Márquez, G. Love in the Time of Chol-
   era.* (German title: Die Liebe in den Zeiten
   der Cholera.)
   R.M. Adams, 453(NYRB):11Oct90–17
   R. González–Echevarría, 676(YR):
   Spring89–472
   S. Plesch, 654(WB):8/1989–1368
García–Márquez, V. The Ballets Russes.
   F. Mason, 441:2Dec90–34
García Ponce, J. Encounters.
   I. Malin, 532(RCF):Fall89–226
García Romero, F. Estructura de la oda ba-
   quilidea.
   J. Irigoin, 555:Vol62Fasc2–332
García Ruiz, V. Victor Ruiz Iriarte: Autor
   dramático. Victor Ruiz Iriarte: Análisis
   semióticos.
   P. Zatlin, 552(REH):May89–139
García Sánchez, J. Lady of the South Wind.
   I. Stavans, 441:4Mar90–24
García Sarriá, F. Estudios de novela española
   moderna.
   D. Henn, 402(MLR):Apr90–482
García Valdés, C.C. – see de Quevedo, F.
Gard, R., ed. Henry James: The Critical Heri-
   tage.
   V.C. Fowler, 177(ELT):Vol32No3–372
Gard, R. – see James, H.
du Gard, R.M. & G. Duhamel – see under Mar-
   tin du Gard, R. & G. Duhamel
Gardam, J. Showing the Flag.*
   D. Durrant, 364:Oct/Nov89–129
Gardenfors, P. & N–E. Sahlin, eds. Decisions,
   Probability and Utility.
   C.B., 185:Oct89–214
Gardi, B. Mali.
   R. Boser-Sarivaxévanis, 2(AfrA):Aug89–
   84
Gardiner, S.C. Old Church Slavonic: An Ele-
   mentary Grammar.
   J. Dingley, 279:Vol35/36–338
Gardner, A. Ava.
   J. Kaufman, 441:18Nov90–29
Gardner, B. The Lesbian Imagination (Victo-
   rian Style).
   V. Blain, 637(VS):Winter90–351
Gardner, H. Art through the Ages. (8th ed)
   (H. de la Croix & R.G. Tansey, eds)
   B.R. Collins, 127:Summer89–190
Gardner, H.M. Eingriffe in das Leben.
   H. Titze, 687:Jan–Mar89–203
Gardner, J. Yeats and The Rhymers' Club.
   A. Bradley, 637(VS):Spring90–537

Gardner, J.F. Women in Roman Law and Soci-
   ety.*
   S. Dixon, 487:Spring89–84
Gardner, S. Blake's Innocence and Experience
   Retraced.
   D. Fuller, 83:Spring89–109
Gardt, A. James Joyce auf Deutsch.
   M. Jahn, 329(JJQ):Fall89–160
Garebian, K. William Hutt.
   A. Hardcastle, 529(QQ):Autumn89–708
Garfield, C.F. & A.R. Ridley. As Ancient is
   this Hostelry.
   F. Fleischmann, 432(NEQ):Dec89–607
Garfield, E.P., ed & trans. Women's Fiction
   from Latin America.
   B.K. Horvath, 532(RCF):Spring89–251
Garfield, J.L., ed. Modularity in Knowledge
   Representation and Natural Language
   Understanding.
   B.L. Pritchett, 350:Dec90–867
Garforth, F.W., ed. Bede's Historia Ecclesias-
   tica.
   C.F. Natunewicz, 124:Mar–Apr90–373
Gargantini Rabbi, S. Du conflit racinien à la
   comédie de moeurs.*
   R. Guichemerre, 535(RHL):Jan–Feb89–160
Garland, N. Not Many Dead.
   A. Sampson, 617(TLS):13–19Apr90–389
Garland, R. The Greek Way of Life.
   P. Cartledge, 617(TLS):11–17May90–508
Garland, R. The Piraeus from the Fifth to the
   First Century B.C.
   R. Osborne, 303(JoHS):Vol109–251
   S.I. Rotroff, 124:Sep–Oct89–69
   G. Shipley, 123:Vol39No2–281
Garlick, K. Sir Thomas Lawrence.
   J. Hayes, 617(TLS):20–26Jul90–771
   A. Stewart, 324:Dec89–73
Garmaise, F. Tough Girls Don't Knit.
   J. Kaufman, 441:15Jul90–19
Garmey, S. Gramercy Park.
   B. Benepe, 576:Mar89–94
Garneau, A.M. Poésies complètes 1955–1987.
   L.H. Forsyth, 627(UTQ):Fall89–192
Garner, H. Postcards From Surfers.*
   D. Durrant, 364:Jun/Jul89–130
Garner, M., ed. Community Languages.
   J.S. Ryan, 464:Vol33Fasc1/2–275
Garner, R. From Homer to Tragedy.
   M. Heath, 617(TLS):15–21Jun90–645
Garner, W. Sleeping Dogs.
   S. Altinel, 617(TLS):24–30Aug90–903
Garnham, A. Mental Models as Representa-
   tions of Discourse and Text.
   A. Franz, 350:Mar90–192
Garnier, E. Plaie rouillée.
   M. Naudin, 102(CanL):Spring89–218
Garnier, P. Les herbes, les arbres, les
   peuples.
   R. Anttila, 159:Vol6No2–279
Garniron, P. & W. Jaeschke – see Hegel, G.W.F.
Garnsey, P. Famine and Food Supply in the
   Graeco–Roman World.
   G.W.M. Harrison, 124:Jan–Feb90–241
   P. Herz, 229:Band61Heft2–135
   D.J. Mattingly, 313:Vol79–174
   R. Seager, 617(TLS):17–23Aug90–878
Garon, S. The State and Labor in Modern
   Japan.*
   K. Taira, 407(MN):Spring89–119
Garrard, J. & C. Inside the Soviet Writers'
   Union.
   J.C. Goldfarb, 441:18Mar90–15

Garrard, M.D. Artemisia Gentileschi.*
  E. Cropper, 551(RenQ):Winter89-864
Garrett, C. Spirit Possession and Popular Religion.*
  D.W. Patterson, 292(JAF):Jul-Sep89-357
Garrett, G. Entered from the Sun.
  A. Goreau, 441:16Sep90-7
Garrison, J.R., B.L. Herman & B.M. Ward, eds. After Ratification.
  J. Larkin, 658:Winter89-272
Garrison, M. & A. Gleason, eds. Shared Destiny.
  W. Taubman, 104(CASS):Spring89-103
Garro, E. Recollections of Things to Come.
  R. Geisdorfer Feal, 238:Mar89-165
der Gartenaere, W. - see under Wernher der Gartenaere
Garvan, B.B. Federal Philadelphia, 1785-1825.
  D.D. Waters, 658:Spring89-81
Garver, E. Machiavelli and the History of Prudence.
  A.J. Parel, 319:Jul90-445
Garver, J.W. Chinese-Soviet Relations 1937-1946.
  W.I. Cohen, 293(JASt):May89-357
Garvey, T.J. Public Sculptor.
  H. Adams, 658:Summer/Autumn89-200
Garvie, A.F. - see Aeschylus
Garza Cuarón, B. El español hablado en la ciudad de Oaxaca, Mexico.
  T.M. Stephens, 238:Sep89-560
Garzya, A. Il mandarino e il quotidiano.
  H. Hofmann, 394:Vol42fasc1/2-129
Gasarian, G. Yves Bonnefoy.*
  M. Bishop, 207(FR):Apr90-878
Gascar, P. Pour le dire avec des fleurs.
  J. Blot, 450(NRF):May89-97
Gasché, R. The Tain of the Mirror.*
  C. Altieri, 149(CLS):Vol26No4-376
Gascoigne, J. Cambridge in the Age of Enlightenment.
  P. Dear, 617(TLS):26Jan-1Feb90-94
Gascou, J. Suétone historien.*
  A.B. Breebaart, 394:Vol42fasc3/4-562
Gascoyne, D. Collected Poems 1988.*
  J. Greening, 493:Spring89-55
Gash, J. The Very Last Gambado.*
  M. Stasio, 441:9Sep90-39
Gaskell, E. Wives and Daughters. (A. Easson, ed)
  H. Abalain, 189(EA):Oct-Dec89-498
Gaskill, W. A Sense of Direction.*
  G. Gordon, 157:No171-49
Gaskins, R.H. Environmental Accidents.
  A.B. Carter, 185:Jul90-901
Gašparíková, V. Slovenská l'udová próza a jej súčasné vývinové tendencie.
  T. Smolińska, 196:Band30Heft3/4-320
Gasparotto, G. Presagi, previsioni e predizioni nel lessico di Virgilio.
  M. Pulbook, 235:Summer89-75
Gasparro, G.S. - see under Sfameni Gasparro, G.
Gasset, J.O. - see under Ortega y Gasset, J.
Gaston, B. Deep Cove Stories.
  M. Kenyon, 376:Sep89-115
Gat, A. The Origins of Military Thought.
  M. Cranston, 617(TLS):6-12Apr90-377
Gateau, J-C. Abécédaire critique.*
  P. Powrie, 208(FS):Oct89-485

Gates, B.T., ed. Critical Essays on Charlotte Brontë.
  M. Reynolds, 617(TLS):10-16Aug90-854
Gates, B.T. Victorian Suicide.
  N. Auerbach, 445(NCF):Dec89-396
  D.E. Hall, 158:Dec89-171
  J.R. Reed, 637(VS):Spring90-520
Gates, H.L., Jr., ed. The Classic Slave Narratives.
  P. Edwards, 538(RAL):Spring89-137
Gates, H.L., Jr. Figures in Black.*
  W. Lubiano, 432(NEQ):Dec89-561
  J.Y. McLendon, 295(JML):Fall88/Winter89-198
Gates, H.L., Jr. The Signifying Monkey.*
  K. Byerman, 395(MFS):Winter89-768
  B. Harlow, 538(RAL):Fall89-575
  W. Lubiano, 432(NEQ):Dec89-561
Gates, R.A. The New York Vision.
  P.R.J., 295(JML):Fall88/Winter89-244
Gati, C. The Bloc that Failed.
  M. Polner, 441:24Jun90-12
Gatrell, S. Hardy the Creator.*
  T. Dawson, 268(IFR):Winter90-54
  R. Schweik, 445(NCF):Dec89-416
  P. Zietlow, 637(VS):Spring90-535
Gatt-Rutter, J. Italo Svevo.
  B. Moloney, 402(MLR):Jan90-215
  E.M. Schächter, 278(IS):Vol44-184
Gatta, J. Gracious Laughter.
  D.E. Stanford, 165(EAL):Vol25No2-211
Gatti, M.I. Massimo il Confessore.
  E. des Places, 555:Vol62Fasc2-353
Gauchet, M. La Révolution des droits de l'homme.*
  J. Starobinski, 453(NYRB):12Apr90-47
Gaudon, J. - see Hugo, V.
Gaudon, J., S. Gaudon & B. Leuilliot, with others - see Hugo, V.
Gaudreault, A. Ce que je vois de mon ciné ...
  I. Hedges, 207(FR):Apr90-923
Gaull, M. English Romanticism.
  A. Bewell, 661(WC):Autumn89-192
  N. Miller, 42(AR):Winter89-105
Gaulmier, J., with J. Boissel & M-L. Concasty - see de Gobineau, J.A.
Gault, P. John Hawkes: La Parole Coupée.
  J. Templeton, 189(EA):Apr-Jun89-236
Gaustad, E.S. Faith of Our Fathers.
  C. Strout, 656(WMQ):Jan89-202
Gauthier, D. Moral Dealing.
  T.W. Pogge, 103:Dec90-492
Gauthier, D.P. Morals by Agreement.*
  D. Copp, 482(PhR):Jul89-411
  R. Hegselmann, 167:Jul89-143
Gauthier, M-M. Émaux méridionaux. (Vol 1)
  C. Nordenfalk, 341:Vol58No2-90
Gauthier, P. Newman et Blondel.
  P. Colin, 192(EP):Jul-Dec89-538
Gautier, T. Correspondance générale de Théophile Gautier.* (Vol 3) (C. Lacoste-Veysseyre & P. Laubriet, eds)
  J. Gaulmier, 535(RHL):Nov-Dec89-1065
Gautier, T. Les Grotesques.* (C. Rizza, ed)
  C. Dédéyan, 535(RHL):Jul-Aug89-731
  P. Whyte, 208(FS):Apr89-221
Gauvin, L. Lettres d'une autre.
  N.B. Bishop, 102(CanL):Autumn-Winter89-272
Gavlovič, H. Hugolín Gavlovič's "Valaská Škola." (G.J. Sabo, ed)
  P. Petro, 574(SEEJ):Fall89-466

Gawlick, G. & L. Kreimendahl. Hume in der deutschen Aufklärung.*
  P. Gorner, 571(ScLJ):Winter89-6
  M. Kuehn, 319:Apr90-301
  N. Waszek, 83:Autumn89-222
Gay, P. Freud.*
  R. Colp, Jr., 77:Winter89-64
  E. Kurzweil, 473(PR):Vol56No3-486
  T.H. Thompson, 455:Mar89-63
Gay, P. A Godless Jew.*
  R.M. Capobianco, 258:Mar89-110
Gay, P. Reading Freud.
  C. Rycroft, 617(TLS):6-12Jul90-725
  J.D. Schwartz, 441:13May90-24
Gay-Lussac, B. La père excommunié.
  F. George, 98:Nov89-884
Gaycken, H-J. Johann Gottfried Herder und seine zeitgenössischen Kritiker.
  G.A. Wells, 83:Autumn89-243
Gaylin, W. Adam and Eve and Pinocchio.
  R. Cherry, 441:22Apr90-30
Gazdar, G. & others. Generalized Phrase Structure Grammar.*
  S. Soames, 482(PhR):Oct89-556
Geach, P.T. - see Wittgenstein, L.
Geach, P.T., K.J. Shah & A.C. Jackson. Wittgenstein's Lectures on Philosophical Psychology 1946-47. (P.T. Geach, ed)
  483:Apr89-275
Gearey, J. - see von Goethe, J.W.
Geary, C.M. Images from Bamum.
  D.H. Ross, 2(AfrA):Aug89-10
Geary, J.S., ed. Historia del Conde Fernán González.*
  P. Rodgers, 240(HR):Summer89-363
  H.M. Wilkins, 238:Mar89-139
Gebhard, D. & S. Zimmerman. The California Architecture of Frank Lloyd Wright.
  P.B. Jones, 46:Oct89-12
Gébler, C. Driving Through Cuba.
  P-L. Adams, 61:Apr90-109
  T. Szulc, 441:18Mar90-5
Gébler, C. Malachy and his Family.
  M. Wormald, 617(TLS):2-8Feb90-115
Geckle, G.L. John Marston's Drama.
  D. Rolle, 38:Band107Heft1/2-228
Geddes, J. - see Beresford, G.
Geddes, V.G. "Various Children of Eve" (AT 758).
  M.A. Mills, 292(JAF):Jan-Mar89-103
Geduld, H.M. - see Wells, H.G.
Gee, M. The Burning Boy.
  T. Aitken, 617(TLS):2-8Nov90-1183
Geeraedts, L. - see "Ulenspiegel"
Geertz, C. Works and Lives.*
  478(P&L):Apr89-221
Geertz, H. - see Kartini, R.A.
Geffray, C. La Cause des armes au Mozambique.
  P. Fry, 617(TLS):9-15Nov90-1202
Geha, J. Through and Through.
  S. Friedman, 441:30Dec90-14
Geiger, G.L. Filippino Lippi's Carafa Chapel.
  D. Franklin, 90:Mar89-229
Geiger, J. Cornelius Nepos and Ancient Political Biography.
  J.L. Moles, 123:Vol39No2-229
  G. Schepens, 394:Vol42fasc1/2-214
Geisdorfer Feal, R. Novel Lives.*
  J. King, 86(BHS):Jan89-115
Geist, S. Interpreting Cézanne.*
  R. Verdi, 90:Dec89-857
  639(VQR):Spring89-67

Gelb, A. Most Likely to Succeed.
  K. Ray, 441:14Oct90-49
Gelbart, N.R. Feminine and Opposition Journalism in Old Regime France.
  S. Davies, 83:Autumn89-208
  M.B. Lacy, 207(FR):Dec89-370
Gelderman, C. Mary McCarthy.*
  S. Rudikoff, 249(HudR):Spring89-46
Gelfer-Jørgensen, M. Medieval Islamic Symbolism and the Paintings in the Cefalù Cathedral.
  Ø. Hjort, 341:Vol58No1-24
Gellert, C.F. C.F. Gellerts Briefwechsel. (J.F. Reynolds, ed)
  E. Meyer-Krentler, 680(ZDP):Band108 Heft2-282
Gelley, A. Narrative Crossings.*
  J.J. Sosnoski, 395(MFS):Summer89-373
Gellinek, C., ed. Europas Erster Baedeker.
  K.F. Otto, Jr., 133:Band22Heft3/4-315
Gellner, E. Relativism and the Social Sciences.*
  A. Flew, 144:Winter-Spring90-155
Gellner, E. State and Society in Soviet Thought.
  639(VQR):Autumn89-134
Gelpi, A. A Coherent Splendor.*
  I.F.A. Bell, 447(N&Q):Jun89-270
  W. Harmon, 301(JEGP):Oct89-565
  S. Matson, 432(NEQ):Sep89-473
  S.E. Olson, 42(AR):Spring89-241
  A. Suberchicot, 189(EA):Jul-Sep89-362
Gelsanliter, D. Jump Start.
  G. Tyler, 441:12Aug90-7
Gendre, A., ed. Ronsard.*
  J. Dupèbe, 535(RHL):Jul-Aug89-700
  P. Ford, 208(FS):Apr89-202
Genequand, C. - see Ibn Rushd
Genet, J. Haute Surveillance.
  P. Bougon, 98:Apr89-301
Genette, G. Seuils.*
  G. Cesbron, 356(LR):Nov89-315
Genette, R.D. Métamorphoses du récit.*
  A. Tooke, 208(FS):Jan89-99
Gengembre, G. La Contre-Révolution ou l'histoire désespérante.
  B. Leuilliot, 450(NRF):Oct89-119
Geniušienė, E. The Typology of Reflexives.*
  A.K. Farmer, 574(SEEJ):Spring89-143
  W.P. Lehmann, 603:Vol13No1-213
Geno, M.G. A la française.*
  J.R. Hightower, Jr., 399(MLJ):Summer89-222
Gentelle, P. Chine, un atlas économique.
  P. Juvenal, 98:Aug-Sep89-714
Gentile, J.S. Cast of One.
  P. Collins, 617(TLS):9-15Mar90-256
Gentile, S., ed. Vita e favole di Esopo.
  R. Coluccia, 379(MedR):Aug89-297
Gentili, B. Poetry and Its Public in Ancient Greece.*
  M.E. Reesor, 529(QQ):Autumn89-704
Gentili, B. & G. Cerri. History and Biography in Ancient Thought.
  S. Hornblower, 123:Vol39No2-398
  D.A. Russell, 303(JoHS):Vol109-236
Gentry, F.G. - see Gottfried von Strassburg
Gentzbittel, M. Madame le proviseur.
  D. Johnson-Cousin, 207(FR):Mar90-759
Geoghegan, V. Utopianism and Marxism.*
  J. Jennings, 521:Jul89-264
George, D.H. Oedipus Anne.*
  P.R.J., 295(JML):Fall88/Winter89-405

George, D.H., ed. Sexton.
J. Mellard, 599:Summer90-302
George, E. The Poetry of Miklós Radnóti.
R.L. Aczel, 575(SEER):Jul89-459
M.D. Birnbaum, 574(SEEJ):Fall89-470
George, E. Well-Schooled in Murder.
M. Stasio, 441:12Aug90-21
George, M. Mystische und religiöse Erfahrung im Denken Vladimir Solov'evs.
A. Pyman, 575(SEER):Apr89-273
George, M. Women in the First Capitalist Society.
M.E. Wiesner, 551(RenQ):Autumn89-574
George, N. The Death of Rhythm and Blues.*
B.L. Cooper, 498:Summer89-117
George, S. Gedichte. (H. Nalewski, ed)
U.K. Goldsmith, 222(GR):Fall89-182
Georgiades, T.G. Nennen und Erklingen.
M.H. Schmid, 417:Oct-Dec89-371
Gérard, A.S., ed. European-Language Writing in Sub-Saharan Africa.*
R. Arnold, 654(WB):1/1989-169
Gerardi, P. A Bibliography of the Tablet Collections of the University Museum.
H. Neumann, 318(JAOS):Apr-Jun88-303
Gerber, D. Grass Fires.
J.W. Grinnell, 573(SSF):Summer88-323
Gerber, H.E., with O.M. Brack, Jr. - see Moore, G.
Gerber, J.C. Mark Twain.
S.I. Bellman, 573(SSF):Fall88-483
J.C. Cawelti, 70:Apr89-71
Gerber, M., ed. Studies in GDR Culture and Society 6.
M.P. Alter, 399(MLJ):Autumn89-373
Gerber, M., ed. Studies in GDR Culture and Society, 7.
I.H.R. McCoy, 399(MLJ):Spring89-90
Gerber, M. & others, eds. Selected Papers from the Thirteenth New Hampshire Symposium on the German Democratic Republic.
M. Silberman, 221(GQ):Fall89-554
Gerber, M.J. King of the World.
D. Blackwell, 441:18Feb90-20
Gerber, P.L. - see Corey, F.
Gerberding, R.A. The Rise of the Carolingians and the "Liber historiae Francorum."
J.M.H. Smith, 589:Apr89-428
Gerbi, A. Nature in the New World.
J.S. Cummins, 86(BHS):Jul89-309
E. Pupo-Walker, 240(HR):Summer89-403
Gerdener, W. Der Purismus im Nynorsk.
P. Trudgill, 562(Scan):May89-110
Gere, C. & G.C. Munn. Artists' Jewellery.
G. Seidmann, 324:Dec89-71
Geremek, B. The Margins of Society in Late Medieval Paris.
B.A. Hanawalt, 589:Oct89-947
Gergen, M.M., ed. Feminist Thought and the Structure of Knowledge.
L.C., 185:Apr90-694
L. Code, 103:Feb90-60
Gerhardie, W. Futility. Memoirs of a Polyglot. God's 5th Column.
J. Symons, 617(TLS):13-19Apr90-387
Gerkens, G. & A. Röver. In Rembrandts Manier.
C.J.W., 90:Jan89-47
C.J.W., 90:Jun89-437
Gerlach, D.R. Proud Patriot.
P.D. Chase, 656(WMQ):Apr89-410
Gerlo, A. Erasmus van Rotterdam.
L.V.R., 568(SCN):Fall-Winter89-71

Germain, S. Jours de colère.
M. Alhau, 450(NRF):Dec89-122
Germain, S. Nuit d'ambre.
P-P. Célérier, 207(FR):Oct89-205
Germond, P. Les invocations à la Bonne Annee au temple d'Edfou.
R.S. Bianchi, 318(JAOS):Jan-Mar88-150
Gernentz, H.J., ed. Untersuchungen zum Russisch-niederdeutschen Gesprächsbuch des Tönnies Fenne, Pskov 1607.
B.J. Koekkoek, 350:Mar90-193
Gerrits, G.H. Inter timorem et spem.
F. Oakley, 589:Apr89-430
Gerritsen, M. Syntaktische verandering in kontrolezinnen.
J.A. van Leuvensteijn, 204(FdL):Dec89-300
Gersh, S. Middle Platonism and Neoplatonism.*
H. Merle, 192(EP):Jan-Mar89-98
Gershenzon, M.O. A History of Young Russia. (J.P. Scanlan, ed & trans)
C. Read, 575(SEER):Apr89-282
Gershon, K. Collected Poems.
D. Hartnett, 617(TLS):21-27Sep90-1007
Gerster, R. Big-Noting.
J. Wieland, 71(ALS):May89-130
Gerstle, G. Working-Class Americanism.
A. Brinkley, 453(NYRB):28Jun90-16
Gerstner, K. & others, eds. Lyökämme kasi kätehen.
H-H. Bartens, 260(IF):Band94-374
Gert, B. Morality.
W.H. Hay, 185:Jan90-411
N. Jecker, 543:Mar90-631
Gervais, G. Verbe Silence.
C. May, 102(CanL):Spring89-200
Gerwing, M. Malogranatum oder der dreifache Weg zur Vollkommenheit.
U. Stargardt, 589:Jan89-164
"Geschichte der Wasserversorgung, 3."
G.E. Rickman, 123:Vol39No2-416
Gethmann-Siefert, A. Die Funktion der Kunst in der Geschichte.
T. Leinkauf, 489(PJGG):Band06Heft1-200
Gethmann-Siefert, A. & O. Pöggeler, eds. Heidegger und die praktische Philosophie.*
P. David, 192(EP):Jul-Dec89-541
Getty, J.A. Origins of the Great Purges.
B. Williams, 242:Vol10No4-483
Getz-Preziosi, P. Sculptors of the Cyclades.*
R.L.N. Barber, 123:Vol39No2-331
E. Schofield, 303(JoHS):Vol109-258
J. Thimme, 229:Band61Heft4-329
Getz-Preziosi, P. with J.L. Davis & E. Oustinoff. Early Cycladic Art in North American Collections.*
R.L.N. Barber, 123:Vol39No2-331
J. Thimme, 229:Band61Heft4-329
Gevrey, F. L'illusion et ses procédés.*
A.K. Mortimer, 475:Vol16No30-288
E. Showalter, Jr., 207(FR):Mar90-706
Geyer, D. Russian Imperialism.*
D.C.B. Lieven, 575(SEER):Apr89-332
Ghirardo, D. Building New Communities.
C. Ward, 46:Nov89-12
Ghiselin, O. The Testimony of Mr. Bones.
A.D. Williams, 441:18Feb90-19
Ghose, R., ed. Protest Movements in South and Southeast Asia.
B. Kerkvliet, 293(JASt):Aug89-676
Giacomelli, G. - see Gori, L. & S. Lucarelli

Giamatti, A.B. Take Time for Paradise.
A. Barra, 441:14Jan90-12
Giampaolini, E.A. Aristocrazia e chiese nella
Marca del centro—nord tra IX e XI secolo.
G. Dameron, 589:Oct89-949
Gianetti, L. & S. Eyman. Flashback.
G.W. Linden, 289:Summer89-119
Giangrande, L. Greek in English.
J—C. Billigmeier, 124:Sep—Oct89-73
S.J. Freebairn-Smith, 123:Vol39No2-367
Giangrande, L. Latin in the Service of Eng-
lish.
L.W. Rutland, 399(MLJ):Spring89-83
Giannetti, G. & M. Bruno. Lisons!
F.I. Andrus, 399(MLJ):Autumn89-360
Giannetti, G. & M. Bruno. Un Kaleidoscope de
Mots.*
F.I. Andrus, 399(MLJ):Winter89-506
Giannone, R. Flannery O'Connor and the
Mystery of Love.
M.J. Friedman, 268(IFR):Winter90-70
J.N. Gretlund, 585(SoQ):Spring90-129
Giantvalley, S. Edward Albee.*
M.C. Roudané, 70:Oct89-155
Gibbins, P. Particles and Paradoxes.*
A. Stairs, 486:Dec89-712
Gibbon, W.M. A Change of Scene.
K. Barker, 611(TN):Vol43No1-45
Gibbons, F. & D. Strom. Neighbors to the
Birds.
42(AR):Winter89-110
Gibbons, J. Code-Mixing and Code Choice.*
C.M. Scotton, 710:Mar89-107
Gibbons, K. A Virtuous Woman.*
T. Rash, 580(SCR):Spring90-131
Gibbs, T. Running Fix.
J. Ellsworth, 441:5Aug90-18
442(NY):20Aug90-91
Gibert, S.P., ed. Security in Northeast Asia.
J.H. Buck, 293(JASt):May89-335
Giboire, C. — see O'Keeffe, G. & A. Pollitzer
Gibson, I. Federico García Lorca.*
D. Mitchell, 364:Aug/Sep89-113
A. Rattansi, 511:Sep89-47
Gibson, J.M. The Philadelphia Shakespeare
Story.
S. Wells, 617(TLS):27Jul-2Aug90-792
Gibson, M. A Doctor's Calling.
T. Goldie, 102(CanL):Winter88-128
Gibson, M. Out in the Open.
P. Booth, 219(GaR):Spring89-161
639(VQR):Autumn89-136
Gibson, M. Workers' Rights.
R. Beehler, 482(PhR):Apr89-247
Gibson, M. & S.M. Wright, eds. Joseph Mayer
of Liverpool.
J.F. Codell, 637(VS):Spring90-499
Gibson, M.E. History and the Prism of Art.*
D. Birch, 541(RES):Nov89-579
P. Drew, 402(MLR):Oct90-928
D.E. Latané, Jr., 577(SHR):Spring89-178
W.D. Shaw, 301(JEGP):Jan89-121
Gibson, R., ed. Studies in French Fiction in
Honour of Vivienne Mylne.
J.C. Hayes, 166:Jan90-178
D. Wood, 402(MLR):Jul90-720
Gibson, W. Neuromancer. Count Zero. Burn-
ing Chrome.
J.R. Wytenbroek, 102(CanL):Summer89-
162
Gide, A. Correspondance avec sa mère, 1880-
1895.* (C. Martin, ed)
R. Jacquelin, 450(NRF):Feb89-144

Gide, A. The Notebooks of André Walter.
C.S. Brosman, 295(JML):Fall88/Winter89-
337
Gide, A. & J. Copeau. Correspondance André
Gide-Jacques Copeau. (Vol 1) (J. Claude,
ed)
G. Durosay, 535(RHL):Jul–Aug89-745
M. Tilby, 208(FS):Jul89-351
Gide, A. & V. Larbaud. Correspondance 1905-
1938. (F. Lioure, ed)
P. Pollard, 617(TLS):15-21Jun90-628
Gide, A. & A. Ruyters. Correspondance. (C.
Martin & V. Martin-Schmets, eds)
P. Pollard, 617(TLS):15-21Jun90-628
Gielgud, J. Backward Glances.
G. Gordon, 511:Aug89-45
Gielgud, J. Early Stages.
42(AR):Fall89-502
Gies, D.T. Theatre and Politics in Nine-
teenth-Century Spain.
D. George, 610:Summer89-202
F.H. Londré, 615(TJ):May89-255
S. Miller, 238:May89-303
R.J. Oakley, 402(MLR):Oct90-1001
N.M. Valis, 639(VQR):Spring89-356
Gies, D.T. — see de Grimaldi, J.
Gies, F. & J. Marriage and the Family in the
Middle Ages.*
J.M. Bennett, 589:Apr89-432
Giesey, R.E. Cérémonial et puissance souver-
aine, France, XVe-XVIIe siècles.
B. Diefendorf, 551(RenQ):Spring89-122
Giffard, I. The Way Things Happen.
B. Thompson, 441:19Aug90-19
Gifford, B. Wild at Heart.
J. Domini, 441:6May90-22
442(NY):4Jun90-103
Gifford, D. The Farther Shore.
R.M. Adams, 453(NYRB):26Apr90-46
Gifford, D., ed. The History of Scottish Liter-
ature. (Vol 3)
M.G.H. Pittock, 571(ScLJ):Winter89-13
Gifford, D., with R.J. Seidman. "Ulysses"
Annotated. (rev)
S. Moore, 532(RCF):Fall89-229
F. Senn, 329(JJQ):Spring90-653
Gifford, T. The Stone Spiral.
I. McMillan, 493:Winter89/90-65
Gigante, M. Filodemo.
D.W.T. Vessey, 123:Vol39No2-184
Gigante, M. & others. La Cultura classica a
Napoli nell' Ottocento.
N. Horsfall, 123:Vol39No2-426
Gigon, O., ed. Aristotelis Opera: Volumen
Tertium.
D. Sider, 124:Sep-Oct89-59
Giguère, R.G. Le Concept de la réalité dans la
poésie d'Yves Bonnefoy.
A. Williams, 207(FR):Mar90-721
Gikandi, S. Reading the African Novel.*
A. Irele, 538(RAL):Fall89-535
Gil Polo, G. Diana enamorada. (F. López
Estrada, ed)
B.M. Damiani, 240(HR):Autumn89-513
Gil y Carrasco, E. El señor de Bembibre.
(J-L. Picoche, ed)
M.A. Rees, 86(BHS):Apr89-184
Gilbert, B.D. La série énumérative.
M. Gómez Díaz, 350:Sep90-634
Gilbert, D. Sandinistas.*
639(VQR):Autumn89-134
Gilbert, F. A European Past.
639(VQR):Winter89-17

Gilbert, K., ed. Inside Black Australia.*
  K. Gallagher, 4:Summer89-58
Gilbert, M. Anything for a Quiet Life.
  P. Raine, 617(TLS):6-12Jul90-732
Gilbert, M. Winston S. Churchill. (Vol 3: The
  Challenge of War; Vol 4: World in Torment.)
  617(TLS):27Apr-3May90-457
Gilbert, M. - see Tory, A.
Gilbert, M.G. "One Flew Over the Cuckoo's
  Nest."
  M.C. Roudané, 587(SAF):Autumn89-248
Gilbert, P. Coming Out From Under.
  S. Walker, 71(ALS):May89-142
Gilbert, S.M. Blood Pressure.*
  M. Kinzie, 491:Jun89-151
Gilbert, S.M. & S. Gubar. No Man's Land.*
  (Vol 1)
  K. Blake, 301(JEGP):Jul89-454
  P.L. Caughie, 620(TSWL):Spring89-111
  K. Fishburn, 594:Spring89-104
  A.W. Fisher-Wirth, 147:Vol6No2-77
  M.E. Gibson, 177(ELT):Vol32No1-129
  A. Herrmann, 141:Fall89-507
  H. Vendler, 453(NYRB):31May90-19
Gilbert, S.M. & S. Gubar. No Man's Land.*
  (Vol 2)
  A. Herrmann, 141:Fall89-507
  C. Patterson, 620(TSWL):Spring89-128
  E.B. Thompson, 395(MFS):Winter89-867
  H. Vendler, 453(NYRB):31May90-19
  L. Wagner-Martin, 392:Spring89-193
  690(VQR):Summer89-84
Gilchrist, E. I Cannot Get You Close Enough.
  S.P. Wells, 441:4Nov90-24
Gilchrist, E. Light Can Be Both Wave and
  Particle.*
  D. Neuhaus, 617(TLS):7-13Sep90-956
Gildea, R. Barricades and Borders.
  P. Morton, 635(VPR):Summer89-81
Gilder, G. Microcosm.*
  J. Fallows, 453(NYRB):1Mar90-14
Gildersleeve, B.L. The Letters of Basil Lan-
  neau Gildersleeve.* (W.W. Briggs, Jr., ed)
  C.R. Phillips 3d, 24:Winter89-636
Gildner, G. The Warsaw Sparks.
  A.Z. Loventhal, 441:29Apr90-39
Gildon, C. Measure for Measure, or Beauty
  the Best Advocate. (E.A. Cairns, ed)
  566:Spring89-195
Giles, J.R. Confronting the Horror.
  T.R. Edwards, 453(NYRB):28Jun90-22
Giles, M. The Poetics of Love.
  C.P. Thompson, 86(BHS):Jan89-202
Giles, P. A Basic Counter-Tenor Method for
  Teacher and Student.
  G. Reynolds, 415:Sep89-571
Giles, R.F., ed. Hopkins Among the Poets.
  N. White, 447(N&Q):Mar89-118
Giles, S. Fred Astaire.
  M. McQuade, 151:Sep89-56
Giles of Rome. Giles of Rome on Ecclesiastical
  Power. (R.W. Dyson, ed & trans)
  T. Renna, 589:Oct89-951
Gili, J., ed. Lo libre dels cavayls que compós
  Ypocras.
  B. Schmid, 547(RF):Band101Heft4-505
Gill, B. The Death of a Joyce Scholar.*
  M.J. O'Shea, 329(JJQ):Spring90-694
Gill, B. Many Masks.*
  A. Adams, 39:Sep89-209
Gill, B. A New York Life.
  C. Seebohm, 441:21Oct90-11

Gill, B.E. White Grease Paint on Black Per-
  formers.
  J.V. Hatch, 610:Autumn89-306
Gill, B.M. Time and Time Again.
  M. Stasio, 441:18Mar90-33
Gill, G. Agatha Christie.
  J. Mortimer, 441:14Oct90-52
Gill, G.E. White Grease Paint on Black Per-
  formers.
  W.L. Fletcher, 612(ThS):Nov88-233
Gill, M.L. Aristotle on Substance.
  L.P. Gerson, 103:Oct90-410
Gill, M.M., B. Wegmann & T. Méndez-Faith. En
  contacto.
  M.J. Treacy, 399(MLJ):Summer89-243
Gill, R. - see Marlowe, C.
Gill, R. - see Shakespeare, W.
Gill, S. William Wordsworth.*
  M. Baron, 175:Autumn89-255
  J. Bate, 661(WC):Autumn89-171
  J.E. Jordan, 445(NCF):Mar90-539
Gill, S.D. Mother Earth.*
  B. Toelken, 649(WAL):Feb90-375
Gillain, A., ed. Le cinéma selon François
  Truffaut.
  E.B. Turk, 207(FR):May90-1084
Gillespie, A.K. & J. Mechling, eds. American
  Wildlife in Symbol and Story.
  S.A. Marks, 292(JAF):Apr-Jun89-243
  R.O. Ribnick, 650(WF):Jan89-72
Gillespie, D.C. Valentin Rasputin and Soviet
  Russian Village Prose.*
  A. Fodor, 104(CASS):Spring-Winter88-
  493
  K. Parthé, 550(RusR):Apr89-222
Gillespie, D.F. The Sisters' Arts.
  P.R. Broughton, 177(ELT):Vol32No3-364
  S. Ferebee, 395(MFS):Winter89-802
Gillespie, D.F. & E. Steele - see Stephen, J.D.
Gillespie, M.A. & M. Lienesch, eds. Ratifying
  the Constitution.
  J.A. Moore, Jr., 173(ECS):Spring90-355
Gillespie, M.A. & T.B. Strong, eds. Nietzsche's
  New Seas.*
  P.F., 185:Apr90-702
Gillespie, S. Poets on the Classics
  J.F. Sullivan, 124:Nov-Dec89-123
Gillette, H., Jr. & Z.L. Miller, eds. American
  Urbanism.
  R.A. Rutherdale, 106:Summer89-89
Gilley, S. Newman and His Age.
  B. Martin, 617(TLS):7-13Dec90-1330
Gillian, A. & M. Loutfi. Récits d'aujourd'hui.
  A.V. Lambros, 207(FR):May90-1088
Gilliatt, P. Lingo.
  L. Duguid, 617(TLS):9-15Mar90-258
Gilliatt, P. To Wit.
  J. Bayley, 617(TLS):23-29Mar90-309
  442(NY):19Nov90-156
Gillies, M. Bartók in Britain.*
  D. Fanning, 415:Jun89-350
  M. Smith, 607:Sep89-33
Gillman, S. Dark Twins.*
  L.J. Budd, 26(ALR):Winter90-93
  R.B. Hauck, 395(MFS):Winter89-739
Gillmor, A.M. Erik Satie.*
  J.B.J., 412:Feb89-71
  R. Orledge, 410(M&L):May89-275
  R. Shattuck, 453(NYRB):15Mar90-32
Gilly, C. Spanien under der Basler Buchdruck
  bis 1600.*
  P.G. Bietenholz, 551(RenQ):Spring89-102

Gilman, C. & M.J. Schneider. The Way to Independence 1840-1920.*
P. Nabokov, 456(NDQ):Spring89-202
Gilman, D. Mrs. Pollifax and the Whirling Dervish.
F.A. Koestler, 441:9Sep90-26
Gilman, E.B. Iconoclasm and Poetry in the English Reformation.*
D. Chambers, 541(RES):Feb89-120
M.L. Hall, 569(SR):Summer89-456
Gilman, S. The Novel According to Cervantes.
A.J. Close, 617(TLS):19-25Jan90-67
Gilman, S.L. Jewish Self-Hatred.*
J. Kornberg, 222(GR):Summer89-140
Gilmore, D.D. Manhood in the Making.
B.L. Benderly, 441:15Apr90-8
R. Brain, 617(TLS):1-7Jun90-590
Gilmore, J. Swinging in Paradise.
D. Lewis, 529(QQ):Autumn89-753
D. Rollins, 627(UTQ):Fall89-244
Gilmore, J.C. The World of the Oregon Fishboat.
D.A. Taylor, 292(JAF):Apr-Jun89-247
Gilmour, D. The Last Leopard.
R. Trevelyan, 364:Apr/May89-140
Gilmour, J.C. Picturing the World.*
A.G. Pleydell-Pearce, 323:Jan89-92
Gilmour, J.D., ed. Sir Thomas Beecham.
R. Anderson, 415:Nov89-683
Gilmour, P., ed. Lasting Impressions.
H. James, 89(BJA):Autumn89-377
Gilot, F. Matisse and Picasso.
L. Liebmann, 441:16Dec90-29
Gilpin, L. The Enduring Navaho.
J. Loughery, 662:Fall89/Winter90-50
Gilson, A. Les Chemins parallèles de Charlélie Couture.
A.J.M. Prévos, 207(FR):Dec89-392
Gilson, D. & M. Smith - see Shackleton, R.
Gilson, E. Linguistics and Philosophy.
S. Baldner, 103:Dec90-495
Gilson, E. Thomist Realism and the Critique of Knowledge.
P. Lee, 438:Winter89-81
Gilson, R. Jean Cocteau, cinéaste.
N. Greene, 207(FR):Apr90-922
Gimpel, G., ed. Weder-Noch.
G.C. Schoolfield, 222(GR):Spring89-92
Gindin, J. John Galsworthy's Life and Art.*
N. Brennan, 295(JML):Fall88/Winter89-335
H. Orel, 301(JEGP):Apr89-258
Ginge, B. Ceramiche etrusche a figure nere.
F.R.S. Ridgway, 123:Vol39No2-341
Gingher, M. Bobby Rex's Greatest Hit.
T. Rash, 580(SCR):Spring90-131
Gingher, M. Teen Angel and Other Stories of Young Love.
R.H. Brinkmeyer, Jr., 573(SSF):Fall88-493
Ginsberg, R., ed. The Philosopher as Writer: The Eighteenth Century.*
W. Goetschel, 221(GQ):Spring89-235
R.W. Perrett, 478(P&L):Oct89-378
K.E. Smith, 83:Autumn89-223
Ginsborg, P. A History of Contemporary Italy.
C. Duggan, 617(TLS):28Sep-4Oct90-1025
Ginsburg, F.D. Contested Lives.*
R. Behar, 385(MQR):Fall90-695
Ginsburg, M.P. Flaubert Writing.*
M. Melaver, 494:Fall89-643
Ginzberg, E. The Medical Triangle.
U.E. Reinhardt, 441:29Apr90-11

Ginzburg, N. The Road to the City.
442(NY):16Jul90-86
Ginzburg, N. Voices in the Evening.*
W. Ferguson, 441:21Jan90-20
Giorgi, G. Antichità classica e Seicento francese.
J-P. Collinet, 535(RHL):Jul-Aug89-713
Gioscio, J. Il dialetto lucano di Calvello.*
H. Lüdtke, 547(RF):Band101Heft1-94
Gioseffi, D., ed. Women on War.
D.J. Austin, 441:7Jan90-16
Giovanardi, C. Linguaggi scientifici e lingua comune nel Settecento.
M. Palermo, 708:Vol14Fasc2-275
di Giovanni, N.T., ed. Celeste Goes Dancing and Other Stories.* In Memory of Borges.
P. Lewis, 565:Autumn89-72
Gipouloux, F. Les Cent Fleurs à l'usine.
E.J. Perry, 293(JASt):Feb89-134
Giraldo, J.J.M. - see under Montes Giraldo, J.J.
Girard, J-Y. Proof Theory and Logical Complexity. (Vol 1)
H. Pfeiffer, 316:Dec89-1493
Girardi, M. & P. Petrobelli, eds. Messa per Rossini.
W. Ashbrook, 410(M&L):Nov89-561
D. Colas, 537:Vol75No2-302
Giraud, Y., ed. Le Paysage à la Renaissance.
F. Berriot, 535(RHL):Sep-Oct89-930
Giraud, Y., ed. Le Premier Livre d'"Amadis de Gaule."*
M.M. McGowan, 208(FS):Jan89-79
Girault, O. & D. Nony. Civilisation et langue françaises.
P.A. Gaeng, 399(MLJ):Summer89-220
Giraut de Borneil. The Cansos and Sirventes of the Troubadour Giraut de Borneil. (R.V. Sharman, ed)
D.D.R. Owen, 617(TLS):5-11Jan90-16
Girfanova, Z.A. Formirovaie norm russkogo literaturnogo jazyka serediny XVIII v.
C.E. Gribble, 574(SEEJ):Fall89-463
Girouard, M. The English Town.
P-L. Adams, 61:Oct90-136
J.M. Crook, 617(TLS):11-17May90-506
G. Darley, 324:Sep90-713
T. Hiss, 441:23Sep90-34
442(NY):17Sep90-110
Giroud, F. Alma Mahler ou l'art d'être aimée.
C. Slawy-Sutton, 207(FR):Dec89-411
Giroux, E.X. A Death for a Darling.
T. Goldie, 102(CanL):Winter88-128
Giroux, R. A Deed of Death.
O. Friedrich, 441:10Jun90-26
Giroux, R. Du fond redouté (1982-1985).
R. Coleman, 168(ECW):Fall89-109
C. May, 102(CanL):Spring89-200
Giroux, R. - see Lowell, R.
Giroux, R. - see Malamud, B.
Gish, R.F. Frontier's End.
M.E. Caldwell, 456(NDQ):Spring89-165
D. Heaberlin, 649(WAL):Aug89-169
L. Owens, 27(AL):Dec89-712
J.J. Wydeven, 395(MFS):Summer89-300
Gislason, D.G., comp. La Chronique musicale, 1873-1876.
F. Lesure, 537:Vol75No1-101
Gíslason, K. Bréf Konráds Gíslasonar. (A. Kristjánsson, ed)
L.A. Pitschmann, 301(JEGP):Oct89-571
Gissing, W. Mississippi Delta Blues.
A.J.M. Prévos, 91:Vol17-185

Gitlin, T. The Sixties.
 J.E. McBride, 529(QQ):Spring89-202
del Giudice, D. Lines of Light.
 P.N. Furbank, 617(TLS):5-11Jan90-18
 I. Thomson, 364:Oct/Nov89-128
Giuliani, L. Bildnis und Botschaft.*
 P. Zanker, 313:Vol79-182
Given-Wilson, C. The English Nobility in the
 Late Middle Ages.
 D.J.D. Boulton, 589:Oct89-953
Gjerdingen, R.O. A Classic Turn of Phrase.
 J. Dunsby, 410(M&L):Aug89-406
 W. Thomson, 413:Summer90-438
Gjertsen, D. The Newton Handbook.
 F.M. Hetzler, 258:Jun89-237
Gladkova, T.L. & others, comps. L'émigration
 russe.
 V. Setchkarev, 574(SEEJ):Summer89-312
Gladstone, W.E. The Gladstone Diaries. (Vols
 9-11) (H.C.G. Matthew, ed)
 P. Clarke, 617(TLS):18-24May90-515
Glaister, L. Honour Thy Father.
 C. Hawtree, 617(TLS):19-25Oct90-1130
Glancey, J. New British Architecture.*
 P.D., 46:Oct89-14
"Glanes d'archéologie, d'histoire et de littér-
 ature creusoises, offerts à Amédée Carriat
 et à Andrée Louradour."
 C. Grisé, 475:Vol16No31-587
Glanville, J. & J.D. Miller. Elvis Don't Like
 Football.
 C. Salzberg, 441:11Nov90-61
Glanville, P. Silver in England.
 J.K.D., Cooper, 39:Feb89-141
 H.H., 90:May89-365
Glaser, H. Das Verschwinden der Arbeit.
 H. Hanke, 654(WB):12/1989-2100
Gläser, R. Phraseologie der englischen
 Sprache.*
 F. Ungerer, 38:Band107Heft3/4-473
 G. Wotjak, 682(ZPSK):Band42Heft2-266
Glasgow, E. Ellen Glasgow's Reasonable
 Doubts.* (J.R. Raper, ed)
 P.R. Matthews, 27(AL):May89-301
 K.L. Seidel, 585(SoQ):Winter90-68
 N. Walker, 395(MFS):Summer89-290
Glass, B. A Guide to the Genetics Collections
 of the American Philosophical Society.
 R. Parsons, 354:Dec89-374
Glass, C. Tribes with Flags.
 C.C. O'Brien, 441:15Apr90-8
 R. Owen, 617(TLS):29Jun-5Jul90-687
 P. Partner, 453(NYRB):19Jul90-25
 442(NY):16Jul90-86
Glass, P. Opera on the Beach.* (R.T. Jones,
 ed)
 R. Samuel, 410(M&L):Nov89-579
Glass, R. Clichés of Urban Doom and Other
 Essays.*
 C. Ward, 46:Feb89-8
Glasscoe, M., ed. The Medieval Mystical Tra-
 dition in England.*
 M-J. Arn, 179(ES):Oct89-450
 S.J. Ogilvie-Thomson, 541(RES):Nov89-
 543
Glasser, P. Singing on the Titanic.*
 R. Curran, 573(SSF):Fall88-497
Glasser, R. Gorbals Voices, Siren Songs.
 A. Cairncross, 617(TLS):20-26Apr90-416
Glassie, H., ed. Irish Folktales.
 W.F.H. Nicolaisen, 292(JAF):Oct-Dec89-
 476

Glassie, H. The Spirit of Folk Art.
 B. Bode, 441:21Jan90-13
Glatthaar, J.T. Forged in Battle.
 J.M. McPherson, 453(NYRB):12Apr90-33
 S.W. Sears, 441:14Jan90-8
Glazebrook, P. The Gate at the End of the
 World.
 J. Bilston, 617(TLS):5-11Jan90-18
Glazer, M., comp. A Dictionary of Mexican
 American Proverbs.
 R.V. Teschner, 238:Mar89-149
Gleason, D.K. Virginia Plantation Homes.
 S. Wilson, Jr., 585(SoQ):Spring90-121
Gleason, J. Oya.
 O. Owomoyela, 538(RAL):Summer89-270
Gleason, J.B., ed. You Can Take It With You.
 E. Spinelli, 399(MLJ):Winter89-487
Gleckner, R.F. Blake and Spenser.*
 A. Elfenbein, 141:Fall89-493
 M.L. Johnson, 301(JEGP):Jul89-429
Gleissner, R. Die Entstehung der ästhet-
 ischen Humanitätsidee in Deutschland.
 R.E. Norton, 221(GQ):Spring89-260
Glen, J.M. Highlander.
 639(VQR):Winter89-30
Glenday, J. The Apple Ghost.*
 W.N. Herbert, 571(ScLJ):Winter89-40
Glendinning, V. The Grown-Ups.*
 C. Dickinson, 441:7Jan90-24
Glendon, M.A. Abortion and Divorce in West-
 ern Law.*
 W. Ver Eecke, 543:Jun90-866
Glenn, J., T. Hermann & H.D. Rodgers - see
 Gong, A.
Glenn, J. & D. Walsh. Catalogue of the Fran-
 cis Trigge Chained Library, St. Wulfram's
 Church, Grantham.
 J. Goldfinch, 354:Dec89-367
 D. McKitterick, 78(BC):Autumn89-301
Glenny, R.E. The Manipulation of Reality in
 Works by Heinrich von Kleist.*
 S.R. Huff, 406:Winter89-494
Glickfeld, C.L. Useful Gifts.*
 G. Oldham, 42(AR):Fall89-500
Glienke, B. Fatale Präzedenz.*
 D.C. Riechel, 563(SS):Winter89-87
 A. Van Hees, 562(Scan):May89-98
Glier, I., ed. Die deutsche Literatur im späten
 Mittelalter (1250-1370).* (Pt 2)
 H-J. Behr, 684(ZDA):Band118Heft3-121
 A. Classen, 564:Sep89-256
 W.C. McDonald, 589:Oct89-955
 B. Schirok, 224(GRM):Band39Heft4-472
 F. Tobin, 221(GQ):Spring89-248
 S.L. Wailes, 301(JEGP):Jul89-367
Glouberman, M. Descartes.*
 C. Wilson, 242:Vol10No3-384
Glover, J. I: The Philosophy and Psychology
 of Personal Identity.*
 A. Brennan, 518:Apr89-106
Glover, J. & others. Ethics of New Reproduc-
 tive Technologies.
 A.B., 185:Jul90-925
 E. Boetzkes, 103:Aug90-311
Glover, J. & J. Silkin, eds. The Penguin Book
 of First World War Prose.
 C.J. Fox, 617(TLS):16-22Feb90-178
Głowiński, M. & J. Sławiński, eds. Poezja pol-
 ska okresu międzywojennego.
 S. Barańczak, 497(PolR):Vol34No1-77
Glück, H. Schrift und Schriftlichkeit.
 E. Feldbusch, 684(ZDA):Band118Heft2-51

Glück, L. Ararat.
S. Dobyns, 441:2Sep90-5
Glymour, C. & others. Discovering Causal Structure.
M. Oaksford, 103:Jan90-19
Goar, R.J. The Legend of Cato Uticensis from the First Century B.C. to the Fifth Century A.D.
J. Briscoe, 313:Vol79-197
M. Griffin, 123:Vol39No2-247
de Gobineau, J.A. Oeuvres.* (Vol 3) (J. Gaulmier, with J. Boissel & M-L. Concasty, eds)
P-L. Rey, 535(RHL):Jan-Feb89-135
Göbl, R. Numismatik.
P. Bastien, 229:Band61Heft7-634
Gochet, P. Ascent to Truth.*
J. Pieters, 258:Mar89-108
A. Weir, 393(Mind):Jul88-496
Godard, B., ed. Gynocritics/La Gynocritique.
L. Hutcheon, 627(UTQ):Fall89-144
G. McGregor, 298:Fall89-146
M. Randall, 529(QQ):Spring89-184
Godard, D. La syntaxe des relatives en français.
S.S. Mufwene, 350:Sep90-635
Godbout, J. An American Story.
B.K. Horvath, 532(RCF):Spring89-266
Goddard, J-C. - see Fichte, J.G.
Goddard, R. In Pale Battalions.
639(VQR):Autumn89-131
Goddard, S.H. The Master of Frankfurt and his Shop.
D. Wolfthal, 551(RenQ):Summer89-328
Goddard, S.H., ed. The World in Miniature.
C. Hartley, 90:Oct89-712
Godden, G.A. Encyclopaedia of British Porcelain Manufacturers.
R. Hildyard, 39:Oct89-285
Godden, R. A House with Four Rooms.*
P. Oakes, 617(TLS):5-11Jan90-5
Godden, R. & J. Mercy, Pity, Peace and Love.
D. Lovatt, 441:3Jun90-22
Goddu, A. The Physics of William of Ockham.
E.D. Sylla, 482(PhR):Apr89-257
Gödel, K. Collected Works of Kurt Gödel. (Vol 1) (S. Feferman & others, eds)
J.L. Bell, 479(PhQ):Apr87-216
B.J. Lucas, 556:Summer89-72
Godfrey, D. - see Innis, H.A.
Godin, M. Après l'Eden.
T.R. Kuhnle, 102(CanL):Autumn-Winter89-270
Godineau, D. Citoyennes tricoteuses.*
J. Rosendaal, 242:Vol10No3-369
Godínez, F. Las lágrimas de David. (E.V. Coughlin & J.O. Valencia, eds)
C.H. Rose, 86(BHS):Apr89-179
Godman, P. Poets and Emperors.*
M. Alberi, 589:Apr89-433
Godman, P. & R. Collins, eds. Charlemagne's Heir.
R. McKitterick, 617(TLS):30Nov-6Dec90-1296
Godsey, F. A Gathering at the River.
S. Pickering, 569(SR):Summer89-lxxxiv
Godwin, F. Our Forbidden Land.
B. Bryson, 617(TLS):19-25Oct90-1122
Godwin, J. Harmonies of Heaven and Earth.*
B. Bujic, 410(M&L):Aug89-392
Godwin, W. The Anarchist Writings of William Godwin. (P. Marshall, ed)
M. Fitzpatrick, 83:Autumn89-217

Goebel, U. & W.T. Zyla, eds. Johann Wolfgang von Goethe.
J.F. Hyde, Jr., 406:Winter89-476
Goebel-Schilling, G. La Littérature entre l'engagement et le jeu.
R. Pensom, 402(MLR):Oct90-943
Goebl, H., ed. Dialectology.
J. Macha, 685(ZDL):3/1989-356
Goedicke, P. The Tongues We Speak.
S. Dobyns, 441:28Jan90-26
Goerdt, W. Russische Philosophie.
G. Ressel, 688(ZSP):Band49Heft2-434
Goethe, J.C. Reise durch Italien im Jahre 1740 (Viaggio per l'Italia). (A. Meier, with H. Hollmer, eds & trans)
E. Koppen, 52:Band24Heft2-191
von Goethe, J.W. Collected Works in Twelve Volumes.
J. Hardin, 617(TLS):2-8Mar90-231
von Goethe, J.W. Faust Part One. (D. Luke, trans)
R.B. Bottigheimer, 221(GQ):Spring89-264
I.H. Washington, 301(JEGP):Apr89-290
von Goethe, J.W. Goethe: Roman Elegies and The Diary. (D. Luke, trans)
R.B. Bottingheimer, 221(GQ):Winter89-104
J.R. Williams, 402(MLR):Oct90-1025
von Goethe, J.W. Scientific Studies. (D. Miller, ed)
F. Burwick, 173(ECS):Fall89-62
W. Riemer, 221(GQ):Fall89-532
von Goethe, J.W. Selected Poems.* (C. Middleton, ed) Essays on Art and Literature.* (J. Gearey, ed) From My Life Poetry and Truth, Parts One to Three.* (T.P. Saine & J.L. Sammons, eds) From My Life Poetry and Truth, Part Four.* (T.P. Saine & J.L. Sammons, eds) [Goethe's Collected Works. (Vols 1, 3, 4 & 5)]
F. Burwick, 173(ECS):Fall89-62
von Goethe, J.W. The Sorrows of Young Werther, Elective Affinities, Novella. (D.E. Wellbery, ed)
F. Burwick, 173(ECS):Fall89-62
E. Dye, 221(GQ):Winter89-111
W. Wittkowski, 166:Jul90-358
von Goethe, J.W. & J.F. Cotta von Cottendorf. Goethe und Cotta: Briefwechsel 1797-1832. (D. Kuhn, ed)
J.F. Hyde, Jr., 406:Winter89-476
"Goethe Yearbook." (Vol 4) (T.P. Saine, ed)
E. Larkin, 221(GQ):Spring89-264
Goffen, R. Giovanni Bellini.
L. Gowing, 441:4Mar90-28
C. Hope, 453(NYRB):19Jul90-28
J. Pope-Hennessy, 617(TLS):16-22Mar90-280
Goffen, R. Piety and Patronage in Renaissance Venice.*
J.G. Bernasconi, 278(IS):Vol43-156
Goffette, G. Éloge pour une cuisine de province.
M-N. Little, 207(FR):Apr90-892
H. Raynal, 450(NRF):Apr89-96
Goffman, D. Izmir and the Levantine World, 1550-1650.
A. Hamilton, 617(TLS):21-27Dec90-1371
"Gogol': Istorija i sovremennost' (k 175-letiju so dnja roždenija)."
R-D. Keil, 688(ZSP):Band49Heft1-173
Golb, N. Les Juifs de Rouen au moyen âge.
I. Robinson, 589:Apr89-435

Gold, B.K. Literary Patronage in Greece and
Rome.*
E.J. Kenney, 229:Band61Heft2-164
W.J. Raschke, 124:Jan-Feb90-244
Gold, I. Sams in a Dry Season.
L. Graeber, 441:30Sep90-28
442(NY):12Nov90-133
Gold, P.S. The Lady and the Virgin.*
K.L. Casey, 242:Vol10No3-372
Goldbarth, A. Popular Culture.
S. Friedman, 441:23Sep90-48
Goldberg, A., ed. Mishna Treatise Eruvin.
J. Goldin, 318(JAOS):Jul-Sep88-471
Goldberg, D. Between Worlds.
L. Thomson, 627(UTQ):Fall89-124
Goldberg, E.L. Patterns in Late Medici Art
Patronage. After Vasari.
C.M. Soussloff, 54:Dec89-697
Goldberg, H. - see Fielding, H.
Goldberg, J. Voice Terminal Echo.*
E. Eldridge, 568(SCN):Spring-Summer89-
1
R. Strier, 551(RenQ):Summer89-347
Goldberg, J. Writing Matter.
N. Forsyth, 617(TLS):8-14Jun90-620
Goldberg, R. & G.J. Anchors.
M.P. Nichols, 441:14Oct90-12
Goldberg, S.M. Understanding Terence.
C. Garton, 122:Jan89-64
M.M. Willcock, 313:Vol79-187
Goldberg, V. Margaret Bourke-White.*
Bourke-White.
J. Loughery, 662:Fall89/Winter90-49
Golde, P., ed. Women in the Field. (2nd ed)
G. Bennett, 203:Vol100No1-124
Golden, J.L. & J.J. Pilotta, eds. Practical
Reasoning in Human Affairs.*
S. Stern-Gillet, 323:May89-189
D.N. Walton, 449:Dec89-702
Golden, M. Children and Childhood in Classi-
cal Athens.
J. Griffin, 453(NYRB):25Oct90-20
Golden, R.L. & C.G. Roland, eds. Sir William
Osler.
G. Jenkins, 87(BB):Mar89-53
Golden, W.T., ed. Science and Technology
Advice to the President, Congress, and
Judiciary.
J.E. Cohen, 31(ASch):Summer89-471
Goldensohn, B. The Marrano.
B. Howard, 491:Sep89-348
Goldfeld, L.N. Moses Maimonides' Treatise on
Resurrection.
N. Roth, 589:Oct89-957
Goldfield, M. The Decline of Organized Labor
in the United States.
B.D. Palmer, 529(QQ):Summer89-556
Goldgar, B.A. - see Fielding, H.
Goldman, A. The Lives of John Lennon.
J. Saari, 42(AR):Winter89-104
Goldman, A.H. Moral Knowledge.*
N. Fotion, 103:Sep90-365
Goldman, A.I. Epistemology and Cognition.*
D. Bruce, 606:Apr89-165
G. Hatfield, 482(PhR):Jul89-386
Goldman, E. The Social Significance of Mod-
ern Drama.*
P. Auslander, 223:Spring89-89
Goldman, M. Acting and Action in Shake-
spearean Tragedy.*
J.A. Bryant, Jr., 569(SR):Summer89-445
Goldman, P., ed. Conflicting Realities.
V. Chamberlin, 593:Spring89-73

Goldman, R.P. - see "The Rāmāyaṇa of Vālm-
īki"
Goldman, W. Hype and Glory.
N. Johnson, 441:22Apr90-12
Goldmann, B. Einheitlichkeit und Eigen-
ständigkeit der "Historia Romana" des
Appian.
K. Brodersen, 313:Vol79-250
C.B.R. Pelling, 123:Vol39No2-202
Goldner, G.R., with L. Hendrix & G. Williams.
European Drawings. (Vol 1)
D. Scrase, 39:Jun89-440
J.B. Shaw, 380:Winter89-368
Goldsmith, E.C. "Exclusive Conversations."
F. Lagarde, 207(FR):May90-1062
J.D. Lyons, 210(FrF):May89-233
Goldsmith, M.E. The Figure of Piers Plowman.
G. Bourquin, 189(EA):Apr-Jun89-211
Goldsmith, R.W. Premodern Financial Systems.
D. Nightingale, 313:Vol79-224
Goldstein, A. & M.J. Jacob. A Forest of Signs.
42(AR):Fall89-501
Goldstein, C. Visual Fact over Verbal Fic-
tion.*
D. De Grazia, 551(RenQ):Winter89-866
Goldstein, E.A. & M.A. Izeman. The New York
Environment Book.
G. Maranto, 441:26Aug90-19
Goldstein, J. Console and Classify.*
P.C. Mullen, 207(FR):Mar90-753
Goldstein, L. The Flying Machine and Modern
Literature.*
W.H., 148:Winter86-126
Goldstein, M.C. A History of Modern Tibet,
1913-1951.
J. Mirsky, 453(NYRB):20Dec90-53
Goldstein, W. Playing for Keeps.
R. Pinsky, 441:1Apr90-18
Goldsworthy, A. Andy Goldsworthy.
M.A. Francis, 617(TLS):8-14Jun90-614
Goldsworthy, P. This Goes With This.
R. Crawford, 490:Autumn89-23
Goldthorpe, R. Sartre.
P.A.Y. Gunter, 478(P&L):Apr89-203
Göllner, T. "Die Sieben Worte am Kreuz" bei
Schütz und Haydn.
G. Fodor, 417:Jan-Mar89-82
Golob, R. & E. Brus, eds. The Almanac of Sci-
ence and Technology.
G. Johnson, 441:13May90-16
Golombek, L. & D. Wilber. The Timurid Archi-
tecture of Iran and Turan.
J.M. Bloom, 576:Sep89-303
Golomstock, I. Totalitarian Art.
T. Hyman, 617(TLS):23-29Nov90-1260
Golsan, R.J. Service inutile.
A. Thiher, 210(FrF):Sep89-378
Golub, J. & others, eds. Activities to Promote
Critical Thinking.
N.R. Comley, 128(CE):Oct89-623
Golub, J. & others, eds. Focus on Collabora-
tive Learning.
T. Nienhuis, 126(CCC):Oct89-355
Golub, M. Secret Correspondence.
R. Bromley, 441:30Sep90-29
Golyšenko, V.S. Mjagkost' soglasnyx v jazyke
vostočnyx slavjan XI-XII vv.
F.V. Gladney, 574(SEEJ):Spring89-150
Gombrich, E.H. Reflections on the History of
Art. (R. Woodfield, ed)
J. Sweetman, 89(BJA):Winter89-77
Gombrich, E.H. The Story of Art. (14th ed)
B.R. Collins, 127:Spring89-90

Gombrich, R. Theravāda Buddhism.
J.W. de Jong, 259(IIJ):Jul89-239
Gombrowicz, W. Diary.* (Vol 1) (J. Kott, ed)
S. Baranczak, 473(PR):Vol56No1-85
Gomes da Costa, A. & others. Estudos sobre
Fernando Pessoa.
J. Parker, 86(BHS):Jul89-301
Gómez, A.E. – see under Enríquez Gómez, A.
Gomez, J.A. & J. Pride. Practice & Improve
Your Spanish. Practice & Improve Your
Spanish Plus.
B.B. Jackson, 399(MLJ):Autumn89-387
Gómez, J.B. – see under Berchez Gómez, J.
Gómez de la Serna, R. El secreto del Acue-
ducto. (C. Richmond, ed)
I. Soldevila-Durante, 238:Dec89-962
Gómez-Heras, J.M.G. El a priori del mundo de
la vida.
P. Trotignon, 542:Oct-Dec89-610
Gómez-Lobo, A. – see Parmenides
Gómez Redondo, F. – see Manuel, J.
Gómez Segade, J.M. Arte actual y arquitec-
tura religiosa en la sociedad contempor-
ánea. Función y símbolo en la arquitectura
eclesial del siglo XX.
M. Cabañas Bravo, 48:Oct-Dec89-475
Gomulka, S. & A. Polonsky, eds. Polish Para-
doxes.
W. Brus, 617(TLS):27Jul-2Aug90-797
Gonda, J. Prajāpati's Rise to Higher Rank.*
J.P. Brereton, 318(JAOS):Apr-Jun88-336
Gonda, J. Rice and Barley Offerings in the
Veda.
K. Mylius, 259(IIJ):Apr89-141
Gong, A. Early Poems. (J. Glenn, J. Hermann
& R.S. Rodgers, eds)
B. Bjorklund, 133:Band22Heft1-87
de Góngora, L. Romances.* (2nd ed) (A. Car-
reño, ed)
M.L. Welles, 240(HR):Summer89-385
Gonick, C. The Great Economic Debate.
A. Tupper, 529(QQ):Spring89-152
González, A. La novela modernista hispano-
americana.
P. Beardsell, 86(BHS):Oct89-394
O.U. Somoza, 238:Mar89-150
Gonzalez, A. & B.P. Sibayan, eds. Evaluating
Bilingual Education in the Philippines
(1974-1985).
S. Jones, 710:Dec89-481
Gonzalez, A.A. Cicerón ante la retórica.
L. Calboli Montefusco, 229:Band61Heft7-
582
González, C. "El cavallero Zifar" y el reino
lejano.
M. Harney, 545(RPh):May90-569
González, C., ed. Libro del caballero Zifar.
M. Harney, 545(RPh):May90-569
González, J.J.M. – see under Martín González,
J.J.
González, J.J.M. & J. Urrea Fernández – see
under Martín González, J.J. & J. Urrea Fer-
nández
González, J.L. Ballads of Another Time.
M.S. Arrington, Jr., 238:Dec89-984
Gonzalez, R., ed. Crossing the River.
J.R. Saucerman, 649(WAL):Aug89-184
Gonzalez, R., ed. Tracks in the Snow.
R.D. Harper, 649(WAL):Feb90-386
González-Cruz, L.F. – see Piñera, V.
González Echevarría, R. La Ruta de Severo
Sarduy.*
S. Moore, 532(RCF):Summer89-242

González Freixas, M.A. Sociedad y tipos en
las novelas de Ramón Mexa y Suárez Inclán.
S. Romeo Fivel-Démoret, 86(BHS):Jan89-
101
González López, P. Els anys daurats del cin-
ema a Barcelona (1906-1923).
P.W. Evans, 86(BHS):Apr89-206
González Muela, J., ed. Libro del caballero
Zifar.
M. Harney, 545(RPh):May90-569
González-Palacios, A. Il Tempio del Gusto.*
W. Rieder, 90:May89-362
González Rodríguez, M.C. Las Unidades Or-
ganizativas Indígenas del Area Indoeuropea
de Hispania.
A.T. Fear, 313:Vol79-242
Gonzalez Salvador, A. Continuidad de lo
Fantástico, por una teoria de la literatura
insólita. (A. Verjat, ed)
R. Baudry, 535(RHL):Jan-Feb89-156
Gonzalez-T., C.A. Unwinding the Silence.
S. Foster, 36:Summer89-122
Gooch, P.W. Partial Knowledge.
B. Hebblethwaite, 483:Apr89-268
Good, G. The Observing Self.
P. Budra, 627(UTQ):Fall89-116
B. Matiko, 178:Sep89-356
S. Rendall, 478(P&L):Oct89-415
Good, M. W.B. Yeats and the Creation of a
Tragic Universe.
T.D., 295(JML):Fall88/Winter89-426
Goodall, J. Through a Window.
V. Hearne, 441:28Oct90-7
P.C. Lee, 617(TLS):30Nov-6Dec90-1299
442(NY):10Dec90-160
Goodden, A. The Complete Lover.*
C. Lazzaro-Weis, 166:Apr90-255
Goode, J. Thomas Hardy.
M. Williams, 447(N&Q):Dec89-536
Goode, J.M. Best Addresses.
E.C. Cromley, 576:Dec89-408
C. Floyd, 47:Jul89-44
Goodheart, E. Pieces of Resistance.*
R. Asselineau, 189(EA):Oct-Dec89-496
Goodman, A. Gilbert and Sullivan's London.
N. Burton, 415:Apr89-218
Goodman, C.M. Jean Stafford.
A. Whitehouse, 441:12Aug90-17
Goodman, D. Criticism in Action.
J.H. Mason, 617(TLS):19-25Jan90-52
Goodman, D. & M. Redclift, eds. The Interna-
tional Farm Crisis.
G. Olney, 617(TLS):20-26Apr90-417
Goodman, D.G. Japanese Drama and Culture
in the 1960s.
J. Raz, 407(MN):Summer89-235
Goodman, J.R. The Legend of Arthur in Brit-
ish and American Literature.
R.J. Schrader, 637(VS):Spring90-492
J.J. Wilhelm, 589:Jul89-708
Goodman, K. Dis/Closures.
S.L. Cocalis, 406:Summer89-230
Goodman, M. The Ruling Class of Judaea.
B.D. Shaw, 313:Vol79-246
M.H. Williams, 123:Vol39No1-88
Goodman, M.F., ed. What Is a Person?
J.B.D., 185:Jan90-444
Goodman, N. & C.Z. Elgin. Reconceptions in
Philosophy and Other Arts and Sciences.*
D. Arrell, 103:Aug90-313
M. Budd, 89(BJA):Autumn89-367
D. Dempster, 289:Winter89-110
[continued]

[continuing]
T. Kulka, 494:Winter89–854
R.A. Sharpe, 521:Oct89–357
Goodrich, D.S. The Reader and the Text.
J. Labanyi, 86(BHS):Apr89–194
Goodrich, P. Legal Discourse.*
G.B., 185:Jan90–451
R.W. Benson, 567:Vol73No1/2–157
Goodridge, C. Hints and Disguises.
B. Costello, 705:Fall89–233
Goodsell, C.T. The Social Meaning of Civic
Space.*
J.L. Meikle, 658:Summer/Autumn89–196
Goodwin, J., ed. British Theatre Design: The
Modern Age.
M. Vaizey, 324:Apr90–375
Goodwin, K. A History of Australian Litera-
ture.
M. Wilding, 506(PSt):May87–123
Goodwyn, J. Edith Wharton.
H. Lee, 617(TLS):25–31May90–547
Goody, J. The Interface between the Written
and the Oral.*
W.C. Watt, 567:Vol75No3/4–279
Goody, J. The Oriental, the Ancient and the
Primitive.
H. Baker, 617(TLS):21–27Sep90–1008
Gool, R. Cape Town Coolie.
M. Jaggi, 617(TLS):7–13Dec90–1326
Goonetilleke, D.C.R.A. Images of the Raj.*
H. Orel, 177(ELT):Vol32No2–214
Gopen, G.D. – see Henryson, R.
Gorak, J. The Alien Mind of Raymond Wil-
liams.
P. Parrinder, 395(MFS):Winter89–821
Gordimer, N. My Son's Story.
G. Annan, 453(NYRB):8Nov90–8
R. Coles, 441:21Oct90–1
D. Papineau, 617(TLS):28Sep–4Oct90–
1037
Gordon, A. & V. Virga, eds. Summer.
H. Rubin, 441:17Jun90–17
Gordon, C.A. A Bibliography of Lucretius.
517(PBSA):Mar89–122
Gordon, D. – see Davies, M.
Gordon, D.R. The Justice Juggernaut.
R.G. Powers, 441:6May90–7
Gordon, E.A. Mark the Music.*
P. O'Connor, 617(TLS):5–11Jan90–14
H. Robinson, 34:Dec89–44
Gordon, F.D. After Winning.
E.I. Perry, 106:Fall89–223
Gordon, G. & D. Hughes, eds. Best Short Sto-
ries, 1989.
D. Durrant, 364:Dec89/Jan90–134
Gordon, H. Dance, Dialogue, and Despair.
J.F. Post, 323:Jan89–98
Gordon, J. "Finnegans Wake."*
B. Benstock, 177(ELT):Vol32No2–264
M.P.L., 295(JML):Fall88/Winter89–358
M.J. O'Shea, 403(MLS):Spring89–78
Gordon, J. She Drove Without Stopping.
M. Spanier, 441:19Aug90–18
Gordon, K.E. Intimate Apparel.
S. Moore, 532(RCF):Summer89–257
Gordon, L. Eliot's Early Years.
W. Bedford, 4:Summer89–70
Gordon, L. Eliot's New Life.*
W. Bedford, 4:Summer89–70
S. Schwartz, 432(NEQ):Sep89–445
Gordon, M. The Other Side.*
S. Mackay, 617(TLS):26Jan–1Feb90–87
J. Thurman, 442(NY):12Mar90–97

Gordon, R.M. The Structure of Emotions.*
M. Cavell, 311(JP):Sep89–493
C.B. McCullagh, 63:Mar89–107
Gordon, S., ed. A Talent for Tomorrow.
C.B. Davies, 128(CE):Jan89–88
Gore, K. – see Sartre, J–P.
Gorelov, A.A., ed. Russkaja literatura i
fol'klor (konec XIX veka).
D.C. Nisula, 574(SEEJ):Fall89–455
Gori, L. & S. Lucarelli. Vocabolario pisto-
iese.* (G. Giacomelli, ed)
P. Manni, 708:Vol12Fasc1–141
Goring, E. A Mischievous Pastime.
D. Hunt, 123:Vol39No1–111
Görisch, R., ed. Perspektiven der Romantik.
H.M.K. Riley, 133:Band22Heft2–165
Gor'kii, M. Iz literaturnogo naslediia.
G. Donchin, 575(SEER):Apr89–280
Görlach, M., ed. Focus on: Scotland.
A. Agutter, 260(IF):Band94–365
Görlach, M. – see Busch, W.
Gorlanov, L.R. Udel'nye krest'iane Rossii
1797–1865 gg.
T.S. Pearson, 550(RusR):Apr89–185
Gorman, J. The Total Penguin.
D. Ackerman, 441:2Dec90–32
Gorman, T.P., A.C. Purves & R.E. Degenhart,
eds. The IEA Study of Written Composition
I.
K.L. Greenberg, 126(CCC):May89–244
Görner, R., ed. Rainer Maria Rilke.
G.C. Schoolfield, 133:Band22Heft3/4–353
Gorny, Y. Zionism and the Arabs, 1882–1948.
N. Heiwan, 390:Jun/Jul89–60
Görög, V. – see Berki, J.
van Gorp, H., ed. Dialogeren met Bakhtin.
W. van Peer, 204(FdL):Mar89–58
Gorst, T., L. Johnman & W.S. Lucas, eds.
Post–war Britain, 1945–64.
B. Appleyard, 617(TLS):9–15Feb90–142
de Gortari, E. Diccionario de la lógica.
A. Guy, 542:Oct–Dec89–650
Gorz, A. Critique of Economic Reason.*
(French title: Métamorphoses du travail.)
P. Kellner, 324:Apr90–370
S. Khilnani, 617(TLS):2–8Mar90–221
Gorz, A. The Traitor. (rev)
S. Khilnani, 617(TLS):2–8Mar90–221
Goscilo, H., ed. Balancing Acts.*
Z. Smardz, 441:21Jan90–20
Goscilo, H. – see Nagibin, Y.
Goscilo, H. & B. Lindsey, eds. Glasnost.
J. Naughton, 617(TLS):14–20Dec90–1357
Gose, E. Mere Creatures.
A. Kertzer, 178:Sep89–352
Goslee, N.M. Scott the Rhymer.
639(VQR):Summer89–87
Goslee, N.M. Uriel's Eye.
J.A.W. Heffernan, 591(SIR):Spring89–156
Gössling, A. Thomas Bernhards frühe Prosa-
kunst.
L.C. De Meritt, 133:Band22Heft3/4–380
Gostin, L., ed. Civil Liberties in Conflict.
B.M.B., 185:Apr90–694
"Gothic and Renaissance Art in Nuremberg,
1300–1550."
J.C. Smith, 589:Jan89–166
"Gotland, tausend Jahre Kultur– und Wirt-
schaftsgeschichte im Ostseeraum."
R. Zeitler, 341:Vol58No4–175
Gotlieb, P. & D. Barbour, eds. Tesseracts².
C. Dean, 102(CanL):Summer89–164

143

Gottcent, J.H. The Bible.*
  D.L. Jeffrey, 627(UTQ):Summer90-569
Gottfried, M. All His Jazz.
  R. Bryden, 441:16Dec90-17
Gottfried, R.S. Doctors and Medicine in Medieval England, 1340-1530.
  M.R. McVaugh, 589:Jan89-168
Gottfried von Strassburg. Tristan und Isolde. (F.G. Gentry, ed)
  A. Classen, 133:Band22Heft3/4-308
Gotthelf, A., ed. Aristotle on Nature and Living Things.*
  G. Haist, 123:Vol39No1-45
Gotthelf, A. & J.G. Lennox, eds. Philosophical. Issues in Aristotle's Biology.*
  G. Haist, 123:Vol39No1-47
  J.M. Rist, 487:Summer89-186
Gottschall, E.M. Typographic Communications Today.*
  P.B. Meggs, 507:Sep/Oct89-174
Göttsche, D. Die Produktivität der Sprachkrise in der modernen Prosa.
  E. Bredeck, 221(GQ):Summer89-399
Gottwald, N.K. The Hebrew Bible.
  J.A. Soggin, 318(JAOS):Jul-Sep88-523
Götze, K-H. Wolfgang Koeppen: "Das Treibhaus."
  P.F. Dvorak, 221(GQ):Summer89-424
van Goudoever, A.P. The Limits of Destalinization in the Soviet Union.*
  S. White, 575(SEER):Apr89-328
Gouhier, H. L'Anti-humanisme au XVIIe siècle.*
  L. Armour, 319:Apr90-299
  G. Malbreil, 535(RHL):Jan-Feb89-106
Gould, C., ed. The Information Web.
  K. Shrader-Frechette, 103:Mar90-110
Gould, C.C. Rethinking Democracy.*
  P. Morriss, 518:Oct89-248
  J. Narveson, 258:Dec89-473
  R. Norman, 291:Vol6No2-235
Gould, J.M. & B.A. Goldman, with K. Millpointer. Deadly Deceit.
  G. Garelik, 441:22Jul90-15
Gould, L.L. & C.H. Roell, eds. William McKinley.
  C.E. Wunderlin, Jr., 87(BB):Sep89-207
Gould, P.C. Early Green Politics.
  J. Greenfield, 637(VS):Winter90-366
Gould, S.J. Time's Arrow, Time's Cycle.*
  R.A. Dodgshon, 242:Vol10No1-104
  J.B. Waugh, 577(SHR):Spring89-173
Gould, S.J. Wonderful Life.*
  R.C. Lewontin, 453(NYRB):14Jun90-3
  J. Secord, 617(TLS):4-10May90-477
Gould, W. - see "Yeats Annual"
Goulder, M.D. Luke.
  J.L. Houlden, 617(TLS):9-15Mar90-260
Goulet, A. Fiction et vie sociale dans l'oeuvre d'André Gide.*
  P. Schnyder, 602:Band20Heft1-141
Goulet, R. La Philosophie de Moïse.
  É. des Places, 555:Vol62Fasc1-153
Goulet-Cazé, M-O. L'ascèse cynique.*
  R. Ferwerda, 394:Vol42fasc1/2-211
  C. Guérard, 192(EP):Jan-Mar89-102
  M.G. Sollenberger, 41:Fall89-328
Gourevitch, V. - see Rousseau, J-J.
de Gournay, M. Fragments d'un discours féminin. (E. Dezon-Jones, ed)
  I. Maclean, 208(FS):Apr89-205
Gove, A.F. The Slavic Akathistos Hymn.
  M. Matejić, 574(SEEJ):Winter89-618

Govenar, A. Meeting the Blues.
  B.L. Cooper, 498:Fall89-102
  E.S., 91:Vol17-194
Gover, C.J. The Positive Image.
  J. Loughery, 662:Fall89/Winter90-48
Govier, K. Between Men.
  P. Koster, 102(CanL):Summer89-188
Govier, T. God, The Devil and the Perfect Pizza.
  A.R. Drengson, 103:Jul90-268
Gowans, L. Cei and the Arthurian Legend.
  M. McCarthy, 447(N&Q):Dec89-497
  P. Noble, 402(MLR):Oct90-897
Gowdy, B. Falling Angels.
  M. Pritchard, 441:27May90-14
Gowers, E. The Complete Plain Words. (rev by S. Greenbaum & J. Whitcut)
  J.W. Ney, 126(CCC):Dec89-489
Gowers, R. Emily Carr.*
  G. Deer, 102(CanL):Spring89-150
Gowing, L. & others. Cézanne: The Early Years, 1859-72.
  R. Cranshaw & A. Lewis, 59:Mar89-129
Gowing, P., ed. Understanding Islam and Muslims in the Philippines.
  G.C. Bentley, 293(JASt):Nov89-935
Goy, R.J. Venetian Vernacular Architecture.
  P. Tabor, 617(TLS):5-11Jan90-15
Goyard-Fabre, S. & R. Sève. Les grandes questions de la philosophie du droit.*
  M. Bastit, 192(EP):Jul-Dec89-540
Goyen, W. Had I a Hundred Mouths.
  P. Lewis, 565:Winter88/89-77
Goyet, F. - see Tabourot, E.
Goyon, J-C. Les Dieux-gardiens et la Genèse de Temples.
  V. Condon, 318(JAOS):Jan-Mar88-149
Goytisolo, J. Juan the Landless.
  A.L. Six, 617(TLS):29Jun-5Jul90-704
Goytisolo, J. Realms of Strife.
  P.J. Smith, 617(TLS):7-13Dec90-1308
Goytisolo, J. Las virtudes del pájaro solitario.
  G.J. Pérez, 238:Sep89-551
Gozak, A. & A. Leonidov. Ivan Leonidov. (C. Cooke, ed)
  D.D. Boles, 505:Apr89-121
  C. Lodder, 90:Sep89-647
Grabar, O. The Formation of Islamic Art. (rev)
  R. Hillenbrand, 463:Spring89-46
Grabar, O. The Illustrations of the Maqamat.
  R. Hillenbrand, 59:Mar89-109
Grabar, O. - see "Muqarnas"
Grabowski, Y., ed. Essays in Polish History and Culture. (Vol 1)
  D. Stone, 104(CASS):Spring89-118
Grace, G.W. The Linguistic Construction of Reality.
  H.R. Battersby, 350:Sep90-635
Gracia, J.J.E. Individuality.*
  J.M.N., 185:Oct89-212
  R. Schumacher, 679:Band20Heft1-162
Gracia, J.J.E., ed. Latin American Philosophy in the Twentieth Century.
  A. Guy, 542:Oct-Dec89-611
Gracia, J.J.E. & I. Jaksic, eds. Filosofía e identidad cultural en América Latina.*
  J.L. Gómez-Martínez, 238:Sep89-558
"Gracián y su época."
  J. Checa, 240(HR):Winter89-97

Gracq, J. Autour des sept collines.*
  F. George, 98:Mar89-115
  D. Pobel, 450(NRF):Mar89-80
  J-P.H. Tétart, 450(NRF):Mar89-82
Graddol, D. & J. Swann. Gender Voices.
  L. Hudson, 617(TLS):9-15Mar90-243
Gradon, P., ed. English Wycliffite Sermons.
  (Vol 2)
  S. Wenzel, 447(N&Q):Sep89-370
Graebner, W. The Engineering of Consent.
  K. Cassidy, 106:Summer89-140
Graf, K. Exemplarische Geschichten.
  C. Daxelmüller, 196:Band30Heft3/4-322
Graf, K. Gmünder Chroniken im 16. Jahrhun-
  dert.*
  K. Gärtner, 680(ZDP):Band108Heft1-128
Graff, G. Professing Literature.*
  K. Cmiel, 271:Winter89-175
  R.G. Collins, 529(QQ):Winter89-948
  M.E. Hazard, 295(JML):Fall88/Winter89-
  176
  J. McGowan, 577(SHR):Spring89-168
  J. Seaton, 580(SCR):Spring90-149
Graff, G. & R. Gibbons, eds. Criticism in the
  University.
  N. Bruss, 128(CE):Jan89-95
Grafton, A. Forgers and Critics.
  H.R. Trevor-Roper, 453(NYRB):6Dec90-26
Grafton, A., G.W. Most & J.E.G. Zetzel - see
  Wolf, F.A.
Grafton, S. "G" is for Gumshoe.
  A. Kozinski, 441:27May90-13
Graham, A.C. Disputers of the Tao. Studies
  in Chinese Philosophy and Philosophical
  Literature.
  T.H. Barrett, 617(TLS):21-27Dec90-1380
Graham, C. Death of a Hollow Man.*
  M. Stasio, 441:4Feb90-26
Graham, D. No Name on the Bullet.*
  C. Reynolds, 649(WAL):Feb90-381
Graham, D.W. Aristotle's Two Systems.
  W. Charlton, 303(JoHS):Vol109-234
  M. Durrant, 518:Jan89-16
  D.W. Hamlyn, 483:Apr89-261
  T.M. Olshewsky, 319:Jul90-439
Graham, E. & others. Her Own Life.
  I. Maclean, 617(TLS):1-7Jun90-587
Graham, F. Happy Talk
  M.C. Janeway, 441:11Mar90-23
Graham, G. Politics in its Place.*
  P. Livet, 192(EP):Jan-Mar89-103
Graham, H. & P. Preston, eds. The Popular
  Front in Europe.
  D.S. Bell, 242:Vol10No2-260
Graham, H.D. The Civil Rights Era.
  D.L. Kirp, 441:22Apr90-43
Graham, I. Goethe.
  C.P. Magill, 402(MLR):Apr90-506
Graham, J. The End of Beauty.*
  R. Jackson, 502(PrS):Fall89-117
Graham, K. Indirections of the Novel.*
  J. Batchelor, 402(MLR):Jan90-157
  B.G. Caraher, 637(VS):Spring90-527
  D.L. Higdon, 177(ELT):Vol32No3-329
Graham, K.W. & N. Johnson, eds. Man and
  Nature.
  K.E. Smith, 83:Autumn89-227
Graham, L. Rebuilding the House.
  N. Perrin, 441:8Jul90-9
Graham, R. Patronage and Politics in Nine-
  teenth Century Brazil.
  P. Cammack, 617(TLS):9-15Nov90-1211

Graham, S.D., ed. Nikolaj Gumilev 1886-1986.
  N. Pollak, 104(CASS):Spring-Winter88-
  434
  A. Pyman, 575(SEER):Oct89-627
  D. Rayfield, 402(MLR):Apr90-539
Graham, W.S. Uncollected Poems.
  C. Hurford, 617(TLS):21-27Dec90-1383
Graham-Brown, S. Images of Women.
  A.E. Coombes & S. Edwards, 59:Dec89-
  510
Grainger, A. The Threatening Desert.
  A. de Waal, 617(TLS):28Sep-4Oct90-1044
Grainger, J.D. The Cities of Seleukid Syria.
  S. Hornblower, 617(TLS):15-21Jun90-648
Gram, M.S., ed. Kant: Disputed Questions.
  (2nd ed)
  R.M., 342:Band80Heft4-498
Gramlich, R. Die Wunder der Freunde Gottes.
  B. Hoffmann, 196:Band30Heft3/4-324
Granada, M.A. Cosmología, religión y política
  en el Renacimiento.
  A. Reix, 542:Oct-Dec89-595
Grancelli, B. Soviet Management and Labor
  Relations.
  A. Åslund, 575(SEER):Apr89-319
de Granda, G. Lingüística e historia.
  L. Hart-Gonzalez, 350:Jun90-413
  J.M. Lipski, 239:Fall89-309
de Granda Gutiérrez, G. Estudios de Lingüís-
  tica Afro-Románica.*
  P. Thiele, 682(ZPSK):Band42Heft6-867
Grandbois, A. Lettres à Lucienne.
  V. Raoul, 102(CanL):Autumn-Winter89-
  249
Grandguillaume, G. Arabisation et politique
  linguistique au Maghreb.
  A. Allouche, 355(LSoc):Sep89-411
Grandin, J.M. Kafka's Prussian Advocate.*
  L. Dietrick, 564:Sep89-276
  P. Perry, 406:Summer89-272
Granfield, D. The Inner Experience of Law.
  J. Boyle, 103:Aug90-316
Granger, B. League of Terror.
  N. Callendar, 441:18Nov90-41
Granger, G-G. Pour la connaissance philoso-
  phique.
  A. Jacob, 192(EP):Jan-Mar89-104
Granick, D. Job Rights in the Soviet Union.
  W. Moskoff, 550(RusR):Oct89-434
  J.L. Porket, 575(SEER):Oct89-651
Granin, D. The Bison.
  O. Wickerhauser, 441:3Jun90-22
Grannes, A. Loan Compounds in Bulgarian
  Reflecting the Turkish Indefinite Izafet-
  Construction.
  V. Friedman, 104(CASS):Spring-Win-
  ter88-517
Gransden, K.W. Virgil: "The Aeneid."
  R. Jenkyns, 617(TLS):23-29Nov90-1268
Grant, B.K., ed. Planks of Reason.
  K. Newman, 707:Winter88/89-68
Grant, E. Memoirs of a Highland Lady. (A.
  Tod, ed)
  J.H. Alexander, 571(ScLJ):Winter89-18
Grant, J. Encyclopedia of Walt Disney's Ani-
  mated Characters.
  J. Canemaker, 507:Mar/Apr89-147
Grant, J.N. Studies in the Textual Tradition
  of Terence.*
  B.A. Victor, 122:Jul89-260
  M.M. Willcock, 313:Vol79-187
Grant, L. Blind Trust.
  M. Stasio, 441:24Jun90-22

Grant, M. The Rise of the Greeks.*
  N.G.L. Hammond, 123:Vol39No1-64
  C.G. Starr, 487:Summer89-187
  I. Weiler, 229:Band61Heft7-631
  639(VQR):Winter89-7
Grant, M. & R. Kitzinger, eds. Civilization of
  the Ancient Mediterranean.*
  C.F. Natunewicz, 124:Sep-Oct89-60
Grant, P. Reading the New Testament.*
  D.L. Jeffrey, 627(UTQ):Summer90-569
Grant, R.W. John Locke's Liberalism.
  R. Ashcraft, 319:Jan90-133
Grant, U.S. Ulysses S. Grant: Memoirs and
  Selected Letters. (M.D. & W.S. McFeely,
  eds)
  G.W. Gallagher, 441:21Oct90-12
  C.V. Woodward, 453(NYRB):8Nov90-29
Grant-Adamson, L. Curse the Darkness.
  P. Craig, 617(TLS):16-22Mar90-298
Grantham, D.W. The Life and Death of the
  Solid South.
  639(VQR):Summer89-81
Granville, H. A Second Self. (V. Surtees, ed)
  B. Fothergill, 617(TLS):29Jun-5Jul90-
  693
Granville-Barker, H. Plays by Harley Gran-
  ville Barker.* (D. Kennedy, ed)
  G. Bas, 189(EA):Oct-Dec89-487
  B. Henderson, 177(ELT):Vol32No1-93
  P. Mudford, 447(N&Q):Jun89-255
  J. Stokes, 677(YES):Vol20-321
Granzotto, G. Christopher Columbus.
  A. Classen, 201:Vol15-330
Grasby, R. Lettercutting in Stone.
  M. Harvey, 324:May90-443
Grass, G. Deutscher Lastenausgleich.
  P. Graves, 617(TLS):15-21Jun90-631
Grass, G. Show Your Tongue.*
  A. Ross, 364:Oct/Nov89-138
Grass, G. Two States - One Nation?
  R. Dahrendorf, 441:30Sep90-9
Grassi, C.A. - see William of Ockham
Grathoff, R., ed. Philosophers in Exile.
  E.F. Kaelin, 103:Dec90-498
Grattarola, P. Un libello antiaugusteo.
  F. Trisoglio, 229:Band61Heft7-624
Grattius. Il "Cynegeticon" di Grattio. (C.
  Formicola, ed & trans)
  N. Horsfall, 123:Vol39No2-213
Gratwick, A.S. - see Terence
Gratz, R.B. The Living City.*
  D. Gantenbein, 45:Jul89-67
  P. Goodman, 47:Sep89-49
Gratzer, W., ed. The Longman Literary Com-
  panion to Science.
  J.A.V. Chapple, 617(TLS):27Apr-3May90-
  452
Grauerholz, J. - see Burroughs, W.
Graulich, M. - see Austin, M.
Grave, S.A. Conscience in Newman's Thought.
  B. Martin, 617(TLS):7-13Dec90-1330
Grave, S.A. A History of Philosophy in Aus-
  tralia.
  J.J.C. Smart, 63:Sep89-345
Gravel, F. Benito.
  N. Bishop, 102(CanL):Winter88-113
Graves, J. The Last Running.
  P-L. Adams, 61:Jul90-105
Graves, R.P. Robert Graves.* (Vol 1)
  M.A. Davis, 295(JML):Fall88/Winter89-
  340

Graves, R.P. Robert Graves. (Vol 2)
  P-L. Adams, 61:Dec90-131
  P. Kemp, 617(TLS):3-9Aug90- 820
  L. Simpson, 441:11Nov90-3
Gravil, R., L. Newlyn & N. Roe, eds. Cole-
  ridge's Imagination.*
  A.C. Goodson, 591(SIR):Spring89-170
Gray, A. Saltire Self-Portraits 4.
  J.C. Hall, 571(ScLJ):Spring89-33
Gray, A. Something Leather. McGrotty and
  Ludmilla, or The Harbinger Report.
  G. Mangan, 617(TLS):6-12Jul90-731
Gray, B. George Eliot and Music.
  A. Jacobs, 617(TLS):9-15Mar90-256
Gray, B. Studies in Chinese and Islamic Art.
  (Vol 2)
  R. Hillenbrand, 463:Spring89-47
Gray, C. The Geo-Politics of Super Power.
  639(VQR):Winter89-24
Gray, C.S. Klaus Rifbjerg.*
  L. Isaacson, 563(SS):Spring/Summer89-
  285
Gray, D. - see Bennett, J.A.W.
Gray, D. - see Coghill, N.
Gray, D. - see "The Oxford Book of Late
  Medieval Verse and Prose"
Gray, F. La Bruyère amateur de caractères.*
  J. Barchilon, 207(FR):Mar90-709
Gray, F.D. Soviet Women.
  R. Daniloff, 441:11Mar90-7
  T. Tolstaya, 453(NYRB):31May90-3
Gray, J. Liberalisms.*
  B. Barry, 358:Feb90-6
Gray, J. Local Boy Makes Good.
  R. Nunn, 108:Winter89-82
Gray, J. The Poems of John Gray.* (I. Flet-
  cher, ed)
  A. Brown, 637(VS):Autumn89-202
  E. Gilcher, 177(ELT):Vol32No1-86
Gray, J.A. & D.S. Lee, eds. The Federal Cyl-
  inder Project.* (Vol 2)
  D.P. McAllester, 187:Winter89-149
Gray, N. The Paintings of David Jones.*
  M.I. James, 90:Nov89-790
Gray, R. The Imperative of Modernity.*
  639(VQR):Autumn89-126
Gray, R. The King's Wife.
  B. Fothergill, 617(TLS):4-10May90-464
Gray, R. Piano.
  R. Crawford, 493:Autumn89-23
Gray, R. Writing the South.*
  J.A.L. Lemay, 677(YES):Vol20-226
  W. Taylor, 301(JEGP):Jan89-133
Gray, S., ed. The Penguin Book of Southern
  African Verse.
  S. Watson, 617(TLS):18-24May90-533
Gray, V. The Character of Xenophon's Hel-
  lenica.
  P. Krentz, 124:Jul-Aug90-531
Gray Díaz, N. Metamorphosis to Animal Form
  in Modern Latin American Narrative.
  P. Hart, 395(MFS):Winter89-778
Grayling, A.C. Berkeley.*
  W. Doney, 482(PhR):Oct89-545
Grayling, A.C. Wittgenstein.*
  G. Gillett, 521:Apr89-187
  M. Proudfoot, 518:Oct89-215
Grayson, D.A. The Genesis of Debussy's "Pel-
  léas et Mélisande."
  R. Nichols, 410(M&L):Nov89-569
Grayson, J. & F. Wigzell, eds. Nikolay Gogol.
  H. McLean, 574(SEEJ):Fall89-453

de Grazia, S. Machiavelli in Hell.*
   N. Rubinstein, 617(TLS):19-25Jan90-70
Gréban, A. Le Mystère de la Passion. (M. de
   Combarieu du Grès & J. Subrenat, eds)
   G.A. Runnalls, 208(FS):Jan89-76
Greco, E. & D. Theodorescu, with others.
   Poseidonia-Paestum III, Forum Nord.
   R.M. Harrison, 313:Vol79-179
   D. Mertens, 229:Band61Heft3-235
Grecu, V.V., ed. Astra 1861-1950.
   D. Deletant, 575(SEER):Apr89-275
Greeley, A.M. All About Women.
   A. Solomon, 441:7Jan90-18
Greeley, A.M. The Catholic Myth.
   R.S. Warner, 441:22Apr90-9
Greeley, A.M. The Search for Maggie Ward.
   K. Ramsland, 441:30Dec90-14
Greeley, A.M. & J. Neusner. The Bible and Us.
   P. Zaleski, 441:2Sep90-9
Greeley, R.E., ed. The Best of Humanism.
   J.G.C., 185:Oct89-215
Green, A. Education and State Formation.
   T. Judt, 617(TLS):14-20Sep90-967
Green, C. Cubism and its Enemies.*
   D. Cottington, 90:Mar89-224
   N.V. Halliday, 39:Sep89-212
Green, E. Banking.
   R.A. Bennett, 441:6May90-16
Green, G. Freud and Nabokov.
   G. Comnes, 532(RCF):Summer89-256
   C. Ross, 395(MFS):Summer89-295
Green, G.K. & J.L. Ornstein-Galicia, eds.
   Mexican-American Language.
   S.N. Cynan, 000:Mar00-169
Green, J. L'Arc-en-ciel.
   R. Stanley, 207(FR):Oct89-206
Green, J. Them.
   I. Buruma, 617(TLS):12-18Oct90-1096
Green, J.A. The Government of England
   under Henry I.
   T.N. Bisson, 589:Apr89-436
Green, J.C.R., A. Rowe & S.M. Hastie, eds &
   trans. Troubled Times.
   G. Connell, 86(BHS):Jul89-297
Green, J.L. & J.O. Harker, eds. Multiple Per-
   spective Analyses of Classroom Discourse.
   E.D. Kuhn, 350:Jun90-415
Green, J.R. Corpus Vasorum Antiquorum.
   (U.S.A., fasc 22)
   B.A. Sparkes, 303(JoHS):Vol109-269
Green, L. The Authority of the State.*
   N. Johnson, 483:Oct89-566
Green, L. Castruccio Castracani.
   W. Gundersheimer, 589:Jan89-171
   J.N. Stephens, 278(IS):Vol43-150
Green, L.D. - see Rainold, J.
Green, M. The Mount Vernon Street Warrens.
   M.S. Kennedy, 441:3Jun90-28
Green, M. The Squanicook Eclogues.
   J. Parini, 473(PR):Vol56No3-510
Green, M.J. Fiction in the Historical Pre-
   sent.*
   D. Schier, 569(SR):Summer89-lxxxviii
Green, O. Art for the London Underground.
   Y.A. Andrews, 441:24Jun90-21
Green, P. Classical Bearings.
   J. Griffin, 617(TLS):23Feb-1Mar90-200
Green, R.M. Religion and Moral Reason.
   P.L. Quinn, 185:Jan90-418
Green-Pedersen, N.J. The Tradition of the
   "Topics" in the Middle Ages.*
   E.P. Bos, 640:May89-81
   N. Lewis, 41:Spring89-147

Greenawalt, K. Religious Convictions and
   Political Choice.
   R. Audi, 185:Jan90-386
Greenaway, P. Fear of Drowning by Numbers.
   J. Roudaut, 450(NRF):Mar89-92
Greenbaum, S. & R. Quirk. A Student's Gram-
   mar of the English Language.
   T. Shippey, 617(TLS):19-25Oct90-1117
Greenbaum, S. & J. Whitcut - see Gowers, E.
Greenberg, C. The Collected Essays of Clem-
   ent Greenberg.* (Vols 1 & 2) (J. O'Brian,
   ed)
   F. Murphy, 569(SR):Summer89-lxxviii
   M. Welish, 473(PR):Vol56No2-301
Greenberg, J.H. Language in the Americas.
   W.F.H. Adelaar, 361:Jul89-249
Greenberg, M. Corneille, Classicism and the
   Ruses of Symmetry.*
   L.W. Riggs, 345(KRQ):Feb89-108
Greenbie, B.B. Space and Spirit in Modern
   Japan.
   H.D. Smith 2d, 293(JASt):Nov89-860
Greenblatt, S., ed. Representing the English
   Renaissance.*
   D. Bevington, 405(MP):May90-400
   J.K. Gardiner, 405(MP):Aug89-83
   M.L. Hall, 569(SR):Summer89-456
   G.W. Pigman 3d, 250(HLQ):Autumn89-501
Greenblatt, S. Shakespearean Negotiations.*
   D. Bevington, 405(MP):Feb90-295
   J. Drakakis, 447(N&Q):Dec89-503
   T. Healy, 567:Sep89-339
   G. Holderness, 402(MLR):Jan90-141
   S. Mullaney, 570(SQ):Winter89-495
   G.W. Pigman 3d, 250(HLQ):Autumn89-501
   D. Porter, 610:Spring89-88
Greenburg, D. Exes.
   B. Levine, 441:21Jan90-9
Greene, A.C. Taking Heart.
   G. Weissmann, 441:8Jul90-10
Greene, D. Insidious Intent.
   G. Kalbouss, 104(CASS):Spring-Winter88-
   462
Greene, D. The Politics of Samuel Johnson.
   617(TLS):24-30Aug90-905
Greene, G. The Captain and the Enemy.*
   J. Mills, 648(WCR):Vol23No2-77
   42(AR):Winter89-114
Greene, G. The Last Word and Other Stories.
   M. Illis, 617(TLS):13-19Jul90-746
Greene, G. Reflections. (J. Adamson, ed)
   C. Hitchens, 617(TLS):21-27Sep90-997
Greene, G. Yours Etc.* (C. Hawtree, ed)
   A. Whitehouse, 441:27May90-15
Greene, J. A Sad Paradise.
   J. Le Saux, 617(TLS):7-13Sep90-954
Greene, J.C. - see Thomson, J.
Greene, J.P., ed. The American Revolution.
   R. Hoffman, 656(WMQ):Apr89-402
Greene, J.P. Pursuits of Happiness.*
   M. Kammen, 432(NEQ):Dec89-639
   639(VQR):Summer89-79
Greene, K. The Archaeology of the Roman
   Economy.*
   K.D. White, 123:Vol39No2-311
Greene, M. The Dialectic of Freedom.
   W.A.D., 185:Apr90-696
Greene, T.L. The Vulnerable Text.
   A.D. Hall, 604:Fall87-61
Greenfeld, J. What Happened Was This.
   F. Wilson, 441:7Oct90-40

Greenfield, J. The Return of Cultural Treasures.
A.C. Danto, 617(TLS):16-22Mar90-286
K.E. Meyer, 441:18Feb90-7
Greenfield, S.B. & D.G. Calder. A New Critical History of Old English Literature.*
H. Gneuss, 38:Band107Heft1/2-149
P.E. Szarmach, 589:Jan89-173
Greengard, C. The Structure of Pindar's Epinician Odes.
L. Pernot, 555:Vol62Fasc2-334
Greenhill, B. & A. Giffard. The British Assault on Finland 1854-1855.
D. Kirby, 575(SEER):Oct89-630
Greenidge, A.H.J. & A.M. Clay, comps. Sources for Roman History 133-70 B.C.
S. Jackson, 235:Summer89-76
Greenwald, E. Realism and the Romance.
L.S. Person, Jr., 27(AL):Dec89-692
K. Vanderbilt, 26(ALR):Spring90-91
Greenwood, J. Shifting Perspectives and the Stylish Style.
L. Gent, 551(RenQ):Summer89-361
A. Kirsch, 405(MP):May90-408
J.V. Mirollo, 401(MLQ):Mar88-76
J. Orrell, 402(MLR):Jul90-694
L. Thomson, 627(UTQ):Fall89-123
Greenwood, L.B. Sherlock Holmes and the Case of Sabina Hall.
639(VQR):Winter89-22
Greer, A. Peasant, Lord, and Merchant.
Y. Frenette, 298:Fall89-140
Greer, G. Daddy, We Hardly Knew You.*
P-L. Adams, 61:Feb90-108
K. Fraser, 442(NY):16Apr90-116
J. Johnston, 441:28Jan90-7
J. Symons, 364:Apr/May89-143
Greer, G. Shakespeare.*
A.F. Kinney, 481(PQ):Fall89-443
K. Tetzeli von Rosador, 156(ShJW):Jahrbuch1989-351
Greer, M.R., with L.K. Stein — see Calderón de la Barca, P.
Gregg, E. The Protestant Succession in International Politics, 1710-1716.
H.M. Scott, 83:Spring89-95
Gregg, K.C. An Index to the Teatro Español Collection in the Biblioteca de Palacio.
S.B. Whitaker, 238:Mar89-142
Grégoire, H-B. L'Abbé Grégoire, éveque des lumières. (F.P. Bowman, ed)
L. Loft, 446(NCFS):Spring-Summer90-559
Grégoire, M. La France et ses immigrés.
A.J.M. Prévos, 207(FR):Oct89-186
Gregor, A. Secret Citizen.
J.F. Cotter, 249(HudR):Autumn89-521
Gregor, F. Die alte ungarische und slowakische Bergbauterminologie mit ihren deutschen Bezügen.*
J. Schütz, 688(ZSP):Band49Heft2-430
Gregorio, L.A. Order in the Court.
D. Beyerle, 547(RF):Band101Heft2/3-340
J. Chupeau, 535(RHL):Jul-Aug89-712
D. Kuizenga, 475:Vol16No30-290
H. Mydlarski, 345(KRQ):Nov89-489
Lady Gregory. Lady Gregory's Journals. (Vol 2) (D.J. Murphy, ed)
R.C. Petersen, 177(ELT):Vol32No2-245
Master Gregory. Magister Gregorius, "The Marvels of Rome." (J. Osborne, trans)
D. Kinney, 589:Oct89-959

Saint Gregory I. Grégoire le Grand, Commentaire sur le Cantique des Cantiques. (R. Bélanger, ed & trans)
M. Reydellet, 555:Vol62Fasc1-168
Gregory, P.N., ed. Traditions of Meditation in Chinese Buddhism.*
P.J. Griffiths, 318(JAOS):Apr-Jun88-346
Greider, W. The Trouble with Money.
J. Taylor, 441:14Jan90-10
Greif, H.K. Historia de Nacimientos.
R.C. Manteiga, 140(CH):Vol11No1&2-120
Greig, A. The Order of the Day.
L. Norfolk, 617(TLS):1-7Jun90-584
Greilsamer, L. Hubert Beuve-Méry.
P. McCarthy, 617(TLS):5-11Oct90-1078
Greimas, A.J. On Meaning.
W.O. Hendricks, 567:Vol75No1/2-95
Greiner, D.J. Domestic Particulars.
E. Carroll, 395(MFS):Winter89-761
Grenberg, B.L. Some Other World to Find.
M. Fisher, 268(IFR):Winter90-67
Grene, D. The Actor in History.
A. Leggatt, 570(SQ):Winter89-511
Grenfell, J. The Time of My Life. (J. Roose-Evans, ed)
A. Chisholm, 617(TLS):2-8Mar90-218
Grenier, R. Pascal Pia ou le droit au Néant.
J. Piel, 98:May89-395
Grennan, E. What Light There Is & Other Poems.
A. Corn, 491:Jan90-287
Grensemann, H. Knidische Medizin.* (Pt 2)
L.A. Jones, 24:Spring89-164
Grenville, K. Joan Makes History.*
M. Hardie, 581:Mar89-113
Grenzmann, L., H. Herkommer & D. Wuttke, eds. Philologie als Kulturwissenschaft.
M. Wehrli, 684(ZDA):Band118Heft1-1
du Grès, M.D. & J. Subrenat — see under de Combarieu du Grès, M. & J. Subrenat
Gresham, D.H. Lenten Lands.
639(VQR):Summer89-88
Gresset, M. Fascination.
M. Backman, 395(MFS):Winter89-751
D.M. Kartiganer, 392:Summer89-317
Gresset, M. & K. Ohashi, eds. Faulkner: After the Nobel Prize.*
C.S. Brown, 569(SR):Fall89-556
M. Kreiswirth, 27(AL):Mar89-125
Greub, S., ed. Expressions of Belief.
N. Barley, 39:Nov89-360
N. Barley, 39:Dec89-433
J. Povey, 2(AfrA):May89-27
Greussing, K., ed. Die Roten am Land.
E. Hobsbawm, 358:Jun90-10
Grévy-Pons, N., E. Ornato & G. Ouy — see de Montreuil, J.
Grew, F. & M. de Neergaard. Shoes and Pattens.
L. von Wilckens, 683:Band52Heft2-293
Grewe, K. Atlas der römischen Wasserleitungen nach Köln.
H. Fahlbusch, 229:Band61Heft6-544
Grey, F. Noel Coward.
R.F. Gross, 615(TJ):May89-263
Grey, J.D., ed. Jane Austen's Beginnings.
J. Bender, 617(TLS):10-16Aug90-854
R. Kiely, 166:Jan90-174
Gribble, C. & L. Parpulova-Gribble. Elementary Bulgarian 1, 2. Intermediate Bulgarian 1.
C.A. Moser, 574(SEEJ):Winter89-640

Gribble, C.E. Reading Bulgarian through Russian.
   C.M. MacRobert, 575(SEER):Oct89-601
   C. Rudin, 399(MLJ):Autumn89-351
Grier, K.C. Culture and Comfort.*
   A. Fabian, 658:Winter89-291
Griesinger, G.A. "Eben komme ich von
   Haydn..." (O. Biba, ed)
   H. Lenneberg, 309:Vol9No4-300
Grieve, P.E. Desire and Death in the Spanish
   Sentimental Romance (1440-1550).*
   I.A. Corfis, 240(HR):Spring89-228
Grieves, K. Sir Eric Geddes.
   T.C. Barker, 617(TLS):2-8Mar90-212
Griffin, C. The Crombergers of Seville.*
   A.J.C. Bainton, 402(MLR):Jul90-681
Griffin, J. Homer: The "Odyssey."*
   M.J. Alden, 303(JoHS):Vol109-210
   L.E. Doherty, 124:Nov-Dec89-124
   J.B. Hainsworth, 123:Vol39No1-3
Griffin, J. Virgil.
   E.A. Schmidt, 229:Band61Heft3-251
Griffin, J. Well-Being.*
   R. Crisp, 518:Jul89-129
   T. Hurka, 393(Mind):Jul88-463
Griffin, K. Alternative Strategies for Eco-
   nomic Development.
   F. Stewart, 617(TLS):26Jan-1Feb90-98
Griffin, L., L.K. Meisel & S.P. Meisel. Clarice
   Cliff.
   C. Buckley, 662:Spring/Summer89-49
   A. Eatwell, 39:Aug89-187
Griffin, M. & J. Barnes, eds. Philosophia
   Togata.
   M. Atkins, 617(TLS):6-12Apr90-380
Griffin, N. Spanish Incunabula in the John
   Rylands University Library of Manchester.*
   D.E. Rhodes, 354:Sep89-278
Griffin, P. Along with Youth.*
   K. Moreland, 577(SHR):Spring89-145
Griffin, R. Rape of the Lock.
   L.M. Porter, 446(NCFS):Spring-
   Summer90-539
Griffin, W. Clive Staples Lewis.
   V. Hyles, 295(JML):Fall88/Winter89-373
Griffith, J.A.G. & M. Ryle, with M.A.J.
   Wheeler-Booth. Parliament.
   G. Drewry, 617(TLS):18-24May90-518
Griffith, N.S. Edward Bellamy.*
   K.M. Roemer, 561(SFS):Jul89-238
Griffiths, E. The Printed Voice of Victorian
   Poetry.*
   T.J. Collins, 637(VS):Summer90-677
Griffiths, J. The Good Spy.
   N. Callendar, 441:25Feb90-35
Griffiths, L. Personification in "Piers Plow-
   man."*
   G. Bourquin, 189(EA):Apr-Jun89-210
Griffiths, M. & M. Whitford, eds. Feminist
   Perspectives in Philosophy.
   K. Lennon, 291:Vol6No2-238
Griffiths, P. Myself and Marco Polo.*
   P-L. Adams, 61:Apr90-108
Griffiths, P.J. On Being Mindless.*
   C.S. Prebish, 318(JAOS):Jan-Mar88-178
Griffiths, R. Le Centre perdu.*
   L. Brockliss, 208(FS):Oct89-472
Griffiths, S. Emigrants, Entrepreneurs, and
   Evil Spirits.
   J-P. Dumont, 293(JASt):May89-433
Griffiths, T.R. & T.A. Joscelyne, eds. Long-
   man Guide to Shakespeare Quotations.
   G. Schmitz, 156(ShJW):Jahrbuch1989-332

Grigg, D. English Agriculture.
   W. Minchinton, 617(TLS):5-11Jan90-20
Grigor'ev, V.P. Slovotvorčestvo i smežnye
   problemy jazyka poèta.
   R. Vroon, 574(SEEJ):Spring89-130
Grigor'ev, V.P. & A.E. Parnis - see Khlebni-
   kov, V.
Grim, W.E. The Faust Legend in Music and
   Literature.
   G. Martin, 465:Spring90-183
de Grimaldi, J. La pata de cabra.* (D.T. Gies,
   ed)
   G.C. Martín, 240(HR):Winter89-105
Grimbert, J.T. "Yvain" dans le miroir.
   K. Busby, 210(FrF):Sep89-351
   N.J. Lacy, 207(FR):Dec89-367
   H.C.R. Laurie, 547(RF):Band101Heft4-471
Grimes, A. Running Mates.
   M. Janeway, 441:5Aug90-15
Grimes, T. A Stone of the Heart.
   H. Wolitzer, 441:20May90-11
Grimké, S. Sarah Grimké: Letters on the
   Equality of the Sexes and Other Essays.
   (E.A. Bartlett, ed)
   K.M., 185:Oct89-216
   J. Ochshorn, 254:Spring90-175
Grimm, H.J. Lexikon zum Artikelgebrauch.
   G. Koss, 685(ZDL):3/1989-351
Grimm, J. Molière.*
   W. Steinsieck, 535(RHL):Jan-Feb89-100
Grimm, J. & V. Elenbergskaja rukopis' 1810.
   (A. Naumenko, trans)
   R. Alsheimer, 196:Band30Heft3/4-326
Grimm, J. & W. The Complete Fairy Tales of
   the Brothers Grimm.* (J. Zipes, ed & trans)
   R.B. Bottigheimer, 292(JAF):Jan-Mar89-
   100
   J. Erickson, 203:Vol100No2-255
   D. Haase, 221(GQ):Spring89-277
   K. Hasselbach, 406:Summer89-265
Grimm, J. & W. Deutsches Wörterbuch. (new
   ed) (Vol 1)
   O. Reichmann, 682(ZPSK):Band42Heft4-
   620
Grimm, J. & W. Unbokannte Märchen von Wil-
   helm und Jacob Grimm.* (H. Rölleke, ed)
   E. Ettlinger, 203:Vol100No1-121
Grimm, J., F-R. Hausmann & C. Miething.
   Einführung in die französische Literatur-
   wissenschaft. (3rd ed)
   R. Zaiser, 547(RF):Band101Heft1-103
Grimm, R. Love, Lust, and Rebellion.*
   W. Wittkowski, 133:Band22Heft1-67
Grimm, R. & J. Hermand, eds. Our "Faust"?*
   A.T. Alt, 406:Winter89-490
Grimm, W. Der Mili.
   42(AR):Winter89-114
Grimmer, D. Die Rezeption von Denis Diderot
   (1713-1784) in Österreich zwischen 1750
   und 1850.
   D.F. Connon, 402(MLR):Oct90-963
   P.H. Meyer, 530:Oct89-155
Grimnes, O.K. Veien inn i krigen.
   M.F. Metcalf, 563(SS):Spring/Summer89-
   280
Grimshaw, J. Philosophy and Feminist Think-
   ing.*
   A.M. Jaggar, 449:Apr89-258
   E.F. Kittay, 482(PhR):Jan89-122
Grimshaw, J.A., Jr., ed. Time's Glory.*
   K. Quinlan, 392:Spring89-197

Grimwood, M. Heart in Conflict.*
  C.S. Brown, 569(SR):Fall89-556
  P.R.J., 295(JML):Fall88/Winter89-324
Grindea, C. - see Tanasescu, D. & G. Bargau-
  anu
Griolet, P. Cadjins et créoles en Louisiane.*
  A. Valdman, 399(MLJ):Summer89-222
Gripp, H. Theodor W. Adorno.
  J. Früchtl, 687:Jan-Mar89-199
Grisé, C.M. & C.D.E. Tolton, eds. Crossroads
  and Perspectives.
  F. Lestringant, 535(RHL):Mar-Apr89-267
Grishman, R. Computational Linguistics.
  G. Russell, 297(JL):Mar89-270
Griswold, C.L., Jr., ed. Platonic Writ-
  ings/Platonic Readings.
  D. Browne, 478(P&L):Oct89-405
  D.W. Conway, 543:Sep89-162
  C. Gill, 123:Vol39No2-252
  J. Mitscherling, 103:Jan90-22
Grizzard, L. If I Ever Get Back to Georgia, I'm
  Gonna Nail My Feet to the Ground.
  M.E. Guthrie, 441:11Nov90-61
Grmek, M.D. Diseases in the Ancient Greek
  World.
  P. De Lacy, 124:Mar-Apr90-378
  J. Scarborough, 617(TLS):5-11Jan90-22
Grmek, M.D. History of AIDS.
  E. Eckholm, 441:18Nov90-14
Grob, F. Faire l'oeuvre de Dieu.
  J-M. Bermès, 531:Jan-Mar89-151
Grobovsky, A.N. Ivan Groznii i Sil'vestr
  (Istoriia odnogo mifa).
  M. Perrie, 575(SEER):Jan89-137
Grodzinsky, F.S. The Golden Scapegoat.
  A.R. Pugh, 268(IFR):Winter90-68
Groen, B.M., J.P. Hinrichs & W.R. Vermeer, eds.
  Nicolaas van Wijk (1880-1941).
  R.F. Feldstein, 574(SEEJ):Winter89-612
Groensteen, T. Animaux en case.
  H. Cronel, 450(NRF):Jul-Aug89-198
Grogin, R.C. The Bergsonian Controversy in
  France, 1900-1914.
  T.A. Goudge, 319:Apr90-308
  A. Shalom, 627(UTQ):Fall89-222
Gromyko, A. Memoirs.* (British title: Memo-
  ries.)
  G. Ball, 441:1Apr90-7
Gromyko, M.M. Traditsionnye normy povede-
  niia i formy obshcheniia russkikh krest'ian
  XIX v.
  C.D. Worobec, 550(RusR):Apr89-186
Groneman, C. & M.B. Norton, eds. "To Toil the
  Livelong Day."
  L.M. Adrian, 106:Summer89-107
Gronewald, M. & others. Kölner Papyri (P.
  Köln). (Vol 6)
  G.O. Hutchinson, 123:Vol39No2-356
Gronow, J. On the Formation of Marxism.
  R. Albritton, 488:Sep89-394
Gronowicz, A. Garbo.
  J. Lahr, 441:24Jun90-10
Grønvold, U. Lund and Slaatto.
  B. Russell, 46:Apr89-12
Groos, A., with others, eds. Magister Regis.
  H. Sauer, 38:Band107Heft1/2-134
Groos, A. & R. Parker. Giacomo Puccini: "La
  bohème."
  D.R.B. Kimbell, 278(IS):Vol43-172
Groos, A. & R. Parker, eds. Reading Opera.*
  R. Donington, 415:Apr89-216
  P.D. Murphy, 590:Dec89-122
  S. Williams, 615(TJ):Oct89-420

Gros, F. Les Secrets du gène.
  C. Devilliers, 531:Jan-Mar89-141
Grose, C. Milton and the Sense of Tradition.*
  R.L. Entzminger, 551(RenQ):Winter89-891
  K.W.F. Stavely, 568(SCN):Fall-Winter89-
  36
Grosholz, E. Shores and Headlands.
  F. Chappell, 219(GaR):Summer89-385
  R.B. Shaw, 491:Aug89-293
  639(VQR):Winter89-27
Gross, H. Rome in the Age of Enlightenment.
  P. Partner, 617(TLS):17-23Aug90-879
Gross, K. & W. Pache, eds. Grundlagen zur
  Literatur in englischer Sprache: Kanada.
  H. Tschachler, 102(CanL):Winter88-157
Gross, L., J.S. Katz & J. Ruby, eds. Image
  Ethics.*
  J.L., 185:Apr90-707
Gross, P. Cat's Whisker.*
  J. Saunders, 565:Autumn89-77
Gross, S. & others - see Hawthorne, N.
Gross, T. - see Mendes, C.
Grosse, S. & U. Rautenberg. Die Rezeption
  mittelalterlicher deutscher Dichtung.
  R. Simek, 602:Band20Heft2-323
Grosseteste, R. De decem mandatis. (R.C.
  Dales & E.B. King, eds)
  C.H. Kneepkens, 640:Nov89-156
Grosshans, H. German Dreams and German
  Dreamers.
  M. Winkler, 221(GQ):Summer89-412
Grossman, D. See Under: LOVE.*
  R. Di Antonio, 268(IFR):Summer89-156
  B. Eisenstein, 376:Dec89-121
  B. Levine, 287:Sep-Oct89-24
  I. Malin, 532(RCF):Fall89-217
  G. Motola, 390:Oct89-37
  S.S. Prawer, 617(TLS):26Jan-1Feb90-86
Grossman, D. The Yellow Wind.*
  G. Levin, 364:Apr/May89-149
Grossman, J.D. Valery Bryusov and the Rid-
  dle of Russian Decadence.
  C. Barnes, 575(SEER):Oct89-613
Grossman, M. "Authors to Themselves."
  T.N. Corns, 447(N&Q):Sep89-394
  J. Di Salvo, 405(MP):Feb90-308
Grossman, M. Colori e lessico.
  J. Heath, 350:Dec90-868
Grossmann, R. Phenomenology and Existen-
  tialism.
  R. McIntyre, 449:Mar89-106
Grossmith, R. The Empire of Lights.
  A. Mars-Jones, 617(TLS):21-27Dec90-
  1381
Grosz, E. Sexual Subversions.
  T. Moi, 358:Jun90-13
Grotjahn, R., C. Klein-Braley & D.K. Steven-
  son, eds. Taking Their Measure.
  Y. Bader, 257(IRAL):Aug89-256
Grottanelli, V.L. The Python Killer.
  D.M. Warren, 538(RAL):Fall89-557
Grotzer, P., ed. Aspekte der Verweigerung in
  der neueren Literatur aus der Schweiz.
  J. Szabó, 680(ZDP):Band108Heft2-309
Grout, D.J. & C.V. Palisca. A History of West-
  ern Music. (4th ed)
  N. Simeone, 415:Aug89-477
Grover, K., ed. Dining in America, 1850-
  1900.*
  S.P. Schoelwer, 658:Winter89-289
Groves, P. Academe.*
  G. Maxwell, 493:Spring89-52
  W. Scammell, 364:Aug/Sep89-92

Grözinger, K.E., S. Mosès & H.D. Zimmermann, eds. Kafka und das Judentum.
 I.M. Goessel, 221(GQ):Summer89-403
Gruber, W.E. Comic Theaters.
 T.J. Reiss, 131(CL):Spring89-183
Grubitzsch, H., H. Cyrus & E. Haarbusch, eds. Grenzgängerinnen.
 M-T. Leuker-Schnelle, 242:Vol10No3-365
Gruenwald, O. & K. Rosenblum-Cale, eds. Human Rights in Yugoslavia.
 M. Scammell, 453(NYRB):19Jul90-37
Gruhn, W., ed. Musikalische Bildung und Kultur.
 W. Pape, 417:Jul-Sep89-275
Grünbaum, A. The Foundations of Psychoanalysis.
 D. Sachs, 482(PhR):Jul89-349
Grunberger, B. New Essays on Narcissism.
 L. Hudson, 617(TLS):23Feb-1Mar90-194
Grundberg, A. Brodovitch.
 C. Frayling, 617(TLS):16-22Mar90-292
Grundlehner, P. The Poetry of Friedrich Nietzsche.*
 A.P. Fell, 529(QQ):Spring89-66
Grünewald, B. Modalität und empirisches Denken.
 W. Becker, 687:Jan-Mar89-190
 M. Zahn, 342:Band80Heft1-100
Grunewald, E. Friedrich Heinrich von der Hagen 1780-1856.
 F. Shaw, 402(MLR):Jul90-796
Grünzweig, W. Das demokratische Kanaan.
 S. Bauschinger, 406:Fall89-382
 B. Fischer, 221(GQ):Winter89-125
Grutman, R. & B. Thomas. Lawyers and Thieves.
 P-L. Adams, 61:Jul90-104
 D. Margolick, 441:5Aug90-21
Grynberg, H. Kadisz.
 M.G. Levine, 497(PolR):Vol34No2-192
Grziwotz, H. Das Verfassungsverständnis der römischen Republik.
 R. Rilinger, 229:Band61Heft4-362
Guang, W. - see under Wu Guang
Guardi, T. - see Titinius
Guarducci, M. La tomba di San Pietro.
 P. Hebblethwaite, 617(TLS):13-19Apr90-390
Guarnieri, R. - see Porete, M.
Gubar, S. & J. Hoff, eds. For Adult Users Only.
 A. Clare, 617(TLS):12-18Jan90-32
Guderzo, M. Bibliografia di Giacomo Zanella.
 E.G. Gerato, 276:Autumn89-358
Gudiol, J. Goya.
 R. Snell, 617(TLS):16-22Mar90-290
Gudiol, J. & S. Alcolea I. Blanch. Pintura Gótica Catalana.
 R. Gibbs, 90:Feb89-155
Gudmundson, L. Costa Rica before Coffee.
 S. Chant, 86(BHS):Apr89-195
Guelzo, A.C. Edwards on the Will.
 D. Weber, 165(EAL):Vol25No3-316
Guenée, B. Entre l'église et l'état.
 H. Kaminsky, 589:Apr89-439
Guénette, D. La Part de l'ode, avec huit petites cosmogonies de Jacques Palumbo.
 C.F. Coates, 207(FR):May90-1100
Guénoun, D. La Levée.
 A. Vasak, 450(NRF):Sep89-114
Guenther, R. Frauenarbeit - Frauenbindung.
 J.F. Gardner, 313:Vol79-228

Guerard, A. Christine/Annette.
 M. De Koven, 473(PR):Vol56No1-157
Guérif, F. François Truffaut.
 A. Thiher, 207(FR):Feb90-568
Guérin, M. Qu'est-ce qu'une oeuvre?*
 G. Cesbron, 356(LR):Feb-May89-101
Guérin, R. Le Temps de la Sottise.
 H. Carn, 450(NRF):Jul-Aug89-189
Guernsey, P. Angel Falls.
 J. Mooney, 441:1Jul90-14
Guerra Cunningham, L. Texto e ideología en la narrativa chilena.
 P. Swanson, 86(BHS):Jan89-100
Guerreschi, J. Montée en première ligne.
 D.C. Spinelli, 207(FR):Apr90-893
Guess, J. Painting the Town.
 W. Tonetto, 581:Jun89-263
de Guevara, L.V. - see under Vélez de Guevara, L.
Guggenheim, M., ed. Women in French Literature.
 A.B. Millstone, 446(NCFS):Spring-Summer90-587
"Guía de Precios, 1986."
 M. Estella, 48:Jan-Mar89-105
Guibbory, A. The Map of Time.*
 T.N. Corn, 506(PSt):May87-108
 D.M. Friedman, 301(JEGP):Apr89-234
Guibert, H. A l'Ami qui ne m'a pas sauvé la vie.
 P. Keegan, 617(TLS):28Sep-4Oct90-1038
Guibert-Sledziewski, E. & J-L. Vieillard-Baron, eds. Penser le sujet aujourd'hui
 A.M. Hjort, 400(MLN):Sep89-942
Guicciardini, F. Le Lettere. (Vol 2) (P. Jodogne, ed)
 M.M. Bullard, 551(RenQ):Spring89-97
Guierre, L. Règles et exercises de prononciation anglaise.
 G. Bourcier, 189(EA):Oct-Dec89-455
Guieu, J-M. & A. Hilton, eds. Emile Zola and the Arts.
 M. Fauvel, 207(FR):Oct89-169
 J. Kaminskas, 529(QQ):Autumn89-732
 W. McClendon, 446(NCFS):Fall-Winter89/90-276
Guilds, J.C., ed. Long Years of Neglect.
 J.L. Idol, 27(AL):Dec89-694
Guilhamet, L. Satire and the Transformation of Genre.*
 F. De Bruyn, 83:Autumn89-228
 F. Doherty, 541(RES):May89-299
 J.V. Guerinot, 568(SCN):Spring-Summer89-4
Guillaud, J. & M. Jerôme Bosch.
 E. Bermejo, 48:Apr-Jun89-230
Guillauma, Y. La Presse en France.
 A.J.M. Prévos, 207(FR):Feb90-595
Guillaume, G. Langages et langue.
 J. Chaurand, 209(FM):Oct89-265
Guillaume, G. Leçons de linguistique de Gustave Guillaume, 1946-1947. (R. Valin, W. Hirtle & A. Joly, eds) (Ser C)
 M.E. Surridge, 320(CJL):Dec89-495
Guillaume, J. & C. Pichois - see de Nerval, G.
Guillaume, J., with J.L. Préat, eds. Nerval, Masques et Visage.
 J. Bony, 535(RHL):Mar-Apr89-305
Guillemay du Chesnay, C-F. - see under Rosidor
Guillén, C. Entre lo uno y lo diverso.
 D-H. Pageaux, 549(RLC):Jan-Mar89-107

Guillén, C. El primer Siglo de Oro.
M.S. Brownlee, 240(HR):Autumn89-506
Guillermoprieto, A. Samba.
J. Ryle, 617(TLS):13-19Jul90-745
442(NY):28May90-110
Guimier, C. Syntaxe de l'adverbe anglais.
J. Hewson, 350:Sep90-636
Guinizelli, G. The Poetry of Guido Guinizelli.
(R. Edwards, ed & trans)
S. Pearce, 382(MAE):1989/1-180
Guiral-Hadziiossif, J. Valence, port méditer-
ranéen au XVe siècle (1410-1525).
R. Burns, 589:Apr89-440
Guiraud-Weber, M. L'aspect du verbe russe.
G.C. Rappaport, 350:Sep90-637
Guiraud-Weber, M. Les propositions sans
nominatif en russe moderne.*
T.M. Nikolaeva, 559:Vol13No2-171
Guitton, J. Un siècle, une vie.
A. Reix, 542:Oct-Dec89-613
Guldan, M.M. Die Tagebücher von Ludwig
Pollak.
M. Moltesen, 90:Sep89-659
Gulen, A. Vis à Vis ma.
K. Kehr, 685(ZDL):3/1989-390
Gullestad, M. Kitchen-Table Society.
J.E. Rasmussen, 563(SS):Winter89-108
Gullette, M.M. Safe at Last in the Middle
Years.*
S. Fogel, 395(MFS):Winter89-764
R.F. Franklin, 27(AL):Oct89-498
639(VQR):Spring89-48
Gullick, J.M. Malay Society in the Late
Nineteenth Century.
A.C. Milner, 293(JASt):Feb89-218
Gullickson, G.L. Spinners and Weavers of
Auffay.
S.M. Bowden, 242:Vol10No2-253
T. Kemp, 83:Autumn89-209
Gumbrecht, H.U. & K.L. Pfeiffer, eds. Stil.*
W. van Peer, 204(FdL):Mar89-61
Gumilev, L.N. Searches for an Imaginary
Kingdom.
C. Lofmark, 575(SEER):Jul89-465
Gumtau, H. - see Morgenstern, C.
Gunderson, M., D.J. Mayo & F.S. Rhame. AIDS.
B.H., 185:Apr90-712
Gunew, S. & J. Mahyuddin, eds. Beyond the
Echo.
A. Corkhill, 71(ALS):Oct89-271
Gunji, T. Japanese Phrase Structure Gram-
mar.
P. Bennett, 297(JL):Mar89-246
B. Saint-Jacques, 320(CJL):Jun89-233
Gunkel, H. Das Märchen im Alten Testament.
W. Brückner, 196:Band30Heft3/4-327
Gunlicks, A.B. & J.D. Treadway, eds. The
Soviet Union under Gorbachev.
B.A. Chotiner, 550(RusR):Jul89-321
Gunn, D. Psychoanalysis and Fiction.*
N. Bradbury, 677(YES):Vol20-362
639(VQR):Winter89-15
Gunn, D. & P. Guyomard, eds. A Young Girl's
Diary.
E. Showalter, 617(TLS):6-12Jul90-724
Gunn, G. The Culture of Criticism and the
Criticism of Culture.*
R.D. Abrahams, 292(JAF):Apr-Jun89-202
P.A. Miller, 577(SHR):Spring89-170
B.W. Shaffer, 271:Winter89-171
Gunn, J., ed. The New Encyclopedia of Sci-
ence Fiction.*
G.K. Wolfe, 561(SFS):Nov89-379

Gunn, J.C. Gunn's Domestic Medicine.
B.B. Sims, 582(SFQ):Vol46No1-89
Gunn, L.R. The Decline of Authority.
639(VQR):Winter89-7
Gunn, R. & C. Minch. Sexual Assault.
529(QQ):Autumn89-780
Gunn, T. Undesirables.*
D. McDuff, 565:Spring89-76
Gunnars, K., ed. Crossing the River.
H.B. Cannon, 649(WAL):May89-77
Gunnars, K. The Prowler.
J. Givner, 647:Spring89-84
B. Szabados, 647:Spring89-80
Gunnarsson, O. Gaga.
P. Lewis, 565:Summer89-66
Gunner, E.M. T.S. Eliot's Romantic Dilemma.
I.V., 295(JML):Fall88/Winter89-320
Günther, H. Schriftliche Sprache.
M.L. Dow, 350:Jun90-372
Günther, H. Das Studium der antiken Archi-
tektur in den Zeichnungen der Hochrenais-
sance.
P. Jacks, 576:Jun89-185
Günther, R. Frauenarbeit - Frauenbindung.
L. Schumacher, 229:Band61Heft8-702
Gunther, R., G. Sani & G. Shabad. Spain After
Franco.
P. Preston, 86(BHS):Apr89-191
Günther, W. Dichter der neueren Schweiz.*
(Vol 3)
P. Spycher, 301(JEGP):Apr89-309
Gupta, R.K. The Great Encounter.*
M.L.P. Patterson, 293(JASt):May89-426
Gura, P.F. The Wisdom of Words.
S.E. Marovitz, 506(PSt):May87-114
Guralnick, P. Searching for Robert Johnson.*
J. Campbell, 617(TLS):27Jul-2Aug90-793
Gurevich, A. Medieval Popular Culture.
G. Zimmermann, 242:Vol10No6-751
Gurganus, A. Oldest Living Confederate Wid-
ow Tells All.*
S.R. Hauer, 585(SoQ):Winter90-59
Gurganus, A.E. The Art of Revolution.*
S.E. Bronner, 222(GR):Spring89-81
E. Schürer, 133:Band22Heft2-185
Gurjewitsch, A.J. Mittelalterliche Volks-
kultur.
A. Classen, 597(SN):Vol61No1-121
Gurnah, A. Dottie.
J. Haynes, 617(TLS):20-26Apr90-430
Gurney, R. La poesía de Juan Larrea.*
J.C. Wilcox, 240(HR):Spring89-259
Gurney, S. Alain-Fournier.*
M. La Vallée-Williams, 295(JML):Fall88/
Winter89-274
Guro, E. Elena Guro: Selected Prose and Po-
etry. (A. Lunggren & N.Å. Nilsson, eds)
E. Bristol, 574(SEEJ):Fall89-460
A. Smith, 575(SEER):Oct89-617
Gurr, A. Playgoing in Shakespeare's London.*
M. Jones, 541(RES):May89-255
Gurr, A. Studying Shakespeare.
M. Coyle, 447(N&Q):Sep89-383
M.T. Rozett, 570(SQ):Winter89-500
G. Schmitz, 156(ShJW):Jahrbuch1989-332
Gurr, A., with J. Orrell. Rebuilding Shake-
speare's Globe.*
E.A.J. Honigmann, 453(NYRB):29Mar90-23
Gurr, D. The Ring Master.
W. Fraser, 102(CanL):Summer89-157
529(QQ):Spring89-213
Gurtler, G.M. Plotinus.
J. Dillon, 103:Jul90-271

Gury, J. - see de Bombelles, M.

Guss, D.M. To Weave and Sing.
  P. Henley, 617(TLS):6-12Apr90-369

Gustafson, D.F. Intention and Agency.
  J. Montmarquet, 449:Apr89-279

Gustafson, R. Plummets and Other Partialities.
  R.E. Conway, 102(CanL):Autumn-Winter89-278

Gustafson, R. Winter Prophecies.*
  M. Jones, 102(CanL):Summer89-186

Gustafson, R.F. Leo Tolstoy.*
  C.J.G. Turner, 104(CASS):Spring-Winter88-473

Gustafsson, L. Bernard Foy's Third Castling.
  G. Kearns, 249(HudR):Summer89-338

Gustafsson, L. Préparatifs de fuite.
  D. Pobel, 450(NRF):Feb89-152

Gustafsson, L. The Stillness of the World Before Bach. (C. Middleton, ed)
  S. Friebert, 199:Spring89-60

Gut, S., ed. Actes du Colloque international Franz Liszt (1811-1886) tenu dans le cadre de l'Université Paris IV-Sorbonne du 27-30 octobre 1986.
  P. Guillot, 537:Vol75No1-114

Gutberlet, D. Die erste Dekade des Livius als Quelle zur gracchischen und sullanischen Zeit.
  S.P. Oakley, 313:Vol79-200

"Gutenberg-Jahrbuch 1989." (H-J. Koppitz, ed)
  J.L. Flood, 617(TLS):5-11Jan90-24

Guthke, K.S. Erkundungen.
  J. Strelka, 221(GQ):Fall89-529

Guthke, K.S. B. Traven.
  R. Furness, 402(MLR):Oct90-1033
  E. Koppen, 52:Band24Heft3-333
  E. Schürer, 221(GQ):Summer89-415
  J.P. Strelka, 133:Band22Heft3/4-369

Guthrie, R.D. Frozen Fauna of the Mammoth Steppe.
  A. Gentry, 617(TLS):30Nov-6Dec90-1299

Gutierrez, D. Subject-Object Relations in Wordsworth and Lawrence.
  D.T.O., 295(JML):Fall88/Winter89-368

Gutiérrez, N.F. - see under de Granda Gutiérrez, G.

Gutiérrez, M.P. - see under Pérez Gutiérrez, M.

Gutiérrez-Cortines Corral, C. Renacimiento y arquitectura religiosa en la antigua diócesis de Cartagena (Reyno de Murcia, Gobernación de Orihuela y Sierra del Segura).
  F. Marías, 48:Apr-Jun89-228

Gutiérrez Díaz-Bernardo, E. - see de Jérica y Corta, P.

Gutman, D. It Ain't Cheatin' If You Don't Get Caught.
  C. Sommers, 441:1Apr90-16

Gutman, R. Architectural Practice.*
  L. Thibault, 47:Feb89-35
  F. Wilson, 47:Feb89-35

Gutman, R. Banana Diplomacy.*
  639(VQR):Winter89-22

Gutman, Y. & others, eds. The Jews of Poland between Two World Wars.
  R.S. Wistrich, 617(TLS):23-29Nov90-1261

Gutmann, A. Democratic Education.*
  G. Sher, 509:Winter89-68

Gutsche, G.J. Moral Apostasy in Russian Literature.*
  R.F. Gustafson, 104(CASS):Spring-Winter88-509
  H. McLean, 550(RusR):Jan89-94
  S. Monas, 574(SEEJ):Spring89-119

Gutting, G. Michel Foucault's Archaeology of Scientific Reason.
  D. Revill, 617(TLS):27Jul-2Aug90-805

Gutwirth, M. Un merveilleux sans éclat.*
  J.P. Collinet, 535(RHL):Jan-Feb89-104
  J. Grimm, 547(RF):Band101Heft2/3-339

Guy, J. Tudor England.*
  W.T. MacCaffrey, 551(RenQ):Winter89-855

Guy, R.K. The Emperor's Four Treasuries.*
  H. Dunstan, 244(HJAS):Dec89-659

Guyer, P. Kant and the Claims of Knowledge.*
  H.E. Allison, 311(JP):Apr89-214
  A. Axiotis, 518:Jan89-22
  S.E., 185:Apr90-704
  R.B. Pippin, 319:Jan90-138

Guyer, P. Kant and the Claims of Reason.
  R.C.S. Walker, 479(PhQ):Jul89-373

Guzmán, M.L. La sombra del caudillo.
  L. Leal, 238:Mar89-151

de Guzman, R.P. & M.A. Reforma, eds. Government and Politics of the Philippines.*
  R. Stauffer, 293(JASt):Feb89-219

Guzzetta, L.F. & others - see under Fava Guzzetta, L. & others

Gvozdev, A. Teatral'naja kritika.
  J. Freedman, 574(SEEJ):Spring89-132

Gwara, J.J., Jr. The Sala Family Archives.
  C.B. Faulhaber, 545(RPh):Aug89-228

Gwin, M.C. Black and White Women of the Old South.*
  C. Mitchell, 582(SFQ):Vol46No2-194

Gwyn, P. The King's Cardinal.
  D. Starkey, 617(TLS):24-30Aug90-898

Gybbon-Monypenny, G.B. - see Ruiz, J.

H.D. Selected Poems. (L.L. Martz, ed)
  639(VQR):Spring89-65

Haakonssen, K., ed. Traditions of Liberalism.
  W.K., 185:Apr90-703
  D.H. Monro, 63:Sep90-061

Haakonssen, K. - see Reid, T.

de Haan, H. & I. Haagsma. Architects in Competition.*
  S. Gutterman, 45:Feb89-67

Haar, J. Essays on Italian Poetry and Music in the Renaissance, 1350-1600.*
  B.J. Blackburn, 317:Spring89-161

Haar, M. Le Chant de la terre.*
  R. Lilly, 319:Jan90-149
  J. Taminiaux, 153:Fall-Winter89-76

Haarmann, H. Language in Ethnicity.*
  D.L. Goyvaerts, 355(LSoc):Sep89-414

Haas, R., ed. Amerikanische Lyrik.
  H. Höhne, 654(WB):4/1989-699

Haase, H. & A. Mádl, eds. Österreichische Literatur des 20. Jahrhunderts.
  E. Middell, 654(WB):1/1989-141

Haasse, H.S. In a Dark Wood Wandering.* (rev) (A. Miller, ed)
  S. Altinel, 617(TLS):6-12Jul90-732

Habegger, A. Henry James and the "Woman Business."*
  D.M. Fogel, 598(SoR):Summer90-697
  H. Lee, 617(TLS):25-31May90-547

Habel, R. - see Morgenstern, C.

Haber, F., K.R. Fuller & D. Wetzel. Robert S. Roeschlaub.
T.J. Noel, 576:Jun89-191
Haberkamp, G. Die Musikhandschriften der Benediktiner-Abtei Ottobeuren.
P.W. Jones, 410(M&L):May89-258
Haberkamp, G. & B. Zuber. Die Musikhandschriften Herzog Wilhelms in Bayern, der Grafen zu Toerring-Jettenbach und der Fürsten Fugger von Babenhausen.
J. Wagstaff, 410(M&L):Aug89-408
Haberland, E. & M. Lamberti. Ibaaddo ka-Ba'iso.
R. Richter, 682(ZPSK):Band42Heft5-695
Haberman, D.C., ed. Bernard Shaw.* (Vol 3)
C.A. Berst, 177(ELT):Vol32No1-71
B.F. Dukore, 610:Autumn89-302
Habermas, J. The Philosophical Discourse of Modernity.* (German title: Der philosophische Diskurs der Moderne.)
D.T.O., 295(JML):Fall88/Winter89-227
R. Shusterman, 494:Fall89-605
G.A. Trey, 153:Summer89-67
Habermas, J. The Structural Transformation of the Public Sphere.
B. Allen, 103:Jun90-228
Habermas, J. The Theory of Communicative Action.* (Vols 1 & 2) (French title: Théorie de l'agir communicationnel. German title: Theorie des kommunikativen Handelns.)
R. Rochlitz, 192(EP):Apr-Jun89-271
F.A. Olafson, 185:Apr90-641
Habicht, C. Cicero the Politician.
T.P. Wiseman, 617(TLS):15-21Jun90-647
Habinek, T.N. The Colometry of Latin Prose.
T. Janson, 229:Band61Heft5-435
Haboush, J.K. A Heritage of Kings.
M.C. Kalton, 293(JASt):Nov89-886
"Hachette Dictionnaire pratique du français."
F.J. Hausmann, 547(RF):Band101Heft1-93
Hacker, H-J. Zur Poetologie des mittelalterlichen Dramas in England.*
S. Kohl, 38:Band107Heft1/2-210
Hacker, P.M.S. Appearance and Reality.
J.M. Hinton, 483:Jan89-116
D. Stern, 518:Jan89-33
M. Tooley, 543:Sep89-164
E. Wright, 393(Mind):Jan89-165
Hacker, P.M.S. Insight and Illusion.
A. Hamilton, 479(PhQ):Apr89-231
Hackett, P. - see Warhol, A.
Hackforth-Jones, P. Barbara Baynton.
S. Sheridan, 71(ALS):May89-118
Hacking, I. The Taming of Chance.
P. Seabright, 617(TLS):14-20Dec90-1339
Hackl, E. Aurora's Motive.
P. Lewis, 565:Autumn89-72
Hackney, R. The Good, the Bad and the Ugly.
A. Coleman, 617(TLS):11-17May90-505
Hacks, P. Liebkind im Vogelnest.
M. Oy, 654(WB):2/1989-314
Hadamczik, D., ed. Theater ... Der Nachwelt Unverloren.
D. Fogg, 610:Spring89-101
Hadamowsky, F. Wien: Theatergeschichte.
W.E. Yates, 402(MLR):Apr90-515
Hadas, R. Pass it On.
L. Rosenberg, 441:6May90-32
Haddad, H. Armelle ou l'éternel retour. Oholiba des songes.
J. Taylor, 617(TLS):7-13Sep90-955
Haddock, B.A. Vico's Political Thought.
V. Jones, 278(IS):Vol43-161

Hadengue, P.S. Petite chronique des gens de la nuit dans un port de l'Atlantique Nord.
J. Taylor, 207(FR):Oct89-207
Hadley, R.V. - see Berenson, B. & I.S. Gardner, with M. Berenson
Haferland, H. Höfische Interaktion.
D.H. Green, 402(MLR):Oct90-1018
Haffenden, J. - see Empson, W.
Haffner, P. Jean Renoir.
A. Thiher, 207(FR):Oct89-192
Hafner, S. & E. Prunč. Thesaurus der slowenischen Volkssprache in Kärnten. (Vol 2)
G. Stone, 575(SEER):Jan89-111
Hagberg, D. Countdown.
N. Callendar, 441:22Jul90-22
Hage, V. & others - see "Deutsche Literatur: Ein Jahresüberblick 1981-1987"
Hagedorn, J. Dogeaters.
B. d'Alpuget, 441:25Mar90-1
Hagège, C. Le comox lhaamen de Colombie Britannique.
P.D. Kroeber, 269(IJAL):Jan89-106
Hagège, C. The Dialogic Species.
D. Papineau, 617(TLS):9-15Nov90-1213
Hagège, C. L'Homme de paroles.
M. Harris, 208(FS):Jan89-116
P. Swiggers, 567:Vol74No1/2-133
Hagenau, B. Der Deutsche Gesamtkatalog.
G. Nattrass, 354:Dec89-369
Hagenbüchle, R. Emily Dickinson.
J. Raab, 27(AL):Dec89-697
Hagerfors, L. The Whales in Lake Tanganyika.*
S. Altinel, 617(TLS):19-25Jan90-66
J. Mellors, 364:Oct/Nov89-133
Hägg, R. & N. Marinatos, eds. The Function of the Minoan Palaces.
C. Sourvinou-Inwood, 123:Vol39No2-335
Haggard, S. Nya.
42(AR):Spring89-249
Hagstrum, J.H. The Romantic Body.*
F. Piquet, 189(EA):Apr-Jun89-215
Hahn, B. & U. Isselstein, eds. Rahel Levin Varnhagen.
T.H. Pickett, 133:Band22Heft2-170
Hahn, H. Das vielfältige Formenmosaik J.S. Bachs in den kleinen Präludien und Fughetten für Klavier. (T. Schicke, ed)
E. Platen, 416:Band4Heft2-187
Hahn, J.W. Soviet Grassroots.*
C. Ross, 550(RusR):Jul89-331
Hahn, L.E. & P.A. Schilpp, eds. The Philosophy of W.V. Quine.*
B. Humphries, 482(PhR):Apr89-242
Hahn, R. Kant's Newtonian Revolution in Philosophy.*
G.G. Brittan, Jr., 319:Oct90-622
von Hahn, W. Fachkommunikation.
K. Kehr, 685(ZDL):1/1989-119
Haid, H. Und olm di weissen Leenen.
K. Kehr, 685(ZDL):3/1989-392
Haig, S. Flaubert and the Gift of Speech.*
D. Kelly, 546(RR):Mar89-328
R.O. Steele, 446(NCFS):Fall-Winter89/90-259
H.H. Weinberg, 131(CL):Summer89-293
Haigh, C., ed. The English Reformation Revised.*
E.T. Dubois, 242:Vol10No5-605
Hailey, A. The Evening News.
D. Murray, 441:6May90-22
Lord Hailsham. A Sparrow's Flight.
P. Clarke, 617(TLS):29Jun-5Jul90-688

Haim, Y. Abandonment of Illusions.
    N. Rejwan, 390:Jun/Jul89-60
Haimo, E. Schoenberg's Serial Odyssey.
    D. Jarman, 617(TLS):5-11Oct90-1071
Haimo, E. & P. Johnson, eds. Stravinsky
    Retrospectives.*
    M. Kielian-Gilbert, 513:Winter89-246
Haimson, L.H., with Z. Galili y Garcia & R.
    Wortman, eds. The Making of Three Russian
    Revolutionaries.
    A. Liebich, 550(RusR):Jan89-67
    H. Shukman, 242:Vol10No5-611
Haines, J. New Poems: 1980-88.
    R. Richman, 441:25Nov90-24
Haines, M. - see Poggi, G.
Hainline, D., ed. New Developments in Com-
    puter-Assisted Language Learning.
    J. Moyne, 710:Mar89-105
Hainsworth, P. Petrarch the Poet.*
    J.L. Smarr, 551(RenQ):Autumn89-546
Hainsworth, P. & others, eds. The Languages
    of Literature in Renaissance Italy.
    J. Bryce, 278(IS):Vol44-158
    B. Richardson, 447(N&Q):Jun89-230
Hajnal, I. A Batthyány-kormány külpoliti-
    kája. (A. Urbán, ed)
    L. Péter, 575(SEER):Apr89-305
Hajny, P.F. & H. Wirbelauer. Lesekurs
    Deutsch.
    J.F. Lalande 2d, 399(MLJ):Summer89-234
Häkli, E. - see Kunze, E.
Hakola, L. In One Person Many People.
    S. Wells, 611(TN):Vol43No2-86
Haksar, V. Civil Disobedience, Threats and
    Offers.*
    G. Richards, 521:Jan89-79
Halberstam, D. Summer of '49.*
    R.B. Heilman, 569(SR):Summer89-475
Halbig, M.C. The Jesuit Theater of Jacob
    Masen.
    T.W. Best, 133:Band22Heft3/4-312
    G.R. Hoyt, 221(GQ):Spring89-257
Haldas, G. Le Coeur de tous.
    F. Mary, 460(NRF):Feb89-146
Hale, B. Abstract Objects.*
    H.W. Noonan, 479(PhQ):Jul89-354
    A. Sweet, 543:Sep89-166
    T. Williamson, 393(Mind):Jul88-487
Hale, J.A. The Broken Window.*
    S. Connor, 402(MLR):Jul90-708
    V.K., 295(JML):Fall88/Winter89-286
    J. Schooler-Riley, 704(SFR):Spring89-97
Hales, P.B. William Henry Jackson and the
    Transformation of the American Landscape.
    J.C. Curtis, 658:Summer/Autumn89-198
Haley, J.M., ed. Pleasure Grounds.
    F. Gutheim, 47:Feb89-38
Haley, S. Getting Married in Buffalo Jump.
    J. Pouw, 102(CanL):Summer89-192
    C. Rooke, 376:Mar89-125
Hall, A. Quiller Barracuda.
    N. Callendar, 441:27May90-27
Hall, C. Running Water.
    T. Cantell, 324:Sep90-717
Hall, D. Fathers Playing Catch with Sons.
    R.B. Heilman, 569(SR):Summer89-475
Hall, D. The Ideal Bakery.
    E.C. Lynskey, 456(NDQ):Spring89-186
Hall, D. In Miserable Slavery.
    M.G. Smith, 617(TLS):11-17May90-489
Hall, D. The One Day.
    J.F. Cotter, 249(HudR):Autumn89-516
    639(VQR):Winter89-26

Hall, D. Poetry and Ambition.
    T. Hansen, 219(GaR):Winter89-815
Hall, D. & P.C. Wykes. Anecdotes of Modern
    Art.
    L. Ellmann, 617(TLS):21-27Sep90-1005
Hall, D.B. & J.B. Hench, eds. Needs and
    Opportunities in the History of the Book:
    America, 1639-1876.
    A. Schreyer, 517(PBSA):Jun89-229
Hall, D.D. Worlds of Wonder, Days of Judg-
    ment.*
    R.P. Gildrie, 165(EAL):Vol25No1-81
Hall, D.L. & R.T. Ames. Thinking Through
    Confucius.*
    J.J. Kupperman, 244(HJAS):Jun89-251
Hall, E. Inventing the Barbarian.
    S. West, 617(TLS):23Feb-1Mar90-200
Hall, F.M., R.S. Stevens & J. Whyman. The
    Kent and Canterbury Hospital 1790-1987.
    F.B. Smith, 637(VS):Winter90-345
Hall, H.G. Richelieu's Desmarets and the
    Century of Louis XIV.
    P. France, 617(TLS):7-13Sep90-953
Hall, J.A. Liberalism.
    D.J. Goldford, 185:Jul90-893
    639(VQR):Summer89-95
Hall, J.A. & J.G. Ikenberry. The State.
    M.B., 185:Jul90-908
Hall, J.W. Paper Products.
    R. Goodman, 441:24Jun90-20
Hall, M.G. The Last American Puritan.*
    F.J. Bremer, 656(WMQ):Apr89-384
    P.J. Gomes, 432(NEQ):Mar89-116
    H. Middlekauff, 656:Summer/Autumn89-
    182
Hall, O. The Art & Craft of Novel Writing.
    S. Bick, 42(AR):Fall89-499
Hall, P. Cities of Tomorrow.
    C. Ward, 46:Feb89-8
Hall, P. Client.
    M. Stasio, 441:15Jul90-26
Hall, P. Juror.
    M. Stasio, 441:30Dec90-26
Hall, R. Captivity Captive.^
    P. Lewis, 565:Summer89-60
Hall, R. Kisses of the Enemy.
    P. Lewis, 565:Summer89-66
Hall, R.A., Jr., ed. Leonard Bloomfield.*
    R.H. Robins, 353:Vol27No1-157
Hall, R.A., Jr. Linguistics and Pseudo-Lin-
    guistics.
    P. Meara, 402(MLR):Jan90-126
Hallal, J. Les Concevables interdits.
    D. Williams, 102(CanL):Autumn-
    Winter89-263
von Hallberg, R. American Poetry and Cul-
    ture, 1945-1980.*
    J.A., 70:Oct89-159
    J. Mellard, 599:Summer90-302
Haller, H.W., ed. The Hidden Italy.*
    M. Chiesa, 228(GSLI):Vol166fasc533-132
    H-E. Keller, 276:Spring89-53
    G. Lepschy, 278(IS):Vol43-169
Haller, R. Questions on Wittgenstein.
    P. Engel, 542:Oct-Dec89-623
    G.L. Hallett, 103:Dec90-500
Hallett, G.L. Language and Truth.*
    J. Hudson, 518:Oct89-220
Halliburton, D. Poetic Thinking.
    K. Ziarek, 153:Fall-Winter89-114

Halliday, E.M. John Berryman and the Thir-
ties.
 K. Davis, 27(AL):Mar89-141
 M. Hofmann, 617(TLS):6-12Apr90-363
Halliday, F. Cold War, Third World.
 H. Brogan, 617(TLS):29Jun-5Jul90-708
 A. Milward, 617(TLS):26Jan-1Feb90-81
Halliday, M.A.K. An Introduction to Func-
tional Grammar.*
 M. Toolan, 179(ES):Jun89-280
Halligan, M. The Hanged Man in the Garden.
 D. Ellison, 581:Dec89-672
Halliwell, S. Aristotle's "Poetics."*
 J.M. Bremer, 303(JoHS):Vol109-233
 R. Janko, 122:Apr89-151
Halliwell, S. - see Aristotle
Hallyn, F. La Structure poétique du monde.
 J. Tribby, 400(MLN):Sep89-956
Halm, W., C. Ortiz Blasco & J. Jones. Contact
Spanish.
 H. Ruiz, 399(MLJ):Spring89-107
Halpenny, F.G. - see "Dictionary of Canadian
Biography"
Halpenny, F.G. & J. Hamelin - see "Dictionary
of Canadian Biography"
Halperin, C.J. Russia and the Golden Horde.
 L. Hughes, 575(SEER):Oct89-628
Halperin, D.M. One Hundred Years of Homo-
sexuality and Other Essays on Greek Love.
 J. Griffin, 453(NYRB):29Mar90-6
 M. Nussbaum, 617(TLS):1-7Jun90-571
Halperin, J. Novelists in Their Youth.
 P.N. Furbank, 617(TLS):23-29Mar90-308
Halperin, J.U. Félix Fénéon.*
 J.F. Codell, 207(FR):Mar90-754
 C. Lloyd, 39:Dec89-431
Halperin, M.H., ed. Nuclear Fallacy.
 S.L., 185:Oct89-224
Halsall, A.W. L'Arte de convaincre.
 P. France, 402(MLR):Jul90-673
Halsey, D. Magnetic North.
 C. Thubron, 441:2Dec90-20
Halsey, M.T. & P. Zatlin, eds. The Contempo-
rary Spanish Theater.
 K.F. Nigro, 615(TJ):Dec89-564
 J. Villegas, 238:Dec89-964
Hamabata, M.M. Crested Kimono.
 M.J. Salter, 441:9Sep90-38
Hamacher, W., N. Hertz & T. Keenan, eds.
Responses: On Paul de Man's Wartime Jour-
nalism.*
 H. Sussman, 400(MLN):Dec89-1172
Hamalian, L. William Saroyan.
 C. Palumbo, 295(JML):Fall88/Winter89-
403
Hamalian, L. - see Saroyan, W.
Hamblin, C.L. Imperatives.*
 I.L. Humberstone, 63:Jun89-239
Hambly, M. Drawing Instruments 1580-1980.
 A. Alpern, 47:Aug89-31
 L. Hellman, 46:Jun89-12
Hambrick-Stowe, C.E. - see Bradstreet, A. &
E. Taylor
Hamburger, M. - see Celan, P.
Hamel, H. Relation du naufrage d'un vaisseau
hollandais sur la côte de l'île de Quelpaert
avec la description du Royaume de Corée,
publiée d'après l'édition française de 1670.
(F. Max, ed)
 M. Detrie, 549(RLC):Jan-Mar89-99
Hamerow, T.S. Reflections on History and
Historians.*
 J.W. Osborne, 577(SHR):Winter89-69

Hamers, J.F. & M.H.A. Blanc. Bilinguality and
Bilingualism.*
 N.C. Dorian, 350:Dec90-869
Hamilton, D.M. "The Tools of My Trade."*
 J. Alhinc, 295(JML):Fall88/Winter89-374
Hamilton, I. In Search of J.D. Salinger.*
 J.J. Benson, 27(AL):Oct89-465
 J. Whalen-Bridge, 395(MFS):Summer89-
299
Hamilton, I. Writers in Hollywood 1915-1951.
 Z. Leader, 617(TLS):15-21Jun90-630
 C. Sigal, 441:27May90-2
Hamilton, J. Arthur Rackham.
 P. Shulman, 441:16Dec90-19
 J.A. Smith, 453(NYRB):20Dec90-67
Hamilton, J.M., with N. Morrison. Entangling
Alliances.
 J. Fallows, 61:Jul90-97
 C. Kelly, 441:29Apr90-39
Hamilton, J.S. Piers Gaveston.
 639(VQR):Autumn89-129
Hamilton-Paterson, J. The Bell-Boy.
 C. Hawtree, 617(TLS):26Jan-1Feb90-87
Hamilton-Paterson, J. Playing with Water.
 W.H. Gass, 441:29Apr90-25
Hamilton-Paterson, J. That Time in Malomba.
 M. Malone, 441:14Oct90-7
 442(NY):12Nov90-134
Hamlyn, D.W. In and Out of the Black Box.
 D. Owens, 617(TLS):24-30Aug90-892
Hamm, J-J. Le Texte stendhalien.*
 G. Falconer, 529(QQ):Summer89-507
 B.A. Soestwohner, 345(KRQ):May89-229
Hammer, R. The Helmsleys.
 C. Salzberg, 441:17Jun90-17
Hammerstein, R. Macht und Klang.*
 S. Olms, 684(ZDA):Band118Heft1-42
Hammerton-Kelly, R.G., ed. Violent Origins.
 J. Rubenstein, 124:Nov-Dec89-113
Hammet, M. - see Reade, C.
Hammond, B. "Gulliver's Travels."
 G. Washington, 566:Autumn89-64
Hammond, F. Girolamo Frescobaldi.*
 R. Judd, 415:Jun89-347
Hammond, G. - see Lovelace, R.
Hammond, J.H. Secret and Sacred.* (C.
Bleser, ed)
 M. Kreyling, 392:Spring89-183
Hammond, J.R. H.G. Wells and the Modern
Novel.
 W.J. Scheick, 177(ELT):Vol32No4-504
Hammond, M. Constraining Metrical Theory.
 B.M. Sietsema, 350:Dec90-870
Hammond, M. & M. Noonan, eds. Theoretical
Morphology.
 L. Bauer, 297(JL):Sep89-502
Hammond, N.G.L. A History of Greece to 322
B.C.* (3rd ed)
 J.H. Croon, 394:Vol42fasc1/2-267
Hammond, N.G.L. & F.W. Walbank. A History
of Macedonia. (Vol 3)
 R.M. Errington, 123:Vol39No2-288
 A. Smith, 235:Winter89-85
Hamnett, B.R. Roots of Insurgency.
 J. Fisher, 86(BHS):Jul89-310
Hamowy, R. The Scottish Enlightenment, and
the Theory of Spontaneous Order.
 D. Gordon, 258:Sep89-357
 D.O. Thomas, 83:Autumn89-204
 W. Zachs, 319:Apr90-304
Hampsher-Monk, I. The Political Philosophy
of Edmund Burke.
 M-C. Révauger, 189(EA):Oct-Dec89-478

Hampshire, S. Innocence and Experience.
A. Morton, 617(TLS):16–22Feb90–164
J.T. Noonan, Jr., 441:25Feb90–28
A. Ryan, 453(NYRB):1Mar90–34
Hampshire-Monk, I. – see Burke, E.
Hampton, H. & S. Fayer, with S. Flynn. Voices of Freedom.
H. Mayer, 441:28Jan90–12
Hampton, J. Hobbes and the Social Contract Tradition.*
S.L. Darwall, 482(PhR):Jul89–401
T. Magri, 242:Vol10No5–597
Hampton, S. & K. Llewellyn, eds. The Penguin Book of Australian Women Poets.
R. Crawford, 493:Autumn89–23
Hamrick, W.S. An Existential Phenomenology of Law.*
H. Paillard, 103:Feb90–64
Hamsun, K. Knut Hamsun: Selected Letters. (Vol 1) (H. Naess & J. McFarlane, eds & trans)
M. Meyer, 617(TLS):29Jun–5Jul90–703
Hamsun, K. Livsfragmenter. (L.F. Larsen, ed)
H.S. Naess, 562(Scan):Nov89–208
Hamzah Fansuri. The Poems of Hamzah Fansuri. (G.W.J. Drewes & L.F. Brakel, eds & trans)
A.H. Johns, 293(JASt):Nov89–934
Hanan, P. The Invention of Li Yu.
D.T. Roy, 293(JASt):May89–359
Hanbury-Tenison, R. Spanish Pilgrimage.
X. Fielding, 617(TLS):12–18Oct90–1108
Hancock, G. Canadian Writers at Work.
P. Easingwood, 677(YES):Vol20–068
Hancock, G. Lords of Poverty.*
N. Hinton, 324:Apr90–370
Hancock, I.F., ed. Diversity and Development in English-Related Creoles.
M. Görlach, 260(IF):Band94–364
Hand, E. Winterlong.
G. Jonas, 441:9Dec90–32
Hand, S. – see Deleuze, G.
Handagard, S. Idar Handagard.
I. Stegane, 172(Edda):1989/2–182
Handel, M.I. War, Strategy and Intelligence.
M. Cranston, 617(TLS):6–12Apr90–377
"Händel-Handbuch." (Vol 4)
R. Wiesend, 417:Jul–Sep89–291
Handke, P. Absence.
E. Tallent, 441:17Jun90–8
Handke, P. The Afternoon of a Writer.* Versuch über die Jukebox.
A. Vivis, 617(TLS):5–11Oct90–1073
Handke, P. Après-midi d'un écrivain.
F Mary, 450(NRF):Apr89–110
Handke, P. Repetition.
I. Malin, 532(RCF):Spring89–260
Handke, P. Slow Homecoming.
J. Schlueter, 573(SSF):Spring89–202
Handler, R. Nationalism and the Politics of Culture in Quebec.
R. Cook, 529(QQ):Summer89–540
Hands, T. Thomas Hardy.
C.E. May, 637(VS):Summer90–670
Handy, C. The Age of Unreason.*
D.B. Henriques, 441:28Oct90–22
Hane, M., ed & trans. Reflections on the Way to the Gallows.*
B. Molony, 293(JASt):May89–387
M.C. Tocco, 407(MN):Autumn89–360
Hanfling, O., ed. Life and Meaning.*
D.Z. Phillips, 483:Apr89–266

Hanfling, O. The Quest for Meaning.
H.P.H., 185:Jan90–443
C. Lyas, 521:Oct89–341
D.Z. Phillips, 483:Apr89–266
639(VQR):Winter89–31
Hanke, I. Alltag und Politik.
J. Rosellini, 406:Spring89–107
Hankey, J. – see Shakespeare, W.
Hankins, J., J. Monfasani & F. Purnell, Jr., eds. Supplementum Festivum.
B.G. Kohl, 551(RenQ):Summer89–292
Hanks, P. & F. Hodges. A Dictionary of Surnames.
E. Battistella, 350:Sep90–638
K.B. Harder, 424:Sep89–285
E.G. Stanley, 447(N&Q):Sep89–373
Hanks, S. The Game That Changed Pro Football.
R. Regen, 441:28Jan90–23
Hänlein-Schäfer, H. Veneratio Augusti.
A. Vassilleiou, 555:Vol62Fasc1–179
Hanley, J. Boy. An End and a Beginning. No Directions.
B. Cheyette, 617(TLS):10–16Aug90–855
Hanna, J.L. Dance, Sex and Gender.
A. Daly, 162(TDR):Winter89–23
Hanna, R. 3d. The Index of Middle English Prose.* (Handlist 1)
H. Gneuss, 38:Band107Heft1/2–169
Hannah, J. Desperate Measures.
J.M. Flora, 649(WAL):May89–69
R.D. Newman, 577(SHR):Fall89–388
Hannay, M.P. Philip's Phoenix.
K. Duncan-Jones, 617(TLS):1–7Jun90–587
Hannesson, J.S. & others – see Sörenson, S.
Hannestad, N. Roman Art and Imperial Policy.*
D.C. Bellingham & A. Watson, 313:Vol79–217
M.A.R. Colledge, 123:Vol39No2–344
Hannick, C., ed. Sprachen und Nationen im Balkanraum.
T. Henninger, 575(SEER):Jul89–448
Hanrahan, B. Flawless Jade.
T. Glyde, 617(TLS):14–20Sep90–980
G. McFall, 441:23Dec90–12
Hanrieder, W.F. Germany, America, Europe.*
G.A. Craig, 453(NYRB):18Jan90–28
Hans, J.S. Imitation and the Image of Man.
M. McCanles, 678(YCGL):No36–168
Hanscombe, G. & V.L. Smyers. Writing for Their Lives.*
S.S. Friedman, 395(MFS):Winter89–864
Hanse, J. Nouveau dictionnaire des difficultés du français moderne.* (2nd ed)
M. Cook, 402(MLR):Apr90–434
Hansel, F. The Letters of Fanny Hensel to Felix Mendelssohn. (M.J. Citron, ed & trans)
R.L. Todd, 410(M&L):Nov89–554
Hansen, A.J. Expatriate Paris.
S. Carnell, 617(TLS):10–16Aug90–860
T. Swick, 441:10Jun90–49
Hansen, B. & N. Davis. Boone.
A. Corn, 441:5Aug90–14
442(NY):8Oct90–117
Hansen, E. & H.F. Nielsen. Irregularities in Modern English.
H. Ulherr, 38:Band107Heft1/2–115
Hansen, E.C. Ludovic Halévy.*
H. Gidel, 535(RHL):Nov–Dec89–1070

Hansen, E.T. The Solomon Complex.
C. Larrington, 382(MAE):1989/2-319
Hansen, H.M. – see Stensen, N.
Hansen, J. The Boy Who Was Buried this
Morning.
M. Stasio, 441:3Jun90-32
Hansen, K.V. & I.J. Philipson, eds. Women,
Class, and the Feminist Imagination.
H. Vendler, 453(NYRB):31May90-19
Hansen, M. – see Mahler, G.
Hansen, M.H. The Athenian Assembly in the
Age of Demosthenes.*
P. Cartledge, 235:Winter88-71
J. Ober, 122:Oct89-322
Hansen, M.H. Three Studies in Athenian De-
mocracy.
M. Menu, 555:Vol62Fasc2-348
Hansen, R. Nebraska.*
K. Ahearn, 649(WAL):Aug89-173
Hansen, U. Conrad Ferdinand Meyer: "Angela
Borgia."*
M.C. Crichton, 301(JEGP):Oct89-594
Hanson, A.M. Die zensurierte Muse.
U. Konrad, 417:Apr-Jun89-180
Hanson, C. – see Mansfield, K.
Hanson, P. Western Economic Statecraft in
East-West Relations.
D.A. Dyker, 575(SEER):Jul89-493
Hanson, P. & M. Kirkwood, eds. Alexander
Zinoviev as Writer and Thinker.
T.G. Marullo, 395(MFS):Winter89-836
Hanson, P.R. Provincial Politics in the French
Revolution.
G. Lewis, 617(TLS):14-20Dec90-1355
Hanson, R.L. The Democratic Imagination in
America.*
S. Friesner, 529(QQ):Summer89-547
Hanto, K.I. Ideologiar i norsk målreising.
K. Haugseth, 563(SS):Winter89-82
Hantos, T. Res publica constituta.
L. Thommen, 229:Band61Heft7-591
Haocheng, Y. – see under Yu Haocheng
Hapgood, R. Shakespeare the Theatre-Poet.
S. Billington, 610:Autumn89-288
N. Curry, 511:Apr89-45
A. Kirsch, 617(TLS):20-26Apr90-421
Harap, L. In the Mainstream.*
M.P.L., 295(JML):Fall88/Winter89-199
Harari, J.V. Scenarios of the Imaginary.*
T.E.D. Braun, 125:Spring89-310
K. Racevskis, 577(SHR):Summer89-295
M-F. Silver, 166:Oct89-76
P. Stewart, 207(FR):Mar90-713
Haraszti, M. The Velvet Prison.*
F.H. Adler, 42(AR):Winter89-103
Haraway, D. Primate Visions.
R. Dunbar, 441:7Jan90-30
C. Geertz, 453(NYRB):8Nov90-19
M. Neve, 617(TLS):20-26Jul90-784
Harben, N. Twentieth-Century English His-
tory Plays.
R.W. Strang, 447(N&Q):Dec89-548
Harcave, S. – see Witte, S.
Harcombe, D. Solomon Islands.
T. Swick, 441:10Jun90-49
Harden, B. Africa.
G. Wheatcroft, 61:Nov90-169
442(NY):22Oct90-143
Harden, E.F. – see Thackeray, W.M.
Harder, A. – see Euripides
Harder, K.B., comp. Names and Their Varie-
ties.
M.R. Miller, 35(AS):Fall89-270

Hardie, P.R. Virgil's "Aeneid."*
E.A. Schmidt, 229:Band61Heft8-672
Hardiman, D. The Coming of the Devi.
D. Haynes, 293(JASt):Aug89-653
Hardin, C.L. Color for Philosophers.*
R. Smook, 103:Jun90-233
J. Westphal, 393(Mind):Jan89-145
Hardin, J. Johann Christoph Ettner.
J.P. Clark, 221(GQ):Fall89-527
Hardin, J. – see "Dictionary of Literary Biog-
raphy"
Hardin, R. Morality within the Limits of Rea-
son.
W. Donner, 103:Mar90-112
Harding, A.J. Coleridge and the Inspired
Word.*
A.C. Goodson, 591(SIR):Spring89-170
Harding, B. – see Hawthorne, N.
Harding, E. & P. Riley. The Bilingual Family.*
O. Garcia, 399(MLJ):Summer89-209
N.H. Hornberger, 355(LSoc):Sep89-459
Harding, G. In Another Europe.
M. Almond, 617(TLS):19-25Jan90-56
Harding, H. China's Second Revolution.
B. Womack, 293(JASt):May89-360
Harding, M.P. The Trouble with Sarah Gul-
lion.
P. Lewis, 565:Summer89-66
Hardison, O.B., Jr. Disappearing Through the
Skylight.*
R.M. Adams, 453(NYRB):26Apr90-46
Hardison, O.B., Jr. Prosody and Purpose in
the English Renaissance.
E.D. Hill, 604:Spring/Summer89-29
Hardman, C. "The Winter's Tale."
R. Knowles, 402(MLR):Apr90-409
Hardouin-Fugier, E. & E. Grafe. French
Flower Painters of the Nineteenth Century.
(P. Mitchell, ed)
B. Scott, 39:Nov89-357
Hardwick, J. An Immodest Violet.
M. Seymour, 617(TLS):23-29Nov90-1258
Hardy, B. The Collected Essays of Barbara
Hardy.* (Vol 1)
C.A. Howells, 677(YES):Vol20-350
Hardy, D. Land and Freedom.
D.L. Pearl, 550(RusR):Jan89-88
Hardy, H. – see Berlin, I.
Hardy, J.E. The Fiction of Walker Percy.*
Z. Abádi-Nagy, 27(AL):Oct89-500
S. Derwin, 400(MLN):Dec89-1223
M.J.F., 295(JML):Fall88/Winter89-390
M. Pearson, 392:Winter88/89-100
Hardy, T. The Collected Letters of Thomas
Hardy.* (Vol 5) (R.L. Purdy and M. Millgate,
eds)
T.R.M. Creighton, 541(RES):Nov89-581
Hardy, T. The Collected Letters of Thomas
Hardy.* (Vol 6) (R.L. Purdy & M. Millgate,
eds)
T.R.M. Creighton, 541(RES):Nov89-581
M. Thorpe, 179(ES):Feb89-94
Hardy, T. The Collected Letters of Thomas
Hardy. (Vol 7) (R.L. Purdy & M. Millgate,
eds)
M. Williams, 447(N&Q):Dec89-536
Hardy, T. Collected Short Stories. (F.B. Pin-
ion, ed)
R.C. Schweik, 177(ELT):Vol32No3-334
Hardy, T. The Mayor of Casterbridge.* (D.
Kramer, ed)
S. Hunter, 677(YES):Vol20-309
M. Thorpe, 179(ES):Feb89-94

Hare, J. & J.D. Lortie – see Lenoir, J.
Hare, P.H., ed. Doing Philosophy Historically.
  A. Kerby, 103:Mar90–115
  A. O'Hear, 484(PPR):Mar90–628
  T.M.R., 185:Apr90–699
Hare, R.M. Essays on Political Morality. Essays in Ethical Theory.
  N. Fotion, 185:Jul90–889
Hare-Mustin, R.T. & J. Marecek, eds. Making a Difference.
  L. Hudson, 617(TLS):1–7Jun90–588
Haren, M. & Y. de Pontfarcy, eds. The Medieval Pilgrimage to St. Patrick's Purgatory.
  K. Simms, 235:Winter89–90
Hareven, T. & A. Plakans, eds. Family History at the Crossroads.
  C.L. Bushman, 658:Summer/Autumn89–175
Harf-Lancner, L., comp. Métamorphose et bestiaire fantastique au Moyen Age.
  M–C. Struyf, 356(LR):Aug89–209
Hargreaves, A.G., ed. Immigration in Post-War France.
  A. Pedley, 402(MLR):Jan90–201
Harich, H. Alexander Epicus.
  N. Adkin, 123:Vol39No1–161
Haring-Smith, T. From Farce to Metadrama.
  C.J. Carlisle, 612(ThS):Nov88–213
Harker, M.F. Henry Peach Robinson.*
  T. Prasch, 637(VS):Winter90–359
Harkness, M. "A Portrait of the Artist as a Young Man."
  M.P. Gillespie, 329(JJQ):Summer90–875
Hari, K.W. Civic Coins and Civic Politics in the Roman East, A.D. 180–275.
  C.J. Howgego, 313:Vol79–243
  N.M. Kennell, 487:Autumn89–276
Harland, C.R. Mark Rutherford.*
  D.F. Hiatt, 178:Jun89–234
  C. Swann, 177(ELT):Vol32No2–236
  K. Wilson, 529(QQ):Autumn89–742
Harland, R. Superstructuralism.*
  D. Dowling, 102(CanL):Winter88–118
  E. Wright, 541(RES):Feb89–142
Harle, G. Die Gestalt des Schönen.*
  G. Bridges, 222(GR):Summer89–136
Harle, J.C. The Art and Architecture of the Indian Subcontinent.
  M. Rabe, 293(JASt):May89–424
  C. Tadgell, 576:Jun89–206
Harle, V., ed. Essays in Peace Studies.
  R.M., 185:Oct89–222
Harley, M.P., ed & trans. A Revelation of Purgatory by an Unknown Fifteenth-Century Woman Visionary.
  E.S. Newlyn, 201:Vol15–333
Harline, C.E. Pamphlets, Printing and Political Culture in the Early Dutch Republic.
  M. Lowry, 551(RenQ):Spring89–105
Harlow, B. Resistance Literature.*
  D. Elam, 454:Winter90–212
  C. Kaplan, 395(MFS):Spring89–181
  N. Lazarus, 454:Spring90–318
  E.S., 295(JML):Fall88/Winter89–199
Harman, A. & W. Mellers, with A. Milner. Man and his Music. (new ed)
  J.H., 412:Nov88–309
Harman, G. Change in View.*
  R. Feldman, 482(PhR):Oct89–552
  C. Hookway, 479(PhQ):Apr89–242
Harman, M., ed. Robert Walser Rediscovered.*
  M. Holona, 133:Band22Heft2–184

Harms, W. & C. Kemp, eds. Deutsche Illustrierte Flugblätter des 16. und 17. Jahrhunderts.* (Vol 4)
  W.E. Schäfer, 224(GRM):Band39Heft1–109
Harms, W. & C. Kemp, eds. Die Sammlungen der hessischen Landes- und Hochschulbibliothek in Darmstadt.
  R. Schenda, 196:Band30Heft3/4–328
Harney, M.J. Intentionality, Sense and the Mind.
  D. Willard, 323:Oct89–299
Harnoncourt, N. Baroque Music Today.
  R. Donington, 410(M&L):Aug89–391
de Haro, P.A. – see under Aullón de Haro, P.
Harootunian, H.D. Things Seen and Unseen.
  K.W. Nakai, 407(MN):Summer89–224
  K. Nobukuni, 293(JASt):Aug89–612
Harper, D. Working Knowledge.
  C.M. Keller, 650(WF):Jan89–79
  E.G. Mishler, 139:Apr/May89–22
Harper, F.E.W. A Brighter Coming Day. (F.S. Foster, ed)
  J. Olney, 441:23Sep90–38
Harper-Bill, C. & R. Harvey, eds. The Ideals and Practice of Medieval Knighthood II.
  D.H. Green, 402(MLR):Jan90–128
Harpham, G.G. The Ascetic Imperative in Culture and Criticism.*
  R. Chambers, 301(JEGP):Apr89–213
  K. Quinlan, 219(GaR):Spring89–200
  T. Rajan, 529(QQ):Summer89–514
  L.S. Koudiez, 567:Vol76No3/4–321
Harpham, G.G. On the Grotesque.
  D.T.O., 295(JML):Fall88/Winter89–184
Harpur, C. Stalwart the Bushranger. (E. Perkins, ed)
  K. Stewart, 71(ALS):May89–122
Harpur, Y. Decoration of Egyptian Tombs of the Old Kingdom.
  K.P. Foster, 124:Nov–Dec89–120
Harrán, D. In Defense of Music.
  D. Leech-Wilkinson, 617(TLS):16–22Mar90–285
Harrán, D. Word-Tone Relations in Musical Thought from Antiquity to the Seventeenth Century.*
  C. Berger, 417:Oct–Dec89–375
  B.J. Blackburn, 317:Spring89–161
  J. Stevens, 410(M&L):Feb89–78
Harrauer, C. Meliouchos.
  J.G. Griffiths, 123:Vol39No1–62
Harries, M. & S. A Pilgrim Soul.*
  B. Elias, 607:Dec89–40
Harries, M. & S. Sheathing the Sword.
  T.W. Burkman, 293(JASt):Feb89–160
Harrington, A. Medicine, Mind, and the Double Brain.
  A. Scull, 637(VS):Spring90–503
Harrington, D.J. & A.J. Saldarini – see "Targum Jonathan of the Former Prophets"
Harrington, W.J. Heroes and Heroines of the Way.
  D. Flanagan, 235:Winter89–93
Harriott, E. American Voices.
  G.S. Armstrong, 610:Autumn89–309
Harris, A., ed. A World Unsuspected.*
  C. Barrow, 577(SHR):Summer89–283
Harris, B.E., ed. The Great Roll of the Pipe for the Fourth Year of the Reign of King Henry III, Michaelmas 1220 (Pipe Roll 64).
  F.A. Cazel, Jr., 589:Jan89–175

Harris, E.T. Henry Purcell's "Dido and
Aeneas."*
  M. Burden, 415:Feb89-85
Harris, J. Jane Austen's Art of Memory.
  J. Bender, 617(TLS):10-16Aug90-854
Harris, J. Samuel Richardson.*
  A. Gibson, 566:Spring89-163
  M. Irwin, 541(RES):May89-269
Harris, J. & G. Higgott. Inigo Jones: Complete
Architectural Drawings.*
  J. Wilton-Ely, 324:Aug90-645
Harris, J.B. & B. Pimsleur. La Vie ailleurs.
  F. Demerson-Baker, 207(FR):Apr90-901
Harris, J.G. Osip Mandelstam.
  C. Isenberg, 104(CASS):Spring-Winter88-
441
  D. Rayfield, 575(SEER):Jul89-457
Harris, K.M. Hypocrisy and Self-Deception in
Hawthorne's Fiction.
  W.B. Dillingham, 587(SAF):Autumn89-244
  R.K. Gollin, 432(NEQ):Mar89-143
  P.F. Gura, 445(NCF):Jun89-101
  J.L. Idol, 594:Fall89-332
  M.V. Murtha, 27(AL):May89-294
  J. Pilditch, 478(P&L):Oct89-413
Harris, M. The Cathay Stories and Other Fic-
tions.
  I. Malin, 532(RCF):Summer89-253
Harris, M. Hemingway's Suitcase.
  M. Paley, 441:17Jun90-9
Harris, M. Our Kind.
  S.B. Hrdy, 441:8Apr90-16
Harris, M. Speed.
  F. Flagg, 441:23Sep90-25
Harris, M. Teaching One-to-One.
  D. George, 128(CE):Apr89-418
Harris, M. & K. Aguero, eds. A Gift of
Tongues.
  L. Goldstein, 271:Fall89-159
Harris, M. & P. Ramat, eds. Historical Devel-
opment of Auxiliaries.
  P.M. Bertinetto, 297(JL):Sep89-537
Harris, M. & N. Vincent, eds. The Romance
Languages.
  T.G. Griffith, 278(IS):Vol44-146
  R. Posner, 353:Vol27No3-557
Harris, M.F. Art on the Road.
  D. Cosentino, 2(AfrA):May89-29
Harris, N. Connecting Times.*
  J.H. Scott, 587(SAF):Spring89-117
Harris, P., ed. Civil Disobedience.
  T.C. Pocklington, 103:Mar90-118
Harris, R. Good and Faithful Servant.
  F. Mount, 617(TLS):21-27Dec90-1369
Harris, R. The Language Machine.*
  N. Love, 494:Winter89-793
  M. Toolan, 355(LSoc):Jun89-269
Harris, R. The Language Myth.* Reading
Saussure.* The Language-Makers.
  N. Love, 494:Winter89-793
Harris, R. Language, Saussure and Wittgen-
stein.*
  W. Bennett, 402(MLR):Jul90-740
  N. Love, 494:Winter89-793
Harris, R., ed. Linguistic Thought in England
1914-1945.*
  L. Zgusta, 350:Jun90-416
Harris, R. The Origin of Writing.
  N. Love, 494:Winter89-793
  W.C. Watt, 567:Vol75No3/4-279
Harris, R. & T.J. Taylor. Landmarks in Lin-
guistic Thought.
  W.P. Lehmann, 350:Sep90-581

Harris, R.C., ed. Historical Atlas of Canada.*
(Vol 1)
  J. Axtell, 656(WMQ):Jan89-170
Harris, R.S. English Studies at Toronto.*
  R.A. Greene, 627(UTQ):Fall89-228
Harris, S. Film, Television, and Stage Music
on Phonograph Records.
  B.L. Cooper, 498:Summer89-120
Harris, S.K. 19th-Century American Women's
Novels.
  L.M. Freibert, 357:Fall90-57
Harris, T. London Crowds in the Reign of
Charles II.
  A. Coleby, 242:Vol10No6-742
Harris, W.V. Ancient Literacy.
  G. Woolf, 617(TLS):6-12Jul90-736
Harris, W.V. Interpretive Acts.*
  R.J. Dingley, 447(N&Q):Dec89-552
  W. Shibles, 603:Vol13No1-195
Harris, Z. Language and Information.
  K. Warmbröd, 103:Mar90-121
Harrison, A., ed. Philosophy and the Visual
Arts.
  P. Humble, 89(BJA):Spring89-180
  G. Iseminger, 290(JAAC):Spring89-191
Harrison, A.H. Christina Rossetti in Context.*
  H.M.A., 636(VP):Summer89-220
  R. Chapman, 445(NCF):Jun89-107
Harrison, A.H. Swinburne's Medievalism.*
  K. McSweeney, 445(NCF):Jun89-109
  R. Rooksby, 447(N&Q):Jun89-253
Harrison, C. Break and Enter.
  M. Stasio, 441:24Jun90-22
Harrison, C. France and Islam in West Africa,
1860-1960.
  J.J. Lafontant, 446(NCFS):Fall-
Winter89/90-284
Harrison, C. Richard's Feet.
  J. Wilcox, 441:21Oct90-31
Harrison, E.R. Darkness at Night.*
  T. Dickinson, 529(QQ):Summer89-549
Harrison, G.B. One Man in His Time.
  F. Teague, 570(SQ):Spring89-128
Harrison, J. The Singing Underneath.*
  B. Howard, 491:May89-107
Harrison, J. The Woman Lit by Fireflies.
  R. Houston, 441:16Sep90-13
Harrison, M. A Temple for Byzantium.
  A.A.M. Bryer, 617(TLS):9-15Feb90-153
Harrison, N.R. Jean Rhys and the Novel as
Women's Text.*
  D.M. McPherson, 395(MFS):Summer89-343
Harrison, P.C., ed. Totem Voices.
  G.H. Bass, 34:Jun89-38
Harrison, R. - see Saba, U.
Harrison, R.J. Spain at the Dawn of History.*
  J. Edmondson, 313:Vol79-240
Harrison, S. Mother Earth Father Sky.
  K. Ramsland, 441:17Jun90-16
Harrison, S.J., ed. Oxford Readings in
Vergil's "Aeneid."
  R. Jenkyns, 617(TLS):23-29Nov90-1268
Harrison, T. V.
  E. Hirsch, 441:18Nov90-24
Harron, M. Don Harron.
  V. Tovell, 108:Fall89-86
Harsent, D. Selected Poems.*
  P. Gross, 493:Autumn89-65
  S. O'Brien, 364:Jun/Jul89-91
Harss, L., ed & trans. Sor Juana's Dream.*
  E. Arenal, 141:Fall89-463
Hart, A. Arafat.
  S.G. Kellman, 390:Jun/Jul89-58

Hart, A. The Life and Times of Hercule
Poirot.
    A. Whitehouse, 441:28Jan90-23
Hart, C. Images of Flight.
    L. Goldstein, 385(MQR):Summer90-472
Hart, C. Joyce, Huston and the Making of
"The Dead."
    D. Kelly, 329(JJQ):Spring90-700
Hart, G. Power, Labor, and Livelihood.
    R. Hefner, 293(JASt):May89-434
Hart, J. Montana - Native Plants and Early
Peoples.
    A.R. Taylor, 269(IJAL):Jul89-359
Hart, K. Your Shadow.
    R. Crawford, 493:Autumn89-23
Hart, K.C. Kitty.
    M.A. Godfrey, 34:May89-41
Hart, L., ed. Making a Spectacle.
    K. Davy, 615(TJ):Oct89-429
    L.P. Ives, 397(MD):Mar89-167
Hart, L. Sam Shepard's Metaphorical Stages.*
    J.S. Dickey, 610:Summer89-220
    R.F.S., 295(JML):Fall88/Winter89-407
Hart, P. The Spanish Sleuth.*
    G. Díaz-Migoyo, 240(HR):Summer89-398
    B. Jordan, 402(MLR):Apr90-483
    I. Stavans, 711(RHM):Jun89-92
Hart, R. Robbed Blind.
    P. Craig, 617(TLS):16-22Mar90-298
Hart, S. Religión, politica y ciencia en la
obra de César Vallejo.
    D. Harris, 402(MLR):Jan90-232
Hart, S.M., ed. "¡No pasarán!"
    O.F. Kenyon, 402(MLR):Oct90-1007
Hart, W.D. The Engines of the Soul.
    J. Edwards, 479(PhQ):Oct89-512
Hart-Davis, D. The House the Berrys Built.
    A. Sampson, 617(TLS):13-19Apr90-389
Hartcup, G. The War of Invention.
    K. Neilson, 529(QQ):Winter89-994
Harte, J. Cuckoo Pounds and Singing Barrows.
    M. Jones, 203:Vol100No1-126
Harth, D. & M. Raether, eds. Denis Diderot
oder die Ambivalenz der Aufklärung.*
    M. Delon, 535(RHL):Jan-Feb89-114
    S. Kupsch-Losereit, 72:Band226Heft1-
    208
Harth, H. - see Bracciolini, P.
Hartigan, R.S. The Future Remembered.
    R.H.B., 185:Oct89-210
Hartle, A.E. Moral Issues in Military Decision
Making.
    A.T. Acerra, 543:Mar90-633
Hartley, G. Textual Politics and the Lan
guage Poets.
    D. Kellogg, 30:Winter90-86
    J. Monroe, 659(ConL):Winter90-542
Hartley, J. Philip Larkin, The Marvell Press
and Me.*
    S. O'Brien, 364:Aug/Sep89-140
    J. Whitworth, 493:Winter89/90-62
Hartman, C. Han Yü and the T'ang Search for
Unity.*
    D.J. Levy, 116:Dec89-149
    D. McMullen, 244(HJAS):Dec89-603
Hartman, D. Conflicting Visions.
    J.E. Young, 441:16Sep90-11
Hartman, E. French Literary Wagnerism.
    B.L. Knapp, 446(NCFS):Fall-Winter89/90-
    295
Hartman, G.H. The Unremarkable Words-
worth.*
    J.D. Gutteridge, 447(N&Q):Mar89-117

Hartmann, J-U., ed & trans. Das Varṇār-
havarṇastotra des Mātṛceṭa.
    J.W. de Jong, 259(IIJ):Jul89-243
Hartmann von Aue. Erec.* (T.L. Keller,
trans)
    P.M. McConeghy, 589:Oct89-964
    K.J. Meyer, 406:Summer89-251
Hartmann von Aue. Erec. (M. Resler, ed &
trans)
    S.M. Johnson, 301(JEGP):Oct89-575
    P.M. McConeghy, 589:Oct89-964
    K.J. Meyer, 406:Summer89-251
Hartnett, D. House of Moon.*
    G. Maxwell, 493:Spring89-52
Hartog, D. Candy from Strangers.
    P.M. St. Pierre, 102(CanL):Spring89-210
Hartog, F. Le XIXe siècle et l'histoire.
    D. Bourel, 531:Jul-Dec89-550
Hartog, F. The Mirror of Herodotus.
    P. Cartledge, 235:Winter88-62
Hartog, H. Heinrich Kaminski.
    R. Stephan, 417:Oct-Dec89-386
de Hartog, J. The Centurion.*
    42(AR):Summer89-375
Hartsfield, M.G., ed. Tall Betsy and Dunce
Baby.
    J.A. Burrison, 292(JAF):Apr-Jun89-226
    E.L. Montenyohl, 582(SFQ):Vol46No2-199
Hartt, F. Art. (2nd ed)
    B.R. Collins, 127:Summer89-190
Hartveit, L. Workings of the Picaresque in
the British Novel.*
    M. Carroll, 295(JML):Fall88/Winter89-244
    A. Ryall, 172(Edda):1989/2-172
Hartwell, D.G., ed. The World Treasury of
Science Fiction.
    J. Updike, 442(NY):26Feb90-126
Harty, J. 3d, ed. Tom Stoppard.
    J.S. Dickey, 615(TJ):May89-266
Harvey, A. Economic Expansion in the
Byzantine Empire, 900-1200.
    M. Angold, 617(TLS):17-23Aug90-879
Harvey, A.D. Literature into History.
    G. Headley, 481(PQ):Summer90-386
Harvey, A.E. Strenuous Commands.
    E. Norman, 617(TLS):21-27Dec90-1379
Harvey, D. The Condition of Postmodernity.
    Z. Bauman, 617(TLS):11-17May90-501
    C. Lock, 627(UTQ):Spring90-433
Harvey, I.E. Derrida and the Economy of Dif-
férance.*
    S.C. Wheeler 3d, 482(PhR):Apr89-273
Harvey, J. The Legend of Captain Space.
    J. Melmoth, 617(TLS):26Jan-1Feb90-87
Harvey, J. Rough Treatment.
    P. Kerr, 617(TLS):25-31May90-558
    M. Stasio, 441:12Aug90-21
Harvey, J. & H. Cantelon, eds. Not Just a
Game.
    G.S. Smith, 529(QQ):Winter89-996
Harvey, P. & J.E. Heseltine. The Oxford Com-
panion to French Literature.
    R. Adams, 453(NYRB):1Feb90-36
Harvey, S. Directed by Vincente Minnelli.
    L. Braudy, 441:4Mar90-7
Harvey, S.A. Asceticism and Society in
Crisis.
    H. Chadwick, 617(TLS):6-12Jul90-737
Harvor, E. If Only We Could Drive Like This
Forever.
    R. Donovan, 198:Spring89-116

Harwood, J. Olivia Shakespear and W.B. Yeats.
R. Foster, 617(TLS):23-29Nov90-1256
Harwood, L. Crossing the Frozen River.*
K. Jebb, 493:Summer89-31
Harwood, R., ed. Dear Alec.
G. Gordon, 511:Apr89-44
Hasan-Rokem, G. & A. Dundes, eds. The Wandering Jew.*
S. Top, 196:Band30Heft1/2-131
Hasford, G. The Phantom Blooper.
C. Salzberg, 441:15Apr90-14
Hashmi, A., ed. The World of Muslim Imagination. Pakistani Literature.
A. Malak, 268(IFR):Summer89-158
Haskell, F. Past and Present in Art and Taste.*
A. Silvers, 290(JAAC):Winter89-94
Haskell, H. The Early Music Revival.*
E. Roche, 410(M&L):Aug89-382
Haskell, M. Love and Other Infectious Diseases.
D. Ephron, 441:8Apr90-9
Haslam, M. Art Nouveau.
90:Aug89-568
Haslam, M.W., ed. Oxyrhynchus Papyri. (Vol 53)
M. Davies, 303(JoHS):Vol109-247
Haspels, J.J.L. Automatic Musical Instruments.
L. Libin, 309:Vol9No2/3-198
Hass, R. Human Wishes.*
M. Boruch, 29(APR):Nov/Dec89-21
Hass, U. Leonhard Schwartzenbachs "Synonyma."
L. Sattler, 682(ZPSK):Band42Heft5-671
Hassan, I. The Postmodern Turn.*
B.K. Horvath, 395(MFS):Summer89-370
D.T.O., 295(JML):Fall88/Winter89-185
A. Thiher, 659(ConL):Summer90-236
Hassel, R.C., Jr. Songs of Death.
P. Happé, 541(RES):Aug89-411
J.R. Siemon, 570(SQ):Spring89-104
Hasselbach, K. Georg Büchner: "Lenz."*
T.R. Nadar, 406:Spring89-127
von Hassell, F. Hostage of the Third Reich. (D. Forbes-Watt, ed)
442(NY):29Jan90-96
von Hassell, F. A Mother's War. (D. Forbes-Watt, ed)
C. Moorehead, 617(TLS):23-29Mar90-313
Hassler, H.L. Toccatas. (S. Stribos, ed)
A. Silbiger, 317:Spring89-172
Hassler, J. North of Hope.
R. Russo, 441:21Oct90-39
Hasting, M. The Devil's Spy.
639(VQR):Autumn89-130
Hasty, O.P. & S. Fusso, eds & trans. America through Russian Eyes, 1874-1926.*
H. Rogger, 550(RusR):Apr89-188
Hatch, N.O. The Democratization of American Christianity.
B. Wilson, 617(TLS):3-9Aug90-831
Hatch, N.O. & H.S. Stout, eds. Jonathan Edwards and the American Experience.
W.U. Solberg, 656(WMQ):Jan89-183
Hattendorf, J.B. England in the War of Spanish Succesion.
J. Black, 83:Autumn89-206
Hattersley, G. Slouching Towards Rotherham.
I. McMillan, 493:Winter89/90-65

Hattersley, R. The Maker's Mark. A Yorkshire Boyhood. (rev)
S. Collini, 617(TLS):17-23Aug90-867
Hattiangadi, J.N. How is Language Possible?*
S. Nicolson, 154:Vol28No3-512
Häublein, G., T. Scherling & G. Häusler. Telefonieren.
I. Henderson, 399(MLJ):Summer89-232
Haubrichs, W. Geschichte der deutschen Literatur von den Anfängen bis zum Beginn der Neuzeit. (Vol 1, Pt 1)
D.H. Green, 402(MLR):Apr90-489
Hauck, G. The Aqueduct of Nemausus.
G.E. Rickman, 123:Vol39No2-416
Hauck, K. & others. Die Goldbrakteaten der Völkerwanderungszeit.* (Vols 1 & 2)
H. Seelow, 684(ZDA):Band118Heft2-60
Haudry, J. La Religion cosmique des Indo-Européens.
M.L. West, 123:Vol39No1-144
Hauenschild, C. Zur Interpretation russischer Nominalgruppen.
H.R. Mehlig, 559:Vol13No2-161
Hauerwas, S. Suffering Presence.
A.A. Grugan, 258:Dec89-485
Hauff, W. Sämtliche Märchen und Novellen.
H. Rölleke, 196:Band30Heft1/2-135
Haug, W. Literaturtheorie im deutschen Mittelalter.*
S. Jaffe, 301(JEGP):Oct89-579
Hauge, O.H. Don't Give Me the Whole Truth.
P. Hager, 563(SS):Winter89-114
Haugen, E. Blessings of Babel.
I. Soto, 402(MLR):Oct90-888
S. Zempel, 563(SS):Spring/Summer89-293
Hauptmann, G. Tagebücher 1897-1905.* (M. Machatzke, ed)
R.C. Cowen, 133:Band22Heft3/4-345
S. Hoefert, 406:Fall89-399
Hauptmann, O.H. & M.G. Littlefield, eds. Escorial Bible I.J.4. (Vol 2)
S. Baldwin, 240(HR):Spring89-226
S.D. Kirby, 304(JHP):Winter89-149
Hauriou, M. Aux sources du droit.
J-L. Dumas, 192(EP):Jul-Dec89-540
Hause, S.C. Hubertine Auclert.*
W.Z. Silverman, 446(NCFS):Spring-Summer90-593
Hausen, M. & others. Eliel Saarinen.
M. Filler, 441:2Dec90-24
Häusler, G. Gespräch.
I. Henderson, 399(MLJ):Summer89-232
Häusler, G., T. Scherling & G. Häublein. Grammatik. Stellensuche.
I. Henderson, 399(MLJ):Summer89-232
Hausman, G. Meditations with The Navajo.
P.K. Kett, 649(WAL):Aug89-161
Hausmann, F-R., ed & trans. Die Gedichte aus Dantes "De vulgari eloquentia."
F. Jensen, 545(RPh):Feb90-486
Hausmann, F-R. – see Villon, F.
Haustrate, G. Bertrand Blier.
J. Anzalone, 207(FR):Feb90-567
Havard, R. Jorge Guillén "Cántico."*
B. Ciplijauskaité, 240(HR):Autumn89-527
Havard, R.G. From Romanticism to Surrealism.
C. Davies, 402(MLR):Oct90-1004
Havel, V. Disturbing the Peace.
R. Brustein, 441:17Jun90-1
P. Sherwood, 617(TLS):23-29Nov90-1262
Havel, V. Letters to Olga June 1979-September 1982.*
J. Malcolm, 453(NYRB):14Jun90-35

Havel, V. Living in Truth. (J. Vladislav, ed)
J. Adler, 617(TLS):23–29Mar90–303
Havelock, E.A. The Muse Learns to Write.*
E.L. Rivers, 131(CL):Winter89–102
W. Rösler, 229:Band61Heft5–385
Havens, L. A Safe Place.
R. Flaste, 441:4Feb90–12
Havens, T.R.H. Fire Across the Sea.*
S. Vlastos, 293(JASt):Feb89–162
Haverkamp-Begemann, E. Creative Copies.
D. Scrase, 39:Dec89–429
Havranek, G. Das Verbalsystem in der Ler-
nersprache.
J.L. Cox, 399(MLJ):Summer89–203
Hawke, D.F. Nuts and Bolts of the Past.
639(VQR):Spring89–46
Hawkes, J. Whistlejacket.*
J. Mellors, 364:Jun/Jul89–133
Hawkes, T. That Shakespeherian Rag.*
D. Ellis, 97(CQ):Vol18No1–86
A.F. Kinney, 481(PQ):Fall89–443
Hawkesworth, W. Leander; Labyrinthus. (S.
Brock, ed)
G. Eatough, 123:Vol39No1–129
R. Green, 447(N&Q):Dec89–498
Hawkin, T. Deutsch Express!
K.E.H. Liedtke, 399(MLJ):Autumn89–371
Hawking, S.W. A Brief History of Time.*
(French title: Une brève histoire du temps.)
T.C. Holyoke, 42(AR):Summer89–363
J. Largeault, 542:Oct–Dec89–650
Hawkins, D. When I Was.
J. Lewis, 364:Oct/Nov89–137
Hawkins, E. Modern Languages in the Cur-
riculum. (rev)
L. Book, 399(MLJ):Autumn89–344
Hawkins, G. & F.E. Zimring. Pornography in a
Free Society.
S.C–M., 185:Apr90–710
A. Clare, 617(TLS):12–18Jan90–32
Hawkins, H. "Measure for Measure."*
S. Billington, 610:Spring89–87
R.J.C. Watt, 541(RES):Nov89–552
Hawkins, H.S., G.A. Greb & G.W. Szilard – see
Szilard, L.
Hawkins, J.A. A Comparative Typology of
English and German.*
M. Markus, 38:Band107Heft1/2–110
Haworth, L. Autonomy.*
N.B. Kapur, 154:Vol28No3–487
Hawthorn, G. – see Sen, A. & others
Hawthorn, J. "Bleak House."*
T.J. Cribb, 541(RES):May89–281
Hawthorn, J. Unlocking the Text.*
T. Docherty, 541(RES):Nov89–598
D. Hewitt, 447(N&Q):Mar89–137
J.A. Varsava, 268(IFR):Summer89–153
Hawthorne, N. Nathaniel Hawthorne: The
Letters, 1853–1856. (T. Woodson & others,
eds)
J.L. Idol, Jr., 301(JEGP):Apr89–261
J.L. Idol, Jr., 573(SSF):Fall88–488
Hawthorne, N. Nathaniel Hawthorne: The
Letters, 1857–1864. (T. Woodson & others,
eds)
J.L. Idol, Jr., 301(JEGP):Apr89–261
Hawthorne, N. The Scarlet Letter. (S. Gross
& others, eds)
D. Hewitt, 447(N&Q):Jun89–273
Hawthorne, N. Young Goodman Brown and
Other Tales. (B. Harding, ed)
M. Gonnaud, 189(EA):Jul–Sep89–367
Hawtree, C. – see Greene, G.

Haxton, B. Traveling Company.
A. Hudgins, 249(HudR):Winter89–675
Hay, G. – see Wedekind, F.
Hay, L., ed. Le Manuscrit inachevé.*
P. Berthier, 535(RHL):Mar–Apr89–343
Haycraft, J. In Search of the French Revolu-
tion.
G. Lewis, 617(TLS):26Jan–1Feb90–93
Hayden, T. Reunion.*
C.J. Fox, 364:Oct/Nov89–126
Haydon, B.R. Neglected Genius. (J. Jolliffe,
ed)
G. Reynolds, 617(TLS):19–25Oct90–1134
Hayes, B., with R. Pack. Run, Bullet, Run.
R. Regan, 441:7Oct90–18
Hayes, D. The Classical Torso in 1980.
G. Harding–Russell, 102(CanL):
Summer89–175
M.T. Lane, 198:Winter89–115
L. McKinney, 526:Summer89–99
Hayes, H., with K. Hatch. My Life in Three
Acts.
P–L. Adams, 61:May90–132
D. Kaufman, 441:6May90–23
Hayes, H.T.P. The Dark Romance of Dian Fos-
sey.
D. Willis, 441:15Jul90–11
Hayley, B. & E. McKay, eds. 300 Years of
Irish Periodicals.*
F. Tipple, 272(IUR):Spring89–197
Hayman, D. Re-Forming the Narrative.*
M.P.L., 295(JML):Fall88/Winter89–246
P. Meisel, 395(MFS):Winter89–852
M. Molaver, 494:Fall89–643
Hayman, H. Between Two Rains.
42(AR):Summer89–373
Hayman, R. Proust.
P. Brooks, 441:23Dec90–8
D. Coward, 617(TLS):26Oct–1Nov90–1144
442(NY):24Dec90–99
Haymes, E.R. The "Nibelungenlied."*
S. Christoph, 125:Fall88–99
G. Gillespie, 402(MLR):Jul90–777
Haymes, E.R. – see "The Saga of Thidrek of
Bern"
Haymes, E.R. & S.C. van D'Elden, eds. The
Dark Figure in Medieval German and Ger-
manic Literature.
G. Gillespie, 402(MLR):Apr90–495
al-Ḥaymī, H.A. A Yemenite Embassy to
Ethiopia, 1647–1649. (E.J. van Donzel, ed
& trans)
C.E. Farah, 318(JAOS):Apr–Jun88–323
Hayner, D. & T. McNamee. Streetwise Chicago.
V.J. Vogel, 424:Dec89–381
Haynes, J. African Poetry and the English
Language.*
T. Ojaide, 538(RAL):Spring89–147
L. Sail, 565:Summer89–75
Hays, M. – see Szondi, P.
Hayter, A. Opium and the Romantic Imagina-
tion. (new ed)
J.D. Gutteridge, 447(N&Q):Sep89–404
Hayter, T. Exploited Earth.
M. Bruce, 324:Apr90–371
Hayton, D. & G. O'Brien – see Simms, J.G.
Hayward, R. The Targum of Jeremiah.
B.L. Visotzky, 508:Jan89–93
Haywood, E., ed. Dante Readings.
P. Shaw, 278(IS):Vol44–153
Haywood, I. The Making of History.*
S. Varey, 83:Autumn89–204

Hazan, B.A. From Brezhnev to Gorbachev.
　M. Rush, 104(CASS):Spring89-84
Hazelton, L. England, Bloody England.
　A. Howard, 617(TLS):23-29Mar90-324
　V. Weissman, 441:18Feb90-21
Hazzard, S. Countenance of Truth.
　M. Howard, 617(TLS):29Jun-5Jul90-686
　P. Lewis, 441:29Apr90-13
Head, A. - see Powys, J.C.
Head, B. La Donna dei Tesori.
　B. Hickey, 538(RAL):Fall89-522
Head, B. A Woman Alone. (C. MacKenzie, ed)
　Tales of Tenderness and Power.
　M. Jaggi, 617(TLS):7-13Dec90-1326
Head, T. & R. Landes, eds. Essays on the
　Peace of God.
　T.N. Bisson, 589:Apr89-442
Headley, J.M. & J.B. Tomaro, eds. San Carlo
　Borromeo.*
　R. Bireley, 551(RenQ):Winter89-848
Headley, L., with W. Hoffman. Loud and Clear.
　C. Salzberg, 441:14Oct90-49
Heal, J. Fact and Meaning.
　P. Snowdon, 617(TLS):4-10May90-476
Heald, S. Controlling Anger.
　P.T.W. Baxter, 617(TLS):18-24May90-532
Heald, T. By Appointment.
　W. Gardner, 324:Jun90-506
Heale, E. "The Faerie Queene."
　P. Thomson, 541(RES):May89-250
Healey, D. The Time of My Life.*
　A. Lewis, 441:23Sep90-9
　J. Newhouse, 442(NY):3Dec90-188
Healy, D. The Suspended Revolution.
　D. Cohen, 617(TLS):23-29Mar90-323
Healy, J. Streets Above Us.
　A-M. Conway, 617(TLS):13-19Apr90-403
Healy, J.M. Endangered Minds.
　R.S. Barth, 441:9Sep90-33
Healy, T.F. Richard Crashaw.
　M.G. Brennan, 447(N&Q):Mar89-105
Heaney, S. The Government of the Tongue.*
　H. Beaver, 472:Vol16No1-104
　W. Bedford, 4:Spring89-72
　M. Boruch, 29(APR):Nov/Dec89-21
Heaney, S. The Haw Lantern.*
　H. Beaver, 472:Vol16No1-104
　B. Howard, 491:Sep89-340
　P.H. Marsden, 272(IUR):Spring89-169
Heaney, S. The Place of Writing.
　S. Deane, 617(TLS):16-22Mar90-275
　H. Hart, 659(ConL):Fall90-383
Heaney, S. Poèmes 1966-1984.
　G. Goffette, 450(NRF):May89-95
Heaney, S. Selected Poems, 1966-1987.
　(British title: New Selected Poems 1966-
　1987.)
　S. Deane, 617(TLS):16-22Mar90-275
　A. Stevenson, 441:11Nov90-11
Heaney, S. Sweeney Astray. Station Island.
　H. Beaver, 472:Vol16No1-104
Heaney, S. - see Wordsworth, W.
Heard, A.H. The Cape of Storms.
　T. Eprile, 441:9Dec90-15
Hearden, P.J. Roosevelts Confronts Hitler.
　G. Adams, Jr., 106:Fall89-245
Hearn, E. Race You Franny.
　J. Buckley, 102(CanL):Autumn-Winter89-
　182
Hearn, T.K., ed. Hume's Philosophy of Reli-
　gion.
　J.C.A. Gaskin, 242:Vol10No3-382

Hearn, V. Adam's Task.
　E. Cobley, 376:Jun89-133
Hearne, B. Beauty and the Beast.*
　H. Carpenter, 441:25Mar90-25
Hearne, B. Choosing Books for Children.
　M. Cart, 441:9Sep90-33
Heater, D. Citizenship.
　M. Goyder, 324:Aug90-640
Heath, J. Ablaut and Ambiguity.*
　H. Wise, 297(JL):Mar89-272
Heath, M. The Poetics of Greek Tragedy.
　S. Halliwell, 303(JoHS):Vol109-231
　N.W. Slater, 478(P&L):Apr89-218
Heath, M. Political Comedy in Aristophanes.*
　A.H. Sommerstein, 303(JoHS):Vol109-222
Heath, M. Unity in Greek Poetics.
　E. Bowie, 617(TLS):6-12Apr90-380
Heath, R. Shadows Round the Moon.
　M. Jaggi, 617(TLS):14-20Sep90-979
Heath, R. The Victorian Peasant. (K. Dock-
　ray, ed)
　P. Perry, 637(VS):Summer90-672
Heath-Stubbs, J. The Game of Love and
　Death.
　T. Gooderham, 617(TLS):16-22Nov90-
　1248
Heaton, T. In Teleki's Footsteps.
　P. Marsden-Smedley, 617(TLS):2-
　8Nov90-1188
Heber, W. Die Arbeiten des Nicolas de Pigage
　in den ehemals kurpfälzischen Residenzen
　Mannheim und Schwetzingen.
　M. Weis, 43:Band19Heft1-97
Hébert, A. Le premier jardin.*
　G. Merler, 102(CanL):Spring89-230
Hebert, E. Live Free or Die.
　M. Gingher, 441:30Dec90-18
Hébert, P., with M. Baszczynski. Le Journal
　intime au Québec.
　Y. Lamonde, 627(UTQ):Fall89-184
　M. O'Neill-Karch, 207(FR):Dec89-365
Hebreo, L. Diálogos de amor. (A. Soria Olme-
　do, ed)
　J.B. Avalle-Arce, 240(HR):Spring89-230
Hecht, A. The Transparent Man. Collected
　Earlier Poems.
　W. Logan, 441:22Jul90-26
Hecht, A. - see Herbert, G.
Hecht, M. La Chanson de Turold.
　C. Beretta, 379(MedR):Apr89-127
　R.F. Cook, 402(MLR):Jul90-724
Hecht, S. & A. Cockburn. The Fate of the
　Forest.*
　J. Hemming, 617(TLS):9-15Mar90-250
van Heck, P. - see Carducci, G.
Heck, T.F. Commedia dell'Arte.
　M.A. Katritzky, 611(TN):Vol43No2-95
Hedin, R. & G. Holthaus, eds. Alaska.
　J.A. Murray, 649(WAL):Aug89-188
Hedley, J. Power in Verse.
　A.M. Esolen, 604:Fall89-49
　J. Rees, 402(MLR):Apr90-405
　D. Shuger, 599:Spring90-141
Hedman, D. Eleganta eskapader.
　R. Jarvi, 563(SS):Spring/Summer89-297
Heeney, B. The Women's Movement in the
　Church of England 1850-1930.
　M.M. Clarke, 637(VS):Spring90-488
Heffernan, C.F. The Phoenix at the Fountain.
　E.G. Stanley, 447(N&Q):Jun89-218
Heffernan, J.A.W. The Re-Creation of Land-
　scape.
　R. Fadem, 591(SIR):Summer89-314

164

Heffernan, M. The Man at Home.
P. Junker, 271:Fall89-154
Heffernan, T.J., ed. The Popular Literature of
Medieval England.*
E.D. Kennedy, 38:Band107Heft1/2-180
Heftrich, E. & J-M. Valentin, eds. Gallo-
Germanica.
U.K. Goldsmith, 678(YCGL):No36-186
Heftrich, E. & H. Wysling, eds. Internation-
ales Thomas-Mann-Kolloquium 1986.
S.R. Cerf, 221(GQ):Summer89-409
Heftrich, E. & H. Wysling - see "Thomas Mann
Jahrbuch"
Hegel, G.W.F. Encyclopédie des sciences phil-
osophiques. (Vol 3) (B. Bourgeois, ed &
trans)
D. Janicaud, 192(EP):Apr-Jun89-259
Hegel, G.W.F. Fragments de la période de
Berne (1793-1796). (R. Legros & F. Vers-
traeten, trans)
J-F. Kervegan, 192(EP):Apr-Jun89-261
Hegel, G.W.F. Gesammelte Werke. (Vol 17) (W.
Jaeschke, ed)
F. Wagner, 489(PJGG):Band96Heft2-414
Hegel, G.W.F. Hegel's Lectures on the Philos-
ophy of Religion. (P.C. Hodgson, ed)
R.L. Perkins, 125:Summer89-387
Hegel, G.W.F. Journal d'un voyage dans les
Alpes bernoises (du 25 au 01 juillet 1796).
P. Somville, 542:Oct-Dec89-636
Hegel, G.W.F. Vorlesungen. (Vol 9) (P. Gar-
niron & W Jaeschke, eds)
F. Wagner, 489(PJGG):Band96Heft2-416
Heger, N. Die Skulpturen der Stadtgebiete
von Aguntum und von Brigantium.
G. Davies, 123:Vol39No2-417
Hegi, U. Floating in My Mother's Palm.
E. Hoagland, 441:18Mar90-5
Heiberg, M. The Making of the Basque Nation.
J. MacClancy, 617(TLS):9-15Mar90-264
Heidegger, M. Gesamtausgabe. (Vol 65) (F-W.
von Herrmann, ed)
M.E. Zimmerman, 617(TLS):16-22Mar90-
296
Heidegger, M. Hegel's Phenomenology of Spir-
it.*
R.L. Siemens, 103:Apr90-138
Heidegger, M. Schelling's Treatise on the
Essence of Human Freedom.
M.G. Vater, 482(PhR):Apr89-260
Heiferman, M. & C. Kismaric. I'm So Happy.
L. Barry, 441:29Apr90-27
Heilbron, J.L. & R.W. Seidel. Lawrence and
His Laboratory. (Vol 1)
D.J. Kevles, 453(NYRB):25Oct90-6
Heilbroner, D. Rough Justice.
M. Chambers, 441:30Sep90-12
Heilbrun, C.G. Hamlet's Mother and Other
Women.
B. Packer, 441:16Sep90-24
H. Vendler, 453(NYRB):31May90-19
Heilbrun, C.G. Writing a Woman's Life.*
L. Simon, 385(MQR):Winter90-133
E.B. Thompson, 395(MFS):Winter89-867
Heilbrun, F. & P. Néagu. Pierre Bonnard Pho-
tographe.
N. Watkins, 90:Apr89-304
Heilenman, L.K., I. Kaplan & C. Tournier.
Voilà!
M-F. Hilgar, 399(MLJ):Winter89-507
Heilman, R.B., ed. Shakespeare: The Trage-
dies.
J.A. Bryant, Jr., 569(SR):Summer89-445

Heim, M. Electric Language.*
D. Ihde, 480(P&R):Vol22No3-219
C. Norris, 131(CL):Summer89-270
Heiman, L., D. Weiner & B. Gutman. When the
Cheering Stops.
S.J. Gould, 453(NYRB):11Oct90-3
Heimlich, J.E. & S.D. Pittelman. Semantic
Mapping.
M.A. Barnett, 399(MLJ):Winter89-488
Heimonet, J-M. Poétiques de l'Ecriture
Bataille/Derrida.*
G. Cesbron, 535(RHL):Mar-Apr89-333
Hein, C. The Distant Lover.*
P. Graves, 617(TLS):27Jul-2Aug90-796
Hein, C. Die fünfte Grundrechenart.
P. Graves, 617(TLS):15-21Jun90-631
Heine, H. Historisch-kritische Gesamtaus-
gabe der Werke.* (Vol 7, Pts 1 & 2) (M.
Windfuhr, ed)
W. Grab, 224(GRM):Band39Heft1-110
Heine, H. The Lazarus Poems. (A. Elliot,
trans)
S.S. Prawer, 617(TLS):28Sep-4Oct90-
1040
"Heine-Jahrbuch 1988." (J.A. Kruse, ed)
R. Robertson, 402(MLR):Jul90-798
"Heine-Jahrbuch." (Vols 26 & 27) (J.A.
Kruse, ed)
E. Feistner, 72:Band226Heft1-126
Heinemann, M.E. Gender and Destiny.*
S.L. Cocalis, 406:Summer89-230
Heinlmann, F. & E. Kienzle - see Erasmus
Heinlein, R.A. Stranger in a Strange Land.
K. Vonnegut, 441:9Dec90-13
Heinrich, R. Kants Erfahrungsraum.
R. Blittkowsky, 489(PJGG):Band96Heft2-
429
W. Sauer, 342:Band80Heft3-357
Heinrichs, W. Threshold of War.*
D.S. Clemens, 293(JASt):May89-337
Heintze, B. Ethnographische Zeichnungen der
Lwimbi/Ngangela (Zentral-Angola).
R.K. Jansen, 2(AfrA):May89-26
Heinze, R-I. Trance and Healing in Southeast
Asia Today.
R.A. O'Connor, 293(JASt):May89-435
Heise, W. Hölderlin.
R. Reschke, 654(WB):12/1989-2090
Hekkanen, E. Medieval Hour in the Author's
Mind.
G. Boire, 102(CanL):Spring89-175
Hekman, S.J. Hermeneutics and the Sociology
of Knowledge.
M. Lynch, 478(P&L):Apr89-178
Helbig, G. Lexikon deutscher Partikeln.
J. Austin, 399(MLJ):Winter89-514
Helbo, A., ed. Approches de l'opéra.
N. Everaert-Desmedt, 567:Vol76No3/4-
275
Helbo, A. Teoría del espectáculo.
B. Seibel, 352(LATR):Spring90-182
Helbo, A. Theory of Performing Arts.
L. Oswald, 567:Vol75No3/4-327
Helbo, A. & others, eds. Théâtre Modes
d'Approche.
E. Fischer-Lichte, 567:Vol75No3/4-317
Held, W.H., Jr., W.R. Schmalstieg & J.E. Gertz.
Beginning Hittite.
C.F. Justus, 159:Vol6No1-111
Heldt, B. Terrible Perfection.*
D.N. Ignashev, 574(SEEJ):Summer89-301
A. Livingstone, 575(SEER):Jul89-460
M. Ziolkowski, 295(JML):Fall88/Winter89-
200

Helgadóttir, G.P., ed. Hrafns saga Sveinbjar-
narsonar.*
   R. Frank, 447(N&Q):Mar89–87
   H. O'Donoghue, 541(RES):Feb89–107
Hellan, L. & K.K. Christensen, eds. Topics in
Scandinavian Syntax.*
   S. Vikner, 452(NJL):Vol12No1–79
Heller, A., ed. Der amerikanische Roman nach
1945.
   B.M., 494:Fall89–644
Heller, A. Beyond Justice.
   H.P.K., 185:Jan90–442
Heller, H–B. Literarische Intelligenz und
Film.*
   J.G. Pankau, 564:Feb89–76
Heller, J. Picture This.
   S. Pinsker, 390:Jan89–33
Heller, L.M. & F.R. Atance, eds. Montaigne.
   M. Debaisieux, 345(KRQ):Feb89–103
Heller, M. Call Me Adirondack.
   K.B. Harder, 424:Dec89–388
Heller, M. & A. Nekrich. Utopia in Power.*
   V. Zaslavsy, 473(PR):Vol56No1–147
Heller, S. & S. Chwast. Graphic Style.*
   S. Gutterman, 507:Mar/Apr89–147
Heller, T. "The Turn of the Screw."
   S.B. Daugherty, 395(MFS):Winter89–729
Heller, W. Die Moskauer "Eiferer für die
Frömmigkeit" zwischen Staat und Kirche
(1642–1652).
   L. Hughes, 575(SEER):Oct89–629
Hellie, R., ed. Ivan the Terrible.
   M. Perrie, 575(SEER):Jul89–471
Hellinga, L. & J. Goldfinch, eds. Bibliography
and the Study of 15th–Century Civilisa-
tion.*
   M.D. Feld, 517(PBSA):Jun89–237
Helliwell, C. Music in the Air.
   M. Kennedy, 415:Jul89–416
Hellmann, M–C. Lampes antiques de la Bib-
liothèque Nationale. (Vol 2)
   D.M. Bailey, 123:Vol39No1–116
Hellmann, M–C., ed. Vrai ou Faux.
   M. Jones, 90:Jun89–423
Hellmann, W. Charles Bally.
   R. Posner, 402(MLR):Jul90–739
Hellmann, W. – see Bally, C.
Hellson, J.C. & M. Gadd. Ethnobotany of the
Blackfoot Indians.
   A.R. Taylor, 269(IJAL):Jul89–359
Helm, P. Eternal God.
   L.L. Garcia, 543:Mar90–634
Helmling, S. The Esoteric Comedies of Car-
lyle, Newman, and Yeats.
   A. Bradley, 637(VS):Spring90–537
   F. McClelland, 445(NCF):Mar90–563
Helms, S. & H. Hopf, eds. Werkanalyse in Bei-
spielen.
   S. Mauser, 416:Band4Heft3–275
Helprin, M., with S. Ravenel, eds. The Best
American Short Stories, 1988.
   T.E. Holt, 219(GaR):Spring89–189
   639(VQR):Summer89–94
Helwig, D. The Bishop.
   J. Pouw, 102(CanL):Summer89–192
Helwig, D. The Hundred Old Names.
   M.A. Jarman, 376:Dec89–125
Helwig, D. A Postcard from Rome.
   A. Munton, 102(CanL):Summer89–150
Helwig, M. Eden.*
   E. Folsom, 529(QQ):Summer89–530
Helwig, M. Talking Prophet Blues.
   S. Scobie, 376:Dec89–126

Hemenway, R. – see Kalstone, D.
Hemingway, E. The Complete Short Stories of
Ernest Hemingway.*
   G. Locklin & C. Stetler, 573(SSF):Fall88–
489
Hemingway, P.S. The Hemingways Past and
Present and Allied Families.
   R.W. Lewis, 234:Fall89–103
Hempel, A. At the Gates of the Animal King-
dom.
   R. Towers, 441:11Mar90–11
Hempel, C.G., H. Putnam & W.K. Essler, eds.
Methodology, Epistemology, and Philosophy.
   B. Mundy, 486:Jun89–361
Hemphill, P. King of the Road.
   P–L. Adams, 61:Jan90–101
   M. Goodman, 441:7Jan90–18
Hemschemeyer, J. The Ride Home.
   R. Schultz, 249(HudR):Spring89–153
Henderson, B. – see Sturges, P.
Henderson, B., with others, eds. The Push-
cart Prize XIV.
   S. Stark, 441:7Jan90–16
Henderson, B., with others, eds. The Pushcart
Prize XV.
   J. Polk, 441:11Nov90–60
Henderson, B., P. Booth & J. Meek, eds. The
Pushcart Prize XIII.*
   J. Allman, 456(NDQ):Summer89–236
Henderson, G.E. Kenneth Burke.
   M. Alcorn, 599:Spring90–132
   C.A. Carter, 223:Fall89–309
Henderson, G.W. Ollie Miss.
   D.R. Noble, 585(SoQ):Summer89–114
Henderson, J. – see Aristophanes
Henderson, K. The Restoration.
   S. Lindsey, 102(CanL):Spring89–215
Henderson, L. The Final Glass.
   N. Callendar, 441:16Sep90–26
Henderson, M.C. Theatre in America.
   D. McDermott, 610:Autumn89–307
Hendrick, G. – see Van Doren, M.
Hendrick, G. & W. – see Salt, H.
Hendrick, R. Anaphora in Celtic and Univer-
sal Grammar.
   R.D. Borsley, 297(JL):Sep89–498
Hendrick, W. & G. Katherine Anne Porter.
(rev)
   R.H. Brinkmeyer, Jr., 392:Spring89–203
   T.F. Walsh, 573(SSF):Summer88–335
Hendricks, G.C. The Second War.
   S.F. Schaeffer, 441:29Apr90–13
Hendrickson, R. Encyclopedia of Word and
Phrase Origins.
   K. Weiss, 710:Dec89–484
Hendriks, A.L. To Speak Simply.
   D. Dabydeen, 493:Spring89–18
Hendriksen, H. Himachali Studies.
   W.L. Smith, 318(JAOS):Jul–Sep88–497
Hendy, M.F. Studies in the Byzantine Mone-
tary Economy, c. 300–1450.*
   C. Foss, 589:Oct89–966
Heng Pek Koon. Chinese Politics in Malaysia.
   S.A. Carstens, 293(JASt):Aug89–677
Henkin, L. Constitutionalism, Democracy, and
Foreign Affairs.
   W. La Feber, 441:5Aug90–10
Henn, D. The Early Pardo Bazán.
   J. Whiston, 402(MLR):Oct90–1003
Henn–Memmesheimer, B. Nonstandard–Mus-
ter.*
   H. Löffler, 685(ZDL):2/1989–214

Henne, H., H. Sitta & H.E. Wiegand – see Muthmann, G.
Hennig, J. Goethes Europakunde.
 H.H.F. Henning, 406:Spring89-124
 J. Hibberd, 133:Band22Heft1-60
Henning, S.D. Beckett's Critical Complicity.
 A. King, 395(MFS):Winter89-812
 J. Pilling, 402(MLR):Apr90-427
Henninger, M.G. Relations.
 A. Santogrossi, 543:Jun90-868
Henninger, T. Balkanische Lexik im Schrift-tum der bulgarischen Wiedergeburt.
 H. Leeming, 575(SEER):Jul89-449
Hennlein, E. Erotik in der phantastischen Literatur.
 M. Nagl, 196:Band30Heft1/2-136
Hennock, E.P. British Social Reform and Ger-man Precedents.
 D.T. Rodgers, 637(VS):Autumn89-203
Henny, S. & J-P. Lehmann, eds. Themes and Theories in Modern Japanese History.*
 M.B. Jansen, 293(JASt):Aug89-613
Henri, A. Wish You Were Here.
 S. O'Brien, 617(TLS):27Jul-2Aug90-803
Henriksen, L.L., with J.A. Boydston. Anzia Yezierska.*
 E.J. Sundquist, 27(AL):Mar89-120
Henry, A. – see "Biblia Pauperum"
Henry, D.O. From Foraging to Agriculture.
 S.J. Gould, 453(NYRB):18Jan90-26
Henry, J. & S. Hutton, eds. New Perspectives on Renaissance Thought.
 P. Burke, 617(TLS):14-20Sep90-984
Henry, P. Montaigne in Dialogue.
 P. Dandrey, 535(RHL):Sep-Oct89-925
 P. Desan, 210(FrF):May89-229
 M. Gutwirth, 207(FR):Oct89-156
 J.J. Supple, 402(MLR):Jan90-180
Henry-Valmore, S. Dieux en exil (Voyage dans la magie antillaise).
 H. Cornel, 450(NRF):Dec89-126
Henryson, R. The Moral Fables of Aesop. (G.D. Gopen, ed & trans)
 S. Mapstone, 541(RES):Feb89-116
 F. Riddy, 447(N&Q):Mar89-83
Henryson, R. The Poems.* (D. Fox, ed)
 A. Samson, 677(YES):Vol20-238
Hensel, F. The Letters of Fanny Hensel to Felix Mendelssohn.* (M.J. Citron, ed & trans)
 N.B. Reich, 451:Summer89-67
Hensellek, W. & P. Schilling. Specimina eines Lexicon Augustinianum (SLA). (Pt 1)
 M. Winterbottom, 123:Vol39No1-142
Henshall, K.G. – see Katai, T.
Henshaw, M. Out of the Line of Fire.*
 Y. Gooneratne, 581:Dec89-652
 J. O'Carroll, 381:Winter89-407
Henstock, M. Fernando De Lucia.
 J.B. Steane, 617(TLS):12-18Oct90-1103
Hentschel, G. Vokalperzeption und natürliche Phonologie.
 A. Kątny, 682(ZPSK):Band42Heft3-404
 M. Skibicki, 688(ZSP):Band49Heft2-400
Henze-Döhring, S. Opera seria, Opera buffa und Mozarts "Don Giovanni."
 W. Seidel, 417:Jan-Mar89-85
Hepburn, J. – see Bennett, A.
Hephaestion. On Metre. (J.M. van Ophuijsen, ed & trans)
 E.K. Borthwick, 123:Vol39No1-134
 S.R. Slings, 394:Vol42fasc3/4-541
 M.L. West, 303(JoHS):Vol109-237

Hepokoski, J.A. Giuseppe Verdi: "Otello."*
 D.R.B. Kimbell, 278(IS):Vol44-182
 D. Lawton, 451:Summer89-59
Heraclitus. Héraclite, Fragments.* (M. Conche, ed & trans)
 Y. Lafrance, 154:Vol28No1-157
Herbert, C. Trollope and Comic Pleasure.*
 H. Rinehart, 529(QQ):Summer89-495
Herbert, D. Engaging Eccentrics.
 M. Dillon, 617(TLS):7-13Sep90-938
Herbert, D.T. & D.M. Smith, eds. Social Prob-lems and the City.
 A. Coleman, 617(TLS):11-17May90-505
Herbert, G. The Essential Herbert. (A. Hecht, ed)
 P. Mariani, 434:Spring90-313
Herbert, G.B. Thomas Hobbes.
 H.J. Johnson, 103:Jul90-274
Herbert, J. Inside Christie's.
 R. Simon, 617(TLS):4-10May90-478
Herbert, K., with K. Candiotti. The John Max Wulfing Collection in Washington Universi-ty.
 H.C. Boren, 124:Jul-Aug90-532
Herbert, M. – see Lawrence, D.H.
Herbert, R.L. Impressionism.*
 C. Lloyd, 39:Jun89-437
Herbert, T. & G.E. Jones, eds. People and Protest.
 A. Howkins, 637(VS):Summer90-657
Herbst, S. Animal Art.
 G. Gessert, 448:Vol27No3-126
Herder, M. Arbetsplatsbibliotek i Sverige.
 J.D. Rudman, 563(SS):Winter89-111
Heres, G., comp. Corpus Speculorum Etruscor-um. (Deutsche Demokratische Republik, fasc 2)
 U. Höckmann, 229:Band61Heft4-347
Herfort-Koch, M. Archaische Bronzeplastik Lakoniens.*
 H. Philipp, 229:Band61Heft4-343
Hergenhan, L., general ed. The Penguin New Literary History of Australia.
 V. O'Sullivan, 71(ALS):May89-126
Hering, W. – see Caesar
Heringer, H.J. Lesen lehren lernen.
 F. Hundsnurscher, 685(ZDL):1/1989-70
 G. Starke, 682(ZPSK):Band42Heft4-534
Herlemann, H., ed. Quality of Life in the Soviet Union.
 V.E. Bonnell, 550(RusR):Apr89-224
Herling, G. The Island.
 G. Hyde, 617(TLS):23-29Nov90-1272
Herman, B.L. Architecture and Rural Life in Central Delaware, 1700-1900.*
 R.B. St. George, 292(JAF):Jul-Sep89-369
 J.M. Vlach, 576:Jun89-200
Herman, G. Ritualized Friendship and the Greek City.
 T.W. Gallant, 121(CJ):Apr-May90-357
 P.W. Sage, 124:Mar-Apr90-364
Herman, J., ed. Latin vulgaire – Latin tar-dif.*
 P. Flobert, 555:Vol62Fasc2-360
Herman, R., Jr. Force of Eagles.
 N. Callendar, 441:15Apr90-19
Herman, W. Understanding Contemporary American Drama.*
 L. Hart, 397(MD):Jun89-324
Herman, W., with S. Troup. The Woodchopper's Ball.
 J.W. Poses, 441:11Mar90-14

Hermand, J. Der alte Traum vom neuen Reich.
S.L. Gilman, 221(GQ):Fall89-544
Hermans, T., ed. The Manipulation of Litera-
ture.*
Y. Chevrel, 549(RLC):Apr-Jun89-259
Hermans, W.F. Au Pair.
R. Todd, 617(TLS):16-22Feb90-180
Hermary-Vieille, C. Le Jardin des Henderson.
A-M. Gronhovd, 207(FR):Apr90-894
Hermenegildo, A. - see Lasso de la Vega, G.L.
Hermogenes. On Types of Style.* (C.W. Woo-
ten, ed & trans)
D.M. Schenkeveld, 394:Vol42fasc1/2-262
Hernadi, P. Interpreting Events.
J. Hurt, 301(JEGP):Jan89-144
Hernández, R. & L. González-del-Valle, eds.
Antología del cuento español 1985.
V. Dean-Thacker, 345(KRQ):Nov89-498
Hernández-Araico, S. Ironía y tragedia en
Calderón.*
J.M. Ruano de la Haza, 86(BHS):Apr89-
181
Hernández de Villaumbrales, P. Peregrinación
de la vida del hombre. (H. Salvador Mar-
tínez, ed)
M. Dunn-Wood, 86(BHS):Jul89-276
Hernton, C.C. The Sexual Mountain and Black
Women Writers.
M. Fabre, 189(EA):Oct-Dec89-499
G. Wilentz, 459:Spring89-78
Hero, A.C. - see Palaiologina, I.E.C.
Herodas. Mimiambi. (I.C. Cunningham, ed)
R.G. Ussher, 123:Vol39No1-17
Herodoto, "Le Storie." (Vol 1) (D.
Asheri, ed; V. Antelami, trans)
S. West, 123:Vol39No2-189
Herodotus. Herodoti "Historiae, I," libros I-IV
continens. (H.B. Rosén, ed)
D. Fehling, 123:Vol39No2-187
Herodotus. The History of Herodotus.* (D.
Grene, trans)
C.D. Hamilton, 124:Sep-Oct89-55
"Herodotus, Book I."* (R.A. McNeal, ed)
T.J. Luce, 124:Mar-Apr90-375
Heron, C. Working in Steel.
D. Frank, 529(QQ):Autumn89-729
Herr, M. Walter Winchell.
P. French, 617(TLS):14-20Sep90-970
D. Johnson, 453(NYRB):22Nov90-16
J. Rascoe, 441:20May90-12
Herraiz, J.J.L. & J. Fernández Jiménez - see
under Labrador Herraiz, J.J. & J. Fernández
Jiménez
de Herrera, A.C. - see under Cohen de Her-
rera, A.
Herrin, J. The Formation of Christendom.*
B. Baldwin, 487:Spring89-88
D.J. Constantelos, 124:Sep-Oct89-64
Herring, P.F. Joyce's Uncertainty Principle.*
S. Brivic, 177(ELT):Vol32No2-268
Herring, R.J. Land to the Tiller.
A. Gupta, 293(JASt):Nov89-787
Herrmann, A. The Dialogic and Difference.
P. Hitchcock, 147:Vol6No3-84
von Herrmann, F-W. - see Heidegger, M.
Herron, C. & G. Kaiser. Vignettes.
B. Ebling 2d, 207(FR):Feb90-590
Herron, J. Universities and the Myth of Cul-
tural Decline.
P. Brantlinger, 141:Fall89-333
Hersant, Y. Italies.
J.P., 98:May89-398
Hersant, Y. - see Bruno, G.

Herschberg-Pierrot, A. Le "Dictionnaire des
idées reçues" de Flaubert.
U. Schulz-Buschhaus, 547(RF):Band101
Heft4-484
M. Wetherill, 402(MLR):Jan90-195
Hersey, G. The Lost Meaning of Classical
Architecture.*
J. Onians, 90:Feb89-158
Hersey, J. Fling.
V. Bourjaily, 441:8Apr90-24
Herskowitz, M. The Quarterbacks.
R.E. Nicholls, 441:7Oct90-20
Herslund, M. Le datif en français.
J.E. Joseph, 350:Dec90-871
Herstein, S. A Mid-Victorian Feminist, Bar-
bara Leigh Smith Bodichon.
R.T. Van Arsdel, 635(VPR):Winter89-164
Hertling, G.H. Theodor Fontanes "Irrungen,
Wirrungen."
W. Paulsen, 222(GR):Spring89-80
Herttrich, E., with W. Martin & T.J. Quigley -
see McCorkle, M.L.
Hertz, D.M. The Tuning of the Word.*
W. Bernhart, 678(YCGL):No36-190
J. Daverio, 451:Spring90-257
Hertzberg, A. The Jews in America.*
J. Higham, 453(NYRB):12Apr90-11
Herz, J.S. The Short Narratives of E.M.
Forster.*
D. Baldwin, 573(SSF):Winter89-102
F.P.W. McDowell, 177(ELT):Vol32No1-105
M. Melaver, 494:Fall89-646
C.J. Summers, 405(MP):Nov89-205
Herzfeld, M. Anthropology through the Look-
ing Glass.*
P.J. Wilson, 242:Vol10No2-249
Herzog, R. & R. Koselleck, eds. Epochensch-
welle und Epochenbewusstsein.
C. Jamme, 489(PJGG):Band96Heft2-442
Herzstein, R.E. Roosevelt & Hitler.
R. Dallek, 441:28Jan90-17
Hesiod. Theogony [and] Works and Days.*
(M.L. West, ed & trans)
R.L. Fowler, 124:Sep-Oct89-60
D. Grene, 235:Winter89-86
J.R. March, 123:Vol39No2-381
Hesketh, P. Netting the Sun.*
S. Kantaris, 493:Autumn89-42
Hess, A. Googie, Fifties Coffee Shop Archi-
tecture.
F.T. Kihlstedt, 576:Jun89-204
Hess, P. Poetik ohne Trichter.
R. Ambacher, 406:Summer89-255
Hess-Lüttich, E.W.B. Angewandte Sprach-
soziologie.
K-H. Jäger, 406:Winter89-494
Hessky, R. Phraseologie.
C. Földes, 72:Band226Heft1-128
K. Günther, 682(ZPSK):Band42Heft1-113
Hester, R., G. Wade & G. Jian. Traits d'Union.
H. Rodina, 399(MLJ):Summer89-224
Heston, W.L. & M. Nasir. The Bazaar of the
Storytellers.
F.W. Pritchett, 293(JASt):Nov89-906
Heth, C., ed. Sharing a Heritage.
M. Herndon, 187:Winter89-182
Hettrich, H. Untersuchungen zur Hypotaxe im
Vedischen.*
H.H. Hock, 350:Sep90-606
Heukenkamp, U., H. Kahlau & W. Kirsten, eds.
Die eigene Stimme.
B. Leistner, 601(SuF):Sep-Oct89-1079

de Heusch, L. Sacrifice in Africa.
D. Ben-Amos, 538(RAL):Summer89-265
Heuser, A. - see MacNeice, L.
von Heusinger, C. Das gestochene Bild, von der Zeichnung zum Kupferstich.*
T. Riggs, 380:Winter89-370
Heward, E. Lord Denning.
J. Campbell, 617(TLS):19-25Oct90-1122
Hewison, R. Future Tense.
M.A. Francis, 617(TLS):17-23Aug90-876
Hewitt, B.G. The Typology of Subordination in Georgian and Abkhaz.
H. Fähnrich, 682(ZPSK):Band42Heft1-115
Hewitt, M.A. The Architect and the American Country House, 1890-1940.
M. Filler, 617(TLS):12-18Oct90-1091
W. Rybczynski, 453(NYRB):20Dec90-24
Hewitt, N., ed. The Culture of Reconstruction.*
N. Greene, 207(FR):Apr90-918
Hewitt, N. The Golden Age of Louis-Ferdinand Céline.
T.C. Spear, 207(FR):May90-1073
A. Thiher, 210(FrF):Jan89-111
Hexter, R.J. Ovid and Medieval Schooling.*
A.E. Samuel, 124:Sep-Oct89-71
Heyck, D., D. Lynn & M.V. González-Widel. Tradición y cambio.
D. Barnwell, 399(MLJ):Spring89-100
M. Handelsman, 399(MLJ):Winter89-532
von Heydebrand, R., D. Pfau & J. Schönert, eds. Zur theoretischen Grundlegung einer Sozialgeschichte der Literatur.
R.C. Holub, 406(FallUU)-077
Heydenreich, L.H. Leonardo-Studien.* (G. Passavant, ed)
F. Zöllner, 90:Apr89-301
Heyer, F. Die Kirche in Däbrä Tabor.
S. Chojnacki, 318(JAOS):Oct-Dec88-667
Heyer, J.H., ed. Jean-Baptiste Lully and the Music of the French Baroque.
E.T. Glasow, 465:Summer90-142
F. Howard, 415:Jul89-410
Heyerdahl, T. Easter Island.*
P.G. Bahn, 617(TLS):19-25Jan90-72
K. Ray, 441:7Jan90-19
Heym, S. Ahasver.
U. Reinhold, 654(WB):3/1989-495
Heym, S. Einmischung. (I. Heym & H. Henniger, eds)
P. Graves, 617(TLS):15-21Jun90-631
Heyworth, P.L. - see Wanley, H.
Hibberd, D. Owen the Poet.*
R. Elkin, 565:Spring89-48
Hibbert, C. Redcoats and Rebels.
J. Shy, 441:30Sep90-42
Hichberger, J.W.M. Images of the Army.
M. Lalumia, 637(VS):Autumn89-192
Hick, J. An Interpretation of Religion.*
G.I. Mavrodes, 103:Apr90-142
Hick, J. & H. Askari, eds. The Experience of Religious Diversity.
E. Hulmes, 242:Vol10No1-99
Hickmann, M., ed. Social and Functional Approaches to Language and Thought.*
J.F. Kess, 320(CJL):Dec89-466
Hicks, E.K. & J.M. Berg, eds. The Genetics of Mental Retardation.
C.N., 185:Jan90-459
Hicks, G. Hong Kong Countdown.
I. Buruma, 453(NYRB):12Apr90-41
Hicks, J. A Market Theory of Money.
W. Godley, 617(TLS):18-24May90-519

Hicks, R. & Ngakpa Chogyam. Great Ocean.
D. Goleman, 441:3Jun90-23
Hiddleston, J., ed. Laforgue aujourd'hui.*
P. Collier, 208(FS):Apr89-224
M.J. Nurnberg, 402(MLR):Jul90-738
Hiddleston, J.A. Baudelaire and "Le Spleen de Paris."*
J. Monroe, 131(CL):Summer89-297
Hiden, J. The Baltic States and Weimar Ostpolitik.
M-L. Hinkkanen-Lievonen, 575(SEER): Jan89-151
T. Kaminski, 104(CASS):Spring89-114
Higginbotham, D. War and Society in Revolutionary America.
R.K. Showman, 656(WMQ):Oct89-821
Higginbotham, V. Spanish Film under Franco.
S.L. Martin-Márquez, 240(HR):Autumn89-535
Higgins, A. Helsingor Station and Other Departures.*
J. Lewis, 364:Dec89/Jan90-140
Higgins, A. Ronda George and Other Precipices.*
J. Lewis, 364:Apr/May89-157
Higgins, G.V. On Writing.
P-L. Adams, 61:Jul90-105
Higgins, G.V. Trust.*
H. Wolitzer, 441:21Jan90-18
Higgins, I., ed. Surrealism and Language.
J. Wilson, 402(MLR):Jan90-132
Higgins, J. Cold Harbour.
B. Hochberg, 441:4Mar90-24
Higgins, J. A History of Peruvian Literature.*
P. Beardsell, 86(BHS):Jan89-99
Higgins, J. Language, Learners and Computers.
C. Chapelle, 710:Sep89-354
Higgins, J. - see Vallejo, C.
Higgins, K.M. Nietzsche's "Zarathustra."*
P. Fenves, 478(P&L):Apr89-215
J. Young, 60:Sep89-349
Higgins, R. Tanagra and the Figurines.*
L. Burn, 303(JoHS):Vol109-263
Higginson, F.H. A Bibliography of the Writings of Robert Graves.* (2nd ed, rev by W.P. Williams)
S. Hills, 78(BC):Spring89-119
Higgitt, J., ed. Early Medieval Sculpture in Britain and Ireland.
L. Karlsson, 341:Vol58No4-172
Higonnet, A. Berthe Morisot.
P. Conisbee, 617(TLS):10-16Aug90-850
A. Truitt, 441:3Jun90-20
Higonnet, P. Sister Republics.*
J. Black, 173(ECS):Spring90-343
Higuera, T.P. - see under Pérez Higuera, T.
Hijiya, J.A. J.W. De Forest and the Rise of American Gentility.
F. Bergmann, 26(ALR):Fall89-95
Hijiya-Kirschnereit, I. Das Ende der Exotik.
F. Coulmas, 407(MN):Summer89-246
Hikmet, N. A Sad State of Freedom.
C. Hurford, 617(TLS):21-27Dec90-1383
Hilberg, R. La Destruction des Juifs d'Europe.
H. Cronel, 450(NRF):Mar89-84
Hildebidle, J. Five Irish Writers.
J.M. Cahalan, 590:Jun90-76
D. Donoghue, 617(TLS):7-13Dec90-1324
J. Lanters, 223:Fall89-333
F.L. Ryan, 268(IFR):Winter90-52

Hildebrandt, D. Pianoforte.
 R. Anderson, 415:Feb89-90
 E. Morris, 442(NY):8Jan90-94
Hildebrandt, R. & U. Knoop, eds. Brüder-
 Grimm Symposion zur Historischen Wortfor-
 schung.
 H. Tiefenbach, 685(ZDL):2/1989-198
Hildermeier, M. Bürgertum und Stadt in Russ-
 land 1760-1870.
 G.E. Munro, 575(SEER):Jul89-474
Hiley, D.R. Philosophy in Question.
 C. Guignon, 543:Sep89-168
 M.K.M., 185:Oct89-213
Hill, A. In Pursuit of Publishing.
 J. Sutherland, 617(TLS):27Apr-3May90-
 442
Hill, A.O. Mother Tongue, Father Time.
 M. Schulz, 567:Vol74No1/2-151
Hill, B. Women, Work and Sexual Politics in
 Eighteenth-Century England.
 L. Jordanova, 617(TLS):26Jan-1Feb90-
 94
Hill, B.W. Robert Harley.
 G.M. Townend, 566:Spring90-224
 639(VQR):Winter89-15
Hill, C. The Collected Essays of Christopher
 Hill.* (Vols 1-3)
 A.M., 125:Winter89-218
Hill, C. Handel's "Imeneo."
 A.V. Joness, 415:Aug89-477
Hill, C. A Tinker and a Poor Man.*
 W.B. Patterson, 569(SR):Summer89-lxxii
Hill, C. A Turbulent, Seditious, and Factious
 People.
 M. Hardman, 402(MLR):Oct90-916
Hill, D.G. Henry Smart (1813-1879).
 G. Reynolds, 415:Sep89-573
Hill, D.M., ed. Human Rights and Foreign Pol-
 icy.
 D.G., 185:Jul90-921
Hill, E.D. Edward, Lord Herbert of Cherbury.
 S. Archer, 568(SCN):Fall-Winter89-53
 C. Malcolmson, 677(YES):Vol20-260
Hill, G. Collected Poems.
 W.W. Werner, 577(SHR):Winter89-97
Hill, J.H. & K.C. Speaking Mexicano.
 P.V. Kroskrity, 350:Mar90-170
Hill, J.M. Celtic Warfare, 1595-1763.
 H.L. Snyder, 173(ECS):Fall89-114
Hill, M.R. & R. McKay. Soviet Product Quality.
 A. McAuley, 575(SEER):Apr89-320
Hill, P., with R. Bennett. Stolen Years.
 P. Hillyard, 617(TLS):31Aug-6Sep90-924
Hill, P. & R. Keynes - see Lopokova, L. & J.M.
 Keynes
Hill, R. Bones and Silence.
 P. Craig, 617(TLS):17-23Aug90-867
 M. Stasio, 441:12Aug90-21
Hill, R. One Small Step.
 P. Raine, 617(TLS):14-20Dec90-1360
Hill, R. Underworld.
 639(VQR):Winter89-21
Hill, R.A. & B. Bair, eds. Marcus Garvey's Life
 and Lessons.
 K. Anyidoho, 538(RAL):Fall89-578
Hill, S. The Accumulation of Small Acts of
 Kindness.*
 S. Kantaris, 493:Autumn89-42
Hill, S. Family.
 D. Leimbach, 441:21Jan90-21
Hill, S.S., ed. Varieties of Religious Experi-
 ence.
 W.H. Daniel, 392:Winter88/89-106

Hill Rigney, B. Margaret Atwood.
 H. Cannon, 649(WAL):Feb90-371
 G. Deer, 102(CanL):Spring89-150
Hillebrandt, A. Kleine Schriften. (R.P. Das,
 ed)
 J.W. de Jong, 259(IIJ):Jul89-205
Hiller, J., ed. Cahiers du Cinéma. (Vol 2)
 H.T.B., 295(JML):Fall88/Winter89-267
Hillerman, T. Coyote Waits.
 P-L. Adams, 61:Sep90-121
 R.F. Gish, 441:24Jun90-12
 442(NY):20Aug90-91
Hillerman, T. Talking God.*
 42(AR):Summer89-374
Hillerman, T. A Thief of Time.*
 J. Brosseau, 456(NDQ):Winter89-214
 W. Engelbrecht, 440:Winter-Spring89-153
Hillesum, E. Lettres de Westerbork. (P.
 Noble, ed & trans)
 L. Kovacs, 450(NRF):Jan89-97
Hillgruber, M. Die zehnte Rede des Lysias.
 D.M. MacDowell, 123:Vol39No2-193
Hilliard, K. Philosophy, Letters, and the Fine
 Arts in Klopstock's Thought.
 D. Pugh, 564:May89-168
Hillier, J. The Art of the Japanese Book.*
 J. Cahill, 463:Autumn89-169
 P.F. Kornicki, 407(MN):Summer89-253
Hillig, G., ed. Hundert Jahre Anton Maka-
 renko.
 J. Dunstan, 575(SEER):Oct89-625
Hillis, R. Limbo River.
 R.O. Butler, 441:23Sep90-40
Hillkirk, J. & G. Jacobson. Grit, Guts, and
 Genius.
 D. Cole, 441:28Oct90-23
Hillman, J. A Blue Fire. (T. Moore, with J.
 Hillman, eds)
 A. Gottlieb, 441:11Mar90-22
Hills, P. The Light of Early Italian Painting.*
 J.G. Bernasconi, 278(IS):Vol44-151
 J.C. Czarnecki, 551(RenQ):Summer89-326
 H.B.J. Maginnis, 54:Mar89-137
 J. White, 589:Jan89-176
Hills, R.L. Papermaking in Britain, 1488-
 1988.
 517(PBSA):Mar89-125
Hilmy, S.S. The Later Wittgenstein.*
 H.O. Mounce, 521:Apr89-176
Hilscher, E. Gerhart Hauptmann.*
 I.M. Goessl, 406:Winter89-507
Hiltebeitel, A. The Cult of Draupadī. (Vol 1)
 F.J. Korom, 292(JAF):Apr-Jun89-214
 B.M. Sullivan, 293(JASt):Feb89-199
Hilton, B. The Age of Atonement.*
 D. Bowen, 637(VS):Spring90-505
Hilton, G.W. American Narrow Gauge Rail-
 roads.
 C.R. Whitney, 441:23Dec90-6
Hilton, J. Performance.
 S. Bassnett, 610:Spring89-105
 C. McCullough, 611(TN):Vol43No1-41
 J. Norwood, 397(MD):Sep89-464
Hilton, N. & T.A. Vogler, eds. Unnam'd Forms.
 M.L. Johnson, 301(JEGP):Jul89-429
 P. Malekin, 541(RES):Nov89-573
Hilton, W. Walter Hilton's Latin Writings.
 (J.P.H. Clark & C. Taylor, eds)
 S. Wenzel, 589:Oct89-969
Hilzinger, S. "Als ganzer Mensch zu leben..."*
 S.L. Cocalis, 406:Summer89-231

Hilzinger, S. Christa Wolf.*
  H.T. Tewarson, 222(GR):Spring89–87
  E. Waldstein, 221(GQ):Summer89–429
Himmelfarb, G. The New History and the Old.*
  H.M. Mackenzie, 106:Summer89–137
Himmelheber, G. Deutsche Möbelvorlagen
  1800–1900.
  S. Jervis, 90:Oct89–719
Himmelsbach, S. L'Épopée ou la "case" vide.
  T.M. Pratt, 402(MLR):Jul90–719
Hinard, F., ed. La Mort, les morts et l'au-
  delà dans le monde romain.
  G. Davies, 123:Vol39No2–325
  Y. Grisé, 487:Winter89–384
Hinchcliffe, P. & E. Jewinski, eds. Magic
  Realism and Canadian Literature.*
  H. Dahlie, 49:Jan89–106
Hinchliffe, A.P., ed. T.S. Eliot: Plays.
  G. Bas, 189(EA):Apr–Jun89–228
Hinchman, L.P. Hegel's Critique of the En-
  lightenment.
  C–A. Scheier, 53(AGP):Band71Heft1–102
Hinckley, K. & B. American Best Sellers.
  J.F. Baker, 441:13May90–17
Hindle, B. & S. Lubar. Engines of Change.
  D.C. Skemer, 658:Spring89–83
Hindman, S.L. Christine de Pizan's "Epistre
  Othéa."*
  N. Margolis, 589:Oct89–971
Hinds, J. Japanese.*
  B. Saint-Jacques, 320(CJL):Jun89–233
Hinds, J., S.K. Maynard & S. Iwasaki Per-
  spectives on Topicalization.*
  N Nagui, 202(JASt):May90 009
Hinds, M. & E–S. Badawi. A Dictionary of
  Egyptian Arabic, Arabic-English.
  P. Cachia, 294:Mar89–82
Hinds, S. The Metamorphosis of Persephone.*
  W.S. Anderson, 229:Band61Heft4–356
  D.F. Kennedy, 313:Vol79–209
Hindus, M. The Crippled Giant.*
  P. Alméras, 535(RHL):Jan–Feb89–153
Hine, D. Arrondissements.
  S. Scobie, 376:Jun89–130
Hine, J.D. Roger North's Writings on Music to
  c. 1703.
  P. Gouk, 410(M&L):Feb89–96
Hines, T.J. The Later Poetry of Wallace Stev-
  ens.
  K. Zlarek, 153:Fall–Winter89–114
Hinnant, C.H. Samuel Johnson.
  L. Basney, 191(ELN):Jun90–74
  L. Lipking, 77:Summer89–251
Hinnant, C.H. Purity and Defilement in "Gul-
  liver's Travels."
  J.I. Fischer, 566:Spring89–168
  B.S. Hammond, 83:Autumn89–233
Hinojosa, R. Claros Varones de Belken/Fair
  Gentlemen of Belken County.*
  J. Bruce-Novoa, 238:Mar89–165
Hinrichs, B. Utopische Prosa als Längeres
  Gedankenspiel.*
  F.P. Ott, 222(GR):Spring89–88
Hinrichs, J.P., ed. Russian Poetry and Liter-
  ary Life in Harbin and Shanghai, 1930–
  1950.
  G.S. Smith, 575(SEER):Jul89–442
Hinrichs, J.P. Zum Akzent im Mittelbulgar-
  ischen.
  H. Leeming, 575(SEER):Apr89–331

Hinsch, W. Erfahrung und Selbstbewusst-
  sein.*
  R. Blittkowsky, 489(PJGG):Band96Heft2–
  428
  B. Merker, 687:Apr–Jun89–383
Hinske, N., ed. Kant-Index. (Vols 1 & 2)
  H. Oberer, 687:Apr–Jun89–380
Hinske, N. La via kantiana alla filosofia
  trascendentale.
  S. Carboncini, 706:Band21Heft2–213
Hinsley, F.H. & C.A.G. Simkins. British Intel-
  ligence in the Second World War.
  Z. Steiner, 617(TLS):24–30Aug90–899
Hintikka, J. & M. The Logic of Epistemology
  and The Epistemology of Logic.
  S.C. Hetherington, 103:Apr90–144
  R.L. Simpson, 543:Dec89–402
Hintikka, M.B. & J. Investigating Wittgen-
  stein.*
  R.J. Fogelin, 482(PhR):Jan89–93
Hinton, L. Havasupai Songs.
  D.J. Gelo, 187:Fall89–539
Hinton, M., with D. Berger. Bass Line.*
  J.K. Skipper, Jr., 498:Summer89–116
Hinton, S. Kurt Weill: "The Threepenny
  Opera."
  P. Brady, 617(TLS):3–9Aug90–818
von Hinüber, O. Das ältere Mittelindisch im
  Überblick.*
  W.L. Smith, 318(JAOS):Jan–Mar88–185
Hinz, E.J., ed. Data and Acta
  D.P. Corbett, 77:Fall89–331
  M. Kenneally, 178:Mar89–104
Hirdina, H. Gestalten für die Serie.
  A. Trebess, 654(WB):10/1989–1739
"Hiroshige: One Hundred Famous Views of
  Edo."* (French title: Hiroshige: Cent vues
  célèbres d'Edo.)
  D. Waterhouse, 244(HJAS):Jun89–285
Hirota, D. No Abode.
  T. Unno, 485(PE&W):Oct89–507
Hirsch, E. The Night Parade.*
  S. Dobyns, 441:28Jan90–26
  A. Hudgins, 249(HudR):Winter89–677
  639(VQR):Autumn89–135
Hirsch, E.D., Jr. Cultural Literacy.*
  J. Seaton, 580(SCR):Spring90–149
Hirsch, F. Harold Prince and the American
  Musical Theatre.
  A. Harris, 441:18Feb90–21
Hirsch, S.R. & J. Harris, eds. Consent and the
  Incompetent Patient.
  H.M.M., 185:Jan90–461
Hirsch, S.W. The Friendship of the Barbari-
  ans.*
  H. Sancisi-Weerdenburg, 394:Vol42
  fasc1/2–186
Hirsh, J.C., ed. Barlam and Iosaphat.*
  H. Sauer, 72:Band226Heft1–167
Hirst, D. Authority and Conflict.*
  42(AR):Spring89–247
Hirst, G. Semantic Interpretation and the
  Resolution of Ambiguity.
  P. Sgall, 603:Vol13No2–484
Hirst, M. Michelangelo and his Drawings.*
  J.B. Shaw, 39:Nov89–356
  W.E. Wallace, 551(RenQ):Autumn89–555
Hirst, M. Michelangelo Draftsman.*
  W.E. Wallace, 380:Spring89–64
Hislop, J. & D. Swannell, eds. The Faber Book
  of Turf.
  J. Roid, 617(TLS):26Oct–1Nov90–1159

Hiss, G. Korrespondenzen.
P. Petersen, 416:Band4Heft2-182
Hiss, T. The Experience of Place.
R. Blythe, 441:12Aug90-3
Hitchberger, J.M.W. Images of the Army.
J. Harris, 39:Aug89-139
Hitchcock, H.W. Marc-Antoine Charpentier.
W. Mellers, 617(TLS):22-28Jun90-670
Hitchcock, H.W. Music in the United States.
(3rd ed)
E. Southern, 91:Vol17-191
Hitchcock, H.W. & S. Sadie, eds. The New
Grove Dictionary of American Music.
P. Dickinson, 410(M&L):May89-233
Hitchens, C. Blood, Class, and Nostalgia.
A. Brinkley, 441:24Jun90-24
P. Smith, 617(TLS):10-16Aug90-845
Hitchens, C. Imperial Spoils.* (British title:
The Elgin Marbles.)
D. Hunt, 303(JoHS):Vol109-279
639(VQR):Autumn89-138
Hitchens, C. The Monarchy.
J. Lively, 617(TLS):16-22Mar90-271
Hittinger, R. A Critique of the New Natural
Law Theory.*
D. Gordon, 258:Mar89-103
H.J.J., 185:Jan90-450
Hjartarson, P., ed. A Stranger to My Time.*
E. Jewinski, 102(CanL):Spring89-159
A.W. Riley, 168(ECW):Fall89-123
Hjortberg, M. Correspondance littéraire
secrète 1775-1793.
J. Lough, 208(FS):Jan89-91
D. Williams, 402(MLR):Oct90-965
Hlasko, M. Killing the Second Dog.
J. Bayley, 453(NYRB):19Jul90-23
O. Conant, 441:17Jun90-8
Hoagland, E. Heart's Desire.*
A. Urquhart, 617(TLS):11-17May90-490
639(VQR):Winter89-30
Hoagwood, T.A. Prophecy and the Philosophy
of Mind.
J. Hall, 340(KSJ):Vol38-175
Hoare, P. Serious Pleasures.
J. Dalley, 617(TLS):6-12Jul90-728
Hobbs, A.S. Beatrix Potter's Art.
T. Harrod, 617(TLS):30Mar-5Apr90-355
Hobby, E. Virtue of Necessity.
C. Hill, 141:Fall89-482
K. Howlett, 566:Spring90-201
Hobe, P. Lovebound.
M. Sandmaier, 441:6May90-18
Hoberman, R. Modernizing Lives.*
I.B.N., 295(JML):Fall88/Winter89-228
Hobgood, B.M., ed. Master Teachers of
Theatre.
R. Hornby, 289:Fall89-117
Hobhouse, J. The Bride Stripped Bare.*
S. Ramljak, 55:Feb89-91
Hobhouse, P. & P. Taylor, eds. The Gardens
of Europe.
L. Yang, 441:2Dec90-40
Hobsbawm, E.J. Echoes of the Marseillaise.
N. Hampson, 617(TLS):15-21Jun90-637
Hobsbawm, E.J. Nations and Nationalism
since 1780.
S. Hoffmann, 441:7Oct90-24
E. Weber, 617(TLS):26Oct-1Nov90-1149
Hobson, A. J.W. Waterhouse.
K. Flint, 617(TLS):19-25Oct90-1134
Hobson, D. The Pride of Lucifer.
M. Massing, 617(TLS):10-16Aug90-846

Hobson, J.A. The Dreaming Brain.*
P. Wild, 456(NDQ):Spring89-217
Hobson, L.W. Walker Percy.
J.N. Gretlund, 392:Winter88/89-91
M. Hargraves, 87(BB):Mar89-56
L.A. Lawson, 585(SoQ):Summer89-117
Hobson, L.W. Understanding Walker Percy.
J.N. Gretlund, 392:Winter88/89-91
L. Lawson, 578:Fall90-107
A. Sternal, 456(NDQ):Spring89-214
Hochberg, H. Logic, Ontology, and Language.*
L.S. Carrier, 606:Sep89-433
Hochman, B. The Art of Frank Norris, Story-
teller.
J.S. Crisler, 27(AL):Oct89-481
M. Lawlor, 26(ALR):Winter90-84
B. Schuyler, 649(WAL):May89-73
T.H. Towers, 395(MFS):Winter89-734
Hochman, B. Character in Literature.
M. Price, 131(CL):Fall89-389
Hochschild, A. The Mirror at Midnight.
G. Wheatcroft, 441:25Nov90-10
Hock, H.H. Principles of Historical Linguis-
tics.*
N. Boretzky, 680(ZDP):Band108Heft3-454
W. van der Wurff, 179(ES):Oct89-441
Hockett, C.F. Refurbishing Our Foundations.*
F. Chevillet, 189(EA):Oct-Dec89-452
F.R. Palmer, 361:Nov89-255
Hockett, C.F. - see Bloomfield, L.
Hockney, D. & P. Joyce. Hockney on Photog-
raphy.
R.B. Woodward, 55:Oct89-132
van Hoddis, J. Dichtungen und Briefe. (R.
Nörtemann, ed)
B. Igel, 601(SuF):Nov-Dec89-1325
W. Paulsen, 133:Band22Heft2-181
Hodges, J.A. New Deal Labor Policy and the
Southern Cotton Textile Industry 1933-
1941.
J. Braeman, 106:Summer89-41
Hodges, R. The Anglo-Saxon Achievement.
P. Wormald, 617(TLS):25-31May90-562
Hodgman, H. Broken Words.*
M. Hardie, 581:Dec89-654
Hodgson, A. The Romances of William Morris.*
R. Sheets, 637(VS):Spring90-525
Hodgson, G. The Colonel.
J. Chace, 441:21Oct90-3
D.M. Kennedy, 61:Nov90-163
Hodgson, G. Economics and Institutions.
P.J. Boettke, 144:Winter-Spring90-10
Hodgson, P.C. God in History.
M.J. De Nys, 543:Dec89-404
Hodgson, P.C. - see Hegel, G.W.F.
Hodgson, T. The Batsford Dictionary of
Drama.
R. Foulkes, 611(TN):Vol43No2-83
Hodnett, E. Five Centuries of English Book
Illustration.
D. McKitterick, 78(BC):Summer89-262
C. Newall, 39:Aug89-138
Hodson, L., ed. Marcel Proust: The Critical
Heritage.*
S. Gillespie, 97(CQ):Vol18No4-446
Hoekstra, A. - see Homer
Hoenigswald, H.M. & L.F. Weiner, eds. Biolog-
ical Metaphor and Cladistic Classification.
W. Kupersmith, 481(PQ):Spring89-272
R. Lass, 297(JL):Sep89-490
Hoensch, J.K. A History of Modern Hungary
1867-1986.
J. Batt, 575(SEER):Jul89-484

Hoerburger, F. Volksmusikforschung.
  A.K. Schaller-Wenzlitschke,
  187:Winter89-177
vom Hofe, G., P. Pfaff & H. Timm, eds. Was
  aber (bleibet) stiften die Dichter?
  W. Larrett, 83:Spring89-120
Höfele, A. Parodie und literarischer Wandel.
  W. Karrer, 38:Band107Heft1/2-245
Hofer, A. Geschichte des Militärmarsches.
  R. Hellyer, 410(M&L):Nov89-548
Hoff, L.K. Hamlet's Choice.
  C.H. Kullman, 580(SCR):Fall90-177
Hoffman, A. The Best of Abbie Hoffman. (D.
  Simon, with A. Hoffman, eds)
  D. Kelly, 441:11Mar90-19
Hoffman, A. Seventh Heaven.
  A. Becker, 441:5Aug90-2
  442(NY):3Sep90-107
Hoffman, A.J. Twain's Heroes, Twain's
  Worlds.
  P. Baender, 27(AL):Dec89-701
  W. Baker, 42(AR):Spring89-244
  E. Emerson, 392:Winter88/89-99
  R.B. Hauck, 395(MFS):Winter89-739
  R.B. Salomon, 445(NCF):Mar90-551
Hoffman, D. Faulkner's Country Matters.
  S. Pinsker, 219(GaR):Winter89-795
Hoffman, D. Hang-Gliding from Helicon.*
  B. Howard, 491:May89-101
Hoffman, E. Lost in Translation.*
  S. Miron, 390:Nov89-60
  42(AR):Summer89-371
Hoffman, F.J. Rationality and Mind in Early
  Buddhism.
  M. Bockover, 485(PE&W):Apr89-214
Hoffman, M.F., ed. Marguerite and William
  Zorach, the Cubist Years: 1915-1918.
  R.K. Tarbell, 662:Fall89/Winter90-52
Hoffman, P. Doubt, Time, Violence.
  S. Romanowski, 475:Vol16No30-292
Hoffman, P.T. Church and Community in the
  Diocese of Lyon, 1500-1789.
  R. Toupin, 589:Vol13No4-411
Hoffman, R. & others, eds. The Economy of
  Early America.
  G.M. Walton, 656(WMQ):Apr89-406
Hoffman, W. By Land, By Sea.
  C. Johnson, 219(GaR):Summer89-406
  639(VQR):Winter89-19
Hoffman, W. Furors Die.
  S. Nesanovich, 441:8Jul90-17
Hoffmann, C. Juden und Judentum im Werk
  deutscher Althistoriker des 19. und 20.
  Jahrhunderts.
  M.H. Williams, 123:Vol39No2-378
Hoffmann, P. Symbolismus.*
  M. Gsteiger, 52:Band24Heft3-323
Hoffmann, R. The Metamict State.
  P. Harris, 639(VQR):Spring89-244
Hoffmann, R.J. & G.A. Larue, eds. Biblical v.
  Secular Ethics.
  J.A.G., 185:Apr90-719
Hoffmann, W. Das "Nibelungenlied."*
  H. Kratz, 133:Band22Heft3/4-306
Hoffmann-Erbrecht, L. Musikgeschichte
  Schlesiens.
  N. Linke, 417:Oct-Dec89-378
Hoffmeier, J.C. Sacred in the Vocabulary of
  Ancient Egypt.
  E. Cruz-Uribe, 318(JAOS):Jan-Mar88-
  159

Hoffmeister, G., ed. Der deutsche Schelmen-
  roman im europäischen Kontext.
  W.G. Marigold, 221(GQ):Spring89-258
  L. Tatlock, 406:Fall89-385
  H. Wagener, 133:Band22Heft2-190
Hoffmeister, G. Deutsche und europäische
  Barockliteratur.*
  M.K. Kremer, 564:Nov89-349
  E.A. Metzger, 133:Band22Heft3/4-313
  M.M. Metzger, 597(SN):Vol61No2-242
  M. Reinhart, 221(GQ):Fall89-525
Hofinger, M. Lexicon Hesiodeum: Index inver-
  sus. Lexicon Hesiodeum cum indice inver-
  so: Lexicon Hesiodeum.
  C.J. Ruijgh, 394:Vol42fasc3/4-571
Hofinger, M. & D. Pinte. Lexicon Hesiodeum
  cum indice inverso: Supplementum.
  C.J. Ruijgh, 394:Vol42fasc3/4-571
Hofman, M. & J. Morehen, comps. Latin Music
  in British Sources c. 1485- c. 1610.*
  H. Benham, 410(M&L):May89-249
Hofmann, E. & A-L. Delacrétaz, eds. Le
  Groupe de Coppet et la Révolution fran-
  çaise.
  T. Unwin, 446(NCFS):Spring-Summer90-
  565
Hofmann, E. & A-L. Delacrétaz - see
  "Annales Benjamin Constant 8-9"
Hofmann, G. Balzac's Horse and Other Sto-
  ries. (C. Middleton, ed & trans)
  P. La Salle, 573(SSF):Summer88-325
  P. Lewis, 565:Autumn89-72
Hofmann, I. Reisen und Erzählen.
  P. Wolfzettel, 547(RF):Band101Heft2/3-
  344
Hofmann, P. That Fine Italian Hand.
  M. Mewshaw, 441:17Jun90-10
Hofstetter, F. Winchester und der spätal-
  tenglische Sprachgebrauch.
  E.G. Stanley, 447(N&Q):Jun89-216
Hoftijzer, J. The Function and Use of the
  Imperfect Forms with Nun Paragogicum in
  Classical Hebrew.
  S. Segert, 318(JAOS):Jan-Mar88-157
Hoftijzer, P.G. Engelse boekverkopers bij de
  Beurs.
  S. Roach, 354:Jun89-163
Hogan, D. Lebanon Lodge.
  D. Durrant, 364:Aug/Sep89-134
Hogan, D.J. Dark Romance.
  K. Newman, 707:Winter88/89-68
Hoge, J.O., ed. Literary Reviewing.*
  M.J.F., 295(JML):Fall88/Winter89-228
Hogg, J., ed. Ms. Grande Chartreuse, I. (Vols
  1 & 3)
  R.B. Marks, 589:Jan89-214
Hogg, R. & C.B. McCully. Metrical Phonology.*
  G.E. Booij, 603:Vol13No1-221
  I. Vogel, 297(JL):Mar89-221
Hoggart, R. A Sort of Clowning. (Vol 2)
  P. Parker, 617(TLS):13-19Jul90-750
Hogsett, C. The Literary Existence of Ger-
  maine de Staël.*
  G.R. Besser, 207(FR):Oct89-164
  N. Senior, 166:Oct89-81
Hogue, W.L. Discourse and the Other.
  R. Martin, 459:Spring89-86
Hoh, L.G. & W.H. Rough. Step Right Up!
  A. Aronson, 441:25Nov90-19
Hohenberger, J. Semitische und Hamitische
  Wortstämme im Nilo-Hamitischen mit
  phonetischen Analysen.
  S. Brauner, 682(ZPSK):Band42Heft6-867

Höhlein, H., P.H. Marsden & C. Pollner. Auswahlbibliographie zum Studium der anglistischen Sprachwissenschaft.
 G. Bourcier, 189(EA):Oct–Dec89–458
Hohmann, C. Thomas Pynchon's "Gravity's Rainbow."*
 B. Duyfhuizen, 454:Fall89–75
 M. Fludernik, 224(GRM):Band39Heft1–118
Höhn, G. Heine-Handbuch.
 J.L. Sammons, 406:Summer89–261
Hohoff, U. E.T.A. Hoffmann: Der Sandmann.
 G.R. Kaiser, 224(GRM):Band39Heft4–476
Høidal, O.K. Quisling.
 P.M. Hayes, 617(TLS):23Feb–1Mar90–195
Hoisington, S.S., ed & trans. Russian Views of "Eugene Onegin."
 A.D.P. Briggs, 402(MLR):Apr90–533
"Hokusai: One Hundred Views of Mount Fuji."*
 W.H. Coaldrake, 293(JASt):Aug89–618
 E. Tinios, 39:May89–368
Holaday, A., with G.B. Evans & T.L. Berger – see Chapman, G.
Holbek, B. Interpretation of Fairy Tales.*
 R.B. Bottigheimer, 221(GQ):Winter89–121
 J. Lindow, 563(SS):Autumn89–404
Holberton, P. Palladio's Villas.
 J. Summerson, 617(TLS):6–12Jul90–730
Holbrook, D. Evolution and the Humanities.*
 J.H. Shea, 125:Fall88–101
Holden, A. Big Deal.
 S. Rushdie, 617(TLS):16–22Nov90–1239
Holden, A.J. – see Chrétien de Troyes
Holden, E. The Nature Notes of an Edwardian Lady.
 P–L. Adams, 61:Jan90–100
Holderness, G., ed. The Shakespeare Myth.*
 D. Devlin, 402(MLR):Jul90–690
 C. Dionne, 147:Vol6No3–66
 H. Mills, 175:Spring89–77
 D. Sedge, 611(TN):Vol43No1–29
 P. Thomson, 610:Summer89–190
Holderness, G., N. Potter & J. Turner. Shakespeare.*
 I. Kamps, 405(MP):Feb90–302
 E.S. Mallin, 551(RenQ):Summer89–359
 P.N. Siegel, 191(ELN):Dec89–65
Holdstock, P. The Blackbird's Song.*
 J–A. Goodwin, 617(TLS):8–14Jun90–617
 D.L. Overmyer, 102(CanL):Summer89–191
Holeczek, H. – see Erasmus
Holes, C. Language Variation and Change in a Modernising Arab State.
 A.S. Kaye, 297(JL):Mar89–275
Holiday, A. Moral Powers.
 D.H., 355(LSoc):Jun89–305
 T.A. Roberts, 518:Oct89–236
van Holk, A., ed. Dutch Contributions to the Tenth International Congress of Slavists.
 D. Shepherd, 575(SEER):Oct89–626
Hölkeskamp, K–J. Die Entstehung der Nobilität.
 R. Develin, 229:Band61Heft4–365
 F. Millar, 313:Vol79–138
Holland, B., ed. Soviet Sisterhood.
 B. Heldt, 104(CASS):Spring89–107
Holland, C. The Bear Flag.
 P–L. Adams, 61:Jul90–104
 S. Altinel, 617(TLS):2–8Nov90–1182
Holland, D. & N. Quinn, eds. Cultural Models in Language and Thought.
 R. Sheffy, 494:Winter89–847

Holland, H. The Struggle.
 G.M. Fredrickson, 453(NYRB):27Sep90–20
 S. Suzman, 441:18Mar90–28
Holland, H.M. Managing Defense.
 J.M. Peek, 293(JASt):Feb89–163
Holland, M.G. The British Catholic Press and the Educational Controversy, 1847–1865.
 J.L. Altholz, 635(VPR):Fall89–130
Holland, N.N. The Brain of Robert Frost.
 R. Wakefield, 27(AL):Oct89–488
Holland–Cunz, B., ed. Feministische Utopien.
 S. Westphal–Wihl, 561(SFS):Mar89–113
Hollander, A. Moving Pictures.*
 L. Ehrlich, 500:Summer89–70
Hollander, J. Harp Lake.*
 S.M. Schultz, 639(VQR):Autumn89–773
 639(VQR):Spring89–64
Hollander, J. Melodious Guile.*
 J. Mellard, 599:Summer90–302
 639(VQR):Spring89–63
Hollander, J. – see Bloom, H.
Hollander, R. Boccaccio's Last Fiction: "Il Corbaccio."
 J. Usher, 382(MAE):1989/2–333
Hölldobler, B. & E.O. Wilson. The Ants.
 T.E. Lovejoy, 441:29Jul90–3
 M. Ridley, 617(TLS):24–30Aug90–894
 J.M. Smith, 453(NYRB):27Sep90–36
Hollein, H. & C. Cooke, eds. Vienna, Dream and Reality.
 P.V., 90:Feb89–162
Höller, H. Ingeborg Bachmann.
 K. Schuhmann, 654(WB):2/1989–347
Hollerman, L. Japan, Disincorporated.
 R.J. Samuels, 293(JASt):Feb89–165
Hollerman, L. Japan's Economic Strategy in Brazil.
 F. Fajnzylber, 293(JASt):Feb89–166
Holley, M. The Poetry of Marianne Moore.*
 R.B.D., 295(JML):Fall88/Winter89–385
 H. Deese, 27(AL):Mar89–140
Hollier, D., ed. A New History of French Literature.
 R. Adams, 453(NYRB):1Feb90–36
 P. France, 617(TLS):2–8Feb90–107
Holliger, C. & others. Chronik Ulrich Bräker.
 G. Braungart, 224(GRM):Band39Heft2–245
Hollinger, D.A. & C. Capper, eds. The American Intellectual Tradition.
 H. Beaver, 617(TLS):25–31May90–549
Hollinghurst, A. The Swimming-Pool Library.*
 S. Moore, 532(RCF):Spring89–246
Hollingworth, C. Front Line.
 C. Wheeler, 617(TLS):13–19Jul90–750
Hollis, A. – see Braun, V.
Hollis, M. The Cunning of Reason.*
 T.E. Wilkerson, 518:Jan89–56
Hollis, P. Ladies Elect.
 J. Damousi, 637(VS):Autumn89–210
Holloway, G. My Ghost In Your Eye.
 D. Kennedy, 493:Autumn89–48
Holloway, J., ed. The Oxford Book of Local Verses.*
 D.H. Stewart, 568(SCN):Fall–Winter89–44
Holloway, J.B. Brunetto Latini.
 P. Armour, 278(IS):Vol44–153
 G. Breuer, 547(RF):Band101Heft4–492
Holloway, J.B. The Pilgrim and the Book.
 H.H. Schless, 589:Oct89–973
Holloway, K.F.C. The Character of the Word.*
 B. Jackson, 459:Winter89–113
Holm, J. Pidgins and Creoles. (Vol 1)
 P. Mühlhäusler, 297(JL):Mar89–250

Holm-Olson, L. Innledning. (A. Kjaer & L. Holm-Olsen, eds)
   K.E. Gade, 563(SS):Spring/Summer89-296
Holman, J. Squabble.
   M. Mifflin, 441:22Jul90-20
Holmberg, A. Word Order and Syntactic Features in the Scandinavian Languages and English.
   J.T. Faarlund, 353:Vol27No1-160
   H. Thráinsson, 452(NJL):Vol12No1-59
Holmberg, H. Glaede over Danmark.
   B.D. Eddy, 563(SS):Winter89-98
Holmes, B. & M. McLean. The Curriculum.
   F. Flower, 324:Dec89-65
Holmes, G. Florence, Rome and the Origins of the Renaissance.*
   A. Molho, 589:Jul89-713
   D. Waley, 278(IS):Vol43-139
Holmes, G., ed. The Oxford Illustrated History of Medieval Europe.
   R. Franklin, 39:Dec89-429
Holmes, J. & R. Lindley. The Values of Psychotherapy.
   D. Ingleby, 617(TLS):6-12Jul90-720
Holmes, J.C. Night Music.
   F. Miele, 363(LitR):Spring90-381
Holmes, J.S. Translated!
   M. Steenmeijer, 204(FdL):Mar89-68
Holmes, J.S. - see Vanderauwera, R.
Holmes, N. Nobody's Fault.
   K. Blickle, 441:14Jan90-31
Holmes, R. Coleridge: Early Visions.*
   P-L. Adams, 61:Jun90-120
   R. Fuller, 364:Dec89/Jan90-106
   B. Leithauser, 442(NY):2Jul90-68
   R.B. Martin, 453(NYRB):6Dec90-43
   J. Wordsworth, 441:17Jun90-11
Holmes, R.L. On War and Morality.
   T. Grassey, 185:Jul90-900
Holmström, L., ed. The Inner Courtyard.
   M. Couto, 617(TLS):14-20Sep90-980
Holmström, R. Karakteristik och värdering.
   M. Fahlgren, 172(Edda):1989/1-88
   G.C. Schoolfield, 562(Scan):Nov89-213
Holoman, D.K. Berlioz.
   J. Rosselli, 617(TLS):4-10May90-475
Holoman, D.K. Catalogue of the Works of Hector Berlioz.*
   F. Lesure, 537:Vol75No2-301
   J. Rushton, 410(M&L):Aug89-410
Holroyd, M. Bernard Shaw.* (Vol 1)
   M. Archer, 157:No171-51
   C.A. Berst, 177(ELT):Vol32No4-471
   H. Fromm, 249(HudR):Summer89-209
   G. Gordon, 511:Jan89-41
   G.K. Larson, 615(TJ):Oct89-426
   C. Murray, 272(IUR):Spring89-165
   J.P. Sisk, 31(ASch):Autumn89-597
   42(AR):Winter89-108
Hölscher, U. "Die Odyssee."
   H. Erbse, 229:Band61Heft6-481
Holst, I. Gustav Holst. (2nd ed)
   A.F.L.T., 412:May89-145
Holstein, W.J. The Japanese Power Game.
   S. Chira, 441:23Sep90-13
   J. Fallows, 453(NYRB):8Nov90-33
Holstun, J. A Rational Millennium.*
   J. Gilsdorf, 656(WMQ):Apr89-382
   C. Hill, 551(RenQ):Autumn89-600
Holt, E.G., ed. The Expanding World of Art, 1874-1902.* (Vol 1)
   P. Greenhalgh, 39:Jun89-440
          [continued]

[continuing]
   R.D. Reck, 207(FR):Feb90-600
   C. Trodd, 89(BJA):Summer89-288
Holt, F.L. Alexander the Great and Bactria.
   P.M. Fraser, 123:Vol39No2-292
Holt, H. A Lot To Ask.
   L. Duguid, 617(TLS):16-22Nov90-1228
Holt, J. Learning All the Time.
   L.E. Beattie, 441:18Feb90-20
Holt, J.C., ed. Domesday Studies.
   W.E. Kapelle, 589:Jul89-620
Holt, J.C. Magna Carta and Medieval Government.
   J. Campbell, 382(MAE):1989/1-149
Holt, T. Goatsong.
   L. Belfer, 441:18Mar90-20
Höltgen, K.J. Aspects of the Emblem.*
   C.W.R.D. Moseley, 402(MLR):Jan90-147
Höltgen, K.J. & others, eds. Tradition und Innovation in der englischen und amerikanischen Lyrik des 20. Jahrhunderts.*
   H-W. Ludwig, 38:Band107Heft3/4-535
Holthusen, H.E. Gottfried Benn.* (Vol 1)
   W. Paulsen, 133:Band22Heft1-79
Holton, G. The Advancement of Science, and Its Burdens.
   G. Gale, 486:Sep89-536
Holton, M. & V.D. Mihailovich. Serbian Poetry from the Beginnings to the Present.
   C. Hawkesworth, 617(TLS):20-26Apr90-429
Holtus, G., ed. Theaterwesen und dramatische Literatur.
   G. von Ruunor, 224(GRM):Band0011eft0 359
Holtus, G. & E. Radtke. eds. Gesprochenes Italienisch in Geschichte und Gegenwart.*
   G. Lepschy, 545(RPh):Nov89-306
Holtus, G. & E. Radtke, eds. Rumänistik in der Diskussion.
   T. Krefeld, 72:Band226Heft1-197
Holtus, G. & E. Radtke, eds. Umgangssprache in der Iberoromania.
   G. Bossong, 545(RPh):Feb90-459
Holub, M. Poems Before and After. Vanishing Lung Syndrome. The Dimensions of the Present Moment and Other Essays. (D. Young, ed)
   O. Reynolds, 617(TLS):4-10May90-467
Holyoake, J. Contextual and Thematic Interference in Montaigne's Essais.
   E. Limbrick, 535(RHL):Jan-Feb89-89
Holz, G. & H. Haarmann - see Wolfenstein, A.
Holz, H. Philosophisch-logische Abhandlung.
   H. Fackeldey, 489(PJGG):Band96Heft2 441
Holzberg, N. Martial.
   H. Szelest, 229:Band61Heft4-358
Holzberger, W.G. & H.J. Saatkamp, Jr. - see Santayana, G.
Holzhey, H. Cohen und Natorp.*
   K-H. Lembeck, 53(AGP):Band71Heft1-109
Hom, K. The Taste of China.
   R. Flaste, 441:2Dec90-14
Hom, M.K. Songs of Gold Mountain.
   F. Wu, 116:Jul88-189
Homan, S., ed. Shakespeare and the Triple Play.
   C.J. Carlisle, 570(SQ):Winter89-505
Homan, S. Shakespeare's Theater of Presence.*
   A.F. Kinney, 481(PQ):Fall89-443
   C.M. Mazer, 610:Summer89-194

Homberger, E. & J. Charmley, eds. The Trou-
bled Face of Biography.*
D. Bair, 77:Winter89-70
N. Page, 506(PSt):Dec89-307
Homer. The Iliad. (R. Fagles, trans)
O. Taplin, 441:7Oct90-1
Homer. Omero, "Odissea," Vol. IV (Libri XIII-
XVI). (A. Hoekstra, ed; G.A. Privitera,
trans)
C.J. Ruijgh, 394:Vol42fasc3/4-521
Homer, W.I. & L. Goodrich. Albert Pinkham
Ryder.
D.M. Lubin, 617(TLS):25-31May90-553
M. Nixon, 441:27May90-15
J. Updike, 453(NYRB):8Nov90-17
Homes, A.M. The Safety of Objects.
B. Levine, 441:2Sep90-16
"Hommages à Henri Le Bonniec, Res sacrae."
P. Flobert, 555:Vol62Fasc1-190
"Hommages à Jozef Veremans."
P. Flobert, 555:Vol62Fasc1-191
Honan, P. Jane Austen.*
E. Gillooly, 147:Vol6No1-87
D. Kaplan, 403(MLS):Spring89-90
S. Morgan, 405(MP):Nov89-191
C.C. Park, 249(HudR):Winter89-647
Honan, P. Authors' Lives.
M. Cart, 441:16Sep90-22
Honderich, T., ed. Morality and Objectivity.
S.R.L. Clark, 479(PhQ):Jan89-98
Honderich, T. A Theory of Determinism.
B. Hannan & K. Lehrer, 262:Mar89-49
C. Hookway, 262:Mar89-79
A. Jack, 393(Mind):Oct89-642
J. Kim, 262:Mar89-29
R. Schacht, 262:Mar89-55
G. Strawson, 262:Mar89-3
M. Tiles, 483:Jan89-109
Honemann, V. & N.F. Palmer, eds. Deutsche
Handschriften 1100-1400.
W. Schröder, 684(ZDA):Band118Heft2-66
Hong, W. Relationship Between Korea and
Japan in Early Period.
S.M. Nelson, 293(JASt):Aug89-636
Hongo, G. The River of Heaven.
R. Schultz, 249(HudR):Spring89-151
Honig, E. & G. Hershatter. Personal Voices.
J.C. Robinson, 293(JASt):Feb89-135
Honigmann, E.A.J. Myriad-Minded Shake-
speare.
A. Barton, 453(NYRB):1Feb90-15
Honigmann, E.A.J. John Weever.*
H.R. Woudhuysen, 354:Jun89-160
Honko, L., ed. Kalevala ja maailman eepok-
set.
A-L. Siikala, 64(Arv):Vol44-204
Honneth, A. & A. Wellmer, eds. Die Frank-
furter Schule und die Folgen.
H. Mörchen, 687:Jan-Mar89-193
Hönnighausen, L. William Faulkner.*
C.S. Brown, 569(SR):Fall89-556
M.A. Cohen, 27(AL):Oct89-496
P.R.J., 295(JML):Fall88/Winter89-325
J.G. Watson, 395(MFS):Summer89-281
Hönnighausen, L., ed. Faulkner's Discourse.*
D.M. Kartiganer, 392:Summer89-317
Hönnighausen, L. The Symbolist Tradition in
English Literature. (G. Hönnighausen, ed &
trans)
T.J. Collins, 637(VS):Summer90-677
Honolka, K. Papageno.
J. Rosselli, 617(TLS):27Jul-2Aug90-801

Honsa, V. Old Spanish Grammar of "La gran
conquista de Ultramar" with Critical Edi-
tion of Book IV, Chapters 126-193.
S.N. Dworkin, 545(RPh):Nov89-317
Hood, A. Three-Legged Horse.
A.E. Johnson, 441:4Feb90-18
Hood, H. Five New Facts About Giorgione.
K. McNeilly, 529(QQ):Autumn89-717
Hood, H. The Motor Boys in Ottawa.*
R. Thacker, 168(ECW):Fall89-23
Hood, S. & G. O'Leary. Questions of Broad-
casting.
S. French, 617(TLS):9-15Feb90-142
J. Thompson, 324:Aug90-642
Hood, W. Cry Spy.
J.A. Cincotti, 441:3Jun90-22
Hoog, M. Paul Gauguin.
R. Kendall, 39:May89-366
Hook, A., ed. The History of Scottish Litera-
ture. (Vol 2)
E. Rothstein, 566:Spring90-215
Hook, D.D. & L. Kahn. Death in the Balance.
P. Weissman, 441:29Jul90-21
Hook, P. & M. Poltimore. Popular Nineteenth
Century Painting.
J.F. Codell, 637(VS):Autumn89-185
Hook, S. Convictions.
P. Wood, 441:26Aug90-14
Hook, S. Out of Step.*
S.P., 295(JML):Fall88/Winter89-176
Hooker, J. Master of the Leaping Figures.*
L. Sail, 565:Summer89-75
Hookway, C. Peirce.
T.H. Engstrom, 479(PhQ):Apr89-248
Hookway, C. Quine.
R.F. Gibson, Jr., 84:Dec89-557
R. Kirk, 518:Jul89-153
G. McCulloch, 393(Mind):Oct89-637
L. Peña, 103:Nov90-449
Hooper, E. Slim.
J. Ryle, 617(TLS):27Apr-3May90-437
Hoose, B. Proportionalism.
D.J.G., 185:Jul90-918
Hoover, M.L. Meyerhold and His Set Design-
ers.
G. McVay, 511:Jun89-44
Hope, A. Londoners' Larder.
V. Pearl, 617(TLS):21-27Dec90-1373
Hope, B., with M. Shavelson. Don't Shoot, It's
Only Me.
J. Kaufman, 441:10Jun90-46
Hope, C. My Chocolate Redeemer.*
J. Mellors, 364:Jun/Jul89-133
Hope, V.M. Virtue by Consensus.
R.S. Downie, 617(TLS):11-17May90-507
Hopkin, A. The Living Legend of Saint Pat-
rick.
P-L. Adams, 61:Apr90-108
Hopkins, D. John Dryden.*
D. Hughes, 402(MLR):Jan90-148
Hopkins, G.M. The Poetical Works of Gerard
Manley Hopkins. (N.H. MacKenzie, ed) The
Early Poetic Manuscripts and Note-Books
of Gerard Manley Hopkins in Facsimile.
(N.H. MacKenzie, ed) Selected Letters. (C.
Phillips, ed)
J. Kelly, 617(TLS):7-13Dec90-1323
Hopkins, J. Emptiness Yoga.
J.W. de Jong, 259(IIJ):Jul89-229
Hopkins, J. - see Saint Anselm
Hopkins, S. Studies in the Grammar of Early
Arabic.
J.A. Bellamy, 318(JAOS):Jan-Mar88-166

Hopkinson, N., ed. A Hellenistic Anthology.
  J. Clack, 124:Jan–Feb90–243
  G.O. Hutchinson, 303(JoHS):Vol109–236
  D.W.T. Vessey, 123:Vol39No2–184
Hopkirk, P. The Great Game.
  C.M. Woodhouse, 617(TLS):11–17May90–
  492
Hopton, A. – see Coppe, A.
Hopwood, D. Tales of Empire.
  B. Wasserstein, 617(TLS):30Mar–5Apr90–
  343
Horak, S.M. The First Treaty of World War I.
  639(VQR):Winter89–8
Horch, H.O. & H. Denkler, eds. Conditio Juda-
  ica.
  M. Pazi, 680(ZDP):Band108Heft4–621
Horder, T.J., J.A. Witkowski & C.C. Wylie, eds.
  A History of Embryology.
  J. Beatty, 486:Mar89–174
Horgan, P. Of America East & West.
  R.F. Gish, 649(WAL):Feb90–394
Horgan, P. A Writer's Eye. Under the Sangre
  de Cristo. A Certain Climate.
  R.F. Gish, 649(WAL):May89–80
Hörig, M. & E. Schwertheim. Corpus Cultus
  Iovis Dolicheni.
  S.R.F. Price, 123:Vol39No1–146
Horio, T. Educational Thought and Ideology
  in Modern Japan.
  V. Kobayashi, 303(JAEt):Aug90–010
  C. Lewis, 407(MN):Spring89–124
Horn, D., with R. Jackson. The Literature of
  American Music in Books and Folk Music
  Collections. (Supp 1)
  E. Southern, 91:Vol17–191
Horn, L.R. A Natural History of Negation.
  B.S. Gillon, 103:May90–181
Horn, W. Die Dresdner Hofkirchenmusik 1720–
  1745.
  B. Baselt, 410(M&L):Nov89–536
  T. Emmerig, 416:Band4Heft2–180
Hornback, B.G. "Middlemarch."
  K.B. Stockton, 637(VS):Autumn89–177
Hornblower, S. Thucydides.*
  P.J. Rhodes, 303(JoHS):Vol109–219
Hornbogen, H. Jakob van Hoddis.
  W. Paulsen, 100;Dand22Heft2–181
Horne, A. Harold Macmillan.* (Vol 2: 1957–
  1986)
  442(NY):26Feb90–132
Horne, D. The Great Museum.*
  D. Rice, 127:Summer89–197
Horne, P., ed. Concordance pascoliane: "Myr-
  icae."
  D. Robey, 402(MLR):Jan90–214
Horner, P.J. The Index of Middle English
  Prose.* (Handlist 3)
  H. Gneuss, 38:Band107Heft1/2–169
Horno–Delgado, A. & others, eds. Breaking
  Boundaries.
  P. de la Fuente, 649(WAL):Nov89–285
Horrocks, G. Generative Grammar.*
  M.O. Tallerman, 297(JL):Mar89–262
  H. Ulherr, 38:Band107Heft3/4–454
"Horror y tragedia en el teatro del Siglo de
  Oro."
  A.L. Mackenzie, 86(BHS):Jul89–279
Horsford, H.C. & L. Horth – see Melville, H.
Horsman, A. The Victorian Novel.
  J. Sutherland, 617(TLS):21–27Dec90–
  1368
Horton, M., with J. & H. Kohl. The Long Haul.
  L. Green, 441:20May90–31

Horvath, B.M. Variation in Australian Eng-
  lish.*
  J.C. Stalker, 710:Mar89–121
Horwich, R. Shakespeare's Dilemmas.
  J.A. Bryant, Jr., 570(SQ):Fall89–355
Horwitz, G.J. In the Shadow of Death.
  P. Hoffmann, 441:11Nov90–24
Hosking, G. The Awakening of the Soviet
  Union.
  K. Fitzlyon, 364:Feb/Mar90–123
  J. Sherr, 617(TLS):16–22Mar90–273
  A.B. Ulam, 441:8Apr90–14
Hösle, V. Hegels System.*
  W. Schmied–Kowarzik, 489(PJGG):
  Band96Heft2–402
Hospital, J.T. Charades.*
  G. Turcotte, 581:Mar89–121
Hossenfelder, M. Die Philosophie der Antike.
  (Vol 3)
  B. Inwood, 53(AGP):Band71Heft1–73
Hossfeld, P. – see Albertus Magnus
Hotchner, A.E. Blown Away.
  J. Pareles, 441:9Sep90–3
Hotchner, A.E. Hemingway and His World.
  P.L. Hays, 234:Spring90–183
  T. Piazza, 441:25Mar90–23
Hotman, F. La Vie de Messire Gaspar de Col-
  ligny Admiral de France.* (E–V. Telle, ed)
  F.M. Higman, 208(FS):Jul89–321
  R. Zuber, 535(RHL):Jan–Feb89–92
Hotzenköcherle, R. Dialektstrukturen im
  Wandel. (R. Schläpfer & N. Bigler, eds)
  W. Koller, 597(SN):Vol61No2–238
Hotzenköcherle, R., ed. Sprachatlas der
  deutschen Schweiz. (Vol 6)
  W. Koller, 597(SN):Vol61No2–238
Hotzenköcherle, R. Die Sprachlandschaften
  der deutschen Schweiz. (N. Bigler & R.
  Schläpfer, with R. Börlin, eds) (Vol 1)
  G. Bellmann, 685(ZDL):1/1989–103
  W. Koller, 597(SN):Vol61No2–238
Houari, K. Confessions d'un immigró.
  A.J.M. Prévos, 207(FR):Oct89–186
de la Houblonnière, R. – see under Ranulphe
  de la Houblonnière
Hough, M. Out of Place.
  A. Salhi, 617(TLS):22–28Jun90–671
Hough, R. and D. Richards. The Battle of
  Britain.*
  P. Smith, 617(TLS):5–11Jan90–6
Houghton, W.E., E.R. Houghton & J.H. Slinger-
  land, eds. The Wellesley Index to Victorian
  Periodicals; 1824–1900.* (Vol 4)
  R.D. Altick, 405(MP):Aug89–101
  B.Q. Schmidt, 635(VPR):Summer89–71
Houle, G. Meter in Music, 1600–1800.*
  D.R. Hurley, 309:Vol9No2/3–163
  E. Linfield, 308:Spring89–222
  E. Schwandt, 410(M&L):Feb89–93
Houlgate, S. Hegel, Nietzsche and the Criti-
  cism of Metaphysics.*
  N. Davey, 323:Oct89–290
  J. Leaman, 402(MLR):Jul90–800
  C.S. Taylor, 518:Jan89–26
Houppermans, S., ed. Recherches sur l'oeuvre
  de Claude Ollier.
  L.S. Roudiez, 535(RHL):Sep–Oct89–944
Houriez, J. La Bible et le sacré dans "Le
  Soulier de satin" de Paul Claudel.
  M. Longstaffe, 208(FS):Jul89–349

House, C. The Outrageous Life of Henry Faulkner.
C.K. Piehl, 392:Winter88/89-107
House, J. & S. Blum-Kulka, eds. Interlingual and Intercultural Communication.
U. Connor, 710:Sep89-337
Houssaye, J. Ecole et vie active.
Y. Palazzeschi, 542:Oct-Dec89-630
Houston, J.P. Victor Hugo. (rev)
J.R. Williams, 207(FR):Mar90-719
Houston, J.P. Joyce and Prose.
R. Gottfried, 329(JJQ):Spring90-690
Houston, J.P. Patterns of Thought in Rimbaud and Mallarmé.*
M-J. Whitaker, 535(RHL):Jan-Feb89-130
Houston, J.P. Shakespearean Sentences.
N.F. Blake, 402(MLR):Apr90-408
A. Graham-White, 615(TJ):Dec89-572
R. McDonald, 551(RenQ):Winter89-881
Houston, L. Necessity.
K. Jebb, 493:Summer89-31
van Hout, R. & U. Knops, eds. Language Attitudes in the Dutch Language Area.
R. De Keyser, 350:Mar90-211
Houtsma, A.J.M., T.D. Rossing & W.M. Wagenaars. Auditory Demonstrations.
E.C. Carterette & R.A. Kendall, 413:Summer90-434
Hove, C. Bones.
S. French, 617(TLS):14-20Sep90-980
C. Sarvan, 268(IFR):Summer89-144
Hoven, H. Malcolm Lowry.
S. Haag, 102(CanL):Autumn-Winter89-168
Hovesen, E. Laegen Ole Worm.
J. Shackelford, 563(SS):Spring/Summer89-269
Hovet, T.R. The Master Narrative.
E. Ammons, 587(SAF):Autumn89-254
Howard, A. Crossman.
J. Turner, 617(TLS):2-8Nov90-1167
Howard, C. Hard City.
F. Handman, 441:26Aug90-15
Howard, D. Defining the Political.
A.B.C., 185:Apr90-693
Howard, D. From Marx to Kant.*
U. Santamaria & A. Manville, 488:Sep89-381
Howard, D. & S. Franklin. Missing the Meaning?
B.B. Wulfeck, 348(L&S):Jul-Sep89-279
Howard, D.R. Chaucer.*
P.S. Baker, 70:Apr89-62
B. Rowland, 439(NM):1989/1-125
Howard, E.J. The Light Years.
J. O'Grady, 617(TLS):27Jul-2Aug90-804
M. Spanier, 441:16Sep90-21
Howard, G. Wheelbarrow Across the Sahara.
P. Marsden-Smedley, 617(TLS):2-8Nov90-1188
Howard, J.E. & M.F. O'Connor, eds. Shakespeare Reproduced.
R.G. Barlow, 615(TJ):Dec89-575
D. Bevington, 405(MP):May90-400
J. Drakakis, 570(SQ):Fall89-342
G. Holderness, 402(MLR):Jan90-141
D. Porter, 610:Spring89-88
Howard, M. British Intelligence in the Second World War.
Z. Steiner, 617(TLS):7-13Dec90-1310
Howard, M. Clausewitz.
B.H. Reid, 242:Vol10No3-381

Howard, M. Monet.
B. Thomson, 617(TLS):2-8Feb90-127
Howard, P. Christoph Willibald Gluck.
J. Hayes, 410(M&L):Feb89-99
Howard, R. No Traveller.
A. Corn, 491:Jan90-292
Howard, R.W. Concepts and Schemata.
M.A. Barnett, 399(MLJ):Winter89-488
Howard, W. Veda Recitation in Vārāṇasī.
J. Kuckertz, 417:Apr-Jun89-192
D. Roche, 187:Winter89-172
Howarth, E. & P. What a Performance!
A. Jacobs, 415:Feb89-91
Howat, R. - see Eigeldinger, J-J.
Howat, R., with C. Helffer - see Debussy, C.
Howatch, S. Glamorous Powers.*
639(VQR):Spring89-58
Howatch, S. Scandalous Risks.
J. Mooney, 441:11Nov90-60
Howatson, M.C., ed. The Oxford Companion to Classical Literature.* (2nd ed)
T. Russell-Cobb, 324:Dec89-66
Howe, A. & R. Waller, eds. En Marge du Classicisme.*
H.G. Hall, 475:Vol16No30-299
H. Mydlarski, 345(KRQ):May89-223
G.E. Rodmell, 83:Spring89-115
Howe, I. Selected Writings 1950-1990.
W. Kendrick, 441:28Oct90-12
Howe, M. The Good Thief.
B. Costello, 473(PR):Vol56No4-671
Howe, N. The Old English Catalogue Poems.*
T.D. Hill, 477(PLL):Fall88-448
C.D. Wright, 301(JEGP):Jan89-85
Howe, V. The Dreams of Zoo Animals.
J.R. Wytenbroek, 102(CanL):Autumn-Winter89-279
Howell, A. Howell's Law.
J. Le Saux, 617(TLS):27Jul-2Aug90-803
Howell, B. Joy Ride.*
639(VQR):Autumn89-131
Howells, C. Sartre.
R.F. Atkinson, 518:Jul89-152
T. Keefe, 402(MLR):Jul90-746
L.S. Kramer, 242:Vol10No2-263
W.L. McBride, 395(MFS):Summer89-358
D. Pollard, 89(BJA):Winter89-93
Howells, C.A. Private and Fictional Words.*
S.E. Grace, 295(JML):Fall88/Winter89-200
L. Monkman, 677(YES):Vol20-357
P. Quartermaine, 447(N&Q):Jun89-277
C. Visser, 102(CanL):Autumn-Winter89-255
Howells, E.M. If Not Literature.* (G.D. Merrill & G. Arms, eds)
L.S. Bergmann, 405(MP):May90-424
J.W. Crowley, 26(ALR):Fall89-90
T. Wortham, 445(NCF):Jun89-124
Howells, M. & K. Skinner. The Ripper Legacy.
L. James, 637(VS):Autumn89-201
Howells, R.J. & others, eds. Voltaire and his World.*
J.A. Perkins, 207(FR):May90-1064
Hoyer, L.G. The Predator.
A. Barrett, 441:14Jan90-11
Hoyers, A.O. Geistliche und Weltliche Poemata. (B. Becker-Cantarino, ed)
M.R. Sperberg-McQueen, 406:Spring89-122
Hoyos, A. Woman, Woman.
S. Foster, 448:Vol27No3-159
Hrabal, B. The Death of Mr. Baltisberger.
A. Thomas, 617(TLS):23-29Nov90-1272

Hrabal, B. Too Loud a Solitude.
    S. Birkerts, 441:9Dec90-11
    442(NY):22Oct90-143
Hsia, R.P-C., ed. The German People and the
    Reformation.*
    R.E. McLaughlin, 551(RenQ):Summer89-
    315
Hsia, R.P-C. Social Discipline in the Refor-
    mation.
    A. Hamilton, 617(TLS):29Jun-5Jul90-690
Hsieh, Y.Y. Victor Segalen's Literary Encoun-
    ter with China.
    M. Détrie, 549(RLC):Jul-Sep89-387
Hsu, C-Y. & K.M. Linduff. Western Chou Civi-
    lization.
    R.L. Thorp, 293(JASt):Nov89-829
Huang Tsung-hsi. The Records of Ming
    Scholars.*   (J. Ching, with C-Y. Fang &
    others, eds & trans)
    D.A. Dilworth, 485(PE&W):Apr89-219
Huannou, A. Essai sur l'esclave.
    A. Ricard, 538(RAL):Summer89-291
Hubbard, S.L. Against All Odds.
    D. Swainson, 529(QQ):Summer89-539
Hubbs, J. Mother Russia.*
    N.K. Moyle, 574(SEEJ):Fall89-474
Huber, C. Die Aufnahme und Verarbeitung
    des Alanus ab Insulis in mittelhoch-
    deutschen Dichtungen.
    D.H. Green, 402(MLR):Oct90-1020
Huber, C. Gottfried von Strassburg: Tristan
    und Isolde.
    B. Schöning, 224(GRM):Band39Heft3-354
Huber, K., ed. Rätisches Namenbuch III.*
    J. Kramer, 545(RPh):Feb90-472
Hubert, M-C. Langage et corps fantasmé dans
    le théâtre des années cinquante.
    M. Autrand, 535(RHL):Mar-Apr89-344
Hubert, R.R. Surrealism and the Book.*
    J. Anzalone, 188(ECr):Summer89-94
    S. Ferguson, 141:Summer89-308
    V.A. La Charité, 210(FrF):May89-249
    S. Winspur, 546(RR):Nov89-628
Hübner, K. Die Wahrheit des Mythos.*
    F. Gniffke, 480(PJGG):Band06Heft1-186
Hübner, M. Zwischen Alkohol und Abstinenz.
    H. Groschopp, 654(WB):10/1989-1750
Hübner, W. Varros Instrumentum vocale im
    Kontext der antiken Fachwissenschaften.
    G. Perl, 229:Band61Heft5-436
Huch, R. Briefe an die Freunde. (M. Braun,
    ed; rev by J. Jessen)
    W. Paulsen, 222(GR):Summer89-139
    W. Paulsen, 564:Feb89-75
Huck, G.J. & A.E. Ojeda, eds. Discontinuous
    Constituency.
    R. Cann, 297(JL):Mar89-257
Hudde, H. & P. Kuon, eds. De l'Utopie à
    l'Uchronie.
    R. Trousson, 475:Vol16No31-592
Huddle, D. Stopping by Home.
    F. Chappell, 219(GaR):Summer89-385
Huddleston, R. English Grammar.*
    N. Houck, 710:Dec89-477
    F.R. Palmer, 353:Vol7No6-1135
Hudgins, A. After the Lost War.*
    E. Pankey, 271:Spring-Summer89-175
Hudson, A. The Premature Reformation.
    P.H. Barnum, 589:Oct89-976
Hudson, A. & M. Wilks, eds. From Ockham to
    Wyclif.
    R.H. Britnell, 242:Vol10No4-488

Hudson, C. Playing in the Sand.*
    J. Mellors, 364:Aug/Sep89-130
Hudson, H.D., Jr. The Rise of the Demidov
    Family and the Russian Iron Industry in the
    Eighteenth Century.*
    G. Munro, 104(CASS):Spring89-123
Hudson, K. Museums of Influence.*
    D. Rice, 127:Summer89-197
Hudson, K. & A. Nicholls. The Cambridge
    Guide to the Historic Places of Britain and
    Ireland. The Cambridge Guide to the Muse-
    ums of Britain and Ireland.
    B.A. Rapple, 174(Eire):Winter89-139
Hudson, M. Our Grandmothers' Drums.*
    C. Bentsen, 441:20May90-13
Hudson, N. Samuel Johnson and Eighteenth-
    Century Thought.
    I. Grundy, 173(ECS):Winter89/90-238
Hudson, P. Travels in Mauritania.
    P. Marsden-Smedley, 617(TLS):2-
    8Nov90-1188
Hudson, S.D. Human Character and Morality.
    A. MacIntyre, 449:Jun89-389
Hudspeth, R.N. - see Fuller, M.
Huebert, R. - see Shirley, J.
Huebler, D. Crocodile Tears.
    G. Gessert, 448:Vol27No2-120
Huebner, S. The Operas of Charles Gounod.
    W. Dean, 617(TLS):12-18Oct90-1103
Huffman, C.C. Elizabethan Impressions.
    P. Morgan, 354:Dec89-366
    V.F. Stern, 551(RenQ):Autumn89-570
Huffman, F.E. Bibliography and Index of
    Mainland Southeast Asian Languages and
    Linguistics.
    D.B. Solnit, 318(JAOS):Jul-Sep88-496
Hugger, P., ed. Stadt und Fest.
    I.M. Goessl, 406:Spring89-118
Huggett, R. Binkie Beaumont.*
    A. Strachan, 511:May89-47
Hughes, A. & P. Trudgill. English Accents
    and Dialects.
    F. Chevillet, 189(EA):Apr-Jun89-207
Hughes, C. & P. Wintour. Labour Rebuilt.
    R. Hutchison, 617(TLS):6-12Jul90-710
Hughes, G. The Antique Collector.
    T. Gunterham, 617(TLS):19-25Oct90-
    1131
Hughes, G. Words in Time.
    639(VQR):Spring89-52
Hughes, H., ed. Achieving Industrialization
    in East Asia.
    Y.W. Kihl, 293(JASt):Nov89-803
Hughes, J. Pastors and Visionaries.*
    G. Rosser, 382(MAE):1989/2-315
Hughes, L.K. The Manyfacèd Glass.*
    M. Shaw, 541(RES):Feb89-136
Hughes, R. Nothing If Not Critical.
    L. Gowing, 617(TLS):14-20Dec90-1354
Hughes, R.S. John Steinbeck.
    J. Ditsky, 649(WAL):Aug89-168
    H. Ostrom, 573(SSF):Winter89-108
Hughes, T. Wolfwatching.*
    P. Gross, 493:Winter89/90-8
Hughes, T.P. American Genesis.*
    42(AR):Fall89-504
Hughes-Hallett, L. Cleopatra.
    J. Ray, 617(TLS):23Feb-1Mar90-192
    J. Updike, 441:10Jun90-9
Hughson, L. From Biography to History.
    S. Derrick, 27(AL):Oct89-483
    A. Kaplan, 432(NEQ):Dec89-586
[continued]

Hughson, L. From Biography to History. [continuing]
    D. Pizer, 301(JEGP):Oct89-556
    J. Rohrkemper, 395(MFS):Summer89-278
Hugill, P.J. & D.B. Dickson, eds. The Transfer and Transformation of Ideas and Material Culture.
    W. Zelinsky, 658:Spring89-101
Huglo, M., ed. Musicologie médiévale.
    J. Caldwell, 410(M&L):Nov89-521
    M. Wittmann, 417:Oct-Dec89-365
Huglo, M. & C. Meyer, comps. The Theory of Music. (Vol 3)
    M-N. Colette, 537:Vol75No2-289
Hugo, V. Correspondance familiale et écrits intimes. (Vol 1) (J. Gaudon, S. Gaudon & B. Leuilliot, with others, eds)
    V. Brombert, 446(NCFS):Fall-Winter89/90-280
    A. Kies, 356(LR):Aug89-218
Hugo, V. Le Rhin, lettres à un ami. (J. Gaudon, ed)
    P. Georgel, 535(RHL):Jul-Aug89-733
Huidobro, M.M. - see under Montes Huidobro, M.
Huisman, B. & F. Ribes. Les philosophes et le droit.
    J-L. Gardies, 542:Oct-Dec89-643
Huizing, K. Das Sein und der Andere.
    P. Trotignon, 542:Oct-Dec89-613
Hülk, W. Als die Helden Opfer wurden.
    P. Whyte, 208(FS):Jan89-96
Hull, D.L. The Metaphysics of Evolution.
    W.A. Rottschaefer, 103:Aug90-319
Hull, D.L. Science as a Process.*
    D.L. Sepper, 543:Sep89-169
Hull, G.T. Color, Sex, and Poetry.*
    J.Y. McLendon, 295(JML):Fall88/Winter89-201
Hull, N.E.H. Female Felons.*
    L. Kealey, 106:Summer89-124
Hüllen, W. & R. Schulze, eds. Understanding the Lexicon.
    B.A. Beatie, 350:Mar90-193
Hulme, F.P. A Dancing Fox.
    W.H. Green, 580(SCR):Spring90-142
Hulme, P. Colonial Encounters.*
    P. Edwards, 83:Spring89-84
Hülsen, C. Il libro Giuliano da Sangallo.
    A. Nesselrath, 683:Band52Heft2-281
Hülser, K. Die Fragmente zur Dialektik der Stoiker. (Vols 2-4)
    J. Barnes, 123:Vol39No2-263
Hulsker, J. Vincent and Theo Van Gogh. (J.M. Miller, ed)
    M. Kimmelman, 441:12Aug90-1
Hülsmann, F., ed. The Erle of Tolous.
    D. Mehl, 72:Band226Heft1-163
    E.G. Stanley, 447(N&Q):Jun89-221
Hulten, P., ed. Futurism and Futurisms.*
    J. Meyers, 364:Apr/May89-119
Hulten, P. Jean Tinguely.
    W. Jeffett, 39:Feb89-136
"The Human Experience."*
    J. Daynard, 441:7Jan90-16
"Human Rights in Iraq."
    E. Mortimer, 453(NYRB):27Sep90-7
    R. Richter, 441:16Dec90-19
"David Hume and the Eighteenth Century."
    M. Malherbe, 192(EP):Jul-Dec89-535
Hume, K. Fantasy and Mimesis.
    K. Sutherland, 148:Winter86-105

Hume, K. Pynchon's Mythography.*
    B. Duyfhuizen, 454:Fall89-75
    M. Fludernik, 224(GRM):Band39Heft1-115
    M.P.L., 295(JML):Fall88/Winter89-398
Hume, R.D. Henry Fielding and the London Theatre 1728-1737.*
    B.A. Goldgar, 566:Spring90-181
    G. Rowell, 610:Summer89-198
Humfrey, P. - see Burckhardt, J.
Humm, P., P. Stigant & P. Widdowson, eds. Popular Fictions.*
    M. Carroll, 295(JML):Fall88/Winter89-177
    M.G. Cooke, 677(YES):Vol20-215
Hummer, T.R. Lower-Class Heresy.*
    R. Mitchell, 502(PrS):Fall89-129
Humphery-Smith, C. Anglo-Norman Armory Two.
    S. Christelow, 589:Jan89-178
Humphrey, T.C. & L.T. "We Gather Together."
    S.E. Newton, 650(WF):Jul89-261
Humphrey, W. No Resting Place.*
    R.E. Morsberger, 649(WAL):Feb90-391
Humphreys, J. Rich in Love.*
    T. Rash, 580(SCR):Spring90-131
Humphreys, K.W. A National Library in Theory and Practice.
    B.J. Enright, 354:Dec89-375
Humphries, J. Losing the Text.*
    I. Winter, 345(KRQ):Feb89-101
Humphries, J. The Puritan and the Cynic.*
    C. Garaud, 207(FR):Mar90-707
Huncke, H. Guilty of Everything.
    J. Herman, 441:10Jun90-22
Hundert, E.M. Philosophy, Psychiatry and Neuroscience.
    G.J. Stack, 543:Mar90-636
Hundsnurscher, F. & E. Weigand, eds. Dialoganalyse.
    R. Thiele, 682(ZPSK):Band42Heft5-675
Hung, W. - see under Wu Hung
Hunger, H. Graeculus perfidus/"Italos itamos."
    J.W. Barker, 589:Oct89-979
Hunger, H. & I. Ševčenko. Des Nikephoros Blemmydes "Basilikos Andrias" und dessen Metaphrase von Georgios Galesiotes und Georgios Oinaiotes.
    A. Kazhdan, 589:Jul89-719
Hunt, D. - see Enlart, C.
Hunt, F., ed. Lessons for Life.
    639(VQR):Winter89-30
Hunt, J.D. Garden and Grove.*
    A.T. Friedman, 576:Mar89-89
Hunt, J.D. William Kent.*
    D. Arnold, 46:Sep89-12
    M.R. Brownell, 173(ECS):Fall89-83
    566:Autumn89-83
Hunt, L. Captain Sword and Captain Pen.
    S. Monod, 158:Mar89-26
Hunt, L.C. A Woman's Portion.
    L. Yelin, 637(VS):Spring90-507
Hunt, M. The Compassionate Beast.
    T. Bay, 441:8Apr90-21
Hunt, P., ed. Children's Literature.
    P. Keating, 617(TLS):14-20Dec90-1361
Hunt, T. Popular Medicine in Thirteenth-Century England.
    V. Nutton, 617(TLS):4-10May90-477
Hunt, T. - see Jeffers, R.
Hunter, J. Image and Word.
    M.D.O., 295(JML):Fall88/Winter89-228

Hunter, J.K. Westmoreland and Portland Places.
658:Summer/Autumn89-207
Hunter, J.P. & M.C. Battestin. Henry Fielding in His Time and Ours.
S. Soupel, 189(EA):Jul-Sep89-367
Hunter, M. Establishing the New Science.
P. Dear, 617(TLS):26Jan-1Feb90-94
Hunter, M. Footprints on the Moon.
M. van Dijk, 108:Spring89-85
Hunter, M. & S. Schaffer, eds. Robert Hooke.
A. Clericuzio, 617(TLS):28Sep-4Oct90-1044
Hunter, M. & R. Thorne, eds. Change at King's Cross.
A. Saint, 617(TLS):26Oct-1Nov90-1147
Hunter, S. Larry Rivers.
C. Rickey, 441:12Aug90-19
Hunting, C. La Femme devant le "tribunal masculin" dans trois romans des Lumières - Challe, Prévost, Cazotte.
P. Hoffmann, 547(RF):Band101Heft1-121
S. Jones, 208(FS):Oct89-468
R. Runte, 166:Oct89-72
Huntington, S.L. The "Pāla-Sena" Schools of Sculpture.
A.W. Norton, 54:Sep89-529
Huntington, S.L., with J.C. Huntington. The Art of Ancient India.
A.W. Norton, 54:Sep89-529
C. Tadgell, 576:Jun89-206
Huot, S. From Song to Book.*
A. Butterfield, 382(MAE):1989/1-165
P.F. Dembowski, 210(FrF):Jan89-85
Huppert, G. After the Black Death.*
T. Harris, 242:Vol10No2-244
le Huray, P. & J. Day, eds. Music and Aesthetics in the Eighteenth and Early Nineteenth Centuries.
83:Autumn89-247
Hurch, B. Über Aspiration.
G.O. Nathan, 050:Sep90-680
T. Stolz, 353:Vol27No6-1139
Hurd, A.E. & P.A. Loeb. An Introduction to Nonstandard Real Analysis.
D.N. Hoover, 316:Jun89-631
Hurford, J.R. Language and Number.
W.N. Francis, 350:Sep90-639
A.S. Kaye, 361:Jul89-257
M. Olsson, 596(SL):Vol42No2-177
Hurford, P. Making Music on the Organ.*
A. Bond, 415:Jan89-47
Hurlburt, L.P. The Mexican Muralists in the United States.
K.A. Marling, 441:7Jan90-13
Hurley, S.L. Natural Reasons.
P. Pettit, 617(TLS):16-22Feb90-168
Hursthouse, R. Beginning Lives.*
C. Swanton, 63:Mar89-109
Hurt, C.D. Information Sources in Science and Technology.
N. Pearson, 87(BB):Sep89-207
Huseman, W.H. La Personalité littéraire de François de la Noue, 1531-1591.*
J.L. Allaire, 207(FR):Dec89-369
J.L. Allaire, 207(FR):Mar90-705
Husserl, E. Gesammelte Werke.
D. Franck, 98:Mar89-180
Hussey, M. The Singing of the Real World.*
J. Marcus, 620(TSWL):Spring89-101
K. Mezei, 677(YES):Vol20-325

el Hussini, M.M. Soviet-Egyptian Relations, 1945-1985.
A.Z. Rubinstein, 550(RusR):Apr89-203
Husson, G. OIKIA.
G. Mussies, 394:Vol42fasc1/2-153
Hutcheon, L. The Canadian Postmodern.
J.M. Kertzer, 627(UTQ):Fall89-147
G. McGregor, 298:Fall89-146
S. Söderlind, 529(QQ):Autumn89-631
Hutcheon, L. A Poetics of Postmodernism.*
E. van Alphen, 494:Winter89-819
H. Bertens, 402(MLR):Jul90-675
E. Cobley, 49:Oct89-197
P. Kitson, 447(N&Q):Dec89-554
G. McGregor, 298:Fall89-146
K.M. Newton, 89(BJA):Summer89-285
Hutchings, R. Soviet Secrecy and Non-Secrecy.
J. Brine, 575(SEER):Apr89-324
Hutchinson, A.C., ed. Critical Legal Studies.
J.S., 185:Jul90-912
Hutchinson, D.S. The Virtues of Aristotle.*
S. Broadie, 482(PhR):Jul89-396
J.A. Novak, 41:Fall89-332
C.M. Young, 487:Autumn89-280
Hutchinson, G.B. The Ecstatic Whitman.*
C.C. Hollis, 70:Apr89-65
Hutchinson, M. The Prince of Wales: Right or Wrong?*
S. Gardiner, 364:Dec89/Jan90-123
Hutchinson, T. & A. Waters. English for Specific Purposes.*
T. Huckin, 710:Mar89-111
Hutchinson, J.C. Albrecht Dürer.
E. Shultz, 441:18Nov90-38
Hutchison, R.A. In the Tracks of the Yeti.
S. Mills, 617(TLS):29Jun-5Jul90-707
Hutchison, T. Before Adam Smith.
P. Divinsky, 529(QQ):Autumn89-765
Hutchison, W.R., ed. Between the Times.
D. Jenkins, 617(TLS):23-29Mar90-326
Huth, A. Such Visitors.*
D. Durrant, 364:Aug/Sep89-134
Hutner, G. Secrets and Sympathy.
N. Baym, 402(MLR):Jul90-712
R.K. Gollin, 27(AL):Oct89-474
J.L. Idol, 591:Fall90-333
Huttar, G.L. & K.J. Gregerson, eds. Pragmatics in Non-Western Perspective.
D.L. Payne, 350:Jun90-417
Hutterer, C.J., W. Kainz & E. Walcher. Weststeirisches Wörterbuch.
A. Rowley, 685(ZDL):2/1989-231
Hüttl-Folter, G. Die "trat/torot"-Lexeme in den altrussischen Chroniken.
P. Rehder, 279:Vol35/36-352
Hutton, L.J. The Christian Essence of Spanish Literature.
A. Sobejano-Morán, 552(REH):Oct89-129
Hutton, R. The British Republic 1649-1660.
J. Miller, 617(TLS):14-20Dec90-1356
Hutton, R. Charles the Second.
L.E. Beattie, 441:11Mar90-19
R. Beddard, 617(TLS):6-12Apr90-378
Hutton, R.H. A Victorian Spectator. (R.H. Tener & M. Woodfield, eds)
C. Baldick, 617(TLS):23-29Mar90-311
Huxley, E., ed. Nine Faces of Kenya.
A. Gurnah, 617(TLS):12-18Oct90-1108
Huy, N.N. & Ta Van Tai - see under Nguyen Ngoc Huy & Ta Van Tai

181

Huỳnh Sanh Thông, ed & trans. To Be Made
Over.
   D-H. Nguyen, 293(JASt):Nov89-936
Huysmans, J-K. La Cathédrale. (P. Cogny,
ed)
   R.B. Antosh, 446(NCFS):Spring-
   Summer90-544
Huysmans, J-K. The Road from Decadence.
(B. Beaumont, ed & trans)
   L.M. Porter, 446(NCFS):Fall-Winter89/90-
   283
Huyssen, A. After the Great Divide.*
   A. Abbas, 125:Fall88-94
   E. van Alphen, 494:Winter89-819
   M. Buskirk, 147:Vol6No2-55
   M.T. Jones, 221(GQ):Summer89-446
Huyssen, A. & K. Scherpe, eds. Postmoderne.
   I. Hoesterey, 221(GQ):Fall89-505
Hwang, S.J.J. Discourse Features of Korean
Narration.
   Ik-sang Eom, 710:Dec89-484
Hyams, N.M. Language Acquisition and the
Theory of Parameters.*
   M.S. Smith, 710:Sep89-347
   L. White, 355(LSoc):Dec89-567
Hyatte, R. & M. Ponchard-Hyatte - see Evrart
de Conty
Hyde, H.M., ed. The "Lady Chatterley's
Lover" Trial.
   T. Paulin, 617(TLS):6-12Jul90-733
Hyde, N. Earthly Delights.
   F. Baveystock, 617(TLS):2-8Feb90-122
Hyde, R. Panoramania!
   G. Speaight, 611(TN):Vol43No2-91
Hyde, R. Wednesday's Children.
   F. Adcock, 617(TLS):2-8Feb90-123
Hyde, T. The Poetic Theology of Love.*
   G. Morgan, 541(RES):Nov89-545
Hyland, P. The Black Heart.*
   C. Thubron, 441:2Dec90-20
Hyland, W.G. The Cold War is Over.
   L.V. Sigal, 441:29Jul90-24
Hyman, J.W. The Light Book.
   M. Fay, 441:8Apr90-20
Hyman, L.J. & S. Green. Going to Chicago.
   S.A. Salzman, 441:19Aug90-18
Hyman, V.R. "To the Lighthouse" and Beyond.
   S. Ferebee, 395(MFS):Winter89-802
Hymes, R.P. Statesmen and Gentlemen.*
   M. Elvin, 293(JASt):May89-361
Hynes, C.J. & B. Drury. Incident at Howard
Beach.
   L. Wolfe, 441:11Feb90-12
Hynes, H.P. Earthright.
   N. Wade, 441:22Apr90-1
Hynes, J. The Art of the Real.
   M. Legris, 268(IFR):Summer89-151
Hynes, J. The Wild Colonial Boy.
   J. Holland, 441:6May90-13
   442(NY):2Jul90-73
Hynes, S. Flights of Passage.*
   A. Ross, 364:Jun/Jul89-138
   J. Wexler, 77:Fall89-339
Hynes, S. A War Imagined.
   M. Imlah, 617(TLS):16-22Nov90-1230

"ISCA Quarterly 3rd Annual Bookworks
Edition." (L. Neaderland, ed)
   G. Gessert, 448:Vol27No1-126
"IUPI: Incipitario unificato della poesia itali-
ana."
   A. Daniele, 379(MedR):Dec89-473

"I Am Here: Two Thousand Years of Southwest
Indian Arts and Culture."
   139:Dec89/Jan90-23
"I libri di Orlando innamorato."
   D. Zancani, 354:Mar89-61
Iamblichus. Iamblichus: The Exhortation to
Philosophy. (T.M. Johnson, trans)
   J.A. Novak, 103:Jan90-24
Iamblichus. The Theology of Arithmetic. (R.
Waterfield, trans)
   S. Seligman, 111:Spring90-14
Ibáñez, M.A.M. - see under Martín Ibáñez,
M.A.
Ibieta, G. Tradition and Renewal in "La glo-
ria de don Ramiro."
   A. McDermott, 86(BHS):Jan89-101
Ibler, R. Textsemiotische Aspekte der Zykli-
sierung in der Lyrik.
   A. Měšťan, 688(ZSP):Band49Heft1-198
Ibn Rushd. Ibn Rushd's Metaphysics. (C.
Genequand, ed & trans)
   E.M. Macierowski, 41:Spring89-144
Ibsch, E. & D.H. Schram, eds. Rezeptionsfor-
schung zwischen Hermeneutik und Empirik.
   P. Hess, 406:Fall89-378
Ibscher, G. Demócrito y sus sentencias sobre
ética y educación.
   J.F. Procopé, 303(JoHS):Vol109-238
Icart, R. La Révolution française à l'écran.
   A.J.M. Prévos, 207(FR):May90-1087
Ichien, M. - see under Mujū Ichien
"Idées et mots au siècle des lumières."
   J.H. Brumfitt, 208(FS):Oct89-471
   J. Voisine, 549(RLC):Oct-Dec89-596
Idema, W.L. The Dramatic Oeuvre of Chu Yu-
tun (1379-1439).
   W. Dolby, 293(JASt):May89-363
Idema, W.L., ed. Leyden Studies in Sinology.
   P.W. Kroll, 318(JAOS):Apr-Jun88-343
Idol, J.L., Jr. A Thomas Wolfe Companion.*
   R. Foster, 580(SCR):Fall89-147
Ifans, D. - see Kilvert, F.
Iffland, J. - see de Quevedo, F.
Ignatieff, M. The Russian Album.
   R.L. Busch, 102(CanL):Spring89-145
   A.C. Wright, 529(QQ):Spring89-135
Ignatow, D. The One in the Many.
   D. Miller, 569(SR):Spring89-283
Ihde, D. Existential Technics.
   D. Janicaud, 192(EP):Apr-Jun89-270
Ihwe, J.F. Konversationen über Literatur.*
   E.A. Kaelin, 606:Jan89-117
Ilefeldt, W.G. Thoughts while Tending Sheep.
   S. Pickering, 569(SR):Spring89-297
   42(AR):Winter89-110
Iles, N. Messages from the Museums of Man.
   J. Saunders, 565:Autumn89-77
Illis, M. The Alchemist.
   L. Duguid, 617(TLS):19-25Jan90-66
Ilson, R., ed. A Spectrum of Lexicography.
   T. Piotrowski, 257(IRAL):May89-165
Imbroscio, C., ed. Requiem pour l'utopie?*
   P. Ronzeaud, 535(RHL):Jul-Aug89-758
Immerwahr, R. - see Schlegel, F.
Imperato, P.J. Arthur Donaldson Smith and
the Exploration of Lake Rudolf.
   K.W. Butzer, 2(AfrA):Nov88-96
"in transition."
   S. Carnell, 617(TLS):10-16Aug90-860
Inchbald, E. Selected Comedies: Elizabeth
Inchbald. (R. Manvell, ed)
   E. Donkin, 615(TJ):Oct89-423

Inden, R. Imagining India.
 C.A. Bayly, 617(TLS):7-13Dec90-1313
Indiana, G. Horse Crazy.*
 A. Mars-Jones, 617(TLS):16-22Nov90-
 1232
Ineichen, G., ed. Romanische Bibliographie
 1985.
 H. Fuchs, 547(RF):Band101Heft2/3-292
Inés de la Cruz, J. A Sor Juana Anthology.
 (A.S. Trueblood, ed & trans)
 E. Arenal, 141:Fall89-463
 J.F. Cotter, 249(HudR):Summer89-315
 P. García, 377:Mar89-55
 K.A. Myers, 385(MQR):Summer90-453
Inez, C. Family Life.*
 R. Schultz, 249(HudR):Spring89-154
Ing, J. Johann Gutenberg and His Bible.
 M.K. Duggan, 354:Jun89-156
Ingalls, R.P. Urban Vigilantes in the New
 South.
 N.R. McMillen, 585(SoQ):Winter90-78
Inge, M.T., ed. Truman Capote.
 J. Sobieraj, 573(SSF):Winter89-104
Inge, T., ed. Naming the Rose.
 M. Viegnes, 395(MFS):Summer89-362
van Ingen, F. Johann Wolfgang Goethe: Götz
 von Berlichingen.
 W. Wittkowski, 221(GQ):Spring89-262
van Ingen, F. - see von Zesen, P.
Ingenhoff, A. Drama oder Epos?
 R.C. Cowen, 406:Summer89-270
 R. Hollinrake, 410(M&L):May89-264
 H.M.K. Riley, 133:Band22Heft2-167
Ingersoll, E.G., J. Kitchen & S.S. Rubin, eds.
 The Post-Confessionals.
 639(VQR):Autumn89-137
Ingold, T., ed. The Social Implications of
 Agrarian Change in Northern and Eastern
 Finland.
 D. Kirby, 575(SEER):Oct89-659
Ingold, T., ed. What Is an Animal?
 P. Bouissac, 567:Vol77No4-497
Ingram, B. & C. King. From Writing to Com-
 posing.
 B.W. Robinett, 399(MLJ):Spring89-84
Ingram, D. Habermas and the Dialectic of
 Reason.*
 R. Rochlitz, 192(EP):Jul-Dec89-542
 M. Westphal, 258:Sep89-359
Ingram, J. The Science of Everyday Life.
 C. Gottlieb, 441:8Apr90-20
Ingram, M. Church Courts.
 J.S. McGee, 551(RenQ):Winter89-857
Ingrao, C.W. The Hessian Mercenary State.
 M. Hughes, 83:Autumn89-201
Ingwersen, S.A. Light and Longing.
 B. Gicovate, 240(HR):Autumn89-539
 C.S. Mathieu, 238:Sep89-555
"Inklings: Jahrbuch für Literatur und Ästhet-
 ik." (Vol 5)
 E. Schenkel, 38:Band107Heft3/4-550
Innes, C.L. Chinua Achebe.
 N. Barley, 617(TLS):18-24May90-533
Innes, S., ed. Work and Labor in Early Amer-
 ica.
 C.G. Steffen, 656(WMQ):Oct89-801
Innis, H.A. Empire and Communications. (D.
 Godfrey, ed)
 R. Collins, 488:Jun89-217
Inoguchi Takashi & Iwai Tomoaki. "Zoku giin"
 no kenkyū.
 G.D. Allinson, 293(JASt):May89-324

Inoue, Y. The Counterfeiter and Other Sto-
 ries.*
 J. Haylock, 364:Jun/Jul89-141
"International Who's Who in Music and Musi-
 cians' Directory." (D.M. Cummings & D.K.
 McIntire, eds)
 A. Jacobs, 617(TLS):15-21Jun90-642
"The International Who's Who 1990-91."
 G. Wheatcroft, 617(TLS):7-13Sep90-941
"Internationales Thomas-Mann-Kolloquium
 1986 in Lübeck."*
 R.A. Nicholls, 564:Sep89-278
"Interpretationen: Dramen des Naturalismus."
 R.C. Cowen, 221(GQ):Spring89-282
"Inventing Ourselves."
 M.K. Blakely, 441:29Apr90-29
Ioffe, O.S. Soviet Civil Law.
 P.B. Maggs, 550(RusR):Apr89-227
Ioffe, O.S. & M.W. Janis, eds. Soviet Law and
 Economy.
 M. Newcity, 550(RusR):Oct89-437
Iorgulescu, M. Eseu despre lumea lui Caragi-
 ale.
 V. Nemoianu, 617(TLS):19-25Jan90-59
Irele, A. In Praise of Alienation.
 R. Bjornson, 538(RAL):Spring89-143
Irigoyen Troconis, M.P. - see Paulus, J.
Irizarry, E. La novelística de Enrique A.
 Laguerre, trayectoria histórica y literaria.
 M. Fernández Olmos, 238:Dec89-966
Irons, C.H., ed. Second Language Acquisition
 R.M. Terry, 399(MLJ):Autumn89-344
Irving, L. Sub/version.*
 L. Wevers, 102(CanL):Autumn-Winter89-
 260
Irvine, R. Baptism for the Dead.
 M. Stasio, 441:29Apr90-18
Irvine, R. Gone to Glory.
 M. Stasio, 441:24Jun90-22
Irving, C. Trial.
 L. Wolfe, 441:18Nov90-20
Irving, J. Garp und wie er die Welt sah.
 W. Wicht, 654(WB):4/1989-646
Irving, J. A Prayer for Owen Meany.*
 C. Rooke, 376:Sep89-115
Irwin, F. - see Noel-Paton, M.H. & J.P. Camp-
 bell
Irwin, G. Three Lives in Mine.
 G.L. Parker, 102(CanL):Autumn-
 Winter89-237
Irwin, M. Against the Meanwhile.
 639(VQR):Summer89-99
Irwin, T. Classical Thought.
 J. Dillon, 235:Winter89-78
Irwin, T. A History of Western Philosophy.
 (Vol 1)
 D.K.W. Modrak, 543:Dec89-405
Irwin, T.H. Aristotle's First Principles.
 J. Barnes, 617(TLS):15-21Jun90-644
 J.D.G. Evans, 235:Winter89-73
Irwin-Zarecka, I. Neutralizing Memory.
 M. Ziomecki, 390:Oct89-44
Isaac, B. The Greek Settlements in Thrace
 until the Macedonian Conquest.
 D. Braund, 123:Vol39No1-148
Isaac, R.J. & V.C. Armat. Madness in the
 Streets.
 D. Mechanic, 441:16Sep90-9
Isaacson, J.M. Seed of Sarah.
 F. Gottlieb, 441:8Jul90-17
Isaksen, J. Ongin rósa er rósa allan dagin.
 W.G. Jones, 562(Scan):Nov89-222

Iseminger, G.L. The Quartzite Border.
  M.E. Caldwell, 456(NDQ):Summer89-246
Isenberg, C. Substantial Proofs of Being.*
  C. Brown, 104(CASS):Spring-Winter88-
  445
  L. Burnett, 575(SEER):Jan89-130
  J.G. Harris, 550(RusR):Jan89-110
Isenberg, M.T. John L. Sullivan and His
  America.
  M. Oriard, 639(VQR):Summer89-540
Isenberg, S.B. India's Bene Israel.
  A. Desai, 453(NYRB):6Dec90-53
Iser, W. Walter Pater.*
  J.B. Bullen, 677(YES):Vol20-306
Iser, W. Prospecting.
  T. Eagleton, 617(TLS):16-22Mar90-294
  M.M. Van de Pitte, 103:Aug90-322
Iser, W. Sterne: "Tristram Shandy."* (German
  title: Laurence Sternes "Tristram Shandy.")
  M. Byrd, 166:Apr90-269
  W. Holtz, 173(ECS):Fall89-93
  M. New, 566:Spring90-185
  P. Wagner, 189(EA):Oct-Dec89-476
Ishiguro, K. The Remains of the Day.*
  M. Kenyon, 376:Dec89-122
  T. Rafferty, 442(NY):15Jan90-102
Ishinomori, S. Japan, Inc.
  J.C. Campbell, 293(JASt):Feb89-167
Islas, A. Migrant Souls.
  D. Unger, 441:20May90-30
Ison, G. Confirm or Deny.
  N. Callendar, 441:25Feb90-35
Ison, G. A Damned Serious Business.
  J. Symons, 617(TLS):22-28Jun90-674
Israel, J.I. Dutch Primacy in World Trade,
  1585-1740.
  J.R. Bruijn, 617(TLS):12-18Jan90-28
  J.H. Elliott, 453(NYRB):1Mar90-26
Israeli, R. Muslims in China.
  E. Naby, 318(JAOS):Jan-Mar88-172
Israeli, R. & A.H. Johns, eds. Islam in Asia.
  (Vol 2)
  E. Naby, 318(JAOS):Jan-Mar88-173
Israeloff, R. In Confidence.
  A. Cooper, 441:8Apr90-20
Israëls, H. Schreber.
  P. Grosskurth, 453(NYRB):18Jan90-36
Issacharoff, M. & R.F. Jones, eds. Performing
  Texts.*
  K. Gore, 208(FS):Jul89-366
  J.R. Leo, 403(MLS):Winter89-91
"The Italianist." (No. 5)
  J. Gatt-Rutter, 278(IS):Vol43-183
Itani, F. Truth or Lies.
  D. Schoemperlen, 526:Summer89-93
Itō Takeo. Life Along the South Manchurian
  Railway.
  J.H. Boyle, 293(JASt):Feb89-136
Itzkowitz, N. - see Thomas, L.V.
Ivantyšynová, T. Češi a Slováci v ideólógii
  ruských slavianofilov (40.-60. roky XIX.
  storočia).
  J.D. Naughton, 575(SEER):Jul89-468
Ivars, A-M. Närpesdialekten på 1980-talet.
  E.B. Holtsmark, 350:Jun90-418
Ives, C., H. Giambruni & S.M. Newman.
  Pierre Bonnard.
  Q. Blake, 617(TLS):1-7Jun90-574
Ives, E.D. George Magoon and the Down East
  Game War.
  J. Santino, 292(JAF):Jul-Sep89-341
Izenberg, J. No Medals for Trying.
  M. Lichtenstein, 441:7Oct90-18

Izenour, G.C. Theatre Technology.
  R. Segrin, 610:Autumn89-299
Izod, J. Hollywood and the Box Office, 1895-
  1986.
  T. Pulleine, 707:Winter88/89-67
  639(VQR):Winter89-29
Izzet, A. - see Kazantzaki, N.

Jaberg, K. & J. Jud. AIS: Atlante linguistico
  ed etnografico dell'Italia e della Svizzera
  meridionale. (G. Sanga, ed)
  V. Della Valle, 708:Vol14Fasc2-277
Jabès, E. From the Desert to the Book. The
  Book of Shares.
  M. Rudman, 441:6May90-30
Jablonski, E. Gershwin.*
  R. Handler, 639(VQR):Spring89-370
Jablonsky, D. The Nazi Party in Dissolution.
  A. Glees, 617(TLS):13-19Apr90-392
Jaccottet, P. Selected Poems.
  L. Sail, 493:Spring89-34
Jack, I. & R. Fowler - see Browning, R.
Jack, M. The Social and Political Thought of
  Bernard Mandeville.
  S.H. Daniel, 566:Autumn89-59
Jack, R.D.S., ed. The History of Scottish Lit-
  erature. (Vol 1)
  E. Archibald, 571(ScLJ):Winter89-1
Jack, R.D.S. Scottish Literature's Debt to
  Italy.*
  R.L. Kindrick, 276:Autumn89-359
Jackman, J.S. Diary of a Confederate Soldier.
  (W.C. Davis, ed)
  P-L. Adams, 61:Dec90-132
Jackson, A. Light Hearts.
  B. Franks, 571(ScLJ):Spring89-38
Jackson, B. Fieldwork.*
  C.L. Briggs, 292(JAF):Apr-Jun89-211
Jackson, B. A History of Afro-American Lit-
  erature. (Vol 1)
  J. Lowe, 578:Spring90-134
Jackson, B. & D. Schaap. Bo Knows Bo.
  M.E. Ross, 441:9Dec90-25
Jackson, B.S. Semiotics and Legal Theory.
  R.M. O'Neil, 567:Vol74No1/2-173
Jackson, D. Among the Sleeping Giants.
  M. Ridge, 656(WMQ):Jul89-632
Jackson, D.C. Great American Bridges and
  Dams.
  R. Jay, 576:Jun89-198
Jackson, F. Conditionals.*
  D. Papineau, 479(PhQ):Oct89-493
  G. Priest, 63:Jun89-236
Jackson, F. Sir Raymond Unwin.
  N. Jackson, 576:Sep89-289
Jackson, H.J. - see Coleridge, S.T.
Jackson, I.V., ed. More Than Drumming. More
  Than Dancing.
  C.A. Waterman, 187:Spring/Summer89-336
Jackson, J.A. Grootka.
  M. Stasio, 441:25Nov90-22
Jackson, J.R.D. Annals of English Verse,
  1770-1835.
  S. Curran, 340(KSJ):Vol38-200
  D.H. Reiman, 591(SIR):Winter89-650
Jackson, P. & L. Lockhart, eds. The Cam-
  bridge History of Iran. (Vol 6)
  J.E. Woods, 589:Apr89-395
Jackson, R. Doctors and Diseases in the Ro-
  man Empire.*
  P. De Lacy, 124:Jan-Feb90-247
  H. King, 313:Vol79-224

Jackson, R. Performance Practice, Medieval to Contemporary.
  P. Holman, 410(M&L):May89-245
  J.T. Winemiller, 309:Vol9No2/3-161
Jackson, R. Victorian Theatre.
  I. Williams, 511:Oct89-47
Jackson, R. & R. Smallwood, eds. Players of Shakespeare, 2.*
  D.I. Rabey, 610:Autumn89-290
Jackson, R.L. Black Literature and Humanism in Latin America.*
  E. Aizenberg, 538(RAL):Summer89-316
  R.S. Sayers, 711(RHM):Jun89-90
  E.L. Steeves, 395(MFS):Summer89-310
Jackson, R.L. & L. Nelson, Jr., eds. Vyacheslav Ivanov.*
  G. Cheron, 574(SEEJ):Summer89-310
Jackson, T.A. Charles Dickens.
  D. Sheridan, 456(NDQ):Winter89-237
Jacob, A. - see More, H.
Jacob, F. The Logic of Life.
  S. Rose, 617(TLS):23Feb-1Mar90-204
Jacob, G. & C. de Givray - see Truffaut, F.
Jacob, H. Silent Revolution.
  M.E.B., 185:Jan90-464
Jacob, H., with others. Literatur in der DDR.
  E. Kaufmann, 654(WB):3/1989-510
  N. Riedel, 133:Band22Heft1-92
Jacob, M. ("L. David") Chroniques d'art 1898-1900. (L.A. Joseph, ed)
  S. Levy, 402(MLR):Jul90-738
Jacob, M.C. The Cultural Meaning of the Scientific Revolution.
  A. Guerrini, 173(ECS):Fall89-111
Jacob, V. Diaries and Letters from India 1895-1900. (C. Anderson, ed)
  A.W. Masters, 617(TLS):6-12Jul90-718
Jacobelli, J., ed. Dove va la lingua italiana?
  G. Rovere, 72:Band226Heft1-193
Jacobo de Junta. Oeuvres.* (Vol 1) (J. Roudil, ed)
  G. Martin, 92(BH):Jul-Dec88-437
Jacoba, B.E. Applied Database Logic I.
  J. Barwise, 316:Jun89-627
Jacobs, E. & R. Worcester. We British.
  J. Vincent, 617(TLS):21-27Sep90-994
Jacobs, F., ed. Western European Political Parties.
  D. Leonard, 617(TLS):5-11Jan90-8
Jacobs, H.A. Incidents in the Life of a Slave Girl, Written by Herself.* (L.M. Child, ed; new ed rev by J.F. Yellin)
  J.H. Silverman, 106:Summer89-99
Jacobs, H.C. Literatur, Musik und Gesellschaft in Italien und Österreich in der Epoche Napoleons und der Restauration.
  P. Ackermann, 416:Band4Heft2-175
  P. Branscombe, 402(MLR):Jan90-257
  U. Mathis, 446(NCFS):Spring-Summer90-569
Jacobs, H.C. Stendhal und die Musik.
  U. Mathis, 446(NCFS):Fall-Winter89/90-293
Jacobs, M. Iseult, We Are Barren.
  R. Anderson, 102(CanL):Autumn-Winter89-178
Jacobs, N. The Korean Road to Modernization and Development.
  R.L. Janelli, 293(JASt):Feb89-188
Jacobs, S.L. & E.E. Petriwsky, eds. Rare Books Slavica in the University of Colorado Libraries, Boulder, Colorado.
  R.H. Davis, Jr., 574(SEEJ):Summer89-320

Jacobsen, C.G., ed. Strategic Power.
  W.F. Kimball, 617(TLS):8-14Jun90-601
Jacobsen, J. The Sisters.*
  S. Gorham, 456(NDQ):Summer89-248
Jacobsen, P.S. & B.F. Leavy. Ibsen's Forsaken Merman.
  M. Carlson, 567:Vol77No4-517
  T.F. Van Laan, 130:Fall89-293
Jacobsen-Brown, J.A. & others. Viva el Español!
  R.F. Novotny, 399(MLJ):Winter89-533
Jacobson, D. Adult Pleasures.*
  P. Lewis, 565:Winter88/89-77
Jacobson, N.P. The Heart of Buddhist Philosophy.
  D.M. Lockett, 485(PE&W):Apr89-217
Jacobson, W.S. The Companion to "The Mystery of Edwin Drood."*
  L. Černy, 38:Band107Heft1/2-241
Jacobus, M. Reading Woman.*
  P.L. Caughie, 477(PLL):Summer88-317
Jacobus, M. Romanticism, Writing, and Sexual Difference.
  A.S. Byatt, 617(TLS):23-29Mar90-310
Jacoby, M. Bibeltradition und Bibelsprache zwischen Mittelalter und 20. Jahrhundert im nordgermanischen Raum.
  E. Bauer, 685(ZDL):2/1989-235
Jacoby, R. The Last Intellectuals.*
  R. Cook, 529(QQ):Summer89-554
  J. Seaton, 580(SCR):Spring90-149
Jacoff, R. - see Freccero, J.
Jacques, G. & J. Lambert, eds. Itinéraires et plaisirs textuels.
  M. Brix, 535(RHL):Jul-Aug89-758
Jacquet, J. & M. Pendanx. A juste titre.
  R.J. Melpignano, 399(MLJ):Winter89-509
Jacquet, M.T. Les mots de l'absence - ou du "Dictionnaire des idées reçues" de Flaubert.
  M. Wetherill, 402(MLR):Jan90-195
Jacquet de La Guerre, E-C. Pièces de clavecin. (C.H. Bates, ed)
  A. Silbiger, 317:Spring89-172
Jaeschke, W. - see Hegel, G.W.F.
Jaffé, D. Rubens' Self Portrait in Focus.
  E. McGrath, 90:Aug89-566
Jaffé, M. Old Master Drawings from Chatsworth.*
  A.S. Harris, 380:Spring89-73
Jäger, A. John McGrath und die 7:84 Company Scotland.*
  H.W. Drescher, 38:Band107Heft1/2-273
Jager, R. Eighty Acres.
  D. Unger, 441:23Dec90-13
al-Jāḥiẓ. Nine Essays of al-Jāḥiẓ. (W.M. Hutchins, trans)
  A.F.L. Beeston, 294:Sep89-200
Jahr, E.H. & O. Lorentz. Morfologi/morphology.
  S. Zempel, 563(SS):Winter89-81
"Jahrbuch für Opernforschung." (Vol 2) (M. Arndt & M. Walter, eds)
  E. Hudson, 410(M&L):May89-266
Jain, B.M. India and the United States, 1961-1963.
  M.L.P. Patterson, 293(JASt):May89-426
Jakle, J.A., R.W. Bastian & D.K. Meyer. Common Houses in America's Small Towns.
  H. Davis, 658:Winter89-283
Jakobson, R. Language and Literature.* (K. Pomorska & S. Rudy, eds)
  A. Carstairs, 478(P&L):Oct89-387
  T.R. Hart, 131(CL):Spring89-170

Jakobson, R. Russian and Slavic Grammar
Studies 1931-1981. (L.R. Waugh & M. Halle,
eds)
 A. Timberlake, 279:Vol35/36-267
Jakobson, R. Selected Writings. (Vol 6) (S.
Rudy, ed)
 T. Eekman, 104(CASS):Spring-Winter88-
489
Jalbert, M. Au beau fixe.
 J.P. Gilroy, 102(CanL):Spring89-187
Jalland, P. & J. Hooper, eds. Women From
Birth to Death.
 J. Gerard, 637(VS):Autumn89-184
Jallier, M. & Y. Lossen. Musique aux Antilles:
Mizik bô kay.
 G. Averill, 187:Winter89-153
Jalloh, C.M. Fichte's Kant-Interpretation and
the Doctrine of Science.
 D. Breazeale, 342:Band80Heft2-238
Jamba, S. Patriots.
 J. Ryle, 617(TLS):14-20Dec90-1359
James, A.R. The Acquisition of a Second
Language Phonology.
 Y. Bader, 257(IRAL):Nov89-357
James, B. The Baseball Book 1990.
 R. Wetzsteon, 441:29Apr90-32
James, C. May Week Was in June.
 D. Davies, 617(TLS):1-7Jun90-576
James, C. Snakecharmers in Texas.*
 P. Lewis, 565:Winter88/89-77
James, C.V., ed. Information China.
 T. Cheek, 293(JASt):Nov89-822
James, D. The House of Janus.
 P. Kerr, 617(TLS):29Jun-5Jul90-705
James, D. Qur'ans of the Mamluks.*
 J.M. Rogers, 90:Sep89-648
James, E. & G. Benjamin. Public Policy and
Private Education in Japan.
 W.K. Cummings, 293(JASt):May89-390
James, F. Semantics of the English Subjunc-
tive.*
 P. Duffley, 320(CJL):Jun89-193
James, H. The Complete Notebooks of Henry
James.* (L. Edel & L.H. Powers, eds)
 J. Batchelor, 677(YES):Vol20-314
James, H. The Critical Muse. (R. Gard, ed)
The Art of Criticism. (W. Veeder & S.M.
Griffin, eds)
 R. Mason, 447(N&Q):Dec89-535
James, H. A German Identity, 1770-1990.*
 G.A. Craig, 453(NYRB):18Jan90-28
James, H. Henry James: Selected Letters.*
(L. Edel, ed)
 N. Bradbury, 677(YES):Vol20-311
 B. Richards, 447(N&Q):Dec89-532
James, H. The Painter's Eye. (J.L. Sweeney,
ed)
 617(TLS):27Apr-3May90-457
James, H. Selected Letters of Henry James to
Edmund Gosse, 1882-1915. (R.S. Moore, ed)
 M. Deakin, 395(MFS):Winter89-733
 J.W. Tuttleton, 177(ELT):Vol32No4-482
 T. Wortham, 445(NCF):Jun89-120
 639(VQR):Summer89-89
James, H. & E. Wharton. Henry James and
Edith Wharton: Letters 1900-1915. (L.H.
Powers, ed)
 H. Lee, 617(TLS):25-31May90-547
 M. Paley, 441:28Jan90-13
James, P.D. Devices and Desires.*
 J. Crist, 441:28Jan90-1
 H. Mantel, 453(NYRB):26Apr90-35

James, T.G.H. Pharaoh's People.
 E.S. Meltzer, 318(JAOS):Apr-Jun88-285
James, W. Manuscript Essays and Notes.
 J.E. Bayley, 619:Summer89-373
James, W. Manuscript Lectures.* (F.H. Burk-
hardt, F. Bowers & I.K. Skrupskelis, eds)
 D.R. Anderson, 619:Fall89-565
James, W. Writings 1902-1910. (B. Kuklick,
ed)
 I.K. Skrupskelis, 619:Winter89-78
Jameson, F. The Ideologies of Theory.
 G. Hentzi, 147:Vol6No1-59
 R. Shusterman, 494:Fall89-605
Jameson, F., ed. Sartre after Sartre.
 P. Petit, 478(P&L):Apr89-195
Jamie, K. The Way We Live.*
 L. Sail, 565:Summer89-75
Jamme, C. & O. Pöggeler, eds. Jenseits des
Idealismus.
 H. Gaskill, 133:Band22Heft3/4-331
Jancar, B. Environmental Management in the
Soviet Union and Yugoslavia.
 P. Frank, 575(SEER):Oct89-647
 D.R. Kelley, 104(CASS):Spring89-121
Jance, J.A. Minor in Possession.
 M. Stasio, 441:29Apr90-18
Janeras, S. Miscel·lánia Papirològica Ramon
Roca-Puig en el seu vuitantè aniversari.
 P.J. Parsons, 123:Vol39No2-421
Jangfeldt, B. - see Mayakovsky, V. & L. Brik
Jangfeldt, B. & R. Kruus - see Severjanin, I.
Janićijević, J. U znaku Moloha - antropološki
ogled a žrtvovanju.
 V. Voigt, 567:Vol73No3/4-363
Janik, A. Essays on Wittgenstein and Wein-
inger.
 T. Nordenstam, 53(AGP):Band71Heft1-115
Janka, W. Schwierigkeiten mit der Wahrheit.
 P. Graves, 617(TLS):15-21Jun90-631
Janko, R. - see Aristotle
Janković, B.M. The Balkans in International
Relations.
 M.S. Anderson, 575(SEER):Jul89-469
Jannaco, C. & M. Capucci. Il Seicento.
 G. Rizzo, 228(GSLI):Vol166fasc533-116
Janney, F. - see Benitez Rojo, A.
Janovic, V. The House of the Tragic Poet.*
 D. O'Driscoll, 493:Summer89-47
Janowitz, A. England's Ruins.
 J. Barrell, 617(TLS):28Sep-4Oct90-1043
Janowitz, T. Esclaves de New York.
 C. Thomas, 98:Dec89-926
Jansky, H. Lehrbuch der türkischen Sprache.
(11th ed) (A. Landmann, ed)
 A. Bassarak, 682(ZPSK):Band42Heft5-678
Janson, H.W. History of Art. (3rd ed) (A.F.
Janson, ed)
 B.R. Collins, 127:Spring89-90
Janssen, M. The Kenyon Review: 1939-1970.
 L.D. Rubin, Jr., 344:Summer90-150
Jansson, H. Per Olov Enquist och det in-
ställda upproret.*
 S. Malmberg, 563(SS):Autumn89-422
Januschek, F., ed. Politische Sprachwissen-
schaft.
 A. Beyrer, 682(ZPSK):Band42Heft1-116
Januszczak, W. Sayonara, Michelangelo.
 P-L. Adams, 61:Nov90-173
 O. Banks, 441:11Nov90-21
Janz, M. Marmorbilder.*
 R. Robertson, 402(MLR):Jul90-795

Jaouiche, H., comp. The Histories of Nishapur by 'Abdalġāfir al-Fārisī (Siyāq Ta'rīḫ Naisābūr): Register der Personen- und Ortsnamen.
  R.W. Bulliet, 318(JAOS):Oct-Dec88-669
"Le Japonisme."
  R.D. Reck, 207(FR):Dec89-387
Japp, U. Literatur und Modernität.
  J.H. Petersen, 52:Band24Heft2-199
Jaquet, F.G.P., ed. Kartini.
  S.E. Wieringa, 293(JASt):May89-436
Jardin, A. Tocqueville.*
  L.D. Mitchell, 95(CLAJ):Dec89-226
  M.K. Spears, 249(HudR):Autumn89-369
Jardin, A. Le Zèbre.
  G.E. Reed, 207(FR):Oct89-208
Jardine, A. & P. Smith, eds. Men in Feminism.*
  C. Slawy-Sutton, 207(FR):May90-1057
Jardine, N. The Birth of History and Philosophy in Science.*
  M.A. Finocchiaro, 319:Oct90-614
  W.R. Shea, 242:Vol10No2-243
Jarman, D., ed. The Berg Companion.
  D. Matthews, 617(TLS):13-19Apr90-398
Jarman, M.A. Killing the Swan.
  D. O'Rourke, 102(CanL):Spring89-206
Jarrell, R. Selected Poems. (W.H. Pritchard, ed)
  A. Broyard, 441:6May90-3
Jarrett, D. The Sleep of Reason *
  C. Peters, 249(HudR):Autumn89-502
Jarrety, M., ed. Valéry, pour quoi?
  P. Gifford, 208(FS):Jan89-110
Jarry, A. Days and Nights [and] The Other Alcestis.
  P. Reading, 617(TLS):5-11Jan90-18
Jarvie, I. Philosophy of the Film.*
  B. Falk, 291:Vol6No1-112
  C. Rostankowski, 290(JAAC):Fall89-384
de Jasay, A. Social Contract, Free Ride.
  K.F.T. Cust, 103:Apr90-129
Jaschok, M. Concubines and Bondservants
  G. Hershatter, 293(JASt):Aug89-589
Jasper, D., ed. The Interpretation of Belief.*
  D. Degrois, 189(EA):Jul-Sep89-349
Jasper, D. The New Testament and the Literary Imagination.
  A. Crépin, 189(EA):Jul-Sep89-365
Jasper, D. The Study of Literature and Religion.
  B. Horne, 617(TLS):6-12Jul90-737
Jasper, R.C.D. The Development of the Anglican Liturgy, 1662-1980.
  T. Baker, 617(TLS):13-19Apr90-390
Jaume, L. Le Discours jacobin et la démocratie.*
  T.E. Kaiser, 173(ECS):Spring90-348
Jauss, H.R. Pour une herméneutique littéraire.
  M. Buffat, 530:Apr89-167
  G. Cesbron, 535(RHL):Sep-Oct89-946
Javadi, H. Satire in Persian Literature.*
  Y. Armajani, 456(NDQ):Spring89-163
Jay, E. - see Oliphant, M.
Jay, K. The Amazon and the Page.
  Y.A. Patterson, 207(FR):Feb90-548
Jay, P. - see Burke, K. & M. Cowley
Jayal, N.G. - see Webb, S. & B.
Jaynes, G.D. & R.M. Williams, Jr. A Common Destiny.*
  J.A. Moss, 441:14Jan90-31

Jayyusi, S.K., ed. The Literature of Modern Arabia.
  S. Noyes, 376:Jun89-130
Jeal, T. The Boy-Man.* (British title: Baden-Powell.)
  I. Buruma, 453(NYRB):15Mar90-17
  Z. Steiner, 441:1Apr90-9
Jeanneret, M. Des mets et des mots.*
  P. Bayley, 402(MLR):Apr90-441
  G. Demerson, 535(RHL):Jul-Aug89-706
  G. Mathieu-Castellani, 549(RLC):Jan-Mar89-113
Jeanrond, W.G. Text and Interpretation as Categories of Theological Thinking.
  N. Biggar, 235:Summer89-81
Jeanson, F. Sartre and the Problem of Morality.
  K.S. Walters, 438:Spring89-241
Jeansonne, G. Gerald L.K. Smith.*
  639(VQR):Spring89-53
Jech, T. Multiple Forcing.
  M. Foreman, 316:Sep89-1112
Jeffares, A.N. W.B. Yeats.*
  P. Levi, 493:Summer89-22
Jeffares, A.N. - see Yeats, W.B.
Jeffers, R. The Collected Poetry of Robinson Jeffers.* (Vol 1) (T. Hunt, ed)
  P.D. Murphy, 649(WAL):May89-82
  L. Wagner-Martin, 115:Spring89-187
  639(VQR):Winter89-28
Jeffers, R. Songs and Heroes. (R.J. Brophy, ed)
  T.A. Hunt, 30:Winter90-80
Jeffers, U. & R. Where Shall I Take You To. (R. Kafka, ed)
  T.A. Hunt, 30:Winter90-80
Jefferson, A. Lotte Lehmann: 1888-1976.
  A. Blyth, 415:Jan89-28
Jefferson, A. Reading Realism in Stendhal.*
  E.J. Talbot, 446(NCFS):Fall-Winter89/90-243
  E. Williamson, 208(FS):Oct89-474
  D. Wood, 242:Vol10No1-85
Jefferson, A. & D. Robey, eds. Modern Literary Theory.* (2nd ed)
  J.R. Bennett, 599:Spring90-126
Jeffery, L.H. The Local Scripts of Archaic Greece. (A.W. Johnston, ed)
  A.G. Woodhead, 617(TLS):13-19Jul90-759
Jeffrey, C.I. El arte narrativo de Rafael Felipe Muñoz.
  A. McDermott, 86(BHS):Jan89-103
Jeffreys-Jones, R. The CIA and American Democracy.*
  639(VQR):Autumn89-134
Jeffries, I. & M. Melzer, eds. The East German Economy.
  S. Gomulka, 575(SEER):Oct89-656
Jehne, M. Der Staat des Dictators Caesar.*
  R. Seager, 123:Vol39No1-84
Jelinek, E. The Piano Teacher.
  J. Mellors, 364:Dec89/Jan90-126
Jelinek, E. Wonderful Wonderful Times.
  A. McRobbie, 617(TLS):2-8Nov90-1183
Jencks, C. Post-Modernism.*
  J.A. Richardson, 289:Winter89-114
Jencks, C. The Prince, the Architects, and the New Wave Monarchy.*
  R. Kimball, 45:Nov89-77
Jenkins, A. Greenheart.
  D. Lehman, 617(TLS):27Apr-3May90-443

Jenkins, A. The Theatre of Tom Stoppard.*
　　B. Crow, 610:Spring89-104
　　S.G. Mullins, 178:Mar89-111
　　K. Worth, 402(MLR):Apr90-431
Jenkins, B. Sir William Gregory of Coole.
　　B.M. Touhill, 635(VPR):Summer89-75
Jenkins, G.H. The Foundations of Modern
　Wales.
　　A. McInnes, 83:Autumn89-209
Jenkins, L. - see Eliot, G.
Jenkins, P. Mrs. Thatcher's Revolution.*
　　639(VQR):Spring89-60
Jenkins, R. Acrobats of the Soul.
　　J. Fisher, 130:Winter89/90-383
Jenkins, R. Guests of War.
　　P. Clarke, 571(ScLJ):Spring89-35
Jenkins, T.A. Gladstone, Whiggery and the
　Liberal Party 1874-1886.
　　P. Stansky, 637(VS):Winter90-352
Jenkins, V. Relative Distances.
　　R. Minkoff, 441:18Nov90-28
Jennett, B. High Technology Medicine.
　　G. Gillett, 291:Vol6No1-114
Jenni, U. Das Skizzenbuch des Jacques
　Daliwe.
　　R.W. Scheller, 600:Vol19No3-206
Jennings, A., P. Lashmar & V. Simson. Scot-
　land Yard's Cocaine Connection.
　　J. Fairleigh, 617(TLS):31Aug-6Sep90-924
Jennings, E. Tributes.*
　　S. Knight, 364:Oct/Nov89-115
　　S. Pugh, 493:Autumn89-60
Jennings, F. Empire of Fortune.
　　J. Ferling, 432(NEQ):Mar89-124
　　R. Middleton, 656(WMQ):Apr89-398
Jennings, K. The Devouring Fungus.
　　L.R. Shannon, 441:2Dec90-75
Jennings, K.M. Balls and Strikes.
　　D. Stetson, 441:1Apr90-13
Jennings, M.W. Dialectical Images.
　　D.T.O., 295(JML):Fall88/Winter89-229
　　K.L. Schultz, 406:Fall89-380
Jens, I. - see Mann, T.
Jensen, F., ed & trans. The Poetry of the
　Sicilian School.*
　　J.H. Levin, 589:Apr89-443
　　R. Russell, 276:Spring89-57
Jensen, J.M. Loosening the Bonds.*
　　L.M. Adrian, 106:Summer89-107
Jensen, J.M. Passage from India.
　　M. Juergensmeyer, 293(JASt):Feb89-201
Jensen, K.O., Ø. Rottem & J. Thon, eds. News
　from the Top of the World.
　　R. Greenwald, 563(SS):Spring/Summer89-
　　261
Jensen, P.A. & others, eds. Text and Con-
　text.*
　　R. Šilbajoris, 104(CASS):Spring-Win-
　　ter88-412
Jenson, R.W. America's Theologian.
　　C.A. Holbrook, 656(WMQ):Jul89-611
Jeremy, D.J. Capitalists and Christians.
　　G. Studdert-Kennedy, 617(TLS):21-
　　27Dec90-1379
Jeremy, M. & M.E. Robinson. Ceremony and
　Symbolism in the Japanese Home.
　　R.A. Jussaume, Jr., 293(JASt):Nov89-861
de Jérica y Corta, P. Cuentos jocosos en dif-
　erentes versos castellanos. (E. Gutiérrez
　Díaz-Bernardo, ed)
　　J.M. Sala Valldaura, 711(RHM):Jun89-83
Jermann, C. Philosophie und Politik.
　　T. Buchheim, 687:Jul-Sep89-552

Saint Jerome. Jérôme, "Commentaire sur
　Jonas." (Y-M. Duval, ed & trans)
　　A. Bastiaensen, 394:Vol42fasc1/2-226
Jerschowa, M. Honigland Bitterland.
　　L. Chamberlain, 617(TLS):5-11Oct90-
　　1073
Jervis, J.L. Cometary Theory in Fifteenth-
　Century Europe.
　　M.H. Shank, 589:Apr89-445
Jessen, J. - see Huch, R.
Jeyifo, B., ed. Contemporary Nigerian Litera-
　ture.
　　O. Maduakor, 538(RAL):Spring89-113
Jhabvala, R.P. Out of India.
　　D. Durrant, 364:Jun/Jul89-130
Jian, M. - see under Ma Jian
Jiaqi, Y. & Gao Gao - see under Yan Jiaqi &
　Gao Gao
Jiles, P. The Jesse James Poems.*
　　S. Glickman, 102(CanL):Autumn-
　　Winter89-148
Jillson, C.C. Constitution Making.
　　H.J. Henderson, 656(WMQ):Oct89-830
Jimack, P. Diderot: "Supplément au Voyage de
　Bougainville."
　　M.L. Perkins, 402(MLR):Oct90-964
Jimenez, M.A. Changing Faces of Madness.*
　　C.K. Warsh, 529(QQ):Summer89-487
Jiménez-Fajardo, S. Multiple Spaces.*
　　G. Connell, 86(BHS):Apr89-188
Jiménez Faro, L. Panorama Antológico de
　Poetisas Españolas (Siglos XV al XX).
　　C. Enríquez de Salamanca, 238:Sep89-550
Jimeno, F.D. - see under Díaz Jimeno, F.
Jin, Z. & Q. Zhou - see "June Four"
Jirō, Y. - see under Yamaguchi Jirō
Jodelle, E. L'Eugène.* (M.J. Freeman, ed)
　　J. Braybrook, 208(FS):Apr89-203
　　L. Zilli, 535(RHL):Sep-Oct89-924
Jodogne, P. - see Guicciardini, F.
Joedicke, J. Weissenhofsiedlung Stuttgart.
　　R. Padovan, 46:Aug89-15
Joeres, R-E.B. & M.J. Maynes, eds. German
　Women in the Eighteenth and Nineteenth
　Centuries.*
　　S.L. Cocalis, 406:Summer89-230
Joffe, C. The Regulation of Sexuality.
　　K.P. Addelson, 254:Summer89-191
Johannesson, K. & others. Heroer på offent-
　lighetens scen.
　　S. Oakley, 562(Scan):May89-85
Johannisse, Y. & G. Lane. La science comme
　mythe.
　　M. Espinoza, 542:Oct-Dec89-651
Johansen, B.F. & others. Ordbog over dansk
　Middelalderlatin/Lexicon Mediae Latinitatis
　Danicae. (Vol 1)
　　J.M. Ziolkowski, 589:Jul89-722
Johanson, C. Women's Struggle for Higher
　Education in Russia, 1855-1900.
　　R.A. Dudgeon, 550(RusR):Oct89-418
　　W.L. Mathes, 104(CASS):Spring89-101
John, N., ed. Strauss: "Salome" and "Elektra."
　Wagner: "Tannhäuser."
　　R. Donington, 415:Jun89-349
John of Salisbury. John of Salisbury's "Enth-
　eticus Maior and Minor." (J. van Laarhov-
　en, ed & trans)
　　J.M. Ziolkowski, 589:Apr89-446
Johnson, A.B. Out of Bedlam.
　　D. Mechanic, 441:16Sep90-9

Johnson, B. Text and Supertext in Ibsen's Drama.
A. Bermel, 34:Jul/Aug89-40
Johnson, B. A World of Difference.*
P.L. Caughie, 477(PLL):Summer88-317
S. Connor, 402(MLR):Jul90-671
D.T.O., 295(JML):Fall88/Winter89-185
J. Pilditch, 478(P&L):Apr89-198
M.P. Spikes, 577(SHR):Spring89-171
J.M. Todd, 131(CL):Summer89-282
Johnson, C. Being and Race.
N. Harris, 395(MFS):Summer89-307
T. Le Clair, 27(AL):Mar89-135
Johnson, C. Middle Passage.
T. Keneally, 441:1Jul90-8
Johnson, C.L. Jane Austen.*
J.P. Brown, 454:Spring90-303
E. Gillooly, 147:Vol6No1-87
C.C. Park, 249(HudR):Winter89-648
L. Speirs, 402(MLR):Jul90-701
S. Tave, 445(NCF):Dec89-399
L. Yelin, 637(VS):Spring90-507
Johnson, D. Health and Happiness.
R.P. Brickner, 441:30Sep90-18
Johnson, D. Iris Murdoch.*
M. Del Sapio, 677(YES):Vol20-342
Johnson, D. & J. Young. The Immigrant Experience.
B. Kroll, 399(MLJ):Autumn89-355
Johnson, D.B. Worlds in Regression.*
C. Ross, 395(MFS):Summer89-295
Johnson, G. Distant Friends.
O. Verderese, 441:9Dec90-24
Johnson, G. Understanding Joyce Carol Oates.*
S.P., 295(JML):Fall88/Winter89-388
Johnson, H. Physical Culture.
R. Kaveney, 617(TLS):8-14Jun90-617
Johnson, J. What Lisa Knew.
R. Coles, 441:8Apr90-1
Johnson, J. & F. Lovell. Poems 1983-1986.
J. Saunders, 565:Autumn89-77
Johnson, J.G. The Book in the Americas.
W.V. Jackson, 263(RIB):Vol39No2-207
Johnson, J.T. The Quest for Peace.
J. Levitt, 529(QQ):Spring89-190
Johnson, L. Lionel Johnson: Selected Letters. (M. Pittock, ed)
G.A. Cevasco, 177(ELT):Vol32No3-348
Johnson, L. The Paintings of Eugène Delacroix. (Vols 5 & 6)
N. Bryson, 617(TLS):30Mar-5Apr90-351
Johnson, L.A. The Expression of Time in "Crime and Punishment."*
R.L. Busch, 104(CASS):Spring-Winter88-512
Johnson, L.J. - see Jordaens, W.
Johnson, L.V. A General for Peace.
J. Levitt, 529(QQ):Spring89-190
Johnson, M. The Body in the Mind.*
G.W. Grace, 567:Vol73No3/4-351
B. King, 320(CJL):Dec89-469
A. Neill, 89(BJA):Winter89-90
Johnson, M.L. The Birds From I Know Where.
W. Zander, 363(LitR):Spring90-399
Johnson, P. Intellectuals.*
C. Marowitz, 34:Jun89-36
J. Seaton, 580(SCR):Spring90-149
Johnson, P. Politics, Innocence, and the Limits of Goodness.
D. George, 291:Vol6No2-243
M. Hughes, 483:Jul89-421
S.E. Marshall, 103:May90-184

Johnson, P., C. Conrad & D. Thomson, eds. Workers versus Pensioners.
P. Laslett, 617(TLS):26Jan-1Feb90-100
P. Willmot & P. Laslett, 358:Feb90-7
Johnson, P. & M. Wigley. Deconstructivist Architecture.
658:Spring89-112
Johnson, P.J., ed. Working the Water.
R. Moonsammy, 658:Spring89-98
Johnson, R. & R. Stam, eds. Brazilian Cinema.
K.S. Larsen, 238:Dec89-975
Johnson, R.W. Heroes and Villains.
J. Vincent, 617(TLS):20-26Jul90-768
Johnson, S. Flying Lessons.
T. Glyde, 617(TLS):14-20Sep90-980
Johnson, S. Rome and Its Empire.
P. Salway, 617(TLS):23-29Mar90-329
Johnson, S. Selections from Johnson on Shakespeare.* (B.H. Bronson & J.M. O'Meara, eds)
M.G.H. Pittock, 83:Spring89-111
Johnson, S.K. The Japanese Through American Eyes.*
J. Tobin, 293(JASt):May89-391
Johnson, S.M. Teachers at Work.
J. Countryman, 441:1Jul90-17
Johnson, S.S., ed. Cadences. (No 1 & 2)
C. Burke, 440:Winter-Spring89-147
Johnson, W. The Snake Game.
E. Hanson, 441:23Dec90-12
Johnson, W.R. Momentary Monsters.*
M. Morford, 24:Summer89-371
Johnston, A. Plants and the Blackfoot.
A.R. Taylor, 269(IJAL):Jul89-359
Johnston, A.F., ed. Editing Early English Drama.
M. Erler, 354:Jun89-158
Johnston, A.W. - see Jeffery, L.H.
Johnston, B. Text and Supertext in Ibsen's Drama.
V. Gottlieb, 402(MLR):Oct90-1041
Johnston, C. Thomas Wolfe.*
R. Foster, 580(SCR):Fall89-147
Johnston, D. Irish Poetry after Joyce.
E.G. Ingersoll, 174(Éire):Fall88-150
Johnston, D. On a Singular Book of Cervidius Scaevola.
W.M. Gordon, 123:Vol39No1-146
W. Waldstein, 229:Band61Heft8-750
Johnston, D. The Rhetoric of "Leviathan."*
P.J. Johnson, 242:Vol10No6-730
J. Sawday, 506(PSt):Sep89-193
Johnston, G. - see Whalley, G.
Johnston, J. The Lord Chamberlain's Blue Pencil.
W. Gaskill, 617(TLS):5-11Oct90-1065
Johnston, J.H. The Poet and the City.
S.E. Larsen, 462(OL):Vol44No3-278
Johnston, M.D. The Spiritual Logic of Ramon Llull.*
J. Biard, 192(EP):Apr-Jun89-249
A. Bonner, 240(HR):Spring89-224
A.V. Esquerra, 319:Jan90-127
Johnston, P. Wittgenstein and Moral Philosophy.
M. Budd, 617(TLS):16-22Feb90-168
Johnston, P.A. Traditio.
F.T. Coulson, 399(MLJ):Summer89-213
J.E. Ziolkowski, 124:Jan-Feb90-249
Johnston, R. Inside Out.
M. Warnock, 617(TLS):26Jan-1Feb90-100

Johnston, R.H. "New Mecca, New Babylon."*
    D.M. Bethea, 550(RusR):Oct89-451
    K. Neilson, 529(QQ):Winter89-966
    G.S. Smith, 575(SEER):Jul89-442
Johnston, W.M. In Search of Italy.*
    J. Hayman, 242:Vol10No3-389
Johnstone, J., with R. Talley. Some of My
    Best Friends Are Crazy.
    M-A.T. Smith, 441:8Jul90-16
Johnstone, P.T. Notes on Logic and Set The-
    ory.
    J.I. Malitz, 316:Mar89-289
Johnstone, R. Belfast.
    P. Craig, 617(TLS):14-20Dec90-1356
Johnstone, R. Eden to Edenderry.*
    S. O'Brien, 493:Autumn89-63
Jolles, C. & W. Müller-Seidel, eds. Die Briefe
    Theodor Fontanes: Verzeichnis und Regis-
    ter. (R. Bachmann, W. Hettsche & J. Neuen-
    dorff-Fürstenau, comps)
    W. Paulsen, 301(JEGP):Jul89-384
Jolley, E. My Father's Moon.*
    M. Hardie, 581:Dec89-654
    42(AR):Summer89-373
Jolley, E. The Sugar Mother.*
    M. Hardie, 581:Mar89-113
    639(VQR):Winter89-21
Jolley, N. The Light of the Soul.
    J. Cottingham, 617(TLS):13-19Jul90-758
Jolliffe, J. - see Haydon, B.R.
Jolly, C., ed. Histoire des bibliothèques
    françaises.* (Vol 2)
    78(BC):Summer89-153
Jonaitis, A. From the Land of the Totem
    Poles.
    V. Wyatt, 2(AfrA):May89-86
Jones, A. Romance "Kharjas" in Andalusian
    Arabic "Muwaššāḥ" Poetry.
    D. Hanlon, 304(JHP):Autumn89-91
Jones, A.H. Ideas and Innovations.*
    W.A. Craik, 541(RES):Nov89-575
Jones, A.R. - see Wordsworth, W.
Jones, A.R.W. Victor Hugo et la Grande-
    Bretagne.
    J.F. Hamilton, 345(KRQ):May89-230
Jones, B. Selected Poems.
    R. Pybus, 565:Winter88/89-67
Jones, B. - see Fauré, G.
Jones, C., ed. Britain in the First Age of
    Party.
    A. McInnes, 83:Spring89-101
Jones, C.P. Culture and Society in Lucian.
    B.P. Reardon, 122:Jul89-271
Jones, D. Adult Education and Cultural
    Development.
    H. Kauppinen, 709:Winter91-122
Jones, D. Concerto.
    N. Callendar, 441:17Jun90-19
Jones, D.C. Empire of Dust.
    A. Marriott, 102(CanL):Summer89-189
Jones, D.G. Balthazar and Other Poems.
    S. Scobie, 376:Mar89-128
Jones, D.G. - see Miron, G.
Jones, D.H. Night Times and Light Times.
    J. Ure, 617(TLS):17-23Aug90-881
Jones, D.J.V. Rebecca's Children.
    J. Stevenson, 617(TLS):13-19Apr90-391
Jones, D.R., ed. Spisok Povremennykh Izdanii.
    R. Service, 575(SEER):Jan89-148
Jones, E. Epicurean Delight.
    M. O'Neill, 441:16Dec90-25
Jones, E. Metropolis.
    Z. Bauman, 617(TLS):11-17May90-501

Jones, E. Reading the Book of Nature.
    P.M. Locke, 543:Mar90-637
Jones, E.H. Native Americans as Shown on
    the Stage, 1753-1916.
    J.H. Stroupe, 130:Fall89-292
Jones, E.L. Growth Recurring.
    J. de Vries, 293(JASt):Feb89-116
Jones, E.P. Where is Home?
    K. Cherry, 441:9Sep90-34
Jones, F.J. The Modern Italian Lyric.*
    T. Harrison, 276:Autumn89-361
    E. Schächter, 278(IS):Vol43-174
    R. West, 345(KRQ):Nov89-503
Jones, G. Selected Poems.
    D. McDuff, 565:Spring89-76
Jones, H. The Epicurean Tradition.
    P. Preuss, 103:Jul90-277
Jones, H. How I Became Hettie Jones.
    S. Brownmiller, 441:11Mar90-12
    442(NY):4Jun90-103
Jones, H. Mutiny on the Amistad.
    J.H. Silverman, 106:Summer89-99
Jones, J.H. - see Empson, W.
Jones, J.T. Wayward Skeptic.*
    M. Amsler, 70:Apr89-72
    J.A. Bryant, Jr., 569(SR):Winter89-153
Jones, K.B. & A.G. Jónasdóttir, eds. The
    Political Interests of Gender.
    N.B., 185:Jul90-923
Jones, K.W. The New Cambridge History of
    India. (Vol 3, Pt 1)
    B. Metcalf, 617(TLS):6-12Jul90-718
Jones, L. Barbed Wire and Mirrors.
    R.F. Anderson, 49:Apr89-86
Jones, L. & V. Kimbrough. Great Ideas.
    J. Kaplan-Weinger, 399(MLJ):Winter89-
    499
Jones, L.B. Ordinary Money.
    M. Gingher, 441:14Jan90-7
    442(NY):26Feb90-131
Jones, M., ed. Fake?
    P-L. Adams, 61:Sep90-121
Jones, M. & K. Kroeber. Wordsworth Scholar-
    ship and Criticism, 1973-84.
    L. Newlyn, 677(YES):Vol20-290
Jones, M.O. Exploring Folk Art.*
    L-M. Ballard, 203:Vol100No2-260
Jones, N. God and the Moneylenders.
    G. Wills, 453(NYRB):18Jan90-22
Jones, N.F. Public Organization in Ancient
    Greece.
    D. Whitehead, 24:Winter89-660
Jones, N.H. Hitler's Herald.
    P. Lewis, 565:Summer89-66
Jones, P.F. The Jews of Britain.
    R.S. Wistrich, 617(TLS):23-29Nov90-1261
Jones, P.V. & K.C. Sidwell. Reading Latin.
    F. Biville, 555:Vol62Fasc2-387
Jones, R. Transparent Gestures.
    S. Dobyns, 441:2Sep90-5
Jones, R. and M. Olwen. Artists in Camera.
    N. Curry, 511:Jul89-44
Jones, R.E., with others. Greek and Cypriot
    Pottery.
    P.P. Betancourt, 303(JoHS):Vol109-263
    A. Johnston, 123:Vol39No1-109
Jones, R.F. Blood Tide.
    N. Callendar, 441:22Jul90-22
Jones, R.T. - see Glass, P.
Jones, R.V. Reflections on Intelligence.
    W. Laqueur, 617(TLS):26Jan-1Feb90-82
Jones, S. Hazlitt.
    G. Lindop, 617(TLS):27Apr-3May90-441

Jones, T. The Improbable Voyage. Some-
wheres East of Suez.
  S. Pickering, 569(SR):Spring89-297
Jones, V. How to Study a Jane Austen Novel.
  J. Wiltshire, 97(CQ):Vol17No4-369
Jones, V., ed. Women in the Eighteenth Cen-
tury.
  C. Lennox-Boyd, 617(TLS):29Jun-
5Jul90-698
Jones, W.G. - see Brandes, G.
Jones, W.R.D. David Williams.
  M. Fitzpatrick, 83:Spring89-99
Jones-Davies, M-T. Shakespeare: le théâtre
du monde.
  K. Muir, 189(EA):Jan-Mar89-100
Jong, E. Any Woman's Blues.
  B. De Mott, 441:28Jan90-13
  D. Montrose, 617(TLS):17-23Aug90-868
de Jong, F., L. Oversteegen & H. Verkuyl.
Betekenis en Taalstructuur.
  J.L.G. Baart, 204(FdL):Mar89-57
de Jong, I.J.F. Narrators and Focalizers.
  A. Bonnafé, 555:Vol62Fasc1-136
  M.M. Willcock, 123:Vol39No2-174
de Jong, J.J.P. Diplomatie of strijd.
  A.R. Kahin, 293(JASt):Nov89-931
Jong Ki-sou. La Corée et l'Occident, diffu-
sion de la culture française en Corée.
  M. Detrie, 549(RLC):Jan-Mar89-99
Jongeneel, E. Michel Butor et le pacte
romanesque.*
  A.A. Inglis, 402(MLR):Oct90-985
Jongman, W. The Economy and Society of
Pompeii.
  J. Banaji, 313:Vol79-229
Jonsen, A.R. & S. Toulmin. The Abuse of
Casuistry.*
  A. Alonso, 548:Mar90-639
  A. MacIntyre, 319:Oct90-634
Jonson, B. The Alchemist. (P. Bement, ed)
  M.J. Haddad, 568(SCN):Fall-Winter89-49
Jonson, B. Sejanus His Fall (P Ayres, ed)
  J.H. Jones, 617(TLS):26Oct-1Nov90-1161
Jönsson, A-M. Johannes Messenius, "Chrono-
logia Sanctae Birgittae."
  P.G. Walsh, 123:Vol39No2-424
Jönsson, H. Gud till ärra, klockan till prat.
  O. Norn, 341:Vol58No1-34
Jönsson, L. On Being Heard in Court Trials
and Police Interrogations.
  B. Nordberg, 452(NJL):Vol12No2-205
Jonsson, M. La Cura dei Monumenti alle Ori-
gini.*
  T.P. Wiseman, 313:Vol79-212
Jönsson, R. My Life as a Dog.*
  M.J. Rosen, 441:8Jul90-8
  442(NY):17Sep90-108
Joost, U. & A. Schöne - see Lichtenberg, G.C.
Joppien, R. & B. Smith. The Art of Captain
Cook's Voyages.* (Vol 3)
  N. Barley, 39:Dec89-430
Jordaens, W. Wilhelm Jordaens's "Avellana."
(L.J. Johnson, ed) Conflictus virtutum et
viciorum. (A. Önnerfors, ed)
  R. Kieckhefer, 589:Apr89-449
Jordan, C. Pulci's "Morgante."*
  L.L. Carroll, 345(KRQ):May89-254
Jordan, C. A Terrible Beauty.*
  A. Bradley, 637(VS):Spring90-537
Jordan, C.S. Second Stories.
  I. Schweitzer, 165(EAL):Vol25No2-217

Jordan, D.W. Foundations of Representative
Government in Maryland, 1632-1715.
  J.D. Krugler, 656(WMQ):Jan89-175
Jordan, E. Alfred Tennyson.
  R. Rooksby, 175:Spring89-83
Jordan, L. The Toy Cupboard.*
  M. Stasio, 441:30Sep90-32
Jordan, R. & H. Love - see Southerne, T.
Jordan, R.A. & S.J. Kalčik, eds. Women's
Folklore, Women's Culture.
  J. Ice, 440:Winter-Spring89-121
Jordan, R.D. The Quiet Hero.
  J. Crewe, 329(JJQ):Spring90-682
Jordan, R.M. Chaucer's Poetics and the Mod-
ern Reader.*
  M. Allen, 569(SR):Fall89-cxxv
  R.A. Shoaf, 401(MLQ):Jun88-187
  D. Williams, 402(MLR):Apr90-401
Jordan, W.B. - see Segal, S.
Jordanova, L.J., ed. Languages of Nature.*
  D. Barnouw, 242:Vol10No5-607
Jørgensen, A. Omkring Per Olov Enquists
skuespil "Fra regnormenes liv."
  P. Vinten-Johansen, 563(SS):Winter89-73
Jørgensen, K.S.R. La Théorie du roman.*
  E.J. Smyth, 208(FS):Oct89-498
Jørgensen, S. Fragments of Legal Cognition.
  J.M.O., 185:Jan90-449
Jos Fernández, M. La Capilla de San Telmo.
  A. Rodríguez G. de Ceballos, 48:Jan-
Mar89-101
Joschko, D. Oswald von Wolkenstein.
  M. Jonas, 680(ZDP):Band108Heft1-117
Joseph, J.E. Eloquence and Power.*
  A. Brakel, 320(CJL):Dec89-451
  S. Romaine, 353:Vol27No3-574
Joseph, L. Curriculum Vitae.*
  L. Upton, 448:Vol27No2-140
Joseph, L. Catherine Pozzi.
  M.C. Weitz, 207(FR):Apr90-898
Joseph, L. - see Pozzi, C.
Joseph, L.A. - see Jacob, M.
Joseph, L.E. Gaia.
  R.B. Parker, 441:8Apr90-17
Joseph, P. & H.J. Ottenheimer. Cousin Joe.
  K. Lornell, 292(JAF):Apr-Jun89-222
  E.S., 91:Vol17-104
Joseph, R. & T.B. The Rose and the Thorn.
  F. Fernea, 538(RAL):Fall89-561
Joshi, R. & R.K. Hebsur, eds. Congress in
Indian Politics.
  G. Prakash, 293(JASt):Nov89-917
Josipovici, G. The Book of God.*
  D.L. Jeffrey, 627(UTQ):Summer90-569
  R. Shankman, 150(DR):Winter88/89-531
Josipovici, G. In the Fertile Land.*
  I. Malin, 532(RCF):Summer89-255
Jost, M. Sanctuaires et cultes d'Arcadie.
  G.J.M.J. te Riele, 394:Vol42fasc1/2-240
Jouanna, J. Hippocrate, "Des Vents," "De
l'Art." (Vol 5, (Pt 1)
  V. Nutton, 123:Vol39No2-185
Jouannet, F. Des tons à l'accent.
  J.A. Blanchon, 350:Dec90-871
Joubert, J. Pensées, jugements et notations.
(R. Tessonneau, ed) Lettres à Pauline de
Beaumont et Louise Angélique de Vinti-
mille.
  O. Houbert, 98:Oct89-771
Jouet, J. Raymond Queneau.
  W.F. Motte, Jr., 207(FR):Oct89-171

Jouffroy, H. La construction publique en Italie et dans l'Afrique romaine.
R.P. Duncan-Jones, 313:Vol79-233
P. Leveau, 555:Vol62Fasc2-379
R.J.A. Wilson, 123:Vol39No2-346
Jouve, N.W. Colette.*
H. Michot-Dietrich, 395(MFS):Summer89-359
Jovanovich, W. The Money Trail.
N. Callendar, 441:15Apr90-19
Jovanovich, W. The World's Last Night.
N. Johnson, 441:9Sep90-30
Jover, J.M. - see Sender, R.J.
Jovicic, V. Once There Was a Man.
M. Junyk, 529(QQ):Spring89-155
Jovino, M.B. - see under Bonghi Jovino, M.
Jowitt, D. Time and the Dancing Image.
L. Garafola, 151:Mar89-74
Joy, L.S. Gassendi the Atomist.*
E.D. James, 208(FS):Oct89-461
R.W.F. Kroll, 319:Apr90-297
F.S. & E. Michael, 242:Vol10No2-254
Joyce, J. James Joyce's Letters to Sylvia Beach, 1921-1940.* (M. Banta & O.A. Silverman, eds)
M.P.L., 295(JML):Fall88/Winter89-357
L. Milesi, 395(MFS):Summer89-323
S. Pinsker, 639(VQR):Summer89-573
Joyce, J. Ulysses. [etchings by R. Motherwell]
R.B. Woodward, 55:Apr89-127
Joyce, J.A. Richard Wright's Art of Tragedy.*
P.R.J., 295(JML):Fall88/Winter89-425
Joyce, P.W. English as We Speak it in Ireland. (2nd ed)
M. Filppula, 272(IUR):Spring89-171
Joyce, W. First Born of an Ass.
R. Fuller, 441:4Mar90-24
Joyes, C. Monet's Table. (British title: Monet's Cookery Notebooks.)
J. Flam, 453(NYRB):17May90-9
M.J. Rosen, 441:20May90-31
B. Thomson, 617(TLS):2-8Feb90-127
Ju-k'ang, T. - see under T'ien Ju-k'ang
Juchem, J.G. - see Ungeheuer, G.
Judd, A. Ford Madox Ford.
G. Vidal, 617(TLS):22-28Jun90-659
Judd, A. Tango.
N. Callendar, 441:19Aug90-17
J. Lewis, 364:Aug/Sep89-142
Judd, B. Formula One.
N. Callendar, 441:15Apr90-19
Judd, D. Give Sorrow Words.
C. Moorehead, 617(TLS):16-22Mar90-297
Judis, J.B. William F. Buckley, Jr.
J.L. De Vitis, 115:Spring89-189
639(VQR):Winter89-19
Judkins, R.A., ed. Iroquois Studies.
E. Tooker, 292(JAF):Apr-Jun89-251
Judovitz, D. Subjectivity and Representation in Descartes.*
T.S. Champlin, 518:Apr89-85
K. Robra, 475:Vol16No8-300
C. Wilson, 242:Vol10No3-387
Jukes, P. A Shout in the Street.
442(NY):27Aug90-94
Juliar, M. Vladimir Nabokov.
J. Grayson, 575(SEER):Jul89-461
Juliet, C. L'Année de l'éveil.
D. Pobel, 450(NRF):Apr89-97
Julliard, J. La Faute à Rousseau.
K.S. Vincent, 242:Vol10No2-237

Jullien, F. Procès ou création.
L. Vandermeersch, 98:Aug-Sep89-588
Jullien, F. La valeur allusive.*
V. Alleton, 98:Aug-Sep89-661
Jun, L.X. - see under Li Xiao Jun
"June Four."* (Z. Jin & Q. Zhou, trans)
J. Mirsky, 453(NYRB):1Feb90-21
Jung, C. Paradiesvögel.
W. Paulsen, 133:Band22Heft1-77
Jung, F. Werke in Einzelausgaben. (Vols 6 & 10) (L. Schulenburg, ed)
W. Paulsen, 133:Band22Heft1-76
Jung, U.O.H. An International Bibliography of Computer-Assisted Language Learning with Annotations in German.
S. Olsen, 399(MLJ):Autumn89-345
Jünger, E. Die Schere.
M. Hulse, 617(TLS):10-16Aug90-842
Junghyo, A. Silver Stallion.
D. Murray, 441:4Feb90-18
Jungius, J. Disputationes Hamburgenses. (C. Müller-Glauser, ed)
H. Breger, 706:Band21Heft1-131
Jungk, P.S. Franz Werfel.
P-L. Adams, 61:Apr90-108
J. Simon, 441:29Apr90-15
A.A. Wallas, 602:Band20Heft1-130
442(NY):2Jul90-74
Junnosuke, M. - see under Masumi Junnosuke
Junor, J. Listening for a Midnight Tram.
C. Brown, 617(TLS):9-15Nov90-1204
Junot, L. At the Court of Napoleon.
E. Morris, 442(NY):23Apr90-110
de Junta, J. - see under Jacobo de Junta
Jur'enen, S. Narušitel' granicy.
N. Perlina, 574(SEEJ):Spring89-136
Jürgensen, K.A., comp. The Bournonville Ballets.
M. Hunt, 151:Jan89-66
Just, R. Women in Athenian Law and Life.
H. King, 617(TLS):30Mar-5Apr90-341
Justice, D. The Semantics of Form in Arabic.
P. Stevens, 399(MLJ):Winter89-493
Justice, D. The Sunset Maker.*
B. Howard, 491:Sep89-342
Justin Martyr. Apologies. (A. Wartelle, ed & trans)
C. Osborne, 303(JoHS):Vol109-271
Justinian. Justinian's "Institutes."* (P. Birks & G. McLeod, trans)
D. Ingsley, 313:Vol79-266
R. Seager, 123:Vol39No2-274

Kabakov, A. No Return.
J. Daynard, 441:11Nov90-60
Kabbani, R. Letter to Christendom.
J. Rizkalla, 364:Feb/Mar90-136
Kabisch, T. Liszt und Schubert.
W. Dömling, 417:Oct-Dec89-383
Kadare, I. Broken April.
S. Altinel, 617(TLS):7-13Dec90-1327
Kadaré, I. Poèmes 1955/1985.
L. Kovacs, 450(NRF):Sep89-110
Kaddour, H. La Fin des vendanges.
L. Ray, 450(NRF):Sep89-96
Kaden, W. Signale des Aufbruchs.
I. Lammel, 654(WB):2/1989-337
Kadir, D. Questing Fictions.*
R.W. Fiddian, 86(BHS):Jan89-111
J.E. Holloway, Jr., 268(IFR):Summer90-143
G. Kirkpatrick, 345(KRQ):May89-249

Kadohata, C. The Floating World.*
    J. Mellors, 364:Dec89/Jan90-126
Kaehler, K.E. Leibniz' Position der Rational-
    ität.
    G.H.R. Parkinson, 706:Band21Heft2-209
Kael, P. Hooked.*
    P. French, 617(TLS):7-13Sep90-948
Kaelin, E.F. Heidegger's "Being and Time."
    R.A. Prier, 478(P&L):Oct89-406
Kaempfer, J. Emile Zola.
    L. Kamm, 207(FR):Feb90-549
Kaes, A. Deutschlandbilder.
    M.E. Geisler, 221(GQ):Summer89-438
Kaes, A. From "Hitler" to "Heimat."*
    C. Koonz, 441:14Jan90-22
Kaeuper, R.W. War, Justice and Public Order.
    J.R. Maddicott, 382(MAE):1989/2-314
Kafitz, D., ed. Dekadenz in Deutschland.
    G.C. Schoolfield, 133:Band22Heft3/4-349
Kafka, B., ed. The James Beard Celebration
    Cookbook.
    M. O'Neill, 441:16Dec90-25
Kafka, F. Der Process. (M. Pasley, ed) Tage-
    bücher. (H-G. Koch, M. Müller & M. Pasley,
    eds)
    R. Robertson, 617(TLS):28Sep-4Oct90-
    1040
Kafka, R. - see Jeffers, U. & R.
Kafker, F.A., with S.L. Kafker. The Encyclo-
    pedists as Individuals.
    R. Rey, 530:Oct89-157
Kagan, D. The Fall of the Athenian Empire.*
    M.R. Crist, 124:Nov-Dec89-133
    H.D. Yunis, 121(CJ):Apr-May90-360
Kagan, J.M. I.V. Cvetaev: Žizn'.
    P. Chester, 574(SEEJ):Fall89-461
Kagan, R.L., ed. Ciudades del Siglo de Oro.
    J. Bury, 90:Oct89-714
Kagan, R.L. Lucrecia's Dreams.
    P. Burke, 617(TLS):30Nov-6Dec90-1296
Kagan, R.L. - see van den Wyngaerde, A.
Kagan, S. Archduke Rudolph, Beethoven's
    Patron, Pupil and Friend.
    K. Korsyn, 415:Nov80-681
Kagarlitsky, B. The Dialectic of Change.
    J. Sherr, 617(TLS):16-22Mar90-273
Kahan, A. Russian Economic History.
    630(VQR):Autumn89-117
Kahn, A. J-K. Huysmans.*
    R.B. Antosh, 446(NCFS):Spring-
    Summer90-544
    Y. Thomas, 207(FR):Oct89-167
Kahrs, E., ed. Kalyāṇamitrārāgaṇam.*
    J. Bronkhorst, 259(IIJ):Apr89-171
Kaige, C. & T. Rayns - see under Chen Kaige
    & T. Rayns
Kaiko, T. Five Thousand Runaways.
    J. Melville, 617(TLS):16-22Nov90-1233
Kaimio, M. Physical Contact in Greek Trag-
    edy.
    E.M. Craik, 303(JoHS):Vol109-230
Kain, P.J. Marx's Method, Epistemology, and
    Humanism.
    R. Hudelson, 488:Jun89-223
Kainz, H.P. Ethics in Context.
    O. O'Neill, 518:Oct89-237
    J.L.S., 185:Jan90-440
Kainz, H.P. Paradox, Dialectic, and System.
    J.B.R., 185:Jan90-457
Kainz, H.P., ed. Philosophical Perspectives on
    Peace.
    M.G., 185:Jan90-464

Kairys, D., ed. The Politics of Law.
    V. Kahn, 153:Summer89-21
Kaiser, K. & H-P. Schwarz, eds. Weltpolitik.
    H. Hanak, 575(SEER):Oct89-665
Kajon, I. Ebraismo e sistema di filosofia in
    Hermann Cohen.
    P. Trotignon, 542:Oct-Dec89-614
Kakonis, T. Criss Cross.
    M. Stasio, 441:4Feb90-26
Kalaidjian, W. Languages of Liberation.
    J. Monroe, 659(ConL):Winter90-542
Kaldor, M., G. Holden & R. Falk, eds. The New
    Détente.
    W.F. Kimball, 617(TLS):8-14Jun90-601
Kalinowski, G. - see Regnerus, C.
Kallendorf, C. - see Petrarch
Kallir, J. Egon Schiele: The Complete Works.
    J. Russell, 441:2Dec90-9
Kallmann, H. A History of Music in Canada
    1534-1914.
    R. Elliott, 529(QQ):Spring89-110
Kalman, L. Abe Fortas.
    S.V. Roberts, 441:11Nov90-19
von Kalnein, W. & S. Anif. Ein Denkmal bay-
    erischer Romantik in Salzburg.
    G. Himmelheber, 683:Band52Heft4-586
Kalnins, M. - see Lawrence, D.H.
Kalstone, D. Becoming a Poet. (R. Hemenway,
    ed)
    T. Gunn, 617(TLS):27Jul-2Aug90-791
    K. Pollitt, 441:14Jan90-3
Kalton, M.C. To Become a Sage.
    D. Baker, 293(JASt):May89-411
Kalupahana, D.J. Nāgārjuna.*
    C. Lindtner, 318(JAOS):Jan-Mar88-176
Kamath, P.M., ed. Indo-U.S. Relations.
    M.L.P. Patterson, 293(JASt):May89-426
Kamens, E. The Three Jewels.
    S. Matisoff, 293(JASt):Nov89-862
    M. Ury, 407(MN):Winter89-485
Kamensky, A. Chagall: The Russian Years
    1907-1922.*
    S. West, 617(TLS):12-18Jan90-38
Kamensky, A. Martiros Saryan.
    M.M. Mudrak, 550(RusR):Oct89-443
Kaminer, W. A Fearful Freedom.
    F.V. Spelman, 441:27May90-8
Kaminski, A. Kith and Kin.*
    B.K. Horvath, 532(RCF):Spring89-269
de Kamiński, J.M. "... Nápred i Názad se ogle-
    dát."
    C.R. Ligota, 575(SEER):Jul89-472
Kaminski, T. The Early Career of Samuel
    Johnson.*
    A.F.T. Lurcock, 447(N&Q):Mar89-113
    D. Womersley, 541(RES):May89-274
Kamioka, K., A. Rahbar & A.A. Hamidi. Com-
    parative Basic Vocabulary of Khonji and
    Lārī: Lārestāni Studies 2.
    P.O. Skjaervø, 318(JAOS):Apr-Jun88-325
Kamioka, K. & M. Yamada. Lārestāni Studies
    1: Lāri Basic Vocabulary.
    P.O. Skjaervø, 318(JAOS):Apr-Jun88-325
Kammen, M. Selvages & Biases.
    S.J. Whitfield, 639(VQR):Spring89-361
Kammen, M. Sovereignty and Liberty.
    R.A. Rutland, 432(NEQ):Sep89-450
Kamp, A. Die politische Philosophie des Aris-
    toteles und ihre metaphysischen Grund-
    lagen.
    E. Schütrumpf, 229:Band61Heft4-293
Kamphoefner, W.D. The Westfalians.
    C.L. Venable, 658:Summer/Autumn89-194

Kamuf, P. Signature Pieces.
   R. Chambers, 210(FrF):Sep89-373
   S.A. Schwartz, 400(MLN):Sep89-936
Kan, Z. — see under Zhong Kan
Kanda, M. Widows of Hiroshima.
   M. Hane, 293(JASt):Aug89-616
Kandell, J. La Capital.
   639(VQR):Spring89-45
Kane, D. The Sino-Jurchen Vocabulary of the
   Bureau of Interpreters.
   K.A. Krippes, 215(GL):Vol29No4-286
Kane, G. Chaucer.
   C.J. Watkin, 148:Winter86-96
Kane, G. — see Langland, W.
Kane, G. & E.T. Donaldson — see Langland, W.
Kane, P. Famine in China, 1959-61.
   R.E. Barrett, 293(JASt):Aug89-591
Kane, R. Free Will and Values.*
   M. Bernstein, 449:Sep89-557
Kane, R. & S.H. Phillips, eds. Hartshorne,
   Process Philosophy, and Theology.
   A.J. Reck, 103:Jun90-237
Kane, S. Spenser's Moral Allegory.
   M.F. Dixon, 627(UTQ):Fall89-118
Kaneko Mitsuharu. Shijin.* (A.D. Syrokomla-
   Stefanowska, ed)
   S. Rabson, 293(JASt):May89-392
Kanet, R.E., ed. The Soviet Union, Eastern
   Europe and the Third World.
   M.E. Yapp, 575(SEER):Oct89-643
Kanev, S.N. Revoliutsiia i anarkhizm.
   P. Avrich, 550(RusR):Jan89-91
Kang, K.W. Hankwuk-e Kye Thong Non.
   K.A. Krippes, 159:Vol6No1-141
Kang, T.W. Gaishi.
   M.B. Grover, 441:28Oct90-22
Kanga, F. Trying to Grow.
   M. Couto, 617(TLS):9-15Mar90-257
Kaniuk, Y. Confessions of a Good Arab.
   B. Zelechow, 390:Dec89-44
Kansteiner, A. — see von Droste-Hülshoff, A.
Kant, I. Critique of Judgment. (W.S. Pluhar,
   trans)
   D. Dutton, 478(P&L):Oct89-426
Kant, I. Geographische und andere naturwis-
   senschaftliche Schriften. (J. Zehbe, ed)
   R. Malter, 342:Band80Heft1-93
Kant, I. I sogni di un visionario spiegati coi
   sogni della metafisica.
   C. La Rocca, 342:Band80Heft1-95
Kant, I. Kant's Latin Writings.* (L.W. Beck,
   with others, eds)
   H. Seigfried, 342:Band80Heft2-208
Kant, I. Metaphysische Anfangsgründe der
   Rechtslehre.
   W. Kersting, 53(AGP):Band71Heft1-100
Kant, I. Primera introduccion a la "Crítica
   del Juicio." (J.L. Zalabardo, trans)
   M. Caimi, 342:Band80Heft4-485
   A. Savile, 89(BJA):Spring89-181
Kant, I. Rechtslehre. (H. Klenner, ed)
   G-W. Küsters, 342:Band80Heft4-483
Kant, I. Teoría y Práctica. (M.F. Pérez López
   & R. Rodríguez Aramayo, trans)
   M. Caimi, 342:Band80Heft4-486
Kant, I. Zum ewigen Frieden.* (M. Buhr & S.
   Dietzsch, eds)
   R.M., 342:Band80Heft4-484
Kantaris, S. Dirty Washing.
   L. Mackinnon, 617(TLS):13-19Jul90-761
Kany, R. Mnemosyne als Programm.*
   M.W. Jennings, 221(GQ):Spring89-286

Kao, S. Lire Valéry.*
   B. Pratt, 345(KRQ):Feb89-113
   C. Voigt, 224(GRM):Band39Heft3-363
Kapitsa, P.L. Pis'ma o nauke. (P. Rubinin,
   ed)
   D. Holloway, 453(NYRB):1Mar90-23
Kaplan, A. & K. Ross, eds. Everyday Life.
   S. Meckling & A. Shuman, 292(JAF):Jul-
   Sep89-347
Kaplan, C. Sea Changes.
   R.B.D., 295(JML):Fall88/Winter89-185
Kaplan, C. & E.C. Rose, eds. Doris Lessing.*
   L.S. Beard, 538(RAL):Summer89-301
Kaplan, C.S. The Party and Agricultural Cri-
   sis Management in the USSR.
   R.D. Laird, 104(CASS):Spring89-97
Kaplan, D. Lewis Hine in Europe.
   J. Sturman, 55:Apr89-127
Kaplan, D.E. & A. Dubro. Yakuza.
   G.A. De Vos, 293(JASt):May89-394
Kaplan, E.A., ed. Postmodernism and its Dis-
   contents.*
   V. Li, 49:Oct89-187
Kaplan, E.A. Rocking Around the Clock.*
   E. Levy, 147:Vol6No2-63
Kaplan, F. Dickens.*
   R. Coles, 639(VQR):Summer89-569
   S. Monod, 637(VS):Spring90-513
   M. Slater, 155:Autumn89-181
Kaplan, F. Sacred Tears.*
   M. Berg, 529(QQ):Spring89-181
   V. Purton, 155:Spring89-51
Kaplan, J. Pearl's Progress.*
   G. Krist, 249(HudR):Winter89-661
Kaplan, J. & R. Atwan, eds. The Best Ameri-
   can Essays, 1990.
   D. Walton, 441:9Dec90-25
Kaplan, J., G. Papajohn & E. Zorn. Murder of
   Innocence.
   L. Green, 441:14Oct90-49
Kaplan, J.A. Unexpected Journeys.*
   M. Manley, 55:Jan89-85
   M. Schor, 62:Dec89-20
Kaplan, K. Report on the Murder of the Gen-
   eral Secretary.
   J. Skvorecký, 453(NYRB):16Aug90-41
Kaplan, R.D. Soldiers of God.
   442(NY):19Feb90-112
Kaplan, Y. From Christianity to Judaism.
   J. Israel, 617(TLS):13-19Jul90-757
Kaplan, Y., H. Méchoulan & R.H. Popkin, eds.
   Menasseh ben Israel and His World.
   G.F. Nuttall, 617(TLS):3-9Aug90-828
Kaplowitt, S.J. The Ennobling Power of Love
   in the Medieval German Lyric.*
   J.A. Schultz, 222(GR):Summer89-141
Kappeler, A., B. Meissner & G. Simon. Die
   Deutschen im russischen Reich und im Sow-
   jetstaat.
   M. McCauley, 575(SEER):Apr89-303
Kappeler, S. The Pornography of Representa-
   tion.*
   A. Soble, 488:Mar89-128
Kara-Murza, A.A. & A.K. Voskresensky, eds.
   Totalitarizm kak istoricheskii fenomen.
   Z. Bauman, 617(TLS):12-18Oct90-1095
Karageorghis, J. & O. Masson, eds. The His-
   tory of the Greek Language in Cyprus.
   J.T. Hooker, 123:Vol39No2-276
Karageorghis, V. & A. Hermary. Etudes Chyp-
   riotes. (Vol 9)
   F. Canciani, 229:Band61Heft7-644

von Karajan, H., with F. Endler. My Autobiography.
  P. Heyworth, 617(TLS):26Jan–1Feb90–92
Karamsin, N. Briefe eines russischen Reisenden. (G. Ziegler, ed)
  R.M., 342:Band80Heft4–487
Karasek, R. & T. Theorell. Healthy Work.
  R. Howard, 441:8Apr90–19
Karbo, K. Trespassers Welcome Here.*
  L. Chamberlain, 617(TLS):25–31May90–558
Karbusicky, V. Grundriss der musikalischen Semantik.
  T. Kneif, 417:Jul–Sep89–288
Karl, F.R. William Faulkner.*
  T.L. McHaney, 392:Summer89–311
  S. Pinsker, 219(GaR):Winter89–795
  W.H. Pritchard, 249(HudR):Winter89–685
Karl, F.R. & L. Davies – see Conrad, J.
Karlin, D. – see Browning, R. & E. Barrett
Karlinsky, S. Russian Drama from Its Beginnings to the Age of Pushkin.
  I.K. Lilly, 104(CASS):Spring–Winter88–495
Karlinsky, S. Marina Tsvetaeva.*
  J.A. Taubman, 104(CASS):Spring–Winter88–477
Karlsen, C.F. The Devil in the Shape of a Woman.*
  P.F. Gura, 639(VQR):Winter90–180
  S. Nissenbaum, 656(WMQ):Jul89–593
Karnow, S. In Our Image.*
  C. Hitchens, 617(TLS):30Mar–5Apr90–342
Karpinski, M. The Theatre of Andrzej Wajda.
  S. Golub, 402(MLR):Oct90–1049
Karpp, P. Ike's Boys.
  B.L. Cooper, 498:Summer89–110
Karsen, S. Ensayos de literatura e historia iberoamericana/Essays on Iberoamerican Literature and History.
  C.J. Alonso, 238:Sep89–557
Kartini, R.A. Letters of a Javanese Princess. (H. Geertz, ed) (A.L. Symmers, trans)
  H.M.J. Maier, 318(JAOS):Jan–Mar88–195
Kartsonis, A.D. Anastasis.
  K. Corrigan, 54:Jun89–312
  D. Kinney, 589:Jul89–723
Karumanchiri Polesini, L. & R.U. Maiguashca. L'italiano d'oggi.
  J. Siracusa, 399(MLJ):Spring89–94
Kasack, W. Dictionary of Russian Literature since 1917.
  R. Russell, 402(MLR):Apr90–540
Kasack, W. Entsiklopedicheskii slovar' russkoi literatury s 1917 goda.
  A. McMillin, 575(SEER):Oct89–618
Kasack, W. Lexikon der russischen Literatur ab 1917: Ergänzungsband.*
  A.F. Zweers, 104(CASS):Spring–Winter88–506
Kasack, W. Schicksal und Gestaltung.
  G.A. Hosking, 688(ZSP):Band49Heft1–193
Kaser, M.C. & E.A. Radice, eds. The Economic History of Eastern Europe 1919–1975. (Vols 1–3)
  D.A. Dyker, 575(SEER):Jul89–481
Käser, R. Die Schwierigkeit, ich zu sagen.
  W. Tschacher, 221(GQ):Winter89–109
Kashner, R. The Graceful Exit.
  E. Stumpf, 441:6May90–23
Kaslow, A.J. & A.J. Pickett 4th. Neighbors.
  F. De Caro, 582(SFQ):Vol46No1–83

Kason, N.M. Breaking Traditions.
  R. Ocasio, 552(REH):Oct89–138
Kasparov, G., with D. Trelford. Unlimited Challenge.
  P. Hoffman, 441:7Oct90–14
Kasper, K., ed. Die Serapionsbrüder von Petrograd.
  G. Schaumann, 654(WB):7/1989–1216
Kasper, M., ed. Language and Culture of the Lusatian Sorbs Throughout Their History.
  C.A. Ferguson, 355(LSoc):Sep89–419
Kassel, R. Die Abgrenzung des Hellenismus in der griechischen Literaturgeschichte.
  W.G. Arnott, 303(JoHS):Vol109–236
Kassel, R. & C. Austin, eds. Poetae Comici Graeci.* (Vol 3, Pt 2)
  H–J. Newiger, 229:Band61Heft1–1
  J.T.M.F. Pieters, 394:Vol42fasc3/4–539
Kassel, R. & C. Austin, eds. Poetae comici Graeci.* (Vol 5)
  W. Luppe, 303(JoHS):Vol109–228
Kasten, I. Frauendienst bei Trobadors und Minnesängern im 12. Jahrhundert.*
  H–H.S. Räkel, 680(ZDP):Band108Heft3–417
Kästner, E. Fabian.
  D.J. Enright, 617(TLS):4–10May90–479
Kastovsky, D. & G. Bauer, with J. Fisiak, eds. Luick Revisited.
  H. Penzl, 350:Mar90–194
Kasulis, T.P. – see Yuasa Yasuo
Kasza, G.J. The State and the Mass Media in Japan, 1918–1945.*
  W.M. Fletcher, 293(JASt):Feb89–168
Katai, T. Literary Life in Tōkyō, 1885–1915.* (K.G. Henshall, ed & trans)
  J. Rubin, 244(HJAS):Jun89–282
Kataoka, T. & R.H. Myers. Defending an Economic Superpower.
  J. Bowen, 293(JASt):Nov89–864
Katō, S. A History of Japanese Literature.
  R. Tsukimura, 678(YCGL):No36–180
Katriel, T. Talking Straight.
  L–R. Bloch, 355(LSoc):Mar89–112
Katz, D.S. Sabbath and Sectarianism in Seventeenth–Century England.*
  R.H. Popkin, 242:Vol10No6–740
Katz, D.S. & J.I. Israel, eds. Sceptics, Millenarians and Jews.
  G.F. Nuttall, 617(TLS):3–9Aug90–828
Katz, I.J. & J.E. Keller, with others, eds. Studies on the "Cantigas de Santa Maria."
  N.J. Dyer, 238:May89–296
  M.E. Schaffer, 240(HR):Winter89–79
Katz, J.J. The Philosophy of Linguistics.
  D. Roberts, 479(PhQ):Jan89–133
Katz, M.B. Reconstructing American Education.
  I.R. Dowbiggin, 106:Fall89–289
Katz, M.B. The Undeserving Poor.
  L.B. Schorr, 441:21Jan90–29
Katz, R. Naked by the Window.
  V. Patrick, 441:10Jun90–24
Katz, R. & C. Dahlhaus, eds. Contemplating Music.* (Vol 1)
  L. Botstein, 451:Fall89–168
  W. Wiora, 417:Jul–Sep89–289
Katz, S.L. Elinor Frost.
  E.J. Ingebretsen, 27(AL):Dec89–704
Katz, W.R. Rider Haggard and the Fiction of Empire.*
  P. Brantlinger, 177(ELT):Vol32No2–217
    [continued]

Katz, W.R. Rider Haggard and the Fiction of Empire. [continuing]
  B. Gasser, 447(N&Q):Sep89-410
  L. Hartveit, 179(ES):Dec89-590
  W. Templeton, 178:Sep89-348
  M. Tucker, 538(RAL):Fall89-584
Kaufman, J. Broken Alliance.
  J. Brent, 390:May89-59
Kaufman, M. Mad Dreams, Saving Graces.*
  I. Irwin-Zarecka, 390:Dec89-28
Kaulbach, F. Immanuel Kants "Grundlegung zur Metaphysik der Sitten."
  U.J. Wenzel, 342:Band80Heft4-472
Kavalek, L. World Cup Chess.
  C. Russ, 617(TLS):26Oct-1Nov90-1159
Kavan, A. My Madness. (B.W. Aldiss, ed)
  S. Roe, 617(TLS):11-17May90-496
Kavanagh, P.J. Finding Connections.
  P. Parker, 617(TLS):6-12Apr90-366
Kavanagh, T.M., ed. The Limits of Theory.
  G. Brahm, Jr., 599:Summer90-316
Kavanagh, T.M. Writing the Truth.*
  J.J. Allison, 188(ECr):Spring89-101
Kavass, I.I. Soviet Law in English.
  E. Huskey, 550(RusR):Jul89-337
Kavka, G.S. Hobbesian Moral and Political Theory.*
  C.A.J. Coady, 518:Jan89-19
  S. Hetcher, 393(Mind):Jul89-435
  L. May, 449:Sep89-560
  A.J. Simmons, 482(PhR):Jul89-404
Kavka, G.S. Moral Paradoxes of Nuclear Deterrence.
  L. Stevenson, 479(PhQ):Apr89-250
Kawabata, Y. The Old Capital.*
  C.L. Chua & T. Yamamoto, 573(SSF):Winter89-96
Kawabata, Y. Palm-of-the-Hand Stories.
  P. Anderer, 293(JASt):Nov89-865
  S.J. Napier, 407(MN):Spring89-113
Kawachi, Y., ed. Calendar of English Renaissance Drama 1558-1642.*
  W. Habicht, 156(ShJW):Jahrbuch1989-385
  K. Smidt, 179(ES):Feb89-86
Kawai, H. The Japanese Psyche.
  C. Schooler, 293(JASt):Nov89-866
Kay, C. Political Constructions.
  C.H. Hinnant, 594:Winter89-452
  R. Kroll, 173(ECS):Fall89-103
  639(VQR):Spring89-49
Kay, D., ed. Sir Philip Sidney.
  M.G. Brennan, 541(RES):May89-252
  A.V. Ettin, 677(YES):Vol20-247
  V. Skretkowicz, 557:Sep89-336
  R. Wymer, 179(ES):Apr89-178
Kay, G.G. The Summer Tree. The Wandering Fire. The Darkest Hour.
  J.R. Wytenbroek, 102(CanL):Autumn-Winter89-262
Kay, T. To Dance with the White Dog.
  C.D. Thompson, 441:30Dec90-14
Kaye, A.S. Nigerian Arabic-English Dictionary.
  M. Woidich, 318(JAOS):Oct-Dec88-663
Kaye, E. Les Correspondants de Charles Weiss.
  F. Bassan, 446(NCFS):Spring-Summer90-557
  A. Kies, 535(RHL):Jul-Aug89-737
Kaye, H.J. - see Kiernan, V.
Kaye, M.M. The Sun in the Morning.
  G.C. Ward, 441:30Sep90-14

Kaysen, S. Far Afield.
  P-L. Adams, 61:Nov90-172
  S. Lee, 441:4Nov90-24
Kazantzaki, N. Ascèse (Salvatores Dei). (A. Izzet, ed)
  F.M., 450(NRF):May89-100
Kazantzis, J. Flame Tree.*
  D. McDuff, 565:Spring89-76
Kazantzis, J. A Poem for Guatemala.
  S. Knight, 364:Apr/May89-129
Kazazis, J.N., ed. Philippikōn Hrētorikai Lexeis.
  I. Rutherford, 123:Vol39No1-137
Kazin, A. A Writer's America.*
  D. Scheese, 658:Winter89-303
  639(VQR):Spring89-49
Kazin, A. & D. Finn. Our New York.
  A. Broyard, 441:14Jan90-9
Kazuko, A.R. Microphones.
  S. Morrissey, 102(CanL):Winter88-146
Kazuko, O. - see under Ono Kazuko
Kealey, E.J. Harvesting the Air.
  J.L. Langdon, 589:Apr89-451
Kean, B.H., with T. Dahlby. M.D.
  J.G. Deaton, 441:11Feb90-20
Keane, P.J. Terrible Beauty.
  C.W. Barrow, 174(Éire):Summer89-146
  J. Stokes, 402(MLR):Jul90-707
Keane, P.J. Yeats's Interactions with Tradition.*
  R. Rooksby, 447(N&Q):Jun89-258
  R. Taylor, 402(MLR):Jan90-160
Kearney, A. John Churton Collins.*
  S. Pickering, 569(SR):Spring89-xliv
Kearney, R. Transitions.*
  B. Benstock, 395(MFS):Summer89-331
  B. Cosgrove, 272(IUR):Spring89-161
Kearns, C.M. T.S. Eliot and Indic Traditions.*
  R. Crawford, 541(RES):Nov89-590
  M. Moran, 27(AL):Mar89-136
  K.E. Roby, 149(CLS):Vol26No1-80
Kearns, M.S. Metaphors of Mind in Fiction and Psychology.*
  J. Batchelor, 402(MLR):Jan90-157
  M. Turner, 405(MP):Aug89-112
  566:Spring89-187
Keating, P. The Haunted Study.*
  J.R. Reed, 637(VS):Summer90-647
Keats, J. The Essential Keats. (P. Levine, ed)
  P. Mariani, 434:Spring90-313
Keaveney, A. Rome and the Unification of Italy.*
  P. Culham, 124:Nov-Dec89-134
  H. Galsterer, 229:Band61Heft3-219
Keaveney, R., with others. Views of Rome from the Thomas Ashby Collection in the Vatican Library.
  M.J. Miller, 380:Autumn89-239
Keay, S.J. Roman Spain.*
  J. Edmondson, 313:Vol79-240
  J.S. Richardson, 123:Vol39No2-318
  639(VQR):Winter89-8
Keck, G.R. & S.V. Martin, eds. Feel the Spirit.
  D.E. McGinty, 91:Vol17-181
Keeble, N.H., ed. John Bunyan.
  G. Midgley, 447(N&Q):Sep89-395
Keeble, N.H. The Literary Culture of Nonconformity in Later Seventeenth-Century England.*
  T.N. Corns, 506(PSt):May89-97
  P. Hammond, 541(RES):Feb89-121
  T.H. Luxon, 551(RenQ):Winter89-893

Keefe, R. & J.A. Walter Pater and the Gods of Disorder.*
  F.C. McGrath, 177(ELT):Vol32No2-220
Keefer, J.K. Reading Mavis Gallant.
  B. Powell, 647:Spring89-77
Keefer, J.K. Transfigurations.
  P. Stevens, 529(QQ):Autumn89-720
Keefer, J.K. Under Eastern Eyes.*
  L. Ricou, 102(CanL):Summer89-140
Keegan, J. The Second World War.*
  P-L. Adams, 61:Feb90-107
  442(NY):23Apr90-116
Keel, A. - see Bjørnson, B.
Keele, A.F. Understanding Günter Grass.*
  L. Caltvedt, 221(GQ):Fall89-553
Keeler, R.F. Newsday.
  J.V. Turk, 441:7Oct90-41
Keeley, E. The Salonika Bay Murder.*
  H. Brogan, 617(TLS):29Jun-5Jul90-708
Keeley, M. A Social-Contract Theory of Organizations.
  J.P. Olsen, 185:Apr90-681
Keeling, N. A Fine and Quiet Place.
  A. Jarman, 376:Jun89-127
  H. Thompson, 102(CanL):Autumn-Winter89-250
Keen, M. The Glory of the English Garden.
  R.I. Ross, 617(TLS):19-25Jan90-74
Keenan, D. & R. Lloyd, eds. Looking for Home.
  D. Jersild, 441:25Nov90-18
Keenan, E.L. Universal Grammar.
  P. Chevillet, 189(EA):Apr-Jun80-00D
  G. Mallinson, 297(JL):Mar89-259
Keene, D. The Pleasures of Japanese Literature.*
  D.E. Mills, 407(MN):Winter89-495
Keene, R. Chess.
  B. Hochberg, 441:21Oct90-24
Kees, W. Fall Quarter. (J. Reidel, ed)
  B. Tauss, 441:25Nov90-18
Kees, W. Reviews and Essays, 1936-55. (J. Reidel, ed)
  M. Boruch, 29(APR):Mar/Apr89-41
Keesing, R.M. Melanesian Pidgin and the Oceanic Substrate
  P. Mühlhäusler, 603:Vol13No2-459
Keesman-Marwitz, A.H. Das Primat der objektiven Zeit.
  M. Astman, 104(CASS):Spring-Winter88-425
  S. Spieker, 575(SEER):Jan89-124
  A.A. Tavis, 574(SEEJ):Fall89-454
Kefala, A. European Notebook.
  W. Tonetto, 581:Dec89-660
Kehler, D. Problems in Literary Research. (3rd ed)
  J.R. Kelly, 87(BB):Jun89-140
Kehoe, D.P. The Economics of Agriculture on Roman Imperial Estates in North Africa.
  S. Spurr, 313:Vol79-235
Keiler, O. & P. Schaefer, eds. Theodor Fontane im literarischen Leben seiner Zeit.
  P. Howe, 402(MLR):Jul90-807
Keinästö, K. Studien zu Infinitivkonstruktionen im mittelhochdeutschen Prosa-Lancelot.
  H. Beckers, 680(ZDP):Band108Heft3-461
Keiser, R. Adonis and Janus. La Forza della Virtù. Claudius and Nebucadnezar.
  W. Braun, 417:Oct-Dec89-390
Keith, S., with A. Tapert. Slim.
  M. Jefferson, 441:24Jun90-13

Keith, W.J. Regions of the Imagination.*
  V.J. Bowes, 529(QQ):Winter89-977
  N. Page, 301(JEGP):Oct89-547
Kekes, J. The Examined Life.*
  P. Butchvarov, 543:Dec89-406
Kekes, J. Moral Tradition and Individuality.
  L. Armour, 103:Apr90-146
  M. Strasser, 543:Jun90-870
Kelikian, A.A. Town and Country under Fascism.
  P. Morgan, 278(IS):Vol43-179
Keller, B. Improvisation in Creative Drama.
  D.E. Kemp, 108:Summer89-88
Keller, H. Zwischen regionaler Begrenzung und universalem Horizont.
  C.R. Bowlus, 589:Jan89-180
Keller, H-E., ed. Romance Epic.
  W.G. van Emden, 382(MAE):1989/1-161
Keller, H-E., with others, eds. Studia Occitanica in memoriam Paul Remy.* (Vol 1)
  K. Klingebiel, 545(RPh):Feb90-501
Keller, H-E., with others, eds. Studia Occitanica in memoriam Paul Remy.* (Vol 2)
  K. Klingebiel, 545(RPh):Feb90-501
  W.D. Paden, 589:Jul89-725
Keller, J.E. Collectanea Hispanica. (D.P. Seniff & M.I. Montoya Ramírez, eds)
  J.S. Geary, 238:Dec89-954
Keller, J.E. Las narraciones breves piadosas versificadas en el castellano y gallego del medievo de Berceo a Alfonso X.* (A.A. Fernández-Vázquez, ed & trans)
  D.W. Belznick, 238:May89-896
Keller, L. Re-Making It New.
  I.F.A. Bell, 447(N&Q):Jun89-270
  P. Douglass, 402(MLR):Jan90-172
  S. Matson, 432(NEQ):Sep89-473
  D. Porter, 27(AL):Mar89-146
  P.C. Willis, 405(MP):Feb90-327
Kellerman, J. Time Bomb.
  V. Patrick, 441:14Oct90-43
Kellermann-Haaf, P. Frau und Politik im Mittelalter.
  T. Ehlert, 680(ZDP):Band108Heft3-442
Kelley, A.V. "To the Lighthouse."*
  S.B., 295(JML):Fall88/Winter89-422
Kelley, J.T., A.R. Kelley & O.H. Pilkey, Jr. Living with the Coast of Maine.
  P. Rosen, 432(NEQ):Dec89-641
Kelley, P. & R. Hudson - see Browning, R. & E.B.
Kelley, T.M. Wordsworth's Revisionary Aesthetics.
  D.H. Bialostosky, 445(NCF):Sep89-237
  J.D. Gutteridge, 447(N&Q):Mar89-116
  L. Lachman, 494:Fall89-646
  D. Morse, 89(BJA):Autumn89-387
  G.W. Ruoff, 661(WC):Autumn89-182
Kelliny, W.W.H. Language Communicative Needs.
  J.N. Davis, 399(MLJ):Winter89-489
Kellner, B., ed. A Gertrude Stein Companion.
  M. Hoffman, 395(MFS):Summer89-279
Kellner, M. Dogma in Medieval Jewish Thought.
  D. Novak, 485(PE&W):Jan89-98
Kellogg, D., with Liu Fei & Tang Min. In Search of China. (D. Stein, ed)
  D.S. Walwyn, 617(TLS):6-12Apr90-369
Kellogg, R., comp. A Concordance to Eddic Poetry.
  H. O'Donoghue, 541(RES):Nov89-601

Kelly, A., ed & trans. The German Worker.
M.J. Neufeld, 242:Vol10No3-378
H. Suhr, 221(GQ):Spring89-283
Kelly, A. Mrs. Coade's Stone.
D.G.C. Allan, 324:Oct90-794
H. Colvin, 617(TLS):14-20Sep90-982
Kelly, A.C. Swift and the English Language.
F.N. Smith, 566:Autumn89-57
S. Soupel, 189(EA):Jan-Mar89-101
Kelly, B. & M. London. The Four Little Drag-
ons.*
S. Winchester, 617(TLS):1-7Jun90-577
Kelly, C. Rousseau's Exemplary Life.*
M. Cranston, 208(FS):Jan89-89
T. L'Aminot, 535(RHL):Jul-Aug89-720
J.C. O'Neal, 207(FR):Dec89-376
Kelly, C., M. Makin & D. Shepherd, eds. Dis-
continuous Discourses in Modern Russian
Literature.
F. Beardow, 402(MLR):Oct90-1052
Kelly, D. Fictional Genders.
T. Dawson, 268(IFR):Summer89-150
Kelly, D. Narrative Strategies in Joyce's
"Ulysses."
J. Heininger, 329(JJQ):Spring90-686
Kelly, F. Frederic Edwin Church and the Na-
tional Landscape.
658:Summer/Autumn89-207
Kelly, G. English Fiction of the Romantic
Period 1789-1830.
J. Thompson, 166:Jan90-176
Kelly, H.A. Chaucer and the Cult of Saint
Valentine.
M.J. Ehrhart, 301(JEGP):Apr89-223
P. Hardman, 677(YES):Vol20-236
J.P. McCall, 589:Apr89-453
Kelly, J. Women, History and Theory.
J. Lewis, 242:Vol10No5-619
Kelly, J.N.D. St. Edmund Hall.
R. Highfield, 617(TLS):2-8Mar90-230
Kelly, K. One Singular Sensation.
D. Kaufman, 441:11Feb90-19
M.B. Siegel, 34:Mar90-34
Kelly, L., ed. Tobias Smollett: The Critical
Heritage.*
J.V. Price, 447(N&Q):Mar89-112
K. Sutherland, 541(RES):Nov89-566
566:Spring89-179
Kelly, M., ed & trans. Jousts of Aphrodite.
D.L. Clayman, 124:Sep-Oct89-72
Kelly, M.T. A Dream Like Mine.*
S.D. Canvin, 529(QQ):Spring89-158
T. Craig, 102(CanL):Summer89-154
Kelly, R. Doctor of Silence.*
42(AR):Winter89-115
Kelly, R. The Flowers of Unceasing Coinci-
dence.
D.C.D. Gansz, 703:Spring89-200
Kelly, R. V.S. Naipaul.
H.S. Mann, 395(MFS):Winter89-870
Kelly, R.J. - see Berryman, J.
Kelly, V. - see Walch, G.
Kelman, J. A Disaffection.*
T. Nairn, 571(ScLJ):Winter89-35
Kelsall, M. Byron's Politics.*
J.K. Chandler, 677(YES):Vol20-294
A. Nicholson, 661(WC):Autumn89-207
Kelsall, M. Studying Drama.
G. Bas, 189(EA):Apr-Jun89-192
Kelsen, H. Die Illusion der Gerechtigkeit.
R. Ferber, 687:Jul-Sep89-557
Kelso, J.A.S. & K.G. Munhall - see Stetson,
R.H.

Kelvin, N. - see Morris, W.
Kemal, S. Kant and Fine Art.*
D. Dutton, 478(P&L):Oct89-428
K.F. Rogerson, 290(JAAC):Spring89-179
H. Williams, 342:Band80Heft4-481
van Kemenade, A. Syntactic Case and Mor-
phological Case in the History of English.
C.L. Allen, 350:Mar90-146
C. Platzack, 353:Vol27No5-948
Kemp, B.R., ed. Reading Abbey Cartularies.
(Vol 1)
W.T. Reedy, 589:Apr89-454
Kemp, I., ed. Hector Berlioz: "Les Troyens."*
I. Keys, 415:Oct89-612
M.B. Tepper, 465:Summer90-149
Kemp, M. The Science of Art.
J.M. Nash, 617(TLS):31Aug-6Sep90-919
Kemp, P. Some Talk Magic.
P.M. St. Pierre, 102(CanL):Spring89-210
Kemp, S. Kipling's Hidden Narratives.*
B. Gasser, 447(N&Q):Dec89-537
D. Hewitt, 184(EIC):Oct89-340
A. Parry, 346(KJ):Jun89-23
Kemp, W. Sermo Corporeus.
H.A. Tummers, 640:Nov89-153
Kemp, W.H. Burgundian Court Song in the
Time of Binchois.
I. Fenlon, 617(TLS):22-28Jun90-670
Kempe, F. Divorcing the Dictator.
M. Massing, 453(NYRB):17May90-43
T. Powers, 441:18Feb90-1
442(NY):21May90-95
Kempen, G., ed. Natural Language Genera-
tion.
L. Proctor, 350:Jun90-418
Kemper, H-G. Deutsche Lyrik der frühen
Neuzeit.* (Vol 1)
D. Ignasiak, 654(WB):10/1989-1752
H-J. Schlütter, 301(JEGP):Apr89-286
J. Van Cleve, 406:Summer89-252
Kemper, R. Gewalt sunder rat vervellet under
seinem laste.
J. Schmidt, 564:Nov89-347
Kempers, A.J.B. - see under Bernet Kempers,
A.J.
Kempf, F.R. Albrecht von Hallers Ruhm als
Dichter.
W. Paulsen, 221(GQ):Winter89-105
Kendall, E. The Runaway Bride.
D. Jacobs, 441:4Nov90-9
Kendall, L. Shamans, Housewives, and Other
Restless Spirits.
E. Ohnuki-Tierney, 293(JASt):Feb89-189
Kendall, R. - see Monet, C.
Kendall, R.D. The Drama of Dissent.*
R.A. Anselment, 677(YES):Vol20-241
T.N. Corns, 506(PSt):May89-97
O.B. Hardison, Jr., 589:Apr89-456
N. Smith, 447(N&Q):Jun89-226
Kende, P. & Z. Strmiska, eds. Equality and
Inequality in Eastern Europe.
A. McAuley, 575(SEER):Apr89-317
Kendle, J. Ireland and the Federal Solution.
J.D. Fair, 637(VS):Spring90-516
Kendrick, C. Milton.*
A.J. Geritz, 125:Winter89-214
Kendrick, L. Chaucerian Play.
G. Olson, 401(MLQ):Sep88-292
J. Schleusener, 405(MP):May90-389
Kendrick, L. The Game of Love.
S. Gaunt, 402(MLR):Jul90-721
S. Kay, 382(MAE):1989/2-331
639(VQR):Spring89-65

Kenneally, M., ed. Cultural Contexts and Literary Idioms in Contemporary Irish Literature.
L. McDiarmid, 617(TLS):13-19Apr90-402
Kenneally, M. Portraying the Self.
M.J. Sidnell, 627(UTQ):Fall89-132
Kennedy, A. Deadly Triplets.
M. Bloom, 441:14Oct90-48
Kennedy, B. Knighthood in the "Morte Darthur."
V. Krishna, 38:Band107Heft1/2-206
J.W. Spisak, 589:Apr89-457
Kennedy, D. Granville Barker and the Dream of Theatre.*
G. Gordon, 511:Aug89-46
Kennedy, D. - see Granville-Barker, H.
Kennedy, E. A Cultural History of the French Revolution.*
J.P. Gilroy, 207(FR):May90-1111
Kennedy, E. Tomorrow's Catholics, Yesterday's Church.*
639(VQR):Spring89-61
Kennedy, G.A., ed. The Cambridge History of Literary Criticism. (Vol 1)
M. Heath, 617(TLS):15-21Jun90-645
Kennedy, J.G. Poe, Death and the Life of Writing.*
R. Regan, 301(JEGP):Jan89-135
L. Weissberg, 27(AL):May89-292
M.J.E. Williams, 405(PoeS):Jun89-22
Kennedy, J.G. & D.M. Fogel, eds. American Letters and the Historical Consciousness.*
R.M.P., 295(JML):Fall89/Winter89-245
Kennedy, L. On My Way to the Club.*
C. de Beaurepaire, 364:Jun/Jul89-142
Kennedy, M. Portrait of Walton.
P. Chipchase, 607:Dec89-41
P. Reed, 617(TLS):12-18Jan90-39
Kennedy, P. The Rise and Fall of the Great Powers.*
G.A. Hosking, 575(SEER):Jan89-135
E.N. Luttwak, 31(ASch):Spring89-289
Kennedy, R.G. Orders from France.* Greek Revival America.*
B. Gill, 442(NY):29Jan90-92
Kennedy, R.G. Rediscovering America.
442(NY):24Dec90-100
Kennedy, T.E. Crossing Borders.
T. Cochran, 441:23Dec90-12
Kennedy, T.E. André Dubus.
F. Baveystock, 617(TLS):6-12Apr90-376
M.B. Gentry, 573(SSF):Summer89-362
Kennelly, B. A Time for Voices.
G. Foden, 617(TLS):17-23Aug90-871
Kenner, H. Historical Fictions.
J. Shulevitz, 441:30Sep90-28
Kenner, H. The Mechanic Muse.*
M.D.O., 295(JML):Fall88/Winter89-229
Kenner, H. A Sinking Island.*
T. Eagleton, 493:Summer89-6
Kenney, S. One Fell Sloop.
M. Slade, 441:14Oct90-48
Kenney, S. Sailing.*
W.H. Pritchard, 249(HudR):Autumn89-486
Kenny, A. The Legacy of Wittgenstein.
R.E. Aquila, 449:Apr89-270
Kenny, A. The Metaphysics of Mind.
P. Carruthers, 617(TLS):27Apr-3May90-454
Kenny, A. Reason and Religion.*
B. Davies, 521:Oct89-349
Kenny, A., ed. Wyclif in his Times.*
W.J. Courtenay, 382(MAE):1989/1-154

Kenny, A. - see Clough, A.H.
Kenny, S.S. - see Farquhar, G.
Kenshur, O. Open Form and the Shape of Ideas.*
T.M. Carr, Jr., 678(YCGL):No36-176
Kent, B. The Spoils of War.
G. Peden, 617(TLS):26Jan-1Feb90-98
Kent, B.D., R. Rainey & P.O. Kristeller - see Kristeller, P.O.
Kent, D., ed. "Lighting Up the Terrain."
J.M. Zezulka, 105:Spring/Summer89-91
Kent, D.A., ed. The Achievement of Christina Rossetti.*
R. Chapman, 445(NCF):Jun89-107
Kent, F.W. & P. Simons, with J.C. Eade. Patronage, Art and Society in Renaissance Italy.*
C.H. Clough, 278(IS):Vol44-161
R. Mackenney, 557:Sep89-329
Kent, G.E. A Life of Gwendolyn Brooks.
J. Wood, 441:18Mar90-21
Kent, N. The Triumph of Light and Nature.*
J.L., 90:Jan89-48
Kenyon, J. The Boat of Quiet Hours.*
G. Kuzma, 271:Winter89-167
Kenyon, N., ed. Authenticity and Early Music.*
R. Donington, 410(M&L):Aug89-386
C. Rosen, 453(NYRB):19Jul90-46
Kenyon, N. Simon Rattle.*
A.F.I.T., 412:May89-145
Kenyon, O. Women Novelists Today.
L.L. Doan, 395(MFS):Summer89-395
C. Hanson, 402(MLR):Jul90-710
Ker, I. John Henry Newman.*
J.C. Livingston, 506(PSt):Dec89-305
Ker, I. & A.G. Hill, eds. Newman after a Hundred Years.
B. Martin, 617(TLS):7-13Dec90-1330
Kerblay, B., ed. L'Evolution des modèles familiaux dans les pays d'Est européen et en URSS.
C. Humphrey, 575(SEER):Oct89-642
Kerik, J., comp. Living with the Land.
A.R. Taylor, 269(IJAL):Jul89-359
Kerkhof, M.P.A. - see Marques de Santillana
Kerlouégan, F. Le "De excidio Britanniae" de Gildas.
P. Flobert, 555:Vol62Fasc2-374
Kerman, C.E. & R. Eldridge. The Lives of Jean Toomer.*
D.B., 295(JML):Fall88/Winter89-413
E. Margolies, 179(ES):Aug89-372
Kerman, J. Contemplating Music.*
J. Levinson, 289:Summer89-113
J. Porter, 187:Fall89-531
F.J. Smith, 309:Vol9No2/3-147
L. Treitler, 317:Summer89-375
Kerman, J. Opera as Drama. (rev)
R. Donington, 415:Dec89-749
C. Hatch, 465:Summer90-135
A.F.L.T., 412:May89-146
Kermode, F. An Appetite for Poetry.*
R.M. Adams, 453(NYRB):1Mar90-38
R. Fuller, 364:Feb/Mar90-115
C. Gallagher, 617(TLS):26Jan-1Feb90-84
Kermode, F. History and Value.*
R. Gill, 447(N&Q):Dec89-556
L. Howe, 141:Fall89-513
G. Viswanathan, 395(MFS):Summer89-377

Kern, G., ed. Zamyatin's "We."
  P. Carden, 550(RusR):Oct89-433
  W.J. Leatherbarrow, 575(SEER):Oct89-621
  R. Russell, 402(MLR):Oct90-1046
Kernan, A. Printing Technology, Letters &
  Samuel Johnson.*
  G.J. Kolb, 301(JEGP):Apr89-241
  J.M. Kuist, 125:Winter89-210
Kerr, J. Fiction against History.
  P. Drew, 617(TLS):20-26Apr90-422
Kerr, L. Suspended Fictions.*
  B.A., 295(JML):Fall88/Winter89-397
  R. Ocasio, 345(KRQ):May89-248
  R. Prieto, 240(HR):Winter89-128
Kerr, P. The Pale Criminal.
  S. Altinel, 617(TLS):29Jun-5Jul90-704
Kerr, P., ed. The Penguin Book of Lies.
  E. Korn, 617(TLS):12-18Oct90-1104
Kerridge, R. In the Deep South.
  C.J. Fox, 364:Jun/Jul89-126
Kerrigan, J. & J. Wordsworth - see Davies,
  H.S.
Kerrigan, W. & G. Braden. The Idea of the
  Renaissance.
  B. Vickers, 617(TLS):30Mar-5Apr90-350
Kersaudy, F. Norway 1940.
  M. Carver, 617(TLS):12-18Jan90-29
Kersey, E.M. Women Philosophers.
  S. Sherwin, 103:Jul90-280
Kershaw, I. The "Hitler Myth."
  O. Bartov, 242:Vol10No3-385
Kershner, R.B. Joyce, Bakhtin, and Popular
  Literature.
  D.J. Cahill, 659(ConL):Fall90-397
  C. Herr, 329(JJQ):Fall89-146
  D.R. Schwarz, 395(MFS):Winter89-798
Kesavan, K.V., ed. Contemporary Japanese
  Politics and Foreign Policy.
  Shimizu Manabu, 285(JapQ):Oct-Dec89-
  462
Kesey, K. The Further Inquiry.
  D. English, 441:9Dec90-3
Kęsik, M. La cataphore.
  C. Thogmartin, 350:Dec90-872
Kessel, F.S., ed. The Development of Lan-
  guage and Language Researchers.
  E. Bialystok, 399(MLJ):Summer89-204
Kesselring, T. Jean Piaget.
  P. Trotignon, 542:Oct-Dec89-630
Kessler, E. Flannery O'Connor and the Lan-
  guage of Apocalypse.*
  L.K. Barnett, 677(YES):Vol20-344
Kessler, R. Moscow Station.
  639(VQR):Summer89-95
Kessler-Harris, A. A Woman's Wage.
  W. Kaminer, 441:28Oct90-23
Kesteloot, L. Comprendre les "Poèmes" de L.S.
  Senghor.
  J. Spleth, 538(RAL):Spring89-145
Kesting, H. - see Liszt, F. & R. Wagner
Kestner, J. Protest and Reform.*
  K. Sutherland, 148:Winter86-105
Kestner, J.A. Mythology and Misogyny.
  D.N. Mancoff, 637(VS):Winter90-335
Ketchian, S. The Poetry of Anna Akhmatova.*
  I. Masing-Delic, 550(RusR):Apr89-220
Ketchum, R.M. The Borrowed Years, 1938-
  1941.
  T. Chaffin, 441:11Feb90-19
Ketterer, D. Imprisoned in a Tesseract.*
  J. Ford, 295(JML):Fall88/Winter89-291
  R. Kaveney, 561(SFS):Nov89-393
  D. Tarrant, 561(SFS):Nov89-390

Kettle, A. Literature and Liberation. (G.
  Martin and W.R. Owens, eds)
  R. Gill, 447(N&Q):Dec89-556
Kettler, A. - see Ballanche, P.S.
Keun, I. Ich lebe in einem wilden Wirbel.* (G.
  Kreis & M.S. Strauss, eds)
  M. Shafi, 133:Band22Heft3/4-368
Kevelson, R. The Law as a System of Signs.
  R.M. O'Neil, 567:Vol74No1/2-173
Kevelson, R. Charles S. Peirce's Method of
  Methods.
  J. Ransdell, 619:Winter89-74
Kévorkian, R.H. Catalogue des "Incunables"
  arméniens (1511-1695) ou chronique de
  l'imprimerie arménienne.
  J.A.C. Greppin, 318(JAOS):Jul-Sep88-521
Key, M.R. & H.M. Hoenigswald, eds. General
  and Amerindian Ethnolinguistics.
  T. Kaufman, 350:Sep90-640
Keyes, R.S. The Male Journey in Japanese
  Prints.
  E.D. Swinton, 293(JASt):Nov89-867
Keyes, S. Collected Poems.
  J. Greening, 493:Spring89-55
Keys, I. Johannes Brahms.
  W. Mellers, 617(TLS):16-22Mar90-285
Keyssar, A. Out of Work.*
  J. Braeman, 106:Summer89-41
Khader, A.B.A-B. Thuburbo Majus, 3.
  R.E. Kolarik, 589:Jul89-643
Khader, A.B.A-B. & others. Thuburbo Majus,
  2.
  R.E. Kolarik, 589:Jul89-643
Khalid, M. The Government They Deserve.
  B. Malwal, 617(TLS):30Nov-6Dec90-1284
Khalidi, T. Classical Arab Islam.
  B. Stowasser, 318(JAOS):Apr-Jun88-318
al-Khalil, S. Republic of Fear.
  A. Edgar, 441:21Oct90-13
  E. Mortimer, 453(NYRB):27Sep90-7
  P. Sluglett, 617(TLS):17-23Aug90-865
Khamchoo, C. & E.B. Reynolds, eds. Thai-
  Japanese Relations in Historical Perspec-
  tive.
  T. Tsurutani, 293(JASt):Nov89-804
Khan, S.R. Profit and Loss Sharing.
  S.J. Burki, 293(JASt):Aug89-654
Khan-Magomedov, S.O. Pioneers of Soviet
  Architecture.*
  A. Delgado, 505:Apr89-121
  C. Lodder, 90:Feb89-157
Khan-Magomedov, S.O. Rodchenko.
  D. Elliott, 550(RusR):Oct89-447
Khapa, N. - see under Tsong Khapa
Khin Yi. The Dobama Movement in Burma
  (1930-1938).
  J. Silverstein, 293(JASt):Feb89-220
Khlebnikov, V. Collected Works of Velimir
  Khlebnikov.* (Vol 1) (C. Douglas, ed)
  R. Cooke, 575(SEER):Apr89-249
  R.B.D., 295(JML):Fall88/Winter89-364
Khlebnikov, V. Ladomir. Stikhotvoreniia i
  poemy. (R. Duganov & S. Lesnevskii,
  comps) Stikhotvoreniia. (R. Duganov, ed)
  Tvoreniia. (V.P. Grigor'ev & A.E. Parnis,
  eds) The King of Time. (C. Douglas, ed)
  R. Cooke, 575(SEER):Apr89-249
Khromov, S.S., ed. Grazhdanskaia voina i
  voennaia interventsiia v SSSR.
  R.G. Suny, 550(RusR):Apr89-213

Khrushchev, N.S. Khrushchev Remembers:
The Glasnost Tapes. (J.L. Schecter, with
V.V. Luchkov, eds & trans)
  A.B. Ulam, 441:28Oct90-13
Khrushchev, S. Khrushchev on Khrushchev.
(W. Taubman, ed)
  G.W. Breslauer, 441:29Jul90-10
  442(NY):27Aug90-95
Khurshid, S. At Home in India.
  M. Yanuck, 293(JASt):Feb89-202
Ki-sou, J. - see under Jong Ki-sou
Kidd, A. The Huron Chief.* (D.M.R. Bentley,
with C.R. Steele, eds)
  C. Ballstadt, 470:Vol27-119
  D. Latham, 102(CanL):Autumn-Winter89-
  141
Kidd, C. & D. Williamson - see "Debrett's
Peerage and Baronetage, 1990"
Kidd, D. Peking Story.*
  S. Pickering, 569(SR):Spring89-297
Kiebuzinska, C. Revolutionaries in the Thea-
tre.
  R. Engle, 610:Spring89-99
  M. Kobialka, 615(TJ):Mar89-123
  P.D. Murphy, 590:Dec89-122
Kiefer, W. The Perpignon Exchange.
  N. Callendar, 441:23Dec90-15
Kieffer, B. The Storm and Stress of Lan-
guage.*
  K.J. Fink, 222(GR):Summer89-134
  T. Salumets, 564:May89-171
Kiely, B., ed. Anthologies de Nouvelles
Irlandaises.
  R. Fréchet, 189(EA):Apr-Jun89-239
Kienzle, W.X. Masquerade.
  M. Stasio, 441:20May90-53
Kiepe, H. Die Nürnberger Priameldichtung.
  I. Glier, 680(ZDP):Band108Heft1-119
Kiernan, K.S. The Thorkelin Transcripts of
"Beowulf."*
  R.H. Bremmer, Jr., 179(ES):Apr89-172
  T.A. Shippoy, 589:Jul89-727
Kiernan, R.F. Saul Bellow.
  K. Opdahl, 395(MFS):Winter89-769
Kiernan, V. History, Classes and Nation
States. (H.J. Kaye, ed)
  P.B. Rich, 242:Vol10No4-480
Kiernan, V.G. The Duel in European History.
  C. Hill, 453(NYRB):14Jun90-55
Kiesel, H. & others - see Lessing, G.E.
Kiessig, M. - see Morgenstern, C.
Kiessling, N.K. The Library of Robert Burton.
  D. McKitterick, 78(BC):Autumn89-301
  R. Robbins, 78(BC):Winter89-550
Kijuk, P.R.D. - see under Dragić Kijuk, P.R.
Kikawada, I.M. & A. Quinn. Before Abraham
Was.
  E. Yamauchi, 318(JAOS):Apr-Jun88-310
Kikuoka, M.T. The Changkufeng Incident.
  J.H. Boyle, 407(MN):Winter89-507
  A.D. Coox, 293(JASt):Aug89-575
Kilbride, P.L. & J.C. Changing Family Life in
East Africa.
  J. Gruber, 617(TLS):1-7Jun90-590
Kilcullen, J. Sincerity and Truth.
  K.R. Weinstein, 543:Mar90-641
Kilgo, J. Deep Enough for Ivorybills.*
  639(VQR):Winter89-31
Kilgore, D. Last Summer.
  M. Phillips, 456(NDQ):Spring89-206
Killens, J.O. Great Black Russian.
  Z. Smardz, 441:18Feb90-20

Killilea, A.G. The Politics of Being Mortal.
  R.M., 185:Jan90-448
  C.A. Rogers, 219(GaR):Fall89-621
Killingsworth, M.J. Whitman's Poetry of the
Body.
  B. Erkkila, 646(WWR):Spring90-194
  T. Gunn, 617(TLS):5-11Jan90-3
  M.J. Hurst, 30:Winter90-84
Killip, C. In Flagrante.
  P. Lewis, 565:Summer89-66
Killy, W., ed. Mythographie der frühen Neu-
zeit.
  G.J.M. Bartelink, 394:Vol42fasc1/2-256
Kilvert, F. The Diary of Francis Kilvert,
June-July 1870. (D. Ifans, ed)
  A.L. Le Quesne, 617(TLS):30Mar-5Apr90-
  348
Kilwardby, R. On Time and Imagination.
  G. Marcil, 589:Oct89-982
Kim, A. Eichhörnchen.
  P. Rollberg, 654(WB):7/1989-1172
Kim, C.S. Faithful Endurance.
  K-O. Kim, 293(JASt):Aug89-637
Kim, I.J. & Y.W. Kihl, eds. Political Change in
South Korea.
  H. Koo, 293(JASt):Nov89-887
Kim, R. & H. Conroy, eds. New Tides in the
Pacific.
  T. Akaha, 293(JASt):Feb89-117
Kimball, R. Tenured Radicals.
  R. Rosenblatt, 441:22Apr90-3
  J. Searle, 453(NYRB):6Dec90-34
Kimbrough, R. - see Conrad, J.
Kimpel, D. & R. Suckale. Die gotische Archi-
tektur in Frankreich, 1130-1270.*
  S. Murray, 589:Jul89-729
Kinahan, F. Yeats, Folklore and Occultism.
  R. Rooksby, 447(N&Q):Dec89-544
Kincaid, J. Lucy.
  T. Davis, 441:28Oct90-11
Kinchin, P. & J., with N. Baxter. Glasgow's
Great Exhibitions, 1888, 1901, 1911, 1938,
1988.*
  P. Greenhalgh, 39:Jun89-440
Kindermann, I. & J., eds. Répertoire Interna-
tional des Sources Musicales A/I/11.
  R. Schaal, 417:Apr-Jun89-177
Kindermann, U., ed. Zwischen Epos and
Drama.
  P.G. Walsh, 123:Vol39No2-423
  J.M. Ziolkowski, 589:Oct89-984
King, A.H. Musical Pursuits.
  P.W. Jones, 410(M&L):May89-263
  S. Sadie, 415:Jun89-351
King, C. The Natural History of Weasels and
Stoats.
  D.W. Macdonald, 617(TLS):12-18Oct90-
  1109
King, D. Trotsky, a Photographic Biography.
  P. Pomper, 104(CASS):Spring89-120
King, F. Confessions of a Failed Southern
Lady.
  C. Mitchell, 582(SFQ):Vol46No2-194
King, F. Lump It or Leave It.
  D. McWhorter, 441:8Jul90-17
King, F. Visiting Cards.
  T. Fitton, 617(TLS):15-21Jun90-653
King, F. - see Ackerley, J.R.
King, J. William Cowper.*
  V. Newey, 83:Spring89-105
King, J. The Last Modern.
  R. Cardinal, 617(TLS):25-31May90-560
  G. Mansell, 324:Oct90-795

King, J., ed. Modern Latin American Fiction.*
P. Standish, 86(BHS):Jan89-109
King, J. "Sur."*
S. Molloy, 86(BHS):Jan89-108
King, J. & N. Torrents, eds. The Garden of the Forking Paths.
A. Avellaneda, 238:Dec89-973
King, J.C. - see Notker der Deutsche
King, K.C. Achilles.
D. Arnould, 555:Vol62Fasc2-331
C.D. Benson, 149(CLS):Vol26No2-177
W.C. Scott, 24:Summer89-339
D.W.T. Vessey, 123:Vol39No1-40
King, L. The Pre-Geography of Snow.
J. Lynes, 102(CanL):Autumn-Winter89-212
King, L., with P. Occhiogrosso. Tell Me More.
C. Wallace, 441:9Sep90-27
King, M., ed. New Italian Women.
J.G. Hendin, 441:4Feb90-18
King, M.L. Venetian Humanism in an Age of Patrician Dominance.*
L. Panizza, 278(IS):Vol43-153
King, N.M.P., L.R. Churchill & A.W. Cross, eds. The Physician as Captain of the Ship.
G.A., 185:Jan90-461
King, S. Four Past Midnight.
A. Solomon, 441:2Sep90-21
King, S. The Stand.
R. Kiely, 441:13May90-3
King, S.B. Passionate Journey.
R.B. Pilgrim, 485(PE&W):Jan89-106
King, T. Medicine River.
J. Butler, 441:23Sep90-29
King, W. Death Was His Koan.
D. Lishka, 293(JASt):Feb89-171
King, W. The Transactioneer (1700).
566:Autumn89-68
King-Farlow, J. & S. O'Connell. Self-Conflict and Self-Healing.
M.K., 185:Jan90-466
Kingdon, J. Island Africa.
H. Kruuk, 617(TLS):29Jun-5Jul90-707
Kingsolver, B. Animal Dreams.
J. Smiley, 441:2Sep90-2
442(NY):10Dec90-158
Kingsolver, B. Holding the Line.
P. Stegner, 441:7Jan90-31
Kingsolver, B. Homeland and Other Stories.*
D. Neuhaus, 617(TLS):7-13Sep90-956
Kingston, B. The Oxford History of Australia. (Vol 3)
F.B. Smith, 617(TLS):9-15Mar90-261
Kinkley, J.C. The Odyssey of Shen Congwen.
L.Y., 295(JML):Fall88/Winter89-407
Kinnamon, K. A Richard Wright Bibliography.
M. Fabre, 70:Oct89-154
Yoshinobu Hakutani, 587(SAF):Spring89-116
Kinneavy, J.L. Greek Rhetorical Origins of Christian Faith.*
G.A. Kennedy, 480(P&R):Vol22No1-74
Kinnell, G. - see Whitman, W.
Kinney, A.F. John Skelton.*
A. Hudson, 541(RES):May89-249
A.D. Weiner, 551(RenQ):Spring89-127
Kinney, A.F. & others, eds. Sidney in Retrospect.
V. Skretkowicz, 557:Sep89-336
Kinney, A.F. & D.S. Collins, eds. Renaissance Historicism.
D. Bevington, 405(MP):May90-400
[continued]

[continuing]
T.N. Corns, 506(PSt):May89-97
M.L. Hall, 569(SR):Summer89-456
G.W. Pigman 3d, 250(HLQ):Autumn89-501
Kinney, D. - see More, T.
Kinsella, J. Covering the Plague.
H.J. Geiger, 441:6May90-23
Kinsella, T. Blood and Family.*
B. O'Donoghue, 493:Summer89-62
W. Scammell, 364:Aug/Sep89-92
Kinsella, T. One Fond Embrace.
B. O'Donoghue, 493:Summer89-62
Kinsella, W.P. The Fencepost Chronicles.
D. Murray, 168(ECW):Spring89-132
Kinsella, W.P. The Future Adventures of Slugger McBatt.
D. Murray, 102(CanL):Autumn-Winter89-227
Kinsella, W.P. Red Wolf, Red Wolf.
D. Murray, 102(CanL):Winter88-141
Kinsley, D. Hindu Goddesses.
E.B. Findly, 318(JAOS):Apr-Jun88-332
P.H. Salus, 567:Vol75No3/4-357
Kinsman, F. Millennium.
F. Cairncross, 617(TLS):9-15Mar90-251
C. Handy, 324:Jul90-565
Kinsolving, W. Bred to Win.
A. Knopf, 441:5Aug90-18
Kintzler, C. Condorcet.*
É. Guibert-Sledziewski, 535(RHL):Jan-Feb89-120
Kinzie, M. - see Vivante, A.
Kiparsky, P. & G. Youmans, eds. Phonetics and Phonology. (Vol 1)
M.H. Kelly, 348(L&S):Apr-Jun89-171
Kipling, R. Early Verse, 1879-1889. (A. Rutherford, ed)
D. Petzold, 38:Band107Heft3/4-528
Kipling, R. Kipling's Japan. (H. Cortazzi & G. Webb, eds)
H. Ballhatchet, 407(MN):Spring89-130
C.F. Beckingham, 346(KJ):Mar89-21
Inoue Eimei, 285(JapQ):Oct-Dec89-465
J. Kirkup, 364:Oct/Nov89-96
M.G. Ryan, 293(JASt):Nov89-854
Kipling, R. The Letters of Rudyard Kipling. (Vols 1 & 2) (T. Pinney, ed)
J. Bayley, 617(TLS):21-27Dec90-1367
Kipperman, M. Beyond Enchantment.*
R. Immerwahr, 564:Nov89-358
Kipps, C. Out of Focus.
S. Oney, 441:18Feb90-21
Király, B.K. & W.S. Dillard, eds. The East Central European Officer Corps 1740-1920s.
J.E.O. Screen, 575(SEER):Jul89-475
Király, P. & A. Hollós, eds. Hungaro-Slavica 1988.
J.I. Press, 402(MLR):Oct90-1042
Kiraly, S. California Rush.
M. Buck, 441:17Jun90-16
Kirby, I.J. Bible Translation in Old Norse.*
E.S. Firchow, 589:Oct89-985
Kirchhof, P. Die Bestimmtheit und Offenheit der Rechtssprache.
W. Otto, 685(ZDL):1/1989-115
Kirk, J.M. & G.W. Schuyler, eds. Central America.
S. Webre, 263(RIB):Vol39No2-208
Kirk, N. The Growth of Working Class Reformation in Mid-Victorian England.
A. Howkins, 637(VS):Summer90-657

Kirk, R. Translation Determined.*
   T. Piotrowski, 257(IRAL):Feb89-70
Kirkham, M. The Imagination of Edward
   Thomas.*
   A. Haberer, 189(EA):Apr-Jun89-228
   A. Heuser, 178:Mar89-99
   P.E. Mitchell, 177(ELT):Vol32No4-506
Kirkland, D. Light Years.
   K. Newman, 707:Autumn89-286
Kirkland, G. & G. Lawrence. The Shape of
   Love.
   A. Macaulay, 441:16Sep90-3
Kirkland, W. The Many Faces of Hull House.
   N.S. Dye, 441:28Jan90-22
Kirkpatrick, B.J. A Bibliography of Katherine
   Mansfield.
   S. Hills, 617(TLS):10-16Aug90-858
Kirkpatrick, R. Dante, "The Divine Comedy."*
   D.H. Higgins, 278(IS):Vol43-136
Kirkpatrick, R. Dante's "Inferno."
   P. Armour, 402(MLR):Jan90-203
   Z.G. Barański, 278(IS):Vol44-149
   L. Pertile, 382(MAE):1989/1-177
Kirn, W. My Hard Bargain.
   V. Sayers, 441:30Sep90-11
   442(NY):24Dec90-99
Kirschenbaum, H. & V.L. Henderson - see
   Rogers, C.
Kirschstein, B. & others - see "Wörterbuch
   der mittelhochdeutschen Urkundensprache"
Kirschten, R. James Dickey and the Gentle
   Ecstasy of Earth.
   R.J. Calhoun, 392:Winter88/89-83
   D. Trouard, 585(SoQ):Winter90-72
Kiš, D. Hourglass.
   R. Di Antonio, 268(IFR):Summer90-146
   C. Newman, 441:7Oct90-14
   442(NY):12Nov90-134
Kiš, D. La Mansarde.
   L. Kovacs, 450(NRF):Jun89-104
Kiškin, L. Alexandr Fillipovič Smirdin.
   S. Gleboff, 574(SEEJ):Spring89-140
Kisor, H. What's That Pig Outdoors?
   C. Lake, 441:3Jun90-14
Kiss, A. Pannonische Architekturelemente
   und Ornamentik in Ungarn.
   H. Dodge, 313:Vol79-242
Kitaj, R.B. First Diasporist Manifesto.*
   T. Hyman, 364:Oct/Nov89-140
Kitarō, N. - see under Nishida Kitarō
Kitcher, P. Vaulting Ambition.*
   R.M. Burian, 311(JP):Jul89-385
Kitching, G. Karl Marx and the Philosophy of
   Praxis.*
   M. Fisk, 125:Summer89-401
Kiteley, B. Still Life with Insects.*
   L. Norfolk, 617(TLS):6-12Apr90-376
Kittay, E.F. Metaphor.*
   D.E. Cooper, 393(Mind):Jul88-479
   P. Somville, 542:Oct-Dec89-636
Kittay, E.F. & D.T. Meyers, eds. Women and
   Moral Theory.*
   S. Wagner, 254:Summer89-186
Kittler, F. Grammophon Film Typewriter.
   G. Winthrop-Young, 564:Feb89-82
Kittredge, W. Owning It All.*
   C. Merrill, 434:Winter89-208
Kittredge, W. & A. Smith, eds. The Last Best
   Place.
   N.P. Arbuthnot, 649(WAL):Nov89-282
   T. Wortham, 445(NCF):Dec89-425
   639(VQR):Summer89-102

Kivy, P. Music Alone.
   S. Davies, 103:Sep90-368
Kivy, P. Osmin's Rage.*
   S. Davies, 63:Sep89-373
   L. Goehr, 103:Jan90-31
Kizaki, S. - see under Satoko Kizaki
Kizer, C. Carrying Over.
   J.F. Cotter, 249(HudR):Autumn89-517
Kjaer, A. & L. Holm-Olsen - see Holm-Olson,
   L.
Kjetsaa, G. Fyodor Dostoyevsky.*
   J. Frank, 249(HudR):Winter89-656
   R. Freeborn, 575(SEER):Apr89-270
Kjetsaa, G. Prinadležnost' Dostoevskomy.
   R. Anderson, 104(CASS):Spring-Win-
   ter88-507
Kjønstad, A. Norwegian Social Law.
   S. Anderson, 563(SS):Spring/Summer89-
   287
Kjørven, J. Robert Frost's Emergent Design.*
   R. Bieganowski, 295(JML):Fall88/
   Winter89-332
Klaar, M. Die Pantöffelchen der Nereide.
   S. Ude-Koeller, 196:Band30Heft1/2-137
Klakowich, R. - see Draghi, G.B.
Klancher, J.P. The Making of English Reading
   Audiences 1700-1832.*
   P. Hamilton, 447(N&Q):Sep89-403
   J. Raven, 541(RES):Feb89-125
   J. Todd, 83:Autumn89-224
Klapisch-Zuber, C. Women, Family, and Ritu-
   al in Renaissance Italy.
   H. Buttors, 551(RenQ):Summer89-297
Klass, P. Other Women's Children.
   M. Dorris, 441:9Sep90-7
Klassen, A.D., C.J. Williams & E.E. Levitt.
   Sex and Morality in the U.S.* (H.J.
   O'Gorman, ed)
   R. Porter, 617(TLS):16-22Feb90-166
Klassen, S. Journey to Yalta.
   C. Levenson, 526:Fall89-94
Klaube, M. Deutschböhmische Siedlungen im
   Karpatenraum.
   C. Goehrke, 575(SEER):Apr89-301
Klaus, H.G., ed. The Rise of Socialist Fiction
   1880-1914.*
   J.H. Wiener, 177(ELT):Vol32No1-84
Klaus, K. Die altindische Kosmologie.
   H.W. Bodewitz, 259(IIJ):Oct89-294
Klaus, K., ed & trans. Das Maitrakanyakāva-
   dāna (Divyāvadāna 38).
   J.P. McDermott, 318(JAOS):Apr-Jun88-
   330
Klawans, H. Newton's Madness.
   J. Cole, 617(TLS):6-12Jul90-721
   G. Hochman, 441:8Apr90-20
Kleberg, L. & H. Lövgren, eds. Eisenstein
   Revisited.
   R. Taylor, 575(SEER):Jan89-154
Kleberg, L. & N.A. Nilsson, eds. Theater and
   Literature in Russia 1900-1930.
   M. Heim, 279:Vol35/36-370
Klegraf, J., ed. Die altenglische Judith.
   U. Schaefer, 38:Band107Heft3/4-515
Kleiber, G. Relatives restrictives et relatives
   appositives.*
   W. Ayres-Bennett, 208(FS):Oct89-501
   J. Chaurand, 209(FM):Oct89-249
Kleiber, W., ed. Symposion Ernst Christmann.
   P. Ernst, 685(ZDL):1/1989-108
   B.J. Koekkoek, 221(GQ):Fall89-514

Klein, A.M. A.M. Klein: Literary Essays and
Reviews.* (U. Caplan & M.W. Steinberg,
eds)
   L. Groening, 102(CanL):Winter88-131
   K. Hoeppner, 178:Mar89-107
Klein, C. Gramercy Park.
   F.D. Reeve, 569(SR):Spring89-xl
Klein, D. Glass.
   139:Dec89/Jan90-68
Klein, D.M. Beauty Sleep.
   L.B. Frumkes, 441:22Jul90-20
Klein, H. J.B. Priestley's Plays.
   A.E. Kalson, 130:Winter89/90-387
Klein, H-A., ed. Hellmut Rosenfeld.
   G. Gillespie, 402(MLR):Apr90-496
Klein, J. Die konklusiven Sprechhandlungen.
   H. Harnisch, 682(ZPSK):Band42Heft3-406
Klein, J. Lectures and Essays. (R.B. William-
son, ed)
   K. Seeskin, 53(AGP):Band71Heft2-250
Klein, M. Determinism, Blameworthiness &
Deprivation.
   R. Kane, 617(TLS):31Aug-6Sep90-927
Klein, M.L. Geniza Manuscripts of Palestinian
Targum to the Pantateuch.
   B.L. Visotzky, 508:Jan89-93
Klein, S.B. Ankoku Butō.
   D.G. Goodman, 407(MN):Winter89-512
Klein, W. Der nüchterne Blick Programmatis-
cher Realismus in Frankreich nach 1848.
   U. Franklin, 446(NCFS):Spring-
   Summer90-552
Klein, Z. Still Among the Living.
   M. Stasio, 441:26Aug90-26
Kleiner, D.E.E. Roman Imperial Funerary Al-
tars with Portraits.
   G. Davies, 313:Vol79-220
   H.R. Goette, 229:Band61Heft2-160
Kleiner, F.S. The Arch of Nero in Rome.
   D. Boschung, 229:Band61Heft2-186
Kleinhenz, C. The Early Italian Sonnet: The
First Century (1220-1321).*
   S. Botterill, 545(RPh):Nov89-341
"Kleist-Jahrbuch 1988/89." (H.J. Kreutzer,
ed)
   D. Horton, 402(MLR):Apr90-508
Klejman, L. Rannjaja Proza Fedora Sologuba.
   M.G. Barker, 558(RLJ):Spring-Fall89-282
Klenner, H. - see Kant, I.
Kleparski, G. Semantic Change and Compo-
nential Analysis.*
   R. Aman, 300:Oct88-215
Klessmann, E. E.T.A. Hoffmann odie die Tiefe
zwischen Stern und Erde.
   G.R. Kaiser, 680(ZDP):Band108Heft2-292
Kligman, G. The Wedding of the Dead.
   M.H. Beissinger, 292(JAF):Jul-Sep89-351
Klíma, I. Love and Garbage.
   J. Naughton, 617(TLS):30Mar-5Apr90-
   338
Klíma, I. My First Loves.*
   B.K. Horvath, 532(RCF):Spring89-263
Kliman, B., ed. "Hamlet."
   F. Teague, 130:Summer89-195
Klinda, F. Orgelregistrierung.
   J. Butt, 410(M&L):Aug89-400
Kline, D. Great Possessions.
   M.E. Guthrie, 441:6May90-23
Klingebiel, K. Bibliographie linguistique de
l'ancien occitan (1960-1982).*
   G. Price, 402(MLR):Jan90-174

Klingebiel, K. Noun + Verb Compounding in
Western Romance.
   D.J. Napoli, 350:Dec90-873
Klinkenberg, J-M. - see Queneau, R. & A.
Blavier
Klinkowitz, J. Rosenberg/Barthes/Hassan.
   B.K. Horvath, 395(MFS):Winter89-861
Klinkowitz, J. Their Finest Hours.
   L. Goldstein, 385(MQR):Summer90-472
Klitgaard, R. Tropical Gangsters.
   T. Clarke, 441:9Sep90-31
Kloesel, C.J.W. & M.H. Fisch - see Peirce, C.S.
Kloesel, C.J.W., M.H. Fisch & others - see
Peirce, C.S.
Klosko, G. The Development of Plato's Politi-
cal Theory.*
   J.D.G. Evans, 518:Oct89-211
Klotz, H. The History of Postmodern Archi-
tecture.*
   A.J. Plattus, 47:Dec89-33
   E. Posner, 45:Feb89-67
   P. Tabor, 46:Apr89-12
Klotz, V. Das europäische Kunstmärchen.*
   J. Feldmann, 400(MLN):Apr89-739
Kluge, G. - see Brentano, C.
Klüver, B. & J. Martin. Kiki's Paris.*
   A. Berman, 55:Oct89-131
Knaipp, F. Hinterglas-Künste.
   U. Ballay, 39:Oct89-287
Knaller, S. Theorie und Dichtung im Werk
Italo Calvinos.
   K. Ackermann, 547(RF):Band101Heft1-
   148
Knape, J. Die ältesten deutschen Überset-
zungen von Petrarcas "Glücksbuch."
   E.J. Morrall, 402(MLR):Apr90-497
Knape, J. - see Messerschmidt, G.
Knapp, B.L. Archetype, Architecture, and the
Writer.*
   J.K.G., 295(JML):Fall88/Winter89-186
Knapp, B.L., ed. Critical Essays on Albert
Camus.
   E. Hughes, 402(MLR):Oct90-982
Knapp, B.L. Jean Genet. (rev)
   H.E. Stewart, 207(FR):Feb90-553
Knapp, B.L. Music, Archetype, and the
Writer.*
   D.A. Powell, 446(NCFS):Fall-
   Winter89/90-296
   P. Stevick, 395(MFS):Summer89-383
   M. Tison-Braun, 188(ECr):Spring89-103
Knapp, B.L. Women in Twentieth-Century
Literature.*
   B. Ciplijauskaité, 403(MLS):Fall89-112
   E.C.R., 295(JML):Fall88/Winter89-230
Knapp, F.P., ed. "Nibelungenlied" und Klage.*
   O. Gschwantler, 684(ZDA):Band118Heft4-
   160
   E.R. Haymes, 221(GQ):Fall89-519
Knapp, J.F. Literary Modernism and the
Transformation of Work.
   J.L. Wilcox, 395(MFS):Winter89-855
Knapp, J.M. & A. Mann. George Frideric
Handel's Chamber Duets.
   C.M.B., 412:May89-142
Knapp, P.A., ed. Assays. (Vols 3 & 4)
   G. Bourquin, 189(EA):Apr-Jun89-209
Knapp, S. Personification and the Sublime.*
   P.H. Fry, 131(CL):Spring89-190
Knappert, J. Proberbs from the Lamu Archi-
pelago and the Central Kenya Coast.
   R. Leger, 685(ZDL):1/1989-129

Kneale, D.J. Monumental Writing.
D. Perkins, 445(NCF):Mar90-543
Knee, S. Hervey Allen (1889-1949).
R.K. Cross, 27(AL):May89-303
Knefelkamp, U. Die Suche nach dem Reich des
Priesterkönigs Johannes.
S. Olms, 684(ZDA):Band118Heft3-115
Kneppe, A. & J. Wiesehöfer. Friedrich Münzer.
E. Badian, 229:Band61Heft7-600
Knetschke, E. & M. Sperlbaum. Zur Orthoepie
der Plosiva in der deutschen Hochsprache.
W. Sendlmeier, 353:Vol27No2-361
Kneuneman, K.P. - see Barthes, R.
Knight, A. The Mexican Revolution.
M.P. Costeloe, 86(BHS):Jul89-311
Knight, A. & K., eds. The Beat Vision.*
A.J. Sabatini, 295(JML):Fall88/Winter89-
186
Knight, D.M. Street of Dreams.
L. Botstein, 617(TLS):19-25Jan90-69
Knight, G.W. Visions and Vices. (J.D. Chris-
tie, ed)
G. Cavaliero, 617(TLS):2-8Nov90-1177
Knight, K.L. Mortal Words.
M. Stasio, 441:12Aug90-21
Knipovič, E.F. Ob Aleksandre Bloke.
D.A. Sloane, 574(SEEJ):Spring89-129
Knoblock, J. - see "Xunzi: A Translation and
Study of the Complete Works"
Knodt, R. Friedrich Nietzsche.*
R. Perkins, 564:Nov89-362
Knoepfle, J. Selected Poems. poems from the
sangamon.
A.C. Bromley, 502(PrS):Winter89-122
Knoepfler, D., ed. Comptes et Inventaires
dans la cité grecque.
M.J. Edwards, 123:Vol39No2-352
Knoop, R.R. Antefixa Satricana.
T.W. Potter, 313:Vol79-179
Knop, C., J. Harris & A. Lévéque. Basic Con-
versational French. (8th ed)
R. Danner, 399(MLJ):Winter89-502
Knorr, W.R. The Ancient Tradition of Geo-
metric Problems."
I. Bulmer-Thomas, 123:Vol39No2-364
Knowles, A.V. Ivan Turgenev.
J.B. Woodward, 402(MLR):Apr90-534
Knowles, G. Patterns of Spoken English.*
F. Chevillet, 189(EA):Apr-Jun89-197
Knowles, R.P., ed. The Proceedings of the
Theatre in Atlantic Canada Symposium.
H. Jones, 178:Jun89-244
B. Peel, 529(QQ):Autumn89-706
Knowles, R.P., ed. The Proceedings of the
Theatre in Atlantic Canada Symposium
(1986).
M. Blagrave, 108:Spring89-87
Knox, E. Paremata.
F. Adcock, 617(TLS):2-8Feb90-123
Knox, E. & H-L. Plus ça change.*
D.B. Perramond, 399(MLJ):Winter89-510
Knox, P.E. Ovid's "Metamorphoses" and the
Traditions of Augustan Poetry.*
S.E. Hinds, 122:Jul89-266
D.F. Kennedy, 313:Vol79-209
Knutson, H. The Triumph of Wit.
J. Clarke, 208(FS):Jul89-327
P.A. Wadsworth, 475:Vol16No30-305
H. Weber, 566:Autumn89-77
D. Whitton, 615(TJ):Dec89-563
R.A. Zimbardo, 401(MLQ):Mar88-65

"Knýtlinga Saga."* (H. Pálsson & P. Edwards,
trans)
P.A. Jorgensen, 301(JEGP):Jan89-54
R. McTurk, 562(Scan):May89-77
Kobak, A. Isabelle.*
42(AR):Summer89-371
Köbler, G. Sammlung kleinerer althochdeut-
scher Sprachdenkmäler.
P.W. Tax, 680(ZDP):Band108Heft3-407
Koch, E. Shah Jahan and Orpheus.*
P.A. Andrews, 39:Oct89-285
R. Hillenbrand, 59:Mar89-109
Koch, E. & F. Trapp, eds. Realismuskonzep-
tionen der Exilliteratur zwischen 1935 und
1940/41.
M. Winkler, 221(GQ):Summer89-419
Koch, E.I., with L.T. Jones. All the Best.
P. Noonan, 441:29Apr90-1
Koch, H., ed. Literatur und Persönlichkeit.
R. Reuss, 72:Band226Heft1-112
Koch, H-G., M. Müller & M. Pasley - see
Kafka, F.
Koch, H.W. In the Name of the Volk.
A. Glees, 617(TLS):13-19Apr90-392
Koch, L.O. Yardbird Suite.
G.L. Starks, Jr., 91:Vol17-183
Kochumuttom, T.A. - see Vasubandhu
Kociancich, V. The Last Days of William
Shakespeare.
A. Feinstein, 617(TLS):24-30Aug90-902
Kocka, J., ed. Bildungsbürgertum im 19.
Jahrhundert. (Pt 4) Bürgertum im 19.
Jahrhundert.
C. Charle, 358:Jun90-8
Kodama, S. - see Pound, E.
Kodera, T. Vincent Van Gogh.
A.S. Byatt, 617(TLS):29Jun-5Jul90-683
Kodish, D. Good Friends and Bad Enemies.*
P.V. Bohlman, 187:Fall89-542
Koditschek, T. Class Formation and Urban
Industrial Scoiety.
H. Porkin, 617(TLS):14-20Sep90-969
Koelb, C. Inventions of Reading.
S. Irlam, 400(MLN):Dec89-1191
Koelb, C. & V. Lokke, eds. The Current in
Criticism.*
J.R. Bonnott, 600:Spring90-120
Koelb, C. & S. Noakes, eds. The Comparative
Perspective on Literature.
G. Lucente, 395(MFS):Winter89-847
J. Monroe, 52:Band24Heft2-209
Koelsch, W.A. Clark University, 1887-1987.
C.C. Bishop, 432(NEQ):Mar89-151
Koenker, D.P. & W.G. Rosenberg. Strikes and
Revolution in Russia, 1917.
R. Pipes, 617(TLS):23-29Mar90-305
Koenker, D.P., W.G. Rosenberg & R.G. Suny,
eds. Party, State, and Society in the Rus-
sian Civil War.
N. Stone, 617(TLS):6-12Apr90-367
Koepke, W. Johann Gottfried Herder.*
H.H.F. Henning, 406:Fall89-393
K. Menges, 564:Nov89-352
H. Reiss, 133:Band22Heft1-62
Koeppen, W. Pigeons on the Grass.*
P.F. Dvorak, 221(GQ):Fall89-551
Koerner, K. Practicing Linguistic Historiog-
raphy.
J.S. Falk, 350:Sep90-641
Koerner, K. Saussurean Studies/Etudes saus-
suriennes.*
W. Bennett, 402(MLR):Jul90-740

Koester, R. Hermann Broch.
G. Brude-Firnau, 564:Nov89-366
D. Horrocks, 402(MLR):Oct90-1030
J.P. Strelka, 133:Band22Heft1-75
Koff, L.M. Chaucer and the Art of Storytelling.
G.R. Keiser, 377:Mar89-60
Kogawa, J. Naomi's Road.
H. Froese-Tiessen, 102(CanL):Autumn-Winter89-251
Koger, L. Farlanburg Stories.
M. Childress, 441:19Aug90-16
Kohak, E. Jan Patočka.
R. Scruton, 617(TLS):5-11Oct90-1054
Kohl, N. Oscar Wilde.
T. Eagleton, 617(TLS):2-8Feb90-124
Kohl, S. Das englische Spätmittelalter.
G. Bourcier, 189(EA):Jul-Sep89-338
Köhler, E. Vorlesungen zur Geschichte der Französischen Literatur. (H. Krauss & D. Rieger, eds)
K. Schnelle, 547(RF):Band101Heft2/3-281
Kohler, S. Miracles in America.
R. Singleton, 441:16Sep90-22
Kohler, S. A Perfect Place.*
S. Roe, 617(TLS):8-14Jun90-617
Kohler, V. Rainy North Woods.
M. Stasio, 441:18Feb90-23
Kohli, A., ed. India's Democracy.
J.R. Roach, 293(JASt):Feb89-203
Kohli, A. The State and Poverty in India.
A. Gupta, 293(JASt):Nov89-787
K.B. Sayeed, 529(QQ):Summer89-544
Köhnke, K. "Hieroglyphenschrift."
H.M.K. Riley, 406:Summer89-260
Köhnke, K.C. Entstehung und Aufstieg des Neukantianismus.
H. Holzhey, 319:Jan90-142
Kohonen, V. Towards Experimental Learning of Elementary English 1.
J.W. Brown, 710:Dec89-486
Kohut, Z.E. Russian Centralism and Ukkrainian Autonomy.
639(VQR):Autumn89-116
Kokare, E. Latviešu un vācu sakāmvārdu paralēles.
P. Grzybek, 196:Band30Heft3/4-331
Kokichi, K. Musui's Story.
M.W. Steele, 293(JASt):Feb89-170
Kokotailo, P. John Glassco's Richer World.*
L. Dudek, 627(UTQ):Fall89-162
A. Pett, 150(DR):Spring89-137
Kołakowski, L. Główne nurty Marksizmu.
B. Zieliński, 497(PolR):Vol34No4-374
Kolakowski, L. Metaphysical Horror.*
T.L.S. Sprigge, 483:Jan89-114
Kolakowski, L. Modernity on Endless Trial.
A.C. Danto, 441:23Dec90-1
T. Nagel, 617(TLS):14-20Dec90-1341
Kolakowski, L. The Presence of Myth.*
K. Harries, 441:14Jan90-24
Z. Janowski, 543:Dec89-408
Kolata, G. The Baby Doctors.
D.J. Kevles, 441:30Sep90-14
Kolb, D. Postmodern Sophistications.
W. Steiner, 617(TLS):21-27Sep90-1005
Kolb, F. Diocletian und die Erste Tetrarchie.
P. Herz, 229:Band61Heft1-48
S. Williams, 123:Vol39No1-152
Kolb, F. Die Stadt im Altertum.*
R. Martin, 229:Band61Heft8-736

Kolb, F. Untersuchungen zur Historia Augusta.
B. Baldwin, 229:Band61Heft7-639
Kolb, P. - see Proust, M.
Kolbe, J. Heller Zauber. (2nd ed)
H. Siefken, 402(MLR):Jul90-810
H.R. Vaget, 222(GR):Fall89-188
Kolchin, P. Unfree Labor.*
P. Dukes, 575(SEER):Apr89-310
R. Munting, 242:Vol10No1-121
Kolin, P.C., ed. American Playwrights since 1945.
E. Ingersoll, 590:Jun90-75
Kolin, P.C., ed. Conversations with Edward Albee.
T.P. Adler, 397(MD):Jun89-321
P.J. Egan, 130:Spring89-103
W. French, 580(SCR):Spring90-158
Kolin, P.C. David Rabe.
P.S. McKinney, 70:Jan89-37
J.L. McMillion, 615(TJ):Oct89-433
L. Morrow, 397(MD):Sep89-456
Kolin, P.C., ed. Shakespeare and Southern Writers.
C.H. Kullman, 580(SCR):Fall90-177
Kolin, P.C. & J.M. Davis, eds. Critical Essays on Edward Albee.*
P.J. Egan, 130:Spring89-103
W. French, 580(SCR):Spring90-158
Kolk, R. Beschädigt Individualität.
W. Wittkowski, 406:Spring89-131
Kolko, G. Confronting the Third World.
639(VQR):Spring89-62
Koller, A. The Stations of Solitude.
J. Shulevitz, 441:22Jul90-21
Kolleritsch, O., ed. Egon Wellesz.*
S. Wollenberg, 415:Sep89-545
Kolm, R. The Plastic Factory.
B.K. Horvath, 532(RCF):Fall89-224
Kolodziej, E.A. Making and Marketing Arms.
E.G. Hollett, 529(QQ):Summer89-536
Koloski, B., ed. Approaches to Teaching Chopin's "The Awakening."
L. Wagner-Martin, 392:Spring89-193
Kolsky, T.A. Jews Against Zionism.
M. Polner, 441:14Oct90-18
Kolve, V.A. Chaucer and the Imagery of Narrative.*
C.J. Watkin, 148:Winter86-96
Kölving, U. & J. Carriat. Inventaire de la "Correspondance littéraire" de Grimm et Meister.*
G. Dulac, 535(RHL):Mar-Apr89-293
Komai, A. & T.H. Rohlich. An Introduction to Japanese Kanbun.
S. Crawcour, 407(MN):Summer89-256
Komar, K.L. Transcending Angels.*
B.L. Bradley, 301(JEGP):Oct89-596
C.S. Brown, 569(SR):Winter89-139
M. Engel, 133:Band22Heft3/4-357
J.M.M., 295(JML):Fall88/Winter89-400
Komesaroff, P.A. Objectivity, Science and Society.
R.J. Faber, 488:Jun89-250
Kommers, D.P. The Constitutional Jurisprudence of the Federal Republic of Germany.
G. Marshall, 617(TLS):21-27Sep90-995
Kondrup, J. Livsvaerker.
S.H. Rossel, 563(SS):Spring/Summer89-291
Koneko, L. Coming Home from Camp.
S. Foster, 448:Vol27No3-155

Koner, P. Solitary Song.*
  W. Sorell, 151:Aug89-44
König, I. "Anonymus Valesianus, Origo Con-
  stantini." (Pt 1)
  B. Baldwin, 229:Band61Heft5-453
Konishi, J. A History of Japanese Literature.
  (Vol 1) (E. Miner, ed)
  E.A. Cranston, 318(JAOS):Oct-Dec88-611
Konishi, J. A History of Japanese Litera-
  ture.* (Vol 2) (E. Miner, ed)
  L.R. Rodd, 318(JAOS):Apr-Jun88-337
Könneker, B. Hartmann von Aue: Der arme
  Heinrich.
  H. Kratz, 133:Band22Heft1-54
Konner, M. Why the Reckless Survive.
  R. Dunbar, 441:29Jul90-11
Konovalov, V.N., ed. Russkaja literaturnaja
  kritika 70-80 gg. XIX veka.
  S.J. Rabinowitz, 574(SEEJ):Spring89-125
Kontje, T.C. Constructing Reality.
  R.L. Crawston, 133:Band22Heft3/4-329
  B. Fischer, 221(GQ):Spring89-271
  R.C. Reimer, 406:Winter89-496
Konvitz, J.W. Cartography in France 1660-
  1848.
  D. Buisseret, 529(QQ):Spring89-162
Konwicki, T. Bohin Manor.
  J. Bayley, 453(NYRB):19Jul90-23
  P. Hampl, 441:15Jul90-7
Koon, G.W., ed. A Collection of Classic
  Southern Humor. A Collection of Classic
  Southern Humor II.
  J.E. Brown, 580(SCR):Fall89-131
Koon, H.P. - see under Heng Pek Koon
Koontz, D.R. The Bad Place.
  K. Ramsland, 441:18Feb90-20
Koopmans, J. & P. Verhuyck. Sermon joyeux
  et truanderie (Villon - Nemo - Ule-
  spiègle).*
  G. Demerson, 535(RHL):Jan-Feb89-87
  S.M. Taylor, 201:Vol15-341
Koopmans, J. & P. Verhuyck, eds. Ulenspiegel
  de sa vie de ses oeuvres.
  E.E. Du Bruck, 201:Vol15-337
  T. Peach, 402(MLR):Oct90-953
Köpeczi, B. Une Enquête linguistique et folk-
  lorique chez les Roumains de Transylvanie
  du Nord 1942-1943.
  I. Taloş, 196:Band30Heft1/2-139
Kopelman, L.M. & J.C. Moskop, eds. Children
  and Health Care.
  R.B., 185:Jul90-924
Koperski, K. The Iconography of Rebirth.
  Ritual Renewal.
  L. Fish, 440:Winter-Spring89-152
Koplow, L. Where Rag Dolls Hide Their Faces.
  S.L. Jamison, 441:24Jun90-21
Koppitz, H-J. - see "Gutenberg-Jahrbuch
  1989"
Kops, B. Barricades in West Hampstead.
  M. Horovitz, 493:Autumn89-56
Korelitz, J.H. The Properties of Breath.*
  S. Pugh, 493:Spring89-47
Korinman, M. Quand l'Allemagne pensait le
  monde.
  U. Raulff, 358:Jun90-6
Kornai, J. The Road to a Free Economy.
  B.P. Bosworth, 441:27May90-17
Körner, K-H. Korrelative Sprachtypologie.*
  E. Schepper, 439(NM):1989/2-221

Körner, K.H. & M. Vitse, eds. Las influencias
  mutuas entre España y Europa a partir del
  siglo XVI.
  F. Meregalli, 547(RF):Band101Heft4-497
Körner, S. & R. Chisholm - see Brentano, F.
Kornis, M. A Félelem dicsérete.
  G. Szirtes, 617(TLS):4-10May90-468
Kornwolf, J.D. "So Good a Design."
  T.C. McDonald, Jr., 656(WMQ):Oct89-808
  P.V. Turner, 576:Dec89-405
Korotich, V., ed. The Best of "Ogonyok."
  G. Webb, 617(TLS):15-21Jun90-632
Kors, A.C. Atheism in France 1650-1729.
  (Vol 1)
  J. McManners, 617(TLS):2-8Nov90-1185
Kors, A.C. & P.J. Korshin, eds. Anticipations
  of the Enlightenment in England, France,
  and Germany.
  J.V. Guerinot, 568(SCN):Fall-Winter89-
  57
Korshin, P., ed. Johnson after Two Hundred
  Years.*
  G.J. Kolb, 301(JEGP):Apr89-241
  M.G.H. Pittock, 83:Spring89-111
  D. Womersley, 541(RES):May89-274
Kort, W.A. Modern Fiction and Human Time.
  N. Simms, 478(P&L):Apr89-190
Kort, W.A. Story, Text and Scripture.
  D.L. Jeffrey, 627(UTQ):Summer90-569
Korte, H. Ordnung und Tabu.
  M. Swales, 402(MLR):Jul90-806
Kortländer, B. & F. Nies, eds. Französische
  Literatur in deutscher Sprache.*
  M. Brody, 549(RLC):Jul-Sep89-400
Kortt, I.R. & J.B. Simčenko. Wörterverzeichnis
  der nganasanischen Sprache. (Vol 1)
  M. Katzschmann, 260(IF):Band94-369
Kos, P. The Monetary Circulation in the
  Southeastern Alpine Region ca. 300 B.C. -
  A.D. 1000.
  B. Prokisch, 229:Band61Heft6-563
Kosáry, D. Culture and Society in Eigh-
  teenth-Century Hungary.
  G.F. Cushing, 575(SEER):Apr89-268
Koselleck, R. Critique and Crisis.
  R.V.S., 185:Oct89-209
Köseoğlu, C. The Topkapı Saray Museum: The
  Treasury. (J.M. Rogers, ed & trans)
  R. Hillenbrand, 59:Mar89-109
Koskoff, E., ed. Women and Music in Cross-
  Cultural Perspective.
  J.C. DjeDje, 187:Fall89-514
Kosloswki, P., R. Spaemann & R. Löw, eds.
  Moderne oder Postmoderne?
  H. Busche, 687:Jan-Mar89-177
Kossmann, O. Polen im Mittelalter. (Vol 2)
  P.W. Knoll, 575(SEER):Jan89-134
Kosta, P. Probleme der Švejk-Übersetzungen
  in den west- und südslavischen Sprachen.
  A. Měšťan, 688(ZSP):Band49Heft1-199
Kostash, M. No Kidding.
  M.P. Maxwell, 529(QQ):Summer89-553
Koster, C.J. Word Recognition in Foreign and
  Native Language.*
  E.A. Levenston, 710:Sep89-336
Koster, J. Domains and Dynasties.
  R.D. Borsley, 297(JL):Sep89-526
Koster, R.M. & G. Sanchez Borbon. In the Time
  of Tyrants.
  C. Krauss, 617(TLS):30Nov-6Dec90-1284
  D. Traxel, 441:4Nov90-24
Koster, S. Ille Ego Qui.
  S.J. Harrison, 123:Vol39No2-399

Kostiainen, A. Loikkarit.
D. Kirby, 575(SEER):Jul89-480
Kostof, S. America by Design.*
N. Boretz, 658:Winter89-302
Kostrzewa, R., ed. Between East and West.
E. Kuryluk, 441:1Apr90-23
Kosztolnyik, Z.J. From Coloman the Learned
to Béla III (1095-1196).
M. Rady, 575(SEER):Apr89-294
Kott, J., ed. Four Decades of Polish Essays.
L. Weschler, 617(TLS):2-8Nov90-1173
Kott, J. - see Gombrowicz, W.
Kötting, B. Die Bewertung der Wiederverheir-
atung (der zweiten Ehe) in der Antike und
in der frühen Kirche.
G. Clark, 123:Vol39No2-410
Kotz, M.L. Rauschenberg/Art and Life.
J. Russell, 441:2Dec90-9
Kotzwinkle, W. The Hot Jazz Trio.
D. Manuel, 441:25Feb90-13
Koudal, J.H. Rasmus Storms nodebog.
B. Nyberg, 64(Arv):Vol44-206
Kovács, A., with K. Benedek. A magyar állat-
mesék katalógusa (AaTh 1-299). (2nd ed)
H-J. Uther, 196:Band30Heft1/2-142
Kovacs, D. The Heroic Muse.*
E.M. Craik, 303(JoHS):Vol109-222
J. Diggle, 24:Summer89-357
W.D. Smith, 124:Nov-Dec89-127
Kovács, S.I., ed. Angol életrajz Zrínyi Mikl-
ósról, London, 1664.
G.F. Cushing, 575(SEER):Jan89-139
Kövecses, Z. Metaphors of Anger, Pride and
Love.*
C. Goddard, 361:Jan89-90
Kowal, D.M. Ribalta y los Ribaltescos.
A. Espinós Díaz, 48:Jan-Mar89-99
Kowalke, K.H., ed. A New Orpheus.*
H.A. Lea, 222(GR):Fall89-183
W. Mann, 607:Mar89-39
617(TLS):27Apr-3May90-457
Kozloff, S. Invisible Storytellers.
B. Covey, 599:Spring90-159
D. Pye, 402(MLR):Apr90-433
Kozlova, M.G. Rossiia i strany iugo-vostoch-
noi Azii.
K. Hitchins, 293(JASt):Feb89-221
Kozulin, A. - see Vygotsky, L.
Krabbenhoft, K. - see Cohen de Herrera, A.
Krabiel, K-D. - see von Eichendorff, J.
Krafchick, M. World Without Heroes.
L. Field, 395(MFS):Summer89-288
Kraft, E. Reservations Recommended.
C. Van Bibber, 441:5Aug90-23
Kraft, H. Mein Indien liegt in Rüschhaus.*
R.E. Panny, 564:Sep89-272
Kraft, K., ed. Zen.
H-J. Kim, 293(JASt):Feb89-119
Kraft-Schwenk, C. Ilse Frapan.
S.L. Cocalis, 406:Summer89-231
Krahnke, K. Approaches to Syllabus Design
for Foreign Language Teaching.
E.M. Guthrie, 399(MLJ):Spring89-78
Krakauer, J. Eiger Dreams.
T. Cahill, 441:10Jun90-48
Krakowian, B. O Nauczaniu Rozumienia Mowy
Obcojęzycznej.
K. Drożdzial-Szelest, 710:Dec89-466
Kramer, B. Papyrus grecs de la Bibliothèque
nationale et universitaire de Strasbourg.
(Nos. 501-800: Index)
J.D. Thomas, 229:Band61Heft8-737
Kramer, D. - see Hardy, T.

Kramer, H., ed. The New Criterion Reader.*
D.D. Todd, 478(P&L):Apr89-194
Kramer, J. Europeans.
639(VQR):Spring89-61
Kramer, J.D. Listen to the Music.
N. Simeone, 415:Sep89-547
Kramer, J.D. The Time of Music.
D. Butler, 413:Summer90-446
Kramer, L.S. Threshold of a New World.
R.D.E. Burton, 208(FS):Apr89-217
A. Demaitre, 242:Vol10No5-630
S. Petrey, 207(FR):May90-1065
Kramer, V.A., ed. The Harlem Renaissance
Re-Examined.
N. Harris, 395(MFS):Summer89-307
Krämling, G. Die systembildende Rolle von
Ästhetik und Kulturphilosophie bei Kant.*
L. Koch, 687:Jul-Sep89-564
K. Konhardt, 342:Band80Heft2-231
Krantz, J. Dazzle.
S. Dundon, 441:16Dec90-18
Kranz, G. Das Architekturgedicht.
G. Goebel-Schilling, 52:Band24Heft1-81
Krashen, S.D. Second Language Acquisition
and Second Language Learning.
E.B. Bernhardt, 399(MLJ):Winter89-483
Krasnobaev, B.I. Ocherki istorii russkoi kul'-
tury XVIII veka.
G. Marker, 550(RusR):Jan89-116
Krasnov, V. Soviet Defectors.*
M. Dewhirst, 575(SEER):Oct89-650
Kratz, A-I. Altonaer Möbel des Rokoko und
Klassizismus.
S. Jervis, 90:Oct89-719
Kratzmann, G. & J. Simpson. Medieval English
Religious and Ethical Literature.*
J.D. Burnley, 541(RES):Feb89-111
Kraus, D. & H. The Gothic Choirstalls of
Spain.
D. Gillerman, 589:Jul89-733
Kraus, F.R. Königliche Verfügungen in Alt-
babylonischer Zeit.
S. Greengus, 318(JAOS):Jan-Mar88-153
Kraus, W. & W. Lütkenhorst. The Economic
Development of the Pacific Basin.
T. Ozawa, 293(JASt):May89-338
Krause, C., ed. The Ties that Bind.
J.B. Kerman, 440:Winter-Spring89-150
Krause, J. What We Bring Home.
P.M. St. Pierre, 102(CanL):Spring89-210
Krause, L.B., K.A. Tee & L. Yuan. The Singa-
pore Economy Reconsidered.
W.G. Huff, 293(JASt):Feb89-222
Krauss, H., ed. Literatur der Französischen
Revolution.
P. Wagner, 166:Jul90-349
Krauss, H. & D. Rieger - see Köhler, E.
Krausse, G.H., ed. Urban Society in Southeast
Asia.
J.A. Hafner, 293(JASt):Feb89-223
Krausz, M., ed. Relativism.
P.A. Roth, 103:Feb90-66
R.M.S., 185:Jul90-905
Kraut, R. Aristotle on the Human Good.
C. Rowe, 617(TLS):11-17May90-507
R.J. Sullivan, 543:Jun90-872
Krauth, N. The Bathing Machine Called the
Twentieth Century.
M. Buck, 441:18Mar90-20
Krautheimer, R. The Rome of Alexander VII,
1655-1667.
P.D. Partner, 278(IS):Vol43-160

Krebs, R. L'idée de "Théâtre National" dans
l'Allemagne des Lumières.
  R. Bauer, 549(RLC):Jul–Sep89–412
Krech, E–M. Vortragskunst.
  E. Ockel, 685(ZDL):1/1989–116
Kreczi, H. Das Bruckner–Stift St. Florian und
das Linzer Reichs–Bruckner–Orchester
(1942–1945).
  W. Kirsch, 417:Apr–Jun89–182
Kreider, I.E. – see Cavaccio, G.
Kreindler, I.T., ed. Sociolinguistic Perspec-
tives on Soviet National Languages.
  S.I. Treskova, 355(LSoc):Sep89–426
Kreis, G. & M.S. Strauss – see Keun, I.
Kreiter–Kurylo, C. Contrary Visions.*
  E.C. Lynskey, 577(SHR):Summer89–285
Kremer, D., ed. Homenagem a Joseph M. Piel
por ocasião de seu 85.° aniversário.
  D. Messner, 547(RF):Band101Heft4–457
Krémer, J–P. Le Désir dans l'oeuvre de Mon-
therlant.
  P. Danger, 535(RHL):Sep–Oct89–941
Kremer, L. & T. Sodmann, eds. Flurnamenfor-
schung im Westmünsterland.
  D. Stellmacher, 685(ZDL):3/1989–387
Kremnitz, G. – see Fabre d'Olivet, A.
Krenzlin, N., ed. Asthetik des Widerstands.
  S. Lange, 654(WB):3/1989–522
Kress, N. Brain Rose.
  G. Jonas, 441:11Feb90–29
Kretzmann, N., ed. Meaning and Inference in
Medieval Philosophy.
  J.J.E. Gracia & J. Kronen, 543:Sep89–170
Kreutzer, H.J. – see "Kleist Jahrbuch
1988/89"
Kreuziger, F.A. The Religion of Science Fic-
tion.
  J.E. Huchingson, 561(SFS):Nov89–388
de Krey, G.S. A Fractured Society.*
  L.K.J. Glasey, 566:Spring89–199
Kreyder, L. L'Enfance des saints et des
autres.*
  G. Jacques, 356(LR):Aug89–220
Krieger, A. & others. The Architecture of
Kallmann McKinnell & Wood.
  C.D. Warren, 45:Apr89–55
Krier, F. La zone frontière du francoproven-
çal et de l'alémanique dans le Valais.*
  I. Werlen, 685(ZDL):2/1989–258
Krier, R. Architectural Composition.
  D. Gosling, 46:Apr89–12
Krinsky, C.H. Gordon Bunshaft of Skidmore,
Owings and Merrill.*
  P. Johnson, 45:May89–79
  B. Russell, 46:Dec89–12
Krisch, T. Konstruktionsmuster und Bedeu-
tungswandel indogermanischer Verben.
  E. Seebold, 260(IF):Band94–333
Krist, G. The Garden State.
  T. Wilhelmus, 249(HudR):Autumn89–493
Kristeller, P.O., comp. Iter Italicum, accedunt
alia itinera. (Index Vol 3) (B.D. Kent, R.
Rainey & P.O. Kristeller, comps)
  J.W. O'Malley, 589:Oct89–987
Kristensson, G. A Survey of Middle English
Dialects 1290–1350.
  N.F. Blake, 677(YES):Vol20–210
  A. Hudson, 541(RES):Feb89–104
  L.M. Matheson, 589:Apr89–459
  E.G. Stanley, 447(N&Q):Sep89–363
Kristeva, J. Black Sun.
  P. Meisel, 441:25Feb90–31

Kristeva, J. Etrangers à nous–mêmes.
  J.M. Laroche, 207(FR):Feb90–580
Kristeva, J. In the Beginning Was Love.
Tales of Love.
  L.W. Rabine, 188(ECr):Spring89–100
Kristeva, J. Les Samouraïs.
  E. Showalter, 617(TLS):28Sep–4Oct90–
1038
Kristiansen, B. Thomas Manns Zauberberg
und Schopenhauers Metaphysik. (2nd ed)
  D.W. Adolphs, 133:Band22Heft1–72
Kristjánsson, A. – see Gíslason, K.
Kritzman, L.D. – see Foucault, M.
Krleža, M. Le Retour de Philippe Latinovicz.
  L. Kovacs, 450(NRF):Feb89–154
von Krockow, C. Die Deutschen in ihrem
Jahrhundert 1890–1990.
  G.A. Craig, 453(NYRB):28Jun90–25
Kroeber, K. Romantic Fantasy and Science
Fiction.
  G. Hirsch, 637(VS):Spring90–522
Kroetsch, R. Excerpts from the Real World.
  M. Jones, 102(CanL):Winter88–119
Kroker, A. & D. Cook. The Postmodern Scene.*
  M.H. Keefer, 102(CanL):Spring89–225
  G. McGregor, 298:Fall89–147
Kroker, A. & M. Body Invaders.
  G. McGregor, 298:Fall89–147
Kroker, A., M. Kroker & D. Crook. Panic En-
cyclopedia.
  W.T. Gordon, 150(DR):Spring89–147
Kröller, E–M. Canadian Travellers in Europe
1851–1900.*
  G. Warkentin, 102(CanL):Spring89–171
Kronick, J.G. American Poetics of History.*
  D.T. O'Hara, 125:Fall88–100
"Kronika: 5–ty Kresowy Baon C.K.M."
  J.T. Hapak, 497(PolR):Vol34No3–265
Kroos, R. Der Schrein des heiligen Servatius
in Maastricht und die vier Zugehörigen
Reliquiare in Brüssel.*
  P. Lasko, 589:Oct89–988
Kropp–Dakubu, M.E., ed. The Languages of
Ghana.*
  I.R. Dihoff, 399(MLJ):Summer89–208
  B. Heine, 353:Vol27No2–369
Kruba, E. & A. Joukovsky, eds. Ukraine
1917–1932.
  D. Saunders, 575(SEER):Apr89–315
Krückmann, P.O. Federico Benkovitch.
  G. Knox, 90:Sep89–655
Kruft, H–W. Geschichte der Architekturthe-
orie.
  D. Wiebenson, 576:Mar89–79
Kruft, H–W. Städte in Utopia, Die Idealstadt
vom 15. bis zum 18. Jahrhundert zwischen
Staatsutopie und Wirklichkeit.
  G. Seibt, 358:Feb90–7
Krugman, P. The Age of Diminished Expecta-
tions.
  P. Passell, 441:28Oct90–26
Krukowski, L. Art and Concept.*
  H. Pardee, 127:Summer89–194
Krumeich, G. Jeanne d'Arc in der Geschichte.
  G. Seibt, 358:Feb90–7
Krummel, D.W. Bibliographical Handbook of
American Music.
  R. Crawford, 187:Spring/Summer89–324
  D. Nicholls, 410(M&L):Feb89–121
Krummel, D.W. The Memory of Sound.
  517(PBSA):Mar89–118

Krummel, D.W. & S. Sadie, eds. Music Printing and Publishing.
  O. Neighbour, 617(TLS):12-18Oct90-1103
Krupat, A. The Voice in the Margin.
  N. Lang, 590:Jun90-78
Kruse, J. Der Tanz der Zeichen.*
  H-D. Dahnke, 654(WB):1/1989-160
Kruse, J.A. - see "Heine-Jahrbuch"
Kruse, J.A. & B. Kortländer, eds. Das Junge Deutschland.*
  G. Benda, 406:Winter89-501
Kruuk, H. The Social Badger.
  T.J. Roper, 617(TLS):12-18Oct90-1109
Kryzanek, M.J. & H.J. Wiarda. The Politics of External Influence in the Dominican Republic.
  G.P. Atkins, 263(RIB):Vol39No1-71
Krzyzanowski, J.R. Advanced Polish.*
  L. Woytak, 399(MLJ):Autumn89-381
Krzyzanowski, J.R., C.Y. Bethin & W.A. Wierzewski. Reading Polish.* (Vol 1)
  L. Woytak, 399(MLJ):Autumn89-381
Krzyzanowski, J.R., Z.K. Mirski & D.W. Roney. Elementary Polish.* Intermediate Polish.*
  L. Woytak, 399(MLJ):Autumn89-381
Krzyzanowski, J.R. & D.W. Roney. Reading Polish.* (Vols 2 & 3)
  L. Woytak, 399(MLJ):Autumn89-381
Kube-McDowell, M.P. The Quiet Pools.
  G. Jonas, 441:8Jul90-22
Kubovy, M. The Psychology of Perspective and Renaissance Art.*
  M.A. Holly, 242:Vol10No3-383
Kucich, J. Repression in Victorian Fiction.*
  N. Armstrong, 445(NCF):Mar90-556
  P.K. Garrett, 301(JEGP):Oct89-541
  J. Sudrana, 158:Sep89-120
Kuczyński, K.A. Polnische Literatur in deutscher Übersetzung von den Anfängen bis 1985.
  D. Arendt, 52:Band24Heft3-336
Kuczynski, P-P. Latin American Debt.
  E.N. Baklanoff, 263(RIB):Vol39No1-72
Kudaka, G. Persona.
  S. Foster, 448:Vol27No3-155
"Kudrun." (B. Murdoch, ed & trans)
  G. Gillespie, 402(MLR):Apr90-494
Kuehl, J. Alternate Worlds.
  S. Moore, 532(RCF):Fall89-227
  B. Stoltzfus, 268(IFR):Summer90-133
Kuehn, M. Scottish Common Sense in Germany, 1768-1800.*
  H.B. Nisbet, 402(MLR):Jan90-242
Kuenzli, R.E., ed. Dada and Surrealist Film.*
  S. Fischer, 207(FR):Mar90-729
Kugler, H. Die Vorstellung der Stadt in der Literatur des deutschen Mittelalters.
  A. Classen, 589:Oct89-990
  S.G. De Maris, 301(JEGP):Jul89-371
  J-D. Müller, 684(ZDA):Band118Heft3-126
  P. Strohschneider, 680(ZDP):Band108 Heft3-434
Kuh, P. An Available Man.
  F. Stanfill, 441:29Jul90-20
Kuhles, D., with E. von Wilamowitz-Moellendorff, eds. Lessing-Bibliographie 1971-1985.
  H.B. Nisbet, 402(MLR):Jul90-791
Kühlmann, W. & W.E. Schäfer, eds. Des Jesaias Romplers von Löwenhalt erstes gebüsch seiner Reim-getiche 1647.*
  G. Dünnhaupt, 406:Fall89-388

Kuhn, A.K. Christa Wolf's Utopian Vision.*
  J. Clausen, 125:Spring89-322
  U. Dersch-Lawson, 221(GQ):Fall89-554
  K.L. Komar, 395(MFS):Summer89-354
  R. Schmidt, 402(MLR):Apr89-529
Kuhn, D. Die Song-Dynastie (960 bis 1279).
  C. Schirokauer, 244(HJAS):Dec89-671
Kuhn, D. - see von Goethe, J.W. & J.F. Cotta von Cottendorf
Kühn, J-H. & U. Fleischer. Index Hippocraticus.* (Fasc 1 & 2)
  J. Mansfeld, 394:Vol42fasc1/2-182
Kühn, J-H. & U. Fleischer. Index Hippocraticus. (fasc 3)
  H. King, 123:Vol39No2-386
Kühn, P. Mit dem Wörterbuch arbeiten.
  D. Herberg, 682(ZPSK):Band42Heft4-536
Kuhn, P.A. Soulstealers.
  C. Hibbert, 441:11Nov90-20
Kühnel, J., H-D. Mück & U. Müller, eds. Mittelalter-Rezeption III.
  A. Classen, 201:Vol15-344
Kuhnen, H-P. Nordwest Palästina in hellenistisch-römischer Zeit.
  M. Goodman, 313:Vol79-245
Kuhrt, A. & S. Sherwin-White, eds. Hellenism in the East.
  M.M. Austin, 303(JoHS):Vol109-255
  E.E. Rice, 123:Vol39No1-80
  R.K. Sherk, 124:Sep-Oct89-73
Kuhse, H. The Sanctity-of-Life Doctrine in Medicine.*
  G. Hunt, 521:Jul89-274
Kuhse, H. & P. Singer. Should the Baby Live?
  K. Dixon, 449:Apr89-256
Kui-kwong, S. - see under Shum Kui-kwong
Kuic, V. - see Simon, Y.R.
Kukathas, C. Hayek and Modern Liberalism.
  B. Barry, 358:Feb90-6
Kuklick, B. - see James, W.
Kula, W., N. Assorodobraj-Kula & M. Kula, eds. Writing Home.* (J. Wtulich, ed & trans)
  T.H. Holloway, 104(CASS):Spring89-89
  J.S. Pula, 497(PolR):Vol34No1-89
Kull, S. Minds at War.*
  S. Plous, 185:Jan90-49
Kultgen, J. Ethics and Professionalism.
  A.I. Applbaum, 185:Apr90-687
"Kultur macht Politik."
  J. Marten, 654(WB):2/1989-341
Kumar, K. & J. Stackhouse. Classical Music of South India.*
  R.K. Wolf, 187:Winter89-175
Kumar, N. The Artisans of Banaras.
  S.B. Freitag, 293(JASt):Aug89-656
Kumar, R. Essays in the Social History of Modern India.
  N.G. Barrier, 293(JASt):Feb89-205
Kumble, S.J. & K.J. Lahart. Conduct Unbecoming.
  S. Zion, 441:25Nov90-27
Kumin, M. In Deep.*
  B. Christophersen, 502(PrS):Winter89-131
  R.B.D., 295(JML):Fall88/Winter89-366
Kumin, M. Nurture.*
  J.F. Cotter, 249(HudR):Autumn89-520
  D.H. George, 219(GaR):Summer89-425
  639(VQR):Autumn89-135
Kümmel, H.M. Nichtliterarische Texte in akkadischer Sprache.
  G.F. Del Monte, 318(JAOS):Apr-Jun88-306

Kummer, I.E. Unlesbarkeit dieser Welt.
  J. Glenn, 221(GQ):Summer89-425
Kundera, M. The Art of the Novel.* (French
  title: L'art du roman.)
  S. Gillespie, 97(CQ):Vol18No2-232
  P. Lewis, 565:Winter88/89-77
  T. Todorov, 494:Winter89-841
Kunert, A.K. Słownik biograficzny konspiracji
  warszawskiej 1939-1944.
  J. Micgiel, 497(PolR):Vol34No3-260
Kunert, G. Fremd Daheim.
  M. Hulse, 617(TLS):5-11Oct90-1064
Kunitz, S. - see Blake, W.
Kunitzsch, P. Über eine "anwā"-Tradition mit
  bisher unbekannten Sternnamen.
  F.J. Ragep, 318(JAOS):Jul-Sep88-496
Kunstadter, P., E.C.F. Bird & S. Sabhasri, eds.
  Man in the Mangroves.
  C. Padoch, 293(JASt):May89-342
Kuntz, P.G. Bertrand Russell.*
  A.C. Lewis, 556:Winter89/90-179
Kunze, E. Deutsch-finnische Literaturbezie-
  hungen.* (E. Häkli, ed)
  G.C. Schoolfield, 133:Band22Heft2-197
Kunze, M. Highroad to the Stake.
  J. Blackwell, 221(GQ):Fall89-523
Kunzle, D. The History of the Comic Strip.
  R. Searle, 441:23Sep90-35
Küper, C. Sprache und Metrum.
  E. Standop, 38:Band107Heft3/4-503
Kupisz, K., G.A. Pérouze & J.Y. Debreuille,
  eds. Le Portrait littéraire.
  G. Cesbron, 356(LR):Nov89-317
Kuppermann, K.O. - see Smith, J.
Kuppner, F. A Concussed History of Scotland.
  I. Bamforth, 617(TLS):16-22Nov90-1232
Kuppner, F. Ridiculous! Absurd! Disgusting!*
  D. Kennedy, 493:Autumn89-48
Kurabayashi, Y. & Y. Matsuda. Economic and
  Social Aspects of the Performing Arts in
  Japan.
  W.J. Baumol, 293(JASt):Nov89-869
Kuralt, C. A Life on the Road.
  S. Simon, 441:28Oct90-12
Kurath, G.P. Half a Century of Dance
  Research.
  C.J. Novack, 187:Winter89-158
Kureishi, H. The Buddha of Suburbia.
  N. Berry, 617(TLS):30Mar-5Apr90-339
  C. Blaise, 441:6May90-20
Kurkela, K. Note and Tone.*
  W.E. Webster, 290(JAAC):Winter89-95
Kurland, P.B. & R. Lerner, eds. The Founders'
  Constitution.*
  D.H. Flaherty, 106:Summer89-81
Kurmann, A. Gregor von Nazianz, "Oratio 4
  gegen Julian."
  W.H.C. Frend, 123:Vol39No2-205
Kurmann, P. La façade de la cathédrale de
  Reims.*
  C. Jacobsson, 341:Vol58No4-176
"Kisho Kurokawa - The Architecture of Sym-
  biosis."
  G. Vorreiter, 46:Oct89-14
Kuromiya, H. Stalin's Industrial Revolution.
  L.H. Siegelbaum, 550(RusR):Apr89-211
Kurth, P. American Cassandra.
  N. Bliven, 442(NY):17Sep90-105
  T. Griffith, 441:29Jul90-12
  G.C. Ward, 453(NYRB):16Aug90-37

Kurtz, M. Stockhausen.
  R. Maconie, 410(M&L):Aug89-441
  N. Osborne, 607:Dec89-37
  P.W. Schatt, 416:Band4Heft3-271
Kurtz, P. Forbidden Fruit.
  J.G.C., 185:Oct89-209
Kuryluk, E. Salome and Judas in the Cave of
  Sex.*
  M-C. Hamard, 189(EA):Oct-Dec89-446
Kurz, P.K. Apokalyptische Zeit.
  H. Suhr, 221(GQ):Summer89-442
Kurzke, H. Thomas Mann.*
  R. Symington, 564:Feb89-71
Kurzman, D. Fatal Voyage.
  W.H. Honan, 441:12Aug90-9
Kurzon, D. It is hereby performed...
  P.M. Tiersma, 603:Vol13No1-245
Kurzweil, E. The Freudians.
  P. Roazen, 627(UTQ):Spring90-454
Kurzweil, R. The Age of Intelligent Machines.
  J.L. Garfield, 441:9Sep90-36
Kushner, D. A Book Dragon.
  M-A. Stouck, 102(CanL):Summer89-194
Küspert, K-C. Vokalsysteme im Westnord-
  ischen.
  M. Bonner, 685(ZDL):3/1989-347
Kussi, P. - see Capek, K.
Kussmaul, A. A General View of the Rural
  Economy of England, 1538-1840.
  R. Houston, 617(TLS):7-13Dec90-1328
Kusz, J. Road Song.
  C. McFadden, 441:16Dec90-12
Kutler, S.I. The Wars of Watergate.
  J.A. Lukas, 441:3Jun90-11
  442(NY):20Aug90-91
Kutnik, J. The Novel as Performance.*
  C. Bode, 224(GRM):Band39Heft3-365
Kutscher, T., with P. Coppens. Les Enfants de
  Sophie.
  J.I. Donohoe, Jr., 102(CanL):Spring89-
  153
Kutzinski, V.M. Against the American Grain.*
  K. Ellis, 240(HR):Spring89-268
Kuzichkin, V. Inside the KGB.
  A. Knight, 617(TLS):7-13Dec90-1309
Kuznecova, A.I. & T.F. Efremova. Slovar'
  morfem russkogo jazyka.
  H.H. Keller, 574(SEEJ):Summer89-323
Kuzniar, A.A. Delayed Endings.*
  R. Gould, 564:May89-173
  D. McCort, 593:Spring89-75
  G. von Molnár, 301(JEGP):Jan89-74
  J.C. Pettey, 591(SIR):Summer89-326
  D. Purdy, 406:Fall89-394
Kuzwayo, E. Sit Down and Listen.
  M. Jaggi, 617(TLS):7-13Dec90-1326
Kvanvig, J.L. The Possibility of an All-
  Knowing God.*
  W. Hasker, 482(PhR):Jan89-125
Kvart, I. A Theory of Counterfactuals.
  F. Jackson, 316:Sep89-1100
  R. Torretti, 160:Jul89-254
Kvetnickij, F. Clavis Poetica.* (B. Uhlen-
  bruch, ed)
  M.J. Okenfuss, 104(CASS):Spring-Win-
  ter88-481
Kvideland, R. & H.K. Sehmsdorf, eds. Scandi-
  navian Folk Belief and Legend.
  K.M. Stokker, 563(SS):Autumn89-411
Kwong, J. Cultural Revolution in China's
  Schools, May 1966-April 1969.
  J. Unger, 293(JASt):Feb89-137
Kyi, A.S.S. - see under Aung San Suu Kyi

Kyle, J., ed. Sign and School.
  J. Albertini, 710:Mar89-94
Kylhammar, M. Maskin och idyll.*
  C.C. Fraser, 563(SS):Winter89-68
Kymlicka, W. Liberalism, Community and Culture.
  J.W. Nickel, 103:Oct90-413
Kyōichi Sonoda - see under Sonoda, K.
Kyte, E.C. Unbeatable Bessie.
  T.C. Holyoke, 42(AR):Winter89-105
Kytö, M., O. Ihalainen & M. Rissanen, eds.
  Corpus Linguistics, Hard and Soft.*
  G. Bourquin, 189(EA):Apr-Jun89-205

Laade, W. Das korsische Volkslied. (Vol 3)
  H. Shields, 187:Fall89-535
van Laarhoven, J. - see John of Salisbury
Labande-Mailfert, Y. & others. Histoire de
  l'abbaye Sainte-Croix de Poitiers.
  P.D. Johnson, 589:Apr89-460
Labarca, A. & J.M. Hendrickson. Nuevas
  Dimensiones.
  C.R. Riess, 399(MLJ):Autumn89-388
Labor, E., R.C. Leitz 3d & I.M. Shepard - see
  London, J.
Laborie, P. L'Opinion française sous Vichy.
  T. Judt, 617(TLS):28Sep-4Oct90-1018
La Bossière, C.R. The Victorian "Fol Sage."
  E. Barton, 268(IFR):Summer89-137
La Botz, D. The Crisis of Mexican Labor.
  I. Roxborough, 263(RIB):Vol39No1-74
Labrador Herraiz, J.J., R. Di Franco & M.T.
  Cacho - see de Rojas, P.
Labrador Herraiz, J.J. & J. Fernández Jimé-
  nez, eds. Cervantes and the Pastoral.*
  C.D. Martínez, 238:May89-300
de La Bretonne, R. - see under Restif de La
  Bretonne
Labro, P. Un Eté dans l'Ouest.
  E. Langlois, 207(FR):Dec89-403
La Capra, D. History, Politics, and the
  Novel.*
  J. Hardin, 133:Band22Heft2-151
  C. Landauer, 478(P&L):Apr89-200
  D. Polan, 494:Fall89-647
  I.V., 295(JML):Fall88/Winter89-246
La Capra, D. Soundings in Critical Theory.
  F.T. Jones, 590:Jun90-79
Lacey, M.J., ed. Religion and Twentieth Cen-
  tury American Intellectual Life.
  D. Jenkins, 617(TLS):23-29Mar90-326
Lachaine, F. Travail au noir.
  P. Haeck, 102(CanL):Spring89-204
La Charité, V.A. The Dynamics of Space.*
  B. Marchal, 535(RHL):Sep-Oct89-934
  D.A. Reynolds, 208(FS):Apr89-223
  M. Robillard, 403(MLS):Fall89-116
Lachet, C. La "Prise d'Orange" ou la parodie
  courtoise d'une épopée.*
  J-P. Martin, 356(LR):Nov89-323
Lachinger, J., A. Schiffkorn & W. Zettl, eds.
  Johannes Urzidil und der Prager Kreis.
  L.J. King, 406:Spring89-116
Lachs, J. Mind and Philosophers.
  A. Kerr-Lawson, 619:Fall89-531
Lachs, J. George Santayana.*
  J.E. Abbott, 619:Summer89-355
Lackey, D.P. The Ethics of War and Peace.
  K.W.K., 185:Apr90-715
Lacorne, D., J. Rupnik & M-F. Toinet, eds.
  The Rise and Fall of Anti-Americanism.
  H. Brogan, 617(TLS):5-11Oct90-1076

Lacoste, J. La philosophie au XXe siècle.
  P. Engel, 98:Mar89-204
Lacoste-Veysseyre, C. & P. Laubriet - see
  Gautier, T.
Lacoue-Labarthe, P. La Fiction du politique.
  J-J. Goux, 153:Fall-Winter89-10
Lacoue-Labarthe, P. Heidegger, Art and Pol-
  itics.
  D.E. Cooper, 617(TLS):23-29Nov90-1269
Lacoue-Labarthe, P. & J-L. Nancy. The Lit-
  erary Absolute.
  I. Balfour, 400(MLN):Apr89-727
Lacouture, J. De Gaulle: The Rebel, 1890-
  1944.
  S.E. Ambrose, 441:11Nov90-1
Lactantius. Lactance, De mortibus persecu-
  torum.* (J.L. Creed, ed & trans)
  M. Reydellet, 555:Vol62Fasc1-166
Lactantius. Lactance, "Epitomé des Institu-
  tions divines." (M. Perrin, ed & trans)
  R. Braun, 555:Vol62Fasc2-372
Lacy, A. The Garden in Autumn.
  B. Neal, 441:2Dec90-40
Lacy, N.J. & others, eds. The Arthurian
  Encyclopedia.*
  D.H. Nelson, 188(ECr):Fall89-111
Lacy, N.J. & G. Ashe. The Arthurian Hand-
  book.*
  D.H. Nelson, 188(ECr):Winter89-106
Lacy, N.J., D. Kelly & K. Busby, eds. The
  Legacy of Chrétien de Troyes. (Vol 1)
  L.C. Brook, 382(MAE):1989/1-168
  T. Hunt, 208(FS):Apr89-195
  R. Middleton, 402(MLR):Apr90-438
Ladany, L. The Communist Party of China
  and Marxism, 1921-1985.
  S. Leys, 453(NYRB):11Oct90-8
  P.M. Mitchell, 293(JASt):Feb89-138
Laden, M-P. Self-Imitation in the Eigh-
  teenth-Century Novel.*
  C.J. Betts, 208(FS):Apr89-215
  S. Davies, 83:Autumn89-235
  M. Fickes, 400(MLN):Sep89-965
  P. Sabor, 677(YES):Vol20-277
  E. Showalter, Jr., 210(FrF):Jan89-97
  S. Soupel, 549(RLC):Jan-Mar89-123
  J. Whatley, 207(FR):Oct89-161
La Fantasie, G.W. & others - see Williams, R.
Lafarga, F., ed. Diderot.*
  M. Boixareu, 535(RHL):Mar-Apr89-286
  D-H. Pageaux, 535(RHL):Nov-Dec89-1060
La Farge, O. Yellow Sun, Bright Sky. (D.L.
  Caffey, ed)
  L. Owens, 649(WAL):Aug89-178
La Fauci, N. Oggetti e soggetti nella forma-
  zione della morfosintassi romanza.
  J.E. Joseph, 350:Dec90-874
Lafay, A. - see Martin du Gard, R. & G. Du-
  hamel
Lafay, J-C. Le Réel et la critique dans "Ma-
  dame Bovary" de Flaubert.
  Y. Leclerc, 535(RHL):Jan-Feb89-124
Madame de Lafayette. The Princess of
  Cleves.
  T.C. Holyoke, 42(AR):Fall89-501
La Feber, W. The American Age.*
  W.F. Kimball, 617(TLS):8-14Jun90-601
Laferrière, D. How to make love to a Negro.
  D.S. Lenoski, 102(CanL):Summer89-236
Lafetá, J.L. - see under Luiz Lafetá, J.
Lafferty, P. The Downing of Flight Six Heavy.
  N. Callendar, 441:22Jul90-22

Laffey, B. Beatrice Lillie.
D. Kaufman, 441:18Feb90–31
Laffineur, R., ed. Thanatos: Les coutumes
funéraires en Égée à l'Age du Bronze.
J. Bouzek, 229:Band61Heft3–271
Laflamme, S. Contribution à la critique de la
persuasion politique.
J. Pestieau, 154:Vol28No3–511
La Fleur, R.A., ed. The Teaching of Latin in
American Schools.*
M. Cleary, 121(CJ):Apr–May90–364
La Fleur, W.R. Buddhism.
M.E. Tucker, 485(PE&W):Oct89–509
Lafont, B. Documents administratifs sumér-
iens provenant du site de Tello et conser-
vés au Musée du Louvre.
T. Gomi, 318(JAOS):Jul–Sep88–522
La Fontaine, J. Child Sexual Abuse.
M. Beard, 617(TLS):14–20Sep90–968
de La Fontaine, J. The Complete Fables of
Jean de La Fontaine. (N. Spector, ed &
trans) Fifty Fables of La Fontaine. (N.R.
Shapiro, trans)
R. Edson, 472:Vol16No1–87
Lafortune, M. Le Roman québécois.
D.M. Hayne, 102(CanL):Autumn–
Winter89–195
La France, M. La fils d'Ariane et autres nou-
velles.
M. Benson, 102(CanL):Autumn–Winter89–
273
Lafrance, Y. Méthode et exégèse en histoire
de la philosophie.
C. Viano, 192(EP):Jul–Dec89–543
Lafrance, Y. Pour interpréter Platon.* (Vol
1)
A.C. Bowen, 487:Autumn89–268
de La Gorce, J., ed. Jean-Philippe Rameau.
S. Bouissou, 537:Vol75No2–297
Lagos, R., ed. Mujeres Poetas de Hispano-
américa.
E. Rivero, 552(REH):May89–145
Lagos-Pope, M-I., ed. Exile in Literature.
C.K. Thompson, 238:Sep89–559
de Lagrave, J-P. Fleury Mesplet (1734–
1794).*
I. Joubert, 102(CanL)·Winter88–194
Lagrée, J. & P-F. Moreau – see Meyer, L.
de La Guerre, E-C.J. – see under Jacquet de
La Guerre, E–C.
de Laguna, A.R. – see under Rodríguez de
Laguna, A.
Lahaise, R. Guy Delahaye et la modernité
littéraire.
A.L. Amprimoz, 102(CanL):Autumn–
Winter89–281
Laidlaw, A. The First Style in Pompeii.
H. von Hesberg, 229:Band61Heft5–464
Laine, E.J., ed. Affective Factors in Foreign
Language Learning and Teaching.*
C. Engber, 710:Mar89–122
Laing, K. Godhorse.
G. Foden, 617(TLS):18–24May90–533
Laing, K. Woman of the Aeroplanes.
E. Ferber, 441:8Jul90–23
Laird, H.A. Self and Sequence.
J. Lucas, 677(YES):Vol20–335
J. Meyers, 639(VQR):Summer89–555
Laitinen, K. Begärets irrvägar.
L. Thompson, 562(Scan):May89–101

Lake, C. Confessions of a Literary Archaeol-
ogist.
P-L. Adams, 61:Jul90–104
D. Leimbach, 441:16Sep90–23
Lake, P. Anglicans and Puritans?
W.S. Hill, 568(SCN):Fall–Winter89–39
Lake, P. Another Kind of Travel.*
D. Mason, 569(SR):Winter89–xxi
Lakoff, G. Women, Fire, and Dangerous
Things.*
T.W. Crusius, 480(P&R):Vol22No4–299
O. Dahl, 353:Vol27No6–1143
O. Flanagan, 35(AS):Winter89–344
B.S. Hartford, 710:Dec89–462
Lakoff, S. & H.F. York. A Shield in Space?
L.J. Korb, 441:4Feb90–9
Lal, B.B. The Romance of Culture in an Urban
Civilization.
A. Coleman, 617(TLS):11–17May90–505
Lalande, D. Jean II Le Meingre, dit Boucicaut
(1366–1421).*
J-L. Picherit, 207(FR):Oct89–153
Lalande, J.F. 2d, ed. Shaping the Future of
Foreign Language Education.
T. Scanlan, 399(MLJ):Summer89–205
Lalić, I.V. Roll Call of Mirrors. The Passion-
ate Measure.
M. Ford, 617(TLS):26Jan–1Feb90–101
Lalli, B.T. – see under Tedeschini Lalli, B.
Lally, M. Juliana's Room.
J. Meek, 456(NDQ):Winter89–227
Lalouette, C. Textes sacrés et textes pro-
fanes de l'ancienne Égypte.
E.S. Meltzer, 318(JAOS):Apr–Jun88–285
Lamacchia, A. Kant in Italia 1950–1979.
C. La Rocca, 342:Band80Heft4–494
de Lamarck, J-B. Système analytique des
connaissance positives de l'homme.
J. Roger, 531:Jul–Dec89–548
Lamarra, A. & L. Procesi – see "Lexicon phil-
osophicum"
Lamb, C. Elia & The Last Essays of Elia. (J.
Bate, ed)
P. Coustillas, 189(EA):Oct–Dec89–479
Lamb, D. Death, Brain Death and Ethics.
K. Gill, 449:Sep89–545
Lamb, D. Down the Slippery Slope.^
S. Marshall, 518:Oct89–240
T.M.R., 185:Jan90–459
Lamb, M.W. Life in Alaska. (D.W. Zimmerman,
ed)
C.M. Petersen, 649(WAL):Nov89–274
Lambek, J. & P.J. Scott. Introduction to
Higher Order Categorical Logic.
J.L. Bell, 316:Sep89–1113
Lambersy, W. Noces noires.
P. Haeck, 102(CanL):Spring89–204
Lambert, A. No Talking after Lights.
C. Hawtree, 617(TLS):9–15Nov90–1214
Lambert, B. Jennie's Story & Under the Skin.
R. Nunn, 108:Fall89–89
Lambert, J. Labiche en Italie d'après ses
carnets de route, 1834.
H. Gidel, 535(RHL):Jul–Aug89–736
Lambert, J.H. Texte zur Systematologie der
Wissenschaftlichen Erkenntnis.
I. Idalovichi, 242:Vol10No6–752
Lambert, J.W. & M. Ratcliffe. The Bodley
Head, 1887–1987.
C. Spadoni, 470:Vol27–135
Lambert, R.S. South Carolina Loyalists in the
American Revolution.
C.J. Vipperman, 656(WMQ):Jan89–198

Lambot, I., ed. Norman Foster: Buildings and Projects. (Vols 2 & 3)
J. Winter, 46:Aug89-12
Lambrecht, J. Das "Heidelberger Kapellinventar" von 1544 (Codex Pal. Germ. 318).
C. Meyer, 537:Vol75No1-107
Lambropoulos, V. Literature as National Institution.
G. Thaniel, 529(QQ):Autumn89-741
Lambropoulos, V. & D.N. Miller, eds. Twentieth-Century Literary Theory.*
J.R. Bennett, 677(YES):Vol20-218
Lambton, A. Pig and Other Stories.
T. Fitton, 617(TLS):7-13Sep90-956
Lamis, A.P. The Two-Party South. (rev)
R.H. Harber, 585(SoQ):Summer89-125
Lamm, N. Torah Umadda.
M. Shulevitz, 441:19Aug90-19
L'Amour, L. The Haunted Mesa.
J. Brosseau, 456(NDQ):Winter89-214
Lampe, P. Die stadtrömischen Christen in den ersten beiden Jahrhunderten.
W.A. Meeks, 229:Band61Heft4-369
di Lampedusa, G.T. Letteratura inglese. (Vol 1)
M. D'Amico, 617(TLS):4-10May90-470
Lampert, H. True Greed.
P. O'Toole, 441:21Jan90-7
M.M. Thomas, 453(NYRB):29Mar90-3
Lampert, L. Nietzsche's Teaching.
A.P. Fell, 529(QQ):Spring89-66
Lamphere, L. From Working Daughters to Working Mothers.
M. Blewett, 432(NEQ):Mar89-148
Lampman, A. The Story of an Affinity. (D.M.R. Bentley, ed)
C. Ballstadt, 470:Vol27-119
L. Early, 102(CanL):Autumn-Winter89-150
Lamprecht, A. Grammatik der englischen Sprache.
D. Nehls, 257(IRAL):Aug89-258
W. Zydatiss, 38:Band107Heft1/2-106
Lamprecht, A. Praslovanština.
G. Fowler, 350:Jun90-419
Lampton, D.M., ed. Policy Implementation in Post-Mao China.
M. Blecher, 293(JASt):Feb89-140
"Lancelot." (Vols 1-9) (A. Micha, ed)
C-A. Van Coolput, 356(LR):Feb-May89-111
Lanczkowski, J., ed. Erhebe dich, meine Seele.
F.L. Borchardt, 221(GQ):Fall89-518
Landa, J. Bürgerliches Schocktheater.
J. Koppensteiner, 221(GQ):Fall89-557
Landau, E.G. Jackson Pollock.
E. Frank, 441:28Jan90-3
H. Kramer, 617(TLS):16-22Mar90-287
Landeira, R. & L.T. González-del-Valle, eds. Nuevos y novísimos.*
I-J. López, 240(HR):Spring89-264
Landes, D.S. L'heure qu'il est.
H. Cronel, 450(NRF):Feb89-149
Landes, J.B. Women and the Public Sphere in the Age of the French Revolution.*
J.R. Censer, 322(JHI):Oct-Dec89-652
V. Folkenflik, 173(ECS):Winter89/90-218
J.H. Stewart, 207(FR):Feb90-536
Landesman, C. Colour and Consciousness.
R. Smook, 103:Jun90-233
J. Westphal, 617(TLS):13-19Jul90-758

Landheer, R., ed. Aspects de linguistique française.
M. Harris, 402(MLR):Oct90-942
B. Peeters, 350:Sep90-643
Landmann, A. - see Jansky, H.
Landolfi, T. An Autumn Story.
G. Annan, 453(NYRB):27Sep90-17
Landon, H.C.R., ed. The Mozart Compendium.
N. Kenyon, 617(TLS):16-22Nov90-1238
Landon, H.C.R. Mozart: The Golden Years, 1781-1791.
J. Keates, 617(TLS):26Jan-1Feb90-92
E. Leinsdorf, 441:25Feb90-7
Landon, H.C.R. 1791.*
A.H. King, 410(M&L):Feb89-105
Landon, H.C.R. & D. Wyn Jones. Haydn.*
A.P. Brown, 410(M&L):Nov89-540
W.D. Sutcliffe, 415:Jul89-410
Landry, T., with G. Lewis. Tom Landry.
R. Blount, Jr., 441:5Aug90-5
Landsberg, M.E., ed. The Genesis of Language.
S.D. Spangehl, 350:Sep90-644
Landy-Houillon, I. & M. Ménard, eds. Burlesque et formes parodiques.*
L. Godard de Donville, 535(RHL):Jul-Aug89-753
H. Stenzel, 547(RF):Band101Heft1-106
Lane, A.J. To "Herland" and Beyond.
M.B. Norton, 441:15Jul90-10
442(NY):4Jun90-104
Lane, D., ed. Labor and Employment in the USSR.
M.P. Sacks, 104(CASS):Spring89-105
Lane, D. Soviet Society under Perestroika.
O. Figes, 617(TLS):5-11Oct90-1056
Lane, M.T. Reckonings.
R. Labrie, 102(CanL):Autumn-Winter89-143
R. Raglan, 526:Winter89-96
B. Whiteman, 198:Summer89-113
Lane, P. Selected Poems.*
A. Brown, 529(QQ):Summer89-526
T. McKeown, 102(CanL):Autumn-Winter89-220
Lane, R. Graham Greene.
J.K.G., 295(JML):Fall88/Winter89-342
Lane, R.C., ed. Bibliography of Works by and about F.I. Tiutchev to 1985.
A.D.P. Briggs, 575(SEER):Jan89-122
Lane, R.F. Philippine Basketry.
M. Symonds, 60:May-Jun89-158
Lang, A.S. Prophetic Woman.*
E. Dreyer, 97(CQ):Vol18No3-334
S.L. Mizruchi, 432(NEQ):Mar89-105
Lang, B. Philosophy and the Art of Writing.
A. Roda, 478(P&L):Apr89-191
Lang, C.D. Irony/Humor.*
P. Gifford, 208(FS):Jul89-368
W.B. Millard, 147:Vol6No3-58
Lang, C.Y. & E.F. Shannon - see Tennyson, A.
Lang, J. Creating Architectural Theory.
R. Geddes & J. Dill, 505:Nov89-115
Lang, J.T. Viking-Age Decorated Wood.
L. Karlsson, 341:Vol58No4-173
Lang, K. Aryadeva's Catuḥśataka.
J.P. McDermott, 318(JAOS):Apr-Jun88-331
Lang, L. Voyage sur la ligne d'horizon.
J.T. Day, 207(FR):May90-1101
Langan, J.D. Hegel and Mallarmé.*
S. Meitinger, 535(RHL):Jan-Feb89-128

Langan, P. A Life with Food.
A. Foster, 617(TLS):27Jul–2Aug90–809
Langbaum, R. The Word from Below.*
S.P., 295(JML):Fall88/Winter89–230
Langdon, H. Claude Lorrain.
P. Conisbee, 617(TLS):30Mar–5Apr90–351
Langdon, J. Horses, Oxen, and Technological Innovation.
B.B. Blaine, 589:Oct89–993
Langdon, P. Orange Roofs, Golden Arches.
F.T. Kihlstedt, 576:Jun89–204
Lange, W–D., ed. Französische Literatur des 20. Jahrhunderts.*
L. Pollmann, 547(RF):Band101Heft2/3–348
Langer, C. Reform nach Prinzipien.
W. Kersting, 687:Jan–Mar89–186
Langer, J.A., ed. Language, Literacy, and Culture.*
J.E. Spratt, 355(LSoc):Dec89–614
Langer, J.A. & A.N. Applebee. How Writing Shapes Thinking.
A.R. Gere, 128(CE):Oct89–617
A.J. Herrington, 126(CCC):Feb89–100
Langer, O. Mystische Erfahrung und spirituelle Theologie.
F. Tobin, 589:Oct89–995
Langer, S.K. Mind. (G. Van Den Heuvel, ed)
F. Sparshott, 529(QQ):Winter89–985
Langer, U. Invention, Death, and Self-Definitions in the Poetry of Pierre de Ronsard.*
A. Gendre, 535(RHL):Mar Apr89–270
I.D. McFarlane, 551(RenQ):Spring89–125
Langeveld, A. Vertalen wat er staat.
R. Landheer, 204(FdL):Mar89–54
Langevin, G. Comme un lexique des abîmes.
C. May, 102(CanL):Spring89–200
Langford, P. Modern Philosophies of Human Nature.*
K. Hart, 63:Sep89–363
Langford, P. A Polite and Commercial People.
L. Colley, 617(TLS):20–26Apr90–415
Langford, R. Don't take your love to town.
H. Dakin, 581:Jun89–260
Langland, E. Anne Brontë.
M. Reynolds, 617(TLS):10–16Aug90–854
Langland, W. Piers Plowman: The A Verision. (rev) (G. Kane, ed) Piers Plowman: The B Version. (rev) (G. Kane & E.T. Donaldson, eds)
P. Hardman, 402(MLR):Oct90–908
D. Pearsall, 191(ELN):Mar90–73
E.G. Stanley, 447(N&Q):Sep89–363
Langley, G., ed. Animal Experimentation.
J.D. Schwartz, 441:8Jul90–17
Langlois, W. Via Malraux. (D. Bevan, ed)
E. Fallaize, 208(FS):Jan89–111
W.C. Putnam 3d, 207(FR):Feb90–554
Langmann, P. Sozialismus und Literatur: Jura Soyfer.
P. Stenberg, 564:May89–180
Langmuir, G.I. History, Religion, and Anti-semitism. Toward a Definition of Antisemitism.
R.I. Moore, 441:23Dec90–10
Langrock, K. Die Sieben Worte Jesu am Kreuz.
G. Feder, 417:Jan–Mar89–84
Lanier, A.R. Living in the U.S.A. (4th ed)
P.B. Nimmons, 399(MLJ):Autumn89–353
Lankamp, R.E. A Study on the Effect of Terminology on L2 Reading Comprehension.
T.A. Waldspurger, 350:Mar90–195

Lankford, G.E., ed. Native American Legends (Southeastern Legends: Tales from the Natchez, Caddo, Biloxi, Chickasaw, and other Nations).
R.E.W. Ghezzi, 292(JAF):Apr–Jun89–249
R.L. Welsh, 650(WF):Jan89–74
Lankheit, K. Der kurpfälzische Hofbildhauer Paul Egell 1691–1752.
P. Volk, 683:Band52Heft4–579
Lanmon, L.W. William Lescaze, Architect.
L. Wodehouse, 576:Jun89–191
"L'année balzacienne, 5."
R. Fortassier, 535(RHL):Jan–Feb89–123
Lannon, F. Privilege, Persecution, and Prophecy.
R.A.H. Robinson, 86(BHS):Jul89–292
Lansbury, C. The Grotto.*
G. Oldham, 42(AR):Spring89–246
Lansdown, H. & A. Spillius, eds. Saturday's Boys.
M. Ford, 617(TLS):16–22Nov90–1239
Lanters, J. Missed Understandings.
J. Baechler, 329(JJQ):Fall89–156
D.R. Schwarz, 395(MFS):Winter89–798
Lantolf, J.P. & A. Labarca, eds. Research in Second Language Learning.*
C. Chaudron, 710:Dec89–464
Lantz, P. L'argent et la mort.
P. Livet, 192(EP):Jul–Dec89–544
La Palombara, J. Democracy, Italian Style.*
G. Bedani, 278(IS):Vol44 190
L. Riall, 97(CQ):Vol18No2–226
Lapidge, M. & R. Sharpe. A Bibliography of Celtic–Latin Literature, 400–1200.
G.H. Brown, 589:Apr89–461
Lapidus, I.M. A History of Islamic Societies.*
N.E. Gallagher, 293(JASt):May89–343
Lapington, S. Legend of True Labour.*
R. Pybus, 565:Winter88/89–67
Laplanche, F. L'Ecriture, le sacré et l'histoire.
J. Le Brun, 531:Jul–Dec89–522
Laponce, J.A. Languages and Their Territories.* (rev)
G. Lessard, 529(QQ):Summer89–489
Lapp, C.E. Cloud Gate.
P.M. St. Pierre, 102(CanL),Spring89–210
Lapsley, R. & M. Westlake. Film Theory.
J.P. McCarthy, 89(BJA):Summer89–273
A. Neill & A. Ridley, 103:Sep90–345
Lapucci, C. Dizionario dei modi di dire della lingua italiana.
G. Lepschy, 617(TLS):28Sep–4Oct90–1026
Laqueur, T. Making Sex,
M. Konner, 441:9Dec90–27
Laqueur, W. The Long Road to Freedom.*
J. Sherr, 617(TLS):16–22Mar90–273
Laqueur, W. Stalin.
D.K. Shipler, 441:18Nov90–3
Laqueur, W., with others. Soviet Union 2000.
L.V. Sigal, 441:29Jul90–24
Lardet, P. & M. Tavoni, eds. Renaissance Linguistics Archive 1350–1700. (2nd Print-Out)
R. Coluccia, 379(MedR):Aug89–301
Lardreau, G. Fictions philosophiques et science-fiction.
P. Trotignon, 542:Oct–Dec89–637
l'Arétin. Lettres.
M–A. Lescourret, 98:May89–335
Large, D.C. Between Two Fires.
D. Johnson, 617(TLS):12–18Oct90–1095
F.J. Prial, 441:25Feb90–30

de Larivey, P. Les Esprits. (M.J. Freeman, ed)
  C. Smith, 208(FS):Jan89-81
Larkin, P. Collected Poems.* (A. Thwaite, ed)
  W. Bedford, 4:Summer89-76
  B. Hardy, 175:Summer89-177
  A. Hudgins, 249(HudR):Winter89-683
  J. Richardson, 491:Mar90-408
  M.J. Salter, 676(YR):Autumn89-129
  D. Wojahn, 219(GaR):Fall89-589
  M. Wood, 472:Vol16No1-165
  639(VQR):Autumn89-135
Larmer, R.A.H. Water Into Wine?
  D. Nagarajan, 529(QQ):Summer89-521
Larmore, C.E. Patterns of Moral Complexity.*
  J. Waldron, 311(JP):Jun89-331
von La Roche, S. Pomona für Teutschlands Töchter. (J. Vorderstemann, ed)
  K. Nyholm, 439(NM):1989/3&4-393
Laronde, A. Cyrène et la Libye hellénistique.
  J.M. Alonso-Núñez, 123:Vol39No2-409
Laroon, M. The Criers and Hawkers of London. (S. Shesgreen, ed)
  S. Coates, 441:23Sep90-51
  T. Russell-Cobb, 324:Jul90-567
Laroque, F. Shakespeare et la fête.
  M.D. Bristol, 570(SQ):Fall89-349
Larose, L. Voyante.
  M. Naudin, 102(CanL):Spring89-218
Larrain, C.J. Die "Sentenzen" des Porphyrios.
  E. Lamberz, 229:Band61Heft8-665
  L. Siorvanes, 123:Vol39No1-137
Larrea, J. Cartas a Gerardo Diego. (E. Cordero de Ciria & J.M. Díaz de Guereñu, eds)
  J.C. Wilcox, 240(HR):Spring89-259
Larreta, A. The Last Portrait of the Duchess of Alba.
  42(AR):Winter89-114
Larsen, J. - see Xue Tao
Larsen, L.F. - see Hamsun, K.
Larsen, N. Quicksand [and] Passing.* (D.E. McDowell, ed)
  J. Campbell, 459:Winter89-117
Larsen, S.B. Mod strømmen.
  G. Callesen, 563(SS):Winter89-111
Larsen, S.U., B. Hagtvet & J.P. Myklebust, eds. Who Were the Fascists?
  H. Ofstad, 262:Dec89-455
Larsen, W. Confessions of a Mail Order Bride.
  C. Kadohata, 441:7Jan90-15
Larson, G.J. & E. Deutsch, eds. Interpreting Across Boundaries.
  J.M. Koller, 485(PE&W):Jul89-338
  D.L. Overmyer, 293(JASt):Aug89-577
  R. Rorty, 485(PE&W):Jul89-332
Larson, K.C. Whitman's Drama of Consensus.*
  J. Loving, 445(NCF):Dec89-402
Larson, P.C., with S.M. Brown, eds. The Spirit of H.H. Richardson on the Midland Prairies.*
  S.K. Robinson, 47:Feb89-36
  D. Waterman, 45:Sep89-59
Larsson, B. La Réception des "Mandarins."
  A. Whitmarsh, 208(FS):Oct89-493
Larthomas, P., with J. Larthomas - see de Beaumarchais, P.A.C.
Laruelle, F. Une biographie de l'homme ordinaire.
  A. Jacob, 192(EP):Jul-Dec89-545
Laruelle, F. Les philosophies de la différence.
  G. Hottois, 540(RIPh):Vol42fasc4-545

Lary, N.M. Dostoevsky and Soviet Film.*
  D.J. Youngblood, 104(CASS):Spring-Winter88-484
de Lasarte, J.A. & others - see under Ainaud i de Lasarte, J. & others
Lascelles, A.J. & J.R. Alberich, eds. Letters from the Carlist War (1874-76).
  R. Carr, 86(BHS):Jul89-291
Lasdun, J. A Jump Start.*
  R. Pybus, 565:Winter88/89-67
Lash, J.P. Dealers and Dreamers.*
  G. Burbank, 106:Fall89-237
Lasker, J. & S. Borg. In Search of Parenthood.
  A. Donchin, 254:Fall89-136
Laslett, P. A Fresh Map of Life.*
  C. Handy, 324:Mar90-296
  P. Willmot & P. Laslett, 358:Feb90-7
Lasnik, H. & J. Uriagereka. A Course in GB Syntax.
  P. Dasgupta, 353:Vol27No3-564
  A.K. Farmer, 350:Dec90-854
  J. Rudanko, 597(SN):Vol61No2-233
Lass, R. The Shape of English.*
  R.M. Hogg, 297(JL):Mar89-264
  J. Pauchard, 189(EA):Apr-Jun89-194
  A. Ward, 382(MAE):1989/2-320
Lasser, W. The Limits of Judicial Power.
  G.R., 185:Apr90-706
Lassman, P. & I. Velody, eds. Max Weber's "Science as a Vocation."
  J.D., 185:Apr90-700
Lasso de la Vega, G.L. Tragedia de la honra de Dido restaurada.* (A. Hermenegildo, ed)
  S.N. McCrary, 345(KRQ):May89-246
Lassonde, J-R. La Bibliothèque Saint-Sulpice 1910-1931.
  L-G. Harvey, 470:Vol27-114
Latane, D.E., Jr. Browning's "Sordello" and the Aesthetics of Difficulty.
  T.P. Walsh, 85(SBHC):Vol16-146
Latham, C. & J. Sakol. "E" is for Elvis.
  K. Tucker, 441:13May90-16
Latham, E.C. - see Stegner, W.
Lathem, E.C., ed. Ray Nash and the Graphic Arts Workshop at Dartmouth College.
  J. Dreyfus, 517(PBSA):Mar89-105
Lathrop, T.A. The Evolution of Spanish.* (2nd ed)
  W.T. Patterson, 238:Mar89-157
"The Latin Riddle Book." (L. Phillips, comp)
  42(AR):Spring89-248
Latraverse, F. La Pragmatique.*
  M. Gueissaz, 531:Jul-Dec89-512
  S. Winter, 596(SL):Vol42No2-184
Latrobe, B.H. Correspondence and Miscellaneous Papers of Benjamin Henry Latrobe. (Vols 1 & 2) (J.C. Van Horne & others, eds)
  C.M. Brown, 656(WMQ):Apr89-419
Latrobe, B.H. Correspondence and Miscellaneous Papers of Benjamin Henry Latrobe. (Vol 3) (J.C. Van Horne & others, eds)
  C.M. Brown, 656(WMQ):Apr89-419
  G. Waddell, 576:Sep89-296
de Lattre, A. La doctrine de la réalité chez Proust.
  A. Daspre, 535(RHL):Jan-Feb89-147
Laubenthal, A. Paul Hindemiths Einakter-Triptychon.*
  G. Allroggen, 416:Band4Heft3-269
Lauber, J. Sir Walter Scott.
  P. Drew, 617(TLS):20-26Apr90-422

Lauber, L. White Girls.
  R. Hoffman, 441:28Jan90-14
  442(NY):19Mar90-109
Laudan, L. La dynamique de la science.
  D. Asselin, 154:Vol28No3-509
Lauer, A.R. Tyrannicide and Drama.
  R. Carter, 402(MLR):Jul90-763
Lauer, B. Das lyrische Frühwerk von Fedor
  Sologub.
  M. Carlson, 550(RusR):Jan89-100
  T. Eekman, 279:Vol37-203
  G. Kalbouss, 104(CASS):Spring-Winter88-
  462
  R.J. Keys, 575(SEER):Jul89-456
Lauer, J.M. & J.W. Asher. Composition
  Research/Empirical Designs.
  B. Bamberg, 126(CCC):Oct89-352
Laughlin, J. Pound as Wuz.*
  C.J. Fox, 364:Apr/May89-159
Laurence, D.H. - see Shaw, G.B.
Laurence, J. A Deepe Coffyn.*
  M. Stasio, 441:18Feb90-23
Laurent, F. L'Oeuvre romanesque de Réjean
  Ducharme.
  M. Archambault, 627(UTQ):Fall89-196
Laurent, J. Le français en cage.
  C. Schmitt, 72:Band226Heft1-180
  D. Trudeau, 207(FR):Oct89-180
Laurent, R. Sigillographie.
  B.B. Ravak, 589:Jan80-150
Laurenti, H. - see "Paul Valéry 5"
Laurentin, R. Le Voou de Louis XIII.
  J-C. Vuillemin, 207(FR):Oct89-188
de Laurettis, T. Technologies of Gender.*
  B. Klinger, 567:Vol75No1/2-165
Lauritzen, P., with R. Wolf. Villas of the
  Veneto.
  D.D. Boles, 505:Feb89-147
Laut, J.P. Der frühe türkische Buddhismus
  und seine literarischen Denkmäler.
  J.W. de Jong, 259(IIJ):Jul89-253
Lauter, P. & others, eds. The Heath Anthol-
  ogy of Literature.
  M. Edmundson, 617(TLS).19-25Oct90-
  1133
Lauter-Bufe, H. Die Geschichte des sikelio-
  tisch-korinthischen Kapitells.
  M. Pfanner, 229:Band61Heft5-425
Lauterbach, A. Before Recollection.*
  M. Junyk, 529(QQ):Spring89-159
Lauth, R. Dostojewski und sein Jahrhundert.*
  P-P. Druet, 258:Jun89-236
Lauth, R. Hegel von der Wissenschaftslehre.
  J. Schreiter, 489(PJGG):Band96Heft1-178
Lauvergnat-Gagnière, C. & G. Demerson, eds.
  Les Chroniques Gargantuines.
  F. Rigolot, 207(FR):May90-1060
Lauvergnat-Gagnière, C. & B. Yon, eds. Le
  Juste et l'Injuste à la Renaissance et à
  l'Age classique.*
  G. Schrenck, 535(RHL):Mar-Apr89-273
Lavandera, B.R. Variación y significado.
  C. Silva-Corvalán, 545(RPh):May90-612
Lavédrine, J., ed. Essais sur le dialogue:
  contrastivités.
  G. Bourcier, 189(EA):Oct-Dec89-459
"Louis Lavelle; Actes du Colloque Interna-
  tional d'Agen, 27-28-29 septembre 1985."
  G. Barthel, 547(RF):Band101Heft2/3-352
Laver, M. & N. Schofield. Multiparty Govern-
  ment.
  D. Leonard, 617(TLS):7-10Sep90-942

Lavers, N. Pop Cultures into Art.*
  P. Hart, 395(MFS):Winter89-778
Lavrentiev, A. Varvara Stepanova.* (J.E.
  Bowlt, ed & trans)
  B. Fer, 59:Sep89-382
  C. Lodder, 90:Sep89-647
  A. Summerfield, 324:Jan90-144
Lawaty, A. Das Ende Preussens in polnischer
  Sicht.
  F.L. Carsten, 575(SEER):Apr89-312
Lawlor, P.M. Le Fonctionnement de la méta-
  phore dans "Les Chants de Maldoror."
  R. Pickering, 208(FS):Jul89-348
Lawner, L. Lives of the Courtesans.*
  J. Gillies, 662:Spring/Summer89-43
Lawrence, D.H. Aaron's Rod. (M. Kalnins, ed)
  D. Carroll, 402(MLR):Jan90-164
  É. Delavenay, 189(EA):Jan-Mar89-111
Lawrence, D.H. The Letters of D.H. Law-
  rence.* (Vol 4) (W. Roberts, J.T. Boulton &
  E. Mansfield, eds)
  É. Delavenay, 189(EA):Jan-Mar89-113
  K.M. Hewitt, 541(RES):May89-291
  P. Hobsbaum, 677(YES):Vol20-333
Lawrence, D.H. Love Among the Haystacks
  and Other Stories.* (J. Worthen, ed)
  É. Delavenay, 189(EA):Jan-Mar89-113
Lawrence, D.H. Memoir of Maurice Magnus.*
  (K. Cushman, ed)
  I.S. MacNiven, 177(ELT):Vol32No3-360
  D.T.O., 295(JML).Fall88/Winter89-368
Lawrence, D.H. The Plumed Serpent. (L.D.
  Clark, ed)
  L. Blanchard, 177(ELT):Vol32No4-518
  D. Carroll, 402(MLR):Jan90-164
  É. Delavenay, 189(EA):Jan-Mar89-112
  K.M. Hewitt, 541(RES):Nov89-588
  D.T.O., 295(JML):Fall88/Winter89-369
Lawrence, D.H. Reflections on the Death of a
  Porcupine and Other Essays.* (M. Herbert,
  ed)
  D. Carroll, 402(MLR):Jan90-164
  C. Jansohn, 72:Band226Heft1-235
Lawrence, D.H. Women in Love.* (D. Farmer,
  L. Vasey & J. Worthen, eds)
  K.M. Hewitt, 541(RES):May89-291
  P. Hobsbaum, 677(YES):Vol20-333
  P. Preston, 447(N&Q):Jun89-262
  R.G. Walker, 177(ELT):Vol32No2-256
Lawrence, E. Through the Garden Gate.
  A. Lacy, 441:10Jun90-13
Lawrence, J. Curriculum Vitae.
  M.J. Sheehan, 115:Spring89-190
Lawrence, K. Springs of Living Water.
  M. Childress, 441:25Mar90-19
Lawrence, L.D. Another Winter, Another
  Spring.
  R.L. Busch, 102(CanL):Spring89-145
Lawrence, V.B. Strong on Music.
  L.W. Levine, 451:Spring90-261
Lawrie, A., H. Matthews & D. Ritchie, eds.
  Glimmer of Cold Brine.
  S.R. Green, 571(ScLJ):Winter89-58
Lawson, A. Anatomy of a Typeface.
  S. Carter, 617(TLS):10-16Aug90-858
Lawson, L. Working Women.
  C.B. Davies, 128(CE):Jan89-88
Lawson, L.A. Following Percy.
  E. Carroll, 395(MFS):Winter89-761
  D.W. Madden, 594:Fall89-344
Lawson, R.H. Franz Kafka.*
  A.P. Foulkes, 301(JEGP):Apr89-302

Lawson, S. Dutch Interiors.
D. Kennedy, 493:Summer89-54
Lawson-Peebles, R. Landscape and Written Expression in Revolutionary America.*
J. Hurt, 402(MLR):Oct90-931
C.Z. Oreovicz, 587(SAF):Autumn89-246
D.A. Ringe, 27(AL):May89-280
Lawton, A. & H. Eagle, eds. Russian Futurism through its Manifestoes, 1912-1928.
639(VQR):Summer89-103
Lawton, D. Chaucer's Narrators.*
C.D. Benson, 589:Jan89-182
C.J. Watkin, 148:Winter86-96
Laybourn, K. Britain on the Breadline.
H. Perkin, 617(TLS):15-21Jun90-637
Layton, M. Some Kind of Hero.
B.H. Pell, 102(CanL):Spring89-165
Lazar, M. & R. Gottesman, eds. The Dove and the Mole.
K. Fickert, 221(GQ):Summer89-401
J.M.M., 295(JML):Fall88/Winter89-362
Lazell, B., D. Rees & L. Crampton, eds. Rock Movers and Shakers.
B.L. Cooper, 498:Fall89-94
Lazer, H., ed. On Louis Simpson.
R. McDowell, 249(HudR):Spring89-163
Lazer, H., ed. What Is A Poet?
J. Payne, 577(SHR):Spring89-191
Lazitch, B., with M.M. Drachkovitch, eds. Biographical Dictionary of the Comintern.* (rev)
A. Brown, 575(SEER):Apr89-332
Lazzaro, C. The Italian Renaissance Garden.
L. Yang, 441:2Dec90-21
Lê, L. Un si tendre vampire. Fuir. Solo.
M. Contat, 98:Dec89-921
Leach, R. Vsevolod Meyerhold.
S. Golub, 402(MLR):Oct90-1049
G. McVay, 511:Sep89-46
Leach, S.S. Subgeometric Pottery from Southern Etruria.
T. Rasmussen, 123:Vol39No2-340
Leak, A.N. The Perverted Consciousness.
R. Goldthorpe, 617(TLS):14-20Dec90-1347
Leaman, O. Averroes and His Philosophy.
T-A. Druart, 543:Mar90-642
D.H. Frank, 319:Jul90-444
Leamon, W. Unheard Melodies.
S. Hearon, 441:29Jul90-26
Leanza, S., ed. Atti della settimana di studi su Flavio Magno Aurelio Cassiodoro.
J.N. Hillgarth, 589:Jul89-734
Lear, E. Selected Letters.* (V. Noakes, ed)
617(TLS):27Apr-3May90-457
Lear, J. Aristotle.*
D.W. Hamlyn, 483:Apr89-261
S.G.S., 185:Jul90-917
C. Shields, 518:Jul89-137
R. Wardy, 123:Vol39No2-258
Leaska, M.A. - see Woolf, V.
Leather, S. The Fireman.
N. Callendar, 441:14Jan90-23
Leatherdale, C. Dracula, the Novel and the Legend.
J. Finné, 189(EA):Oct-Dec89-483
Leatherdale, C. The Origins of Dracula.
J. Finné, 189(EA):Oct-Dec89-485
Leavey, J.P., Jr. & G.L. Ulmer. Glassary.*
K. Hart, 63:Jun89-243
Leavis, Q.D. Collected Essays.* (Vol 2) (G. Singh, ed)
J. Updike, 442(NY):30Jul90-85

Leavitt, D. Equal Affections.*
J. Mellors, 364:Jun/Jul89-133
W.H. Pritchard, 249(HudR):Autumn89-485
Leavitt, D. A Place I've Never Been.
W. Martin, 441:26Aug90-11
Leavy, J. Squeeze Play.
M. Perlman, 441:22Apr90-24
Lebacqz, K. Justice in an Unjust World.
P.T.M., 185:Oct89-205
Lebacqz, K. Six Theories of Justice.
P.T.M., 185:Oct89-206
Lebell, S. Naming Ourselves, Naming Our Children.
E.D. Lawson, 424:Dec89-391
Le Blanc, C. & S. Blader, eds. Chinese Ideas about Nature and Society.
W.J. Peterson, 293(JASt):May89-365
Le Blanc, G. & C. Beausoleil, eds. La Poésie acadienne 1948-1988.
R. Boudreau, 627(UTQ):Fall89-180
Le Blanc, R.D. The Russianization of Gil Blas.
C. Emerson, 104(CASS):Spring-Winter88-492
Le Blond, R.E., Jr., with M. Madden. From Chaos to Fragility.
D. Hering, 151:Dec89-68
Le Boeuffle, A. Astronomie, Astrologie.*
P. Flobert, 555:Vol62Fasc1-158
Le Bourdellès, H. L'Aratus Latinus.
F. Kerlouégan, 555:Vol62Fasc1-185
Lebowitz, N. Kierkegaard.
D. Brezis, 192(EP):Apr-Jun89-264
Lebrecht, N., ed. Mahler Remembered.*
L. Mintz, 390:Dec89-35
Le Brun, A. Sade, aller et détours.
C.V. Michael, 166:Jul90-356
Lebrun, R.A. Joseph de Maistre.
E. Lehouck, 627(UTQ):Fall89-135
E. Zawisza, 529(QQ):Winter89-970
Lebsanft, F. Studien zu einer Linguistik des Grusses.
W. Raible, 547(RF):Band101Heft2/3-298
Lecker, R. An Other I.
W.L. Schissel, 395(MFS):Winter89-781
Le Clair, T. The Art of Excess.
S. Moore, 532(RCF):Fall89-227
J. Tabbi, 659(ConL):Winter90-553
Le Clair, T. In the Loop.*
W.B. Stengel, 27(AL):Mar89-132
Leclerc, A. Origines.
L. Enjolras, 207(FR):May90-1102
Leclerc, Y. La Spirale et le monument.
E.N. Meyer, 446(NCFS):Spring-Summer90-542
Le Clézio, J.M.G. Haï.
H. Cronel, 450(NRF):Jan89-90
Le Clézio, J.M.G. Printemps et autres saisons.
D. Pobel, 450(NRF):Oct89-112
Le Clézio, J.M.G. Le Rêve mexicain ou la pensée interrompue.
H. Cronel, 450(NRF):Jan89-90
D. Pierson, 207(FR):Mar90-745
Le Compte, J. Moon Passage.*
42(AR):Spring89-250
Le Comte, E. I, Eve.
E. Schoenberg, 391:Mar89-37
639(VQR):Winter89-20
Lecoq, A-M. François Ier imaginaire.
J.M. Massing, 90:Sep89-652
Ledbetter, D. Harpsichord and Lute Music in 17th-Century France.*
D. Maple, 415:Jan89-26

Leder, S., with A. Abbott. The Language of Exclusion.
  A.H. Harrison, 27(AL):Mar89-112
Lederer, H. Handbook of East German Drama 1945-1985.
  J. Rosellini, 406:Spring89-107
Lederer, W. The Kiss of the Snow Queen.
  G. Boyes, 203:Vol100No1-127
"L'Édition du livre populaire."
  D. Saint-Jacques, 470:Vol27-108
Le Doeuff, M. L'Étude et le rouet.
  T. Moi, 358:Jun90-13
Lee, A.R., ed. First Person Singular.
  W. Berry, 569(SR):Spring89-li
  J. Pilling, 402(MLR):Apr90-422
Lee, C.C. & C.C. Soufas - see under Castro
Lee, C. & C.C. Soufas
Lee, C.H. & S. Naya, eds. Trade and Investment in Services in the Asia-Pacific Region.
  J.E. Vestal, 293(JASt):Nov89-805
Lee, C-S. Japan and Korea.
  D.C. Hellmann, 293(JASt):Aug89-638
Lee, D. The Difficulty of Living on Other Planets.
  E. Nicol, 102(CanL):Autumn-Winter89-228
Lee, D. Language, Children, and Society.
  S. Romaine, 355(LSoc):Dec89-565
Lee, G.F. From Exile to Redemption.*
  M.P.L., 295(JML):Fall88/Winter89-408
  R.H. Wolf, 508:Jan89-85
Lee, H. Willa Cather.*
  S. Rudikoff, 111:06Mar90-31
Lee, H., ed. The Secret Self/2.
  G. Bas, 189(EA):Oct-Dec89-491
Lee, J.B. Rediscovered Sheep.
  S. Scobie, 376:Dec89-126
Lee, J.J. Ireland 1912-1985.
  D. Fitzpatrick, 617(TLS):8-14Jun90-604
Lee, L.O-F., ed. Lu Xun and His Legacy.
  R.E. Hegel, 318(JAOS):Apr-Jun88-338
Lee, L.O-F. Voices from the Iron House.*
  L.Y., 295(JML):Fall88/Winter89-376
Lee, L-Y. Rose.*
  R. Mitchell, 502(PrS):Fall89-129
Lee, M., Jr. Great Britain's Solomon.
  K.M. Brown, 617(TLS):10-16Aug90-852
Lee, M., R. McLaurin & C-I. Moon. Alliance Under Tension.
  D.S. Macdonald, 293(JASt):Aug89-639
Lee, N. - see Debussy, C.
Lee, P.N.S. Industrial Management and Economic Reform in China, 1949-1984.
  J. Frankenstein, 293(JASt):Aug89-592
Lee, S. The God Project.
  N. Callendar, 441:14Jan90-23
Lee, S. & others. Law, Blasphemy and the Multi-Faith Society.
  D. Pannick, 617(TLS):4-10May90-471
Lee, S. & P. Stanford. Believing Bishops.
  E. Norman, 617(TLS):22-28Jun90-663
Lee, S.H. The Philosophical Theology of Jonathan Edwards.
  C.A. Holbrook, 656(WMQ):Oct89-810
Lee, S.J. The European Dictatorships, 1918-1945.
  H. Hanak, 575(SEER):Oct89-654
Lee, V. Love and Strategy in the Eighteenth-Century French Novel.*
  F.A. Spear, 345(KRQ):Feb89-109
Lee, Y-B. West Goes East.
  M. Deuchler, 293(JASt):Nov89-888

Leech, G.N. Meaning and the English Verb. (2nd ed)
  N.R. Norrick, 603:Vol13No1-251
Leech-Wilkinson, D. Machaut's Mass.
  R. Woodley, 617(TLS):9-15Nov90-1210
Leed, R.L. & L. Paperno - see Zhitkov, B.
Lees, G. Oscar Peterson.*
  R. Waddell, 441:12Aug90-17
van Leeuwen, T.A.P. The Skyward Trend of Thought.
  D. Dunster, 46:Aug89-15
  W.H. Jordy, 47:Jun89-39
Le Fanu, M. The Cinema of Andrei Tarkovsky.*
  R. Bates, 97(CQ):Vol18No3-339
Lefanu, S. In the Chinks of the World Machine.
  V. Hollinger, 561(SFS):Jul89-223
Le Fanu, W. A Catalogue of Books Belonging to Dr. Jonathan Swift.
  M.J. Jannetta, 354:Sep89-279
Le Fanu, W. Nehemiah Grew, M.D., F.R.S.
  M. Hunter, 617(TLS):14-20Sep90-984
Le Faye, D. - see Austen-Leigh, W. & R.A.
Lefebvre, C. & P. Muysken. Mixed Categories.
  M. Baker, 350:Mar90-142
Lefebvre, J. "Isabelle" von André Gide oder die Überwindung des verräumlichten Lebens.
  C. Foucart, 72:Band226Heft1-212
  P. Schnyder, 602:Band20Heft1-141
Lefebvre, J-P. Der gute Trommler.*
  L. Netter, 549(RLC):Jan-Mar89-126
Lefèvre, R. Le Recoeil des Histoires de Troyes.* (M. Aeschbach, ed)
  F. Vielliard, 554:Vol108No2/3-395
Leff, L.J. Hitchcock and Selznick.*
  M.A. Anderegg, 456(NDQ):Winter89-211
Leff, L.J. & J.L. Simmons. The Dame in the Kimono.
  J. Charyn, 441:28Jan90-19
  Z. Leader, 617(TLS):25-01May90-551
  R. Schickel, 61:Feb90-103
Leffland, E. The Knight, Death and the Devil.
  T. Keneally, 441:11Feb90-8
Lefkovitz, L.H. The Character of Beauty in the Victorian Novel.*
  T.E. Morgan, 620(TSWL):Spring89-140
Lefkowitz, M.R. Women in Greek Myth.
  J. Cahill, 487:Summer89-165
  A.J.L. van Hooff, 394:Vol42fasc3/4-503
Lefort, C. Democracy and Political Theory.*
  M.B., 185:Jul90-908
Lefort, C. Essais sur le politique.
  P. Livet, 192(EP):Jan-Mar89-105
Legatt, M. The Illustrated Dictionary of Western Literature.*
  C.M. Wright, 649(WAL):May89-90
Leggatt, A. English Drama: Shakespeare to the Restoration, 1590-1660.
  W.C. Carroll, 627(UTQ):Fall89-120
  S. McCafferty, 447(N&Q):Sep89-378
Leggatt, A. "King Lear."
  M. Neill, 402(MLR):Jul90-692
Leggatt, A. Shakespeare's Political Drama.*
  W.C. Carroll, 627(UTQ):Fall89-120
  G. Holderness, 402(MLR):Jan90-141
Legge, G. The Shoe.
  K. Jamie, 617(TLS):4-10May90-480
Legge, J.D. Intellectuals and Nationalism in Indonesia.
  H.A. Poeze, 293(JASt):Aug89-678

Leggett, B.J. Wallace Stevens and Poetic Theory.*
  R.W.B., 295(JML):Fall88/Winter89-410
Le Gloannec, A-M. La Nation orpheline.
  G.A. Craig, 453(NYRB):18Jan90-28
Le Goff, J. Your Money or Your Life.*
  (French title: La Bourse et la vie.)
  J.W. Baldwin, 589:Oct89-998
Legris, R. & others. Le Théâtre au Québec,
  1825-1980.
  L.E. Doucette, 627(UTQ):Fall89-188
Le Guin, M.W. A Home-Concealed Woman.
  (C.A. Le Guin, ed)
  L.T. Ulrich, 441:9Dec90-24
Le Guin, U. Buffalo Gals and Other Animal
  Presences.
  L. Tuttle, 617(TLS):18-24May90-534
Le Guin, U.K. Tehanu.
  442(NY):23Jul90-88
Lehfeldt, W. Sprjaženie ukrainskogo glagola.
  A.L. Ščarandin & S.I. Alatorceva,
  688(ZSP):Band49Heft2-419
Lehiste, I. Lectures on Language Contact.*
  P. Meara, 361:Nov89-249
Lehman, A. & G.B. Bogliolo, eds. Herman Mel-
  ville.
  R. Asselineau, 189(EA):Oct-Dec89-498
Lehman, D., ed. Ecstatic Occasions, Expedi-
  ent Forms.*
  B.C., 295(JML):Fall88/Winter89-255
Lehman, D. The Perfect Murder.
  P. Craig, 617(TLS):21-27Sep90-1006
Lehmann, R.P.M. - see "Beowulf"
Lehmann, W.P. A Gothic Etymological Dictio-
  nary.*
  R.B. Howell, 406:Summer89-249
Lehmann, W.P., ed. Language Typology 1985.
  M. Haspelmath, 603:Vol13No2-488
  A.S. Kaye & F. Müller-Gotama, 320(CJL):
  Mar89-104
  G. Mallinson, 297(JL):Sep89-541
Lehmann-Langholz, U. Kleiderkritik in mit-
  telalterlicher Dichtung.
  D. Peil, 680(ZDP):Band108Heft3-444
Lehmberg, S.E. The Reformation of Cathe-
  drals.*
  N. Llewellyn, 90:Sep89-653
Lehnert-Rodiek, G. Zeitreisen.
  R. Borgmeier, 52:Band24Heft1-103
Lehr, G., ed. Come and I Will Sing You.
  D. Melhorn-Boe, 187:Winter89-171
Lehrberger, J. & L. Bourbeau. Machine
  Translation.
  J. Pinkham, 350:Mar90-180
Lehrer, J. The Sooner Spy.
  N. Callendar, 441:11Mar90-33
Lehrer, K. Theory of Knowledge.
  J.O. Young, 103:Oct90-416
Lehrer, W. GRRRHHHH.
  G. Gessert, 448:Vol27No2-126
Lehtiranta, J. Yhteissaamelainen sanasto.
  L. Campbell, 350:Dec90-875
Leibacher-Ouvrard, L. Libertinage et utopies
  sous le règne de Louis XIV.
  A. Rosenberg, 166:Oct89-88
Leibfried, E. Fabel.
  I. Köhler-Zülch, 196:Band30Heft3/4-333
Leibowitz, H. Fabricating Lives.*
  H. Beaver, 617(TLS):23-29Mar90-308
Leibrock, F. Aufklärung und Mittelalter.
  O. Ehrismann, 684(ZDA):Band118Heft4-
  178
  E. Mason, 402(MLR):Jul90-787

Leichty, E. Catalogue of the Babylonian
  Tablets in the British Museum. (Vol 6)
  M.A. Dandamayev, 318(JAOS):Jan-
  Mar88-165
Leigh, D. The Wilson Plot.*
  639(VQR):Autumn89-133
Leigh, R.A. - see Rousseau, J-J.
Leighten, P. Re-Ordering the Universe.*
  639(VQR):Autumn89-139
Leighton, A. Elizabeth Barrett Browning.*
  S. Shatto, 677(YES):Vol20-300
Leighton, L.G., ed & trans. Russian Romantic
  Criticism.
  C. Emerson, 149(CLS):Vol26No4-368
  H. Goscilo, 574(SEEJ):Spring89-120
Leimbach, M. Dying Young.
  M. Heinemann, 617(TLS):20-26Jul90-782
  J. McCorkle, 441:14Jan90-22
Leimbach, R. Militarische Musterrhetorik.
  T.F. Scanlon, 124:Mar-Apr90-367
Leiner, W. Das Deutschlandbild in der fran-
  zösischen Literatur.
  J. Jurt, 358:Jun90-7
Leiner, W., ed. Horizons européens de la lit-
  térature française au XVIIe siècle.
  M-O. Sweetser, 475:Vol16No31-589
Leinfellner, W. & F. Wurketis, eds. The Tasks
  of Contemporary Philosophy/Die Aufgaben
  der Philosophie in der Gegenwart.
  P. Engel, 192(EP):Apr-Jun89-267
Leino, P. Language and Metre.
  I. Lehiste, 350:Mar90-138
Leiris, M. A Cor et à cri.*
  A.P. Colombat, 207(FR):Dec89-404
Leiris, M. Images de marque.
  A.P. Colombat, 207(FR):Mar90-746
Leiris, M. Nights as Day and Days as Night.*
  I. Malin, 532(RCF):Spring89-265
Leisi, E. Rilkes Sonette an Orpheus.
  O.H. Olzien, 224(GRM):Band39Heft1-112
  M. Vos, 221(GQ):Summer89-405
Leiss, W., S. Kline & S. Jhally. Social Commu-
  nication in Advertising.*
  T. Goldie, 102(CanL):Winter88-128
Leitch, T.M. What Stories Are.*
  R. Siegle, 125:Fall88-88
Leitch, V.B. American Literary Criticism from
  the Thirties to the Eighties.*
  W.E. Cain, 128(CE):Mar89-320
  J.A. Steele, 27(AL):Oct89-507
  G. Webster, 395(MFS):Summer89-270
Leites, E., ed. Conscience and Casuistry in
  Early Modern Europe.
  M.H.W., 185:Oct89-216
Leith, P. & P. Ingram, eds. The Jurisprudence
  of Orthodoxy.
  L. Green, 518:Oct89-254
  N. Lacey, 291:Vol6No1-119
Leithauser, B. Hence.*
  W.H. Pritchard, 249(HudR):Autumn89-488
Leitner, G., ed. The English Reference Gram-
  mar.
  F.W. Gester, 38:Band107Heft1/2-100
Lejeune, C. Age poétique, âge politique.*
  J. Labat, 207(FR):May90-1104
Lejeune, P. On Autobiography. (P.J. Eakin,
  ed)
  M. Sheringham, 617(TLS):16-22Feb90-
  178
Lekisch, B. Tahoe Place Names.
  B. Julyan, 424:Sep89-290
Leland, C.T. The Book of Marvels.
  K. Ray, 441:14Jan90-30

Leland, J. A Guide to Hemingway's Paris.
    A. De Fazio 3d, 234:Spring90-180
Lelchuk, A. Brooklyn Boy.
    D. Stern, 441:7Jan90-24
Lem, S. Eden.*
    J. Clute, 617(TLS):9-15Feb90-149
Lemaire, R. Passions et Positions.
    R. Pensom, 208(FS):Jul89-319
Lemaître, J-L. L'obituaire du chapitre col-
    légial Saint-Honore de Paris. Répertoire
    des documents nécrologiques français.
    (supp)
    G. Constable, 589:Jul89-735
Lemaître, N. Le Rouergue flamboyant.
    P. Jansen, 531:Jul-Dec89-517
Leman-Stefanovic, I. The Event of Death.
    B. Warren, 63:Jun89-250
Lemay, J.A.L., ed. Deism, Masonry, and the
    Enlightenment.*
    W.B. Carnochan, 677(YES):Vol20-281
    K. Craven, 149(CLS):Vol26No2-161
Lemay, J.A.L. "New England's Annoyances."*
    J.R. Kelly, 517(PBSA):Mar89-121
Lemay, J.A.L. - see Franklin, B.
Lemerle, P., ed. Actes de Kutlumus.
    R.W. Allison, 589:Oct89-998
Lemire, M. - see "Dictionnaire des oeuvres
    littéraires du Québec"
Lemmings, D. Gentlemen and Barristers.
    G. Holmes, 617(TLS):10-16Aug90-851
Lemnius, S. Amorum Libri IV. (L. Mundt, ed &
    trans)
    L.V.R., 568(SCN):Fall-Winter89-69
Lemoine, P. La Château de Versailles.
    J. Dubu, 475:Vol16No30-310
Lemsine, A. Beneath a Sky of Porphyry.
    I. Hill, 617(TLS):13-19Apr90-404
Lenard, Y. Chantal.
    A. Sonnenfeld, 207(FR):May90-1105
Lenard, Y. Parole et Pensée. (5th ed)
    G. Crouse, 399(MLJ):Autumn89-361
Lencek, R.L. The Structure and History of the
    Slovene Language.
    R. Greenberg, 279:Vol35/36-285
"L'Encyclopédie et ses lectures."
    C. Lebedel, 530:Apr89-170
Lendle, O. & others. Mediterrane Kulturen
    und ihre Ausstrahlung auf das Deutsche.
    J. Udolph, 685(ZDL):1/1989-74
L'Engle, M. Two-Part Invention.
    639(VQR):Spring89-68
Leniashin, V., ed. Soviet Art 1920s-1930s.
    C. Lodder, 90:Sep89-647
Lenman, B. The Jacobite Cause.
    M G H Pittock, 571(ScLJ):Spring89-5
Lenneberg, H. Witnesses and Scholars.
    G.B. Stauffer, 317:Fall89-657
Lennon, J.M., ed. Conversations with Norman
    Mailer.
    P. Bufithis, 395(MFS):Summer89-302
Lennon, J.M., ed. Critical Essays on Norman
    Mailer.
    M.D.O., 295(JML):Fall88/Winter89-378
Lennox-Boyd, C., R. Dixon & T. Clayton.
    George Stubbs.
    D. Bindman, 617(TLS):16-22Mar90-289
Lenoir, J. Oeuvres. (J. Hare & J.D. Lortie,
    eds)
    D.M. Hayne, 627(UTQ):Fall89-198
Lenoir, Y. Folklore et Transcendance dans
    L'Oeuvre Americaine de Béla Bartók (1940-
    1945).*
    S. Erdely, 187:Fall89-511

Lentin, A., ed. Enlightened Absolutism
    (1760-1790).
    H. Dunthorne, 83:Autumn89-202
Lentricchia, F. After the New Criticism.
    J.R. Bennett, 599:Spring90-119
Lentricchia, F. Ariel and the Police.*
    I.F.A. Bell, 677(YES):Vol20-322
Lentricchia, F. & T. McLaughlin, eds. Critical
    Terms for Literary Study.
    G.G. Harpham, 617(TLS):17-23Aug90-872
Lentricchia, M. No Guarantees.
    D. Huddle, 441:15Jul90-20
Lenz, E. & B. Myerhoff. The Feminization of
    America.
    E.I. Perry, 106:Fall89-223
Lenz, J.M.R. Werke und Briefe in drei Bän-
    den.* (S. Damm, ed)
    D. Hill, 402(MLR):Jan90-247
Leo de Belmont, L.A. El concepto de la vida
    en el teatro de Lope de Vega, William
    Shakespeare, Calderón de la Barca.
    J-P. Leroy, 549(RLC):Jul-Sep89-411
de León, J.L.P. - see under Ponce de León,
    J.L.
de León, L. Fray Luis de León: Poesía.* (D.
    Fernández-Morera & G. Bleiberg, eds)
    D.G. Walters, 86(BHS):Jan89-201
Leonard, E. Get Shorty.
    W. Balliett, 442(NY):3Sep90-106
    N. Ephron, 441:29Jul90-1
    D. Papineau, 617(TLS):30Nov-6Dec90-
    1287
Leonard, E. Killshot.*
    639(VQR):Autumn89-130
Leonard, H. The Eye of Jazz.
    T. Piazza, 441:4Mar90-26
Leonard, H. Out After Dark.
    J. Lewis, 364:Dec89/Jan90-140
Leonard, I.A. Colonial Travelers in Latin
    America.
    M.P. Costeloe, 86(BHS):Jul89-310
Leonard, J.S. & C.E. Wharton. The Fluent
    Mundo.*
    J.V. Brogan, 27(AL):May89-317
Leonard, T., ed. Radical Renfrew
    D. Dunn, 617(TLS):11-17May90-494
Leonardi, C. & G. Orlandi, eds. Aspetti della
    letteratura latina nel secolo XIII.
    J.M. Ziolkowski, 589:Apr89-462
Leonardi, R. & D.A. Wertman. Italian Chris-
    tian Democracy.
    R. Ward-Jackson, 617(TLS):18-24May90-
    518
Leoni, F. Vocabulario Australitaliano.
    J.S. Ryan, 464:Vol33Fasc1/2-275
Leopardi, G. Poesie e prose. (Vol 1) (M.A.
    Rigoni, with C. Galimberti, eds)
    E. Bigi, 228(GSLI):Vol166fasc534-278
Leopold, T. Somebody Sing.
    S. Ferguson, 441:2Sep90-16
Le Pan, D. Weathering It.
    M.T. Lane, 198:Spring89-104
    T. McKeown, 102(CanL):Autumn-
    Winter89-220
Lepore, E., ed. New Directions in Semantics.
    D.E.B. Pollard, 307:Dec89-217
Lepore, E., ed. Truth and Interpretation.*
    J. Butterfield, 482(PhR):Jan89-107
Leppard, R. Authenticity in Music.*
    J.H.B., 412:Feb89-64
    T. Carter, 410(M&L):Aug89-384
    C. Willner, 415:Oct89-611

Leppert, R. & S. McClary, eds. Music and Society.*
  G.D. Booth, 414(MusQ):Vol74No3-439
Leppmann, W. Rilke.
  C.S. Brown, 569(SR):Winter89-139
Leproux, G-M. Recherches sur les peintres-verriers parisiens de la Renaissance 1540-1620, No. 62 of Hautes Études Médiévales.
  M. Archer, 90:May89-362
Lepschy, A.L., J. Took & D.E. Rhodes, eds. Book Production and Letters in the Western European Renaissance.*
  M.M. Wright, 278(IS):Vol43-144
Lerch, I. Fragmente aus Cambrai.
  C. Berger, 417:Jul-Sep89-278
  D. Hiley, 416:Band4Heft1-92
  M. Popin, 537:Vol75No2-291
Lerer, S. Boethius and Dialogue.*
  S. Davis, 41:Spring89-133
  A.M. Wilson, 123:Vol39No2-240
Le Rider, J. & G. Raulet, eds. Verabschiedung der (Post-)Moderne?
  F.A. Lubich, 221(GQ):Summer89-444
Lerner, L. The Frontiers of Literature.
  A. Neill, 89(BJA):Autumn89-381
Lerner, L.S. - see under Schwartz Lerner, L.
Lerner, M. Wrestling with the Angel.
  G. Weissmann, 441:8Jul90-10
Lerner, R. The Thinking Revlutionary.*
  R. Buel, Jr., 656(WMQ):Jan89-200
Leroux, J. La sémantique des théories physiques.
  G. Stahl, 542:Oct-Dec89-653
Leroy, G. & A. Roche. Les Écrivains et le Front Populaire.
  G. Cesbron, 356(LR):Feb-May89-122
Lerski, G. Poland's Secret Envoy, 1939-1945.
  J. Nowak, 497(PolR):Vol34No3-263
Le Saux, F.H.M. Lazamon's "Brut."
  M. Fries, 617(TLS):24-30Aug90-904
Le Shan, E. It's Better to be Over the Hill than Under It.
  H. Knight, 441:9Dec90-25
Leslau, W. Comparative Dictionary of Ge'ez (Classical Ethiopic).
  A.S. Kaye, 361:Sep89-89
Leśmian, B. Skrzypek opętany. (R.H. Stone, ed)
  P.J. Drozdowski, 574(SEEJ):Fall89-463
Lessing, D. The Fifth Child.*
  P. Lewis, 565:Winter88/89-77
  W. Phillips, 473(PR):Vol56No1-143
Lessing, G.E. Werke und Briefe. (Vol 11, Pts 1 & 2) (H. Kiesel & others, eds)
  H.B. Nisbet, 402(MLR):Jul90-791
"Lessing Yearbook XIX 1987." (R.E. Schade, ed)
  E. Glass, 221(GQ):Winter89-106
"Lessing Yearbook XX 1988." (R.E. Schade, ed)
  S.D. Martinson, 173(ECS):Spring90-336
Lester, D.G. Irish Research.*
  M.F. Funchion, 174(Éire):Fall88-152
Lester, G.A. The Index of Middle English Prose.* (Handlist 2)
  H. Gneuss, 38:Band107Heft1/2-169
Lester, G.A. Sir John Paston's "Grete Boke."
  H. Gneuss, 38:Band107Heft1/2-172
Lester, J. Conrad and Religion.*
  R.G. Hampson, 402(MLR):Jan90-159
  R.F. Peterson, 395(MFS):Summer89-321
Lester, J. Lovesong.
  A.K. Rippis, 390:Feb/Mar89-62

Lestringant, F. - see Marot, C.
Lestringant, F. & D. Ménager, eds. Études sur la "Satyre Ménippée."*
  M. Jeanneret, 208(FS):Apr89-204
Le Sueur, M. Little Brother of the Wilderness. Sparrow Hawk.
  J. Spaeth, 456(NDQ):Winter89-241
Lethbridge, R. & T. Keefe, eds. Zola and the Craft of Fiction.
  J.F. McMillan, 617(TLS):7-13Dec90-1317
Letley, E. From Galt to Douglas Brown.
  G. Tulloch, 571(ScLJ):Winter89-20
Létoublon, F. Il allait, pareil à la nuit.
  J-L. Perpillou, 555:Vol62Fasc2-330
  C.J. Ruijgh, 394:Vol42fasc1/2-146
Létoublon, F. Fonder une cité.
  P. Demont, 555:Vol62Fasc2-341
"Let's Get Acquainted."
  S.M. Sloan, 574(SEEJ):Spring89-151
Letwin, O. Ethics, Emotion and the Unity of the Self.*
  A. Lyon, 483:Oct89-569
Leung, K.C. Hsü Wei as Drama Critic.
  J.L. Faurot, 116:Dec89-153
Leunig, M. There's no place like home. A Piece of Cake.
  M. Hardie, 616:Vol10No2-55
van Leuvensteijn, J.A., ed. Uitgangspunten en toepassingen.
  C. van Bree, 204(FdL):Jun89-156
Lev, D.S. Legal Aid in Indonesia.
  J. Mackie, 293(JASt):Feb89-233
Levelt, W.J.M. Speaking.
  D. Sperber, 617(TLS):9-15Feb90-143
Levenson, C. Arriving at Night.*
  D. Lewis, 529(QQ):Summer89-528
Levenson, C. The Return.
  E. Bartlett, 493:Spring89-64
Levenson, J.C. & others - see Adams, H.
Levenson, J.L. "Romeo and Juliet."
  M. Wiggins, 447(N&Q):Sep89-386
Levenson, M.H. A Geneology of Modernism.
  P.L. Caughie, 620(TSWL):Spring89-111
Levenson, T. Ice Time.*
  42(AR):Summer89-368
Lever, J.W. The Tragedy of State.
  M.J. Haddad, 568(SCN):Fall-Winter89-47
Lever, Y. Histoire générale du cinéma au Québec.
  D. Clandfield, 627(UTQ):Fall89-255
Leverenz, D. Manhood and the American Renaissance.
  R.K. Martin, 646(WWR):Winter90-143
Levey, M., ed. The Soul of the Eye.
  R. Snell, 617(TLS):23-29Nov90-1260
Levey, M. Giambattista Tiepolo.*
  C. Whistler, 278(IS):Vol43-167
Levi, A.H.T. - see Erasmus
Levi, G. Inheriting Power.
  R. Boenig, 568(SCN):Fall-Winter89-53
Levi, M. Of Rule and Revenue.
  K. Stanton, 185:Jan90-430
Levi, P. Collected Poems.*
  R. Feld, 472:Vol16No1-7
  D. Sampson, 249(HudR):Autumn89-507
Levi, P. The Drowned and the Saved.* (Italian title: I sommersi e i salvati.)
  I. Klein, 400(MLN):Jan89-263
  P. Lewis, 565:Winter88/89-77
Levi, P. The Mirror Maker.
  H. Denman, 617(TLS):9-15Mar90-248
  I. Kapp, 441:4Feb90-15

Levi, P. Other People's Trades.*
   R.S. Peckham, 364:Oct/Nov89-124
   S. Siporin, 390:Oct89-60
Levi, P. Boris Pasternak.
   H. Gifford, 453(NYRB):31May90-26
   G. Josipovici, 617(TLS):9-15Feb90-135
Levi, P. Shadow and Bone.* Goodbye to the
   Art of Poetry.*
   P. Scupham, 493:Autumn89-45
Levi, P. The Sixth Day and Other Tales.
   R. Gordon, 617(TLS):23-29Nov90-1271
Levi, P. To the Goat.
   D. Constantine, 493:Spring89-61
Levi, P. The Wrench.
   P. Lewis, 565:Winter88/89-77
Levi, P. - see Connolly, C.
Lévi-Strauss, C. Anthropology and Myth.
   K.Z. Moore, 295(JML):Fall88/Winter89-
   231
Lévi-Strauss, C. The Jealous Potter.*
   M. Folch-Serra, 529(QQ):Autumn89-698
   D.H., 355(LSoc):Jun89-302
   R.A. Segal, 292(JAF):Apr-Jun89-207
Leviant, C. The Man Who Thought He Was
   Messiah.
   H. Mittelmark, 441:16Dec90-18
Levick, B. Claudius.
   B. Knox, 61:Apr90-98
   H. Lloyd-Jones, 453(NYRB):6Dec90-49
Levillain, H. Sur deux versants.*
   G. Cesbron, 356(LR):Nov89-338
Levin, B. Now Read On
   E.S. Turner, 617(TLS):12-18Oct90-1104
Levin, D. California Street.
   M. Stasio, 441:28Oct90-41
Levin, E. The History of American Ceramics.*
   E.P. Denker, 658:Summer/Autumn89-180
Levin, E. Sex and Society in the World of the
   Orthodox Slavs, 900-1700.
   L. Hughes, 617(TLS):5-11Jan90-22
Levin, G. The Thyssen-Bornemisza Collec-
   tion: Twentieth-Century American Paint-
   ing.
   D.F. Jenkins, 39:Jun89-440
Levin, H. Playboys and Killjoys *
   W.W. Combs, 130:Winter89/90-385
   N. Rhodes, 447(N&Q):Sep89-376
   A.J. Sabatini, 295(JML):Fall88/Winter89-
   262
   L. Salingar, 402(MLR):Apr90-399
   E.L. Steeves, 403(MLS):Summer89-81
   R.W. Tobin, 207(FR):Mar90-700
Levin, I. & U. Masing, eds. Armenische
   Märchen.
   E. Ettlinger, 203:Vol100No1-123
Levin, J.D. Ossian v russkoj literature.
   C. Heithus, 52:Band24Heft2-218
Levin, J.H. Rustico di Filippo and the Flor-
   entine Lyric Tradition.
   H.W. Storey, 276:Summer89-221
Levin, M. Feminism and Freedom.
   M.E. Morton, 529(QQ):Summer89-563
Levin, M. Settling the Score.
   42(AR):Summer89-374
Levin, M. When the Eiffel Tower was New.
   J.F. Codell, 207(FR):May90-1118
Levin, M.R. Republican Art and Ideology in
   Late Nineteenth-Century France.
   V. Jirat-Wasiutynski, 529(QQ):Spring89-
   131
Levin, P. Temples and Fields.
   D. Allen, 249(HudR):Summer89-328
   L. Upton, 152(UDQ):Summer89-124

Levin, S.R. Metaphoric Worlds.*
   M. Johnson, 290(JAAC):Summer89-287
   J.C. McKusick, 661(WC):Autumn89-195
Levinas, E. Collected Philosophical Papers.
   T. O'Connor, 323:May89-186
Levine, A. & J.J. McGann - see Lord Byron
Levine, G. Darwin and the Novelists.
   A.D. Culler, 301(JEGP):Oct89-544
   A.L. Harris, 268(IFR):Winter90-65
   L. Sterrenburg, 637(VS):Spring90-487
   F.M. Turner, 445(NCF):Dec89-412
   639(VQR):Spring89-48
Levine, G., ed. One Culture.
   J.R. Kincaid, 301(JEGP):Jul89-447
   F. McConnell, 637(VS):Spring90-496
Levine, I.A. Left-Wing Dramatic Theory in
   the American Theatre.
   R.K. Bank, 610:Summer89-217
"Jack Levine."
   A. Barnet, 441:21Jan90-20
Levine, L.W. Highbrow/Lowbrow.*
   T. Druckrey, 147:Vol6No1-81
   H. Fromm, 219(GaR):Spring89-179
   J. Hurt, 402(MLR):Oct90-934
   42(AR):Winter89-113
   639(VQR):Summer89-97
Levine, M. Deep Cover.
   C. Salzberg, 441:15Apr90-15
Levine, M.P. Hume and the Problem of Mira-
   cles.*
   483:Jul89-427
Levine, P. A Walk with Tom Jefferson.*
   L. Gregerson, 491:Dec89-236
   R. Schultz, 249(HudR):Spring89-149
Levine, P. - see Keats, J.
Levine, R.S. Conspiracy and Romance.
   G. Dekker, 183(ESQ):Vol35No1-69
Levins, R. & R. Lewontin. The Dialectical
   Biologist.
   P. Kitcher, 482(PhR):Apr89-262
Levins Morales, A. & R. Morales. Getting
   Home Alive.
   R. Benmayor, 36:Fall-Winter90-107
Levinson, M. Keats's Life of Allegory.*
   M. Allott, 447(N&Q):Sep89-405
   J.C. Robinson, 661(WC):Autumn89-201
   J. Stillinger, 445(NCF):Dec89-390
   R.S. White, 175:Summer89-168
Levinson, M. & others. Rethinking Histori-
   cism.
   T. McFarland, 617(TLS):6-12Apr90-381
Levinson, S. Constitutional Faith.
   K. Nutting, 185:Oct89-185
Levinson, S. & S. Mailloux, eds. Interpreting
   Law and Literature.
   V. Kahn, 153:Summer89-21
Levison, B. Strange Smells of a Cat.
   E. Bartlett, 493:Spring89-64
Levith, M.J. Shakespeare's Italian Settings
   and Plays.
   639(VQR):Summer89-82
Levitt, M.P. Modernist Survivors.*
   C.K. Columbus, 395(MFS):Winter89-858
Levon, O.U. Caverns.
   A. Bendixen, 441:21Jan90-28
Lévy, A. - see "Fleur en Fiole d'Or (Jin Ping
   Mei cihua)"
Levy, B. Quakers and the American Family.
   J.D. Marietta, 656(WMQ):Jul89-613
Levy, C., ed. Socialism and the Intelligentsia
   1880-1914.
   J. Greenfield, 637(VS):Winter90-366
   J.J. Schwarzmantel, 242:Vol10No4-482

Levy, D. Ophelia and the Great Idea.*
 R.S. Peckham, 364:Apr/May89-156
Levy, D. Political Order.
 C.O. Schrag, 323:May89-194
Levy, D.J. Chinese Narrative Poetry: The
 Late Han Through T'ang Dynasties.
 J.R. Allen, 116:Dec89-139
Lévy, F.P. & M. Ségaud. Anthropologie de
 l'espace.
 M. Detienne, 98:Apr89-211
Levy, L.W. Original Intent and the Framers'
 Constitution.
 H.J. Powell, 656(WMQ):Oct89-828
 639(VQR):Spring89-61
Levy, P. Finger Lickin' Good.
 A. Ross, 617(TLS):8-14Jun90-608
Levy, R. Scottish Nationalism at the Cross-
 roads.
 C. Harvie, 617(TLS):30Mar-5Apr90-342
Levy, S.H. The Targum of Ezekiel.
 B.L. Visotzky, 508:Jan89-93
Levy, T. Le Droit chemin.
 L. Lê, 98:Oct89-807
Levy, Y., I.M. Schlesinger & M.D.S. Braine.
 Categories and Processes in Language
 Acquisition.*
 J.F. Kess, 350:Dec90-875
Lewalski, B.K., ed. Renaissance Genres.*
 R.J. Du Rocher, 577(SHR):Winter89-81
Lewicki, R. Prezekład wobec zjawisk podst-
 andardowych.
 J. Wawrzyńczyk, 559:Vol13No2-180
Lewin, D. Generalized Musical Intervals and
 Transformations.*
 N. Böker-Heil, 416:Band4Heft3-273
 R. Cohn, 309:Vol9No1-47
 J.R. Hughes, 411:Oct89-325
Lewin, M. The Gorbachev Phenomenon.*
 G.A. Hosking, 575(SEER):Jul89-488
 T. McDaniel, 550(RusR):Jul89-327
Lewin, R. Bones of Contention.
 S. Rose, 617(TLS):23Feb-1Mar90-204
Lewis, A., J. Turner & S. McQuillin. The Opu-
 lent Interiors of the Gilded Age.
 W. Seale, 576:Mar89-100
Lewis, A.W. Le Sang royal.
 P. Jansen, 531:Jul-Dec89-531
Lewis, B. Le Langage politique de l'Islam.
 N. Jensé, 531:Jul-Dec89-528
Lewis, B. Race and Slavery in the Middle
 East.
 D.B. Davis, 453(NYRB):11Oct90-35
 R. Irwin, 617(TLS):21-27Dec90-1371
 M. Zonis, 441:5Aug90-20
Lewis, C., with J. Marx. Inside Track.
 M. Bloom, 441:15Jul90-19
Lewis, C.A. Blood Evidence.
 K. Ray, 441:22Jul90-21
Lewis, C.S. The Essential C.S. Lewis. (L.W.
 Dorsett, ed)
 639(VQR):Summer89-86
Lewis, D. On the Plurality of Worlds.*
 J.E. Tomberlin, 449:Mar89-117
Lewis, D. Philosophical Papers. (Vol 2)
 F. Jackson, 311(JP):Aug89-433
 E.J. Lowe, 393(Mind):Jul88-484
Lewis, G. Australian Movies and the Ameri-
 can Dream.
 C. Ward, 500:Fall89/Winter90-123
Lewis, G. For Instruction and Recreation.
 S.C., 324:Mar90-303
Lewis, G. Eva Gore-Booth and Esther Roper.
 J. Lavin, 174(Éire):Fall89-140

Lewis, H.W. Technological Risk.
 J.A. Paulos, 441:25Nov90-11
Lewis, J.W. & X. Litai. China Builds the Bomb.
 T.W. Robinson, 293(JASt):Aug89-593
Lewis, M. Liar's Poker.*
 M. Bradham, 617(TLS):9-15Feb90-140
Lewis, M.A. Treading the Ebony Path.*
 E. Aizenberg, 538(RAL):Spring89-120
Lewis, N. The Ides of March.
 A. Vassileiou, 555:Vol62Fasc1-173
Lewis, N. Life in Egypt under Roman Rule.*
 H. Heinen, 229:Band61Heft2-176
Lewis, N. To Run Across the Sea.
 R. Fraser, 617(TLS):26Jan-1Feb90-97
Lewis, P. Fielding's Burlesque Drama.*
 B.A. Goldgar, 566:Spring90-181
Lewis, P. The National.
 S. Wall, 617(TLS):14-20Dec90-1352
Lewis, P. & N. Wood, eds. John Gay and the
 Scriblerians.
 J.V. Guerinot, 566:Spring90-188
Lewis, R.E., N.F. Blake & A.S.G. Edwards.
 Index of Printed Middle English Prose.*
 H. Gneuss, 38:Band107Heft1/2-169
Lewis, R.W.B. & N. — see Wharton, E.
Lewis, S. The Art of Matthew Paris in the
 "Chronica majora."*
 M. Camille, 589:Jul89-735
Lewis, W. Creatures of Habit and Creatures
 of Change. (P. Edwards, ed) Tarr. (P.
 O'Keeffe, ed)
 J. Symons, 617(TLS):15-21Jun90-628
Lewis, W. The Essential Wyndham Lewis.* (J.
 Symons, ed)
 F. Upjohn, 364:Aug/Sep89-141
Lewis, W. The Vulgar Streak [and] Rotting
 Hill. (P. Edwards, ed)
 P. O'Keeffe, 148:Winter86-124
Lewy, G. Peace and Revolution.
 J. Narveson, 185:Apr90-685
"Lexicon Iconographicum Mythologiae Clas-
 sicae." (Vol 4)
 H. Lloyd-Jones, 617(TLS):15-21Jun90-
 644
"Lexicon philosophicum." (Pt 3) (A. Lamarra
 & L. Procesi, eds)
 A. Heinekamp, 706:Band21Heft1-129
LEXUS, with others, comps. Dutch at your
 Fingertips.
 W. Christian, 399(MLJ):Summer89-214
Leydet, F. The Coyote. (rev)
 M. Pettis, 649(WAL):May89-82
Leyerle, J. & A. Quick, eds. Chaucer.*
 J. Norton-Smith, 447(N&Q):Mar89-79
Leymarie, J. Gauguin.
 E. Darragon, 98:Apr89-228
Lezama Lima, J. Paradiso.
 D. Zalacain, 238:Mar89-164
L'Hermitte, R. Marr, Marrisme, Marristes.*
 V.M. Du Feu, 575(SEER):Jan89-111
L'Hermitte, R. Science et perversion idéolo-
 gique.
 A. Liberman, 559:Vol13No1-77
L'Heureux, J. Comedians.
 L.G. Sexton, 441:18Feb90-13
Li Ang. The Butcher's Wife.*
 N. Tisdall, 364:Oct/Nov89-141
Li, K.T. The Evolution of Policy Behind Tai-
 wan's Development Success.
 F.S.T. Hsiao, 293(JASt):May89-367
Li, P.S. The Chinese in Canada.
 M. Horn, 529(QQ):Autumn89-726

Li Xiao Jun. The Long March to the Fourth of June.
  D. Davin, 617(TLS):23-29Mar90-304
Li Xueqin. Eastern Zhou and Qin Civilizations.*
  D.W. Goodrich, 318(JAOS):Jul-Sep88-507
Li Yu. The Carnal Prayer Mat.
  A.C. Yu, 441:15Jul90-3
Liang-chieh, T-S. - see under Tung-shan Liang-chieh
Libby, R.T. The Politics of Economic Power in Southern Africa.
  529(QQ):Spring89-211
de Libéra, A. La philosophie médiévale.
  F. Pironet, 540(RIPh):Vol43fasc2-317
Liberaki, M. Trois étés.
  S. Basch, 450(NRF):Jan89-96
Liberman, A. The Artist in His Studio.*
  S.H. Madoff, 55:Apr89-128
Librandi, R. - see Saint Alfonso
Licastro, E. Ugo Betti.
  J. Gatt-Rutter, 278(IS):Vol43-182
Lichtblau, M.I., ed. La emigración y el exilio en la literatura hispánica del siglo veinte.
  K. Oyarzún, 593:Summer89-140
  C.K. Thompson, 238:Sep89-559
Lichtenberg, G.C. Georg Christoph Lichtenberg, Briefwechsel. (U. Joost & A. Schöne, eds)
  H-G. Werner, 680(ZDP):Band108Heft2-284
Lichtmann, M.R. The Contemplative Poetry of Gerard Manley Hopkins.
  G.B. Tennyson, 445(NCF):Mar90-575
Liddy, G.G. The Monkey Handlers.
  A. Gottlieb, 441:14Oct90-36
"L'idée de Renaissance dans l'Occident moderne."
  M. Hugues, 549(RLC):Jan-Mar89-115
Lidén, F. Between Water and Heaven.
  E.S. O'Brien, 563(SS):Winter89-104
Lie, A.R. with R. Robinson. Night and Fog.
  P-L. Adams, 61:Aug90-92
  J. Shulevitz, 441:18Mar90-21
Lieb, M. The Sinews of Ulysses.
  R. Shafer, 500:Jun90-81
Lieber, M. Maurice Grevisse und die französische Grammatik.
  F.J. Hausmann, 547(RF):Band101Heft2/3-297
Lieber, R. An Integrated Theory of Autosegmental Processes.
  K. Rice, 320(CJL):Mar89-59
Lieberman, D. The Province of Legislation Determined.
  B. Simpson, 617(TLS):7-13Sep90-944
Lieberman, L. The Creole Mephistopheles.
  J.F. Cotter, 249(HudR):Autumn89-514
  M.A. Jarman, 376:Jun89-131
  R. Smith, 344:Winter90-213
  639(VQR):Summer89-99
Lieberman, P. & S.E. Blumstein. Speech Physiology, Speech Perception, and Acoustic Phonetics.
  M. Fourakis, 353:Vol27No3-570
  S. Hawkins, 297(JL):Sep89-533
Lieberthal, K. & M. Oksenberg. Policy Making in China.*
  J.K. Kallgren, 293(JASt):Nov89-830
Liebertz-Grün, U. Das andere Mittelalter.
  H. Thomas, 680(ZDP):Band108Heft1-107
Liebeschuetz, J.H.W.G. Barbarians and Bishops.
  C. Kelly, 617(TLS):8-14Jun90-621

Liebfried, E. Schiller.
  W. Wittkowski, 133:Band22Heft2-158
Liebling, A.J. A Neutral Corner. (F. Warner & J. Barbour, eds)
  A. Barra, 441:4Nov90-25
Liebowitz, R.D., ed. Gorbachev's New Thinking.
  S.J. Linz, 550(RusR):Jul89-333
Liebs, E. Kindheit und Tod.*
  J. Zipes, 221(GQ):Fall89-501
Lienert, E. "Frau Tugendreich."
  I. Kasten, 224(GRM):Band39Heft3-357
Lienhard, S. Die Abenteuer des Kaufmanns Siṃhala.
  O.V. Hinüber, 259(IIJ):Apr89-164
van Lier, L. The Classroom and the Language Learner.
  R.R. Day, 710:Sep89-349
  J. Hellebrandt, 350:Sep90-656
  J. Walz, 399(MLJ):Spring89-80
"The Life of Mr. Richard Savage (1727)."
  566:Autumn89-72
"Life-sustaining Treatment."
  G.A., 185:Jan90-460
Lifton, R.J. & E. Markusen. The Genocidal Mentality.
  I. Buruma, 453(NYRB):25Oct90-15
  S. Tobias, 441:27May90-19
Light, L., comp. The Bible in the Twelfth Century.
  M. Gibson, 354:Sep89-273
Light, S. Shūzō Kuki and Jean-Paul Sartre.*
  P.A.M., 206(JML):Fall88/Winter89-919
Lightbown, R. Sandro Botticelli.
  A. Lillie, 617(TLS):16-22Mar90-278
Lightbown, R. Mantegna.*
  D. Ekserdjian, 90:Mar89-228
  J. Woods-Marsden, 589:Oct89-1001
Lightfoot, M. & N. Martin, eds. The Word for Teaching is Learning.
  G. Summerfield, 126(CCC):May89-238
Lightfoot-Klein, H. Prisoners of Ritual.
  M. Köhner, 441:15Apr90-5
Lightman, A. & R. Brawer. Origins.
  J. Gleick, 61:Sep90-113
  D. Overbye, 441:16Sep90-23
Lightstone, J.N. Society, the Sacred, and Scripture in Ancient Judaism.
  I.M. Zeitlin, 627(UTQ):Fall89-224
Lillie, A. & D. Brown, with others - see Clark, N.
Lilly, P.R., Jr. Words in Search of Victims.
  L. McCaffery, 659(ConL):Winter90-564
Lim Chong Yah & others. Policy Options for the Singapore Economy.
  W.G. Huff, 293(JASt):Nov89-937
Lima, J.L. - see under Lezama Lima, J.
Lima, R. Vallé-Inclán.*
  639(VQR):Spring89-53
Limentani, U. & M. Capucci, eds. Studi Secenteschi. (Vol 27)
  E. Speciale, 276:Autumn89-364
Lin, S-F. & S. Owen, eds. The Vitality of the Lyric Voice.*
  J-P. Diény, 318(JAOS):Jul-Sep88-449
Linck, E.S. & J.G. Roach. EATS.
  C. Reynolds, 649(WAL):Nov89-275
Lincoln, C.E. & L.H. Mamiya. The Black Church in the African American Experience.
  J. Forbes, 441:23Dec90-1
Lincoln, E.J. Japan.
  L. Hollerman, 293(JASt):Feb89-172

Lincoln, H.B. The Italian Madrigal and Related Repertories.*
  I. Fenlon, 415:Dec89-744
Lincoln, L., with others. Assemblage of Spirits.
  G.A. Corbin, 2(AfrA):Nov88-94
Lincoln, W.B. Red Victory.
  J.A.C. Greppin, 441:25Feb90-12
  N. Stone, 617(TLS):6-12Apr90-367
Lindahl, C. Earnest Games.*
  J. Mann, 38:Band107Heft1/2-197
Lindberg, E.J. Om skrömt, magi och gammal klokskap. Tugga beck, slå blod, skåda i brännvin.
  J. Gustafson, 64(Arv):Vol44-207
Lindberg, K.V. Reading Pound Reading.*
  J.G. Kronick, 223:Summer89-195
  M. Melaver, 494:Winter89-856
Lindenbaum, P. Changing Landscapes.*
  M.L. Hall, 569(SR):Summer89-456
Linder, L. - see Potter, B.
Lindfors, B. - see Tutuola, A.
Lindgren, T. Merab's Beauty and Other Stories.*
  A.G. Mojtabai, 441:11Mar90-20
Lindholm, C. Charisma.
  D.E. Cooper, 617(TLS):6-12Jul90-721
Lindley, D. Thomas Campion.*
  J. Stevens, 557:Mar89-68
Lindon, J. Studi sul Foscolo "inglese."
  C.P. Brand, 278(IS):Vol44-175
Lindow, J., L. Lönnroth & G.W. Weber, eds. Structure and Meaning in Old Norse Literature.*
  K.E. Gade, 563(SS):Spring/Summer89-266
  A. Liberman, 301(JEGP):Apr89-276
Lindroth, S. Les Chemins du savoir en Suède de la fondation de l'Université d'Upsal à Jacob Berzelius. (J-F. Battail, ed & trans)
  C. Smith, 562(Scan):Nov89-197
Lindsay, M. Requiem for a Sexual Athlete.
  R. Calder, 571(ScLJ):Spring89-57
Lindsey, L. The Growth Experiment.
  P. Passell, 441:25Mar90-17
Lindstrom, N. Jewish Issues in Argentine Literature.
  R. Di Antonio, 268(IFR):Winter90-50
Ling, P.J. America and the Automobile.
  T.C. Barker, 617(TLS):23-29Mar90-312
Lingard, J. The Women's House.
  A. Clyde, 441:21Jan90-21
Lingeman, R. Theodore Dreiser.* (Vol 1)
  E. Margolies, 179(ES):Aug89-372
Lingeman, R. Theodore Dreiser. (Vol 2)
  A. Kazin, 441:30Sep90-1
Linggard, R. Electronic Synthesis of Speech.
  D. O'Shaughnessy, 320(CJL):Jun89-210
Lingis, A. Deathbound Subjectivity.
  K.A. Bryson, 103:Jul90-283
Lingis, A. Phenomenological Explanations.*
  C. Chalier, 192(EP):Jan-Mar89-106
Link-Salinger, R., ed. Of Scholars, Savants, and their Texts.
  J.A. Buijs, 103:Jun90-240
Link-Salinger, R., ed-in-chief. A Straight Path.
  J.A. Buijs, 319:Oct90-609
Linker, K. Love for Sale.
  M. Lavin, 441:5Aug90-3
Linklater, J., ed. The Red Hog of Colima.*
  D. Durrant, 364:Dec89/Jan90-134
Links, J.G. - see Constable, W.G.

Linowes, D.F. Privacy in America.
  J.B. Rule, 441:4Mar90-34
Linskill, J. - see Riquier, G.
Lintner, B. Outrage. (2nd ed)
  P. Carey, 617(TLS):6-12Jul90-717
Lioure, F. - see Gide, A. & V. Larbaud
Lioutas, A. Attische schwarzfigurige Lekanai und Lekanides.
  H.A. Shapiro, 229:Band61Heft4-374
Lipiński, E. Studia Phoenicia, VI.
  H. Hurst, 123:Vol39No2-305
Lipman, E. Then She Found Me.
  R. Cohen, 441:27May90-5
  442(NY):16Jul90-86
Lipman, J. Frank Lloyd Wright and the Johnson Wax Building.
  R.G. Wilson, 576:Jun89-192
Lipman, M. Philosophy Goes to School.
  H.S., 185:Apr90-709
Lipmann, A. Divinely Elegant.
  R. Minkoff, 441:13May90-25
Lippert, C.B. Eighteenth-Century English Porcelain in the Collection of the Indianapolis Museum of Art.
  A. Dawson, 90:May89-363
  R. Hildyard, 39:Jun89-442
Lippman, E.A., ed. Musical Aesthetics. (Vol 2)
  L. Botstein, 451:Fall89-168
Lippy, C.H. The Christadelphians in North America.
  B. Wilson, 617(TLS):18-24May90-531
Lipschutz, I.H. La Pintura española y los románticos franceses.
  J.A. Tomlinson, 446(NCFS):Fall-Winter89/90-274
Lipset, S.M. Continental Divide.
  J.M. Cameron, 453(NYRB):16Aug90-25
  M. Ignatieff, 441:13May90-41
  G. Martin, 617(TLS):2-8Nov90-1189
Lipset, S.M. North American Cultures.
  J.M. Cameron, 453(NYRB):16Aug90-25
Lipton, E. Looking into Degas.*
  A. McCauley, 54:Mar89-144
  P.H. Salus, 567:Vol75No3/4-357
Lira, G.G. - see under Gálvez Lira, G.
Lish, G. Extravaganza.*
  I. Malin, 532(RCF):Summer89-247
Liska, G. Rethinking US-Soviet Relations.
  D.N.M., 185:Apr90-718
Lisle, L. Louise Nevelson.
  M. Brenson, 441:25Mar90-15
Lispector, C. The Passion According to G.H.*
  I. Malin, 532(RCF):Summer89-251
Lista, G. Futurism.
  J. Meyers, 364:Apr/May89-119
Lister, R. British Romantic Painting.
  A. Kidson, 617(TLS):16-22Feb90-160
Lister, R. Catalogue Raisonné of the Works of Samuel Palmer.*
  L. Stainton, 90:Nov89-787
Liszt, F. Franz Liszt: Tagebuch 1827.* (D. Altenburg & R. Kleinertz, eds)
  D. Torkewitz, 417:Jan-Mar89-91
Liszt, F. & R. Wagner. Franz Liszt - Richard Wagner: Briefwechsel. (H. Kesting, ed)
  S. Gut, 537:Vol75No2-304
Litchfield, R.B. Emergence of a Bureaucracy.*
  H.M. Scott, 83:Autumn89-207
Littell, N.M. My Roosevelt Years. (J. Dembo, ed)
  G. Adams, Jr., 106:Fall89-245

Littell, R. The Once and Future Spy.
  N. Callendar, 441:27May90-27
Little, C.E. Greenways for America.
  J.M. La Belle, 441:25Nov90-11
Little, C.E. - see Bromfield, L.
Little, D. The Scientific Marx.
  R. Hudelson, 482(PhR):Jul89-421
Little, D., H. Ó Murchú & D. Singleton, comps.
  A Functional-Notional Syllabus for Adult
  Learners of Irish.
  N. Stenson, 174(Éire):Fall88-154
Little, G.C. A Well-Tuned Harp.
  D. Sampson, 249(HudR):Autumn89-512
Little, J.P. Simone Weil.
  K.A. Reader, 402(MLR):Oct90-980
Littlejohn, A. Company to Company.
  L.F. Kenman, 399(MLJ):Winter89-500
Littlejohns, R. Wackenroder-Studien.*
  E. Waniek, 406:Summer89-264
Litvin, V. The Soviet Agro-Industrial Com-
  plex.*
  C.S. Kaplan, 104(CASS):Spring89-104
Litwack, L.F. & A. Meier, eds. Black Leaders
  of the Nineteenth Century.
  639(VQR):Winter89-17
Liu, A. Wordsworth.
  P.J. Manning, 591(SIR):Fall89-515
Liu Binyan. Le cauchemar des mandarins
  rouges. (J-P. Béja, ed & trans)
  P. de Beer, 98:Aug-Sep89-709
Liu Binyan. China's Crisis, China's Hope.
  J. Mirsky, 617(TLS):16-22Nov90-1225
Liu Binyan. A Higher Kind of Loyalty.
  F. MacFarquhar, 441:27May90-0
  J. Mirsky, 453(NYRB):26Apr90-23
Liu Binyan, with Ruan Ming & Xu Gang. "Tell
  the World."
  J. Mirsky, 453(NYRB):26Apr90-23
Liu, J.J.Y. Language - Paradox - Poetics.
  (R.J. Lynn, ed)
  D. Palumbo-Liu, 293(JASt):Nov89-832
  Zhang Longxi, 116:Jul88-190
Livadie, C.A. - see under Albore Livadie, C.
Lively, A. The Burnt House.*
  J. Mellors, 364:Aug/Sep89-130
Lively, A. Parliament.
  M. Foot, 617(TLS):20-26Jul90-767
Lively, P. Pack of Cards.*
  639(VQR):Autumn89-129
Lively, P. Passing On.*
  R. Bausch, 441:11Feb90-12
  J. Mellors, 364:Jun/Jul89-133
  442(NY):19Mar90-109
Livesay, D. The Self-Completing Tree.
  B. Mitchell, 168(ECW):Spring89-73
Livesey, M. Homework.
  C. Verderese, 441:6May90-22
Livi, F. Ungaretti, Pea e altri - Lettere agli
  amici "egiziani" - Carteggi inediti con
  Jean-Léon e Henri Thuile.
  A. Fongaro, 535(RHL):Nov-Dec89-1071
Livingston, E. The Ethnomethodological
  Foundations of Mathematics.
  T. Tymoczko, 316:Sep89-1104
Livingston, J.C. Matthew Arnold and Chris-
  tianity.*
  E.B. Greenwood, 506(PSt):May87-117
Livingston, P. Literary Knowledge.*
  M. Benton, 89(BJA):Summer89-274
  G. Brahm, Jr., 599:Summer90-316
  P. Dumouchel, 154:Vol28No2-346
  R. Zwaan, 204(FdL):Jun89-158

Livingstone, D. Keeping Heart.*
  S. Kantaris, 493:Autumn89-42
  S. Knight, 364:Oct/Nov89-115
Livingstone, D. Saving Grace.
  J. Saunders, 565:Autumn89-77
Livingstone, M. Pop Art.
  A. Mars-Jones, 617(TLS):30Nov-6Dec90-
  1293
Livingstone, N.C. & D. Halevy, with others.
  Inside the PLO.
  B. Schweid, 441:29Apr90-20
Livy. Tite-Live, "Histoire Romaine."* (Vol 8,
  Bk 8) (R. Bloch & C. Guittard, eds & trans)
  P.M. Martin, 555:Vol62Fasc2-369
  S.P. Oakley, 123:Vol39No2-395
Livy. Tito Livio, "Historia de Roma desde la
  fundación de la ciudad (Ab urbe condita)."
  (Vol 1) (A. Fontán, ed & trans)
  S.P. Oakley, 123:Vol39No2-394
Lixl, A. Ernst Toller und die Weimarer Re-
  publik 1918-1933.
  H. Schmidt, 406:Summer89-273
Lixl-Purcell, A., ed. Women in Exile.
  S.L. Pentlin, 221(GQ):Fall89-546
Lize, E. & E. Wahl, eds. Inédits de correspon-
  dances littéraires.
  R. Waldinger, 207(FR):Apr90-875
Ljung, M. Skinheads, Hackers & Lama Ankor.
  R.H. Southerland, 350:Mar90-196
Llewellyn, S. Death Roll.*
  N. Callendar, 441:27May90-27
Llompart, P.G. - see Castaldo, J.B.
Lloréns Barber, R. Refranero de los frutos del
  campo.
  R. Wright, 86(BHS):Jan89-199
Llosa, M.V. - see under Vargas Llosa, M.
Lloyd, A.B. Herodotus, Book II.
  S. West, 123:Vol39No2-191
Lloyd, A.C. The Anatomy of Neoplatonism.
  A. Sheppard, 617(TLS):31Aug-6Sep90-
  927
Lloyd, A.L., K.K. Purdy & O. Springer. Wör-
  terverzeichnisse zu dem etymologischen
  Wörterbuch des Althochdeutschen. (Vol 1)
  E.A. Ebbinghaus, 215(GL):Vol29No2-135
Lloyd, A.L. & O. Springer. Etymologisches
  Wörterbuch des Althochdeutschen. (Vol 1)
  E.A. Ebbinghaus, 215(GL):Vol29No2-135
  C. van Kerckvoorde, 221(GQ):Spring89-
  247
Lloyd, C. Explanation in Social History.
  C.B. McCullagh, 63:Mar89-116
Lloyd, G.E.R. Polarity and Analogy.
  H. King, 303(JoHS):Vol109-225
Lloyd, G.E.R. The Revolutions of Wisdom.
  J. Dillon, 24:Fall89-499
  J.G. Landels, 123:Vol39No2-361
  J.P. Oleson, 124:Sep-Oct89-53
Lloyd, J. Light and Liberty.
  R. Davenport-Hines, 617(TLS): 14-
  20Sep90-969
Lloyd, P.M. From Latin to Spanish.* (Vol 1)
  W. Mettmann, 547(RF):Band101Heft4-470
  M. Torreblanca, 240(HR):Summer89-357
  M.T. Ward, 238:Sep89-562
  R. Wright, 86(BHS):Oct89-373
Lloyd, R. "Madame Bovary."
  R. Huss, 617(TLS):2-8Mar90-231
Lloyd, R. - see Mallarmé, S.
Lloyd Thomas, D.A. In Defence of Liberalism.
  A. Collier, 518:Jan89-52
  W.A. Galston, 185:Apr90-676
  D.H. Monro, 63:Jun89-254

Llull, R. Raymond Lulle, "Arbre des exemples." (A. Llinarès, trans)
    A. Bonner, 545(RPh):Feb90-482
Llull, R. Raimundus Lullus, "Opera Latina," 14. (A. Madre, ed)
    J.N. Hillgarth, 589:Apr89-465
Llull, R. Selected Works of Ramon Llull (1232-1316).* (A. Bonner, ed & trans)
    C.J. Wittlin, 545(RPh):Aug89-235
Lo Ch'in-shun. Knowledge Painfully Acquired.* (I. Bloom, ed & trans)
    R.E. Hegel, 116:Jul88-197
    S-C. Huang, 485(PE&W):Jul89-364
Lobanov-Rostovsky, N. Revolutionary Ceramics.
    J. Milner, 617(TLS):31Aug-6Sep90-919
Lobner, C.D. James Joyce's Italian Connection.
    M.T. Reynolds, 329(JJQ):Spring90-665
Lobo Antunes, A. Fado Alexandrino.
    A. Dorfman, 441:29Jul90-15
Lo Cascio, V. & Co Vet, eds. Temporal Structure in Sentence and Discourse.
    E. Hinrichs, 359:Apr89-243
Locher, R. & B. Sigel, eds. Domus Tiberiana.
    M. Royo, 229:Band61Heft2-184
Lock, F.P. Burke's Reflections on the Revolution in France.
    R. Zimmer, 489(PJGG):Band96Heft2-431
Locke, J. Some Thoughts Concerning Education. (J.W. & J.S. Yolton, eds)
    L. Stone, 617(TLS):2-8Mar90-229
Lockett, T.A. & G.A. Godden. Davenport, China, Earthenware, Glass.
    T. Hughes, 324:Jun90-505
Locklin, G. The Death of Jean-Paul Sartre and Other Poems. Children of a Lesser Demagogue. A Constituency of Dunces.
    J.H. Maguire, 649(WAL):May89-93
Lockman, Z. & J. Beinin, eds. Intifada.
    D. McDowall, 617(TLS):9-15Nov90-1203
Lockridge, K.A. The Diary, and Life, of William Byrd II of Virginia, 1674-1744.*
    C. Swanson, 106:Summer89-119
Lockwood, L. Music in Renaissance Ferrara, 1400-1505.
    T. Carter, 278(IS):Vol43-147
Lockwood, M. Mind, Brain and the Quantum.
    D. Papineau, 617(TLS):23Feb-1Mar90-193
Lockwood, M.J. A Study of the Poems of D.H. Lawrence.
    D.T.O., 295(JML):Fall88/Winter89-369
Lockyer, R. The Early Stuarts.
    A. Fletcher, 617(TLS):2-8Mar90-230
Lodge, A., ed. Le Plus Ancien Registre de comptes des consuls de Montferrand en provençal auvergnat 1259-1272.
    S. Kay, 208(FS):Jan89-73
Lodge, D. After Bakhtin.
    J. Bayley, 617(TLS):10-16Aug90-839
Lodge, D. Nice Work.*
    P. Lewis, 565:Summer89-66
Loening, T.C. The Reconciliation Agreement of 403/402 B.C. in Athens.
    J.T. Roberts, 124:Jul-Aug90-525
Loest, E. The Monument.
    P. Lewis, 565:Winter88/89-77
Loewe, M. The Pride that Was China.
    J. Rawson, 617(TLS):7-13Sep90-952
Loewe, R., ed & trans. The Rylands Haggadah.
    J. Backhouse, 39:Nov89-360

Loewen, H., ed. Why I am a Mennonite.
    E. Friesen, 102(CanL):Spring89-155
Lofaro, M.A. & J. Cummings, eds. Crockett at Two Hundred.
    S. Armitage, 585(SoQ):Winter90-75
    T. Wortham, 445(NCF):Dec89-423
Löffler, H., ed. Das Deutsch der Schweizer.
    D. Stellmacher, 685(ZDL):3/1989-370
Löfstedt, B., L. Holtz & A. Kibre - see Smaragdus
Loftis, J. Renaissance Drama in England and Spain.*
    L. Barroll, 405(MP):Feb90-293
    L. Fothergill-Payne, 240(HR):Winter89-90
Logan, A-M. The Collections of the Detroit Institute of Arts: Dutch and Flemish Drawings and Watercolours.
    M. Royalton-Kisch, 90:Jun89-428
    J. Spicer, 380:Spring89-70
Logan, G.M. & G. Teskey, eds. Unfolded Tales.
    D.J.G., 604:Fall89-55
Logan, R.K. The Alphabet Effect.*
    W.C. Watt, 567:Vol75No3/4-279
Logsdon, L. & C.W. Mayer, eds. Since Flannery O'Connor.*
    G. Monteiro, 573(SSF):Summer88-328
Lohmann, D. Die Andromache-Szenen der "Ilias."
    M.M. Willcock, 123:Vol39No2-174
Loizou, A. The Reality of Time.*
    B. Hale, 323:Jan89-99
Lokke, K. Gérard de Nerval.*
    L.M. Porter, 210(FrF):Jan89-105
Lólos, Y.B. The Late Helladic I Pottery of the Southwestern Peloponnesos and its Local Characteristics.
    E. French, 303(JoHS):Vol109-261
Lomas, M. The Peepshow Girl.
    S. Pugh, 493:Autumn89-60
Lomasky, L.E. Persons, Rights, and the Moral Community.*
    J.W. Nickel, 393(Mind):Oct89-652
Lomax, D.W. & R.J. Oakley - see Lopes, F.
Lomax, M. The Peepshow Girl.*
    S. Knight, 364:Oct/Nov89-115
Lomax, M. Stage Images and Traditions: Shakespeare to Ford.*
    V. Bourgy, 189(EA):Oct-Dec89-470
    M. Charney, 551(RenQ):Spring89-140
    C. Dymkowski, 541(RES):Feb89-119
    G. Holderness, 402(MLR):Jan90-141
    D. Stevens, 615(TJ):Mar89-115
Lomba Fuentes, J. El Oráculo de Narciso.
    M. Kerkhoff, 160:Jan89-161
Lombardo, S. & D. Rayor - see Callimachus
Lombreglia, R. Men under Water.
    W. Ferguson, 441:15Apr90-14
    R. Towers, 453(NYRB):17May90-38
Lomotey, K., ed. Going to School.
    A. Hacker, 453(NYRB):22Nov90-19
London, J. The Letters of Jack London.* (E. Labor, R.C. Leitz 3d & I.M. Shepard, eds)
    D.L. Walker, 649(WAL):May89-91
    C.N. Watson, Jr., 27(AL):Dec89-684
    T. Williams, 395(MFS):Summer89-272
    T. Wortham, 445(NCF):Jun89-123
Long, A.A. Hellenistic Philosophy. (2nd ed)
    A. Dalzell, 41:Spring89-131
Long, A.A. & D.N. Sedley. The Hellenistic Philosophers.*
    G.B. Kerferd, 123:Vol39No1-49
    P. Louis, 555:Vol62Fasc2-346

Long, H.A. Personal and Family Names.
E.D. Lawson, 424:Mar89-93
Long, J.W. From Privileged to Dispossessed.
639(VQR):Summer89-82
Long, T. Repetition and Variation in the
Short Stories of Herodotus.*
J.M. Bigwood, 487:Summer89-172
Longenbach, J. Modernist Poetics of History.*
G. Bornstein, 401(MLQ):Mar88-82
T.H. Jackson, 468:Spring&Fall89-253
J. Korg, 125:Fall88-73
L.S. Rainey, 405(MP):Aug89-106
Longenbach, J. Stone Cottage.*
G. Bornstein, 401(MLQ):Mar88-82
N. Grene, 447(N&Q):Dec89-546
W. Harmon, 301(JEGP):Oct89-565
Longeon, C., ed. La Farce des Théologastres.
K. Cameron, 402(MLR):Oct90-952
Longhurst, C.A. & others, eds. A Face Not
Turned to the Wall.
P.J. Smith, 402(MLR):Jan90-222
"Longman Dictionary of Contemporary Eng-
lish." (new ed) (D. Summers & others, eds)
E. Standop, 38:Band107Heft1/2-130
Longuet Marx, A. Proust, Musil, Partage
d'écritures.
R. Smadja, 549(RLC):Jul-Sep89-426
Longum, L. Drømmen om det frie menneske.*
F. Hermundsgard, 563(SS):Autumn89-419
Lönnroth, E. Den stora rollen
H.A. Barton, 563(SS):Autumn89-426
Lonsdale, R., ed. Eighteenth-Century Women
Poets.*
W. Vestlo, 050:Fab00-0
H. Vendler, 453(NYRB):31May90-19
Lopate, P. Against Joie de Vivre.*
J. Saari, 42(AR):Fall89-498
Lopera, J.Á. - see under Álvarez Lopera, J.
Lopes, F. The English in Portugal, 1367-87.
(D.W. Lomax & R.J. Oakley, eds & trans)
J. Edwards, 402(MLR):Jul90-775
Lopez, C.A. & others - see Franklin, B.
Lopez, D. La Plume et l'épée.
D. Kuizenga, 207(FR):Apr90-871
J. Marmier, 475:Vol16No30-314
Lopez, D.S., Jr., ed. Buddhist Hermeneutics.
J.R. McRae, 293(JASt):Feb89-120
Lopez, D.S., Jr. The Heart Sutra Explained.
J.I. Cabezón, 293(JASt):Feb89-206
Lopez, D.S., Jr. A Study of Svätantrika.
J.W. de Jong, 259(IIJ):Jul89-226
López, I-J. Caballero de novela.
C.A. Longhurst, 86(BHS):Jul89-291
N.M. Valis, 240(HR):Winter89-110
López, F.G. - see under González López, F.
López Criado, F. El erotismo en la novela
ramoniana.
W.M. Sherzer, 552(REH):Oct89-136
López de Ayala, P. Libro de la caça de las
aves.* (J.G. Cummins, ed)
D. Hook, 304(JHP):Winter90-178
López de Ayala, P. Rimado de Palacio.* (G.
Orduna, ed)
P. Rodgers, 238:May89-297
López Estrada, F. - see Gil Polo, G.
López Morales, H. Enseñanza de la lengua
materna.
J.R. Lodares, 548:Jan-Jun89-183
López Morales, H. - see de Torres Naharro, B.
López Moreda, S. Los grupos lexemáticos de
"facio" y "ago" en el latín arcaico y clásico.
H. Rosén, 229:Band61Heft2-111

López Román, J.E. La obra literaria de Vi-
cente Palés Matos.
P. Hulme, 86(BHS):Jul89-313
López-Vázquez, A.R. - see under Rodríguez
López-Vázquez, A.
Lopinski, M., M. Moskit & M. Wilk. Konspira.
M.T. Kaufman, 441:24Jun90-12
Lopokova, L. & J.M. Keynes. Lydia and May-
nard.* (P. Hill & R. Keynes, eds)
P. Rose, 441:22Jul90-11
442(NY):9Jul90-92
Loraux, N. The Invention of Athens.
P.W. Sage, 124:Sep-Oct89-67
Loraux, N. Tragic Ways of Killing a Woman.*
J. Cahill, 487:Summer89-165
G. Cockburn, 123:Vol39No2-398
Lorca, F.G. Antología poética. (A.A. Ander-
son, ed)
E.A. Southworth, 86(BHS):Apr89-188
Lorca, F.G. Canciones y Primeras canciones.
(P. Menarini, ed)
H.T. Young, 240(HR):Spring89-262
Lorca, F.G. La Désillusion du monde. (Y.
Véquaud, ed & trans)
J.P., 98:Oct89-813
Lorca, F.G. Poema del cante jondo. (C. De
Paepe, ed)
H. Sonneville, 356(LR):Aug89-224
Lorca, F.G. El público. (M.C. Millán, ed)
A.A. Anderson, 00(DH3).Jul89-296
L.H. Klibbe, 240(HR):Winter89-119
Lorca, F.G. Romancero gitano. (H. Ramsden,
ed)
D. Harris, 402(MLR):Oct90-1008
Lord, B.B. Legacies.
L. Mathews, 441:15Apr90-9
J. Mirsky, 453(NYRB):26Apr90-23
Lord, G.D. Classical Presences in Seven-
teenth-Century English Poetry.*
W. Frost, 131(CL):Fall89-395
J.V. Guerinot, 568(SCN):Spring-
Summer89-4
P. Hammond, 677(YES):Vol20-257
W. Kupersmith, 301(JEGP):Jul89-399
A. Patterson, 149(CLO):Vol20No1-71
Lorenz, K. The Waning of Humaneness.
J. Holloway, 97(CQ):Vol18No2-215
S. Rose, 617(TLS):23Feb-1Mar90-204
Lorenzo, L.G. - see under García Lorenzo, L.
Lorenzo, R., ed. Crónica troiana.
J. Weiss, 589:Apr89-463
Lorenzo-Rivero, L. Estudios literarios sobre
Mariano J. de Larra.
M.A. Rees, 86(BHS):Apr89-183
Lorenzo-Rivero, L. Larra.
J.R. Rosenberg, 552(REH):Oct89-134
Lornell, K. "Happy in the Service of the
Lord."
J.C. Downey, 585(SoQ):Winter90-80
Lortat-Jacob, B., ed. L'improvisation dans
les musiques de tradition orale.
M. Benamou, 187:Fall89-551
Lortie, J.D., with P. Savard & P. Wyczynski.
Les Textes poétiques du Canada français,
1606-1867. (Vol 1)
D.M. Hayne, 627(UTQ):Fall89-178
Lorusso, E.N.S. - see McAlmon, R.
Łoś, M. Communist Ideology, Law and Crime.
W.J. Wagner, 497(PolR):Vol34No2-178
Loskutoff, Y. La Sainte et la Fée.
J. Barchilon, 475:Vol16No30-316
R. Zuber, 535(RHL):Mar-Apr89-281

Loss, A.K. W. Somerset Maugham.*
    J.K.G., 295(JML):Fall88/Winter89-381
Lossky, V. Marina Tsvétaeva.
    A. Smith, 575(SEER):Apr89-287
"Lost Crops of the Incas."
    J.E. Butler, 441:29Apr90-39
Loster-Schneider, G. Der Erzähler Fontane.
    J. Chew, 222(GR):Summer89-142
    W. Paulsen, 133:Band22Heft2-178
    W. Wittkowski, 406:Spring89-131
Losurdo, D. Autocensura e compromesso nel
    pensionero politico di Kant.
    L. Ucciani, 192(EP):Jul-Dec89-546
Losurdo, D. Hegel, Marx e la tradizione liber-
    ale.
    P. Trotignon, 542:Oct-Dec89-601
Lotito, B.A. Entre nosotros.
    E. Spinelli, 399(MLJ):Summer89-242
Loudon, I. Medical Care and the General
    Practitioner 1750-1850.
    F.B. Smith, 637(VS):Winter90-345
Lough, J. France on the Eve of Revolution.*
    B.G. Garnham, 83:Spring89-78
    P. Jansen, 535(RHL):Jul-Aug89-723
Loukomski, G. The Palaces of Tsarskoe Selo.
    C. McCorquodale, 39:Feb89-140
Lourié, V. Poems. (T.R. Beyer, Jr., ed)
    T. Pachmuss, 574(SEEJ):Winter89-625
Lourié, V. Stikhotvoreniia. (T.R. Beyer, Jr.,
    ed)
    G.S. Smith, 575(SEER):Jul89-442
Louvish, S. The Last Trump of Avram Blok.
    T. Aitken, 617(TLS):24-30Aug90-902
"The Love Songs of the Carmina Burana."
    (E.D. Blodgett & R.A. Swanson, trans)
    D.A. Traill, 124:Sep-Oct89-75
Loveday, L. Explorations in Japanese Socio-
    linguistics.
    K. Shiokawa, 355(LSoc):Sep89-430
Lovegrove, J. The Hope.
    P. Reading, 617(TLS):9-15Feb90-149
Lovelace, R. Selected Poems. (G. Hammond,
    ed)
    M.G. Brennan, 447(N&Q):Mar89-105
Loveland, A.C. Lillian Smith.*
    C.M. Perry, 580(SCR):Spring90-173
Lovell, B. Astronomer by Chance.
    W.G. Kolata, 441:3Jun90-23
Lovenduski, J. & J. Woodall. Politics and
    Society in Eastern Europe.
    R.K. Kindersley, 575(SEER):Jan89-162
Loverance, R. Byzantium.
    M. Dimaio, Jr., 124:Mar-Apr90-374
Lovesey, P. Bertie and the Seven Bodies.
    P. Craig, 617(TLS):1-7Jun90-593
    M. Stasio, 441:21Jan90-35
Lovin, R.W. & F.E. Reynolds, eds. Cosmogony
    and Ethical Order.
    M. Taber, 485(PE&W):Oct89-514
Lovis, G., ed. Contes fantastiques du Jura.
    M-L. Tenèze, 196:Band30Heft1/2-143
Low, A.D. The Sino-Soviet Confrontation
    Since Mao Zedong.*
    L.E. Williams, 104(CASS):Spring89-110
Low, D.A. Robert Burns.*
    S. Mapstone, 541(RES):May89-275
Lowden, J. Illuminated Prophet Books.
    C. Mango, 90:Dec89-852
Lowe, D. Russian Writing since 1953.*
    P.M. Mitchell, 295(JML):Fall88/Winter89-
    201
    L. Weeks, 550(RusR):Oct89-445
Lowe, D. & R. Meyer - see Dostoevsky, F.

Lowe, D.A. - see Dostoevsky, F.
Lowe, G.S. Women in the Administrative Rev-
    olution.
    H.J. Maroney, 529(QQ):Summer89-562
Löwe, H-D. Die Lage der Bauern in Russland
    1880-1905.
    N. Stone, 617(TLS):6-12Apr90-367
Lowe, P. & C.W. Stansfield, eds. Second Lan-
    guage Proficiency Assessment.
    A.O. Hadley, 399(MLJ):Winter89-489
Lowe, V. Alfred North Whitehead.* (Vols 1 &
    2) (J.B. Schneewind, ed)
    A.W. Masters, 617(TLS):7-13Dec90-1329
Lowe-Evans, M. Crimes Against Fecundity.
    J. Chadwick, 329(JJQ):Spring90-668
    B.K. Scott, 174(Éire):Fall89-139
Lowell, R. Collected Prose.* (R. Giroux, ed)
    J. McCue, 4:Summer89-63
Lowell, S. Ganado Red.
    M. Kenyon, 376:Mar89-125
    P. Powell, 219(GaR):Fall89-609
Lowen, J. Cynthia Ozick.
    E. New, 508:Sep89-288
Lowenstein, T. Filibustering in Samsåra.
    L. Sail, 565:Summer89-75
Lowenthal, D. The Past Is a Foreign Country.
    S.P. Schoelwer, 658:Winter89-306
Lowenthal, E. - see Shakespeare, W.
Lowitt, R. The New Deal and the West.
    J. Braeman, 106:Summer89-41
Lowry, G.D. & M.C. Beach. An Annotated and
    Illustrated Checklist of the Vever Collec-
    tion.
    B.W. Robinson, 463:Winter89/90-225
Lowry, G.D., with S. Nemazee. A Jeweler's
    Eye.
    B.W. Robinson, 463:Winter89/90-225
Lowry, M. & G. Noxon. The Letters of Mal-
    colm Lowry and Gerald Noxon 1940-1952.
    (P. Tiessen, ed)
    C. Ackerley, 102(CanL):Autumn-
    Winter89-167
    K. Scherf, 627(UTQ):Fall89-156
    B.W. Shaffer, 395(MFS):Winter89-811
Lowry, S.T. The Archaeology of Economic
    Ideas.*
    T. Pekáry, 229:Band61Heft6-551
Loy, D. Nonduality.
    S.B. King, 293(JASt):Aug89-578
Loy, R. The Dust Roads of Monferrato.
    T. Parks, 617(TLS):9-15Nov90-1215
Loyer, F. & J. Delhaye. Victor Horta, Hôtel
    Tassel, 1893-1895.
    S. Levine, 576:Sep89-287
Lozano Marco, M.A. - see Miró, G.
Lubenow, W.C. Parliamentary Politics and the
    Home Rule Crisis.
    J. Vincent, 637(VS):Autumn89-195
Lubich, F.A. Die Dialektik von Logos und
    Eros im Werk von Thomas Mann.
    Ü. Gökberk, 222(GR):Spring89-86
Lubin, G. - see Sand, G.
Lübke, C. Regesten zur Geschichte der Slaven
    an Elbe und Oder (vom Jahr 900 an). (Pts
    1-4)
    G. Stone, 575(SEER):Apr89-293
Lucan. Lucan's "Civil War." (P.F. Widdows,
    trans)
    H. Lloyd-Jones, 453(NYRB):18Jan90-39
Lucanio, P. Them or Us.
    P. Rist, 106:Summer89-111

Lucas, C., ed. The French Revolution and the Creation of Modern Political Culture. (Vol 2)
  J. Starobinski, 453(NYRB):12Apr90–47
Lucas, C., ed. The Sociolinguistics of the Deaf Community.
  S. Fischer, 350:Dec90–837
Lucas, J. England and Englishness.
  J. Bayley, 617(TLS):23Feb–1Mar90–187
Lucas, J. Modern English Poetry from Hardy to Hughes.*
  V.S., 295(JML):Fall88/Winter89–256
Lucas, J. Tables.
  A. Enders, 441:10Jun90–53
Lucas, J.R. The Future.
  P. Horwich, 617(TLS):22–28Jun90–672
Lucas, M. The Southern Vision of Andrew Lytle.*
  A.E. Elmore, 580(SCR):Fall90–167
  A. Foata, 585(SoQ):Winter90–71
Lucas, R. Evenings at Mongini's and Other Stories.
  S. Chew, 617(TLS):2–8Mar90–214
Lucash, F.S., ed. Justice and Equality.
  S.R., 185:Oct89–204
Lucchesi, J. & R.K. Shull. Musik bei Brecht.
  J. Schebera, 654(WB):1/1989–171
Luce, S.L. Céline and his Critics.
  P. Alméras, 535(RHL):Jan–Feb89–152
  P.J. Lapaire, 345(KRQ):May89–238
  I. Piette, 356(LR):Feb–May89–124
Lucente, G.L. Beautiful Fables.*
  C. Klopp, 276:Summer89–224
  M.L. McLaughlin, 278(IS):Vol44–177
  B. Merry, 345(KRQ):Nov89–500
  J. Smith, 402(MLR):Jan90–219
Lucie-Smith, E. Sculpture since 1945.
  W. Jeffett, 39:Feb89–136
Luck, C.D. The Field of Honour.*
  E.R. Sicher, 575(SEER):Jan89–165
Luck, G. – see Tibullus
Luckhardt, U. Lyonel Feininger.
  S. West, 617(TLS):16–22Mar90–291
Ludewig, G. Stadthannoversches Wörterbuch. (D. Stellmacher, ed)
  E. Piirainen, 685(ZDL):3/1989–380
Ludlum, R. The Bourne Ultimatum.
  N. Callendar, 441:11Mar90–33
Ludvigson, S. The Beautiful Noon of No Shadow.
  W.H. Green, 580(SCR):Spring90–142
Ludwig, P. Studien zum Motettenschaffen der Schüler Palestrinas.
  M. Just, 416:Band4Heft2–175
Lueders, E. The Wake of the General Bliss.
  K. Wilson, 649(WAL):Aug89–174
Luedtke, L.S. Nathaniel Hawthorne and the Romance of the Orient.
  R. Irwin, 617(TLS):29Jun–5Jul90–702
Luelsdorff, P.A., ed. Orthography and Phonology.*
  E. Hajičová, 603:Vol13No1–202
  J. Panevová, 361:Jul89–255
Lugarini, L. Critica della ragione e universo della culture.
  G.V. Di Tommaso, 342:Band80Heft4–495
Lugin, I.A. – see under Cheron, F.I.
Lühr, R. Expressivität und Lautgesetz im Germanischen.
  E. Seebold, 684(ZDA):Band118Heft4–147
Luiz Lafetá, J. Figuração da intimidade.
  D. Treece, 86(BHS):Jul89–316

Lukacs, J. Confessions of an Original Sinner.
  P. Theroux, 441:20May90–14
Lukan, W. & D. Medakovic, eds. Vuk Stefanović Karadžić, 1787–1987.
  C. Hawkesworth, 575(SEER):Jan89–117
Lukezic, J. & T. Schwarz. False Arrest.
  S. Fried, 441:18Feb90–17
Lullies, R. & W. Schiering, eds. Archäologenbildnisse.
  J.M. Cook, 123:Vol39No2–428
Lulofs, T.J. & H. Ostrom. Leigh Hunt.*
  S. Monod, 158:Mar89–26
Lumiansky, R.M. & D. Mills, eds. The Chester Mystery Cycle.* (Vol 2)
  A.F. Johnston, 447(N&Q):Sep89–371
"Les Lumières en Hongrie, en Europe centrale et en Europe orientale."
  D-H. Pageaux, 549(RLC):Jan–Mar89–121
Lummis, C. Letters from the Southwest. (J.W. Byrkit, ed) Some Strange Corners of Our Country.
  P. Wild, 649(WAL):Aug89–189
Lummis, T. & J. Marsh. The Woman's Domain.
  C. Bingham, 617(TLS):19–25Oct90–1124
Lumsden, M. Existential Sentences.
  C. Lyons, 297(JL):Mar89–267
  G. Milsark, 350:Dec90–850
"Lun Zhongguo chuantong wenhua."
  J. Thoraval, 98:Aug–Sep89–558
Lunan, D., ed. Starfield.
  J. Clute, 617(TLS):23Feb–1Mar90–202
Lund, M. Reading Thackeray.*
  R.E. Lougy, 637(VS):Autumn89–197
Lundbaek, K. T.S. Bayer (1694–1738).
  S.W. Durrant, 318(JAOS):Apr–Jun88–349
Lundquist, J. Jack London.*
  J. Alhinc, 295(JML):Fall88/Winter89–374
Lundstrom, R.F. William Poel's "Hamlets."
  C.J. Carlisle, 612(ThS):Nov88–213
  J. Hankey, 611(TN):Vol43No1–27
Lundström, S. Zur Textkritik der "Tusculanen."*
  J-M. André, 555:Vol62Fasc1–165
Lunenfold, M. Keepers of the City.*
  A. MacKay, 86(BHS):Jul89–276
  S.T. Nalle, 551(RenQ):Summer89–303
Lunggren, A. & N.Å. Nilsson – see Guro, E.
Lungu, D.D. Romania and the Great Powers 1933–1940.
  E. Weber, 617(TLS):19–25Jan90–58
Lunn, A.J.E. Développement économique de la Nouvelle France, 1712–1760.*
  T. Crowley, 529(QQ):Spring89–150
Luntley, M. Language, Logic, and Experience.*
  J. Heal, 518:Apr89–100
Luo, Z-P. A Generation Lost.
  G. Feldman, 441:11Mar90–9
Lupack, B.T. Plays of Passion, Games of Chance.
  S. Fogel, 395(MFS):Winter89–764
  L. McCaffery, 659(ConL):Winter90–564
Luper-Foy, S., ed. The Possibility of Knowledge.
  F.W. Kroon, 63:Mar89–102
Luper-Foy, S., ed. Problems of International Justice.
  T.N., 185:Oct89–220
Lupica, M. Limited Partner.
  M. Lichtenstein, 441:14Oct90–48
Luporini, C. Filosofi vecchi e nuovi.
  C. La Rocca, 342:Band80Heft3–364

Lupton, T. All for Money. (M.G.P. Concolato, ed)
  K. Duncan–Jones, 447(N&Q):Mar89–92
Luque, M.I.R. – see under Ramírez Luque, M.I.
Lurati, O. & I. Pinana. Le parole di una valle.
  G. Sanga & E.F. Tuttle, 545(RPh):Nov89–283
Lurie, A. Don't Tell the Grown–Ups.
  P–L. Adams, 61:Apr90–108
  R. Brown, 441:11Mar90–13
  H. Carpenter, 617(TLS):8–14Jun90–607
  J.A. Smith, 453(NYRB):26Apr90–45
  442(NY):7May90–110
Lurie, A. The Truth about Lorin Jones.
  D. Flower, 249(HudR):Spring89–137
  J. Saari, 42(AR):Winter89–106
Lüsebrink, H.J. – see Raynal, G. & D. Diderot
Lush, R. A Grass Pillow.
  G. Harding–Russell, 102(CanL):Summer89–175
Lusignan, S. Parler vulgairement.
  W.W Kibler, 589:Jan89–183
  F. Vielliard, 531:Jul–Dec89–502
  F. Vielliard, 554:Vol108No2/3–387
de Lussy, F. L'Univers formel de la poésie chez Valéry [ou] La recherche d'une morphologie généralisée.
  N. Celeyrette–Pietri, 535(RHL):Mar–Apr89–327
  C.M. Crow, 208(FS):Jul89–353
Lust, B., ed. Studies in the Acquisition of Anaphora. (Vol 1)
  M. Labelle, 320(CJL):Dec89–474
  S. Romaine, 353:Vol27No5–966
Lust, B., ed. Studies in the Acquisition of Anaphora. (Vol 2)
  M. Labelle, 320(CJL):Dec89–474
Lust, J. Western Books on China Published Up to 1850 in the Library of the School of Oriental and African Studies, University of London.
  F. Wood, 78(BC):Summer89–268
Lustbader, E.V. White Ninja.
  N. Callendar, 441:25Feb90–35
Lustig, I.S. & F.A. Pottle – see Boswell, J.
Lütkehaus, L. Schopenhauer – Metaphysischer Pessimismus und "soziale Frage."
  M. Hielscher, 489(PJGG):Band96Heft1–198
Lutts, R.H. The Nature Fakers.
  K. Ray, 441:8Apr90–21
Lutz, H. "Indianer" und "Native Americans."
  E.P. Hamp, 269(IJAL):Jul89–382
Lutz, J. Flame.
  I. Sinclair, 617(TLS):24–30Aug90–903
Lutz, J.G. Chinese Politics and Christian Missions.
  S.W. Barnett, 293(JASt):Nov89–833
Lützeler, P.M. Geschichte in der Literatur.*
  E. Geulen, 400(MLN):Apr89–737
  G.P. Knapp, 221(GQ):Winter89–107
  F. Piedmont, 406:Winter89–495
Lützeler, P.M. Zeitgeschichte in Geschichten der Zeit.
  H. Emmel, 301(JEGP):Apr89–304
  C. Koelb, 406:Spring89–135
  H. Wagener, 221(GQ):Summer89–413
Lutzker, M. Research Projects for College Students.
  K.B. Lovejoy, 126(CCC):May89–247
Luxton, S. The Hills that Pass By.
  G.V. Downes, 102(CanL):Autumn–Winter89–187

L'vov, N. & I. Prach. A Collection of Russian Folk Songs. (M.H. Brown, with M. Mazo, eds)
  R. Reeder, 292(JAF):Apr–Jun89–220
  F. Wigzell, 575(SEER):Apr89–266
Lycan, W.G. Judgement and Justification.*
  C. Misak, 518:Apr89–107
Lycos, K. Plato on Justice and Power.
  D. Browne, 63:Sep89–352
Lydenberg, R. Word Cultures.*
  D. Seed, 677(YES):Vol20–341
Lyle, S. The Year I Owned the Yankees.
  M. Caruso, 441:1Apr90–11
Lyman, F. The Greenhouse Trap.
  N. Wade, 441:22Apr90–1
Lynch, A. The Soviet Study of International Relations.
  S. Shenfield, 575(SEER):Apr89–329
Lynch, G. Stephen Leacock.*
  D.J. Dooley, 627(UTQ):Fall89–153
  C. Spadoni, 529(QQ):Winter89–983
Lynch, J. Bourbon Spain 1700–1808.
  J.H. Elliott, 453(NYRB):1Mar90–26
  H. Kamen, 617(TLS):23–29Mar90–330
Lynch, J. The Secret Diary of Laura Palmer.
  A. Stanley, 441:28Oct90–35
Lynch, O.M., ed. Divine Passions.
  D. Quigley, 617(TLS):5–11Oct90–1059
Lyne, R.O.A.M. Further Voices in Vergil's "Aeneid."*
  K. Galinsky, 24:Spring89–171
Lyne, R.O.A.M. Words and the Poet.
  D. West, 617(TLS):19–25Jan90–71
Lynn, D.H. The Hero's Tale.
  M. Magalaner, 395(MFS):Winter89–849
Lynn, K.S. Hemingway.*
  L. Butts, 573(SSF):Summer88–334
  K. Moreland, 577(SHR):Spring89–145
  S.P., 295(JML):Fall88/Winter89–347
Lynn, L.H. & T.J. McKeown. Organizing Business.
  L.W. Farnsworth, 293(JASt):May89–395
Lynn, R. Educational Achievement in Japan.
  C. Lewis, 407(MN):Spring89–124
  M.I. White, 293(JASt):May89–396
Lynn, R.J. – see Liu, J.J.Y.
Lynn–George, M. Epos.
  S. Lowenstam, 124:Jan–Feb90–238
  J.D. Smart, 123:Vol39No1–1
Lyon, T.J., ed. This Incomperable Lande.
  A. Ronald, 649(WAL):Nov89–270
Lyon, T.J. & others, eds. A Literary History of the American West.
  H.P. Simonson, 448:Vol27No3–136
Lyons, C.R., ed. Critical Essays on Henrik Ibsen.*
  J. Chamberlain, 563(SS):Spring/Summer89–273
Lyons, L. & D. Perlo. Jazz Portraits.
  G.L. Starks, Jr., 91:Vol17–183
Lyons, R. These Modern Nights.
  639(VQR):Winter89–26
Lyons, R. A Wilderness of Faith and Love.
  L. Rackstraw, 455:Sep89–67
Lyotard, J–F. The Differend.
  A. Bresnick, 147:Vol6No2–42
  T.R., 185:Jul90–913
  C.J. Stivale, 207(FR):Mar90–722
Lyotard, J–F. Heidegger et "les juifs."
  A. Ronell, 153:Fall–Winter89–63
Lyotard, J–F. The Lyotard Reader. (A. Benjamin, ed)
  W. Steiner, 441:4Mar90–15

Lyotard, J-F. Peregrinations.*
R. Bogue, 478(P&L):Apr89-209
Lysias. Lisia, Apologia per l'uccisione di
Eratostene - Epitafio. (G. Avezzù, ed)
T.K. Stephanopoulos, 229:Band61Heft1-
19
Lyte, C. Frank Kingdom-Ward.
A. Urquhart, 617(TLS):19-25Jan90-74
Lytle, A. From Eden to Babylon. (M.E. Brad-
ford, ed)
A.E. Elmore, 580(SCR):Fall90-167
Lytle, A. Southerners and Europeans.*
A. Foata, 585(SoQ):Summer89-118
J. Hurt, 402(MLR):Oct90-931
639(VQR):Winter89-10
Lytle, A. & A. Tate. The Lytle-Tate Letters.*
(T.D. Young & E. Sarcone, eds)
J.E. Brown, 580(SCR):Fall90-158
M.R. Winchell, 106:Fall89-280

Ma Jian. La Mendiante de Shigatze.
L. Kovacs, 450(NRF):May89-101
Maas, P. In a Child's Name.
J. Barthel, 441:11Nov90-12
Maaskant-Kleibrink, M. Settlement Excava-
tions at Borgo Le Ferriere "Satricum." (Vol
1)
T.W. Potter, 313:Vol79-179
Mabee, B. Die Poetik von Sarah Kirsch.
C. Weedon, 402(MLR):Oct90-1034
Mabileau, A. & others. Local Politics and
Participation in Britain and France.
J. Hayward, 617(TLS):7-13Sep90-942
MacAdam, A.J. Textual Confrontations.*
R.W. Fiddian, 86(BHS):Jan89-110
H.R.M., 295(JML):Fall88/Winter89-202
R. Prieto, 400(MLN):Mar89-509
MacAdams, W. Ben Hecht.
J. Crist, 441:1Apr90-21
Macafee, C. Glasgow.
A. Agutter, 260(IF):Band94-362
McAllister, L. The Blue House.*
L. Inbar, 102(CanL):Summer89-180
McAlmon, R. Village. (E.N.S. Lorusso, ed)
J.R. Mellow, 441:22Jul90-9
McAlpine, M. The Other Side of Silence.
L. McMullen, 529(QQ):Winter89-963
McArthur, M. Stolen Writings.*
M. May, 177(ELT):Vol32No3-384
McArthur, M.S.H. Report on Brunei in 1904.
J.F. Warren, 293(JASt):Feb89-225
Macaulaitis-Cooke, J. & M. Scheraga. The
Complete ESL/EFL Resource Book.
C.F. McCreary, 399(MLJ):Summer89-216
McAuslan, I. & P. Walcot, eds. Virgil.
R. Jenkyns, 617(TLS):23-29Nov90-1268
MacAvoy, R.A. Lens of the World.
G. Jonas, 441:2Sep90-18
Macazaga Ordoño, C. Los nahuatlismos de la
Academia.
W. Bright, 545(RPh):May90-610
McBain, E. Three Blind Mice.
M. Stasio, 441:5Aug90-29
McBain, E. Vespers.
M. Stasio, 441:7Jan90-29
MacBain, W., ed. De sainte Katerine.*
H. Shields, 208(FS):Oct89-452
MacBeth, G. Anatomy of a Divorce.*
D. McDuff, 565:Spring89-76
MacBeth, G. Collected Poems 1958-1982.
T. Dooley, 617(TLS):26Jan-1Feb90-101

McCabe, B. The Other McCoy.
I. Bamforth, 617(TLS):4-10May90-480
Maccabée-Iqbal, F. Desafinado.
P. Merivale, 102(CanL):Autumn-
Winter89-229
McCaffery, S. North of Intention.
K. Jirgens, 102(CanL):Summer89-144
R.P. Knowles, 168(ECW):Fall89-144
MacCaig, N. Collected Poems.*
J. Greening, 493:Spring89-55
McCall, D. Triphammer.
P. Barker, 441:4Feb90-14
McCallion, J. Tough Roots.*
G.V. Downes, 102(CanL):Autumn-
Winter89-187
MacCallum, H. Milton and the Sons of God.*
R.J. Du Rocher, 301(JEGP):Apr89-237
McCalman, I. Radical Underworld.*
P. Edwards, 538(RAL):Fall89-573
McCann, D.R. Form and Freedom in Korean
Poetry.
M.R. Pihl, 293(JASt):Nov89-889
McCann, G. Woody Allen.
K. Quinn, 441:1Jul90-14
MacCannell, J.F. Figuring Lacan.
S. Mills, 506(PSt):May89-90
A. Thiher, 207(FR):Apr90-882
McCardie, A., ed. The Collins Book of Love
Poems.
A.S. Byatt, 617(TLS):31Aug-6Sep90-913
McCarey, P. Hugh MacDiarmid and the Rus-
sians.*
A. Riach, 478(P&L):Apr89-207
McCarey, P. & A. Riach. For What It Is.
T. Nairn, 571(ScLJ):Spring89-54
McCarney, S. Memory Loss.
G. Gessert, 448:Vol27No3-129
McCarthy, F. Eric Gill.*
A. Adams, 39:Sep89-209
R. Cork, 90:Sep89-660
P. Davey, 46:Mar89-12
M. Kelly, 364:Feb/Mar90-125
McCarthy, G. Edward Albee.*
C. Johnson, 295(JML):Fall88/Winter89-
275
McCarthy, M. How I Grew.
M.J.F., 295(JML):Fall88/Winter89-376
S. Rudikoff, 249(HudR):Spring89-46
McCarthy, M. The Origins of the Gothic Re-
vival.*
J. Frew, 576:Dec89-400
McCarthy, M.L. The Crisis of Philosophy.
H. Meynell, 103:Dec90-502
McCarthy, P. Albert Camus, "The Stranger."
C. Robinson, 447(N&Q):Dec89-559
C.A. Viggiani, 478(P&L):Apr89-182
McCarthy, P., C. Elkins & M.H. Greenberg, eds.
The Legacy of Olaf Stapledon.
J. Huntington, 395(MFS):Winter89-810
McCarthy, T. Seven Winters in Paris.
W. Scammell, 617(TLS):18-24May90-522
McCartney, D. The Dawning of Democracy
1800-1870.
J. Hill, 235:Summer89-86
McCartney, G. Confused Roaring.*
A. Blayac, 189(EA):Oct-Dec89-489
D. Bradshaw, 541(RES):Aug89-440
M.P.L., 295(JML):Fall88/Winter89-417
McCaughrean, G. Fires' Astonishment.
J. O'Grady, 617(TLS):13-19Apr90-403
McCauley, M., ed. Gorbachev and Perestroika.
O. Figes, 617(TLS):5-11Oct90-1056

McCauley, M., ed. The Soviet Union under Gorbachev.*
 B.A. Chotiner, 550(RusR):Jul89-321
McCauley, M. & P. Waldron. The Emergence of the Modern Russian State, 1855-81.
 R.P. Bartlett, 575(SEER):Oct89-631
McCauley, S. The Object of My Affection.
 M. De Koven, 473(PR):Vol56No1-157
McClatchy, J.D. The Rest of the Way.
 R. Richman, 441:25Nov90-24
McClatchy, J.D. White Paper.*
 639(VQR):Autumn89-136
McClellan, D. Simone Weil.
 P. McCarthy, 617(TLS):13-19Jul90-747
McClendon, C.B. The Imperial Abbey of Farfa.*
 B. Ward-Perkins, 90:Feb89-154
McCloskey, D.N. The Rhetoric of Economics.*
 C.R. Miller, 544:Winter89-101
McCloskey, M.A. Kant's Aesthetic.*
 D. Dutton, 478(P&L):Oct89-428
 E. Schaper, 290(JAAC):Spring89-180
McClure, B. - see "Paris, 1979-1989"
McConnel, P. Sing Soft, Sing Loud.*
 P. Glasser, 455:Sep89-69
 L. Wagner-Martin, 573(SSF):Summer89-354
McConnell, F., ed. The Bible and Narrative Tradition.
 S. Helmling, 569(SR):Summer89-462
McConnell, F. The Frog King.
 M. Stasio, 441:12Aug90-21
McConnell, G. Stehekin.
 42(AR):Winter89-110
McCooey, C. - see Strange, J.
McCool, G.A. - see Clarke, W.N.
McCord, M. William Ockham.
 F. Inciarte, 489(PJGG):Band96Heft2-382
McCorkle, J. Ferris Beach.
 R. Loewinsohn, 441:7Oct90-10
McCorkle, M.L. Johannes Brahms Thematisch-Bibliographisches Werkverzeichnis. (E. Herttrich, with W. Martin & T.J. Quigley, eds)
 D. Brodbeck, 317:Summer89-418
MacCormac, E.R. A Cognitive Theory of Metaphor.*
 M. Danesi, 567:Vol77No4-521
McCormack, E. Inspecting the Vaults and Other Stories.*
 D. Durrant, 364:Feb/Mar90-133
 S. Fogel, 168(ECW):Spring89-137
McCormack, G. & Y. Sugimoto, eds. Modernization and Beyond.*
 A. Walthall, 293(JASt):Nov89-872
McCormick, C.H. This Nest of Vipers.
 J.M. Forsythe, 585(SoQ):Summer90-117
McCormick, E.H. The Friend of Keats.
 R. Lansdown, 617(TLS):23Feb-1Mar90-188
McCormick, P.J. Fictions, Philosophics and the Problems of Poetics.
 M. Fischer, 103:Feb90-70
 D. Novitz, 290(JAAC):Fall89-382
 D.E.B. Pollard, 307:Dec89-225
 E. Sankowski, 289:Fall89-111
McCormick, T.J. America's Half-Century.
 W.F. Kimball, 617(TLS):8-14Jun90-601
McCort, D. States of Unconsciousness in Three Tales by C.F. Meyer.
 J. Osborne, 402(MLR):Jul90-809
 G.W. Reinhardt, 133:Band22Heft3/4-342

MacCoull, L.S.B. Dioscorus of Aphrodito.
 D.J. Constantelos, 124:Mar-Apr90-372
McCracken, G. Culture and Consumption.
 E.J. Arnold, 292(JAF):Oct-Dec89-487
 T.H. Witkowski, 658:Spring89-79
McCracken, K. The Constancy of Objects.
 M.T. Lane, 198:Autumn89-111
McCrary, S.N. "El último godo" and the Dynamics of "Urdrama."*
 D.W. Bleznick, 552(REH):May89-137
 R.L. Fiore, 345(KRQ):Nov89-495
McCray, S. Advanced Principles of Historical Linguistics.
 M.L. Bender, 350:Mar90-199
McCrone, K.E. Playing the Game.
 D. Rubinstein, 637(VS):Winter90-358
McCrory, M. The Fading Shrine.
 P. Craig, 617(TLS):6-12Jul90-732
McCrum, M. Thomas Arnold, Headmaster.*
 W. James, 324:Mar90-301
 C. Sprawson, 364:Feb/Mar90-121
McCrumb, S. If Ever I Return, Pretty Peggy-O.
 M. Stasio, 441:20May90-53
McCrumb, S. The Windsor Knot.
 E. Budd, 441:14Oct90-48
McCulloch, H.Y., Jr. Narrative Cause in the "Annals" of Tacitus.
 P.H. Schrijvers, 394:Vol42fasc1/2-221
McCulloch, M. The Novels of Neil M. Gunn.*
 M. Reizbaum, 395(MFS):Winter89-796
McCullough, C. The First Man in Rome.
 C.E. Rinzler, 441:4Nov90-19
McCullough, H.C. Bungo Manual.
 A. Gatten, 407(MN):Winter89-522
McCullough, H.C. - see "The Tale of the Heike"
McCumber, J. Poetic Interaction.
 J. Mitscherling, 103:Jun90-245
McCutchan, P. Convoy of Fear.
 N. Callendar, 441:23Dec90-15
McDannel, C. & B. Lang. Heaven.
 639(VQR):Spring89-46
McDannell, C. The Christian Home in Victorian America, 1840-1900.
 L.N. Primiano, 292(JAF):Jul-Sep89-371
McDermott, J. Kingsley Amis.
 K. Wilson, 395(MFS):Winter89-817
MacDiarmid, H. A Drunk Man Looks at the Thistle. (K. Buthlay, ed)
 P. Crotty, 571(ScLJ):Winter89-23
McDiarmid, L. Auden's Apologies for Poetry.
 K. Bucknell, 617(TLS):3-9Aug90-819
McDiarmid, L. Saving Civilization.
 G. Monteiro, 675(YER):Summer89-61
McDiarmid, M.P. & J.A.C. Stevenson - see "Barbour's Bruce"
McDonald, A.P., ed. Shooting Stars.*
 P. Rist, 106:Summer89-111
MacDonald, C. The Killing of SS Obergruppenführer Reinhard Heydrich, 27 May 1942.
 J. Bowen, 364:Dec89/Jan90-142
 A. Glees, 617(TLS):13-19Apr90-392
Macdonald, C. Mind-Body Identity Theories.
 H. Steward, 617(TLS):4-10May90-476
McDonald, F. & E.S. Requiem.
 R.L. Hatzenbuehler, 656(WMQ):Jul89-625
Macdonald, G. & P. Pettit. Semantics and Social Science.
 L.H. Simon & R.A. Strikwerda, 449:Dec89-688

MacDonald, G. & C. Wright, eds. Fact, Science and Morality.*
B. Hale, 393(Mind):Apr89-307
McDonald, I. Mercy Ward.*
D. Dabydeen, 493:Spring89-18
MacDonald, I. The New Shostakovich.
S. Karlinsky, 617(TLS):7-13Sep90-949
H. Robinson, 441:25Nov90-16
McDonald, J. The "New Drama" 1900-1914.*
M.M. Morgan, 610:Summer89-207
MacDonald, J.F. One Nation Under Television.
P. Keepnews, 441:2Sep90-17
Macdonald, L. 1914.
639(VQR):Autumn89-117
MacDonald, M. Brahms.
W. Mellers, 617(TLS):16-22Mar90-285
MacDonald, M. John Foulds and His Music.
W. Mellers, 617(TLS):30Mar-5Apr90-353
MacDonald, M. Schoenberg.
A.F.L.T., 412:May89-146
MacDonald, M., comp. Dmitri Shostakovich. (2nd ed)
A.F.L.T., 412:May89-146
MacDonald, M. Ronald Stevenson.
W. Mellers, 617(TLS):12-18Jan90-39
McDonald, M. "We Are Not French."
D. Johnson, 617(TLS):19-25Oct90-1119
McDonald, P. Biting the Wax.
N. Corcoran, 617(TLS):16-22Feb90-179
Macdonald, R.R. The Burial-Places of Memory.*
K.W. Gransden, 403(MLR):Jan90-131
McDonald, W. After the Noise of Saigon.*
639(VQR):Winter89-87
McDonald, W.A., W.D.E. Coulson & J. Rosser. Excavations at Nichoria in Southwest Greece. (Vol 3)
S. Hiller, 229:Band61Heft6-534
Macdonell, D. Theories of Discourse.*
S. Mills, 506(PSt):May89-90
McDonnell, J. & P. Healy. Gold-Tooled Book-bindings Commissioned by Trinity College Dublin in the Eighteenth Century.
M.M. Foot, 354:Sep89-280
D. McKitterick, 78(BC):Spring89-118
J. Morris, 90:Sep89-656
D. Pearson, 83:Spring89-95
MacDonogh, G. A Good German.
R. Overy, 617(TLS):29Jun-5Jul90-699
McDonogh, G.W. Good Families of Barcelona.
J-L. Marfany, 86(BHS):Apr89-193
McDougal, S.Y., ed. Dante Among the Moderns.*
J.H. McGregor, 678(YCGL):No36-183
McDougall, B.S. - see Bei Dao
MacDougall, E.B., ed. Ancient Roman Villa Gardens.*
B. Bergmann, 576:Dec89-387
Macdougall, N. James IV.
K.M. Brown, 617(TLS):10-16Aug90-852
McDowall, D. Palestine and Israel.*
A. Hertzberg, 453(NYRB):25Oct90-41
B. Morris, 441:25Mar90-12
McDowall, R. Double Exposure: Take Two.
D. Kaufman, 441:3Jun90-23
McDowell, D.E. - see Larsen, N.
McDowell, D.E. & A. Rampersad, eds. Slavery and the Literary Imagination.
W. Berry, 569(SR):Fall89-591
MacDowell, D.M. Spartan Law.*
M. Gagarin, 124:Sep-Oct89-65
MacDowell, D.M. - see Andocides

McDowell, G.L. Curbing the Courts.
A.S.R., 185:Oct89-218
MacDowell, J. Cara Massimina.
S. Whiteside, 617(TLS):16-22Mar90-293
McDowell, R. Quiet Money.
D. Mason, 569(SR):Winter89-xxi
Macé, G. Le Dernier des Égyptiens.
C-P. Pérez, 450(NRF):Jun89-101
McElrath, J.R., Jr. Frank Norris and "The Wave."
J.R. Kelly, 517(PBSA):Jun89-253
G.A. Love, 26(ALR):Spring90-94
B. Schuyler, 649(WAL):May89-73
McElroy, C.J. Jesus and Fat Tuesday, and Other Stories.
P.K. Collier, 502(PrS):Spring89-109
R. Hemley, 459:Spring89-82
McElroy, G.C., with H.L. Gates, Jr. Facing History.
R. Dorment, 453(NYRB):27Sep90-54
McEnery, J.H. Epilogue in Burma 1945-48.
M. Morland, 617(TLS):30Nov-6Dec90-1284
McEwan, I. The Child in Time.*
P. Lewis, 565:Winter88/89-77
McEwan, I. The Innocent.
J. Banville, 453(NYRB):6Dec90-22
G. Stade, 441:3Jun90-1
J. Symons, 617(TLS):11-17May90-497
McEwan, N. Perspectives in British Historical Fiction Today.
M.P.L., 295(JML):Fall88/Winter89-246
G. Viswanathan, 395(MFS):Summer89-377
McEwen, G. Afterworlds.*
B. Pell, 628(UWR):Vol22No1-101
McEwen, T. McX.
J.K. Crane, 441:9Dec90-20
S. Whiteside, 617(TLS):13-19Apr90-403
Macey, D.A.J. Government and Peasant in Russia 1861-1906.*
J. Pallot, 575(SEER):Jul89-476
McFadden, D. Canadian Sunset.
T. Goldie, 102(CanL):Winter88-128
McFadden, D. Gypsy Guitar.*
J. Doyle, 102(CanL):Spring89-154
McFadden, R.D. & others. Outrage.
E. Goodman, 441:29Jul90-7
McFall, L. Happiness.
R.K., 185:Jul90-904
P. Miller, 103:Aug90-328
McFall, L. The One True Story of the World.
R. Sassone, 441:3Jun90-22
McFarland, D. The Music Room.
S. Amidon, 617(TLS):31Aug-6Sep90-916
J. Humphreys, 441:6May90-11
R. Towers, 453(NYRB):16Aug90-46
McFarland, R.E. & W. Studebaker, eds. Idaho's Poetry.
J.H. Maguire, 649(WAL):Aug89-183
McFarland, T. Romantic Cruxes.
J. Bate, 191(ELN):Jun90-79
E.D. Mackerness, 447(N&Q):Jun89-245
W. Ruddick, 677(YES):Vol20-285
J. Whale, 661(WC):Autumn89-188
McFarland, T. & S. Ranawake, eds. Hartmann von Aue.
D.H. Green, 402(MLR):Jan90-236
McFeely, M.D. & W.S. - see Grant, U.S.
McGahern, J. Amongst Women.
J. Banville, 453(NYRB):6Dec90-22
R.R. Cooper, 441:9Sep90-44
L. Duguid, 617(TLS):18-24May90-535
442(NY):24Dec90-99

McGann, J.J. The Beauty of Inflections.
  T. Tessier, 189(EA):Apr-Jun89-191
McGann, J.J. Social Values and Poetic Acts.*
  M. Fischer, 88:Summer89-32
  W.V. Harris, 478(P&L):Oct89-381
McGann, J.J. - see Lord Byron
McGee, A. The Elizabethan "Hamlet."
  M.L. Ranald, 551(RenQ):Summer89-357
  J. Rees, 541(RES):Aug89-412
  E. Sams, 447(N&Q):Mar89-99
  W. Schrickx, 179(ES):Feb89-88
McGee, J.S. - see Bunyan, J.
McGee, P. Paperspace.*
  S. Pinsker, 177(ELT):Vol32No1-122
  C. Shloss, 395(MFS):Autumn89-617
MacGill-Eain, S. - see under MacLean, S.
McGing, B.C. The Foreign Policy of Mithri-
dates VI Eupator King of Pontus.
  E. Olshausen, 229:Band61Heft1-67
McGing, B.C. - see Parke, H.W.
McGinn, C. Wittgenstein on Meaning.*
  P.A. Boghossian, 482(PhR):Jan89-83
  C. Wright, 393(Mind):Apr89-289
McGinn, M. Sense and Certainty.*
  J. Hornsby, 393(Mind):Oct89-635
  M. Williams, 479(PhQ):Oct89-520
McGinn, R., ed. Studies in Austronesian Lin-
guistics.
  J.T. Collins, 293(JASt):Feb89-226
McGough, R. Selected Poems 1967-1987.
  S. O'Brien, 617(TLS):27Jul-2Aug90-803
McGowan, J.P. Representation and Revela-
tion.*
  J. McMaster, 301(JEGP):Apr89-252
McGowan, M. Marieluise Fleisser.
  H.T. Tewarson, 222(GR):Fall89-186
McGrane, B. Beyond Anthropology.
  G. Lienhardt, 617(TLS):19-25Jan90-68
McGrath, A. The Intellectual Origins of the
European Reformation.*
  F. Oakley, 589:Oct89-1008
McGrath, F.C. The Sensible Spirit.*
  D. Schwanitz, 38:Band107Heft1/2-247
McGrath, P. The Grotesque.*
  I. Malin, 532(RCF):Fall89-221
McGrath, P. Spider.
  K. Dunn, 441:23Sep90-14
McGrath, R.L. & B.J. MacAdam. "A Sweet
Foretaste of Heaven."
  658:Summer/Autumn89-207
McGrath, T. Selected Poems: 1938-1988.*
  C. Buckley, 649(WAL):May89-83
  D. Jacobson, 29(APR):May/Jun89-27
  D. Wakoski, 219(GaR):Winter89-804
McGraw, E. Bodies at Sea.
  J.R. Moehringer, 441:18Mar90-20
McGregor, G. The Noble Savage in the New
World Garden.
  P. Lapp, 529(QQ):Winter89-981
  R.E. Meyer, 27(AL):May89-281
MacGregor, J.M. The Discovery of the Art of
the Insane.*
  P-L. Adams, 61:Mar90-116
  L. Hudson, 617(TLS):23-29Mar90-323
  D. Kuspit, 62:Summer90-23
McGregor, M.F. The Athenians and Their Em-
pire.*
  P. Cartledge, 235:Winter88-68
McGuane, T. Keep the Change.*
  J. Clute, 617(TLS):25-31May90-558
McGuckian, M. On Ballycastle Beach.*
  C. Bedient, 472:Vol16No1-195
                              [continued]

[continuing]
  J. Drexel, 434:Winter89-179
  G.M. McCarthy, 272(IUR):Spring89-175
McGuinness, B. Wittgenstein. (Vol 1)
  N. Malcolm, 521:Apr89-162
  J.P. Stern, 483:Jul89-409
McGuirk, B. & R. Cardwell, eds. Gabriel Gar-
cía Márquez.*
  B.A., 295(JML):Fall88/Winter89-335
  G.R. McMurray, 238:Mar89-155
  D.L. Shaw, 86(BHS):Jan89-116
McGuirk, R. Colloquial Arabic of Egypt.
  P. Stevens, 399(MLJ):Winter89-493
McGushin, P. Sallust, "The Conspiracy of
Catiline."
  J.L. Moles, 123:Vol39No2-393
Mácha, K. Glaube und Vernunft. (Pt 2)
  J. Kalvoda, 104(CASS):Spring89-115
Machado, A. Solitudes, Galleries, and Other
Poems.*
  J.A. Jiménez, 552(REH):Jan89-138
  G. Ribbans, 86(BHS):Jul89-294
  N. Valis, 403(MLS):Summer89-89
McHale, B. Postmodernist Fiction.*
  E. van Alphen, 494:Winter89-819
  S.B., 295(JML):Fall88/Winter89-247
  T. Docherty, 541(RES):Nov89-597
  M. Hite, 454:Spring90-324
  L. Olsen, 70:Jan89-36
MacHale, D. George Boole.
  V. Putnam, 316:Jun89-619
Machan, T. Individuals and Their Rights.
  S.D. Warner, 543:Jun90-873
Machan, T.R., ed. Commerce and Morality.
  M.J. Brandon, 185:Jan90-432
Machan, T.R. The Moral Case for the Free
Market Economy.
  R.G.F., 185:Jul90-910
Machann, C. & F.D. Burt, eds. Matthew Arnold
in His Time and Ours.*
  W.E. Buckler, 637(VS):Autumn89-188
  G.B. Tennyson, 445(NCF):Sep89-254
Machatzke, M. - see Hauptmann, G.
de Machaut, G. "Le Jugement du roy de Be-
haigne" and "Remède de Fortune." (J.I.
Wimsatt, W.W. Kibler & R.A. Baltzer, eds)
  R. Morris, 402(MLR):Oct90-948
Machiavelli, N. Florentine Histories.
  639(VQR):Summer89-103
Machin, G.I.T. Politics and the Churches in
Great Britain 1869 to 1921.*
  J.L. Altholz, 635(VPR):Summer89-77
Machin, R. & C. Norris, eds. Post-Structur-
alist Readings of English Poetry.*
  S. Bassnett, 307:Dec89-234
  S. Moulthrop, 677(YES):Vol20-221
  E. Wright, 541(RES):Feb89-142
McHugh, H. Shades.*
  M. Boruch, 29(APR):Mar/Apr89-41
McHugh, H. To the Quick.*
  R. Jackson, 502(PrS):Fall89-117
Maciejewska, I., ed. Meczenstwo i zaglada
Zydow w zapisach literatury polskiej.
  M. Adamczyk-Garbowska, 508:Sep89-273
McIlvanney, W. In Through the Head.
  J. Hendry, 571(ScLJ):Winter89-66
  B. Turner, 493:Summer89-57
McIlvanney, W. Walking Wounded.*
  D. Durrant, 364:Apr/May89-154
  G. Telfer, 571(ScLJ):Winter89-31
McInerney, J. Story of My Life.*
  D. Flower, 249(HudR):Spring89-134

236

MacInnes, J.W. The Comic as Textual Practice in "Les Fleurs du Mal."
　L.M. Porter, 446(NCFS):Spring–Summer90–530
McIntosh, A., M.L. Samuels & M. Benskin, with others. A Linguistic Atlas of Late Medieval English.* Guide to "A Linguistic Atlas of Late Medieval English."
　A. Lutz, 38:Band107Heft3/4–495
McIntosh, M.K. Autonomy and Community.
　L. Attreed, 589:Jan89–187
MacIntyre, A. Three Rival Versions of Moral Enquiry.
　J. Teichman, 441:12Aug90–14
MacIntyre, A. Whose Justice? Which Rationality?*
　J. Annas, 509:Fall89–388
　B. Barry, 185:Oct89–160
　A. Hartle, 319:Jul90–470
　C. Larmore, 311(JP):Aug89–437
　W.I. Matson, 483:Oct89–564
Macintyre, D.B. Duncan Ban Macintyre's "Ben Dorain."
　D. McDuff, 565:Spring89–76
McJimsey, G. Harry Hopkins.*
　J. Braeman, 106:Summer89–41
Mack, C.R. Pienza.
　J.G. Bernasconi, 278(IS):Vol44–160
　C.W. Westfall, 576:Mar89–85
Mack, J., ed. Ethnic Jewelry.
　R.K. Liu, 2(AfrA):May89–25
Mack, P. & M.C. Jacob, eds. Politics and Culture in Early Modern Europe.
　L.A. McKenzie, 242:Vol10No1–89
Mack, S. Ovid.
　N. Goldman, 124:Nov–Dec89–130
　639(VQR):Spring89–66
McKay, A. Human Bones.
　L. Drew, 198:Autumn89–118
McKay, A. in the house of winter.
　R. Anderson, 102(CanL):Autumn–Winter89–178
MacKay, A. Society, Economy and Religion in Late Medieval Castile.
　J. Edwards, 86(BHS):Jul89–275
Mackay, C. The Sound of the Sea.*
　M. Addison, 571(ScLJ):Winter89–49
MacKay, C.H. Soliloquy in Nineteenth-Century Fiction.
　N. Bradbury, 541(RES):Aug89–425
　B. Westburg, 637(VS):Summer90–661
McKay, D. Allies of Convenience.
　M. Hughes, 83:Spring89–91
McKay, E.N. The Impact of the New Pianofortes on Classical Keyboard Style.
　R. Burnett, 410(M&L):Aug89–407
McKay, F. The Life of James K. Baxter.
　F. Adcock, 617(TLS):14–20Sep90–978
Mackay, J. Quebec Hill; or, Canadian Scenery. (D.M.R. Bentley, ed)
　C. Ballstadt, 470:Vol27–119
McKay, K.M. Many Glancing Colours.
　W.D. Shaw, 627(UTQ):Winter89/90–358
McKay, S.L. Teaching Grammar.
　Y. Bader, 257(IRAL):Feb89–72
McKee, A. Strike from the Sky. (rev)
　P. Smith, 617(TLS):5–11Jan90–6
McKee, P. & H. Kauppinen. The Art of Aging.
　M.H. Bornstein, 290(JAAC):Spring89–194
MacKendrick, P. The Philosophical Books of Cicero.
　T.P. Wiseman, 617(TLS):15–21Jun90–647

McKenna, M. A Handbook of Modern Spoken Breton.
　J. Le Dû, 547(RF):Band101Heft2/3–309
McKenna, W. W.J. Turner.
　D. Hibberd, 617(TLS):7–13Sep90–948
Mackensen, M., with others. Eine befestigte spätantike Anlage vor den Stadtmauern von Resafa.
　F.W. Deichmann, 229:Band61Heft7–614
MacKenzie, C. – see Head, B.
MacKenzie, J.J. & M.T. El-Ashry. Air Pollution's Toll on Forests and Crops.
　S. Mills, 617(TLS):11–17May90–490
MacKenzie, J.M. The Empire of Nature.*
　639(VQR):Autumn89–139
MacKenzie, N.H. – see Hopkins, G.M.
Mackenzie, P.T. The Problems of Philosophers.
　W. Davie, 103:Sep90–373
McKeon, M. The Origins of the English Novel 1600–1740.*
　H.P. Abbott, 301(JEGP):Jan89–99
　J.A. Downie, 566:Spring89–161
　M. Irwin, 541(RES):May89–269
　J. Tylus, 551(RenQ):Spring89–156
　W.B. Warner, 153:Spring89–62
McKeon, R. Rhetoric.* (M. Backman, ed)
　W.R. Fisher, 480(P&R):Vol22No3–221
　G.A. Press, 319:Jan90–151
McKeown, J.C. Ovid, Amores. (Vol 1)
　A. Ramírez de Verger, 229:Band01Heft5–388
Mackerras, C. Western Images of China.
　D.S. Walwyn, 617(TLS):6–12Apr90–369
Mackey, D. Philip K. Dick.
　P. Fitting, 561(SFS):Jul89–233
McKibben, B. The End of Nature.*
　T. O'Riordan, 617(TLS):9–15Mar90–250
McKibbin, R. The Ideologies of Class.
　H. Perkin, 617(TLS):15–21Jun90–637
Mackie, J.L. Selected Papers.* (J. & P. Mackie, eds)
　F. Recanati, 192(EP):Jul–Dec89–548
McKim-Smith, G., G. Andersen-Bergdoll & R. Newman. Examining Velázquez.*
　R. Mulcahy, 90:Oct89–716
McKinnoll, J. – see "Viga Glums Saga with the Tales of Ogmund Bash and Thorvald Chatterbox"
McKinney, I. Quick and Slow Fire. Six O'Clock Mine Report.
　D. McNamara, 236:Spring–Summer89–42
MacKinnon, C.A. Feminism Unmodified.
　V. Kahn, 153:Summer89–21
　C. Pateman, 185:Jan90–398
Mackinnon, L. Shakespeare the Aesthete.
　H. Mills, 175:Spring89–77
MacKinnon, S.R. & O. Friesen, eds. China Reporting.
　N.C. Wiest, 293(JASt):Feb89–141
Mackintosh, C.R. The Architectural Papers. (P. Robertson, ed)
　S. Harries, 617(TLS):10–16Aug90–856
Macklin, J. The Window and the Garden.
　P. Hart, 395(MFS):Summer89–364
McKnight, R. I Get on the Bus.
　K. Brailsford, 441:16Sep90–22
　R. Gibson, 617(TLS):24–30Aug90–902
　442(NY):16Jul90–85
McKnight, R. Moustapha's Eclipse.
　G. Johnson, 219(GaR):Summer89–406
　J. Klinkowitz, 455:Mar89–69

McKnight, S.A. Sacralizing the Secular.
  B.P. Copenhaver, 319:Oct90−611
McKusick, J.C. Coleridge's Philosophy of Language.*
  A.C. Goodson, 591(SIR):Spring89−170
McLane, J.B. & G.D. McNamee. Early Literacy.
  B.E. Cullinan, 441:1Jul90−17
McLane−Iles, B. Uprooting and Integration in the Writings of Simone Weil.
  W. Gealy, 521:Oct89−344
McLaughlin, B. Theories of Second−Language Learning.
  I. Soto, 402(MLR):Oct90−888
  T. Vogel, 710:Dec89−472
McLaughlin, B.P. & A.O. Rorty, eds. Perspectives on Self−Deception.
  L.H. Steffen, 185:Jan90−438
McLaughlin, J. Jefferson and Monticello.
  S.R. Hauer, 580(SCR):Fall89−149
  R. Lavenstein, 45:Mar89−63
  J. Lewis, 656(WMQ):Apr89−417
  R.G. Wilson, 47:Apr89−44
McLean, G.F. & H. Meynell, eds. Person and Society.
  J.B.D., 185:Jan90−444
Maclean, M. Narrative as Performance.
  D.M. Betz, 446(NCFS):Fall−Winter89/90−263
  M. Melaver, 494:Fall89−648
Maclean, N. A River Runs through It.
  F. Tuohy, 617(TLS):10−16Aug90−841
MacLean, S. [S. MacGill−Eain] From Wood to Ridge/O Choille gu Bearradh.
  C. Craig, 617(TLS):28Sep−4Oct90−1041
McLeish, K. Longman Guide to Shakespeare's Characters.
  G. Schmitz, 156(ShJW):Jahrbuch1989−332
MacLeish, R. Crossing at Ivalo.
  N. Callendar, 441:27May90−27
McLeod, A., ed. New Women's Fiction.
  F. Adcock, 617(TLS):2−8Feb90−123
MacLeod, D. My Son the Lawyer is Drowning.
  M. Gilman, 616:Vol10No2−56
MacLeod, R., ed. Government and Expertise.*
  H. Parris, 637(VS):Summer90−676
MacLeod, R. & P.F. Rehbock, eds. Nature in Its Greatest Extent.
  K.G. Dugan, 293(JASt):Feb89−121
McLeod, W.H. Who Is a Sikh?
  S. Khilnani, 617(TLS):19−25Jan90−68
McLintock, D., A. Stevens & F. Wagner, eds. Geistliche und weltliche Epik des Mittelalters in Österreich.
  H. Bekker, 201:Vol15−347
McLuhan, M. & E. Laws of Media.*
  L. Dubinsky, 150(DR):Spring89−127
  J. Fekete, 627(UTQ):Fall89−248
MacLulich, T.D. Between Europe and America.
  B. Godard, 529(QQ):Summer89−511
  W.J. Keith, 627(UTQ):Fall89−146
  A. Knoenagel, 102(CanL):Spring89−227
McLure, R. Sarraute: "Le Planétarium."
  V. Minogue, 402(MLR):Apr90−462
Maclure, S. A History of Education in London 1870−1990.
  T. Wingate, 324:Sep90−712
McLynn, F. Burton.
  R. Irwin, 617(TLS):12−18Oct90−1089
McLynn, F. Crime and Punishment in 18th Century England.
  J. Styles, 617(TLS):25−31May90−561
McLynn, F. Stanley.*
  A. Knopf, 441:30Dec90−14

McMahon, K. Causality and Containment in Seventeenth−Century Chinese Fiction.
  K. Carlitz, 293(JASt):May89−368
McManners, J., ed. The Oxford Illustrated History of Christianity.
  E. Norman, 617(TLS):21−27Sep90−1003
McManus, J. Ghost Waves.*
  I. Malin, 532(RCF):Spring89−250
McManus, P.F. & P.M. Gass. Whatchagot Stew.
  K. Ray, 441:4Feb90−19
McMillan, D. & M. Fehsenfeld. Beckett in the Theatre.
  P. Davies, 402(MLR):Jan90−170
  L. Oppenheim, 210(FrF):Sep89−372
  W.B. Worthen, 615(TJ):Dec89−561
Macmillan, H. & S. Marks, eds. Africa and Empire.
  W.R. Louis, 617(TLS):16−22Feb90−174
McMillan, J. The Traverse Theatre Story.
  J. Farrell, 511:Jan89−42
McMillan, J.B. & M.B. Montgomery, eds. Annotated Bibliography of Southern American English.
  S.R. Hauer, 585(SoQ):Winter90−83
MacMillan, M. Women of the Raj.
  C. Hoyser, 637(VS):Summer90−655
McMillen, S. & G. Garrett, eds. Eric Clapton's Lover.
  G. Gilliland, 441:23Sep90−53
McMillin, S. The Elizabethan Theatre and "The Book of Sir Thomas More."*
  E.A.J. Honigmann, 677(YES):Vol20−242
McMullen, D. State and Scholars in T'ang China.
  P.K. Bol, 293(JASt):Feb89−142
Macmullen, R. Constantine.
  R. Braun, 555:Vol62Fasc1−175
MacMullen, R. Corruption and the Decline of Rome.*
  P. Culham, 124:Jul−Aug90−532
  W. McCuaig, 529(QQ):Autumn89−705
McMurray, G.R., ed. Critical Essays on Gabriel García Márquez.*
  R.L. Williams, 573(SSF):Fall88−485
McMurray, G.R. Spanish−American Writing since 1941.*
  C. Carrasquillo, 295(JML):Fall88/Winter89−202
McMurrin, S.M., ed. The Tanner Lectures on Human Values, VIII.
  A.P. Iannone, 242:Vol10No4−484
McMurtry, L. Anything for Billy.*
  C. Reynolds, 649(WAL):May89−65
McMurtry, L. Buffalo Girls.
  S.F. Schaeffer, 441:7Oct90−3
McMurtry, L. Texasville.
  R.C. Reynolds, 577(SHR):Winter89−92
McNab, N. & J.T. Novak. The Pig Farmer.
  G. Gessert, 448:Vol27No3−133
McNamara, R.S. Out of the Cold.*
  W.F. Kimball, 617(TLS):8−14Jun90−601
McNaughton, D. Moral Vision.
  M.V., 185:Jul90−906
McNaughton, P.R. The Mande Blacksmiths.
  K. Ezra, 2(AfrA):May89−12
McNaughton, T., ed. In Deadly Earnest.
  F. Adcock, 617(TLS):2−8Feb90−123
Macnaughton, W.R. Henry James: The Later Novels.*
  J.P. Dyson, 178:Mar89−95
McNeal, R.A. − see "Herodotus, Book I"

McNeal, R.H. Stalin.
D. Brower, 550(RusR):Apr89-208
639(VQR):Winter89-16
MacNeice, L. Selected Literary Criticism of
Louis MacNeice.* (A. Heuser, ed)
W. Blazek, 295(JML):Fall88/Winter89-377
K. Hoeppner, 178:Mar89-107
R. Marsack, 541(RES):May89-295
MacNeice, L. Selected Prose of Louis
MacNeice. (A. Heuser, ed)
G. Mangan, 617(TLS):31Aug-6Sep90-914
McNeil, B., ed. Biography and Geneology
Master Index 1988.
K.B. Harder, 424:Sep89-294
McNeil, I., ed. An Encyclopaedia of the His-
tory of Technology.
C. Freeman, 324:May90-440
MacNeil, J.N. Tales Until Dawn.*
M. Thorpe, 102(CanL):Spring89-212
McNeil, M., I. Varcoe & S. Yearley, eds. The
New Reproductive Technologies.
R. Cullen, 617(TLS):7-13Sep90-943
MacNeil, R. Wordstruck.*
M. Wormald, 617(TLS):6-12Apr90-366
McNeile, H.C. Bulldog Drummond. The Black
Gang. The Third Round. The Final Count.
The Female of the Species. The Return of
Bulldog Drummond.
A. Higgins, 364:Oct/Nov89-142
McNeill, D. Psycholinguistics.
S. Fillenbaum, 350:Jun90-388
T. Scovel, 399(MLJ):Spring90-70
McNeillie, A. - see Woolf, V.
McNerney, K., ed. On Our Own Behalf.*
C.G. Bellver, 238:May89-319
N.L. Molinaro, 573(SSF):Spring89-204
McNerney, K. Understanding Gabriel García
Márquez.
V. Smith, 402(MLR):Jul90-774
McNichol, S. Virginia Woolf and the Poetry of
Fiction.
A. Pratt, 268(IFR):Summer90-135
McNicklo, D. Wind from an Enemy Sky.
D.E. Hailey, Jr., 456(NDQ):Spring89-184
McNight, K. Moustapha's Eclipse.
E. Lesser, 434:Autumn89-98
MacNiven, D. Bradley's Moral Psychology.
J.W. Allard, 518:Apr89-90
S.G., 185:Apr90-701
D. Lamb, 521:Oct89-353
MacNiven, I. - see Durrell, L. & H. Miller
McNutt, R. We Wanna Boogie.
B.L. Cooper, 498:Summer89-107
Maconie, R. - see Stockhausen, K.
McPartland, M. All in Good Time.*
A. Shipton, 415:Aug89-479
McPhail, R. & D.E. Ward. Morality and
Agency.
W.N., 185:Jan90-441
McPhee, J. Looking for a Ship.
P. Theroux, 441:23Sep90-3
McPheron, W. Edward Dorn.
C. White, 649(WAL):Aug89-163
Macpherson, J. James Macpherson/Džejms
Makferson: The Poems of Ossian/Poèmy
Ossiana.
C. Heithus, 52:Band24Heft2-218
McPherson, J.M. Battle Cry of Freedom.
E.L. Ayers, 639(VQR):Autumn89-735
McPherson, S. Streamers.
M. Boruch, 29(APR):Mar/Apr89-41
J.D. McClatchy, 491:Apr89-29
639(VQR):Spring89-63

Macquarrie, J. Jesus Christ in Modern
Thought.
A. Race, 617(TLS):16-22Nov90-1241
MacQueen, J. The Rise of the Historical
Novel.
P. Drew, 617(TLS):20-26Apr90-422
MacQueen, J. & W. - see Bower, W.
McQueen, R. Blind Trust.
D. Swainson, 529(QQ):Summer89-542
McQuillan, K. Deadly Safari.
M. Stasio, 441:8Apr90-26
McQuiston, L. Women in Design.
J. Chiti, 662:Spring/Summer89-51
Macready, S. & F.H. Thompson, eds. Roman
Architecture in the Greek World.
G.B. Waywell, 123:Vol39No2-415
MacRéamoinn, S. Vatacáin II agus an Réabh-
lóid Chultúrtha.
R. Ó Glaisne, 174(Éire):Fall88-156
Macrorie, K. The I-Search Paper.
S.B. Smith, 126(CCC):Oct89-360
McSherry, F., Jr., C. Waugh & M. Greenberg,
eds. Civil War Women.
42(AR):Winter89-113
McSparran, F., ed. Octovian.*
O.D. Macrae-Gibson, 541(RES):May89-246
M. Mills, 382(MAE):1989/2-324
MacSween, A. & M. Sharp. Prehistoric Scot-
land.
R. Mercer, 617(TLS):10-16Aug90-852
McSweeney, K. Invisible Man.
T. Carmichael, 627(UTQ):Fall89-137
G. Clarke, 402(MLR):Oct90-938
McTaggart, J.M.E. The Nature of Existence.*
(Vols 1 & 2; Vol 2 ed by C.D. Broad)
H.W. Breunig, 393(Mind):Jul89-463
McTear, M. Children's Conversation.
H. Dahlbäck, 596(SL):Vol42No2-187
MacVean, J. - see Blackburn, T.
McVeigh, J. Kontinuität und Vergangenheits-
bewältigung in der österreichischen Litera-
tur nach 1945.
M-R. Kecht, 221(GQ):Fall89-555
W.G. Sebald, 402(MLR):Apr90-531
J. Strelka, 680(ZDP):Band108Heft4-634
Macvey, J.W. Time Travel.
C. Bailyn, 441:26Aug90-15
McWatters, K-G. & C.W. Thompson, eds. Sten-
dhal et l'Angleterre.*
G. Strickland, 208(FS):Apr89-218
C. Weiand, 535(RHL):Mar-Apr89-304
McWhiney, G. Cracker Culture.
A.V. Huff, Jr., 392:Spring89-205
McWhirter, D. Desire and Love in Henry
James.
D.M. Fogel, 598(SoR):Summer90-697
H. Lee, 617(TLS):25-31May90-547
McWilliam, G.H. - see Boccaccio, G.
McWilliams, T.S. The New South Faces the
World.
D.W. Grantham, 585(SoQ):Winter90-77
639(VQR):Summer89-79
Madden, B. & M. Klein. Damned Yankees.
M. Whitton, 441:1Apr90-11
Madden, D. & P. Bach, eds. Rediscoveries II.
42(AR):Winter89-112
Maddox, B. Nora.*
R.A. Battaglia, 31(ASch):Autumn89-615
M.R. Callaghan, 305(JIL):Jan89-59
N. Miller, 42(AR):Winter89-105
B.K. Scott, 305(JIL):Jan89-57
Madell, G. Mind and Materialism.
D. Taylor, 518:Jul89-172

Madge, T. Beyond the BBC.
S. French, 617(TLS):9–15Feb90–142
Madigan, P. Christian Revelation and the Completion of the Aristotelian Revolution.
D.B. Burrell, 543:Sep89–172
Madison, G.B. The Hermeneutics of Postmodernity.
T.R., 185:Jul90–915
J. Wallulis, 103:Sep90–375
Madre, A. – see Llull, R.
Madrid, J.F. – see under Fernández Madrid, J.
Madrid, L. Cervantes y Borges.
J.S. Chittenden, 238:May89–309
D.L. Shaw, 86(BHS):Jan89–105
Madsen, A. Chanel.
V. Glendinning, 617(TLS):16–22Nov90–1229
W. Hochswender, 441:3Jun90–22
Madsen, A. Silk Roads.
D. Pryce-Jones, 617(TLS):1–7Jun90–577
Maehlum, B. Språklige variasjonsmønstre hos innflyttere i Oslo.
E. Haugen, 355(LSoc):Sep89–433
K. Haugseth, 563(SS):Spring/Summer89–294
Maffei, S. De' teatri antichi e moderni e altri scritti teatrali. (L. Sannia Nowé, ed)
M. Mari, 228(GSLI):Vol166fasc535–456
von Magdeburg, M. – see under Mechthild von Magdeburg
Magee, B. Aspects of Wagner. (rev)
G. Seaman, 242:Vol10No4–494
A. Whittall, 410(M&L):Aug89–419
Mager, N.H. & S.K. The Morrow Book of New Words.
J. Algeo, 35(AS):Fall89–256
"Magie et littérature."
R.L. Blair, 111:Spring90–13
Magini, R. Saint Copperblack.
A.L. Amprimoz, 102(CanL):Autumn-Winter89–276
de Maglahães, T.C. – see under Calvet de Maglahães, T.
Magliola, R. Derrida on the Mend.*
S. Sim, 148:Winter86–114
Magnarelli, S. Reflections/Refractions.
P. Hart, 395(MFS):Winter89–778
Magnien-Simonin, C. – see Rougeart, J.
Magnino, D. Appiani Bellorum Civilium Liber Tertius.
P.W. de Neeve, 394:Vol42fasc1/2–204
Magno, C.T. & D.V. Erdman – see Blake, W.
Magnus, A. – see under Albertus Magnus
Magnuson, P. Coleridge and Wordsworth.*
K.R. Johnston, 445(NCF):Jun89–93
M. Jones, 529(QQ):Winter89–975
Magny, J. Eric Rohmer.
C.P. James, 207(FR):Oct89–195
Magris, C. Danube.*
M. Ignatieff, 453(NYRB):15Feb90–3
Magris, C. Inferences from a Sabre.
J. O'Faolain, 617(TLS):9–15Nov90–1215
Maguire, H. Earth and Ocean.
L. Brubaker, 589:Jul89–737
J. Lowden, 90:Mar89–225
L. Rodley, 303(JoHS):Vol109–274
Maguire, N.K., ed. Renaissance Tragicomedy.
J.D. Cox, 130:Winter89/90–379
E.M. Waith, 551(RenQ):Autumn89–576
Maguire, R. The Journals of Rochfort Maguire 1852–1854. (J. Bockstoce, ed)
P.N. Limerick, 617(TLS):12–18Jan90–27

Mah, H. The End of Philosophy, the Origin of "Ideology."
L.S. Stepelevich, 319:Apr90–305
Mahaffey, V. Reauthorizing Joyce.
Z. Bowen, 177(ELT):Vol32No2–262
B. Cheyette, 617(TLS):5–11Jan90–17
P. McGee, 223:Fall89–315
C. Rossman, 329(JJQ):Spring90–662
C. Shloss, 395(MFS):Autumn89–617
Mahdi, M., ed. The Thousand and One Nights (Alf layla wa layla), from the Earliest Known Sources.*
H.H. Biesterfeld, 196:Band30Heft3/4–335
Maheux-Forcier, L. Isle of Joy.*
M.J. Green, 102(CanL):Autumn-Winter89–193
Mahfouz, N. Palace Walk.
E. Hower, 441:4Feb90–11
G. Strawson, 617(TLS):27Apr–3May90–435
Mahfouz, N. Qushtumur.
S. El-Gabalawy, 268(IFR):Winter90–57
Mahjoub, J. Navigation of a Rainmaker.
S. French, 617(TLS):14–20Sep90–980
Mahler, G. Gustave Mahler Briefe. (M. Hansen, ed)
E.F.K., 412:Nov88–312
Mahmud, 'U.A. Arabic in the Southern Sudan.
A.S. Kaye, 318(JAOS):Jan–Mar88–175
Mahon, D. & N. Turner. The Drawings of Guercino in the Collection of Her Majesty the Queen at Windsor Castle.
D. Ekserdjian, 617(TLS):5–11Jan90–15
Mahon, J.W. & T.A. Pendleton, eds. "Fanned and Winnowed Opinions."
T.H. Howard-Hill, 541(RES):Nov89–557
J. McLauchlan, 447(N&Q):Sep89–385
Mahoney, D.F. Der Roman der Goethezeit (1774–1829).
J.K. Fugate, 406:Winter89–511
G. Hoffmeister, 221(GQ):Spring89–267
G. Marahrens, 166:Jan90–169
Mahoney, R. The Early Arrival of Dreams.
O. Schell, 441:28Oct90–15
Mahood, M.M. – see Shakespeare, W.
Maia, C.D. História do galego-português.*
A. Veiga Arias, 548:Jul–Dec89–459
Maiden, J. The Trust.
S. Lee, 581:Jun89–249
Maier, C.S., ed. Changing Boundaries of the Political.
H–G. Betz, 242:Vol10No3–379
Maier, C.S. In Search of Stability.
D.C. Coleman, 242:Vol10No4–490
Maier, C.S. The Unmasterable Past.*
C. Landauer, 390:Dec89–53
A.J. Nicholls, 617(TLS):2–8Feb90–110
639(VQR):Spring89–43
Maillet, A. Garrochés en paradis. Le Huitième Jour.
H.R. Runte, 102(CanL):Winter88–147
Maillet, A. Mariaagelas/Maria, daughter of Gélas.
J. Harrison, 102(CanL):Spring89–193
H. Murray, 102(CanL):Winter88–143
Maillet, A. Les Montréalais.
A.L. Amprimoz, 102(CanL):Autumn-Winter89–276
Mailloux, P. A Hesitation before Birth.*
J. Pilling, 402(MLR):Apr90–523
Maine, B., ed. Dos Passos: The Critical Heritage.
S. Stevens, 97(CQ):Vol18No2–223

240

Maini, D.S. Henry James. (2nd ed)
  G. Caramello, 395(MFS):Summer89-267
  P. Sicker, 177(ELT):Vol32No4-520
Mainstone, R.J. Hagia Sophia.*
  T.F. Mathews, 576:Jun89-181
  L. Rodley, 303(JoHS):Vol109-273
Mair, C. David Angus.
  P.S. Bagwell, 324:Apr90-373
Mair, G. To Kill a King.
  N. Lemann, 453(NYRB):17May90-18
Mair, V. Painting and Performance.
  K.J. De Woskin, 293(JASt):Nov89-806
Mair, V.H. Four Introspective Poets.
  D. Holzman, 116:Jul88-182
Mairs, N. Carnal Acts.
  L. Graham, 441:2Sep90-7
Maitland, F.W. Domesday Book and Beyond.
  (2nd ed)
  W.E. Kapelle, 589:Jul89-620
Maitland, S. Three Times Table.
  A-M. Conway, 617(TLS):8-14Jun90-616
Maja-Pearce, A. How Many Miles to Babylon?
  A. Bery, 617(TLS):3-9Aug90-830
Majewski, H.F. Paradigm and Parody.
  R. Chadbourne, 446(NCFS):Spring-
    Summer90-524
Major, C. Fun & Games.
  K. Brailsford, 441:20May90-30
Major, N. Joan Sutherland. (2nd ed)
  E. Forbes, 415:Mar89-161
Makashin, S.A. & L.R. Lanskii. Gertsen i
  zapad.
  J. Beecher, 550(RusR):Jan89-87
Makdisi, J.S. Beirut Fragments.
  A. Edgar, 441:16Sep90-41
  442(NY):12Nov90-134
Makec, J.W. The Customary Law of the Dinka
  People of Sudan.
  P.N. Kok, 617(TLS):21-27Sep90-1008
Makkreel, R.A. & F. Rodi - see Dilthey, W.
Makogonenko, G.P. Gogol' i Puškin.
  R D. Keil, 688(ZSP):Band49Heft1-173
Makogonenko, G.P. Lermontov i Puškin.
  S. Driver, 674(SEEJ):Fall89-450
Makowsky, V.A. Caroline Gordon.*
  J.E. Brown, 580(SCR):Fall90-158
  D.E. Stanford, 569(SR):Fall89-572
Maksudov, S., ed. Neuslyshannye golosa.
  J. Bushnell, 550(RusR):Apr89-210
Malachy, T. Molière: Les Métamorphoses du
  carnaval.*
  C. Abraham, 475:Vol16No31-598
  I. Landy-Houillon, 535(RHL):Mar-Apr89-
    279
  R W. Tobin, 207(FR):Oct89-160
Malamud, B. The People and Uncollected
  Stories.* (R. Giroux, ed)
  B. Cheyette, 617(TLS):9-15Feb90-148
Malan, R. My Traitor's Heart.
  V. Crapanzano, 441:21Jan90-3
  D. Papineau, 617(TLS):4-10May90-482
  442(NY):7May90-110
Malaxecheverria, I. El bestiario esculpido en
  Navarra.
  R. Burkard, 552(REH):Jan89-130
Malaxecheverria, I., ed. Bestiario Medieval.
  A.I. Robledo, 552(REH):Jan89-129
Malcolm, J. The Journalist and the Murderer.
  F.W. Friendly, 441:25Feb90-1
Malcolm, N. Nothing is Hidden.*
  D. Pears, 482(PhR):Jul89-379

Maleczek, W. Petrus Capuanus, Kardinal,
  Legat am vierten Kreuzzug, Theologe
  (1214†).
  R.C. Figueira, 589:Oct89-1003
"Maledicta." (Vol 9)
  U. Kutter, 196:Band30Heft1/2-146
Maletic, V. Body - Space - Expression.*
  E.D. Chapple, 567:Vol75No3/4-365
"Kazimir Malevich 1878-1935."
  C. Lodder, 90:Sep89-646
Malherbe, M. Thomas Hobbes, ou l'oeuvre de
  la raison.*
  K. Schuhmann, 242:Vol10No5-595
Malherbe, M. & J-M. Pousseur - see Bacon, F.
Malicet, M., ed. Cahiers de textologie 1.
  A. Séailles, 535(RHL):Mar-Apr89-341
Malingrey, A-M. - see Palladius
Malkiel, Y. A Tentative Autobibliography.
  E.A. Ebbinghaus, 215(GL):Vol29No3-222
Malkin, I. Religion and Colonization in
  Ancient Greece.
  R. Parker, 123:Vol39No2-271
Mallarmé, S. Poésies. (P. Citron, ed)
  L.J. Austin, 208(FS):Jul89-346
Mallarmé, S. Selected Letters of Stéphane
  Mallarmé.* (R. Lloyd, ed & trans)
  E.A. Howe, 446(NCFS):Spring-Summer90-
    558
  S. Tokatlian, 207(FR):May90-1067
Mallet, J. L'art roman de l'ancien Anjou.
  B.S. Bachrach, 589:Jul89-740
Mallinckrodt, A M The Environmental Dia-
  logue in the GDR.
  T. Fiedler, 099(MLJ).Winter89-515
Mallinson, G.J. Molière: "L'Avare."
  C.J. Gossip, 402(MLR):Oct90-956
Mallinson, J. I Will Bring You Berries.*
  H. Thompson, 102(CanL):Autumn-
    Winter89-250
Mallon, B. Children Dreaming.
  C. Moorehead, 617(TLS):16-22Mar90-297
Mallory, W.E. & P. Simpson-Housley, eds.
  Geography and Literature.
  J. Stevens, 295(JML):Fall88/Winter89-
    231
Malmstad, J.E., ed. Andrew Bely.*
  G. Donchin, 575(SEER):Apr90-291
  O. Hayward, 126:Winter89-217
  P.M. Mitchell, 295(JML):Fall88/Winter89-
    288
Malone, J.L. The Science of Linguistics in the
  Art of Translation.*
  M. Doherty, 353:Vol27No6-1156
Malone, M.P. & R.W. Etulain. The American
  West.
  P.N. Limerick, 617(TLS):27Jul-2Aug90-
    794
Maloney, J.C. The Mundane Matter of the
  Mental Language.
  P. Engel, 617(TLS):17-23Aug90-880
Malouf, D. The Great World.
  R. Brain, 617(TLS):6-12Apr90-375
  I. Buruma, 453(NYRB):19Jul90-43
Malti-Douglas, F. Structures of Avarice.
  K. Lacey, 318(JAOS):Jul-Sep88-493
  J. Sadan, 196:Band30Heft3/4-338
Mälzer, G. Die Inkunabeln der Universitäts-
  bibliothek Würzburg.
  L.V. Gerulaitis, 589:Apr89-466
Mamczarz, I., ed. Problèmes, interférences
  des genres au théâtre et les fêtes en
  Europe.
  L. Picciola, 549(RLC):Jan-Mar89-111

Mamone, S. Firenze e Parigi due capitali dello spettacolo per una regina.
S. Mazzoni, 228(GSLI):Vol166fasc534-290
de Man, P. Critical Writings, 1953-1978.* (L. Waters, ed)
R.M. Adams, 453(NYRB):1Mar90-38
de Man, P. The Resistance to Theory.*
F. McCombie, 447(N&Q):Jun89-280
Manca, G. - see Alain-Fournier
Manchester, M.L. The Philosophical Foundations of Humboldt's Linguistic Doctrines.
L. Zgusta, 361:Aug89-363
Mancini, H., with G. Lees. Did They Mention the Music?
G. Dyer, 441:11Feb90-25
Mancini, I. Guida alla Critica della ragion pura. (Vol 1)
C. Esposito, 342:Band80Heft1-98
de Mandach, A. Naissance et développement de la chanson de geste en Europe. (Vol 5)
M.J. Ailes, 382(MAE):1989/1-163
W.G. van Emden, 208(FS):Oct89-453
J-L.G. Picherit, 589:Oct89-1007
Mandel, E. The Family Romance.*
L. Mathews, 168(ECW):Spring89-155
Mandel, E. & D. Taras, eds. A Passion for Identity.
G. Laforest, 298:Winter89/90-172
Mandel, U. Kleinasiatische Reliefkeramik der mittleren Kaiserzeit.
M.A.R. Colledge, 123:Vol39No2-420
Mandelbaum, D.G. Women's Seclusion and Men's Honor.
P. Jeffery, 293(JASt):Aug89-657
Mandelbaum, K. "A Chorus Line" and the Musicals of Michael Bennett.*
M.B. Siegel, 34:Mar90-34
Mandelbaum, M. Purpose and Necessity in Social Theory.
J.A.W. Gunn, 529(QQ):Spring89-207
S. James, 482(PhR):Apr89-252
M. Martin, 518:Apr89-118
Mandell, N. & A. Duffy, eds. Reconstructing the Canadian Family.
S. Boyd, 529(QQ):Winter89-999
Mandel'shtam, N. Kniga tret'ia.
D. Fanger, 550(RusR):Apr89-219
Mander, C. Emily Murphy.
G. Whitlock, 102(CanL):Summer89-168
Mandracci, V.C. - see under Comoli Mandracci, V.
Mandrell, B., with G. Vecsey. Get to the Heart.
S. Liveten, 441:21Oct90-25
Manén, L. Bel Canto.
D. Galliver, 410(M&L):Feb89-119
Maner, M. The Philosophical Biographer.
C.N. Parke, 481(PQ):Fall89-527
Manero Sorolla, M.P. Introducción al estudio del petrarquismo en España.
J. Cammarata, 240(HR):Winter89-87
A.J. Cruz, 547(RF):Band101Heft2/3-365
R.M. Price, 86(BHS):Jul89-277
Manes, C. Green Rage.
J. Gorman, 441:29Jul90-22
Manetti, G. Le teorie del segno nell' antichità classica.
T.A. Sebeok, 567:Vol73No1/2-133
Mangan, K.N., ed. Lenore Tawney.
A. Barnet, 441:22Jul90-21
Manhire, B., ed. Six by Six.
F. Baveystock, 617(TLS):2-8Feb90-122

Manicas, P.T. A History and Philosophy of the Social Sciences.
D.A. Hollinger, 385(MQR):Winter90-123
Manion, M.M., V.F. Vines & C. de Hamel. Medieval and Renaissance Manuscripts in New Zealand Collections.
J. Griffiths, 617(TLS):15-21Jun90-650
Mañjuśrimitra. Primordial Experience.
L. Nordstrom, 485(PE&W):Jul89-355
Mankowitz, W. Exquisite Cadaver.
J. Clute, 617(TLS):17-23Aug90-868
Manley, F. Within the Ribbons.*
D. Durrant, 364:Feb/Mar90-133
Manley, J. Atlas of Prehistoric Britain.
P.J. Fowler, 617(TLS):19-25Jan90-72
Mann, A. Theory and Practice.
A. Maisel, 415:Nov89-685
Mann, G. Erinnerungen und Gedanken.
F.A. Lubich, 222(GR):Spring89-94
Mann, G. Reminiscences and Reflections.
G.A. Craig, 441:16Sep90-15
442(NY):8Oct90-117
Mann, I. Dialektika khudozhestvennogo obraza.
R. Sobel, 575(SEER):Jan89-121
Mann, M. & D. Dalby, eds. A Thesaurus of African Languages.
P.R. Bennett, 538(RAL):Summer89-318
Mann, P. Hugo Ball.*
D.L. Hoffmeister, 406:Summer89-274
Mann, S. At Twelve.
639(VQR):Spring89-68
Mann, S. Holding On.
R. Owen, 617(TLS):29Jun-5Jul90-687
Mann, T. Briefwechsel mit Autoren. (H. Wysling, ed)
H. Lehnert, 462(OL):Vol44No3-267
H. Siefken, 402(MLR):Jul90-810
Mann, T. Pro and Contra Wagner.
G. Bridges, 222(GR):Winter89-42
Mann, T. Tagebücher 1944-1946. (I. Jens, ed) Aufsatze, Reden, Essays. (Vol 3) (H. Matter, ed)
H. Lehnert, 462(OL):Vol44No3-267
Mann, T. Tagebücher 1946-1948. (I. Jens, ed)
F. Schirrmacher, 358:Feb90-7
Mann, T. & J. Ponten. Dichter oder Schriftsteller? (H. Wysling, with W. Pfister, eds)
H. Lehnert, 462(OL):Vol44No3-267
"Thomas Mann Jahrbuch." (Vol 1) (E. Heftrich & H. Wysling, eds)
H. Siefken, 402(MLR):Oct90-1028
Manning, H. Walking the Beach to Bellingham.
S. Pickering, 569(SR):Spring89-297
Manning, J. - see Palmer, T.
Mannocci, L. The Etchings of Claude Lorrain.
P.D. Massar, 90:Oct89-717
Mannoni, M. Ce qui manque à la vérité pour être dire.
A. Reix, 542:Oct-Dec89-631
Manolescu, N. Despre poezie.
V. Nemoianu, 617(TLS):19-25Jan90-59
Mansar, A. Nicolas de Staël.
R. Cardinal, 617(TLS):13-19Jul90-749
Manser, A. & G. Stock, eds. The Philosophy of F.H. Bradley.
F. Schoeman, 637(VS):Spring90-523
Mansfeld, J., ed & trans. Die Vorsokratiker.*
D. Arnould, 555:Vol62Fasc2-335

Mansfield, K. The Collected Letters of Kath-
erine Mansfield. (Vol 1) (V. O'Sullivan & M.
Scott, eds)
K. Williamson, 447(N&Q):Mar89-121
Mansfield, K. The Collected Letters of Kath-
erine Mansfield.* (Vol 2) (V. O'Sullivan &
M. Scott, eds)
M.J.F., 295(JML):Fall88/Winter89-379
K. Williamson, 447(N&Q):Mar89-121
Mansfield, K. The Critical Writings of Kath-
erine Mansfield.* (C. Hanson, ed)
M.P.L., 295(JML):Fall88/Winter89-380
Mansfield, K. The Poems of Katherine Mans-
field. (V. O'Sullivan, ed)
C.K. Stead, 617(TLS):2-8Feb90-123
Manteiga, R.C., C. Galerstein & K. McNerney,
eds. Feminine Concerns in Contemporary
Spanish Fiction by Women.*
M.E.W. Jones, 238:Sep89-549
Mantel, H. Fludd.*
J. Mellors, 364:Oct/Nov89-133
Manuel, J. Cinco tratados. (R. Ayerbe-
Chaux, ed)
H.O. Bizzarri, 304(JHP):Winter90-175
Manuel, J. Libro del Conde Lucanor. (F.
Gómez Redondo, ed)
J. England, 402(MLR):Jan90-223
Manuel, P. Popular Musics of the Non-West-
ern World.
G.D. Booth, 414(MusQ):Vol74No3-439
Manuel II Palaeologus. Manuelis Palaelologi,
Dialogum de matrimonio "Peri gamoy." (C.
Bevegni, ed)
E. des Places, 555:Vol63Fasc3-066
Manvell, R. Elizabeth Inchbald.
E. Donkin, 615(TJ):Oct89-423
Manvell, R. - see Inchbald, E.
Manz, B.F. The Rise and Rule of Tamerlane.
R. Irwin, 617(TLS):12-18Jan90-28
Manzini, E. The Material of Invention.
139:Dec89/Jan90-69
Manzoni, A. Scritti sulla lingua. (T. Matar-
rese, ed)
D. Zancani, 402(MLR):Oct90-994
Mappin, S. Heart Murmurs.
D. Ellison, 581:Dec89-672
Maracle, L. I Am Woman.
A. Grant, 137:Winter90-64
Maraini, D. La lunga vita di Marianna Ucrìa.
M. D'Amico, 617(TLS):28Sep-4Oct90-1039
Maranhão, T. Therapeutic Discourse and So-
cratic Dialogue.
B.E. Goldfarb, 24:Spring89-161
Marani, P.C. Leonardo e i Leonardeschi a
Brera.
D.A. Brown, 90:Jul89-491
Maravall, J.A. La literatura picaresca desde
la historia social (siglos XVI y XVII).*
F. Baasner, 72:Band226Heft1-213
M. Horányi, 547(RF):Band101Heft1-151
Marcaduri, M. & T. Nikol'skaja - see Teren-
t'ev, I.
Marceau, W. Henri Bergson et Joseph Malè-
gue.
S. Fraisse, 535(RHL):Nov-Dec89-1078
M.M. Jones, 402(MLR):Apr90-453
R.J. Sealy, 446(NCFS):Fall-Winter89/90-
304
March, A. Selecció de poemes/Selected Poems.
A. Terry, 86(BHS):Jul89-303
March, J., comp. Willa Cather Handbook. (M.
Arnold, ed)
D. Brunvand, 649(WAL):Aug89-193

March, J.R. The Creative Poet.
J.H. Molyneux, 123:Vol39No2-180
S.D. Olson, 124:Jan-Feb90-247
March, M., ed. Child of Europe.
M. Hofmann, 617(TLS):9-15Nov90-1197
Marchal, B. La Religion de Mallarmé.
U. Franklin, 446(NCFS):Fall-
Winter89/90-302
Marchalonis, S. The Worlds of Lucy Larcom,
1824-1893.
J.A. Berkman, 357:Fall90-61
Marchand, J. Le Premier Mouvement.
T.R. Kuhnle, 102(CanL):Autumn-
Winter89-270
Marchand, P. Marshall McLuhan.
L. Dubinsky, 150(DR):Spring89-127
G.W., 102(CanL):Autumn-Winter89-301
Marchello-Nizia, C. - see Tibaut
Marchenko, A. To Live Like Everyone Else.*
O. Figes, 617(TLS):6-12Apr90-368
Marchessault, J. Des Cailloux blancs pour les
forêts obscures.
K.L. Kellett, 102(CanL):Winter88-138
Marchessault, J. Demande de travail sur les
nébuleuses.
A-M. Picard, 108:Summer89-86
Marchetta, A. Orosio e Ataulfo nell'ideologia
dei rapporti romano-barbarici.
J.F. Drinkwater, 123:Vol39No1-92
Marciales, M. - see de Rojas, F.
Marcil-Lacoste, L. & others. Egalité et dif-
férence des sexes.
L. Poissant, 154:Vol28No2-338
Marco, M.A.L. - see under Lozano Marco, M.A.
Marconi, D. L'eredità di Wittgenstein.
T. Williamson, 518:Jan89-30
Marcos, J.M. De García Márquez al postboom.
L. King, 86(BHS):Jan89-118
Marcovich, M. Alcestis Barcinonensis.
N. Horsfall, 123:Vol39No2-220
Marcus, D. Jephthah and His Vow.
S.B. Parker, 318(JAOS):Apr-Jun88-312
Marcus, G. Lipstick Traces.*
D. Diederichsen, 62:Nov89-25
Marcus, G.E. & M.M.J. Fischer. Anthropology
as Cultural Critique.
F.A. Hanson, 488:Jun89-237
Marcus, J. Georg Lukács and Thomas Mann.*
H.F. Pfanner, 406:Fall89-400
Marcus, J., ed. Virginia Woolf and Blooms-
bury.*
P.L. Caughie, 454:Fall89-106
E.C.R., 295(JML):Fall88/Winter89-423
Marcus, J. Virginia Woolf and the Languages
of Patriarchy.*
P.L. Caughie, 454:Fall89-106
D. McManus, 295(JML):Fall88/Winter89-
423
Marcus, L.S. The Politics of Mirth.*
N.W. Bawcutt, 541(RES):May89-262
C.C. Brown, 677(YES):Vol20-263
S.N. Zwicker, 401(MLQ):Dec87-388
Marcus, L.S. Puzzling Shakespeare.*
J.R. Siemon, 141:Fall89-475
Marcus, M. Italian Film in the Light of Neo-
realism.
Z.G. Barański, 278(IS):Vol44-189
Marcus Aurelius. The "Meditations" of Mar-
cus Aurelius Antoninus; and A Selection
from the Letters of Marcus and Fronto.
(A.S.L. Farquharson & R.B. Rutherford,
trans)
M. Atkins, 617(TLS):6-12Apr90-380

Marcuse, H. Hegel's Ontology and the Theory of Historicity.
  K.R. Dove, 482(PhR):Jul89–419
Marek, M. Two-Fisted Management.
  J. Shulevitz, 441:28Oct90–23
Marenbon, J. Later Medieval Philosophy (1150–1350).*
  S. MacDonald, 53(AGP):Band71Heft1–84
  A.A. Maurer, 319:Apr90–288
Marer, P. & W. Siwiński, eds. Creditworthiness and Reform in Poland.
  A. Åslund, 575(SEER):Apr89–318
Margarito, M.C. – see under Capel Margarito, M.
Margolin, J-C. – see Mathieu-Castellani, G.
Margolis, H. Patterns, Thinking, and Cognition.
  G. Harman, 185:Oct89–200
Margolis, J. Science without Unity.*
  P. Milne, 518:Jan89–62
  J. Van Evra, 103:Oct90–418
Margolis, J., M. Krausz & R.M. Burian, eds. Rationality, Relativism and the Human Sciences.
  J. Dunphy, 63:Mar89–117
Margolis, J. & T. Rockmore – see Farías, V.
Margolis, R.J. Risking Old Age in America.
  H.L. Sheppard, 441:21Jan90–36
Mariani, P. Dream Song.
  C. Kizer, 441:25Feb90–14
  B. Leithauser, 442(NY):30Apr90–109
Marías, J. La felicidad humana.
  A. Donoso, 240(HR):Winter89–115
"Marie de France: Fables."* (H. Spiegel, ed & trans)
  P. Carnes, 292(JAF):Apr–Jun89–223
de Marigny, A., with M. Herskowitz. A Conspiracy of Crowns.
  E.S. Turner, 617(TLS):13–19Jul90–750
Marin, L. Food for Thought.
  T. Cave, 617(TLS):5–11Jan90–21
Marin, L. Portrait of the King.
  F. Lagarde, 475:Vol16No30–296
Marinelli, P.V. Ariosto and Boiardo.*
  C. Jordan, 551(RenQ):Summer89–334
  M.J. Murrin, 276:Winter89–466
Marinetti, F.T. The Futurist Cookbook. (L. Chamberlain, ed)
  M.J. Rosen, 441:21Jan90–24
Marinetti, F.T. Taccuini 1915–1921. (A. Bertoni, ed)
  S.W. Vinall, 402(MLR):Jan90–217
Marinetti, F.T. – see Andreoli-de-Villers, J-P.
Marino, A. Comparatisme et théorie de la littérature.
  J-P. Cometti, 98:Mar89–199
Marinoni, M.C. La versione valdese del libro di Tobia.
  L. Borghi Cedrini, 379(MedR):Apr89–129
Mariotti, S., ed. Livio Andronico e la traduzione artistica.
  D. Briquel, 555:Vol62Fasc1–162
  N. Horsfall, 313:Vol79–184
Mariscal de Rhett, B., ed. La muerte ocultada.
  M. da Costa Fontes, 545(RPh):Feb90–497
Markert, L.W. Arthur Symons.
  A. Brown, 637(VS):Autumn89–202
  B. Morris, 177(ELT):Vol32No3–344
Markham, E.A., ed. Hinterland.
  G. Foden, 617(TLS):2–8Mar90–236
Markham, E.A. Towards the End of a Century.
  G. Foden, 617(TLS):2–8Mar90–236

Markhof, W. Renaissance oder Substitition?
  F. Abel, 72:Band226Heft1–189
Markie, P.J. Descartes's Gambit.*
  P. Hoffman, 484(PPR):Sep89–199
Markkanen, R. Cross-Language Studies in Pragmatics.
  T.W. Du Bois, 355(LSoc):Dec89–618
Markley, R. Two-Edg'd Weapons.
  H. Love, 402(MLR):Oct90–920
  E. Pollack, 223:Fall89–323
Markoe, G. Phoenician Bronze and Silver Bowls from Cyprus and the Mediterranean.
  J.V. Canby, 318(JAOS):Oct–Dec88–657
Markolin, C. Die Grossväter sind die Lehrer.
  K.Q. Johnson, 221(GQ):Fall89–560
Markovits, A.S. & M. Silverstein, eds. The Politics of Scandal.
  K.G., 185:Jan90–466
Markovna, N. Nina's Journey.
  B. Finkelstein, 441:11Feb90–19
Marks, E., ed. Critical Essays on Simone de Beauvoir.*
  D.A. MacLeay, 207(FR):Feb90–555
  A. Whitmarsh, 208(FS):Oct89–493
Marks, F.W. 3d. Wind Over Sand.
  G. Adams, Jr., 106:Fall89–245
Marks, P.M. And Die in the West.
  P.N. Limerick, 441:23Sep90–14
Marks, S.K. "Sir Charles Grandison."*
  L.A. Chaber, 166:Oct89–77
Markus, M., ed. Historical English.
  W.N. Francis, 350:Mar90–197
Marland, H. Medicine and Society in Wakefield and Huddersfield 1780–1870.
  F.B. Smith, 637(VS):Winter90–345
Marlatt, D. A.N.A. Historic.
  P. Imbert, 102(CanL):Autumn–Winter89–199
  J. Ruzesky, 376:Sep89–116
Marling, K.A. George Washington Slept Here.
  T. Martin, 42(AR):Spring89–243
  W.B. Rhoads, 658:Summer/Autumn89–202
  T. Wortham, 445(NCF):Dec89–422
Marlowe, C. The Complete Works of Christopher Marlowe. (Vol 2) (R. Gill, ed)
  J.H. Jones, 617(TLS):26Oct–1Nov90–1161
Marmor, T.R., J.L. Mashaw & P.L. Harvey. America's Misunderstood Welfare State.
  G. Sanger, 441:11Nov90–61
Marot, C. L'Adolescence clémentine;* L'Enfer; Déploration de Florimond Robertet; Quatorze Psaumes. (F. Lestringant, ed)
  G. Schrenck, 535(RHL):Nov–Dec89–1049
Marotta, G. Modelli e misure ritmiche.
  I. Vogel, 350:Mar90–198
Marotti, G. Black Characters in the Brazilian Novel.
  M.S. Arrington, Jr., 238:Sep89–561
Marples, D.R. The Social Impact of the Chernobyl Disaster.*
  M. McCauley, 575(SEER):Oct89–658
Marquand, D. The Unprincipled Society.
  R. Bellamy, 242:Vol10No2–227
Marqués, S. La lengua que heredamos.
  G.D. Bills, 238:Mar89–160
Márquez, G.G. – see under García Márquez, G.
Marquis, A.G. Alfred H. Barr, Jr.*
  B.B. Stretch, 55:Oct89–131
Marr, D. American Worlds Since Emerson.*
  R.B. Goodman, 27(AL):Mar89–111
  D. Van Leer, 125:Spring89–307
  R.F. Sayre, 481(PQ):Fall89–530

Marres, R. In Defense of Mentalism.
S.G. Smith, 543:Sep89-173
Marrey, B. Louis Bonnier 1856-1946.
A. Saint, 46:Aug89-14
Marrinan, M. Painting Politics for Louis-Philippe.*
N. McWilliam, 90:Apr89-302
Marrs, S. The Welty Collection.
W.U. McDonald, Jr., 585(SoQ):Winter90-81
S. Wright, 569(SR):Fall89-cvi
Mars-Jones, A. Venus Envy.
L. Sage, 617(TLS):13-19Jul90-747
Marschak, B. Silberschätze des Orients.
J.M. Rogers, 90:May89-359
Marschall, R. America's Great Comic-Strip Artists.
M. Cart, 441:18Feb90-21
Marsden, H. & R. Inglesfield - see Brontë, A.
Marsden-Smedley, P. A Far Country.
D. Murphy, 617(TLS):12-18Oct90-1108
Marsh, D. The Germans.
D. Binder, 441:11Nov90-18
G.A. Craig, 453(NYRB):18Jan90-28
Marsh, D. The New Germany.
M. Burleigh, 617(TLS):27Jul-2Aug90-796
Marsh, J. The Legend of Elizabeth Siddal.
K. Flint, 617(TLS):19-25Oct90-1134
Marsh, J. Jane and May Morris.*
R. Sheets, 637(VS):Spring90-525
Marsh, J.L. Post-Cartesian Meditations.
M.J. De Nys, 543:Sep89-174
Marsh, R. Images of Dictatorship.
D. Rayfield, 617(TLS):2-8Mar90-237
Marsh, R.J. Soviet Fiction since Stalin.*
D. Brown, 104(CASS):Spring-Winter88-524
Marshall, D. The Surprising Effects of Sympathy.*
P.J., 185:Apr90-704
R.C. Rosbottom, 166:Jan90-153
R. Runte, 478(P&L):Apr89-193
Marshall, M.F. - see Rowe, E.S.
Marshall, M.H.B. Verbs, Nouns, and Postpositives in Attic Prose.*
P. Monteil, 555:Vol62Fasc1-145
Marshall, O. The Divided World.
F. Baveystock, 617(TLS):2-8Feb90-122
Marshall, P. Soul Clap Hands and Sing.
J. Pettis, 459:Summer89-114
Marshall, P. - see Godwin, W.
Marshall, R.L. The Music of Johann Sebastian Bach.
D. Hush, 414(MusQ):Vol74No3-451
Marshall, S., ed. Women in Reformation and Counter-Reformation Europe.
B. Scribner, 617(TLS):9-15Feb90-151
Marshall-Andrews, B. The Palace of Wisdom.
C. Holland, 441:21Jan90-28
Marsland, S.E. The Birth of the Japanese Labor Movement.
S.J. Ericson, 293(JASt):Nov89-870
S.S. Large, 407(MN):Autumn89-358
Marston, J.G. King and Congress.*
D. Ammerman, 656(WMQ):Jan89-190
Martel, G. Imperial Diplomacy.
D.E. Torrance, 529(QQ):Summer89-545
Martelli, M. - see Adembri, B. & others
Marten, H. The Art of Knowing.
T.R. Spivey, 27(AL):May89-309

Martial. Epigrams of Martial Englished by Divers Hands.* (J.P. Sullivan & P. Whigham, eds)
P. Howell, 123:Vol39No1-30
S. Mandell, 121(CJ):Feb-Mar90-266
H.A. Mason, 97(CQ):Vol17No4-297
Martin, A., ed. Forgiveness.
S. Stark, 441:19Aug90-18
Martin, A. The Knowledge of Ignorance.*
C. Clark-Evans, 345(KRQ):May89-233
Martin, A. The Mask of the Prophet.
V. Brombert, 617(TLS):16-22Nov90-1231
Martin, A. La titulature épigraphique de Domitien.
R. Urban, 229:Band61Heft6-569
Martin, A. - see Yeats, W.B.
Martin, A.L. The Jesuit Mind.
T. McCoog, 551(RenQ):Autumn89-564
Martin, C., ed. André Gide 8.
D.H. Walker, 208(FS):Jul89-350
Martin, C. The Legacy.
H. Murray, 102(CanL):Winter88-143
Martin, C. Love Me, Love Me Not.
M.J. Green, 102(CanL):Autumn-Winter89-193
Martin, C. - see Gide, A.
Martin, C. - see de Maupassant, G.
Martin, C. & V. Martin-Schmets - see Gide, A. & A. Ruyters
Martin, C. & G. Parker. The Spanish Armada.*
639(VQR):Winter89-9
Martin, C.C. Godchildren.
M. Stasio, 441:8Apr90-26
Martin, D. The Telling Line.
B. Alderson, 617(TLS):30Mar-5Apr90-355
P. Campbell, 324:May90-442
Martin, D. Tongues of Fire.
H. O'Shaughnessy, 617(TLS):3-9Aug90-821
Martin, D.M. - see under Moyano Martin, D.
Martín, E. Federico García Lorca, heterodoxo y mártir.*
I-J. López, 345(KRQ):Feb89-120
E.A. Southworth, 86(BHS):Jul89-296
Martin, E. The Woman in the Body.
R. Behar, 385(MQR):Fall90-696
Martin, G. Arithmetic and Combinatorics (J. Wubnig, ed & trans)
A. Broadie, 342:Band80Heft1-122
Martin, G. The Companion to Twentieth-Century Opera.
W. Dean, 415:Dec89-750
A.F.L.T., 412:May89-146
Martin, G. Journeys Through the Labyrinth.
M. Deas, 617(TLS):30Mar-5Apr90-336
Martin, G. & W.R. Owens - see Kettle, A.
Martin, H. Le Métier de prédicateur à la fin du Moyen Age: 1350-1520.
N. Lemaître, 531:Jul-Dec89-515
Martin, H.C. W.B. Yeats.*
K. Worth, 541(RES):May89-289
Martin, J. To Rise Above Principle.
R.W. Lewis, 456(NDQ):Winter89-248
Martín, J.D-M. - see under Díaz-Modesto Martín, J.
Martin, J.W. Religious Radicals in Tudor England.
A. Hamilton, 617(TLS):27Apr-3May90-448
Martin, L. & K. Segrave. Anti-Rock.
B.L. Cooper, 498:Summer89-108
Martin, L.H. Hellenistic Religions.
P.N. Boulter, 124:Sep-Oct89-54

Martin, L.H., H. Gutman & P.H. Hutton, eds. Technologies of the Self.
D. Latané, 147:Vol6No1–39
Martín, L.V.D. – see under Díaz Martín, L.V.
Martin, M.W. Self-Deception and Morality.*
A.R. Miller, 449:Jun89–394
Martin, M.W., ed. Self-Deception and Self-Understanding.
F. Recanati, 192(EP):Jul–Dec89–549
Martin, P. New and Selected Poems.
W. Tonetto, 581:Jun89–263
Martin, P.W. Mad Women in Romantic Writing.*
R. Ivy, 402(MLR):Jan90–155
M.R. Wedd, 661(WC):Autumn89–213
Martin, R. Architecture et urbanisme.
V. Kockel, 229:Band61Heft2–179
Martin, R. Fashion and Surrealism.*
R.J. Belton, 662:Fall89/Winter90–34
Martin, R. The Past Within Us.
S. Fuller, 103:Aug90–326
Martin, R. Qu'en carapaces de mes propres ailes.
P. Coleman, 168(ECW):Fall89–109
Martin, R.H. – see Traversagni, L.G.
Martin, R.M. The Meaning of Language.*
D.E. Over, 518:Apr89–101
Martin, S.E. The Japanese Language Through Time.*
B. Saint-Jacques, 320(CJL):Jun89–233
Martin, V. Mary Reilly.
J. Crowley, 441:4Feb90–7
E. Showalter, 617(TLS):1–7Jun90–586
Martin, W. Recent Theories of Narrative.
T.B. Farrell, 480(P&R):Vol22No4–303
Martin, W.R. Alice Munro.*
E. Savoy, 49:Jan89–101
B. Trehearne, 529(QQ):Winter89–973
I.V., 295(JML):Fall88/Winter89–387
L.M. York, 168(ECW):Fall89–139
Martin du Gard, R. & G. Duhamel. Témoins d'un temps troublé. (A. Lafay, ed)
P. de Gaulmyn, 535(RHL):Sep–Oct89–940
Martín Gaite, C. Behind the Curtains.
I. Stavans, 441:22Jul90–20
Martin-Gistucci, M-G. Bourget et l'Italie.
J-P. de Nola, 549(RLC):Jul–Sep89–424
Martín González, J.J. Monumentos religiosos de la ciudad de Valladolid (Conventos y Seminarios).
M. Estella, 48:Oct–Dec89–479
Martín González, J.J. & J. Urrea Fernández. Monumentos religiosos de la ciudad de Valladolid (Catedral, Parroquias, Cofradías y Santuarios).
M. Estella, 48:Oct–Dec89–479
Martín Ibáñez, M.A. Antonio Carnicero Mancio, pintor.
I. Mateo Gómez, 48:Apr–Jun89–231
Martín Morán, J.M. Ginevra y Finea.*
E.M. Gerli, 240(HR):Winter89–86
Martín y Coll, A. Tonos de Palacio y canciones comunes. (J. Sagasta Galdos, ed)
A. Silbiger, 317:Spring89–172
Martindale, A. Simone Martini.*
F. Ames-Lewis, 557:Sep89–316
J. Gardner, 90:Jul89–487
D. Gordon, 59:Sep89–370
R. Simon, 39:Jun89–435
Martindale, C. John Milton and the Transformation of Ancient Epic.*
M. Mueller, 678(YCGL):No36–184

Martindale, C., ed. Ovid Renewed.
W.S. Anderson, 124:Sep–Oct89–56
F. Blessington, 566:Autumn89–76
W. von Koppenfels, 156(ShJW):Jahrbuch1989–382
Martindale, J., ed. English Humanism: Wyatt to Cowley.
C. Malcolmson, 677(YES):Vol20–260
Martinet, A. Fonction et dynamiques des langues.
B. Peeters, 350:Dec90–876
Martínez, C.F. – see under Fernández Martínez, C.
Martínez, H.S. – see under Salvador Martínez, H.
Martínez, J.M. – see under Montoya Martínez, J.
Martínez, T.E. – see under Eloy Martínez, T.
Martínez Colomer, V. El Valdemaro (1972). (G. Carnero, ed)
P. Deacon, 86(BHS):Jul89–286
Martínez de Aguirre, J. Arte y monarquía en Navarra 1328–1425.
R.S. Janke, 90:Oct89–710
Martínez Marzoa, F. Desconocida raíz común.
A. Savile, 89(BJA):Spring89–181
Marting, D.E., ed. Women Writers of Spanish America.
K.F. Nigro, 238:Mar89–148
"Simone Martini: Atti del Convegno." (1985)
R. Simon, 39:Jun89–435
Martino, P. Arbiter.
K-H. Ziegler, 229:Band61Heft2–169
Martinson, H. Wild Bouquet.
R-M.G. Oster, 563(SS):Winter89–113
Marton, K. The Polk Conspiracy.
M. Janeway, 441:28Oct90–3
442(NY):12Nov90–134
Martone, M. Safety Patrol.
A. Bukoski, 448:Vol27No1–136
W. Cummins, 573(SSF):Summer88–321
Martos, J-F. Histoire de l'Internationale Situationniste.
L. Jenny, 98:Oct89–765
Martz, J.D., ed. United States Policy in Latin America.
H. Brogan, 617(TLS):29Jun–5Jul90–708
G. Marcella, 263(RIB):Vol39No1–75
Martz, L.L. – see H.D.
Marubbi, M. Vincenzo Civerchio.*
J. Shell, 551(RenQ):Spring89–99
Maruya, S. Rain in the Wind.
J. Melville, 617(TLS):16–22Nov90–1233
M. Ury, 441:29Jul90–29
Marvan, J. České stupňováni.
C.E. Townsend, 279:Vol35/36–344
Marvell, A. Selected Poetry and Prose.* (R. Wilcher, ed)
M.L.K. Lally, 568(SCN):Spring–Summer89–13
Marvick, E.W. Louis XIII.*
J.M. Hayden, 77:Winter89–68
Marwil, J. Frederic Manning.*
D. Hewitt, 447(N&Q):Jun89–261
Marx, A.L. – see under Longuet Marx, A.
Marx, L. The Pilot and the Passenger.*
P. Lukacs, 31(ASch):Autumn89–600
R. Miller, 432(NEQ):Mar89–121
A.E. Monfried, 505:Sep89–183
Marx, W. Ethos und Lebenswelt.
K. Düsing, 687:Jan–Mar89–182

Marx, W., ed. Zur Selbstbegründung der Phil-
osophie seit Kant.
  E.L. Gennat, 489(PJGG):Band96Heft2-426
Marx, W. & J.F. Drennan, eds. The Middle
English Prose Complaint of Our Lady and
Gospel of Nicodemus.*
  K. Bitterling, 38:Band107Heft3/4-526
Mary, G. - see Le comte de Creutz
Marzoa, F.M. - see under Martínez Marzoa, F.
Mas, M. La escritura material de José Angel
Valente.
  M. Persin, 240(HR):Spring89-263
Mas i Vives, J. El teatre a Mallorca a l'època
romàntica.
  J-L. Marfany, 86(BHS):Apr89-192
Masayuki, F. - see under Fukuoka Masayuki
Masefield, P. Divine Revelation in Pali Bud-
dhism.*
  C.S. Prebish, 318(JAOS):Apr-Jun88-333
Masi, M. - see Boethius
Maslowski, T. - see Cicero
Maso, C. The Art Lover.
  W. Ferguson, 441:24Jun90-20
Mason, A. The Racket.
  J-A. Goodwin, 617(TLS):9-15Nov90-1214
Mason, A. The War against Chaos.
  P. Lewis, 565:Winter88/89-77
Mason, B.A. Love Life.*
  G Johnson, 219(GaR):Summer89-406
  J. Saari, 42(AR):Summer89-366
Mason, B.A. Spence + Lila.*
  G. Krist, 340(HudR):Spring89-127
  42(AR):Spring89-249
Mason, H.T., ed. Seventh International Con-
gress on the Enlightenment.
  R. Niklaus, 402(MLR):Jan90-186
Mason, H.T. - see "Studies on Voltaire and
the 18th Century"
Mason, J.D. Wisecracks.
  D.W. McCaffrey, 456(NDQ):Spring89-187
  D.B. Wilmeth, 615(TJ):Dec89-565
Mason, J.D., Jr. - see Wheatley, P.
Mason, J.K. Medico-Legal Aspects of Repro-
duction and Parenthood.
  R. Cullen, 617(TLS):7-13Sep90-943
Mason, M. - see Blake, W.
Mason, P. The City of Men.*
  J. Dremmel, 394:Vol42fasc1/2-240
Mason, R. Art Education and Multicultural-
ism.
  M. Stokrocki, 709:Spring90-184
Mason, R.A., ed. Scotland and England, 1286-
1815.
  R. Mitchison, 83:Autumn89-212
Mason, S. The Great English Nude.
  S. Whiteside, 617(TLS):6-12Jul90-732
Mason, T., ed. Sport in Britain.
  D. Papineau, 617(TLS):2-8Feb90-114
Maspero, F. Le Figuier.
  J.M. Laroche, 207(FR):Dec89-405
Mass, J.P. Lordship and Inheritance in Early
Medieval Japan.
  C. Steenstrup, 407(MN):Winter89-501
"Massacre in Beijing."
  J. Mirsky, 453(NYRB):1Feb90-21
Massey, I. Find You the Virtue.
  G.G. Harpham, 478(P&L):Apr89-197
  W.A. Kumbier, 141:Summer89-301
  S. Pinsker, 219(GaR):Summer89-395
Massey, M. Women in Ancient Greece and
Rome.
  S.J. Freebairn-Smith, 123:Vol39No2-367
  F. Mench, 124:Jan-Feb90-254

Massie, A. A Question of Loyalties.*
  M. Elliott, 364:Dec89/Jan90-130
Massie, S. Pavlovsk.
  O. Bernier, 441:4Nov90-21
  L. Hughes, 617(TLS):14-20Dec90-1354
Massó, R.C. & others - see under Cerdà Massó,
R. & others
Masson, J.M. Final Analysis.
  C. Tavris, 441:21Oct90-7
Masson, O. & T.B. Mitford. Les inscriptions
syllabiques de Kouklia-Paphos.*
  C.J. Ruijgh, 394:Vol42fasc3/4-568
Masson, P. Le Disciple et l'insurgé.
  W. Redfern, 208(FS):Jan89-102
"Masterpieces from the Louvre: French
Bronzes and Paintings from the Renaissance
to Rodin."
  C. Avery, 39:Dec89-429
Masters, A. Literary Agents.
  J. Hunter, 639(VQR):Winter89-161
Masters, B. Gary.
  P. Lomas, 617(TLS):24-30Aug90-893
Masters, H. Strickland.
  G.M. Henry, 441:11Feb90-18
Masters, O. The Home Girls.
  M. Perlman, 441:12Aug90-16
  442(NY):27Aug90-94
Masters, R.D. The Nature of Politics.
  D. Miller, 617(TLS):5-11Jan90-8
Mastretta, A. Mexican Bolero.
  A.C. Sussman, 441:26Aug90-14
Masui, M., ed. A New Rime Index to "The
Canterbury Tales."
  D.G. Stanley, 447(N&Q):Sep89-369
Masui, M. Studies in Chaucer's Language of
Feeling.
  E.G. Stanley, 447(N&Q):Sep89-369
Masumi Junnosuke. Postwar Politics in
Japan, 1945-1955.
  S.R. Reed, 293(JASt):Feb89-174
Matar, F. Sadam Hussein.
  E. Mortimer, 453(NYRB):27Sep90-7
Matarrese, T. - see Manzoni, A.
Matejka, L. - see "Cross Currents"
Matera, L. The Good Fight.
  M. Stasio, 441:21Jan90-35
Mather, I. & C. Two Mather Biographies.
(W.J. Scheick, ed)
  J. Canup, 165(EAL):Vol25No3-323
Mather, R.B. The Poet Shen Yüeh (441-513).
  P.F. Rouzer, 293(JASt):May89-369
  K-Y. Wang, 116:Dec89-142
Matheson, A. & P. Cadell, eds. "For the
Encouragement of Learning."
  A. Bell, 78(BC):Winter89-445
Matheson, P. - see Müntzer, T.
Matheus, M. Hafenkrane.
  B.S. Hall, 589:Jan89-186
Mathews, A. Muesli at Midnight.
  D. Montrose, 617(TLS):6-12Jul90-731
Mathews, H. Cigarettes.*
  R. Hadas, 473(PR):Vol56No2-310
Mathews, H. The Orchard.
  S. Moore, 532(RCF):Spring89-276
Mathews, T. Reading Apollinaire.
  M. Davies, 208(FS):Oct89-486
  P. Read, 402(MLR):Apr90-456
Mathieu, D., ed. Organ Substitution Technol-
ogy.
  L.L.H., 185:Oct89-227

Mathieu, J–C. & M. Collot, eds. Passages et Langages de Henri Michaux.
  G. Cesbron, 356(LR):Feb–May89–125
  C.A. Hackett, 208(FS):Jul89–357
  J. Pierrot, 535(RHL):Jul–Aug89–752
Mathieu–Castellani, G. Eros baroque.
  C. Grisé, 475:Vol16No30–319
Mathieu–Castellani, G., ed. Les Méthodes du discours critique dans les études seiziémistes. (rev by J–C. Margolin)
  I. Piette, 356(LR):Nov89–326
Mathieu–Castellani, G. Montaigne, L'Écriture de l'Essai.
  M. Adam, 542:Oct–Dec89–596
  D.A. Fein, 207(FR):Oct89–157
  O. Millet, 535(RHL):Sep–Oct89–926
Mathis, E. Out of the Shadows.
  M. Stasio, 441:30Sep90–32
Mathis, G. Analyse Stylistique du "Paradis Perdu" de John Milton.*
  L. Miller, 391:May89–83
  M.A. Radzinowicz, 551(RenQ):Spring89–146
  I. Simon, 541(RES):May89–266
Mathis, P. Face à l'ordre des lois (l'énigme du désir).
  P. Somville, 542:Oct–Dec89–637
Matilal, B.K. Logic, Language and Reality.
  P.K. Sen, 393(Mind):Jan89–150
Matoré, G. Le Vocabulaire et la société du XVIe siècle.
  P. Desan, 207(FR):Oct89–184
  J. O'Brien, 402(MLR):Apr90–440
Matossian, M.K. Poisons of the Past.
  A. Wear, 617(TLS):23Feb–1Mar90–191
Matsuo, H. The Logic of Unity.
  R. Pilgrim, 485(PE&W):Jul89–357
"Matsuri: Festival and Rite in Japanese Life."
  R.B. Pilgrim, 293(JASt):Nov89–871
Matte, E.J. French and English Verbal Systems.
  T.J. Cox, 207(FR):Apr90–907
Mattei, C.R. – see under Ramos Mattei, C.
Mattei, J–F. L'ordre du monde.
  P. Trotignon, 542:Oct–Dec89–615
Matteo, S. Textual Exile.
  566:Autumn89–71
Matter, H. – see Mann, T.
Matter, W.D. If It Takes All Summer.
  639(VQR):Summer89–82
Mattera, P. Prosperity Lost.
  D. Diamond, 441:28Oct90–22
Matterson, S. Berryman and Lowell.*
  W.V. Davis, 27(AL):Dec89–723
Matthen, M., ed. Aristotle Today.
  D.W. Hamlyn, 483:Apr89–261
  R.J. Hankinson, 487:Spring89–75
Matthew, H.C.G. Gladstone, 1809–1874.*
  P. Clarke, 617(TLS):18–24May90–515
Matthew, H.C.G. – see Gladstone, W.E.
Matthew, J.R. Testimony.
  M. Hanzimanolis, 577(SHR):Winter89–94
Matthews, C. Hardball.
  639(VQR):Winter89–23
Matthews, D. Beethoven.
  A.F.L.T., 412:May89–146
Matthews, G. One True Thing.
  R. Russo, 441:25Mar90–27
Matthews, G. & K. Everest – see Shelley, P.B.
Matthews, L.J. & D.E. Brown, eds. The Parameters of Military Ethics.
  T.G., 185:Apr90–716

Matthews, M.R., ed. The Scientific Background to Modern Philosophy.
  C. Wilson, 103:Jun90–243
Matthews, R., ed. Informal Justice?
  J.M., 185:Apr90–706
Matthews, W. Blues If You Want.
  F. Chappell, 344:Summer90–168
Matthiae, P. I tesori di Ebla.
  M–H. Gates, 318(JAOS):Jul–Sep88–518
Matthias, J. & V. Vučković – see "The Battle of Kosovo"
Matthiessen, P. Far Tortuga. Under the Mountain Wall. The Snow Leopard. The Cloud Forest.
  C.J. Fox, 364:Aug/Sep89–128
Matthiessen, P. Killing Mister Watson.
  J. Clute, 617(TLS):31Aug–6Sep90–916
  R. Hansen, 441:24Jun90–7
  442(NY):17Sep90–108
Matthiessen, P. On the River Styx.*
  D. Durrant, 364:Dec89/Jan90–134
Mattina, A. – see Seymour, P.J.
Mattox, H.E. The Twilight of Amateur Diplomacy.
  639(VQR):Autumn89–133
Mattusch, C.C. Greek Bronze Statuary.
  639(VQR):Summer89–101
Maturana, H.R. & F.J. Varela. Der Baum der Erkenntnis.
  J. Schopman, 679:Band20Heft1–166
Maugham, W.S. The Razor's Edge. A Writer's Notebook. The Narrow Corner. Cakes and Ale.
  G. Vidal, 453(NYRB):1Feb90–39
Maughan-Brown, D. Land, Freedom, and Fiction.
  R.A. Berger, 538(RAL):Spring89–111
Maunder, R. Mozart's Requiem.
  P. Moseley, 410(M&L):Nov89–545
Maung, U.M. – see under U Maung Maung
Maunoury, J–L. Le Saut de l'ange.*
  K. Fleurant, 207(FR):Oct89–209
de Maupassant, G. Monsieur Parent. (C. Martin, ed) Mont–Oriol. (P. Bonnefis, ed)
  G. Woollen, 208(FS):Oct89–482
de Maupassant, G. Mont–Oriol. (P. Bonnefis, ed)
  R. Killick, 402(MLR):Jul90–737
Maupin, A. Sure of You.* Tales of the City; More Tales of the City; Further Tales of the City.
  T. Glyde, 617(TLS):9–15Mar90–258
Maurais, J., ed. Politique et Aménagement linguistiques.
  M. Etxebarria, 548:Jan–Jun89–195
Maurer, M. Aufklärung und Anglophilie in Deutschland.
  R. Baasner, 72:Band226Heft1–120
Maurer, P. Les modifications temporelles et modales du verbe dans le papiamento de Curaçao (Antilles Néerlandaises).
  G.A. Lorenzino, 350:Dec90–877
Maurer, P. & T. Stolz, eds. Varia Creolica.
  M. Perl, 682(ZPSK):Band42Heft3–407
Mauriac, C. L'Oncle Marcel.
  G.R. Besser, 207(FR):Apr90–884
Mauriac, F. & J. Rivière. Correspondance 1911–1925. (J.E. Flower, ed)
  D.H. Walker, 402(MLR):Jul90–744
Mauriello, A. – see Fortini, P.
Mavor, R. Dr. Mavor and Mr. Bridie.
  D. Hutchison, 571(ScLJ):Winter89–29

Mawdsley, E. The Russian Civil War.
   I. Getzler, 575(SEER):Jan89-149
Max, F. - see Hamel, H.
Maxton, H. The Puzzle Tree Ascendant.
   B. O'Donoghue, 493:Summer89-62
Maxwell, G. Tale of the Mayor's Son.
   T. Dooley, 617(TLS):7-13Sep90-954
Maxwell, G.S. The Romans in Scotland.
   P. Salway, 617(TLS):23-29Mar90-329
Maxwell, M. & J.P. Berni. Comment ça va?
   J.T. Mitchell, 399(MLJ):Winter89-510
Maxwell, W. The Outermost Dream.*
   J.D. Remy, 219(GaR):Winter89-826
May, C.N. In the Name of War.
   42(AR):Summer89-368
May, G. "Les Mille et une nuits" d'Antoine
   Galland ou le Chef-d'oeuvre invisible.*
   R. Cardinal, 208(FS):Oct89-468
May, H.F. Coming to Terms.*
   T. Nieman, 31(ASch):Spring89-308
May, J. The Greenpeace Book of the Nuclear
   Age.
   D. Berreby, 441:29Jul90-21
May, J.M. Trials of Character.*
   A.E. Douglas, 24:Fall89-512
   J.G.F. Powell, 123:Vol39No2-223
May, K.M. Nietzsche and Modern Literature.*
   M. Winkler, 478(P&L):Oct89-382
May, L. The Morality of Groups.
   J.P. Dougherty, 543:Sep89-176
   G. Graham, 518:Oct89-240
   L.G.L., 185:Jan90-446
May, R. Logical Form.
   A. Cormack, 361:Jan89-75
Mayakovsky, V. & L. Brik. Love is the Heart
   of Everything. (B. Jangfeldt, ed)
   R.B., 295(JML):Fall88/Winter89-381
Mayberry, R. & N. Francisco Martínez de la
   Rosa.
   J. Dowling, 238:Dec89-960
Mayer, A. Everyday Situations in French.
   A. Caprio, 399(MLJ):Summer89-225
Mayer, A.J. Why Did the Heavens Not Dark-
   en?*
   R.S. Wistrich, 617(TLS):23-29Nov90-1261
   639(VQR):Summer89-97
Mayer, B. Eduard Mörike.*
   L.B. Jennings, 406:Summer89-267
Mayer, C., ed. Augustinus-Lexikon. (Vol 1,
   Pts 1-3)
   A.C. Dionisotti, 313:Vol79-259
Mayer, C.A. Lucien de Samosate et la Renais-
   sance française.
   A. Chevrel-Giorgi, 549(RLC):Jul-Sep89-
   406
Mayer, F. - see Flecknoe, R.
Mayer, F.H., ed & trans. The Yanagita Kunio
   Guide to the Japanese Folk Tale.
   R.H. Minear, 318(JAOS):Jan-Mar88-146
Mayer, F.H. - see "Ancient Tales in Modern
   Japan"
Mayer, G.L. The Definite Article in Contem-
   porary Standard Bulgarian.
   C.V. Chvany, 279:Vol37-197
   E.A. Scatton, 574(SEEJ):Winter89-635
Mayer, M. The Greatest-Ever Bank Robbery.
   R. Brownstein, 441:28Oct90-28
   442(NY):24Dec90-99
Mayle, P. A Year in Provence.*
   B. Fussell, 441:13May90-8
   442(NY):2Jul90-74
Maynard, S.K. Japanese Conversation.
   H. Yamada, 350:Dec90-877

Mayne, J. Private Novels, Public Films.
   D. Pye, 402(MLR):Apr90-433
Maynor Bikai, P. The Phoenician Pottery of
   Cyprus.
   G. Maass-Lindemann, 229:Band61Heft8-
   727
Mayo, B. The Philosophy of Right and Wrong.
   T.L. Carson, 482(PhR):Jan89-135
Mayo, P.J. The Morphology of Aspect in Sev-
   enteenth-Century Russian (Based on Texts
   of the Smutnoe Vremja).
   A. Grannes, 559:Vol13No1-71
   D.S. Worth, 104(CASS):Spring-Winter88-
   528
Mayor, A. Borderlines.
   M. Stasio, 441:4Nov90-30
Mayrhofer, M. Etymologisches Wörterbuch des
   Altindoarischen. (Vol 1, fasc 1-3)
   W.P. Lehmann, 215(GL):Vol29No3-206
Mayrhofer, M. & R. Schmitt, eds. Iranisches
   Personennamenbuch. (Vol 2, fasc 2)
   P. Huyse, 259(IIJ):Oct89-311
Mays, J.C.C. - see Devlin, D.
Mazal, O. Lehrbuch der Handschriftenkunde.
   M. Steinmann, 684(ZDA):Band118Heft1-12
Mazarr, M.J. Semper Fidel.
   42(AR):Winter89-110
Mazlish, B. A New Science.
   S. Collini, 617(TLS):25-31May90-564
Mazouer, C. - see Poisson, R.
Mazzotta, G. The World at Play in Boccaccio's
   "Decameron."*
   M. Marcus, 276:Summer89-227
Mead, R. Malaysia's National Language and
   the Legal System.
   M.B. Hooker, 293(JASt):Feb89-227
Mead, S.J. Maverick Writers.
   J. Milton, 649(WAL):Feb90-385
Mead, W.B. Two Spectacular Seasons.
   A. Barra, 441:1Apr90-18
Meade, R.C., Jr. Red Brigades.
   C. Duggan, 617(TLS):12-18Jan90-30
Meadows, C. Ārya-Śura's Compendium of the
   Perfections.
   J.W. de Jong, 259(IIJ):Jul89-234
Meagher, R.E. Mortal Vision.
   D.J. Conacher, 235:Winter89-83
Meara, P., ed. Spoken Language.*
   J. John, 257(IRAL):May89-166
   K. Krahnke, 710:Mar89-113
Meara, P., ed. Vocabulary in a Second Lan-
   guage.
   S.M. Gass, 710:Mar89-121
Méasson, A. Du char ailé de Zeus à l'Arche
   d'Alliance.
   R. Ferwerda, 394:Vol42fasc1/2-203
Mebus, G. & others. Sprachbrücke, Deutsch
   als Fremdsprache.
   S.E. Lindenau, 399(MLJ):Summer89-233
Mecarelli, P. "Il zabaione musicale" di Adri-
   ano Banchieri.
   D. Butchart, 410(M&L):Feb89-88
Méchoulan, H. Hispanidad y judaísmo en
   tiempos de Espinoza.
   A. Guy, 92(BH):Jul-Dec88-456
Mechthild von Magdeburg. Ich tanze, wenn du
   mich führst. (M. Schmidt, ed & trans)
   F. Tobin, 133:Band22Heft3/4-310
Meckier, J. Hidden Rivalries in Victorian
   Fiction.*
   M.M. Clarke, 301(JEGP):Jul89-442
   L. Davis, 637(VS):Autumn89-180
   [continued]

Meckier, J. Hidden Rivalries in Victorian Fiction. [continuing]
  R. Ivy, 677(YES):Vol20-302
  L. Myrick, 577(SHR):Summer89-278
  E. Noel, 158:Jun89-69
Meckier, B.W. Papa Was a Farmer.
  639(VQR):Winter89-18
Medawar, J. A Very Decided Preference.
  M.F. Perutz, 453(NYRB):16Aug90-12
Medawar, P.B. The Threat and the Glory. (D. Pyke, ed)
  M.F. Perutz, 453(NYRB):16Aug90-12
de' Medici, L. The Heritage of Italian Cooking.
  R. Flaste, 441:2Dec90-14
de Medina, J.P. - see under Polo de Medina, J.
Medrich, A. Cocolat.
  R. Flaste, 441:2Dec90-14
Medvedev, R. & G. Chiesa. Time of Change.
  A. Brumberg, 441:12Aug90-9
Medvedev, Z.A. The Legacy of Chernobyl.
  G. Garelik, 441:22Jul90-15
  D. Holloway, 453(NYRB):19Jul90-4
  D. Weiner, 617(TLS):3-9Aug90-815
Medvedev, Z.A. Soviet Agriculture.
  C.S. Kaplan, 550(RusR):Jul89-334
Mee, M. Margaret Mee in Search of Flowers of the Amazon Forests.* (T. Morrison, ed)
  M. Lambourne, 39:Dec89-432
Meech-Pekarik, J. The World of the Meiji Print.*
  Susumu Takiguchi, 463:Spring89-48
  E. Tinios, 39:Nov89-359
Meek, H.A. Guarino Guarini and His Architecture.*
  B. Boucher, 39:Dec89-428
  D. Del Pesco, 576:Dec89-396
  M.D. Pollak, 54:Dec89-699
  E.C. Robison, 551(RenQ):Winter89-868
  D. Shawe-Taylor, 90:Feb89-156
Meek, J. McFarlane Boils the Sea.*
  C. McCullough, 571(ScLJ):Winter89-44
Meek, J. Stations.
  W. Harmon, 472:Vol16No1-136
Meeks, W.A. The Moral World of the First Christians.
  L. Thomas, 124:Jul-Aug90-533
Meer, F. Higher Than Hope.
  G.M. Fredrickson, 453(NYRB):27Sep90-20
  G.M. Gerhart, 441:11Mar90-17
  C.C. O'Brien, 617(TLS):23Feb-1Mar90-189
Meerhoff, K. Rhétorique et poétique au XVIe siècle en France.*
  G.P. Norton, 551(RenQ):Summer89-339
  P.J. Smith, 531:Jul-Dec89-505
Meggs, P.B. Type & Image.
  K.F. Schmidt, 507:May/Jun89-149
Megill, A. Prophets of Extremity.*
  P. Bonilla, 295(JML):Fall88/Winter89-232
  F.J. Wetz, 687:Jul-Sep89-561
Mehl, A. Seleukos Nikator und sein Reich. (Vol 1)
  F.W. Walbank, 303(JoHS):Vol109-254
Mehl, D. Geoffrey Chaucer.*
  P. Boitani, 38:Band107Heft1/2-188
  J.W. Nicholls, 677(YES):Vol20-234
Mehl, D. Shakespeare's Tragedies.* (German title: Die Tragödien Shakespeares.)
  F.D. Hoeniger, 570(SQ):Spring89-112
  K.E. McLuskie, 610:Summer89-191
  K.P. Steiger, 156(ShJW):Jahrbuch1989-384

Mehra, P. A Dictionary of Modern Indian History, 1707-1947. (rev)
  A.T. Embree, 293(JASt):Aug89-659
Mehring, M. The Screenplay.
  D. Johnson, 453(NYRB):22Nov90-16
Mehrotra, R.R. Sociolinguistics in Hindi Contexts.
  M.L. Apte, 355(LSoc):Sep89-436
Mehta, G. Raj.*
  639(VQR):Autumn89-131
Mehta, R.C., ed. Essays in Musicology.
  S. Slawek, 187:Winter89-169
Meidal, B. - see Strindberg, A.
Meier, A., with H. Hollmer - see Goethe, J.C.
Meier, B. The Modes of Classical Vocal Polyphony.
  C.C. Judd, 415:Sep89-541
Meier, C. La politique et la grâce.
  F. Wolff, 192(EP):Apr-Jun89-272
Meier, G. Im Anfang war des Wort Die Spracharchäologie als neue Diziplin der Gesteswissenschaften.
  D.H., 355(LSoc):Sep89-460
Meier, H. Etymologische Aufzeichnungen.
  C. Schmitt, 547(RF):Band101Heft1-90
Meier, H. Carl Schmitt, Leo Strauss und "Der Begriff des Politischen."
  R. Brague, 192(EP):Jan-Mar89-107
Meier, T.K. Defoe and the Defense of Commerce.*
  J. McVeagh, 566:Spring89-183
Meier-Brügger, E. Fermo e Lucia e "I Promessi Sposi" come situazione comunicativa.
  H. Blank, 72:Band226Heft1-227
Meier-Brügger, M., ed. Lexikon des frühgriechischen Epos. (Pt 12)
  W.J. Verdenius, 394:Vol42fasc3/4-516
Meiggs, R. Trees and Timber in the Ancient Mediterranean World.
  G.W. Houston, 121(CJ):Oct-Nov89-63
Meijs, W., ed. Corpus Linguistics and Beyond.
  G. Bourquin, 189(EA):Apr-Jun89-205
Meikle, S. Essentialism in the Thought of Karl Marx.*
  C. Sciabarra, 144:Winter-Spring90-61
de Meilhan, G.S. - see under Sénac de Meilhan, G.
Mein, M. Proust et la chose envolée.
  B. Rogers, 535(RHL):Sep-Oct89-939
Meindl, D. & F.W. Horlacher, with M. Christadler, eds. Mythos und Aufklärung in der amerikanischen Literatur/Myth and Enlightenment in American Literature.
  B. Scheer-Schäzler, 38:Band107Heft3/4-538
Meisami, J.S. Medieval Persian Court Poetry.*
  M.R. Menocal, 131(CL):Summer89-289
Meisel, J.M., ed. Adquisición de lenguaje - Aquisição de linguagem.
  J.F. Lee, 710:Dec89-459
Meisel, P. The Myth of the Modern.*
  J.J. Conlon, 177(ELT):Vol32No4-490
  J. Gindin, 301(JEGP):Apr89-254
  E. Goodheart, 191(ELN):Sep89-72
  M. Green, 363(LitR):Spring90-403
  W. Harris, 401(MLQ):Jun88-194
  E. Lobb, 529(QQ):Summer89-505
  D.T.O., 295(JML):Fall88/Winter89-232
  J-M. Rabaté, 189(EA):Jul-Sep89-351
  R. Rooksby, 447(N&Q):Dec89-558
Meiser, G. Lautgeschichte der umbrischen Sprache.
  D. Langslow, 229:Band61Heft2-167

Meisig, K. Das Śrāmaṇyaphala-Sūtra.
   C. Vogel, 259(IIJ):Oct89-320
Meisling, P. Agnetes latter.*
   L. Isaacson, 563(SS):Autumn89-416
Meissner, K. Mālushāhī and Rājulā.*
   M.C. Shapiro, 318(JAOS):Oct-Dec88-636
Meister, M.W. & M.A. Dhaky, eds. Encyclopae-
   dia of Indian Temple Architecture.* (Vol 1,
   Pt 2)
   J.F. Mosteller, 318(JAOS):Jan-Mar88-187
   J.M. Richards, 46:Jun89-12
Meister, M.W. & M.A. Dhaky, eds. Encyclopae-
   dia of Indian Temple Architecture. (Vol 2,
   Pt 1)
   J.M. Richards, 46:Jun89-12
Meixner, U. Handlung, Zeit, Notwendigkeit.
   J-L. Gardies, 316:Dec89-1487
Melada, I. Sheridan Le Fanu.
   D.E. Hall, 158:Dec89-171
Melanson, H., comp. Literary Presses in Can-
   ada, 1975-1985.
   M. Rueter, 470:Vol27-102
Melberg, A. Fördömda realister.
   J. Lutz, 563(SS):Winter89-93
Mel'čuk, I.A. Dependency Syntax.
   J.E. Miller, 297(JL):Mar89-242
Mel'čuk, I.A. Poverxnostnyj sintaksis russkix
   čislovyx vyraženij.
   G. Fowler, 574(SEEJ):Spring89-149
Mel'čuk, I.A. & N.V. Pertsov. Surface Syntax
   of English.
   G. Dourciei, 189(EA):Apr-Jun89-196
Melden, A.I. Rights in Moral Lives.
   C Wellman, 185:Oct89-100
Mele, A.R. Irrationality.*
   F. Jackson, 484(PPR):Mar90-635
Melhem, D.H. Gwendolyn Brooks.
   T.A. Higgins, 295(JML):Fall88/Winter89-
   296
McIhorn, L. Light and Flaky.
   G. Gessert, 448:Vol27No2-124
Meli, F. South Africa Belongs to Us.
   G.M. Fredrickson, 453(NYRB):27Sep90-20
Melis, A.R. - see under Riera Melis, A.
Mell, D.C., Jr., T.E.D. Braun & L.M. Palmer,
   eds. Man, God, and Nature in the Enlight-
   enment.
   A. Ingram, 402(MLR):Apr90-414
Meller, H. Patrick Geddes.
   P. Searby, 617(TLS):11-17May90-503
Mellers, W. Vaughan Williams and the Vision
   of Albion.*
   B. Adams, 414(MusQ):Vol74No4-629
   D. Matthews, 607:Dec89-39
Melli, E., ed. I cantari di Fiorabraccia e Uli-
   vieri.
   S. Grossvogel, 589:Jul89-743
Mellon, J., ed. Bullwhip Days.*
   W. Berry, 569(SR):Fall89-591
Mellor, A.K., ed. Romanticism and Feminism.
   C. Burroughs, 615(TJ):May89-251
   M. Ferguson, 340(KSJ):Vol38-187
Mellor, A.K. Mary Shelley.*
   L. Claridge, 594:Winter89-454
   L. Langbauer, 661(WC):Autumn89-210
   639(VQR):Spring89-55
Melman, Y. & D. Raviv. The Imperfect Spies.
   W. Laqueur, 617(TLS):26Jan-1Feb90-82
Melnyk, D. Naked Croquet.
   H. Prest, 102(CanL):Spring89-167

Meltzer, F. Salomé and the Dance of Writing.*
   M.E. Hazard, 295(JML):Fall88/Winter89-
   233
   S. Melville, 290(JAAC):Winter89-91
Melville, H. The Essential Melville. (R.P.
   Warren, ed)
   P. Mariani, 434:Spring90-313
Melville, H. The Writings of Herman Melville.*
   (Vol 15: Journals) (H.C. Horsford & L.
   Horth, eds)
   H. Cohen, 617(TLS):24-30Aug90-901
Melville, J. Ellen and Edy.*
   S. Watt, 637(VS):Autumn89-206
Melville, J. A Tarnished Phoenix.
   S. Altinel, 617(TLS):24-30Aug90-903
Melville, P. Shape-shifter.
   L. Doughty, 617(TLS):23Feb-1Mar90-203
Melvin, P.M. The Organic City.
   R.A. Rutherdale, 106:Summer89-89
Melvoin, R. New England Outpost.
   639(VQR):Summer89-80
Melzer, S.E. Discourses of the Fall.*
   G. Ferreyrolles, 535(RHL):Mar-Apr89-275
Memmi, A. Le Pharaon.
   R. Linkhorn, 207(FR):Dec89-407
Ménard, P., ed. Le Roman de Tristan en
   prose.* (Vol 1)
   G.N. Bromiley, 382(MAE):1989/1-172
Menarini, P. - see Lorca, F.G.
Mencken, H.L. The Diary of H.L. Mencken.*
   (C.A. Fecher, ed)
   J.K. Galbraith, 453(NYRB):28Jun90-41
Mencken, H.L. H.L. Mencken's "Smart Set"
   Criticism. (W.H. Nolte, ed)
   W. Blazek, 295(JML):Fall88/Winter89-382
Mendelson, E. Introduction to Mathematical
   Logic. (3rd ed)
   J. Corcoran & W. Park, 316:Jun89-618
Mendelson, E. - see Auden, W.H.
Mendelson, E. - see Auden, W.H. & C. Isher-
   wood
Mendelson, S.H. The Mental World of Stuart
   Women.*
   C. Cross, 242:Vol10No1-126
   M.A. O'Donnell, 566:Autumn89-81
   R.M. Warnicke, 551(RenQ):Spring89-152
Mendelssohn, F. Felix Mendelssohn: A Life in
   Letters.* (R. Elvers, ed)
   B. Gilliam, 415:Sep89-542
Mendenhall, G.E. The Syllabic Inscriptions
   from Byblos.
   S. Izre'el, 318(JAOS):Jul-Sep88-519
Mendenhall, T.C. An American Scientist in
   Early Meiji Japan. (R. Rubinger, ed)
   H. Ballhatchet, 407(MN):Autumn89-356
Mendes, C. Fight for the Forest. (T. Gross,
   ed)
   J. Hemming, 617(TLS):9-15Mar90-250
Mendès, C. Le Roi vierge.
   M. Pakenham, 208(FS):Oct89-481
Mendes Pinto, F. The Travels of Mendes
   Pinto. (R.D. Catz, ed & trans)
   J.S. Cummins, 617(TLS):9-15Mar90-262
   S. Schwartz, 441:4Mar90-41
   J.D. Spence, 453(NYRB):12Apr90-38
Méndez Dosuna, J. Los dialectos del Noro-
   este.
   C.J. Ruijgh, 394:Vol42fasc1/2-155
Mendus, S. & D. Edwards, eds. On Toleration.
   B. Baxter, 518:Jan89-53
   R.J.K., 185:Jan90-445

Mendus, S. & J. Rendall, eds. Sexuality and
Subordination.*
   M.K. Clarke, 637(VS):Summer90–649
Mendyk, S.A.E. "Speculum Britanniae."
   M. Hunter, 617(TLS):9–15Feb90–153
Menefee, S. I'm Not Thousandfurs.
   S. Foster, 448:Vol27No3–156
Ménétra, J–L. Journal of My Life. (D. Roche,
ed)
   R. Waller, 83:Spring89–116
Meng, W. – see under Wang Meng
Mengel, E. Geschichtsbild und Romankonzep-
tion.
   F–W. Neumann, 38:Band107Heft1/2–233
Menges, C.C. Inside the National Security
Council.*
   639(VQR):Autumn89–133
Menke–Eggers, C. Die Souveränität der
Kunst.
   R. Rochlitz, 98:Dec89–937
   P. Trotignon, 542:Oct–Dec89–638
Mennemeier, F.N. Literatur der Jahrhundert-
wende. (Vol 1)
   M. Gsteiger, 52:Band24Heft3–323
Mennemeier, F.N. Literatur der Jahrhundert-
wende. (Vol 2)
   M. Gsteiger, 52:Band24Heft3–323
   M. Swales, 402(MLR):Jul90–806
Menninghaus, W. Unendliche Verdopplung.
   T. Pfau, 400(MLN):Apr89–729
Menocal, M.R. The Arabic Role in Medieval
Literary History.*
   C.S.F. Burnett, 240(HR):Summer89–359
   M. McCarthy, 447(N&Q):Dec89–490
Mensching, E. Caesars Bellum Gallicum.
   R. Chevallier, 229:Band61Heft7–624
Menyuk, P. Language Development.
   P.D. Seaman, 350:Jun90–420
Menzel, H. Die römischen Bronzen aus
Deutschland. (Vol 3)
   G. Heres, 229:Band61Heft7–657
de Méo, P., ed. Perspectives sur Sartre et
Beauvoir.
   A. Zielonka, 345(KRQ):Feb89–116
Meo–Zilio, G. & S. Mejía. Diccionario de ges-
tos: Españae Hispanoamérica.
   M. Rector, 567:Vol73No1/2–177
Mercer, M. Goodnight Disgrace.
   J. Wasserman, 102(CanL):Autumn–
Winter89–257
Mercer, N., ed. Language and Literacy from
an Educational Perspective. (Vol 2)
   J. Battenburg, 350:Jun90–421
Mercer, P. "Hamlet" and the Acting of Re-
venge.*
   J. Limon, 570(SQ):Fall89–365
Merchant, I. Hullabaloo in Old Jeypore.*
   G. Adair, 707:Winter88/89–67
Meredith, P., ed. The Mary Play from the N–
Town Manuscript.*
   C. Gauvin, 189(EA):Oct–Dec89–461
   P. Happé, 677(YES):Vol20–240
Meredith, W., ed. Poets of Bulgaria.
   D. O'Driscoll, 493:Summer89–47
Merek, J. Blackbird.
   N. Callendar, 441:19Aug90–17
Mérimée, P. Notes d'un voyage dans le Midi
de la France. Notes d'un voyage dans
l'Ouest de la France. Notes d'un voyage en
Auvergne. Notes d'un voyage en Corse.
(P–M. Auzas, ed)
   V.D.L., 605(SC):15Jul90–411

Mérimée, P. Nouvelles. (M. Crouzet, ed)
   P.W.M. Cogman, 208(FS):Oct89–476
Merino, C.C. – see under Codoñer Merino, C.
Merkel, I. & A.G. Debus, eds. Hermeticism and
the Renaissance.*
   C.G. Nauert, Jr., 551(RenQ):Autumn89–
550
Merkelbach, R. Nikaia in der römischen
Kaiserzeit.
   S. Mitchell, 123:Vol39No1–153
Merkl, P.H., ed. The Federal Republic of Ger-
many at Forty.
   G.A. Craig, 453(NYRB):18Jan90–28
Merle, R. The Idol.*
   M. Elliott, 364:Dec89/Jan90–130
Merleau–Ponty, M. Le primat de la perception
et ses conséquences philosophiques.
   P. Trotignon, 542:Oct–Dec89–615
"Maurice Merleau–Ponty à la Sorbonne."
   P. Trotignon, 542:Oct–Dec89–616
Merllié, F. Michel Tournier.*
   J.E. Flower, 402(MLR):Oct90–986
Mermier, G.R. – see Beroul
Mermier, G.R. – see Viret, P.
Mermin, D. Elizabeth Barrett Browning.
   K. Millard, 617(TLS):30Mar–5Apr90–354
Merod, J. The Political Responsibility of the
Critic.*
   W.E. Cain, 580(SCR):Fall89–124
   J. Clifford, 128(CE):Sep89–517
   K. Racevskis, 577(SHR):Summer89–270
Merrifield, R. The Archaeology of Ritual and
Magic.
   J. Hutchings, 203:Vol100No1–128
Merrill, G.D. & G. Arms – see Howells, E.M.
Merrill, J. The Inner Room.*
   J.D. McClatchy, 491:Apr89–29
   D. Sampson, 249(HudR):Autumn89–510
   K.A. Weisman, 529(QQ):Winter89–959
Merrill, L.L. The Romance of Victorian Natu-
ral History.
   F. Kirchhoff, 125:Winter89–218
   H. Ritvo, 637(VS):Spring90–491
Merrim, S., ed. Feminist Perspectives on Sor
Juana Inés de la Cruz.
   K.A. Myers, 385(MQR):Summer90–453
Mervaud, C. Voltaire et Frédéric II.
   J. Renwick, 402(MLR):Oct90–958
Mervaud, C. & S. Menant, eds. Le Siècle de
Voltaire.
   M. Cook, 402(MLR):Apr90–444
van der Merwe, P. Origins of the Popular
Style.
   W. Mellers, 617(TLS):7–13Sep90–949
Merwin, W.S. The Rain in the Trees.*
   M. Boruch, 29(APR):Nov/Dec89–21
Merwin, W.S. Regions of Memory.
   S.A.S., 295(JML):Fall88/Winter89–383
Merwin, W.S. Selected Poems.*
   A. Turner, 199:Spring89–78
   D. Wakoski, 219(GaR):Winter89–804
Merwin, W.S. – see Wyatt, T.
Merzbacher, D. Meistergesang in Nürnberg um
1600.
   D–R. Moser, 196:Band30Heft3/4–339
Mescherskaya, E. Comrade Princess.
   L. Chamberlain, 617(TLS):16–22Mar90–
274
Meschery, J. A Gentleman's Guide to the
Frontier.
   J. Kennedy, 441:24Jun90–20

Message, J., J. Roman & E. Tassin, eds. A quoi pensent les philosophiques?
   M. Adam, 542:Oct-Dec89-619
Messenger, A. His and Hers.*
   B. Redford, 677(YES):Vol20-270
Messenger, P.M., ed. The Ethics of Collecting Cultural Property.
   K.E. Meyer, 441:18Feb90-7
Messerschmidt, G. Brissonetus (1559). (J. Knape, ed)
   P. Schäffer, 133:Band22Heft3/4-311
Messervy, J.M. & S. Abell. Contemplative Gardens.
   L. Yang, 441:2Dec90-40
Messina, A.M. Race and Party Competition in Britain.
   G. Peele, 617(TLS):7-13Dec90-1311
Messina, G. Index Parmenideus.
   É. des Places, 555:Vol62Fasc1-138
Messina, M. A House in the Shadows.
   L. Lawner, 441:22Apr90-31
Messing, G.M. A Glossary of Greek Romany as Spoken in Agia Varvara (Athens).
   T. Kaufman, 350:Sep90-645
   P. Mackridge, 575(SEER):Oct89-600
"Mest om järn."
   L. Karlsson, 341:Vol58No4-174
Měšťan, A. Geschichte der tschechischen Literatur im 19. und 20. Jahrhundert.
   H. Rösel, 688(ZSP):Band49Heft1-194
Měšt'an, A. & V. Měšt'anová. Wörterbuch zu Karel Hynek Mácha: "Máj."
   R.B. Pynsent, 575(SEER):Oct89-662
Mosuro, E. - see Dilthey, W.
Mészáros, I. Philosophy, Ideology and Social Science.*
   N. Funk, 482(PhR):Oct89-573
Mészöly, M. Volt egyszer egy Közép-Európa.
   R. Aczel, 617(TLS):4-10May90-468
Metcalf, J. Adult Entertainment.*
   L. Zeidner, 441:18Feb90-9
Metcalf, J., ed. The Bumper Book.*
   I.S. MacLaren, 102(CanL):Spring89-196
Metcalf, J., ed. Carry On Bumping.
   W.E. Swayze, 627(UTQ):Fall89-141
Metcalf, J. What Is a Canadian Literature?
   W.E. Swayze, 627(UTQ):Fall89-141
Metcalf, P. "Golden Delicious" and "Firebird."
   J. Byrne, 532(RCF):Summer89-243
Metcalf, P. I-57.
   R. Buckeye, 532(RCF):Spring89-247
   D. Kadlec, 703:Spring89-187
Metcalf, T.R. An Imperial Vision.
   R.E. Frykenberg, 637(VS):Summer90-652
   R. Head, 324:Jan90-146
   R. Llewellyn-Jones, 46:Oct89-14
   M. Wortman, 45:Oct89-69
Metraux, D. The History and Theology of Soka Gakkai.
   H.B. Earhart, 293(JASt):Aug89-619
   R.F. Young, 407(MN):Winter89-513
Mets, D.R. Master of Air Power.
   Lord Zuckerman, 453(NYRB):29Mar90-33
Mette, A. & B. Seidensticker - see Mette, H.J.
Mette, H.J. Kleine Schriften. (A. Mette & B. Seidensticker, eds)
   W.G. Arnott, 123:Vol39No2-373
Metz, T. Black Monday.
   639(VQR):Spring89-60
Metzger, E.A. & R.E. Schade, eds. Sprachgesellschaften - Galante Poetinnen.
   L. Adev, 402(MLR):Oct90-1023

Metzger, H. La méthode philosophique en histoire des sciences. (G. Freudenthal, ed)
   D. Merllié, 542:Oct-Dec89-589
Meulenbeld, G.J. & D. Wujastyk, eds. Studies on Indian Medical History.
   K.G. Zysk, 259(IIJ):Oct89-322
Mewshaw, M. Playing Away.
   T. Cahill, 441:10Jun90-48
Meyer, A. Stand Up and Be Counted.
   G. Peele, 617(TLS):7-13Dec90-1311
Meyer, A.G. The Feminism and Socialism of Lily Braun.
   S.L. Cocalis, 406:Summer89-231
Meyer, B. The Open Room.
   C. Morton, 526:Fall89-102
Meyer, C.F. A Linguistic Study of American Punctuation.
   K.S. Campbell, 126(CCC):May89-242
Meyer, D., ed. Lives on the Line.
   L. Olsen, 395(MFS):Summer89-314
Meyer, D. Sex and Power.
   T. Steuernagel, 563(SS):Autumn89-429
Meyer, E. Aṅkālaparamēcuvari.
   S.B. Steever, 318(JAOS):Jan-Mar88-193
Meyer, E. & L.Z. Smith. The Practical Tutor.
   D. George, 128(CE):Apr89-418
Meyer, G., ed. Die altfranzösische Vita der heiligen Valeria.
   H. Shields, 208(FS):Jul89-318
Meyer, H. Spiegelungen.
   R. Salter, 133:Band22Heft3/4-298
Meyer, H. & R. Suntrup. Lexikon der mittelalterlichen Zahlenbedeutungen.*
   M.S. Batts, 301(JEGP):Oct89-573
   H. Freytag, 224(GRM):Band39Heft2-237
   M. Hardt, 547(RF):Band101Heft2/3-312
Meyer, K.E., ed. Pundits, Poets, and Wits.
   D.R. Boldt, 441:23Sep90-62
Meyer, L. La Philosophie interprète de l'Écriture sainte. (J. Lagrée & P-F. Moreau, eds & trans)
   P. Macherey, 531:Jan-Mar89-152
Meyer, M. Ernst Jünger.
   M. Hulse, 617(TLS).10-16Aug90-842
Meyer, M., ed. De la métaphysique à la rhétorique.*
   G. Leroux, 154:Vol28No4-686
Meyer, M. Not Prince Hamlet.*
   N. Curry, 511:Aug89-47
   P. Vansittart, 364:Aug/Sep89-123
Meyer, M., ed. Questions and Questioning.
   W.S. Chisholm, 350:Sep90-646
Meyer, P. Find What the Sailor Has Hidden.
   C. Ross, 395(MFS):Winter89-757
Meyer-Krentler, E. Willkomm und Abschied.
   T. Sebastian, 400(MLN):Apr89-734
   F. Stock, 52:Band24Heft1-85
Meyer zur Capellen, J. Gentile Bellini.
   C.L. Joost-Gaugier, 54:Jun89-315
Meyerbeer, G. Briefwechsel und Tagebücher. (Vol 4) (H. & G. Becker, eds)
   P. Kast, 417:Oct-Dec89-387
Meyerbeer, G. Giacomo Meyerbeer: A Life in Letters. (H. & G. Becker, eds)
   D. Charlton, 617(TLS):22-28Jun90-670
Meyerhoff, D. Traditioneller Stoff und individuelle Gestaltung.
   A.M.V. Taalman Kip, 394:Vol42fasc3/4-525
Meyering, S.L., ed. Charlotte Perkins Gilman.*
   S.B. Brill, 26(ALR):Winter90-83

Meyers, A. Tender Death.
   M. Stasio, 441:15Jul90–26
Meyers, C. Teaching Students to Think Criti-
cally.
   N.R. Comley, 128(CE):Oct89–623
Meyers, J., ed. The Craft of Literary Biog-
raphy.
   G. Jeansonne, 77:Winter89–63
Meyers, J. Hemingway.*
   K. Moreland, 577(SHR):Spring89–145
Meyers, J. D.H. Lawrence.
   P-L. Adams, 61:Aug90–92
   J. Symons, 617(TLS):7–13Sep90–940
Meyers, J., ed. The Legacy of D.H. Lawrence.*
   D. Mehl, 72:Band226Heft1–234
Meyers, J. Manic Power.*
   H.B., 295(JML):Fall88/Winter89–213
   S. Wright, 569(SR):Winter89–xiv
Meyn, B. The Abalone Heart.
   D.C. Gessaman, 649(WAL):Aug89–191
Meyrick, C., ed. The Bloodstream.
   S. Carnell, 617(TLS):16–22Feb90–179
Mezei, K., with P. Matson & M. Hole. Bibliog-
raphy of Criticism on English and French
Literary Translations in Canada, 1950–
1986, Annotated/Bibliographie de la cri-
tique des traductions littéraires anglaises
et françaises au Canada, de 1950 à 1986,
avec commentaires.
   E.D. Blodgett, 470:Vol27–106
   C. Partridge, 402(MLR):Oct90–907
Micha, A. Essais sur le cycle du Lancelot-
Graal.*
   E. Baumgartner, 554:Vol108No4–559
   E. Kennedy, 382(MAE):1989/1–169
Micha, A. – see "Lancelot"
Michael, C. – see Thomas, A–L.
Michael, C.V. Negritude.
   A.J. Arnold, 538(RAL):Fall89–563
Michael, J. Emerson and Skepticism.*
   R.E. Burkholder, 27(AL):May89–289
   R.W. Butterfield, 402(MLR):Oct90–933
   M. Fischer, 478(P&L):Oct89–379
Michael, J. A Ruling Passion.
   M. Wolf, 441:22Apr90–24
Michael, N.C., comp. "Pericles."
   R. Hillman, 570(SQ):Spring89–117
Michaelis, D. Boy, Girl, Boy, Girl.
   D. Leimbach, 441:7Jan90–18
Michaels, L. Shuffle.
   A. Broyard, 441:9Sep90–14
Michaels, W.B. The Gold Standard and the
Logic of Naturalism.*
   P.R.Y., 295(JML):Fall88/Winter89–187
Michalczyk, J.J. The Italian Political Film-
makers.
   B. Lawton, 276:Summer89–230
Michalet, C–A. Le Drôle de drame du cinéma
mondial.
   J.A. Lambeth, 207(FR):Mar90–730
Michaud, A.A. La Femme de Sath.
   A. Whitfield, 102(CanL):Autumn–
   Winter89–265
Michaud, Y. Locke.
   P. Carrive, 192(EP):Jul–Dec89–549
Michaux, H. Emergences–Resurgences.
   W. Greenberg, 207(FR):Apr90–895
Michel, C. Charles–Nicholas Cochin et le
livre illustré au XVIIIe siècle.
   R. Wrigley, 90:Jan89–42
Michelet, J. Michelet in Liguria. (T. Di
Scanno, ed & trans)
   A.L. Lepschy, 402(MLR):Oct90–971

Micheli, L.M., comp. "Henry VIII."
   J.D. Cox, 570(SQ):Winter89–509
Michelini, A.N. Euripides and the Tragic Tra-
dition.
   J. Diggle, 24:Summer89–357
   R. Hamilton, 124:Sep–Oct89–54
Michell, G. The Penguin Guide to the Monu-
ments of India. (Vol 1)
   G.H.R. Tillotson, 617(TLS):10–16Aug90–
   856
Michener, J.A. The Eagle and the Raven.
   C. Salzberg, 441:30Sep90–28
Michie, H. The Flesh Made Word.*
   T.E. Morgan, 620(TSWL):Spring89–140
   J. Todd, 677(YES):Vol20–298
Michio, M., Itō Mitsutoshi & Tsujinaka Yut-
aka – see under Muramatsu Michio, Itō
Mitsutoshi & Tsujinaka Yutaka
Micou, P. The Music Programme.*
   A. Donald, 441:3Jun90–42
Middlebrook, D.W. & D.H. George – see Sexton,
A.
Middlebrook, D.W. & M. Yalom, eds. Coming to
Light.
   L. Goldstein, 271:Fall89–159
Middlemas, K. Power, Competition and the
State. (Vol 2)
   J. Turner, 617(TLS):12–18Oct90–1094
Middleton, C. Two Horse Wagon Going By.
   M.M. Clark, 577(SHR):Winter89–98
Middleton, C. – see von Goethe, J.W.
Middleton, C. – see Gustafsson, L.
Middleton, C. – see Hofmann, G.
Middleton, S. Changes and Chances.
   P. Binding, 617(TLS):1–7Jun90–585
Middleton, T. & T. Dekker. The Roaring Girl.
(P.A. Mulholland, ed)
   N.W. Bawcutt, 541(RES):Nov89–559
   L. Hutson, 447(N&Q):Jun89–237
Midgley, M. Wisdom, Information and Wonder.*
   T.R. Foster, J. Losco & P. Miller, 185:
   Jul90–902
   P. Mackenzie, 103:Apr90–149
Mieder, W. International Proverb Scholarship.
   D. Ben–Amos, 292(JAF):Jul–Sep89–353
Mieder, W. Tradition and Innovation in Folk
Literature.*
   D. Haase, 221(GQ):Winter89–121
   N. Ingwersen, 406:Winter89–492
   W.F.H. Nicolaisen, 196:Band30Heft1/2–
   147
Mielsch, H. Die römische Villa.*
   J. Percival, 123:Vol39No1–158
Miemitz, B. Nominalgruppen als Textverweis-
mittel.
   T. Henninger, 575(SEER):Jul89–498
Mierau, E., ed. Russen in Berlin: 1918–1933.
   T.R. Beyer, Jr., 574(SEEJ):Summer89–312
Mierzejewski, A.C. The Collapse of the Ger-
man War Economy, 1944–1945.
   Lord Zuckerman, 453(NYRB):29Mar90–33
   639(VQR):Spring89–63
Migeotte, L. L'emprunt public dans les cités
grecques.
   H.W. Pleket, 487:Summer89–177
Miguel, N.S. – see under Salvador Miguel, N.
Mihura, M. The Independent Act.*
   D. Gagen, 86(BHS):Oct89–389
   M.T. Halsey, 238:Mar89–163
Mikkelson, G. & M. Winchell – see Rasputin, V.
Mikosch, I. Die Präpositionen in gesprochener
Sprache.*
   A. Liberman, 215(GL):Vol29No1–60

254

Mila, M. Massimo Mila alla Scala. (R. Gara-
vaglia & A. Sinigaglia, eds)
  H. Sachs, 617(TLS):15-21Jun90-642
Milanich, J.T. & S. Milbrath, eds. First En-
counters.
  J.H. Elliott, 453(NYRB):1Mar90-26
Milbauer, A.Z. & D.G. Watson, eds. Reading
Philip Roth.*
  J.H. Justus, 587(SAF):Spring89-115
  D.W. Madden, 594:Summer89-210
Milburn, R. Early Christian Art and Archi-
tecture.*
  D. Kinney, 576:Jun89-180
Miles, B. Ginsberg.*
  C. Hitchens, 617(TLS):9-15Mar90-255
Miles, D. Francis Place, 1771-1854.
  D. Nicholls, 637(VS):Autumn89-183
Miles, E. More Tales of the Big Bend.
  J.F. Nagy, 292(JAF):Apr-Jun89-230
Miles, H.A.D. & D.B. Brown, with others. Sir
David Wilkie of Scotland (1785-1841).
  T. Stimson, 83:Autumn89-243
Miles, P. & M. Smith. Cinema, Literature and
Society.
  J. Izod, 677(YES):Vol20-359
  R. Maltby, 447(N&Q):Mar89-129
Miles, R. The Female Form.*
  K. Fishburn, 594:Spring89-104
  J. Simons, 541(RES):May89-303
  E.B. Thompson, 395(MFS):Summer89-393
Milon, R. The Women's History of the World.
  S. Tillotson, 529(QQ):Summer89-559
Milhouse, J. & R.D. Hume - see Downes, J.
Miliaras, B.A. Pillar of Flame.*
  E. Delavenay, 189(EA):Jan-Mar89-109
Miliband, R. Divided Societies.
  Z. Bauman, 617(TLS):12-18Jan90-30
Mill, J.S. "On Liberty" with "The Subjection
of Women" and "Chapters on Socialism." (S.
Collini, ed)
  B. Barry, 358:Feb90-6
Millán, M.C. - see Lorca, F.G.
Millar, J.R., ed. Politics, Work, and Daily Life
in the USSR.
  M. McAuley, 575(SEER):Apr89-327
  W. Moskoff, 104(CASS):Spring89-108
Millar, M. Vanish in an Instant.
  P. Craig, 617(TLS):1-7Jun90-593
de Mille, A. Portrait Gallery.
  P-L. Adams, 61:Sep90-131
  L. Shea, 441:26Aug90-8
Miller, A. Banished Knowledge.
  D. Elkind, 441:18Nov90-22
Miller, A. Timebends.*
  B. Bawer, 31(ASch):Winter89-140
  B.F. Dukore, 610:Summer89-219
  D. Miller, 569(SR):Spring89-283
  M.D.O., 295(JML):Fall88/Winter89-383
  529(QQ):Winter89-1003
Miller, A. The Untouched Key.
  R. Dinnage, 617(TLS):6-12Jul90-720
  A. Storr, 441:18Mar90-10
Miller, A. - see Haasse, H.S.
Miller, C. Emily Dickinson.*
  J.F. Diehl, 620(TSWL):Spring89-133
  L. Lane, Jr., 106:Summer89-130
Miller, C.L. Blank Darkness.*
  M. Mortimer, 131(CL):Fall89-408
Miller, D. The Icarus Paradox.
  C. Harris, 441:28Oct90-23
Miller, D. Market, State and Community.
  G. Hawthorn, 617(TLS):2-8Feb90-112
Miller, D. - see von Goethe, J.W.

Miller, D., M. Bracher & D. Ault, eds. Critical
Paths.*
  M. Fischer, 403(MLS):Spring89-93
  A.K. Mellor, 88:Fall89-98
  K.E. Smith, 83:Autumn89-231
  B. Wilkie, 301(JEGP):Jan89-106
Miller, D.A. The Novel and the Police.*
  P.K. Garrett, 301(JEGP):Oct89-541
  M.P. Ginsburg, 149(CLS):Vol26No1-76
  R. Hull, 594:Spring89-108
  R.R. Thomas, 405(MP):Feb90-319
Miller, D.L. The Poem's Two Bodies.
  D. Cheney, 604:Winter89-4
Miller, D.N. Fear of Fiction.
  R.H. Wolf, 508:Jan89-85
Miller, D.N., ed. Recovering the Canon.
  R.H. Wolf, 508:Jan89-85
Miller, E.H. Walt Whitman's "Song of Myself."
  T. Gunn, 617(TLS):5-11Jan90-3
  J.P. Warren, 646(WWR):Winter90-141
Miller, F.J. A Handbook of Russian Verbs.
  M.I. Levin, 558(RLJ):Spring-Fall89-277
Miller, G. Sancho.
  F. Manley, 102(CanL):Autumn-Winter89-
216
Miller, H. Letters to Emil. (G. Wickes, ed)
  A.F. Hill, 441:4Feb90-19
Miller, H.H. Colonel Parke of Virginia.
  L.E. Beattie, 441:1Jul90-15
Miller, J. American Odalisque.*
  M. Boruch, 29(APR):Mar/Apr80-41
Miller, J., ed. The Don Giovanni Book.
  J. Kerrigan, 617(TLS):3-9Aug90-817
Miller, J., ed. Hot Type.
  A. Dawid, 152(UDQ):Fall89-107
Miller, J. One, by One, by One.
  E.N. Evans, 441:29Apr90-7
  442(NY):9Jul90-92
Miller, J. Rousseau, Dreamer of Democracy.
  P. Carrive, 192(EP):Jul-Dec89-550
Miller, J. & L. Mylroie. Saddam Hussein and
the Crisis in the Gulf.
  B. Lewis, 453(NYRB):20Dec90-44
  M. Zonis, 441:11Nov90-7
Miller, J.B. My Life in Action Painting.
  J.K. Peters, 441:22Jul90-20
Miller, J.D. The Baseball Business.
  L. Rukeyser, 441:1Apr90-13
Miller, J.G. Françoise Sagan.
  M. Rosello, 210(FrF):Jan89-117
Miller, J.H. The Ethics of Reading.*
  S. Connor, 402(MLR):Oct90-891
  J. Neubauer, 149(CLS):Vol26No1-87
  M.W. Redfield, 153:Summer89-35
Miller, J.H. Versions of Pygmalion.
  B. Harrison, 617(TLS):9-15Nov90-1200
Miller, J.M. - see Hulsker, J.
Miller, J.M. & J.H. Hayes. A History of An-
cient Israel and Judah.*
  J. Van Seters, 318(JAOS):Apr-Jun88-309
Miller, J.T. Poetic License.*
  A.C. Spearing, 589:Jan89-189
Miller, K. Authors.
  C. Gallagher, 617(TLS):26Jan-1Feb90-84
Miller, L. John Milton and the Oldenburg
Safeguard.
  J.M. Patrick, 568(SCN):Spring-Summer89-
6
Miller, L.B., with S. Hart - see Peale, C.W.
Miller, M. Letchworth.
  J.S. Curl, 324:May90-441

Miller, M. A Thousand and One Coffee Morn-
ings.*
B. Thompson, 441:24Jun90-14
Miller, M.C. Boxed In.*
H. Fromm, 219(GaR):Spring89-179
E. Levy, 147:Vol6No2-63
Miller, M.C. Coyote Cafe.
R. Flaste, 441:10Jun90-53
Miller, M.C., ed. Seeing Through Movies.
M. Covino, 441:19Aug90-21
Miller, M.J. Turn Up the Contrast.
A. Nothof, 627(UTQ):Fall89-257
V. Tovell, 108:Fall89-86
Miller, N.K. Subject to Change.*
M.N. Evans, 210(FrF):Sep89-370
L.R. Huffer, 147:Vol6No2-71
Miller, R. American Apocalypse.
T. Hine, 441:15Jul90-13
Miller, R.A. Nihongo.*
A.M. Niyekawa, 399(MLJ):Autumn89-377
B. Saint-Jacques, 320(CJL):Jun89-236
Miller, R.C. Virginia Woolf.
S. Ferebee, 395(MFS):Winter89-802
Miller, R.W. Fact and Method.
R. Campbell, 185:Jul90-897
Miller, S. Family Pictures.
J. O'Grady, 617(TLS):21-27Dec90-1381
J. Smiley, 441:22Apr90-1
P. Storace, 453(NYRB):16Aug90-22
Miller, S.W. Concise Dictionary of Acronyms
and Initialisms.
L.A. Ramsey, 710:Dec89-483
Miller, W.B., ed. The Selected Papers of
Charles Willson Peale and His Family. (Vol
2)
639(VQR):Winter89-17
Miller, W.L. & others. How Voters Change.
G. Peele, 617(TLS):7-13Dec90-1311
Millet, G.C. Dino Campana fuorilegge.
M. King, 276:Summer89-244
Millett, K. The Loony-Bin Trip.
R. Dinnage, 441:3Jun90-12
Millett, M. The Romanization of Britain.
S.E. Cleary, 617(TLS):31Aug-6Sep90-928
Millgate, J. Scott's Last Edition.*
F. Robertson, 541(RES):Feb89-133
M.A. Weinstein, 301(JEGP):Jan89-114
517(PBSA):Mar89-117
Millgate, M., ed. New Essays on "Light in Au-
gust."
C.S. Brown, 569(SR):Fall89-556
Millhauser, S. The Barnum Museum.
J. Cantor, 441:24Jun90-16
Millington, M. Reading Onetti.*
P. Martínez Arévalo, 345(KRQ):May89-
252
Millman, J. The Effigy.
F.A. Koestler, 441:9Dec90-24
Millman, L. Last Places.
P-L. Adams, 61:Mar90-117
T. Cahill, 441:10Jun90-48
442(NY):26Feb90-132
Millman, L. The Wrong-Handed Man.
S. Pinsker, 573(SSF):Fall88-496
Millon, H.A. & C.H. Smyth. Michelangelo Ar-
chitect: The Façade of San Lorenzo and the
Drum and Dome of St. Peter's.
W.E. Wallace, 380:Spring89-64
Milloy, J.S. The Plains Cree.
G.W., 102(CanL):Autumn-Winter89-301

Mills, D. The Idea of Loyalty in Upper Canada
1784-1850.
G. Patterson, 529(QQ):Autumn89-725
G.W., 102(CanL):Autumn-Winter89-302
Mills, J. Towards the End.
L. Doughty, 617(TLS):16-22Feb90-181
Mills, J.A. Hamlet on Stage.*
C.J. Carlisle, 612(ThS):Nov88-213
Mills, M., ed. Horn Childe and Maiden Rimnild.
N.F. Blake, 72:Band226Heft1-164
Mills, W. The Arkansas.
J. Kilgo, 569(SR):Fall89-cxviii
Milly, J. - see Proust, M.
Milne, L. - see Rudnitsky, K.
Milner, J. The Studios of Paris.*
R. Kendall, 39:May89-366
B.A. MacAdam, 55:Jan89-85
R.D. Reck, 207(FR):Feb90-599
Milnes, R. - see Orrey, L.
Milolo, K. L'image de la femme chez les ro-
mancières de l'Afrique noire francophone.*
J.V. Arnold, 538(RAL):Spring89-122
Miloslavskij, I.G. Kratkaja prakticeskaja
grammatika russkogo jazyka.
V.A. Friedman, 399(MLJ):Autumn89-384
Milosz, C. The Collected Poems, 1931-1987.*
P.J.M. Robertson, 529(QQ):Winter89-954
W.W. Werner, 577(SHR):Fall89-382
Miłosz, C. Kroniki.
J.T. Baer, 497(PolR):Vol34No1-75
Milroy, L. Language and Social Networks.*
(2nd ed)
M.A. Kaplan, 355(LSoc):Jun89-275
Milroy, L. Observing and Analysing Natural
Language.
S. Romaine, 353:Vol27No2-372
Milsap, R., with T. Carter. Almost Like a
Song.
S. Liveten, 441:10Jun90-45
Milstein, N. & S. Volkov. From Russia to the
West.
J.R. Oestreich, 441:12Aug90-20
Milton, C. Lawrence and Nietzsche.*
E. Delavenay, 189(EA):Jan-Mar89-108
K.M. Hewitt, 541(RES):Nov89-588
M. Storch, 677(YES):Vol20-336
Milward, P. Biblical Influences in Shake-
speare's Great Tragedies.*
C. Freer, 570(SQ):Spring89-106
Testsumaro Hayashi, 577(SHR):Winter89-
86
Minco, M. An Empty House. The Fall.
R. Friedman, 617(TLS):15-21Jun90-654
Miner, E. - see Konishi, J.
Miner, S.M. Between Churchill and Stalin.*
639(VQR):Summer89-97
Miners, N. Hong Kong Under Imperial Rule,
1912-1941.
T-L. Lee, 293(JASt):Feb89-143
Minervini, V. & M.L. Indini - see de San
Pedro, D.
Ming, Z. - see under Zhou Ming
Mingay, G.E., ed. The Agrarian History of
England and Wales. (Vol 6)
W. Minchinton, 617(TLS):5-11Jan90-20
Minh-ha, T.T. - see under Trinh T. Minh-ha
Minhinnick, R. The Looters.
S. Carnell, 617(TLS):16-22Feb90-179
Mink, L.O. Historical Understanding.* (B.
Fay, E.O. Golub & R.T. Vann, eds)
P.F., 185:Oct89-213
T. Postlewait, 615(TJ):Dec89-557

Minnis, A.J. Medieval Theory of Authorship.*
(2nd ed)
E.E. Du Bruck, 201:Vol15-358
Minnis, A.J. & A.B. Scott, with D. Wallace,
eds. Medieval Literary Theory and Criti-
cism c. 1100-c. 1375.
B. O'Donoghue, 506(PSt):Dec89-303
Minor, R.N. Radhakrishnan.
T. Organ, 485(PE&W):Apr89-224
D.R. Tuck, 293(JASt):Aug89-660
Minoru, N. - see under Nakano Minoru
Minot, S. Lust and Other Stories.*
K. Bucknell, 617(TLS):9-15Feb90-148
R. Wilson, 219(GaR):Winter89-829
42(AR):Fall89-505
Minow-Pinkney, M. Virginia Woolf and the
Problem of the Subject.*
J. Marcus, 620(TSWL):Spring89-101
E.C.R., 295(JML):Fall88/Winter89-424
Minta, S. García Márquez.*
P.T.S., 295(JML):Fall88/Winter89-336
Minter, D. - see Faulkner, W.
Mintz, M.M. The Generals of Saratoga.
P-L. Adams, 61:Dec90-130
Miodunka, W. & J. Wróbel. Poland in Polish.
A. Barańczak, 574(SEEJ):Summer89-330
Miquelon, D. New France 1701-1744.
T. Crowley, 529(QQ):Spring89-150
Y. Frenette, 298:Fall89-140
M. Power, 628(UWR):Vol22No1-99
Mirbeau, O. Le Jardin des supplices. (M.
Delon, ed)
R. Carr, 208(FS):Oct89-481
Mirbeau, O. Sketches of a Journey.
E. Weber, 617(TLS):23-29Mar90-312
Mirkowska, G. & A. Salwicki. Algorithmic
Logic.
E. Engeler, 316:Sep89-1105
Miró, G. Niño y grande. (C. Ruiz Silva, ed)
M.G.R. Coope, 402(MLR):Apr90-479
Miró, G. Novelas cortas. (M.A. Lozano Marco,
ed)
E.L. King, 240(HR):Winter89-112
"Miroirs de la ville."
G. Ponnau, 549(RLC):Jul-Sep89-403
Miron, D. & D. Laor, eds. U.N. Gnessin - Meḥ-
qarim uteudot.
A. Balaban, 508:May89-177
Miron, G. The March to Love. (D.G. Jones,
ed)
J. Harrison, 102(CanL):Spring89-193
Mirrer-Singer, L. The Language of Evalua-
tion.*
T.A. Lathrop, 238:Mar89-140
D.G. Pattison, 382(MAE):1989/1-182
J. Szertics, 240(HR):Summer89-365
J.C. Zamora, 552(REH):May89-136
Mirsky, D.S. Uncollected Writings on Russian
Literature. (G.S. Smith, ed)
K. Lantz, 104(CASS):Spring-Winter88-468
Misfeldt, J. the half-finished christ.*
B.H. Pell, 102(CanL):Spring89-165
Mishima, Y. Acts of Worship.
P-L. Adams, 61:Feb90-109
F. Misurella, 441:21Jan90-21
Mishima, Y. The Sea of Fertility.
J. Fallows, 61:Sep90-117
Mishler, E.G. The Discourse of Medicine.
R.M. Arnold, 355(LSoc):Mar89-116
Miska, J., comp. Canadian Studies on Hun-
garians, 1886-1986.
N.F. Dreisziger, 298:Summer89-153

Misra, U. The Raj in Fiction.
K.S.N. Rao, 395(MFS):Summer89-387
Mistry, R. Swimming Lessons and Other Sto-
ries from Firozsha Baag.*
P.J. Bailey, 455:Dec89-61
B. Holmes, 198:Winter89-109
Mistry, R. Tales from Firozsha Baag.
A. Malak, 102(CanL):Winter88-101
Mitchell, A. A Fragile Paradise.
S. Mills, 617(TLS):9-15Mar90-250
Mitchell, B. Old English Syntax.*
V. Adams, 300:Apr88-88
Mitchell, B. On Old English.
T.A. Shippey, 447(N&Q):Dec89-488
E.G. Stanley, 382(MAE):1989/2-317
Mitchell, C., ed. Changing Perspectives in
Latin American Studies.
T.M. Davies, Jr., 263(RIB):Vol39No2-209
D.W. Foster, 238:Sep89-559
Mitchell, D.J. Succession.
D.E. Smith, 298:Summer89-146
Mitchell, E. People Etcetera.*
L. Sail, 565:Summer89-75
Mitchell, J. Scott, Chaucer, and Medieval
Romance.*
R. Beckett, 571(ScLJ):Spring89-7
H-J. Diller, 72:Band226Heft1-175
Mitchell, J. & A. Oakley, eds. What is Femi-
nism?
J. Pedersen, 242:Vol10No3-366
Mitchell, J.H. Living at the End of Time.
J.R. Stilgoe, 441:13May90-33
Mitchell, J.L. Gay Hunter.
J. Cluto, 617(TLS):23Feb-1Mar90-302
Mitchell, L.C., ed. New Essays on "The Red
Badge of Courage."
J. Cazemajou, 189(EA):Jul-Sep89-361
Mitchell, L.G. - see Burke, E.
Mitchell, P. - see Hardouin-Fugier, E. & E.
Grafe
Mitchell, S., ed. Victorian Britain.*
G.B. Tennyson, 445(NCF):Jun89-117
W. Thesing, 637(VS):Spring90-490
Mitchell, T. Colonizing Egypt.*
M. Crinson, 46:Jan89-14
Mitchell, T.J. Violence and Piety in Spanish
Folklore.
S. Brandes, 292(JAF):Jul-Sep89-338
M.G. Paulson, 238:May89-301
Mitchell, T.N. - see Cicero
Mitchell, W.J.T. Iconology.*
M. Bull, 90:Jun89-435
C. Gandelman, 678(YCGL):No36-171
E. Piltz, 341:Vol58No1-43
Mitchison, N.A. Peter Brian Medawar: 28
February 1915 - 2 October 1987.
M.F. Perutz, 453(NYRB):16Aug90-12
Mitford, J. Grace Had an English Heart.*
T.C. Holyoke, 42(AR):Fall89-496
Mitias, M.H., ed. Aesthetic Quality and Aes-
thetic Experience.
J. Jobes, 103:Nov90-452
Mitias, M.H. What Makes an Experience Aes-
thetic?
D. Simak, 103:May90-187
Mitsis, P. Epicurus' Ethical Theory.*
M.E. Reesor, 103:Jun90-248
S.A. White, 319:Oct90-605
Mitsuharu, K. - see under Kaneko Mitsuharu
Mitterand, H., ed. Émile Zola, Carnets d'en-
quêtes.
C. Becker, 535(RHL):Jan-Feb89-139

Mittler, E. & W. Werner. Codex Manesse.
  R. Watson, 39:Feb89-133
Mittman, B.G. Spectators on the Paris Stage in the Seventeenth and Eighteenth Centuries.
  A.M. Hjort, 345(KRQ):Feb89-127
Mizener, A.F. F. Scott Fitzgerald.
  R.M.P., 295(JML):Fall88/Winter89-330
Mizruchi, S.L. The Power of Historical Knowledge.
  N. Bradbury, 677(YES):Vol20-313
  E. Carton, 445(NCF):Jun89-104
  A. Kaplan, 432(NEQ):Dec89-586
  N.E. Stafford, 27(AL):May89-297
Mladenović, Ž. Traganja za Vukom.
  E.D. Goy, 575(SEER):Jan89-116
Mlynarczyk, G. Ein Franziskanerinnenkloster im 15. Jahrhundert.
  P.L. Nyhus, 589:Oct89-1011
Moamín. Libro de los animales que cazan (Kitāb al-Yawāriḥ).* (J.M. Fradejas Rueda, ed)
  D.P. Seniff, 240(HR):Spring89-221
Moat, J. Firewater and The Miraculous Mandarin.
  T. Gooderham, 617(TLS):16-22Nov90-1248
Moates, M.M. A Bridge of Childhood.
  E. Pall, 441:4Mar90-24
Moatti, C., ed. André Malraux 7.
  M. Autrand, 535(RHL):Mar-Apr89-329
  E. Fallaize, 208(FS):Jan89-111
Moatti, C. Le Prédicateur et ses masques.*
  M. Tison-Braun, 535(RHL):Mar-Apr89-330
Mobärg, M. English "Standard" Pronunciations.
  R.K.S. Macaulay, 350:Dec90-878
Mochon, J.D. Clara.
  J.P. Gilroy, 102(CanL):Spring89-187
Mocquais, P-Y. Hubert Aquin, ou la quête interrompue.
  P. Merivale, 102(CanL):Autumn-Winter89-229
Model, A. Metaphysik und reflektierende Urteilskraft bei Kant.
  W. Steinbeck, 342:Band80Heft3-360
Modert, J. - see Austen, J.
Modiano, M. Domestic Disharmony and Industrialization in D.H. Lawrence's Early Fiction.*
  É. Delavenay, 189(EA):Jan-Mar89-110
Modiano, P. Remise de peine.*
  S. Petit, 207(FR):Dec89-408
Modiano, P. Vestiaire de l'enfance.*
  M. Alhau, 450(NRF):Jun89-102
  M. Naudin, 207(FR):Feb90-581
Modiano, P. Voyage de noces.
  R. Buss, 617(TLS):9-15Nov90-1215
Modiano, R. Coleridge & the Concept of Nature.*
  R.F. Storch, 591(SIR):Summer89-303
Modleski, T., ed. Studies in Entertainment.
  J.K. Forte, 615(TJ):Mar89-116
Modleski, T. The Women Who Knew Too Much.
  M.A. Anderegg, 456(NDQ):Winter89-211
Modlin, C.E. - see Anderson, S.
Moebs, T.T. U.S. Reference-iana: 1841-1899.
  P.S. Koda, 87(BB):Sep89-205
Moeller, J., H. Liedloff & B.B. Sharon. Deutsch Heute. (4th ed)
  I.H.R. McCoy, 399(MLJ):Autumn89-372

Moeran, B. Language and Popular Culture in Japan.
  P. Popham, 617(TLS):12-18Jan90-40
Moerman, M. Talking Culture.*
  J.J. Errington, 350:Sep90-566
Moessner, L. Early Middle English Syntax.
  W.N. Francis, 350:Sep90-646
Moffat, D., ed. The Soul's Address to the Body.*
  C. Franzen, 447(N&Q):Mar89-79
  E. Kooper, 179(ES):Jun89-270
  C.A. Lees, 382(MAE):1989/1-150
  O.S. Pickering, 72:Band226Heft1-155
Moffat, G. Rage.
  P. Craig, 617(TLS):11-17May90-496
Moffat, G. The Storm Seekers.
  P.N. Limerick, 617(TLS):12-18Jan90-27
Mofolo, T. Chaka.
  B. Hickey, 538(RAL):Fall89-522
Mogen, D., M. Busby & P. Bryant, eds. The Frontier Experience and the American Dream.
  F. Erisman, 585(SoQ):Spring90-115
Mohamad, G. The "Cultural Manifesto" Affair.
  J. Mackie, 293(JASt):Feb89-233
Mohanti, P. Changing Village, Changing Life.
  R. Nayar, 617(TLS):19-25Oct90-1120
Möhn, D., ed. Die Fachsprache der Windmüller und Windmühlenbauer.
  J.B. Berns, 685(ZDL):2/1989-248
Möhn, D. & R. Pelka. Fachsprachen.
  K. Kehr, 685(ZDL):1/1989-118
  V.A. Tatarinov, 682(ZPSK):Band42Heft1-118
Mohr, M.M. & M.S. MacLean, eds. Working Together.
  S. Stotsky, 128(CE):Nov89-750
Mohr, R.D. Gays/Justice.
  D. Van De Veer, 185:Jan90-426
Möhren, F. Wort- und sachgeschichtliche Untersuchungen an französischen landwirtschaftlichen Texten, 13., 14. und 18. Jahrhundert.
  B. von Gemmingen, 72:Band226Heft1-176
Moi, T. Sexual/Textual Politics.*
  D. Fuss, 50(ArQ):Winter89-95
Moir, A. & D. Jessel. Brainsex.
  L. Hudson, 617(TLS):9-15Mar90-243
Moisan, A. Répertoire des noms propres de personnes et de lieux cités dans les chansons de geste françaises et les oeuvres étrangères dérivées.*
  B. Guidot, 547(RF):Band101Heft1-110
Mok, E.M. Chinese for Beginners and Advanced Beginners.
  C.Y. Ning, 399(MLJ):Summer89-211
Moked, G. Particles and Ideas.
  R. Dégremont, 542:Oct-Dec89-599
Molander, M. - see Le comte de Creutz
Moldenhauer, J.J. - see Thoreau, H.D.
Mole, J. Passing Judgements.*
  E. Longley, 493:Winter89/90-22
Moles, R.N. Definition and Rule in Legal Theory.
  N. Lacey, 291:Vol6No1-119
Molesworth, C. Marianne Moore.
  K. Pollitt, 441:26Aug90-8
de Molina, L. On Divine Foreknowledge. (A.J. Freddoso, ed & trans)
  S. MacDonald, 543:Sep89-177
de Molina, T. - see under Tirso de Molina
Molinaro, J.A. Matteo Maria Boiardo.
  C. Ross, 276:Summer89-232

Molinaro, U. A Full Moon of Women.
　A. Johnson, 441:2Sep90-24
Molinaro, U. Thirteen.
　I. Malin, 532(RCF):Fall89-219
Mollat, M. Die Armen im Mittelalter. (2nd ed)
　A. Classen, 597(SN):Vol61No1-123
Möller, H. Vernunft und Kritik.
　W. Goetschel, 221(GQ):Spring89-235
Møller, P.U. Postlude to the Kreutzer Sonata.
　R.F. Christian, 575(SEER):Oct89-609
　D.T. Orwin, 104(CASS):Spring-Winter88-467
Mollica, A., ed. A Touch of ... Class!
　H.J. Siskin, 399(MLJ):Autumn89-346
Molloy-Olund, B. In Favor of Lightning.*
　E. Pankey, 271:Spring-Summer89-175
　C. Wright, 434:Winter89-193
von Molnár, G. Romantic Vision, Ethical Context.*
　J. Neubauer, 301(JEGP):Apr89-293
　D. Purdy, 406:Fall89-394
　H.M.K. Riley, 133:Band22Heft2-163
Molnar, M. Body of Words.
　J.D. Elsworth, 575(SEER):Jan89-129
von Moltke, H.J. Letters to Freya 1939-1945.* (German title: Briefe an Freya 1939-1945.) (B.R. von Oppen, ed & trans)
　V.R. Berghahn, 441:1Jul90-10
　G.A. Craig, 453(NYRB):28Jun90-25
　442(NY):27Aug90-94
Momeyer, R.W. Confronting Death.
　A G K., 185:Jul90-927
Momigliano, A. On Pagans, Jews, and Christians.
　S.J.D. Cohen, 124:Nov-Dec89-134
Monaghan, J., ed. Grammar in the Construction of Texts.
　S.A. Thompson, 350:Mar90-200
Monahan, A.P. Consent, Coercion, and Limit.*
　T. Renna, 589:Jul89-745
Monange, S. Le Récit du scribe.
　M. Alhau, 450(NRF):Oct89-114
Monballin, M. Gracq, création et recréation de l'espace.
　G. Cesbron, 356(LR):Feb-May89-128
Moñer, M. Cervantès.
　M. McKendrick, 86(BHS):Oct89-379
Moñer, M. Cervantes conteur.
　Y. Jehenson, 304(JHP):Autumn89-107
Monet, C. Monet by Himself. (R. Kendall, ed)
　J. Flam, 453(NYRB):17May90-9
　B. Thomson, 617(TLS):2-8Feb90-127
　442(NY):26Feb90-132
Monette, P. Afterlife.
　J. Viorst, 441:4Mar90-7
Monga, L. In the Very Heart of Man.
　C.D. Noble, 276:Autumn89-366
Mongrédien, G., ed. Comédies et pamphlets sur Molière.
　R. Guichemerre, 535(RHL):Jan-Feb89-100
　H.G. Hall, 208(FS):Oct89-466
Monk, P. Struggles with the Image.
　G. McGregor, 298:Fall89-146
Monk, R. Ludwig Wittgenstein.
　A.C. Danto, 617(TLS):19-25Oct90-1115
　A. Kenny, 441:30Dec90-9
Monna, A.D.A. Zwerftocht met middeleeuwse Heiligen.
　D. Nicholas, 589:Jul89-746
Monnerie, A. Le français au présent.
　E. McKee, 399(MLJ):Spring89-87

Monschein, Y. Der Zauber des Fuchsfee, Enstehung und Wandel eines "Femme-fatale"-Motivs in der chinesischen Literatur.
　W.H. Nienhauser, Jr., 116:Dec89-141
Montagné, G. Tu vois ce que je veux dire ...
　A.J.M. Prévos, 207(FR):Dec89-392
Montagu, J. Alessandro Algardi.*
　M.M. Estella, 48:Jul-Sep89-380
Montagu, J. Roman Baroque Sculpture.
　J. Connors, 453(NYRB):12Apr90-23
　N. Penny, 617(TLS):16-22Mar90-277
Montagu, M.W. Embassy to Constantinople. (C. Pick, ed)
　566:Spring90-214
Montague, J. Mount Eagle. The Figure in the Cave and Other Essays. (A. Quinn, ed)
　S. O'Brien, 617(TLS):27Apr-3May90-443
de Montaigne, M.E. Essais. (P. Villey, ed)
　M. Adam, 542:Oct-Dec89-596
Montalban, M.Z. The Angst-Ridden Executive.
　M. Stasio, 441:25Nov90-22
Montanari, E. La sezione linguistica del "Peri hermeneias" di Aristotele.* (Vol 1)
　M. Baratin, 555:Vol62Fasc2-382
Montandon, A., ed. E.T.A. Hoffmann et la musique.
　U. Weisstein, 52:Band24Heft3-315
Montaner, M.E. Guía para la lectura de "Cien años de soledad."*
　R.W. Fiddian, 402(MLR):Jan90-234
　K McNerney, 238:Mar90 155
de Montclos, J-M.P. - see under Pérouse de Montclos, J-M.
Montecino, M. Big Time.
　M. Pellecchia, 441:9Sep90-26
Montefiore, H. Christianity and Politics.
　E. Norman, 617(TLS):1-7Jun90-576
Montefiore, J. Feminism and Poetry.*
　R.B.D., 295(JML):Fall88/Winter89-256
Monteiro, G. Robert Frost and the New England Renaissance.
　J.T. Gage, 402(MLR):Jan90-162
　E.J. Ingebretsen, 27(AL):Dec89-704
Montell, W.L. Killings.*
　C. Joyner, 582(SFQ):Vol46No1-88
Montero, J. La controversia sobre las "anotaciones" herrerianas.
　R.M. Price, 86(BHS):Oct89-377
　J.L. Suárez García, 304(JHP):Autumn89-101
Montero, O. The Name Game.
　R. Ocasio, 238:Dec89-971
Montero Cartelle, E., ed & trans. Liber minor de coitu.
　H.R. Lemay, 589:Apr89-467
Montes, H. - see Neruda, P.
Montes Giraldo, J.J. Dialectología general e hispanoamericana.
　J.M. Lipski, 239:Fall89-271
Montes Huidobro, M. Exilio.
　G. Schmidhuber, 352(LATR):Spring90-172
Montes Huidobro, M. Persona.*
　P. Meléndez, 352(LATR):Spring90-161
Montgomery, L.M. Akin to Anne. (R. Wilmshurst, ed)
　E.R. Epperly, 102(CanL):Autumn-Winter89-165
Montgomery, L.M. The Selected Journals of L.M. Montgomery. (Vol 2) (M. Rubio & E. Waterston, eds)
　L. Boone, 102(CanL):Autumn-Winter89-163

Monti, N. Africa Then.
　　A.E. Coombes & S. Edwards, 59:Dec89–
　　510
Montias, J.M. Vermeer and His Milieu.*
　　L. Gowing, 617(TLS):16–22Feb90–159
Montigel, U. Der Körper im humoristischen
　　Roman.
　　A. Duţu, 52:Band24Heft2–216
　　A. Scott–Prelorentzos, 564:Nov89–348
Montoya Martínez, J. – see de Berceo, G.
de Montreuil, J. Opera. (Vol 3 ed by N.
　　Grévy–Pons, E. Ornato & G. Ouy; Vol 4 ed
　　by E. Ornato, G. Ouy & N. Pons)
　　J.R. Berrigan, 589:Oct89–981
Montupet, J. The Lacemaker.*
　　639(VQR):Summer89–92
Moody, T.W. & R.A.J. Hawkins, with M.
　　Moody – see Arnold–Forster, F.
Mookerjee, R.N. Art for Social Justice.
　　T.H. Towers, 395(MFS):Winter89–734
Moon, B. The Grapefruit Tree.
　　G. Cook, 198:Autumn89–115
Moon, B. Harvest.
　　K. Thompson, 150(DR):Winter88/89–526
Moon, B. Seeds.
　　B.H. Pell, 102(CanL):Spring89–165
Moon, J.D., ed. Responsibility, Rights and
　　Welfare.*
　　P.H. Werhane, 518:Oct89–250
　　D.Z., 185:Jan90–447
Moon, M. The Children's Book of Mary (Bel–
　　son) Elliot.*
　　J. Barr, 354:Mar89–75
Moon, M. John Harris's Books for Youth 1801–
　　1843.*
　　J. Barr, 354:Sep89–285
Moon, P. The British Conquest and Dominion
　　of India.*
　　R.E. Frykenberg, 637(VS):Summer90–652
Mooney, J.E. Maps, Globes, Atlases and
　　Geographies through the Year 1800.
　　B.B. McCorkle, 432(NEQ):Dec89–636
Mooney, T. Traffic and Laughter.
　　D. Glover, 441:16Dec90–9
Mooneyham, L.G. Romance, Language, and
　　Education in Jane Austen's Novels.
　　B. Roth, 594:Spring89–111
Moor, A. Architectural Glass.
　　139:Dec89/Jan90–68
Moor, R. Der Pfaffe mit der Schnur.
　　J. Köhler, 196:Band30Heft1/2–151
Moorcock, M. Casablanca.
　　W. Steiner, 617(TLS):23Feb–1Mar90–202
Moore, A.W. The Infinite.
　　R. Penrose, 617(TLS):26Oct–1Nov90–1155
Moore, B. The Color of Blood.*
　　K. McNeilly, 529(QQ):Autumn89–717
　　E. Mozejko, 102(CanL):Spring89–147
Moore, B. Lies of Silence.
　　J. Banville, 453(NYRB):6Dec90–22
　　S. Deane, 617(TLS):20–26Apr90–430
　　F. Prose, 441:2Sep90–1
Moore, C.N. The Maiden's Mirror.
　　M.R. Wade, 301(JEGP):Jul89–377
Moore, C.W., W.J. Mitchell & W. Turnbull, Jr.
　　The Poetics of Gardens.
　　D. Clarke, 47:Dec89–118
　　P. Davey, 46:May89–14
　　A.E. Monfried, 505:Jul89–103
Moore, D.D., ed. East European Jews in Two
　　Worlds.
　　R.S. Wistrich, 617(TLS):23–29Nov90–1261

Moore, E.H. Moated Sites in Early North East
　　Thailand.
　　D.J. Welch, 293(JASt):May89–437
Moore, G. George Moore on Parnassus.* (H.E.
　　Gerber, with O.M. Brack, Jr., eds)
　　W.E. Davis, 395(MFS):Winter89–794
　　J.W. Weaver, 177(ELT):Vol32No1–67
Moore, G., with J. Hyams. My Time at Tif–
　　fany's.
　　G. Lois, 441:2Dec90–45
Moore, G.E. The Early Essays.* (T. Regan,
　　ed)
　　N. Griffin, 556:Summer89–80
Moore, J.N. – see Elgar, E.
Moore, L. Like Life.
　　S. McCauley, 441:20May90–7
　　A. Vaux, 617(TLS):31Aug–6Sep90–917
Moore, M.B. & M.Z.P. Philippides. The Athe–
　　nian Agora.* (Vol 23)
　　A.W. Johnston, 303(JoHS):Vol109–267
Moore, R. Broken Ghosts.
　　D. O'Rourke, 102(CanL):Spring89–206
Moore, R.S. – see James, H.
Moore, S. William Gaddis.
　　T. LeClair, 395(MFS):Winter89–773
Moore, S.D. Literary Criticism and the
　　Gospels.
　　B. Horne, 617(TLS):6–12Jul90–737
Moore, T. The Style of Connectedness.*
　　S.B., 295(JML):Fall88/Winter89–398
　　B. Duyfhuizen, 454:Fall89–75
Moore, T., with J. Hillman – see Hillman, J.
Moore, W. Schrödinger.*
　　J. Bernstein, 442(NY):5Nov90–142
　　D. Teresi, 441:7Jan90–14
　　S. Toulmin, 453(NYRB):28Jun90–48
Moore–Blunt, J. – see Plato
Moores, P.M. Vallès: "L'Enfant."
　　C. Lloyd, 208(FS):Jan89–100
　　W. Redfern, 402(MLR):Apr90–451
Moormann, E.M. La pittura parietale romana
　　come fonte di conoscenza per la scultura
　　antica.
　　R. Ling, 123:Vol39No2–419
Moosa, M. The Maronites in History.
　　R.M. Haddad, 318(JAOS):Apr–Jun88–314
Moose, R. The Wreath Ribbon Quilt.
　　E.C. Lynskey, 577(SHR):Winter89–95
Moosmüller, S. Soziophonologische Variation
　　im gegenwärtigen Wiener Deutsch.
　　G. Lerchner, 682(ZPSK):Band42Heft4–540
Mora, J.F. – see under Ferrater Mora, J.
Morabito, R., ed. Griselda.
　　C. Lee, 379(MedR):Apr89–136
Moraga, C. Giving Up the Ghost.
　　S. Foster, 448:Vol27No3–160
Morales, A. Gramáticas en contacto.
　　J.M. Lope Blanch, 545(RPh):Nov89–322
Morales, A.L. & R. Morales – see under Levins
　　Morales, A. & R. Morales
Morales, H.L. – see under López Morales, H.
Morales, J.L.O. – see under Onieva Morales,
　　J.L.
Morales Folguera, J.M. La Málaga de los Bor–
　　bones.
　　W. Rincón García, 48:Jul–Sep89–381
Morán, J.M.M. – see under Martín Morán, J.M.
Moran, R. Life on the Rim.
　　G.S. Lensing, 580(SCR):Fall89–137
Morán de la Estrella, F. Cartapacio de Fran–
　　cisco Morán de la Estrella. (R.A. Di Franco,
　　J.J. Labrador Herraiz & C.A. Zorita, eds)
　　C. Maurer, 304(JHP):Winter89–158

Morand, P. New York.
  F-E. Dorenlot, 207(FR):Mar90-747
Morani, M. - see Nemesius of Emesa
Moravec, H. Mind Children.*
  R. Penrose, 453(NYRB):1Feb90-3
Moravia, A. The Voyeur.
  R. Hadas, 473(PR):Vol56No2-310
Morby, J.E. Dynasties of the World.
  C. Russell, 617(TLS):7-13Dec90-1314
Mörchen, H. Adorno und Heidegger.
  F. Dallmayr, 153:Fall-Winter89-82
Mordden, E. Medium Cool.
  P. Biskind, 441:7Oct90-41
Mordden, E. Opera Anecdotes.
  A.F.L.T., 412:May89-146
Mordecai, P. & B. Wilson, eds. Her True-True
Name.
  L. Doughty, 617(TLS):23Feb-1Mar90-203
More, H. The Immortality of the Soul. (A.
Jacob, ed)
  S. Hutton, 319:Jul90-453
More, T. In Defense of Humanism.* (D. Kin-
ney, ed)
  J.N. Wall, 541(RES):Feb89-117
Morea, P. Personality.
  D. Cohen, 617(TLS):3-9Aug90-832
Moreau, F. Six études de métrique.
  C. Scott, 208(FS):Jul89-365
Moreau, M. Amours à en mourir.
  J. Taylor, 532(RCF):Spring89-247
Moreda, S.L. - see under López Moreda, S.
Morel, N. L'homme aux rapts.
  A. Minazzoli, 98:Nov89-858
Morelli, G. - see Aleixandre, V.
Morency, P. Quand nous serons.
  J. Le Blanc, 102(CanL):Autumn-
  Winter89-268
Moreno de Alba, J.G. El español en América.
  J.M. Lipski, 239:Fall89-271
Moreno de Alba, J.G. Minucias del lenguaje.
  R. Rodríguez-Ponga, 548:Jul-Dec89-482
Moretti, F. The Way of the World.*
  J. Hardin, 221(GQ):Winter89-97
  T.L. Jeffers, 125:Winter89-207
  A.K. Wettlaufer, 147:Vol6No3-48
Morfey, W. Painting the Day.
  J.F. Codell, 637(VS):Spring90-499
Morgan, A.L. - see Stieglitz, A & A. Dove
Morgan, C.M. Redneck Liberal.
  J. Braeman, 106:Summer89-41
Morgan, E. The Descent of Woman. The
Aquatic Ape.
  S. Rose, 617(TLS):23Feb-1Mar90-204
Morgan, E. Themes on a Variation.*
  D. McDuff, 565:Spring89-76
Morgan, E.S. Inventing the People.
  S. Innes, 639(VQR):Autumn89-770
  D.S. Lutz, 656(WMQ):Jul89-596
Morgan, E.S. Parties.
  R. Schultz, 249(HudR):Spring89-155
  639(VQR):Winter89-28
Morgan, J. Godly Learning.*
  L.A. Cellucci, 568(SCN):Spring-
  Summer89-15
Morgan, J. & A. Richards. A Paradise out of a
Common Field.
  A. Urquhart, 617(TLS):10-16Aug90-857
Morgan, L. The Miniature Wall Paintings of
Thera.
  K.P. Foster, 124:Mar-Apr90-376
Morgan, M.L. Platonic Piety.
  A.W. Price, 617(TLS):26Oct-1Nov90-1156

Morgan, N. Early Gothic Manuscripts. (Vol 2)
  B.J. Davis, 377:Mar89-56
  C.M. Kaufmann, 39:Aug89-138
Morgan, P., comp. Shadow and Shine.
  K. Stewart, 71(ALS):May89-122
Morgan, R. At the Edge of the Orchard Coun-
try.*
  T. Kooser, 502(PrS):Summer89-126
Morgan, R. Women and Sexuality in the Nov-
els of Thomas Hardy.
  P.J. Casagrande, 268(IFR):Summer89-147
  A.M. Duckworth, 219(GaR):Fall89-616
  N. Page, 445(NCF):Mar90-571
  A. Sisson, 594:Summer89-211
  P. Widdowson, 637(VS):Winter90-368
  M. Williams, 447(N&Q):Dec89-536
Morgan, R., with J. Barton. Biblical Interpre-
tation.*
  A.D.H. Mayes, 235:Summer89-76
Morgan, S. Homeboy.
  D. Mason, 441:6May90-13
Morgan, S. My Place.*
  42(AR):Summer89-371
Morgan, T. Literary Outlaw.
  A. Ansen, 532(RCF):Spring89-240
  L.K. Pietschner, 27(AL):Dec89-710
Morgan, T. An Uncertain Hour.*
  T. Judt, 617(TLS):28Sep-4Oct90-1018
Morgan, T.A., J.F. Lee & B. Van Patten, eds.
Language and Language Use.
  T. Dvorak, 710:Dec89-480
Morgan, W. An American Icon.*
  T. Wortham, 445(NCF):Dec89-422
Morgan, W.N. Prehistoric Architecture in
Micronesia.
  M. Wortman, 45:Oct89-71
Morgenstern, C. Werke und Briefe. (Vol 1 ed
by M. Kiessig, Vol 5 ed by R. Habel, Vol 6
ed by H. Gumtau)
  R. Furness, 402(MLR):Oct90-1028
Morhange-Motchane, M. Thematic Guide to
Piano Literature.
  C. Timbrell, 510:Winter88/89-63
Morin, E. Penser l'Europe.
  J. Lambeth, 207(FR):Feb90-603
Morin, E., C. Lefort & C. Castoriadis. Mai 68.
  A.J.M. Prévos, 207(FR):Mar90-758
Morine, D.E. Good Dirt.
  M. Nichols, 441:25Nov90-11
Morisot, B. The Correspondence of Berthe
Morisot.* (D. Rouart, ed; newly ed by K.
Adler & T. Garb)
  N.M. Mathews, 662:Spring/Summer89-46
Morley, J., ed. Current Perspectives on Pro-
nunciation.*
  W. Acton, 710:Dec89-479
Morley, R. The Pleasures of Age.
  B. Levine, 441:10Jun90-46
Morley, S. Out in the Midday Sun.
  J.R. Taylor, 511:Mar89-45
Morley, W.F.E. Queen Anne Pamphlets.
  W.J. Cameron, 470:Vol27-131
Moro, G. - see Franco, N.
Morone, J.A. The Democratic Wish.
  A. Tonelson, 441:23Dec90-5
Morone, J.G. & E.J. Woodhouse. Averting
Catastrophe.
  D.G. Haglund, 529(QQ):Summer89-517
Morone, J.G. & E.J. Woodhouse. The Demise of
Nuclear Energy?*
  A.B. Stewart, 42(AR):Summer89-363
Morpurgo, J.E. Master of None.
  P. Parker, 617(TLS):20-26Apr90-416

Morrell, R.E. – see Mujū Ichien
Morres, P. Vallès: "L'Enfant."
  A. Lebugle, 446(NCFS):Fall–Winter89/90–
  273
Morrill, J., ed. Oliver Cromwell and the Eng-
lish Revolution.
  J. Miller, 617(TLS):14–20Dec90–1356
Morris, C.B., ed. "Cuando yo me muera ..."
  J. Crosbie, 402(MLR):Oct90–1005
Morris, C.R. The Coming Global Boom.
  A. Smith, 441:24Jun90–1
Morris, D. Animal Watching.
  D. Attenborough, 441:2Dec90–44
Morris, D. Thomas Hearne and His Landscape.
  G. Reynolds, 617(TLS):16–22Feb90–160
Morris, H. Last Things in Shakespeare.*
  J.A. Bryant, Jr., 569(SR):Summer89–445
Morris, I. Burial and Ancient Society.*
  R. Garland, 123:Vol39No1–66
Morris, I. Mr. Collins Considered.*
  M. Kirkham, 83:Autumn89–226
  D. Le Faye, 541(RES):May89–277
  J. Wiltshire, 97(CQ):Vol17No4–369
Morris, J. The Venetian Empire.
  C. Moorehead, 617(TLS):24–30Aug90–905
Morris, J. & P. Wakefield. Ireland.
  C. Thubron, 441:2Dec90–20
Morris, J.N. A Schedule of Benefits.
  M. Kinzie, 491:Jun89–151
Morris, M., ed. The Faber Book of Contempo-
rary Carribbean Short Stories.
  D. Dabydeen, 617(TLS):14–20Sep90–979
Morris, M. Nothing to Declare.
  S. Pickering, 569(SR):Spring89–297
Morris, M. The Waiting Room.*
  W. Brandmark, 617(TLS):27Apr–3May90–
  456
Morris, M.E. The Last Kamikaze.
  N. Callendar, 441:23Dec90–15
Morris, M.E. Sword of the Shaheen.
  N. Callendar, 441:14Jan90–23
Morris, M.M. Vanished.*
  G. Davenport, 569(SR):Summer89–468
Morris, R. The Edges of Science.
  D. Voss, 441:21Oct90–25
Morris, R.D. Composition with Pitch-Classes.
  J. Peel, 308:Fall89–400
  A. Whittall, 410(M&L):Feb89–134
Morris, R.J. Class, Sect and Party.
  H. Perkin, 617(TLS):14–20Sep90–969
Morris, T.V. Anselmian Explorations.
  B. Leftow, 258:Dec89–483
Morris, T.V. The Logic of God Incarnate.
  W.H. Austin, 449:Dec89–706
  A. Millar, 479(PhQ):Apr89–245
Morris, W. The Collected Letters of William
Morris. (Vol 1) (N. Kelvin, ed)
  G. Weales, 219(GaR):Spring89–203
Morris, W. The Collected Letters of William
Morris.* (Vol 2) (N. Kelvin, ed)
  W.E. Fredeman, 405(MP):Nov89–200
  G. Weales, 219(GaR):Spring89–203
Morris, W. William Morris by himself. (G.
Naylor, ed)
  139:Dec89/Jan90–68
Morris–Suzuki, T. Beyond Computopia.*
  M. Ivy, 293(JASt):Aug89–620
Morrison, D. Grape and Grain.
  B. Franks, 571(ScLJ):Spring89–38
Morrison, D.R. Bibliography of Editions,
Translations, and Commentary on Xeno-
phon's Socratic Writings, 1600–Present.
  G.H. Whitaker, 123:Vol39No2–387

Morrison, J.J. & C. Nelson, with others – see
Wing, D.
Morrison, K.F. "I am You."*
  D.B. King, 125:Spring89–312
Morrison, T. Beloved.*
  R. Hadas, 473(PR):Vol56No2–310
Morrison, T. – see Mee, M.
Morrissey, K. Batoche.
  S. Scobie, 376:Dec89–126
Morrow, B. Some Sunday.
  S. Moore, 532(RCF):Spring89–253
Morrow, J. Only Begotten Daughter.
  J. Butler, 441:18Mar90–8
Morrow, K.D. Greek Footwear and the Dating
of Sculpture.
  E.B. Harrison, 487:Autumn89–265
Morrow, N. Dreadful Games.
  J.J. Montelaro, 26(ALR):Winter90–78
Morse, D. American Romanticism.*
  K. Carabine, 447(N&Q):Mar89–132
Morse, E.W. Freshwater Saga.
  C.E.S. Franks, 529(QQ):Summer89–558
Morson, G.S., ed. Bakhtin.*
  F. Stockholder, 104(CASS):Spring–Win-
  ter88–502
Morson, G.S. Hidden in Plain View.*
  R.F. Gustafson, 550(RusR):Jan89–97
  C. Popkin, 104(CASS):Spring–Winter88–
  526
  A. Wijzenbroek, 204(FdL):Mar89–66
Morson, G.S., ed. Literature and History.*
  P. Seyffert, 104(CASS):Spring–Winter88–
  500
von Morstein, P. On Understanding Works of
Art.*
  W. Cooper, 154:Vol28No4–682
Mort, F. Dangerous Sexualities.
  C.C., 185:Jul90–924
  B. Haley, 637(VS):Winter90–330
Mort, G. Into the Ashes.
  I. McMillan, 493:Winter89/90–65
Mortier, R., J. Marchand & J. Renwick – see de
Voltaire, F.M.A.
Mortimer, J. Rumpole a la Carte.
  D.E. Westlake, 441:2Dec90–12
Mortimer, J. Summer's Lease.
  G. Krist, 249(HudR):Spring89–131
Mortimer, J. Titmuss Regained.
  R. Plunket, 441:29Apr90–9
  J.K.L. Walker, 617(TLS):9–15Mar90–257
  442(NY):4Jun90–102
Mortimer, M. Assia Djebar.
  A. Lippert, 207(FR):Oct89–175
Morton, B.N. & D.C. Spinelli. Beaumarchais.
  R. Niklaus, 208(FS):Oct89–469
Morton, C. The Merzbook.
  K. Jirgens, 102(CanL):Summer89–137
  E.D. Rutland, 529(QQ):Summer89–490
Mortzfeld, P. – see Szarota, E.M.
Moscovici, S. La machine à faire des dieux.
  J–M. Gabaude, 542:Oct–Dec89–644
Moseley, C. A Century of Emblems.
  O. Reynolds, 617(TLS):15–21Jun90–651
Moseley, C.W.R.D. Shakespeare's History
Plays.
  R. Knowles, 402(MLR):Apr90–409
Moser, C. Clyde Connell.
  S.V. Donaldson, 585(SoQ):Summer89–111
Moser, C.A., ed. The Russian Short Story.*
  R.J. Keys, 575(SEER):Jul89–462
Moser, M. Counterpoint.
  L. Wevers, 102(CanL):Spring89–181

Moses, S. Spuren der Schrift.
    S. Samples, 221(GQ):Spring89-266
Mosey, D. The Wisden Book of Captains on
    Tour.
    A.L. Le Quesne, 617(TLS):26Oct-1Nov90-
    1159
Mosher, S.W. China Misperceived.
    M.B. Young, 441:11Nov90-63
Moshi, L.J. Tuimarishe Kiswahilli Chetu.
    G.D. Little, 350:Mar90-201
Mosino, F. Glossario del calabrese antico
    (sec. XV).
    S. Luongo, 545(RPh):Nov89-310
    P. Zolli, 708:Vol12Fasc1-136
Mosino, F. Testi calabresi antichi (sec. xv).
    (A. Piromalli, ed)
    S. Luongo, 545(RPh):Nov89-310
Moskowitz, A.F. The Sculpture of Andrea and
    Nino Pisano.*
    B.M., 278(IS):Vol44-156
    D. Stott, 589:Apr89-468
Moskowitz, D. & J. Pheby - see "The Oxford-
    Duden Pictorial French and English Dictio-
    nary"
Mosley, W. Devil in a Blue Dress.
    M. Stasio, 441:5Aug90-29
    442(NY):17Sep90-110
Moss, A. & C. Holder. Improving Student
    Writing.
    A. Young, 126(CCC):Feb89-104
Moss, C. Elephant Memories.
    42(AR):Summer89-368
Moss, D. The Politics of Left-Wing Violence
    in Italy, 1969-1985.
    C. Duggan, 617(TLS):12-18Jan90-30
Moss, J., ed. Future Indicative.*
    F. Davey, 627(UTQ):Fall89-138
    G. McGregor, 298:Fall89-146
    S. Söderlind, 529(QQ):Autumn89-631
Moss, J. A Reader's Guide to the Canadian
    Novel. (2nd ed)
    529(QQ):Spring89-210
Moss, M.E. Benedetto Croce Reconsidered.
    E.G. Caserta, 276:Winter89-469
    V. Jones, 278(IS):Vol44-178
    C. Lyas, 89(BJA):Winter89-75
    J.R. Woodhouse, 402(MLR):Jan90-221
Moss, R. Shouting at the Crocodile.
    G.M. Gerhart, 441:30Dec90-10
Moss, R.W. The American Country House.
    M. Filler, 617(TLS):12-18Oct90-1091
    W. Rybczynski, 453(NYRB):20Dec90-24
Moss, S. The Intelligence of Clouds.*
    R.B. Shaw, 491:Aug89-285
Moss, T. Pyramid of Bone.
    639(VQR):Summer89-100
Mosse, G.L. Fallen Soldiers.
    I. Buruma, 453(NYRB):25Oct90-15
Mostovskaia, N.N. I.S. Turgenev i russkaia
    zhurnalistika 70-kh godov XIX veka.
    A. Pogorelskin, 550(RusR):Apr89-189
Moszynska, A. Abstract Art.
    R. Cardinal, 617(TLS):13-19Jul90-749
Mota, M. & P. Tiessen - see Noxon, G.
Mote, F.W. & D. Twitchett, eds. The Cam-
    bridge History of China. (Vol 7, Pt 1)
    C.O. Hucker, 293(JASt):Feb89-145
Motion, A. Natural Causes.*
    R. Pybus, 565:Winter88/89-67
Motion, A. The Pale Companion.*
    J. Mellors, 364:Oct/Nov89-133
Motley, W. The American Abraham.*
    J-M. Santraud, 189(EA):Oct-Dec89-493

Motojirō, A. - see under Akashi Motojirō
de Motolinia, T. Historia de los Indios de la
    Nueva España.* (G. Baudot, ed)
    D. Treece, 86(BHS):Jul89-310
Motrošilova, N.V., ed. Studien zur Geschichte
    der westlichen Philosophie.
    E. van der Zweerde, 687:Oct-Dec89-705
Motsch, W., ed. Satz, Text, sprachliche Hand-
    lung.
    W. Heinemann, 682(ZPSK):Band42Heft4-
    542
Motta, F.C. The Theatrical Writings of Fab-
    rizio Carini Motta.
    A. Aronson, 615(TJ):May89-257
Mouer, R. & Y. Sugimoto. Images of Japanese
    Society.
    M. Picone, 293(JASt):Nov89-873
Moughtin, J.C., ed. The Work of Z.R. Dmo-
    chowski.
    J.M. Vlach, 2(AfrA):Feb89-16
Mouliéras, A., ed & trans. Les Fourberies de
    Si Djeh'a.
    U. Marzolph, 196:Band30Heft1/2-153
Moulton, G.E., with T.W. Dunlay, eds. The
    Journals of the Lewis and Clark Expedi-
    tion.* (Vols 2-4)
    J.L. Allen, 656(WMQ):Jul89-630
Mouré, E. Furious.
    R. Labrie, 102(CanL):Autumn-Winter89-
    143
    R. Raglan, 526:Winter89-96
Moureau, F., ed. Les Presses grises.
    D.J. Adams, 402(MLR):Jul90-718
    D. Bourel, 531:Jul-Dec89-548
Mous, P.H.J., ed. The Southern Version of
    Cursor Mundi.* (Vol 4)
    C. Houswitschka, 201:Vol15-361
Moutote, D. Maîtres livres de notre temps.
    W.C. Putnam 3d, 207(FR):Dec89-380
Moutoussamy-Ashe, J. Viewfinders.
    J. Loughery, 662:Fall89/Winter90-49
Moutsopoulos, E.A. Les structures de l'imagi-
    naire dans la philosophie de Proclus.*
    M. Erler, 229:Band61Heft7-577
Mouzelis, N.P. Politics in the Semi-Periphery.
    G. Stokes, 575(SEER):Oct89-665
Mowl, T. & B. Earnshaw, John Wood *
    R. Adam, 46:May89-12
    C. Stevenson, 90:Sep89-656
Moyano Martin, D., ed. Handbook of Latin
    American Studies. (No. 48)
    P. Howard, 263(RIB):Vol39No1-75
Moyer, K. Tumbling.
    G. Krist, 249(HudR):Spring89-131
    M. Kuznets, 455:Jun89-69
Moyers, B. & others. Global Dumping Ground.
    R.H. Boyle, 441:25Nov90-14
Moyes, M.R. - see Rolle, R.
Moyes, P. Black Girl, White Girl.*
    P. Craig, 617(TLS):1-7Jun90-593
Moyle, R. Tongan Music.
    A.L. Kaeppler, 187:Spring/Summer89-354
Moynihan, D.P. On the Law of Nations.
    R. Rosenblatt, 441:26Aug90-1
    442(NY):10Dec90-160
Moyse-Faurie, C. & M-A. Néchérö-Jorédié.
    Dictionnaire Xârâcùù-Français (Nouvelle-
    Calédonie).
    R. Blust, 350:Mar90-201
Możejko, E., ed. Between Anxiety and Hope.
    J.R. Krzyżanowski, 104(CASS):Spring-
    Winter88-444
    G. Woodcock, 102(CanL):Spring89-183

Możejko, E., with B. Briker & P. Dalgård, eds.
Vasily Pavlovich Aksënov.*
   R.L. Chapple, 104(CASS):Spring–Winter88–488
Mozet, N. – see Sand, G.
Mozzarelli, C., ed. "Familia" del principe e famiglia aristocratica.
   G. Castelnuovo, 402(MLR):Jul90–754
Mrozek, S. Les distributions d'argent et de nourriture dans les villes italiennes du Haut–Empire romain.
   P. Garnsey, 313:Vol79–232
   P. Herz, 229:Band61Heft4–371
Msimang, C.T. Folktale Influence on the Zulu Novel.
   S. Schmidt, 196:Band30Heft1/2–154
Mück, H–D. – see Oswald von Wolkenstein
Muckenhaupt, M. Text und Bild.
   I. Pufahl, 350:Mar90–202
Muckle, J. A Guide in the Soviet Curriculum.
   J. Dunstan, 575(SEER):Jan89–159
Mudge, B.K. Sara Coleridge, A Victorian Daughter.*
   442(NY):19Feb90–112
Muela, J.G. – see under González Muela, J.
Mufson, S. Fighting Years.
   G. Wheatcroft, 441:25Nov90–10
Mugerauer, R. Heidegger's Language and Thinking.*
   B.E.B., 185:Jan90–454
   B. Baugh, 478(P&L):Oct89–416
Múgica, L.F. – see under Fernando Múgica; L.
Mühlhäusler, P. Pidgin & Creole Linguistics.*
   J.C. Clements, 710:Mar89–109
Mühlhäusler, P. & R. Harré. Pronouns and People.
   R. Hudson, 617(TLS):19–25Oct90–1118
Muir, E. Selected Prose.* (G.M. Brown, ed)
   S. Manning, 97(CQ):Vol18No4–401
Muir, E. The Truth of the Imagination.* (P.H. Butter, ed)
   H. Hewitt, 571(ScLJ):Winter89–26
Muir, F., ed. The Oxford Book of Humorous Prose.
   H. Jacobson, 617(TLS):8–14Jun90–605
Muir, K. Shakespeare.
   J.A. Bryant, Jr., 569(SR):Summer89–445
Mujica, B. Iberian Pastoral Characters.*
   J.A. Jones, 86(BHS):Apr89–175
Mujū Ichien. Sand & Pebbles (Shasekishū). (R.E. Morrell, ed & trans)
   R.J. Corless, 318(JAOS):Jan–Mar88–145
Mukand, J., ed. Sutured Words.*
   E.G. Olmstead, 456(NDQ):Winter89–233
Mukarovsky, H.G., ed. Leo Reinisch – Werk und Erbe.
   S. Brauner, 682(ZPSK):Band42Heft5–679
Mukerji, C. A Fragile Power.
   D. Kevles, 617(TLS):22–28Jun90–664
   D. Nelkin, 441:8Apr90–18
Mukherjee, A. The Gospel of Wealth in the American Novel.*
   P.R.J., 295(JML):Fall88/Winter89–247
   J. Tavernier–Courbin, 178:Jun89–237
Mukherjee, B. Jasmine.*
   S. Curtis, 617(TLS):27Apr–3May90–436
Mukherjee, B. The Middleman and Other Stories.*
   D. Durrant, 364:Oct/Nov89–129
   J. Harrison, 529(QQ):Autumn89–714

Mulcahy, R. Spanish Paintings in the National Gallery of Ireland.
   N.A. Mallory, 90:Feb89–158
   I. Mateo Gómez, 48:Oct–Dec89–480
Muldoon, P. Madoc.
   L. Mackinnon, 617(TLS):12–18Oct90–1105
Muldoon, P. Meeting the British.*
   C. Bedient, 472:Vol16No1–195
   J. Drexel, 434:Winter89–179
Muldoon, P. Selected Poems 1968–1986.*
   C. Bedient, 472:Vol16No1–195
Muldoon, P. – see Lord Byron
Mulhall, S. On Being in the World.
   D.E. Cooper, 617(TLS):23–29Nov90–1269
Mulholland, P.A. – see Middleton, T. & T. Dekker
Mullally, E. The Artist at Work.
   T. Hunt, 402(MLR):Oct90–947
Mullaly, E. Desperate Stages.*
   M. Blagrave, 108:Spring89–87
   M. Day, 102(CanL):Summer89–146
Mullan, J. Sentiment and Sociability.
   K.L. Cope, 594:Summer89–214
   D. Orchin, 223:Spring89–92
   A. Varney, 447(N&Q):Dec89–517
Mullaney, S. The Place of the Stage.*
   R.D. Abrahams, 292(JAF):Apr–Jun89–202
   D. Bevington, 405(MP):Feb90–295
   J. Drakakis, 551(RenQ):Autumn89–580
   E. Eldridge, 568(SCN):Spring–Summer89–17
   A. Leggatt, 529(QQ):Autumn89–711
   A. Thompson, 611(TN):Vol43No3–140
Mullen, E.J. & D.H. Darst. Sendas literarias: Hispano–América. (P.A. Evans, ed)
   J.B. McInnis, 399(MLJ):Spring89–99
Mullen, R. Anthony Trollope.
   R. Shannon, 617(TLS):31Aug–6Sep90–912
Müller, A.W. Praktisches Folgern und Selbstgestaltung nach Aristoteles.
   T. Frerking, 438:Winter89–111
Müller, B. Diccionario del español medieval. (fasc 1–3)
   W. Mettmann, 547(RF):Band101Heft2/3–302
Müller, C. Hans Holbein d.J. Zeichnungen aus dem Kupferstichkabinett der Öffentlichen Kunstsammlung Basel.
   C. Andersson, 90:Jun89–426
Muller, C. Langue française, linguistique quantitative, informatique.
   B. Cerquiglini, 545(RPh):Nov89–300
Müller, G. Jean Pauls Exzerpte.
   J.W. Smeed, 402(MLR):Apr90–509
Müller, H. Geschichte zwischen Kairos und Katastrophe.
   I.S. Immel, 221(GQ):Fall89–536
Muller, J.M. Rubens.*
   O. Millar, 617(TLS):30Mar–5Apr90–351
Muller, J.Z. The Other God that Failed.
   A.J. Hoover, 242:Vol10No5–618
Müller, K. Schlossgeschichten.*
   C. Kahrmann, 400(MLN):Apr89–742
Muller, K. – see Benya, R.
Müller, K. & I. Huber, eds. Zur Physiologie der bildenden Kunst.
   N. Lübbren, 662:Fall89/Winter90–42
Müller, K–D., ed. Bertolt Brecht.*
   A.C. Ulmer, 406:Spring89–137
Müller, L. Die kranke Seele und das Licht der Erkenntnis.
   A. Dumont, 654(WB):12/1989–2108

Muller, M. Trophies and Dead Things.
 M. Stasio, 441:4Nov90-30
Müller, R. Polis und Res publica.
 K. Christ, 229:Band61Heft3-245
Müller, U. & P. Wapnewski, eds. Richard Wag-
 ner Handbuch.*
 H.R. Vaget, 222(GR):Summer89-138
 I. Vetter, 417:Jan-Mar89-92
Müller-Funk, W., ed. Jahrmarkt der Gerech-
 tigkeit.
 W. Koepke, 221(GQ):Summer89-417
Müller-Glauser, C. - see Jungius, J.
Müller-Salget, K. - see Frisch, M.
Mullins, R.B. Pulling Leather. (J.E. Roush &
 L. Clayton, eds)
 R.A. Roripaugh, 649(WAL):Nov89-268
Mülsch, E-C. Zwischen Assimilation und Jüd-
 ischem Selbstverständnis.
 R. Lloyd, 402(MLR):Oct90-975
Mulvihill, J. Thomas Love Peacock.
 N.A. Joukovsky, 340(KSJ):Vol38-192
Mumtaz, K.K. Architecture in Pakistan.
 G.H.R. Tillotson, 617(TLS):10-16Aug90-
 856
Munck, J.L. The Kornilov Revolt.
 B. Pearce, 575(SEER):Jan89-147
Munday, A. & others. Sir Thomas More. (V.
 Gabrieli & G. Melchiori, eds)
 J.H. Jones, 617(TLS):26Oct-1Nov90-1161
Mundler, O. The Travel Diary of Otto Mund-
 ler. (B. Fredericksen & C. Dowd, eds)
 H. Brigstocke, 90:Sep89-658
Mundt, L. - see Lemnius, S.
"Mundus Foppensis (1691) [and] The Levellers
 (1745)."
 C. Thomas, 566:Autumn89-66
Mungello, D.E. Curious Land.*
 M. Détrie, 549(RLC):Jul-Sep89-387
Mungoshi, C. The Setting Sun and the Rolling
 World.*
 P. Benson, 363(LitR):Spring90-396
Munich, A.A. Andromeda's Chains.
 M. Warner, 617(TLS):9-15Mar90-244
Munich, A.A. - see "Browning Institute
 Studies"
Munich, A.A. & J. Maynard - see "Browning
 Institute Studies"
Munier, R. Contre l'image.
 L. Lurçat, 450(NRF):Jun89-108
Münk, H.J. Der Freiburger Moraltheologe Fer-
 dinand Geminian Wanker (1758-1824) und
 Immanuel Kant.
 L. Hauser, 342:Band80Heft4-488
Munné, J.C.Z. & J.M. Guitart - see under Zam-
 ora Munné, J.C. & J.M. Guitart
Muno, J. Jeu de rôles.
 L. Lazar, 207(FR):Dec89-409
Muñoz, D. & others, eds. Política de la pob-
 lación marginal.
 C. Boyle, 352(LATR):Fall89-158
Muñoz, E.M. Crazy Love.
 M.S. Arrington, Jr., 238:Dec89-984
Muñoz, E.M. El discurso utópico de la sex-
 ualidad en Manuel Puig.
 P. Bacarisse, 86(BHS):Jan89-117
 L. Kerr, 238:May89-311
 B. Torres Caballero, 240(HR):Summer89-
 405
Muñoz, F. El teatro regional de Yucatán.
 D.H. Frischmann, 352(LATR):Spring90-
 185
de Muñoz, M.B. - see under Bertrand de Muñ-
 oz, M.

Muñoz Garcia, A. Alberti de Saxonia Quaes-
 tiones in artem veterem.
 J. Biard, 192(EP):Apr-Jun89-250
Munro, A. The Folk Music Revival in Scot-
 land.
 L. Coates, 595(ScS):Vol29-95
Munro, A. Friend of My Youth.
 P. Craig, 617(TLS):19-25Oct90-1130
 B. Mukherjee, 441:18Mar90-1
 R. Towers, 453(NYRB):17May90-38
Munro, A. The Progress of Love.*
 B. Haviland, 473(PR):Vol56No1-151
Munro, J.S. Mademoiselle de Scudéry and the
 "Carte de Tendre."*
 E.T. Dubois, 535(RHL):Jul-Aug89-711
 I. Maclean, 208(FS):Jan89-83
Munter, R. A Dictionary of the Print Trade in
 Ireland, 1550-1775.*
 W.R. Eshelman, 87(BB):Jun89-142
Müntzer, T. The Collected Works of Thomas
 Müntzer. (P. Matheson, ed & trans)
 A. Hamilton, 617(TLS):14-20Sep90-983
Munz, P. Our Knowledge of the Growth of
 Knowledge.*
 J. Forge, 63:Sep89-359
"Muqarnas." (Vol 2) (O. Grabar, ed)
 N. Hanna, 318(JAOS):Jul-Sep88-490
Murakami, H. A Wild Sheep Chase.*
 J. Melville, 617(TLS):16-22Nov90-1233
Muramatsu Michio, Itô Mitsutoshi & Tsujinaka
 Yutaka. Sengo Nihon no atsuryoku dantai.
 G.D. Allinson, 293(JASt):May89-324
Murano, V., with W. Hoffer. Cop Hunter.
 D.J. Carroll, 441:14Oct90-51
Muraro, M. Venetian Villas.
 C. Kolb, 576:Sep89-285
Murase, M. Masterpieces of Japanese Screen
 Painting.
 E. Seidensticker, 441:16Dec90-26
Murat, M. Robert Desnos, les grands jours du
 poète.
 M. Davies, 402(MLR):Oct90-977
Murdoch, B. Fighting Songs and Warring
 Words.
 G. Ewart, 617(TLS):6-12Jul90-734
Murdoch, B. - see "Kudrun"
Murdoch, I. The Message to the Planet.*
 P-L. Adams, 61:Mar90-116
 A. Broyard, 441:4Feb90-3
Murfin, R.C., ed. Joseph Conrad, "Heart of
 Darkness."
 J. Halperin, 395(MFS):Winter89-786
 639(VQR):Autumn89-120
Murnaghan, S. Disguise and Recognition in
 the "Odyssey."*
 M.J. Alden, 303(JoHS):Vol109-211
 M. Lloyd, 235:Winter88-61
 W.C. Scott, 24:Summer89-339
Murphy, B. American Realism and American
 Drama, 1880-1940.*
 R.N.C., 295(JML):Fall88/Winter89-263
 G. Cologne-Brookes, 541(RES):Aug89-432
 T. D'haen, 179(ES):Apr89-187
 J. Fisher, 397(MD):Sep89-453
Murphy, B.A. Fortas.
 J.A. Stein, 31(ASch):Summer89-478
Murphy, D.J. - see Lady Gregory
Murphy, H. Murder Times Two.
 M. Stasio, 441:18Mar90-33
Murphy, J. & J. Hampton. Forgiveness and
 Mercy.
 G.W. Rainbolt, 185:Jan90-413

Murphy, J.G. & J.L. Coleman. Philosophy of Law. (rev)
T. Dare, 103:May90–189
Murphy, J.J. – see Quintilian
Murphy, K. Hector Berlioz and the Development of French Music Criticism.
K. Reeve, 309:Vol9No2/3–219
Murphy, M.C. Women Writers and Australia.
S. Sheridan, 71(ALS):May89–118
Murphy, O.T. Charles Gravier de Vergennes, Comte de Vergennes.
J.M.J. Rogister, 83:Spring89–82
Murphy, P., J. Williams & E. Dunning. Football on Trial.
M. Ford, 617(TLS):16–22Nov90–1239
Murphy, P.E. Triadic Mysticism.
S.B. Goodman, 318(JAOS):Apr–Jun88–330
Murphy, R. New Selected Poems.* The Mirror Wall.*
B. O'Donoghue, 493:Summer89–62
Murphy, R. Realism and Tinsel.*
T. Pulleine, 707:Summer89–212
Murphy, R. & R. Altman. Grammar in Use.
P.B. Nimmons, 399(MLJ):Winter89–501
Murphy, S. The Measure of Miranda.
G. Campbell, 529(QQ):Spring89–153
Murphy, T. After Tragedy.
U. Dantanus, 272(IUR):Spring89–180
Murray, B. Journey into Space.
D. King-Hele, 617(TLS):28Sep–4Oct90–1044
Murray, C. In Pursuit.
639(VQR):Summer89–96
Murray, I., ed. Oscar Wilde.
T. Eagleton, 617(TLS):2–8Feb90–124
Murray, I.H. Jonathan Edwards.
W.U. Solberg, 656(WMQ):Jan89–183
Murray, L. Michelangelo.
A. Hughes, 278(IS):Vol43–157
Murray, L.A. The Boys Who Stole the Funeral.
M. Imlah, 617(TLS):18–24May90–521
Murray, L.A. The Daylight Moon.*
R. Calder, 571(ScLJ):Spring89–45
M. Imlah, 617(TLS):18–24May90–521
Murray, M. Changelings.
B.K. Horvath, 532(RCF):Spring89–258
Murray, P. Marx's Theory of Scientific Knowledge.*
D. Little, 518:Jan89–29
Murray, R.W. Phonological Strength and Early Germanic Syllable Structure.
Seiichi Suzuki, 361:Nov89–252
Murray, S. Building Troyes Cathedral.*
V. Paul, 576:Jun89–184
Murray, S. Fetch Out No Shroud.
P. Craig, 617(TLS):23Feb–1Mar90–203
Murray, T. Theatrical Legitimation.*
M.G. Brennan, 447(N&Q):Jun89–239
J. Crewe, 551(RenQ):Winter89–888
H.W. Deutsch, 615(TJ):May89–253
E. Forman, 610:Summer89–196
P. Hyland, 568(SCN):Fall–Winter89–45
B. Norman, 475:Vol16No30–323
C. Perricone, 125:Winter89–204
Murray, W. The Getaway Blues.
M. Stasio, 441:26Aug90–26
Murry, J.M. Defending Romanticism. (M. Woodfield, ed)
M. Di Battista, 617(TLS):13–19Apr90–388
Murtagh, W.J. Keeping Time.
P. Chase-Harrell, 432(NEQ):Sep89–468
M.A. Tomlan, 576:Dec89–409

Murtha, T. Short Stories of Thomas Murtha. (W. Murtha, ed)
A. Weiss, 102(CanL):Autumn–Winter89–259
Murthy, S.L. The Novels of William Styron.
E. Carroll, 395(MFS):Winter89–761
Musgrave, M. The Music of Brahms.
D. Brodbeck, 310:Summer89–403
C. Schachter, 411:Mar/Jul89–187
Musgrave, S. The Dancing Chicken.
P. Demers, 102(CanL):Autumn–Winter89–184
Musgrove, J. – see Fletcher, B.
Musicant, I. The Banana Wars.
T. Rosenberg, 441:16Sep90–23
Musselwhite, D.E. Partings Welded Together.*
N. Bradbury, 541(RES):Aug89–425
M.W. Carpenter, 529(QQ):Spring89–178
Mustazza, L. "Such Prompt Eloquence."
R. Trubowitz, 568(SCN):Fall–Winter89–35
Musto, R.G. – see Petrarch
Mutahi, E.K. Sound Change and the Classification of the Dialects of Southern Mt. Kenya.
R. Leger, 685(ZDL):1/1989–128
Mutgé Vives, J. La ciudad de Barcelona durante el reinado de Alfonso el Benigno (1327–1336).
P. Freedman, 589:Oct89–1012
Muthmann, G. Rückläufiges deutsches Wörterbuch.* (H. Henne, H. Sitta & H.E. Wiegand, eds)
C.J. Wells, 402(MLR):Oct90–1012
Muybridge, E. & M. Klett. One City/Two Visions.
A. Grundberg, 441:2Dec90–71
Mwanzi, H. Notes on Leonard Kibera and Sam Kahiga's "Potent Ash."
C.P. Sarvan, 538(RAL):Spring89–129
Myer, V.G. Charlotte Brontë.
H. Glen, 402(MLR):Jan90–154
K.M. Hewitt, 447(N&Q):Jun89–250
M. Smith, 82:Vol19No7–324
Myerowitz, M. Ovid's Games of Love.
J. den Boeft, 394:Vol42fasc1/2–219
Myers, A.R. London in the Age of Chaucer.
R.H. Jones, 589:Oct89–1013
Myers, E. & G. Adamson, eds. Continental, Latin-American and Francophone Women Writers.
K. McKinney, 395(MFS):Summer89–361
M. Whitford, 208(FS):Jul89–370
Myers, G.E. William James.*
P. Carrive, 192(EP):Apr–Jun89–266
Myers, J. & M. Simms. Longman Dictionary and Handbook of Poetry.
B. Cottle, 541(RES):Aug89–398
E.G. Stanley, 447(N&Q):Jun89–213
Myers, K. The Catskills.
658:Spring89–110
Myers, L. When Life Falls It Falls Upside Down.
F.A. Koestler, 441:7Oct90–40
Myers, P. Deadly Crescendo.
N. Callendar, 441:18Nov90–41
Myers, P. Deadly Sonata.
N. Callendar, 441:25Feb90–35
Myers, R. & M. Harris, eds. Fakes and Frauds: Varieties of Deception in Print and Manuscript.
J.P. Feather, 617(TLS):27Apr–3May90–446

Myers, R. & M. Harris, eds. Pioneers in Bibliography.*
  J. Hewish, 354:Sep89-272
  517(PBSA):Sep89-405
Myers, S.H. The Bluestocking Circle.
  T. Castle, 617(TLS):14-20Dec90-1345
Myers, T. Walking Point.
  M.G. Porter, 27(AL):May89-327
Myers, W. Milton and Free Will.*
  W.E. Broman, 478(P&L):Apr89-179
Myerson, J. & D. Shealy, with M.B. Stern - see Alcott, L.M.
Mylius, K. Geschichte der Literatur im alten Indien.*
  H.W. Bodewitz, 259(IIJ):Oct89-300
Mylius, K. Mallanāga Vātsyāyana.
  J.M. Verpoorten, 259(IIJ):Apr89-160
Mynors, R.A.B. - see Vergil
Myres, J.N.L. The English Settlements.
  T. Hahn, 589:Jan89-191
Myron, M-R. & J. Smetana. Nouvelles Perspectives. (3rd ed)
  T. Scanlan, 207(FR):Apr90-899

Naar, J. Design for a Livable Planet.
  N. Wade, 441:22Apr90-1
Nabb, M. The Marshal and the Madwoman.*
  639(VQR):Spring89-59
Nabb, M. The Marshal's Own Case.
  M. Stasio, 441:5Aug90-29
Nabhan, G.P. Enduring Seeds.
  P. Wild, 456(NDQ):Spring89-219
Nabokov, P. & R. Easton. Native American Architecture.
  P.B. Jones, 46:Dec89-12
  M.J. Schneider, 456(NDQ):Spring89-208
Nabokov, V. Selected Letters, 1940-1977.*
  (D. Nabokov & M.J. Bruccoli, eds)
  Z. Zinik, 617(TLS):9-15Mar90-245
Nádas, P. Évkönyv.
  R. Aczel, 617(TLS):4-10May90-468
Nadel, A. Invisible Criticism.*
  R.B. Dandridge, 27(AL):Mar89-128
Nadel, I.B. Joyce and the Jews.
  J. Berman, 390:Dec89-57
  B. Cheyette, 617(TLS):5-11Jan90-17
  C.D. Lobner, 395(MFS):Winter89-801
  D. Manganiello, 329(JJQ):Fall89-152
Nadler, S.M. Arnauld and the Cartesian Philosophy of Ideas.*
  Z. Janowski, 543:Mar90-643
Nadolny, S. Selim oder Die Gabe der Rede.
  J.J. White, 617(TLS):5-11Oct90-1073
Naess, H. & J. McFarlane - see Hamsun, K.
Nagarajan, S. & S. Vishwanathan, eds. Shakespeare in India.*
  J. Singh, 615(TJ):Mar89-113
Nagel, J. & H.S. Villard. Hemingway in Love and War.
  A. De Fazio 3d, 234:Spring90-182
Nagel, T. The View from Nowhere.*
  S. Bernecker, 687:Apr-Jun89-399
  C. Peacocke, 482(PhR):Jan89-65
Nagel, T. What Does It All Mean?*
  G. Bourne, 518:Apr89-91
Nägele, R. Reading After Freud.*
  W. Goetschel, 221(GQ):Winter89-98
  A.A. Kuzniar, 564:Feb89-64
Nagibin, Y. Arise and Walk.
  L. Chamberlain, 617(TLS):14-20Dec90-1359

Nagibin, Y. The Peak of Success and Other Stories. (H. Goscilo, ed)
  R.N. Porter, 558(RLJ):Spring-Fall89-286
Nagl-Docekal, H. & H. Vetter, eds. Todes des Subjekts?
  T. Bettendorf, 687:Apr-Jun89-390
Nagy, A.N. Between.
  D. O'Driscoll, 493:Summer89-47
Naharro, B.D. - see under de Torres Naharro, B.
Nahaylo, B. & V. Swoboda. Soviet Disunion.
  N. Lubin, 441:15Jul90-16
Nahm, A.C. Korea.
  J.B. Duncan, 293(JASt):Nov89-892
Naifeh, S. & G.W. Smith. The Mormon Murders.*
  D. Johnson, 453(NYRB):15Mar90-28
Naifeh, S. & G.W. Smith. Jackson Pollock.
  E. Frank, 441:28Jan90-3
  H. Kramer, 617(TLS):16-22Mar90-287
Naipaul, V.S. The Enigma of Arrival.*
  J. Piedra, 153:Spring89-34
Naipaul, V.S. India.
  J.T. Hospital, 441:30Dec90-1
  F. Kanga, 617(TLS):5-11Oct90-1059
Naipaul, V.S. A Turn in the South.*
  C.J. Fox, 364:Jun/Jul89-126
  B. Griffith, 249(HudR):Autumn89-523
  R. King, 598(SoR):Winter90-236
  G. Oldham, 42(AR):Spring89-247
  639(VQR):Autumn89-132
Naisbitt, J. & P. Aburdene. Megatrends 2000.
  J. Fallows, 61:Jul90-97
  S. Loe, 441:7Jan90-20
Najita, T. Visions of Virtue in Tokugawa Japan.*
  R.B. Minear, 244(HJAS):Jun89-259
Nakagawa, H., ed. Diderot: Le XVIIIe siècle en Europe et au Japon.
  D.F. Connon, 242:Vol10No6-748
  J.P. Seguin, 530:Apr89-162
Nakai, K.W. Shogunal Politics.
  H. Bolitho, 407(MN):Autumn89-354
  P. Nosco, 293(JASt):May89-399
Nakamura, H. Indian Buddhism.
  C. Hallisey, 293(JASt):Aug89-661
Nakamura, J., ed. Writers for Young Adults. (3rd ed)
  A. Hildebrand, 87(BB):Dec89-257
Nakano Minoru, ed. Nihon-gata seisaku kettei no hen'yō.
  G.D. Allinson, 293(JASt):May89-324
Nakayama, C. Behind the Waterfall.
  J. Banerjee, 617(TLS):14-20Dec90-1360
  D. Plante, 441:3Jun90-29
Nakhimovsky, A.D. & R.L. Leed. Advanced Russian.* (2nd ed)
  W.V. Tuman, 399(MLJ):Spring89-96
Nalewski, H. - see George, S.
Namenwirth, S.M. Gustav Mahler.
  J. Williamson, 410(M&L):May89-269
Namjoshi, S. Because of India. The Mothers of Maya Diip. Feminist Fables.
  K. Jamie, 617(TLS):14-20Sep90-978
Nance, J.J. Final Approach.
  E. Weiner, 441:4Nov90-24
Nanda, B.R. Gandhi.
  R. Nayar, 617(TLS):8-14Jun90-603
Napier, E.R. The Failure of Gothic.*
  R. Beecham, 541(RES):Aug89-423
  W.L. Jones, 179(ES):Apr89-184
  I. Weber, 38:Band107Heft1/2-231
  D. Worrall, 83:Spring89-107

Napoli, D.J. Predication Theory.
   S. Rothstein, 350:Sep90-598
Naquin, S. & E.S. Rawski. Chinese Society in the Eighteenth Century.*
   P. Duara, 244(HJAS):Jun89-241
Narayan, R.K. The World of Nagaraj.
   J. Moynahan, 441:15Jul90-8
   W. Walsh, 617(TLS):23-29Mar90-328
   442(NY):27Aug90-94
Narayanan, V. The Way and the Goal.
   T.K. Stewart, 293(JASt):Nov89-907
Nardelli, F.P. - see under Petrucci Nardelli, F.
Nardin, J. He Knew She Was Right.*
   R.C. Terry, 637(VS):Summer90-659
Narogin, M. Doin Wildcat.
   H. Dakin, 581:Jun89-260
Narten, J. Der Yasna Haptanhāiti.
   H. Schmeja, 259(IIJ):Apr89-152
Narveson, J. The Libertarian Idea.
   R.G. Frey, 103:Nov90-455
   D. Herzog, 144:Winter-Spring90-74
   E. Mack, 185:Jan90-419
Nasar, J.L., ed. Environmental Aesthetics.
   P. Dickens, 89(BJA):Summer89-270
   B. Russell, 46:Mar89-12
Nascimbeni, G. Montale.
   J.R. Woodhouse, 402(MLR):Jul90-756
Nash, C. The Dinosaurs Ball.
   P. Reading, 617(TLS):6-12Jul90-732
Nash, C. World-Games.
   P.R.J., 295(JML):Fall88/Winter89-248
   M. Yong, 677(YES):Vol20-363
Nash, G.B. Forging Freedom.
   W.E. Martin, Jr., 656(WMQ):Jul89-589
Nash, O. Loving Letters from Ogden Nash.
   (L.N. Smith, ed)
   R. Kelly, 441:11Feb90-7
Nash, R. - see Tasso, T.
Nash, R.F. The Rights of Nature.*
   J.B.C., 185:Jan90-462
Nash, S. Paul Valery's "Album de vers anciens."
   R. Chambers, 546(RR):Jan89-153
Nash, W. English Usage.
   R. Sampson, 179(ES):Oct89-460
Naslund, S.J. Ice Skating at the North Pole.
   E. Lesser, 434:Autumn89-98
Nasr, S.H. - see Schuon, F.
Nater, H.F. The Bella Coola Language.
   B. Galloway, 269(IJAL):Jan89-97
Nath, P., ed. Fresh Reflections on Samuel Johnson.*
   A. Pailler, 189(EA):Oct-Dec89-475
Nathan, I. & Lord Byron. A Selection of Hebrew Melodies, Ancient and Modern by Isaac Nathan and Lord Byron. (F. Burwick & P. Douglass, eds)
   R. Siemens, 661(WC):Autumn89-204
Nathan, K.S. & M. Pathmanathan, eds. Trilateralism in Asia.
   T. Ozawa, 293(JASt):May89-338
Nathan, R.B. Katherine Mansfield.
   A. Smith, 402(MLR):Apr90-426
Natoli, J., ed. Literary Theory's Future(s).
   J.R. Bennett, 599:Spring90-126
   L. Sage, 617(TLS):18-24May90-523
Natoli, J., ed. Tracing Literary Theory.*
   J.R. Bennett, 599:Spring90-126
   K.Z. Moore, 295(JML):Fall88/Winter89-233

Nattiez, J-J. Proust as Musician.*
   C. Ayrey, 415:Sep89-544
   P. Newman-Gordon, 207(FR):May90-1069
Nattiez, J-J. - see Boulez, P.
Nau, H.R. The Myth of America's Decline.
   P. Kennedy, 453(NYRB):28Jun90-31
   R. Kuttner, 617(TLS):16-22Nov90-1226
Naudé, G. Lettres de Naudé à Grémonville.* (K.W. & P.J. Wolfe, eds)
   R. Zuber, 535(RHL):Mar-Apr89-275
Naughton, J.T. - see Bonnefoy, Y.
Naumann, B. Einführung in die Wortbildungslehre des Deutschen. (2nd ed)
   U. Püschel, 685(ZDL):3/1989-353
Naumann, B. Grammatik der deutschen Sprache zwischen 1781 und 1856.* (W. Binder & others, eds)
   R. Bergmann & C. Moulin, 680(ZDP):Band108Heft3-458
Naumann, M., ed. Die Geschichte ist offen.
   P. Graves, 617(TLS):15-21Jun90-631
Naumann, M., ed. Lexikon der französischen Literatur.
   K. Schnelle, 654(WB):8/1989-1393
Naumann, U. Charlotte von Kalb.
   S.L. Cocalis, 406:Summer89-230
Naumoff, L. Rootie Kazootie.
   R. Daniell, 441:11Mar90-28
   442(NY):21May90-95
Navajas, G. Mimesis y cultura en la ficción.*
   J. Labanyi, 86(BHS):Jul89-289
Navajas, G. Teoría y práctica de la novela española posmoderna.
   C. Alborg, 240(HR):Summer89-399
   D.K. Herzberger, 238:Sep89-552
Navarre, Y. Louise.
   R.A. Kingcaid, 532(RCF):Fall89-220
Navarro, A. & J. Ribalta - see Valera, J.
Naylor, G. - see Morris, W.
Nead, L. Myths of Sexuality.
   S.P. Casteras, 662:Fall89/Winter90-35
   J.A. Kestner, 620(TSWL):Spring89-135
   M. Pointon, 59:Mar89-115
Neaderland, L. Missing Persons.
   G. Gessert, 448:Vol27No3-132
Neaderland, L. - see "ISCA Quarterly 3rd Annual Bookworks Edition"
Neal, B. Biscuits, Spoonbread, and Sweet Potato Pie.
   R. Flaste, 441:10Jun90-12
Near, H., with D. Richardson. Fire in the Rain ... Singer in the Storm.
   M. Mifflin, 441:5Aug90-10
Neary, I. Political Protest and Social Control in Pre-war Japan.
   Kojita Yasunao, 285(JapQ):Oct-Dec89-459
Nebbiai-Dalla Guarda, D. La bibliothèque de l'abbaye de Saint-Denis en France du IXe au XVIIIe siècle.
   D. Williman, 589:Jan89-194
Needham, J., with others. Science and Civilisation in China. (Vol 5, Pt 7)
   F. Kierman, 318(JAOS):Oct-Dec88-647
Needham, P. The Printer and the Pardoner.
   A.S.G. Edwards, 517(PBSA):Mar89-103
Needham, R. Mamboru.
   D. Hicks, 293(JASt):Feb89-228
Neef, A. Mühsal ein Leben lang.
   H.M. Nickel, 654(WB):8/1989-1404
Neeft, C.W. Protocorinthian Subgeometric Aryballoi.
   A. Johnston, 123:Vol39No1-112

Neel, J. Plato, Derrida and Writing.
  D.R. Lachterman, 480(P&R):Vol22No4–310
  C. Moran, 126(CCC):May89–234
Nees, L. The Gundohinus Gospels.
  G. Henderson, 589:Apr89–471
Negri, S. The Other Side of Now.
  D. Chorlton, 496:Winter89/90–43
Neher, A. Faust et le Maharal de Prague.*
  R.Y. Dufour, 192(EP):Jan–Mar89–108
Nehls, D., ed. Interlanguage Studies.
  J. John, 257(IRAL):Feb89–67
Neill, P., ed. Maritime America.
  A. Witty, 658:Winter89–273
Neill, W. Making Tracks.
  R. Calder, 571(ScLJ):Spring89–57
  B. Turner, 493:Summer89–57
Neils, J. The Youthful Deeds of Theseus.
  K. Hitzl, 229:Band61Heft2–148
Nekvapil, J. & O. Šoltys, eds. Teoretické
  otázky jazykovědy.
  D. Short, 575(SEER):Jan89–165
Nelde, P.H., ed-in-chief. Wortatlas der deut-
  schen Umgangssprachen in Belgien.
  D. Karch, 133:Band22Heft3/4–386
Nelken, H. Pamiętnik z getta w Krakowie.
  J. Maurer, 497(PolR):Vol34No2–190
Nellen, K. & J. Němec – see Patočka, J.
Nellen, K. & I. Srubar – see Patočka, J.
Nelms, B.F., ed. Literature in the Classroom.
  A.R. Gere, 128(CE):Oct89–617
Nelson, B. Workers on the Waterfront.*
  A. Brinkley, 453(NYRB):28Jun90–16
Nelson, C. & E. Folsom, eds. W.S. Merwin.*
  S.A.S., 295(JML): Fall88/Winter89–000
Nelson, C. & L. Grossberg, eds. Marxism and
  the Interpretation of Culture.*
  T.B., 395(MFS):Summer89–367
  M.F., 185:Jul90–917
Nelson, C. & M. Seccombe, comps. British
  Newspapers and Periodicals 1641–1700.*
  J. Feather, 447(N&Q):Sep89–396
  M. Harris, 354:Dec89–378
  S.E. Noble, 566:Spring90–227
Nelson, J.G. Elkin Mathews.
  J. Sutherland, 617(TLS):27Apr–3May90–
  442
Nelson, J.S., A. Megill & D.N. McCloskey, eds.
  Language and Argument in Scholarship and
  Public Affairs.
  C.C. Arnold, 480(P&R):Vol22No2–151
Nelson, J.S., A. Megill & D.N. McCloskey, eds.
  The Rhetoric of the Human Sciences.
  C.R. Miller, 544:Winter89–101
Nelson, K. The Art of Reciting the Qu'ran.*
  R.B. Qureshi, 187:Fall89–523
Nelson, K., ed. Narratives from the Crib.
  J.S. Falk, 350:Sep90–558
Nelson, K.E. & A. van Kleeck, eds. Children's
  Language. (Vol 6)
  A.G. Walker, 350:Mar90–203
Nelson, L., Jr. – see Cavalcanti, G.
Nelson, P.D. William Alexander, Lord Stirling.
  G.A. Billias, 656(WMQ):Jul89–621
Nelson, R.J. Willa Cather and France.*
  M. Doane, 649(WAL):May89–89
  J.W. Hall, 594:Summer89–217
  A. Romines, 27(AL):Mar89–119
  D. Stineback, 106:Fall89–219
Nelson, R.J. The Logic of Mind. (2nd ed)
  S.N. Thomas, 543:Mar90–644
Nelson, R.L. Partners with Power.
  L.T. Perera, 432(NEQ):Sep89–453

Nelson, W., with B. Shrake. Willie.*
  R. Dwyer, 649(WAL):Aug89–184
Nemerov, H. The Oak in the Acorn.*
  J.A. Hiddleston, 447(N&Q):Jun89–280
  J.M.M., 295(JML):Fall88/Winter89–396
Nemerov, H. War Stories.*
  L. Goldstein, 385(MQR):Summer90–472
Nemesius of Emesa. Nemesius, "De Natura
  Hominis." (M. Morani, ed)
  A. Meredith, 123:Vol39No1–39
Nemetz, P.N., ed. The Pacific Rim.
  T. Ozawa, 293(JASt):May89–338
Nemoianu, V. A Theory of the Secondary.*
  M.I. Spariosu, 400(MLN):Dec89–1195
Nenola, A. Miessydäminen nainen – naisnäk-
  ökulmia kulttuuriin.
  S. Knuuttila, 64(Arv):Vol44–208
"Neo-Confucian Terms Explained." (W-T.
  Chan, trans)
  C. Hansen, 485(PE&W):Apr89–203
Neog, M. Early History of the Vaiṣṇava Faith
  and Movement in Assam.
  T.K. Stewart, 318(JAOS):Apr–Jun88–334
Nepo, M. Fire without Witness.
  639(VQR):Summer89–99
Nepveu, P. L'Ecologie du réel.
  N.B. Bishop, 627(UTQ):Fall89–213
Néraudau, J-P. L'Olympe du Roi-Soleil.
  F. Assaf, 475:Vol16No30–326
Nerdinger, W. Theodor Fischer.
  P.B. Jones, 46:May89–12
Nerdinger, W. & F. Zimmermann. Die Archi-
  tekturzeichnung.
  R.M., 90:Feb89–161
Nersessian, V. Armenian Illuminated Gospel-
  Books.
  M. Wenzel, 39:Apr89–292
Neruda, P. Selected Poems. (N. Tarn, ed)
  S. O'Brien, 493:Summer89–44
Neruda, P. Veinte poemas de amor y una
  canción desesperada. (H. Montes, ed)
  C. Perriam, 402(MLR):Jan90–234
de Nerval, G. Oeuvres Complètes. (Vol 1) (J.
  Guillaume & C. Pichois, eds)
  R. Sieburth, 617(TLS):17–23Aug90–869
Nesfield, W.E. A Deuce of an Uproar.
  A. Symondson, 46:Nov89–14
Nesfield-Cookson, B. William Blake.
  A. Lincoln, 541(RES):Feb89–128
Nespor, M. & I. Vogel. Prosodic Phonology.*
  S.H. Weinberger, 710:Mar89–114
Nespoulous-Neuville, J. Léopold Sédar Sen-
  ghor.
  C.L. Dehon, 207(FR):Feb90–559
  J. Spleth, 538(RAL):Fall89–523
Nestorova, T. American Missionaries among
  the Bulgarians (1858–1912).
  R.J. Crampton, 575(SEER):Apr89–309
Nettelbeck, C.W., ed. War and Identity.
  K. Chadwick, 208(FS):Apr89–233
  R. Davison, 402(MLR):Apr90–459
Nettels, E. Language, Race, and Social Class
  in Howells's America.*
  A. Delbanco, 445(NCF):Jun89–112
  R. Kephart, 392:Spring89–211
  A.F. Stein, 401(MLQ):Mar88–80
  T.H. Towers, 395(MFS):Winter89–734
Netter, F.H. Atlas of Human Anatomy.
  L.K. Altman, 441:13May90–14
Nettl, B. The Study of Ethnomusicology.
  N.A. Jairazbhoy, 317:Fall89–625

Nettl, B., with others. The Radif of Persian Music.
  M. Caton, 187:Spring/Summer89-349
Neubauer, J. The Emancipation of Music from Language.*
  R. Monelle, 131(CL):Winter89-104
  C. Stanger, 678(YCGL):No36-193
Neuhart, J., M. Neuhart & R. Eames. Eames Design.
  C. Frayling, 617(TLS):16-22Mar90-292
  R. Leigh, 324:May90-438
Neuman, S. & S. Kamboureli, eds. A Mazing Space.*
  R.E. Davies, 105:Fall/Winter89-66
  C.A. Howells, 102(CanL):Spring89-177
  G. McGregor, 298:Fall89-146
Neuman, S. & I.B. Nadel, eds. Gertrude Stein and the Making of Literature.
  M. Hoffman, 395(MFS):Summer89-279
Neumann, D. Objects and Spaces.
  M.E. Winters, 350:Mar90-205
Neumann, D. Studentinnen aus dem Russischen Reich in der Schweiz.
  J.J. Tomiak, 550(RusR):Apr89-190
Neumann, F. Ornamentation and Improvisation in Mozart.*
  A. Newman, 414(MusQ):Vol74No4-623
Neumann, W. & B. Techtmeier, eds. Bedeutungen und Ideen in Sprachen und Texten.
  T. Schippan, 682(ZPSK):Band42Heft4-530
Neumeyer, D. The Music of Paul Hindemith.*
  C.M. Joseph, 308:Fall89-417
Neuner, G. & others. Deutsch aktiv Neu.
  B. Lewis, 399(MLJ):Winter89-516
Neuschäfer, B. Origenes als Philologe.
  N.G. Wilson, 123:Vol39No1-136
Neuschel, K.B. Word of Honor.
  639(VQR):Autumn89-116
Neutsch, E. Claus und Claudia.
  R. Bernhardt, 654(WB):10/1989-1704
Neve, C. Unquiet Landscape.
  M. James, 617(TLS):12-18Oct90-1102
Nevill, T. – see Stockhausen, K.
Neville, R.C. The Puritan Smile.*
  J. Berthrong, 485(PE&W):Apr89-212
Nevo, R. Shakespeare's Other Language.
  J. Drakakis, 447(N&Q):Jun89-231
New, M., ed. Approaches to Teaching Sterne's "Tristram Shandy."
  J. Stedmond, 166:Jul90-354
New, W.H., ed. Dictionary of Literary Biography. (Vol 68)
  S. Latham, 470:Vol27-104
New, W.H. Dreams of Speech and Violence.*
  H. Tiffin, 102(CanL):Summer89-131
New, W.H. A History of Canadian Literature.
  P. Easingwood, 402(MLR):Oct90-941
"New Chatto Poets Number Two."
  D. Kennedy, 493:Autumn89-48
"The New Czech Poetry." (E. Osers, trans)
  D. O'Driscoll, 493:Summer89-47
"The New Testament in Greek." (Vol 3: The Gospel according to St. Luke. [Pt 2])
  J.N. Birdsall, 123:Vol39No2-198
"The New York Public Library Desk Reference."
  E. Lucaire, 441:13May90-17
Newall, C. The Art of Lord Leighton.
  C. Mullen, 617(TLS):7-13Sep90-947
Newall, C. Victorian Watercolours.
  L. Lambourne, 39:Apr89-292
Newbury, C. The Diamond Ring.
  R. Oliver, 617(TLS):16-22Feb90-174

Newby, E. What the Traveller Saw.
  A. Youngman, 441:15Apr90-15
Newby, I.A. Plain Folk in the New South.
  639(VQR):Autumn89-115
Newby, L. Sino-Japanese Relations.
  W.E. Sharp, Jr., 293(JASt):Nov89-834
Newdigate, B.H. Book Production Notes.
  517(PBSA):Mar89-125
Newell, R.H. Objectivity, Empiricism and Truth.
  P.A. Roth, 488:Jun89-244
Newhouse, J. War and Peace in the Nuclear Age.*
  42(AR):Summer89-369
Newkirk, T., ed. Only Connect.
  N.R. Comley, 128(CE):Feb89-192
Newman, B. Barnett Newman: Selected Writings and Interviews. (J.P. O'Neill, ed)
  J. Russell, 441:2Dec90-9
Newman, B. & I.O. Evans, eds. Anthology of Armageddon.
  C.J. Fox, 617(TLS):16-22Feb90-178
Newman, G. The Rise of English Nationalism.*
  D. Jarrett, 83:Autumn89-219
Newman, J. The Journalist in Plato's Cave.
  C. Meyers, 103:Nov90-458
Newman, J. John Updike.
  R.M. Luscher, 27(AL):May89-325
  W.R. Macnaughton, 587(SAF):Spring89-124
  W.T.S., 395(MFS):Winter89-771
Newman, J.H. The "Via Media" of the Anglican Church. (H.D. Weidner, ed) John Henry Newman: Prayers, Poems, Meditations. (A.N. Wilson, ed)
  B. Martin, 617(TLS):7-13Dec90-1330
Newman, J.K. The Classical Epic Tradition.*
  M. Murrin, 122:Apr89-172
  C. Schaar, 597(SN):Vol61No1-117
Newman, K. The Night Mayor.
  C. Greenland, 617(TLS):23Feb-1Mar90-202
  G. Jonas, 441:21Oct90-35
Newman, L.F., ed. Hunger in History.
  D. Arnold, 617(TLS):17-23Aug90-878
Newman, L.M. – see Craig, E.G.
Newman, R.D. Understanding Thomas Pynchon.*
  B. Duyfhuizen, 454:Fall89-75
Newman, R.D. & W. Thornton, eds. Joyce's "Ulysses."*
  J.J.M., 295(JML):Fall88/Winter89-359
  L. Milesi, 395(MFS):Summer89-323
Newman, R.M. An English-Hausa Dictionary.
  W. Burgess, 617(TLS):27Apr-3May90-451
Newman, W.S. Beethoven on Beethoven.
  W. Rothstein, 415:Jul89-406
Newmark, K., ed. Phantom Proxies.
  C.D. Minahen, 446(NCFS):Spring-Summer90-577
Newmeyer, F.J., ed. Linguistics.* (Vols 1-3) [entry in prev was of Vols 1-4]
  K. Bardovi-Harlig, 710:Dec89-474
Newmeyer, F.J. The Politics of Linguistics.*
  L.G. Kelly, 320(CJL):Mar89-111
  T.J. Taylor, 350:Mar90-159
Newnham, R. About Chinese. (rev)
  D. Barnes, 399(MLJ):Winter89-494
Newsom, R. A Likely Story.
  B.A. Boehm, 395(MFS):Summer89-376
  G. Currie, 290(JAAC):Summer89-297
Newsom, V. Midnight Snow.
  S. Lee, 581:Jun89-249

Newson, J. & H. Buchbinder. The University Means Business.
M. Abbott, 529(QQ):Winter89–947
Newton, J.L. Women, Power, and Subversion.
D. Elam, 454:Winter90–212
Newton, K.M., ed. Twentieth-Century Literary Theory.
P. Kitson, 447(N&Q):Dec89–554
Newton, M. Hunting Humans.
B. Gewen, 441:13May90–16
Newton, R. Diane Wakoski.
R.J. Bertholf, 470:Vol27–139
Newton, S.M. The Dress of the Venetians 1495–1525.
L. von Wilckens, 683:Band52Heft4–573
Newton-Smith, W.H. The Rationality of Science.
C. Mitcham, 438:Winter89–106
Ng, M–S. The Russian Hero in Modern Chinese Fiction.
M. Anderson, 293(JASt):May89–370
Ngo Kim Chung & Nguyen Duc Nghinh. Propriété privée et propriété collective dans l'ancien Vietnam.
T.B. Lam, 293(JASt):Feb89–229
Ng'ombe, J. Sugarcane with Salt.
S. French, 617(TLS):14–20Sep90–980
Nguyen Ngoc Huy & Ta Van Tai. The Le Code.
A. Woodside, 293(JASt):Feb89–231
Niall, B. Martin Boyd.
S. McKernan, 581:Sep89–531
C. Munro, 71(ALS):May89–138
Niatum, D., ed. Harper's Anthology of 20th Century Native American Poetry.
R.W. Lewis, 456(NDQ):Spring89–221
639(VQR):Winter89–27
Nicephorus Phocas. Le traité sur la guérilla (De velitatione) de l'empereur Nicéphore Phocas (963–969). (G. Dagron & H. Mihăescu, eds; G. Dagron & J–C. Cheynet, trans)
G.T. Dennis, 303(JoHS):Vol109–275
W.E. Kaegi, 589:Jan89–194
Ničeva, K. Bălgarska frazeologija.
T. Henninger, 575(SEER):Apr89–260
Nicholas, D. The Metamorphosis of a Medieval City.*
L. Attreed, 589:Apr89–473
Nicholas, R.L. Unamuno, narrador.
C.A. Longhurst, 402(MLR):Jul90–768
G. Roberts, 238:Dec89–961
G. Seda Rodríguez, 711(RHM):Dec89–187
Nicholas, R.L., M. Canteli Dominicis & E. Neale-Silva. Motivos de Conversación. (2nd ed)
I. Wherritt, 399(MLJ):Autumn89–090
Nicholas, S., ed. Convict Workers.
F.B. Smith, 617(TLS):9–15Mar90–261
Nicholas of Methone. Nicholas of Methone, "Refutation of Proclus' Elements of Theology." (A.D. Angelou, ed)
A. Kazhdan, 589:Jan89–196
Nicholls, D. American Experimental Music, 1890–1940.
P. Griffiths, 617(TLS):25–31May90–552
Nicholls, D. Deity and Domination.
E. Norman, 617(TLS):5–11Jan90–22
Nicholls, G. "Measure for Measure."
M. Wiggins, 447(N&Q):Sep89–386
Nichols, A. The Poetics of Epiphany.*
J. McGowan, 577(SHR):Summer89–280
Nichols, B. & G. Loescher, eds. The Moral Nation.
T.M.R., 185:Jul90–921

Nichols, G. Lazy Thoughts of a Lazy Woman.
E. Bartlett, 493:Winter89/90–48
G. Foden, 617(TLS):2–8Mar90–236
Nichols, J.B. The Uneasy Alliance.
S.A., 185:Oct89–225
Nichols, J.D., ed. An Ojibwe Text Anthology.
A. Mattina, 350:Dec90–879
Nichols, M.P. Socrates and the Political Community.*
J.B. Allis, 41:Fall89–323
Nichols, R., ed. Ravel Remembered.*
J.B. Jones, 410(M&L):Feb89–128
510:Winter88/89–62
Nicholson, C., ed. Alexander Pope.
C. Chapin, 566:Autumn89–61
Nicholson, G. What We Did on Our Holidays.
C. Hawtree, 617(TLS):19–25Jan90–66
Nicholson, L.J., ed. Feminism/Postmodernism.
P.D. Murphy, 590:Jun90–83
H. Vendler, 453(NYRB):31May90–19
Nickel, J.W. Making Sense of Human Rights.
T. Hurka, 518:Jan89–54
Nicolai, F. "Kritik ist überall, zumal in Deutschland, nötig." (W. Albrecht, ed)
P.M. Mitchell, 301(JEGP):Jan89–68
de Nicolás, A.T. Powers of Imagining.
T. O'Reilly, 86(BHS):Apr89–173
Nicolas, J. La Révolution française dans les Alpes Dauphiné et Savoie, 1789–1799.
V.D.L., 605(SC):15Jul90–409
Nicolet, C. L'inventaire du monde.
J. Desanges, 555:Vol62Fasc2–309
Nicolle, D.C. Arms and Armour of the Crusading Era, 1050–1350.
K. De Vries, 589:Oct89–1016
Niderst, A., ed. Pierre Corneille.*
M. Defrenne, 535(RHL):Jan–Feb89–93
Nieciuński, W. & T. Żukowski, eds. Studia nad ładem społecznym.
Z. Bauman, 617(TLS):12–18Oct90–1095
Niederehe, H–J. & B. Schlieben-Lange, eds. Die Frühgeschichte der romanischen Philologie: von Dante bis Diez.*
Y. Malkiel, 603:Vol13No1–248
Niederehe, H–J. & I. Wolf, eds. Français du Canada – français de France.
K. Bochmann, 682(ZPSK):Band42Heft5–670
Niederman, S. A Quilt of Words.
J.N. Lensink, 649(WAL):Feb90–387
Niehüser, W. Redecharakterisierende Adverbiale.
S. Schuetze-Coburn, 350:Mar90–205
Niel, J–B. Vous qui passez dans l'ombre.*
É. de la Héronnière, 450(NRF):Sep89–99
Nielsen, A. The Summer of the Paymaster.
P. Hoover, 441:18Nov90–47
Nielsen, E.K. Jeg vil synge en sang.
W.K. McNeil, 292(JAF):Apr–Jun89–239
Nielsen, H.F. The Germanic Languages.
E.H. Antonsen, 159:Vol6No2–287
C. von Kerckvoorde, 350:Sep90–647
Nielsen, J.P., with L.L. Albertsen & J. Kjaer, eds. Antifaschismus in deutscher und skandinavischer Literatur.
P. Houe, 563(SS):Winter89–95
Nielsen, K. Marxism and the Moral Point of View.
G.G. Brenkert, 103:Feb90–73
S. Ross, 185:Jan90–422
Nielsen, K. Why Be Moral?
J. van Ingen, 185:Apr90–670

Niemann, L. Boomer.
    H. Junker, 617(TLS):7-13Sep90-943
Niemeier, J-P. Kopien und Nachahmungen im
Hellenismus.
    P. Kranz, 229:Band61Heft2-182
Niemeier, W-D. Die Palaststilkeramik von
Knossos.
    P.A. Mountjoy, 303(JoHS):Vol109-262
Niemöller, K.W. & V. Zaderackij, eds. Bericht
über das Internationale Dmitri-Schostako-
witsch-Symposion Köln 1985.
    T. Emmerig, 416:Band4Heft3-277
Nies, F. & K. Stierle, eds. Französische Klas-
sik.*
    R. Baustert, 547(RF):Band101Heft2/3-331
Niewöhner, F. Veritas sive Varietas.
    H.B. Nisbet, 402(MLR):Oct90-1024
Nigel of Canterbury. Miracles of the Virgin
Mary, in Verse/Miracula sancte Dei geni-
tricis Virginis Marie, versifice. (J. Ziol-
kowski, ed)
    D. Carlson, 589:Apr89-475
Nightingale, F. Ever Yours, Florence Night-
ingale.* (M. Vicinus & B. Nergaard, eds)
    N. Auerbach, 441:25Mar90-16
    N. Bliven, 442(NY):14May90-105
Nightingale, P. Journey through Darkness.*
    M.P.L., 295(JML):Fall88/Winter89-387
Niiniluoto, I. Truthlikeness.
    D. Pearce, 316:Mar89-297
Nikulin, N. Netherlandish Paintings in Soviet
Museums.
    J.O. Hand, 90:Jan89-39
Niles, B. A Window on Provence.
    A. Youngman, 441:9Sep90-27
Niles, J.D., ed. Old English Literature in
Context.
    H. Gneuss, 38:Band107Heft1/2-155
Nilson, A.T. Svenskt i USA.
    A. Gustavsson, 64(Arv):Vol44-210
Nilsson, N.Å., ed. The Slavic Literatures and
Modernism.*
    P. Austin, 104(CASS):Spring-Winter88-
417
Nilus. Nilus Ancyranus, "Narratio." (F.
Conca, ed)
    P. Pattenden, 123:Vol39No1-138
Nimis, S.A. Narrative Semiotics in the Epic
Tradition.
    S.M. Goldberg, 124:Mar-Apr90-362
    T.J. Winnifrith, 123:Vol39No2-397
Nimmo, W.F. Behind a Curtain of Silence.
    T. Hasegawa, 293(JASt):Aug89-622
Nin, A. & H. Miller. A Literate Passion.* (G.
Stuhlmann, ed)
    M.J.F., 295(JML):Fall88/Winter89-214
"Nineteenth Century Short Title Catalogue."
(Ser 1, Phase 1)
    D.H. Reiman, 591(SIR):Winter89-650
Nipperdey, T. Deutsche Geschichte 1866-
1918. (Vol 1)
    R.J. Evans, 617(TLS):5-11Oct90-1079
Nirenburg, S., ed. Machine Translation.
    G. Sampson, 361:Dec89-327
Nirk, E. Estonian Literature. (2nd ed)
    D. Kirby, 575(SEER):Oct89-625
Nisbet, A.M. & V-A. Massena. L'Empire à
table.
    R.W. Tobin, 207(FR):May90-1117
Nisbet, P. El Lissitzky, 1890-1941.
    V. Margolin, 574(SEEJ):Summer89-318

Nischik, T-M. Das volkssprachliche Natur-
buch im späten Mittelalter.*
    H. Meyer, 684(ZDA):Band118Heft2-79
Nish, I., ed. Contemporary European Writing
on Japan.
    M. Cooper, 407(MN):Summer89-258
Nishida Kitarō. Intuition and Reflection in
Self-Consciousness.
    D.A. Dilworth, 407(MN):Summer89-247
    J.C. Maraldo, 485(PE&W):Oct89-465
    T.T. Tominaga, 293(JASt):Feb89-177
Nishida Kitarō. Last Writings.*
    J.C. Maraldo, 485(PE&W):Oct89-465
    T.T. Tominaga, 293(JASt):Feb89-177
Nite, N.N. Rock On Almanac.
    B.L. Cooper, 498:Winter89-88
Nitecki, M.H., ed. Evolutionary Progress.
    M. Vicedo, 103:May90-192
Nitze, P.H., with A.M. Smith & S.L. Rearden.
From Hiroshima to Glasnost.*
    W.F. Kimball, 617(TLS):8-14Jun90-601
Nixon, R. In the Arena.
    M. Kempton, 453(NYRB):14Jun90-26
    E.R. May, 617(TLS):28Sep-4Oct90-1024
    R. Morris, 441:29Apr90-3
Nixon, R. 1999.*
    639(VQR):Winter89-24
Nixon, W. Strategic Compromise.
    N. Callendar, 441:16Sep90-26
Nizan, P. The Conspiracy.
    P. McCarthy, 617(TLS):14-20Sep90-964
    J. Weightman, 453(NYRB):25Oct90-29
Njeri, I. Every Good-Bye Ain't Gone.
    P-L. Adams, 61:Mar90-116
    M. Wolitzer, 441:4Feb90-9
Noakes, V. - see Lear, E.
Nobach, C. Untersuchungen zu George
Onslows Kammermusik.
    F. Krummacher, 417:Oct-Dec89-384
Noble, C.A.M. Modern German Dialects.
    L. Zehetner, 685(ZDL):3/1989-358
Noble, J.V. The Techniques of Painted Attic
Pottery. (rev)
    A.W. Johnston, 303(JoHS):Vol109-267
    E. Moignard, 123:Vol39No2-412
Noble, P. - see Hillesum, E.
Nocera, M. & others, eds. I registri della cat-
ena del comune di Savona: Registro II
(Parte I).
    S.A. Epstein, 589:Apr89-489
Noddings, N. Women and Evil.
    M. Midgley, 617(TLS):16-22Feb90-166
Nodier, C. Jean Sbogar. (J. Sgard & others,
eds)
    J-R. Dahan, 535(RHL):Jul-Aug89-726
Noel-Paton, M.H. & J.P. Campbell. Noel Paton
1821-1901. (F. Irwin, ed)
    K. Flint, 617(TLS):19-25Oct90-1134
Noguchi, T.T. & A. Lyons. Physical Evidence.
    J. Curtin, 441:22Jul90-20
Noiray, J. - see Zola, E.
Nokes, D. Raillery and Rage.
    F. De Bruyn, 83:Autumn89-228
Nolan, M. Foundations.
    J.T. Goodwin, 102(CanL):Winter88-155
Nolan, P. The Political Economy of Collective
Farms.
    A. Hussain, 293(JASt):Nov89-835
Nold, J. Willing Victims.
    G.V. Downes, 102(CanL):Autumn-
    Winter89-187

Nolin, B. & P. Forsgren, eds. The Modern
Breakthrough in Scandinavian Literature
1870-1905.
M. Robinson, 562(Scan):Nov89-224
Noll, P. In the Face of Death.
B. Bawer, 441:21Jan90-41
Nolte, W.H. - see Mencken, H.L.
Nomachi, K. The Nile.
P-L. Adams, 61:Aug90-92
Nony, D. & A. André, eds. La Littérature
française.
J.A. Storme, 399(MLJ):Winter89-511
Noonan, H.W. Personal Identity.*
V.F. Daues, 543:Jun90-875
Noonan, P. What I Saw at the Revolution.*
W. Sheed, 441:4Feb90-1
Nooteboom, C. The Knight Has Died.
L. Simon, 441:9Sep90-20
Norall, F. Bourgmont.
P.N. Limerick, 617(TLS):12-18Jan90-27
Norcross, E. & E. Dickinson. A Poet's Parents.
(V.R. Pollak, ed)
M.E.K. Bernhard, 432(NEQ):Jun89-305
T. Wortham, 445(NCF):Jun89-124
Nordan, L. The All-Girl Football Team.
G. Johnson, 219(GaR):Summer89-406
Nordbustad, F. Iraqw Grammar.
G. Gilligan, 350:Jun90-422
Nordhaus, J. A Bracelet of Lies.
D. Chorlton, 496:Winter89/90-43
Nordhjem, D. What Fiction Means.*
T. Docherty, 541(RES):Nov89-597
M. Nøjgaard, 402(OL):Vol44No3-281
G. Smith, 677(YES):Vol20-213
Nordland, G. Richard Diebenkorn.*
M.I. James, 90:Mar89-232
Norman, G. Bouncing Back.
H.G. Summers, Jr., 441:19Aug90-14
Norman, J. Chinese.
J.A. Matisoff, 293(JASt):Nov89-836
G. Sampson, 297(JL):Mar89-229
Norman, M. These Good Men.
J. McGinniss, 441:14Jan00-7
Norman, P. The Age of Parody.
A. Howard, 617(TLS):23-29Mar90-324
Norman, R. Free and Equal.*
D.R. Mapel, 185:Oct89-184
F.E. McDermott, 521:Jan90-75
Nörr, D. Causa mortis.*
O. Behrends, 229:Band61Heft8-685
Norris, C. The Deconstructive Turn.*
S. Sim, 148:Winter86-114
Norris, C. Derrida.*
T. Docherty, 541(RES):Nov89-598
D. Gorman, 478(P&L):Apr89-204
C. Howells, 208(FS):Jul89-363
D.T.O., 295(JML):Fall88/Winter89-234
R. Selden, 677(YES):Vol20-223
Norris, C. Paul de Man.*
M.W. Redfield, 153:Summer89-35
Norris, D., ed. Miloš Crnjanski and Modern
Serbian Literature.
B. Johnson, 402(MLR):Oct90-1055
Norris, H. Water into Wine.
M. Kuznets, 455:Jun89-69
R.C. Sethi, 573(SSF):Fall88-498
Norris, K. Islands.
D. Prescosky, 168(ECW):Fall89-95
Norris, L. The Girl from Cardigan.*
V. Perlman, 573(SSF):Winter89-101
Norris, L. Sequences.
J. Meek, 456(NDQ):Winter89-227

Norris, P. British By-Elections.
G. Peele, 617(TLS):7-13Dec90-1311
Norris, W. & J.E. Strain, eds. Charles Carpen-
ter Fries.
E. Tschirner, 399(MLJ):Winter89-490
Norrish, P. New Tragedy and Comedy in
France 1945-70.
D. Bradby, 402(MLR):Oct90-987
Norrish, P. - see Adamov, A.
Nörtemann, R. - see van Hoddis, J.
North, J.S. The Waterloo Directory of Irish
Newspapers and Periodicals, 1800-1900.*
(Phase 2)
517(PBSA):Mar89-123
North, N. Continuo Playing on the Lute,
Archlute and Theorbo.
A. Rooley, 410(M&L):Nov89-530
North, R. Roger North's "The Musical Gram-
marian" and "Theory of Sounds." (M. Chan
& J. Kassler, eds)
P. Gouk, 415:Jun89-348
North, S.B., ed. Studies in Medieval French
Language and Literature Presented to Brian
Woledge in Honour of his 80th Birthday.*
K. Busby, 382(MAE):1989/2-328
A.J. Holden, 402(MLR):Jan90-176
E. Kennedy, 208(FS):Oct89-457
North, S.M. The Making of Knowledge in Com-
position.
R.L. Larson, 126(CCC):Feb89-95
R. Lloyd-Jones, 126(CCC):Feb89-98
J.C. Raymond, 126(CCC):Feb89-93
Norton, A. Reflections on Political Identity.
D.A.C., 185:Jun90-440
Norton, B.G. Why Preserve Natural Variety?
P.S.W., 185:Oct89-210
Noske, F. Sweelinck.
M. Desmet, 537:Vol75No1-111
J. Harper, 415:Feb89-89
C. Stembridge, 410(M&L):May89-252
Nosov, V.D. "Ključ" k Gogolju - opyt chudo-
žestvennogo čtenija.
K-D. Keil, 688(ZSP):Band49Heft1-173
Nossiter, B.D. Fat Years and Lean.
J.K. Galbraith, 441:19Aug90-11
Nostwich, T.D. - see Dreiser, T.
"Notai genovesi in Oltremare." (M. Balard,
ed)
A.E. Laiou, 589:Jan89-115
Nöth, W. Handbuch der Semiotik.
D. Nehls, 257(IRAL):Aug89-263
Notker der Deutsche. Boethius, "De consola-
tione Philosophiae."* (Bks 1 & 2) (P.W.
Tax, ed)
H. Mayer, 680:Jan89 199
Notker der Deutsche. Boethius, "De consola-
tione Philosophiae." (Bk 3) (P.W. Tax, ed)
N.F. Palmer, 402(MLR):Jul90-779
H.D. Schlosser, 133:Band22Heft3/4-303
Notker der Deutsche. Notker Latinus zum
Martianus Capella.* (J.C. King, ed)
H. Mayer, 589:Jan89-199
301(JEGP):Jan89-60
Novak, D. Jewish-Christian Dialogue.
J. Sacks, 617(TLS):20-26Apr90-424
Novak, J., ed. On Masaryk.
H. Declève, 192(EP):Jul-Dec89-551
Novak, M. Free Persons and the Common
Good.
D.J.G., 185:Jul90-918
Novara, A. Poésie virgilienne de la mémoire.
S.J. Harrison, 123:Vol39No2-390
P. Heuzé, 555:Vol62Fasc2-362

Nove, A. Glasnost' in Action.*
   J. Sherr, 617(TLS):16–22Mar90–273
Novick, P. That Noble Dream.*
   639(VQR):Spring89–43
Novitz, D. Knowledge, Fiction & Imagination.*
   P. Lamarque, 478(P&L):Oct89–365
   I. Newman, 518:Jul89–190
   A. Segal, 63:Jun89–246
   N. Warburton, 89(BJA):Winter89–81
Novitz, D. & B. Willmott, eds. Culture and
   Identity in New Zealand.
   R. Shannon, 617(TLS):2–8Feb90–121
Nowak, H. Powědamy Dolnoserbski – Gutes
   Niedersorbisch.
   C. Wukasch, 574(SEEJ):Winter89–637
Nowé, L.S. – see under Sannia Nowé, L.
Noxon, G. "On Malcolm Lowry" and Other
   Writings. (M. Mota & P. Tiessen, eds)
   C. Ackerley, 102(CanL):Autumn–
   Winter89–167
Noyer-Weidner, A., ed. Literatur zwischen
   immanenter Bedingtheit und äusserem
   Zwang.
   G. Güntert, 547(RF):Band101Heft1–141
Noyes, H. China Born.
   D.S. Walwyn, 617(TLS):6–12Apr90–369
Nozick, R. The Examined Life.*
   442(NY):29Jan90–96
Nriagu, J.O. Lead and Lead Poisoning in An-
   tiquity.
   G.W. Houston, 121(CJ):Oct–Nov89–63
Nugent, N. The Government and Politics of
   the European Community.
   D. Leonard, 617(TLS):18–24May90–518
Nugent, S. Big Mouth.
   S. Mills, 617(TLS):7–13Dec90–1315
Null, G. Clearer, Cleaner, Safer, Greener.
   N. Wade, 441:22Apr90–1
Numbers, R.L., ed. Medicine in the New World.
   J. Duffin, 106:Summer89–128
Numbers, R.L. & T.L. Savitt, eds. Science and
   Medicine in the Old South.
   T.F. Waites, 585(SoQ):Spring90–119
Nunan, D. The Learner-Centred Curriculum.
   M–A. Reiss, 399(MLJ):Winter89–491
   P.D. Seaman, 350:Jun90–423
Nunes, M.L. Becoming True to Ourselves.
   J.C. Haggstrom, 538(RAL):Fall89–545
Nunn, P.G. Victorian Women Artists.*
   S.P. Casteras, 662:Fall89/Winter90–35
   R.T. Van Arsdel, 635(VPR):Summer89–88
Nurser, J. The Reign of Conscience.
   R.J. Schoeck, 637(VS):Autumn89–204
Nussbaum, A.J. Head and Horn in Indo-Euro-
   pean.
   D.A. Ringe, Jr., 318(JAOS):Jan–Mar88–
   186
Nussbaum, B. Good Intentions.
   R. Lewin, 441:4Nov90–20
Nussbaum, F. & L. Brown, eds. The New Eigh-
   teenth Century.*
   A. Ingram, 402(MLR):Apr90–414
   J. Peavoy, 478(P&L):Apr89–213
   S. Soupel, 189(EA):Jul–Sep89–345
   H. Weber, 141:Winter89–107
Nussbaum, M.C. The Fragility of Goodness.*
   M. Barabas, 521:Jan89–63
   R.T. Runia, 394:Vol42fasc1/2–132
   P.B. Woodruff, 484(PPR):Sep89–205
Nusser, K–H. Kausale Prozesse und sinner-
   fassende Vernunft.*
   A. Pieper, 687:Jan–Mar89–172

Nuttall, A.D. A New Mimesis.
   J.A. Bryant, Jr., 569(SR):Summer89–445
Nuttgens, P., ed. Mackintosh and his Con-
   temporaries in Europe and America.*
   C. McCorquodale, 39:Sep89–212
Nuyts, J. & G. de Schutter, eds. Getting One's
   Words into Line.
   B.J. Hoff, 204(FdL):Sep89–224
Nydell, M.K. Understanding Arabs.
   P. Stevens, 399(MLJ):Autumn89–348
Nye, A. Feminist Theory and the Philosophies
   of Man.*
   K. Lennon, 291:Vol6No2–238
Nye, J.S., Jr. Bound to Lead.
   M.R. Beschloss, 441:15Apr90–13
   P. Kennedy, 453(NYRB):28Jun90–31
   R. Kuttner, 617(TLS):16–22Nov90–1226
Nye, J.S., Jr., G.T. Allison & A. Carnesale,
   eds. Fateful Visions.
   S.L., 185:Oct89–223
Nye, N.S. Yellow Glove.
   P. Booth, 219(GaR):Spring89–161
Nye, R. The Life and Death of My Lord Gilles
   de Rais.
   P.J. Kleeb, 617(TLS):21–27Sep90–999
Nyíri, J.C., ed. From Bolzano to Wittgen-
   stein/Von Bolzano zu Wittgenstein.
   P. Engel, 192(EP):Apr–Jun89–267
Nyíri, J.C. & B. Smith, eds. Practical Knowl-
   edge.*
   T. Whittock, 89(BJA):Spring89–191
Nykrog, P. L'Amour et la rose.*
   P. Barrette, 207(FR):Apr90–869
Nykrog, P. La Recherche du don perdu.*
   G. Brée, 207(FR):Oct89–170
Nyquist, M. & M.W. Ferguson, eds. Re-mem-
   bering Milton.*
   T.N. Corns, 447(N&Q):Sep89–394
   D.N.C. Wood, 627(UTQ):Fall89–126

Oakes, G. Weber and Rickert.
   J.D., 185:Apr90–701
Oakes, G. – see Rickert, H.
Oakeshott, M. The Voice of Liberal Learn-
   ing.* (T. Fuller, ed)
   T. Hall, 543:Sep89–159
   J. Searle, 453(NYRB):6Dec90–34
Oakley, S.P. Scandinavian History 1520–
   1970.
   D.D. Aldridge, 562(Scan):May89–109
Oates, J.C. Because it is Bitter, and Because
   it is My Heart.
   M. Robinson, 441:22Apr90–7
   P. Storace, 453(NYRB):16Aug90–22
   442(NY):28May90–109
Oates, J.C. I Lock My Door Upon Myself.
   P–L. Adams, 61:Nov90–173
   C. Kimble, 441:11Nov90–68
Oates, J.C. You Must Remember This.*
   S. Pinsker, 577(SHR):Spring89–193
   P. Stevens, 529(QQ):Autumn89–720
Oates, S.B. William Faulkner.*
   C.S. Brown, 569(SR):Fall89–556
   P.R.J., 295(JML):Fall88/Winter89–325
Oberer, H. – see Doflein, E.
Oberer, H. & G. Geismann – see Ebbinghaus,
   J.
Oberhuber, K. Poussin, the Early Years in
   Rome.
   M. Bull, 59:Dec89–516

Oberman, H.A. Luther.
A. Hamilton, 617(TLS):30Mar-5Apr90-
348
442(NY):26Feb90-132
O'Brian, J. - see Greenberg, C.
O'Brian, P. The Letter of Marque.
N. Callendar, 441:7Oct90-39
O'Brien, D. Pour interpréter Empédocle.
D. Pralon, 555:Vol62Fasc1-139
O'Brien, E. Lantern Slides.
L. Doughty, 617(TLS):8-14Jun90-616
D. Leavitt, 441:24Jun90-9
O'Brien, F.J. Stealth Strike.
N. Callendar, 441:18Nov90-41
O'Brien, G. Anglo-Irish Politics in the Age of
Grattan and Pitt.
P.D.G. Thomas, 83:Spring89-96
O'Brien, G. Diesel Mystic.
F. Baveystock, 617(TLS):2-8Feb90-122
O'Brien, G. Ruckers.
C. Hogwood, 617(TLS):21-27Dec90-1378
O'Brien, G. The Village of Longing [and]
Dancehall Days.*
P. Finn, 441:15Apr90-15
O'Brien, J. - see "Akutagawa and Dazai: In-
stances of Literary Adaptation"
O'Brien, M. The Daphne Decisions.
M. Stasio, 441:29Apr90-18
O'Brien, M. Rethinking the South.
R.L. Meyer, 585(SoQ):Spring90-118
639(VQR):Winter89-8
O'Brien, P.M. T.E. Lawrence.
E. Gilcher, 177(ELT):Vol32No2-241
J. Meyers, 07(DD).Mar09-84
O'Brien, S. Willa Cather.*
M.A. Peterman, 106:Fall89-211
O'Brien, T. Chasing After Danger.
S. Hynes, 617(TLS):24-30Aug90-900
O'Brien, T. If I Die in a Combat Zone.
H. Brogan, 617(TLS):29Jun-5Jul90-708
O'Brien, T. The Screening of America.
M. Covino, 441:19Aug90-21
O'Brien, T. The Things They Carried.
R.R. Harris, 441:11Mar90-8
J. Loose, 617(TLS):29Jun-5Jul90-705
442(NY):4Jun90-102
Obuchowski, C.W. The Franco-File.*
R.A. Hartzell, 207(FR):Feb90-585
de Oca, J.A.S.M. - see under Silveira y Montes
de Oca, J.A.
O'Callaghan, J.F. The Cortes of Castile-León,
1188-1350.
E.H. Shealy, 377:Jul89-147
Ochester, E. Changing the Name to Ochester.
W. Harmon, 472.Vol16No1-136
Ochs, E. Culture and Language Development.
G.B. Milner, 350:Dec90-834
Ochs, E. & B.B. Schieffelin. Acquiring Con-
versational Competence.
G.W. Shugar, 355(LSoc):Dec89-581
Ochs, S.J. Desegregating the Altar.
M.E. Marty, 441:23Sep90-46
Ochsenwald, W. Religion, Society and the
State in Arabia.
M.C. Wilson, 318(JAOS):Oct-Dec88-665
Ochwald, C. Ernst Barlach, Hugo Körtzinger
und Hermann Reemtsma.
R. Low, 683:Band52Heft3-443
William of Ockham. Guillelmus de Ockham,
"Tractatus de quantitate" et "Tractatus de
corpore Christi." (C.A. Grassi, ed)
T.M. Tomasic, 589:Jul89-711

Ocón Alonso, D. Tímpanos románicos españ-
oles.
J. Huidobro Pérez-Villamil, 48:Oct-
Dec89-478
O'Connell, M.R. John Ireland and the Ameri-
can Catholic Church.
J.M. O'Toole, 432(NEQ):Sep89-461
O'Connell, R.J. The Origin of the Soul in St.
Augustine's Later Works.
J.M. Rist, 258:Jun89-221
O'Connell, R.L. Of Arms and Men.*
M. Cranston, 617(TLS):6-12Apr90-377
O'Connor, F. Collected Works. (S. Fitzgerald,
ed)
F. Crews, 453(NYRB):26Apr90-49
M.J. Friedman, 268(IFR):Summer89-139
B. Griffith, 569(SR):Fall89-575
H. McDonald, 31(ASch):Autumn89-622
O'Connor, G. Sean O'Casey.*
J. Countryman, 615(TJ):Dec89-560
O'Connor, J.L. & H., with S.M. Bowler. Harvey
and Jessie.
T. Martin, 42(AR):Summer89-365
O'Connor, M. John Davidson.*
N.H. MacKenzie, 529(QQ):Spring89-140
O'Connor, P. Memoirs of a Public Baby.
G. Annan, 453(NYRB):1Feb90-19
O'Connor, S. Tokens of Grace.
C. Kimble, 441:5Aug90-18
O'Connor, T.H. South Boston, My Home Town.
W.J. Reid, 432(NEQ):Sep89-477
Ó Cuilleanáin, C. Religion and the Clergy in
Boccaccio's "Decameron."
R. Hastings, 278(IS):Vol43-132
Oda, M. The Bomb.
I. Buruma, 453(NYRB):25Oct90-15
C. Lansbury, 441:12Aug90-10
Odaka, K., K. Ono & F. Adachi. The Automo-
bile Industry in Japan.
D. Ostrom, 293(JASt):Nov89-874
O'Daly, G. Augustine's Philosophy of Mind.
G. Madec, 229:Band61Heft5-443
R.J. O'Connell, 319:Jan90-125
Oddie, G. Likeness to Truth.
I. Niiniluoto, 316:Mar89-290
Odell, L. & D. Goswami, eds. Writing in Non-
academic Settings
S. Watson, 580(SCR):Fall89-133
Odelman, E., ed. Prosules de la messe, 2.*
[shown in prev under title Corpus troporum
VI.]
P. Jeffery, 589:Jan89-120
Odendahl, T. Charity Begins at Home.
K. Teltsch, 441:19Aug90-19
Odier, D. Cannibal Kiss.
M.E. Ross, 441:15Apr90-15
442(NY):8Jan90-99
O'Donnell, E.E. The Annals of Dublin.
H.B. Clarke, 272(IUR):Spring89-182
O'Donnell, G., P.C. Schmitter & L. Whitehead,
eds. Transiciónes desde un Gobierno Auto-
ritario.
C.T. Powell, 358:Jun90-5
O'Donnell, L. A Wreath for the Bride.
M. Stasio, 441:21Jan90-35
O'Donnell, P. Passionate Doubts.
E.B. Safer, 677(YES):Vol20-356
O'Donnell, P. & R.C. Davis, eds. Intertextu-
ality and Contemporary American Fiction.
M.L. McGill, 400(MLN):Dec89-1197
O'Donnell, W.H. - see Yeats, W.B.

O'Donoghue, B. The Absent Signifier.
C. Hurford, 617(TLS):21–27Dec90–1383
O'Donoghue, B. Poaching Rights.
R. Pybus, 565:Winter88/89–67
O'Donoghue, H. – see Woolf, R.
Odoyevsky, V.F. Pyostrye skazki. (N. Cornwell, ed)
P. Kindlon, 402(MLR):Jul90–813
R.D. Le Blanc, 574(SEEJ):Winter89–620
O'Driscoll, D. Hidden Extras.*
R. Pybus, 565:Winter88/89–67
Odrowąż–Pieniążek, J., ed. Blok–Notes Muzeum Literatury im Adama Mickiewicza, No. 9.
J.T. Baer, 497(PolR):Vol34No4–371
Oellers, N., ed. Germanistik und Deutschunterricht im Zeitalter der Technologie.
W. Paulsen, 221(GQ):Fall89–563
Oesch, H., with M. Haas & H.P. Haller. Aussereuropäische Musik. (Pt 2)
B. Nettl, 187:Winter89–147
Oesterreich, P.L. Person and Handlungsstil.
D. Birnbacher, 687:Apr–Jun89–397
"Oeuvres et Critiques." (Vol 11)
G. Cesbron, 356(LR):Nov89–321
O'Ferrall, F. Catholic Emancipation, Daniel O'Connell and the Birth of Irish Democracy 1820–30.
L. Carruthers, 272(IUR):Spring89–193
Offer, A. The First World War.
D. French, 617(TLS):18–24May90–536
O'Flaherty, J.C., T.F. Sellner & R.M. Helm, eds. Studies in Nietzsche and the Judaeo–Christian Tradition.
M. Boulby, 564:Sep89–274
J.P. Stern, 301(JEGP):Apr89–295
O'Flaherty, W.D., ed & trans. Textual Sources for the Study of Hinduism.
F.X. Clooney, 293(JASt):Nov89–909
Ogden, D.H. Performance Dynamics and the Amsterdam Werkteater.*
T. Postlewait, 130:Winter89/90–377
"Ogni anno un Maggio nuovo."
E. Hobsbawm, 358:Jun90–10
Ogilvie–Thomson, S.J., ed. Walter Hilton's "Mixed Life."*
M. Rigby, 541(RES):Feb89–113
Ognjanowa, E., ed. Märchen aus Bulgarien.
I. Köhler–Zülch, 196:Band30Heft3/4–341
O'Gorman, F. British Conservatism.
A. Morvan, 189(EA):Jan–Mar89–105
O'Gorman, F. Voters, Patrons and Parties.
L. Colley, 617(TLS):20–26Apr90–415
O'Gorman, H.J. – see Klassen, A.D., C.J. Williams & E.E. Levitt
O'Gorman, J.F., ed. Aspects of American Printmaking, 1800–1950.
K. Martinez, 658:Spring89–88
O'Gorman, J.F. H.H. Richardson.*
A. Saint, 46:Mar89–12
O'Gorman, J.F. & others. Drawing Toward Building.
K. Curran, 576:Jun89–194
O'Grady, D. Alexander Pope and Eighteenth–Century Italian Poetry.
J. Lindon, 402(MLR):Jan90–213
L.A. Zaina, 278(IS):Vol43–168
O'Grady, T. Motherland.*
A. Davis–Goff, 441:13May90–28
O'Grady, W. Principles of Grammar and Learning.
S. Carroll, 320(CJL):Mar89–89
L. Eubank, 710:Sep89–332

O'Grady, W. & M. Dobrovolsky, eds. Contemporary Linguistics.
L.J. Brinton, 320(CJL):Mar89–78
J.L. Malone, 350:Sep90–573
Ogren, K.J. The Jazz Revolution.
A.V. Hewat, 617(TLS):2–8Feb90–129
Ogunbiyi, Y., ed. Perspectives on Nigerian Literature. (Vols 1 & 2)
J.O.J. Nwachukwu–Agbada, 538(RAL): Summer89–297
Ohala, J.J. & J.J. Jaeger, eds. Experimental Phonology.*
A. Bell, 350:Dec90–826
G. Hudson, 710:Sep89–357
G. Meinhold, 682(ZPSK):Band42Heft3–408
O'Hanlon, R. Into the Heart of Borneo.
S. Pickering, 569(SR):Spring89–297
O'Hara, D.T. The Romance of Interpretation.*
D.G. Marshall, 131(CL):Spring89–204
O'Hara, D.T. Lionel Trilling.
P.A. Bové, 659(ConL):Fall90–373
O'Hara, D.T., ed. Why Nietzsche Now?
A.P. Fell, 529(QQ):Spring89–66
O'Hara, J.E. John Cheever.
V.C. Wang, 573(SSF):Summer89–364
O'Hara, J.J. Death and the Optimistic Prophecy in Vergil's "Aeneid."
R. Jenkyns, 617(TLS):23–29Nov90–1268
Ohashi, R. Zeitlichkeitsanalyse der Hegelschen Logik.
A. Halder, 489(PJGG):Band96Heft2–445
O'Hear, A. The Element of Fire.
D. Cockburn, 483:Apr89–272
D. Collinson, 89(BJA):Autumn89–368
D.D. Todd, 478(P&L):Oct89–399
O'Hehir, D. Home Free.
M. Kinzie, 491:Jun89–151
Ohl, J.K. Hugh S. Johnson and the New Deal.
J. Braeman, 106:Summer89–41
Ohlin, B., comp. Correspondance Littéraire Secrète, 29 juin–28 décembre 1776.* (G. von Proschwitz, ed)
P. Jansen, 535(RHL):Mar–Apr89–290
Ohly, F. Süsse Nägel der Passion.
B. Murdoch, 402(MLR):Oct90–1017
Ohly, R. Swahili–English Slang Pocket–Dictionary.
S. Brauner, 682(ZPSK):Band42Heft6–868
Ohly, S. & P. Schmitt, eds. Wörterbuch der Mittelhochdeutschen Urkundensprache. (fasc 1 & 2)
U. Goebel, 589:Jan89–200
U. Goebel, 589:Jul89–748
J. West, 235:Winter88–84
Ohly, S. & P. Schmitt, eds. Wörterbuch der mittelhochdeutsch Urkundensprache. (Vol 1, Pt 1)
N.R. Wolf, 684(ZDA):Band118Heft1–22
Ohmae, K. The Borderless World.
H.H. Segal, 441:2Sep90–10
Ohmann, R. Politics of Letters.*
J. Clifford, 128(CE):Sep89–517
K. Cmiel, 271:Winter89–175
D.T.O., 295(JML):Fall88/Winter89–234
Oikonomides, N. A Collection of Dated Byzantine Lead Seals.*
T.E. Gregory, 589:Jul89–749
Oinas, F.J. Essays on Russian Folklore and Mythology.*
D.E. Bynum, 104(CASS):Spring–Winter88–475

van Oirsouw, R.R. The Syntax of Coordination.
 A. Neijt, 361:Aug89–343
 L. Schwartz, 350:Dec90–844
Okada, S. Edmund Blunden and Japan.
 A. Head, 175:Summer89–171
 J. Kirkup, 364:Apr/May89–146
O'Keefe, C. Black Snow Days.
 G. Jonas, 441:13May90–35
O'Keeffe, G. & A. Pollitzer. Lovingly, Georgia. (C. Giboire, ed)
 A. Barnet, 441:18Nov90–29
O'Keeffe, P. – see Lewis, W.
Okenfuss, M.J. – see Tolstoi, P.
Okken, L. Das goldene Haus und die goldene Laube.*
 T. Kerth, 133:Band22Heft1–53
 S. Olms, 684(ZDA):Band118Heft3–119
Okrent, D. & S. Wulf. Baseball Anecdotes.*
 R.B. Heilman, 569(SR):Summer89–475
Okrent, M. Heidegger's Pragmatism.
 D. Frede, 484(PPR):Mar90–619
 J. Protevi, 319:Oct90–631
 M.A. Weinstein, 242:Vol10No2–265
Okruhlik, K. & J. Brown, eds. The Natural Philosophy of Leibniz.
 G. Sayre–McCord, 486:Mar89–173
Oksaar, E., ed. Soziokulturelle Perspektiven von Mehrsprachigkeit und Spracherwerb.
 H. Terborg, 355(LSoc):Dec89–591
Oksaar, E. Spracherwerb im Vorschulalter.* (2nd ed)
 B. Reimann, 682(ZPSK):Band42Heft3–410
Olafson, F.A. Heidegger and the Philosophy of Mind.
 J. Haugeland, 484(PPR):Mar90–633
 T.R. Schatzki, 319:Jul90–466
 J.M.B. Waugh, 577(SHR):Summer89–293
Olafsson, E.H. Fridas visor och folkets visor.
 I. Massengale, 563(SS):Winter89–89
Olbrich, J. Aktionen–Installationen–Copy Art–Mail Art.
 G. Gessert, 448:Vol27No3–126
Olby, R.C. & others, eds. Companion to the History of Modern Science.
 B. Pippard, 617(TLS):27Apr–3May90–452
Oldfield, S. Women against the Iron Fist.
 C. Townshend, 617(TLS):23Feb–1Mar90–192
Oldham, J. The Poems of John Oldham.* (H.F. Brooks, with R. Selden, eds)
 C. Gullans, 568(SCN):Fall–Winter89–42
 I. Jack, 447(N&Q):Mar89–110
Olds, S. The Matter of this World.
 R. Pybus, 565:Winter88/89–67
O'Leary, P. Sir James Mackintosh.
 A. Bell, 617(TLS):2–8Mar90–212
Olen, J. Moral Freedom.
 J. Narveson, 103:Apr90–152
 M.J. Zimmerman, 185:Jan90–415
Olender, M. Les Langues du Paradis.
 J. Starobinski, 358:Feb90–11
Olesch, R. Thesaurus Linguae Dravaenopolabicae. (Vols 2 & 3)
 G. Stone, 575(SEER):Jan89–110
Olesch, R. Thesaurus linguae Dravaenopolabicae. (Vol 4)
 A. Slupski, 688(ZSP):Band49Heft2–428
 G. Stone, 575(SEER):Jan89–110
Olesch, R. & H. Rothe, eds. Slavistische Studien zum X. Internationalen Slavistenkongress in Sofia 1988.
 W. Busch, 688(ZSP):Band49Heft2–385

Oleson, J.P. Bronze Age, Greek and Roman Technology.
 G.W. Houston, 121(CJ):Oct–Nov89–63
Oleson, J.P. Greek and Roman Water–Lifting Devices.
 G.W. Houston, 121(CJ):Oct–Nov89–63
Olins, W. Corporate Identity.
 C. Frayling, 617(TLS):16–22Mar90–292
 P. Gorb, 324:Jan90–140
Mrs. Oliphant. Miss Marjoribanks. Phoebe Junior.
 T.C. Holyoke, 42(AR):Fall89–500
Oliphant, B.J. Dead in the Scrub.
 M. Stasio, 441:29Apr90–18
Oliphant, M. The Autobiography of Margaret Oliphant. (E. Jay, ed)
 J. Briggs, 617(TLS):9–15Nov90–1196
Oliva, P. Solon – Legende und Wirklichkeit.
 L. Hardwick, 123:Vol39No2–407
 E. Ruschenbusch, 229:Band61Heft5–444
Olivelle, P. Renunciation in Hinduism.
 J.W. de Jong, 259(IIJ):Jul89–212
Oliver, D. Kind.
 R. Caddel, 493:Summer89–35
 J. Saunders, 565:Autumn89–77
Oliver, E.R. Journal of an Aleutian Year.
 C. Servid, 649(WAL):Aug89–182
Oliver, M. Dream Work.
 G. Kuzma, 502(PrS):Spring89–111
Oliver, M. House of Light.
 R. Richman, 441:25Nov90–24
Olivera, M.A. Study in Lilac.
 E. Bou, 238:May89–319
Olken, I.T. With Pleated Eye and Garnet Wing.
 M.L. McLaughlin, 278(IS):Vol43–188
Oller, N. La fiebre del oro.
 J. Marti–Olivella, 240(HR):Autumn89–537
Ollier, C. Disconnection.
 A. Johnson, 441:28Jan90–22
Ollier, M–L. Lexique et concordance de Chrétien de Troyes d'après la copie Guiot.
 F.R.P. Akehurst, 589:Jan89–202
Ollier, M–L., ed. Masques et déguisements dans la littérature médiévale.
 R. Blumenfeld–Kosinski, 546(RR):Nov89–626
Olmedo, A.S. – see under Soria Olmedo, A.
Olmstead, R. A Trail of Heart's Blood Wherever We Go.
 M. Malone, 441:5Aug90–6
 442(NY):1Oct90–110
Olsen, B.A. The Proto–Indo–European Instrument Noun Suffix *tlom and its Variants.
 M. Menu, 555:Vol62Fasc2–328
Olsen, B.M. L'étude des auteurs classiques latins aux XIe et XIIe siècles.* (Vol 3, Pt 1)
 M.E. Milham, 487:Autumn89–281
 E. des Places, 555:Vol62Fasc1–157
Olsen, G.M., ed. Industrial Change and Labour Adjustment in Sweden and Canada.
 G. Teeple, 529(QQ):Winter89–971
Olsen, J. "Doc."*
 D. Johnson, 453(NYRB):15Mar90–28
Olsen, L. Elipse of Uncertainty.*
 J. Ford, 295(JML):Fall88/Winter89–248
Olsen, M.A., ed. Libro del Cauallero Çifar.*
 M. Harney, 545(RPh):May90–569
Olsen, S. Wortbildung im Deutschen.
 H. Vater, 603:Vol13No1–236

Olsen, S.H. The End of Literary Theory.
  A. Haberer, 189(EA):Oct–Dec89–450
Olson, C. The Collected Poems of Charles
  Olson.* (G.F. Butterick, ed)
  D. Wood, 295(JML):Fall88/Winter89–388
Olson, C. & R. Creeley. Charles Olson and
  Robert Creeley: The Complete Correspon-
  dence. (Vols 7 & 8) (G. Butterick, ed)
  R.B.D., 295(JML):Fall88/Winter89–312
  J. Gardiner, 30:Winter90–81
Olson, K.R. An Essay on Facts.
  P.L. Peterson, 484(PPR):Mar90–610
  D–H. Ruben, 518:Jul89–161
Olson, P.A. The "Canterbury Tales" and the
  Good Society.*
  H. Cooper, 541(RES):Feb89–114
  J.M. Ganim, 301(JEGP):Jan89–89
  D. Pearsall, 677(YES):Vol20–230
  P. Rogers, 529(QQ):Summer89–503
Olson, T. Dorit in Lesbos.
  S. Birkerts, 441:22Apr90–38
Olsson, H. La concurrence entre "il, ce" et
  "cela (ça)" comme sujet d'expressions
  impersonnelles en français contemporain.*
  C. Heldner, 597(SN):Vol61No1–89
Oltra Tomás, J.M. La parodia como referente
  en "La Pícara Justina."*
  M. Joly, 92(BH):Jul–Dec88–445
Olwell, C. Gardening from the Heart.
  A. Lacy, 441:10Jun90–13
Olzien, O.H. Rainer Maria Rilke, Wirklichkeit
  und Sprache.
  A. Stahl, 224(GRM):Band39Heft4–481
Omaggio, A.C. & others. Kaléidoscope. (2nd
  ed)
  G. Morain, 399(MLJ):Summer89–225
O'Malley, J.W. – see Erasmus
O'Malley, M. Keeping Watch.
  D. Walton, 441:5Aug90–19
O'Malley, P. Biting at the Grave.
  N. Bliven, 442(NY):29Oct90–130
  R. Foster, 441:15Apr90–6
O'Meally, R., ed. New Essays on "Invisible
  Man."*
  G. Clarke, 402(MLR):Oct90–938
  R. Willett, 447(N&Q):Dec89–560
O'Meara, D. Pythagoras Revived.
  L.P. Schrenk, 543:Jun90–877
O'Meara, D.J., ed. Studies in Aristotle.
  H. Mendell, 41:Fall89–340
O'Meara, J.J. Eriugena.*
  J. Marenbon, 382(MAE):1989/2–317
  P.J.W. Miller, 319:Jul90–442
Onakkoor, G. Orchid.
  E.J. Higgins, 95(CLAJ):Jun90–451
Ondaatje, M., ed. The Faber Book of Contem-
  porary Canadian Short Stories.
  C. Bold, 617(TLS):19–25Oct90–1130
"One Dinner a Week and Travels in the East."
  E.M. Casey, 635(VPR):Summer89–86
O'Neal, H. "Life is Painful, Nasty & Short ...
  In My Case It Has Only Been Painful &
  Nasty."
  L. Shea, 441:25Nov90–19
O'Neill, E. Selected Letters of Eugene O'Neill.
  (T. Bogard & J.R. Bryer, eds)
  B.F. Dukore, 610:Autumn89–304
  S.A. Black, 27(AL):May89–310
  M. Manheim, 130:Summer89–179
  J. Veitch, 432(NEQ):Dec89–601
O'Neill, E. The Unknown O'Neill.* (T. Bogard,
  ed)
  J. Veitch, 432(NEQ):Dec89–601

O'Neill, F. Roman Circus.
  N. Callendar, 441:14Jan90–23
O'Neill, J. The Communicative Body.
  D.H. Davis, 103:Dec90–505
O'Neill, J. – see de Villena, E.
O'Neill, J.P. – see Newman, B.
O'Neill, M. Percy Bysshe Shelley. The Human
  Mind's Imaginings.
  A. Leighton, 617(TLS):30Mar–5Apr90–354
O'Neill, M. The Stripped Bed.
  T. Dooley, 617(TLS):2–8Mar90–236
O'Neill, P. Wilkie Collins.
  C.A. Howells, 447(N&Q):Dec89–529
  P. Thoms, 529(QQ):Winter89–979
O'Neill, P., ed. Critical Essays on Günter
  Grass.*
  S. Mews, 222(GR):Summer89–143
O'Neill, P. Ireland and Germany.
  H. Kosok, 38:Band107Heft3/4–540
O'Neill, T. Merchants and Mariners in Medi-
  eval Ireland.
  W.K. O'Riordan, 272(IUR):Spring89–196
Onetti, J.C. C'est alors que.
  M. Alhau, 450(NRF):Jul–Aug89–194
Onfray, M. Georges Palante.
  F. George, 98:Oct89–743
Ong, W.J. Oralität und Literalität.
  A. Hartmann, 196:Band30Heft1/2–155
Onians, J. Bearers of Meaning.*
  R. Padovan, 46:Nov89–12
Onieva Morales, J.L. Como dominar la gramá-
  tica estructural del español.
  J.F. Ford, 238:May89–314
Onieva Morales, J.L. Diccionario básico de
  terminología gramatical.
  O. Ozete, 238:May89–314
Oniga, R. I composti nominali latini.
  D.J. Napoli, 350:Sep90–648
Önnerfors, A. – see Jordaens, W.
Önnerfors, A. & C. Schaar – see Axelson, B.
Ono Kazuko. Chinese Women in a Century of
  Revolution, 1850–1950. (J. Fogel, ed)
  C. Gilmartin, 293(JASt):Aug89–595
Ono, M. Morphologische Untersuchungen zur
  deutschen Sprache in einem Stadtbuch der
  Prager Neustadt vom 16. bis 18. Jahrhun-
  dert.*
  K–P. Wegera, 680(ZDP):Band108Heft1–138
Onwuanibe, R.C. A Critique of Revolutionary
  Humanism.
  N. Gibson, 147:Vol6No2–92
Ooi Jin Bee. Depletion of Forest Resources in
  the Philippines.
  J.F. Eder, 293(JASt):Aug89–679
van Ophuijsen, J.M. – see Hephaestion
Opie, I., R. Opie & B. Alderson. The Treasures
  of Childhood.
  L. Marcus, 441:22Apr90–26
Opie, I. & M. Tatem, eds. A Dictionary of
  Superstitions.
  J.R. Porter, 617(TLS):5–11Jan90–22
Opll, F. Stadt und Reich im 12. Jahrhundert
  (1125–1190).
  M.B. Dick, 589:Jan89–204
Oppel, F.N. Mask and Tragedy.*
  J. Neubauer, 149(CLS):Vol26No4–366
  L. Santoro, 272(IUR):Spring89–188
von Oppen, B.R. – see von Moltke, H.J.
Oppenheim, F.M., ed. The Reasoning Heart.
  R.S. Corrington, 619:Winter89–80
Oppenheim, F.M. Royce's Mature Philosophy
  of Religion.*
  R.S. Corrington, 319:Jan90–146

Oppenheim, L., ed. Three Decades of the
French New Novel.*
　　N.M. Leov, 345(KRQ):May89-235
　　C. Rigolot, 207(FR):Feb90-538
Oppenheimer, J. Private Demons.
　　N. Walker, 395(MFS):Summer89-290
Oppenheimer, J. Barbara Walters.
　　M. Dowd, 441:25Mar90-14
Oppenheimer, M. & R.H. Boyle. Dead Heat.
　　S.J. Gould, 441:22Apr90-15
Oppler, E.C. Picasso's Guernica.
　　R. Cembalest, 55:May89-111
Opul'skij, A. Žitija svjatyx v tvorčestve
russkix pisatelej XIX veka.*
　　J.B. Dunlop, 104(CASS):Spring-Winter88-
522
Orcibal, J., with J. Le Brun & I. Noye – see
Fénelon, F.D.D.
Ordiz, F.J. El mito en la obra narrativa de
Carlos Fuentes.
　　W.B. Faris, 240(HR):Summer89-407
Ordoño, C.M. – see under Macazaga Ordoño, C.
Orduna, G. – see López de Ayala, P.
Orel, H. The Unknown Thomas Hardy.*
　　S. Hunter, 677(YES):Vol20-309
Orel, H., ed. Victorian Short Stories.*
　　F. Kersnowski, 573(SSF):Fall88-490
　　L.K. Uffelman, 635(VPR):Winter89-163
Orenstein, A. – see Ravel, M.
Organ, T.W. Third Eye Philosophy.
　　R.N. Minor, 485(PE&W):Oct89-511
"Origo Characteris Sclavonici."
　　H. Leeming, 575(SEER):Jul89-452
Oring, D., ed. Folk Groups and Folklore Gen-
res.
　　B. Allen, 582(SFQ):Vol46No1-81
Orkin, M. Disinvestment, the Struggle, and
the Future.
　　M.B.R., 185:Oct89-220
Orlando, F. Lecture freudienne de "Phèdre."
　　J-L. Backès, 535(RHL):Jan-Feb89-138
Orlando, L. Palermo. (O. Fotia & A. Coccuzzo,
eds)
　　M. Clark, 617(TLS):28Sep-4Oct90-1026
Orlean, S. Saturday Night.
　　S. Simon, 441:6May90-9
Orledge, R. Charles Koechlin.
　　W. Mellers, 617(TLS):2-8Mar90-216
Orlich, R. Die Parodiemessen von Orlando di
Lasso.
　　M. Just, 416:Band4Heft2-177
　　B. Meier, 417:Oct-Dec89-380
Orlova, A. Tchaikovsky.
　　J. Warrack, 617(TLS):9-15Nov90-1210
Orlove, B.S., M.W. Foley & T.F. Love, eds.
State, Capital, and Rural Society.
　　S. Plattner, 263(RIB):Vol39No2-211
Orlowsky, U. Literarische Subversion bei
E.T.A. Hoffmann.
　　G.R. Kaiser, 224(GRM):Band39Heft4-476
Ormond, L. J.M. Barrie.*
　　R.M.P., 295(JML):Fall88/Winter89-282
Ormsby, F., ed. Northern Windows.
　　A. Haberer, 189(EA):Jul-Sep89-357
Ornato, E., G. Ouy & N. Pons – see de Mont-
reuil, J.
Ornish, N. Pioneer Jewish Texans.
　　S. Shapiro, 441:29Jul90-20
Ornstein-Galicia, J., ed. Form and Function
in Chicano English.
　　P. Benitez-Pérez, 238:Dec89-978
　　O. Santa Ana A., 350:Jun90-424

Orr, J. The Making of the Twentieth-Century
Novel.*
　　M.P.L., 295(JML):Fall88/Winter89-249
Orr, L. Semiotic and Structuralist Analyses
of Fiction.
　　J.J. Sosnoski, 395(MFS):Summer89-373
Orrell, J. The Human Stage.*
　　R.A. Foakes, 551(RenQ):Winter89-879
　　A. Gurr, 570(SQ):Winter89-248
　　D. Smith, 615(TJ):Dec89-573
Orrey, L. Opera. (rev by R. Milnes)
　　A.F.L.T., 412:May89-146
Orrieux, C. Zénon de Caunos, "parépidèmos,"
et le dessin grec.*
　　R. Lonis, 555:Vol62Fasc1-149
Orso, S.N. Art and Death at the Spanish
Habsburg Court.
　　J.H. Elliott, 453(NYRB):1Mar90-26
Ortega, J., with C. Elliott, eds. Gabriel Gar-
cía Márquez and the Powers of Fiction.*
　　G.R. McMurray, 268(IFR):Summer89-133
　　L. Olsen, 395(MFS):Summer89-314
Ortega y Gasset, J. Espíritu de la letra. (R.
Senabre, ed)
　　J. Butt, 86(BHS):Jul89-298
Ortiz de Urbina, J. Parameters in the Gram-
mar of Basque.
　　E. Manandise, 350:Sep90-590
Ortiz Rojas, J.J. Sulma.
　　F. González Cajiao, 352(LATR):Spring90-
163
Ortolani, B., ed. International Bibliography
of the Theatre: 1984.
　　S. Brock, 611(TN):Vol43No2-90
Orton, D.A., ed. Where to Fish, 1990-1991.
　　J. Swift, 617(TLS):10-16Aug90-857
Ortona, E. Anni d'America la Cooperazione
1967-1975.
　　J.L. Harper, 617(TLS):25-31May90-546
Osa, O. Foundation.
　　A. Abarry, 500(RAL):Spring89-150
Osborn, C. A Sense of Touch.
　　J. Mellors, 364:Aug/Sep89-130
Osborne, B. & D. Swainson. Kingston.
　　M. Angus, 529(QQ):Autumn89-723
Osborne, C. The Complete Operas of Richard
Strauss.+
　　M. Kennedy, 415:Apr89-217
Osborne, C. Rethinking Early Greek Philoso-
phy.*
　　D.H. Frank, 319:Jan90-119
　　A.P.D. Mourelatos, 41:Spring89-111
Osborne, J. The Meininger Court Theatre
1866-1890.*
　　R.K. Sarlos, 615(TJ):Dec89-570
Osborne, L. Paris Dreambook. The Angelic
Game.
　　L. Brandon, 617(TLS):5-11Oct90-1072
Osborne, R. Classical Landscape with Fig-
ures.*
　　V. Hunter, 121(CJ):Dec89-Jan90-148
　　J.E. Jones, 303(JoHS):Vol109-249
Osborne, R. Conversations with von Karajan.
　　R. Dyer, 441:5Aug90-12
　　P. Heyworth, 617(TLS):26Jan-1Feb90-92
Osers, E. – see "The New Czech Poetry"
O'Shaughnessy, B. The Will.
　　W.E. Morris & R.C. Richardson,
449:Dec89-677
O'Shea, J. Music and Medicine.
　　S. Harries, 617(TLS):4-10May90-475
O'Shea, M.J. James Joyce and Heraldry.*
　　J.G.C., 70:Oct89-159

Osherow, J. Looking for Angels in New York.
639(VQR):Summer89-98
Osmańczyk, E.J. Encyclopedia of the United Nations and International Agreements.
M.K. Dziewanowski, 497(PolR):Vol34No3-266
Ospovat, A.L. & V.A. Tunimanov, comps. Živye kartiny.
R.D. Le Blanc, 574(SEEJ):Winter89-620
Ossenkop, D. Hugo Wolf.
E. Sams, 415:Jun89-348
J. Williamson, 410(M&L):Nov89-568
Ossola, C. Dal "Cortegiano" all' "Uomo di Mondo."
C.H. Clough, 402(MLR):Jan90-207
Ostenfeld, E. Ancient Greek Psychology and the Modern Mind-Body Debate.*
L. Parker, 124:Nov-Dec89-115
Oster, J. Internal Affairs.
M. Stasio, 441:4Feb90-26
Oster, P. The Mexicans.*
42(AR):Summer89-369
Oster, R.E. A Bibliography of Ancient Ephesus.
S.R.F. Price, 123:Vol39No1-148
Österberg, J. Self and Others.
B. Keenan, 103:May90-196
Osterle, H.D., ed. Bilder von Amerika.*
T.F. Barry, 406:Summer89-247
I.E. Hunt, 221(GQ):Summer89-437
L.L. Miller, 564:Feb89-81
H-P. Rodenberg, 125:Fall88-86
K-H. Schoeps, 133:Band22Heft3/4-375
Ostiguy, L. & R. Sarrasin. Phonétique comparée du français et de l'anglais nord-américains.
B. Rochet, 320(CJL):Jun89-217
Ostriker, A. The Imaginary Lover.
J. McCombs, 102(CanL):Spring89-202
Ostriker, A.S. Stealing the Language.*
A. Kaminsky, 141:Fall89-505
J. McCombs, 102(CanL):Spring89-202
Ostrovsky, E. Under the Sign of Ambiguity.*
H. Levillain, 535(RHL):Mar-Apr89-328
Ostrovsky, V. & C. Hoy. By Way of Deception.
D. Wise, 441:7Oct90-12
Ostwald, M. "Anagke" in Thucydides.
S. Lattimore, 124:Jul-Aug90-535
Ostwald, M. From Popular Sovereignty to the Sovereignty of Law.*
M. Gagarin, 24:Summer89-367
N.F. Jones, 41:Spring89-118
E. Lévy, 303(JoHS):Vol109-241
D.M. Lewis, 123:Vol39No2-279
N. Robertson, 487:Winter89-365
O'Sullivan, J.C. Joyce's Use of Colors.*
M.J. O'Shea, 295(JML):Fall88/Winter89-359
O'Sullivan, V., ed. The Unsparing Scourge.
K. Stewart, 71(ALS):May89-122
O'Sullivan, V. - see Mansfield, K.
O'Sullivan, V. & M. Scott - see Mansfield, K.
Oswald von Wolkenstein. Streuüberlieferung.* (H-D. Mück, ed)
M. Jonas, 680(ZDP):Band108Heft1-114
Otman, G. Essais.
E.M. Guthrie, 399(MLJ):Summer89-227
Otman, G. La rue est à nous.
R.J. Melpignano, 399(MLJ):Winter89-509
O'Toole, P. The Five of Hearts.
F. MacCarthy, 441:12Aug90-18
442(NY):9Jul90-92

Ott, G. Teatro.
R. Perales, 352(LATR):Spring90-188
Ott, U., G. Schuster & M. Pehle, eds. Harry Graf Kessler.
E.M. Chick, 221(GQ):Summer89-399
Ottenberg, H-G. Carl Philipp Emanuel Bach.*
J.R. Stevens, 410(M&L):Feb89-98
Ottewill, D. The Edwardian Garden.*
H. Jordan, 324:Dec89-68
Otto, M. Tom Doesn't Visit Us Anymore.
J. Buckley, 102(CanL):Autumn-Winter89-182
Otto, R. Publishing for the People.
P. Carden, 574(SEEJ):Fall89-476
Ottosen, K. L'antiphonaire latin au moyen-âge.
J.M. McCulloh, 589:Apr89-477
Oudemans, T.C.W. & A.P.M.H. Lardinois. Tragic Ambiguity.*
R.G.A. Buxton, 303(JoHS):Vol109-216
den Ouden, B. & M. Moen, eds. New Essays on Kant.
T. Vinci, 103:Feb90-57
Oudot, S. & D. Gobert. Conversational French.
G. Normand, 207(FR):Mar90-737
C. Philibert, 399(MLJ):Summer89-228
Oughton, J. Mata Hari's Last Words.
S. Scobie, 376:Sep89-123
"Our Common Future."
M. Valiante, 529(QQ):Spring89-23
Ousby, I., ed. The Cambridge Guide to Literature in English.*
566:Spring90-226
Ousby, I. The Englishman's England.
J. Barrell, 617(TLS):28Sep-4Oct90-1043
Ousterhout, A.M. A State Divided.
B.H. Newcomb, 656(WMQ):Jan89-194
Outram, D. The Body and the French Revolution.*
V. Folkenflik, 173(ECS):Winter89/90-218
Ovadiah, R. & A. Hellenistic, Roman and Early Byzantine Mosaic Pavements in Israel.
W. Raeck, 229:Band61Heft4-377
Overall, C. Ethics and Human Reproduction.*
J.C. Callahan, 103:Oct90-421
A. Donchin, 254:Fall89-136
M. Yeo, 154:Vol28No4-655
Overing, J., ed. Reason and Morality.
F.A. Hanson, 488:Jun89-237
Overy, P. & others. The Rietveld Schröder House.*
S. Gutterman, 45:Sep89-59
Ovid. The Love Poems. (A.D. Melville, trans) Ovid's Poetry of Exile. (D.R. Slavitt, trans)
R. Jenkyns, 617(TLS):15-21Jun90-646
Ovid. P. Ovidio Nasone: "Remedia Amoris." (P. Pinotti, ed)
E. Fantham, 124:Jul-Aug90-534
Ovid. Selections from Ovid's "Metamorphoses." (W.S. Anderson & M.P. Frederick, eds)
B.R. Nagle, 124:Mar-Apr90-368
Owen, A.L.R. Conservation Under F.D.R.
J. Braeman, 106:Summer89-41
Owen, F. & D.B. Brown. Collector of Genius.*
M. Cormack, 90:Feb89-159
Owen, S. Mi-lou.
M. Backstrom, 116:Dec89-146
R.B. Kershner, 219(GaR):Fall89-602
Owren, H. Herders Bildungsprogramm und seine Auswirkungen im 18. und 19. Jahrhundert.
R.S. Leventhal, 222(GR):Spring89-82

Owusu, K., ed. Storms of the Heart.
   F. Jussawalla, 538(RAL):Fall89-581
Oxenhorn, H. Tuning the Rig.
   M. Kumin, 441:22Apr90-13
"The Oxford Book of Late Medieval Verse and
   Prose."* (D. Gray, ed)
   S. Kohl, 38:Band107Heft1/2-199
"The Oxford Dictionary of Art." (I. Chilvers &
   H. Osborne, with D. Farr, eds)
   D. Collinson, 89(BJA):Winter89-78
   C. McCorquodale, 39:Sep89-212
"The Oxford-Duden Pictorial French and Eng-
   lish Dictionary." (D. Moskowitz & J. Pheby,
   eds)
   M. Cook, 402(MLR):Jul90-718
"The Oxford-Duden Pictorial Serbo-Croat &
   English Dictionary." (V. Boban & J. Pheby,
   eds)
   J.L. Conrad, 399(MLJ):Autumn89-385
"Oxford Studies in Ancient Philosophy." (Vol
   4) (M. Woods, ed)
   D.W. Graham, 242:Vol10No1-103
"Oxford Studies in Ancient Philosophy." (Vol
   6) (J. Annas, ed)
   P. Hall, 543:Mar90-619
"Oxford Studies in Ancient Philosophy."
   (Supp Vol 1988) (J. Annas & R. Grimm, eds)
   T.V. Upton, 543:Jun90-849
Oxnam, R.B. Cinnabar.
   R.S. Nathan, 441:11Mar90-25
Oz, A. The Slopes of Lebanon.
   L. Anderson, 441:4Feb90-14
   A. Hourani, 617(TLS):8-9Mar90-219
Ozete, O. & S.D. Guillen. Contigo.
   G.D. Greenia, 238:Mar89-161
Ozick, C. Metaphor & Memory.*
   S. Pinsker, 390:May89-45
   I. Stavans, 287:Sep-Oct89-25
   I. Stavans, 532(RCF):Fall89-222
Ozick, C. The Shawl.*
   S. Miron, 390:Oct89-61
Ozment, S., ed. Three Behaim Boys.
   P-L. Adams, 61:Jun90-120
   S.C. Ogilvie, 617(TLS):17-23Aug90-879
Ozouf, M. Festivals and the French Revolu-
   tion.*
   D. Peel, 529(QQ):Winter89-964
Ozouf, M. L'Homme régénéré.
   G. Lewis, 617(TLS):26Jan-1Feb90-93

Pabst, A. Divisio regni.
   D. Braund, 123:Vol39No1-151
Pachet, P. La force de dormir.
   J-Y. Pouilloux, 98:Dec89-974
   S. Rappaport, 450(NRF):Sep89-105
Pachmuss, T. Russian Literature in the Baltic
   Between the World Wars.
   J. Silenieks, 104(CASS):Spring-Winter88-
   454
   G.S. Smith, 575(SEER):Jul89-442
   V. Terras, 574(SEEJ):Fall89-472
Pacht, O. Book Illumination in the Middle
   Ages.*
   W. Cahn, 589:Jul89-750
Pack, E. Städte und Steuern in der Politik
   Julians.
   G.W. Bowersock, 229:Band61Heft3-270
Pack, R. Before it Vanishes.
   P. Mariani, 344:Winter90-207
   L. Rosenberg, 441:6May90-32

Packalen, M.S. Pokolenie 68.
   T. Witkowski, 104(CASS):Spring-Win-
   ter88-420
Packer, G. The Village of Waiting.
   E. Gillies, 617(TLS):26Jan-1Feb90-97
   42(AR):Winter89-110
Packer, J.G. Margaret Drabble.
   C. Doreski, 87(BB):Sep89-204
Packer, N.H. In My Father's House.
   E. Current-Garcia, 577(SHR):Spring89-
   188
de Paco, M. - see Sastre, A.
Pacosz, C. This is Not a Place to Sing. Notes
   from the Red Zone.
   S. Foster, 448:Vol27No3-157
Padel, R. Summer Snow.
   V. Rounding, 617(TLS):7-13Sep90-954
Paden, W.D., ed & trans. The Medieval Pas-
   tourelle.
   M.R. Blakeslee, 589:Oct89-1018
Paden, W.D., ed. The Voice of the Trobairitz.
   D.D.R. Owen, 617(TLS):5-11Jan90-16
Paden, W.E. Religious Worlds.
   A. Denman, 42(AR):Spring89-241
Padfield, P. Himmler.
   R.J. Evans, 617(TLS):24-30Aug90-899
Padilla, H. Self-Portrait of the Other.
   R. González Echevarría, 441:18Feb90-22
Padrón, J.J. On the Cutting Edge.
   M. Mantero, 238:Dec89-982
Paduano, G. & M. Fusillo - see Apollonius
Paehlke, R.C. Environmentalism and the
   Future of Progressive Politics.*
   A.B.C., 185:Apr90-715
Paetzold, H. Ästhetik des deutschen Idealis-
   mus.
   T. Leinkauf, 489(PJGG):Band96Heft1-200
Pagden, A., ed. The Languages of Political
   Theory in Early-Modern Europe.*
   M. Francis, 242:Vol10No6-739
Pagden, A. Spanish Imperialism and the
   Political Imagination.
   J. Lynch, 617(TLS):13-19Apr90-400
Page, C. The Owl and the Nightingale.
   D. Fallows, 617(TLS):13-19Apr90-398
Page, C. Voices and Instruments of the Mid-
   dle Ages.*
   G. Seaman, 242:Vol10No3-387
Page, C. & D. Varrod. Goldman.
   A.J.M. Prévos, 207(FR):Dec89-392
Page, G. Footwork.
   S. Lee, 581:Jun89-249
Page, G. Winter Vision.
   R. Olmstead, 441:17Jun90-10
Page, K. Island Paradise.*
   J. Mellors, 364:Aug/Sep89-130
Page, N. A Byron Chronology.*
   M.G.H. Pittock, 447(N&Q):Dec89-521
Page, N. A Dickens Chronology.*
   R. Mason, 447(N&Q):Dec89-525
   S. Monod, 637(VS):Spring90-513
   A.S. Watts, 155:Spring89-55
Page, N. E.M. Forster.
   J. Haegert, 395(MFS):Winter89-808
   K. Watson, 447(N&Q):Dec89-539
Page, N., ed. Dr. Johnson: Interviews and
   Recollections.
   A.F.T. Lurcock, 447(N&Q):Mar89-113
Page, N. Muriel Spark.
   L. Sage, 617(TLS):21-27Sep90-998
Page, T. & V.W. - see Thomson, V.
Pagels, E. Adam, Eve, and the Serpent.*
   J.F. Cotter, 249(HudR):Spring89-165

Paglia, C. Sexual Personae.
R. Clare, 617(TLS):20–26Apr90–414
T. Teachout, 441:22Jul90–7
H. Vendler, 453(NYRB):31May90–19
Pagliaro, H. Selfhood and Redemption in Blake's Songs.
P.H. Butter, 677(YES):Vol20–288
L.M. Trawick, 403(MLS):Spring89–84
Pagnoulle, C. David Jones.*
A. Cazade, 189(EA):Oct–Dec89–492
B. Eeckhout, 179(ES):Apr89–169
R. Pybus, 565:Winter88/89–67
Painter, G.D. Marcel Proust.* (rev)
J. Weightman, 453(NYRB):18Jan90–10
Paknadel, F., ed. La Méditerrannée au XVIIIe siècle.
S. Davies, 83:Spring89–98
Pal, L.A. State, Class and Bureaucracy.
G.E. Dirks, 529(QQ):Autumn89–760
Palaiologina, I.E.C. A Woman's Quest for Spiritual Guidance. (A.C. Hero, ed & trans)
A.E. Laiou, 589:Apr89–478
Palau i Fabre, J. Picasso Cubism (1907–1917).
J. Russell, 441:2Dec90–9
Palazzolo–Nöding, B. Drei Substandardregister im Französischen.
J. Langenbacher–Liebgott, 72:Band226 Heft1–187
Palencia–Roth, M. Myth and the Modern Novel.
B.A., 295(JML):Fall88/Winter89–249
Paley, V.G. The Boy Who Would Be a Helicopter.
D. Elkind, 441:29Apr90–11
Palii, P. V nemetskom plenu [together with] Vashchenko, N.V. Iz zhizni voennoplennogo.
J.A. Armstrong, 550(RusR):Jan89–107
Palisca, C.V., ed. Norton Anthology of Western Music.
N. Simeone, 415:Aug89–477
Palladio, A. Scritti sull'Architettura (1554–1579). (L. Puppi, ed)
A. Beyer, 683:Band52Heft4–575
Palladius. Palladios, Dialogue sur la vie de Jean Chrysostome. (A–M. Malingrey, ed & trans)
É. des Places, 555:Vol62Fasc2–352
Palliser, C. The Quincunx.*
M. Malone, 441:4Mar90–12
442(NY):5Mar90–106
Pallone, D., with A. Steinberg. Behind the Mask.
D. Cole, 441:22Jul90–21
Pallottino, M. Etruskologie.
H. Lehmann, 229:Band61Heft5–462
Palmer, A. Bernadotte.
J. Ure, 617(TLS):12–18Oct90–1090
Palmer, A. Concept and Object.
O. Hanfling, 521:Jul89–255
P.M. Sullivan, 393(Mind):Jul89–465
F.A. Watts, 518:Oct89–222
Palmer, A. & V. Who's Who in Bloomsbury.
N. Griffin, 556:Summer89–80
Palmer, L.R. Die griechische Sprache.
C.J. Ruijgh, 394:Vol42fasc3/4–511
Palmer, M. Sun.*
D. Allen, 249(HudR):Summer89–327
M. Boruch, 29(APR):Mar/Apr89–41
S.M. Schultz, 639(VQR):Autumn89–773
S. Yenser, 491:Aug89–295
639(VQR):Summer89–98

Palmer, N. Nettie Palmer: Her Private Journal "Fourteen Years." (V. Smith, ed)
C. Wallace–Crabbe, 71(ALS):Oct89–262
Palmer, R.R. – see de Tocqueville, H. & A.
Palmer, S.H. Police and Protest in England and Ireland 1780–1850.
D. Philips, 637(VS):Winter90–338
Palmer, T. Dream Science.
R. Cohen, 441:22Apr90–18
Palmer, T. The Emblems of Thomas Palmer. (J. Manning, ed)
C.W.R.D. Moseley, 402(MLR):Jul90–688
Palmer, W. The Good Republic.
C. Hawtree, 617(TLS):24–30Aug90–902
Palmer, W.J. The Detective and Mr. Dickens.
M. Stasio, 441:16Dec90–33
Palmquist, S.R. A Complete Index to Kemp Smith's Translation of Immanuel Kant's "Critique of Pure Reason."
L.W. Beck, 342:Band80Heft1–121
Palomero, M.P. – see under Pepa Palomero, M.
Palomo, M.D. – see under del Pilar Palomo, M.
Pálsson, H. & P. Edwards – see "Knýtlinga Saga"
Paludan, P.S. "A People's Contest."*
W.E. Parrish, 389(MQ):Winter90–281
Pamuk, O. The White Castle. Kara Kitap.
S. Altinel, 617(TLS):12–18Oct90–1087
Pan, L. Sons of the Yellow Emperor.
A.J. Nathan, 441:9Dec90–26
Panaccione, A., ed. The Memory of May Day.
E. Hobsbawm, 358:Jun90–10
Panagiotou, S., ed. Justice, Law and Method in Plato and Aristotle.
R.F. Stalley, 123:Vol39No2–256
Pancrazi, J–N. Le Passage des princes.
J. Labat, 207(FR):Apr90–896
Pandey, S.M. The Hindi Oral Epic.
J.B. Flueckiger, 293(JASt):May89–427
Pándi, P. "Gespenster" gehen in Ungarn um.
G.F. Cushing, 575(SEER):Jul89–483
Pandolfi, V., ed. La Commedia dell'Arte.
K. Hecker, 610:Autumn89–288
Panek, L.L. An Introduction to the Detective Story.
R.P. Moses, 295(JML):Fall88/Winter89–250
Panetta, V.J. – see Denis, J.
Pang, E–S. In Pursuit of Honor and Power.
G.P. Browne, 263(RIB):Vol39No1–76
Pang Pu. Wenhua de minzuxing yu shidaixing.
J. Thoraval, 98:Aug–Sep89–558
Pangle, T.L., ed. The Roots of Political Philosophy.*
C.J. Rowe, 123:Vol39No2–194
Pangle, T.L. The Spirit of Modern Republicanism.*
J.P. Diggins, 619:Summer89–370
M.R. Zinman, 543:Dec89–409
639(VQR):Summer89–79
Pangle, T.L. – see Strauss, L.
Panichas, G.A. & C.G. Ryn, eds. Irving Babbitt in Our Time.
J.A. Bryant, Jr., 569(SR):Winter89–153
Panikar, P.G.K. & C.R. Soman. Health Status of Kerala.
P.K.B. Nayar, 293(JASt):Nov89–910
Panitz, E. Leben für Leben.
E. Mehnert, 654(WB):1/1989–117
Pankhurst, J., M.S. Smith & P. Van Buren, eds. Learnability and Second Languages.
R. De Keyser, 350:Sep90–649

Pannenberg, W. Metaphysik und Gottesge-
danke.
    P. Clayton, 543:Sep89-179
Panshin, A. & C. The World Beyond the Hill.
    G. Jonas, 441:11Feb90-29
Pantaleoni, H. On the Nature of Music.
    A.D. Shapiro, 187:Spring/Summer89-339
Paolella, A. Retorica e racconto.
    V. Kirkham, 589:Oct89-1019
Papachryssanthou, D., ed. Actes de Xéno-
phon.
    R.W. Allison, 589:Oct89-1021
Papadopoulos, C. L'Expression du temps dans
l'oeuvre romanesque et autobiographique
de Marguerite Yourcenar.
    C.F. Farrell, Jr. & E.R. Farrell, 188(ECr):
    Winter89-108
Papadopoulos, T., ed. Meletai kai ypomnē-
mata.
    J. Rosser, 589:Oct89-1023
Papanghelis, T.D. Propertius.*
    M. Wyke, 313:Vol79-165
Papanicolaou Christensen, A. & others. Hama:
Fouilles et recherches de la Fondation
Carlsberg 1931-1938. (Vol 3, Pt 3)
    K.S. Freyberger, 229:Band61Heft7-652
    R. Higgins, 303(JoHS):Vol109-261
Pape, M. Mendelssohns Leipziger Orgelkon-
zert 1840.
    W.J. Gatens, 410(M&L):Aug89-414
    R.L. Todd, 415:Jun89-374
Paperno, I. Chernyshevsky and the Age of
Realism.
    C. Popkin, 104(CASS):Spring-Winter88-
    438
    W.G. Wagner, 550(RusR):Apr89-201
Papin, B. Sens et fonction de l'utopie tahi-
tienne dans l'oeuvre politique de Diderot.
    L. Loty, 530:Apr89-154
    W.E. Rex, 207(FR):Feb90-546
Papin, L. L'autre scène.
    D. Coward, 402(MLR):Apr90-461
    N. Greene, 210(FrF):Sep89-369
    K. Schoell, 547(RF):Band101Heft1-137
Papineau, D. Reality and Representation.*
    F.J. Clendinnen, 63:Jun89-234
Papini, G.A. - see Carducci, G.
Papp, D.S. - see Rusk, D., with R. Rusk
Paquette, R.L. Sugar is Made With Blood.
    639(VQR):Spring89-45
Parade, L., ed. Kulturarbeit konkret.
    K. Spieler, 654(WB):4/1989-676
Paradin, C. Devises Heroïques.
    O. Reynolds, 617(TLS):15-21Jun90-651
Paradowska, M. Polacy w Meksyku i Ameryce
Środkowej.
    A.A. Hetnal, 497(PolR):Vol34No1-87
Parain-Vial, J. Gabriel Marcel.
    P. Trotignon, 542:Oct-Dec89-616
Paratte, H-D. Alexander Voisard.
    A.L. Amprimoz, 345(KRQ):Feb89-117
Paré, F., ed. Théorèmes et canons.
    E. Guild, 208(FS):Jul89-323
Paré, Y. Les Oiseaux de glace.
    A. Whitfield, 102(CanL):Autumn-
    Winter89-265
Parent, W. - see Thomson, J.J.
Parente, J.A., Jr. Religious Drama and the
Human Tradition.
    L.V.R., 568(SCN):Spring-Summer89-31
Paretsky, S. Burn Marks.
    E. Budd, 441:17Jun90-17
    P. Craig, 617(TLS):21-27Dec90-1382

Pareyson, L. L'estetica di Kant.
    C. La Rocca, 342:Band80Heft2-228
Parfionovich, Y. & V. Dylykova - see Roerich,
Y.N. & others
Parfit, D. Reasons and Persons.
    R.M. Adams, 482(PhR):Oct89-439
Pariente, A., ed. En torno a Góngora.*
    J. Gornall, 86(BHS):Apr89-179
Parini, J. The Last Station.
    M. Seymour, 441:22Jul90-1
Parins, M.J., ed. Malory: The Critical Heri-
tage.
    P.J.C. Field, 447(N&Q):Dec89-496
Paris, B. Louise Brooks.*
    P. O'Connor, 617(TLS):27Apr-3May90-
    458
"Paris et le phénomène des capitales littér-
aires, carrefour ou dialogue des cultures."
    T. de Vulpillières, 549(RLC):Jan-Mar89-
    112
"Paris, 1979-1989."* (B. McClure, trans)
    C. Ellis, 47:Jan89-34
Parizeau, L. Périples autour d'un langage.
    F. Gallays, 627(UTQ):Fall89-216
Park, D. Oranges from Spain.
    K. Joughin, 617(TLS):27Jul-2Aug90-804
Park, D. The David Park Scroll.
    G. Gessert, 448:Vol27No3-134
Park, E. & J.P. Carlhian. A New View from
the Castle.
    S. Gutterman, 46:Feb89-67
Park, K. Doctors and Medicine in Early Re-
naissance Florence.
    P. Denley, 278(IS):Vol44-157
Parke, H.W. Sibyls and Sibylline Prophecy in
Classical Antiquity. (B.C. McGing, ed)
    R.A. Tomlinson, 303(JoHS):Vol109-241
Parker, B. Creation.
    42(AR):Spring89-247
Parker, B. Invisible Matter and the Fate of
the Universe.
    B. Sharp, 441:7Jan90-19
Parker, B.L. A Precious Seeing.
    P. Honan, 447(N&Q):Mar89-101
    N. Rhodes, 402(MLR):Apr90-411
Parker, C. The English Historical Tradition
since 1850.
    H. Kearney, 617(TLS):12-18Oct90-1092
Parker, D. & R. Evans. The Coast of Illyria.
    A. Mackie, 617(TLS):25-31May90-548
Parker, F.R. Black Votes Count.
    M. Barone, 441:22Jul90-14
Parker, G. The Military Revolution.
    639(VQR):Winter89-7
Parker, N. Portrayals of Revolution.
    N. Hampson, 617(TLS):15-21Jun90-637
Parker, P. Ackerley.*
    G. Ewart, 364:Oct/Nov89-122
    S. Hampshire, 453(NYRB):18Jan90-34
    C. McGrath, 442(NY):9Apr90-97
Parker, P. For Starters.
    S. Hornby, 324:Mar90-297
Parker, P. Literary Fat Ladies.
    C. Belsey, 677(YES):Vol20-225
    M.W. Carpenter, 529(QQ):Autumn89-778
    R.J. Du Rocher, 604:Spring/Summer89-31
    J.S. Herz, 627(UTQ):Fall89-115
    M. Quilligan, 570(SQ):Fall89-369
    R.R. Wilson, 178:Dec89-502
Parker, P. & G. Hartman, eds. Shakespeare
and the Question of Theory.*
    D. Ellis, 97(CQ):Vol18No1-86

Parker, R.B. Stardust.
  D. Papineau, 617(TLS):30Nov-6Dec90-
    1287
  R.G. Powers, 441:8Jul90-8
  442(NY):20Aug90-91
Parker, R.D. The Unbeliever.*
  B. Costello, 432(NEQ):Jun89-310
  L. Keller, 405(MP):May90-430
  B.M., 494:Fall89-648
  L.M. Steinman, 27(AL):May89-319
Parker, S.J. Understanding Vladimir Nabokov.
  C. Ross, 395(MFS):Summer89-295
  W.W. Rowe, 574(SEEJ):Fall89-459
Parker, S.T. Romans and Saracens.*
  A. Chastagnol, 555:Vol62Fasc2-377
  R. Schick, 318(JAOS):Apr-Jun88-317
Parker, T. Life after Life.
  I. Bamforth, 617(TLS):23-29Mar90-324
Parker, W.H., ed & trans. Priapea.
  J.J. Winkler, 124:Mar-Apr90-370
Parker-Hale, M.A. G.F. Handel.
  C.M.B., 412:May89-142
Parkin, A. Dancers in a Web.
  M. Jones, 102(CanL):Summer89-186
Parkinson, D.B. Constructing the Social Con-
    text of Communication.*
  D. Reynolds, 355(LSoc):Mar89-144
Parkinson, G.H.R., ed. An Encyclopaedia of
    Philosophy.
  A.R. White, 518:Jul89-156
Parkinson, T. Poets, Poems, Movements.
  M. Jennings, 649(WAL):Feb90-380
Parks, G. Voices in the Mirror.
  P-L. Adams, 61:Dec90-132
  M.E. Dyson, 441:9Dec90-19
Parks, R. The Western Hero in Film and Tele-
    vision.
  P. Skenazy, 649(WAL):Aug89-188
Parks, S. The Elizabethan Club of Yale Uni-
    versity and its Library.
  T.A.B., 179(ES):Apr89-170
  P. Davison, 541(RES):Feb89-143
Parks, T. Family Planning.*
  C. Fein, 441:7Jan90-19
  442(NY):19Feb90-112
Parlett, D. The Oxford Guide to Card Games.
  S. Rushdie, 617(TLS):16-22Nov90-1239
Parma Armani, E. Perin del Vaga, l'anello
    mancante.
  D. Ekserdjian, 90:Jul89-492
  L. Wolk-Simon, 54:Sep89-515
Parmenides. Le deux chemins de Parménide.
  (N-L. Cordero, ed & trans) Parménides.
  (A. Gómez-Lobo, ed & trans) The Frag-
    ments of Parmenides. (A.H. Coxon, ed &
    trans)
  M. Kerkhoff, 160:Jan89-161
Parmenides. Parmenides of Elea: Fragments.
  (D. Gallop, ed & trans)
  A. Barker, 41:Fall89-313
  M. Kerkhoff, 160:Jan89-161
Parmet, H.S. Richard Nixon and His America.
  E.R. May, 617(TLS):28Sep-4Oct90-1024
  R.N. Smith, 441:7Jan90-3
Parodi, M. Il Conflitto dei Pensieri.
  G.R. Evans, 640:Nov89-153
Parodi, S. Cose e parole nei "Viaggi" di Pietro
    Della Valle.
  J.R. Woodhouse, 402(MLR):Oct90-994
Paroissien, D. - see Dickens, C.
Parotti, P. Fires in the Sky.
  P-L. Adams, 61:Oct90-136

Parotti, P. The Trojan Generals Talk.
  E. Fuller, 569(SR):Fall89-cxv
  M. Kuznets, 455:Jun89-69
Parpaglia, P.P. Per una Interpretazione della
    Lex Cornelia de Edictis Praetorum del 67
    A.C.
  A. Lintott, 313:Vol79-265
  W. Selb, 229:Band61Heft6-567
Parpulova-Gribble, L. & C. Gribble. Advanced
    Bulgarian 1, 2.
  C.A. Moser, 574(SEEJ):Winter89-640
Parpulova-Gribble, L. & C. Rudin. Intermedi-
    ate Bulgarian 2.
  C.A. Moser, 574(SEEJ):Winter89-640
Parr, J., ed. Still Running ...
  M. Gillett, 529(QQ):Spring89-132
Parr, J.A. "Don Quixote."
  J. Iffland, 304(JHP):Autumn89-103
  E. Urbina, 238:Sep89-543
Parret, H. & H-G. Ruprecht, eds. Exigences et
    perspectives de la sémiotique.*
  S.E. Larsen, 567:Vol75No1/2-123
Parrinder, P. The Failure of Theory.*
  T. Docherty, 541(RES):May89-300
  S.P., 295(JML):Fall88/Winter89-250
  R. Rooksby, 447(N&Q):Jun89-282
  J. Wallace, 147:Vol6No1-102
Parrinder, P. James Joyce.
  U. Schneider, 38:Band107Heft1/2-253
Parris, M. Inca-Kola.
  D. Murphy, 617(TLS):2-8Nov90-1188
Parris, P.B. Waltzing in the Attic.
  J.A. Goudie, 441:4Nov90-25
Parrish, S.M. - see Coleridge, S.T.
Parrish, T. Roosevelt and Marshall.
  D. Murray, 441:25Feb90-25
Parrish, T.M. & R.A. Willingham, Jr. Confed-
    erate Imprints.*
  G. Wilson, 517(PBSA):Mar89-116
Parry, A.M. The Language of Achilles and
    Other Papers.
  J. Griffin, 617(TLS):23Feb-1Mar90-200
Parry, D.M. Hegel's Phenomenology of the
    "We."
  P.M. Locke, 543:Dec89-413
Parry, G. The Seventeenth-Century.
  566:Spring90-224
Parry, G.J.R. A Protestant Vision.*
  E. Dubois, 242:Vol10No1-113
Parry, L. Textiles of the Arts and Crafts
    Movement.
  J. Harris, 39:Oct89-286
Parsa, M. Social Origins of the Iranian Revo-
    lution.
  M. Yapp, 617(TLS):24-30Aug90-890
Parsons, M.J. How We Understand Art.*
  G. Mayes, 89(BJA):Winter89-73
Parsons, P.J. - see Turner, E.G.
Parsons, W. The Power of the Financial Press.
  R.M. Solow, 441:4Mar90-9
Part, A. The Making of a Mandarin.
  J. Campbell, 617(TLS):3-9Aug90-822
"Les Particules énonciatives en russe contem-
    porain." (Pt 3)
  M. Kirkwood, 575(SEER):Oct89-662
Partnoy, A. The Little School.
  C. Gardner, 448:Vol27No1-140
Partnoy, A., ed. You Can't Drown the Fire.*
  C. Gardner, 448:Vol27No1-140
Parton, A. - see Yablonskaya, M.N.
Partridge, E. Frank Honywood, Private.
  J. Wieland, 71(ALS):May89-130

Partridge, F. Hanging On.
   A. Chisholm, 617(TLS):5–11Oct90–1062
Partridge, M. Alexander Herzen.
   E. Acton, 402(MLR):Apr90–534
   R.M. Davison, 575(SEER):Oct89–606
Pasco, A.H. Novel Configurations.*
   P. Brady, 478(P&L):Apr89–172
   A. Dezalay, 535(RHL):Jul–Aug89–740
   M. Tilby, 208(FS):Oct89–498
Pasenow, H–J. Die konjunktionale Hypotaxe
   in der Nikonchronik.
   R. Marti, 559:Vol13No1–55
Pasierbsky, F. Deutsche Sprache im Reforma-
   tionszeitalter. (E. Büchler & E. Dirksch-
   neider, ed)
   H. Penzl, 685(ZDL):3/1989–350
Pasler, J., ed. Confronting Stravinsky.*
   M. Kielian–Gilbert, 513:Winter89–246
Pasley, M. – see Kafka, F.
Pasley, M. & H. Rodlauer – see Brod, M. & F.
   Kafka
Pasquali, A. Un amour irrésolu.
   J. Roudaut, 450(NRF):Apr89–99
Passavant, G. – see Heydenreich, L.H.
Passek, J–L., ed. D'un cinéma l'autre.
   M–N. Little, 207(FR):Dec89–397
Passin, H. – see Cohen, T.
Passmann, D.F. "Full of Improbable Lies."
   S. Soupel, 189(EA):Jan–Mar89–101
Passty, J.N. Eros and Androgyny.
   A.R. Bensen, 395(MFS):Winter89–795
   L.P. De La Vars, 177(ELT):Vol32No3–352
Pastan, L. The Imperfect Paradise.*
   B. Howard, 491:Sep89–345
Pasternak, B. Deviat' sot Piatyi God: The
   Year Nineteen–Five.
   G. McVay, 402(MLR):Oct90–1048
Pasternak, B. Second Nature. Poems 1955–
   1959 [and] An Essay in Autobiography.
   G. Josipovici, 617(TLS):9–15Feb90–135
Pasternak, E. Boris Pasternak: The Tragic
   Years 1930–1960.
   H. Gifford, 453(NYRB):31May90–26
   G. Josipovici, 617(TLS):9–15Feb90–135
Pastor, R.A. Condemned to Repetition.*
   W.G. Lovell, 529(QQ):Spring89–198
Patai, D., ed. Looking Backward, 1988–1888.
   639(VQR):Summer89–104
Pateman, C. The Disorder of Women.
   J. Waldron, 617(TLS):1–7Jun90–588
Pateman, C. The Sexual Contract.
   W. Kymlicka, 103:Nov90–461
   S.M. Okin, 185:Apr90–658
Pateman, T. Language in Mind and Language
   in Society.*
   S. Baird, 360:Mar90–206
   R.D. Borsley, 361:May89–95
   F. D'Agostino, 488:Sep89–398
Paterson, J.M. Anne Hébert.*
   C.F. Coates, 207(FR):May90–1059
Paterson, L.M. & S.B. Gaunt, eds. The Trou-
   badours and the Epic.*
   P.V. Davies, 382(MAE):1989/1–176
   G. Hesketh, 208(FS):Apr89–196
Patetta, L. L'architettura del Quattrocento a
   Milano.
   R. Schofield, 90:Feb89–155
Patocka, F. Das österreichische Salzwesen.*
   H–R. Fluck, 685(ZDL):2/1989–234

Patočka, J. Le Monde naturel et le mouvement de l'existence humaine.* (H. Decleve,
   ed) Kunst und Zeit. (K. Nellen & I. Srubar,
   eds) Die natürliche Welt als philoso-
   phisches Problem. (K. Nellen & J. Němec,
   eds) Ketzerische Essais zur Philosophie
   der Geschichte und ergänzende Schriften.
   (K. Nellen & J. Němec, eds)
   R. Scruton, 617(TLS):5–11Oct90–1054
Patočka, J. Philosophy and Selected Writings.
   D.T. O'Connor, 103:Jun90–250
Patrides, C.A. & J. Wittreich, eds. The Apoc-
   alypse in English Renaissance Thought and
   Literature.
   D.K. Hedrick, 478(P&L):Oct89–418
Patsch, H. Alle Menschen sind Künstler.
   H. Eichner, 133:Band22Heft2–161
Patten, B. Grinning Jack.
   S. O'Brien, 617(TLS):27Jul–2Aug90–803
Patten, B. Storm Damage.
   J. Whitworth, 493:Summer89–56
"Patterns of Life, Patterns of Art."
   R.W. Lewis, 456(NDQ):Spring89–223
Patterson, A. Pastoral and Ideology.*
   W.W. Batstone, 405(MP):Nov89–170
   A.V. Ettin, 401(MLQ):Jun88–190
   S. Gillespie, 97(CQ):Vol18No3–322
   N. Gross, 124:Nov–Dec89–131
   R. Jenkyns, 184(EIC):Jan89–65
   A. Low, 551(RenQ):Summer89–332
   D. Norbrook, 301(JEGP):Oct89–534
Patterson, D. Literature and Spirit.
   C. Emerson, 395(MFS):Summer89–380
   C. Emerson, 478(P&L):Oct89–380
Patterson, L. Negotiating the Past.*
   D. Brewer, 589:Jul89–751
   R.J. Goldstein, 141:Summer89–327
Patterson, M.R. Authority, Autonomy, and
   Representation in American Literature,
   1776–1865.
   D. Barone, 165(EAL):Vol25No1–88
   W.R. Everdell, 594:Winter89–458
Patterson, T.G. Meeting the Communist
   Threat.
   630(VQR):Winter89–22
Patteson, R.F. A World Outside.*
   H. Bertens, 295(JML):Fall88/Winter89–
   293
Pattison, R. The Triumph of Vulgarity.*
   L. White, 577(SHR):Spring89–182
Pattoni, M.P. L'autenticità del "Prometeo
   Incatenato" di Eschilo.
   M. Davies, 123:Vol39No1–11
Patty, J.S. Dürer in French Letters.
   B.L. Knapp, 446(NCFS):Spring–Summer90–
   550
Patty, J.S., ed. Perspectives on French Ro-
   manticism.
   D.G. Charlton, 402(MLR):Jan90–192
Patzer, A. Bibliographia Socratica.
   M. Winiarczyk, 229:Band61Heft4–351
Paul, B. He Huffed and He Puffed.*
   639(VQR):Summer89–93
Paul, E.F. Equity and Gender.
   J.K., 185:Apr90–711
Paul, E.F., ed. Totalitarianism at the Cross-
   roads.
   O. Figes, 617(TLS):5–11Oct90–1056
Paul, J.M. The Victorian Heritage of Virginia
   Woolf.*
   L. Goldstein, 635(VPR):Summer89–74
   J.M. Stein, 403(MLR):Oct90–929

Paul, M. & M. Rae, eds. New Women's Fiction. (Vol 3)
 F. Adcock, 617(TLS):2-8Feb90-123
Paul, P. Murder Under the Microscope.
 I. Sinclair, 617(TLS):6-12Apr90-371
Paul, R. Vorstudien zu einem Wörterbuch zur Bergmannssprache in den sieben niederungarischen Bergstädten während der frühneuhochdeutschen Sprachperiode.
 E. Neuss, 685(ZDL):2/1989-243
Paulhan, J. La vie est pleine de choses redoutables.
 L. Jenny, 98:Dec89-915
Paulin, T., ed. The Faber Book of Political Verse.*
 H. Buckingham, 565:Winter88/89-45
Paulin, T., ed. The Faber Book of Vernacular Verse.
 T. Shippey, 617(TLS):9-15Nov90-1198
Paulin, T. Fivemiletown.*
 R. Pybus, 565:Winter88/89-67
Paulini, H.M. August Wilhelm Schlegel und die Vergleichende Literaturwissenschaft.
 U. Weisstein, 678(YCGL):No36-164
Paulson, M.G. The Possible Influence of Montaigne's "Essais" on Descartes' "Traité des passions."
 M. Gutwirth, 207(FR):Oct89-156
Paulson, M.G. The Queen's Encounter.
 J. Pizer, 475:Vol16No30-329
Paulson, M.G. & T. Alvarez-Detrell. Cervantes, Hardy and "La fuerza de la sangre."
 P. Gethner, 475:Vol16No30-331
Paulson, S.M. Flannery O'Connor.
 M.J. Friedman, 268(IFR):Summer89-139
 M.B. Gentry, 573(SSF):Spring89-208
Paulson, W.R. Enlightenment, Romanticism, and the Blind in France.*
 B. Rigby, 208(FS):Apr89-216
Paulson, W.R. The Noise of Culture.
 W.J. Ong, 405(MP):Nov89-215
Paulston, C.B., ed. International Handbook of Bilingualism and Bilingual Education.*
 R.V. Teschner, 399(MLJ):Summer89-210
Paulus, J. "Julio Paulo, Sentencias a su hijo." (Bk 1) (M.P. Irigoyen Troconis, ed & trans)
 H.L.W. Nelson, 229:Band61Heft5-419
Pauwels, A. Immigrant Dialects and Language Maintenance in Australia.
 S. Gal, 355(LSoc):Sep89-399
Pauwels, J.R. Women, Nazis, and Universities.
 S.L. Cocalis, 406:Summer89-230
Pauza, M., ed. Zur Problematik der transzendentalen Phänomenologie.
 J. Sivak, 542:Oct-Dec89-617
Pavel, T. Le mirage linquistique.* Univers de la fiction.
 J. Bouveresse, 98:Mar89-169
Pavel, T.G. Fictional Worlds.*
 T. Docherty, 677(YES):Vol20-211
 D. Dowling, 102(CanL):Winter88-118
 F. Merrell, 153:Spring89-2
Pavese, C. Stories.
 F. Girelli-Carasi, 577(SHR):Spring89-196
Pavić, M. Dictionary of the Khazars.* (French title: Le Dictionnaire Khazar.)
 I. Gorak, 152(UDQ):Winter90-93
 G. Kearns, 249(HudR):Summer89-339
 I. Stavans, 287:May-Jun89-29
 P. Vansittart, 364:Apr/May89-151
 639(VQR):Spring89-58
Pavic, M. Landscape Painted with Tea.
 J. Baumbach, 441:16Dec90-11

Pavlova, Ž. Imperatorskaja biblioteka Ermitaža, 1762-1917.
 E. Kasinec, 574(SEEJ):Fall89-477
Paxman, J. Friends in High Places.
 J. Vincent, 617(TLS):21-27Sep90-994
Payerle, G. Unknown Soldier.*
 W.J. Keith, 102(CanL):Spring89-179
Payne, J. Colloquial Hungarian.* (2nd ed)
 M. Pereszlényi-Pintér, 399(MLJ): Winter89-520
Payne, J.R. - see Cotter, J.S., Jr.
Payne, M. The Most Respectable Place in the Territory.
 G.W., 102(CanL):Autumn-Winter89-287
Payne, P. Robert Musil's "The Man without Qualities."
 A. Classen, 221(GQ):Fall89-541
Payne, P. Revelation.
 639(VQR):Winter89-19
Payne, R.O. Geoffrey Chaucer.* (2nd ed)
 C. Brewer, 447(N&Q):Sep89-367
de Paz, E.M.D. - see under Domínguez de Paz, E.M.
Paz, O. The Collected Poems of Octavio Paz, 1957-1987.* (E. Weinberger & others, eds & trans)
 J.D. McClatchy, 491:Apr89-29
 J. Wilson, 364:Jun/Jul89-117
 M. Wood, 493:Autumn89-27
Paz, O. Sor Juana.
 E. Arenal, 141:Fall89-463
 J.F. Cotter, 249(HudR):Summer89-318
 P. García, 377:Mar89-55
 T.R. Hart, 131(CL):Fall89-397
 K.A. Myers, 385(MQR):Summer90-453
 J. Wilson, 364:Jun/Jul89-117
 639(VQR):Spring89-52
Pazi, M., ed. Max Brod 1884-1984.
 H.O. Horch, 680(ZDP):Band108Heft2-300
Pazzi, R. Searching for the Emperor.*
 N. Jones, 364:Jun/Jul89-144
Peach, T. Nature et Raison.
 J. Brunel, 535(RHL):Jan-Feb89-89
Peach, T. - see Toutain, C.
Peacock, M. Take Heart.*
 D. Wojahn, 219(GaR):Fall89-589
 639(VQR):Autumn89-137
Peacock, N. Molière: "L'École des femmes."
 C.J. Gossip, 402(MLR):Oct90-955
Peacock, S.J. Jane Ellen Harrison.*
 R. Ackerman, 637(VS):Summer90-669
 M.R. Lefkowitz, 31(ASch):Summer89-464
Peacocke, A. & G. Gillett, eds. Persons and Personality.
 B.J. Garrett, 393(Mind):Jan89-154
 R.B.S., 185:Jul90-912
Peacocke, C. Thoughts.*
 A. Appiah, 482(PhR):Jan89-110
 J. Campbell, 393(Mind):Jan89-135
 M.F. Egan, 486:Jun89-359
Peak, D. The Cotoneaster Factor.
 J. O'Grady, 617(TLS):8-14Jun90-616
Peale, C.W. The Selected Papers of Charles Willson Peale and His Family. (Vol 2, Pts 1 & 2) (L.B. Miller, with S. Hart, eds)
 R.M. Peck, 658:Spring89-84
Pearce, D., N. Markandya & E.B. Barbier. Blueprint for a Green Economy.
 T. Burke, 324:Feb90-221
Pearce, M. The Mamur Zapt and the Donkey-Vous.
 P. Craig, 617(TLS):29Jun-5Jul90-709

Pearce, M. The Mamur Zapt and the Return of the Carpet.
  N. Callendar, 441:23Dec90-15
Pearce, R.H. Gesta Humanorum.*
  T. Martin, 191(ELN):Dec89-75
Pearlman, M., ed. American Women Writing Fiction.
  S. Armitage, 649(WAL):Nov89-284
  B.K. Scott, 677(YES):Vol20-366
Pearlman, M. & K.U. Henderson. Inter/View.
  A. Johnson, 441:23Sep90-55
Pears, D. The False Prison. (Vol 1)
  D. Bolton, 393(Mind):Jan89-160
  A. Janik, 319:Jul90-468
  D. McQueen, 518:Jul89-149
  S. Mulhall, 521:Oct89-327
  K. Puhl, 479(PhQ):Oct89-503
  B.A. Worthington, 242:Vol10No6-740
Pears, D. The False Prison.* (Vol 2)
  A. Janik, 319:Jul90-468
  S. Mulhall, 521:Oct89-327
  D. Stern, 103:Feb90-75
Pears, D. Motivated Irrationality.
  J. Church, 393(Mind):Jul88-471
Pears, I. The Discovery of Painting.*
  R. Paulson, 173(ECS):Fall89-87
  639(VQR):Autumn89-139
Pearsall, D. "The Canterbury Tales."*
  V. Di Marco, 38:Band107Heft1/2-192
  S. Mapstone, 447(N&Q):Jun89-222
  C.J. Watkin, 148:Winter80-90
Pearsall, D. & N. Zeeman - see Salter, E.
Pearsall, D.A., ed. Manuscripts and Readers in Fifteenth-Century England.
  H. Gneuss, 38:Band107Heft1/2-172
Pearsall, D.A., ed. Manuscripts and Texts.*
  J.D. Burnley, 541(RES):Feb89-111
  H. Gneuss, 38:Band107Heft1/2-172
  A. Hudson, 382(MAE):1989/1-155
  O.S. Pickering, 72:Band226Heft1-151
"Logan Pearsall Smith: An Anthology." (E. Burman, ed)
  M. Shelden, 617(TLS):5-11Jan90-17
Pearson, D.W., comp. "Two Gentlemen of Verona."
  T.H. Howard-Hill, 40(AEB):Vol3No1-20
Pearson, J. Façades.
  617(TLS):9-15Mar90-266
Pearson, J. The Prostituted Muse.
  H. Love, 402(MLR):Oct90-920
Pearson, L. The Greek Historians of the West.
  G.L. Cawkwell, 123:Vol39No2-244
  A. Foley, 124:Nov-Dec89-135
  K. Meister, 229:Band61Heft6-520
  L.J. Sanders, 487:Winter89-375
  F.W. Walbank, 313:Vol79-183
Pearson, N.W., Jr. Goin' to Kansas City.*
  H. Brofsky, 187:Spring/Summer89-334
Pearson, R. Stendhal's Violin.*
  E.J. Talbot, 446(NCFS):Fall-Winter89/90-245
  C.W. Thompson, 208(FS):Oct89-475
Pearson, R., ed. Vtoroi Vserossiiskii S"ezd Konstitutsionno-Demokraticheskoi Partii, 5-11 Ianvaria 1906 g.
  R. Service, 575(SEER):Jan89-148
Pearson, T.S. Russian Officialdom in Crisis.*
  639(VQR):Autumn89-115
Peart-Binns, J.S. Bishop Hugh Montefiore.
  E. Norman, 617(TLS):1-7Jun90-576
Peary, D., ed. Cult Baseball Players.
  M. Gallagher, 441:29Apr90-39

Pease, D.E. Visionary Compacts.*
  J. Michael, 223:Spring89-85
  J.P. Warren, 577(SHR):Summer89-282
Pease, W.D. Playing the Dozens.
  M. Stasio, 441:28Oct90-41
Peattie, M.R. Nan'yō.*
  D.C. Purcell, Jr., 293(JASt):Feb89-179
Peavler, T.J. Individuations.
  J.J. Sosnoski, 395(MFS):Summer89-373
Peck, H.D., ed. The Green American Tradition.
  J. Ballowe, 456(NDQ):Summer89-239
  L. Buell, 27(AL):Dec89-726
  F. Garber, 659(ConL):Winter90-558
Peck, J. & M. Coyne. How to Study a Shakespeare Play.*
  G. Schmitz, 156(ShJW):Jahrbuch1989-332
Peck, M.S. A Bed by the Window.
  M.K. Blakely, 441:2Sep90-6
Peck, R.N. The Horse Hunters.
  639(VQR):Summer89-92
Pecker Berio, T., ed. La trascrizione.
  A. Beaumont, 410(M&L):Feb89-122
Pecora, V. Self and Form in Modern Narrative.
  V. Luftig & M. Wollaeger, 329(JJQ):Spring90-673
Pecoraro, W. & C. Pisacane. L'avverbio.
  M. Palermo, 708:Vol12Fasc1-143
Peddie, J. Invasion.
  H.W. Bonario, 121(CJ):Feb-Mar90-267
Pedersen, J.S. The Reform of Girls' Secondary and Higher Education in Victorian England.*
  J. Perkin, 242:Vol10No6-736
Pederson, L. & others, eds. Linguistic Atlas of the Gulf States. (Vol 1)
  E.W. Schneider, 685(ZDL):2/1989-208
Pedley, J.G. Paestum.
  D. Ridgway, 617(TLS):31Aug-6Sep90-928
Pedroia, L. - see Casti, G.B.
Peeler, D.P. Hope Among Us Yet.
  G. Burbank, 106:Fall89-237
Peer, L.H., ed. The Romantic Manifesto.
  J.R. Rosenberg, 402(MLR):Oct90-900
van Peer, W. Stylistics and Psychology.
  G. Lerchner, 682(ZPSK):Band42Heft9-417
Peeters, B. Tintin and the World of Hergé.
  A. Higgins, 364:Feb/Mar90-127
Peeters, B. Paul Valéry, une vie d'écrivain?
  J. Baetens, 98:Oct89-809
  M.J., 450(NRF):Sep89-103
Pegels, C.C. & others. Management and Industry in China.
  M.A. Von Glinow, 293(JASt):Nov89-838
Péguy, C. Oeuvres en prose complètes.* (Vol 1)
  F. Gerbod, 535(RHL):Mar-Apr89-320
Péguy, C. Oeuvres en prose complètes. (Vol 2) (R. Burac, ed)
  F. Gerbod, 535(RHL):Nov-Dec89-1073
  N. Wilson, 208(FS):Jul89-354
Peirce, C.S. C.S. Peirce: Textes anticartésiens. (J. Chenu, ed & trans)
  A. De Tienne & C.J.W. Kloesel, 619:Summer89-341
Peirce, C.S. Writings of Charles S. Peirce. (Vols 1, 2 & 4) (C.J.W. Kloesel, M.H. Fisch & others eds)
  W.B. Ewald, 617(TLS):8-14Jun90-599

Peirce, C.S. Writings of Charles S. Peirce.*
(Vol 3) (C.J.W. Kloesel & M.H. Fisch, eds)
C. Chauviré, 98:Apr89-282
W.B. Ewald, 617(TLS):8-14Jun99-599
Peires, J.B. The Dead Will Arise.
C. Hope, 617(TLS):17-23Aug90-866
Peiss, K. & C. Simmons, eds. Passion and
Power.
J.S., 185:Apr90-712
Pekhlivanova, K.I. & M.N. Lebedeva. Gram-
matika Russkogo yazyka e Illyustratsiyakh.
(2nd ed)
W.V. Tuman, 399(MLJ):Autumn89-383
Pelckmans, P. Hemsterhuis sans rapports.
M. Delon, 535(RHL):Jul-Aug89-722
A. Strugnell, 402(MLR):Apr90-447
Pelen, M.M. Latin Poetic Irony in the "Roman
de la Rose."*
J. Hill, 382(MAE):1989/2-329
Peletz, M.G. A Share of the Harvest.
L.L. Thomas, 293(JASt):Nov89-939
Pelikan, J. The Melody of Theology.*
M.E. Hussey, 42(AR):Summer89-364
639(VQR):Spring89-67
Pellegrin, J. Réversibilité de Baudelaire.
K. Harrington, 446(NCFS):Spring-
Summer90-533
Pellegrin, P. Aristotle's Classification of
Animals.*
C. Witt, 482(PhR):Oct89-543
Pellegrino, E.D. & D.C. Thomasma. For the
Patient's Good.
D. Van De Veer, 185:Jan90-434
Pellerin, G. Ni le lieu ni l'heure.
M. Benson, 102(CanL):Autumn-Winter89-
273
Pelletier, C. Once Upon a Time on the Banks.*
442(NY):8Jan90-99
Pelletiere, S.C., D.V. Johnson 2d & L.R.
Rosenberger. Iraqi Power and US Security
in the Middle East.
E. Mortimer, 453(NYRB):27Sep90-7
Pelling, C.B.R., ed. Characterization and
Individuality in Greek Literature.
M. Heath, 617(TLS):15-21Jun90-645
Pelling, C.B.R. - see Plutarch
Pellón, G. & J. Rodríguez-Luis, eds. Upstarts,
Wanderers or Swindlers.*
J.A. Jones, 86(BHS):Apr89-176
Pelrine, D.M. African Art from the Rita and
John Grunwald Collection.
B. Frank, 2(AfrA):Aug89-32
Peltenburg, E.J. & others. Lemba Archaeo-
logical Project.* (Vol 1)
S. Hood, 123:Vol39No2-334
F.G. Maier, 303(JoHS):Vol109-257
Pelteret, D.A.E. Catalogue of English Post-
Conquest Vernacular Documents.
J. Green, 617(TLS):21-27Dec90-1386
Pemble, J. The Mediterranean Passion.*
T. Follini, 97(CQ):Vol17No4-381
Pencak, W. & C.E. Wright, eds. Authority and
Resistance in Early New York.
M.L. Lustig, 656(WMQ):Jul89-606
Penfield, J. The Media.*
C.P. Richardson, 399(MLJ):Autumn89-346
Penfield, J., ed. Women and Language in
Transition.*
M.M. Talbot, 353:Vol27No2-375
Penfield, J. & J.L. Ornstein-Galicia. Chicano
English.*
E.W. Schneider, 38:Band107Heft1/2-124

Pénisson, B. Henri d'Hellencourt.
I. Joubert, 102(CanL):Winter88-134
Penley, C., ed. Feminism and Film Theory.
A. Neill & A. Ridley, 103:Sep90-345
Penn, W. The Papers of William Penn. (Vol 2
ed by R.S. & M.M. Dunn, with others; Vols 3
& 4 ed by M.S. Wokeck & others; Vol 5 ed by
E.B. Bronner & D. Fraser)
S.V. James, 656(WMQ):Jan89-165
Penna, S. Un peu de fièvre.
F. Mary, 450(NRF):Mar89-89
Penna, S. Poesie.
P. Robb, 617(TLS):23-29Mar90-327
Penner, J. Natural Order.
F. Busch, 441:26Aug90-6
Pennington, M.C., ed. Teaching Languages
With Computers.
G.T. Diller, 207(FR):Dec89-412
Penrose, R. The Emperor's New Mind.*
J.M. Smith, 453(NYRB):15Mar90-21
Pensabene, P., ed. Marmi Antichi.
J.C. Fant, 313:Vol79-222
Pentland, D.H. & H.C. Wolfart. Bibliography of
Algonquian Linguistics.
E.P. Hamp, 269(IJAL):Jul89-382
Penuel, A.M. Psychology, Religion, and Ethics
in Galdós' Novels.*
J. Whiston, 402(MLR):Apr90-478
Penwarden, C. Little Gregory.
R. Cobb, 617(TLS):28Sep-4Oct90-1028
Pepa Palomero, M. Poetas de los 70.
J. Cano Ballesta, 240(HR):Summer89-396
Peperzak, A.T. Philosophy and Politics.*
H.S. Harris, 488:Sep89-396
Pépin, P-Y. La Terre émue.
J.P. Gilroy, 102(CanL):Spring89-187
Peppe, L. Sulla Giurisdizione in Populos Li-
beros del Governatore Provinciale al Tempo
di Cicerone.
A. Lintott, 313:Vol79-194
Pepper, S. & N. Adams. Firearms and Fortifi-
cations.*
C.H. Clough, 278(IS):Vol43-159
Pepper, T. & J. Kobal. The Man Who Shot
Garbo.
K. Newman, 707:Autumn89-286
Pepys, S. The Pepys Ballads. (W.G. Day, ed)
R. Zim, 447(N&Q):Sep89-398
Pera, M. Hume, Kant e l'induzione.
C. La Rocca, 342:Band80Heft3-354
Percy, T. & J. Bowle. Cervantine Correspon-
dence. (D. Eisenberg, ed)
J.J. Allen, 240(HR):Spring89-234
F. Pierce, 402(MLR):Apr90-477
Perdue, C.L., Jr., ed. Outwitting the Devil.
K.F. Stone, 582(SFQ):Vol46No2-202
Perec, G. Un cabinet d'amateur.
J-Y. Pouilloux, 98:Apr89-263
Perec, G. L'infra-ordinaire.*
J. Piel, 98:Nov89-903
Perec, G. Things. A Man Asleep.
D. Gunn, 617(TLS):10-16Aug90-841
Perec, G. W or the Memory of Childhood.*
R. Jancu, 390:Aug/Sep89-61
Pereira, J. My Dear Mr. Bell. (C.P. Cloughly,
J.G.L. Burnby & M.P. Earles, eds)
W.H. Brock, 635(VPR):Summer89-84
Perelman, B. The First World.
W. Marsh, 456(NDQ):Winter89-225
Perelman, S.J. Don't Tread on Me.* (P. Crow-
ther, ed)
S.P., 295(JML):Fall88/Winter89-392

Pereszlényi-Pintér, M. Advanced Hungarian 1.
  J. Victor-Rood, 399(MLJ):Winter89-521
Pereszlényi-Pintér, M. & J.N. Ludányi. Elementary Hungarian 1. Elementary Hungarian 2. Intermediate Hungarian I.
  J. Victor-Rood, 399(MLJ):Winter89-520
Pereszlényi-Pintér, M. & J.N. Ludányi. Intermediate Hungarian 2. Reading Hungarian 1.
  J. Victor-Rood, 399(MLJ):Winter89-521
Péret, B. Oeuvres complètes. (Vol 4)
  M-C. Dumas, 535(RHL):Jul-Aug89-746
Peretz, D. Intifada.
  D. McDowall, 617(TLS):9-15Nov90-1203
Pérez, A.J. Poética de la prosa de J.L. Borges.*
  B.J. McGuirk, 86(BHS):Jan89-106
Pérez, J.B. Fases de la poesía creacionista de Gerardo Diego.
  H.T. Young, 593:Fall89-221
Pérez, O.B. - see under Barrero Pérez, O.
Pérez, R. Severo Sarduy and the Religion of the Text.
  P. Rozencvaig, 711(RHM):Dec89-195
Pérez Firmat, G. Literature and Liminality.*
  J. Labanyi, 86(BHS):Jul89-288
Pérez Galdós, B. The Golden Fountain Cafe.
  L.B. Osborne, 441:25Mar90-22
Pérez Galdós, B. Our Friend Manso.* (R. Russell, trans)
  J. Rutherford, 86(BHS):Jul89-290
Pérez Galdós, B. Torquemada. (F.M. López-Morillas, trans)
  J. Lowe, 86(BHS):Apr89-185
Pérez Gutiérrez, M. La estética musical de Ravel.
  A. Fernández, 410(M&L):Nov89-574
Pérez Higuera, T. La Puerta del Reloj de la catedral de Toledo.
  J. Huidobro Pérez-Villamil, 48:Apr-Jun89-229
Pérez-Ramos, A. Francis Bacon's Idea of Science and the Maker's Knowledge Tradition.
  R. Kennington, 543:Dec89-414
Pérez Sánchez, A.E. La Nature morte espagnole.
  E. Bermejo, 48:Oct-Dec89-476
Pérez Sánchez, A.E. & E.A. Sayre. Goya and the Spirit of the Enlightenment.* (Spanish title: Goya y el espíritu de la ilustración.)
  P.E. Muller, 380:Winter89-374
  A. Stewart, 324:Dec89-73
  J.A. Tomlinson, 127:Fall89-260
Pérez-Tibi, D. Dufy.
  E. Cowling, 617(TLS):12-18Oct90-1102
Perina, R.M. & R. Russell, eds. Argentina en el mundo (1973-1987).
  A. Vacs, 263(RIB):Vol39No1-77
Perkell, J.S. & D.H. Klatt, eds. Invariance and Variability in Speech Processes.
  D.R. Ladd, 353:Vol27No1-166
Perkin, H. The Rise of Professional Society.*
  D. Cannadine, 453(NYRB):15Feb90-25
Perkins, D. A History of Modern Poetry: Modernism and After.*
  A. Robinson, 541(RES):May89-288
  V.S., 295(JML):Fall88/Winter89-257
Perkins, E. - see Harpur, C.
Perkins, R.L., ed. International Kierkegaard Commentary.
  J.H. Thomas, 323:Oct89-301

Perl, J. Paris without End.*
  R.C. Cafritz, 90:Sep89-661
  E.M. Gomez, 55:May89-112
  D.D. Todd, 290(JAAC):Fall89-394
  639(VQR):Spring89-67
Perlemuter, V. & H. Jourdan-Morhange. Ravel according to Ravel.*
  R. Howat, 415:May89-284
Perlin, J. A Forest Journey.
  S. Mills, 617(TLS):11-17May90-490
Perlman, H.H. The Dancing Clock.
  P. Hampl, 441:1Apr90-20
Perlmann, M.L. Der Traum in der literarischen Moderne.
  P.F. Dvorak, 221(GQ):Summer89-397
  R.H. Lawson, 406:Summer89-271
Perloff, M. The Dance of the Intellect.*
  W. Pratt, 131(CL):Spring89-202
  M. Schiralli, 289:Fall89-123
Perloff, M. The Futurist Moment.*
  W. Bohn, 131(CL):Spring89-200
  J. Meyers, 364:Apr/May89-119
Perloff, M. The Poetics of Indeterminacy.
  R. Chambers, 546(RR):Nov89-630
Perloff, M., ed. Postmodern Genres.
  P.D. Murphy, 590:Jun90-83
Perneczky, G. The Story of the Colourful Ribbons.
  G. Gessert, 448:Vol27No3-132
Pernicone, V. - see Boccaccio, G.
Pernoud, R. Couleurs du moyen âge.
  W.B. Clark, 589:Apr89-480
Pérol, J. Pouvoir de l'ombre.
  D. Pobel, 450(NRF):Dec89-118
Perosa, M.L.P. - see under Premuda Perosa, M.L.
Pérouse de Montclos, J-M. - see De L'orme, P.
Perović, M.R., ed. Iskustva prošlosti.
  C.H. Krinsky, 576:Mar89-98
Perr, H. Making Art Together Step-by-Step.
  J.A. Hobbs, 709:Spring90-186
Perraudin, M. Heinrich Heine.
  R. Robertson, 402(MLR):Jul90-798
Perrault, C. Contes. (R. Zuber, ed)
  J. Barchilon, 475:Vol16No30-362
  P. Sellier, 535(RHL):Jan-Feb89-102
  M. Slater, 208(FS):Apr89-208
  J.M. Zarucchi, 207(FR):Mar90-714
Perrault, C. Pensées chrétiennes de Charles Perrault. (J. Barchilon & C. Velay-Vallantin, eds)
  M. Koppisch, 207(FR):Feb90-544
  J.L. Pallister, 568(SCN):Spring-Summer89-22
Perreiah, A.R. Paul of Venice.
  I. Boh, 589:Jan89-206
Perret, M. Le Signe et la mention.
  S.N. Rosenberg, 207(FR):Feb90-592
Perrett, R.W. Death and Immortality.*
  B. Warren, 63:Jun89-250
Perrie, M. The Image of Ivan the Terrible in Russian Folklore.*
  D.E. Bynum, 574(SEEJ):Spring89-137
Perrin, M. - see Lactantius
Perrin, N. A Reader's Delight.*
  R. Asselineau, 189(EA):Oct-Dec89-500
Perrot, M., ed. A History of Private Life. (Vol 4)
  R. Shattuck, 441:1Apr90-24
Perry, A. Bethlehem Road.
  M. Stasio, 441:5Aug90-29
Perry, A. The Face of a Stranger.
  R. Herbert, 441:18Nov90-40

Perry, B., ed. American Ceramics.
  P. Hunter-Stiebel, 139:Dec89/Jan90-20
Perry, M.J. Morality, Politics and Law.
  J. Shklar, 185:Jan90-427
Perry, P. On the Bus.
  D. English, 441:9Dec90-3
Perry, T.A. The Moral Proverbs of Santob de
  Carrión.
  D.J. Lasker, 242:Vol10No5-627
  D.S. Severin, 551(RenQ):Autumn89-562
  B. Taylor, 240(HR):Winter89-82
Perry, T.D. Professional Philosophy.
  R.A. Watson, 449:Jun89-403
Persico, J.E. Casey.
  M.R. Beschloss, 441:7Oct90-11
Persius. The "Satires" of Persius.* (G. Lee,
  trans; W. Barr, ed)
  S.H. Braund, 123:Vol39No1-29
Person, J.E., Jr., ed. Literature Criticism
  from 1400 to 1800. (Vols 5 & 6)
  S. Soupel, 189(EA):Jul-Sep89-365
Person, L.S., Jr. Aesthetic Headaches.*
  V. Hyles, 594:Summer89-219
  J. McIntosh, 445(NCF):Jun89-99
  J. McWilliams, 27(AL):Mar89-109
Pertschuk, M. & W. Schaetzel. The People
  Rising.*
  L. Sager, 453(NYRB):25Oct90-23
Perucho, J. Libro de caballerías.
  J. Martí-Olivella, 240(HR):Autumn89-537
Perucho, J. Natural History.*
  I. Fonseca, 617(TLS):16-22Feb90-180
Perutz, L. By Night Under the Stone Bridge.*
  (French title: La Nuit sous le pont de
  pierre.)
  P-L. Adams, 61:Jun90-121
  A. Clyde, 441:27May90-16
  D. Durrant, 364:Dec89/Jan90-134
Perutz, L. Leonardo's Judas.* The Marquis of
  Bolibar.*
  P. Vansittart, 364:Apr/May89-151
Peruzzi, E. Studi leopardiani, II.
  M. Marti, 228(GSLI):Vol166fasc533-144
Perysinakis, I.N. E ennoia toy ploytoy stēn
  Istoriē toy Erodotoy.
  J.T. Hooker, 303(JoHS):Vol109-218
Pesando, F. Oikos e ktesis.
  R.A. Tomlinson, 303(JoHS):Vol109-264
Pesce, D. The Affinities and Medieval Trans-
  position.
  S. Fuller, 308:Fall89-439
Pesenti, T. Professori e promotori di medicina
  nello studio di Padova dal 1405 al 1509.
  K. Park, 589:Jan89-207
Pesetsky, B. Confessions of a Bad Girl.*
  P.J. Bailey, 455:Dec89-61
  R. Orodenker, 573(SSF):Summer89-355
Peteneva, Z.M. Jazyk i stil' russkix bylin.
  J. Bailey, 574(SEEJ):Winter89-619
Peter, J. Vladimir's Carrot.*
  E. Brater, 130:Summer89-184
  J. Fisher, 397(MD):Jun89-318
  V.K., 295(JML):Fall88/Winter89-263
Péter, L. & R.B. Pynsent, eds. Intellectuals
  and the Future in the Habsburg Monarchy,
  1890-1914.
  R.J.W. Evans, 575(SEER):Oct89-634
Peter of Ailly. Concepts and Insolubles.
  (P.V. Spade, ed & trans)
  I. Boh, 438:Winter89-101
Peterman, M. Robertson Davies.*
  D. Brydon, 178:Mar89-116
  J.S. Grant, 168(ECW):Fall89-135

Peters, C. Thackeray's Universe.*
  G.A. Hudson, 594:Winter89-460
  W. Hughes, 454:Fall89-102
  G.C. Sorensen, 541(RES):May89-280
Peters, E. The Potter's Field.
  T.J. Binyon, 617(TLS):26Jan-1Feb90-86
  M. Stasio, 441:30Dec90-26
Peters, H.F.M. & W. Hulstijn, eds. Speech Mo-
  tor Dynamics in Stuttering.
  E. Abberton, 361:May89-87
Peters, M. The House of Barrymore.
  B. Nightingale, 441:25Nov90-3
Peters, T.F. Transitions in Engineering.
  E.C. Robison, 576:Jun89-197
Peters, U. Religiöse Erfahrung als literar-
  isches Faktum.
  D.H. Green, 402(MLR):Jan90-129
Peters, W.H. & others. Effective English
  Teaching.
  S. Stotsky, 128(CE):Nov89-750
Petersen, A.F. Why Children and Young Ani-
  mals Play.
  M. Menu, 555:Vol62Fasc2-344
Petersen, B.T., ed. Convergences.
  N.R. Comley, 128(CE):Feb89-192
Petersen, K.H., ed. Criticism and Ideology.
  C. Nwankwo, 538(RAL):Fall89-532
Petersen, R. & C. – see Yamasaki, T.
Petersen, S. Marktweiber und Amazonen.
  M-T. Leuker-Schnelle, 242:Vol10No3-368
Peterson, B.L., Jr. Contemporary Black Amer-
  ican Playwrights and Their Plays.*
  R. Engle, 70:Apr89-69
Peterson, C.L. The Determined Reader.*
  L.G. Zatlin, 158:Mar89-24
Peterson, G.B., ed. The Tanner Lectures on
  Human Values. (Vol 9)
  483:Oct89-573
Peterson, L.H. Victorian Autobiography.*
  K.H. Beetz, 635(VPR):Summer89-78
Peterson, L.S. Juanita Brooks.
  W. Mulder, 649(WAL):Aug89-159
Peterson, M. A Time of War.
  D. Fitzpatrick, 441:27May90-14
Peterson, M.D. & R.C. Vaughen, eds. The Vir-
  ginia Statute for Religious Freedom.
  J. Ryder, 619:Spring89-221
Peterson, M.J. Family, Love, and Work in the
  Lives of Victorian Gentlewomen.*
  M.K. Clarke, 637(VS):Summer90-649
  M. Rapoport, 358:Feb90-8
Peterson, S. Daniel Defoe.
  P.N. Furbank, 566:Autumn89-63
  J.A. Stoler, 166:Jan90-161
Peterson, S. The Living Tradition of Maria
  Martinez.
  139:Dec89/Jan90-24
Peterson, V.L. Idea y representación literaria
  en la narrativa de René Marqués.
  E. Irizarry, 238:May89-309
Peterson, W.F. The Berlin Liberal Press in
  Exile.
  M. Goth, 221(GQ):Summer89-420
Petöfi, J.S., ed. Text and Discourse Consti-
  tution.
  M. Velcic, 567:Vol74No1/2-165
Petr, J. & I. Popjordanov, eds. 40 let vědecké
  a kulturní spolupráce ČSSR a BLR.
  D. Short, 575(SEER):Oct89-667
Petr, J. & Z. Urban, eds. Slavistický odkaz
  F.L. Čelakovského.
  D. Short, 575(SEER):Apr89-261

Petrarch. Letters on Familiar Matters. (A.S. Bernardo, ed & trans)
C.H. Rawski, 276:Spring89-59
Petrarch. Francesco Petrarca, "Canzoniere." (G. Regn, ed)
F-R. Hausmann, 547(RF):Band101Heft1-138
Petrarch. The Revolution of Cola di Rienzo.* (M.E. Cosenza, ed) (2nd ed rev by R.G. Musto)
L.V.R., 568(SCN):Spring-Summer89-29
Petrarch. Selected Letters. (C. Kallendorf, ed)
D.H. Smith, 123:Vol39No1-162
Petrat, N. Hausmusik des Biedermeier im Blickpunkt der zeitgenössischen musikalischen Fachpresse (1815-1848).
U. Konrad, 417:Apr-Jun89-178
Petrea, M.D. Ernesto Sábato.
S. Bacarisse, 86(BHS):Jan89-113
Petrey, S. Realism and Revolution.
M. Melara, 446(NCFS):Spring-Summer90-573
Petrić, V. Constructivism in Film.
J. Izod, 677(YES):Vol20-359
R. Taylor, 575(SEER):Jan89-155
D.J. Youngblood, 550(RusR):Oct89-446
Petrignani, S. The Toy Catalogue.
P. Curry, 617(TLS):7-13Dec90-1327
Petrillo, R. Itinerario del primo Verga, 1864-74.
A. Pallotta, 593:Summer89-142
D. Tench, 276:Summer89-234
Petrioli Tofani, A. & G. Smith. Sixteenth-Century Tuscan Drawings from the Uffizi.
C.M. Goguel, 90:Oct89-712
Petrobelli, P., M. Di Grigorio Casati & C.M. Mossa - see Verdi, G.
Petrocchi, G. La Selva del Protonotario.
M. Marti, 228(GSLI):Vol166fasc533-126
Petroski, H. The Pencil.
J. Adkins, 441:4Feb90-21
J. Bell, 617(TLS):9-15Nov90-1201
C. Murphy, 61:Jan90-74
J. Updike, 442(NY):4Jun90-99
Petrovics-Ofner, L. Broken Places.
P. L. Adams, 61:Sep90-121
Petrucci Nardelli, F. - see Bronzino, A.
Petry, A.H. A Genius in His Way.
E. Brown, 27(AL):Oct89-478
M. Kreyling, 573(SSF):Fall88-479
R.O. Stephens, 26(ALR):Winter90-89
Petsopoulos, Y. - see Atasoy, N. & J. Raby
Pett, S. Sirens.
B. Kent, 441:19Aug90-22
Pettersson, T. Att söka sanningen.*
M. Mazzarella, 563(SS):Winter89-92
Pettersson, T. Literary Interpretation.
S. Davies, 478(P&L):Oct89-384
P. Kitson, 447(N&Q):Dec89-554
R. Stecker, 290(JAAC):Summer89-294
Petyt, K.M. Dialect and Accent in Industrial West Yorkshire.*
J.C. Beal, 355(LSoc):Sep89-443
Petzl, G., ed. Die Inschriften von Smyrna. (Vol 2, Pt 1)
D.J. Geagan, 229:Band61Heft5-448
D.M. Lewis, 123:Vol39No2-350
A.G. Woodhead, 303(JoHS):Vol109-243
Petzoldt, L. & S. de Rachewiltz, eds. Der Dämon und sein Bild.
J. Jech, 196:Band30Heft3/4-047

Petzoldt, L. & S. de Rachewiltz, eds. Studien zur Volkserzählung.
S. Top, 196:Band30Heft3/4-344
Peucker, B. Lyric Descent in the German Romantic Tradition.
J.F. Fetzer, 221(GQ):Winter89-99
K.L. Komar, 222(GR):Fall89-187
Peyer, B.C., ed. The Singing Spirit.
C.D. Thompson, 441:11Feb90-18
Peyser, J. Leonard Bernstein.*
R.S. Clark, 249(HudR):Spring89-101
Pfaff, F. Twenty-five Black African Filmakers.
R. Bell-Metereau, 538(RAL):Summer89-284
Pfanner, H., ed. Kulturelle Wechselbeziehungen im Exil/Exile Across Cultures.*
U.K. Faulhaber, 222(GR):Summer89-137
Pfeffer, P.F. A. Philip Randolph, Pioneer of the Civil Rights Movement.
C.G. Fraser, 441:23Sep90-49
D. Pinckney, 453(NYRB):22Nov90-29
Pfeiffer, B.B., ed. Frank Lloyd Wright: His Living Voice.
R.G. Wilson, 576:Jun89-192
Pfeiffer, H., H.R. Jauss & F. Gaillard, eds. Art social und art industriel.
G. Handwerk, 52:Band24Heft3-320
Pfister, M. The Theory and Analysis of Drama.
M. Carlson, 567:Vol76No3/4-267
Pfitzner, H. Hans Pfitzner: Sämtliche Schriften. (Vol 4) (B. Adamy, ed)
J. Williamson, 410(M&L):Feb89-124
Pflanze, O. Bismarck and the Development of Germany.
J.J. Sheehan, 617(TLS):16-22Nov90-1223
Pflaum, R. Grand Obsession.
Y. Baskin, 441:7Jan90-32
Pflüger, K. & H. Herbst. Schreibers Papiertheater.
K. Vania, 196:Band30Heft1/2-156
Pfrommer, M. Studien zu alexandrinischer und grossgriechischer Toreutik frühhellenistischer Zeit.
D.W.J. Gill, 123:Vol39No1-114
Phan, M. O. Les Amours illégitimes, histoires de séduction en Languedoc (1676-1786).
M. Cottret, 531:Jul-Dec89-537
Phelan, S. Identity Politics.
L. Pineau, 103:Oct90-423
Philip, M. Godwin's Political Justice.
F. Ferguson, 173(ECS):Winter89/90-234
Philip, N., ed. A New Treasury of Poetry.
C.A. Duffy, 617(TLS):3-9Aug90-833
Philip, N. - see Yeats, W.B.
Philip, N. & V. Neuburg - see Dickens, C.
Philipe, A. Le Regard de Vincent.
M-T. Noiset, 207(FR):Oct89-210
Philippon, A. Jean Eustache.
J. Anzalone, 207(FR):Dec89-395
Philippon, A. André Téchiné.
J.J. Michalczyk, 207(FR):Feb90-566
Phillips, C. The Final Passage.
T. Nolan, 441:29Apr90-38
Phillips, C. - see Hopkins, G.M.
Phillips, D.Z. Faith After Foundationalism.
C. Lyas, 483:Jul89-419
Phillips, E. Emily Dickinson.
V. Pollak, 27(AL):Oct89-477
Phillips, E. Hope Springs Eternal.
C. Rooke, 376:Mar89-136

Phillips, G.D. Fiction, Film, and Faulkner.
  A. Bleikasten, 395(MFS):Winter89–748
  R. Fadiman, 392:Summer89–333
  D. Polan, 27(AL):May89–314
Phillips, H., with others. Modern Thai Litera-
  ture, with an Ethnographic Interpretation.
  C.J. Compton, 293(JASt):May89–439
Phillips, J.H. Poet of the Colours.
  C. Hanna, 71(ALS):Oct89–273
Phillips, J.K., F.M–V. Klein & R.N. Liscinsky.
  Quoi de neuf?
  J–C. Seigneuret, 399(MLJ):Spring89–88
Phillips, K.P. The Politics of Rich and Poor.
  K. Scharfenberg, 61:Jun90–117
  G. Wills, 453(NYRB):19Jul90–3
  D.H. Wrong, 441:24Jun90–1
  442(NY):23Jul90–88
Phillips, L. – see "The Latin Riddle Book"
Phillips, M. The "Memoir" of Marco Parenti.
  G. Brucker, 589:Jul89–753
Phillips, M. – see Blake, W.
Phillips, M.R. George MacDonald.
  L. Smith, 571(ScLJ):Spring89–22
Phillips, R. & N. Foy. The Random House Book
  of Herbs.
  L. Yang, 441:2Dec90–21
Phillips, S.H. Aurobindo's Philosophy of
  Brahman.*
  E.B. Findly, 318(JAOS):Jan–Mar88–183
Philo, G. Seeing and Believing.
  P. Whitehead, 617(TLS):14–20Sep90–968
Philo of Alexandria. Filone d'Alessandria, La
  filosofia mosaica. (K. Reggiani & R. Radice,
  trans; R. Radice, ed)
  E. des Places, 555:Vol62Fasc1–152
"The Philosophy of Science of Ruđer
  Bošković."
  M. Carrier, 489(PJGG):Band96Heft2–421
Philpin, C.H.E., ed. Nationalism and Popular
  Protest in Ireland.
  S.H. Palmer, 242:Vol10No5–616
Phinney, E., P.E. Bell & B. Romaine. Cam-
  bridge Latin Course Unit 1.* (3rd ed)
  A. Shaw, 124:Sep–Oct89–62
Phipps, F. Let Me Be Lost.*
  L. Milesi, 395(MFS):Summer89–323
Phocas, P. Gide et Guéhenno polémiquent.*
  G. Leroy, 535(RHL):Jan–Feb89–156
Photius. Epistulae et Amphilochia. (Vol 6,
  fasc 1) (L.G. Westerink, ed)
  L. Siorvanes, 123:Vol39No1–139
Physick, J. – see Whinney, M.
Piacentino, E.J. T.S. Stribling.*
  F. Hobson, 27(AL):Mar89–121
Picabia, L. & A. Zribi–Hertz. Découvrir la
  grammaire française.
  B.K. Barnes, 207(FR):Oct89–182
Picard, M. An Introduction to the Compara-
  tive Phonetics of English and French in
  North America.
  W. Cichocki, 207(FR):Apr90–909
  B. Rochet, 320(CJL):Jun89–217
Piccirilli, L. Temistocle, Aristide, Cimone,
  Tucidide di Melesia fra politica e propa-
  ganda.
  M. Jehne, 229:Band61Heft2–171
Pichl, R. & others, eds. Grillparzer und die
  Europäische Tradition.*
  K. Schaum, 133:Band22Heft2–175
Pichois, C. Baudelaire.*
  O. Conant, 441:25Mar90–23
Pichois, C. & J. Ziegler. Baudelaire.*
  R. Pouilliart, 535(RHL):Mar–Apr89–308

Pick, C. – see Montagu, M.W.
Pick, D. Faces of Degeneration.
  E. Weber, 617(TLS):30Mar–5Apr90–335
Pickard, N. Bum Steer.
  M. Stasio, 441:4Mar90–35
Picken, L. Music from the Tang Court. (Vols
  2 & 3)
  J.S.C. Lam, 187:Spring/Summer89–345
Picker, M. Johannes Ockeghem and Jacob
  Obrecht.
  D. Fallows, 410(M&L):May89–247
Pickering, O.S., ed. The South English Minis-
  try and Passion Edited from St. John's Col-
  lege, Cambridge, MS. B.6.*
  K. Bitterling, 38:Band107Heft3/4–525
  T.J. Heffernan, 589:Jul89–755
Pickering, S.F., Jr. Still Life.
  S. Slosberg, 441:23Sep90–49
Pickles, J.D. & J.L. Dawson, eds. A Concor-
  dance to John Gower's "Confessio Aman-
  tis."*
  C. Gauvin, 189(EA):Oct–Dec89–465
  H. White, 382(MAE):1989/1–153
Picoche, J–L. – see Gil y Carrasco, E.
Picon, A. Claude Perrault, 1613–1688, ou la
  curiosité d'un classique.
  R.W. Berger, 576:Dec89–394
Picón–Garfield, E., ed & trans. Women's Fic-
  tion from Latin America.
  639(VQR):Winter89–14
Picón–Garfield, E. Women's Voices from Latin
  America.
  H.R.M., 295(JML):Fall88/Winter89–203
Picone, M., ed. Il giuoco della vita bella.
  C. Calenda, 379(MedR):Aug89–288
Pieczonka, A. Sprachkunst und bildende
  Kunst.
  G. Kranz, 52:Band24Heft3–335
Piedmont, R.M. Beiträge zum französischen
  Sprachbewusstsein im 18. ten Jahrhundert.
  J–P. Saint–Gerand, 209(FM):Oct89–257
Piekarski, V., ed. Westward the Women.
  N. German, 577(SHR):Fall89–389
Pienkos, A.T. The Imperfect Autocrat.*
  J.M.P. McErlean, 104(CASS):Spring89–116
Pienkos, D.E. One Hundred Years Young.*
  S.A. Blejwas, 497(PolR):Vol34No4–379
Pierce, D.M. Down in the Valley.
  M. Stasio, 441:26Aug90–26
Pierce, J.J. Foundations of Science Fiction.
  P. Parrinder, 561(SFS):Jul89–231
Piercy, M. Available Light.
  S. Pugh, 493:Spring89–47
Piercy, M., ed. Early Ripening.
  L. Sail, 565:Summer89–75
Pierman, C.J. The Age of Krypton.
  W. Harmon, 472:Vol16No1–136
Pierrehumbert, J.B. & M.E. Beckman. Japa-
  nese Tone Structure.
  Haruo Kubozono, 348(L&S):Oct–Dec89–
  373
  D.R. Ladd, 297(JL):Sep89–519
Piersen, W.D. Black Yankees.
  D.M. Jacobs, 656(WMQ):Apr89–396
Pierson, G.W. The Founding of Yale.
  W.A. Koelsch, 432(NEQ):Dec89–622
Pierson, P. Commander of the Armada.
  J.H. Elliott, 453(NYRB):1Mar90–26
Pierson, W.D. Black Yankees.
  W.J. Bolster, 432(NEQ):Mar89–133
  P. Edwards, 538(RAL):Fall89–573
Pietilä–Castrén, L. Magnificantia publica.
  J. Briscoe, 123:Vol39No1–149

Pietralunga, M. Beppe Fenoglio and English Literature.
  E. Saccone, 400(MLN):Jan89–256
Pietsch, H.C. Grundlagen des Cembalospiels.
  B. Billeter, 416:Band4Heft2–181
Piette, I. Littérature et Musique.*
  U. Weisstein, 678(YCGL):No36–197
Pifer, C.S. & J. Sandoz, Jr. Son of Old Jules.
  J.J. Wydeven, 649(WAL):Feb90–388
Pigault–Lebrun. L'Enfant du carnaval, histoire remarquable et surtout véritable, pour servir de supplément aux Rhapsodies du jour.
  J.F. Jones, Jr., 173(ECS):Spring90–368
Pigeaud, J. Folie et cures de la folie chez les médecins de l'antiquité gréco-romaine.*
  J. Boulogne, 555:Vol62Fasc1–148
Piggott, S. Ancient Briton and the Antiquarian Imagination.
  M. Hunter, 617(TLS):9–15Feb90–153
Pigman, G.W. 3d. Grief and English Renaissance Elegy.
  J. Egan, 568(SCN):Spring–Summer89–13
Piguet, J–C. – see Ansermet, E.
Pilrainen, I.T. Das Stadt– und Bergrecht von Banská Štiavnica/Schemnitz.*
  E. Neuss, 685(ZDL):2/1989–243
Pike, D.E. Vietnam and the Soviet Union.*
  H. Gelman, 104(CASS):Spring89–86
  S.K. Gupta, 550(RusR):Jul89–344
Pikulik, L. E.T.A. Hoffmann als Erzähler.*
  C.E. Schweitzer, 400.Summer89–266
  G. Vitt–Maucher, 196:Band30Heft1/2–158
Pikulik L, H Kurzenberger & G Guntermann, eds. Deutsche Gegenwartsdramatik.* (Vols 1 & 2)
  R.C. Conard, 406:Winter89–503
  L.C. De Meritt, 221(GQ):Summer89–435
  K–H. Schoeps, 301(JEGP):Oct89–604
de Pilar Palomo, M. La poesía en la Edad de Oro (Barroco).
  M.L. Welles, 240(HR):Spring89–232
Pilcher, R. September.
  B. Plain, 441:6May90–14
Pilkington, M. Gurney, Ireland, Quilter and Warlock.
  S. Banfield, 415:Oct89–614
Pilnyak, B. "Chinese Story" and Other Tales by Boris Pilnyak.*
  G.L. Browning, 574(SEEJ):Fall89–458
Pilzer, P.Z., with R. Dietz. Other People's Money.*
  J.K. Galbraith, 453(NYRB):18Jan90–15
Pimlott, B., A. Wright & T. Flower, eds. The Alternative.
  J. Vincent, 617(TLS):20–26Jul90–768
Piñal, F.A. – see under Aguilar Piñal, F.
Pinchard, B. Métaphysique et sémantique.
  O. Boulnois, 192(EP):Jul–Dec89–517
Pincher, C. The Spycatcher Affair.
  639(VQR):Spring89–62
Pinchon, J. Morphosyntaxe du français.
  W.J. Ashby, 320(CJL):Mar89–77
Pinciss, G.M. Literary Creations.
  J.G. Fink, 615(TJ):Oct89–417
Pincoffs, E.L. Quandaries and Virtues.*
  L.H. Hunt, 482(PhR):Apr89–249
  R. Paden, 321:Mar89–79
Pindell, T. Making Tracks.
  E. Zotti, 441:9Sep90–27
Pinder–Wilson, R. Studies in Islamic Art.
  R. Hillenbrand, 59:Mar89–109
  R. Hillenbrand, 463:Spring89–47

Pine, R. The Dandy and the Herald.
  R. Gagnier, 177(ELT):Vol32No3–341
Piñera, V. Una caja de zapatos vacía. (L.F. González–Cruz, ed)
  T. Kapcia, 86(BHS):Apr89–196
Pingenot, B.E. Siringo.
  R.L. Buckland, 649(WAL):Feb90–386
Pinget, R. The Apocrypha.
  J.T. Naughton, 577(SHR):Winter89–74
Pinget, R. Monsieur Songe.
  A. Whitehouse, 441:21Jan90–20
Pinget, R. Du Nerf.
  G. Craig, 617(TLS):9–15Nov90–1215
Pingree, D., ed. Picatrix.
  W. Shumaker, 589:Jul89–757
Pingree, D. – see Vettius Valens
Pini, I., ed. Corpus der minoischen und mykenischen Siegel. (Vol 11)
  J. Boardman, 229:Band61Heft4–373
Pinion, F.B. – see Hardy, T.
Pinkard, T. Democratic Liberalism and Social Union.*
  W.A. Galston, 185:Apr90–676
Pinkard, T. Hegel's Dialectic.*
  125:Summer89–421
Pinkus, B. The Jews of the Soviet Union.
  R.S. Wistrich, 617(TLS):23–29Nov90–1261
Pinkus, B. & I. Fleischhauer. Die Deutschen in der Sowjetunion.
  M. McCauley, 575(SEER):Apr89–303
Pinkwart, D. & W. Stammnitz. Peristylhäuser westlich der unteren Agora.
  J.J. Coulton, 123:Vol39No2–412
Pinney, T. – see Kipling, R.
Pinotti, P. – see Ovid
Pinsker, H. & W. Ziegler, eds & trans. Die altenglischen Rätsel des Exeterbuchs.*
  R. Gleissner, 38:Band107Heft1/2–140
Pinsker, S. The Uncompromising Fictions of Cynthia Ozick.*
  S.E. Marovitz, 295(JML):Fall88/Winter89–389
  E. New, 508:Sep89–288
Pinsky, R. The Want Bone.
  E. Hirsch, 441:18Nov90–24
Pinter, H. The Dwarfs.
  M. Imlah, 617(TLS):5–11Oct90–1072
  D. Kaufman, 441:18Nov90–28
Pinto, F.M. – see under Mendes Pinto, F.
Pipes, D. Greater Syria.
  M. Yapp, 617(TLS):21–27Sep90–996
Pipes, D. The Rushdie Affair.
  E. Mortimer, 441:22Jul90–3
Pipes, R. The Russian Revolution.
  R. Hingley, 441:7Oct90–7
Pipili, M. Laconian Iconography of the Sixth Century B.C.*
  S. Woodford, 303(JoHS):Vol109–265
Pippin, R. Hegel's Idealism.
  T. Pinkard, 543:Jun90–831
Pippin, R., A. Feenberg & C.P. Webel, eds. Marcuse.
  S. Sim, 89(BJA):Summer89–282
Pirandello, L. Collected Plays of Luigi Pirandello. (Vol 1)
  R. Bates, 97(CQ):Vol18No4–420
Pirandello, L. Tonight We Improvise and "Leonora, Addio."
  M.R. Vitti–Alexander, 276:Spring89–64
Pire, F. Questions de psychologie.
  J–M. Gabaude, 542:Oct–Dec89–632
Pirie, D.B. – see Empson, W.

Pirogova, L.I. Conjugation of Russian Verbs. (2nd ed)
D.M. Fiene, 399(MLJ):Winter89-527
Piromalli, A. - see Mosino, F.
Pirotte, J-C. Les Contes bleus du Vin.
F. Mary, 450(NRF):May89-99
Pisarczyk, K. Slawische Ortsnamen ⟩ Deutsche Ortsnamen - Personenamen.
J. Udolph, 688(ZSP):Band49Heft1-214
Pisemsky, A. Nina; The Comic Actor; An Old Man's Sin.
P. Chester, 574(SEEJ):Summer89-307
Pistorius, A. Cutting Hill.
P-L. Adams, 61:Aug90-92
Pitoni, G.O. Notitia de' contrapuntisti e compositori di musica. (C. Ruini, ed)
G. Dixon, 410(M&L):May89-254
H. Lenneberg, 309:Vol9No4-299
Pitt, D.G. E.J. Pratt: The Master Years, 1927-1964.*
S.E. Billingham, 529(QQ):Autumn89-735
Pitt, J.C., ed. Theories of Explanation.
M. Espinoza, 542:Oct-Dec89-654
Pitter, R. Collected Poems.
T. Gooderham, 617(TLS):16-22Nov90-1248
Pittock, M. - see Johnson, L.
Pivčević, E. Change and Selves.
A.W. Moore, 617(TLS):27Jul-2Aug90-805
de Pizan, C. - see under Christine de Pizan
Pizer, D. Dos Passos' "U.S.A."
R.J. Reising, 395(MFS):Summer89-275
Pizzo, S., M. Fricker & P. Muolo. Inside Job.*
J.K. Galbraith, 453(NYRB):18Jan90-15
Place, M. The Confusion of Anglers.
I. McMillan, 493:Winter89/90-65
Place, R. The Romans.
S.J. Freebairn-Smith, 123:Vol39No2-367
Plachy, S. Sylvia Plachy's Unguided Tour.
R. Lippincott, 441:18Nov90-28
Plain, B. Harvest.
W. Schott, 441:30Sep90-35
Planché, J.R. Plays by James Robinson Planché. (D. Roy, ed)
D. Mayer, 611(TN):Vol43No1-33
Plangg, G.A. & M. Iliescu, eds. Akten der Theodor Gartner-Tagung (Rätoromanisch und Rumänisch) in Vill/Innsbruck 1985.
D. Messner, 547(RF):Band101Heft2/3-306
Plante, D. The Native.
C. Rooke, 376:Jun89-128
639(VQR):Winter89-20
Plathe, A. Klaus Mann und André Gide.*
P. Schnyder, 547(RF):Band101Heft2/3-351
R. Theis, 52:Band24Heft3-331
Plato. Early Socratic Dialogues. (T.J. Saunders, ed)
A. Ford, 124:Jul-Aug90-534
D.J. de Vries, 394:Vol4fasc1/2-191
Plato. Phaedrus. (C.J. Rowe, ed & trans)
G.B. Kerferd, 303(JoHS):Vol109-226
Plato. Platonis Epistulae.* (J. Moore-Blunt, ed)
S.R. Slings, 394:Vol42fasc1/2-192
Plato. Plato's "Symposium." (A. Nehamas & P. Woodruff, trans)
J.S. Zembaty, 103:Jan90-34
Platt, J. Zabawy Przyjemne i Pożyteczne 1770-1777.
M. Tomaszewski, 549(RLC):Jan-Mar89-130

Platz, N.H. Die Beeinflussung des Lesers.
W. Klooss, 38:Band107Heft1/2-236
Plautus. Bacchides.* (J. Barsby, ed & trans)
F. Muecke, 313:Vol79-185
Plaza, M. Ecriture et folie.
H. Rey-Flaud, 535(RHL):Jan-Feb89-172
Pleasants, H. - see Wieck, F.
Pleck, E. Domestic Tyranny.
C.H. Sommers, 473(PR):Vol56No1-164
Pleines, J-E., ed. Kant und die Pädagogik.
E. Hufnagel, 342:Band80Heft1-117
Pleket, H.W. & R.S. Stroud. Supplementum Epigraphicum Graecum. (Vol 34)
P.M. Fraser, 123:Vol39No2-421
Pley, H. De sneeuwpoppen van 1511.
J. Reynaert, 204(FdL):Dec89-306
Plimpton, G., ed. The Paris Review Anthology. The Writer's Chapbook.
D. Kirby, 441:4Mar90-11
Plimpton, G., ed. Writers at Work. (Vol 8)
42(AR):Winter89-109
"Plotinus." [Loeb, Vols 6 & 7] (A.H. Armstrong, trans)
M.J. Atkinson, 123:Vol39No2-389
J. Bussanich, 124:Jul-Aug90-528
É. des Places, 555:Vol62Fasc2-351
Plotkin, C.H. The Tenth Muse.
G.B. Tennyson, 445(NCF):Mar90-574
Plourde, S., with others. Vocabulaire philosophique de Gabriel Marcel.*
J. Colette, 192(EP):Jan-Mar89-114
Plouzeau, M., ed. "Parise la Duchesse:" Chanson de geste du XIIIe siècle.*
L.S. Crist, 589:Apr89-481
Plumb, J.H. The American Experience.
639(VQR):Autumn89-116
Plumptre, G. Garden Ornament.
R.I. Ross, 617(TLS):19-25Jan90-74
Plunka, G.A. Peter Shaffer.
D.A. Klein, 130:Summer89-188
J.C. Trewin, 157:No173-38
Plunkett, J. The Boy on the Back Wall and Other Essays.
J.M. Cahalan, 174(Éire):Fall88-153
Plunkett, J. The Circus Animals.
S. Leslie, 617(TLS):21-27Dec90-1381
Plutarch. Life of Antony. (C.B.R. Pelling, ed)
J.M. Carter, 313:Vol79-211
C.D. Hamilton, 124:Jul-Aug90-529
R. Seager, 123:Vol39No2-201
Pluto, T. Loose Balls.
C. Paikert, 441:23Dec90-13
Ply, M.S. & D.H. Winchell. Writer, Audience, Subject.
R.F. Lunsford, 580(SCR):Fall90-192
Pocock, J.G.A. The Ancient Constitution and the Feudal Law.
S.A. Conrad, 242:Vol10No1-117
Pocock, J.G.A. The Machiavellian Moment. Virtue, Commerce and History.
J-F. Spitz, 98:May89-307
Pocock, T. Alan Moorehead.
J. Ryle, 617(TLS):9-15Feb90-140
Podlecki, A.J. The Early Greek Poets and Their Times.
A.M.V. Taalman Kip, 394:Vol42fasc3/4-504
Podossinov, A. Ovids Dichtung als Quelle für die Geschichte des Schwarzmeergebiets.
D. Braund, 123:Vol39No1-141
M. Mirković, 229:Band61Heft3-258

"The Poem of My Cid (Poema de Mio Cid)." (P.
Such & J. Hodgkinson, trans)
    J.N.H. Lawrance, 86(BHS):Jul89−272
    J.T. Snow, 238:May89−316
"Poetry World 2."
    D.J. Enright, 617(TLS):12−18Jan90−40
Pogge, T.W. Realizing Rawls.
    W.J. Norman, 103:Nov90−465
Poggenburg, R.P. Charles Baudelaire.
    P. Burrell, 446(NCFS):Fall−Winter89/90−
    292
    J. Ziegler, 535(RHL):Mar−Apr89−310
Poggi, G. Il Duomo di Firenze. (M. Haines, ed)
    D.F. Zervas, 90:Sep89−649
Pogorelsky, A. The Double or My Evenings in
Little Russia.
    J.M. Mills, 574(SEEJ):Summer89−302
Pohl, A. Untersuchungen zur Wortbildung.
    W. Lubaszewski, 688(ZSP):Band49Heft1−
    218
Pohl, A. & A. de Vincenz, eds. Deutsch−Pol−
nische Sprachkontakte.*
    M. Gehrmann, 682(ZPSK):Band42Heft3−
    401
Pohle, F. Das mexikanische Exil.
    A. Stephan, 406:Fall89−401
Pohorský, M. − see Čapek, K.
Pointer, R.W. Protestant Pluralism and the
New York Experience.
    B.E. Steiner, 656(WMQ):Jan89−186
Pointon, M., ed. Pre−Raphaelites Re−Viewed.
    P.L. Sawyer, 637(VS):Summer90−664
Poirier, C. − see "Dictionnaire du français
plus"
Poirier, R. The Renewal of Literature.*
    C. Biggs, 147:Vol6No1−71
Poirion, D., ed. Jérusalem, Rome, Constanti−
nople.
    F. Bonney, 531:Jan−Mar89−155
Poirion, D. Résurgences.
    E.B. Vitz, 589:Apr89−483
Poissant, C. Passer la nuit.
    L.E. Doucette, 108:Spring89−84
Poisson, G. Monsieur de Saint−Simon.
    P. Hourcade, 535(RHL):Jan−Feb89−108
Poisson, R. "Le Baron de la Crasse" et
"L'Après−soupé des auberges." (C.
Mazouer, ed)
    J. Clarke, 208(FS):Oct89−466
    P. Hourcade, 475:Vol16No30−321
Poizat, B. Groupes stables.
    J. Loveys, 316:Dec89−1494
Pol Stock, M. Dualism and Polarity in the
Novels of Ramón Pérez de Ayala.
    W. Newberry, 593:Fall89−223
Polan, D.B. The Political Language of Film
and the Avant−Garde.*
    T.C., 295(JML):Fall88/Winter89−269
Polasky, J. Revolution in Brussels 1787−
1793.
    J. Black, 83:Autumn89−214
von Polenz, P., J. Erben & J. Goossens, eds.
Kontroversen, alte und neue. (Vol 4)
    D. Stellmacher, 260(IF):Band94−367
Polesini, L.K. & R.U. Maiguashca − see under
Karumanchiri Polesini, L. & R.U. Maiguashca
Poliakoff, M.B. Combat Sports in the Ancient
World.*
    S. Instone, 303(JoHS):Vol109−256
    H.W. Pleket, 123:Vol39No1−107
Polianskii, N. MID.
    M. McCauley, 575(SEER):Jul89−500

Politien, A. Les Silves. (P. Galand, ed &
trans)
    R. Friedman, 551(RenQ):Winter89−835
Polkinghorne, D.E. Narrative Knowing and
the Human Sciences.*
    B. Johnstone, 480(P&R):Vol22No2−145
Pollack, D. The Fracture of Meaning.
    H. Ooms, 244(HJAS):Jun89−266
Pollack, R−G. George S. Kaufman.
    D.B. Wilmeth, 615(TJ):Dec89−565
Pollak, V.R. − see Norcross, E. & E. Dickinson
Pollard, A. & S. McBride. The Lanscape of the
Brontës.
    J.A. Kestner, 620(TSWL):Spring89−135
Pollard, E.B. Visual Arts Research.
    A. Dutta, 709:Spring90−191
Pollard, J.G., ed. Italian Medals.
    R. Falkiner, 39:Feb89−140
Pollard, M. Dublin's Trade in Books, 1550−
1800.
    J. Raven, 617(TLS):8−14Jun90−618
Pollard, S. Britain's Prime and Britain's
Decline.
    M.J. Wiener, 637(VS):Spring90−539
· Pollini, J. The Portraiture of Gaius and Lu−
cius Caesar.
    R. Brilliant, 124:Jan−Feb90−256
    R. Hannah, 123:Vol39No1−119
    R.R.R. Smith, 313:Vol79−213
Pollitt, J.J. Art in the Hellenistic Age.*
    H. von Hesberg, 229:Band61Heft6−539
    S.G. Miller, 54:Sep89−510
Pollner, C. Englisch in Livingston.
    G. Leitner, 000:Oct00−010
Pollock, G. Vision and Difference.
    J.A. Isaak, 59:Sep89−362
Pollock, J.L. How to Build a Person.
    C. Macdonald, 617(TLS):23−29Nov90−
    1270
Pollock, J.L. Technical Methods in Philoso−
phy.
    P.K. Moser, 103:Aug90−331
Pollock, S.I. − see "The Rāmāyaṇa of Vālmīki"
Polo, G.G. − see under Gil Polo, G.
Polo de Medina, J. Poesía: Hospital de incur−
ables. (F.J. Diez de Revenga, ed)
    J. Checa, 240(HR):Summer89−388
    R.M. Price, 86(BHS):Jul89−283
Polowy, T. The Novellas of Valentin Raspu−
tin.
    D. Gillespie, 402(MLR):Oct90−1048
    K. Parthé, 574(SEEJ):Winter89−627
Polt, J.H.R. Batilo.
    E.V. Coughlin, 238:Dec89−959
    S−A. Kitts, 402(MLR):Jul90−766
Pomathios, J−L. Le Pouvoir politique et sa
représentation dan l'"Énéide" de Virgile.
    P.R. Hardie, 123:Vol39No1−26
Pombo, A. Des crimes insignifiants.
    M. Alhau, 450(NRF):Mar89−91
Pomerantsev, K. Skvoz' smert'.
    G.S. Smith, 575(SEER):Jul89−442
Pomeroy, S.B. Frauenleben im klassischen
Altertum.
    G. Müller, 654(WB):1/1989−165
Pommer, R., D. Spaeth & K. Harrington. In the
Shadow of Mies.*
    R. Kimball, 45:Nov89−77
    R. Padovan, 46:Apr89−14
Pommier, R. Roland Barthes, ras le bol!*
    R. Shryock. 345(KRQ):May89−240
Pomorska, K. & S. Rudy − see Jakobson, R.
Ponce, J.G. − see under García Ponce, J.

Ponce de León, J.L. El arte de la conversación. El arte de la composición. (4th ed)
    H. Ruiz, 399(MLJ):Autumn89-391
Pons, P. D'Edo à Tōkyō, Mémoires et modernités.
    H. Cronel, 450(NRF):Jan89-94
Ponting, C. 1940.
    H. Strachan, 617(TLS):27Apr-3May90-439
Poole, A. "Coriolanus."
    M. Neill, 402(MLR):Jul90-692
Poole, A. Tragedy.*
    M.E. Reesor, 529(QQ):Summer89-494
    F. Rosslyn, 97(CQ):Vol18No2-208
Poole, C. Among the Sioux of Dakota.
    D.R. Miller, 650(WF):Jan89-78
Poole, F.F. The Rock Garden: Stories.
    F. Adcock, 617(TLS):2-8Feb90-123
Poole, R. Richard Hughes.
    R.M.P., 295(JML):Fall88/Winter89-353
Poole, T.R. Identifying Antique British Silver.
    A.B.B., 90:May89-365
Poore, D. No Timber Without Trees.
    M. Bruce, 324:Apr90-371
Poovey, M. Uneven Developments.*
    M.M. Clarke, 637(VS):Spring90-488
    R. Felski, 141:Fall89-455
    J.P.R., 185:Apr90-711
    L.M. Shires, 454:Fall89-99
Pope, A. Poems in Facsimile.
    566:Spring90-210
Pope, S.L. Catching the Light.
    K. Morton, 441:5Aug90-18
Pope-Hennessy, J., with L.B. Kanter. The Robert Lehman Collection.* (Vol 1)
    R.B. Simon, 551(RenQ):Spring89-118
Popham, M.R., with others. The Minoan Unexplored Mansion at Knossos.
    S. Hiller, 229:Band61Heft7-605
Popkin, J.D. Revolutionary News.
    G. Lewis, 617(TLS):14-20Dec90-1355
Popkin, R.H. Isaac La Peyrère (1596-1676).
    P. Burke, 242:Vol10No1-115
    I.C. Jarvie, 488:Sep89-345
Popkin, R.H. & C.B. Schmitt, eds. Scepticism from the Renaissance to the Enlightenment.
    R.A. Watson, 319:Jul90-447
Popkin, R.H. & M.A. Signer - see Spinoza, B.
Popova, T.V., ed. Slavjanskaja morfonologija.
    F.Y. Gladney, 574(SEEJ):Winter89-637
Popović, T. Prince Marko.
    J.L. Conrad, 104(CASS):Spring-Winter88-531
    E.C. Hawkesworth, 575(SEER):Oct89-605
Poppendieck, J. Breadlines Knee-Deep in Wheat.
    J. Braeman, 106:Summer89-41
Porete, M. Le Mirouer des simples ames. (R. Guarnieri, ed) Speculum simplicium animarum. (P. Verdeyden, ed)
    L. Löfstedt, 439(NM):1989/2-233
    K. Ruh, 684(ZDA):Band118Heft1-16
Porod, R. Der Literat Curtius.
    S. Borzsák, 229:Band61Heft5-441
Porphyry. Porphyry's Launching-Points to the Realm of Mind. (K.S. Guthrie, trans)
    M. Miller, 124:Jul-Aug90-540
    J.A. Novak, 103:Jan90-25
Porphyry. Porphyry's Letters to His Wife Marcella. (A. Zimmern, trans)
    J.A. Novak, 103:Jan90-25

Portefaix, L. Sisters Rejoice.
    C.S. Hamilton, 124:Jul-Aug90-536
Porteous, J.D. The Mells.
    A. Rayburn, 424:Jun89-189
Porter, C. Larissa Reisner.
    B. Heldt, 575(SEER):Apr89-289
Porter, D., J. Robertson & I.C. Smith, eds. I Can Sing, Dance, Rollerskate and Other Short Stories by Scottish Writers.
    C. Gow, 571(ScLJ):Spring89-51
Porter, D.H. Horace's Poetic Journey.*
    A.J. Woodman, 123:Vol39No2-208
Porter, D.H. Only Connect.*
    P.E. Easterling, 303(JoHS):Vol109-230
Porter, E. & J. Iceland.
    P-L. Adams, 61:Feb90-108
Porter, H.A. Stealing the Fire.
    K. Byerman, 395(MFS):Winter89-768
Porter, H.F. January, February, June, or July.
    C. Rooke, 376:Sep89-119
Porter, I. Operation Autonomous.
    D. Pryce-Jones, 617(TLS):19-25Jan90-58
Porter, J.A. Shakespeare's Mercutio.
    C.H. Kullman, 580(SCR):Fall90-177
Porter, J.R. & J. Bélisle. La Sculpture ancienne au Québec.
    J. Castel-Vanderburgh, 627(UTQ):Fall89-240
Porter, K.A. Letters of Katherine Anne Porter. (I. Bayley, ed)
    R. Price, 441:27May90-1
Porter, L. The Banished Prince.
    M. Hinden, 130:Summer89-197
    J.A. Robinson, 27(AL):Dec89-716
Porter, L. & L.M., eds. Aging in Literature.
    I. Sobkowska-Ashcroft & L. Berman, 549(RLC):Jan-Mar89-109
Porter, M.E. The Competitive Advantage of Nations.
    R.B. Reich, 617(TLS):31Aug-6Sep90-925
    L.C. Thurow, 441:27May90-7
Porter, P. - see Bell, M.
Porter, P. & A. Boyd. Mars.
    D. Houston, 493:Summer89-51
Porter, R. Four Contemporary Russian Writers.
    D. Rayfield, 617(TLS):2-8Mar90-237
Porter, R. Mind-Forg'd Manacles.
    W.B. Ober, 566:Spring89-186
    J. Wiltshire, 97(CQ):Vol18No2-198
Porter, R. A Social History of Madness.
    42(AR):Winter89-109
Porter, R. & D. In Sickness and in Health.
    D.A. Bennahum, 173(ECS):Spring90-333
Porter, R. & M. Teich, eds. Romanticism in National Context.*
    M. Stocker, 478(P&L):Oct89-394
Porter, R. & S. Tomaselli, eds. The Dialectics of Friendship.
    R. Dinnage, 617(TLS):2-8Feb90-114
Porter, R.P. Forked Tongue.
    A. Hacker, 453(NYRB):22Nov90-19
Pörtl, K., ed. Reflexiones sobre el Nuevo Teatro Español.*
    K. Kohut, 72:Band226Heft1-218
Porxomovskij, V.J., ed. Afrikanskoe istoručeskoe jazykoznanie - problemy rekonstrukcii.
    S. Brauner, 682(ZPSK):Band42Heft6-869
Posner, R.A. Cardozo.
    P.A. Freund, 441:4Nov90-31

Posner, R.A. Law and Literature.
  V. Kahn, 153:Summer89–21
  B. Lang, 478(P&L):Oct89–421
  639(VQR):Spring89–66
Posner, R.A. The Problems of Jurisprudence.
  C. Woodard, 441:9Sep90–15
Posse, A. The Dogs of Paradise.
  G. Brotherston, 617(TLS):29Jun–5Jul90–
  704
  A. Coleman, 441:18Mar90–22
  G. Wills, 453(NYRB):22Nov90–6
Post, J.F. The Faces of Existence.*
  D. Gordon, 258:Dec89–489
  N. Unwin, 518:Jul89–162
van der Post, L. The Lost World of the Kala-
hari.
  42(AR):Spring89–248
van der Post, L., with J-M. Pottiez. A Walk
with a White Bushman.
  S. Pickering, 569(SR):Spring89–297
Postan, M.M. & E. Miller, with C. Postan, eds.
The Cambridge Economic History of Europe.
(Vol 2) (2nd ed)
  K.L. Reyerson, 589:Oct89–1025
Poster, M. – see Baudrillard, J.
Posthumus, J. A Description of a Corpus of
Anglicisms.
  B. Carstensen, 685(ZDL):1/1989–120
Postigliola, A., ed. Storia e ragione.
  D. Morineau, 535(RHL):Jul–Aug89–716
Postman, N. Die Verweigerung der Hörigkeit.
  M. Hofmann, 654(WB):2/1989–346
Poteet, M., ed. Textes de l'exode.*
  Y. Frenette, 298:Fall89–140
Potempa, G. Thomas Mann.
  H. Lehnert, 462(OL):Vol44No3–267
Potichnyj, P.J. & H. Aster, eds. Ukrainian–
Jewish Relations in Historical Perspective.
  A.S. Korros, 550(RusR):Oct89–415
Potok, C. The Gift of Asher Lev.
  B. Morton, 617(TLS):2–8Nov90–1182
  N. Stiller, 441:13May90–29
Potrebenko, H. Life, Love and Unions.
  J. Kuropatwa, 102(CanL):Spring89–161
Pott, H.G., ed. Johann Christian Günther (Mit
einem Beitrag zu Lohensteins "Agrippina").
  U. Rogonor, 680(ZDP):Band100Heft4–018
Potter, B. The Journal of Beatrix Potter,
1881–1897.* (L. Linder, ed)
  J.A. Smith, 453(NYRB):14Jun90–19
Potter, B. Beatrix Potter's Letters.* (J. Tay-
lor, ed)
  S.G. Lanes, 441:4Mar90–14
  J.A. Smith, 453(NYRB):14Jun90–19
Potter, D. Ticket to Ride.* Blackeyes. The
Singing Detective. Pennies from Heaven.
  P. Delany, 150(DR):Winter88/89–511
Potter, J. The Long Lost Journey.*
  M-K. Wilmers, 441:18Nov90–11
Potter, L. Secret Rites and Secret Writing.
  C. Hill, 617(TLS):12–18Jan90–42
Potter, N.T. & M. Timmons, eds. Morality and
Universality.
  H.J. Gensler, 449:Sep90–555
Pötters, W. Chi era Laura?
  J.L. Smarr, 551(RenQ):Autumn89–546
Potthast, B. Die Mosquitoküste im Span-
nungsfeld britischer und spanischer Politik
1502–1821.
  O.C. Stoetzer, 263(RIB):Vol39No2–211
Pouchain, G. Promenades en Bretagne et Nor-
mandie avec un guide nommé Stendhal.
  V.D.L., 605(SC):15Oct89–81

Pouilloux, J., P. Roesch & J. Marcillet–Jau-
bert. Salamine de Chypre XIII. (Vol 2)
  R.S. Bagnall, 229:Band61Heft4–360
Poulet, J. & others. Julio Cortázar.
  S. Boldy, 86(BHS):Jan89–112
Poulsen, R.C. Misbegotten Muses.
  B.W. Dippie, 649(WAL):Nov89–283
Poulsen, R.C. The Mountain Man Vernacular.
  L. Deringer, 35(AS):Winter89–365
Pound, E. Lettres de Paris.
  L. Mackinnon, 617(TLS):12–18Jan90–43
Pound, E. Ezra Pound and Japan.* (S. Koda-
ma, ed)
  H. Hirata, 407(MN):Winter89–498
  R. John, 4:Summer89–27
Pound, E. Pound/The Little Review.* (British
title: "The Little Review.") (T.L. Scott &
M.J. Friedman, with J.R. Bryer, eds)
  L. Mackinnon, 617(TLS):12–18Jan90– 43
  F. Upjohn, 364:Dec89/Jan90–108
Pound, O. & R. Spoo, eds. Ezra Pound and
Margaret Cravens.*
  B.K. Scott, 620(TSWL):Spring89–125
Poupart, J-M. Beaux Draps.
  E. Cobley, 102(CanL):Winter88–115
  E. Cobley, 102(CanL):Spring89–184
Powe, B.A. The Ice Eaters.
  B.N.S. Gooch, 102(CanL):Summer89–174
Powe, B.W. The Solitary Outlaw.*
  P.J.M. Robertson, 529(QQ):Autumn89–680
Powell, A. Athens and Sparta.*
  P. Cartledge, 123:Vol39No1–77
  S. Hodkinson, 000(JeHU).Vol109–251
  M.L. Lang, 124:Nov–Dec89–116
Powell, A. Classical Sparta.
  T.J. Figueira, 124:Jan–Feb90–250
Powell, A. Miscellaneous Verdicts.
  P.N. Furbank, 617(TLS):18–24May90–524
Powell, C. Turner in the South.*
  U. Seibold, 683:Band52Heft1–137
  A. Staley, 90:Nov89–777
Powell, D. Tom Paine.*
  A. Zakai, 242:Vol10No3–371
Powell, E. Collected Poems.
  S. Collini, 617(TLS):17–23Aug90–867
Powell, E. Kingship, Law and Society.
  M.T. Clanchy, 617(TLS):23–29Mar90–330
Powell, E.A. Thomas Cole.
  J. Russell, 441:2Dec90–74
Powell, H. Trammels of Tradition.*
  R.E. Schade, 221(GQ):Fall89–524
Powell, I. It Was Fever That Made the World.
  M. Kinzie, 491:Jun89–151
Powell, J.G.F. – see Cicero
Powell, J.M. Anatomy of a Crusade, 1213–
1221.
  D.E. Queller, 589:Jan89–207
Powell, K. & others. Femmes D'esprit.
  P-L. Adams, 61:Nov90–172
Powell, R.J., ed. The Blues Aesthetic.
  S.F. Young, 585(SoQ):Winter90–85
Powell, W.S., ed. Dictionary of North Carolina
Biography. (Vol 3)
  639(VQR):Autumn89–126
Power, M.S. Crucible of Fools.
  T. Gooderham, 617(TLS):9–15Nov90–1214
Powers, D.S. Studies in Qur'ān and Hadīth.*
  F.J. Ziadeh, 318(JAOS):Jul–Sep88–487
Powers, J.F. Morte D'Urban. Prince of Dark-
ness and Other Stories.
  A.P. Hinchliffe, 148:Winter86–122

Powers, J.F. Wheat That Springeth Green.
D. Flower, 249(HudR):Spring89–139
639(VQR):Winter89–19
Powers, L.H., ed. Leon Edel and Literary Art.*
W. Blazek, 295(JML):Fall88/Winter89–318
Powers, L.H. – see James, H. & E. Wharton
Powys, J.C. The Letters of John Cowper Powys to Hal W. and Violet Trovillion. (P. Roberts, ed) The Letters of John Cowper Powys to Ichiro Hara. (A. Head, ed)
G. Cavaliero, 617(TLS):2–8Nov90–1177
Poyer, D. The Gulf.
N. Callendar, 441:23Sep90–16
Poyser, J. In a Lonely Place.
M. Casserley, 617(TLS):16–22Mar90–293
Pozner, V. Parting With Illusions.
W. Goodman, 441:4Mar90–15
G. Webb, 617(TLS):30Nov–6Dec90–1282
Pozzi, C. Oeuvre Poétique. (L. Joseph, ed) Agnès.
M.C. Weitz, 207(FR):Apr90–898
Pradervand–Amiet, B. L'Ancienne Académie de Lausanne.
M. Kiene, 683:Band52Heft2–278
Pradon, J. Phèdre et Hippolyte.* (O. Classe, ed)
A. Rathé, 475:Vol16No30–273
Praeger, M. Les romans de Robert Pinget.*
A.C. Pugh, 402(MLR):Apr90–464
J–C. Vareille, 535(RHL):Mar–Apr89–347
Prangwatthanakun, S. & P. Cheesman. Lan Na Textiles: Yuan Lue Lao.
M. Roseman, 293(JASt):Nov89–940
Prasad, H.M. The Dramatic Art of Eugene O'Neill.
R.H. Wainscott, 615(TJ):Mar89–120
Prater, D. A Ringing Glass.*
C.S. Brown, 569(SR):Winter89–139
Prauss, G., ed. Handlungstheorie und Transzendentalphilosophie.
W. Steinbeck, 342:Band80Heft1–114
Prawer, S.S. Frankenstein's Island.*
G.W. Field, 564:Sep89–271
Préaud, M. Claude Mellan.
S. Laveissière, 90:Sep89–654
Préaud, M. & others. Dictionnaire des éditeurs d'estampes à Paris sous l'Ancien Régime.
R. Wrigley, 90:Jan89–42
Préaud, M. & B. Brejon de Lavergnée. L'oeil d'or, Claude Mellan.
S. Laveissière, 90:Sep89–654
Prédal, R. Jean–Pierre Mocky.
N. Greene, 207(FR):Apr90–922
Preisler, B. Linguistic Sex Roles in Conversation.
S. Ehrlich, 320(CJL):Jun89–198
J. Holmes, 355(LSoc):Jun89–293
Premuda Perosa, M.L., ed. Jules Vallès giornalista.
R. Ripoll, 535(RHL):Jul–Aug89–742
Prendergast, C. The Order of Mimesis.*
A. Bresnick, 454:Fall89–95
G. Falconer, 131(CL):Spring89–194
J.P. Gilroy, 446(NCFS):Fall–Winter89/90–237
R.A. Hartzell, 207(FR):Apr90–877
Prenshaw, P.W. Elizabeth Spencer.
M.R. Winchell, 569(SR):Fall89–580
Press, J.I. Aspects of the Phonology of the Slavonic Languages.*
H. Leeming, 575(SEER):Jul89–450

Presser, J. Ashes in the Wind.
639(VQR):Summer89–96
Prest, M. Model Theory and Modules.
T.G. Kucera, 316:Sep89–1115
Preston, D.R. Perceputal Dialectology.
T.C. Frazer, 350:Sep90–650
Preston, J. Queen Bess.
W. Wasserstein, 441:8Apr90–13
Prestwich, M. Edward I.
639(VQR):Spring89–53
Prévost, P. Le prélude non mesuré pour clavecin (France 1650–1700).
M. Rollin, 537:Vol75No2–295
Prévost, R., S. Gagné & M. Phaneuf. L'Histoire de l'alcool au Québec.
V. Raoul, 102(CanL):Autumn–Winter89–241
Price, A.W. Love and Friendship in Plato and Aristotle.
M. Nussbaum, 617(TLS):16–22Feb90–165
Price, E.J. China Journal, 1889–1900.* (R.H. Felsing, ed)
639(VQR):Autumn89–124
Price, R. Alabi's World.
E.J. Hobsbawm, 453(NYRB):6Dec90–46
Price, R. Clear Pictures.*
C.W. Lewis, 569(SR):Fall89–c
G. Oldham, 42(AR):Summer89–366
Price, R. A Common Room.*
M.P.L., 295(JML):Fall88/Winter89–395
Price, R. A Social History of Nineteenth Century France.
J. Kolbert, 207(FR):Dec89–390
Price, R. The Tongues of Angels.
P. West, 441:13May90–13
Price, S. Primitive Art in Civilized Places.
J. Coote, 617(TLS):2–8Mar90–235
Prickett, S. England and the French Revolution.
M. Cumming, 173(ECS):Spring90–373
V. Newey, 402(MLR):Oct90–923
Prickett, S. Words and "The Word."
D.L. Jeffrey, 627(UTQ):Summer90–569
D. Womersley, 541(RES):Feb89–105
Priebe, R.K., ed. Ghanaian Literatures.
T. Knipp, 538(RAL):Fall89–540
Priebe, R.K. Myth, Realism, and the West African Writer.
D. Izevbaye, 538(RAL):Fall89–537
Priest, C. The Quiet Woman.
B. Richards, 617(TLS):23–29Mar90–328
Priest, G. In Contradiction.*
N.C.A. da Costa & S. French, 479(PhQ):Oct89–498
Priest, S., ed. Hegel's Critique of Kant.
K. Hartmann, 323:May89–192
D. Knowles, 518:Jan89–25
E. Schaper, 479(PhQ):Jul89–366
Priestman, M. Detective Fiction and Literature.
D. Lehman, 617(TLS):21–27Dec90–1382
Prieto, A. El discurso criollista en la formación de la Argentina moderna.
C.R. Carlisle, 263(RIB):Vol39No1–78
Prieto, A. La poesía española del siglo XVI.
A. Porqueras Mayo, 240(HR):Summer89–374
Prieto, J.L.R. – see under Rave Prieto, J.L.
Prignitz, I. – see Fühmann, F.
Prince, G. Dictionary of Narratology.*
C. Barrow, 577(SHR):Summer89–289
W. Martin, 395(MFS):Summer89–374
[continued]

[continuing]
42(AR):Winter89-112
478(P&L):Apr89-221
Principato, A. Il Raggio nella cripta.
R.A. Francis, 402(MLR):Oct90-960
Pringle, D. & others. The Red Tower (al-Burj
al-Ahmar).
J. Rosser, 589:Apr89-487
Pringle, T. Tycoon.
G. Gilliland, 441:12Aug90-16
Prini, P. Storia dell'esistenzialismo da Kier-
kegaard a oggi.
P. Trotignon, 542:Oct-Dec89-603
"Der Prinzipal."
K. Birkin, 410(M&L):Aug89-434
"Priorités pour l'université."
H.B. Sutton, 207(FR):May90-1120
Pritchard, B.W., ed. Antonio Caldera.*
H. Federhofer, 417:Jan-Mar89-88
Pritchard, J.B. Tell Es-Sa'idiyeh: Excava-
tions on the Tell, 1964-1966.
S.M. Paley, 318(JAOS):Jan-Mar88-151
Pritchard, W.H. Randall Jarrell.
A. Broyard, 441:6May90-3
Pritchard, W.H. - see Jarrell, R.
Pritchett, M. The Venus Tree.
A.H. Petry, 573(SSF):Summer89-353
Pritchett, V.S. At Home and Abroad.*
J. Bayley, 453(NYRB):8Nov90-3
M.J. Dugeja, 219(GaR):Winter89-821
Pritchett, V.S. A Careless Widow and Other
Stories.*
J. Bayley, 453(NYRB):8Nov90-3
F. Tuohy, 364:Dec89/Jan90-118
Pritchett, V.S. Chekhov.*
A. Cattaneo, 34:Jul/Aug89-42
T. Dunn, 511:Mar89-45
G. McVay, 575(SEER):Oct89-610
M. Meyer, 364:Apr/May89-132
D. Mills, 157:No173-39
639(VQR):Spring89-50
Pritchett, V S. The Complete Short Stories.
V. Cunningham, 617(TLS):23-29Nov90-
1255
Pritchett, V.S. Lasting Impressions.
J. Bayley, 453(NYRB):8Nov90-3
V. Cunningham, 617(TLS):23-29Nov90-
1255
Probst, R.E. Response and Analysis.
A.R. Gere, 128(CE):Oct89-617
Probyn, C.T. English Fiction of the Eigh-
teenth Century 1700-1789.
J. McLaverty, 447(N&Q):Mar89-110
A. Morvan, 189(EA):Jul-Sep89-343
R. Stephanson, 166:Oct89-67
K. Sutherland, 541(RES):Nov89-566
Probyn, C.T. Jonathan Swift, "Gulliver's
Travels."
566:Spring90-208
"Proceedings of the PMR Conference."
Z.P. Thundy, 201:Vol15-364
Prochazka, T., Jr. Saudi Arabian Dialects.
D. Odden, 350:Dec90-880
Proclus. Commentary on Plato's "Parmen-
ides."* (J.M. Dillon, ed; G.R. Morrow & J.M.
Dillon, trans)
É. des Places, 555:Vol62Fasc1-155
L. Siorvanes, 303(JoHS):Vol109-274
Proclus. Proclo Licio Diadoco, I manuali. (C.
Faraggiana di Sarzana, ed & trans)
É. des Places, 555:Vol62Fasc1-156

Proclus. Proclus, "Elementatio theologica,"
translata a Guillielmo del Moerbecca.* (H.
Boese, ed)
E.M. Macierowski, 589:Oct89-962
Proclus. Proclus, "Théologie Platonicienne,"
Livre V. (H.D. Saffrey & L.G. Westerink,
eds)
L. Siorvanes, 123:Vol39No2-206
Proddow, P. & D. Healy. American Jewelry.
J. Stancliffe, 39:Feb89-139
Proffer, C.R. The Widows of Russia and Other
Writings.*
A. McMillin, 575(SEER):Jan89-131
Proffitt, N. Edge of Eden.
T. Fleming, 441:3Jun90-19
Profitlich, U., ed. Dramatik der DDR.
S. Hoefert, 564:May89-184
Pronzini, B. & M.H. Greenberg - see Estleman,
L.D.
Propertius. Sexti Properti "Elegiarum" Libri
IV.* (P. Fedeli, ed)
J. den Boeft, 394:Vol42fasc3/4-558
Propp, V. Die historischen Wurzeln des Zaub-
ermärchen.
A. Hartmann, 196:Band30Heft1/2-160
Prosch, H. Michael Polanyi.*
R. Brownhill, 323:Oct89-303
von Proschwitz, G. - see Ohlin, B.
Prosdocimo de' Beldomandi. "Brevis summula
proportionum quantum ad musicam perti-
nent" and "Parvus tractatulus de modo
monochordum dividendi."
F. Hammond, 589:Oct89-1026
"Prose et prosateurs de la Renaissance."*
B.C. Bowen, 535(RHL):Nov-Dec89-1050
Prott, L.V. & P.J. O'Keefe. Law and the Cul-
tural Heritage. (Vol 3)
A.C. Danto, 617(TLS):16-22Mar90-286
Proulx, B. Le Roman du territoire.
D. Trudel, 102(CanL):Spring89-220
Proulx, E.A. Heart Songs and Other Stories.*
L. Cumming, 617(TLS):9-15Feb90-148
M.A. Jarman, 376:Jun89-128
L. Rackstraw, 455:Sep89-67
Proulx, M. Le Sexe des etoiles.
A. Whitfield, 102(CanL):Autumn-
Winter89-265
Proust, J. Questions de forme.*
J. Gayon, 342:Band80Heft4-489
Proust, M. Against Sainte-Beuve and Other
Essays.
S. Gillespie, 97(CQ):Vol18No4-446
Proust, M. Un Amour de Swann.* (M. Rai-
mond, ed)
A. Finch, 208(FS):Jan89-104
G. Joly-Tupinier, 535(RHL):Sep-Oct89-
936
Proust, M. "Bricquebec." (R. Bales, ed)
D.W. Alden, 617(TLS):8-14Jun90-618
Proust, M. Correspondance. (Vol 18) (P. Kolb,
ed)
F. Steegmuller, 617(TLS):14-20Dec90-
1347
Proust, M. Du côté de chez Swann.* (A. Com-
pagnon, ed) Du côté de chez Swann. (J.
Milly, ed) A la recherche du temps perdu.
(Vol 1) (J-Y. Tadié, ed)
A. Finch, 208(FS):Jan89-104
Proust, M. Selected Letters.* (Vol 2) (P.
Kolb, ed)
J. Weightman, 453(NYRB):18Jan90-10

Proust, M. & G. Gallimard. Correspondance: 1912-1922.* (P. Fouché, ed)
P-L. Rey, 450(NRF):Oct89-111
Provencher, J. C'était l'hiver.
D. Trudel, 102(CanL):Spring89-220
Provvedi-Fournier, D. Immagini d'Italia. Italia allo specchio.
A.P. Esposito, 399(MLJ):Autumn89-375
Prozesky, M., ed. Christianity amidst Apartheid.
P. Collins, 617(TLS):3-9Aug90-831
Prunty, W. Balance as Belief.
F. Chappell, 344:Summer90-168
Pryor, J.H. Geography, Technology, and War.
B.M. Kreutz, 589:Oct89-1027
Przeworski, A. Capitalism and Social Democracy.
E.J. Girdner, 488:Mar89-135
Przyboś, J. L'Entreprise mélodramatique.*
F.P. Bowman, 210(FrF):Sep89-357
J-M. Thomasseau, 535(RHL):Nov-Dec89-1062
Przybylski, R. An Essay on the Poetry of Osip Mandelstam.*
C.R. Isenberg, 550(RusR):Jan89-113
D. Rayfield, 575(SEER):Apr89-286
Ptak, R. Cheng Hos Abenteuer im Drama und Roman der Ming-Zeit.
W. Schlepp, 318(JAOS):Jan-Mar88-141
Pu, P. - see under Pang Pu
Pucci, P. Odysseus Polutropos.*
W.C. Scott, 24:Summer89-339
Pucci, S.L. Diderot and a Poetics of Science.*
H. Cohen, 207(FR):Dec89-373
Pucciarelli, E., ed. I cristiani e il servizio militare.*
E. Heck, 229:Band61Heft7-629
Puértolas, J.R. - see under Rodríguez Puértolas, J.
Puffett, D., ed. Richard Strauss: "Salome." Richard Strauss: "Elektra."
M. Tanner, 617(TLS):15-21Jun90-642
Pugh, A.R. The Birth of "A la recherche du temps perdu."
R. Bales, 208(FS):Apr89-229
W.C. Carter, 207(FR):Dec89-382
E. Hughes, 402(MLR):Apr90-454
L.M. Porter, 395(MFS):Summer89-356
B. Rogers, 535(RHL):Nov-Dec89-1076
R. Zaiser, 547(RF):Band101Heft4-490
Pugh, S. Garden - nature - language.
D.D.C. Chambers, 566:Spring90-219
S. Gillespie, 97(CQ):Vol18No3-322
Puhle, A. Persona.
H.A. Gärtner, 229:Band61Heft5-432
Puhvel, J. Comparative Mythology.*
J.W. de Jong, 259(IIJ):Jul89-206
Pullinger, K. When the Monster Dies.* Tiny Lies.
D. Durrant, 364:Aug/Sep89-134
Pullum, G.K. & W.A. Ladusaw. Phonetic Symbol Guide.*
D.H., 355(LSoc):Mar89-145
Pulos, A.J. The American Design Adventure: 1940-1975.
R. Flinchum, 139:Aug/Sep89-23
H. Gottfried, 47:Oct89-44
Pulsford, P. Lee's Ghost.
J-A. Goodwin, 617(TLS):31Aug-6Sep90-916
Pump, A. & S., with G. Le Roy. The Loaves and Fishes Party Cookbook.
R. Flaste, 441:10Jun90-53

Puncuh, D. & A. Rovere, eds. I registri della catena del comune di Savona: Registro I.
S.A. Epstein, 589:Apr89-489
Puntel, K. Die Struktur künstlerischer Darstellung.
A.J. Camigliano, 406:Spring89-124
Puntel, L.B., ed. Der Wahrheitsbegriff.
P. Brauch, 489(PJGG):Band96Heft1-217
Puppi, L. - see Palladio, A.
Purdy, A. - see Aquin, H.
Purdy, J. The Candles of Your Eyes and Thirteen Other Stories.
B. Christophersen, 573(SSF):Fall88-492
Purdy, R.L. & M. Millgate - see Hardy, T.
Puri, N. Political Elite and Society in the Punjab.
P. Wallace, 293(JASt):Feb89-208
Purich, D. Our Land.
E.J. Peters, 529(QQ):Spring89-203
Purnelle, G. Aristote, "De Animea."
P. Louis, 555:Vol62Fasc2-346
Purnelle-Simart, C. & G. Purnelle. Ovide, "Ars amatoria, Remedia amoris, De medicamine."
A.A.R. Henderson, 123:Vol39No1-141
Pursglove, M. D.V. Grigorovich.*
R.A. Peace, 575(SEER):Jan89-127
Purves, A.C. Writing Across Languages and Cultures.
A. Raimes, 126(CCC):Dec89-491
Purvis, J. Hard Lessons.
M. Pugh, 617(TLS):2-8Mar90-218
Puschmann, R. Heinrich von Kleists Cäcilien-Erzählung.
S.R. Huff, 406:Winter89-498
Putnam, H. Representation and Reality.*
M. Talbot, 393(Mind):Jul89-453
Putnam, M.C.J. Artifices of Eternity.*
D.H. Porter, 122:Apr89-165
Putnis, P. Steele Rudd's Australia.
K. Stewart, 71(ALS):May89-122
Puttfarken, T. Roger de Piles' Theory of Art.*
G. Cowart, 475:Vol16No30-335
Putu Wijaya. Bomb. (E. Rafferty & L.J. Sears, eds)
W.H. Frederick, 293(JASt):May89-444
Putzel, S. Reconstructing Yeats.
T.D., 295(JML):Fall88/Winter89-427
Pye, L.W. The Mandarin and the Cadre.
P.R. Moody, Jr., 293(JASt):Nov89-839
Pye-Smith, C. Travels in Nepal.
C. Thubron, 441:2Dec90-20
Pyke, D. - see Medawar, P.B.
Pykett, L. Emily Brontë.
M. Reynolds, 617(TLS):10-16Aug90-854
Pynchon, T. Vineland.
D. Cowart, 344:Fall90-176
Z. Leader, 617(TLS):2-8Feb90-115
B. Leithauser, 453(NYRB):15Mar90-7
T. Rafferty, 442(NY):19Feb90-108
S. Rushdie, 441:14Jan90-1
Pyne, S.J. Fire on the Rim.*
D. Scheese, 649(WAL):Feb90-379
Pynsent, R., ed. Decadence and Innovation.
R. Morgan, 617(TLS):9-15Mar90-263
Pynsent, R.B., ed. T.G. Masaryk. (Vol 2)
T. Judt, 358:Feb90-7
T. Judt, 617(TLS):26Jan-1Feb90-79
Pyrse, M. - see Austin, M.

Qian Zhongshu. Cinq essais de poétique.* (N.
Chapuis, ed & trans)
  V. Alleton, 98:Aug–Sep89–661
Quacquarelli, A. Reazione pagana e trasfor-
mazione della cultura (fine IV secolo d.C.).
  A. Chastagnol, 555:Vol62Fasc1–174
"Quaderni Petrarcheschi I."
  A. Noyer–Weidner, 547(RF):Band101
Heft4–448
Quadflieg, H. Die Short Story der Nineties.
  C. Melchior, 177(ELT):Vol32No4–501
Quammen, D. Bloodlines.
  E. Lesser, 434:Autumn89–98
"Quanguo dangxiao xitong zhonggong dangshi
xueshu taolunhui zhuanti baogao he fayan
huibian."
  M. Schoenhals, 293(JASt):Aug89–563
Quarles, B. Black Mosaic.
  M. Drimmer, 656(WMQ):Jul89–604
Quarrington, P. Whale Music.
  M. Mifflin, 441:25Feb90–12
Quart, B.K. Woman Directors.
  S.G. Kellman, 390:Dec89–34
Queller, D.E. The Venetian Patriciate.*
  J. Martin, 529(QQ):Spring89–165
Queneau, R. Oeuvres complètes. (Vol 1) (C.
Debon, ed)
  M. Sheringham, 617(TLS):27Apr–3May90–
455
Queneau, R. & A. Blavier. Lettres croisées,
1949–1976. (J–M. Klinkenberg, ed)
  C. Shorley, 208(FS):Oct89–492
Quesnel, M. Baudelaire – solaire et clandes-
tin.
  K.A. Ott, 547(RF):Band101Heft1–128
Quétel, C. Escape from the Bastille.
  A. Forrest, 617(TLS):14–20Dec90–1355
Quétel, C. History of Syphilis.
  M. Holub, 617(TLS):5–11Oct90–1051
de Quevedo, F. El buscón. (A. Basanta, ed)
  J.A. Jones, 86(BHS):Jan89–203
de Quevedo, F. El buscón. (J. Iffland, ed)
  D.W. Bleznick, 238:Dec89–958
de Quevedo, F. Sátiras lingüísticas y literar-
ias (en prosa). (C.C. García Valdés, ed)
  R. Moore, 86(BHS):Apr89–178
de Quevedo, F. Sentencias filosóficas. (A.V.
Ebersole, ed)
  D.W. Bleznick, 238:Dec89–958
Quick, B. Northern Edge.
  D. Freedman, 441:22Jul90–20
Quigley, C. Close To The Floor.
  V.R. Brown, 582(SFQ):Vol46No2–188
Quigley, J. Palestine and Israel.
  A. Hertzberg, 453(NYRB):25Oct90–41
  D. McDowall, 617(TLS):9–15Nov90–1203
Quigley, J. "What Does Joan Say?"
  M. Ivins, 441:18Mar90–6
Quine, W.V. Pursuit of Truth.
  B. van Fraassen, 617(TLS):10–16Aug90–
853
Quine, W.V. Quiddities.*
  617(TLS):10–16Aug90–853
Quinet, E. La Grèce moderne et ses rapports
avec l'antiquité, [suivi du] Journal de
Voyage (inédit). (W. Aeschimann & J.
Tucoo–Chala, eds)
  O.A. Haac, 446(NCFS):Fall–Winter89/90–
285
Quinlan, K. John Crowe Ransom's Secular
Faith.
  M.R. Winchell, 580(SCR):Fall90–194
Quinn, A. – see Montague, J.

Quinn, D.P. An Examination of Kant's Treat-
ment of Transcendental Freedom.
  M.J.D., 185:Apr90–703
Quintilian. Quintilian on the Teaching of
Speaking and Writing. (J.J. Murphy, ed)
  A.A. Lunsford, 126(CCC):May89–229
Quirini, B.Z. – see under Zannini Quirini, B.
Quirk, L.J. Fasten Your Seat Belts.
  C. Rickey, 441:11Mar90–19
Quirk, R. Words at Work.
  N.E. Enkvist, 452(NJL):Vol12No1–91
Quirk, R. & G. Stein. English in Use.
  T. Shippey, 617(TLS):19–25Oct90–1117
Quiroga, H. The Exiles and Other Stories.
(J.D. Danielson, with E.K. Gambarini, eds &
trans)
  M.S. Peden, 238:May89–317
Quogan, A. The Touch of a Vanished Hand.
  P. Craig, 617(TLS):17–23Aug90–867
Qvist, P.O. Jorden är vår arvedel.
  B. Steene, 563(SS):Winter89–102

Raaflaub, K. Die Entdeckung der Freiheit.*
  R. Seager, 303(JoHS):Vol109–250
Raaflaub, K.A., ed. Social Struggles in Ar-
chaic Rome.*
  K–J. Hölkeskamp, 229:Band61Heft4–304
  F. Millar, 313:Vol79–138
van Raalte, M. Rhythm and Metre.*
  S.R. Slings, 394:Vol43fasc3/4–608
Raban, J. Hunting Mister Heartbreak.
  D. Rieff, 617(TLS):23–29Nov90–1260
Rabbets, J. From Hardy to Faulkner.
  G. Harrington, 395(MFS):Winter89–874
  C.E. May, 637(VS):Summer90–670
Rabbi, S.G. – see under Gargantini Rabbi, S.
Rabe, S.G. Eisenhower and Latin America.
  T.H. Cohn, 106:Fall89–255
  J. Tillapaugh, 263(RIB):Vol39No1–79
Rabel, R.G. Between East and West.*
  B. Heuser, 575(SEER):Oct89–639
Rabel–Jullien, C. – see Allégret, M.
Råberg, M. Visioner och verklighet.
  T. Hall, 341:Vol58No1–37
Rabil, A., Jr., ed. Renaissance Humanism.
  J. Kraye, 575(SEER):Jul89–460
Rabin, O. Tri žizni.
  N. Perlina, 574(SEEJ):Spring89–136
Rabinbach, A. The Human Motor.
  R. Howard, 441:16Dec90–7
Rabine, L.W. Reading the Romantic Heroine.*
  F. Bartkowski, 131(CL):Fall89–401
  L. Kintz, 591(SIR):Spring89–152
Rabinow, P. French Modern.
  T.M.R., 185:Jul90–914
Rabinowitz, P.J. Before Reading.*
  C.M. Bauschatz, 478(P&L):Oct89–388
  B. Foley, 454:Fall89–92
Rabinowitz, R. The Spiritual Self in Everyday
Life.
  J. Conforti, 165(EAL):Vol25No2–213
Raby, P. Oscar Wilde.
  B. Bashford, 177(ELT):Vol32No3–336
  T. Eagleton, 617(TLS):2–8Feb90–124
  D. Lawler, 637(VS):Spring90–532
  R.K. Miller, 395(MFS):Winter89–790
  639(VQR):Summer89–88
Race, W.H. Classical Genres and English Po-
etry.
  W. Allen, 569(SR):Summer89–lxxvi

"Race Relations Survey, 1988-9." (C. Cooper, general ed)
  A. Sampson, 617(TLS):17-23Aug90-866
Rach, R. Just Listen 'N Learn German Plus.
  J.L. Fox, 399(MLJ):Winter89-517
Rach, R. Practice and Improve Your German. Practice and Improve Your German Plus.
  C. Hall, 399(MLJ):Winter89-518
Rachels, J. Created from Animals.
  J. Waldron, 617(TLS):14-20Sep90-984
  R. Wright, 441:29Jul90-27
Rachilde. La Tour d'Amour.
  J-P.H. Tétart, 450(NRF):Jan89-87
Racine, D., ed. Saint-John Perse.* (Vol 1)
  H. Levillain, 535(RHL):Jul-Aug89-751
  M-N. Little, 207(FR):Apr90-883
Racine, J. Bérénice. (A. Delbée & G. Forestier, eds)
  R.W. Tobin, 475:Vol16No30-277
Racine, J. Phaedra.* (R. Wilbur, trans)
  J. Saunders, 565:Autumn89-77
Rácz, I., ed. Tanulmányok Erdély történetérol.
  P. Longworth, 575(SEER):Jul89-485
Radcliff-Umstead, D. Carnival Comedy and Sacred Play.*
  J.I. Cope, 400(MLN):Jan89-242
Radcliff-Umstead, D. The Exile Into Eternity.*
  D.L. Bastianutti, 529(QQ):Summer89-498
  C. Federici, 345(KRQ):May89-255
  J. Kelly, 278(IS):Vol44-188
Radcliffe, J. - see Damigeron
Radcliffe, S. Fontane: "Effi Briest."*
  W. Paulsen, 133:Band22Heft2-177
Raddall, T.H. Courage in the Storm.
  J. Buckley, 102(CanL):Autumn-Winter89-182
Radelli, G. Italia in prospettiva.
  A.P. Esposito, 399(MLJ):Autumn89-375
Rader, B.A. & H.G. Zettler, eds. The Sleuth and the Scholar.
  E. Lauterbach, 395(MFS):Summer89-346
Radford, A. Transformational Grammar: A First Course.
  B. Aarts, 179(ES):Oct89-456
  M. Baltin, 350:Sep90-569
  J. Erickson, 353:Vol27No6-1128
  R. Freidin, 297(JL):Sep89-509
  C. Pooser, 710:Dec89-482
Radford, C., C. Shorley & M. Hossain. Signposts to French Literature.
  J. Cruickshank, 208(FS):Oct89-497
Radford, J. The Progress of Romance.*
  T. Goldie, 102(CanL):Winter88-128
Radforth, I. Bushworkers and Bosses.
  P. Campbell, 529(QQ):Spring89-164
Radice, R. - see Philo of Alexandria
Radke, G. Zur Entwicklung der Gottesvorstellung und der Gottesverehrung in Rom.
  R. Schilling, 229:Band61Heft3-198
Radnitzky, G. & W.W. Bartley 3d, eds. Evolutionary Epistemology, Theory of Rationality, and the Sociology of Knowledge.
  R. Curtis, 488:Mar89-95
  D.H. Helman, 518:Apr89-94
Radu, K. The Cost of Living.
  H. Prest, 102(CanL):Spring89-167
Radu, K. Letter to a Distant Father.
  S. Morrissey, 102(CanL):Winter88-146
Raeff, M. Russia Abroad.
  J. Woll, 441:29Apr90-21
Raev, S. - see "Gottfried Böhm"

Rafael, V.L. Contracting Colonialism.
  J-P. Dumont, 293(JASt):Nov89-941
Raffaelli, R., ed. Rappresentazioni della morte.
  R. Garland, 123:Vol39No2-245
Rafferty, E. & L.J. Sears - see Putu Wijaya
Rafferty, K. City on the Rocks.*
  I. Buruma, 453(NYRB):12Apr90-41
  J. Mirsky, 441:22Apr90-35
Raffin, T.A., J.N. Shurkin & W. Sinkler 3d. Intensive Care.
  R.F.W., 185:Jul90-928
Raforth, B.A. & D.L. Rubin, eds. The Social Construction of Written Communication.
  P. Bizzell, 126(CCC):Dec89-483
Ragache, G. & J-R. La Vie quotidienne des écrivains et des artistes sous l'occupation.
  R.J. Golsan, 207(FR):Apr90-917
Ragan, D.P. William Faulkner's "Absalom, Absalom!"
  P.R.J., 295(JML):Fall88/Winter89-326
Ragans, R. ArtTalk.
  S. Hagaman, 709:Winter90-124
Ragland-Sullivan, E. Jacques Lacan and the Philosophy of Psychoanalysis.*
  R. Stott, 529(QQ):Spring89-195
Rahmstorf, G., ed. Wissensrepräsentation in Expertensystemen.
  E. & J. Dölling, 682(ZPSK):Band42Heft5-682
Rai, A. Orwell and the Politics of Despair.*
  F.S., 185:Jan90-453
Raible, W., ed. Romanistik, Sprachtypologie und Universalienforschung.
  M. Haspelmath, 350:Jun90-425
Raible. W., ed. Zwischen Festtag und Alltag.
  P. Morf, 196:Band30Heft3/4-312
  W. van Peer, 204(FdL):Mar89-63
Railing, P. From Science to Systems of Art.
  J. Milner, 617(TLS):31Aug-6Sep90-919
Raimond, M. - see Proust, M.
Raina, B. Dickens and the Dialectic of Growth.*
  T.J. Cribb, 541(RES):May89-281
Raine, C. Haydn and the Valve Trumpet.
  C. Rawson, 617(TLS):15-21Jun90-627
Raine, K. The Presence.*
  J. Greening, 493:Spring89-55
  D. McDuff, 565:Spring89-76
Raine, K. Selected Poems.
  J. Greening, 493:Spring89-55
  J. MacVean, 4:Summer89-39
Rainold, J. John Rainold's Oxford Lectures on Aristotle's "Rhetoric."* (L.D. Green, ed & trans)
  W.W. Fortenbaugh, 303(JoHS):Vol109-235
Raio, G. Ermeneutica e teoria del simbolo.
  P. Somville, 542:Oct-Dec89-638
Raison, T. Tories and the Welfare State.
  J. Campbell, 617(TLS):7-13Dec90-1312
Raith, J. Sprachgemeinschaftstyp, Sprachkontakt, Sprachgebrauch.
  H. Scheuringer, 685(ZDL):3/1989-363
Raith, J., R. Schulze & K-H. Wandt, eds. Grundlagen der Mehrsprachigkeitsforschung.
  G. Lerchner, 682(ZPSK):Band42Heft4-532
Rajab, J. Palestinian Costume.
  U. Roberts, 60:Nov-Dec89-158
Rajagopalachari, M. The Novels of Bernard Malamud.
  K. Opdahl, 395(MFS):Winter89-759

Rajan, R.S. Towards a Critique of Cultural Reason.
  M. McGhee, 89(BJA):Summer89-279
Rajaratnam, S. The Prophetic and the Political. (C.H. Chee & O. ul Haq, eds)
  T.J. Bellows, 293(JASt):Aug89-670
Räkel, H-H.S. Der deutsche Minnesang.*
  W. Hofmeister, 602:Band20Heft1-129
  J.A. Schultz, 222(GR):Summer89-141
Raleigh, D.J. - see Babine, A.
Ramage, E.S. The Nature and Purpose of Augustus' "Res Gestae."*
  D. Flach, 229:Band61Heft7-635
  D. Kienast, 24:Spring89-177
  B.M. Levick, 313:Vol79-204
Ramanujan, A.K. & S.H. Blackburn, eds. Another Harmony.
  F.J. Korom, 318(JAOS):Jan-Mar88-189
Ramaswamy, S. Explorations.
  R.E. McDowell, 538(RAL):Fall89-531
Ramat, A.G., O. Carruba & G. Bernini, eds. Papers from the 7th International Conference on Historical Linguistics.*
  F. Chevillet, 189(EA):Apr-Jun89-203
Ramat, P. Linguistic Typology.* (Italian title: Linguistica Tipologica.)
  F. Chevillet, 189(EA):Apr-Jun89-198
  G. Mallinson, 545(RPh):Feb90-443
Ramat, P., H-J. Niederehe & K. Koerner, eds. The History of Linguistics in Italy.
  L. Zgusta, 361:Sep89-73
"The Rāmāyaṇa of Vālmīki." (Vol 1) (R.P. Goldman, trans)
  J.W. de Jong, 259(IIJ):Jul90-106
"The Rāmāyaṇa of Vālmīki." (Vol 2) (S.I. Pollock, trans)
  D.L. Gitomer, 293(JASt):Feb89-206
  J.W. de Jong, 259(IIJ):Jul89-195
Ramazani, V.K. The Free Indirect Mode.
  C.F. Coates, 446(NCFS):Spring-Summer90-540
  L.R. Furst, 188(ECr):Fall89-112
Rambach, P. & S. Gardens of Longevity in China and Japan.
  M. Keswick, 46:Sep89-14
  M. Treib, 576:Mar89-90
Rambo, A.T., K. Gillogly & K.L. Hutterer, eds. Ethnic Diversity and the Control of Natural Resources in Southeast Asia.
  H.L. Lefferts, Jr., 293(JASt):Feb89-232
Ramers, K.H. Vokalquantität und qualität im Deutschen.
  B.J. Koekkoek, 350:Mar90-207
Ramírez, F.A., ed. Tratado de la comunidad (Biblioteca de El Escorial MS. & II-8).
  R. Rohland de Langbehn, 304(JHP):Winter89-153
  B. Taylor, 402(MLR):Oct90-999
Ramírez Luque, M.I. Arte y belleza en la Estética de Hegel.
  C. Cordura, 160:Jul89-247
Ramke, B. The Language Student.
  G.E. Murray, 502(PrS):Spring89-112
Ramondino, F. & A.F. Müller. Dadapolis.
  P. Robb, 617(TLS):5-11Oct90-1080
Ramos Mattei, C. Ethical Self-Determination in Don José Ortega y Gasset.
  A. Donoso, 240(HR):Spring89-257
Rampelberg, R-M. - see Bodin, J.
Rampersad, A. The Life of Langston Hughes.* (Vol 2)
  W. Shear, 389(MQ):Winter90-283

Ramratnam, M. W.B. Yeats and the Craft of Verse.
  T.R. Whitaker, 677(YES):Vol20-317
Ramsay, A. & W. Mungkandi, eds. Thailand-U.S. Relations.
  C.D. Neher, 293(JASt):Aug89-681
Ramsden, H. Lorca's "Romancero gitano."
  D. Harris, 402(MLR):Oct90-1006
Ramsden, H. - see Lorca, F.G.
Ramsey, B. & M. Waldvogel. The Quilts of Tennessee.*
  J.A. Ice, 582(SFQ):Vol46No2-192
Ramsey, C. & H. Sleeper. Architectural Graphic Standards. (8th ed)
  S. Kliment & C. Kean, 45:Nov89-75
Ramsey, M. Professional and Popular Medicine in France, 1770-1830.
  E. & R. Peschel, 446(NCFS):Fall-Winter89/90-290
Ramsey, S.R. The Languages of China.*
  D. Barnes, 399(MLJ):Summer89-212
  W.S. Coblin, 318(JAOS):Oct-Dec88-644
  R. Hymes, 355(LSoc):Sep89-448
Ranade, A.D. Stage Music of Maharashtra.
  A.E. Arnold, 187:Fall89-545
Ranald, M.L. Shakespeare and His Social Context.
  H. Castrop, 156(ShJW):Jahrbuch1989-360
  P. Edwards, 677(YES):Vol20-263
  C.R. Swift, 570(SQ):Fall89-357
Ranalli, G., with M. Sorkin & A. Vidler. Buildings and Projects.
  D. Kesler, 45:Sep89-55
  D. London, 47:Jun89-40
Rand, H. Paul Manship.
  S. Rather, 127:Winter89-360
Randall, D. The Sin Eater.*
  S. Pugh, 493:Autumn89-60
Randall, D.B.J. "Theatres of Greatness."*
  M. Garrett, 541(RES):Nov89-561
  M.H. Wikander, 125:Fall88-80
Randall, W.S. Benedict Arnold.
  P. Maier, 441:26Aug90-12
  J. Rakove, 61:Oct90-128
Randel, D.M., ed. The New Harvard Dictionary of Music.*
  J. Caldwell, 410(M&L):Feb89-72
Randolph, J. Collected Letters of John Randolph of Roanoke to Dr. John Brockenbrough, 1812-1833. (K. Shorey, ed)
  639(VQR):Winter89-17
von Randow, E. Valente Substantive des Englischen.
  H. Czepluch, 353:Vol27No6-1132
  T. Herbst, 38:Band107Heft3/4-455
Ranke, K., ed. Enzyklopädie des Märchens.* (Vol 5, Pts 1-5)
  P. Assion, 196:Band30Heft1/2-125
Ranke-Heinemann, U. Eunuchs for Heaven.
  H. Chadwick, 617(TLS):22-28Jun90-663
Ranke-Heinemann, U. Eunuchs for the Kingdom of Heaven.
  J. Berry, 441:30Dec90-8
Rankin, H.D. Antisthenes Sokratikos.
  F.D. Caizzi, 229:Band61Heft2-100
Rankin, H.D. Celts and the Classical World.
  J.F. Drinkwater, 123:Vol39No1-100
  G. Woolf, 313:Vol79-236
Rankin, N. Dead Man's Chest.*
  J. Hunter, 177(ELT):Vol32No4-494
Ransel, D.L. Mothers of Misery.*
  S.C. Ramer, 550(RusR):Oct89-416

Ransmayr, C. The Last World.* (German title: Die letzte Welt.)
M. Hofmann, 617(TLS):15-21Jun90-654
R. Irwin, 441:27May90-12
Ransom, R.L. Conflict and Compromise.
D. Macleod, 617(TLS):9-15Nov90-1211
Ranulphe de la Houblonnière. La prédication de Ranulphe de la Houblonnière. (N. Bériou, ed)
P.B. Roberts, 589:Oct89-1029
Rao, M.S.A., ed. Studies in Migration.
S. Vatuk, 293(JASt):Aug89-662
Rapaczynski, A. Nature and Politics.
R. Ashcraft, 319:Jan90-133
Rapaport, H. Heidegger & Derrida.
D. Cook, 103:Oct90-427
N. Lukacher, 153:Fall-Winter89-128
Raper, J.R. - see Glasgow, E.
Raphael, F. Somerset Maugham.
617(TLS):23Feb-1Mar90-204
Raphael, S. An Oak Spring Sylva.
P. Dietz, 441:25Mar90-26
Raphaël, S.J., with P. Proctor. Sally.
J. Cohen, 441:1Jul90-15
Rapoport, L. Confrontations.
I. Halperin, 390:Apr89-64
Rapoport, L. Stalin's War Against the Jews.
D.K. Shipler, 441:18Nov90-3
Rapp, F. & R. Wiehl, eds. Whitehead's Metaphysics of Creativity.* (German title: Whiteheads Metaphysik der Kreativität.)
B. Hendley, 103:Nov90-468
Rasch, R. - see Fokker, A.D.
Raschke, W.J., ed. The Archaeology of the Olympics.
D. Arnould, 555:Vol62Fasc2-329
V.J. Matthews, 123:Vol39No2-297
D.G. Romano, 124:Mar-Apr90-363
Harun-Or-Rashid. The Foreshadowing of Bangladesh.
R. Ahmed, 293(JASt):Aug89-664
Rasico, P.D. Els menorquins de la Florida.
P.G. Broad, 345(KRQ):Nov89-506
Raskin, B. Current Affairs.
L. Wertheimer, 441:16Sep90-41
Raskin, V. & I. Weisner. Language and Writing.*
J.M. Swales, 710:Sep89-352
Rasky, H. Stratas.
W. Albright, 465:Summer90-147
Rasmussen, D., ed. Der Weltumsegler und seine Freunde.
T.P. Saine, 221(GQ):Spring89-270
Rasputin, V. Siberia on Fire.* (G. Mikkelson & M. Winchell, eds & trans)
J. Bayley, 453(NYRB):15Mar90-26
Rastier, F. Sémantique interprétative.*
P. Laurendeau, 320(CJL):Dec89-485
C. Morinet, 567:Vol73No1/2-151
Rath, R., H. Immesberger & J. Schu, eds. Textkorpora 2. Kindersprache.
E. Strassner, 685(ZDL):3/1989-390
Rath, W. Not am Mann.
F.M. Sharp, 221(GQ):Summer89-431
Rathjen, F. "... Schlechte Augen."
A. Palme, 329(JJQ):Summer90-882
Rathkolb, O., ed. Gesellschaft und Politik am Beginn der Zweiten Republik.
F.L. Carsten, 575(SEER):Oct89-664
Rathmayr, R. Die russischen Partikeln als Pragmalexeme.*
B. Kunzmann-Müller, 682(ZPSK):Band42 Heft1-120

Ratner, R.S. & J.L. McMullan, eds. State Control.
R.B., 185:Apr90-708
Rattner, J. Dichtung und Humanitat.
H. Knust, 406:Spring89-121
Ratushinskaya, I. Grey Is the Color of Hope.
639(VQR):Spring89-54
Ratushinskaya, I. In the Beginning.
V. Rounding, 617(TLS):30Mar-5Apr90-340
Ratz, N. Der Identitätsroman.*
W. Koepke, 133:Band22Heft3/4-322
Rau, W. - see Weller, F.
Raudszus, G. Die Zeichensprache der Kleidung.
D. Peil, 680(ZDP):Band108Heft3-444
Rauh, G. Tiefenkasus, thematische Relationen und Thetarollen.
K.G. Ottósson, 603:Vol13No2-495
Raun, T.U. Estonia and the Estonians.
M-L. Hinkkanen-Lievonen, 575(SEER): Apr89-299
Raupp, H-J. Untersuchungen zu Künstlerbildnis und Künstlerdarstellung in der Niederlanden im 17. Jahrhundert.
M. Russell, 39:Feb89-134
Rausch, R. & I. Deutsche Phonetik für Ausländer.
M. Pétursson, 685(ZDL):3/1989-395
Rauschenbach, B. - see Schmidt, A. & W. Michels
Rautenberg, U. Das "Volksbuch vom armen Heinrich."
W.G. Ganser, 680(ZDP):Band108Heft1-129
Rave Prieto, J.L. Arte religioso en Marchena.
M. Estella, 48:Jan-Mar89-104
Ravel, M. A Ravel Reader.* (French title: Lettres, écrits, entretiens.) (A. Orenstein, ed)
J. Rosselli, 617(TLS):5-11Oct90-1071
Raven, S. Bird of Ill Omen.
J. Lewis, 364:Dec89/Jan90-140
Raven, S. In the Image of God.
T. Fitton, 617(TLS):16-22Mar90-293
Ravenel, S., ed. New Stories from the South: The Year's Best, 1988.*
T.E. Holt, 219(GaR):Spring89-189
Ravenel, S., ed. New Stories from the South: The Year's Best, 1989.
R. Sassone, 441:7Jan90-16
Raviv, D. & Y. Melman. Every Spy a Prince.
D. Wise, 441:8Jul90-1
Rawlence, C. The Missing Reel.
K. Brownlow, 441:18Nov90-15
D. Coward, 617(TLS):1-7Jun90-575
Rawles, S. & M.A. Screech, with others. A New Rabelais Bibliography: Editions of Rabelais before 1626.*
D.J. Shaw, 402(MLR):Jan90-178
J. Veyrin-Forrer & B. Moreau, 354: Dec89-363
Rawlinson, P. The Jesuit Factor.
P. Hebblethwaite, 617(TLS):18-24May90-531
Rawlyk, G.A., ed. Canadian Baptists and Christian Higher Education.
T. Sinclair-Faulkner, 150(DR): Winter88/89-529
Raworth, T. Tottering State.*
K. Jebb, 493:Summer89-31
Rawson, C.J. Order from Confusion Sprung.*
M.E. Novak, 83:Spring89-112

Rawson, E. Intellectual Life in the Late Roman Republic.*
P. Flobert, 555:Vol62Fasc2-375
Rawson, H. Wicked Words.
D. Menaker, 441:13May90-14
Ray, B. Hyderabad and British Paramountcy, 1858-1883.
K. Leonard, 293(JASt):Nov89-911
Ray, D. Sam's Book.*
R. Mitchell, 502(PrS):Fall89-129
Ray, D.L., with L. Guzzo. Trashing the Planet.
D.B. Botkin, 441:30Sep90-29
Ray, G.N. Books as a Way of Life. (G.T. Tanselle, ed)
517(PBSA):Jun89-246
Ray, M. - see Conrad, J.
Ray, R.H., ed. Approaches to Teaching Shakespeare's "King Lear."*
R.A. Cohen, 570(SQ):Winter89-502
Raya, G. Verga e i Treves.
N. Patruno, 276:Summer89-236
Rayan, K. Text and Sub-Text.
P. Kitson, 447(N&Q):Mar89-135
Raymo, C. In the Falcon's Claw.
J. Crace, 441:4Mar90-26
Raymond, D. I Was Dora Suarez.
M. Stasio, 441:4Nov90-30
Raymond, F., ed. Jules Verne 5.
S. Vierne, 535(RHL):Jul-Aug89-737
Raymond, M.B. & M.R. Sullivan - see Browning, E.B. & M.R. Mitford
Raynal, G. & D. Diderot. Die Geschichte beider Indien. (H.J. Lüsebrink, ed)
J. Chouillet, 535:Apr89-155
Raynal, H. Sur toi l'or de la nuit.
M-N. Little, 207(FR):May90-1106
Rayner, A. Comic Persuasion.
R. Simard, 610:Spring89-90
R.A. Zimbardo, 401(MLQ):Mar88-65
Raz, J. The Morality of Freedom.*
C. Audard, 98:Jun-Jul89-540
R.E. Ewin, 63:Dec89-494
J.M. Fischer, 482(PhR):Apr89-254
C. Kolbley, 258:Mar89-106
L.E. Lomasky, 144:Winter-Spring90-86
Razzi, L.M. & G. Bonfadini. Il dialetto di Salò.
M. Moretti, 545(RPh):Feb90-455
Rdyé, M., J. Mougenot & J. Royer. La Télé des allumés, 1960-1975.
A.J.M. Prévos, 207(FR):Feb90-601
Re, L. Calvino and the Age of Neorealism.
L. Sage, 617(TLS):5-11Oct90-1060
Read, A. & D. Fisher. Kristallnacht.
A. Glees, 617(TLS):13-19Apr90-392
Read, E. A Time of Cicadas.
L. Manning, 526:Fall89-100
Read, P.P. On the Third Day.
D.J. Enright, 617(TLS):19-25Oct90-1130
Read, S. Relevant Logic.
G. Stahl, 542:Oct-Dec89-656
Reade, B. Aubrey Beardsley.
C. Newall, 39:Feb89-137
Reade, C. Plays by Charles Reade.* (M. Hammet, ed)
G. Bas, 189(EA):Oct-Dec89-487
Reader, J. Missing Links.
S. Rose, 617(TLS):23Feb-1Mar90-204
Reading, P. Perduta Gente.*
T. Whitworth, 493:Autumn89-40
Reading, P. Shitheads.
C. Hurford, 617(TLS):21-27Dec90-1383

Reagan, R. An American Life.
M. Dowd, 441:18Nov90-1
F. Fitz Gerald, 442(NY):24Dec90-91
K.S. Lynn, 617(TLS):21-27Dec90-1370
G. Wills, 453(NYRB):20Dec90-3
Reale, G. & others. L'opera letteraria di Agostino tra Cassiciacum e Milano.
G. Bonner, 123:Vol39No2-238
Reaney, J. Take the Big Picture.
H. Froese-Tiessen, 102(CanL):Autumn-Winter89-251
Reardon, D.C. Aborted Women.
N.D., 185:Jul90-926
Rearick, W.R. The Art of Paolo Veronese 1528-1588.
C. Dempsey, 617(TLS):5-11Jan90-15
Reaver, J.R., ed. Florida Folktales.
P.A. Bulger, 292(JAF):Apr-Jun89-228
Reavis, D.J. Conversations with Moctezuma.
J.G. Castañeda, 441:25Feb90-10
Reber, A.S., ed. The Penguin Dictionary of Psychology.
D.H., 355(LSoc):Mar89-146
Rebhorn, W.A. Foxes and Lions.
P. Bondanella, 551(RenQ):Autumn89-559
S. de Pretis, 547(RF):Band101Heft2/3-358
J.H. Whitfield, 402(MLR):Jan90-205
Recanati, F. Meaning and Force.*
A. Ross, 393(Mind):Oct89-649
Recht, R., ed. Les Bâtisseurs des Cathédrales Gothiques.
A. Saint, 617(TLS):9-15Mar90-265
"La Hacha de voyage."
L. Godard de Donville, 535(RHL):Jan-Feb89-164
Recker, J.A.M. "Appelle-moi Pierrot."*
C. Morlet Chantalat, 535(RHL):Jan-Feb89-101
H. Mydlarski, 345(KRQ):Nov89-489
K.W. Wolfe, 568(SCN):Fall-Winter89-51
Z. Youssef, 475:Vol16No30-337
Reckford, K.J. Aristophanes' Old-and-New Comedy.* (Vol 1)
D.M. MacDowell, 123:Vol39No1-16
F. Muecke, 303(JoHS):Vol109-223
M.X. Zelenak, 130:Spring89-98
Reddè, M. Prospection des vallees du nord de la Libye (1979-1980).
C. Tarditi, 229:Band61Heft7-654
Reddy, M.T. Sisters in Crime.
J.A. Roberts, 395(MFS):Winter89-869
Redekop, C. Mennonite Society.
B. Godlee, 617(TLS):18-24May90-531
Redfern, W. Puns.
M.L. Apte, 35(AS):Summer89-181
Redford, B. The Converse of the Pen.*
B. Beatty, 83:Autumn89-236
Redford, D.B. Akhenaten, The Heretic King.
E.S. Meltzer, 318(JAOS):Apr-Jun88-285
Redgrove, P. The Black Goddess.
J. Ramsay, 493:Winter89/90-44
Redgrove, P. The First Earthquake.*
J.P. Ward, 493:Winter89/90-42
Redgrove, P. The Moon Disposes. In the Hall of the Saurians.
J. Saunders, 565:Autumn89-76
Redhead, B. The Inspiration of Landscape.
T. Cantell, 324:Jul90-570
Rediker, M. Between the Devil and the Deep Blue Sea.
P.A. Gilje, 656(WMQ):Apr89-390
[continued]

Rediker, M. Between the Devil and the Deep
Blue Sea. [continuing]
　R. Ritchie, 432(NEQ):Mar89-141
　566:Spring90-220
Redmond, C. In Bed with Sherlock Holmes.
　T. Goldie, 102(CanL):Winter88-128
Redmond, J., ed. Themes in Drama, 7.
　G. Bas, 189(EA):Apr-Jun89-192
Redmond, J., ed. Themes in Drama, 9.
　G. Bas, 189(EA):Apr-Jun89-192
　R. Jackson, 611(TN):Vol43No1-39
Redner, H. The Ends of Philosophy.
　R. Grigg, 63:Dec89-491
"Odilon Redon; the Woodner Collection."
　D. Scrase, 39:Jul89-65
Redona, P.V.B., with G.A. dell'Acqua & G.
Vezzoli – see under Begni Redona, P.V.,
　with G.A. dell'Acqua & G. Vezzoli
Redondi, P. Galileo Heretic.* (French title:
Galilée hérétique.)
　M.A. Finocchiaro, 319:Jan90-130
Redondo, F.G. – see under Gómez Redondo, F.
Redondo Cantera, M.J. El sepulcro en España
en el siglo XVI.
　M.M. Estella, 48:Jul-Sep89-379
Redshaw, T.D., ed. Hill Field.
　S. O'Brien, 617(TLS):27Apr-3May90-443
Rée, J. Philosophical Tales.*
　A. Montefiore, 447(N&Q):Dec89-557
　D. Shaw, 518:Oct89-217
"Réécritures 3."
　J-C. Margolin, 531:Jul-Dec89-504
Reed, C. Henry Chapman Mercer and the Mor-
avian Pottery and Tile Works.
　R. Hildyard, 39:Sep89-212
　J.R., 90:May89-366
Reed, G.F. Obsessional Experience and Com-
pulsive Behaviour.
　J.O. Wisdom, 488:Jun89-228
Reed, I. The Free-Lance Pallbearers.* The
Terrible Twos.*
　A. Lively, 617(TLS):18-24May90-534
Reed, I. New and Collected Poems.*
　S.J. Jones, 649(WAL):Nov89-259
Reed, I. The Terrible Threes.*
　B.K. Horvath, 532(RCF):Fall89-213
　S.J. Jones, 649(WAL):Nov89-259
Reed, J. Madness.
　H. Lomas, 364:Feb/Mar90-142
　L. Mackinnon, 617(TLS):22-28Jun90-673
Reed, J. Nineties. Dicing for Pearls.
　L. Mackinnon, 617(TLS):22-28Jun90-673
Reed, J.R. Decadent Style.
　J. Hunter, 301(JEGP):Jan89-129
Reed, P. Sartre: "Les Mains sales."
　W. Redfern, 402(MLR):Jul90-748
Reed, P. Sartre: "La Nausée."
　D.A. MacLeay, 207(FR):Dec89-385
　P. Thody, 402(MLR):Apr90-460
Reed, W.H. Elgar as I Knew Him. (2nd ed)
　A.F.L.T., 412:May89-145
Reeder, R. – see Akhmatova, A.
Reeg, U. Schreiben in der Fremde.
　H. Suhr, 221(GQ):Fall89-562
Rees, A.L. & F. Borzelli. The New Art History.
　M. Erickson, 709:Summer90-251
Rees, E.A. State Control in Soviet Russia.
　L.T. Lih, 550(RusR):Jan89-102
　C. Merridale, 575(SEER):Jan89-157
Rees, G. Francis Bacon's Natural Philosophy.
　C. Walton, 319:Apr90-289

Rees-Davies, J., comp. Bibliography of the
Early Clarinet.
　R. Andrewes, 415:Dec89-746
Reesink, G.P. Structures and Their Functions
in Usan.
　D.H., 355(LSoc):Mar89-146
Reeve, A.L. From Hacienda to Bungalow.
　J. Caufield, 576:Jun89-201
Reeve, C.D.C. Philosopher-Kings.*
　M.L. Morgan, 543:Dec89-417
Reeve, C.D.C. Socrates in the Apology.
　W. Uzgalis, 103:Nov90-471
Reeve, D. Golkar of Indonesia.
　J. Mackie, 293(JASt):Feb89-233
Reeve, W.C. In Pursuit of Power.*
　K. Arens, 221(GQ):Winter89-120
　J. Gearey, 301(JEGP):Jan89-76
　J.M. Grandin, 406:Fall89-395
　W. Wittkowski, 133:Band22Heft3/4-334
Reeves, G. T.S. Eliot.
　L. Unger, 675(YER):Fall90-102
Reeves, M. & W. Gould. Joachim of Fiore and
the Myth of the Eternal Evangel in the
Nineteenth Century.*
　V. Hyde, 111:Fall90-6
　R. ap Roberts, 301(JEGP):Jul89-445
　N. Sagovsky, 97(CQ):Vol18No1-105
Reeves, R. Peeping Thomas.
　M. Stasio, 441:30Sep90-32
Regan, T. Bloomsbury's Prophet.*
　N. Griffin, 556:Summer89-80
　T. Vichy, 189(EA):Jul-Sep89-354
Regan, T. – see Moore, G.E.
Regehr, E. Arms Canada.
　M. Bradfield, 298:Spring89-146
　E.G. Hollett, 529(QQ):Summer89-536
Regis, E. Great Mambo Chicken and the
Transhuman Condition.
　A. Kohn, 441:28Oct90-29
"Register of Early Music."
　A.F.L.T., 412:May89-146
Regn, G. – see Petrarch
Regnerus, C. Demonstratio logicae verae
ivridica. (G. Kalinowski, ed)
　J.S. Freedman, 53(AGP):Band71Heft1-94
van Regteren Altena, I.Q. Jacques de Gheyn.*
　C.J.W., 90:Jan89-47
　C.J.W., 90:Jun89-437
Rehder, P., ed. Einführung in die slavischen
Sprachen.
　L.R. Micklesen, 279:Vol35/36-335
　D. Weiss, 688(ZSP):Band49Heft1-202
Reich, K. Die Vollständigkeit der Kantischen
Urteilstafel. (3rd ed)
　R.M., 342:Band80Heft4-498
Reich, W., comp. Jan Dismas Zelenka.
　S. Oschmann, 417:Jan-Mar89-80
Reich-Ranicki, M. Thomas Mann and His
Family.
　C.J. Fox, 364:Dec89/Jan90-115
Reichard, G. August Wilhelm Schlegels "Ion."
　G.K. Hart, 133:Band22Heft3/4-330
Reichel, J. Der Spruchdichter Hans Rosen-
plüt.*
　I. Glier, 680(ZDP):Band108Heft1-119
Reichenberger, K.& R. Bibliographisches
Handbuch der Calderón-Forschung. (Vols 1
& 3)
　A.L. Mackenzie, 86(BHS):Apr89-180
Reichholf, C. Gerhard Amanshausers Ironie
und Satire.
　A. Reiter, 406:Fall89-404

Reichler—Beguelin, M—J. Les noms latins du type "mēns."
M. Fruyt, 555:Vol62Fasc2-357

Reichman, H. Railwaymen and Revolution: Russia, 1905.
R.G. Robbins, Jr., 242:Vol10No1-123

Reichman, R. Getting Computers to Talk Like You and Me.
R.E. Sanders & C. Iacobucci, 355(LSoc): Mar89-121

Reid, A. Southeast Asia in the Age of Commerce, 1450-1680.* (Vol 1)
D.P. Chandler, 293(JASt):Nov89-942

Reid, B., ed. Alexander Pope (1688-1744).
566:Spring90-211

Reid, B.L. First Acts.
R.G. Benson, 569(SR):Spring89-lvii

Reid, C. Edmund Burke and the Practice of Political Writing.
W.A. Speck, 506(PSt):May87-112

Reid, C., ed. The Poetry Book Society Anthology 1989-1990.
T. Dooley, 617(TLS):6-12Jul90-734

Reid, J.H. Heinrich Böll.*
K.G. Knight, 447(N&Q):Jun89-279
S. Mandel, 395(MFS):Summer89-351

Reid, M. Ask Sir James.*
F.B. Smith, 637(VS):Winter90-345

Reid, N. T'es fou l'artiste.
K.L. Kellett, 102(CanL):Autumn—Winter89-202

Reid, T. Practical Ethics. (K. Haakonssen, ed)
R.D. Downie, 617(TLS):17-23Aug90-880

Reidel, J. – see Kees, W.

van Reijen, W. & G.S. Noerr. Vierzig Jahre Flaschenpost.
J. Früchtl, 687:Jan-Mar89-199

Reilly, B.F. The Kingdom of León—Castilla under King Alfonso VI, 1065-1109.*
M. Lunenfeld, 589:Jul89-758

Reilly, C.W. English Poetry of the Second World War.
J.G. Watson, 447(N&Q):Mar89-130

Reilly, E.J., ed. Approaches to Teaching Swift's "Gulliver's Travels."*
S. Soupel, 189(EA):Jan-Mar89-116

Reilly, P. The Literature of Guilt.
566:Autumn89-65

Reilly, R. Wedgwood.
J.K. des Fontaines, 324:Feb90-218
N. McKendrick, 617(TLS):10-16Aug90-851

Reiman, D.H. Intervals of Inspiration.
J. Clubbe, 445(NCF).Sep89-233
S.M. Sperry, 340(KSJ):Vol38-184

Reiman, D.H. Romantic Texts and Contexts.
K. Everest, 677(YES):Vol20-295
A.D. Knerr, 340(KSJ):Vol38-190

Reinders, J.S. Violence, Victims and Rights.
J.B., 185:Apr90-708

Reiner, H. Duty and Inclination.
T.E. Hill, Jr., 342:Band80Heft2-243

Reinhard, J. Burning the Prairie.*
M. Vinz, 456(NDQ):Summer89-255

Reinhold, M. From Republic to Principate.
R.L. Bates, 124:Jan-Feb90-241
J. Carter, 123:Vol39No2-204
J.W. Rich, 313:Vol79-251

Reinsma, L.M. "Aelfric": An Annotated Bibliography.
H. Gneuss, 38:Band107Heft1/2-159
T.H. Leinbaugh, 589:Jul89-760

Reisel, J. Zeitgeschichtliche und theologisch-scholastische Aspekte im "Daniel von dem blühenden Tal" des Stricker.
J. Margetts, 402(MLR):Jul90-782

Reising, R.J. The Unusable Past.*
J.A.L. Lemay, 677(YES):Vol20-226

Reisner, M. Cadillac Desert.
P.N. Limerick, 617(TLS):27Jul-2Aug90-794

Reisner, M. & S. Bates. Overtapped Oasis.
G. Maranto, 441:2Sep90-17

Reiss, N. Speech Art Taxonomy as a Tool for Ethnographic Description.
S.J. Sigman, 355(LSoc):Mar89-126

Reiter, W. Aemilius Paullus.
A.E. Astin, 123:Vol39No1-149
L—M. Günther, 229:Band61Heft5-447

Reith, H.R. René Descartes.*
M. Phillips, 192(EP):Jan-Mar89-112

von Reitzenstein, W—A. Lexikon bayerischer Ortsnamen.*
G. Schlimpert, 682(ZPSK):Band42Heft2-269

Rembert, J.A.W. Swift and the Dialectical Tradition.
A.B. England, 566:Spring89-169
A.C. Kelly, 301(JEGP):Oct89-539

Rémi-Giraud, S., ed. L'infinitif.
B. Peeters, 350:Jun90-425

Remington, F. Frederic Remington Selected Letters. (A.P. & M.D. Splete, eds)
F. Erisman, 640(WAL):Feb90-373

Remini, R. The Life of Andrew Jackson.
639(VQR):Spring89-54

Rempel, R.A., with others – see Russell, B.

"Die Renaissance im Deutschen Südwesten zwischen Reformation und Dreissigjährigen Krieg."
P.O. Kristeller, 551(RenQ):Spring89-101

Renart, J. The "Lai de l'ombre."* (M.E. Winters, ed)
M. Boulton, 589:Apr89-490

Rendall, J., ed. Equal or Different.
M.M. Clarke, 637(VS):Spring90-488

Rendell, R. Collocted Storica.
P. Wolfe, 573(SSF):Winter89-95

Rendell, R. Going Wrong.
P. Craig, 617(TLS):21-27Dec90-1382
R.W. Winks, 441:14Oct90-42

Rener, F.M. Interpretatio.
J. Sturrock, 617(TLS):12-18Jan90-40

Rener, M., ed. Petri Presbyteri Carmina.
T.A—P. Klein, 229:Band61Heft8-680

Renfrew, C. Archaeology and Language.*
E.A. Ebbinghaus, 215(GL):Vol29No3-213
S. Lindsey, 102(CanL):Spring89-215
B. Vine, 124:Mar-Apr90-359

Renfrew, C.B. & others. Democracy.
K.G., 185:Jan90-447

Rengakos, A. Form und Wandel des Machtdenkens der Athener bei Thukydides.*
P.J. Rhodes, 303(JoHS):Vol109-219

Renoir, A. A Key to Old Poems.
A.S.G. Edwards, 402(MLR):Jul90-679

Renoir, J. Entretiens et propos.
A. Thiher, 207(FR):Dec89-396

Renoir, J. Renoir on Renoir.
A. Sarris, 441:25Mar90-11

Rensch, R. Harps and Harpists.*
O. Ellis, 415:Oct89-614

Rentschler, E., ed. West German Filmmakers on Film.
T. Elsaesser, 707:Spring89-140

Rentto, J-P. Prudentia Iuris.
G.L. Froelich, 543:Dec89-418
Repici, L. La natura e l'anima.
R.W. Sharples, 123:Vol39No2-261
Rescher, N. Moral Absolutes.
J.P. Dougherty, 543:Dec89-420
Rescher, N. A Philosophical Inquiry into the
Nature and the Rationale of Reason.
T.V. Upton, 543:Jun90-878
Resler, M. - see Hartmann von Aue
Resnick, M. Second Contact.
G. Jonas, 441:13May90-35
Ressler, S. Joseph Conrad.
A. Hunter, 447(N&Q):Dec89-538
Z. Najder, 497(PolR):Vol34No1-82
D.R. Schwarz, 395(MFS):Summer89-318
639(VQR):Winter89-10
Restagno, E., ed. Petrassi.
J.C.G. Waterhouse, 410(M&L):May89-277
Restif de La Bretonne. Monsieur Nicolas. (P.
Testud, ed)
D. Coward, 617(TLS):30Mar-5Apr90-348
Restif de La Bretonne. Les Nuits de Paris ou
le Spectateur-nocturne. (M. Delon, ed)
I-O. Gacem, 535(RHL):Jan-Feb89-118
Restuccia, F.L. Joyce and the Law of the
Father.
C. Froula, 329(JJQ):Summer90-871
P. McGee, 223:Fall89-315
Rétat, P. Les Journaux de 1789.*
M. Cook, 402(MLR):Apr90-447
Cardinal de Retz. Mémoires. (S. Bertière, ed)
J. Marmier, 475:Vol16No30-265
Reutersvärd, O. Otto G. Carlsund i fjärrper-
spektiv.
A. Fant, 341:Vol58No2-91
Revel, J. & A. Farge. Logiques de la foule.
P. Higonnet, 617(TLS):28Sep-4Oct90-
1028
Revell, D. The Gaza of Winter.
B. Howard, 491:May89-109
S.M. Schultz, 639(VQR):Autumn89-773
L. Upton, 448:Vol27No2-140
Revelli, M. Lavorare in Fiat.
D. Frigessi, 358:Feb90-7
de Revenga, F.J.D. - see under Díez de
Revenga, F.J.
de Revenga, F.J.D. & M. de Paco - see under
Díez de Revenga, F.J. & M. de Paco
Reventlow, H., W. Sparn & J. Woodbridge, eds.
Historische Kritik und biblischer Kanon in
der deutschen Aufklärung.
F. Laplanche, 531:Jul-Dec89-525
Reverand, C.D. 2d. Dryden's Final Poetic
Mode.
P. Hammond, 566:Spring90-190
J.E. Lewis, 173(ECS):Winter89/90-211
G. Parfitt, 402(MLR):Oct90-917
639(VQR):Summer89-86
Revkin, A. The Burning Season.
J. Brooke, 441:19Aug90-7
Revueltas, J. Human Mourning.
D. Unger, 441:25Feb90-24
Rewald, J. Cézanne and America.*
C. Lloyd, 39:Dec89-431
Rewald, J. Seurat.
J. Russell, 441:2Dec90-9
Rex, W.E. The Attraction of the Contrary.*
S. Davies, 208(FS):Oct89-472
P. France, 242:Vol10No2-245
T.M. Kavanagh, 210(FrF):Jan89-101
M.R. Morris, 207(FR):Mar90-712
R. Niklaus, 83:Autumn89-238

Rexroth, D., ed. Der Komponist Hans Werner
Henze.
S. Wiesmann, 417:Jan-Mar89-98
Rexroth, K. World Outside the Window.*
R.B.D., 295(JML):Fall88/Winter89-400
Rey, A.D. - see under Domínguez Rey, A.
Rey Rosa, R. Dust on Her Tongue.*
D. Durrant, 364:Aug/Sep89-134
Reyes, R., ed. Poesía española del siglo XVIII.
J.H.R. Polt, 240(HR):Autumn89-523
Reyle, U. & C. Rohrer, eds. Natural Language
Parsing and Linguistic Theories.*
E.J. Briscoe, 297(JL):Sep89-535
de Reyniès, N. Le Mobilier Domestique, Vo-
cabulaire Typlolgique.
S. Jervis, 90:May89-364
Reynolds, B.H. Space, Time and Crisis.
E. Acosta-Belén, 711(RHM):Dec89-189
E. Irizarry, 238:May89-309
D.L. Shaw, 402(MLR):Apr90-487
Reynolds, C. The Politics of War.
M. Cranston, 617(TLS):6-12Apr90-377
Reynolds, C.J. Thai Radical Discourse.
A. Turton, 293(JASt):May89-440
Reynolds, D.S. Beneath the American Renais-
sance.*
N. Fredricks, 223:Summer89-201
G. Johnson, 639(VQR):Spring89-349
M.J. Killingsworth, 646(WWR):Summer89-
32
J. McIntosh, 587(SAF):Autumn89-243
H. Parker, 401(MLQ):Sep88-298
S. Railton, 445(NCF):Sep89-247
G. Scharnhorst, 594:Summer89-221
M. Schueller, 27(AL):Mar89-104
Reynolds, G. English Portrait Miniatures.*
(rev)
S. Foister, 90:Nov89-782
Reynolds, J. & R. Tannenbaum. Jews and
God-Fearers at Aphrodisias.*
A.G. Woodhead, 303(JoHS):Vol109-243
Reynolds, J.F. - see Gellert, C.F.
Reynolds, K. Girls Only?
C. Lennox-Boyd, 617(TLS):5-11Oct90-
1065
Reynolds, L.J. European Revolutions and the
American Literary Renaissance.
B. Erkkila, 445(NCF):Mar90-534
L.L. Willis, 594:Winter89-462
Reynolds, M., ed. Erotica.
H. Williams, 617(TLS):21-27Dec90-1372
Reynolds, M. Hemingway: The Paris Years.
J.D. Bloom, 441:7Jan90-19
J. Campbell, 617(TLS):2-8Feb90-108
A. De Fazio 3d, 234:Spring90-178
Reynolds, M. The Young Hemingway.*
K. Moreland, 577(SHR):Spring89-145
Reynolds, M.S. "The Sun Also Rises."*
W. Balassi, 587(SAF):Spring89-123
Reynolds, P. "As You Like It."
R. Knowles, 402(MLR):Apr90-409
Reynolds, R. A Searcher's Path.
P. Dickinson, 410(M&L):Aug89-442
Reynolds-Cornell, R. Witnessing an Era.*
D.L. Drysdall, 208(FS):Apr89-203
R. Zuber, 535(RHL):Mar-Apr89-271
Reznek, L. The Nature of Disease.*
M. Evans, 521:Jul89-267
Rezvani. Le 8e Fléau.
C. Dauvergne-Green, 207(FR):May90-
1107

von Rezzori, G. The Snows of Yesteryear.*
P-L. Adams, 61:Jan90-100
M. Ignatieff, 453(NYRB):15Feb90-3
de Rhett, B.M. - see under Mariscal de Rhett,
B.
Rhoads, D.A. Shakespeare's Defense of
Poetry.
H.F. Plett, 156(ShJW):Jahrbuch1989-366
Rhode, D.L., ed. Theoretical Perspectives on
Sexual Difference.
L. Hudson, 617(TLS):1-7Jun90-588
Rhodes, D.E. Catalogue of Books Printed in
Spain and of Spanish Books Printed Else-
where in Europe before 1601 Now in the
British Library. (2nd ed)
C. Griffin, 617(TLS):2-8Mar90-232
Rhodes, D.E., ed. Catalogue of Seventeenth
Century Italian Books in the British
Library. Short-Title Catalogue of Books
Printed in Italy and of Italian Books Print-
ed in Other Countries from 1465 to 1600
Now in the British Library: Supplement.
U. Limentani, 278(IS):Vol43-162
Rhodes, R. A Hole in the World.
R. Banks, 441:28Oct90-14
Rial, H.V. - see under Vázquez Rial, H.
Rials, S. La Déclaration des droits de l'homme
et du citoyen.*
J. Starobinski, 453(NYRB):12Apr90-47
Ribaillier, J. - see William of Auxerre
Ribard, J. Le Moyen Age.
P.H. Stäblein, 545(RPh):Aug90-000
Ribon, M. L'art et la nature.
P. Somville, 542:Oct-Dec89-639
Ricapito, J.V., ed. Tri-linear Edition of
"Lazarillo de Tormes" of 1554.*
R.L. Fiore, 238:Mar89-140
Ricard, A. L'invention de théâtre.
G. Moore, 538(RAL):Summer89-286
Ricard, A. Naissance du roman africain.
J-N. Vignonde, 538(RAL):Summer89-288
Ricardou, J. Révolutions miniscules, précédé
de "Révélations miniscules, en guise de
préface, à la gloire de Jean Paulhan."* La
Cathédrale de Sens.*
J. Baetens, 400(MLN):Sep89-960
Ricco, R. & F. Maresca, with J. Weissman.
American Primitive.*
M. Moorman, 55:May89-111
Rice, A. The Witching Hour.
P. McGrath, 441:4Nov90-11
Rice, B. Daniel.
D. Kosub, 198:Winter89-113
S. Scobie, 376:Sep89-123
Rice, B. Trafficking.
C. Salzberg, 441:7Jan90-9
Rice, C. Nordi's Gift.
A. Cooper, 441:25Nov90-19
Rice, C. Russian Workers and the Socialist-
Revolutionary Party through the Revolution
of 1905-1907.
M. Melancon, 550(RusR):Apr89-197
Rice, C.J., ed. Protokoly Vtorogo (Ekstren-
nogo) S"ezda Partii Sotsialistov-Revoliuts-
ionerov.
R. Service, 575(SEER):Jan89-148
Rice, E. Captain Sir Richard Francis Burton.
P-L. Adams, 61:Jul90-105
A. Burgess, 441:20May90-1
Rice, J.A. Middle English Romance.
S. Crane, 589:Apr89-491
Rice, L. Stone Heart.
A. McDermott, 441:1Jul90-13

Rice, M. Egypt's Making.
J. Ray, 617(TLS):25-31May90-562
Rice, P. & C. Gowing. British Studio Ceramics
in the 20th Century.
O. Watson, 39:Nov89-361
Rice, P. & P. Waugh. Modern Literary Theory.
W. Baker, 599:Summer90-338
Rice, S. He Included Me. (L. Westling, ed)
J.D. Cain, 441:27May90-15
Rich, A. Time's Power.*
A. Hudgins, 249(HudR):Winter89-681
S. Kantaris, 493:Autumn89-42
639(VQR):Autumn89-137
Rich, S. & L. Mayer. People I Have Shot.
V. Mallet, 617(TLS):1-7Jun90-578
Richard, C. Lettres americaines.
J. Templeton, 189(EA):Jul-Sep89-358
Richard, J-P. L'État des choses.
R. Buss, 617(TLS):17-23Aug90-870
Richard, L. Le Nazisme et la culture.
J-J. Goux, 153:Fall-Winter89-10
Richard, M. Propositional Attitudes.
M.J. Cresswell, 103:Oct90-430
Richard, P-M. Découverte du français fam-
ilier et argotique.
D. Nehls, 257(IRAL):Nov89-358
Richard-Amato, P. Making It Happen.
P.A. McCollum, 351(LL):Sep89-439
Richards, B. Transport in Cities.
T. Bendixson, 324:Aug90-644
Richards, D.A. Nights Below Station Street.*
G. Noonan, 198.3:Summer89-118
Richards, D.G. The Hero's Quest for the Self.
R. Koester, 406:Winter89-506
S. Mandel, 395(MFS):Summer89-351
Richards, G. Human Evolution.
G.E.V., 185:Apr90-698
Richards, I.A. Selected Letters. (J. Con-
stable, ed)
D.J. Enright, 617(TLS):3-9Aug90-821
Richards, J. Happiest Days.*
J.A. Mangan, 637(VS):Winter90-361
Richards, J., ed. Imperialism and Juvenile
Literature.
C. Nelson, 637(VS):Spring90-506
Richards, J.L. Mathematical Visions.
T. Banchoff, 637(VS):Summer90-662
Richards, R.J. Darwin and the Emergence of
Evolutionary Theories of Mind and Behav-
ior.*
D.C. Dennett, 486:Sep89-540
M. Ruse, 319:Jan90-144
Richardson, A. A Mental Theater.
J.K. Brown, 340(KSJ):Vol38-195
P.A. Cantor, 661(WC):Autumn89-198
Richardson, H. - see Burns, P.
Richardson, J. Existential Epistemology.*
L. Stevenson, 484(PPR):Sep89-210
Richardson, J. Judith Gautier.
M.C. Hawthorne, 620(TSWL):Spring89-137
Richardson, J. Wallace Stevens: The Later
Years, 1923-1955.*
J.V. Brogan, 27(AL):Oct89-491
C.R. Wagner, 705:Spring89-74
Richardson, J. Vanishing Lives.*
A.H. Harrison, 637(VS):Winter90-339
K. McSweeney, 445(NCF):Jun89-109
T.L. Meyers, 177(ELT):Vol32No4-529
Richardson, J. Wacousta; or, The Prophecy.
(D. Cronk, ed)
M.A. Peterman, 470:Vol27-116

Richardson, J.S. Hispaniae.*
  P.J.J. Vanderbroeck, 394:Vol42fasc1/2-
  242
Richardson, L., Jr. Pompeii.
  R. Brilliant, 24:Winter89-672
  D.E.E. Kleiner, 576:Sep89-284
  R. Ling, 90:Feb89-153
  D.L. Thompson, 124:Jul-Aug90-537
Richardson, R. Death, Dissection and the
  Destitute.*
  R. Cooter, 637(VS):Winter90-327
Richardson, R.A. & B.H. MacDonald, comps.
  Science and Technology in Canadian His-
  tory.
  S. Zeller, 470:Vol27-112
Richardson, W. "Zolotoe Runo" and Russian
  Modernism.
  D.M. Bethea, 574(SEEJ):Spring89-127
  G. Donchin, 575(SEER):Apr89-277
Riché, P. Gerbert d'Aurillac.
  J.T. Hallenbeck, 589:Apr89-491
Richel, V.C. The German Stage, 1767-1890.
  R.C. Cowen, 221(GQ):Fall89-530
  S. Williams, 610:Summer89-200
Richetti, J.J. Daniel Defoe.*
  D. Blewett, 173(ECS):Fall89-76
  M.M. Boardman, 405(MP):Nov89-187
Richie, D. Different People.*
  P. McCarthy, 407(MN):Spring89-132
Richie, D. Tokyo Nights.
  J. Haylock, 364:Apr/May89-106
Richler, M. Solomon Gursky Was Here.
  P-L. Adams, 61:May90-132
  J. Clute, 617(TLS):15-21Jun90-653
  F. Prose, 441:8Apr90-7
Richman, R., ed. The Direction of Poetry.
  R. McDowell, 249(HudR):Winter89-603
Richmond, C. - see Gómez de la Serna, R.
Richmond, I. & C. Venesoen, eds. Présences
  féminines.
  N. Hepp, 547(RF):Band101Heft1-115
Richter, C. Writing to Survive. (H. Richter,
  ed)
  E.W. Gaston, Jr., 395(MFS):Summer89-292
Richter, D. Das fremde Kind.*
  J. Zipes, 221(GQ):Fall89-501
Richter, D.H., ed. The Critical Tradition.
  J.R. Bennett, 402(MLR):Jul90-669
Richter, H., ed. Writing to Survive.
  C.L. Adams, 649(WAL):Aug89-181
Richter, M. Les deux "Cimes" de Rimbaud,
  "Dévotion" et "Rêve."
  L. Forestier, 535(RHL):Jan-Feb89-131
Richter, M. Medieval Ireland.
  639(VQR):Spring89-45
Richter-Schröder, K. Frauenliteratur und
  weibliche Identität.*
  T.E. Goldsmith-Reber, 564:Feb89-79
Rickels, L.A. Aberrations of Mourning.
  S.L. Gilman, 221(GQ):Spring89-287
Rickert, H. The Limits of Concept Formation
  in Natural Science.* (G. Oakes, ed & trans)
  H.P. Rickman, 488:Sep89-401
Ricketts, M. Mircea Eliade.
  S. Cain, 390:Nov89-27
Ricketts, P.T., ed. Actes du premier Congrès
  International de l'Association Internation-
  ale d'Etudes Occitanes.
  S.B. Gaunt, 382(MAE):1989/1-174
  S. Kay, 208(FS):Apr89-199
  D.A. Monson, 589:Oct89-1031
Rickman, H.P. Dilthey Today.
  B.E.B., 185:Jan90-456

Ricks, C. T.S. Eliot and Prejudice.*
  W. Bedford, 4:Summer89-70
  W. Scammell, 493:Summer89-38
  M. Wood, 453(NYRB):15Feb90-32
Ricks, C., ed. The New Oxford Book of Victo-
  rian Verse.*
  P. Davis, 97(CQ):Vol18No1-73
  S. Lavabre, 189(EA):Jul-Sep89-349
  A. Nichols, 577(SHR):Summer89-276
Ricks, C. Tennyson.
  617(TLS):27Apr-3May90-457
Ricks, C. - see Tennyson, A.
Ricks, C. & L. Michaels, eds. The State of the
  Language.
  J. Sturrock, 617(TLS):2-8Feb90-113
Ricks, D. The Shade of Homer.
  E. Keeley, 617(TLS):27Apr-3May90-455
Rico, D. Kovacsland.
  M. Goodman, 441:13May90-34
Rico, F., ed. Lazarillo de Tormes.*
  E.C. Riley, 240(HR):Autumn89-507
Rico, F. Problemas del "Lazarillo."
  E.C. Riley, 240(HR):Autumn89-507
Ricoeur, P. A l'école de la phénoménologie.
  J. Colette, 192(EP):Jan-Mar89-113
Ricoeur, P. Lectures on Ideology and Utopia.*
  (G.H. Taylor, ed)
  F.H. Adler, 42(AR):Winter89-102
Ricoeur, P. Time and Narrative.* (French
  title: Temps et Récit.) (Vols 1 & 2)
  T. Postlewait, 615(TJ):Dec89-557
  T.G. Taylor, 290(JAAC):Fall89-380
Ricoeur, P. Time and Narrative. (Vol 3)
  W.V. Harris, 478(P&L):Apr89-201
  T. Postlewait, 615(TJ):Dec89-557
  T.G. Taylor, 290(JAAC):Fall89-380
  M.J. Valdes, 529(QQ):Autumn89-746
Ricou, L. Everyday Magic.*
  J-P. Durix, 102(CanL):Spring89-223
  S. Strömqvist, 307:Apr89-81
Riddel, J. The Inverted Bell.
  K. Ziarek, 153:Fall-Winter89-114
Riddell, J., ed. The Communist International
  in Lenin's Time.
  F.L. Carsten, 575(SEER):Jan89-150
Riddell, P. The Thatcher Decade.
  P. Jenkins, 453(NYRB):12Apr90-30
Riddy, F. Sir Thomas Malory.
  M. Andrew, 402(MLR):Apr90-404
  J.A. Burrow, 447(N&Q):Mar89-82
  P.J.C. Field, 382(MAE):1989/1-160
Ridgely, R.S. & G. Tudor. The Birds of South
  America. (Vol 1)
  M. Kelsey, 617(TLS):29Jun-5Jul90-707
Ridler, A. New and Selected Poems.
  D. McDuff, 565:Spring89-76
Ridler, A. Selected Poems.
  J. Greening, 493:Spring89-55
Ridley, P. Flamingoes in Orbit.
  R. Kaveney, 617(TLS):22-28Jun90-674
Riede, D.G. Matthew Arnold and the Betrayal
  of Language.*
  P.A. Dale, 637(VS):Autumn89-189
  C.D. Ryals, 301(JEGP):Apr89-250
  E.T. Tyler, 405(MP):May90-421
Riedel, F.W., ed. Joseph Martin Kraus und
  Italien.
  S. Staral, 417:Jan-Mar89-76
Riedel, N. Internationale Günter-Kunert-
  Bibliographie.* (Vol 1)
  J. Rosellini, 406:Winter89-510

Riedel, N., ed. Uwe Johnsons Frühwerk im Spiegel der deutschsprachigen Literaturkritik.
L.L. Miller, 564:Nov89-370
B. Neumann, 133:Band22Heft2-193
Riedl, P.A. & M. Seidel, eds. Die Kirchen von Siena.* (Vol 1)
J. Beck, 551(RenQ):Spring89-117
Riedman, M. The Pinnipeds.
T. Halliday, 617(TLS):30Nov-6Dec90-1299
Riegl, A. El culto moderno a los monumentos.
A. Savile, 89(BJA):Spring89-181
Riem, A. L'Universo Terra in "Voss" di Patrick White. The Labyrinths of the Self.
A.M. Stewart, 71(ALS):Oct89-268
Riemen, A., ed. Ansichten zu Eichendorff.
R. Littlejohns, 402(MLR):Jan90-253
van Riemsdijk, H. & E. Williams. Introduction to the Theory of Grammar.*
S. Franks, 710:Dec89-481
Riera Melis, A. La Corona de Aragón y el Reino de Mallorca en el primer cuarto del Siglo XIV.* (Vol 1)
B. Leroy, 92(BH):Jul-Dec88-440
Ries, F.W.D. The Dance Theatre of Jean Cocteau.
M. Autrand, 535(RHL):Mar-Apr89-327
Riese-Hubert, R. Surrealism and the Book.
M. Antle, 400(MLN):Sep89-949
Riethmüller, A. Ferruccio Busonis Poetik.
A. Beaumont, 410(M&L):Nov89-571
Rifey, C.D. Word and Figure.*
W.K. Chapman, 345(KRQ):May89-228
Rifkin, G. & G. Harrar. The Ultimate Entrepreneur.
A.D. Chandler, Jr., 432(NEQ):Dec89-598
Rifkin, J., ed. The Green Lifestyle Handbook.
N. Wade, 441:22Apr90-1
Rifkin, J. Time Wars.*
K-M. Wu, 485(PE&W):Oct89-516
Rigaud, N.J. La Veuve dans la Comédie Anglaise au temps de Shakespeare 1600-1625.*
R.A. Houlbrooke, 677(YES):Vol20-245
Rigaudis, M. Ito-san.
J. Kirkup, 617(TLS):14-20Dec90-1360
"Rigaud's Views of Stowe Gardens."
P.D., 46:Sep89-12
Rigby, P. Original Sin in Augustine's "Confessions."*
R.J. O'Connell, 319:Jan90-125
Rigby, T.H. Political Elites in the USSR.
O. Figes, 617(TLS):10-16Aug90-844
Riggio, T.P. - see Dreiser, T. & H.L. Mencken
Riggs, D. Ben Jonson.*
A. Bermel, 34:Jan90-38
T.C. Holyoke, 42(AR):Spring89-243
G. O'Connor, 511:Oct89-46
639(VQR):Summer89-87
Righetti, A. Il ritratto, l'epitaffio, il clavicordo.
M. Chalaby, 85(SBHC):Vol16-149
Righi, G. A.M.S. Boezio.
H. Merle, 192(EP):Jul-Dec89-554
Rigney, B.H. - see under Hill Rigney, B.
Rigolot, F. Les Métamorphoses de Montaigne.
R.M. Berrong, 400(MLN):Sep89-953
E.J. Campion, 207(FR):Mar90-706
Rigoni, M.A., with C. Galimberti - see Leopardi, G.

Rigoulot, P. Des Français au Goulag, 1917-1984.
J.A. Getty, 550(RusR):Oct89-431
Rigsbee, D. The Hopper Light.*
A. Bromley, 219(GaR):Spring89-209
Riis, T.L. Just Before Jazz.
P. O'Connor, 617(TLS):2-8Feb90-129
Rijksbaron, A., H.A. Mulder & C.C. Wakker, eds. In the Footsteps of Raphael Kühner.
H.M. Hoenigswald, 350:Dec90-880
Rike, R.L. Apex Omnium.
R.J. Penella, 124:Jan-Feb90-252
Rikoon, J.S. Threshing in the Midwest, 1820-1940.
P. Benes, 292(JAF):Oct-Dec89-505
G.C. Fite, 658:Winter89-279
Riley, D. "Am I That Name?"
R. Felski, 141:Fall89-455
D. Fuss, 50(ArQ):Winter89-95
Riley, H.M.K. Die weibliche Muse.*
B. Becker-Cantarino, 301(JEGP):Jan89-71
J. Blackwell, 133:Band22Heft2-172
S.L. Cocalis, 406:Summer89-230
C. Fell, 564:Sep89-263
Riley, J. Liberal Utilitarianism.
P. Weirich, 518:Jul89-182
Riley, J.C. Sickness, Recovery and Death.
A. Wear, 617(TLS):23Feb-1Mar90-191
Riley-Smith, J. The Crusades.*
R.S. Avi-Yonah, 589:Jul89-763
Rilke, R.M. Letters on Cézanne. (C. Rilke, ed)
C.S. Brown, 569(SR):Winter89-139
R. Gray, 97(CQ):Vol18No4-440
Rilke, R.M. Letters to Merline, 1919-1922.
L. Chamberlain, 617(TLS):29Jun-5Jul90-703
Rilke, R.M. New Poems (1908): The Other Part.* Sonnets to Orpheus.* Between Roots. Duino Elegies.
C.S. Brown, 569(SR):Winter89-139
Rimbaud, A. Une saison en enfer. (P. Brunel, ed)
C.A. Hackett, 535(RHL):Mar-Apr89-312
Rimer, J.T. Pilgrimages.
L.R. Rodd, 407(MN):Summer89-223
W.J. Tyler, 293(JASt):Aug89-625
Rimer, J.T. A Reader's Guide to Japanese Literature.
M.H. Childs, 407(MN):Winter89-497
Rimmon-Kenan, S., ed. Discourse in Psychoanalysis and Literature.*
N. Segal, 208(FS):Apr89-237
Rinaldi, S. Das Bergell.*
F. Krier, 685(ZDL):2/1989-265
Rinaldi, S.M. & D. Luciano, eds. Toeput a Treviso, Lodewijk Toeput, Ludovico Pozzoserrato, pittore neerlandese nella civiltà veneta del tardo Cinquecento.
K. Andrews, 90:Jul89-492
Rincón, J.S. - see under Salazar Rincón, J.
Rindo, R.J. Suburban Metaphysics.
R. Burgin, 441:29Apr90-38
Rinear, D.L. The Temple of Momus.
W.B. Durham, 610:Spring89-92
Ringbom, H. The Role of the First Language in Foreign Language Learning.*
C. Blackshire-Belay, 350:Sep89-651
Ringbom, S. Stone, Style and Truth.*
I. Sjöström, 341:Vol58No4-181
Ringger, K. & C. Weiand, eds. Stendhal und Deutschland.
M. Erman, 535(RHL):Jan-Feb89-122

Ringler, W.A., Jr. & M. Flachmann – see Baldwin, W.
Ringmacher, C.U. The Ringmacher Catalogue (1773).
  H. Lenneberg, 309:Vol9No2/3-227
Rintoul, H. refugees.
  M. van Dijk, 108:Spring89-85
Rio, M. Archipelago.
  V. Weissman, 441:15Apr90-14
Rio, M. Merlin.
  J.A. Reiter, 207(FR):May90-1108
Riordan, J., ed. Soviet Education.
  J.J. Tomiak, 575(SEER):Oct89-648
Ripley, C.P., ed. The Black Abolitionist Papers.* (Vol 2)
  J.W.S. Walker, 529(QQ):Summer89-480
Ripley, J., ed. Gilbert Parker and Herbert Beerbohm Tree Stage "The Seats of the Mighty."
  M. Day, 102(CanL):Summer89-146
Ripley, M. Angel Hunt.
  P. Craig, 617(TLS):21-27Dec90-1382
Ripp, V. Pizza in Pushkin Square.
  P. Goldberg, 441:30Dec90-15
Rippmann, I. & W. Labuhn, eds. "Die Kunst – eine Tochter der Zeit."
  J.L. Sammons, 680(ZDP):Band108Heft2-295
Riquelme, J.P. Teller and Tale in Joyce's Fiction.
  U. Schneider, 38:Band107Heft1/2-253
Riquelme, J.P. – see Senn, F.
de Riquer, M. Estudios sobre el amadís de Gaula.
  F. Pierce, 86(BHS):Oct89-376
Riquier, G. Les Epîtres de Guiraut Riquier, troubadour du XIIIe siècle. (J. Linskill, ed)
  P.V. Davies, 382(MAE):1989/2-332
Risco, A. La obra narrativa de Vicente Risco.
  C. Davies, 86(BHS):Oct89-383
Riskin, M.W. The Woman Upstairs.*
  L. Abbey, 102(CanL):Winter88-110
Rist, J.M. Platonism and Its Christian Heritage.
  L.G. Westerink, 487:Winter89-382
Ristoff, D. Updike's America.
  W.T.S., 395(MFS):Winter89-771
Ristory, H. Post-franconische Theorie und Früh-Trecento.
  M. Everist, 410(M&L):Nov89-522
Ritchie, A.T. The Two Thackerays.
  R.E. Lougy, 637(VS):Autumn89-197
Ritchie, C. My Grandfather's House.
  P. Barclay, 102(CanL):Summer89-160
Ritchie, E., ed. The Dolphin's Arc.
  D. Chorlton, 496:Winter89/90-43
Ritchin, F. In Our Own Image.
  R. Ranck, 441:4Nov90-25
Ritsos, Y. Selected Poems 1938-1988. (K. Friar & K. Myrsiades, eds & trans) Exile and Return.
  R. Beaton, 617(TLS):14-20Dec90-1358
Rittenberg, S.A. Ethnicity, Nationalism, and the Pakhtuns.
  D. Gilmartin, 293(JASt):Nov89-913
Ritter, E. Ritter in Residence.
  T.L. Cottrell, 529(QQ):Summer89-477
Ritter, H.W. Rom und Numidien.
  D. Braund, 229:Band61Heft4-367
  C.R. Whittaker, 313:Vol79-195
Ritti, T. Hierapolis, Scavi e ricerche I, Fonti letterarie ed epigrafiche.
  C. Dobias-Lalou, 555:Vol62Fasc1-151

de la Riva, B. – see under Bonvesin de la Riva
Rivard, D. Torque.
  L. Domina, 448:Vol27No3-152
  M. Halliday, 152(UDQ):Summer89-102
  D. Sampson, 249(HudR):Autumn89-511
Rive, R. Advance, Retreat.
  T. Eprile, 441:7Jan90-9
Rive, R. – see Schreiner, O.
Rivelaygue, J. – see Schelling, F.W.
Rivera, I. This Migrant Earth.
  A. Ramírez, 238:Mar89-166
Rivers, J.W. When the Owl Cries, Indians Die. The Lady in Once-White Shoes.
  W.H. Green, 580(SCR):Spring90-142
Rivers, W., M.M. Azevedo & W.H. Heflin, Jr. Teaching Spanish. (2nd ed)
  T.V. Higgs, 399(MLJ):Summer89-244
Rivers, W.M., ed. Interactive Language Teaching.*
  J.W. Larson, 399(MLJ):Spring89-78
Rivers, W.M. Teaching French.* (2nd ed)
  C.R. Hancock, 399(MLJ):Spring89-89
Rivet, A.L.F. Gallia Narbonensis.*
  J.F. Drinkwater, 123:Vol39No2-317
Rivière, J-C. Sens et poésie.
  K. Klingebiel, 545(RPh):Nov89-325
Rix, A. – see Ball, W.M.
Rizachēs, T. & G. Touratsogou. Epigraphes Anō Machedonias. (Vol A)
  K. Buraselis, 229:Band61Heft3-208
Rizk, B.J. El nuevo teatro latinoamericano.*
  C.M. Boyle, 86(BHS):Oct89-398
Rizvi, S.A.A. A Socio-Intellectual History of the Isnā 'Asharī Shī'īs in India.
  M.H. Fisher, 293(JASt):Feb89-209
Rizza, C. – see Gautier, T.
Rizzon, B. Pearl S. Buck.
  D.W. Petrie, 395(MFS):Winter89-756
Robb, D.S. George MacDonald.
  L. Fasick, 637(VS):Autumn89-194
  D. Groves, 447(N&Q):Jun89-254
  L. Smith, 571(ScLJ):Spring89-22
Robb, G. Baudelaire lecteur de Balzac.
  J. Gale, 446(NCFS):Fall-Winter89/90-260
Robbins, K. – see "The Blackwell Biographical Dictionary of British Political Life in the Twentieth Century"
Robbins, T. Skinny Legs and All.
  J. Queenan, 441:15Apr90-12
Robert, P-E. – see Dabit, E.
Robert, R., ed. Contes parodiques et licencieux du 18e siècle.
  G. Campbell, 166:Oct89-73
  S. Davies, 83:Spring89-118
Roberto, E. La Gorgone dans "Morts sans sépulture" de Sartre.
  G. Prince, 207(FR):Feb90-557
Roberts, B. Plantation Homes of the James River.
  S. Wilson, Jr., 585(SoQ):Summer90-126
Roberts, B. Cecil Rhodes.
  639(VQR):Winter89-18
Roberts, C.H. & T.C. Skeat. The Birth of the Codex.*
  L. Carruthers, 189(EA):Jul-Sep89-337
Roberts, D. Jean Stafford.
  M.V. Davidson, 395(MFS):Summer89-297
  J.J. Firebaugh, 27(AL):May89-312
  639(VQR):Spring89-54

Roberts, D.D. Benedetto Croce and the Uses
   of Historicism.
   H.S. Harris, 319:Jan90-148
   V. Jones, 278(IS):Vol44-178
Roberts, G., ed. Gerard Manley Hopkins: The
   Critical Heritage.*
   N. White, 447(N&Q):Mar89-118
Roberts, G. Unamuno.*
   R.W. Fiddian, 86(BHS):Apr89-186
Roberts, J. A Dictionary of Michelangelo's
   Watermarks.
   W.E. Wallace, 380:Spring89-64
Roberts, J. German Philosophy.
   R. Ackermann, 518:Apr89-88
   B. Doniela, 63:Jun89-241
   E. Schaper, 402(MLR):Apr90-514
Roberts, J. & A.G. Watson - see "John Dee's
   Library Catalogue"
Roberts, J.G. Mitsui. (2nd ed)
   K. van Wolferen, 617(TLS):31Aug-
   6Sep90-926
Roberts, J.R. Richard Crashaw.
   R. Ellrodt, 189(EA):Apr-Jun89-214
Roberts, J.R. George Herbert. (rev)
   D. Treviño Benet, 391:May89-86
Roberts, L. Black Wings.
   S. Burris, 598(SoR):Spring90-456
Roberts, M. Biblical Epic and Rhetorical
   Paraphrase in Late Antiquity.
   A.I. Rossi, 589:Apr89-493
Roberts, M. In the Red Kitchen.
   L. Doughty, 617(TLS):6-12Apr90-975
Roberts, M.S. & D. Gallagher - see Dufrenne,
   M.
Roberts, P., ed. The Best of Plays and Players
   1953-1968.
   A. Cameron, 610:Spring89-102
Roberts, P. - see Powys, J.C.
ap Roberts, R. The Ancient Dialect.
   W. Baker, 184(EIC):Jul89-254
   E. Block, Jr., 445(NCF):Jun89-96
   F. Kaplan, 191(ELN):Jun90-81
   M. Timko, 637(VS):Winter90-336
Roberts, W., J.T. Boulton & E. Mansfield - see
   Lawrence, D.H.
Robertson, A. Atkinson Grimshaw.*
   J. Treuherz, 90:Nov89-789
Robertson, J.C. The Hidden Cinema.*
   A. Smith, 707:Autumn89-283
Robertson, M. Greek, Etruscan and Roman
   Vases in the Lady Lever Art Gallery, Port
   Sunlight.
   D.W.J. Gill, 39:Apr89-293
   G. Waywell, 123:Vol39No1-156
Robertson, M.L.C. Soviet Policy Towards
   Japan.
   J.J. Stephan, 407(MN):Spring89-122
   J.A. Yager, 293(JASt):Nov89-808
Robertson, P. - see Mackintosh, C.R.
Robertson, S. Exodus to Alford.
   H. Henderson, 571(ScLJ):Spring89-29
Robichez, G. J-J. Lefranc de Pompignan.
   T.E.D. Braun, 208(FS):Apr89-213
Robidoux, R. La Création de Gérard Bessette.*
   A. Hayward, 529(QQ):Spring89-183
Robinet, A. G.W. Leibniz Iter Italicum (mars
   1689-mars 1690).
   D. Bertoloni Meli, 706:Band21Heft2-211
   B. Pinchard, 192(EP):Apr-Jun89-243
Robinson, A. Instabilities in Contemporary
   British Poetry.*
   A. Golding, 447(N&Q):Dec89-549
                           [continued]

[continuing]
   E. Longley, 493:Winter89/90-22
   R. Marsack, 402(MLR):Apr90-432
Robinson, A. Satyajit Ray.
   E. Hower, 441:25Mar90-22
   A. Ross, 364:Oct/Nov89-138
Robinson, B.W. & others. The Keir Collection.
   J.M. Rogers, 90:Dec89-858
Robinson, C. & J. Herschman. Architecture
   Transformed.*
   B.L. Michaels, 576:Jun89-195
Robinson, D. Stanley Spencer.
   J. Russell, 441:2Dec90-74
Robinson, D. War Story.
   639(VQR):Spring89-58
Robinson, H., ed. Visibly Female.
   P. Mathews, 662:Fall89/Winter90-44
Robinson, J. Wayward Women.
   C. Moorehead, 617(TLS):13-19Jul90-745
Robinson, K.S. Pacific Edge.
   G. Jonas, 441:9Dec90-32
Robinson, M. Mother Country.*
   G. MacKerron, 617(TLS):5-11Jan90-9
Robinson, M. Strindberg and Autobiography.
   C.C. Fraser, 563(SS):Winter89-68
   K-Å. Kärnell, 562(Scan):May89-90
Robinson, P. Gallows View.
   M. Stasio, 441:30Dec90-26
Robinson, P. This Other Life.
   K. Jebb, 493:Summer89-31
Robinson, R. Georgia O'Keeffe.*
   W. Steiner, 617(TLS):16-22Mar90-281
Robinson, R. with J. Slevin. Black on Red.
   A. Blakely, 550(RusR):Apr89-206
Robinson, R.D., ed. Foreign Capital and
   Technology in China.
   R. Stross, 293(JASt):Aug89-596
Robinson, T. Stones of Aran.*
   C. Moorehead, 617(TLS):24-30Aug90-905
Robinson, W.S. Brains and People.
   R. Fellows, 518:Jul89-174
   W. Seager, 100:Jun90-252
Robisheaux, T. Rural Society and the Search
   for Order in Early Modern Germany.
   B. Scribner, 617(TLS):9-15Feb90-151
Robison, J.C. Peter Taylor.
   M. Kreyling, 573(SSF):Spring89-206
Roblès, E. Albert Camus et la trève civile.
   A.D. Ranwez, 207(FR):Apr90-898
Roblès, E. Norma ou l'exil infini.
   M-N. Little, 207(FR):Dec89-410
Robson, G.M. Aspects of Verdi.
   W. Dean, 415:Nov89-682
Robson, J.M., ed. Origin and Evolution of the
   Universe.
   D.A. Hanes, 529(QQ):Summer89-551
   E.R. MacCormac, 518:Jul89-186
Roca, S.G., ed. Socialist Cuba.
   R. Moncarz, 263(RIB):Vol39No2-212
Rocard, M. The Children of the Sun.
   C.R. Shirley, 649(WAL):Feb90-377
Rocchi, G.D. - see under Daverio Rocchi, G.
Rochberg, G. The Aesthetics of Survival. (W.
   Bolcom, ed)
   S. Blaustein, 513:Winter89-286
Roche, D. La Culture des apparences.
   A. Forrest, 617(TLS):23-29Mar90-312
Roche, D. The People of Paris.
   C. Jones, 83:Spring89-81
Roche, D. - see Ménétra, J-L.
Roche, J.D. - see under Domínguez Roche, J.

Roche, M.W. Dynamic Stillness.
    J.L. Sammons, 406:Summer89-256
    J. Simons, 133:Band22Heft2-162
Rocher, L., ed. Ezourvedam.*
    W.H. Maurer, 318(JAOS):Apr-Jun88-326
Rocher, L. The Purāṇas.*
    W.H. Maurer, 318(JAOS):Oct-Dec88-633
Rocher, L. - see van Buitenen, J.A.B.
Lord Rochester. The Poems of John Wilmot,
    Earl of Rochester. (K. Walker, ed)
    P.G. Reeve, 580(SCR):Spring90-177
Rochon, E. Le traversier.
    M. Benson, 102(CanL):Autumn-Winter89-
    273
Rockmore, T. Hegel's Circular Epistemology.*
    J. Grondin, 192(EP):Jan-Mar89-115
    125:Summer89-425
Rodari, F. Le collage, Papiers collés, papiers
    déchirés, Papiers découpés.
    D. Caron, 98:Mar89-201
Rodden, J. The Politics of Literary Reputa-
    tion.*
    D. Trotter, 617(TLS):30Mar-5Apr90-336
Rödding, D. - see Börger, E.
Rödel-Kappl, C. Analogie und Sprachwandel
    im Vergleich zweier verwandter Sprachen.
    J. Dingley, 279:Vol37-199
Röder, T. Auf dem Weg zur Bruckner-Sym-
    phonie.
    M. Sonntag, 309:Vol9No2/3-189
Rodgers, E. Beyond the Barrier.
    P-L. Adams, 61:Sep90-122
    M.W. Browne, 441:3Jun90-17
Rodgers, E. From Enlightenment to Realism.*
    P.A. Bly, 402(MLR):Jan90-231
    T.A. Sackett, 238:Sep89-545
Rodis-Lewis, G., ed. Méthode et métaphys-
    ique chez Descartes. La Science chez Des-
    cartes.
    D.A. Cress, 319:Jul90-449
Roditi, E. Oscar Wilde. (rev)
    W. Harmon, 569(SR):Winter89-148
Rodman, H., S.H. Lewis & S.B. Griffith. The
    Sexual Rights of Adolescents.
    J.H., 185:Oct89-220
Rodman, H.A. Destiny Express.
    A. Hislop, 617(TLS):15-21Jun90-653
    D. Mason, 441:4Mar90-13
Rodmell, G.E. - see Sedaine, M-J.
Rodowick, D.N. The Crisis of Political Mod-
    ernism.*
    W. Fisher, 707:Spring89-139
Rodríguez, C.E. Puerto Ricans.
    A.C. Vidal, 441:11Feb90-22
Rodríguez, E., ed. Novelas amorosas de di-
    versos ingenios del siglo XVII.
    P.J. Smith, 402(MLR):Jan90-226
Rodríguez, G. La iglesia de El Salvador de
    Santa Cruz de la Palma.
    A. López-Yarto Elizalde, 48:Jan-Mar89-
    100
Rodriguez, J. Oddsplayer.
    L. Torres, 649(WAL):Nov89-278
Rodríguez, M.C.G. - see under González Rodrí-
    guez, M.C.
Rodríguez Alfageme, I., ed. Los clásicos como
    pretexto.
    J.M. Alonso-Núñez, 123:Vol39No2-428
Rodríguez de Laguna, A., ed. Images and
    Identities.*
    L.E. Roses, 36:Spring89-124

Rodríguez G. de Ceballos, A. La iglesia y el
    convento de San Esteban de Salamanca.
    A. Bustamante García, 48:Apr-Jun89-227
Rodríguez López-Vázquez, A. Andrés de
    Claramonte y "El burlador de Sevilla."*
    P.W. Evans, 86(BHS):Jul89-281
    J.M. Ruano de la Haza, 402(MLR):Apr90-
    471
Rodríguez López-Vázquez, A. - see de Clara-
    monte, A.
Rodríguez Puértolas, J. Literatura fascista
    española.
    M. Lentzen, 547(RF):Band101Heft4-501
Roe, N. Wordsworth and Coleridge.*
    J.D. Gutteridge, 447(N&Q):Sep89-404
    J.A. Hodgson, 591(SIR):Fall89-499
    A.J. Sambrook, 677(YES):Vol20-289
    S.M. Sperry, 191(ELN):Dec89-71
    639(VQR):Winter89-12
Roe, S. Women Reading Women's Writing.*
    R.B.D., 295(JML):Fall88/Winter89-234
Roebling, I. Wilhelm Raabes doppelte Buch-
    führung.
    S. Radcliffe, 402(MLR):Jan90-262
Roediger, D.R. & P.S. Foner. Our Own Time.
    J-A. Mort, 441:11Mar90-15
Roehmann, F.L. & F.R. Wilson, eds. The Biol-
    ogy of Music Making.
    B. Gowen, 510:Spring89-50
Roell, C.H. The Piano in America, 1890-1940.
    C. Ehrlich, 415:Oct89-610
Roemer, J.E. Value, Exploitation and Class.
    A.N., 185:Oct89-211
Roeper, T. & E. Williams, eds. Parameter Set-
    ting.*
    S. Romaine, 355(LSoc):Dec89-572
Roerich, Y.N. & others. Tibetan-Russian-
    English Dictionary with Sanskrit Parallels.
    (Y. Parfionovich & V. Dylykova, eds)
    B. Galloway, 259(IIJ):Oct89-333
Roger, D. & P. Bull, eds. Conversation.
    T. Scovel, 399(MLJ):Autumn89-378
Roger, J. Buffon.
    C. Jones, 617(TLS):20-26Apr90-411
Rogers, C. Carl Rogers: Dialogues. The Carl
    Rogers Reader. (H. Kirschenbaum & V.L.
    Henderson, eds)
    L. Hudson, 617(TLS):6-12Jul90-723
Rogers, E.S. & T.J., eds. In Retrospect.*
    M.I. Lightblau, 240(HR):Spring89-267
Rogers, F.R., with M.A. Rogers. Painting and
    Poetry.
    S.Z. Levine, 567:Vol75No1/2-181
Rogers, J.M. - see Çağman, F. & Z. Tanindi
Rogers, J.M. - see Köseoğlu, C.
Rogers, J.M. - see Tezcan, H.
Rogers, J.M. - see Tezcan, H. & S. Delibaş
Rogers, K.M. & W. McCarthy, eds. The Meridi-
    an Anthology of Early Women Writers.
    M.E. Mulvihill, 566:Spring89-175
Rogers, L. Singing Rib.
    R. Labrie, 102(CanL):Autumn-Winter89-
    143
Rogers, N. Whigs and Cities.
    L. Colley, 617(TLS):20-26Apr90-415
Rogers, P., ed. The Oxford Illustrated History
    of English Literature.
    F.J.M. Blom, 179(ES):Feb89-74
    B. Cottle, 541(RES):May89-298
    J. Pafford, 447(N&Q):Sep89-374
Rogers, T.N.R. Too Far from Home.
    J.L. Halio, 573(SSF):Winter89-97

Rogers, W.E. The Three Genres and the Interpretation of Lyric.
J. Mellard, 599:Summer90-302
Rogers, W.E. Upon The Ways.*
J.W. Nicholls, 677(YES):Vol20-234
Rogerson, H.D. & others. Words for Students of English.
W.R. Slager, 399(MLJ):Summer89-217
Rogerson, K.F. Kant's Aesthetics.
C. Haskins, 290(JAAC):Fall89-387
Rognon, F. Les Primitifs nos contemporains.
J-D. Pénel, 542:Oct-Dec89-591
Rogues, J-P. S'écarter du sujet.
F. Mary, 450(NRF):Jul-Aug89-190
Rohatyn, D. The Reluctant Naturalist.
T. Szubka, 258:Jun89-235
Rohmer, E. Die literarische Glosse.
G.J. Carr, 402(MLR):Apr90-518
Rohr, K.I. Geldbezeichnungen im Neufranzösischen unter besdonderer Berücksichtigung des Argot.
F. Lebsanft, 209(FM):Oct89-268
Rohrbach, G. Studien zur Erforschung des mittelhochdeutschen Tagelieds.*
M. Schiendorfer, 680(ZDP):Band108Heft3-409
Rohse, E. Der frühe Brecht und die Bibel.
A. Tatlow, 133:Band22Heft1-83
Roiphe, A. A Season for Healing.
B. Zelechow, 390:Aug/Sep89-43
Roiz Lucas de Senna, M. Dissertação sobre as Ilhas de Cabo Verde 1818. (A. Carreira, ed)
P.E.H. Hair, 86(BHS):Oct89-394
de Rojas, F. Celestina.* (M. Marciales, ed)
K. Kish, 304(JHP):Autumn89-79
de Rojas, F. Celestina. (D.S. Severin, ed)
R.L. Fiore, 238:Sep89-567
G. Hoffmeister, 547(RF):Band101Heft1-150
Rojas, J.J.O. - see under Ortiz Rojas, J.J.
de Rojas P. Cancionero de Pedro de Rojas. (J.J. Labrador Herraiz, R. Di Franco & M.I. Cacho, eds)
A. de Colombí Monguió & L. Monguió, 304(JHP):Winter89-155
Rojo, A.D. - see under Benítez Rojo, A.
Rokach, A. & A. Millman. Focus on Flowers.
A. Lacy, 441:10Jun90-33
Rokem, F. Theatrical Space in Ibsen, Chekhov and Strindberg.
S.B. Garner, Jr., 615(TJ):May89-259
M. Robinson, 562(Scan):May89-89
Rokkan, E. - see Sandel, C.
Madame Roland. The Memoirs of Madame Roland.
G. Lewis, 617(TLS):26Jan-1Feb90-93
Roland, A. In Search of Self in India and Japan.
C. Nakane, 293(JASt):May89-344
Oshikawa Fumiko, 285(JapQ):Jul-Sep89-338
Roland, J.G. Jews in British India.
A. Desai, 453(NYRB):6Dec90-53
Rolbein, S. Nobel Costa Rica.
639(VQR):Summer89-102
Rollason, D. Saints and Relics in Anglo-Saxon England.
R. McKitterick, 617(TLS):27Apr-3May90-448
Rolle, R. Richard Rolle's "Expositio super novem lectiones mortuorum." (M.R. Moyes, ed)
A.S.G. Edwards, 589:Oct89-1033
Rolle, R. The World of the Scythians.
A. Sherratt, 617(TLS):26Jan-1Feb90-95
Rölleke, H. - see Grimm, J. & W.
Rolleston, J. Narratives of Ecstasy.*
K. Weissenberger, 301(JEGP):Oct89-587
Rollfinke, D. & J. The Call of Human Nature.*
E. Friedrichsmeyer, 133:Band22Heft1-91
R. Furness, 402(MLR):Jan90-265
Rollin, J-F. - see Tchouang Tseu (Zhuang Zi)
Rollin, M., ed. Oeuvres des Gallot.
D. Kirsch, 417:Oct-Dec89-389
Rollings, A. In Your Own Sweet Time.
A. Brumer, 441:11Feb90-16
Rollyson, C. Lillian Hellman.*
T.P. Adler, 397(MD):Sep89-454
Rollyson, C. Nothing Ever Happens to the Brave.
J. O'Reilly, 441:30Dec90-6
Rolston, H. Science and Religion.
J. Painter, 63:Sep89-369
Rolston, H. 3d. Environmental Ethics.
R. Elliot, 63:Dec89-493
P.S. Wenz, 185:Oct89-195
Roman, C. Foreplay.
A. Rice, 441:25Mar90-13
Román, J.E.L. - see under López Román, J.E.
Roman, Z. Gustav Mahler's American Years, 1907-1911.
G. Martin, 465:Spring90-176
"Romanesque and Gothic: Essays for George Zarnecki."*
H.R. Loyn, 39:Apr89-294
Romanillos, J.L. Antonio de Torres, Guitar Maker.
G. Wade, 415:Feb89-90
Romanyshyn, R.D. Technology as Symptom and Dream.
B. Rotman, 617(TLS):6-12Jul90-722
Romero, F.G. - see under García Romero, F.
Romodanovskaja, E.K. Povesti o gordom care v rukopisnoj tradicii XVII-XIX vekov. (L.A. Dmitriev, ed)
N.W. Ingham, 574(SEEJ):Spring89-118
Rompkey, R. Soame Jenyns.
E. Hepple, 83:Autumn89-229
Ronan, C.E. & B.B.C. Oh, eds. East Meets West.
K. Lundbaek, 293(JASt):Aug89-597
Ronell, A. Dictations.*
L. Weissberg, 222(GR):Summer89-135
Ronell, A. The Telephone Book.
R. Coover, 441:3Jun90-15
A.M. Lippit, 400(MLN):Dec89-1200
Rönisch, S., ed. DDR-Literatur im Gespräch.
G. Krieger, 654(WB):10/1989-1742
Ronzeaud, P. Peuple et représentations sous le règne de Louis XIV.
M. Alcover, 207(FR):Feb90-598
G. Le Coat, 475:Vol16No31-600
Rooke, L. A Good Baby.
D. Bauer, 441:30Sep90-12
442(NY):19Nov90-155
Rooke, L. How I Saved the Province.
J. Ruzesky, 376:Sep89-120
Roome, A. A Second Shot in the Dark.
P. Craig, 617(TLS):21-27Dec90-1382
Rooney, A., ed. The Tretyse off Huntyng (Cambridge University Library MS Ll.1.18, fols 48r-55v).
R. Hands, 589:Oct89-1034
Rooney, E. Seductive Reasoning.
L. Sage, 617(TLS):18-24May90-523
Roose-Evans, J. - see Grenfell, J.

Roosen, W. Daniel Defoe and Diplomacy.*
    J. McVeagh, 566:Spring89-183
Roosevelt, S. Keeper of the Gate.
    J. Kaufman, 441:4Nov90-25
Root, J. Weaving the Sheets.
    W. Harmon, 472:Vol16No1-136
Root-Bernstein, R.S. Discovering.
    B. Barnes, 617(TLS):9-15Mar90-259
    M. Bartusiak, 441:28Jan90-24
van Rooyen, J.C.W. Censorship in South Afri-
ca.
    D.P. Kunene, 538(RAL):Summer89-306
Roper, J.H. C. Vann Woodward, Southerner.*
    F. Shivers, 577(SHR):Summer89-291
Roper, L. The Holy Household.
    M. Aston, 617(TLS):27Apr-3May90-448
Rorabaugh, W.J. Berkeley at War.
    L. Botstein, 617(TLS):19-25Jan90-69
Rorty, R. Contingency, Irony, and Solidarity.*
    L.P. Gerson, 627(UTQ):Spring90-449
    D.R. Lachterman, 125:Summer89-391
    J. Ramazani, 147:Vol6No3-40
    R. Shusterman, 494:Fall89-605
Rosa, A. Victor Hugo, l'éclat d'un siècle.
    A. Ubersfeld, 535(RHL):Mar-Apr89-311
Rosa, R.R. - see under Rey Rosa, R.
Rosas, Y. Villasandino y su hablante lírico.
    F. Colecchia, 552(REH):Jan89-136
Roscoe, P. Beneath the Western Slopes.
    L. Abbey, 102(CanL):Winter88-110
Rose, C.H. & T. Oelman - see Enríquez Gómez,
A.
Rose, D. Black American Street Life.
    B. Jackson, 292(JAF):Jul-Sep89-339
Rose, G.J. Trauma and Mastery in Life and
Art.*
    G. Zeiger, 219(GaR):Winter89-828
Rose, J. The Edwardian Temperament, 1895-
1919.*
    J. Batchelor, 541(RES):May89-286
Rose, M. Lives on the Boundary.*
    J.J. Royster, 126(CCC):Oct89-349
    J.F. Trimmer, 128(CE):Nov89-759
Rose, M.B. The Expense of Spirit.
    L. Helms, 615(TJ):Oct89-416
    S. Stockton, 223:Summer89-197
Rose, M.B., ed. Women in the Middle Ages and
the Renaissance.*
    M.L. Trivison, 345(KRQ):May89-222
Rose, X. Widow's Journey.
    J. Moore, 441:11Nov90-69
Rosebury, B. Art and Desire.
    N. Bradbury, 677(YES):Vol20-362
    S.M. Sperry, 395(MFS):Winter89-845
    D. Townsend, 290(JAAC):Fall89-389
Rosecrance, R. America's Economic Resur-
gence.
    P. Kennedy, 453(NYRB):28Jun90-31
    R. Kuttner, 441:6May90-15
Rosellini, A., ed. La "Geste Francor" di Vene-
zia.
    A.J. Holden, 554:Vol108No4-562
Rosello, M. L'Humour noir selon André Breton.
    M. Autrand, 535(RHL):Mar-Apr89-325
Rosemain, J. La Musique dans la Société
Antillaise, 1635-1902: Martinique, Guade-
loupe.
    G. Averill, 187:Winter89-153
Rosemont, H., Jr., ed. Explorations in Early
China Cosmology.
    D. Harper, 318(JAOS):Apr-Jun88-354
Rosen, C. Sonata Forms. (rev)
    W. Drabkin, 415:Nov89-684

Rosen, E. Three Imperial Mathematicians.
    P.W. Knoll, 497(PolR):Vol34No4-382
Rosén, H.B. Early Greek Grammar and
Thought in Heraclitus.
    M. Menu, 555:Vol62Fasc2-334
    A.C. Moorhouse, 123:Vol39No2-404
Rosén, H.B. - see Herodotus
Rosen, L. Bargaining for Reality.
    M. Lazreg, 318(JAOS):Apr-Jun88-320
Rosen, N. John and Anzia.
    B. Probst, 441:28Jan90-23
Rosen, S. The Ancients and the Moderns.
    M. Reinhold, 124:Jul-Aug90-538
Rosen, S. Hermeneutics as Politics.*
    A.J. Cascardi, 540(RIPh):Vol42fasc4-541
Rosen, S. The Quarrel Between Philosophy
and Poetry.*
    B. Gibbs, 89(BJA):Summer89-278
Rosenbaum, A.S., ed. Constitutionalism.*
    O.J., 185:Jan90-450
Rosenbaum, S.P. Victorian Bloomsbury.*
    N. Griffin, 556:Summer89-80
Rosenberg, A. Movement in Slow Time.
    J. Ruzesky, 376:Sep89-120
Rosenberg, A. & G.E. Myers, eds. Echoes from
the Holocaust.
    T.L.C., 185:Jan90-465
Rosenberg, D., ed. Congregation.*
    L. Wieder, 473(PR):Vol56No2-325
Rosenberg, D., ed. Testimony.
    E. Milton, 441:28Jan90-27
Rosenberg, D. - see "The Book of J"
Rosenberg, J. King and Kin.*
    D. Damrosch, 508:Sep89-257
Rosenberg, J.F. The Thinking Self.*
    P. Kitcher, 482(PhR):Jan89-115
    A. Marras, 484(PPR):Sep89-214
Rosenberg, M. Coming Around (Another Axis
Cycle).
    G. Gessert, 448:Vol27No1-131
Rosenberg, N.V. Bluegrass.
    T.A. Adler, 292(JAF):Apr-Jun89-210
    L. Martin, 187:Fall89-520
Rosenberg, P. & M.C. Stewart, with T. Lefran-
çois. French Paintings 1500-1825: The
Fine Arts Museums of San Francisco.
    H. Opperman, 39:Jan89-65
Rosenberg, S., ed. Advances in Applied Psy-
cholinguistics.
    G.D. Prideaux, 361:Aug89-356
Rosenberg, S. A Soviet Odyssey.*
    G.W., 102(CanL):Autumn-Winter89-301
Rosenberg, S.N. & S. Danon - see Gace Brulé
Rosenblat, A. - see "Amadís de Gaula"
Rosenblatt, A. Virginia Woolf for Beginners.*
    J. Marcus, 620(TSWL):Spring89-101
Rosenblatt, P. The Sun in Capricorn.
    J. Polk, 441:11Mar90-18
Rosenblum, D. Christina Rossetti.
    S. Donaldson, 85(SBHC):Vol16-156
Rosenblum, N.L., ed. Liberalism and the Moral
Life.
    G. Crowder, 617(TLS):4-10May90-476
    E.R. Gill, 103:Oct90-433
Rosenblum, R. & A. Grundberg. Mike and Doug
Starn.
    L.E. Nesbitt, 441:9Dec90-25
Rosenblum, S.P. Performance Practices in
Classical Piano Music.
    M. Tan, 415:Apr89-215
Rosenfeld, B.A. A History of Non-Euclidean
Geometry.
    R. Torretti, 160:Jul89-250

Rosengarten, H. & M. Smith – see Brontë, C.
Rosenman, E.B. The Invisible Presence.*
    N.T. Justicia, 177(ELT):Vol32No3-367
    J. Marcus, 620(TSWL):Spring89-101
Rosenstone, R.A. Mirror in the Shrine.*
    H. Ballhatchet, 407(MN):Spring89-130
    C.A. Gerstle, 293(JASt):Nov89-876
    D. McLeod, 432(NEQ):Dec89-594
    Nakanishi Shōzō, 285(JapQ):Jul-Sep89-
    341
    S. Pickering, 569(SR):Spring89-297
Rosenstrauch, H. Buchhandelsmanufaktur
und Aufklärung.
    A. Košenina, 406:Winter89-488
Rosenstrauch-Königsberg, E., ed. Literatur
der Aufklärung 1765-1800.
    G. Mieth & H-J. Malles, 654(WB):5/1989-
    876
Rosenthal, A.L. A Good Look at Evil.
    R. Fellows, 291:Vol6No1-109
Rosenthal, B.G., ed. Nietzsche in Russia.*
    P. Bonila, 295(JML):Fall88/Winter89-203
    J. Goodliffe, 478(P&L):Oct89-410
    R.J. Keys, 575(SEER):Jul89-464
Rosenthal, D.M. & F. Shehadi, eds. Applied
Ethics and Ethical Theory. (Vol 1)
    J.P.D., 185:Apr90-691
Rosenthal, H.M. The Consolations of Philoso-
phy. (A.L. Rosenthal, ed)
    P.J. Bagley, 543:Jun90-879
    J. McCarthy, 103:Apr90-155
Rosenthal, M. Constable.
    M Cormack, VolMar90-230
Rosenthal, M. Franz Marc.
    S. West, 617(TLS):16-22Mar90-291
Rosenthal, M.L. The Poet's Art.*
    P. Levi, 541(RES):Nov89-595
    S.P., 295(JML):Fall88/Winter89-258
Rosenwald, L. Emerson and the Art of the
Diary.*
    A.J. von Frank, 27(AL):May89-288
    J. Myerson, 432(NEQ):Sep89-459
Roses, L.E. Voices of the Storyteller.*
    J. Ferrán, 238:Mar89-152
    T.J. Peavler, 593:Winter89/90-307
Rosidor [C-F. Guillemay du Chesnay]. Les
Valets de chambre nouvellistes.* (M.C.
Djelassi, ed)
    C.J. Gossip, 402(MLR):Apr90-445
    O. Välikangas, 597(SN):Vol61No2-247
Rosińska, G. Optyka w xv wieku/Fifteenth-
Century Optics.
    E. Hilfstein, 589:Jan89-209
Roskies, D.G., ed. The Literature of Destruc-
tion.
    M. Roshwald, 268(IFR):Summer89-135
Roskill, M. The Interpretation of Pictures.
    N. Bryson, 54:Dec89-704
    639(VQR):Autumn89-139
Rosmarin, L.A. Saint-Evremond.
    A. Niderst, 475:Vol16No31-603
Rosovsky, H. The University.
    L.B. Salamon, 441:22Apr90-3
Rosowski, S.J. The Voyage Perilous.*
    M.A. Peterman, 106:Fall89-211
Ross, A., ed. Universal Abandon?
    M. Hite, 454:Spring90-324
    G. Meyerson, 49:Oct89-192
    B. Robbins, 395(MFS):Winter89-856
Ross, A. – see Vaughan, K.

Ross, A. & D. Robins. The Life and Death of a
Druid Prince.
    P-L. Adams, 61:Sep90-123
    M.W. Browne, 441:17Jun90-10
Ross, C. Local Government in the Soviet
Union.
    R.J. Hill, 575(SEER):Jan89-161
Ross, D.O., Jr. Virgil's Elements.*
    K. Galinsky, 24:Spring89-171
    M.C.J. Putnam, 122:Oct89-349
Ross, H. Film as Literature, Literature as
Film.
    Z.B., 295(JML):Fall88/Winter89-269
Ross, J.C. – see Shadwell, T.
Ross, L. Environmental Policy in China.
    J.P. Burns, 293(JASt):Aug89-598
Ross, M.C. Skáldskaparmál.
    J. Frankis, 562(Scan):May89-75
    K.E. Gade, 301(JEGP):Apr89-274
Ross, R.S. The Indochina Tangle.
    M. Gurtov, 293(JASt):Nov89-840
Ross, S.M. Fiction's Inexhaustible Voice.
    A. Bleikasten, 395(MFS):Winter89-748
    S. Pinsker, 219(GaR):Winter89-795
Ross, V. Homecoming.*
    N. Bailey, 102(CanL):Winter88-111
    M. Junyk, 529(QQ):Spring89-159
Rossabi, M. Khubilai Khan.
    E. Endicott-West, 244(HJAS):Dec89-664
    J.M. Smith, Jr., 293(JASt):May89-372
Rossebastiano Bart, A. Antichi vocabolari
plurilingui d'uso popolare.
    P. Zolli, 708:Vol12Fasc1-137
Rossen, J., ed. Indóponduni Winner.
    C. Hanson, 402(MLR):Jul90-710
    M. Knochel, 395(MFS):Summer89-342
Rossen, J. Philip Larkin.
    T. Paulin, 617(TLS):20-26Jul90-779
Rossen, J. The World of Barbara Pym.*
    S.A.S., 295(JML):Fall88/Winter89-397
Rossen, J.M. Songs of Bellona Island (Na
Taungua o Mungiki).
    J.W. Love, 187:Fall89-555
Rosset, C. Le Principe do cruauté.
    M. Jarrety, 450(NRF):Jan89-92
Rossi, F. I manoscritti del Fondo Torrefranca
del Conservatorio Benedetto Marcello.
    P.W. Jones, 410(M&L):May89-258
Rossi, J. Spravochnik po GULagu.
    R.A. Rothstein, 550(RusR):Oct89-429
Rossi, M. Le origini della filosofia greca. (L.
Rossi, ed)
    C. Viano, 192(EP):Jul-Dec89-556
Rossi, M. & A. Rovetta. Pittura in Alto Lario
tra Quattro e Cinquecento.
    D.A. Brown, 551(RenQ):Autumn89-554
    E. Welch, 90:Dec89-853
Rossner, J. His Little Women.
    C. McFadden, 441:22Apr90-11
Rosso, C. Procès à La Rochefoucauld et à la
maxime.*
    M.S. Koppisch, 210(FrF):Jan89-95
Rosso, C. Les Tambours de Santerre.*
    S. Dunn, 546(RR):Jan89-151
Rosswurm, S. Arms, Country, and Class.
    C.S. Olton, 656(WMQ):Apr89-409
Rostenberg, L. The Library of Robert Hooke.
    D. McKitterick, 78(BC):Autumn89-301
Rostom, K.A., ed. Arab-Canadian Writing.
    J. Werner-King, 268(IFR):Winter90-64

Roston, M. Renaissance Perspectives in Lit-
erature and the Visual Arts.*
  E.B. Gilman, 551(RenQ):Winter89-871
  C. Jordan, 191(ELN):Dec89-67
Roston, M., R. Paulson & M. Novak. Reading
Hogarth.
  S. Shesgreen, 566:Autumn89-74
Rot, S. Old English. (2nd ed)
  W. Viereck, 685(ZDL):1/1989-97
Rotberg, R.I., with M.F. Shore. The Founder.*
  D. Kennedy, 637(VS):Spring90-530
Roth, H.H. Boundaries of Love.
  A. St. George, 441:9Dec90-24
Roth, J. Tarabas, A Guest On Earth.
  T. Palmer, 577(SHR):Winter89-79
Roth, P. Deception.
  G. Annan, 453(NYRB):31May90-7
  W. Steiner, 617(TLS):31Aug-6Sep90-917
  F. Weldon, 441:11Mar90-3
Roth, P. The Facts.*
  J. Lewis, 364:Aug/Sep89-117
  B. Lyons, 573(SSF):Fall88-481
  S. Pickering, 569(SR):Spring89-297
  S. Pinsker, 390:Jan89-59
  639(VQR):Winter89-16
Roth, P.A. Meaning and Method in the Social
Sciences.*
  G. MacDonald, 311(JP):Aug89-442
Roth-Rubi, K. & H.R. Sennhauser. Verena-
münster Zurzach. (Vol 1)
  J. Rychener, 229:Band61Heft5-468
Rothe, A. Der literarische Titel.
  R. Stillers, 547(RF):Band101Heft4-461
Rothenberg, J. New Selected Poems: 1970-
1985.*
  L. Levis, 29(APR):Jan/Feb89-14
Rothgeb, J. – see Schenker, H.
Rothman, B.K. The Tentative Pregnancy.
  K.P. Addelson, 254:Summer89-191
Rothschild, M. Wondermonger.
  D. Dawson, 441:16Sep90-18
Rothstein, E. & F.M. Kavenik. The Designs of
Carolean Comedy.
  A.M., 125:Spring89-322
  C. Spencer, 130:Summer89-198
Rotola, A.C. – see Stoquerus, G.
Rotter, A.J. The Path to Vietnam.*
  D.G. Marr, 293(JASt):Aug89-682
Rotter, E. Abendland und Sarazenen.
  D. Metlitzki, 589:Jan89-211
Rouart, D. – see Morisot, B.
Rouart, M-F. Le Mythe du Juif Errant dans
l'Europe du XIXe siècle.
  A. Blum, 446(NCFS):Spring-Summer90-
567
Rouaud, J. Les Champs d'honneur.
  R. Buss, 617(TLS):16-22Nov90-1233
Roubaud, J. Le Grand Incendie de Londres.*
  C. Bobin, 450(NRF):Apr89-101
Rouben, C. – see de Bussy-Rabutin, R.
Roudané, M.C., ed. Conversations with Arthur
Miller.
  T.P. Adler, 397(MD):Jun89-321
  J.H. Lutterbie, 615(TJ):Dec89-567
Roudané, M.C. Understanding Edward Albee.*
  W. French, 580(SCR):Spring90-158
  L. Hart, 397(MD):Jun89-324
Roudaut, J. Lieu de composition.
  R. Blin, 450(NRF):Oct89-107
Roudaut, J. Une Ombre au tableau.
  H. Raynal, 450(NRF):Apr89-104
Roudil, J. – see Jacobo de Junta

Rougeart, J. Oeuvres complètes (1578). (C.
Magnien-Simonin, ed)
  K. Cameron, 402(MLR):Jul90-729
Roumani, J. Albert Memmi.
  H. Bouraoui, 538(RAL):Spring89-126
  M. Mortimer, 295(JML):Fall88/Winter89-
381
Round, N.G. – see Tirso de Molina
Rouner, L.S., ed. Human Rights and World's
Religions.
  D.G., 185:Jul90-919
Rouse, J. Knowledge and Power.
  D.A. Hollinger, 385(MQR):Winter90-123
Roush, J.E. & L. Clayton – see Mullins, R.B.
Rousseau, F-O. La Gare de Wannsee.
  G.E. Reed, 207(FR):May90-1109
Rousseau, G.S. & R. Porter, eds. Sexual
Underworlds of the Enlightenment.*
  H.A. Chalmers, 141:Fall89-490
  A. Hammond, 166:Oct89-86
  S. Soupel, 189(EA):Jul-Sep89-346
  42(AR):Winter89-109
Rousseau, G.S. & P. Rogers, eds. The Endur-
ing Legacy.
  V. Carretta, 173(ECS):Winter89/90-231
  C. Chapin, 566:Spring90-191
  M. Kelsall, 402(MLR):Jan90-149
Rousseau, J-J. Correspondance complète.*
(Vol 46) (R.A. Leigh, ed)
  J. Bloch, 208(FS):Apr89-214
  J-L. Lecercle, 535(RHL):Mar-Apr89-291
Rousseau, J-J. The First and Second Dis-
courses, Together with the Replies to Crit-
ics and Essay on the Origin of Language.
(V. Gourevitch, ed & trans)
  C.E. Butterworth, 543:Sep89-181
Rousseau, N. Connaissance et langage chez
Condillac.*
  M. Hobson, 208(FS):Jul89-329
Roussel, R. The Conversation of the Sexes.*
  A. Forster, 568(SCN):Spring-Summer89-
19
Rousselle, A. Porneia.
  J.F. Gardner, 123:Vol39No2-329
Rousset, J. Le lecteur intime – De Balzac au
journal.*
  R. Amossy, 494:Fall89-650
  G. Cesbron, 356(LR):Feb-May89-104
Roussineau, G., ed. Perceforest.* (Pt 4)
  B. Guidot, 547(RF):Band101Heft1-112
  E. Kennedy, 208(FS):Jan89-74
  J.H.M. Taylor, 589:Apr89-496
Routley, R., with others. Relevant Logics and
Their Rivals. (Pt 1)
  D.H. Cohen, 316:Mar89-293
Rouveret, A. – see Chomsky, N.
de Rouville, H. La Musique anglaise.
  J. Michon, 189(EA):Oct-Dec89-447
Roux, A. & M. French Country Cooking.
  A. Williams, 617(TLS):27Jul-2Aug90-809
Roviello, A-M. L'institution kantienne de la
liberté.
  P. Guenancia, 342:Band80Heft4-493
Rovine, H. Silence in Shakespeare.
  J.L. Halio, 570(SQ):Fall89-354
  J.P. Rice, 615(TJ):Oct89-418
Rovner, E. Teatro.
  M. Inés Cincinnati, 352(LATR):Fall89-155
Rowan, A. Catalogues of Architectural Draw-
ings in the Victoria and Albert Museum:
Robert Adam.
  I. Gow, 90:Nov89-785
Rowe, C.J. – see Plato

Rowe, D.W. Through Nature to Eternity.
　M. Andrew, 402(MLR):Apr90-404
　S. Delany, 401(MLQ):Mar88-73
　L.J. Kiser, 405(MP):Feb90-291
　D. Mehl, 447(N&Q):Sep89-367
Rowe, E.S. The Poetry of Elizabeth Singer
　Rowe. (M.F. Marshall, ed)
　J.F. Sena, 566:Autumn89-70
Rowe, G.E. Distinguishing Jonson.
　L.A. Beaurline, 405(MP):Feb90-305
　L. Danson, 131(CL):Summer89-291
　P. Hyland, 447(N&Q):Dec89-506
　W.D. Kay, 301(JEGP):Jul89-407
Rowe, J.G., ed. Aspects of Late Medieval
　Government and Society.*
　R.B. Dobson, 179(ES):Feb89-84
　C. Gauvin, 189(EA):Oct-Dec89-464
　S. Mapstone, 447(N&Q):Jun89-223
Rowe, K.E. Saint and Singer.*
　S. Bush, Jr., 677(YES):Vol20-269
　M. Schuldiner, 250(HLQ):Spring89-295
Rowe, P.G. Design Thinking.*
　R. Geddes & J. Dill, 505:Nov89-115
Rowe, W. Rulfo: "El llano en llamas."
　P. Standish, 402(MLR):Apr90-486
Rowell, G. The Art of Adventure.*
　Y.A. Andrews, 441:14Jan90-30
Rowell, M. The Captured Imagination.*
　W.J., 90:Apr89-305
Rowen, H.H. & A. Lossky. Political Ideas and
　Institutions in the Dutch Republic.
　H. Dunthorne, 83:Autumn89-218
Rowlands, M., M.T. Larsen & K. Kristiansen,
　eds. Centre and Periphery in the Ancient
　World.
　S.E. Alcock, 123:Vol39No1-97
　G. Woolf, 313:Vol79-236
Rowley, R. The Sea of Affliction.*
　G.M. McCarthy, 272(IUR):Spring89-175
Rowse, A.L. The Controversial Colensos.
　G. Palmer, 617(TLS):2-8Feb90-120
Rowse, A.L. Friends and Contemporaries.*
　P. Vansittart, 364:Aug/Sep89-123
Rowson, S. Charlotte Temple.
　D. Seed, 83:Spring89-110
Roy, C. The Distant Friend.
　J. Marcus, 441:10Dec90 10
　442(NY):19Nov90-156
Roy, C.D., ed. Iowa Studies in African Art.
　(Vol 2)
　P.M. Peek, 2(AfrA):Nov88-27
Roy, D. - see Planché, J.R.
Roy, G. Enchantment and Sorrow.
　A. Hayward, 529(QQ):Spring89-177
Roy, G. Ma chère petite soeur.
　J-G. Hudon, 627(UTQ):Fall89-200
Roy, S. Philosophy of Economics.
　M. Bacharach, 617(TLS):18-24May90-520
Royer, J. Depuis l'amour.
　C. May, 102(CanL):Spring89-200
Royle, E. Modern Britain.
　V.G. Kiernan, 242:Vol10No6-738
Royster, C. - see Sherman, W.T.
Rozett, M.T. The Doctrine of Election and the
　Emergence of Elizabethan Tragedy.*
　J.A. Bryant, Jr., 569(SR):Summer89-445
Rozier, J., ed. The Granite Farm Letters.
　639(VQR):Summer89-88
Rubens, B. Kingdom Come.
　S. Altinel, 617(TLS):2-8Mar90-214
Rubens, P.P. Lettere Italiane. (I. Cotta, ed)
　90:Jan89-48

Rubenstein, R. Boundaries of the Self.*
　E.G. Friedman, 532(RCF):Summer89-254
Rubin, A., ed. Marks of Civilization.
　K. Stevenson, 2(AfrA):Feb89-10
Rubin, D. After the Raj.*
　M.M. Mahood, 541(RES):Feb89-139
Rubin, L.D., Jr. The Edge of the Swamp.
　R.L. Phillips, Jr., 585(SoQ):Winter90-64
　T.D. Young, 580(SCR):Spring90-172
Rubin, M. Charity and Community in Medieval
　Cambridge.
　S.F. Roberts, 589:Apr89-498
Rubin, W. Picasso and Braque.
　J. Golding, 453(NYRB):31May90-8
Rubin-Dorsky, J. Adrift in the Old World.*
　J. Clendenning, 445(NCF):Sep89-244
　W.L. Hedges, 27(AL):Mar89-106
　T. Martin, 405(MP):May90-417
Rubinger, R. - see Mendenhall, T.C.
Rubinin, P. - see Kapitsa, P.L.
Rubinstein, D. Before the Suffragettes.
　S. Graver, 635(VPR):Spring89-34
Rubinstein, H., ed. The Oxford Book of Mar-
　riage.
　A. Motion, 617(TLS):16-22Mar90-296
Rubio, J. & E. Waterston - see Montgomery,
　L.M.
Ruchner, J. & M. Schlup, eds. Aspects du
　livre neuchâtelois.
　B. Gagnebin, 535(RHL):Mar-Apr89-334
Rucker, R. The Hollow Earth.
　G. Jonas, 441:2Sep90 10
Rucquoi, A. Valladolid au Moyen Age.
　(Spanish title: Valladolid en la edad
　media.)
　C. Estow, 589:Oct89-1035
　B. Leroy, 92(BH):Jul-Dec88-443
Rudavsky, T., ed. Divine Omniscience and
　Omnipotence in Medieval Philosophy.
　B. Weiss, 318(JAOS):Jul-Sep88-494
Rudd, I. & S. Fischler. The Sporting Life.
　M. Mehler, 441:29Jul90-21
Rudd, N. & T. Wiedemann - see Cicero
Rudd, S. In Australia, or The Old Selection.
　(R. Fotheringham, ed)
　K. Stewart, 71(ALS):May89-122
Ruddick, S. Maternal Thinking.*
　C. Townshend, 617(TLS):23Feb-1Mar90-
　192
Rudé, G. The French Revolution.*
　639(VQR):Summer89-81
Ruderman, D. Kabbalah, Magic, and Science.
　A.A. Aciman, 390:Oct89-49
Rudes, B.A. Tuscarora Roots, Stems, and Par-
　ticles.*
　J. Scancarelli, 269(IJAL):Oct89-478
Rudes, B.A. & D. Crouse. The Tuscarora Leg-
　acy of J.N.B. Hewitt.*
　J. Scancarelli, 269(IJAL):Oct89-478
Rudnitsky, K. Russian and Soviet Theater
　1905-1932. (L. Milne, ed)
　J. Fisher, 130:Fall89-291
　C. Lodder, 90:Sep89-647
Rudnytsky, P.L. Freud and Oedipus.
　D. Barnouw, 242:Vol10No5-609
Rudolf von Biberach. De septem itineribus
　aeternitatis.* (M. Schmidt, ed) Die sieben
　strassen zu got.* (M. Schmidt, ed & trans)
　[shown in prev under von Biberach, R.]
　B. McGinn, 589:Jan89-213
Rudolph, L.I. & S.H. In Pursuit of Lakshmi.
　A. Gupta, 293(JASt):Nov89-787
　J. Manor, 293(JASt):Nov89-916

Rudolph, W. & A. Calinescu, eds. Ancient Art from the V.G. Simkhovitch Collection.
A.W. Johnston, 123:Vol39No2-413
Rudy, S. - see Jakobson, R.
Rudzka, B. Wśród Polaków. (Pt 2)
C.Y. Bethin, 399(MLJ):Summer89-235
Rudzka, B. & Z. Goczolowa. Wśród Polaków. (3rd ed) (Pt 1)
C.Y. Bethin, 399(MLJ):Summer89-235
Rueda, J.M.F. - see under Fradejas Rueda, J.M.
Ruff, I. Edenville.
P. Kerr, 617(TLS):18-24May90-535
Rüffer, N. Konfigurationalität.
G. Fowler, 350:Jun90-426
Ruggiero, K.H. And Here the World Ends.
D. Nasatir, 263(RIB):Vol39No1-80
Ruggle, G. Ignoramus. (E.F.J. Tucker, ed)
G. Eatough, 123:Vol39No1-129
R. Green, 447(N&Q):Dec89-498
Ruh, K., ed. Abendländische Mystik im Mittelalter.*
R. Imbach, 684(ZDA):Band118Heft1-6
Ruh, K., ed. Franziskanisches Schrifttum im deutschen Mittelalter. (Vol 2)
K.O. Seidel, 684(ZDA):Band118Heft2-86
Ruh, K. & others, eds. Die deutsche Literatur des Mittelalters: Verfasserlexikon. (2nd ed) (Vol 5)
N.F. Palmer, 402(MLR):Apr90-492
Ruh, K. & others, eds. Die deutsche Literatur des Mittelalters: Verfasserlexikon. (2nd ed) (Vol 6)
N.F. Palmer, 402(MLR):Oct90-1022
Ruhl, C. On Monosemy.
B.M. Birch, 350:Dec90-881
Ruhlen, M. A Guide to the World's Languages.* (Vol 1)
D.E. Ager, 402(MLR):Jan90-125
Rühmkorf, P. Einmalig wie wir alle.
J. Hieber, 358:Feb90-7
Ruini, C. - see Pitoni, G.O.
Ruiz, J. [Arcipreste de Hita] Libro de buen amor. (G.B. Gybbon-Monypenny, ed)
N.J. Dyer, 238:Sep89-539
Ruiz, V.G. - see under García Ruiz, V.
Ruiz Silva, C. - see Miró, G.
Ruiz Veintemilla, J.M., ed. Diario de los literatos de España.
I.L. McClelland, 86(BHS):Oct89-382
Rukmani, T.S., ed & trans. Yogavārttika of Vijñānabhikṣu.
J. Borelli, 318(JAOS):Oct-Dec88-638
Rüland, J., ed. Urban Government and Development in Asia.
R.W. Jones, 293(JASt):Nov89-809
Rule, J. A Hot-Eyed Moderate.
G. Whitlock, 102(CanL):Summer89-168
Rule, J. Memory Board.*
E. Johnston, 102(CanL):Autumn-Winter89-200
Rule, J. Theme for Diverse Instruments.
E. Fishel, 441:2Sep90-17
Rumens, C. From Berlin to Heaven.
S. O'Brien, 617(TLS):5-11Jan90-19
Rumens, C. The Greening of the Snow Beach.*
S. Pugh, 493:Spring89-47
W. Scammell, 364:Aug/Sep89-92
Rumford, B.T. & C.J. Weekley. Treasures of American Folk Art.
139:Dec89/Jan90-24
Rummel, E. - see Erasmus

Rumrich, J.P. Matter of Glory.*
G. Campbell, 402(MLR):Apr90-412
C.C. Newman, 391:Mar89-34
P. Stevens, 301(JEGP):Jul89-417
Runciman, W.G. A Treatise on Social Theory. (Vol 2)
A.L. Stinchcombe, 185:Jul90-897
Runyan, W.M. Life Histories and Psychobiography.
J.E. Gedo, 77:Fall89-332
Runyan, W.M., ed. Psychology and Historical Interpretation.
J.E. Gedo, 77:Fall89-332
Ruotolo, L.P. The Interrupted Moment.*
N.T. Justicia, 177(ELT):Vol32No3-367
J. Marcus, 620(TSWL):Spring89-101
Rupe, C.J. La dialéctica del amor en la narrativa de Juan Valera.*
A.A. Fox, 552(REH):Jan89-135
Rupp, H. & C.L. Lang, eds. Deutsches Literatur-Lexikon. (Vol 10) (3rd ed)
P.M. Mitchell, 301(JEGP):Jan89-56
Rupp, J.E. Lealao Chinantec Syntax.
T. Kaufman, 350:Dec90-882
Rupp, L.J. & V. Taylor. Survival in the Doldrums.
J.K.D., 185:Jan90-463
Ruppert, J. D'Arcy McNickle.
C. White, 649(WAL):Aug89-163
Rusbridger, J. The Intelligence Game.
W. Laqueur, 617(TLS):26Jan-1Feb90-82
Rüsen, J., E. Lämmert & P. Glotz, eds. Die Zukunft der Aufklärung.
W. Goetschel, 221(GQ):Spring89-235
Rush, C. Two Christmas Stories. Into the Ebb.
I. Hood, 571(ScLJ):Winter89-33
Rushdie, S. The Satanic Verses.*
S. Aravamudan, 153:Summer89-3
C. Hampshire, 381:Autumn89-161
J. Harrison, 529(QQ):Autumn89-714
G.G. Hospital, 529(QQ):Autumn89-662
A. Malak, 49:Oct89-176
W.H. Pritchard, 249(HudR):Autumn89-491
639(VQR):Summer89-91
Rusinko, S. British Drama 1950 to the Present.
J. Wilders, 617(TLS):5-11Jan90-14
Rusk, D., with R. Rusk. As I Saw It. (D.S. Papp, ed)
J.L. Gaddis, 441:1Jul90-3
J. Mirsky, 453(NYRB):16Aug90-29
Ruskin, J. & C.E. Norton. The Correspondence of John Ruskin and Charles Eliot Norton.* (J.L. Bradley & I. Ousby, eds)
J. Clubbe, 637(VS):Winter90-353
R.E. Fitch, 301(JEGP):Apr89-248
L.J. Workman, 432(NEQ):Dec89-572
Ruspoli, M. The Cave of Lascaux.
J. Canemaker, 507:Sep/Oct89-174
Russell, A. No Sign of Murder.
M. Upchurch, 441:11Nov90-68
Russell, B. The Collected Papers of Bertrand Russell. (Vol 8) (J.G. Slater, ed)
B. Linsky, 154:Vol28No4-675
Russell, B. The Collected Papers of Bertrand Russell. (Vol 9 ed by J.G. Slater, with B. Frohmann; Vol 13 ed by R.A. Rempel, with others)
483:Jan89-123
Russell, B. Bertrand Russell on God and Religion. (A. Seckel, ed)
S. Andersson, 556:Summer89-94

Russell, C. Poets, Prophets, and Revolution-
aries.
   C. Robinson, 447(N&Q):Jun89-285
Russell, H.L. Rush to Nowhere.
   42(AR):Winter89-116
Russell, J.B. The Prince of Darkness.*
   K.V., 185:Jan90-465
Russell, J.M. Atlanta 1847-1890.
   S. Wilson, Jr., 585(SoQ):Summer89-127
   639(VQR):Winter89-9
Russell, J.S. The English Dream Vision.
   K.L. Lynch, 301(JEGP):Jul89-393
   R.P. McGerr, 115:Spring89-188
Russell, K. A British Picture.
   M. Wood, 617(TLS):12-18Jan90-33
Russell, P. The Salt Point.
   S. Ferguson, 441:6May90-22
Russell, P.A. Lay Theology in the Reforma-
tion.
   J.M. Stayer, 551(RenQ):Winter89-843
Russell, R. Blind Spot.
   M. Stasio, 441:16Dec90-33
Russell, R. Russian Drama of the Revolu-
tionary Period.
   E.J. Czerwinski, 130:Fall89-289
   C. Marsh, 575(SEER):Oct89-619
"Russia — the Land, the People."*
   D. Farrell, 104(CASS):Spring89-102
Russo, J.P. I.A. Richards.*
   J. Culler, 617(TLS):9-15Mar90-246
Russom, G. Old English Metre and Linguistic
Theory.*
   M. Griffith, 383(MAE):1989/1-140
   W. Obst, 38:Band107Heft3/4-506
   S.D. Spangehl, 350:Jun90-427
Rutherford, A. - see Kipling, R.
Rutherford, R.B. The "Meditations" of Marcus
Aurelius.
   M. Atkins, 617(TLS):6-12Apr90-380
Ruthven, M. A Satanic Affair.
   A. Gurnah, 617(TLS):2-8Mar90-221
   A. Knoenagel, 200(IFR):Summer90-190
Rutkowski, K. Braterstwo albo śmierć.
   R. Koropeckyj, 497(PolR):Vol34No4-367
Rutz, W. Cities and Towns in Indonesia.
   R. Provencher, 293(JASt):Aug89-683
Ruzicka, W.T. Faulkner's Fictive Architec-
ture.
   P.R.J., 295(JML):Fall88/Winter89-326
Ryals, C.D. & K.J. Fielding - see Carlyle, T. &
J.W.
Ryan, A. Bertrand Russell.*
   R. Harrison, 556:Summer89-64
Ryan, C. The Capricorn Quadrant.
   N. Callendar, 441:16Sep90-26
Ryan, M. God Hunger.*
   M. Boruch, 29(APR):Nov/Dec89-21
   S. Burris, 598(SoR):Spring90-456
Ryan, M., ed. Ireland and Insular Art A.D.
500-1200.
   L. Karlsson, 341:Vol58No4-172
Ryan, M. & R. Prentice. Social Trends in the
Soviet Union from 1950.
   V.E. Bonnell, 550(RusR):Apr89-224
Ryavec, K.W. United States-Soviet Relations.
   T.R. Maddux, 550(RusR):Jul89-343
   A. Milward, 617(TLS):26Jan-1Feb90-81
Ryback, T.W. Rock Around the Bloc.
   L. Doružka, 617(TLS):7-13Sep90-950
   442(NY):23Apr90-116
Rybakov, A. Children of the Arbat.* (French
title: Les Enfants de l'Arbat.)
   J. Blot, 450(NRF):Mar89-88

Rybczynski, W. The Most Beautiful House in
the World.*
   M. Filler, 453(NYRB):1Feb90-26
   D. Gantenbein, 45:Oct89-69
Ryckmans, P. - see Confucius
Rydén, M. & S. Brorström. The Be/Have Vari-
ation with Intransitives in English.*
   G. Bourcier, 189(EA):Oct-Dec89-458
   R. Sampson, 179(ES):Oct89-458
   H. Ulherr, 38:Band107Heft3/4-468
   A. Ward, 541(RES):Nov89-601
Ryder, A. Alfonso the Magnanimous.
   D. Abulafia, 617(TLS):20-26Jul90-773
Ryder, F.G., ed. German Romantic Stories.
   H.M.K. Riley, 133:Band22Heft3/4-337
Ryder, R.D. Animal Revolution.
   J. Serpell, 617(TLS):16-22Feb90-167
Rykwert, J., N. Leach & R. Tavernor - see
Alberti, L.B.
Rylance, R., ed. Debating Texts.*
   J.R. Bennett, 677(YES):Vol20-218
Ryman, G. The Child Garden.
   G. Jonas, 441:21Oct90-35
Rymkiewicz, J.M. Umschlagplatz.*
   M. Adamczyk-Garbowska, 508:Sep89-273
Ryn, C.G. Will, Imagination and Reason.
   J.A. Bryant, Jr., 569(SR):Winter89-153
Rywkin, M., ed. Russian Colonial Expansion
to 1917.
   B. Jelavich, 550(RusR):Apr89-196
   S.F. Jones, 575(SEER):Oct89-635
Rzepka, C.J. The Self as Mind.*
   F. Garber, 340(KSJ):Vol38-173

Sa'adah, A. The Shaping of Liberal Politics in
Revolutionary France.
   G. Lewis, 617(TLS):14-20Dec90-1355
Saame, O. El principio de razón en Leibniz.
   B. Orio de Miguel, 706:Band21Heft1-127
Saari, H. Re-enactment.
   J.J. Goldstein, 488:Jun89-247
Saarikoski, P. Dances of the Obscure.
   J. Saunders, 565:Autumn89-77
de Saavedra, A. [Duque de Rivas]. Romances
históricos. (S. García-Castañeda, ed)
   O. Chú-Pund, 240(HR):Autumn89-525
Saavedra, L. Clarín, una interpretación.
   Y. Lissorgues, 711(RHM):Jun89-86
Saavedra, M.D. - see under de Cervantes
Saavedra, M.
Saba, G. - see de Viau, T.
Saba, U. Umberto Saba: An Anthology of His
Poetry and Criticism. (R. Harrison, ed &
trans)
   L. Baffoni-Licata, 276:Spring89-56
Sabaliūnas, L. Lithuanian Social Democracy
in Perspective, 1893-1914.
   D. Kirby, 617(TLS):27Jul-2Aug90-797
Sabato, E. L'écrivain et la catastrophe.
   J. Colette, 192(EP):Jul-Dec89-557
Sabin, M. The Dialect of the Tribe.
   B.B., 295(JML):Fall88/Winter89-251
   P. Parrinder, 301(JEGP):Jul89-452
   L.P. Ruotolo, 131(CL):Winter89-108
Sabiston, E.J. The Prison of Womanhood.*
   J. McMaster, 627(UTQ):Fall89-128
   J. Matus, 178:Dec89-498
Sabo, G.J. - see Gavlovič, H.
Sabor, P., ed. Horace Walpole: The Critical
Heritage.
   A. Ingram, 677(YES):Vol20-280
                                    [continued]

Sabor, P., ed. Horace Walpole: The Critical
Heritage. [continuing]
    P. Rogers, 83:Autumn89-212
    J. Smitten, 541(RES):Nov89-569
Sabor, P. & M.A. Doody - see Burney, F.
Saborit, I.T. - see under Terradas i Saborit, I.
Sabsay, S., M. Platt & others. Social Setting,
Stigma, and Communicative Competence.
    P. Davies, 355(LSoc):Mar89-128
Saccenti, M., ed. Carducci e la letteratura
italiana.
    A. Brambilla, 228(GSLI):Vol166fasc536-
569
Saccenti, M., ed. La Colonia Renia.
    M. Mari, 228(GSLI):Vol166fasc534-293
Saccone, E. Conclusioni anticipate su alcuni
racconti e romanzi del Novecento.
    J. Smith, 402(MLR):Jan90-219
Sachdev, P., ed. International Handbook on
Abortion.
    N.D., 185:Jul90-927
Sachs, A. Running to Maputo.
    T. Eprile, 441:9Dec90-15
Sachs, H. Music in Fascist Italy.*
    R. Fearn, 410(M&L):Feb89-130
Sacks, M. The World We Found.
    S. Gardner, 617(TLS):2-8Mar90-227
    W.S. Robinson, 103:Apr90-157
Sacks, O. Seeing Voices.*
    A. Burgess, 617(TLS):19-25Jan90-53
    J. Ryle, 358:Feb90-8
    W. Tumin, 324:May90-439
Sacks, P.M. The English Elegy.*
    A.V. Ettin, 191(ELN):Sep89-69
Sackville-West, V. The Letters of Vita Sack-
ville-West to Virginia Woolf. (L. De Salvo
& M.A. Leaska, eds)
    J. Marcus, 620(TSWL):Spring89-101
Sackville-West, V. Saint Joan of Arc.
    617(TLS):9-15Mar90-266
Sacré, J. Une fin d'après-midi à Marrakech.
    R. Jacquelin, 450(NRF):Jan89-86
Sacré, R., ed. The Voice of the Delta.
    A.J.M. Prévos, 91:Vol17-185
Saddlemyer, A. & C. Smythe, eds. Lady Greg-
ory, Fifty Years After.*
    M. Demoor, 177(ELT):Vol32No4-509
Sadie, S., ed. The Grove Concise Dictionary
of Music.
    M. Kennedy, 410(M&L):Nov89-517
Sadie, S., ed. History of Opera.
    J. Tyrrell, 617(TLS):13-19Apr90-398
Sadie, S. & A. Hicks, eds. Handel Tercenten-
ary Collection.
    D.R.B. Kimbell, 410(M&L):Aug89-404
    C. Willner, 415:Nov89-678
Sadikov, O.N., ed. Soviet Civil Law.
    P.B. Maggs, 550(RusR):Apr89-227
Sadler, L. Welsh Syntax.*
    R.D. Borsley, 353:Vol27No6-1125
    M. Rockel, 682(ZPSK):Band42Heft3-411
    M.O. Tallerman, 297(JL):Mar90-260
Sadoff, I. Emotional Traffic.
    P. Harris, 639(VQR):Spring89-236
Sadovnikov, D. Riddles of the Russian People.
    F. Wigzell, 575(SEER):Jul89-499
Sadrin, A. "Great Expectations."
    M. Cardwell, 155:Spring89-50
    R. Mason, 447(N&Q):Dec89-525
    S. Monod, 637(VS):Spring90-513
Sadrin, A. L'être et l'avoir dans les romans
de Charles Dickens.
    J. Dobrinsky, 189(EA):Oct-Dec89-482

Sáenz, G. El pleyto y querella de los guajolo-
tes.
    V.B. Levine, 238:Sep89-554
Sáenz, T.D. Pintura española del último ter-
cio del siglo XVI en Madrid.
    I. Mateo Gómez, 48:Apr-Jun89-231
Sáez, A. Cuentos. (J. Belmonte Serrano, ed)
    V.P. Dean-Thacker, 345(KRQ):Nov89-498
Safer, E.B. The Contemporary American Comic
Epic.
    V. Hyles, 27(AL):Oct89-497
    J.M. Krafft, 395(MFS):Winter89-774
    S. Moore, 532(RCF):Spring89-275
    D. Seed, 402(MLR):Oct90-939
    S. Trachtenberg, 587(SAF):Autumn89-251
Safer, M. Flashbacks.
    N. Lemann, 441:15Apr90-3
    J. Mirsky, 453(NYRB):16Aug90-29
    442(NY):28May90-110
Saffrey, H.D. & L.G. Westerink - see Proclus
"The Saga of Thidrek of Bern." (E.R. Haymes,
trans)
    S. Jefferis, 221(GQ):Fall89-516
Sagan, D. Biospheres.
    G. Maranto, 441:18Mar90-16
Sagan, F. Sarah Bernhardt - Le rire incas-
sable.
    C. Slawy-Sutton, 207(FR):Dec89-411
Sagarra, E., ed. Deutsche Literatur in sozial-
geschichtlicher Perspektive.
    L. Löb, 402(MLR):Oct90-1035
Sagasta Galdos, J. - see Martín y Coll, A.
Saggs, H.F. Civilization before Greece and
Rome.
    A.R. Burn, 123:Vol39No2-406
Sagoff, M. The Economy of the Earth.*
    D. Knowles, 518:Oct89-242
de Sagredo, D. Medidas del Romano.*
    J. Bury, 90:Jan89-43
Sahlins, P. Boundaries.
    H. Kamen, 617(TLS):13-19Apr90-400
Sahni, J. Moghul Microwave.
    R. Flaste, 441:2Dec90-14
Said, E. & C. Hitchens, eds. Blaming the Vic-
tims.
    S.H. Buccleugh, 577(SHR):Fall89-373
Saikaku, I. The Great Mirror of Male Love.
    I. Buruma, 617(TLS):20-26Apr90-413
Saine, T.P. Von der Kopernikanischen bis zur
Französischen Revolution.
    R. Baasner, 52:Band24Heft2-214
    H.B. Nisbet, 402(MLR):Jan90-245
Saine, T.P. - see "Goethe Yearbook"
Saine, T.P. & J.L. Sammons - see von Goethe,
J.W.
Sainsbury, R.M. Paradoxes.
    B. Linsky, 518:Jul89-164
Saint, A., ed. Politics and the People of Lon-
don.
    R. Pinker, 617(TLS):11-17May90-504
Saint, A. Towards a Social Architecture.
    S. Pepper, 576:Sep89-291
    R. Thorne, 59:Mar89-136
St. Aubyn, F.C. Arthur Rimbaud, Updated
Edition.
    G. Browning, 446(NCFS):Fall-
Winter89/90-266
    U. Franklin, 207(FR):May90-1066
de Saint-Cheron, P. Rencontre avec Elie
Wiesel.
    J. Kolbert, 207(FR):Apr90-885

St. Clair, W. The Godwins and the Shelleys.*
R. Fuller, 364:Oct/Nov89-118
442(NY):8Jan90-100
de Saint-Exupéry, A. Wartime Writings 1939-
1944.*
L. Goldstein, 385(MQR):Summer90-472
Saint-Fleur, J. Logiques de la représenta-
tion, essai d'épistémologie wittgenstein-
ienne.
P. Engel, 542:Oct-Dec89-624
St. George, E.Y. Lions in the Afternoon.
B. Rendall, 647:Fall89-79
St. George, R.B., ed. Material Life in America,
1600-1860.
P. Chase-Harrell, 432(NEQ):Sep89-468
B. Mergen, 658:Summer/Autumn89-178
Saint-Gérand, J-P. L'Intelligence et l'Émo-
tion.
R.T. Denommé, 446(NCFS):Fall-
Winter89/90-249
St. John, J. William Heinemann.
J. Sutherland, 617(TLS):27Apr-3May90-
442
St. Just, M. - see Williams, T.
Saint-Martin, F. La fiction du réel.
B. Godard, 102(CanL):Winter88-123
St.-Pierre, C. Sur les pas de la mer.
A.L. Amprimoz, 102(CanL):Autumn-
Winter89-276
de Saint Pierre, M. Le Milieu de l'été.
D. O'Connell, 207(FR):Oct89-211
Saintsbury, E. George MacDonald.
J. Smith, 571(ScLJ):Spring89-22
Sajama, S & M Kemppinen A Historical
Introduction to Phenomenology.
S. Cunningham, 53(AGP):Band71Heft1-
112
Sajavaara, K., ed. Applications of Cross-
Language Analysis.
C. Engber, 710:Mar89-123
Sakai, K. Sekai to Jiga - Leibniz Keijijōgaku
Ronkô.
A. Tanaka, 706:Band21Heft1-124
Sakellaridou, E. Pinter's Female Portraits.
R. Knowles, 677(YES):Vol20-346
S.H. Merritt, 397(MD):Mar89-171
P Mudford, 447(N&Q):Jun89-265
Sakharov, A. Gorki, Moskva, Dalye Vezde.
Trevoga i Nadezhda.
D. Remnick, 453(NYRB):16Aug90-3
Sakharov, A. Memoirs.
P-L. Adams, 61:Sep90-123
J.H. Billington, 441:17Jun90-1
E. Gellner, 617(TLS):17-23Aug90-863
D. Remnick, 453(NYRB):16Aug90-3
442(NY):3Sep90-108
Sakharov, A. Moscow and Beyond.
M.D. Shulman, 441:30Dec90-3
Sakkas, J. Ilias.
N.A. Basbanes, 441:27May90-15
R. Jolly, 581:Dec89-667
Sakwa, R. Soviet Communists in Power.
P. Ashin, 550(RusR):Oct89-425
Salam-Liebich, H. The Architecture of the
Mamluk City of Tripoli.
N. Hanna, 318(JAOS):Jul-Sep88-489
Salamand, G. Paulin de Barral libertin dau-
phinois.
V.D.L., 605(SC):15Jul90-413
Šalamun, T. Selected Poems. (C. Simic, ed)
S. Friebert, 199:Spring89-60
Salaris, C. Storia del futurismo.
A.J. Tamburri, 276:Summer89-238

Salat, S., with F. Labbé. Fumihiko Maki.
M. Treib, 576:Sep89-304
G. Vorreiter, 46:Nov89-12
Salazar Rincón, J. El mundo social del "Qui-
jote."*
W. Ferguson, 240(HR):Summer89-381
E. Ruiz-Fornells, 238:Sep89-542
Sälde, A-M. Bo Beskows glasmålningar i
Skara domkyrka och deras relation till
efterkrigstidens franska glasmåleri.
L. Karlsson, 341:Vol58No2-92
Sale, K. The Conquest of Paradise.
W.H. McNeill, 441:7Oct90-28
G. Wills, 453(NYRB):22Nov90-6
442(NY):12Nov90-134
Sale, R. Closer to Home.
A.J. Sambrook, 677(YES):Vol20-284
R.K.R. Thornton, 83:Autumn89-223
Salerno, J. & S.J. Rivele. The Plumber.
T. Jacoby, 441:18Feb90-11
de Sales, F. & J. de Chantal. Letters of Spir-
itual Direction. (W.M. Wright & J.F. Power,
eds)
R. Boenig, 568(SCN):Fall-Winter89-53
Salgádo, G. & G.K. Das, eds. The Spirit of D.H.
Lawrence.
K.M. Hewitt, 541(RES):Nov89-588
Salgado, S. An Uncertain Grace.
A. Grundberg, 441:2Dec90-71
de Salinas, J. Poesías humanas.* (H. Bonne-
ville, ed)
S.B. Vranich, 402(MLR):Jul90-762
Salisbury, H.E. Disturber of the Peace.
C. Wheeler, 617(TLS):9-15Feb90-140
Salisbury, H.E. Tiananmen Diary.*
J. Mirsky, 453(NYRB):1Feb90-21
Sallis, J. Delimitations.
J.T. Bagwell, 153:Spring89-97
Salloum, S. Malcolm Lowry: Vancouver Days.*
S. Vice, 168(ECW):Fall89-118
529(QQ):Spring89-214
Salm, P. Pinpoint of Eternity.*
R.E. Schade, 678(YCGL):No36-170
Salmen, W. & N.J. Schneider, eds. Der musik-
alische Satz.
D. de la Motte, 416:Band4Heft2-169
H.W. Zimmermann, 416:Band4Heft2-167
Salmon, C., ed. Literary Migrations.
P.H. Lee, 293(JASt):Aug89-579
Salmon, N. & S. Soames, eds. Propositions and
Attitudes.
P. Loptson, 103:Sep90-377
Salmon, V. & E. Burness, eds. A Reader in the
Language of Shakespearean Drama.*
N.F. Blake, 156(ShJW):Jahrbuch1989-372
R. McDonald, 570(SQ):Fall89-360
H. Suhamy, 189(EA):Oct-Dec89-469
A. Ward, 447(N&Q):Jun89-234
Salomies, O. Die römischen Vornamen.
A.R. Birley, 123:Vol39No1-93
Salomon, R. - see Bhaṭṭa, N.
Salomon, R.B. Desperate Storytelling.
P. Merivale, 149(CLS):Vol26No2-179
K.Z. Moore, 295(JML):Fall88/Winter89-
251
C. Ross, 395(MFS):Summer89-295
Salomon-Bayet, C., ed. Pasteur et la révolu-
tion pastorienne.
A. Pichot, 192(EP):Jul-Dec89-552
Salrach, J.M. Historia de Catalunya, 2.
T.N. Bisson, 589:Jul89-764

Salt, H. The Savour of Salt. (G. & W. Hendrick, eds)
P. Singer, 453(NYRB):15Feb90−41
Salter, E. English and International. (D. Pearsall & N. Zeeman, eds)
M. Camille, 90:Nov89−781
Salter, J. Dusk and Other Stories.*
F. Baveystock, 617(TLS):25−31May90−558
Salter, L., with E. Levy & W. Leiss. Mandated Science.
A. Flores, 103:Sep90−381
Salter, M.J. Unfinished Painting.
M. Boruch, 29(APR):Nov/Dec89−21
J.F. Cotter, 249(HudR):Autumn89−518
D. Lehman, 385(MQR):Winter90−140
Salter, R. Hannah.
H. Murray, 102(CanL):Winter88−143
Saltini, V. Le Livre de Li Po.
G. Goffette, 450(NRF):Nov89−123
Salvador, A.G. − see under Gonzalez Salvador, A.
"Luis Salvador Carmona en Valladolid."
M. Estella, 48:Jan−Mar89−100
Salvador Martínez, H. − see Hernández de Villaumbrales, P.
Salvador Miguel, N., ed. Cancionero de Estúñiga.
S.G. Armistead, 240(HR):Summer89−368
C. Gariano, 238:May89−298
J. Whetnall, 402(MLR):Apr90−467
Salvaggio, R. Enlightened Absence.
R. Janes, 566:Spring90−193
Salvatore, A.T. Greene and Kierkegaard.
H−P. Breuer, 395(MFS):Summer89−337
di Salvo, T.J. El arte cuentistico de Vicente Blasco Ibáñez.
R. Landeira, 238:Sep89−547
Salwak, D., ed. Philip Larkin.
J. Whitworth, 493:Winter89/90−62
639(VQR):Spring89−66
Salwak, D. − see Amis, K.
Salwen, P. Upper West Side Story.
R. Siegel, 441:25Feb90−25
Salzano, E. − see "An Atlas of Venice"
Salzberg, J., ed. Critical Essays on Bernard Malamud.
B. Lyons, 573(SSF):Summer88−330
S.P., 295(JML):Fall88/Winter89−379
D. Walden, 587(SAF):Spring89−120
Salzman, J. & others, eds. The Cambridge Handbook of American Literature.*
L.K. Barnett, 677(YES):Vol20−228
Sambrook, J. − see Thomson, J.
Sammells, N. Tom Stoppard.
J.S. Dickey, 615(TJ):May89−266
K.E. Kelly, 130:Summer89−193
Sammons, J.L. Wilhelm Raabe.*
J.S. Chew, 222(GR):Fall89−183
H.S. Daemmrich, 301(JEGP):Jan89−79
Sammons, J.T. Beyond the Ring.
M. Oriard, 639(VQR):Summer89−540
Sampford, C. The Disorder of Law.
A. Altman, 103:May90−198
Sampson, A. The Midas Touch.
A.J. Sherman, 617(TLS):19−25Jan90−69
Sampson, G. Writing Systems.
E.P. Hamp, 269(IJAL):Jul89−384
W.C. Watt, 567:Vol75No3/4−279
Samson, J., ed. Chopin Studies.
V.K. Agawu, 410(M&L):Nov89−556
J.B.J., 412:May89−142
[continued]

[continuing]
H. Krebs, 308:Fall89−429
R.L. Todd, 415:May89−281
Samson, J. The Music of Chopin.
C. Schachter, 411:Mar/Jul89−187
Samson, J., A. Carpentier & others. Actes.
T. Goldie, 102(CanL):Winter88−128
Samuel, A.E. The Promise of the West.*
É. des Places, 555:Vol62Fasc2−351
Samuels, A. The Plural Psyche.
S. Wilson, 617(TLS):19−25Jan90−54
Samuels, E., with J.N. Samuels. Bernard Berenson: The Making of a Legend.*
D. Garstang, 39:Feb89−135
M. Goldstein, 569(SR):Spring89−xxxiv
Sanborn, M. Mark Twain: The Bachelor Years.
D. Walton, 441:22Apr90−25
Sánchez, A.E.P. − see under Pérez Sánchez, A.E.
Sánchez, A.E.P. & E.A. Sayre − see under Pérez Sánchez, A.E. & E.A. Sayre
Sánchez, J.F. − see under Fernández Sánchez, J.
Sánchez, J.G. − see under García Sánchez, J.
Sánchez, L.R. La importancia de llamarse Daniel Santos.
A. Figueroa, 711(RHM):Dec89−197
Sanchez−Eppler, B. Habits of Poetry; Habits of Resurrection.*
T. Kapcia, 86(BHS):Oct89−395
Sand, G. Correspondance. (Vol 21) (G. Lubin, ed)
L.J. Austin, 208(FS):Jan89−97
Sand, G. Elle et Lui. (T. Bodin, ed)
J. Gaulmier, 535(RHL):Jan−Feb89−127
Sand, G. Lélia. (B. Didier, ed)
F. Massardier−Kenney, 446(NCFS):Fall−Winter89/90−252
Sand, G. Nanon. (N. Mozet, ed)
F. Massardier−Kenney, 207(FR):Dec89−378
Sandbank, S. After Kafka.
K. Fickert, 268(IFR):Winter90−48
Sandel, C. Selected Short Stories. (B. Wilson, ed & trans) The Silken Thread. (E. Rokkan, ed & trans)
M. Wells, 562(Scan):May89−104
Sandel, M.J. Liberalism and the Limits of Justice.
J−P. Dupuy, 98:Jun−Jul89−542
Sander, R. The Trinidad Awakening.
B. King, 538(RAL):Summer89−313
Sanders, C.R. & others − see Carlyle, T. & J.W.
Sanders, D. Clover.
J. Sullivan, 441:20May90−30
Sanders, H. Das Subjekt der Moderne.
P. Vandevelde, 356(LR):Nov89−329
Sanders, J.B. La Correspondance d'André Antoine.*
W. Asholt, 547(RF):Band101Heft2/3−347
J. Robichez, 535(RHL):Jul−Aug89−743
Sanders, J.B. − see Zola, E.
Sanders, L.C. The Development of Black Theater in America.
M.B. Wilkerson, 34:Jan90−41
P.M. Yancy, 27(AL):Mar89−134
T. Youngs, 397(MD):Sep89−458
Sanders, L.J. Dionysius I of Syracuse and Greek Tyranny.
D. Konstan, 124:Sep−Oct89−70
R.G. Lewis, 123:Vol39No2−285

Sanders, W. Gutes Deutsch – besseres Deutsch.
R.M.G. Nickisch, 301(JEGP):Apr89–281
Sanders, W. "The Winter's Tale."*
S. Billington, 610:Spring89–87
J. Rees, 541(RES):Nov89–554
K. Tetzeli von Rosador, 156(ShJW):Jahrbuch1989–357
M. Willems, 189(EA):Oct–Dec89–470
Sandhöfer-Sixel, J. Modalität und gesprochene Sprache.
W.V. Davies, 402(MLR):Apr90–487
Sandiford, K.A. Measuring the Moment.
P. Edwards, 538(RAL):Fall89–568
Sandler, L.F. Gothic Manuscripts 1285–1385.*
M. Camille, 54:Mar89–134
Sandler, R. – see Frye, N.
Sandler, S. Distant Pleasures.
P.G. Reeve, 580(SCR):Fall90–188
Sandon, H. & J. Grainger's Worcester Porcelain.
T. Hughes, 324:Jun90–505
Sandor, M. A Night of Music.
R. Minkoff, 441:21Jan90–20
Sands, M. The Eighteenth-Century Pleasure Gardens of Marylebone 1737–1777.
P. Borsay, 83:Autumn89–211
P. Ranger, 447(N&Q):Jun89–243
P. Ranger, 611(TN):Vol43No1–38
Sandstrom, A R & P E. Traditional Papermaking and Paper Cult Figures of Mexico.
E. Socolov, 292(JAF):Jul–Sep89–355
Sandström, S. Anchorage of Imagination.
M.R. Lagerlöf, 341:Vol58No1–42
van der Sandt, R.A. Context and Presupposition.
R. Blutner, 682(ZPSK):Band42Heft4–549
N. Burton-Roberts, 297(JL):Sep89–437
Sandulescu, C.G. The Language of the Devil.
P. Van Caspel, 395(MFS):Summer89–328
Sandweiss, M.A. Laura Gilpin.
J. Loughery, 662:Fall89/Winter90–51
Sanford, L.T. Strong at the Broken Places.
M. Sandmaier, 441:9Sep90–34
Sanga, G. – see Jaberg, K. & J. Jud
Sangsue, D. Le Récit excentrique *
H.U. York, 210(FrF):Jan89–104
Sani, B. Rosalba Carriera.*
F. Russell, 90:Dec89–857
Sankoff, D., ed. Diversity and Diachrony.
S. Clarke, 320(CJL):Mar89–97
Sankovitch, T.A. French Women Writers and the Book.
R.D. Cottrell, 210(FrF):May89–251
P.M. Gathercole, 207(FR):Apr90–865
A.R. Larsen, 188(ECr):Summer89–95
Sannia Nowé, L. – see Maffei, S.
de San Pedro, D. "Càrcer d'amor," "Carcer d'amore."* (V. Minervini & M.L. Indini, eds)
J.T. Snow, 589:Jul89–744
de San Pedro, D. Diego de San Pedro's "Cárcel de Amor."* (I.A. Corfis, ed)
J.J. Gwara, 382(MAE):1989/2–334
O.T. Impey, 240(HR):Summer89–371
C. Parrilla García, 304(JHP):Winter90–187
B. Schmid, 547(RF):Band101Heft2/3–364
D.S. Severin, 86(BHS):Oct89–375
de San Pedro, D. Diego de San Pedro's "Tractado de amores de Arnalte y Lucenda."* (I.A. Corfis, ed)
O.T. Impey, 545(RPh):May90–632

Sansone, D. Greek Athletics and the Genesis of Sport.
B.K. Gold, 124:Jul–Aug90–542
Santas, G. Plato and Freud.
C. Gill, 123:Vol39No2–255
Santato, G. Alfieri e Voltaire.
A. Fabrizi, 228(GSLI):Vol166fasc535–462
Santayana, G. Persons and Places.* (W.G. Holzberger & H.J. Saatkamp, Jr., eds)
D.T.O., 295(JML):Fall88/Winter89–403
Santayana, G. The Sense of Beauty. (W.G. Holzberger & H.J. Saatkamp, Jr., eds)
W.E. Arnett, 619:Fall89–538
Santema, A. Literatuur en Kennis.
M. den Buurman, 204(FdL):Sep89–228
Marqués de Santillana. Comedieta de Ponça. (M.P.A. Kerkhof, ed)
V.A. Burrus, 240(HR):Winter89–84
Santirocco, M.S. Unity and Design in Horace's "Odes."*
A.J. Woodman, 123:Vol39No2–208
Santner, E.L. Friedrich Hölderlin.*
A.A. Kuzniar, 222(GR):Spring89–79
Santoro, M. Ariosto e il Rinascimento.
D. Robey, 617(TLS):5–11Jan90–16
Santos, R., ed. And We Sold the Rain.
E. Echevarria, 573(SSF):Summer89–359
D. Unger, 441:7Jan90–16
Santos, S. The Southern Reaches.
L. Rosenberg, 441:6May90–32
R. Smith, 344:Winter90–213
L. Upton, 160(UDQ):Summer90–124
"The Sanuto Sixteenth-Century Venetian Globe Cores."
H. Kelsey, 250(HLQ):Spring89–308
Saperstein, M. Moments of Crisis in Jewish-Christian Relations.
J. Sacks, 617(TLS):20–26Apr90–424
Sapia, Y. Valentino's Hair.
C.M. Fowler, 36:Summer89–115
Sapir, B. – see Dan, L.O.
Sapontzis, S.F. Morals, Reasons, and Animals.
R.G. Frey, 185:Oct89–191
"Sappho of Lesbos: The Poems." (T. Duquesne, trans)
T. Moi, 617(TLS):31Aug–6Sep90–919
Sarabianov, D.V. Russian Art.
J. Milner, 617(TLS):31Aug–6Sep90–919
S.F. Starr, 441:22Jul90–13
Sarah, R. Becoming Light.*
R.J. Merrett, 102(CanL):Autumn-Winter89–223
Sarduy, S. Maitreya.
S. Moore, 532(RCF):Summer89–242
Sargent, M. & J. Hogg, eds. The "Chartae" of the Carthusian General Chapter, Paris, Bibliothèque Nationale Ms. Latin 10888. (Pt 2)
R.B. Marks, 589:Jan89–214
Sarner, M., S.A. Schane & T.D. Terrell. Cahier d'exercices.
K. Jansma, 207(FR):Feb90–584
Saroyan, W. Madness in the Family.* (L. Hamalian, ed)
W. Buchanan, 573(SSF):Summer89–362
Sarraute, N. You Don't Love Yourself.
G. Danto, 441:18Nov90–7
Sarriá, F.G. – see under García Sarriá, F.
Sarton, M. The Education of Harriet Hatfield.*
V. Rounding, 617(TLS):9–15Mar90–258
Sarton, M. The Silence Now.
639(VQR):Summer89–99

Sartre, J–P. The Family Idiot. (Vol 3)
R. Huss, 617(TLS):2–8Mar90–231
Sartre, J–P. Huis clos. (K. Gore, ed)
T. Keefe, 402(MLR):Apr90–460
W. Redfern, 208(FS):Jul89–358
Sartre, J–P. Mallarmé, or the Poet of Noth-
ingness.*
P. Dayan, 208(FS):Oct89–480
D. Schier, 569(SR):Winter89–xii
Sartre, J–P. Vérité et existence. (A. Elkaïm-
Sartre, ed)
R. Goldthorpe, 617(TLS):14–20Dec90–
1347
Sartre, J–P. What Is Literature? and Other
Essays.
W. Fowlie, 569(SR):Summer89–lxxx
di Sarzana, C.F. – see under Faraggiana di
Sarzana, C.
Sasse, G. Die aufgeklärte Familie.
D. Jonnes, 133:Band22Heft3/4–326
S.D. Martinson, 221(GQ):Spring89–259
Sassoon, B. Fantasies.
K. Olson, 441:3Jun90–22
Sassoon, D. Contemporary Italy.
G. Bedani, 278(IS):Vol43–186
Sassower, R. Philosophy of Economics.
L.A. Boland, 488:Jun89–231
Sastre, A. La taberna fantástica. (M. de
Paco, ed)
J.E. Lyon, 86(BHS):Apr89–190
Sather, L.B., comp. Norway.*
S. Lyngstad, 562(Scan):May89–114
Sather, L.B. & A. Swanson. Sweden.
K. Brookfield, 562(Scan):May89–117
Satō Seizaburō & Matsuzaki Tetsuhisa. Jimintō
seiken.
G.D. Allinson, 293(JASt):May89–324
Satoko Kizaki. The Phoenix Tree.
G. Johnson, 441:26Aug90–14
Sattelmeyer, R. Thoreau's Reading.
R. Thomas, 27(AL):Oct89–476
Satter, R. Doing Justice.
P–L. Adams, 61:Mar90–115
C.E. Rinzler, 441:18Mar90–10
Satterthwait, W. At Ease with the Dead.
M. Stasio, 441:3Jun90–32
Satterthwait, W. Miss Lizzie.*
S. Altinel, 617(TLS):14–20Sep90–970
Saul, J. Heron and Quin.
P. Baker, 617(TLS):16–22Feb90–181
Saul, N. Scenes from Provincial Life.
M. Altschul, 589:Jan89–215
Saulnier, L. & N. Stratford. La Sculpture
oubliée de Vézelay.
F. Niehoff, 683:Band52Heft3–426
Saumarez Smith, C. The Building of Castle
Howard.
K. Downes, 617(TLS):30Mar–5Apr90–349
Saunders, A. The Sixteenth-Century French
Emblem Book.*
A. Adams, 402(MLR):Jul90–725
D.G. Coleman, 557:Jun89–227
D. Russell, 551(RenQ):Summer89–342
Saunders, R.H. & E.G. Miles. American Colo-
nial Portraits, 1700–1776.*
M.M. Lovell, 658:Spring89–69
Saunders, T.J. – see Plato
Sauter, H. & E. Loos – see d'Holbach, P.T.
Savage, C.C. Architecture of the Private
Streets of St. Louis.
A. Miller, 576:Mar89–93

Savage, H., Jr. & E.J. André and François
André Michaux.
N.J.H. Smith, 77:Winter89–67
Savan, B. Science under Siege.
I. Winchester, 627(UTQ):Fall89–232
Savard, M. Le Sourire des chefs.*
B. Belyea, 102(CanL):Autumn–Winter89–
175
Savel'ev, S.N. Ideinoe bankrotstvo bogoiska-
tel'stva v Rossii v nachale XX veka.
B.G. Rosenthal, 550(RusR):Apr89–194
Savignon, S.J. & M.S. Berns, eds. Initiatives
in Communicative Language Teaching.
T.L. Ballman, 399(MLJ):Summer89–206
Savile, A. Aesthetic Reconstructions.*
S. Ross, 103:Sep90–383
C. Wilde, 290(JAAC):Fall89–379
Savile, G. The Works of George Savile, Mar-
quis of Halifax. (M.N. Brown, ed)
P. Rogers, 617(TLS):30Mar–5Apr90–349
Saville, J. 1848.
B.S. Millard, 637(VS):Autumn89–179
Savinio, A. Childhood of Nivasio Dolcemare.*
(French title: Enfance de Nivasio Dolce-
mare.)
S. Basch, 450(NRF):Sep89–108
D. Day, 577(SHR):Fall89–386
G. Kearns, 249(HudR):Summer89–343
Savitzkaya, E. Sang de chien.
F. Mary, 450(NRF):Jul–Aug89–196
Savoca, g., comp. Concordanza del "Poema
paradisiaco" di Gabriele D'Annunzio.
J.R. Woodhouse, 402(MLR):Oct90–996
Savoca, G. & A. D'Aquino, comps. Concor-
danza della "Chimera" di Gabriele D'An-
nunzio.
J.R. Woodhouse, 402(MLR):Oct90–996
Savran, D. In Their Own Words.
P.C. Kolin, 397(MD):Jun89–327
Savran, G.W. Telling and Retelling.
A. Bach, 508:Sep89–264
Sawatsky, J. The Insiders.
H.L. Leung, 529(QQ):Summer89–535
Sawicki, L. Verb-Valency in Contemporary
Polish.
W.R. Schmalstieg, 215(GL):Vol29No1–76
Sawyer, C.H. The J. Alfred Prufrock Murders.
G.S. Winchell, 580(SCR):Fall89–143
Sawyer, P., ed. Domesday Book.
W.E. Kapelle, 589:Jul89–620
Sawyer, P. Ruskin's Poetic Argument.
J. Loesberg, 506(PSt):May87–119
Sawyer, W., K. Watson & A. Adams, eds. Eng-
lish Teaching from A to Z.
R.L. Houghton, 97(CQ):Vol18No4–413
Sawyer-Lauçanno, C. An Invisible Specta-
tor.*
S. Gray, 364:Feb/Mar90–141
S.E. Olson, 42(AR):Fall89–496
Sax, B. The Frog King.
A. Wawn, 617(TLS):14–20Dec90–1361
Sax, B. The Romantic Heritage of Marxism.
J. Rosellini, 406:Spring89–107
Saxby, T.J. The Quest for the New Jerusalem.
E.G.E. van der Wall, 319:Oct90–617
Saxon, A.H. P.T. Barnum.*
M.G. Butler, 441:21Jan90–21
Sayer, P. Howling at the Moon.
M. Casserley, 617(TLS):23Feb–1Mar90–
203
Sayre, H.M. The Object of Performance.
S. Hiller, 617(TLS):2–8Feb90–127

Sayre—McCord, G., ed. Essays on Moral Realism.*
    M.T., 185:Jul90–906
Scaglione, A.D. The Liberal Arts and the Jesuit College System.
    A.L. Martin, 276:Autumn89–369
Scalapino, R.A. & D. Kim, eds. Asian Communism.
    W.R. Heaton, 293(JASt):Nov89–810
Scammell, W. Eldorado.*
    L. Sail, 565:Summer89–75
Scamp, J. Photios historien des lettres.
    E. des Places, 555:Vol62Fasc1–156
Scanlan, J.P. – see Gershenzon, M.O.
Scanlan, M. Traces of Another Time.
    E. Svarny, 617(TLS):21–27Sep90–1006
Scanlon, T.F. Spes frustrata.
    J. Ginsburg, 124:Jan–Feb90–248
    J. Korpanty, 229:Band61Heft5–438
    G.M. Paul, 123:Vol39No2–233
Scarbrough, G. Invitation to Kim.
    E. Francisco, 598(SoR):Autumn90–920
Scarce, R. Eco-Warriors.
    G. Maranto, 441:25Nov90–14
Scardigli, B., with P. Delbianco – see di Damasco, N.
Scarisbrick, D., ed. Antique Jewellery and Watch Prices.
    J. Stancliffe, 39:Feb89–140
Scarisbrick, D. & others. Jewellery.
    G.S., 324:Dec89–72
Scarpat Bellincioni, M. Studi Senecani e altri scritti.
    J–M. Andre, 555:Vol62Fasc2–072
Scarron, P. Le Virgile travesti. (J. Serroy, ed)
    E. Woodrough, 402(MLR):Oct90–954
Scarry, E., ed. Literature and the Body.
    A.C. Vila, 400(MLN):Sep89–927
    R.R. Warhol, 478(P&L):Oct89–397
Scatton, E.A. – see Velcheva, B.
Schade, J.A. The Selected Poems of Jens August Schade. (A. Taylor, ed & trans)
    P. Houe, 563(SS):Winter89–91
Schade, R.E. Studies in Early German Comedy, 1500–1650.
    J.W. Rbst, 221(GQ):Spring89–250
Schade, R.E. – see "Lessing Yearbook"
Schaeder, B. Germanistische Lexikographie.
    D. Herberg, 682(ZPSK):Band42Heft1–122
Schaefer, A. Die Schopenhauer-Welt.
    M. Hielscher, 489(PJGG):Band96Heft1–198
Schaefer, F. The Scapeweed Goat.*
    C. Reynolds, 649(WAL):Feb90–393
Schaeffer, R. Warpaths.
    J.L. Gaddis, 61:Mar90–111
Schaeffner, A., with A. Coeuroy. Le jazz.
    A.J.M.P., 91:Vol17–189
Schaeken, J. Die Kiever Blätter.* (A.A. Barentsen, B.M. Groen & R. Sprenger, eds)
    H. Birnbaum, 279:Vol35/36–340
Schäfer, J. Early Modern English Lexicography.
    N. Osselton, 617(TLS):9–15Nov90–1201
Schäfer, L. Karl R. Popper.
    G. Engel, 679:Band20Heft2–380
Schaffer, D., ed. Two Centuries of American Planning.
    A. Saint, 46:Feb89–8
Schaffer, K. Women and the Bush.
    S. Sheridan, 71(ALS):May89–118
Schaill, W.S. Cabot Station.
    N. Callendar, 441:23Dec90–15

Schak, D.C. A Chinese Beggars' Den.
    R.P. Weller, 293(JASt):Feb89–146
Schaller, H.W. Bulgaristik in Deutschland.
    T. Henninger, 575(SEER):Apr89–259
Schaller, M. Douglas MacArthur.*
    M.A. Barnhart, 293(JASt):Nov89–811
Schama, S. The Embarrassment of Riches.*
    G. Watson, 473(PR):Vol56No3–507
Schanzer, G.O. The Persistence of Human Passions.*
    J. King, 86(BHS):Jan89–114
Schapelhouman, M. Netherlandish Drawings circa 1600 in the Rijksmuseum.
    M. Royalton-Kisch, 90:Jun89–428
Scharfman, R.L. Engagement and the Language of the Subject in the Poetry of Aimé Césaire.
    J.M. Dash, 188(ECr):Summer89–93
    G.N. Onyeoziri-Miller, 529(QQ):Spring89–144
Scharfstein, B–A. Of Birds, Beasts, and Other Artists.
    A. Berleant, 103:Jan90–37
Scharlemann, R. Inscriptions and Reflections.
    J. Harold, 543:Jun90–882
Schärmeli, Y. Königsbrauch und Dreikönigsspiele im welschen Teil des Kantons Freiburg.
    K. Schoell, 547(RF):Band101Heft2/3–323
Schatz, T. The Genius of the System.*
    E. Buscombe, 707:Summer89–212
Schatzberg, W., R.A. Waite & J.K. Johnson, eds. The Relations of Literature and Science.*
    S. Soupel, 189(EA):Jul–Sep89–367
Schavelzon, I. La Fin des choses.
    J. Taylor, 207(FR):Feb90–582
Schechner, R. Performance Theory.
    T. Whittock, 89(BJA):Autumn89–378
Schecter, J.L., with V.V. Luchkov – see Khrushchev, N.S.
Schefer, J.L. Le Greco ou l'éveil des ressemblances.
    A. Minazzoli, 98:Mar80–174
Schoffor, C. Roman Cinerary Urns in Stockholm Collections.
    G. Davies, 010:Vol70–000
Schefold, K. & F. Jung. Die Urkönige, Perseus, Bellerophon, Herakles und Theseus in der klassischen und hellenistischen Kunst.
    S. Woodford, 303(JoHS):Vol109–268
Scheibe, S. & others. Vom Umgang mit Editionen.
    P. Goldammer, 654(WB):4/1989–689
Scheick, W.J. – see Mather, I. & C.
Scheick, W.J. & J.R. Cox, eds. H.G. Wells.
    J. Huntington, 177(ELT):Vol32No3–323
    R.M.P., 561(SFS):Jul89–243
Scheindlin, R.P. Wine, Women, and Death.
    S.A. Bonebakker, 318(JAOS):Oct–Dec88–673
Schele, L. & D. Freidel. A Forest of Kings.
    L.E. Beattie, 441:16Dec90–18
Scheler, M., ed. Berliner Anglistik in Vergangenheit und Gegenwart 1810–1985.
    H. Gneuss, 38:Band107Heft1/2–93
    G. Haenicke, 72:Band226Heft1–231
Schell, J. History in Sherman Park.
    639(VQR):Winter89–25
Schell, O. Discos and Democracy.*
    B. Stavis, 293(JASt):Feb89–148

Schelling, F.W. Bruno ou Du principe divin et naturel des choses. (J. Rivelaygue, ed)
P. David, 192(EP):Apr–Jun89–258
Schelling, F.W.J. The Philosophy of Art.
J.P. Lawrence, 103:May90–201
Scheman, L.R., ed. The Alliance for Progress.
M.C. Needler, 263(RIB):Vol39No2–212
Schenck, M.J.S. The Fabliaux.*
N.J. Lacy, 210(FrF):Jan89–91
R.S. Sturges, 345(KRQ):Nov89–486
J. Tattersall, 208(FS):Apr89–197
Schenda, R., with H. ten Doornkaat. Sagenerzähler und Sagensammler der Schweiz.
U. Brunold-Bigler, 196:Band30Heft3/4–349
Schenker, H. Counterpoint.* (J. Rothgeb, ed)
W. Drabkin, 411:Mar/Jul89–197
H. Federhofer, 417:Jul–Sep89–287
Scheps, W. & J.A. Looney. Middle Scots Poets.*
K. Bitterling, 38:Band107Heft1/2–214
Scher, S.P., ed. Literatur und Musik.
G. Flaherty, 678(YCGL):No36–194
Scherer, C. & J. Le Théâtre classique.*
J. Dubu, 535(RHL):Jul–Aug89–715
Scherer, J. Dramaturgies d'Oedipe.*
M. Anderson, 610:Summer89–186
Scherer, J.L., ed. USSR. (Vol 11, 1987)
A. Brown, 575(SEER):Apr89–333
Scherf, W. Die Herausforderung des Dämons.
L. Bluhm, 196:Band30Heft3/4–352
Scherfig, H. Stolen Spring.* The Missing Bureaucrat.
B.K. Horvath, 532(RCF):Summer89–239
Scherpe, K.R. & L. Winckler, eds. Frühe DDR-Literatur.
G. Müller-Waldeck, 654(WB):9/1989–1574
Scherr, B.P. Maxim Gorky.
A. Barratt, 402(MLR):Apr90–538
G. McVay, 575(SEER):Oct89–612
T. Yedlin, 558(RLJ):Spring-Fall89–284
Scherr, B.P. Russian Poetry.
R. Aizlewood, 575(SEER):Apr89–267
E. Klenin, 279:Vol35/36–366
D.S. Worth, 574(SEEJ):Fall89–448
Scheuring, H.L. Die Drachenfluss-Werft von Nanking.
R. Ptak, 318(JAOS):Jul–Sep88–508
Scheuringer, H. Sprachstabilität und Sprachvariabilität im nördlichen oberösterreichischen Innviertel und im angrenzenden Niederbayern.
J. Macha, 685(ZDL):3/1989–368
Scheurleer, P.L. & M.J. Klokke. Ancient Indonesian Bronzes.
L. de Guise, 60:Sep–Oct89–156
Schevill, M.B. Costume as Communication.*
W. Stanley, 203:Vol100No2–261
Schezen, R. Visions of Ancient America.
S. Coates, 441:26Aug90–15
Schiavone, A. Giuristi e nobili nella Roma repubblicana.
E. Rawson, 313:Vol79–193
D. Schanbacher, 229:Band61Heft3–212
Schibli, R. Die ältesten russischen Zeitungsübersetzungen (Vesti-Kuranty) 1600–1650.
F. Otten, 559:Vol13No3–330
Schicke, T. – see Hahn, H.
Schiebinger, L. The Mind Has No Sex?
C. Geertz, 453(NYRB):8Nov90–19
L. Hudson, 617(TLS):9–15Mar90–243

Schieffelin, B.B. & E. Ochs, eds. Language Socialization Across Cultures.
S. Romaine, 353:Vol27No6–1162
G.W. Shugar, 355(LSoc):Dec89–581
Schiendorfer, M., ed. mine sinne di sint mine.
J. Schulz-Grobert, 684(ZDA):Band118 Heft3–138
Schier, F. Deeper into Pictures.*
D. Raffman, 482(PhR):Oct89–576
Schiff, Z. & E. Ya'ari. Intifada. (I. Friedman, ed & trans)
R. Owen, 617(TLS):29Jun–5Jul90–687
M. Widlanski, 441:18Mar90–3
Schiffer, S. Remnants of Meaning.*
M.J. Cresswell, 353:Vol27No5–953
K. Sterelny, 393(Mind):Oct89–623
Schiffer, S. & S. Steele, eds. Cognition and Representation.
R.J. Bogdan, 103:Jan90–39
Schiffrin, D. Discourse Markers.
M. Owen, 297(JL):Mar89–255
Schildt, J. & others. Zum Sprachwandel in der deutschen Literatursprache des 16. Jahrhunderts.*
H. Penzl, 685(ZDL):2/1989–200
K-P. Wegera, 680(ZDP):Band108Heft1–138
Schillebeeckx, E. The Church With a Human Face.
R. Penaskovic, 577(SHR):Spring89–184
Schilling, B. Virtuose Klaviermusik des 19. Jahrhunderts am Beispiel von Charles Valentin Alkan (1813–1888).
W. Rathert, 417:Apr–Jun89–186
Schilling, J. Arnold von Lübeck.
H. Freytag, 680(ZDP):Band108Heft3–424
Schimmel, A. And Muhammad Is His Messenger.
M. Swartz, 318(JAOS):Jul–Sep88–492
Schindel, U., ed. Demosthenes.
S. Usher, 303(JoHS):Vol109–227
Schine, C. To the Birdhouse.
L. Smith, 441:20May90–15
P. Storace, 453(NYRB):16Aug90–22
442(NY):4Jun90–103
Schinkel, K.F. Collection of Architectural Designs Including Designs Which Have Been Executed and Objects Whose Execution was Intended.
J.S. Curl, 324:Apr90–377
Schipper, K. Comment on crée un lieu-saint local.
M. Detienne, 98:Apr89–211
Schirmacher, E. Stadtvorstellungen.
H-G. Lippert, 43:Band19Heft1–94
von Schirnding, A. Begegnungen mit Ernst Jünger.
M. Hulse, 617(TLS):10–16Aug90–842
Schlagel, R.H. From Myth to the Modern Mind. (Vol 1)
J. De Groot, 41:Fall89–319
Schlager, K., ed. Das Erbe deutscher Musik. (Vol 88)
H. Hucke, 417:Jan–Mar89–101
Schläpfer, R. & N. Bigler – see Hotzenköcherle, R.
Schlebecker, J.T. The Many Names of Country People.
E.D. Lawson, 424:Sep89–292
Schleberger, E. Die indische Götterwelt.
H. von Stietencron, 196:Band30Heft1/2–162
Schlee, G. Identities on the Move.
P. Spencer, 617(TLS):9–15Mar90–264

Schlegel, F. Kritische Friedrich-Schlegel-Ausgabe. (Section 3, Vol 24) (R. Immer-wahr, ed)
G. Heinrich, 654(WB):4/1989-682
Schlegel, J-L. - see Schmitt, C.
Schleier, E. - see Boskovits, M.
Schleiermacher, F.D.E. Herméneutique. (C. Berner, ed & trans)
R. Rochlitz, 98:Nov89-839
Schleifer, E. - see Vinaver, C.
Schleifer, R. A.J. Greimas and the Nature of Meaning.*
R. Harris, 541(RES):Nov89-541
S.E. Larsen, 567:Vol75No1/2-123
B. Readings, 223:Fall89-329
Schleifman, N. Undercover Agents in the Russian Revolutionary Movement.
A.E. Pogorelskin, 550(RusR):Oct89-421
Schlesier, K.H. The Wolves of Heaven.
J.A. Grim, 292(JAF):Jan-Mar89-118
Schlesinger, C. & J. Willoughby. The Thrill of the Grill.
R. Flaste, 441:10Jun90-12
Schlesinger, G.N. New Perspectives on Old-Time Religion.
M.J. Ferreira, 518:Jul89-187
Schless, H.H. Chaucer and Dante.
C.J. Watkin, 148:Winter86-96
Schlichtmann, M. - see Estudillo, J.M.
Schlobach, J., ed. Correspondances littér-aires inédites.*
R. Waldinger, 207(FR):Apr90-875
Schlobinski, P. Stadtsprache Berlin.*
H. Schmidt, 680(ZDP).Band40Heft4 664
de Schloezer, B., with M. Scriabine. Scriabin.*
C.J. Barnes, 402(MLR):Jul90-815
C. Emerson, 574(SEEJ):Summer89-316
A. Pople, 410(M&L):Feb89-127
G.R. Seaman, 575(SEER):Jan89-153
Schlosser, H.D. & H.D. Zimmermann, eds. Poetik.
O. Melin, 301(GQ):Fall80-511
Schlossstein, S. The End of the American Century.
J. Fallows, 453(NYRB):1Mar90-14
C.V. Prestowitz, Jr., 441:18Feb90-24
Schlueter, J. & J.K. Flanagan. Arthur Miller.*
T.P. Adler, 397(MD):Jun89-321
J.H. Lutterbie, 615(TJ):Dec89-567
Schmalstieg, W.R. A Lithuanian Historical Syntax.*
T.G. Fennell, 215(GL):Vol29No2-131
Schmeja, H. Interpretationen aus dem Rig-veda.
H. Falk, 259(IIJ):Oct89-287
J.S. Klein, 350:Mar90-207
Schmeling, M. Der labyrinthische Diskurs - Vom Mythos zum Erzählmodell.*
Y. Chevrel, 549(RLC):Apr-Jun89-278
G. Gillespie, 131(CL):Fall89-387
Schmid, B. Les "traducions valencianes" del "Blanquerna" (València 1521) i de la "Scala Dei" (Barcelona 1523).
A.M. Perrone Capano Compagna, 379(MedR):Apr89-158
Schmid, W., ed. Mythos in der Slawischen Moderne.
J.T. Baer, 574(SEEJ):Fall89-473
Schmid-Cadalbert, C. Der "Ortnit AW" als Brautwerbungsdichtung.*
W. Dinkelacker, 680(ZDP):Band108Heft1-103

Schmid-Cadalbert, C., ed. Das ritterliche Basel.
A. Classen, 597(SN):Vol61No2-240
Schmid-Cadalbert, C. - see Dieth, E.
Schmid-Kowarzik, W., ed. Objektivationen des Geistigen.
A. Bharati, 489(PJGG):Band96Heft1-220
Schmidgall, G. Shakespeare & Opera.
W. Weaver, 441:23Dec90-9
Schmidt, A. & N. Altwicker, eds. Max Hork-heimer heute.
A. Wüstehube, 687:Jan-Mar89-196
Schmidt, A. & W. Michels. Arno Schmidt: Der Briefwechsel mit Wilhelm Michels. (B. Rauschenbach, ed)
M.M. Schardt, 680(ZDP):Band108Heft2-306
Schmidt, A.V.C. The Clerkly Maker.*
M. Andrew, 677(YES):Vol20-229
T. Turville-Petre, 541(RES):Nov89-548
Schmidt, E.A. Zeit und Geschichte bei Aug-ustin.
F.G. Maier, 229:Band61Heft5-397
Schmidt, H. Maverick Marine.
P. Karsten, 106:Fall89-286
M. Slackman, 77:Spring89-154
Schmidt, H. Men and Powers.
G.A. Craig, 453(NYRB):18Jan90-28
B. Denitch, 441:8Apr90-28
R.J. Evans, 617(TLS):27Jul-2Aug90-796
Schmidt, H. Wörterbuchprobleme.*
S. Clausing, 133:Band22Heft1-97
Schmidt, H.J. The Rose Thieves.
J. Polshek, 441:10Dec90-10
Schmidt, H-P., with W. Lentz & S. Insler. Form and Meaning of Yasna 33.
H. Schmeja, 259(IIJ):Apr89-157
Schmidt, J. & T. Simon. Frontiers.*
E.U. Irving, 399(MLJ):Summer89-219
Schmidt, J.A. If There Are No More Heroes, There Are Heroines.
O. Carlin, 176:Vol16No30-330
L. Picciola, 535(RHL):Nov-Dec89-1054
Schmidt, L.E. Holy Fairs.
G.W.S. Barrow, 617(TLS):10-16Aug90-852
Schmidt, M. The Love of Strangers.*
D. Davie, 4:Winter89/Spring90-160
P. Gross, 493:Autumn89-65
S. O'Brien, 364:Feb/Mar90-111
Schmidt, M. Reading Modern Poetry.*
E. Longley, 493:Winter89/90-22
Schmidt, M. - see Mechthild von Magdeburg
Schmidt, M. - see Rudolf von Biberach
Schmidt, P. William Carlos Williams, the Arts, and Literary Tradition.*
T.H. Crawford, 27(AL):Dec89-720
639(VQR):Summer89-86
Schmidt-Biggemann, W. Theodizee und Tat-sachen.
W. Goetschel, 221(GQ):Spring89-235
Schmiedt, H. Karl May.
G.K. Hart, 221(GQ):Winter89-126
Schmits, G. Jean Pellerin.
V.D.L., 605(SC):15Jul90-410
Schmitt, C. Théologie politique. (J-L. Schle-gel, ed & trans)
H. Cronel, 450(NRF):Nov89-124
Schmitt, C.B., Q. Skinner & E. Kessler, eds. The Cambridge History of Renaissance Phi-losophy.
M.J.B. Allen, 551(RenQ):Autumn89-543
M.L. Colish, 319:Jan90-128

[continued]

Schmitt, C.B., Q. Skinner & E. Kessler, eds.
The Cambridge History of Renaissance Philosophy. [continuing]
S. Gaukroger, 63:Sep89–347
L. Panizza, 278(IS):Vol44–138
Schmitt, M.C. Peter Weiss, "Die Ästhetik des Widerstands."*
J.E. Michaels, 406:Spring89–138
Schmitt, P., ed. "Liber ordinis rerum" (Esse-Essencia-Glossar).
G.A.R. de Smet, 684(ZDA):Band118Heft1–24
Schmitz, D. Eden.
F. Chappell, 344:Summer90–168
T. Hoagland, 146:Winter89–138
Schmitz, F. Wittgenstein et la philosophie des mathématiques.
P. Engel, 542:Oct–Dec89–624
Schmitz, H-P. Fürstenau heute.
E. Emmerig, 416:Band4Heft3–279
Schmitz, W., ed. Max Frisch.
W. Paulsen, 564:Nov89–367
A.D. White, 680(ZDP):Band108Heft2–304
Schmitz, W. Wirtschaftliche Prosperität, soziale Integration und die Seebundpolitik Athens.
G. Audring, 229:Band61Heft7–633
Schnapp, J.T. The Transfiguration of History at the Center of Dante's "Paradise."*
P. Armour, 382(MAE):1989/1–179
W.A. Stephany, 589:Jan89–216
J. Took, 278(IS):Vol43–138
Schneebaum, T. Where the Spirits Dwell.
S. Pickering, 569(SR):Spring89–297
Schneewind, J.B. – see Lowe, V.
Schneider, E.W. American Earlier Black English.
W. Wolfram, 350:Mar90–121
Schneider, H. Der Musikverleger Heinrich Philipp Bossler, 1744–1812.
P.W. Jones, 410(M&L):May89–259
Schneider, H.J., ed. Deutsche Idyllentheorien im 18. Jahrhundert.
G. Finney, 221(GQ):Fall89–510
Schneider, K. Gotische Schriften in deutscher Sprache.* (Vol 1)
C.W. Edwards, 402(MLR):Jan90–239
Schneider, K. Sophia Lectures on "Beowulf."
R. Frank, 133:Band22Heft3/4–302
Schneider, L. Paradox and Society. (J. Weinstein, ed)
S.H. Daniel, 566:Autumn89–59
Schneider, L. – see Shakespeare, W.
Schneider, M. Cathedral of Birds.
I. McMillan, 493:Winter89/90–65
Schneider, M. Vengeance of the Victim.*
G.O. De Stefanis, 276:Summer89–240
Schneider, M.J. & I. Stern, eds. Modern Spanish and Portuguese Literatures.
W.W. Moseley, 399(MLJ):Autumn89–389
Schneider, M.W. Poetry in the Age of Democracy.
V.J. Emmett, Jr., 389(MQ):Autumn89–141
E.J. Higgins, 95(CLAJ):Dec89–229
J.J. Savory, 637(VS):Spring90–509
G.B. Tennyson, 445(NCF):Sep89–256
Schneider, N., ed. Georg Heym, 1887–1912.
M. Rogister, 402(MLR):Apr90–522
Schneider, P. Deutsche Ängste.
P. Carrier, 402(MLR):Oct90–1039
Schneider, P-P. Die "Denkbücher" Friedrich Heinrich Jacobis.*
D. Bell, 83:Autumn89–242

Schneider, R., ed. Die moralisch-belehrenden Artikel im altrussischen Sammelband Merilo pravednoe.
J. Reinhart, 688(ZSP):Band49Heft2–401
Schneider, S. The Art of Low-Calorie Cooking.
R. Flaste, 441:2Dec90–14
Schnell, R. Die Literatur der Bundesrepublik.*
K. Pezold, 654(WB):1/1989–145
Schnitzler, A. Arthur Schnitzler Tagebuch 1879–1892.* (W. Welzig & others, eds)
A. Obermayer, 564:Nov89–364
Schnyder, P. Pré-textes.
W. Gorgé, 602:Band20Heft1–138
Schodek, D.L. Landmarks in American Civil Engineering.*
R. Jay, 576:Jun89–198
Schodt, F.L. Inside the Robot Kingdom.
W. Kelly, 407(MN):Spring89–133
Schoeck, R.J. Erasmus Grandescens.
L.V.R., 568(SCN):Fall–Winter89–70
Schoeman, F., ed. Responsibility, Character and the Emotions.*
D. Carr, 518:Oct89–229
R.C. Roberts, 543:Dec89–421
Schoenbaum, S. William Shakespeare.
I. Boltz, 156(ShJW):Jahrbuch1989–384
Schoenberg, A. Preliminary Exercises in Counterpoint. (L. Stein, ed)
A.F.L.T., 412:May89–146
Schoenberg, H.O. A Mandate for Terror.
Y. Rabi, 390:Aug/Sep89–62
Schoeser, M. & C. Rufey. English And American Textiles from 1790 to the Present.
P. Byrom, 324:Mar90–299
B. Nevill, 617(TLS):30Mar–5Apr90–352
Schofer, P. & D. Rice. Autour de la littérature.*
M. McCluney, 399(MLJ):Summer89–229
Schofield, M.A. Eliza Haywood.
E. Hepple, 83:Autumn89–229
Scholem, B. & G. Mutter und Sohn im Briefwechsel 1917–1946. (I. Shedletzky & T. Sparr, eds)
J. Adler, 617(TLS):28Sep–4Oct90–1016
Scholem, G. Walter Benjamin.
G. McNamee, 456(NDQ):Spring89–190
Scholes, R. Protocols of Reading.
R.M. Adams, 453(NYRB):1Mar90–38
W. Steiner, 617(TLS):7–13Sep90–957
Scholes, R., N.R. Comley & G.L. Ulmer. Text Book.
K. Cope, 400(MLN):Dec89–1202
Schömbucher, E. Die Vāḍabalija in Andhra Pradesh und in Orissa–Aspekte der wirtschaftlichen und sozialen Organisation einer maritimen Gesellschaft.
S.B. Steever, 318(JAOS):Jan–Mar88–194
Schöne, A. Götterzeichen, Liebeszauber, Satanskult.
F. Amrine, 221(GQ):Winter89–117
Schöne, A., ed. Kontroversen, alte und neue.* (Vol 1)
F. Patocka, 685(ZDL):3/1989–339
Schöning, U. Complexity and Structure.
S.R. Mahaney, 316:Sep89–1106
Schönzeler, H-H. Furtwängler.
M. Tanner, 617(TLS):27Apr–3May90–453
Schoolfield, G.C. Elmer Diktonius.
V. Zuck, 563(SS):Winter89–85
Schopen, B. The Desert Look.
M. Stasio, 441:24Jun90–22

Schopenhauer, A. Philosophische Vorles-
ungen. (V. Spierling, ed)
R. Margreiter, 489(PJGG):Band96Heft1-
195
Schöpflin, G. & N. Wood, eds. In Search of
Central Europe.
G.M. Tamás, 617(TLS):10-16Aug90-843
Schopp, C. Alexander Dumas.*
639(VQR):Summer89-90
Schopp, C. - see Dumas, A.
Schor, N. Breaking the Chain.*
P.L. Caughie, 477(PLL):Summer88-317
Schor, N. Reading in Detail.*
C. Bernheimer, 188(ECr):Spring89-98
P.Z. Brand, 290(JAAC):Spring89-193
P.L. Caughie, 477(PLL):Summer88-317
Schor, S. The Great Letter E.
S. Stark, 441:25Feb90-24
Schott, M. Ben.
K. Ray, 441:15Jul90-18
Schott, R.M. Cognition and Eros.
R. Hahn, 103:Feb90-79
Schöttker, D. & W. Wunderlich, eds. Hermen
Bote.
V. Honemann, 196:Band30Heft1/2-166
Schouls, P.A. Descartes and the Enlighten-
ment.*
J. Cottingham, 103:Feb90-81
Schoultz, L. National Security and United
States Policy Toward Latin America.
D.G. Haglund, 639(QQ):Spring89-192
Schrader, B. & J. Schebera. The "Golden"
Twenties.
R. Salter, 221(GQ):Fall89-537
Schrader, S. Arriving At Work.
P. Glasser, 455:Sep89-69
Schraft, C. Instead of You.
J. Vandenburgh, 441:23Sep90-23
Schrag, C.O. Communicative Praxis and the
Space of Subjectivity.*
J.L. Marsh, 323:May89-180
Schram, S.R., ed. Foundations and Limits of
State Power in China.
R.R. Thompson, 293(JASt):Feb89-149
Schreiber, L.A. Midstream.
J. Smiley, 441:7Jan90-10
Schreiner, O. 1899.
B. Hickey, 538(RAL):Fall89-522
Schreiner, O. Olive Schreiner Letters.* (Vol
1) (R. Rive, ed)
L.S. Bergmann, 405(MP):May90-424
J.A. Berkman, 177(ELT):Vol32No2-226
C. Clayton, 402(MLR):Apr90-421
D. Driver, 538(RAL):Fall89-519
Schriber, M.S. Gender and the Writer's Imagi-
nation.*
L. Bartlett, 594:Summer89-223
A. Delbanco, 445(NCF):Jun89-112
S.F. Fishkin, 27(AL):Mar89-108
C. Goodman, 587(SAF):Spring89-121
Schrijvers, P.H. Eine medizinische Erklärung
der männlichen Homosexualität aus der
Antike.
J. Bremmer, 394:Vol42fasc1/2-234
Schröder, J. Gottfried Benn und die Deut-
schen.
M.W. Roche, 221(GQ):Summer89-411
Schröder, J. Lexikon deutscher Präposition-
en.*
G. Koss, 685(ZDL):3/1989-351
Schroder, T. The National Trust Book of Eng-
lish Domestic Silver 1500-1900.*
A.B.B., 90:May89-365

Schroder, T.B. The Gilbert Collection of Gold
and Silver.
J.K.D. Cooper, 39:Jun89-442
Schröder, W., ed. Wolfram Studien. (Vol 9)
M.E. Kalinke, 301(JEGP):Jul89-365
Schroeder, D.P. Haydn and the Enlighten-
ment.
J.H. Johnson, 617(TLS):30Nov-6Dec90-
1295
Schroeder, P.R. The Presence of the Past in
Modern American Drama.
M.G. Bower, 27(AL):Dec89-718
Schubert, A. Der Strukturgedanke in Hegels
"Wissenschaft der Logik."
E. Schadel, 489(PJGG):Band96Heft1-194
Schubert, K. Metataxis.
B. Sigurd, 596(SL):Vol42No2-181
Schubert, K., with D. Maxwell, eds. Interlin-
guistics.
P. Hopkins, 350:Dec90-883
Schueller, H.M. The Idea of Music.
L. Goehr, 290(JAAC):Spring89-188
Schuetz, M., ed. Architectural Practice in
Mexico City.
C. Bargellini, 576:Sep89-302
Schuhmacher, W.W. The Linguistic Aspect of
Thor Heyerdahl's Theory.
S.G. Thomason, 350:Mar90-208
Schuiskii, V. Vincenzo Brenna.
V. Antonow, 43:Band19Heft1-100
Schulberg, B. Love, Action, Laughter and
Other Sad Tales.
M. Buck, 441:4Feb90-10
Schulenburg, L. - see Jung, F.
Schüler, W. Grundlegungen der Mathematik in
tranzendentaler Kritik.
P. Schroeder-Heister, 316:Jun89-622
Schuller, W. Frauen in der römischen
Geschichte.*
S. Dixon, 487:Spring89-84
Schulman, G. Marianne Moore.*
R.W.B., 295(JML):Fall88/Winter89-386
Schulman, S. After Delores.
R. Kaveney, 617(TLS):27Apr-3May90-456
Schulman, S. People in Trouble.
C. Bram, 441:8Jul90-16
Schultze, B., ed. Die literarische Überset-
zung.
Y. Chevrel, 549(RLC):Apr-Jun89-259
S. Greif, 680(ZDP):Band108Heft2-310
Schulz, B. Letters and Drawings of Bruno
Schulz.* (J. Ficowski, ed)
I. Stavans, 287:May-Jun89-29
42(AR):Winter89-111
Schulz, P.S. America the Beautiful Cookbook.
R. Flaste, 441:2Dec90-14
Schulz, R. Puškin i Kazot/Pouchkine et Caz-
otte.
R-D. Keil, 52:Band24Heft1-100
Schulze, B., ed. Die literarische Übersetzung.
F. Apel, 52:Band24Heft2-210
Schulze-Busacker, E. Proverbes et expres-
sions proverbiales dans la littérature nar-
rative du moyen âge français.
M. Coppens d'Eeckenbrugge, 356(LR):Feb-
May89-114
L. Morini, 379(MedR):Aug89-283
Schumacher, H., ed. Verben in Feldern.
B. Schaeder, 257(IRAL):May89-159
Schumann, C. & R. Briefwechsel. (Vol 2) (E.
Weissweiler, with S. Ludwig, eds)
M. Struck, 417:Jul-Sep89-291

Schuon, F. The Essential Writings of Frithjof Schuon. (S.H. Nasr, ed)
   H. Smith, 485(PE&W):Oct89-497
Schürer, E. The History of the Jewish People in the Age of Jesus Christ (175 B.C. – A.D. 135).* (Vol 3) (2nd ed) (G. Vermes, F. Millar & M. Goodman, eds)
   B. Isaac, 313:Vol79-244
Schürmann, R. Heidegger on Being and Acting.
   R. Gasché, 153:Fall-Winter89-101
Schürmann, R., ed. The Public Realm.
   P. Trotignon, 542:Oct-Dec89-645
   D.Z., 185:Jan90-446
Schurz, G., ed. Erklären und Verstehen in der Wissenschaft.
   R. Stranzinger, 679:Band20Heft2-387
Schuster-Šewc, H. Historisch-etymologisches Wörterbuch der ober- und niedersorbischen Sprache. (Vol 3)
   G. Stone, 575(SEER):Oct89-602
Schutz, B.M. The Things We Do For Love.
   639(VQR):Summer89-93
Schütz, E. Romane der Weimarer Republik.*
   E. Schürer, 222(GR):Spring89-84
"Schütz Jahrbuch 7/8." (W. Breig, with others, eds)
   K. Huber, 417:Jul-Sep89-276
Schutzner, S. Medieval and Renaissance Manuscript Books in the Library of Congress. (Vol 1)
   J. Griffiths, 617(TLS):15-21Jun90-650
Schuyler, J. Selected Poems.*
   L. Gregerson, 491:Feb90-351
   J. Loose, 617(TLS):22-28Jun90-673
   R. Wasserman, 29(APR):Nov/Dec89-5
Schüz, M. Die Einheit des Wirklichen.
   W. Farr, 489(PJGG):Band96Heft1-222
Schwaderer, R. Idillio campestre.
   E. Kanduth, 547(RF):Band101Heft1-145
Schwalbe, M.L. The Psychosocial Consequences of Natural and Alienated Labor.
   L.A. Scaff, 488:Jun89-229
Schwartz, B. The Ascent of Pragmatism.
   S.L. Mayer, 441:21Jan90-21
Schwartz, B. First Principles, Second Thoughts.
   E.J. Peters, 529(QQ):Spring89-203
Schwartz, B. The New Right and the Constitution.
   K.M. Sullivan, 441:28Oct90-30
Schwartz, B. George Washington.
   T. Wortham, 445(NCF):Dec89-421
Schwartz, B.F. The Civil Works Administration, 1933-1934.
   J. Braeman, 106:Summer89-41
Schwartz, G. & M.J. Bok. Pieter Saenredam.
   A. Saint, 617(TLS):5-11Oct90-1070
Schwartz, H. Century's End.
   442(NY):5Mar90-107
Schwartz, H. Lilith's Cave.
   R. Di Antonio, 390:Jan89-63
   42(AR):Summer89-372
Schwartz, J. Jewish Settlement in Judea after the Bar-Kochba War until the Arab Conquest 135 C.E.-640 C.E.
   S.J.D. Cohen, 318(JAOS):Apr-Jun88-311
Schwartz, J. & others. Papyrus grecs de la Bibliothèque nationale et universitaire de Strasbourg. (Nos. 661-680 & 821-840)
   J.D. Thomas, 229:Band61Heft8-737

Schwartz, J. & others. Papyrus grecs de la Bibliothèque nationale et unversitaire de Strasbourg. (Nos. 841-860)
   J.D. Thomas, 229:Band61Heft3-263
Schwartz, J.L. & C.L. Schlundt. French Court Dance and Dance Music.
   N. Raviart Guilcher, 537:Vol75No2-293
   E. Schwandt, 410(M&L):Feb89-94
Schwartz, L. That Sense of Constant Readjustment.
   S.A.S., 295(JML):Fall88/Winter89-290
Schwartz, L.H. Creating Faulkner's Reputation.
   N. Baym, 301(JEGP):Oct89-557
   C.S. Brown, 569(SR):Fall89-556
   B. Foley, 454:Winter90-218
   R. Godden, 392:Summer89-339
   J.H. Justus, 578:Spring90-129
   V. Strandberg, 395(MFS):Summer89-283
Schwartz, L.S. Leaving Brooklyn.*
   B. & L. Quart, 390:Nov89-62
Schwartz, N.L. The Blue Guitar.
   I.C., 185:Jul90-909
Schwartz, P. Georges Perec.
   W.F. Motte, Jr., 210(FrF):Sep89-360
Schwartz, R. – see Weimann, R.
Schwartz, S. "A Mixed Multitude."
   M.J. Westerkamp, 656(WMQ):Apr89-388
Schwartz Lerner, L. Quevedo: Discurso y representación.*
   D.W. Bleznick, 238:Dec89-958
   R.M. Price, 86(BHS):Apr89-177
Schwartzkopf, C. German Americans.
   H. Langner, 682(ZPSK):Band42Heft5-684
Schwartzkopff, C. Deutsch als Muttersprache in den Vereinigten Staaten. (Pt 3)
   H. Fix, 685(ZDL):3/1989-361
Schwarz, D.R. Conrad: The Later Fiction.
   J. Batchelor, 136:Spring89-75
Schwarz, D.R. Reading Joyce's "Ulysses."*
   J. Batchelor, 136:Spring89-75
   R.A. Battaglia, 594:Summer89-224
Schwarz, D.R. The Transformation of the English Novel: 1890-1930.
   M. Magalaner, 395(MFS):Winter89-849
Schwarz, E. Literatur aus vier Kulturen.
   B.L. Bradley, 133:Band22Heft3/4-300
Schwarz, H-P., ed. Die Architektur der Synagoge.
   C.H. Krinsky, 576:Sep89-294
Schwarz, P.J. Twice Condemned.
   639(VQR):Autumn89-116
Schwarz, R.L. Broken Images.
   S. Bagchee, 675(YER):Fall90-105
Schwarz, W. Principles of Lawful Politics.
   P. Foulkes, 483:Jul89-423
Schwarze, C., ed. Bausteine für eine italienische Grammatik. (Vol 2)
   G. Lepschy, 545(RPh):Feb90-452
Schwarze, C. Grammatik der italienischen Sprache.
   G. Lepschy, 402(MLR):Oct90-990
Schwarze, C. & D. Wunderlich, eds. Handbuch der Lexikologie.*
   C. Gansel, 682(ZPSK):Band42Heft4-544
Schwarzkopf, E. On and Off the Record.
   A.F.L.T., 412:May89-145
Schwarzlose, R.A. The Nation's Newsbrokers. (Vol 1)
   R.B. Smith, 441:18Mar90-23

Schwarzlose, R.A. The Nation's Newsbrokers. (Vol 2)
N. Hiley, 617(TLS):13-19Jul90-756
R.B. Smith, 441:18Mar90-23
Schweda-Nicholson, N., ed. Languages in the International Perspective.*
S.K. Sonntag, 355(LSoc):Sep89-439
Schwede, R. Wilhelminische Neuromantik - Flucht oder Zuflucht?
H. Schreckenberger, 221(GQ):Spring89-285
Schwegel, J., ed. The Baby Name Countdown.
E.D. Lawson, 424:Sep89-299
Schweickard, W. Die "cronaca calcistica."
F. Marri, 547(RF):Band101Heft2/3-300
R. Neumann, 72:Band226Heft1-195
Schweier, U. Zum Flexionsakzent in der grossrussischen Literatursprache des 16. und des 17. Jahrhunderts.
D.J. Birnbaum, 559:Vol13No3-319
Schweikert, U., with G. Schweikert - see Tieck, L.
Schweikle, G. Germanisch-deutsche Sprachgeschichte im Überblick.
S. Žepić, 680(ZDP):Band108Heft1-136
Schweitzer, M.M. Custom and Contract.
E. Nellis, 106:Summer89-121
S.V. Salinger, 656(WMQ):Jan89-178
Schwemmer, O., ed. Über Natur.
D. Ginev, 670(BandD0Heft2 389
Schwerin, D. Cat and I.
A. Barnot, 441(B4Jun90 21
Schwerteck, H. Strukturen baskischer Verbformen.
C. Perlick, 683(ZPSK):Band42Heft1-124
Schwertheim, E., ed. Die Inschriften von Hadrianoi und Hadrianeia.
B. Rémy, 229:Band61Heft5-450
A.G. Woodhead, 303(JoHS):Vol109-243
Schwilk, H., ed. Das Echo der Bilder.
M. Hulse, 617(TLS):10-16Aug90-842
Schwinge, E-R. Goethe und die Poesie der Griechen.
J.F. Hyde, Jr., 406:Winter89-476
Schwinger, W. Krzysztof Penderecki.
P. Patterson, 415:Sep89-547
Schwoerer, L.G. Lady Rachel Russell
R.M. Warnicke, 551(RenQ):Spring89-152
Schwok, R. Interprétations de la politique étrangère de Hitler.
R.R. Thalmann, 531:Jul-Dec89-541
Sciascia, L. The Council of Egypt.
D. Day, 577(SHR):Fall89-386
Scindia, V.R., with M. Malgonkar. The Last Maharani of Gwalior.
S.S. Dulai, 293(JASt):Feb89-210
Scliar, M. The Enigmatic Eye.*
R. Di Antonio, 268(IFR):Winter90-59
Sclippa, N. Texte et idéologie.
D. Wood, 208(FS):Jul89-336
Scobbie, I., ed. Aspects of Modern Swedish Literature.
B. Steene, 562(Scan):Nov89-220
Scobie, S. The Ballad of Isabel Gunn.*
K. Hoeppner, 102(CanL):Summer89-135
Scofield, M. T.S. Eliot: The Poems.
B. Bergonzi, 402(MLR):Jan90-168
F. McCombie, 447(N&Q):Dec89-541
Scorsese, M. Scorsese on Scorsese. (D. Thompson & I. Christie, eds)
M. Wood, 617(TLS):12-18Jan90-33

Scoto, G. Omelia sul prologo di Giovanni. (M. Cristiani, ed)
H.J. Ryan, 589:Oct89-952
Scott, A. Tracks Across Alaska.
J.M. Hamilton, 441:9Sep90-10
Scott, B.K. James Joyce.*
M.B., 295(JML):Fall88/Winter89-360
J. Hunter, 177(ELT):Vol32No1-120
T.C. Ware, 174(Eire):Summer89-153
Scott, B.K., ed. New Alliances in Joyce Studies.
J.P. Riquelme, 329(JJQ):Winter90-414
C. Shloss, 395(MFS):Autumn89-617
Scott, C. A Queston of Syllables.*
M. Gauthier, 535(RHL):Mar-Apr89-315
H. Suhamy, 549(RLC):Jul-Sep89-419
Scott, C. The Riches of Rhyme.
J.S.T. Garfitt, 402(MLR):Oct90-944
J-H. Périvier, 207(FR):Apr90-864
Scott, D. Pictorialist Poetics.
D. Kinloch, 208(FS):Apr89-225
S. Stern-Gillet, 89(BJA):Summer89-284
A.V. Williams, 207(FR):May90-1114
Scott, D. Playing for England.
M. Wormald, 617(TLS):21-27Sep90-1007
Scott, D.B. The Singing Bourgeois.
A. Jacobs, 617(TLS):9-15Mar90-256
Scott, G. Heroine.*
M. Meigs, 102(CanL):Autumn-Winter89-222
Scott, G. Spaces Like Stairs.
C. Norton, 618:Fall89-70
Scott, G.G. The Open Door.
T. Swick, 441:10Jun90-49
Scott, H.F. & W.F. Soviet Military Doctrine.
J. Snyder, 550(RusR):Jul89-347
Scott, J. Arrogance.
S. Bradfield, 441:19Aug90-14
Scott, J.W. Gender and the Politics of History.*
J. Lewis, 242:Vol10No5-619
L.F. Rakow, 125:Spring89-321
Scott, M. The Black Swans.
S. Lee, 581:Jun89-249
Scott, M. The Female Advocate.
J. Egan, 568(SCN):Spring-Summer89-12
Scott, M. The Great Caruso.*
J. Steane, 415:Jul89-415
Scott, M., ed. Harold Pinter.*
S.H. Merritt, 397(MD):Sep89-459
Scott, M.J.W. James Thomson, Anglo-Scot.
E. Rothstein, 566:Spring89-191
Scott, M.W. & S.L. Williamson, eds. Shakespearean Criticism. (Vol 6)
M. Steppat, 156(ShJW):Jahrbuch1989-380
Scott, P. Knowledge and Nation.
T. Judt, 617(TLS):14-20Sep90-967
Scott, P.D. Coming to Jakarta.
R. Labrie, 102(CanL):Autumn-Winter89-143
A.C. Morrell, 198:Spring89-111
Scott, T. Thomas Müntzer.
A. Hamilton, 617(TLS):14-20Sep90-983
Scott, T.L. & M.J. Friedman, with J.R. Bryer - see Pound, E.
Scott, W. Scott's Interleaved Waverley Novels. (I.G. Brown, ed)
F. Robertson, 541(RES):Feb89-133
Scott, W. The Two Drovers and Other Stories. (G. Tulloch, ed)
C. Lamont, 571(ScLJ):Spring89-10

Mme. Scottez–De Wambrechies. Boilly 1761–
1845.
  B. Scott, 39:Jul89–65
Scotus, J.D. Jean Duns Scot, "Sur la connais-
sance de Dieu et l'univocité de l'étant."
(O. Boulnois, ed & trans)
  B. Pinchard, 192(EP):Jul–Dec89–527
Scragg, L. Discovering Shakespeare's Mean-
ing.
  M. Coyle, 447(N&Q):Sep89–383
  H. Mills, 175:Spring89–77
Screech, M.A. Looking at Rabelais.
  K. Cameron, 402(MLR):Jul90–729
Scriven, M. Paul Nizan.*
  T.B., 395(MFS):Summer89–367
Scruton, R. The Philosopher on Dover Beach.
  J. Vincent, 617(TLS):20–26Jul90–768
Scruton, R. Sexual Desire.
  A. O'Hear, 393(Mind):Jul88–493
Scully, D. The Catholic Question, Ireland and
England 1798–1822.
  R.E. Ward, 174(Éire):Summer89–155
Scully, T., ed. The "Viandier" of Taillevent.
  L.E. Doucette, 627(UTQ):Fall89–113
Scupham, G. The Good Voyage.
  E. Bartlett, 493:Spring89–64
Scupham, P. The Air Show.*
  S. Knight, 364(Apr/May89–129
Scurla, H. Die Brüder Grimm.
  D. Haase, 406:Spring89–127
Seabrook, J. The Myth of the Market.
  T. Burke, 324:Oct90–793
  D.R. Harrod, 617(TLS):15–21Jun90–634
Seager, R. Ammianus Marcellinus.*
  H. Forte, 313:Vol79–258
  J. Szidat, 229:Band61Heft3–261
Seale, P. Asad of Syria.*
  S. Bakhash, 453(NYRB):27Sep90–49
Sealey, R. The Athenian Republic.*
  P. Cartledge, 235:Winter88–70
  M.H. Hansen, 229:Band61Heft8–744
Sealts, M.M., Jr. Melville's Reading.* (rev)
  L.C. Johnson, 27(AL):May89–285
Seaman, G. Journey to the North.
  J.A. Berling, 293(JASt):Aug89–599
Seanor, D. & N. Fotion, eds. Hare and Crit-
ics.*
  S. Mendus, 483:Apr89–269
  J. Wolff, 518:Oct89–201
Searing, H. & G. Wright. James Stewart Pol-
shek.
  C.D. Warren, 45:Apr89–55
Searle, J.R. Intentionalität.
  M. Tichy, 687:Apr–Jun89–393
Searle, J.R. & D. Vanderveken. Foundations
of Illocutionary Logic.
  J.M. Sadock, 316:Mar89–300
Sears, E. The Ages of Man.*
  M.H. Bornstein, 290(JAAC):Spring89–194
Sears, P. Tour.
  F. Skloot, 448:Vol27No1–132
Seary, P. Lewis Theobald and the Editing of
Shakespeare.
  P. Rogers, 617(TLS):9–15Nov90–1200
Seaton, D. The Art Song.
  I. Ledsham, 410(M&L):Nov89–528
Seavey, O. Becoming Benjamin Franklin.*
  M. Breitwieser, 656(WMQ):Oct89–816
Sebba, G. The Dream of Descartes. (R.A.
Watson, ed)
  D.J. Fitz Gerald, 319:Jan90–132
Seca, J–M. Vocations Rock.
  A.J.M. Prévos, 498:Winter89–87

Séchan, T. Le Roman de Renaud.
  A.J.M. Prévos, 207(FR):Dec89–392
Seckel, A. – see Russell, B.
"Secret Visions of the Fifth Dalai Lama."
  T.R. Blurton, 463:Winter89/90–226
Sedaine, M–J. Le Philosophe sans le savoir.
(G.E. Rodmell, ed)
  C. Bonfils, 535(RHL):Jul–Aug89–719
  J. Dunkley, 83:Spring89–118
  W.D. Howarth, 208(FS):Jul89–331
  R. Niklaus, 402(MLR):Apr90–446
Seddon, K. Time.
  F. Beets, 540(RIPh):Vol43fasc1–168
  P.M. Huby, 518:Jan89–60
Seddon, Q. The Silent Revolution.
  B. Green, 324:Dec89–67
Seebass, T., comp. Musikhandschriften der
Bodmeriana.
  U. Konrad, 417:Jan–Mar89–78
Seed, D. The Fictional Labyrinths of Thomas
Pynchon.*
  B. Duyfhuizen, 454:Fall89–75
  J.M. Mellard, 27(AL):Mar89–131
Seeger, A. Why Suyá Sing.
  B. Nettl, 309:Vol9No2/3–209
Seehase, G., ed. Englische Literatur im Über-
blick.
  C. Jansohn, 72:Band226Heft1–137
Seel, H. Lexikologische Studien zum Pennsyl-
vaniadeutschen.
  W. Enninger, 685(ZDL):1/1989–109
Seel, M. Die Kunst der Entzweiung.*
  U. Müller, 489(PJGG):Band96Heft1–151
Seelbach, U. Späthöfische Literatur und ihre
Rezeption im späten Mittelalter.
  F. Tobin, 221(GQ):Fall89–520
Seelbach, U. – see Wernher der Gartenaere
Seeskin, K. Dialogue and Discovery.*
  P.W. Gooch, 487:Autumn89–270
Segade, J.M.G. – see under Gómez Segade, J.M.
Segal, C. La musique du sphinx.
  S. Murnaghan, 303(JoHS):Vol109–232
Segal, C. Orpheus.
  639(VQR):Summer89–86
Segal, C. – see Conte, G.B.
Segal, G. Rethinking the Pacific.
  S. Winchester, 617(TLS):1–7Jun90–577
Segal, L. Slow Motion.
  R. Porter, 617(TLS):1–7Jun90–589
Segal, N. Narcissus and Echo.*
  C. Cazenobe, 535(RHL):Nov–Dec89–1057
  W.R. Everdell, 594:Summer89–228
  G. May, 207(FR):Dec89–364
Segal, N. The Unintended Reader.*
  C. Cazenobe, 535(RHL):Nov–Dec89–1057
  P. Kamuf, 173(ECS):Winter89/90–223
Segal, R.A. Joseph Campbell.
  W.G. Doty, 577(SHR):Winter89–68
Segal, S. A Prosperous Past. (W.B. Jordan,
ed)
  S. Koslow, 127:Fall89–265
Segeberg, H. Literarische Technik–Bilder.
  W. Riemer, 221(GQ):Winter89–122
  E. Schürer, 301(JEGP):Oct89–598
Segoviano, C. & S., eds. Lengua, literatura,
civilización en la clase de español.
  G.D. Greenia, 238:Dec89–979
Segrè, C.G. Italo Balbo.
  P. Morgan, 278(IS):Vol44–183
Seguí, A.F. Lo psicopatológico en las novelas
de Ernesto Sábato.
  J. Küpper, 547(RF):Band101Heft1–154

Seibert, W. & U. Stollenwerk. Schritte–Pasos–
Passi–Steps–Pas.
    J.F. Lalande 2d, 399(MLJ):Summer89–234
Seidel, F. These Days.
    D. Stap, 441:14Oct90–20
Seidel, K.L. The Southern Bell in the Ameri-
can Novel.*
    C. Mitchell, 582(SFQ):Vol46No2–194
Seidel, K.O. Mittelniederdeutschen Hand-
schriften aus Bielefelder Bibliotheken.*
    N.F. Palmer, 402(MLR):Apr90–494
Seidel, M. Exile and the Narrative Imagina-
tion.*
    P. Goetsch, 38:Band107Heft1/2–271
Seidel, W. Werk und Werkbegriff in der Mus-
ikgeschichte.
    B. Bujic, 410(M&L):Feb89–73
Seidensticker, D. Tokyo Rising.
    I. Buruma, 453(NYRB):28Jun90–14
    J. McInerney, 441:1Apr90–3
    442(NY):4Jun90–103
Seidler, V.J. Kant, Respect and Injustice.*
    G. Weiler, 488:Sep89–377
Seidmann, G. Nathaniel Marchant, Gem En-
graver 1739–1816.
    D.G.C. Allan, 324:Sep90–716
Seifert, S. & A.A. Volgina. Heine-Bibliogra-
phie 1965–1982.
    J.L. Sammons, 406:Spring89–129
Seiler, R.M., ed. Walter Pater.*
    B. Richards, 506(PSt):May89–102
Seizaburō, S. & Matousaki Tetsuhisa – see
under Satō Seizaburō & Matsuzaki Tetsuhisa
Selbmann, R., ed. Zur Geschichte des deut-
schen Bildungsromans.
    J. Hardin, 221(GQ):Spring89–268
Selbourne, D. Death of the Dark Hero.
    N. Malcolm, 617(TLS):4–10May90–465
Selby, J.E. The Revolution in Virginia, 1775–
1783.
    E.W. Carp, 656(WMQ):Jul89–617
    639(VQR):Summer89–81
Seldon, R. Practicing Theory and Reading
Literature.
    W. Baker, 599:Summer90–338
Selden, R., ed. The Theory of Criticism.*
    J.R. Bennett, 402(MLR):Jul90–669
Selig, K-L. & R. Somerville, eds. Florilegium
Columbianum.
    S. Prete, 276:Winter89–473
Selinger, B. Le Guin and Identity in Contem-
porary Fiction.
    H.R.M., 295(JML):Fall88/Winter89–371
Selkirk, E.O. Phonology and Syntax.*
    E. Broselow, 710:Mar89–91
Sell, A.P.F. Defending and Declaring the
Faith.
    D. Bowen, 637(VS):Spring90–505
Sell, A.P.F. The Philosophy of Religion:
1875–1980.
    T.E. Burke, 518:Jan89–63
Sellars, W. The Metaphysics of Epistemology.
(P.V. Amaral, ed)
    B. Aune, 103:Nov90–473
Selle, I., ed. Frankreich meines Herzens.
    K. Kohut, 224(GRM):Band39Heft1–114
Sellers, S., ed. Writing Differences.
    639(VQR):Spring89–48
Sellier, G. Jean Grémillon.
    H.A. Garrity, 207(FR):Mar90–731
Selling, G. A.T. Gellerstedt och det Stockholm
som går.
    J. Sjöström, 341:Vol58No1–39

Selling, J.A., ed. Personalist Morals.
    G.M.B., 185:Apr90–718
Sells, P. Lectures on Contemporary Syntactic
Theories.
    P. Jacobson, 316:Jun89–628
Sellstrom, A.D. Corneille, Tasso and Modern
Poetics.*
    C.B. Kerr, 546(RR):Jan89–149
van Selm, B. Een Menighte Treffelijcke Boec-
ken.*
    D. McKitterick, 78(BC):Autumn89–301
    F. de Marez Oyens, 517(PBSA):Sep89–390
    S. Roach, 78(BC):Winter89–560
Selman, R.L. & L.H. Schultz. Making a Friend
in Youth.
    M.J. West, 441:5Aug90–6
Selous, T. The Other Woman.*
    R. Gunther, 402(MLR):Oct90–983
    S. Rava, 207(FR):May90–1077
    42(AR):Summer89–371
Seltmann, F. Schattenspiel in Kerala.
    S.B. Steever, 318(JAOS):Jan–Mar88–192
Selwyn, V. & others, eds. Poems of the
Second World War. More Poems of the
Second World War.
    G. Ewart, 617(TLS):6–12Jul90–734
Selzer, R. Imagine a Woman.
    M.J. Gerber, 441:18Nov90–32
Semenko, I. Poētika pozdnego Mandel'štama.
    J.G. Harris, 104(CASS):Spring–Winter88–
519
Sémon, M., ed. Cahiers Léon Tolstoï, 0.
    A.V. Knowles, 575(SEER):Jan89–126
Sen, A. On Ethics and Economics.*
    D. Gauthier, 482(PhR):Oct89–569
Sen, A. & others. The Standard of Living.*
(G. Hawthorn, ed)
    D. Gauthier, 482(PhR):Oct89–569
Sena, J.F. The Best–Natured Man.*
    P. Roberts, 677(YES):Vol20–272
Senabre, R. – see Ortega y Gasset, J.
Sénac de Meilhan, G. Des principes et des
causes de la Révolution en France.* (M.
Delon, ed)
    N. Hampson, 208(FS):Jul89–333
Sender, R.J. Míster Witt en el Cantón. (J.M.
Jover, ed)
    D. Gagen, 402(MLR):Apr90–480
    M.E.W. Jones, 238:May89–304
    A. Trippett, 86(BHS):Oct89–386
Senderovich, S. & M. Sendich, eds. Anton
Chekhov Rediscovered.
    J.L. Conrad, 104(CASS):Spring–Winter88–
448
    T. Eekman, 550(RusR):Apr89–184
Seneca. L. Annaei Senecae, Tragoediae, In-
certorum auctorum Hercules [OEtaeus] Oc-
tavia.* (O. Zwierlein, ed)
    J. Delz, 229:Band61Heft6–501
    J.G. Fitch, 122:Jul89–236
    H. Zehnacker, 555:Vol62Fasc1–160
Seneca. Seneca's "Hercules Furens."* (J.G.
Fitch, ed)
    M. Billerbeck, 487:Spring89–79
    E. Fantham, 313:Vol79–210
Seneca. Seneca's "Phaedra."* (A.J. Boyle, ed
& trans)
    E. Fantham, 313:Vol79–210
    K. Heldmann, 229:Band61Heft5–394
Senelick, L. The Age and Stage of George L.
Fox, 1825–1877.*
    C.D. Johnson, 658:Winter89–286
    D. Mayer, 610:Autumn89–293

Senf, C.A. The Vampire in Nineteenth-Century English Literature.
  E. Lauterbach, 395(MFS):Summer89-322
Senft, G. Kilivila.*
  M.R. Hale, 350:Dec90-884
Senghor, L.S. Oeuvre poétique. Ce que je crois.
  R. Shattuck & S. Ka, 453(NYRB):20Dec90-11
Seniff, D.P., ed. Libro de la montería.
  B. Taylor, 304(JHP):Autumn89-98
Seniff, D.P. & M.I. Montoya Ramírez - see Keller, J.E.
Senkman, L. La identidad judía en la literatura argentina.
  I. Stavans, 508:May89-184
Senn, F. Joyce's Dislocutions. (J.P. Riquelme, ed)
  U. Schneider, 38:Band107Heft1/2-253
de Senna, M.R.L. - see under Roiz Lucas de Senna, M.
Sensibar, J.L. Faulkner's Poetry.
  K. Butterworth, 392:Summer89-347
Seoane, M.C. - see under Cruz Seoane, M.
Sepänmaa, Y. The Beauty of Environment.
  W.H. Clark, Jr., 289:Summer89-123
Sepper, D.L. Goethe contra Newton.*
  A.E. Shapiro, 319:Oct90-621
Serafine, M.L. Music as Cognition.
  R. Cox, 290(JAAC):Winter89-86
Serafini, A. Linus Pauling.
  R. Olby, 617(TLS):26Jan-1Feb90-96
Serebrennikov, A., comp. Ubiistvo Stolypina.
  R. Pearson, 575(SEER):Jan89-142
Sereni, V. Selected Poems.
  C. Wilmer, 617(TLS):14-20Dec90-1358
Sérieyx, H. Le Zéro Mépris.
  A.J. Strange, 207(FR):Mar90-751
de la Serna, R.G. - see under Gómez de la Serna, R.
Serpa, F., ed. Il Punto su Virgilio.*
  S.J. Harrison, 313:Vol79-204
Serpa, M.A., J.R. Curry & F. Vergara. Aquí, allá y acullá. (2nd ed)
  F. Nuessel, 399(MLJ):Spring89-101
Serrà Campins, A. El teatre burlesc mallorquí, 1701-1850.
  J-L. Marfany, 86(BHS):Jul89-305
Serrano, J.B. - see under Belmonte Serrano, J.
Serroy, J., ed. La France et l'Italie au temps de Mazarin.
  F. Assaf, 475:Vol16No30-342
Serroy, J., ed. Jean Pellerin (1885-1921), Actes du colloque du centenaire et pastiches poétiques.
  Y-A. Favre, 535(RHL):Nov-Dec89-1070
Serroy, J. - see Scarron, P.
Servadio, G. La storia di R.
  J. Landry, 617(TLS):2-8Nov90-1183
Servera Baño, J., ed. En torno a San Juan de la Cruz.
  C.P. Thompson, 402(MLR):Jan90-224
Service, G. Golden Inches. (J.S. Service, ed)
  T. Bown, 617(TLS):16-22Mar90-274
  J.K. Fairbank, 453(NYRB):20Dec90-77
Sessions, S., with P. Meyer. Dark Obsession.
  J. Crewdson, 441:25Feb90-3
Sessions, W.A. Henry Howard, Earl of Surrey.*
  S.K. Heninger, Jr., 604:Fall87-63
Sestan, E. La Firenze di Vieusseux e di Capponi. (G. Spadolini, ed)
  A. Moz, 276:Winter89-477

Setaioli, A. Seneca e i Greci.
  K. Abel, 229:Band61Heft2-126
  C.D.N. Costa, 123:Vol39No2-237
Seth, V. All You Who Sleep Tonight.
  L. Mackinnon, 617(TLS):21-27Sep90-1007
Seth, V. The Golden Gate.*
  K. Hellerstein, 473(PR):Vol56No4-677
Seton-Watson, M. Scenes from Soviet Life.
  R. Pittman, 575(SEER):Apr89-292
Settis, S., ed. Memoria dell'antico nell'arte italiana.
  H-W. Kruft, 229:Band61Heft5-470
Settle, M.L. Celebration.
  B. Haviland, 473(PR):Vol56No1-151
Seubold, G. Heideggers Analyse der neuzeitlichen Technik.
  C. Jamme, 489(PJGG):Band96Heft1-191
  E. Weinmayr, 687:Jan-Mar89-174
Seuren, P.A.M. Discourse Semantics.
  P. Werth, 361:Aug89-321
Ševčenko, I. & N.P., eds & trans. The Life of Saint Nicholas of Sion.
  D.D. Abrahamse, 589:Jan89-219
Sève, R. Leibniz et l'école moderne du droit naturel.
  G. Fraysse, 542:Oct-Dec89-599
"Seventeenth-Century Writings on the Kievan Caves Monastery."
  P.A. Rolland, 550(RusR):Oct89-413
Severin, D.S. - see de Rojas, F.
Severjanin, I. Pis'ma k Avguste Baranovoj, 1916-1938. (B. Jangfeldt & R. Kruus, eds)
  R. Masing-Delic, 104(CASS):Spring-Winter88-419
  G.S. Smith, 575(SEER):Jul89-442
Sevin, D. & I. Zur Diskussion. (3rd ed)
  J.F. Lalande 2d, 399(MLJ):Spring89-91
Sewell, D.R. Mark Twain's Languages.*
  A. Burns, 392:Spring89-206
  B.M., 494:Fall89-641
  L.C. Mitchell, 301(JEGP):Jan89-140
Sexton, A. Selected Poems of Anne Sexton. (D.W. Middlebrook & D.H. George, eds)
  M. Kinzie, 491:Jun89-151
Seyffert, P. Soviet Literary Structuralism.
  T.G. Winner, 104(CASS):Spring-Winter88-409
Seymour, G. The Running Target.
  N. Callendar, 441:11Mar90-33
Seymour, H. Baseball.
  R. González Echevarría, 441:1Apr90-10
  S.J. Gould, 453(NYRB):11Oct90-3
Seymour, M. The Reluctant Devil.
  R. Clare, 617(TLS):4-10May90-480
Seymour, M. A Ring of Conspirators.*
  D.M. Fogel, 598(SoR):Summer90-697
Seymour, P.J. The Golden Woman. (A. Mattina, ed)
  E.P. Hamp, 269(IJAL):Jan89-96
  K. Kroeber, 269(IJAL):Jan89-94
Seymour-Smith, M. Rudyard Kipling.*
  P. Mason, 346(KJ):Dec89-40
Sfameni Gasparro, G. Misteri e culti mistici di Demetra.
  K. Dowden, 303(JoHS):Vol109-240
  E. Kearns, 123:Vol39No1-61
Sfez, L. Critique de la communication.
  P. Livet, 192(EP):Jul-Dec89-558
Sgard, J. & others - see Nodier, C.
Shackelford, R. - see Dallapiccola, L.

Shackleton, R. Essays on Montesquieu and on the Enlightenment. (D. Gilson & M. Smith, eds)
R. Bonnel, 207(FR):Apr90–873
Shackleton Bailey, D.R. Onomasticon to Cicero's Speeches.
K.B. Harder, 424:Jun89–197
Shackleton Bailey, D.R. – see Cicero
Shadbolt, M. Monday's Warriors.
T. Aitken, 617(TLS):29Jun–5Jul90–705
Shadwell, T. The Squire of Alsatia. (J.C. Ross, ed)
A.H. Scouten, 566:Spring89–195
Shaffer, E. Erewhons of the Eye.*
O. Leaman, 89(BJA):Summer89–281
L. Ormond, 90:Jun89–434
Shafir, G. Land, Labor and the Origins of the Israeli-Palestinian Conflict 1882–1914.
B. Wasserstein, 617(TLS):30Mar–5Apr90–343
Shafruddin, B.H. The Federal Factor in the Government and Politics of Peninsular Malaysia.
S. Barraclough, 293(JASt):Feb89–235
Shah, D.K. As Crime Goes By.
M. Stasio, 441:9Sep90–39
Shahar, S. Childhood in the Middle Ages.
L. Pollock, 617(TLS):9–15Nov90–1212
Shaheen, N. Biblical References in Shakespeare's Tragedies.
C. Lewis, 570(SQ):Spring89–108
Shahîd, I. Rome and the Arabs.* Byzantium and the Arabs in the Fourth Century.*
R. Browning, 313:Vol79–248
Shailor, B.A. Catalogue of Medieval and Renaissance Manuscripts in the Beinecke Rare Book and Manuscript Library, Yale University. (Vol 1)
A.S.G. Edwards, 517(PBSA):Sep89–385
H. Gneuss, 38:Band107Heft1/2–167
Shailor, B.A. Catalogue of Medieval and Renaissance Manuscripts in the Beinecke Rare Book and Manuscript Library, Yale University. (Vol 2)
A.I. Doyle, 40(AEB):Vol3No2–68
A.S.G. Edwards, 517(PBSA):Sep89–385
H. Gneuss, 38:Band107Heft1/2–167
Shailor, B.A. The Medieval Book.
M.P. Brown, 354:Sep89–274
K. Gould, 517(PBSA):Jun89–233
Shaitanov, I.O., ed. Anglia v pamflete.
I. Burova, 566:Autumn89–83
Shaked, S., D. Shulman & G.G. Strousma, eds. Gilgul.
J.W. de Jong, 259(IIJ):Jul89–208
Shakespeare, N. The Vision of Elena Silves.*
J. Mellors, 364:Oct/Nov89–133
Shakespeare, W. The Bantam Shakespeare: The Complete Works. (D. Bevington & others, eds)
J.A. Roberts, 570(SQ):Summer89–239
Shakespeare, W. The Comedy of Errors. (T.S. Dorsch, ed)
S. Billington, 610:Summer89–195
Shakespeare, W. The Complete King Lear, 1608–1623. (M. Warren, ed)
E.A.J. Honigmann, 453(NYRB):25Oct90–58
Shakespeare, W. The Complete Works: Modern-Spelling Edition.* (S. Wells & G. Taylor, general eds)
H.W. Gabler, 156(ShJW):Jahrbuch1989–344
B. Vickers, 541(RES):Aug89–402

Shakespeare, W. The Complete Works, Original-Spelling Edition.* (S. Wells & G. Taylor, general eds)
C.B. Evans, 301(JEGP):Jul89–401
H.W. Gabler, 156(ShJW):Jahrbuch1989–344
Shakespeare, W. Henry IV, Part I. A Midsummer Night's Dream. Romeo and Juliet. (R. Gill, ed of all)
G. Schmitz, 156(ShJW):Jahrbuch1989–332
Shakespeare, W. King Lear.* (J.S. Bratton, ed) Othello. (J. Hankey, ed)
L. Cookson, 541(RES):May89–260
Shakespeare, W. La Komedio de Eraroj. (W. Auld & A.M. Simeonov, trans)
M. Boulton, 447(N&Q):Jun89–224
Shakespeare, W. The Merchant of Venice.* (M.M. Mahood, ed)
L. Danson, 570(SQ):Summer89–240
K. Duncan-Jones, 447(N&Q):Mar89–98
W. Montgomery, 541(RES):May89–256
Shakespeare, W. Sämtliche Werke. (Vols 1–3, 5th ed; E. Lowenthal, ed. Vol 4, 4th ed; L. Schneider, ed)
D. Feldmann, 156(ShJW):Jahrbuch1989–371
Shakespeare, W. Shakespeare Made Easy: "Henry IV Part One." Shakespeare Made Easy: "The Tempest." Shakespeare Made Easy: "A Midsummer Night's Dream." (A. Durband, ed of all)
G. Schmitz, 156(ShJW):Jahrbuch1989–332
Shakespeare, W. & W. Rowley, with others. The Birth of Merlin, or The Childe Hath Found His Father.
S. Schoenbaum, 617(TLS):2–8Feb90–124
"Shakespeare Survey." (Vol 38) (S. Wells, ed)
R. Fricker, 38:Band107Heft1/2–220
"Shakespeare Survey." (Vol 40) (S. Wells, ed)
A. Yearling, 610:Spring89–91
Shalk, E., ed. Culture, Society and Religion in Early Modern Europe.
P.F. Grendler, 551(RenQ):Spring89–92
Shammas, A. Arabesques.
A. Balaban, 385(MQR):Winter90–145
G. Levin, 364:Apr/May89–149
B. Zelechow, 390:Dec89–44
Shamsul, A.B. From British to Bumiputera Rule.
M. Peletz, 293(JASt):May89–442
Shanes, E. Turner's Human Landscape.
P. Rogers, 617(TLS):7–13Sep90–947
Shanker, S.G. Wittgenstein and the Turning-Point in the Philosophy of Mathematics.*
P.K. Moser, 242:Vol10No1–124
M. Steiner, 316:Sep89–1098
Shankman, S. Now Let's Talk of Graves.
B.J. Rahn, 441:11Nov90–25
Shanor, R.R. The City That Never Was.*
D. Dunster, 46:Aug89–15
P. Goodman, 47:Jul89–39
Shântâ, N. La voie jaina.
J. Cort, 293(JASt):May89–430
Shanzer, D. A Philosophical and Literary Commentary on Martianus Capella's "De nuptiis Philologiae et Mercurii," Book 1.*
S. Gersh, 589:Apr89–501
Shapard, R. & J. Thomas, eds. Sudden Fiction International.
G.S. Bourdain, 441:7Jan90–16
Shapcott, J. Electroplating the Baby.*
S. Pugh, 493:Spring89–47
W. Scammell, 364:Aug/Sep89–92

Shapiro, A. Happy Hour.
  K. Hellerstein, 473(PR):Vol56No4-677
Shapiro, D. We Danced All Night.
  J. Lahr, 441:11Feb90-10
Shapiro, G. Nietzschean Narratives.
  D.W. Conway, 543:Jun90-883
Shapiro, I. & G. Reeher, eds. Power, In-
  equality, and Democratic Politics.
  W.N., 185:Jan90-448
Shapiro, K. Reports of My Death.
  E. Toynton, 441:13May90-25
Shapiro, K. The Younger Son.
  D. Miller, 569(SR):Spring89-283
Shapiro, M. The Shadow in the Sun.
  L. Abrams, 441:9Sep90-19
Shapiro, M.J. The Politics of Representation.
  A. Keenan, 400(MLN):Dec89-1206
  J. Rieder, 77:Fall89-337
Shapiro, N.R. – see "Fables from Old French:
  Aesop's Beast and Bumpkins"
Shapiro, S., ed. Intensional Mathematics.
  H.T. Hodes, 486:Mar89-177
Sharkey, J. Death Sentence.
  B. Lowry, 441:14Oct90-50
Sharkey, M., ed. The Illustrated Treasury of
  Australian Humour.
  G. Turcotte, 616:Vol10No2-57
Sharkey, T. Jack the Ripper.
  L. James, 637(VS):Autumn89-201
Sharma, B.R., ed. Puṣpasūtra.
  W. Howard, 259(IIJ):Apr89-147
Sharma, K. Bhakti and the Bhakti Movement.
  D.N. Lorenzen, 293(JASt):Aug89-665
Sharma, S. Lions in the Path.
  J.E. Funston, 284:Fall89-223
Sharman, R.V. – see Giraut de Borneil
Sharon, A., with D. Chanoff. Warrior.*
  A. Margalit, 453(NYRB):26Apr90-38
Sharp, E. The Making of a Schoolgirl.
  T.C. Holyoke, 42(AR):Summer89-367
Sharpe, E.J. Comparative Religion.
  M.S. Costello, 485(PE&W):Jul89-362
Sharpe, J.A. Early Modern England.
  R. Porter, 173(ECS):Fall89-109
  G. Walker, 242:Vol10No1-108
Sharpe, K. Criticism and Compliment.*
  H. Abalain, 189(EA):Oct-Dec89-473
  D. Lindley, 141:Summer89-313
  D. Norbrook, 541(RES):Nov89-560
  G. Walker, 242:Vol10No2-256
Sharpe, K. & S.N. Zwicker, eds. Politics of
  Discourse.*
  G.W. Pigman 3d, 250(HLQ):Autumn89-501
  N. Smith, 141:Summer89-322
Sharrad, P. Raja Rao and Cultural Tradition.
  K.S.N. Rao, 395(MFS):Summer89-387
Sharrock, R., ed. The Green Man Revisited.
  G. Bas, 189(EA):Oct-Dec89-490
Shatto, S. The Companion to "Bleak House."
  T. Braun, 447(N&Q):Sep89-408
  S. Monod, 637(VS):Spring90-513
Shattuck, C.H. Shakespeare on the American
  Stage. (Vol 2)
  L. Helms, 141:Summer89-311
  D.B. Wilmeth, 610:Spring89-94
Shatz, M.S. & J.E. Zimmerman, eds & trans.
  Signposts.
  C. Read, 575(SEER):Apr89-282
Shatzmiller, J. Shylock Reconsidered.
  G. Wills, 453(NYRB):18Jan90-22
Shaughnessy, E.L. Eugene O'Neill in Ireland.
  J.E. Barlow, 27(AL):Oct89-501

Shaumyan, S. A Semiotic Theory of Language.
  R. Harris, 567:Vol74No1/2-121
  J. Hearne, 297(JL):Mar89-239
Shaver, A., with A. Cash, eds & trans. Tris-
  tan and the Round Table.
  C. Kleinhenz, 276:Spring89-71
Shaw, A., ed. Energy Design for Architects.
  M.S. Stubbs, 47:Mar89-54
Shaw, B.A. & N. Vera-Godwin, eds. Critical
  Perspectives on Gabriel García Márquez.*
  G. Pontiero, 86(BHS):Jan89-115
Shaw, D. Molière: "Les Précieuses ridicules."*
  W.D. Howarth, 208(FS):Apr89-207
  P.A. Wadsworth, 207(FR):Apr90-871
Shaw, G.B. Bernard Shaw: Collected Letters.*
  (Vol 4) (D.H. Laurence, ed)
  A. Turco, Jr., 177(ELT):Vol32No3-317
Shaw, G.B. Bernard Shaw on the London Art
  Scene, 1885-1950. (S. Weintraub, ed)
  R. Dorment, 617(TLS):8-14Jun90-614
  M. Vaizey, 324:Oct90-796
Shaw, G.B. Bernard Shaw's Letters to Sieg-
  fried Trebitsch.* (S.A. Weiss, ed)
  L.J. Wolf, 610:Autumn89-301
Shaw, J.B. & G. Knox. Italian Eighteenth-
  Century Drawings in the Robert Lehman
  Collection.
  D. Scrase, 39:Jun89-441
Shaw, M. David Kindersley.
  M. Harvey, 324:May90-443
Shaw, M., ed. The Modern Presidency.
  639(VQR):Winter89-22
Shaw, P. The War against the Intellect.
  J. Seaton, 580(SCR):Spring90-149
  639(VQR):Autumn89-133
Shaw, W., ed. Sir Frederick Ouseley and St.
  Michael's, Tenbury.
  W.J. Gatens, 410(M&L):Aug89-426
  G. Reynolds, 415:Jun89-374
Shaw, W.D. The Lucid Veil.*
  P. Davis, 97(CQ):Vol18No1-73
Shaw, Y-M., ed. Changes and Continuities in
  Chinese Communism.
  M.C. Morgan, 293(JASt):Aug89-600
"Shaw: The Annual of Bernard Shaw Studies."
  (Vol 5) (S. Weintraub, ed)
  J-C. Amalric, 189(EA):Apr-Jun89-225
"Shaw: The Annual of Bernard Shaw Studies."
  (Vol 7) (A. Turco, Jr., ed)
  B.B., 295(JML):Fall88/Winter89-406
  A.M. Gibbs, 677(YES):Vol20-316
  N. Grene, 447(N&Q):Mar89-119
  L.J. Wolf, 610:Autumn89-301
"Shaw: The Annual of Bernard Shaw Studies."
  (Vol 8) (S. Weintraub, ed)
  A.P. Barr, 637(VS):Winter90-357
  N. Grene, 447(N&Q):Jun89-256
  B. Henderson, 177(ELT):Vol32No2-248
Shawcross, J.T. "Paradise Regain'd."
  M.A. Mikolajczak, 568(SCN):Fall-
  Winter89-34
Shawcross, W. Kowtow!*
  I. Buruma, 453(NYRB):12Apr90-41
Shawcross, W. The Shah's Last Ride.*
  639(VQR):Spring89-60
Shay, A. Nelson Algren's Chicago.
  T.R. Edwards, 453(NYRB):28Jun90-22
Shcheglov, Y. & A. Zholkovsky. Poetics of
  Expressiveness.*
  M. Sosa, 104(CASS):Spring-Winter88-458
Shea, S. Victims.
  T. Goldie, 102(CanL):Winter88-128

Shearman, P. The Soviet Union and Cuba.
  N. Miller, 575(SEER):Apr89-330
Shechner, M. After the Revolution.*
  M.P.L., 295(JML):Fall88/Winter89-203
Shedletzky, I. & T. Sparr - see Scholem, B. &
  G.
Sheed, W. Essays in Disguise.
  P. Klass, 441:18Mar90-17
Sheehan, H. Marxism and the Philosophy of
  Science. (Vol 1)
  T. Carver, 488:Jun89-241
Sheehan, J.J. German History, 1770-1866.
  T. Childers, 441:11Nov90-15
  G.A. Craig, 453(NYRB):28Jun90-25
  R.J. Evans, 617(TLS):4-10May90-463
Sheehan, N. A Bright Shining Lie.*
  H. Brogan, 617(TLS):29Jun-5Jul90-708
  T. Vuong-Riddick, 529(QQ):Autumn89-
  769
Sheehan, T. Karl Rahner.
  W.V. Dych, 258:Dec89-487
Sheehy, G. The Man Who Changed the World.
  P. Taubman, 441:16Dec90-9
Sheehy, H. Margo.
  W.L. Taitte, 441:28Jan90-28
Sheets-Pyenson, S. Cathedrals of Science.
  H. Ritvo, 637(VS):Spring90-491
Sheffield, C. Summertide.
  G. Jonas, 441:25Mar90-30
Shekerjian, D. Uncommon Genius.
  E. Regis, 441:11Feb90-9
Shelden, M. Friends of Promise.*
  N. Annan, 453(NYRB):15Feb90-10
  R. Fuller, 364:Apr/May89-134
Shelden, M. Memories of Midnight.
  M. Buck, 441:19Aug90-18
Sheleff, L.S. Ultimate Penalties.
  R.T. Anderson, 115:Winter89-91
Shelemay, K.K. Music, Ritual, and Falasha
  History.
  A.A. Moorefield, 187:Winter89-179
Shell, M. The End of Kinship.
  B.M., 494:Winter89-857
  M. Rose, 570(SQ):Spring89-97
Shelley, M. The Journals of Mary Shelley
  1814-1844.* (P.R. Feldman & D. Scott-Kil-
  vert, eds)
  A.G. Fredman, 301(JEGP):Jul90-404
  P. Morgan, 179(ES):Jun89-278
Shelley, M.W. The Letters of Mary Wollstone-
  craft Shelley.* (Vol 3) (B.T. Bennett, ed)
  W. Keach, 661(WC):Autumn89-208
  M.K. Stocking, 340(KSJ):Vol38-181
  D. Womersley, 447(N&Q):Dec89-523
Shelley, P.B. The Poems of Shelley. (Vol 1)
  (G. Matthews and K. Everest, eds)
  A. Leighton, 617(TLS):30Mar-5Apr90-354
Shelmerdine, C.W. The Perfume Industry of
  Mycenaean Pylos.
  K. Kilian, 229:Band61Heft5-456
Shelnutt, E. Recital in a Private Home.
  W. Harmon, 472:Vol16No1-136
Shen Tong, with M. Yen. Almost a Revolution.
  J. Shapiro, 441:18Nov90-14
Shengold, L. Soul Murder.*
  J. Lear, 617(TLS):24-30Aug90-893
  C. Rycroft, 453(NYRB):1Mar90-47
Shennan, A. Rethinking France.
  J. Hayward, 617(TLS):29Jun-5Jul90-700
Shepard, J. Lights Out in the Reptile House.
  L. Freed, 441:25Feb90-27
Shepherd, A. Wintu Texts.
  D. Hymes, 350:Sep90-651

Shepherd, S. Spenser.
  K. Farley, 604:Fall89-52
Sheppard, A. Aesthetics.*
  P. Lewis, 89(BJA):Spring89-178
  E.E. Selk, 290(JAAC):Winter89-93
Sheppard, C.D. Creator of the Santa Fe Style.
  J. Caufield, 576:Sep89-300
Sher, A. Middlepost.*
  A. Rattansi, 511:Oct89-48
  42(AR):Summer89-373
Sher, G. Desert.*
  J.E. Bickenbach, 529(QQ):Summer89-519
  J. Lamont, 63:Mar89-114
Sherbo, A. The Birth of Shakespeare Stud-
  ies.*
  A.F. Kinney, 481(PQ):Fall89-443
  P. Wenzel, 38:Band107Heft1/2-225
Shercliff, W.H. Morality to Adventure.
  J. Barr, 354:Sep89-285
  C. Hurst, 78(BC):Summer89-261
Shergold, N.D. & J.E. Varey, eds. Genealogía,
  origen y noticias de los comediantes de
  España.
  J.M. Díez Borque, 304(JHP):Autumn89-
  112
  A.L. Mackenzie, 86(BHS):Apr89-183
Shergold, N.D. & J.E. Varey. Representaciones
  palaciegas: 1603-1699.
  A.L. Mackenzie, 86(BHS):Apr89-177
Shergold, N.D. & J.E. Varey, with C. Davis.
  Teatros y comedias en Madrid: 1699-1719.*
  A.L. Mackenzie, 86(BHS):Jul89-284
Sheridan, D., ed. Wartime Women.
  M. Lefkowitz, 617(TLS):1-7Jun90-591
Sheridan, S. Christina Stead.
  P.F. Edelson, 395(MFS):Winter89-872
Sheriff, M.D. Fragonard.
  H. Wine, 617(TLS):17-23Aug90-876
Sherk, R.K., ed & trans. The Roman Empire:
  Augustus to Hadrian.
  D. Braund, 313:Vol79-223
  H. Freis, 229:Band61Heft8-748
  T.E.J. Wiedemann, 123:Vol39No2-314
"Cindy Sherman: Untitled Film Stills."
  A. Grundberg, 441:2Dec90-71
Sherman, J. Shaping the Flame.
  D. Kosub, 198:Winter89-113
  S. Scobie, 376:Sep89-123
Sherman, K. The Book of Salt.
  C. Levenson, 529(QQ):Summer89-531
Sherman, N. The Fabric of Character.
  C.D.C. Reeve, 185:Jul90-894
Sherman, S.W. Sarah Orne Jewett.
  M. Littenberg, 357:Spring90-65
Sherman, W.T. William Tecumseh Sherman:
  Memoirs. (C. Royster, ed)
  G.W. Gallagher, 441:21Oct90-12
  C.V. Woodward, 453(NYRB):8Nov90-29
Sherover, C.M. Heidegger, Kant and Time.
  J. Protevi, 319:Oct90-631
Sherry, N. The Life of Graham Greene.* (Vol
  1)
  J. Mills, 648(WCR):Vol23No2-77
  J. Symons, 364:Aug/Sep89-111
Sherry, R. Studying Women's Writing.
  T. Moi, 172(Edda):1989/4-361
Sherry, V. The Uncommon Tongue.*
  D. Gervais, 677(YES):Vol20-349
  T.H.J., 295(JML):Fall88/Winter89-351
  A.V.C. Schmidt, 541(RES):May89-297
Shershow, S.C. Laughing Matters.
  W.E. Gruber, 131(CL):Summer89-280

Sherwood, F. Everything You've Heard is True.
  J.L. Halio, 573(SSF):Summer89-361
Sherzer, D. & J., eds. Humor and Comedy in Puppetry.
  M.B. Helstien, 292(JAF):Apr-Jun89-237
Shesgreen, S. - see Laroon, M.
Shevelow, K. Women and Print Culture.
  C.N. Thomas, 173(ECS):Spring90-330
Shields, C. The Orange Fish.
  J. Giltrow, 648(WCR):Vol23No3-57
Shields, C. Swann.*
  C. Addison, 102(CanL):Summer89-158
  G. Campbell, 529(QQ):Spring89-153
  D. Wilson, 617(TLS):16-22Nov90-1232
Shields, H., ed. Ballad Research.
  G.D. Zimmermann, 235:Winter88-80
Shields, J.C. - see Wheatley, P.
Shigihara, S., ed. Reger-Studien 2.
  H. Steger, 417:Oct-Dec89-369
Shikatani, G. Selected Poems and Texts.
  S. Scobie, 376:Dec89-127
Shillingsburg, M.J. At Home Abroad.
  L.J. Budd, 395(MFS):Summer89-265
  G.C. Carrington, Jr., 26(ALR):Winter90-94
  639(VQR):Spring89-67
Shillingsburg, P.L. Scholarly Editing in the Computer Age.*
  517(PBSA):Jun89-243
Shillingsburg, P.L. - see Thackeray, W.M.
Shilstone, F.W. Byron and the Myth of Tradition.
  F.L. Beaty, 580(SCR):Fall89-136
  M. Kelsall, 445(NCF):Mar90-548
Shilts, R. And the Band Played On.
  G.S. Smith, 529(QQ):Summer89-244
Shiman, L.L. Crusade Against Drink in Victorian England.
  D.W. Gutzke, 637(VS):Autumn89-186
Shinn, W.T., Jr. The Decline of the Russian Peasant Household.
  K. Brooks, 550(RusR):Apr89-205
Shipley, G. A History of Samos 800-188 B.C.
  T.J. Figueira, 303(JoHS):Vol109-252
  P. Herrmann, 229:Band61Heft6-511
  A.J. Papalas, 124:Sep-Oct89-57
Shipley, W., ed. In Honor of Mary Haas.
  W. Bright, 350:Jun90-375
Shirer, W.L. 20th Century Journey. (Vol 3)
  A. Brinkley, 441:21Jan90-15
Shirley, C.R. & P.W. Understanding Chicano Literature.
  A. Paredes, 649(WAL):Aug89-167
Shirley, J. The Cardinal.* (E.M. Yearling, ed) The Lady of Pleasure.* (R. Huebert, ed)
  W. Zunder, 179(ES):Feb89-89
Shishuo, Y. - see under Yuan Shishuo
Shive, D.M. Naming Achilles.*
  W.C. Scott, 24:Summer89-339
  M.M. Willcock, 123:Vol39No2-174
  J. Williams, 124:Sep-Oct89-66
Shklar, J.N. Montesquieu.*
  J.P. Diggins, 173(ECS):Fall89-121
  J. Jennings, 521:Jul89-264
Shlaim, A. Collusion across the Jordan.
  639(VQR):Winter89-24
Shloss, C. In Visible Light.*
  M.D.O., 295(JML):Fall88/Winter89-178
  M. Orvell, 454:Fall89-89
Shneidman, N.N. Soviet Literature in the 1980s.
  D. Rayfield, 617(TLS):2-8Mar90-237
Shoaf, R.A. - see Chaucer, G.

Shoemaker, S. Identity, Cause, and Mind.*
  F. Jackson, 482(PhR):Oct89-550
Shokoohy, M., with M. Bayani-Wolpert & N.H. Shokoohy. Bhadresvar.
  S.S. Blair, 576:Dec89-390
Shokoohy, M. & N.H. Hisar-i Furuza.
  S.S. Blair, 576:Dec89-390
Shomette, D.G. & R.D. Haslach. Raid on America.
  S. Hornstein, 656(WMQ):Oct89-806
Shone, R. Walter Sickert.
  N.V. Halliday, 39:Dec89-433
  K. McConkey, 90:Apr89-304
Shopen, T., ed. Languages and Their Speakers. Languages and Their Status.
  A. Brakel, 320(CJL):Dec89-445
  F. Nuessel, 35(AS):Summer89-176
Shor, I. Critical Thinking and Everyday Life.
  N.R. Comley, 128(CE):Oct89-623
Shore, P. Nuclear Dreams.
  G. Gessert, 448:Vol27No2-118
Shore, W., ed. Louder than Words.
  D. Rifkind, 441:29Apr90-26
Shorey, K. - see Randolph, J.
Short, J.R. The Humane City.
  A. Coleman, 617(TLS):11-17May90-505
Short, K.R.M., ed. Western Broadcasting over the Iron Curtain.
  E.M. Robson, 575(SEER):Oct89-666
Shoumatoff, A. The World is Burning.
  J. Brooke, 441:19Aug90-7
Shoven, J.B., ed. Government Policy Towards Industry in the United States and Japan.
  L.H. Lynn, 293(JASt):Aug89-626
Showalter, E. Sexual Anarchy.
  J.K. Weinberg, 441:26Aug90-9
Shreve, S.R. A Country of Strangers.*
  639(VQR):Autumn89-131
Shrosbree, C. Public Schools and Private Education.
  I. Britain, 637(VS):Spring90-515
Shturman, D. The Soviet Secondary School.
  J.Y. Muckle, 575(SEER):Oct89-659
Shue, V. The Reach of the State.*
  T.P. Bernstein, 293(JASt):May89-373
Shuger, D.K. Sacred Rhetoric.
  C. Kallendorf, 568(SCN):Spring-Summer89-3
Shuldham-Shaw, P., E.B. Lyle & P.A. Hall, eds. The Greig-Duncan Folk Song Collection. (Vol 3)
  D. Buchan, 571(ScLJ):Spring89-19
Shulman, R. Social Criticism and Nineteenth-Century American Fictions.*
  N. Baym, 301(JEGP):Jan89-138
  S.B. Girgus, 70:Jan89-34
  D.H. Hirsch, 401(MLQ):Jun88-173
  A. Kaplan, 432(NEQ):Dec89-586
  M.D.O., 295(JML):Fall88/Winter89-178
Shum Kui-kwong. The Chinese Communists' Road to Power.
  P.J. Seybolt, 293(JASt):May89-375
Shumaker, P. The Circle of Totems.
  639(VQR):Winter89-28
Shuman, A. Storytelling Rights.
  S. Hobbs, 203:Vol100No1-122
Shuman, R.B. William Inge. (rev)
  C. Cagle, 389(MQ):Spring90-423
Shusterman, R. T.S. Eliot and the Philosophy of Criticism.*
  R. Bush, 191(ELN):Sep89-74
  J.X. Cooper, 27(AL):Mar89-137
                                    [continued]

[continuing]
G.S. Jay, 125:Spring89-315
P. Lamarque, 89(BJA):Autumn89-384
M. Lewis, 518:Apr89-120
M. Melaver, 494:Fall89-651
I. Robinson, 521:Jul89-259
Shuttle, P. Adventures with My Horse.*
S. Pugh, 493:Spring89-47
W. Scammell, 364:Aug/Sep89-92
Sichelschmidt, G. Theodor Fontane.
W. Paulsen, 133:Band22Heft2-177
Sicher, E. Style and Structure in the Prose of
Isaak Babel'.*
P. Carden, 550(RusR):Jan89-109
J. Curtis, 575(SEER):Apr89-288
M. Friedberg, 104(CASS):Spring-Win-
ter88-436
Sichrovsky, P. Born Guilty.
M. Birnbach, 639(VQR):Autumn89-767
Sickler, M. The Judaic State.
R.L.R., 185:Apr90-719
Siddons, A.R. King's Oak.
G. Lyons, 441:4Nov90-33
Sidebotham, S.E. Roman Economic Policy in
the Erythra Thalassa 30B.C.-A.D.217.*
P. Turner, 313:Vol79-249
Sidel, R. On Her Own.
J. Moore, 441:29Jul90-21
Sidelle, A. Necessity, Essence, and Individu-
ation.
W.R. Carter, 103:Nov90-476
A. Rein, 617(TLS)·11-17May90-507
Sidney, P. The Countess of Pembroke's Arca-
dia 1590. (V. Skretkowicz, ed)
M.G. Brennan, 541(RES):May89-252
A.V. Ettin, 677(YES):Vol20-247
M. McCanles, 551(RenQ):Spring89-133
R. Wymer, 179(ES):Apr89-178
Sidorchenko, L.V. Alexander Pope.
I. Burova, 566:Spring89-190
Siebenmann, G. Ensayos de literatura his-
panoamericana.
W.B. Berg, 547(RF):Band101Heft2/3-389
F.M. Rodríguez-Arenas, 711(RHM):Jun89-
88
Siebers, T. The Ethics of Criticism.*
C. Baldick, 301(JEGP):Oct89-531
W.E. Cain, 131(CL):Summer89-284
T. Docherty, 677(YES):Vol20-211
J. Phelan, 405(MP):May90-435
Siedlecki, J. Losy Polaków w ZSRR w latach
1939-1986.
J.R. Krzyżanowski, 497(PolR):Vol34No3-
259
K.R. Sword, 575(SEER):Jul89-489
Sieff, M. On Management.
J. Harvey-Jones, 324:Sep90-711
Siegel, B., ed. The American Writer and the
University.
S. Fogel, 395(MFS):Winter89-764
Siegel, B. A Death in White Bear Lake.
A. Vachss, 441:29Jul90-13
Siegel, F.F. The Roots of Southern Distinc-
tiveness.
M. Snay, 106:Summer89-135
Siegel, H. Educating Reason.
R.R., 185:Oct89-230
Siegel, H. Relativism Refuted.
J. Dunphy, 63:Mar89-117
M. Krausz, 484(PPR):Jun90-841
R. Nola, 84:Sep89-419
Siegel, J.T. Solo in the New Order.
S.O. Robson, 293(JASt):Aug89-684

Siegel, L. Laughing Matters.
S.H. Blackburn, 292(JAF):Oct-Dec89-502
E. Gerow, 485(PE&W):Jul89-327
Siegel, R.K. Intoxication.
M. Gossop, 617(TLS):19-25Jan90-54
Siegelbaum, L.H. Stakhanovism and the Poli-
tics of Productivity in the USSR, 1935-
1941.*
W.B. Husband, 550(RusR):Apr89-204
Siemon, J.R. Shakespearean Iconoclasm.*
J.A. Bryant, Jr., 569(SR):Summer89-445
Sieverding, N. Der ritterliche Kampf bei
Hartmann und Wolfram.*
M.H. Jones, 402(MLR):Jul90-780
Siewert, K. Glossenfunde.
J.M. Jeep, 350:Sep90-652
Sifakis, G.M. Gia mia poiētikē toy ellēnikoy
dēmotikoy tragoydioy.
R. Beaton, 303(JoHS):Vol109-278
Sigal, L.V. Fighting to the Finish.
O. Cary, 407(MN):Summer89-233
A. Iriye, 293(JASt):May89-401
Sigmund, P.E. Liberation Theology at the
Crossroads.
M. Davidson, 441:15Apr90-18
Sigmundsson, S. Islensk samheitaorðabók.
D.A. Hill, 563(SS):Winter89-80
Sigsworth, E.M. Montague Burton.
E.S. Turner, 617(TLS):15-21Jun90-636
Sigsworth, E.M., ed. In Search of Victorian
Values.
E. Langland, 158:Jun89-71
Sijpesteijn, P.J. & P.A. Verdult, eds. Papyri
in the Collection of the Erasmus University
(Rotterdam).
D.J. Thompson, 303(JoHS):Vol109-246
Silbiger, A., ed. Frescobaldi Studies.
G.S.J., 412:Nov88-308
R. Jackson, 410(M&L):Feb89-89
R. Judd, 415:Jun89-347
Siler, T. Breaking the Mind Barrier.
G. Johnson, 441:30Dec90-7
Silius. Sili Italici "Punica." (J. Delz, ed)
P. McGushin, 24:Fall89-518
M.D. Reeve, 123:Vol09No2-215
A. Smith, 235:Winter88-67
Silk, M. Spiritual Politics *
C.S. Byrum, 577(SHR):Summer89-268
Silkin, J. Selected Poems.
D. Houston, 493:Summer89-51
Sill, B, C. & J. A Field Guide to Little-known
and Seldom-seen Birds of North America.
42(AR):Winter89-110
Sillars, S. Art and Survival in First World
War Britain.*
R. Cork, 39:Nov89-358
Silli, P., ed. Testi Costantiniani nelle fonti
letterarie.
R. Klein, 229:Band61Heft2-178
Sillitoe, A. Last Loves.
D.A.N. Jones, 617(TLS):18-24May90-535
Sillitoe, L. Windows on the Sea and Other
Stories.
D. Johnson, 453(NYRB):15Mar90-28
Sillitoe, L. & A. Roberts. Salamander.
D. Johnson, 453(NYRB):15Mar90-28
Silman, R. Beginning the World Again.
J. Penner, 441:4Nov90-29
Silva, C.R. - see under Ruiz Silva, C.
Silva, M.D.S. - see under de Fátima Sousa e
Silva, M.

Silveira y Montes de Oca, J.A. Los romances
hispánicos contenidos en "El ingenioso hi-
dalgo don Quijote de la Mancha."
 I.A. Corfis, 238:May89-299
Silver, I. Ronsard and the Hellenic Renais-
sance in France.* (Vol 2, Pt 3)
 P. Ford, 208(FS):Oct89-460
 M-M. Fragonard, 535(RHL):Mar-Apr89-
 268
 J.C. Nash, 207(FR):Apr90-870
 A. Scholar, 402(MLR):Jan90-179
Silver, K.E. Esprit de Corps.
 T. Hilton, 617(TLS):16-22Mar90-289
Silver, P.W. La casa de Anteo.
 J.C. Wilcox, 400(MLN):Mar89-503
Silvera, M., ed. Fireworks.
 R. Buchanan, 102(CanL):Summer89-182
Silverberg, R. & K. Haber, eds. Universe 1.
 G. Jonas, 441:13May90-35
Silverman, D.L. Art Nouveau in Fin-de-
Siècle France.
 R. Thomson, 617(TLS):16-22Mar90-288
Silverman, G. Happy Divorce.
 R. Friedman, 617(TLS):10-16Aug90-855
Silverman, H.J., ed. Continental Philosophy I.
 M. Kelly, 402(MLR):Oct90-890
Silverman, H.J. Inscriptions.*
 C. Howells, 323:May89-182
 D. Pollard, 478(P&L):Apr89-187
 R.L. Zimmerman, 290(JAAC):Winter89-97
Silverman, H.J. & D. Welton, eds. Postmod-
ernism and Continental Philosophy.
 A. Nye, 103:May90-204
 J. Rodman, 89(BJA):Summer89-276
 G. Shapiro, 290(JAAC):Spring89-186
Silverman, K. The Acoustic Mirror.*
 B.E. Strong, 367(L&P):Vol35No3-64
Silverman, M. Moderna Sátira Brasileira.
 B.J. Chamberlain, 238:Sep89-560
Silverthorne, E. Marjorie Kinnan Rawlings.
 K.M. McCarthy, 395(MFS):Summer89-293
Silvester, P.J. A Left Hand Like God.*
 T. Piazza, 441:4Feb90-18
Simard, J. Les Arts sacrés au Québec.
 A. Chartier, 207(FR):Apr90-912
Simard, S. Mythe et reflet de la France.
 A. Chartier, 207(FR):Oct89-183
 D.M. Hayne, 627(UTQ):Fall89-191
Simcox, K. Wilfred Owen.
 P.E. Firchow, 70:Oct89-152
Simenon, G. The Door.
 442(NY):23Jul90-88
Simic, C. The Book of Gods and Devils.
 D. Kirby, 441:23Dec90-16
Simic, C. The Uncertain Certainty.
 W. Marsh, 456(NDQ):Winter89-224
Simic, C. - see Campion, T.
Simic, C. - see Šalamun, T.
Simmel, G. Philosophie de la modernité.
 M. Adam, 542:Oct-Dec89-620
Simmel, G. La Philosophie de l'Argent. La
Tragédie de la Culture et autres essais. La
Philosophie de l'Amour.
 I. Joseph, 98:May89-380
Simmen, E., ed. Gringos in Mexico.
 C.R. Shirley, 649(WAL):Feb90-377
Simmerman, J. Once Out of Nature.
 F. Chappell, 344:Summer90-168
 D. Chorlton, 496:Winter89/90-43
Simmie, S. & B. Nixon. Tiananmen Square.
 J. Mirsky, 453(NYRB):1Feb90-21
Simmons, J. Vision and Spirit.*
 M.R.B., 185:Oct89-217

Simmons, S. Driving the Angels Out.
 F. Manley, 102(CanL):Autumn-Winter89-
 216
Simms, J., ed. Life by Other Means.
 M. Walters, 617(TLS):9-15Mar90-248
Simms, J.G. War and Politics in Ireland,
1649-1730. (D. Hayton & G. O'Brien, eds)
 P.D.G. Thomas, 83:Spring89-96
Simms, K. From Kings to Warlords.*
 D.W. Cashman, 589:Oct89-1037
Simo, M.L. Loudon and the Landscape.*
 P.D., 46:Sep89-14
 639(VQR):Summer89-102
Simon, B. Tragic Drama and the Family.
 P.D. Murphy, 590:Dec89-122
 N.M. Tischler, 130:Winter89/90-384
Simon, C. L'acacia.
 F. Bon, 98:Dec89-980
 G. Craig, 617(TLS):16-22Feb90-180
Simon, D., with A. Hoffman - see Hoffman, A.
Simon, D.F. & M. Goldman, eds. Science and
Technology in Post-Mao China.
 J. Sigurdson, 293(JASt):Nov89-842
Simon, D.F. & D. Rehn. Technological Innova-
tion in China.
 R.P. Suttmeier, 293(JASt):Aug89-602
Simon, G. Nationalismus und Nationalitäten-
politik in der Sowjetunion.
 M. McCauley, 575(SEER):Apr89-303
Simon, J.L. The Economic Consequences of
Immigration.
 N. Glazer, 441:14Jan90-28
Simon, K. Etchings in an Hourglass.
 D. Grumbach, 441:19Aug90-3
Simon, R. Road Show.
 N. Lemann, 441:30Sep90-13
Simon, S. The Future of Asian-Pacific Secu-
rity Collaboration.
 L.W. Farnsworth, 293(JASt):Aug89-580
Simon, Y. The Road to Vichy, 1918-1938.*
(rev)
 J. Fletcher, 208(FS):Jul89-371
Simon, Y.R. The Definition of Moral Virtue.*
(V. Kuic, ed)
 D.B., 185:Jul90-905
Simoni, A.E.C. Catalogue of Books from the
Low Countries, 1601-1621, in the British
Library.
 D. McKitterick, 617(TLS):20-26Jul90-786
Simonnot, P. Homo Sportivus.
 H. Cronel, 450(NRF):May89-102
Simonova, M.S. Krizis agrarnoi politiki tsar-
izma nakanune pervoi Rossiiskoi revoliu-
tsii.
 D.A.J. Macey, 550(RusR):Jan89-92
Simons, D. Hyperion. The Fall of Hyperion.
 G. Jonas, 441:25Mar90-30
Simons, F.W. & P. Kent, eds. Patronage, Art
and Society in Renaissance Italy.
 T. Tuohy, 39:Feb89-139
Simons, G., ed. Eco-Computer.
 T. Lougheed, 529(QQ):Autumn89-770
Simons, J. Diaries and Journals of Literary
Women from Fanny Burney to Virginia
Woolf.
 L. Duguid, 617(TLS):20-26Jul90-770
Simonsen, T. - see Brooks, S.
Simonsen, H.P. Prairies Within.*
 J.W. Dietrichson, 172(Edda):1989/2-177
Simonson, R. & S. Walker, eds. Multi-Cultural
Literacy.
 S. Weiland, 271:Fall89-142

Simpson, B. The Great Dismal.
P-L. Adams, 61:Mar90-116
442(NY):21May90-96
Simpson, D. The Politics of American English,
1776-1850.*
E. Green, 591(SIR):Spring89-161
J.A.L. Lemay, 677(YES):Vol20-283
Simpson, D. Wordsworth's Historical Imagina-
tion.*
J.D. Gutteridge, 447(N&Q):Mar89-117
G. Harrison, 401(MLQ):Dec87-392
P.J. Manning, 141:Winter89-111
C. Salvesen, 541(RES):Feb89-132
Simpson, H. Four Bare Legs in a Bed and
Other Stories.
S. Roe, 617(TLS):13-19Jul90-746
Simpson, J. Inside Iran.
639(VQR):Winter89-23
Simpson, J. Spoils of Power.
N. Ward, 529(QQ):Autumn89-761
Simpson, K. The Protean Scot.*
R. Crawford, 571(ScLJ):Winter89-8
D. Duncan, 166:Oct89-90
Simpson, L. Collected Poems.*
R. McDowell, 249(HudR):Spring89-158
R. Moran, 580(SCR):Spring90-169
D. Wakoski, 219(GaR):Winter89-804
Simpson, L. In the Room We Share.
S. Dobyns, 441:2Sep90-5
Simpson, L.P. Mind and the American Civil
War.
C.V. Woodward, 452(NYRB):15Mar90-30
Simpson, M. Anywhere But Here.
W. Kelley, 473(FR):Vol56No4-683
Simpson, P., ed. The Given Condition.
R.W. Dasenbrock, 538(RAL):Spring89-107
Simpson, P. - see Curnow, A.
Simpson, P. - see Smithyman, K.
Simpson-Cooke, J. Future Rivers.*
R.J. Merrett, 102(CanL):Autumn-
Winter89-223
von Simson, Ö.G. Sacred Fortress.
H. Maguire, 589:Oct89-1048
Sin, A.S. - see under Szaszkóné Sin, A.
Sinclair, A., comp. The War Decade.*
J. Mellors, 364:Feb/Mar90-117
Sinclair, A. War Like a Wasp.*
J. Mellors, 364:Feb/Mar90-117
Sinclair, I. Flesh Eggs & Scalp Metal.*
R. Caddel, 493:Summer89-35
Sinclair, J. - see "Collins COBUILD English
Language Dictionary"
Sinclair, J.M., ed-in-chief. Collins COBUILD
English Grammar.
T. Shippey, 617(TLS):19-25Oct90-1117
Sinclair, K.V., comp. French Devotional Texts
of the Middle Ages. (2nd supp)
A.J. Holden, 402(MLR):Jul90-722
Sinclair, K.V. Prières en ancien français.*
B.J. Levy, 208(FS):Oct89-456
Sinclair, R.K. Democracy and Participation in
Athens.*
E. David, 242:Vol10No3-390
M.H. Hansen, 123:Vol39No1-69
D.G. Kyle, 124:Sep-Oct89-63
D. Lateiner, 121(CJ):Apr-May90-359
Sinclair, T.A. Eastern Turkey.
C. Mango, 617(TLS):28Sep-4Oct90-1045
Sinclair, U. The Lost First Edition of Upton
Sinclair's "The Jungle." (G. De Gruson, ed)
D. Roediger, 389(MQ):Autumn89-138
Sinclair-Stevenson, C. - see Vizinczey, S.

Sinden, D., ed. The Everyman Book of Theat-
rical Anecdotes.
P. Hartnoll, 611(TN):Vol43No1-41
Singer, B.C.J. Society, Theory and the French
Revolution.
N. Parker, 83:Spring89-77
Singer, C. Histoire d'âme.
C.F. Demaray, 207(FR):Mar90-749
Singer, H. & R.B. Rudell, eds. Theoretical
Models and Processes of Reading. (3rd ed)
H. Günther, 353:Vol27No3-572
Singer, I. The Nature of Love.* (Vol 3)
D.T.O., 295(JML):Fall88/Winter89-235
Singer, I.B. The King of the Fields.*
639(VQR):Spring89-57
Singer, I.B. & R. Burgin. Conversations with
Isaac Bashevis Singer.
R.H. Wolf, 508:Jan89-85
Singerman, A.J. L'abbe Prévost.*
C.J. Betts, 208(FS):Jan89-88
R. Granderoute, 535(RHL):Jan-Feb89-117
Singerman, P. An American Hero.
D. Smith, 441:19Aug90-19
Singh, G. - see Leavis, Q.D.
Singh, K., ed. The Writer's Sense of the
Past.*
K.O. Arthur, 71(ALS):Oct89-270
Singh, M. This My People.
I. Merchant, 441:15Jul90-9
Singleton, C.S. - see Boccaccio, G.
Singleton, F., ed. Environmental Problems in
the Soviet Union and Eastern Europe.
D.R. Weiner, 550(RusR):Apr89-223
Singleton, M.W. God's Courtier.
D.H. Burden, 184(EIC):Jul89-247
D.R. Dickson, 568(SCN):Spring-
Summer89-9
N.H. Keeble, 447(N&Q):Sep89-392
M.C. Schoenfeldt, 301(JEGP):Jul89-411
Sinn, F. Stadtrömische Marmorurnen.
G. Davies, 313:Vol79-220
Sinnott-Armstrong, W. Moral Dilemmas.
R.A. Duff, 479(PhQ):Apr89-240
D. McNaughton, 518:Oct89-244
Sinor, D., ed. The Cambridge History of Early
Inner Asia.
D. Morgan, 617(TLS):3-9Aug90-840
Siraisi, N.G. Avicenna in Renaissance Italy.
P.G. Sobol, 551(RenQ):Winter89-828
Sirc, L. Between Hitler and Tito.
R. Kindersley, 617(TLS):6-12Apr90-368
Sirinelli, J-F. Intellectuels et passions fran-
çaises.
P. Brooks, 617(TLS):5-11Oct90-1075
Siroën, J-M. L'Économie mondiale.
P. Monzani, 531:Jul-Dec89-552
Sirr, P. Talk, Talk.
B. O'Donoghue, 493:Summer89-62
Siskin, C. The Historicity of Romantic Dis-
course.*
J. Engell, 445(NCF):Sep89-229
J.E. Hogle, 340(KSJ):Vol38-162
M. Russett, 400(MLN):Dec89-1210
D.P. Watkins, 141:Fall89-502
Sisòkò, F-D. The Epic of Son-Jara.
J. Knappert, 203:Vol100No1-125
Sissa, G. Greek Virginity.
H. King, 617(TLS):30Mar-5Apr90-341
Sisson, C.H. On the Look-out.*
G. Ewart, 364:Dec89/Jan90-139
Sisson, R. & S. Wolpert, eds. Congress and
Indian Nationalism.
G. Prakash, 293(JASt):Nov89-917

343

"SITE."
S. Izenour, 47:Oct89-41
"K. Janson Sitewell's Book of Spoofs."
42(AR):Fall89-504
Sittig, D. "Vyl wonders machet minne."
W.E. Jackson, 201:Vol15-366
Sitwell, S. & W. Blunt. Great Flower Books:
1700-1900.
L. Yang, 441:2Dec90-21
Six, A.L. Juan Goytisolo.
J. Labanyi, 617(TLS):6-12Jul90-733
Sizemore, C.W. A Female Vision of the City.
K. Ford, 617(TLS):29Jun-5Jul90-702
Sjönell, B.S. Strindbergs Taklagsöl - ett
prosaexperiment.
S.C. Brantly, 563(SS):Spring/Summer89-
275
Skaff, W. The Philosophy of T.S. Eliot.*
S. Bagchee, 675(YER):Spring90-83
R. Crawford, 541(RES):May89-293
R.F.S., 295(JML):Fall88/Winter89-320
Skal, D.J. Hollywood Gothic.
K. Quinn, 441:30Dec90-15
Skelton, B. Weep No More.
J. Dalley, 617(TLS):5-11Jan90-5
J. Lewis, 364:Dec89/Jan90-120
Skelton, R. Celtic Contraries.
D. Donoghue, 617(TLS):7-13Dec90-1324
Skelton, R. Fires of the Kindred.
J.R. Wytenbroek, 102(CanL):Autumn-
Winter89-279
Skelton, R. The Memoirs of a Literary Block-
head.*
G. Woodcock, 102(CanL):Autumn-
Winter89-275
Skelton, R. Openings.
R. Nash, 526:Summer89-102
Skelton, R. The Parrot Who Could.*
G. Boire, 102(CanL):Spring89-175
Skemp, S. William Franklin.
E. Wright, 441:30Sep90-15
Skenazy, P. James M. Cain.
D. Fine, 649(WAL):Feb90-383
D. Geherin, 395(MFS):Winter89-752
Skillman, J. Worship of the Visible Spectrum.
O. Siporin, 649(WAL):May89-88
Skimin, R. Gray Victory.
639(VQR):Spring89-56
Skinner, J. A Guide to Forgetting.
R.B. Shaw, 491:Aug89-291
Skinner, Q., ed. The Return of Grand Theory
in the Human Sciences.
T.E. Huff, 488:Mar89-120
Skira, P. Still Life.
L. Gowing, 617(TLS):20-26Jul90-772
Sklar, L. Philosophy and Spacetime Physics.
R. Di Salle, 486:Dec89-714
Sklepowich, E. Death in a Serene City.
M. Stasio, 441:28Oct90-41
Skoda, F. Médecin ancienne et métaphore.
R.J. Durling, 229:Band61Heft2-166
Skogan, W.G. Disorder and Decline.
J. Lardner, 441:16Dec90-14
Skorupski, J. John Stuart Mill.
A. Ryan, 617(TLS):13-19Apr90-399
Skovron, A. The Rearrangement.
W. Tonetto, 581:Dec89-660
Skretkowicz, V. - see Sidney, P.
Skupinska-Løvset, I. Funerary Portraiture of
Roman Palestine.
R. Rebuffat, 555:Vol62Fasc1-184
Skutsch, O. - see Ennius

Škvorecký, J. The End of Lieutenant Bor-
uvka.
T.J. Binyon, 617(TLS):30Nov-6Dec90-
1300
K. Marton, 441:18Feb90-14
Škvorecký, J. Sins for Father Knox.* The
Return of Lieutenant Boruvka.
T.J. Binyon, 617(TLS):30Nov-6Dec90-
1300
Škvorecký, J. Talkin' Moscow Blues. (S. Sol-
ecki, ed)
G. Woodcock, 627(UTQ):Fall89-169
617(TLS):27Apr-3May90-457
Skwara, E.W. Hans Sahl, Leben und Werk.
K. Weissenberger, 133:Band22Heft1-88
Slater, E. The Problem of "The Reign of King
Edward III."
M.W.A. Smith, 447(N&Q):Dec89-500
Slater, J.G. - see Russell, B.
Slater, J.G., with B. Frohmann - see Russell,
B.
Slater, W.J. - see Aristophanes of Byzantium
Slavitt, D.R. Lives of the Saints.
M. Mifflin, 441:11Feb90-18
442(NY):29Jan90-95
Slawek, S.M. Sitār Technique in Nibaddh
Forms.
S.L. Marcus, 187:Winter89-167
Slawson, D.A. Secret Teachings in the Art of
Japanese Gardens.
B. Bognar, 293(JASt):Aug89-627
Slawson, W. Sound Color.*
P. Lansky, 308:Spring89-191
Sleeman, M.G. & G.A. Davies. Variations on
Spanish Themes.
E.F.K., 412:Feb89-70
Sleeper, J. The Closest of Strangers.
A. Hacker, 453(NYRB):22Nov90-19
J.A. Lukas, 441:9Sep90-11
Sljivic-Simsic, B. Serbo-Croatian Just for
You.
M.J. Elson, 399(MLJ):Winter89-529
Sljivic-Simsic, B. & R.F. Price. Advanced
Serbo-Croatian 1. Advanced Serbo-Croa-
tian 2. Reading Serbo-Croatian 1 & 2.
M.J. Elson, 399(MLJ):Winter89-529
Sljivic-Simsic, B. & K. Vidakovic. Elementary
Serbo-Croatian 1.* Elementary Serbo-
Croatian 2.* Intermediate Serbo-Croatian
1.*
M.J. Elson, 399(MLJ):Winter89-529
Sloan, B. The Pioneers of Anglo-Irish Fic-
tion, 1800-1850.
H. Pyle, 541(RES):May89-276
Sloan, J. George Gissing.
J. Korg, 637(VS):Summer90-674
Sloane, D.A. Aleksandr Blok and the Dynam-
ics of the Lyric Cycle.
A. Pyman, 402(MLR):Apr90-535
Sloane, D.E.E. "Adventures of Huckleberry
Finn."
J.E. Bassett, 392:Spring89-209
G.C. Carrington, Jr., 26(ALR):Fall89-85
Sloane, T.O. Donne, Milton, and the End of
Humanist Rhetoric.*
M. Trousdale, 402(MLR):Oct90-915
Slob, E. Luxuria.
H. Kloft, 229:Band61Heft6-561
Slobin, D.I., ed. The Cross-Linguistic Study
of Language Acquisition.
P. Fletcher, 297(JL):Sep89-473
S. Romaine, 355(LSoc):Dec89-577

Slobin, D.I. & K. Zimmer, eds. Studies in Turkish Linguistics.*
J. Kornfilt, 603:Vol13No1-171
Slobin, G.N., ed. Aleksej Remizov.
J.G. Tucker, 104(CASS):Spring-Winter88-431
Sloboda, J.A., ed. Generative Processes in Music.*
E. Graebner, 410(M&L):May89-242
S. McAdams, 413:Winter89-195
Slocum, J., ed. Machine Translation Systems.
J. Pinkham, 350:Mar90-209
Slodnjak, A. & J. Kos, eds. Pisma Matija Čopa.
H.R. Cooper, Jr., 574(SEEJ):Fall89-468
Slonimsky, N. Perfect Pitch.*
E.S., 414(MusQ):Vol74No3-455
Sloterdijk, P. Critique of Cynical Reason.
W.G. Regier, 223:Spring89-94
M. Westphal, 258:Dec89-479
Sloterdijk, P. Versprechen auf Deutsch.
P. Graves, 617(TLS):15-21Jun90-631
Slotte, P., ed. Denotationsbyte i ortnamn.
E. Gunnemark, 424:Mar89-100
Sluka, J.A. Hearts and Minds, Water and Fish.
T. Hadden, 617(TLS):20-26Jul90-769
Słupski, Z., ed. Selective Guide to Chinese Literature, 1900-1949. (Vol 2)
P.F. Williams, 116:Jul88-194
Slusser, G.E., C. Greenland & E.S. Rabkin, eds. Storm Warnings.*
T.J. Remington, 455:Jun90-67
Slusser, G.E. & E.S. Rabkin, eds. Aliens.* Mindscapes.
T.J. Remington, 455:Jun89-67
Slusser, G.E. & E.S. Rabkin, eds. Intersections.
C.D. Malmgren, 561(SFS):Nov89-384
T.J. Remington, 455:Jun89-67
Slusser, R.M. Stalin in October.*
S.F. Jones, 575(SEER):Apr89-316
P. Pomper, 550(RusR):Oct89-423
Slyomovics, S. The Merchant of Art.
G. Canova, 196:Band30Heft3/4-354
M. Galley, 292(JAF):Jul-Sep89-344
H.T. Norris, 294:Mar89-83
Small, C. Music of the Common Tongue.*
E.S. Meadows, 187:Spring/Summer89-348
Small, C. The Printed Word.
517(PBSA):Mar89-114
Smallman, B. The Piano Trio.
E. Sams, 617(TLS):20-26Jul90-778
Smallwood, A.J. Fielding and the Woman Question.
M.C. Battestin, 166:Apr90-264
Smaragdus. Liber in partibus Donati. (B. Löfstedt, L. Holtz & A. Kibre, eds)
P. Flobert, 555:Vol62Fasc2-383
V. Law, 640:May89-77
J. Marenbon, 589:Apr89-502
Smarr, J.L. Boccaccio and Fiammetta.*
M. Cottino-Jones, 276:Autumn89-371
Smarr, J.L. - see Boccaccio, G.
Smart, C. The Poetical Works of Christopher Smart. (Vol 3) (M. Walsh, ed)
J.P. Vander Motten, 179(ES):Apr89-183
Smart, C. The Poetical Works of Christopher Smart. (Vol 4) (K. Williamson, ed)
J.P. Vander Motten, 179(ES):Apr89-183
566:Spring89-196
Smart, C.M., Jr. Muscular Churches.
T. Burgess, 324:Jul90-566

Smart, E. In the Meantime. (A. Van Wart, ed) Juvenilia. Autobiographies.
L.L. Tostevin, 102(CanL):Autumn-Winter89-169
Smart, E. Necessary Secrets.* (A. Van Wart, ed)
J. Mills, 168(ECW):Spring89-161
Smart, J.J.C. Essays Metaphysical and Moral.*
D.B., 185:Oct89-207
Smart, P. Ecrire dans la maison du père.
P. Hébert, 627(UTQ):Fall89-218
Smart, W.B. Old Utah Trails.
R. Burrows, 649(WAL):Aug89-158
Smeed, J.W. Don Juan.
J. Kerrigan, 617(TLS):3-9Aug90-817
Smeed, J.W. German Song and its Poetry, 1740-1900.*
E. West, 410(M&L):Feb89-109
Smerlas, F. & V. Carucci. By a Nose.
M. Mehler, 441:7Oct90-20
Smets, P-F. Albert Camus dans le premier silence ... et au-delà.
J. Kolbert, 207(FR):May90-1075
Smidak, E.F. Isaak-Ignaz Moscheles.
J. Warrack, 617(TLS):23-29Mar90-322
"Smide 88."
L. Karlsson, 341:Vol58No4-174
Smidt, K. Unconformities in Shakespeare's Early Comedies.
H. Castrop, 156(ShJW):Jahrbuch1989-360
S. Thomas, 570(SQ):Summer89-230
Smiley, J. Ordinary Love & Good Will.*
(British title: Ordinary Love.)
W. Brandmark, 617(TLS):27Apr-3May90-456
Smit, D.W. The Language of a Master.*
G. Caramello, 395(MFS):Summer89-267
S.B. Daugherty, 26(ALR):Winter90-88
Smith, A. Explorers of the Amazon.
S. Mills, 617(TLS):7-13Dec90-1315
Smith, A. The Roaring '80s.
639(VQR):Spring89-59
Smith, A.L., Jr. Hitler's Gold.
A.J. Sherman, 617(TLS):23-29Mar90-313
Smith, B. Costly Performances.
D. Windham, 460(NYRD):19Jul90-12
Smith, B., ed. Culture and History.
S. Ingle, 447(N&Q):Jun89-266
Smith, B., ed. Truth, Liberty, Religion.
W.R. Ward, 83:Spring89-88
Smith, B. & H.B. Reynolds, eds. The City as a Sacred Center.
S. Naquin, 293(JASt):Nov89-812
Smith, B.H. Contingencies of Value.*
W.E. Cain, 478(P&L):Oct89-376
S. Connor, 402(MLR):Oct90-891
G.G. Harpham, 533:Summer89-134
L. Howe, 141:Fall89-513
R. Shusterman, 290(JAAC):Spring89-182
M. Slote, 543:Mar90-646
42(AR):Fall89-503
Smith, B.R. Ancient Scripts and Modern Experience on the English Stage 1500-1700.
A.F. Kinney, 130:Fall89-287
Smith, C. The Lives of the Dead.
S. Morgan, 441:23Sep90-15
Smith, C. St. Bartholomew's Church.
M.J. Crosbie, 47:Nov89-37

Smith, C., with M. Bermejo Marcos, E. Chang-
Rodríguez & others – see "Collins Spanish–
English English–Spanish Dictionary/Collins
Diccionario Español–Inglés Inglés–Español"
Smith, C.R. Interior Design in 20th–Century
America.
 J. Montague, 576:Mar89–101
Smith, C.S. – see under Saumarez Smith, C.
Smith, D. Cuba Night.
 S. Burris, 598(SoR):Spring90–456
 H. Vendler, 442(NY):2Apr90–113
Smith, D. Diplomacy of Fear.
 F. Harbutt, 106:Fall89–288
Smith, D. The Everyday World as Problematic.
 G. McGregor, 298:Fall89–147
Smith, D. & D. Bottoms, eds. The Morrow
Anthology of Younger American Poets.*
 R. McDowell, 249(HudR):Winter89–598
Smith, D.B. Ladder to the Moon.* Living in
the Cave of the Mouth.*
 M.T. Lane, 198:Winter89–115
Smith, D.M. Italy and Its Monarchy.*
 J. Joll, 453(NYRB):14Jun90–8
Smith, E.A. Lord Grey, 1764–1845.
 B. Hilton, 617(TLS):3–9Aug90–827
Smith, E.A.T., ed. Blueprints for Modern Liv-
ing.
 K.W. Forster, 441:25Mar90–28
Smith, E.B. The Presidencies of Zachary Tay-
lor and Millard Fillmore.
 R.K. Ratzlaff, 389(MQ):Winter90–284
Smith, F. Joining the Literacy Club.
 D. Gorrell, 126(CCC):May89–241
Smith, G., ed. On Walter Benjamin.*
 L. Vieth, 478(P&L):Oct89–390
Smith, G. Reagan and Thatcher.
 F. Mount, 617(TLS):21–27Dec90–1369
Smith, G.B. Soviet Politics.
 R. Sakwa, 575(SEER):Oct89–653
Smith, G.E.K. Looking at Architecture.
 M. Filler, 441:2Dec90–22
Smith, G.S. – see Mirsky, D.S.
Smith, H. The New Russians.
 S.F. Starr, 441:9Dec90–9
Smith, H. The Power Game.
 T.C. Holyoke, 42(AR):Spring89–242
 639(VQR):Winter89–24
Smith, H.D. 2d. Kiyochika.
 F. Baekeland, 407(MN):Summer89–251
Smith, H.E. & R.B. – see Twain, M.
Smith, I.C. The Dream.
 G. Maxwell, 617(TLS):11–17May90–495
Smith, I.C. Selected Stories.
 B. Morton, 617(TLS):7–13Sep90–956
Smith, I.C. The Village and Other Poems.
 J.H. Alexander, 571(ScLJ):Winter89–46
 G. Maxwell, 617(TLS):11–17May90–495
Smith, J. Don't Leave Me This Way.
 P. Craig, 617(TLS):17–23Aug90–867
Smith, J. Misogynies.*
 H. Mantel, 364:Aug/Sep89–122
Smith, J. New Orleans Mourning.
 M. Stasio, 441:4Mar90–35
Smith, J. Off the Record.* (M. Fink, ed)
 R.S. Denisoff, 498:Summer89–119
 C.T. Morrissey, 498:Fall89–105
Smith, J. Captain John Smith: A Select Edi-
tion of His Writings. (K.O. Kupperman, ed)
 C. Mulford, 585(SoQ):Summer89–120
Smith, J. Translating Sleep.
 S. Scobie, 376:Sep89–123

Smith, J. & others, eds. Racism, Sexism, and
the World–System.
 N.B., 185:Jul90–922
Smith, J.A. Franklin and Bache.
 E. Wright, 441:30Sep90–15
Smith, J.E. Lucius D. Clay.
 S.E. Ambrose, 441:29Jul90–13
Smith, J.H. The Spirit and Its Letter.
 H. Reiss, 402(MLR):Jul90–802
 C. Sills, 319:Oct90–625
Smith, J.H. & W. Kerrigan, eds. Images in Our
Souls.*
 J. Maxfield, 478(P&L):Apr89–219
 P.A. Roth, 290(JAAC):Spring89–184
Smith, J.L. Sea of Troubles.
 M. Stasio, 441:29Apr90–18
Smith, J.S. Patenting the Sun.
 M. Caldwell, 441:6May90–15
 442(NY):18Jun90–96
Smith, J.W. Essays on Ultimate Questions.
 J.E. Malpas, 63:Sep89–361
Smith, J.W. The Progress and Rationality of
Philosophy as a Cognitive Enterprise.
 J. Fox, 63:Dec89–489
Smith, K. The Bright Particulars.*
 J. Lynes, 102(CanL):Autumn–Winter89–
212
Smith, K. Wormwood.*
 R. Pybus, 565:Winter88/89–67
Smith, K., with D. Wait. Inside Time.
 M. Crucefix, 493:Autumn89–33
 A. Rudolf, 364:Jun/Jul89–121
Smith, K.J.M. James Fitzjames Stephen.*
 J.W. Bicknell, 637(VS):Spring90–495
Smith, L. Fair and Tender Ladies.*
 T. Rash, 580(SCR):Spring90–131
Smith, L., ed. Heartlands.
 42(AR):Summer89–370
Smith, L. Me and My Baby View the Eclipse.
 E. Canin, 441:11Feb90–11
Smith, L., ed. Ukiyoe – Images of Unknown
Japan.
 Susumu Takiguchi, 463:Spring89–48
Smith, L.B. Treason in Tudor England.
 B. Cottret, 531:Jul–Dec89–535
Smith, L.D. Behaviorism and Logical Positiv-
ism.
 L. Addis, 606:Mar89–345
Smith, L.E., ed. Discourse Across Cultures.
 Y. Bader, 257(IRAL):Aug89–255
Smith, L.N. – see Nash, O.
"Logan Pearsall Smith: An Anthology" – see
under Pearsall
Smith, L.Z., ed. Audits of Meaning.
 R. Penticoff, 126(CCC):Oct89–350
Smith, M. & H. Rosengarten – see Brontë, C.
Smith, M. & W. Ulmer, eds. Ezra Pound.
 M. Schiralli, 289:Fall89–123
Smith, M.D. & J.L. Locke, eds. The Emergent
Lexicon.
 J.S. Falk, 350:Dec90–885
Smith, M.P. Spirit World.
 F. De Caro, 582(SFQ):Vol46No1–83
Smith, N. Perfection Proclaimed.
 639(VQR):Autumn89–122
Smith, O. The Politics of Language 1791–
1819.
 E. Green, 591(SIR):Spring89–161
Smith, P. The Book of Nasty Legends. The
Book of Nastier Legends.
 R.W. Brednich, 196:Band30Heft1/2–170

Smith, P. Discerning the Subject.*
C. Altieri, 577(SHR):Summer89-255
J. Clifford, 128(CE):Sep89-517
Smith, P. Killing the Spirit.
G.I. Maeroff, 441:18Mar90-27
442(NY):28May90-111
Smith, P. A Reader's Guide to the Short Sto-
ries of Ernest Hemingway.
234:Fall89-102
Smith, P. & O.R. Jones. The Philosophy of
Mind.*
H.M. Robinson, 393(Mind):Apr89-311
Smith, P.A. W.B. Yeats and the Tribes of
Danu.
C. Holdsworth, 177(ELT):Vol32No1-108
Smith, P.C. - see Gadamer, H-G.
Smith, P.E. 2d & M.S. Helfand - see Wilde, O.
Smith, P.H. & others, eds. Letters of Dele-
gates to Congress, 1774-1789. (Vol 15)
639(VQR):Autumn89-128
Smith, P.J. Quevedo on Parnassus.*
M.E. Barnard, 240(HR):Autumn89-518
R. Moore, 402(MLR):Jan90-225
Smith, P.J. Voyage et Écriture.*
G. Jondorf, 208(FS):Oct89-458
G. de Rocher, 210(FrF):Jan89-92
Smith, P.J. Writing in the Margin.
R. El Saffar, 304(JHP):Winter89-160
Smith, Q. The Felt Meanings of the World.
P. Butchvarov, 449:Apr89-281
F. Dunlop, 323:May89-187
Smith, R. Nemesis.
T. Carpenter, 441:29Jul90-1
Smith, R.A. Sports & Freedom.
M. Onigman, 432(NEQ):Dec89-634
Smith, R.J. The Gothic Bequest.*
R. Jann, 637(VS):Spring90-511
Smith, R.W. The Space Telescope.
D. King-Hele, 617(TLS):27Jul-2Aug90-
808
L.M. Lederman, 441:8Apr90-3
Smith, S. Horatio McCulloch.
D.B. Brown, 90:Sep89-658
Smith, S. A Poetics of Women's Autobiogra-
phy.
L. Anderson, 506(PSt):Sep89-198
H.M. Buss, 49:Jul89-98
K. Straub, 141:Spring89-207
Smith, S. Edward Thomas.*
R. Bouyssou, 189(EA):Jul-Sep89-355
Smith, S.A. - see "Free Speech Yearbook"
Smith, S.B. Hegel's Critique of Liberalism.
P. Franco, 185:Jan90-424
Smith, S.B. In All His Glory.
C. Buckley, 441:4Nov90-1
Smith, S.G. The Concept of the Spiritual.
R. Marres, 543:Mar90-647
Smith, S.G. Saltire Self-Portraits 3.
J.C. Hall, 571(ScLJ):Spring89-33
Smith, S.S. - see Crapsey, A.
Smith, T.C. Native Sources of Japanese In-
dustrialization, 1750-1920.*
J.L. McClain, 293(JASt):Nov89-877
Smith, V., ed. Australian Poetry 1988.
S. Lee, 581:Jun89-249
Smith, V. Self-Discovery and Authority in
Afro-American Narrative.
R.K. Barksdale, 301(JEGP):Apr89-265
W. Hall, 402(MLR):Jan90-173
N. Harris, 395(MFS):Summer89-307
R. Martin, 459:Summer89-104
Smith, V. - see Palmer, N.

Smith, W. Real Life Drama.
M. Gussow, 441:30Dec90-11
Smith, W.F. Modern Technology in Foreign
Language Education.
E.G. Joiner, 399(MLJ):Summer89-207
K.E. Kintz, 207(FR):Dec89-415
Smith, W.J. & F.D. Reeve - see Voznesensky,
A.
Smith, W.S. & E. Morales Dominguez, eds.
Subject to Solution.
W.R. Duncan, 263(RIB):Vol39No1-81
Smither, E. A Pattern of Marching.
L. Norfolk, 617(TLS):2-8Feb90-122
Smither, H.E. The Oratorio in the Classical
Era.*
H. Loos, 417:Apr-Jun89-184
Smithers, G.V., ed. Havelok.*
F.M. Biggs, 301(JEGP):Jan89-87
D. Mehl, 72:Band226Heft1-161
Smithyman, K. Selected Poems. (P. Simpson,
ed)
L. Norfolk, 617(TLS):2-8Feb90-122
Smoke, R., with W. Harman. Paths to Peace.
J.M., 185:Apr90-717
Smolińska, T. Jo wóm trocha połosprawiom ...
Wspólcześni gawędziarze ludowi na Śląsku.
Z wybranych problemów dawnej i współ
czesnej sztuki opowiadania.
D. Simonides, 196:Band30Heft3/4-355
Omolka, H.H. Untersuchungen zur Umgangs-
sprache in Nordhessen.
D. Stellmacher, 685(ZDL):2/1989-232
Smollett, T. The Adventures of Ferdinand
Count Fathom.* (J.C. Beasley & O.M. Brack,
eds)
K.L. Cope, 594:Winter89-442
639(VQR):Spring89-50
Smollett, T. The History and Adventures of
an Atom. (R.A. Day, ed)
P. Rogers, 617(TLS):8-14Jun90-606
Smoor, P. Kings and Bedouins in the Palace of
Aleppo as reflected in Ma'arri's Works.
J.E. Montgomery, 294:Mar89-81
Smout, T.C. & S. Wood. Scottish Voices, 1745-
1060.
T.M. Devine, 617(TLS):28Sep-4Oct90-
1042
Smuts, R.M. Court Culture and the Origins of
a Royalist Tradition in Early Stuart Eng-
land.*
J.C. Robertson, 557:Mar89-71
G. Walker, 242:Vol10No2-256
Smyllie, J.S. The Fifth Sun.
S. Altinel, 617(TLS):4-10May90-480
Smyth, J.V. A Question of Eros.
S. Soupel, 189(EA):Apr-Jun89-214
Snead, J.A. Figures of Division.*
J.E. Bassett, 401(MLQ):Dec87-396
R. Belflower, 541(RES):Aug89-439
Sneck, S. Assessment of Chronography in
Finnish-English Telephone Conversation.
C. Engber, 710:Mar89-122
Snellgrove, D. Indo-Tibetan Buddhism.*
J.W. de Jong, 259(IIJ):Jul89-219
Snider, C. Blood and Bones.
G. Locklin, 649(WAL):Aug89-193
Snigurowicz, D., comp. L'Art musical, 1860-
1870, 1872-1894.
F. Lesure, 537:Vol75No1-101
Snodgrass, A.M. An Archaeology of Greece.*
K. Branigan, 303(JoHS):Vol109-248
D.B. Small, 124:Nov-Dec89-129

Snodgrass, W.D. Selected Poems, 1957–1987.*
  L. Levis, 29(APR):Jan/Feb89–9
  W. Logan, 472:Vol16No1–72
Snodgrass, W.D. & D. McGraw. W.D.'s Midnight
Carnival.
  639(VQR):Spring89–66
"Snorri Sturluson's Edda." (A. Faulks, trans)
  H. O'Donoghue, 541(RES):Feb89–107
"Snorri Sturluson's Edda: Prologue and Gylfa-
ginning."* (A. Faulkes, ed)
  J. Simpson, 203:Vol100No2–256
Snow, P. The Star Raft.
  D. Brautigam, 293(JASt):Nov89–843
Snowden, F.M. The Facist Revolution in Tus-
cany, 1919–1922.
  A. Kelikian, 617(TLS):9–15Mar90–263
Snyder, J.M. The Woman and the Lyre.
  D.H. Kelly, 124:Jul–Aug90–537
Snyder, K.J. Dietrich Buxtehude.
  S. Daw, 415:Apr89–215
  K. Elcombe, 410(M&L):Aug89–398
  G.B. Stauffer, 317:Fall89–657
Snyder, R.W. The Voice of the City.
  M.C. Curtis, 441:4Mar90–25
Snyder, S.H. Brainstorming.*
  M. Gossop, 617(TLS):19–25Jan90–54
Sŏ Chŏngju. Selected Poems of Sŏ Chŏngju.
  A.S–H. Lee, 293(JASt):Nov89–891
Sobel, M. The World They Made Together.
  W.D. Jordan, 656(WMQ):Apr89–394
  C. Lounsbury, 658:Summer/Autumn89–187
Soble, A., ed. Eros, Agape and Philia.
  C. Williams, 103:Jun90–255
Soble, A. The Structure of Love.
  R.C. Solomon, 103:Nov90–478
Sochor, Z.A. Revolution and Culture.
  A. Kelly, 453(NYRB):6Dec90–60
"sociolinguistica." (Vol 1) (U. Ammon, K.J.
Mattheier & P.H. Nelde, eds)
  K. Bochmann, 682(ZPSK):Band42Heft5–
  687
Socken, P.G. Myth and Morality in "Alexandre
Chenevert" by Gabrielle Roy.
  R. Benson, 627(UTQ):Fall89–202
  D. Essar, 102(CanL):Summer89–171
Socknat, T.P. Witness Against War.
  J. Levitt, 529(QQ):Spring89–190
Socolow, E. Laughing at Gravity.
  K.E. Duffin, 472:Vol16No1–41
Soderlund, J.R., ed. William Penn and the
Founding of Pennsylvania, 1680–1684.
  S.V. James, 656(WMQ):Jan89–165
Soeteman, A. Logic in Law.
  J.G., 185:Jan90–452
Soffer, W. From Science to Subjectivity.*
  R.A. Watson, 319:Oct90–615
Soja, C. – see under Ch'oe Soja
Sojka, G.S. Ernest Hemingway.
  Z.B., 295(JML):Fall88/Winter89–348
Sojourner, M. Sisters of the Dream.
  J.B. Hemesath, 649(WAL):Feb90–389
Sokolova, L. Dancing for Diaghilev.
  M. McQuade, 151:Sep89–56
Sokolove, M.Y. Hustle.
  F. King, 441:11Nov90–9
Sokolowski, R., ed. Edmund Husserl and the
Phenomenological Tradition.
  J.G. Hart, 543:Dec89–423
Sokolowski, R. Moral Action.*
  K. Torell, 323:Jan89–96
Solà, J. Qüestions controvertides de sintaxi
catalana.
  M. Wheeler, 86(BHS):Oct89–390

Solalinde, A.G. Poemas breves medievales.
(I.A. Corfis, ed)
  J.E. Connolly, 240(HR):Autumn89–502
Solecki, S. – see Škvorecký, J.
Solin, H. & O. Salomies. Repertorium nominum
gentilium, et cognominum Latinorum.
  T.J. Cadoux, 123:Vol39No2–327
Sollers, P. Event.
  J.T. Naughton, 577(SHR):Winter89–74
Sollers, P. Le Lys d'or.
  J.T. Letts, 207(FR):Mar90–749
  C–P. Pérez, 450(NRF):Jun89–103
Sollors, W. Beyond Ethnicity.*
  M. Shapiro, 677(YES):Vol20–355
Solms, H–J. Die morphologischen Veränder-
ungen der Stammvokale der starken Verben
im Frühneuhochdeutschen.
  M. Durrell, 680(ZDP):Band108Heft3–463
Solms, W. & C. Oberfeld, eds. Das selbstver-
ständliche Wunder.
  S. Neumann, 196:Band30Heft1/2–171
Solodow, J.B. The World of Ovid's "Metamor-
phoses."
  K. Galinsky, 24:Fall89–515
  A.M. Keith, 487:Autumn89–273
  S. Lundström, 229:Band61Heft3–255
  D.V. McCaffrey, 124:Sep–Oct89–69
Solomita, S. Forced Entry.
  A. Pagnozzi, 441:14Oct90–47
Solomon, B.S. Green Architecture and the
Agrarian Garden.
  M.J. Darnall, 45:Mar89–63
Solomon, C. Emergency Messages.
  D. Blaise, 532(RCF):Spring89–249
Solomon, M. Beethoven Essays.*
  W. Drabkin, 410(M&L):Nov89–550
  K. Korsyn, 415:Jul89–407
Solomon, M., ed & trans. The Mirror of Coitus.
  J.J. Gwara, 304(JHP):Winter90–181
Solomon, R.C. Continental Philosophy since
1750.*
  D. Breazeale, 319:Jul90–460
  B. Doniela, 63:Jun89–241
  J. Rée, 518:Jul89–144
Solotaroff, R. Bernard Malamud.
  C. Stetler, 573(SSF):Summer89–363
Solotorevsky, M. Literatura paraliteratura.
  D.W. Foster, 263(RIB):Vol39No2–213
Solow, B.L. & S.L. Engerman, eds. British
Capitalism and Caribbean Slavery.
  J. Walvin, 656(WMQ):Oct89–814
Solway, D. Modern Marriage.
  M. Bowering, 102(CanL):Autumn–
  Winter89–181
Somcynsky, J–F. Les Visiteurs du pole nord.
  M.B. Yoken, 399(MLJ):Winter89–512
Somers, R.M. – see Wright, A.F.
Somerwil–Ayrton, S.K. Poverty and Power in
the Early Works of Dostoevskij.
  A.R. Durkin, 395(MFS):Winter89–839
Somfai, L. – see Bartók, B.
Sommer, E. & M., eds. Similes Dictionary.
  K.B. Harder, 424:Sep89–294
Sommer, R. Fawn Bones.
  R.E. Conway, 102(CanL):Autumn–
  Winter89–278
Sommer, S. Still Lives.*
  42(AR):Summer89–375
Sondrup, S.P. & D. Chisholm, comps. Verskon-
kordanz zu Goethes "Faust, erster Teil."*
  J.W. Marchand, 301(JEGP):Apr89–291

Song, B–S. The Sanjo Tradition of Korean
Kŏmun'go Music.
    R.C. Provine, 187:Fall89–537
Song, C. Frameless Windows, Squares of
Light.
    R.B. Shaw, 491:Aug89–289
Song, C–H. Chosŏn Sahoesa Yŏn'gu.
    F. Kawashima, 293(JASt):Feb89–190
Sonn, R.D. Anarchism and Cultural Politics in
Fin de Siècle France.*
    E.L. Newman, 446(NCFS):Spring–
    Summer90–572
Sonnabend, H. Fremdenbild und Politik.
    S. Mitchell, 313:Vol79–196
    D.J. Thompson, 123:Vol39No1–86
Sonnichsen, C.L. Pilgrim in the Sun.
    J.R. Milton, 649(WAL):May89–75
Sonoda, K. Health and Illness in Changing
Japanese Society.* [shown in prev under
Kyōichi Sonoda]
    S.O. Long, 293(JASt):Aug89–629
Sontag, S. AIDS and Its Metaphors.*
    W. Koestenbaum, 676(YR):Spring89–466
    639(VQR):Summer89–97
Sontag, S. & others. Cage Cunningham Johns.
    J. Johnston, 441:16Dec90–13
Sophocles. Oedipus Rex.* (R.D. Dawe, ed)
    S. Wiersma, 394:Vol42fasc3/4–529
Sopiee, N., Chew Lay See & Lim Siang Jin, eds.
ASEAN at the Crossroads.
    E. Colbert, 293(JASt):Feb89–236
Şora, M. Sarea pămîntului.
    V. Nemoianu, 617(TLS):19–25Jan90–59
Sorabji, R., ed. Aristotle Transformed
    D. Konstan, 103:Sep90–387
Sorabji, R., ed. Philoponus and the Rejection
of Aristotelian Science.
    H.J. Blumenthal, 319:Apr90–284
    A. Madigan, 258:Jun89–233
Sordello. The Poetry of Sordello. (J.J. Wil-
helm, ed & trans)
    S.B. Gaunt, 382(MAE):1989/1–181
    W.D. Paden, 276:Spring89–65
    L. Shepard, 589:Jan89–220
Sorensen, C. Over the Mountains Are Moun-
tains.
    R. Janelli, 293(JASt):Nov89–893
Sørensen, D. Theory Formation and the Study
of Literature.*
    J. Paccaud, 189(EA):Oct–Dec89–449
Sørensen, K. & R. Jørgensen. La Théorie du
Roman.
    A. Kablitz, 547(RF):Band101Heft2/3–314
Sorensen, R.A. Blindspots.
    W.E. Morris, 518:Jul89–166
Sørensen, V. Seneca.
    E.E. Batinski, 41:Fall89–351
Sörenson, S. Ensk-íslensk orðabók. (J.S.
Hannesson & others, eds)
    K. Wolf, 563(SS):Winter89–78
Sorescu, M. The Youth of Don Quixote.*
    J. Saunders, 565:Autumn89–77
Soria Olmedo, A. Les "Dialoghi d'amore" de
León Hebreo.
    J.B. Avalle-Arce, 240(HR):Spring89–230
Soria Olmedo, A., ed. Lecciones sobre Fede-
rico García Lorca.*
    A. Josephs, 345(KRQ):May89–250
    R. Warner, 86(BHS):Apr89–187
Soria Olmedo, A. – see Hebreo, L.
Soriano, O. Winter Quarters.
    A. Manguel, 617(TLS):13–19Apr90–404
    I. Stavans, 441:7Jan90–18

Sorley, C.H. The Collected Poems of Charles
Hamilton Sorley.* (J.M. Wilson, ed)
    J. Stallworthy, 541(RES):Aug89–436
Sorolla, M.P.M. – see under Manero Sorolla,
M.P.
Sorrell, T. Hobbes.*
    J. Hampton, 482(PhR):Jul89–408
Sorrentino, G. Misterioso.
    H. Coale, 441:14Jan90–31
    J. Loose, 617(TLS):25–31May90–558
Sōseki, N. The Miner.* (J. Rubin, trans)
    W.E. Naff, 293(JASt):Feb89–175
Sosin, J.M. English America and Imperial
Inconstancy.
    A. Murdoch, 566:Spring89–198
Soskice, J.M. Metaphor and Religious Lan-
guage.*
    S.M. Cahn, 449:Apr89–274
    A. Millar, 479(PhQ):Apr87–224
Sosnowski, S. La orilla inminente.
    I. Stavans, 508:May89–184
Sosnowski, S., ed. Augusto Roa Bastos y la
producción cultural americana.
    S. Bacarisse, 86(BHS):Jan89–114
Sotis, G. Walt Whitman in Italia.
    R.J. Rodini, 276:Spring89–68
Soto, G. Lesser Evils.
    G. Haslam, 649(WAL):May89–92
Soto Bruna, M.J. Individuo y Unidad.
    J.M. Oritz Ibarz, 706:Band21Heft1–128
Soubiran, J. Essai sur la versification dra-
matique des Romains.
    C.J. Ruiigh, 394:Vol42fasc3/4–544
Souilh, J. Gluck.*
    A. Adams, 39:Sep89–209
    F. Spalding, 90:Nov89–791
Souiller, D. Le Dialectique de l'ordre et de
l'anarchie dans les oeuvres de Shakespeare
et de Calderón.
    J-P. Leroy, 549(RLC):Jul–Sep89–408
Soulez, P. Bergson politique.
    D. Bourel, 531:Jul–Dec89–550
Soulez, P., ed. Les philosophes et la guerre
de 14.
    P. Trotignon, 542:Oct–Dec89–619
Soumagne, L. Brut vom Bäcker.
    K. Kehr, 685(ZDL):3/1989–301
Soumagne, L. En't Jebett jenomme.
    K. Kehr, 685(ZDL):3/1989–390
Soupel, S. – see Sterne, L.
Souritz, E. Soviet Choreographers in the
1920s. (S. Banes, ed & trans)
    C. Crisp, 441:23Sep90–41
Sournia, J–C. A History of Alcoholism.
    R. Davenport-Hines, 617(TLS):29Jun–
    5Jul90–701
Sourvinou-Inwood, C. Studies in Girls' Tran-
sitions.
    R. Osborne, 123:Vol39No2–272
de Sousa, R. The Rationality of Emotion.*
    S. Burns, 154:Vol28No3–499
    M. Cavell, 311(JP):Sep89–493
    W. Lyons, 484(PPR):Mar90–631
    A. Mele, 518:Jan89–39
    D. Walton, 480(P&R):Vol22No4–302
Souster, R. Asking for More. Collected
Poems. (Vol 6)
    A. Brown, 526:Fall89–98
Souster, R. Eyes of Love.
    T. McKeown, 102(CanL):Autumn–
    Winter89–220

Southam, B., ed. Jane Austen: The Critical Heritage.* (Vol 2)
  A.O.J. Cockshut, 541(RES):Feb89-135
  J. Wiltshire, 97(CQ):Vol17No4-369
Southerne, T. The Works of Thomas Southerne.* (R. Jordan & H. Love, eds)
  R.D. Hume, 405(MP):Feb90-275
  D. Womersley, 447(N&Q):Dec89-511
Southwell, S.B. Kenneth Burke and Martin Heidegger.
  N.R. Orringer, 403(MLS):Winter89-88
Souza, G.B. The Survival of Empire.*
  R. Ptak, 318(JAOS):Apr-Jun88-355
Sova, M. A Practical Czech Course for English-Speaking Students.
  L.A. Janda, 399(MLJ):Winter89-497
"Sovetskaja klassika 20-x-30-x godov na sovremennoj scene: Stenogramma konferencii."
  J. Freedman, 574(SEEJ):Winter89-614
Sowa, W. Der Staat und das Drama.
  H.M.K. Riley, 133:Band22Heft3/4-335
Sowayan, S.A. Nabaṭi Poetry.
  S. Somekh, 318(JAOS):Oct-Dec88-666
Sowell, T. Preferential Policies.
  A. Hacker, 441:1Jul90-7
Sowerby, R. - see Vergil
Soyinka, W. Art, Dialogue, and Outrage.
  J. Gibbs, 538(RAL):Fall89-509
Soyinka, W. Isara.*
  P. Benson, 363(LitR):Spring90-397
  J. Haynes, 617(TLS):23-29Mar90-307
Soyinka, W. Mandela's Earth and Other Poems.
  D. Dabydeen, 493:Spring89-18
  J. Haynes, 617(TLS):23-29Mar90-307
  639(VQR):Spring89-63
Spacks, P.M. Desire and Truth.
  J. Todd, 617(TLS):7-13Sep90-953
Spadafora, D. The Idea of Progress in Eighteenth-Century Britain.
  J. Clark, 617(TLS):21-27Sep90-1004
Spade, P.V. - see Peter of Ailly
Spade, P.V. & G.A. Wilson - see Wyclif, J.
Spadolini, G. - see Sestan, E.
Spaeth, A. The Hong Kong Foreign Correspondents Club.
  P. Popham, 617(TLS):20-26Jul90-781
Spaethling, R. Music and Mozart in the Life of Goethe.*
  G. Flaherty, 301(JEGP):Jan89-69
  C.S. Stanger, 400(MLN):Apr89-747
  D. Vincent, 564:Sep89-260
Spagnuolo Vigorita, T. Exsecranda pernicies.
  E.L. Will, 124:Nov-Dec89-114
Spain, C. Praying for Rain.
  C. Kino, 441:23Sep90-30
Spalding, F. Stevie Smith.*
  42(AR):Fall89-503
Spalding, L. Daughters of Captain Cook.*
  C. Lillard, 102(CanL):Autumn-Winter89-211
Spalla, G., ed. Liguria.
  S. Gruber, 576:Dec89-403
Spallone, P. & D. Steinberg, eds. Made to Order.
  A. Donchin, 254:Fall89-136
Spaltenstein, F. Commentaire des élégies de Maximien.
  A.P. Orbán, 394:Vol42fasc1/2-235
Spanbauer, T. Faraway Places.
  J.H. Maguire, 649(WAL):Aug89-174

Spann, P.O. Quintus Sertorius and the Legacy of Sulla.*
  H.C. Boren, 124:Jan-Feb90-239
  J.S. Richardson, 313:Vol79-197
Spanos, W.V. Repetitions.
  D.T.O., 295(JML):Fall88/Winter89-188
Sparham, G., ed & trans. The Tibetan Dhammapada.
  J.W. de Jong, 259(IIJ):Jul89-249
Spark, M. A Far Cry from Kensington.*
  42(AR):Winter89-115
Spark, M. Symposium.
  G. Annan, 453(NYRB):20Dec90-22
  J. Martin, 441:25Nov90-8
  L. Sage, 617(TLS):21-27Sep90-998
Sparks, A. The Mind of South Africa.
  A. Sampson, 617(TLS):17-23Aug90-866
  L. Thompson, 453(NYRB):14Jun90-12
  G. Wheatcroft, 441:13May90-26
  442(NY):18Jun90-96
Sparks, R.C. To Treat or Not to Treat?
  E.G-R., 185:Jan90-460
Sparshott, F. Off the Ground.*
  639(VQR):Summer89-104
Sparwenfeld, J.G. Lexicon Slavonicum. (Vol 1) (U. Birgegard, ed)
  H. Leeming, 575(SEER):Jul89-452
Spear, F.A. Bibliographie de Diderot. (Vol 2)
  A. Strugnell, 402(MLR):Oct90-962
  R.P. Thomas, 207(FR):May90-1065
Spear, K. Sharing Writing.
  A.R. Gere, 128(CE):Oct89-617
  D. Lipscomb, 126(CCC):Feb89-103
Speare, A., Jr., P.K.C. Liu & C-L. Tsay. Urbanization and Development.
  J.F. Williams, 293(JASt):Feb89-150
Spearing, A.C. Readings in Medieval Poetry.*
  G. Jack, 179(ES):Feb89-83
  A.V.C. Schmidt, 382(MAE):1989/1-147
  S. Wenzel, 301(JEGP):Jul89-390
  D. Williams, 402(MLR):Apr90-401
Spears, H. The Word for Sand.
  S. Scobie, 376:Jun89-132
Spears, M.K. American Ambitions.*
  G. Core, 639(VQR):Winter89-155
  P.R.J., 295(JML):Fall88/Winter89-236
  M.R. Winchell, 580(SCR):Spring90-180
Spears, R.A. The Slang and Jargon of Drugs and Drink.
  R. Aman, 300:Oct88-215
"The Spectator." (D.F. Bond, ed)
  J.A. Downie, 506(PSt):Dec89-296
Spector, N. - see de La Fontaine, J.
Spector, R.D. Backgrounds to Restoration and Eighteenth-Century English Literature.
  K.M. Blair, 40(AEB):Vol3No1-24
Spector, R.D. Tobias George Smollett.
  J.C. Beasley, 166:Jan90-168
Spector, R.H. Eagle Against the Sun.
  A.D. Coox, 293(JASt):May89-403
"Spectrum Guide to Kenya." "Spectrum Guide to Pakistan."
  T. Swick, 441:10Jun90-49
Spehner, N. Ecrits sur la science-fiction.
  A.B. Evans, 561(SFS):Jul89-240
Speier, H-M., ed. Celan Jahrbuch I.
  M. Winkler, 221(GQ):Summer89-426
Speirs, R. Out of the Blue.
  D.E. Smith, 298:Summer89-146
Spellman, C.C. Paint the Wind.
  K. Olson, 441:18Feb90-20

Spelman, E.V. Inessential Woman.*
    L. Simon, 385(MQR):Winter90-133
    I.M. Young, 185:Jul90-898
Spence, A. The Magic Flute.
    J. Campbell, 617(TLS):8-14Jun90-616
Spence, J.D. The Search for Modern China.
    J.K. Fairbank, 453(NYRB):31May90-16
    L. Jaivin, 617(TLS):27Jul-2Aug90-795
    V. Schwarcz, 441:13May90-1
Spence, S. Rhetorics of Reason and Desire.
    J.J. O'Donnell, 24:Summer89-379
Spencer, C. La Tragédie du Prince.
    R. Horville, 535(RHL):Mar-Apr89-278
    H. Phillips, 208(FS):Apr89-210
    M-O. Sweetser, 475:Vol16No30-346
    K.W. Wolfe, 568(SCN):Fall-Winter89-50
Spencer, E. Fire in the Morning. The Light in
    the Piazza. The Voice at the Back Door.
    Jack of Diamonds Other Stories. The Salt
    Line.
    M.R. Winchell, 569(SR):Fall89-580
Spencer, F. Piltdown. The Piltdown Papers,
    1908-1985.
    C. Grigson, 617(TLS):14-20Dec90-1343
    N. Wade, 441:11Nov90-14
    Lord Zuckerman, 453(NYRB):8Nov90-12
Spencer, H., ed. The Liberated Page.
    K.F. Schmidt, 507:Jul/Aug89-345
Spencer, J.M. Sacred Symphony.
    D.E. McGinty, 91:Vol17-181
Spencer, L. Bitter Sweet.
    A.Z. Leventhal, 441:11Mar90-18
Spencer, R.H. The Doveroaun File.
    N. Callendar, 441:27May90-27
Spencer, S. Secret Anniversaries.
    C. Muske, 441:22Jul90-12
Spencer, S. & B. Millington - see Wagner, R.
Spender, D. Writing a New World.
    S. Sheridan, 71(ALS):May89-118
Spengemann, W.C. A Mirror for Americanists.
    M. Clark, 165(EAL):Vol25No2-208
    639(VQR):Autumn89-122
"Spenser Studies." (Vol 6) (P. Cullen & T.P.
    Roche, Jr., eds)
    P. Thomson, 541(RES):May89-250
Speranza, A., ed. Maurice Scève nelle "Vies
    des Poëtes françois" di Guillaume Colletet.
    I.D. McFarlane, 402(MLR):Jul90-730
Sperber, D. On Anthropological Knowledge.
    S.R. Barrett, 488:Mar89-103
Sperber, D. & D. Wilson. Relevance.*
    S.C. Levinson, 297(JL):Sep89-455
Sperry, S.M. Shelley's Major Verse.
    N. Brown, 445(NCF):Sep89 240
    L. Lachman, 494:Fall89-652
    F.W. Shilstone, 580(SCR):Spring90-174
    639(VQR):Summer89-100
Spicker, S.F. & others, eds. The Use of Human
    Beings in Research.
    D.T., 185:Jul90-928
Spiegel, H. - see "Marie de France: Fables"
Spiel, H. Die hellen und die finsteren Zeiten.
    S. Beller, 617(TLS):30Mar-5Apr90-340
Spielrein, S. Entre Freud et Jung.
    P. Babin, 98:Oct89-747
Spierling, V. - see Schopenhauer, A.
Spilias, T. & S. Messinis, eds. Reflections.
    A. Corkhill, 71(ALS):Oct89-271
Spilman, R. Hot Fudge.
    D. Mason, 441:29Jul90-16
Spina, L. Il cittadino alla tribuna.*
    C. Orrieux, 555:Vol62Fasc1-146

Spinelli, E. & M. Rosso-O'Laughlin. Encuen-
    tros.*
    L. Guzmán, 238:Sep89-564
Spinoza, B. Ethique. (B. Pautrat, trans)
    O. Merzoug, 98:Apr89-259
Spinoza, B. A Loving Salutation to the Seed
    of Abraham among tre Jews, wherever they
    are scattered up and down upon the Face of
    tre Earth. (R.H. Popkin & M.A. Signer, eds)
    J-P. Osler, 192(EP):Apr-Jun89-253
Spires, E. Annonciade.*
    F. Chappell, 219(GaR):Summer89-385
    639(VQR):Summer89-100
Spires, J.C. Running Amok.
    K.G. Heider, 293(JASt):May89-443
Spires, R.C. Transparent Simulacra.
    M. Bieder, 395(MFS):Winter89-842
Spitzer, A.B. The French Generation of 1820.
    L.S. Kramer, 242:Vol10No5-612
    E. Weber, 242:Vol10No6-743
Spitzer, L. Die Familie Höchst. (H. Adolf, ed)
    E. Schürer, 221(GQ):Summer89-410
Spitzer, L. Leo Spitzer: Representative
    Essays. (A.K. Forcione, H. Lindenberger &
    M. Sutherland, eds)
    T.R. Hart, 131(CL):Spring89-170
    C. Landauer, 31(ASch):Autumn89-618
Spitzmüller, A. Memoirs of Alexander Spitz-
    müller, Freiherr von Harmersbach (1862-
    1953). (C. de Bussy, ed & trans)
    D.E. Emerson, 104(CASS):Spring89-111
Spivak, C. Merlin's Daughters.
    J.K.G., 295(JML):Fall89/Winter90-180
Spivak, G.C. In Other Worlds.*
    D.T.O., 295(JML):Fall88/Winter89-236
    E. Wright & D. Chisholm, 541(RES):
    May89-305
Spivey, N.J. The Micali Painter and his Fol-
    lowers.
    E. Moignard, 303(JoHS):Vol109-265
    F.R.S. Ridgway, 123:Vol39No2-341
Spivey, T.R. Beyond Modernism.
    P. Stevick, 395(MFS):Summer89-383
Splete, A.P. & M.D. - see Remington, F.
Splett, J., with others, eds. das hymelreich
    ist gleich einem verporgen schatz in einem
    acker ... Die hochdeutschen Übersetzungen
    von Matthäus 13, 44-52 in mittelalter-
    lichen Handschriften.
    D. Duckworth, 402(MLR):Apr90-493
Sponberg, A. & H. Hardacre, eds. Maitreya,
    the Future Buddha.
    L.O. Gómez, 293(JASt):May89-345
Spongberg, S.A. A Reunion of Trees.
    L. Yang, 441:2Dec90-21
Sponheuer, B. Musik als Kunst und Nicht-
    Kunst.*
    W. Seidel, 416:Band4Heft1-86
Sponza, L. Italian Immigrants in Nineteenth
    Century Britain.
    B. Porter, 637(VS):Winter90-348
Spooner, A. Lingo.
    S.J. Freebairn-Smith, 123:Vol39No2-367
Sportes, M. L'Appât.
    R. Cobb, 617(TLS):28Sep-4Oct90-1028
Spoto, D. Lenya.*
    H. Robinson, 34:Dec89-44
Spoto, D. Madcap.
    G. O'Brien, 453(NYRB):20Dec90-6
    G. Weales, 441:22Apr90-20
Spotts, F. - see Woolf, L.

Spotts, F. & T. Wieser. Italy, a Difficult Democracy.
    G. Bedani, 278(IS):Vol43-186
Sprague, C. Re-Reading Doris Lessing.*
    C. Hanson, 677(YES):Vol20-344
    H.R.M., 295(JML):Fall88/Winter89-372
    M. Thorpe, 538(RAL):Spring89-132
Sprague, L.F., ed. Agreeable Situations.*
    I.M.G. Quimby, 658:Winter89-269
Spraul, H. Untersuchungen zur Satzsemantik russischer Sätze mit freien Adverbialen.
    T. Henninger, 575(SEER):Jan89-112
Sprigge, T.L.S. The Rational Foundations of Ethics.*
    M. Hollis, 483:Jan89-113
    M.T. Nelson, 518:Jan89-49
    D. Schmidtz, 185:Apr90-671
    J. Shand, 323:Jan89-94
    R.J. Wallace, 479(PhQ):Oct89-509
Springer, C. The Marble Wilderness.
    N. Broude, 405(MP):Aug89-95
    C.M.S. Johns, 242:Vol10No1-127
    J.H. Whitfield, 278(IS):Vol44-174
Sprinker, M. Imaginary Relations.*
    J. Frow, 131(CL):Fall89-405
    D. Kellner, 290(JAAC):Fall89-390
    G. Levine, 405(MP):Nov89-212
Sprinkle, P.H. Murder in the Charleston Manner.
    M. Stasio, 441:15Jul90-26
Sprintzen, D. Camus.
    E.F. Gray, 395(MFS):Winter89-833
    R.E. Lauder, 103:Feb90-83
    C. Toloudis, 207(FR):Feb90-558
Spronk, K. Beatific Afterlife in Ancient Israel and the Ancient Near East.
    M.S. Smith & E.M. Bloch-Smith, 318(JAOS):Apr-Jun88-277
Sproxton, B., ed. Trace.*
    F.W. Kaye, 502(PrS):Winter89-128
Spufford, F., ed. The Chatto Book of Cabbages and Kings.
    T. Tanner, 617(TLS):9-15Feb90-150
Spufford, P., with W. Wilkinson & S. Tolley. Handbook of Medieval Exchange.*
    L.V. Gerulaitis, 201:Vol15-369
Spurling, H. Paul Scott.
    J.K.L. Walker, 617(TLS):2-8Nov90-1175
Spurr, R. Enter the Dragon.
    R.S. Ross, 293(JASt):May89-376
Squier, C.L. John Fletcher.
    E.C. Bartels, 551(RenQ):Spring89-142
Squier, S.M. Virginia Woolf and London.
    J. Marcus, 620(TSWL):Spring89-101
Squire, J.R., ed. The Dynamics of Language Learning.*
    N.R. Comley, 128(CE):Oct89-623
Squire, L.R. Memory and Brain.
    P.S. Churchland, 486:Sep89-539
Squires, M. & K. Cushman, eds. The Challenge of D.H. Lawrence.
    J. Symons, 617(TLS):7-13Sep90-940
Srzednicki, J. The Democratic Perspective.
    R.E. Ewin, 63:Sep89-367
Staal, F. The Fidelity of Oral Tradition and the Origins of Science.
    J. Bronkhorst, 259(IIJ):Oct89-303
    D. Pingree, 318(JAOS):Oct-Dec88-637
Staal, F. Universals.
    G. Cardona, 293(JASt):Aug89-666
Staal, J.D.W. The New Patterns in the Sky.
    E.J. Dwyer, 124:Jul-Aug90-541

Stacey, J. Brave New Families.
    J. Rieder, 441:18Nov90-9
Stacey, P.F. Boulez and the Modern Concept.*
    M. Fischer, 537:Vol75No1-121
    D. Jarman, 410(M&L):Nov89-578
Stacey, S. Body of Opinion.
    M. Stasio, 441:18Feb90-23
Stachel, J. - see Einstein, A.
Stack, G.J. Lange und Nietzsche.
    M. Kerkhoff, 160:Jan89-200
Stackhouse, K.A. - see Alas, L.
von Staden, H., ed & trans. Herophilus.
    J. Scarborough, 617(TLS):26Jan-1Feb90-96
    D. Sider, 124:Jul-Aug90-540
Stadnikova, E.B. Vlijanie akcentnoj sistemy na fonologičeskuju (na materiale istorii dvux fonem "tipa o" v russkom jazyke).
    D.J. Birnbaum, 559:Vol13No1-64
Staebler, W.W. Architectural Detailing in Contract Interiors.
    C. Boyne, 46:May89-12
Madame de Staël. Delphine.* (Vol 1) (S. Balayé & L. Omacini, eds)
    M. Gutwirth, 207(FR):Apr90-876
    M. de Rougemont, 535(RHL):Nov-Dec89-1062
Štaerman, E.M. & others. Die Sklaverei in den westlichen Provinzen des römischen Reiches im 1.-3. Jahrhundert.
    B.M. Levick, 123:Vol39No2-315
Stafford, D. The Silent Game.
    W.K. Wark, 529(QQ):Autumn89-738
Stafford, F. The Sublime Savage.*
    J.H. Pittock, 571(ScLJ):Winter89-9
Stafford, J. & I. Young. The Ricky Nelson Story.
    B.L. Cooper, 498:Winter89-77
Stafford, R.A. Scientist of Empire.
    J.A.V. Chapple, 617(TLS):13-19Jul90-751
Stafford, W. Socialism, Radicalism and Nostalgia.*
    S. Sayers, 242:Vol10No1-119
Stahl, A.M., ed. The Medal in America.
    658:Spring89-111
Stahl, H-P. Propertius: "Love" and "War."*
    M. Wyke, 313:Vol79-165
Stahl, M. Aristokraten und Tyrannen im archaischen Athen.
    R. Sealey, 229:Band61Heft1-65
Stainer, P. The Honeycomb.*
    S. Pugh, 493:Autumn89-60
Staines, D., ed. Stephen Leacock.*
    L.K. MacKendrick, 168(ECW):Fall89-130
    G. Noonan, 102(CanL):Autumn-Winter89-233
Staley, T.F. An Annotated Critical Bibliography of James Joyce.
    C. Burns, 400(MLN):Dec89-1226
    M. Groden, 329(JJQ):Winter90-411
Staller, J. Frontier New York.
    M. Esterow, 55:May89-112
Stalley, R. The Cistercian Monasteries of Ireland.*
    M.T. Davis, 589:Apr89-504
    H.R. Loyn, 39:Feb89-136
Stalley, R.F. An Introduction to Plato's "Laws."
    T.L. Pangle, 41:Fall89-321
Stallings, B. Banker to the Third World.
    T.H. Cohn, 106:Fall89-255

Stallybrass, P. & A. White. The Politics and Poetics of Transgression.*
  R.D. Abrahams, 292(JAF):Apr-Jun89-202
Stålmarck, T. Tankebyggare, 1753-1762.
  A. Swanson, 563(SS):Spring/Summer89-271
Stalnaker, R. Inquiry.
  G. Forbes, 606:Apr89-171
Stambaugh, J. The Real is Not the Rational.*
  D.L. Reeves, 323:May89-199
Stambaugh, J.E. The Ancient Roman City.
  P. Gros, 229:Band61Heft7-649
  D.E.E. Kleiner, 576:Sep89-284
  G.M. Woloch, 121(CJ):Dec89-Jan90-151
Stambovsky, P. The Depictive Image.
  M. Johnson, 290(JAAC):Summer89-287
Stammerjohann, H., ed. Tema-Rema in Italiano/Theme-Rheme in Italian/Thema-Rhema im Italienischen.
  G. Lepschy, 545(RPh):May90-602
  E. Radtke, 72:Band226Heft1-192
Stampp, K.M. America in 1857.
  H. Brogan, 441:11Nov90-22
Standish, P. - see Fuentes, C.
"Stanford Slavic Studies."* (Vol 1) (L. Fleishman & others, eds)
  C. Isenberg, 550(RusR):Apr89-216
Stangerup, H. The Seducer.
  P. Keegan, 617(TLS):15-21Jun90-654
Stankiewicz, E. Grammars and Dictionaries of the Slavic Languages from the Middle Ages up to 1850.
  H. Leeming, 575(SEER):Apr89-257
Stannard, M. Denying England.
  I. McMillan, 493:Winter89/90-65
Stannard, M. Evelyn Waugh: The Early Years 1903-1939.*
  B. Stovel, 49:Jan89-97
Stanton, D.C., ed. The Female Autograph.
  H.M. Buss, 49:Jul89-98
  L. Moore, 529(QQ):Spring89-170
Stanton, J. Never Say Die!
  J. Webber, 529(QQ):Summer89-538
Stanton, M. The Country I Come From.*
  E. Lesser, 434:Autumn89-98
Stanton, M. Tales of the Supernatural.*
  M. Boruch, 29(APR):Nov/Dec89-21
  B. Howard, 491:May89-103
Stanworth, M., ed. Reproductive Technologies.
  A. Donchin, 254:Fall89-136
Stap, D. A Parrot Without a Name.
  G. Plimpton, 453(NYRB):25Oct90-3
Stapanian, J.R. Mayakovsky's Cubo-Futurist Vision.*
  R. Aizlewood, 575(SEER):Jan89-129
  H. Stephan, 104(CASS):Spring-Winter88-460
Stape, J.H. & A.N. Thomas. Angus Wilson.
  B.C. Bloomfield, 78(BC):Autumn89-416
  J. Rossen, 70:Apr89-70
  L. Wood, 354:Jun89-174
Stapledon, O. & A. Miller. Talking Across the World.* (R. Crossley, ed)
  C.C. Smith, 395(MFS):Summer89-400
Stappers, L. Substitutiv und Possessiv im Bantu. (H-I. Weier, ed)
  K.H. Schmidt, 685(ZDL):1/1989-127
Starcky, L.C. Paris, Mobilier national: Dessins de Van der Meulen et de son atelier.
  M. Royalton-Kisch, 90:Jun89-430
Stark, S. The Outskirts.
  639(VQR):Spring89-56

Starke, F. Die keilschrift-luwischen Texte in Umschrift.
  G. Mauer, 318(JAOS):Jul-Sep88-525
Starkey, D. - see Wormald, J.
Starkey, P. From the Ivory Tower.
  P. Cachia, 294:Sep89-209
Starn, F. Soup of the Day.
  P-L. Adams, 61:May90-132
  J.A. Goudie, 441:29Apr90-31
Starnes, T.C. Christoph Martin Wieland.
  W. Albrecht, 654(WB):12/1989-2104
  W.D. Wilson, 133:Band22Heft3/4-318
Starobinski, J. The Living Eye.
  W. Fowlie, 569(SR):Fall89-cxx
  P.L. Rudnytsky, 580(SCR):Spring90-178
Starobinski, J. La remède dans le mal.*
  M. Jarrety, 450(NRF):Sep89-100
  J. Terrasse, 166:Jan90-172
Starobinski, J. Jean-Jacques Rousseau.*
  A. Demaitre, 577(SHR):Fall89-379
  J.A. Perkins, 478(P&L):Apr89-175
Starosta, S. The Case for Lexicase.*
  F.K. Ameka, 603:Vol13No2-506
Starr, F.S., ed. Russia's American Colony.
  N.E. Saul, 550(RusR):Jan89-86
Starr, K. Material Dreams.
  J. Fallows, 61:Mar90-108
Starr, S.F. New Orleans UnMasqued.
  F. De Caro, 582(SFQ):Vol46No2-190
Starr, W.C. & R.C. Taylor, eds. Moral Philosophy.
  E.J. Kremer, 103:May90-207
Stasny, J.F., ed. Victorian Poetry.
  P. Morgan, 635(VPR):Fall89-130
Stasz, C. American Dreamers.
  C.N. Watson, Jr., 27(AL):Dec89-684
Staten, H. Wittgenstein and Derrida.
  S. Sim, 148:Winter86-114
Staten, J.C. Conscience and the Reality of God.
  42(AR):Fall89-504
Staten, V. Unauthorized America.
  T. Swick, 441:10Jun90-49
States, B.O. The Rhetoric of Dreams.*
  A. Storr, 249(HudR):Autumn89-497
Stati, S. Cinque miti della parola.
  R. Galassi, 545(RPh):Feb90-447
Statius. Silvae IV. (K.M. Coleman, ed & trans)
  M.J. Dewar, 123:Vol39No1-33
Staton, J. & others. Dialogue Journal Communication.
  A. Shuman, 355(LSoc):Dec89-621
Staub, E. The Roots of Evil.
  Z. Bauman, 617(TLS):6-12Jul90-722
Stäuble, M. & A. - see Bertola, A.D.
Stauder, T. Umberto Ecos "Der Name der Rose."
  K. Ackermann, 547(RF):Band101Heft2/3-362
  P.F. Schmitz, 204(FdL):Dec89-308
Stauth, C. The Franchise.
  C. Paikert, 441:27May90-15
Stavely, K.W.F. Puritan Legacies.*
  G. Campbell, 402(MLR):Apr90-412
  D. Griffin, 141:Winter89-103
  R.I. Headley, 391:May89-81
  J.G. Turner, 551(RenQ):Autumn89-593
Stavis, B. China's Political Reforms.
  B. Womack, 293(JASt):Aug89-603
Stavrakis, P.J. Moscow and Greek Communism, 1944-1949.
  N. Clive, 617(TLS):26Jan-1Feb90-82

Staw, J.A. & M. Swander. Parsnips in the Snow.
A. Lacy, 441:10Jun90–13
Stead, C.K. Pound, Yeats, Eliot and the Modernist Movement.*
R. Spoo, 468:Spring&Fall89–249
Stead, C.K. Sister Hollywood.*
J. Mellors, 364:Oct/Nov89–133
Steadman, J.M. Milton and the Paradoxes of Renaissance Heroism.*
G. Campbell, 402(MLR):Apr90–412
Steadman, M. Angel Child.
J.E. Brown, 580(SCR):Fall89–131
von Stechow, A. & W. Sternefeld. Bausteine syntaktischen Wissens.
P. Das Gupta, 353:Vol27No5–941
Steedman, C. Childhood, Culture and Class in Britain.
G. Avery, 617(TLS):11–17May90–504
Steedman, C., C. Urwin & V. Walkerdine, eds. Language, Gender, and Childhood.
J. Miller, 355(LSoc):Dec89–598
Steel, D. Message from Nam.
E. Goodman, 441:10Jun90–14
Steel, J. Paul Nizan.*
W. Redfern, 402(MLR):Jan90–200
"Steel in Housing."
M. Stacey & A. Brookes, 46:Dec89–12
Steele, H.M. Realism and the Drama of Reference.
M. Deakin, 395(MFS):Winter89–733
F.G. See, 27(AL):May89–298
Steele, I.K. The English Atlantic, 1675–1740.
B.S. Schlenther, 83:Spring89–86
Steele, J. The Representation of the Self in the American Renaissance.*
M.J. Killingsworth, 646(WWR):Summer89–32
Steele, R. & T. Threadgold, eds. Language Topics.*
F. Chevillet, 189(EA):Jul–Sep89–333
Steele, R.W. Propaganda in an Open Society.
J. Braeman, 106:Summer89–41
Steele, S. The Content of Our Character.
P.J. Williams, 441:16Sep90–12
Steele, T. Missing Measures.
D.E. Stanford, 598(SoR):Summer90–708
Steele, T. Sapphics Against Anger and Other Poems.
K. Hellerstein, 473(PR):Vol56No4–677
Steen, R. Der hjertet banker.
O. Høidal, 563(SS):Autumn89–431
van der Steen, W.J. & P.J. Thung. Faces of Medicine.
J.W., 185:Oct89–226
Steene, B. Ingmar Bergman.
A. Weinstein, 563(SS):Autumn89–425
Stéfan, J. Litanies du Scribe.
F.M., 450(NRF):May89–99
Stéfan, J. A la Vieille Parque.
P. Di Meo, 450(NRF):Oct89–104
Stefanini, R. – see Bonvesin de la Riva
Stefenelli, A. Die lexikalischen Archaismen in den Fablen von La Fontaine.*
W. Ayres-Bennett, 208(FS):Jul89–326
D. Beyerle, 72:Band226Heft1–203
Steffen, L.H. Self-Deception and the Common Life.
R.M., 185:Apr90–692
Steffens, R. Zur Graphemik domanialer Rechtsquellen aus Mainz (1315–1564).
M. Bürgisser, 685(ZDL):2/1989–241

Stegane, I. Det nynorske skriftlivet.
S.J. Walton, 562(Scan):Nov89–217
Steger, W. & J. Bowermaster. Saving the Earth.
N. Wade, 441:22Apr90–1
Steggink, O. – see Saint Teresa
Stegmann, T., ed. Ein Spiel von Spiegeln.
H. Bihler, 547(RF):Band101Heft1–157
Stegmann, T. – see Tàpies, A.
Stegmüller, W. Die Entwicklung des neuen Strukturalismus seit 1973.
J. Leroux, 154:Vol28No4–677
Stegmüller, W. Theorie und Erfahrung. (Pt 3)
W. Diederich, 167:May89–363
Stegner, W. Collected Stories of Wallace Stegner.
A. Tyler, 441:18Mar90–2
Stegner, W. On the Teaching of Creative Writing. (E.C. Latham, ed)
D.G. Myers, 569(SR):Spring89–xlvii
639(VQR):Summer89–84
Steiger, K.P. Die Geschichte der Shakespeare-Rezeption.*
M. Brunkhorst, 156(ShJW):Jahrbuch1989–378
Stein, A. The House of Death.*
K. Dunn, 570(SQ):Summer89–245
Stein, B. Thomas Munro.
P.J. Marshall, 617(TLS):31Aug–6Sep90–929
Stein, B. The New Cambridge History of India. (Vol 1, Pt 2)
K.N. Chaudhuri, 617(TLS):31Aug–6Sep90–929
Stein, C. The Secret of the Black Chrysanthemum.
L.M. Steinman, 27(AL):May89–319
Stein, D. – see Kellogg, D., with Liu Fei & Tang Min
Stein, E. Wordsworth's Art of Allusion.
B. Wilkie, 445(NCF):Dec89–393
Stein, G. The English Dictionary before Cawdrey.
H. Gneuss, 38:Band107Heft3/4–478
Stein, G. & C. Van Vechten. The Letters of Gertrude Stein and Carl Van Vechten.* (E. Burns, ed)
S. Benstock, 620(TSWL):Spring89–121
C. Caramello, 365:Spring/Summer88–163
Stein, H. Die romanischen Wandmaleriern in der Klosterkirche Prüfening.*
P. Lasko, 90:Mar89–226
Stein, K. The Poetry of a Grown Man.
D. Galef, 27(AL):Dec89–725
Stein, L. – see Schoenberg, A.
Stein, M. Christian den Fjerdes Billedverden.
H-O. Boström, 341:Vol58No1–32
Stein, R.L. Victoria's Year.*
R.D. Altick, 301(JEGP):Jul89–437
L. Hartveit, 179(ES):Dec89–588
D.E. Latané, Jr., 636(VP):Spring89–101
L. Poston, 405(MP):Aug89–98
Steinbach, M. Here Lies the Water.
K. Blickle, 441:19Aug90–18
Steinbach, M. Reliable Light.
J. Dunford, 441:23Sep90–48
Steinbeck, J. The Grapes of Wrath.*
E.L. Galligan, 569(SR):Fall89–cxxii
J.R. Millichap, 395(MFS):Winter89–753
Steinbeck, J. The Harvest Gypsies.
J.D. Houston, 649(WAL):Aug89–153

Steinbeck, J. Working Days.* (R. De Mott, ed)
   B. Baker, 42(AR):Summer89-365
   E.L. Galligan, 569(SR):Fall89-cxxii
   J.D. Houston, 649(WAL):Aug89-153
   J.R. Millichap, 395(MFS):Winter89-753
Steinberg, D.J., ed. In Search of Southeast
   Asia. (rev)
   M. Aung-Thwin, 293(JASt):Aug89-686
Steinberg, G. All or Nothing.
   C. Browning, 617(TLS):19-25Oct90-1125
Steinberg, L. La Sexualité du Christ dans
   l'art de la Renaissance et son refoulement
   moderne.*
   A. Reinbold, 531:Jul-Dec89-521
Steinberger, P.J. Logic and Politics.*
   P. Franco, 185:Jan90-424
Steinbrügge, L. Das moralische Geschlecht.*
   P.H. Meyer, 530:Apr89-168
Steinecke, H. Romanpoetik von Goethe bis
   Thomas Mann.*
   J.P. Strelka, 133:Band22Heft3/4-321
Steiner, G. Real Presences.*
   S. Solecki, 627(UTQ):Spring90-451
   R.S. Stein, 364:Dec89/Jan90-137
Steiner, W. Pictures of Romance.
   M. Melaver, 494:Fall89-652
   S. Melville, 290(JAAC):Winter89-91
Steinhardt, N. Escale in timp şi spaţiu.
   V. Nemoianu, 617(TLS):19-25Jan90-59
Steinlein, R. Die domestizierte Phantasie.*
   R.E. Lorbe, 406:Fall89-090
   I. Tomkowiak, 196:Band30Heft1/2-173
   J. Zipes, 221(GQ):Fall89-501
Steinman, L.M. Made in America.*
   C. Brookeman, 447(N&Q):Mar89-134
   L. Goldstein, 301(JEGP):Jan89-148
   P.R.Y., 295(JML):Fall88/Winter89-258
Steinsaltz, A. - see "The Talmud"
van Stekelenburg, D. Michael Albinus "Dan-
   tiscanus" (1610-1653).
   J. Hardin, 133:Band22Heft2-157
Stella, F. Working Space *
   P.H. Salus, 567:Vol75No3/4-357
Steller, G.W. Journal of a Voyage with Ber-
   ing, 1741-1742. (O.W. Frost, ed)
   P.N. Limerick, 61(TLS):12-18Jan90-27
Stellmacher, D. Wer spricht Platt?
   H. Löffler, 685(ZDL):2/1989-216
Stellmacher, D. - see Ludewig, G.
Stelzle, R. Der musikalische Satz der Notre-
   Dame-Conductus.
   M. Popin, 537:Vol75No2-292
Stem, S. Designing Furniture.
   139:Dec89/Jan90-68
Stempel, T. Framework.
   A. Graham, 219(GaR):Summer89-423
Stendhal. The Pink and the Green.
   639(VQR):Winter89-21
Stenerson, D.C., ed. Critical Essays on H.L.
   Mencken.
   D. Fowler, 70:Oct89-156
Stengel, R. January Sun.
   T. Eprile, 441:13May90-25
Stenger, K.L. Die Erzählstruktur von Fried-
   rich Theodor Vischers "Auch Einer."*
   L.B. Jennings, 564:May89-177
Stenger, W. "Gebt dem Kaiser, was des Kaiser
   ist..!"
   M. Goodman, 313:Vol79-245
Stensen, N. Niels Stensens korrespondence i
   dansk oversaettelse. (H.M. Hansen, ed)
   W.G. Jones, 562(Scan):Nov89-195

Stenzel, H. Molière und der Funktionswandel
   der Komödie im 17. Jahrhundert.
   I. MacLean, 547(RF):Band101Heft4-476
   U. Schulz-Buschhaus, 602:Band20Heft1-
   134
Stenzel, H. & H. Thoma, eds. Die französische
   Lyrik des 19. Jahrhunderts.*
   R. Lloyd, 208(FS):Oct89-484
Stenzi, J. - see Corelli, A.
Stephan, I., R. Venske & S. Weigel. Frauenli-
   teratur ohne Tradition?
   M.E. Goozé, 221(GQ):Summer89-428
Stephan, J.J. & V.P. Chichkanov, eds. Sovi-
   et-American Horizons on the Pacific.
   A.P. Allison, 550(RusR):Oct89-440
Stephen, J. Definitions of a Horse.
   R. Kaveney, 617(TLS):19-25Oct90-1132
Stephen, J.D. Julia Duckworth Stephen: Sto-
   ries for Children, Essays for Adults. (D.F.
   Gillespie & E. Steele, eds)
   P.R. Broughton, 177(ELT):Vol32No1-125
Stephens, C.R., ed. The Fiction of Anne
   Tyler.
   A.H. Petry, 578:Fall90-113
Stephens, M. Lost in Seoul.
   L. Downer, 441:25Feb90-39
Stephenson, G. Elizabeth Barrett Browning
   and the Poetry of Love.
   K. Millard, 617(TLS):30Mar-5Apr90-354
Stepto, R.B. - see Wright, J.
Steptoe, A. The Mozart-Da Ponte Operas.*
   H.C.R. Landon, 415:Jul89-411
   J. Rushton, 410(M&L):Nov89-543
Sterba, J.P. How to Make People Just.
   T.R.M., 185:Jan90-442
Sterchi, B. Cow.
   J. Crowley, 441:8Jul90-9
Sterling, C. The Mafia.
   C. Duggan, 617(TLS):23Feb-1Mar90-190
Sterling, C. Octopus.
   S. Raab, 441:28Jan90-11
Stern, D.N. Diary of a Baby.
   L. Bernstein, 441:9Sep90-34
Stern, F.C., ed. The Revolutionary Poet in
   the United States.
   M. McKenzie, 649(WAL):Nov89-288
Stern, G. Literatur im Exil.
   P.M. Lützeler, 221(GQ):Fall89-544
Stern, G. Lovesick.*
   L. Gregerson, 491:Dec89-233
   R. Jackson, 502(PrS):Fall89-117
Stern, J. The Hidden Damage.
   R. Overy, 617(TLS):29Jun-5Jul90-699
Stern, J. & M. Elvis World.
   P. Rist, 106:Summer89-111
Stern, J. & M. The Encyclopedia of Bad Taste.
   S. Heller, 441:23Dec90-13
Stern, J. & M. Sixties People.
   S. Liveten, 441:11Mar90-18
Stern, J.P. Soviet Oil and Gas Exports to the
   West.
   M.J. Bradshaw, 104(CASS):Spring89-98
Stern, M.B. Nicholas Gouin Dufief of Phil-
   adelphia.
   N. Barker, 78(BC):Winter89-557
Stern, R. Hegel, Kant and the Structure of
   the Object.
   J. Lear, 617(TLS):23-29Nov90-1270
Stern, S.L. & T. Schoenhaus. Toyland.
   H. Rogan, 441:2Sep90-17
Sternberg, M. The Poetics of Biblical Narra-
   tive.*
   J.C. Nohrnberg, 678(YCGL):No36-143

Sternberg, R.J. & J. Kolligian, Jr., eds. Competence Considered.
M. Csikszentmihalyi, 441:1Apr90–22
Sterne, L. Leben und Ansichten von Tristram Shandy, Gentleman. (Vols 1–6) (M. Walter, trans)
W.G. Day, 566:Autumn89–70
Sterne, L. Laurence Sterne: "Le Roman politique," "Le Journal à Eliza." (S. Soupel, ed & trans)
R.A. Day, 189(EA):Jul–Sep89–347
Sterne, L. Tristram Shandy. [photocollages by J. Baldessari]
R.B. Woodward, 55:Apr89–127
Sternfeld, R. & H. Zyskind. Meaning, Relation, and Existence in Plato's "Parmenides."
D.C. Lindemuth, 480(P&R):Vol22No3–216
Sternfield, J. The Look of Horror.
M.E. Ross, 441:25Nov90–19
Sterngold, J. Burning Down the House.
J. Train, 441:21Oct90–13
Sternlicht, S. – see Colum, P.
Stetser, C. Hierograms.
G. Gessert, 448:Vol27No1–126
Stetson, R.H. R.H. Stetson's Motor Phonetics. (J.A.S. Kelso & K.G. Munhall, eds)
A. Löfqvist, 348(L&S):Jan–Mar89–73
Stetz, M.D. & M.S. Lasner. England in the 1880s.
E. Gilcher, 177(ELT):Vol32No3–350
639(VQR):Spring89–48
Steuermann, E. The Not Quite Innocent Bystander. (C. Steuermann, D. Porter & G. Schuller, eds)
D. Jarman, 617(TLS):30Mar–5Apr90–353
Stevens, A. On Jung.
J–R. Staude, 617(TLS):6–12Jul90–725
Stevens, C.J. Lawrence at Tregerthen.
K. Widmer, 395(MFS):Winter89–807
Stevens, J. The Marathon Monks of Mount Hiei.
H.B. Earhart, 407(MN):Summer89–244
Stevens, J. Words and Music in the Middle Ages.*
D.G. Hughes, 317:Summer89–403
J. Yudkin, 589:Jul89–765
Stevens, J.E. America's National Battlefield Parks.
T. Swick, 441:10Jun90–49
Stevens, M. Four Middle English Mystery Cycles.*
B.B. Adams, 301(JEGP):Jan89–93
A.H. Nelson, 191(ELN):Dec89–62
Stevens, P. Stepwives.
M. Stasio, 441:26Aug90–26
Stevens, S. Rosalía de Castro and the Galician Revival.*
C. Rodiek, 547(RF):Band101Heft2/3–387
Stevens, W. Opus Posthumous. (rev) (M.J. Bates, ed)
G.S. Lensing, 705:Fall89–226
L. Mackinnon, 617(TLS):25–31May90–552
H. Vendler, 442(NY):12Nov90–124
Stevens, W. "Sur Plusieurs Beaux Sujets." (M.J. Bates, ed)
N.P. Arbuthnot, 496:Fall89–57
G.S. Lensing, 705:Fall89–226
L. Mackinnon, 617(TLS):25–31May90–552
Stevenson, A. The Other House.
C. Wills, 617(TLS):2–8Nov90–1184
Stevenson, A. Selected Poems, 1956–1986.*
S. Knight, 364:Oct/Nov89–115

Stevenson, A., with others. Bitter Fame.*
L. Gordon, 493:Winter89/90–60
H. Mantel, 364:Oct/Nov89–120
Stevenson, D. The Origins of Freemasonry.* The First Freemasons.*
M.C. Jacob, 173(ECS):Spring90–322
Stevenson, J. Yoshitoshi's Women.
P.J. Graham, 293(JASt):Feb89–180
Stevenson, P.R. Cross a Wide River.
J.C. Alhinc, 649(WAL):Nov89–277
Stewart, A. Greek Sculpture.
J. Boardman, 441:30Sep90–38
Stewart, D.B. The Making of a Modern Japanese Architecture: 1868 to the Present.*
A.P. Leers, 47:Apr89–43
M. Treib, 576:Sep89–304
Stewart, G.T. The Origins of Canadian Politics.
P. Crunican, 529(QQ):Summer89–533
Stewart, J. Shetland Place Names.
W.F.H. Nicolaisen, 424:Mar89–108
Stewart, M.A., ed. Studies in the Philosophy of the Scottish Enlightenment.
R.S. Downie, 617(TLS):11–17May90–507
Stewart, P. Half-Told Tales.*
P. Koch, 535(RHL):Jul–Aug89–721
Stewart, R. Plumbers.
M. Vinz, 456(NDQ):Summer89–255
Stewart, S. George Herbert.
C.F. Main, 551(RenQ):Spring89–144
C. Malcolmson, 677(YES):Vol20–260
Stewart, W.D. Edward Warren. (B. Barbour, ed)
L.S. Peterson, 649(WAL):May89–67
Sticca, S. The Planctus Mariae in the Dramatic Tradition of the Middle Ages.
M.B. McNamee, 377:Mar89–59
Stich, K.P., ed. Reflections.
S. Neuman, 627(UTQ):Fall89–149
Stief, A. Die Aeneisillustrationen von Girodet–Trioson.
A. Gier, 52:Band24Heft1–89
Stieglitz, A. & A. Dove. Dear Stieglitz, Dear Dove. (A.L. Morgan, ed)
P. Cummings, 90:Jun89–434
Stiff, R.L.A. Flowers from the Royal Gardens of Kew.
M. Lambourne, 39:Dec89–432
Stilgoe, J.R. Borderland.*
K.T. Jackson, 505:May89–121
Stillman, D. English Neo–Classical Architecture.
J. Summerson, 46:Jan89–12
Stillman, P.G., ed. Hegel's Philosophy of Spirit.
H.S. Harris, 488:Mar89–118
Stimpson, C.R. Where the Meanings Are.
C. Belsey, 141:Fall89–518
Stine, P.C., ed. Issues in Bible Translation.
B.M. Sietsema, 350:Jun90–428
Stineman, E.L. Mary Austin.
M. Graulich, 357:Fall90–59
Stipe, R.E. & A.J. Lee, eds. The American Mosaic.
M.A. Tomlan, 576:Dec89–409
Stirling, J. The Asking Price.
R. Singleton, 441:25Mar90–22
Stites, R. Revolutionary Dreams.*
A. Kelly, 453(NYRB):6Dec90–60
Stith, J.E. Redshift Rendezvous.
G. Jonas, 441:21Oct90–35
Stitt, P. The World's Hieroglyphic Beauty.
T. Barr, 295(JML):Fall88/Winter89–258

Stivale, C.J. Oeuvre de sentiment, oeuvre de combat.
  P.M. Moores, 208(FS):Oct89-479
Stoces, F. Signes immortels, recueil de poèmes lyriques de la Chine ancienne.*
  M. Détrie, 549(RLC):Jul-Sep89-387
Stock, B. Listening for the Text.
  M.T. Clanchy, 617(TLS):13-19Jul90-757
Stock, M.P. - see under Pol Stock, M.
Stockenström, G., ed. Strindberg's Dramaturgy.
  M. Robinson, 562(Scan):Nov89-203
  639(VQR):Summer89-84
Stocker, M. Apocalyptic Marvell.*
  E.S. Donno, 125:Fall88-76
  J.F.S. Post, 551(RenQ):Spring89-149
Stocker, M. Royalist and Realist.*
  N. Penny, 90:Nov89-788
Stockhausen, K. Stockhausen on Music.* (R. Maconie, ed)
  S. Bradshaw, 415:May89-286
  N. Osborne, 607:Dec89-37
  A. Whittall, 410(M&L):Nov89-577
Stockhausen, K. Towards a Cosmic Music. (T. Nevill, ed & trans)
  K. Potter, 617(TLS):23-29Mar90-322
Stockholder, K. Dream Works.*
  B.M., 494:Winter89-857
  V. Traub, 570(SQ):Spring89-100
Stocking, G.W., Jr., ed. Malinowski, Rivers, Benedict and Others.
  I.C. Jarvie, 488:Sep89-345
Stocking, G.W., Jr. Victorian Anthropology.*
  I.C. Jarvie, 488:Sep89-345
Stocks, K. Emily Dickinson and the Modern Consciousness.
  W. Branch, 447(N&Q):Sep89-413
  W. Martin, 26(ALR):Fall89-93
  D.H. Oberhaus, 27(AL):May89-299
Stoddard, W.S. Sculptors of the West Portals of Chartres Cathedral.
  D. Kahn, 589:Apr89-506
Stoekl, A. Politics, Writing, Mutilation.
  M. Richman, 131(CL):Summer89-278
Stoessel, F. Die Vorgeschichte des griechischen Theaters.
  P. Demont, 555:Vol62Fasc2-343
Stokes, J., M.R. Booth & S. Bassnett. Bernhardt, Terry, Duse.*
  N. Auerbach, 637(VS):Autumn89-205
  L. Fitzsimmons, 611(TN):Vol43No3-141
  J. McDonald, 610:Summer89-205
  C.M. Mazer, 177(ELT):Vol32No3-355
  S.J. Rudolph, 615(TJ):Oct89-426
Stokes, M. & T.L. Burton, eds. Medieval Literature and Antiquities.
  E. Kooper, 179(ES):Feb89-80
  C. von Nolcken, 541(RES):May89-243
Stokes, M.C. Plato's Socratic Conversations.*
  B.E. Goldfarb, 24:Spring89-161
  P.W. Gooch, 487:Autumn89-270
  K. Quandt, 122:Jan89-60
  R.W. Sharples, 303(JoHS):Vol109-224
Stol, M. Letters from Collections in Philadelphia, Chicago and Berkeley.
  W.L. Moran, 318(JAOS):Apr-Jun88-307
Stoljar, M.M. Poetry and Song in Late Eighteenth-Century Germany.
  G. Busch, 402(MLR):Jan90-250
Stoll, A.K. - see de Vega Carpio, L.

Stoll, D. Is Latin America Turning Protestant?
  H. O'Shaughnessy, 617(TLS):3-9Aug90-831
Stoller, P. The Taste of Ethnographic Things. Fusion of the Worlds.
  J. Gleason, 617(TLS):9-15Feb90-141
Stoltzfus, B. Red White & Blue.
  M. Praeger, 268(IFR):Summer89-148
Stoltzfus, B. Alain Robbe-Grillet.
  M.P.L., 295(JML):Fall88/Winter89-401
Stolz, B.A., I.R. Titunik & L. Dolezel, eds. Language and Literary Theory.
  F. Stockholder, 104(CASS):Spring-Winter88-502
Stone, B.D. & B.S. Alt. Uncle Sam's Brides.
  A. Banks, 441:8Jul90-29
Stone, H. Royal DisClosure.
  P. Koch, 207(FR):Feb90-543
  A. Zanger, 475:Vol16No30-350
Stone, H. - see Dickens, C.
Stone, I.F. The Trial of Socrates.*
  D.K. Glidden, 319:Oct90-601
  T.H. Irwin, 509:Spring89-184
  C. Orwin, 31(ASch):Winter89-146
  W. Poznar, 577(SHR):Fall89-375
  G. Welty, 577(SHR):Summer89-264
Stone, J. The Passionate Bibliophile.
  J. Fletcher, 581:Mar89-106
Stone, L. Road to Divorce.
  N. McKendrick, 441:4Nov90-12
Stone, L. Starting with Serge.
  F. Loewinsohn, 441:18Feb90-16
Stone, N. & M. Glenny. The Other Russia.
  G.S. Smith, 617(TLS):15-21Jun90-632
Stone, R.D. The Voyage of the Sanderling.
  R. Finch, 441:23Sep90-18
Stone, R.H. - see Leśmian, B.
Stone, R.M. Dried Millet Breaking.
  M. Kilson, 292(JAF):Jul-Sep89-343
  J.L. Mbele, 538(RAL):Fall89-555
Stoneburner, B.C., comp. Hawaiian Music.
  E. Tatar, 187:Spring/Summer89-342
Stonehill, B. The Self-Conscious Novel.*
  M. Beja, 405(MP):May90-428
  G. Comnes, 532(RCF):Spring89-267
  M. Ilie, 454:Spring90-394
Stoneman, P. Elizabeth Gaskell.
  N. Auerbach, 620(TSWL):Spring89-131
Stoquerus, G. De Musica Verbali Libri Duo. (A.C. Rotola, ed & trans)
  O.B. Ellsworth, 377:Jul89-150
Storey, C. An Annotated Bibliography and Guide to Alexis Studies.*
  W.G. van Emden, 208(FS):Jul89-316
  K.D. Uitti, 589:Oct89-1039
Storey, G. Charles Dickens: "Bleak House."*
  T.J. Cribb, 541(RES):May89-281
Storey, G., K. Tillotson & N. Burgis - see Dickens, C.
Storey, M. Byron and the Eye of Appetite.*
  G.M. Ridenour, 591(SIR):Summer89-321
Storey, M., ed. Poetry and Ireland since 1800.
  P.M. Diskin, 447(N&Q):Sep89-408
  L. McDiarmid, 617(TLS):13-19Apr90-402
Storey, M. - see Clare, J.
Storey, R. Pierrots on the Stage of Desire.*
  J.L. Caplan, 591(SIR):Summer89-329
Storey, R., comp. Primary Sources for Victorian Studies; an Updating.
  R.A. Colby, 635(VPR):Summer89-89

"Storiografia della critica francese nel Seicento."
  F. Graziani, 549(RLC):Jan-Mar89-117
  B. Tocanne, 535(RHL):Jan-Feb89-106
Stork, P. Index of Verb-Forms in Herodotus on the Basis of Powell's "Lexicon."
  M.H.B. Marshall, 123:Vol39No1-133
Storm, T., H. Brinkmann & L. Brinkmann. Theodor Storm - Hartmuth und Laura Brinkmann, Briefwechsel.*
  C.A. Bernd, 301(JEGP):Jul89-383
Storni, A. Selected Poems.* (M. Freeman, ed)
  J. Shreve, 238:Sep89-568
Storr, A. Churchill's Black Dog, Kafka's Mice, and Other Phenomena of the Human Mind.*
  H. Fromm, 249(HudR):Autumn89-479
  639(VQR):Summer89-102
Storr, A. Solitude.
  H. Fromm, 249(HudR):Autumn89-479
Story, D. & J. Clayton. Building the Blackfish.
  J. Gardner, 432(NEQ):Sep89-456
Stouck, D. - see Wilson, E.
Stout, J. Ethics after Babel.*
  T.D. Whitmore, 185:Oct89-180
Stove, D.C. The Rationality of Induction.*
  H.E. Kyburg, Jr., 449:Jun89-396
Stovel, N.F. Margaret Drabble.
  J. Campbell, 268(IFR):Winter90-47
Stover, L. Robert A. Heinlein.*
  R. Asselineau, 189(EA):Apr-Jun89-238
Strachan, M. Sir Thomas Roe 1581-1644.
  G. Parker, 617(TLS):6-12Apr90-378
Strachan, P. Pagan.
  P. Herbert, 617(TLS):18-24May90-530
Strada, V., ed. Rossija/Russia, 5.
  J. Graffy, 575(SEER):Apr89-269
Stradling, R.A. Philip IV and the Government of Spain, 1621-1665.*
  639(VQR):Winter89-9
Straight, M. Nancy Hanks.
  M.A. Godfrey, 34:May89-41
Straight, S. Aquaboogie.
  A. Boaz, 441:18Nov90-28
Strane, S. A Whole-Souled Woman.
  V. Hamilton, 441:29Apr90-17
Strange, J. Despatches from the Home Front. (C. McCooey, ed)
  A. Chisholm, 617(TLS):2-8Mar90-218
von Strassburg, G. - see under Gottfried von Strassburg
van Straten, R. Iconclass Indexes. (Vols 1 & 3)
  C. Hourihane, 90:Mar89-226
Stratos, N.A., ed. Byzantion. (Vol 1)
  M. Arbagi, 589:Apr89-509
Stratton, R. Smack Goddess.
  J. Atlas, 441:9Dec90-7
Straub, K. Divided Fictions.*
  P.R. Backscheider, 405(MP):Aug89-93
  J. Epstein, 141:Fall89-486
Straub, P. Houses without Doors.
  W. Kendrick, 441:30Dec90-6
Strauss, F.J. Die Erinnerungen.*
  G.A. Craig, 453(NYRB):18Jan90-28
Strauss, G. & G. Zifonun. Die Semantik schwerer Wörter im Deutschen.
  U. Schröter, 682(ZPSK):Band42Heft1-127
Strauss, L. The Rebirth of Classical Political Rationalism.* (T.L. Pangle, ed)
  A. Udoff, 543:Mar90-648
  639(VQR):Autumn89-132

Strauss, W.A. On the Threshold of a New Kabbalah.
  C. Koelb, 395(MFS):Winter89-828
Strawson, G. Freedom and Belief.*
  J. Christman, 393(Mind):Jul88-481
Strawson, P.F. Skepticism and Naturalism.
  J.D. Kenyon, 521:Jul89-246
Street, R.L. & J.N. Cappella, eds. Sequence and Pattern in Communicative Behavior.
  J.P. Folger, 355(LSoc):Mar89-131
Streeten, P., ed. Beyond Adjustment.
  G. Rosen, 293(JASt):Feb89-122
Streicher, G. Minnesangs Refrain.
  I. Bennewitz, 680(ZDP):Band108Heft1-101
Streitberger, W.R., ed. Jacobean and Caroline Revels Accounts, 1603-1642.
  G. McMullan, 447(N&Q):Jun89-236
Strelka, J.P., ed. Ernst Schönwiese.
  H. Steinecke, 133:Band22Heft2-188
Streller, S. Wortweltbilder.
  M. Franz, 654(WB):2/1989-333
Stribling, T.S. The Forge. The Store. Unfinished Cathedral.
  M.E. Summerlin, 392:Winter88/89-103
Stribos, S. - see Hassler, H.L.
Strieber, W. Billy.
  R. Fuller, 441:19Aug90-18
Striedter, J. Literary Structure, Evolution, and Value.
  P. Seyffert, 104(CASS):Spring-Winter88-415
  D. Shepherd, 402(MLR):Oct90-1054
Strindberg, A. The Roofing Ceremony and The Silver Lake.* (D.M. & M. Paul, trans)
  C.C. Fraser, 563(SS):Winter89-68
Strindberg, A. August Strindbergs brev, 16 mai 1907-12 juli 1908. (B. Meidal, ed)
  M. Robinson, 562(Scan):Nov89-185
Strohbach, M. Johann Christoph Adelung.
  U. Püschel, 685(ZDL):1/1989-76
Strohm, R. Essays on Handel and Italian Opera.
  P. Rogers, 83:Autumn89-245
Strohm, R. Music in Late Medieval Bruges.
  P. Higgins, 317:Spring89-150
  A. Wathey, 410(M&L):Feb89-79
Strohschneider, P. Ritterromantische Versepik im ausgehenden Mittelalter.*
  C. Rischer, 680(ZDP):Band108Heft3-415
Ströker, E. Husserls transzendentale Phänomenologie.
  D. Lohmar, 489(PJGG):Band96Heft2-437
Ströker, E. Phänomenologische Studien.
  D. Lohmar, 489(PJGG):Band96Heft2-440
Strong, D.H. Dreamers and Defenders.
  P. Wild, 649(WAL):Aug89-160
Strong, R. Lost Treasures of Britain.
  H.R. Woudhuysen, 617(TLS):7-13Dec90-1322
Strosetzki, C. Literatur als Beruf.*
  K. Kohut, 72:Band226Heft1-215
Stroud, B. The Significance of Philosophical Scepticism.
  G. De Pierris, 449:Sep89-531
Stroupe, J.H., ed. Critical Approaches to O'Neill.
  R.H. Wainscott, 615(TJ):Mar89-120
Stroyan, K.D., with W.A.J. Luxemburg. Introduction to the Theory of Infinitesimals.
  D.N. Hoover, 316:Jun89-631
Stroynowski, J., ed. Who's Who in the Socialist Countries of Europe.
  A. Brown, 617(TLS):2-8Feb90-112

Struc, R. & J.C. Yardley, eds. Franz Kafka
(1883–1983).*
    C. Koelb, 564:Feb89–68
Strumingher, L.S. The Odyssey of Flora Tris-
tan.
    M. Rice–De Fosse, 446(NCFS):Spring–
    Summer90–594
Struve, N. Osip Mandel'shtam.
    J. Graffy, 575(SEER):Oct89–663
Stuard, S.M., ed. Women in Medieval History
and Historiography.
    J.M. Bennett, 589:Jan89–221
Stuart, R.C. United States Expansionism and
British North America, 1775–1871.*
    J. Potter, 106:Fall89–273
Stuart, S.P. Men in Trouble.
    42(AR):Winter89–115
Stuart–Fox, M., ed. Contemporary Laos.
    C.F. Keyes, 293(JASt):Feb89–216
Stuart–Smith, S., ed. An Enitharmon Anthol-
ogy.
    T. Gooderham, 617(TLS):16–22Nov90–
    1248
Stubbs, M. Educational Linguistics.
    F.W. Gester, 38:Band107Heft1/2–119
Stuckey, C.F. & W.P. Scott, with S.G. Lindsay.
Berthe Morisot, Impressionist.*
    N.M. Mathews, 662:Spring/Summer89–46
Stuckey, S. Slave Culture.
    J.H. Silverman, 106:Summer89–99
"Studi di lingua e letteratura lombarda
offerti a Maurizio Vitale."*
    R. Stefanini, 276:Autumn90–070
"Studi e Richerche, I: Le fonti musicali in
Italia."
    M–N. Colette, 537:Vol75No2–287
"Studien zur Alten Geschichte Siegfried Lauf-
fer zum 70. Geburtstag am 4. August 1981
dargebracht von Freunden, Kollegen und
Schülern."
    J–C. Richard, 555:Vol62Fasc2–386
"Studies in Eighteenth-Century Culture."*
(Vol 16) (O.M. Brack, Jr., ed)
    K.E. Smith, 83:Autumn89–227
"Studies in the Eighteenth Century, 6." (C.
Duckworth & H. Le Grand, eds)
    K.E. Smith, 83:Autumn89–227
"Studies on Voltaire and the 18th Century."
(Vol 242)
    M. Delon, 535(RHL):Jan–Feb89–111
"Studies on Voltaire and the 18th Century."*
(Vol 245) (H.T. Mason, ed)
    T. L'Aminot, 535(RHL):Jan–Feb89–112
"Studies on Voltaire and the Eighteenth Cen-
tury." (Vol 249) (H.T. Mason, ed)
    D. Williams, 402(MLR):Jan90–184
Studwell, W.E. Adolphe Adam and Léo
Delibes.
    A.F.L.T., 412:Feb89–66
Stuhlmann, G. – see Nin, A. & H. Miller
Stuip, R.E.V., ed. Franse literatuur van de
Middeleeuwen.
    D. Hogenelst, 204(FdL):Dec89–297
Stump, E. – see Boethius
Stumpf, V.O. Josiah Martin.
    C.W. Troxler, 656(WMQ):Jan89–196
de Stúñiga, L. Lope de Stúñiga: Poesías (Edi-
tion critique). (J. Battesti–Pelegrín, ed)
    N.G. Ground, 86(BHS):Apr89–169
"Le Stupéfait."
    E. Maakaroun, 98:Oct89–785
Stupples, P. Pavel Kuznetsov.
    J. Milner, 617(TLS):31Aug–6Sep90–919

Sturges, P. Five Screenplays by Preston
Sturges.* (B. Henderson, ed)
    G. O'Brien, 453(NYRB):20Dec90–6
Sturges, P. Preston Sturges. (S. Sturges, ed)
    P–L. Adams, 61:Oct90–134
    G. O'Brien, 453(NYRB):20Dec90–6
    J.A. Shulevitz, 441:9Sep90–27
Sturgess, K. Jacobean Private Theatre.*
    G. Bas, 189(EA):Oct–Dec89–471
    M. Marrapodi, 568(SCN):Fall–Winter89–46
"Snorri Sturluson's Edda" – see under Snorri
Sturm, D. Community and Alienation.
    N.L.S., 185:Oct89–206
Sturm, D., ed. Deutsch als Fremdsprache
weltweit.
    U. Scheck, 564:Nov89–339
Sturm–Maddox, S. Petrarch's Metamorphoses.*
    F. Mouret, 549(RLC):Jul–Sep89–404
Sturtevant, K. Our Sisters' London.
    T. Swick, 441:10Jun90–49
Styan, J.L. Restoration Comedy in Per-
formance.*
    J. Ogden, 83:Autumn89–230
Styron, W. Darkness Visible.
    V. Glendinning, 441:19Aug90–1
Suárez, F. Donoso Cortés y la fundación de El
Heraldo y El Sol.
    A.H. Clarke, 86(BHS):Jul89–287
Suárez, J.I. Pontos Essenciais do Português
Comercial.
    R.A. Proto–Rodas, 238:Sep89–566
Suarez, V. Latin Jazz.
    E.M. Muñoz, 36:Fall–Winter89–189
Suárez–Galbán, E., ed. José Lezama Lima.
    A. Moreiras, 240(HR):Spring89–270
Suasso, F. Dichter, dame, diplomaat.
    L. Burnett, 575(SEER):Oct89–607
Subirats–Rüggeberg, C. Sentential Comple-
mentation in Spanish.*
    M. Suñer, 240(HR):Spring89–219
Sublet, J. – see "Cahiers d'Onomastique
Arabe"
Subrahmanyam, S. The Political Economy of
Commerce.
    K.N. Chaudhuri, 617(TLS):31Aug–
    6Sep90–929
"Sub Saharan Africa: From Crisis to Sustain-
able Growth."
    R. Oliver, 617(TLS):30Mar–5Apr90–342
Subtelny, O. Domination of Eastern Europe.*
    J.T. Lukowski, 575(SEER):Apr89–295
Succi, D., ed. Capricci Veneziani del Sette-
cento.
    M. Levey, 90:Oct89–717
Such, P. & J. Hodgkinson – see "The Poem of
My Cid (Poema de Mio Cid)"
Suchlicki, J. Historical Dictionary of Cuba.
    J.R. Benjamin, 263(RIB):Vol39No1–83
Suckow, R. A Ruth Suckow Omnibus.
    R.W. Meyer, 649(WAL):May89–77
    639(VQR):Summer89–91
Sudjic, D. Cult Heroes.
    J. Gerston, 441:29Apr90–35
Sugarman, S. Piaget's Construction of the
Child's Reality.
    M. Chapman, 353:Vol27No6–1152
Sugden, J. Sir Francis Drake.
    K. Andrews, 617(TLS):27Jul–2Aug90–806
Sugiyama, S. Japan's Industrialization in the
World Economy 1858–99.*
    L. Grove, 407(MN):Winter89–506
Sukenick, R. In Form.
    42(AR):Fall89–505

Suleiman, E.N. Private Power and Centralization in France.
   H.G. Thorburn, 529(QQ):Summer89-482
Suleiman, S.R. Subversive Intent.
   P. Meisel, 441:5Aug90-25
Sullivan, C., ed. Women Photographers.
   A. Grundberg, 441:2Dec90-71
Sullivan, E.J. Catalogue of Spanish Paintings.
   R. Studing, 568(SCN):Spring-Summer89-22
Sullivan, E.W. 2d, ed. The First and Second Dalhousie Manuscripts.
   J.B. Gabel, 517(PBSA):Mar89-101
   N. Rhodes, 402(MLR):Oct90-913
Sullivan, E.W. 2d & D.J. Murrah, eds. The Donne Dalhousie Discovery.
   J.B. Gabel, 517(PBSA):Mar89-101
   P.A. Parrish, 568(SCN):Spring-Summer89-9
Sullivan, J.P. & P. Whigham - see Martial
Sullivan, L.H. A System of Architectural Ornament.
   M. Filler, 441:2Dec90-24
Sullivan, N.J. The Minors.
   R. Regen, 441:24Jun90-21
Sullivan, P. Unfinished Conversations.
   S. MacNeille, 441:28Jan90-23
Sullivan, R. Christopher Caudwell.
   R. Currie, 89(BJA):Winter89-85
   V.N. Paananen, 115:Winter89-90
   P. Stansky, 301(JEGP):Oct89-553
Sullivan, R.J. Immanuel Kant's Moral Theory.*
   M. Gregor, 543:Mar90-650
Sullivan, T. Mad Hannah Rafferty.
   P. Reading, 617(TLS):13-19Apr90-403
Sullivan, W. Allen Tate.*
   J.E. Brown, 580(SCR):Fall90-158
   D. Fowler, 392:Winter88/89-110
   R.B. Heilman, 569(SR):Spring89-289
   R.C. Petersen, 585(SoQ):Winter90-60
   639(VQR):Spring89-52
Sullivan, W.L. Listening for Coyote.
   G.A. Love, 649(WAL):May89-87
   S. Pickering, 569(SR):Spring89-297
Sulloway, A.G. Jane Austen and the Province of Womanhood.
   J. Bender, 617(TLS):10-16Aug90-854
   J. Todd, 166:Jul90-359
Sultan, S. Eliot, Joyce and Company.*
   Z.B., 295(JML):Fall88/Winter89-214
   J-M. Rabaté, 189(EA):Jul-Sep89-351
   A. Robinson, 677(YES):Vol20-330
Sultana, D. The Journey of Sir Walter Scott to Malta.*
   O. Friggieri, 549(RLC):Jan-Mar89-128
   J. Millgate, 541(RES):May89-307
Summers, A. Angels and Citizens.
   R.P. Greenburg, 637(VS):Winter90-342
Summers, C.J. & T-L. Pebworth, eds. "Bright Shootes of Everlastingnesse."*
   N.H. Keeble, 447(N&Q):Sep89-391
   J.F.S. Post, 551(RenQ):Spring89-149
Summers, C.J. & T-L. Pebworth, eds. "The Muses Common-Weale."
   V. Kahn, 551(RenQ):Autumn89-598
Summers, D. The Judgment of Sense.*
   D. Carrier, 89(BJA):Winter89-74
   D. Koenigsberger, 242:Vol10No2-258
   D.B. Kuspit, 54:Jun89-317
   A. Moss, 83:Spring89-104
   J. Took, 551(RenQ):Winter89-859

Summers, D. & others - see "Longman Dictionary of Contemporary English"
Summers, J.H. Dreams of Love and Power.*
   J.A. Bryant, Jr., 569(SR):Summer89-445
Summerson, J. Georgian London.* (rev)
   S. Gutterman, 45:Sep89-59
   566:Spring90-221
Summerson, J. The Unromantic Castle.
   M. Filler, 441:2Dec90-22
   A. Hollinghurst, 617(TLS):17-23Aug90-877
Sumner, L.W. The Moral Foundation of Rights.*
   J.E. Bickenbach, 483:Jan89-120
   D. Copp, 154:Vol28No1-131
   T. Hurka, 154:Vol28No1-117
   R. Martin, 185:Jan90-408
   P. Vallentyne, 518:Apr89-110
Sumner, M. "The Centerpiece."
   G. Gessert, 448:Vol27No1-124
Sumption, J. The Hundred Years War. (Vol 1)
   M. Prestwich, 617(TLS):28Sep-4Oct90-1029
"Sundays at Moosewood Restaurant."
   R. Flaste, 441:2Dec90-73
Sundberg, J. The Science of the Singing Voice.
   E.C. Carterette, 413:Winter89-187
Sundelius, B., ed. The Neutral Democracies and the New Cold War.
   J.L. Voorhis, 563(SS):Spring/Summer89-284
Sunderland, J. John Hamilton Mortimer.
   M. Butlin, 90:Nov89-785
Sunstein, E.W. Mary Shelley.*
   L. Claridge, 594:Winter89-454
   P.H. Michaelson, 166:Jul90-360
Suolinna, K. & K. Sinikara. Juhonkylä.
   M. Junnonaho, 64(Arv):Vol44-211
Super, R.H. The Chronicler of Barsetshire.*
   D.D. Stone, 445(NCF):Sep89-250
   S. Tave, 385(MQR):Spring90-296
   R.C. Terry, 637(VS):Summer90-659
Supervielle, J. "La Fable du monde" suivi de "Oublieuse Mémoire."
   J.A. Hiddleston, 208(FS):Jul89-356
Supičić, I. Music in Society.* (rev)
   C. Ehrlich, 410(M&L):May89-240
   S. Feld, 187:Spring/Summer89-321
Suppe, F. The Semantic Conception of Theories and Scientific Realism.
   R.H. Schlagel, 543:Jun90-885
Supple, J.J. Arms versus Letters.
   F. Lestringant, 535(RHL):Jan-Feb89-88
Supple, J.J. Racine: "Bérénice."*
   H.T. Barnwell, 208(FS):Apr89-209
"A Supplement to the Oxford English Dictionary." (Vol 4) (R.W. Burchfield, ed)
   G. Stein, 38:Band107Heft3/4-482
"Sur Aragon 'Le Libertinage'."
   G. Cesbron, 535(RHL):Jan-Feb89-155
"Sur les écrits posthumes de Sartre."
   J. Lefranc, 192(EP):Jul-Dec89-560
Surdich, L. La cornice di amore.
   A. Scolari, 379(MedR):Apr89-139
"Surrogate Parenting."
   N.D., 185:Jul90-926
Surtees, V. - see Granville, H.
Surtz, E. & V. Murphy, eds. The Divorce Tracts of Henry VIII.*
   D. Loades, 551(RenQ):Autumn89-566

Surtz, R.E., J. Ferrán & D.P. Testa, eds. Américo Castro.
    J.L. Gómez-Martínez, 238:Dec89-954
Susie, D.A. In the Way of Our Grandmothers.
    R. Davis-Floyd, 650(WF):Jan89-69
Suskin, S. Opening Night on Broadway.
    D. Kaufman, 441:30Dec90-15
Süskind, P. The Double Bass.
    P. Lewis, 565:Winter88/89-77
Sutcliffe, S. Champagne.
    639(VQR):Spring89-68
Sutherland, C. Monica.
    L.E. Beattie, 441:12Aug90-17
Sutherland, C.H.V. Roman History and Coinage 44BC-AD 69.*
    C.E. King, 123:Vol39No2-312
Sutherland, D.E. The Confederate Carpetbaggers.
    639(VQR):Spring89-43
Sutherland, J. The Stanford Companion to Victorian Literature.
    J.R. Reed, 637(VS):Summer90-647
    639(VQR):Autumn89-118
Sutherland, J. Mrs. Humphry Ward.
    J. Keates, 617(TLS):9-15Nov90-1195
    J.H. Murray, 441:18Nov90-30
Sutter, A. Göttliche Maschinen.
    H. Breger, 706:Band21Heft2-215
Sutton, A. & D. Sheehan. Ideas in Weaving.
    139.Dec89/Jan90-34
Sutton, P., ed. Dreamings.
    H. Murphy, 09:Nov89-361
Sutton, W.A. - see Anderson, S.
Suvin, D. Positions and Presuppositions in Science Fiction.
    C.C. Smith, 395(MFS):Summer89-400
Suzuki, Y., ed. The Japanese Financial System.
    R.S. Ozaki, 293(JASt):May89-404
Svahnström, G. & K. Måleri på Gotland 1530-1830.
    M. Lindgren, 341:Vol58No4-179
Svanberg, J. Furstebilder från folkungatid.
    I. Pegelow, 341:Vol58No4-178
Svarny, E. "The Men of 1914."*
    B. Bergonzi, 402(MLR):Jan90-168
Svedberg, O. Arkitekternas århundrade.
    A. Fant, 341:Vol58No1-39
Švejcer, A.D. Contemporary Sociolinguistics.*
    D. Jutronić-Tihomirović, 355(LSoc):Jun89-280
    Ž. Muljačić, 685(ZDL):1/1989-81
Švejcer, A.D. Übersetzung und Linguistik.
    K. Henschelmann, 72:Band226Heft1-107
    B. Herting, 682(ZPSK):Band42Heft3-413
Švejcer, A.D. & L.B. Nikol'skij. Introduction to Sociolinguistics.*
    D. Jutronić-Tihomirović, 355(LSoc):Jun89-280
    Ž. Muljačić, 685(ZDL):1/1989-81
Svensén, B. Handbok i lexikografi.
    S-G. Malmgren, 452(NJL):Vol12No1-95
Svensson, Ö. Saxon Place-Names in East Cornwall.*
    G. Bourcier, 189(EA):Apr-Jun89-195
    J. Insley, 685(ZDL):3/1989-388
Swaim, K.M. Before and After the Fall.*
    J.T. Miller, 551(RenQ):Summer89-365
Swales, M., ed. German Poetry - an Anthology from Klopstock to Enzensberger.*
    P. Guenther, 635(VPR):Summer89-75

Swallow, M. Teaching Little Fang.
    D. Singmaster, 617(TLS):23-29Nov90-1271
Swann, B. & A. Krupat, eds. I Tell You Now.
    J. De Flyer, 456(NDQ):Spring89-168
Swann, B. & A. Krupat, eds. Recovering the Word.
    J. De Flyer, 456(NDQ):Spring89-171
    H.D. Wong, 650(WF):Jan89-75
Swanson, P. José Donoso: The "Boom" and Beyond.
    P. Bacarisse, 86(BHS):Apr89-195
Swanson, W.R. The Christ Child Goes to Court.
    K.J. Uva, 441:23Sep90-49
Swanton, M.J. English Literature before Chaucer.
    D.G. Calder, 589:Jul89-769
    P.J. Lucas, 447(N&Q):Mar89-78
    C. von Nolcken, 541(RES):May89-243
    K. Reichl, 72:Band226Heft1-144
    D.G. Scragg, 38:Band107Heft3/4-510
    E.G. Stanley, 382(MAE):1989/1-143
Swarthout, G. The Homesman.
    W. Baker, 42(AR):Winter89-107
    N.O. Nelson, 649(WAL):May89-70
Swarzenki, H. & N. Netzer. Catalogue of Medieval Objects in the Museum of Fine Arts, Boston.
    B.S., 90:May89-365
Swearington, R. Siberia and the Soviet Far East.*
    A.F. Allison, 550(RusR):Oct89-440
Sweeney, J.L. - see James, H.
Sweeney, M. Blue Shoes.*
    S. O'Brien, 493:Autumn89-63
Sweetman, D. The Love of Many Things.
    A.S. Byatt, 617(TLS):29Jun-5Jul90-683
Sweetman, D. Van Gogh.
    M. Kimmelman, 441:12Aug90-1
Sweetman, J. The Oriental Obsession.*
    M. Crinson, 46:Jan89-14
    R. Hillenbrand, 463:Winter89/90-218
    G.T. Scanlon, 39:Jun89-441
Sweetser, M-O. La Fontaine.*
    C. Grisé, 402(MLR):Apr90-444
    A. Pizzorusso, 535(RIIL):Jan-Feb89-104
Swenarton, M. Artisans and Architects.
    J.D. Kornwolf, 576:Dec89-402
    P. Stansky, 637(VS):Spring90-518
Swenson, M. In Other Words.*
    L. Gregerson, 491:Jul89-233
Swidlicki, A. Political Trials in Poland 1981-1986.
    K.R. Sword, 575(SEER):Jul89-491
Swietlicki, C. Spanish Christian Cabala.*
    D.E. Carpenter, 345(KRQ):Nov89-494
    J.A. Jones, 86(BHS):Oct89-378
Swift, E. Mother of Pearl.
    R. Short, 441:2Sep90-17
Swift, J. Service is No Inheritance, or Rules to Servants, according to the Rev. J. Swift, To be Read Constantly One Night Every Week upon Going to Bed. (S. Draghici, ed)
    D.C. Mell, 566:Spring89-182
Swift, K.E. Morfología del caquinte (arawk preandino).
    D.L. Payne, 350:Dec90-886
"Swift, Temple and the du Cros Affair." (Pt 1)
    C.T. Probyn, 566:Autumn89-69
"Swift, Temple and the du Cros Affair." (Pt 2)
    A. Morvan, 189(EA):Jan-Mar89-102
    C.T. Probyn, 566:Autumn89-69

Swiggers, P. Grammaire et théorie du langage au dix-huitième siècle.
  G. Hassler, 682(ZPSK):Band42Heft2-274
Swinburne, R. The Evolution of the Soul.*
  P. Kitcher, 449:Dec89-708
Swindells, J. Victorian Writing and Working Women.*
  P.G. Gurney, 158:Dec89-174
  K. Sutherland, 148:Winter86-105
Swingle, L.J. The Obstinate Questionings of English Romanticism.
  G. Bornstein, 661(WC):Autumn89-190
  G. Crossan, 447(N&Q):Sep89-401
  J. Engell, 445(NCF):Sep89-229
  C.D. Ryals, 402(MLR):Apr90-416
  S.M. Sperry, 340(KSJ):Vol38-184
Switten, M.L. The "Cansos" of Raimon de Miraval.
  N. van Deusen, 545(RPh):Nov89-356
Switzer, B., with B. Shrake. Bootlegger's Boy.
  F.E. Halpert, 441:7Oct90-21
Syberberg, H-J. Vom Glück und Unglück der Kunst in Deutschland nach dem Letzten Kriege.
  I. Buruma, 453(NYRB):20Dec90-34
Sychrava, J. Schiller to Derrida.
  A. Gelley, 617(TLS):20-26Jul90-783
Sykes, C.J. The Hollow Men.
  F.M. Hechinger, 441:9Dec90-28
Sykes, C.J. ProfScam.*
  J. Seaton, 580(SCR):Spring90-149
Syllaba, T. & S. Heřman. A. Teodorov-Balan na univerzitě v Praze.
  R.B. Pynsent, 575(SEER):Apr89-311
Sylvan, D. & B. Glassner. A Rationalist Methodology for the Social Sciences.
  P.A. Roth, 488:Mar89-104
Syme, R. The Augustan Aristocracy.*
  H. Galsterer, 313:Vol79-201
  P.M. Swan, 487:Summer89-180
  U. Vogel-Weidemann, 229:Band61Heft3-222
Syme, R. Roman Papers.* (Vols 2 & 3) (A.R. Birley, ed)
  H.W. Benario, 121(CJ):Dec89-Jan90-150
Syme, R. Roman Papers. (Vols 4 & 5) (A.R. Birley, ed)
  H.W. Benario, 121(CJ):Dec89-Jan90-150
  J-C. Richard, 229:Band61Heft3-246
Symmons, S. Goya.*
  A. Stewart, 324:Dec89-73
Symonds, J. The King of the Shadow Realm.
  F. MacCarthy, 617(TLS):5-11Jan90-5
Symons, A. Selected Letters, 1880-1935.* (K. Beckson & J.M. Munro, eds)
  A. Johnson, 445(NCF):Mar90-568
Symons, J. Death's Darkest Face.
  P. Craig, 617(TLS):25-31May90-559
  R. Hill, 441:28Oct90-18
Symons, J. - see Lewis, W.
Sypnowich, C. The Concept of Socialist Law.
  T.D. Campbell, 617(TLS):20-26Apr90-417
Syrokomla-Stefanowska, A.D. - see Kaneko Mitsurharu
Syska-Lamparska, R.A. Stanisław Brzozowski.
  J.J. Baer, 497(PolR):Vol34No2-186
Sysyn, F.E. Between Poland and the Ukraine.*
  R.P. Bartlett, 575(SEER):Apr89-298
Syverson-Stork, J. Theatrical Aspects of the Novel.*
  F. Pierce, 86(BHS):Apr89-176

Szabolcsi, M. & J. Kóvacs, with M. Culyás, eds. Change in Language and Literature.
  D.M. Roskies, 678(YCGL):No36-162
Szambien, W. Le Musée d'Architecture.
  B. Bergdoll, 90:Jun89-433
Szambien, W. Symétrie, goût, caractère.
  R. Middleton, 90:Jan89-44
Szanto, G. The Underside of Stones.
  D. Goodwin, 441:29Jul90-20
Szarmach, P.E., ed. Studies in Earlier Old English Prose.*
  D.G. Calder, 301(JEGP):Apr89-217
  H. Gneuss, 38:Band107Heft1/2-155
Szarmach, P.E. & B.F. Huppé, eds. The Old English Homily and its Backgrounds.
  H. Gneuss, 38:Band107Heft1/2-155
Szarota, E.M. Das Jesuitendrama im deutschen Sprachgebiet. (Vol 4) (P. Mortzfeld, comp)
  R.J. Alexander, 406:Summer89-254
Szarota, E.M. Stärke, Dein Name Sei Weib!
  K. Hecker, 610:Autumn89-292
Szaszkóné Sin, A., ed. Magyarország történeti helységnévtára.*
  M. Rady, 575(SEER):Jul89-482
Szczepanski, J.J. Kadencja.
  S. Baranczak, 560:Winter89-42
Szczesny, G. Bertolt Brechts "Leben des Galilei."*
  H. Schmidt, 564:May89-178
Szczypiorski, A. The Beautiful Mrs. Seidenman.
  J. Bayley, 453(NYRB):19Jul90-23
  V. Rounding, 617(TLS):3-9Aug90-829
  L. Segal, 441:18Feb90-10
Szemerényi, O. Einführung in der vergleichende Sprachwissenschaft. (3rd ed)
  K.H. Schmidt, 685(ZDL):3/1989-344
Szeps, C. Edmond Géraud à l'aube du romantisme.
  C. Crossley, 402(MLR):Jul90-735
  J.M. Vest, 446(NCFS):Fall-Winter89/90-239
Szilard, L. Toward a Livable World. (H.S. Hawkins, G.A. Greb & G.W. Szilard, eds)
  J.M. Pearson, 529(QQ):Autumn89-756
Szirtes, G. Metro.*
  S. Knight, 364:Apr/May89-129
Szittya, P.R. The Antifraternal Tradition in Medieval Literature.*
  J.A. Alford, 589:Jan89-222
  J.B. Friedman, 301(JEGP):Jul89-396
Szondi, P. Introduction à l'herméneutique littéraire.
  R. Rochlitz, 98:Nov89-839
Szondi, P. Theory of the Modern Drama.* (M. Hays, ed & trans)
  P. Auslander, 223:Spring89-89
Szpyra, J. The Phonology-Morphology Interface.
  C.Y. Bethin, 350:Sep90-594
Szuchman, M.D. Order, Family, and Community in Buenos Aires, 1810-1860.
  C.J. Little, 263(RIB):Vol39No2-214
Szulc, A. Historische Phonologie des Deutschen.*
  P. Freeouf, 133:Band22Heft3/4-387
  W. Neumann, 682(ZPSK):Band42Heft2-271
Szulc, T. Then and Now.
  A. Howard, 441:8Jul90-11
Szumigalski, A. Dogstones.*
  S. Gingell, 168(ECW):Spring89-69

Szwajger, A.B. I Remember Nothing More.
  A. Brumberg, 617(TLS):14–20Dec90–1342
Szymanek, B. Categories and Categorization in Morphology.
  A. Carstairs, 297(JL):Sep89–506

Tabātabā'ī, H.M. Karāj in Islamic Law.
  F.J. Ziadeh, 318(JAOS):Jul–Sep88–488
Tabātabā'i, S.M.H. A Shi'ite Anthology. (W.C. Chittick, ed & trans)
  A.A. Sachedina, 318(JAOS):Apr–Jun88–320
Tabor, S. Sylvia Plath.*
  N. Corcoran, 677(YES):Vol20–348
  L. Wagner-Martin, 470:Vol27–142
Tabourot, E. Les Bigarrures du Seigneur des Accords.* (Bk 1) (F. Goyet, ed)
  M.J. Freeman, 557:Jun89–231
Tabucchi, A. Indian Nocturne.*
  G. Krist, 249(HudR):Winter89–665
Tabucchi, A. Little Misunderstandings of No Importance.
  A.H. Carter 3d, 573(SSF):Summer88–327
Tacchella, J-C. & R. Thérond. Les Années éblouissantes.
  H.A. Garrity, 207(FR):May90–1086
Tacey, D.J. Patrick White.
  L. Kramer, 581:Jun89–247
Tadié, J-Y – see Proust, M.
Taeger, A. Die Kunst, Medusa zu töten.*
  S.L. Cocalis, 406:Summer89–230
  M.K. Flavell, 402(MLR):Apr90–519
  D. Millet-Gérard, 549(RLC):Jan–Mar89–110
Tagg, J. The Burden of Representation.
  J. Harris, 59:Jun89–247
Taguieff [Taguiev], P-A. La force du préjugé.*
  A. Jacob, 192(DP):Jul–Dec80–661
Tahir, U.M.M. – see under Ungku M.M. Tahir
Taibo, P.I. 2d. An Easy Thing.
  M. Stasio, 441:21Jan90–35
Tainter, J.A. The Collapse of Complex Societies.
  R. Rousselle, 124:Jul–Aug90–542
Tait, H. & P.G. Coole. Catalogue of Watches in the British Museum. (Vol 1)
  R. Garnier, 39:Feb89–138
Taittinger, C. Monsieur Cazotte monte à l'echafaud.
  M. Cook, 402(MLR):Jul90–734
Tajima, M., comp. Old and Middle English Language Studies.
  G. Jack, 159:Vol6No1–151
  J.R.J. North, 603:Vol13No2–518
Tajima, M. The Syntactic Development of the Gerund in Middle English.*
  R.L. Thomson, 215(GL):Vol29No1–64
Takahatake, T. Young Man Shinran.*
  S.H. Kanda, 485(PE&W):Jul89–359
Takashi, I. & Iwai Tomoaki – see under Inoguchi Takashi & Iwai Tomoaki
Takeda, K. The Dual Image of the Japanese Emperor.
  B-A. Shillony, 407(MN):Autumn89–375
Takeo, I. – see under Itō Takeo
Tala, K.I. An Introduction to Cameroon Oral Literature. A Field Guilde to Oral Literature.
  T. Ojaide, 538(RAL):Summer89–275
Talbot, M. Antonio Vivaldi.
  J.W. Hill, 410(M&L):May89–256

"The Tale of the Heike."* (H.C. McCullough, trans)
  P. Varley, 293(JASt):May89–397
Tallack, D., ed. Literary Theory at Work.*
  A. Jefferson, 208(FS):Jul89–367
  R. Lawson-Peebles, 541(RES):May89–302
  I.V., 295(JML):Fall88/Winter89–237
Tallián, T. Béla Bartók.
  D.C., 412:May89–145
Tallis, R. In Defence of Realism.
  R. Gill, 447(N&Q):Dec89–556
"The Talmud."* (Vol 1) (A. Steinsaltz, commentary) (I.V. Berman, ed & trans)
  S. Reif, 617(TLS):20–26Apr90–424
Tambiah, S.J. Magic, Science, Religion and the Scope of Rationality.
  D. Hymes, 617(TLS):7–13Sep90–951
Tambiah, S.J. Sri Lanka.*
  C. Hallisey, 318(JAOS):Jul–Sep88–498
Tambling, J. Dante and Difference.
  Z.G. Barański, 278(IS):Vol44–149
  T. Barolini, 551(RenQ):Autumn89–537
  J. Took, 402(MLR):Jul90–751
Tames, G. Eye on Washington.
  D. Murray, 441:11Nov90–60
Tammel, J.W., comp. The Pilgrims and Other People from the British Isles in Leiden 1576–1640.
  A. Hamilton, 617(TLS):26Oct–1Nov90–1157
Tammi, P. Problems of Nabokov's Poetics.*
  P. Meyer, 104(CASS):Spring–Winter88–470
Tamplin, R. Seamus Heaney.
  S. Deane, 617(TLS):16–22Mar90–275
Tam'Si, T.U. – see under Tchicaya U Tam'Si
Tan Zongji & others. Shinian hou de ping-shuo.
  M. Schoenhals, 293(JASt):Aug89–563
Tanabe, W.J. Paintings of the Lotus Sutra.*
  O. Impey, 39:Dec89–434
  M. Symmonds, 60:Jan–Feb89–149
Tanasescu, D. & G. Bargauanu. Lipati. (C. Grindea, ed)
  J. Chissell, 415:Feb89–89
  S. Nicholls, 607:Jun89–65
Tancred-Sheriff, P., ed. Feminist Research.
  G. McGregor, 298:Fall89–147
Tanitch, R. Guinness.
  G. Gordon, 511:Apr89–44
Tanizaki, J. A Cat, a Man, and Two Women.
  P-L. Adams, 61:Dec90–133
  E. Hanson, 441:9Dec90–33
Tanizaki, J. Childhood Years.*
  K.K. Ito, 293(JASt):Feb89–181
  M. Morris, 617(TLS):24–30Aug90–901
Tankard, J.B. & M.R. Van Valkenburgh. Gertrude Jekyll.*
  A.E. Monfried, 505:Jul89–103
Tannen, D., ed. Coherence in Spoken and Written Discourse.
  R.J. Vann, 710:Mar89–102
Tannen, D., ed. Linguistics in Context.
  N. Besnier, 350:Sep90–562
  M. Rost & N. Dittmar, 710:Sep89–329
Tannen, D. You Just Don't Understand.
  R. Rose, 441:5Aug90–8
Tannen, M. After Roy.
  442(NY):1Jan90–84
Tannen, M. Second Sight.
  W. Kelley, 473(PR):Vol56No4–683

Tannenbaum, A.G. Pierre Bayle's "Philosoph-
ical Commmentary."
　F. Lagarde, 207(FR):Apr90-872
　S.G.M. O'Cathasaigh, 208(FS):Jul89-328
Tannenbaum, M. Conversations with Stock-
hausen.*
　S. Bradshaw, 415:May89-286
　R. Maconie, 410(M&L):Feb89-136
Tanner, H.H. & others, eds. Atlas of Great
Lakes Indian History.
　J. Axtell, 656(WMQ):Jan89-170
Tanner, M. - see Furtwängler, W.
Tanner, R.L. The Humor of Irony and Satire
in the Tradiciones Peruanas.*
　J. Cuervo Hewitt, 552(REH):May89-141
Tanner, S.L. Paul Elmer More.*
　J.A. Bryant, Jr., 569(SR):Winter89-153
Tanner, T. Jane Austen.*
　J. Wiltshire, 97(CQ):Vol17No4-369
Tanner, T. Scenes of Nature, Signs of Men.*
　J. Cazemajou, 189(EA):Oct-Dec89-496
　T.D., 295(JML):Fall88/Winter89-252
　S.B. Girgus, 26(ALR):Fall89-92
　L. Kelly, 402(MLR):Jul90-711
　B.M., 494:Fall89-644
　S. Moore, 532(RCF):Spring89-272
Tanning, D. Birthday.
　R.L. Belton, 662:Spring/Summer89-40
Tanselle, G.T. Textual Criticism since Greg.*
　L. Hunter, 402(MLR):Oct90-895
Tanselle, G.T. - see Ray, G.N.
Tao, J-S. Two Sons of Heaven.
　H. Franke, 293(JASt):Feb89-151
Tao, X. - see under Xue Tao
"The Taoist I Ching." (T. Cleary, trans)
　K. Smith, 318(JAOS):Apr-Jun88-350
Tàpies, A. Ein Spiel von Spiegeln. (T. Steg-
mann, ed)
　J. Hösle, 52:Band24Heft1-69
Taplin, K. By the Harbour Wall.
　T. Gooderham, 617(TLS):16-22Nov90-
1248
Taplin, O. Greek Fire.
　P. Cartledge, 617(TLS):11-17May90-508
Tappan, D.W. & W.M. Mould, eds. French
Studies in Honor of Philip A. Wadsworth.*
　W.C. Marceau, 475:Vol16No30-353
Tarallo, F. & T. Alkmin. Falares Crioulos.
　M. Perl, 682(ZPSK):Band42Heft6-871
Taralon, J., A. Prache & N. Blondel. Inven-
taire général des monuments et richesses
artistiques de la France: Les Vitraux de
Bourgogne, Franche Comté et Rhone-Alpes.
　M.H. Caviness, 90:Jan89-78
Tarbox, K. The Art of John Fowles.
　C. Sprague, 395(MFS):Winter89-818
Tarcov, N. Locke's Education for Liberty.*
　G.B. Herbert, 543:Mar90-651
Tardieu, J. On vient chercher Monsieur Jean.
　D. Coward, 617(TLS):13-19Jul90-748
Targan, B. Falling Free.
　E. Lotozo, 441:4Mar90-24
"Targum Jonathan of the Former Prophets."
(D.J. Harrington & A.J. Saldarini, trans)
　B.L. Visotzky, 508:Jan89-93
Tarkovsky, A. Sculpting in Time.
　J.R.B., 148:Winter86-197
Tarlinskaja, M. Shakespeare's Verse.
　A. Graham-White, 615(TJ):Dec89-572
　B.M., 494:Winter89-857
　R. McDonald, 570(SQ):Fall89-360
Tarn, N. - see Neruda, P.

Tarnanidis, I.C. The Slavonic Manuscripts
Discovered in 1975 at St. Catherine's
Monastery on Mount Sinai.
　A. Alekseev, 279:Vol37-190
Tarnawski, W. Conrad the Man, the Writer,
the Pole.
　I.P. Pulc, 136:Spring89-72
Tarr, R.L. Thomas Carlyle.
　W. Baker, 40(AEB):Vol3No2-71
　A. Bell, 617(TLS):13-19Jul90-762
Tarrant, H. Scepticism or Platonism?
　J. Glucker, 303(JoHS):Vol109-272
Tarrant, R.J., ed. Seneca's "Thyestes."
　T. Hirschberg, 229:Band61Heft3-259
Tarrío Varela, A. Literatura gallega.
　I. Stern, 711(RHM):Jun89-94
Tarski, A. Logic, Semantics, Metamathemat-
ics.
　I. Grattan-Guinness, 316:Mar89-281
Tartler, G. Orient Express.
　L. Chamberlain, 617(TLS):19-25Jan90-59
Tasso, T. Jerusalem Delivered.* (R. Nash, ed
& trans)
　L. Rhu, 276:Spring89-69
Tata, S. Shanghai, 1949.
　442(NY):8Oct90-118
Tatalovich, R. & B.W. Daynes, eds. Social
Regulatory Policy.
　J.P. Burke, 185:Apr90-686
Tatar, M. The Hard Facts of the Grimms'
Fairy Tales.*
　D. Haase, 301(JEGP):Oct89-594
　J. Schmidt, 268(IFR):Winter90-72
　D. Ward, 292(JAF):Jan-Mar89-97
Tatarkiewicz, W. Geschichte der Ästhetik.
(Vol 3) [entry in prev was of Vols 1 & 2]
　R. Reschke, 654(WB):3/1989-517
Tate, A. Collected Poems: 1919-1976.
　J.E. Brown, 580(SCR):Fall90-158
Tate, T. Child Pornography.
　M. Beard, 617(TLS):14-20Sep90-968
Tatilon, C. Traduire pour une pédagogie de la
traduction.
　P. Léon, 320(CJL):Jun89-201
"The Tatler."* (D.F. Bond, ed)
　J.A. Downie, 506(PSt):Dec89-296
　G.J. Kolb, 405(MP):Nov89-184
　S. Varey, 83:Autumn89-234
Tatton-Brown, V. Ancient Cyprus.
　D. Bolger, 123:Vol39No1-155
Tatum, J. Xenophon's Imperial Fiction.
　P.A. Stadter, 24:Winter89-665
Tatz, M. Asaṅga's Chapter of Ethics with the
Commentary of Tsong-Kha-Pa, The Basic
Path to Awakening, The Complete Bodhis-
attva.
　J.W. de Jong, 259(IIJ):Jul89-215
Taubken, H. Die Mundarten der Kreise Ems-
land und Grafschaft Bentheim. (Pt 1)
　D. Stellmacher, 685(ZDL):3/1989-376
Taubman, W. - see Khrushchev, S.
Taulbert, C.L. Once Upon a Time When We
Were Colored.
　R.L. Bray, 441:18Feb90-9
Tavard, G.H. Poetry and Contemplation in St.
John of the Cross.
　A.L. Cilveti, 403(MLS):Fall89-114
　J. Mandrell, 240(HR):Autumn89-511
Tavoni, M., ed. Renaissance Linguistics
Archive 1350-1700.* (1st Print-Out)
　R. Coluccia, 379(MedR):Aug89-301

Tavor, E. Scepticism, Society and the Eighteenth-Century Novel.*
  L.E. Warren, 566:Spring89-174
Tawaststjerna, E. Sibelius, 1904-1914. (Vol 2)
  A. Swanson, 563(SS):Spring/Summer89-279
Tax, P.W. - see Notker der Deutsche
Taylor, A. Book Catalogues. (2nd ed rev by W.P. Barlow, Jr.)
  J.F. Fuggles, 354:Jun89-169
Taylor, A. Coleridge's Defense of the Human.*
  P.M. Zall, 591(SIR):Spring89-168
Taylor, A. To School Through the Fields.
  P. Hampl, 441:1Apr90-20
Taylor, A. - see Schade, J.A.
Taylor, B., ed. Michael Dummett: Contributions to Philosophy.
  K. Bach, 103:Apr90-160
  L.E. Johnson, 63:Sep89-355
Taylor, B.B. Le Corbusier: The City of Refuge.
  C. Ellis, 47:Aug89-32
Taylor, C. Human Agency and Language.
  R. Brown, 488:Mar89-109
Taylor, C. Philosophical Papers.
  M.E. Rosen, 311(JP):May89-270
Taylor, C. Sources of the Self.
  J. Waldron, 617(TLS):23-29Mar90-325
  B. Williams, 453(NYRB):8Nov90-45
Taylor, D. Hardy's Metres and Victorian Prosody.*
  S. Hunter, 402(MLR):Jul90-705
  F. Tietjen, 447(VQR):Spring90-62
Taylor, D.J. A Vain Conceit.*
  J. Mellors, 364:Dec89/Jan90-138
Taylor, G. Players and Performances in the Victorian Theatre.
  J. Wilders, 617(TLS):9-15Mar90-256
Taylor, G. Pride, Shame and Guilt.*
  B. Elevitch, 449:Apr90-253
Taylor, G. Reinventing Shakespeare.*
  A. Barton, 453(NYRB):1Feb90-15
  A. Kirsch, 617(TLS):20-26Apr90-421
Taylor, G.H. - see Ricoeur, P.
Taylor, H. Gender, Race, and Region in the Writings of Grace King, Ruth McEnery Stuart, and Kate Chopin.
  B.C. Ewell, 27(AL):Dec89-700
  B. Harrison, 585(SoQ):Winter90-66
  M. Schueller, 395(MFS):Winter89-741
  L. Wagner-Martin, 392:Spring89-193
Taylor, H. Scarlett's Women.*
  A.H. Petry, 585(SoQ):Spring90-125
Taylor, J. English Historical Literature in the Fourteenth Century.*
  C. Gauvin, 189(EA):Oct-Dec89-463
  N. Saul, 382(MAE):1989/2-327
  G.B. Stow, 589:Jul89-771
  T. Turville-Petre, 541(RES):May89-245
Taylor, J. - see Potter, B.
Taylor, J.B. In the Secret Theatre of Home.
  S. Mitchell, 637(VS):Winter90-344
Taylor, J.G. & T.J. Lyon, general eds. A Literary History of the American West.*
  C. Merrill, 434:Winter89-208
Taylor, J.R. Linguistic Categorization.
  N. Smith, 617(TLS):9-15Feb90-143
Taylor, K., with K. Mumby. The Poisoned Tree.
  J. Fairleigh, 617(TLS):31Aug-6Sep90-924
Taylor, M., ed. Lads.
  J. Keates, 617(TLS):18-24May90-536

Taylor, M., ed. Rationality and Revolution.
  B.M. Downing, 185:Apr90-679
  P.B. Rich, 242:Vol10No2-266
Taylor, M.C. Altarity.*
  B. Martin, 478(P&L):Apr89-185
Taylor, P. See How They Run.
  H. Goodman, 441:30Sep90-13
Taylor, P.M., ed. Britain and the Cinema in the Second World War.
  639(VQR):Winter89-30
Taylor, R. & I. Christie, eds. The Film Factory.*
  D.J. Youngblood, 574(SEEJ):Summer89-314
Taylor, R.L. The Confucian Way of Contemplation.
  T.J. Kodera, 293(JASt):Nov89-878
Taylor, S. The Mighty Nimrod.*
  C.J. Fox, 364:Feb/Mar90-139
Taylor, S.J. Stalin's Apologist.
  F.D. Gray, 441:24Jun90-3
Tchernia, A. Le Vin de l'Italie romaine.*
  R.J. Rowland, Jr., 124:Mar-Apr90-365
Tchicaya U Tam'Si. The Madman and the Medusa.
  I. Malin, 532(RCF):Fall89-223
Tchouang Tseu (Zhuang Zi). Les Tablettes intérieures. (J-F. Rollin, ed & trans)
  M. Détrie, 549(RLC):Jul-Sep89-387
Tchoukovskaïa, L. Entretiens avec Anna Akhmatova.
  J. Russell, 453(NYRB):15Feb90-12
Teachout, T., ed. Beyond the Boom.
  H. Goodman, 441:18Dec90-19
Teague-Jones, R. The Spy Who Disappeared. Adventures in Persia.
  C.M. Woodhouse, 617(TLS):11-17May90-492
Tebbel, J. Between Covers.*
  G.L. Parker, 470:Vol27-143
  P.T.S., 295(JML):Fall88/Winter89-179
Tec, N. In the Lion's Den.
  S. Shapiro, 441:3Jun90-23
Tedeschini Lalli, B. - see Whitman, W.
Teichman, J. Pacifism and the Just War.*
  P. Rule, 63:Sep89-365
Teichman, J. Philosophy and the Mind.
  K. Pfeifer, 103:Aug90-332
Teichmann, R. Larra.*
  P. Deacon, 402(MLR):Apr90-478
Teicholz, T. The Trial of Ivan the Terrible.
  R.E. Herzstein, 441:25Nov90-6
Teitler, H.C. "Notarii" and "Exceptores."*
  H. Freis, 394:Vol42fasc1/2-252
Tejerina-Canal, S. La muerte de Artemio Cruz.
  S. Boldy, 86(BHS):Apr89-207
Telle, E-V. - see Hotman, F.
Telushkin, J. An Eye for an Eye.
  S. Altinel, 617(TLS):24-30Aug90-903
Temmer, M. Samuel Johnson and Three Infidels.*
  R. Waldinger, 478(P&L):Apr89-188
Temperley, N., ed. The Lost Chord.
  A. Jacobs, 617(TLS):9-15Mar90-256
Temple, R.K.G. Quand la Chine nous précédait.
  K. Chemla, 98:Aug-Sep89-715
Ten, C.L. Crime, Guilt and Punishment.*
  C. Ripley, 518:Apr89-113
Tener, R.H. & M. Woodfield - see Hutton, R.H.
Tennant, E. Sisters and Strangers.
  P. Craig, 617(TLS):13-19Jul90-746

Tennant, E. Two Women of London.* The Bad
Sister.
    B. Dickson, 571(ScLJ):Winter89-37
Tennant, E.C. The Habsburg Chancery Lan-
guage in Perspective.
    N.R. Wolf, 133:Band22Heft1-96
Tennant, N. Anti-Realism and Logic.*
    N. Griffin, 518:Jan89-35
    W.D. Hart, 316:Dec89-1485
    M. Luntley, 479(PhQ):Jul89-361
    192(EP):Apr-Jun89-274
Tennenhouse, L. Power on Display.*
    A.F. Kinney, 481(PQ):Fall89-443
    M.S., 615(TJ):May89-254
    R. Strier, 141:Spring89-200
Tennyson, A. The Letters of Alfred Lord
Tennyson.* (Vols 1 & 2) (C.Y. Lang & E.F.
Shannon, eds)
    M. Shaw, 541(RES):Feb89-136
Tennyson, A. The Poems of Tennyson.* (2nd
ed) (C. Ricks, ed)
    J. Kolb, 405(MP):May90-419
Tennyson, B., ed. Impressions of Cape Breton.
    M. Thorpe, 102(CanL):Spring89-212
Teotónio Almeida, O. "Mensagem."
    J. Parker, 86(BHS):Jul89-301
Tepper, S.S. Raising the Stones.
    G. Jonas, 441:21Oct90-35
de Terán, L.S. Joanna.
    D. Davies, 617(TLS):25-31May90-559
Teraoka, A.A. The Silence of Entropy or
Universal Discourse.*
    L. Kohn, 400(MLN):Apr89-749
Terborg-Penn, R., S. Harley & A.B. Rushing,
eds. Women in Africa and the African Di-
aspora.
    C.H. Bruner, 538(RAL):Summer89-308
Terence. The Brothers.* (A.S. Gratwick, ed &
trans) The Self-Tormenter. (A.J. Brothers,
ed & trans)
    F. Muecke, 313:Vol79-185
Terent'ev, I. Sobranie sočinenij. (M. Marca-
duri & T. Nikol'skaja, eds)
    G.J. Janecek, 574(SEEJ):Winter89-630
Saint Teresa. Libro de la vida. (O. Steggink,
ed)
    T. O'Reilly, 86(BHS):Apr89-175
"Terminologie und Typologie mittelalterlicher
Sachgüter: Das Beispiel der Kleidung."
    E. Brüggen & J. Bumke, 684(ZDA):Band118
    Heft3-99
Ternes, E. Einführung in die Phonologie.
    G. Meinhold, 682(ZPSK):Band42Heft3-414
    H. Penzl, 685(ZDL):2/1989-188
Terracini, L. I codici del silenzio.
    M. Grazia Profeti, 547(RF):Band101Heft4-
    495
Terradas i Saborit, I. El Cavaller de Vidrà.
    J-L. Marfany, 86(BHS):Oct89-391
Terrasse, M. Bonnard at Le Cannet.*
    N. Watkins, 90:Apr89-304
Terrell, T.D. & others. Deux Mondes.
    K. Jansma, 207(FR):Feb90-584
    E.G. Joiner, 399(MLJ):Autumn89-364
Terrell, T.D. & others. Dos Mundos.
    M.D. Finnemann, 399(MLJ):Spring89-106
Terrell, T.D. & others. Kontakte: A Communi-
cative Approach.
    M.P. Alter, 399(MLJ):Spring89-92
Terry, A. Sobre poesia catalana contempor-
ània.
    D. Keown, 86(BHS):Jul89-304

Terry, G.M., comp. East European Languages
and Literatures. (Vol 4)
    P.J. Mayo, 402(MLR):Apr90-531
Terry, R.C., ed. Trollope.*
    S.M. Smith, 541(RES):Aug89-430
Tertullian. De Idololatria.* (J.H. Waszink &
J.C.M. van Winden, eds & trans)
    R.D. Sider, 24:Winter89-675
Tertullian. Tertullien, "Les Spectacles" (De
spectaculis.)* (M. Turcan, ed & trans)
    J.C.M. van Winden, 394:Vol42fasc1/2-223
Tertz, A. Goodnight!*
    R. Hingley, 617(TLS):4-10May90-479
    442(NY):26Feb90-130
Tesh, S.N. Hidden Arguments.
    R.H.B., 185:Oct89-228
Tesich, N. Shadow Partisan.
    P.J. Bailey, 455:Dec89-61
    D. Galef, 448:Vol27No2-137
Tessonneau, R. - see Joubert, J.
Testud, P. - see Restif de La Bretonne
Tétreau, F. Le Lit de Procruste.
    D.W. Russell, 102(CanL):Autumn-
    Winter89-247
Tetreault, R. The Poetry of Life.*
    H. Donnelly, 541(RES):Nov89-576
Tétu, M. La Francophonie.
    B. Hourcade, 207(FR):Mar90-752
Tewarson, H.T. Rahel Levin Varnhagen.
    T.H. Pickett, 221(GQ):Spring89-275
Texier, C. Panic Blood.
    S. Bradfield, 441:15Apr90-16
Tezcan, H. The Topkapı Saray Museum: Car-
pets. (J.M. Rogers, ed & trans)
    R. Hillenbrand, 59:Mar89-109
Tezcan, H. & S. Delibaş. The Topkapı Saray
Museum: Costumes, Embroideries and Other
Textiles. (J.M. Rogers, ed)
    R. Hillenbrand, 59:Mar89-109
    J. Raby, 90:May89-360
Thackara, J., ed. Design After Modernism.*
    A.E. Monfried, 505:Sep89-183
    139:Dec89/Jan90-69
Thacker, C. Historic Gardens.
    H.J., 324:Dec89-69
Thacker, C. & others, eds. Larousse Garden-
ing and Gardens.
    A. Urquhart, 617(TLS):27Apr-3May90-
    440
Thackeray, W.M. Vanity Fair. (P.L. Shil-
lingsburg, ed) The History of Henry
Esmond. (E.F. Harden, ed)
    J. Sutherland, 617(TLS):15-21Jun90-652
Thagard, P. Computational Philosophy of
Science.
    D. Ross, 103:Jul90-285
Thalmann, W.G. Conventions of Form and
Thought in Early Greek Epic Poetry.*
    N. Postlethwaite, 303(JoHS):Vol109-212
Thaon, M. & others. Science-Fiction et Psy-
chanalyse.
    M. Angenot, 561(SFS):Jul89-218
Thapar, V. & F.S. Rathore. Tigers.
    J. Seidensticker, 441:26Aug90-3
Thayer, E.L. Casey at Bat.*
    R.B. Heilman, 569(SR):Summer89-475
"Theater and Society in French Literature."
    F.P. Bowman, 210(FrF):Sep89-355
Theile, N.R. Buddhism and Christianity in
Japan.*
    S.H. Kanda, 485(PE&W):Jan89-95
Theoharis, A.G. & J.S. Cox. The Boss.
    A.L. Hamby, 77:Summer89-253

Theoharis, T.C. Joyce's "Ulysses."
  C. Barrow, 174(Éire):Summer89-148
  P.A. McCarthy, 177(ELT):Vol32No3-375
  J.L. McDonald, 268(IFR):Summer89-134
  R.D. Reck, 329(JJQ):Winter90-419
  P. Van Caspel, 395(MFS):Summer89-328
Theophrastus. Théophraste, "Recherches sur
  les plantes, Tome I:" Livres I-II. (S.
  Amigues, ed & trans)
  R.W. Sharples, 123:Vol39No2-197
Theoret, F. Entre Raison et déraison.
  N.B. Bishop, 102(CanL):Autumn-
  Winter89-272
Théoret, M. Les discours de Cicéron.
  M. Baratin, 555:Vol62Fasc1-160
Thério, A., ed. Conteurs québécois 1900-
  1940.
  M.E. Ross, 627(UTQ):Fall89-181
Thernstrom, M. The Dead Girl.
  A. Boyer, 441:14Oct90-49
Theroux, A. An Adultery.* Three Wogs.
  Darconville's Cat.
  M. Pinker, 152(UDQ):Winter90-101
Theroux, P. Chicago Loop.
  J. Clute, 617(TLS):6-12Apr90-376
Theroux, P. My Secret History.*
  I. Thomson, 364:Jun/Jul89-128
Theroux, P. Riding the Iron Rooster.*
  K. Gernant, 293(JASt):May89-377
Theroux, P. Sandstorms.
  S. Mackey, 441:24Jun90-14
Theuerkauff, C. Nachmittelalterliche Elfen-
  beine.
  M. Estella, 48:Jan-Mar89-102
Theweleit, K. Male Fantasies.* (Vol 1)
  M.E. Papke, 367(L&P):Vol35No4-55
Thickstun, M.O. Fictions of the Feminine.*
  E.V. Beilin, 604:Winter89-7
  D. McColley, 70:Jul89-110
  M.A. Schofield, 402(MLR):Apr90-406
Thiele, S. Die Verwicklungen im Denkens
  Wittgensteins.
  I. Idalovichi, 242:Vol10No1-97
Thierry, A. - see d'Aubigné, T.A.
Thierry, J-M. & P. Donabédian, with N.
  Thierry. Armenian Art.
  C. Mango, 617(TLS):20-26Jul90-772
Thierry, S. - see Chevalier, D., P. Chevalier &
  P-F. Bertrand
Thierry of Chartres. The Latin Rhetorical
  Commentaries by Thierry of Chartres. (K.M.
  Fredborg, ed)
  P.G. Walsh, 123:Vol39No2-423
  J.O. Ward, 544:Autumn89-360
Thody, P. French Caesarism from Napoleon I
  to Charles de Gaulle.
  T.H. Jones, 207(FR):May90-1116
Thody, P. Marcel Proust.
  E. Hughes, 208(FS):Jul89-352
  A.H. Pasco, 210(FrF):Sep89-377
  L.M. Porter, 395(MFS):Summer89-356
  M. Slater, 402(MLR):Jan90-198
Thom, F. The Gorbachev Phenomenon.
  J. Sherr, 617(TLS):16-22Mar90-273
Thom, R. Esquisse d'une sémiophysique.
  J. Largeault, 542:Oct-Dec89-656
Thoma, H. Die öffentliche Muse.
  J.J. Goblot, 535(RHL):Mar-Apr89-300
  G. Pauls, 356(LR):Feb-May89-115
Thomas, A. La variation phonétique.*
  W. Cichocki, 320(CJL):Dec89-454

Thomas, A-L. Essai sur le caractère, les
  moeurs, et l'esprit des femmes dans les
  différents siècles (1772). (C. Michael, ed)
  F. Moureau, 530:Apr89-169
Thomas, A.R., ed. Methods in Dialectology.
  J.M. Fayer, 399(MLJ):Autumn89-379
Thomas, B. The Big Wheel.
  T. Hibbert, 617(TLS):31Aug-6Sep90-918
Thomas, B. Clown Prince of Hollywood.
  M.E. Ross, 441:15Jul90-19
Thomas, B. Cross-Examinations of Law and
  Literature.*
  B. Lee, 402(MLR):Jan90-151
Thomas, B. An Underground Fate.
  H-P. Breuer, 395(MFS):Summer89-337
  D. Erdinast-Vulcan, 447(N&Q):Dec89-547
  R. Stevenson, 402(MLR):Jul90-709
  P. Stratford, 627(UTQ):Fall89-134
Thomas, C. La Reine scélérate.
  P. Saint-Amand, 98:Oct89-805
Thomas, C.G. Paths from Ancient Greece.
  R. Stoneman, 123:Vol39No2-376
Thomas, D. & D.K. Jackson. The Poe Log.*
  J.L. Dameron & T.C. Carlson, 495(PoeS):
  Dec88-44
Thomas, D. & J. Compton Mackenzie.
  J.G. Watson, 447(N&Q):Mar89-125
Thomas, D.A.L. - see under Lloyd Thomas,
  D.A.
Thomas, D.M. Lying Together.
  A. Goreau, 441:8Jul90-3
  C. Rumens, 617(TLS):13-19Jul90-746
Thomas, D.M. Memories and Hallucinations.*
  S. Pickering, 569(SR):Spring90-297
Thomas, E.M. The Animal Wife.
  M. Johnson, 441:14Oct90-24
  442(NY):8Oct90-147
Thomas, F. & O. Johnston. Too Funny for
  Words.
  J. Canemaker, 507:May/Jun89-161
Thomas, G. The Impact of Illyrian Movement
  on the Croatian Lexicon.
  T.F. Magner, 574(SEEJ):Fall89-466
Thomas, G. The Moral Philosophy of T.H.
  Green.
  D.M.A. Campbell, 518:Jul89-147
  G. Stock, 479(PhQ):Oct89-518
Thomas, H., ed. Berryman's Understanding.
  M. Hofmann, 617(TLS):6-12Apr90-363
Thomas, H. Un Retour par la vie.*
  W. Cloonan, 207(FR):Dec89-412
Thomas, H., with M. Thomas. Under Storm's
  Wing.
  P.E. Mitchell, 177(ELT):Vol32No1-80
Thomas, J. Le dépassement du quotidien dans
  l'"Énéide," les "Métamorphoses" d'Apulée et
  le "Satiricon."*
  W. Kissel, 229:Band61Heft8-742
Thomas, J.P. Private Religious Foundations
  in the Byzantine Empire.
  D.J. Constantelos, 589:Oct89-1041
Thomas, K. Gender and Subject in Higher
  Education.
  E. Hinds, 324:Oct90-792
Thomas, L. Et Cetera, Et Cetera.
  T. Bay, 441:21Oct90-25
Thomas, L. Living Morally.
  S.G. Clarke, 103:Jul90-288
Thomas, L.V. Elementary Turkish. (N. Itz-
  kowitz, ed)
  D.R. Magrath, 399(MLJ):Spring89-108

Thomas, M.M. Hanover Place.
L. Auchincloss, 453(NYRB):26Apr90–21
J. Martin, 441:7Jan90–10
Thomas, M.W. The Lunar Light of Whitman's
Poetry.*
C.C. Hollis, 70:Apr89–65
T. Oggel, 599:Spring90–146
Thomas, P., ed. The Red Jeep and Other
Landscapes.
F. Cogswell, 102(CanL):Autumn–
Winter89–183
Thomas, P. The Welsher.*
M.E. Turner, 102(CanL):Autumn–
Winter89–253
Thomas, P.D.G. The Townshend Duties Crisis.
R.R. Johnson, 656(WMQ):Apr89–399
Thomas, R. Japan.
K. van Wolferen, 617(TLS):31Aug–
6Sep90–926
Thomas, R. Twilight at Mac's Place.
R. Lourie, 441:21Oct90–30
Thomas, R. A Woman of Our Times.
K. Blickle, 441:9Dec90–24
Thomas, R.S. The Echoes Return Slow.*
D. McDuff, 565:Spring89–76
Thomas, V. The Moral Universe of Shake-
speare's Problem Plays.*
P. Happé, 447(N&Q):Mar89–100
Thomas, W. Die Erforschung des Tocharischen
(1960–1984).*
P. Kosta, 260(IF):Band94–343
Thomas, W.K. & W.U. Ober. A Mind For Ever
Voyaging.
D. Perkins, 445(NCF):Mar90–543
J. Thompson, 150(DR):Spring89–143
Thompson, A. "King Lear."
R.A. Cohen, 570(SQ):Winter89–502
M. Elliott, 447(N&Q):Dec89–501
M. Lomax, 402(MLR):Jan90–145
Thompson, A. & J.O. Shakespeare, Meaning
and Metaphor.*
A.F. Kinney, 481(PQ):Fall89–443
B.M., 494:Winter89–857
D. Novitz, 290(JAAC):Winter89–92
H.F. Plett, 156(ShJW):Jahrbuch1989–366
Thompson, B. The Art of Graphic Design.*
C. Pearlman, 55:May89–111
Thompson, B. Bradbury Thompson.
P.B. Meggs, 507:May/Jun89–149
Thompson, C. & A. Sonnenschein. Down and
Dirty.
F.E. Halpert, 441:7Oct90–21
Thompson, C.P. The Strife of Tongues.
639(VQR):Summer89–89
Thompson, D. & I. Christie – see Scorsese, M.
Thompson, D.J. Memphis under the Ptole-
mies.*
J.F. Oates, 24:Fall89–509
Thompson, E.A. Who Was Saint Patrick?
J.F. Kelly, 589:Oct89–1043
Thompson, E.M. Understanding Russia.*
A. Barker, 104(CASS):Spring89–95
Thompson, F.M.L., ed. The Cambridge Social
History of Britain, 1750–1950.
D. Cannadine, 617(TLS):7–13Sep90–935
Thompson, F.M.L. The Rise of Respectable
Society.*
D. Cannadine, 453(NYRB):15Feb90–25
R.W. Davis, 637(VS):Summer90–668
G. Woodcock, 569(SR):Summer89–lxxxvi
Thompson, H.S. Songs of the Doomed.
R. Rosenbaum, 441:25Nov90–7

Thompson, J. Between Self and World.*
L.V. Graves, 594:Fall89–346
C.C. Park, 249(HudR):Winter89–645
L. Speirs, 402(MLR):Jul90–701
Thompson, J. Past Reckoning.
P. Craig, 617(TLS):16–22Mar90–298
Thompson, J. – see Trollope, A.
Thompson, J.J. Robert Thornton and the Lon-
don Thornton Manuscript.*
E. Wilson, 382(MAE):1989/1–158
Thompson, J.J. Tennessee Williams' Plays.
T.P. Adler, 397(MD):Jun89–319
Thompson, K. Breaking the Glass Armor.
A. Neill & A. Ridley, 103:Sep90–345
Thompson, K. Married Love.
D.S. Lenoski, 102(CanL):Spring89–236
Thompson, L. A History of South Africa.
G.M. Fredrickson, 453(NYRB):27Sep90–20
L. Hahn, 441:15Jul90–12
Thompson, L.A. Romans and Blacks.
M. Beard, 617(TLS):19–25Jan90–71
A. Lintott, 235:Winter89–89
Thompson, L.B. Dorothy Livesay.
529(QQ):Spring89–215
Thompson, M.G. The Death of Desire.
R. Skelton, 323:May89–188
Thompson, M.W. Feeding the Beast.
A. Feinberg, 441:29Jul90–9
Thompson, P. The Structure of Biological
Theories.
J. Collier, 103:Apr90–163
Thompson, P., C. Itzin & M. Abenstern. I
Don't Feel Old.
P. Willmott, 617(TLS):26Oct–1Nov90–
1148
Thompson, R.J. Everlasting Voices.
F.L. Ryan, 268(IFR):Winter90–52
Thompson, T.L. & R. Sheldon, eds. Soviet
Society and Culture.
A.G. Meyer, 550(RusR):Apr89–218
Thomsen, C.W., ed. Grundzüge der Geschichte
des europäischen Hörspiels.*
H. Priessnitz, 38:Band107Heft3/4–544
Thomsen, M. The Saddest Pleasure.
T. Cahill, 441:10Jun90–48
Thomsen, M-L. The Sumerian Language.
T. Jacobsen, 318(JAOS):Jan–Mar88–123
Thomsen, R. Ambition and Confucianism.
K. Turner, 293(JASt):Aug89–604
Thomson, A. Barbary and Enlightenment.
A. Gunny, 83:Spring89–93
Thomson, A. The Life and Times of Charles-
Marie Widor, 1844–1937.*
R. Nichols, 415:Jan89–27
Thomson, A. Widor.
W.J. Gatens, 410(M&L):Feb89–120
Thomson, D. Silver Light.
W. Hjortsberg, 441:1Apr90–8
J. Loose, 617(TLS):10–16Aug90–855
Thomson, G. Needs.*
R. Keshen, 185:Oct89–179
Thomson, J. "Liberty," "The Castle of Indo-
lence," and Other Poems.* (J. Sambrook,
ed)
D.A. Low, 447(N&Q):Dec89–515
Thomson, J. The Plays of James Thomson,
1700–1748. (J.C. Greene, ed)
J. Sambrook, 566:Spring89–192
Thomson, J.J., ed. On Being and Saying.
J. Bogen, 518:Apr89–92

Thomson, J.J. Rights, Restitution, and Risk.
(W. Parent, ed)
M.B. Naylor, 449:Jun89-399
H.M. Smith, 482(PhR):Jul89-414
Thomson, R. Degas: The Nudes.*
R. Kendall, 39:May89-366
Thomson, R.M. Catalogue of the Manuscripts
of Lincoln Cathedral Chapter Library.
T. Webber, 617(TLS):8-14Jun90-618
Thomson, V. Music with Words.*
42(AR):Fall89-502
Thomson, V. Selected Letters of Virgil Thom-
son. (T. & V.W. Page, eds)
P. Dickinson, 415:Jul89-414
Thon, M.R. Meteors in August.
R. Sassone, 441:21Oct90-24
Thông, S.H. - see under Huỳnh Sanh Thông
Thoreau, D. The Book of Numbers.
M. Stasio, 441:29Apr90-18
Thoreau, H.D. Cape Cod. (J.J. Moldenhauer,
ed)
J. Myerson, 40(AEB):Vol3No1-29
Thorlby, A. Leo Tolstoy: "Anna Karenina."*
L. Trott, 575(SEER):Jan89-125
C.J.G. Turner, 104(CASS):Spring-Win-
ter88-428
Thornburg, M.K.P. The Monster in the Mirror.
R. Beecham, 541(RES):Aug89-423
Thornbury, C. - see Derryman, J.
Thorniley, D. The Rise and Fall of the Soviet
Rural Communist Party, 1927-30.
C. Merridale, 575(SEER):Oct89-638
Thornton, L. Imagining Argentina.
I. Malin, 532(RCF):Spring89-271
Thornton, L. Under the Gypsy Moon.
S. Ruta, 441:14Oct90-14
Thornton, K. We Shall Live Again.
W. Westerman, 292(JAF):Jan-Mar89-122
Thorp, N. The Glory of the Page.
J. Backhouse, 39:Dec89-428
Thorpe, A. Meeting Montaigne.
L. Mackinnon, 617(TLS):17-23Aug90-871
Thorpe, E. Black Dance.
P. Brinson, 324:Mar90-207
Thorpe, T.B. A New Collection of Thomas
Bangs Thorpe's Sketches of the Old South-
west. (D.C. Estes, ed)
R. Dodge, 649(WAL):Nov89-273
Thrift, S. & B. Shapiro. The Game According
to Syd.
B. James, 441:1Apr90-14
Thubron, C. Behind the Wall.*
K. Gernant, 293(JASt):May89-377
Thubron, C. Falling.*
J. Mellors, 364:Dec89/Jan90-126
Thuillier, G. & J. Tulard. Les Écoles histor-
iques.
P. Higonnet, 617(TLS):28Sep-4Oct90-
1028
Thuillier, J. Nicolas Poussin.
M. Bull, 59:Dec89-516
Thun, H. Dialoggestaltung im Deutschen und
Rumänischen.
J. Erfurt, 682(ZPSK):Band42Heft5-688
Thurm, M. Henry in Love.
R. Sassone, 441:4Mar90-18
de Thurocz, J. Chronica Hungarorum, I. (E.
Galántai & J. Kristó, eds)
G. Chaix, 549(RLC):Jan-Mar89-132
Thurston, C. The Romance Revolution.*
C. Belsey, 402(MLR):Oct90-906

Thwaite, A. A.A. Milne.
N. Auerbach, 441:23Sep90-12
H. Carpenter, 617(TLS):8-14Jun90-607
J.A. Smith, 453(NYRB):27Sep90-3
Thwaite, A. - see Larkin, P.
Tibaut. Le roman de la poire.* (C. Mar-
chello-Nizia, ed)
S. Huot, 589:Jan89-223
Tibullus. Albi Tibulli Aliorumque Carmina.
(G. Luck, ed)
J.L. Butrica, 123:Vol39No2-211
Tichi, C. Shifting Gears.*
T. Goldie, 102(CanL):Winter88-129
M.D.O., 295(JML):Fall88/Winter89-179
Tickell, P., ed. The Indonesian Press.
J. Mackie, 293(JASt):Feb89-233
Tickner, L. The Spectacle of Women.
J. Beckett & D. Cherry, 59:Mar89-121
D.S. Gardner, 54:Dec89-700
Tidrick, K. Empire and the English Character.
A. Lively, 617(TLS):28Sep-4Oct90-1022
Tieck, L. Schriften. (Vol 11) (U. Schweikert,
with G. Schweikert, eds)
R. Paulin, 402(MLR):Apr90-509
Tiedemann, R. - see Benjamin, W.
Tiemroth, J.E. Det labyrintiske sind.
P.M. Mitchell, 563(SS):Spring/Summer89-
296
T'ien Ju-k'ang. Male Anxiety and Female
Chastity.
P.S. Ropp, 293(JASt):Aug89-605
Tierney, F.M. & G. Clever, eds. Nine-
teenth-Century Narrative Poetry.
I.S. MacLaren, 105:Spring/Summer89-81
Tierney, P. The Highest Altar.
R.T. Zuidema, 441:7Jan90-29
Tierney, R. The Stone Veil.
M. Stasio, 441:8Apr90-26
Tiessen, P. - see Lowry, M. & G. Noxon
Tiger, L. Men in Groups. (2nd ed)
R. Porter, 617(TLS):1-7Jun90-589
Tigerman, S. The Architecture of Exile.
D. Kesler, 45:Sep89-57
Tigges, W., ed. Explorations in the Field of
Nonsense.
J-J. Lecercle, 189(EA):Oct-Dec89-446
Tikkanen, B. The Sanskrit Gerund.
J.S. Klein, 350:Mar90-210
Tikkanen, H. The Thirty Years' War.*
K.O. Dana, 563(SS):Autumn89-421
T. Palmer, 577(SHR):Winter89-77
Tiles, J.E. Dewey.*
J. Welchman, 319:Jul90-465
Tilghman, B.R. But Is It Art?
H. Pardee, 127:Summer89-194
Tilghman, C. In a Father's Place.
J. Casey, 441:6May90-12
R. Towers, 453(NYRB):16Aug90-45
Tillian, K. Die Kärntner Dehnung.
H. Tatzreiter, 685(ZDL):3/1989-369
Tillinghast, D. Women Hoping for Rain.*
M.G. Harris, 580(SCR):Fall89-141
Tillman, B. Warriors.
N. Callendar, 441:22Jul90-22
Tillotson, G.H.R. The Rajput Palaces.*
C. Russell, 47:Mar89-57
Tillyard, S.K. The Impact of Modernism 1900-
1920.
B. Kennedy, 89(BJA):Summer89-286
S. Watney, 90:Jan89-45
Timerman, J. Cuba.
D. Rieff, 441:21Oct90-9

Timko, M. Carylye and Tennyson.
M. Peckham, 445(NCF):Mar90-566
R. Tarr, 637(VS):Winter90-331
Timko, M., F. Kaplan & E. Guiliano – see
"Dickens Studies Annual"
Timm, E. Graphische und phonische Struktur
des Westjiddischen unter besonderer Ber-
ücksichtigung der Zeit um 1600.
M.G. Heide, 680(ZDP):Band108Heft1-152
B. Simon, 682(ZPSK):Band42Heft4-547
Timms, E. Karl Kraus, Apocalyptic Satirist.*
P. Pabisch, 301(JEGP):Jul89-388
Timms, E. & P. Collier, eds. Visions and
Blueprints.*
M.P.L., 295(JML):Fall88/Winter89-189
S. Sayers, 242:Vol10No5-624
Timms, E. & D. Kelley, eds. Unreal City.*
S.E. Larsen, 462(OL):Vol44No3-278
Tinder, G. The Political Meaning of Chris-
tianity.
W.S. Coffin, 441:18Feb90-18
Tinkler-Villani, V. Visions of Dante in Eng-
lish Poetry.*
F.M. Keener, 173(ECS):Winter89/90-216
Tinniswood, A. A History of Country House
Visiting.
J.M. Robinson, 46:Dec89-14
Tintner, A.R. The Book World of Henry
James.*
G. Caramello, 395(MFS):Summer89-267
F. Golffing, 473(PR):Vol56No3-518
Tintner, A.R. The Pop World of Henry James.*
S.B. Daugherty, 26(ALR):Winter90-90
S.B. Daugherty, 395(MFS):Winter89-729
Tippett, B. "Gulliver's Travels."
D. Bywaters, 566:Spring90-209
Tirado, I.A. Young Guard!
R.A. Wade, 550(RusR):Apr89-215
Tirso de Molina. Damned for Despair (El con-
denado por desconfiado).* (N.G. Round, ed
& trans)
V.G. Williamsen, 238:Mar89-163
Tirso de Molina. La Santa Juana. (Pt 2)
(X.A. Fernández, ed)
R.L. Hathaway, 304(JHP):Winter89-165
Tirso de Molina. El vergonzoso en palacio.
(F. Florit Durán, ed)
M. Wilson, 86(BHS):Jan89-202
Tise, L.E. Proslavery.
W.D. Jordan, 432(NEQ):Mar89-136
W. Stanton, 656(WMQ):Jul89-601
Tišma, A. Le Kapo.
L. Kovacs, 450(NRF):Dec89-123
Tisseron, S. Psychanalyse de la bande dessi-
née.
M. Fauvel, 207(FR):Feb90-537
Tissier, A., ed. Recueil de Farces (1450-
1550).* (Vol 3)
H. Arden, 207(FR):Mar90-703
E.E. Du Bruck, 201:Vol15-371
A. Hindley, 402(MLR):Oct90-949
Tissier, A., ed. Recueil de Farces (1450-
1550). (Vol 4)
A. Hindley, 402(MLR):Oct90-949
"Titian."
F. Haskell, 453(NYRB):16Aug90-8
Titinius. Titinio e Atta, Fabula togata, i
frammenti. (T. Guardi, ed)
P. Flobert, 555:Vol62Fasc2-362
Titley, N.M. Persian Miniature Painting and
its Influence on the Art of Turkey and In-
dia.
A. Schimmel, 318(JAOS):Jan-Mar88-174

Titon, J.T. Powerhouse for God.*
B. Sutton, 187:Fall89-527
Titone, R. Cinque millenni di insegnamento
delle lingue.
M. Danesi, 710:Sep89-359
Tiwari, K.N., ed. Suffering.
G. Chemparathy, 318(JAOS):Jul-Sep88-
500
Tlili, M. Lion Mountain.
R. Irwin, 617(TLS):14-20Dec90-1359
"Tlumačal'ny slounik belaruskaj movy."
K. Müller, 682(ZPSK):Band42Heft1-132
Toaff, E. Perfidi Giudei Fratelli Maggiori.
A.A. Aciman, 390:Nov89-32
Tobin, F. Meister Eckhart.*
F. Brunner, 192(EP):Jan-Mar89-118
R. Kieckhefer, 589:Jan89-226
Tobin, R.W., ed. Littérature et gastronomie.
L.A. Gregorio, 475:Vol16No30-356
Tobin, Y., ed. The Prague School and Its Leg-
acy, in Linguistics, Literature, Semiotics,
Folklore, and the Arts.
M.J. Elson, 350:Dec90-887
S. Levin, 215(GL):Vol29No2-133
de Tocqueville, H. & A. The Two Tocque-
villes, Father and Son. (R.R. Palmer, ed &
trans)
A.J. Arscott, 529(QQ):Summer89-485
Tod, A. – see Grant, E.
Todd, J., ed. A Dictionary of British and
American Women Writers 1660-1800.
C. Salmon, 447(N&Q):Mar89-109
Todd, J. Feminist Literary Criticism.
C.A. Rogers, 219(GaR):Spring89-210
Todd, J. Feminist Literary History.*
R. Felski, 141:Fall89-455
D. Fuss, 50(ArQ):Winter89-95
E.H. Schor, 478(P&L):Oct89-403
Todd, J. Sensibility.*
R. Ferguson, 83:Spring89-108
Todd, J. The Sign of Angellica.*
J.C. Beasley, 566:Spring90-200
P.M. Spacks, 166:Jul90-364
Todd, J. – see Wollstonecraft, M.
Todd, J. & M. Butler – see Wollstonecraft, M.
Todd, L. Pidgins and Creoles.
T. Shippey, 617(TLS):19-25Oct90-1117
Todd, M. Christian Humanism and the Puritan
Social Order.
W.J. Bouwsma, 551(RenQ):Autumn89-568
Todd, R. The Opacity of Signs.
M. Elsky, 301(JEGP):Apr89-233
S. Gottlieb, 541(RES):Nov89-563
Todd, W.B. & A. Bowden. Tauchnitz Interna-
tional Editions in English 1841-1955.*
E. Gilcher, 177(ELT):Vol32No4-498
D. McKitterick, 78(BC):Winter89-555
J. Stephens, 354:Sep89-290
Todd, W.M. 3d. Fiction and Society in the Age
of Pushkin.*
W. Arndt, 104(CASS):Spring-Winter88-
450
P.G. Reeve, 580(SCR):Fall90-188
R. Reid, 575(SEER):Oct89-608
Todesco, F. Riforma della metafisica e sapere
scientifico.
A. Clericuzio, 319:Jan90-136
Todorov, T. Mikhail Bakhtin.
R.D. Abrahams, 292(JAF):Apr-Jun89-202
F. Stockholder, 104(CASS):Spring-Win-
ter88-502
Todorov, T. The Conquest of America.
J. Piedra, 153:Spring89-34

Todorov, T. Literature and Its Theorists.
R. Dutton, 89(BJA):Autumn89-382
D.T.O., 295(JML):Fall88/Winter89-237
Toer, P.A. The Fugitive.
I. Buruma, 453(NYRB):19Jul90-43
K. Swenson, 441:20May90-12
Tofani, A.P. & G. Smith - see under Petrioli
Tofani, A. & G. Smith
Toffler, A. Powershift.
D. Cole, 441:4Nov90-25
Togeby, K. & others. Grammaire française, 5.
D. Gaatone, 545(RPh):Nov89-301
Toker, L. Nabokov.
C. Ross, 395(MFS):Winter89-757
Tolchin, N.L. Mourning, Gender, and Creativity in the Art of Herman Melville.*
N. Baym, 301(JEGP):Apr89-263
B. Harvey, 432(NEQ):Mar89-130
C. Sten, 27(AL):May89-286
Toledano, R. Francesco di Giorgio Martini.
P.C. Marani, 90:Oct89-710
Tolkien, J.R.R. The Letters of J.R.R. Tolkien.
(H. Carpenter, ed)
617(TLS):24-30Aug90-905
Tolstaya, T. On the Golden Porch.*
A. Fitzlyon, 364:Aug/Sep89-138
G. Krist, 249(HudR):Winter89-663
P. Lewis, 565:Autumn89-72
Tolstoi, P. The Travel Diary of Peter Tolstoi.
(M.J. Okenfuss, ed & trans)
S.H. Baron, 550(RusR):Jan89-84
Tolstoy, N. Auf der Suche nach Merlin.
W. Wunderlich, 196:Band30Heft1/2-177
Tomalin, C. The Invisible Woman.
S. Wall, 617(TLS):2-8Nov90-1177
Tomalin, C. Katherine Mansfield.*
D. Baldwin, 573(SSF):Fall88-480
Tomás, J.M.O. - see under Oltra Tomás, J.M.
Tomaselli, K., ed. Rethinking Culture.
D. Coplan, 538(RAL):Summer89-278
Tomaszewski, J., E. Smułkowa & H. Majecki,
eds. Studia polsko-litewsko-białoruskie.
J. Dingley, 575(SEER):Oct89-622
Tomiš, K. Časovost' literatury.
J.D. Naughton, 575(SEER):Oct89-623
Tomlin, B.W. & M.A. Molot. 1986/Talking
Trade.
M. Bradfield, 298:Spring89-146
Tomlin, E.W.F. T.S. Eliot.*
R. Crawford, 447(N&Q):Dec89-541
Tomlin, R.S., ed. Coherence and Grounding in
Discourse.
G. Bourcier, 189(EA):Oct-Dec89-454
G. Redeker, 603:Vol13No1-226
Tomlins, C.L. The State and the Unions.
J. Braeman, 106:Summer89-41
Tomlinson, C. Collected Poems.
B. Howard, 502(PrS):Summer89-119
J.D. McClatchy, 491:Apr89-29
Tomlinson, C. The Return.*
R. Pybus, 565:Winter88/89-67
Tomlinson, G. Monteverdi and the End of the
Renaissance.*
D. Baumann, 417:Apr-Jun89-185
J. Haar, 317:Fall89-647
T. Knighton, 557:Sep89-324
Tomlinson, J. Public Policy and the Economy
since 1900.
G. Peden, 617(TLS):18-24May90-520
Tomlinson, J.A. Francisco Goya.
R. Snell, 617(TLS):16-22Mar90-290

Tommola, X. Aspektual'nost' v finskom i rus-
skom jazykax.
I. Press, 559:Vol13No2-178
Tompkins, J.M.S. William Morris.*
F. Kirchhoff, 637(VS):Winter90-365
Tong, S., with M. Yen - see under Shen Tong,
with M. Yen
Tonkin, P. The Coffin Ship.
N. Callendar, 441:7Oct90-39
Tooke, A.J. - see Flaubert, G. & M. du Camp
Toolan, M.J. Narrative.
D.E. Hardy, 350:Sep90-653
W. Jenkins, 599:Summer90-335
J.J. Weber, 307:Dec89-232
Toole, J.K. The Neon Bible.
M. Childress, 617(TLS):30Mar-5Apr90-
338
Tooley, M. Abortion and Infanticide.
M. Wreen, 449:Dec89-690
Tooley, M. Causation.*
E. Fales, 484(PPR):Mar90-605
P. Menzies, 63:Jun89-230
A. Morton, 518:Jul89-157
Toombs, S.E. James Thurber.
J. Griffin, 573(SSF):Spring89-209
S.P., 295(JML):Fall88/Winter89-413
Toomer, J. Cane. (D.T. Turner, ed)
J. Booth, 447(N&Q):Dec89-561
van den Toorn, P.C. Stravinsky and "The Rite
of Spring."*
T.A. Greer, 308:Spring89-198
B. Northcott, 415:Feb89-83
A. Pople, 410(M&L):Aug89-430
Topping, N. & M.D. Seymour. Conversations
with Nadine Gordimer.
D. Papineau, 617(TLS):28Sep-4Oct90-
1037
Topsfield, V. The Humour of Samuel Beckett.
P.H. Solomon, 395(MFS):Winter89-815
Torchiana, D.T. Backgrounds for Joyce's
"Dubliners."*
K.P. Müller, 38:Band107Heft1/2-263
Torgovnick, M. Gone Primitive.
A.C. Danto, 441:24Jun90-33
Tørnsø, K. Djaevletro og folkemagi.
T. Hall, 563(SS):Autumn89-412
de Toro, A., ed. Gustave Flaubert.*
L. Bottineau, 535(RHL):Nov-Dec89-1066
U. Dethloff, 547(RF):Band101Heft1-132
Torraca, L. Duride de Samo.
P. Pédech, 229:Band61Heft6-556
de la Torre, B.R. Thomas Buckingham and the
Contingency of Futures.
M.T. Clark, 589:Jul89-692
Torrente Ballester, G. Ifigonia y otros cuen-
tos.
A.G. Loureiro, 238:Sep89-548
Torrente Ballester, G. Yo no soy yo, eviden-
temente.
G.J. Pérez, 238:Mar89-147
Torres, D. Studies on Clarín.*
R. Eberenz, 547(RF):Band101Heft1-154
C. Richmond, 240(HR):Spring89-251
Torres, V.B. - see Calderón de la Barca, P.
de Torres Naharro, B. Comedias.* (H. López
Morales, ed)
J. Lihani, 86(BHS):Apr89-172
Torrevejano, M. Razón y Metafísica en Kant.
M. Caimi, 342:Band80Heft4-491
Torrey, G.E., ed. General Henri Berthelot and
Romania.
D. Deletant, 575(SEER):Oct89-637

Tory, A. Surviving the Holocaust. (M. Gilbert, ed)
  I. Deák, 453(NYRB):8Nov90-52
  J. Shulevitz, 441:20May90-31
  R.S. Wistrich, 617(TLS):23-29Nov90-1261
Tostevin, L.L. 'sophie.
  D. McCance, 137:Spring89-58
  D.E. Smyth, 648(WCR):Vol23No2-70
Toth, E. Kate Chopin.
  S. O'Brien, 441:30Dec90-10
Totman, C. The Green Archipelago.
  W.W. Farris, 293(JASt):Aug89-630
  J. Robertson, 407(MN):Winter89-504
Tottie, G. & I. Bäcklund, eds. English in Speech and Writing.
  K-D. Barnickel, 38:Band107Heft3/4-469
Touati, A-M.L. The Great Trajanic Frieze.
  F.A. Lepper, 123:Vol39No2-418
  R.R.R. Smith, 313:Vol79-213
Toulmin, S. Cosmopolis.
  T.K. Rabb, 617(TLS):29Jun-5Jul90-689
  Q. Skinner, 453(NYRB):12Apr90-36
  W. Steiner, 441:4Mar90-15
Toulouse, T. The Art of Prophesying.*
  M.P. Kramer, 301(JEGP):Oct89-554
Toumayan, A. La Littérature et la hantise du Mal.
  C. Bernard, 446(NCFS):Fall-Winter89/90-255
  C. Lloyd, 208(FS):Oct89-483
  J-L. Pire, 356(LR):Nov89-333
  M. Scott, 402(MLR):Apr90-448
Tourbin, D. The Port Dalhousie Stories.
  N. Bailey, 102(CanL):Winter88-111
Tourgée, A.W. The Invisible Empire.
  639(VQR):Summer89-93
Tourneur, C. The Revenger's Tragedy. (R.A. Foakes, ed)
  R.G. Barlow, 568(SCN):Fall-Winter89-48
Tournier, M. The Golden Droplet.*
  R. Hadas, 473(PR):Vol56No2-310
Tournier, M. Le Médianoche amoureux.
  S. Petit, 207(FR):Feb90-583
Tournier, M. The Wind Spirit.*
  42(AR):Winter89-108
  42(AR):Summer89-372
Toussaint, J-P. The Bathroom.* (French title: La Salle de bain.)
  P-L. Adams, 61:Apr90-109
  P. Erens, 441:29Apr90-38
  Y. Leclerc, 98:Nov89-889
Toussaint, J-P. L'appareil-photo.* Monsieur.
  Y. Leclerc, 98:Nov89-889
Toutain, C. La Tragédie d'Agamemnon. (T. Peach, ed)
  C. Smith, 208(FS):Oct89-460
Touzot, J., ed. Lectures du "Sagouin."
  J. Flower, 402(MLR):Jan90-199
Tovey, D.F. Essays in Musical Analysis.
  K. Korsyn, 415:Aug89-472
Tovey, D.F. Symphonies and Other Orchestral Works. Concertos and Choral Works. Chamber Music.
  A.F.L.T., 412:May89-146
"Toward Civilization: A Report on Arts Education."
  S. Hope, 289:Summer89-85
  J.W. Hutchens, 289:Summer89-96
  K.V. Mulcahy, 289:Summer89-92
  R.A.S., 289:Summer89-83

Towell, J.E. & H.E. Sheppard, eds. Acronyms, Initialisms & Abbreviations Dictionary 1988.
  K.B. Harder, 424:Sep89-294
Townend, G. - see Caesar
Townsend, C.E. & D.T. Kliment. Reading Czech 1. Reading Czech 2.
  L.A. Janda, 399(MLJ):Winter89-497
Townsend, C.E. & T. McAuley. Advanced Czech 1.* Advanced Czech 2.*
  L.A. Janda, 399(MLJ):Winter89-497
Townsend, C.E., T. McAuley & P. Kussi. Intermediate Czech 2.*
  L.A. Janda, 399(MLJ):Winter89-497
Townsend, C.E. & E. McKee. Elementary Czech 1.* Elementary Czech 2.* Intermediate Czech 1.*
  L.A. Janda, 399(MLJ):Winter89-497
Townsend, K. Sherwood Anderson.*
  E. Margolies, 179(ES):Aug89-372
Townsend, S. Rebuilding Coventry.
  B. Kent, 441:22Apr90-24
Townshend, C., ed. Consensus in Ireland.
  J. McGarry, 174(Éire):Summer89-141
Trabant, J. Apeliotes oder der Sinn der Sprache.
  E. Escoubas, 192(EP):Apr-Jun89-263
Trace, A. Furnace of Doubt.*
  A.R. Durkin, 395(MFS):Winter89-839
Tracy, C. English Gothic Choir-Stalls, 1200-1400.*
  P. Williamson, 589:Jul89-775
Tracy, C. A Portrait of Richard Graves.*
  F. Doherty, 541(RES):Aug89-446
  P. Millard, 178:Mar89-94
  P. Sabor, 677(YES):Vol20-279
Tracy, N. Navies, Deterrence, and American Independence.
  J. Gwyn, 656(WMQ):Oct89-823
Tracy, S.C. Langston Hughes and the Blues.
  J. McCluskey, Jr., 27(AL):Oct89-487
Tracy, W. Letters of Credit.*
  517(PBSA):Jun89-252
Träger, C., ed. Wörterbuch der Literaturwissenschaft.*
  D. Harth, 72:Band226Heft1-110
  H. Henne, 685(ZDL):1/1989-78
Trager, J. Park Avenue.
  R.F. Shepard, 441:29Jul90-21
Trager, P. The Villas of Palladio.
  C. Kolb, 576:Sep89-285
Tragesser, R.S. Husserl and Realism in Logic and Mathematics.
  R. McIntyre, 484(PPR):Mar90-624
Trahern, J.B., ed. Standardizing English.
  B. Trouth, 350:Sep90-654
Traill, J.S. Demos and Trittys.
  K.H. Kinzl, 123:Vol39No1-67
  R.S. Stroud, 303(JoHS):Vol109-253
Train, J. Valsalva's Maneuver.
  442(NY):29Jan90-96
Trainer, Y. Everything Happens at Once.
  P.M. St. Pierre, 102(CanL):Spring89-210
Trainer, Y. Landscape Turned Sideways.
  S. Scobie, 376:Mar89-128
Trakl, G. Song of the West.
  D. Sampson, 249(HudR):Autumn89-509
Tranel, B. The Sounds of French.*
  A.W. Grundstrom, 207(FR):Apr90-910
  J. Pauchard, 189(EA):Jul-Sep89-336
"La Transitivité."
  A.R. Tellier, 189(EA):Apr-Jun89-201

Transue, P.J. Virginia Woolf and the Politics of Style.*
  K. Mezei, 677(YES):Vol20-325
  J. Marcus, 620(TSWL):Spring89-101
Tranter, J. Under Berlin.
  R. Crawford, 493:Autumn89-23
Trapido, B. Temples of Delight.
  R. Kaveney, 617(TLS):9-15Nov90-1214
Trapnell, W.H. Eavesdropping in Marivaux.*
  C. Bonfils, 535(RHL):Sep-Oct89-932
  D.F. Connon, 83:Autumn89-239
  S. Harvey, 402(MLR):Apr90-445
  R. Howells, 208(FS):Jan89-87
  M-P. Laden, 210(FrF):Jan89-98
  C. Miething, 547(RF):Band101Heft2/3-343
Trapnell, W.H. The Treatment of Christian Doctrine by Philosophers of the Natural Light from Descartes to Berkeley.
  R. Hutchison, 208(FS):Oct89-462
Trassard, J-L. Territoire.
  Y. Leclair, 450(NRF):Jul-Aug89-190
Traub, A., ed. Sándor Veress.
  J. Hunkemöller, 417:Jan-Mar89-76
Traub, J. Too Good to Be True.
  A. Feinberg, 441:29Jul90-9
  442(NY):1Oct90-111
Trautmann, T.R. Lewis Henry Morgan and the Invention of Kinship.
  D.H., 355(LSoc):Jun89-303
  I.C. Jarvie, 488:Sep89-345
  G. Park, 106:Summer89-141
Traver, N. Kife.
  U. Kelly, 441:7Jan90-19
Travers, M.E. The Devotional Experience in the Poetry of John Milton.
  R. Trubowitz, 568(SCN):Spring-Summer89-7
Traversagni, L.G. The "Epitoma Margarite Castigate Eloquentie" of Laurentius Guilielmus Traversagni de Saona.* (R.H. Martin, ed & trans)
  J. Chomarat, 555:Vol62Fasc1-187
Traversari, G. La statuaria ellenistica del Museo archeologico di Venezia.
  A. Linfert, 229:Band61Heft5-460
  J. Marcadé, 555:Vol62Fasc1-179
Travisano, T.J. Elizabeth Bishop.*
  B. Costello, 432(NEQ):Jun89-310
  L. Keller, 405(MP):May90-430
"III Rëscontr antërnassional dë studi an sla lenga e la literatura piemontëisa."
  T. Telmon, 547(RF):Band101Heft1-96
Treat, J.W. Pools of Water, Pillars of Fire.
  A.V. Liman, 407(MN):Spring89-115
  M. Marcus, 395(MFS):Summer89-397
  M. Mizenko, 293(JASt):Aug89-631
Trefousse, H.L. Andrew Johnson.*
  E.L. McKitrick, 453(NYRB):17May90-8
Treitler, L. Music and the Historical Imagination.*
  J.R. Ronsheim, 42(AR):Fall89-497
Tremain, R. Restoration.*
  F. King, 441:15Apr90-7
Tremblay, F.A. Bibliotheca Lexicologiae Medii Aevii. (Vol 1)
  A.S.G. Edwards, 40(AEB):Vol3No1-17
Tremblay, M. Albertine, in Five Times.*
  J. Wasserman, 102(CanL):Autumn-Winter89-257
Tremblay, M. Le coeur découvert, roman d'amours.
  I. Oore, 102(CanL):Spring89-221

Tremblay, M. Dark Forms Gliding.
  M. Anderson, 376:Sep89-121
Tremblay, M. The Real World? Bonjour, là, bonjour.
  L. Rae, 108:Winter89-83
Trendall, A.D. The Red-Figured Vases of Paestum.
  B.A. Sparkes, 303(JoHS):Vol109-270
Trénet, C. Mes jeunes années racontées par ma mère et par moi. Boum!
  A.J.M. Prévos, 207(FR):Dec89-391
Trenner, F. Richard Strauss: Werkverzeichnis.*
  A.F.L.T., 412:May89-146
Trevor, W. Family Sins and Other Stories.
  J. Conarroe, 441:3Jun90-9
  P. Craig, 617(TLS):26Jan-1Feb90-87
  R. Towers, 453(NYRB):17May90-38
Trevor, W., ed. The Oxford Book of Irish Short Stories.
  C. Bohner, 305(JIL):Sep89-58
  G.S. Frear, 174(Éire):Winter89-133
Trevor, W. The Silence in the Garden.
  D. Flower, 249(HudR):Spring89-138
  639(VQR):Winter89-19
Trevor-Roper, H. Catholics, Anglicans and Puritans.
  M.R. O'Connell, 242:Vol110No3-375
  W.B. Patterson, 569(SR):Summer89-lxxii
  J.M. Rosenheim, 405(MP):Nov89-176
  J.H. Sims, 568(SCN):Fall-Winter89-33
Tribe, L.H. Abortion.
  A. Quindlen, 441:8Jun90-7
Tricomi, A.H. Anticourt Drama in England, 1603-1642.
  A. Leggatt, 551(RenQ):Autumn89-582
Trigg, R. Ideas of Human Nature.
  483:Jul89-426
Triggs, K. The Stars and the Stillness.
  L. Smith, 571(ScLJ):Spring89-22
Trigoboff, J. The Bone Orchard.
  M. Stasio, 441:3Jun90-32
Trillin, C. Enough's Enough.
  M. Kington, 441:28Oct90-9
Trim, J. & others. ganz spontan!
  R.H. Buchheit, 399(MLJ):Autumn89-374
Trinh T. Minh-ha. Woman, Native, Other.
  L. Wagner-Martin, 659(ConL):Fall90-392
Trippett, A.M. Adjusting to Reality.*
  D. Gagen, 402(MLR):Apr90-480
  D. Henn, 86(BHS):Apr89-190
Trisoglio, F. La lettera Ciceroniana come specchio di umanità.*
  J. Beaujeu, 555:Vol62Fasc1-164
Trissino, G.G. Scritti linguistici.* (A. Castelvecchi, ed)
  N. Maraschio, 708:Vol14Fasc2-270
Tristan, F. L'Ange dans la machine. La Retournement du gant.
  J. Taylor, 617(TLS):7-13Sep90-955
Tritle, A.L. Phocion the Good.
  G. Dobesch, 229:Band61Heft6-514
  R.A. Knox, 123:Vol39No1-79
  J.F. Lazenby, 303(JoHS):Vol109-254
Troconis, M.P.I. - see under Irigoyen Troconis, M.P.
Trodd, A. Domestic Crimes in the Victorian Novel.
  N. Auerbach, 445(NCF):Dec89-396
  D.E. Hall, 158:Dec89-171
Troesser, M. Moderieren im Hörfunk.
  F. Unger, 682(ZPSK):Band42Heft2-276

Troitsky, A. Tusovka.
L. Doružka, 617(TLS):7-13Sep90-950
Trollope, A. Cousin Henry. (J. Thompson, ed)
P. Coustillas, 189(EA):Oct-Dec89-481
Trollope, J. A Village Affair.*
42(AR):Fall89-505
Troncoso Durán, D. La narrativa de Juan
García Hortelano.
B. Jordan, 86(BHS):Jul89-300
Trotter, D. Circulation.*
E. Langland, 158:Jun89-71
Trotter, D.A. Medieval French Literature and
the Crusades (1100-1300).
L.S. Crist, 402(MLR):Apr90-437
S. Kay, 208(FS):Apr89-196
W.W. Kibler, 589:Oct89-1044
Trousson, R. Jean-Jacques Rousseau, I.
A. Rosenberg, 627(UTQ):Winter89/90-356
J. Still, 402(MLR):Oct90-960
Trower, P. Unmarked Doorways.
M.A. Jarman, 376:Dec89-127
Troyat, H. Chekhov.*
G. Woodcock, 569(SR):Spring89-308
de Troyes, C. - see under Chrétien de Troyes
Trubačeva, O.N., ed. Ètimologičeskij slovar'
slavjanskich jazykov.
J. Schütz, 688(ZSP):Band49Heft2-398
Trudgill, P. Dialects in Contact.*
B. Glauser, 38:Band107Heft3/4-492
T. Klingler, 710:Mar89-118
Trudgill, P. The Dialects of England.
T. Shippey, 617(TLS):19-25Oct90-1117
Trueblood, A.S. Letter and Spirit in Hispanic
Writers: Renaissance to Civil War.
F. Pierce, 86(BHS):Jul89-277
Trueblood, A.S. - see Inés de la Cruz, J.
Truffaut, F. François Truffaut: Correspon-
dence 1945-1984.* (French title: Corres-
pondance. British title: François Truffaut:
Letters.) (G. Jacob & C. de Givray, eds)
J. Barnes, 453(NYRB):11Oct90-14
D. Potter, 441:27May90-1
F. Raphael, 617(TLS):25-31May90-551
L. Spaas, 207(FR):Oct89-197
Truhlar, R. Utensile Paradise.
D.A. Precosky, 102(CanL):Summer89-193
Truitt, A. Daybook. Turn.
M. Zurmuehlen, 709:Winter91-124
Truman, M. Murder at the National Cathedral.
M. Stasio, 441:28Oct90-41
Trump, D.J., with C. Leerhsen. Trump: Sur-
viving at the Top.
M. Lewis, 441:2Sep90-3
R. Pleming, 617(TLS):30Nov-6Dec90-1286
Truscott, L.K. 4th. Rules of the Road.
J. Glenn, 441:16Sep90-22
Truscott, M.R. Brats.
J. Glenn, 441:21Jan90-21
Truscott, S. Just Listen 'n Learn Spanish
Plus.
M. Sabló-Yates, 399(MLJ):Summer89-245
Trussler, S. - see Etherege, G.
Trussler, S. - see Farquhar, G.
Trussler, S. - see Wycherley, W.
Trypanis, C., ed & trans. The Penguin Book
of Greek Verse.
M. Colakis, 124:Mar-Apr90-370
Tsai Chin. Daughter of Shanghai.
B.D. Sanders, 441:14Jan90-31
Tsang, S.Y-S. Democracy Shelved.
K.L. MacPherson, 293(JASt):Nov89-844

Tschumi, B. Cinegrammé Folie Le Parc de la
Villette.
D. Kesler, 45:Sep89-55
Tseu, T. (Zhuang Zi) - see under Tchouang
Tseu (Zhuang Zi)
Tsivian, Y. & others, eds. Silent Witnesses.
M. Le Fanu, 617(TLS):27Apr-3May90-458
Tsong Khapa. Tsong Khapa's Speech of Gold
in the "Essence of True Eloquence." (R.A.F.
Thurman, trans)
R. Kornman, 318(JAOS):Jul-Sep88-503
Tsuchiya, K. Democracy and Leadership.
S.C. de Jong, 293(JASt):Aug89-687
Tsung-hsi, H. - see under Huang Tsung-hsi
Tsur, R. How Do the Sound Patterns Know
They Are Expressive? The Road to Kubla
Khan.
B.M., 494:Fall89-654
Tsuruta, K. & T. Goossen, eds. Nature and
Identity in Canadian and Japanese Litera-
ture.
S. Buckley, 407(MN):Spring89-107
D. Fahy, 293(JASt):May89-405
Tsutsui, W.M. Banking Policy in Japan.
S. Takagi, 293(JASt):Nov89-880
Tsvetayeva, M. Selected Poems.*
J. Saunders, 565:Autumn89-77
Tuana, N., ed. Feminism and Science.
C. Geertz, 453(NYRB):8Nov90-19
Tucci, N. The Rain Came Last & Other
Stories.
L. Venuti, 441:29Jul90-23
Tuccille, J. Rupert Murdoch.
L. Green, 441:4Mar90-25
Tuchman, G., with N.E. Fortin. Edging Women
Out.*
P.T. Srebrnik, 637(VS):Spring90-497
D. Trotter, 445(NCF):Dec89-407
Tuck, R. Hobbes.
M.L. Morgan, 543:Mar90-652
Tucker, E.F.J. - see Ruggle, G.
Tucker, H.F. Tennyson and the Doom of
Romanticism.*
J.J. Baker, 141:Fall89-498
H.B. Bryant, 580(SCR):Spring90-170
A. Day, 184(EIC):Oct89-326
L. Erickson, 405(MP):Nov89-195
K. McSweeney, 402(MLR):Jan90-152
D. Mermin, 301(JEGP):Apr89-246
L.H. Peterson, 191(ELN):Dec89-73
Tucker, J.G. Innokentij Annenskij and the
Acmeist Doctrine.*
C. Cavanagh, 104(CASS):Spring-Win-
ter88-452
Tucker, P.H. Monet in the '90s.
J. Flam, 453(NYRB):17May90-9
Tucker, R.C. Stalin in Power.
D.K. Shipler, 441:18Nov90-3
Tucker, R.W. & D.C. Hendrickson. Empire of
Liberty.
R. Dallek, 441:1Jul90-11
E.L. McKitrick, 453(NYRB):6Dec90-57
Tufnell, O., with G.T. Martin & W.A. Ward.
Studies on Scarab Seals. (Vol 2)
J.M. Weinstein, 318(JAOS):Jul-Sep88-517
Tufte, E.R. Envisioning Information.
R. Ranck, 441:5Aug90-19
Tugendhat, E. Self-Consciousness and Self-
Determination.* (German title: Selbstbe-
wusstsein und Selbstbestimmung.)
C. Larmore, 482(PhR):Jan89-104
Tulloch, G. - see Scott, W.

Tully, J., ed. Meaning and Context.
  J. Arscott, 150(DR):Spring89-149
  D.H., 185:Jul90-916
  M.L. Morgan, 543:Dec89-425
  I. Shapiro, 103:Jul90-291
Tuman, M.C. A Preface to Literacy.
  J. Clifford, 126(CCC):May89-239
Tung-shan Liang-chieh. The Record of
Tung-shan. (W.F. Powell, trans)
  K. Kraft, 318(JAOS):Apr-Jun88-340
Tuquoi, J-P. Emmanuel d'Astier. (L. Aubrac,
  ed)
  K. Bieber, 207(FR):Oct89-191
Turcan, M. - see Tertullian
Turchetta, G. Dino Campana.
  M. King, 276:Summer89-244
Turco, A., Jr. - see "Shaw: The Annual of
Bernard Shaw Studies."
Turk, E.B. Child of Paradise.*
  A. Gillain, 207(FR):May90-1085
Turnbull, G. A Winter Journey.
  R. Pybus, 565:Winter88/89-67
Turner, A. Swallows and Martins of the
World.
  R.W. Ashford, 617(TLS):19-25Jan90-74
Turner, D.T. - see Toomer, J.
Turner, E. The Spirit and the Drum.*
  B.A. Babcock, 538(RAL):Fall89-558
Turner, E.G. Greek Manuscripts of the An-
cient World.* (Fasc 2) (2nd ed) (P.J. Par-
sons, ed)
  J. Irigoin, 555:Vol62Fasc2-316
Turner, F. Genesis.
  D. Allen, 249(HudR):Summer89-321
Turner, G. Film as Social Practice.
  A. Neill & A. Ridley, 103:Sep90-346
Turner, J.F. Howard Finster.
  E.J. Sozanski, 441:6May90-23
Turner, J.G. One Flesh.*
  R.A. Houlbrooke, 677(YES):Vol20-245
  D. McColley, 70:Jul89-110
  M.L. Williamson, 141:Fall89-480
Turner, L. & J. Alan. Frantz Fanon, Soweto
and American Black Thought.
  N. Gibson, 147:Vol6No2-92
Turner, M. Playing the Numbers.
  S. Morrissey, 102(CanL):Autumn-
  Winter89-161
Turnley, D., P. Turnley & M. Liu. Beijing
Spring.*
  J. Mirsky, 453(NYRB):1Feb90-21
Turow, S. The Burden of Proof.
  P. Maas, 441:3Jun90-1
  R. Towers, 453(NYRB):16Aug90-45
Tursman, R. Peirce's Theory of Scientific
Discovery.
  J. McCarthy, 619:Spring89-191
  P. Sullivan, 319:Apr90-307
Turull, A. Pere Quart: poeta del nostre
temps.
  D. Keown, 86(BHS):Jul89-304
Tuska, J. The American West in Film.
  J. Maddock, 649(WAL):May89-97
Tutuola, A. The Wild Hunter in the Bush of
the Ghosts. (B. Lindfors, ed) The Village
Witch Doctor and Other Stories.
  J. Haynes, 617(TLS):18-24May90-534
Tuzet, H. Mort et résurrection d'Adonis.
  A. Pizzorusso, 535(RHL):Jul-Aug89-755

Twain, M. Mark Twain's Letters.* (Vol 1)
  (E.M. Branch, M.B. Frank & K.M. Sanderson,
  eds)
  L.J. Budd, 395(MFS):Summer89-265
  A. Gribben, 26(ALR):Fall89-82
  H.H. Kolb, Jr., 639(VQR):Summer89-550
  J. Raban, 617(TLS):21-27Sep90-991
  M. Sargent, 392:Spring89-187
  J. Steinbrink, 27(AL):Mar89-102
  T. Wortham, 445(NCF):Jun89-125
Twain, M. Mark Twain's Letters. (Vol 2)
  (H.E. & R.B. Smith, eds)
  J. Raban, 617(TLS):21-27Sep90-991
Tweedale, G. Sheffield Steel and America.
  C. Freeman, 637(VS):Winter90-355
"12,000 Words."
  J. Algeo, 35(AS):Fall89-256
Twiggs, J. Transferences.
  G. Davenport, 569(SR):Summer89-468
Twitchell, J.B. Dreadful Pleasures.
  K. Newman, 707:Winter88/89-68
Twitchett, D. & M. Loewe, eds. The Cambridge
History of China.* (Vol 1)
  C.S. Goodrich, 318(JAOS):Jul-Sep88-457
Tydeman, W. English Medieval Theatre 1400-
1500.*
  A.F. Johnston, 447(N&Q):Sep89-372
Tyerman, C. England and the Crusades,
1095-1588.
  639(VQR):Spring89-43
Tylee, C.M. The Great War and Women's Con-
sciousness.
  M. Lefkowitz, 617(TLS):1-7Jun90-591
Tyler, A. Breathing Lessons.*
  D. Flower, 249(HudR):Spring89-133
  639(VQR):Spring89-56
Tyler, R., ed & trans. Japanese Tales.
  P. Knecht, 292(JAF):Apr-Jun89-224
Tyler, T.R. Why People Obey the Law.
  R. Hood, 617(TLS):14-20Dec90-1344
Tynan, K. The Life of Kenneth Tynan.^
  S. Friedman, 42(AR):Fall89-495
  K. Garobian, 529(QQ):Spring89-134
Tynan, K. Profiles.
  D. Kaufman, 441:21Oct90-25
  M. Meyer, 364:Dec89/Jan90-122
Tynes, M. Borrowed Beauty.
  S. Morrissey, 102(CanL):Winter88-146
Tyrrell, J. Czech Opera.*
  P.A. Autexier, 537:Vol75No1-117
  N. Simeone, 415:Jul89-413
Tysdahl, B. Maurits Hansens fortellerkunst.
  A. van Marken, 172(Edda):1989/1-82
Tyson, A. Mozart.*
  C. Eisen, 410(M&L):Feb89-101
Tytell, J. Ezra Pound.*
  M.P.L., 295(JML):Fall88/Winter89-394
Tzonis, A. Hermes and the Golden Thinking
Machine.
  M. Stasio, 441:25Nov90-22

U Maung Maung. Burmese Nationalist Move-
ments 1940-1948.
  M. Morland, 617(TLS):30Nov-6Dec90-
  1284
Ubeikaitė, A. Lietuvių kalbotyra 1917-1929.
  W.R. Schmalstieg, 574(SEEJ):Fall89-471
Uchida, F.Y. L'Enigme onomastique et la cré-
ation romanesque dans "Armance."*
  C. Bernard, 210(FrF):May89-243
  G. Strickland, 208(FS):Apr89-218

Udoff, A., ed. Kafka and the Contemporary Critical Performance.*
  R. Heinemann, 395(MFS):Winter89–826
  M.P.L., 295(JML):Fall88/Winter89–362
Ueda, M., ed. Explorations.
  Leung Yiu–nam, 149(CLS):Vol26No3–287
Ueding, G. Klassik und Romantik.
  G. Hoffmeister, 221(GQ):Winter89–113
Uffenbeck, L.A. & E. Fudakowska – see de Balzac, Madame H.
Uglione, R., ed. Atti del convegno nazionale di studi su la donna nel mondo antico, Torino 21–22–23 Aprile 1986.
  G. Clark, 123:Vol39No1–103
Ugrinsky, A., ed. Friedrich von Schiller and the Drama of Human Existence.
  B.E.B., 185:Jan90–456
  J. Simons, 221(GQ):Fall89–533
Uhlenbruch, B. – see Kvetnickij, F.
Ulansey, D. The Origins of the Mithraic Mysteries.
  J.D. North, 617(TLS):27Jul–2Aug90–807
Ulbert, T., with others. Resafa II: Die Basilika des Heiligen Kreuzes in Resafa–Sergiupolis.* [shown in prev under sub–title]
  W. Djobadze, 318(JAOS):Oct–Dec88–659
"Ulenspiegel." (L. Geeraedts, ed)
  R. Tenberg, 196:Band30Heft1/2–178
Ulibarri, S. El Cóndor and Other Stories.
  L. Torres, 649(WAL):Nov89–278
Ullman, L. Dreams by No One's Daughter.*
  C. Wright, 434:Winter89–193
Ullmann–Margalit, E., ed. Science in Reflection.
  A. Fuhrmann, 242:Vol10No5–625
Ulloa, J.C. Sobre José Lezama Lima y sus lectores.*
  B. Torres Caballero, 240(HR):Autumn89–541
Ulrich, L.T. A Midwife's Tale.
  C.N. Degler, 441:4Mar90–12
Ulrich, M. Thetisch und Kategorisch.
  M. Gawełko, 260(IF):Band94–358
Ultee, M., ed. Adapting to Conditions.
  H.L. Snyder, 173(ECS):Fall89–114
Umegaki, M. After the Restoration.
  G. Akita, 407(MN):Summer89–229
  J.C. Baxter, 293(JASt):Aug89–633
Umiker–Sebeok, J. & T.A. Sebeok, eds. Monastic Sign Language.
  D. Brentari, 350:Sep90–655
Umiker–Sebeok, J. & T.A. Sebeok, eds. The Semiotic Web 1986.
  G. Mounin, 567:Vol73No3/4–301
Umphrey, M. The Lit Window.
  639(VQR):Winter89–28
"Un'altra Italia nelle bandiere dei lavoratori."
  E. Hobsbawm, 358:Jun90–10
Underhill, N. Testing Spoken Language.*
  M. Wesche, 320(CJL):Dec89–497
Underwood, M. Rosa's Dilemma.
  P. Craig, 617(TLS):1–7Jun90–593
Underwood, R.A. Shakespeare on Love.
  L. Daniel, 580(SCR):Fall89–150
Ungeheuer, G. Kommunikationstheoretische Schriften I. (J.G. Juchem, ed)
  M. Lissek, 682(ZPSK):Band42Heft1–133
Unger, R.M. The Critical Legal Studies Movement.
  V. Kahn, 153:Summer89–21

Unger–Hamilton, C. & P. van der Spek, eds. The Great Symphonies, The Great Orchestras, The Great Conductors.
  N. Simeone, 415:Sep89–547
Ungku M.M. Tahir. Modern Malay Literary Culture.
  A. Sweeney, 293(JASt):Nov89–923
"Universidad de Sevilla: Patrimonio monumental y artístico."
  M. Estella, 48:Jan–Mar89–103
Uno Chiyo. Confessions of Love.
  N. Irving, 617(TLS):16–22Mar90–293
  Y. McClain, 293(JASt):Nov89–881
Unterkircher, F., ed & trans. Bestiarium.
  W.B. Clark, 589:Oct89–1045
Unverricht, H., ed. Musik des Ostens 10.
  N. Linke, 417:Jul–Sep89–277
Unwin, T. Constant, "Adolphe."*
  P. Delbouille, 535(RHL):Jan–Feb89–136
Uotila, T.E. & M. Korhonen – see Wichmann, Y.
Updike, D. Out on the Marsh.*
  D. Durrant, 364:Jun/Jul89–130
Updike, J. Just Looking.*
  R. Wollheim, 617(TLS):25–31May90–553
  442(NY):8Jan90–100
Updike, J. Rabbit at Rest.
  Z. Leader, 617(TLS):26Oct–1Nov90–1145
  J.C. Oates, 441:30Sep90–1
  G. Wills, 453(NYRB):25Oct90–11
  442(NY):22Oct90–143
Updike, J. S.*
  S. Pinsker, 577(SHR):Summer89–287
Updike, J. Self–Consciousness.*
  J. Lewis, 364:Aug/Sep89–117
Uphaus, R.W., ed. The Idea of the Novel in the Eighteenth Century.
  B. Roth, 594:Winter89–464
"Upp till kamp."
  E. Hobsbawm, 358:Jun90–10
Upton, C., S. Sanderson & J. Widdowson. Word Maps.
  F. Chevillet, 189(EA):Apr–Jun89–208
  M. Görlach, 685(ZDL):2/1989–204
  W.A.K., 300:Oct88–223
Upton, D. Holy Things and Profane.*
  J.R. Gundersen, 656(WMQ):Apr89–379
  F.D. Nichols, 576:Jun89–203
  F.D. Nichols, 656(WMQ):Apr89–378
Upton, D. & J.M. Vlach, eds. Common Places.*
  T. Carter, 576:Jun89–202
Upton, L. No Mercy.
  A. Brumer, 441:11Feb90–16
Upward, A. Scented Leaves from a Chinese Jar.
  J. Saunders, 565:Autumn89–77
Urbach, E.E. The World and Wisdom of the Rabbis of the Talmud: The Sages.
  L.E. Goodman, 485(PE&W):Apr89–225
Urbach, P. Francis Bacon's Philosophy of Science.
  J. Agassi, 488:Mar89–89
  R. Ariew, 53(AGP):Band71Heft3–350
  C. Walton, 319:Apr90–289
  M. Williams, 479(PhQ):Jul89–357
Urbán, A. Batthyány Lajos miniszterelnöksége.
  L. Péter, 575(SEER):Apr89–305
Urbán, A. – see Hajnal, I.
Urban, J.B. Moscow and the Italian Communist Party.
  S. Gundle, 278(IS):Vol43–177
Urban, P., ed. Anton Čechov.
  G. McVay, 575(SEER):Oct89–611

de Urbina, J.O. – see under Ortiz de Urbina,
J.
Urdang, C. The Woman Who Read Novels and
Peacetime.
    A. Brumer, 441:25Nov90–18
Urdang, L. & F.R. Abate. Loanwords Dictio-
nary.*
    G. Cannon, 35(AS):Fall89–261
Ureland, P.S., ed. Die Leistung der Stratafor-
schung und der Kreolistik.
    H. & R. Kahane, 545(RPh):Nov89–297
Ureland, P.S., ed. Sprachkontakt in der
Hanse.
    L. Johanson, 452(NJL):Vol12No1–93
    G. Lötzsch, 682(ZPSK):Band42Heft2–277
    D. Stellmacher, 685(ZDL):2/1989–218
Urkowitz, S. Shakespeare's Revision of "King
Lear."
    J. Wasson, 130:Spring89–102
Urman, D. The Golan.
    E.M. Meyers, 318(JAOS):Jan–Mar88–162
Urquhart, F. Full Score.
    D. Durrant, 364:Oct/Nov89–129
Urquhart, J. The Whirlpool.
    T.M. Disch, 441:18Mar90–16
Urry, J. None But Saints.
    B. Godlee, 617(TLS):18–24May90–531
Uscatescu, G. Prospettive estetiche europee.
    P. Somville, 542:Oct–Dec89–639
Utley, R.M. Billy the Kid.
    G. Johnson, 441·7Jan90–19
Utley, R.M. Cavalier in Buckskin.
    639(VQR):Summer89–90
"Utotombo."
    L.T. Wells, Jr., 2(AfrA):Nov88–29
Utt, R.L. Textos y con-textos de Clarín.
    S. Miller, 238:Sep89–546

Väänänen, V. Le journal-épître d'Egérie.*
    R. de Dardel, 439(NM):1989/2–207
    D. Löfstedt, 616(RPh):Feb90–448
Vachon, A. Toute la terre à décorer.
    R. Sarkonak, 102(CanL):Winter88–149
Vachss, A. Blossom.
    M. Stasio, 441:15Jul90–26
Vaes, G. Le Regard romanesque.
    G. Michaux, 356(LR):Aug89–226
Vaggione, R.P. – see Eunomius
Vaid, J., ed. Language Processing in Bilin-
guals.
    S. Cavazos Pena, 399(MLJ):Autumn89–
349
Vaillant, J.G. Black, French and African.
    R. Oliver, 617(TLS):14–20Sep90–966
    A. Rampersad, 441:21Oct90–26
    R. Shattuck & S. Ka, 453(NYRB):20Dec90–
11
Vaillot, R. Voltaire en son temps. (Vol 2)
    J.C. Nicholls, 207(FR):Dec89–371
Vajda, M. – see Weöres, S.
Vakhtin, B. The Sheepskin Coat & an Abso-
lutely Happy Village.
    K. Karbo, 441:18Mar90–12
Valdés, C.C.G. – see under García Valdés, C.C.
Valdes, G. Comiendo Lumbre/Eating Fire.
    S. Foster, 448:Vol27No3–158
Valdes, J.M., ed. Culture Bound.*
    M. Berns, 710:Mar89–106
Valdés, M.J. Phenomenological Hermeneutics
and the Study of Literature.*
    G. Handwerk, 52:Band24Heft1–77
[continued]

[continuing]
    W.W. Holdheim, 678(YCGL):No36–174
    J. Walker, 529(QQ):Spring89–187
Valdivieso, J.H. & L.T. Negocios y comuni-
caciones.
    V. Arizpe, 399(MLJ):Spring89–103
Valdman, A., ed. Proceedings of the Sympos-
ium on the Evaluation of Foreign Language
Proficiency.
    H.J. Siskin, 207(FR):Oct89–217
    W.F. Smith, 399(MLJ):Spring89–81
Valender, J. – see Altolaguirre, M.
Valens, V. – see under Vettius Valens
Valenti, J., with R. Naclerio. Swee'pea and
Other Playground Legends.
    N. George, 441:23Dec90–9
Valentin, J–M., ed. "Monarchus Poeta."*
    M.M. Metzger, 564:Sep89–258
Valentin, J–M., ed. Das österreichische
Volkstheater im europäischen Zusammen-
hang 1830–1880.
    P. Branscombe, 402(MLR):Jan90–258
Valentine, D. The Phoenix Program.
    M. Safer, 441:21Oct90–19
Valentine, J. Home. Deep. Blue.
    S. Gorham, 466(NDQ):Summer89–248
    A. Turner, 199:Spring89–78
Valenzuela, L. Open Door.
    B.K. Horvath, 532(RCF):Spring89–243
Valenzuela, L. Other Weapons.
    M.J. Metzger, 271:Winter89–161
Valera, J. Pepita Jiménez. (A. Navarro & J.
Ribalta, eds)
    M. Hemingway, 402(MLR):Oct90–1000
Valéry, P. Cahiers, 1894–1914.* (Vol 1) (N.
Celeyrette–Pietri & J. Robinson–Valéry,
eds) [entry in prev was of Vols 1 & 2]
    K.H.R. Anderson, 402(MLR):Apr90–455
    C.M. Crow, 208(FS):Apr89–226
    J. Lawler, 207(FR):May90–1070
"Paul Valéry 5." (H. Laurenti, ed)
    C. Davis, 208(FS):Apr89–227
    I. Piette, 356(LR):Nov89–337
Valesio, P. Ascoltare il silenzio.
    M. Chan, 544:Autumn89–368
Valette, J–P. & R. Contacts. (4th ed)
    G. Normand, 207(FR):Feb90–586
Valette, J–P., R.M. Valette & T. Carrera-
Hanley. Situaciones: Intermediate Spanish.
    C.M. Cherry, 399(MLJ):Spring89–102
Valin, R., W. Hirtle & A. Joly – see Guillaume,
G.
Valins, M. Housing for Elderly People.
    M.C. Comerio, 47:Jul89–37
Valis, N.M. Leopoldo Alas (Clarín).*
    C. Richmond, 240(HR):Spring89–251
della Valle, P. The Pilgrim. (G. Bull, ed &
trans)
    R. Irwin, 617(TLS):2–8Mar90–228
del Valle, R. Eva the Fugitive.
    W. Ferguson, 441:23Sep90–48
Vallejo, A.B. – see under Buero Vallejo, A.
Vallejo, C. César Vallejo: A Selection of his
Poetry. (J. Higgins, ed & trans)
    D. Harris, 402(MLR):Jan90–232
    S.M. Hart, 86(BHS):Jul89–313
    L. Sail, 565:Summer89–75
Vallois, M–C. Fictions Féminines.*
    A. Amend, 535(RHL):Jul–Aug89–724
    C. Hogsett, 446(NCFS):Spring-Summer90–
588

Vallone, A. Antidantismo politico e dantismo letterario.
J. Took, 402(MLR):Oct90-993
Valverde, J.F. - see under Fernández Valverde, J.
Vamplew, W. Pay Up and Play the Game.*
D. Underdown, 637(VS):Summer90-654
Vanamali, R. & others, eds. Critical Theory and African Literature.
F.B.O. Akporobaro, 538(RAL):Spring89-140
Vanasse, A. La Vie à rebours.
K.L. Kellett, 102(CanL):Autumn-Winter89-202
Van Caspel, P. Bloomers of the Liffey.
J. Hurt, 301(JEGP):Jan89-131
Vance, E. From Topic to Tale.*
D. Maddox, 589:Jan89-231
M. Melaver, 494:Fall89-655
Vance, E. Mervelous Signals.*
B.M., 494:Winter89-851
Vance, N. Irish Literature.
D. Donoghue, 617(TLS):7-13Dec90-1324
Vance, S. Spook.
B. Lott, 441:14Oct90-22
Vance, T.J. An Introduction to Japanese Phonology.
G.S. Nathan, 350:Dec90-888
Van Cleave, W.R. & S.T. Cohen. Nuclear Weapons, Policies, and the Test Ban Issue.
P.A.W., 185:Oct89-225
Van Cleve, J.W. The Merchant in German Literature of the Enlightenment.*
T.G. Sauer, 406:Fall89-392
J. Whaley, 402(MLR):Jan90-243
Van Coolput, C-A. Aventures querant et le sens du monde.
A. Leupin, 589:Jan89-227
Vande Kopple, W. Clear and Coherent Prose.
P. Arrington & F. Farmer, 126(CCC):Dec89-486
Vandenbroeck, P. Jheronimus Bosch.
A. Arnould, 90:Jun89-425
Vandenbroeck, P. "Over Wilden en Narren, Boeren en Bedelaars."
E.M., 90:Jan89-48
E.M., 90:Jun89-437
M. Russell, 39:Jan89-66
Van den Broek, R., T. Baarda & J. Mansfeld, eds. Knowledge of God in the Graeco-Roman World.
A.H. Armstrong, 123:Vol39No2-401
Van Den Heuvel, G. - see Langer, S.K.
Vanderauwera, R. Dutch Novels Translated into English.* (J.S. Holmes, ed)
M. Scholz, 678(YCGL):No36-188
Vanderbilt, K. American Literature and the Academy.*
H. Beaver, 677(YES):Vol20-324
K. Cmiel, 271:Winter89-175
P.R.Y., 295(JML):Fall88/Winter89-180
Vanderbroeck, P.J.J. Popular Leadership and Collective Behavior in the Last Roman Republic (ca. 80-50 B.C.).*
K-J. Hölkeskamp, 313:Vol79-191
J.W. Rich, 123:Vol39No1-83
Van der Elst, G. Aspekte zur Entstehung der neuhochdeutschen Schriftsprache.
E. Neuss, 685(ZDL):1/1989-101
Vanderhaeghe, G. Homesick.
D. Bauer, 441:17Jun90-15

Vander Meulen, D.L. Where Angels Fear to Tread.
517(PBSA):Mar89-118
Vanderwood, P.J. & F.N. Samponaro. Border Fury.
R.E. Snyder, 577(SHR):Fall89-391
Van De Veer, D. Paternalistic Intervention.
C.L. Ten, 63:Mar89-119
Van Doren, M. The Selected Letters of Mark Van Doren.* (G. Hendrick, ed)
M.D. Aeschliman, 473(PR):Vol56No2-305
S.J. Kahn, 639(VQR):Autumn89-755
Van Dusen, K. But But.
S. Scobie, 376:Dec89-128
Van Duyn, M. Near Changes.
E. Hirsch, 441:18Nov90-24
Van Els, T. & others. Applied Linguistics and the Learning and Teaching of Foreign Languages.
S.S. Magnan, 399(MLJ):Spring89-81
Van Helden, A. Measuring the Universe.
W.A. Wallace, 551(RenQ):Winter89-839
Van Horne, J.C. & others - see Latrobe, B.H.
Van Leer, D. Emerson's Epistemology.*
D. Marr, 125:Winter89-196
Van Miegroet, H.J. De invloed van de vroege Nederlandse schilderkunst in de eerste helft van de 15de eeuw op Konrad Witz.
L.C., 90:Jan89-48
L.C., 90:Jun89-436
Vannier, F. Finances publiques et richesses privées dans le discours athénien aux Ve et IVe siècles.
M. Nouhaud, 555:Vol62Fasc2-349
Vansant, J. Against the Horizon.
K.L. Komar, 395(MFS):Summer89-354
D.C.G. Lorenz, 221(GQ):Fall89-556
Vansittart, P., ed. Voices of the Revolution.
C.J. Fox, 364:Aug/Sep89-143
G. Lewis, 617(TLS):26Jan-1Feb90-93
Van Slyke, L.P. Yangtze.
J.K. Ocko, 293(JASt):Nov89-845
Van Spanckeren, K. & J.G. Castro, eds. Margaret Atwood.
W.L. Schissel, 395(MFS):Winter89-781
Van Steenberghen, F. Études philosophiques. (2nd ed)
T-A. Druart, 543:Sep89-183
Van Trump, J.D. Majesty of the Law.
J.K. Ochsner, 576:Dec89-406
Vanvugt, E. Le Sabot plein de sang.
L. Gillet, 358:Feb90-8
Van Walleghen, M. Blue Tango.
J.F. Cotter, 249(HudR):Autumn89-519
T. Hoagland, 146:Winter89-138
Van Wart, A. - see Smart, E.
Van Winckel, N. Bad Girl, with Hawk.
639(VQR):Winter89-28
Vaquera, M.L.C. - see under Calero Vaquera, M.L.
Vaquero, M. Tradiciones orales en la historiografía de fines de la Edad Media.
L. Chalon, 304(JHP):Winter90-185
Vaquero, M. - see de Arredondo, G.
Varas, A., ed. Soviet-Latin American Relations in the 1980s.
H. Desfosses, 550(RusR):Jul89-345
Vareille, K.W. Socialité, sexualité et les impasses de l'histoire.
T. Alvarez-Detrell, 446(NCFS):Fall-Winter89/90-251
K. Wren, 208(FS):Apr89-220
Varela, A.T. - see under Tarrio Varela, A.

Varey, J.E. & N.D. Shergold, with C. Davis. Los arriendos de los corrales de comedias de Madrid: 1587–1719.
  J.J. Allen, 304(JHP):Autumn89–111
  E. Ruiz-Fornells, 238:Dec89–958
  D.L. Smith, 402(MLR):Apr90–476
Varey, S. Henry Fielding.*
  R. Stamper, 594:Fall89–349
Vargas Llosa, M. In Praise of the Stepmother.
  R.M. Adams, 453(NYRB):11Oct90–17
  A. Burgess, 441:14Oct90–11
  J. Updike, 442(NY):1Oct90–107
Vargas Llosa, M. The Storyteller.*
  J. Butt, 617(TLS):13–19Apr90–404
Vargas Llosa, M. The War of the End of the World.
  R.M. Adams, 453(NYRB):11Oct90–17
Vargish, T. The Providential Aesthetic in Victorian Fiction.*
  L.G. Zatlin, 158:Mar89–24
Varinlioğlu, E., ed. Die Inschriften von Keramos.*
  A.G. Woodhead, 303(JoHS):Vol109–243
Varnado, S.L. Haunted Presence.*
  D. Ketterer, 561(SFS):Nov89–397
Varnedoe, K. A Fine Disregard.
  P-L. Adams, 61:Aug90–93
  J. Golding, 617(TLS):14–20Dec90–1353
  442(NY):4Jun90–104
Varnedoe, K. Vienna 1900.*
  S.J., 90:Feb89–162
Varnedoe, K.T. Gustave Caillebotte.*
  R. Kendall, 39:May89–366
Varnhagen von Ense, K.A. Werke in fünf Bänden. (Vols 1–3) (K. Feilchenfeldt, ed)
  T.H. Pickett, 133:Band22Heft2–169
Varriano, J. Italian Baroque and Rococo Architecture.*
  J. Wilton-Ely, 278(IS):Vol44–170
Varro. Varron, "Satires Ménippées."* (fasc 8) (J-P. Cèbe, ed & trans)
  R. Astbury, 123:Vol39No1–140
Vaschenko, N.V. – see under Palii, P.
Vasconcellos, L.P. Dicionário de teatro.
  D. George, 352(LATR):Spring90–184
Vasconcellos, M., ed. Technology as Translation Strategy, II.
  B.A. Shaw, 399(MLJ):Summer89–246
Vasilenko, E. & E. Lamm. Russian on Your Own. (2nd ed) Learning to Read Russian. Learning to Speak Russian. Russian-English Vocabulary.
  J.J. Rinkus, 399(MLJ):Winter89–528
Vasilevič, G. Wörterbuch des Bibliotheks-wesens: Russisch-Deutsch/Deutsch-Russisch.
  W. Busch, 688(ZSP):Band49Heft2–395
Vásquez, M.S., ed. Homenaje a Ramón J. Sender.
  J. Fernández Jiménez, 140(CH): Vol11No1&2–123
  G. Navajas, 238:Sep89–547
  A. Trippett, 86(BHS):Oct89–385
Vassalli, S. La chimera.
  A.L. Lepschy, 617(TLS):5–11Oct90–1074
Vassanji, M.G. The Gunny Sack.
  S. French, 617(TLS):14–20Sep90–980
Vasubandhu. A Buddhist Doctrine of Experience. (T.A. Kochumuttom, ed & trans) Seven Works of Vasubandhu. (S. Anacker, ed & trans)
  B.C. Hall, 318(JAOS):Jan–Mar88–180

Vaughan, K. Journals 1939–1977.* (A. Ross, ed)
  S. Spender, 364:Dec89/Jan90–110
Vaughan, W.E., ed. A New History of Ireland. (Vol 5)
  A. Macintyre, 617(TLS):4–10May90–464
Vaughan Williams, R. & R. Douglas. Working with Vaughan Williams.
  A. Frogley, 415:Mar89–159
Vaughn, S. Sweet Talk.
  J. Olshan, 441:4Feb90–27
Vázquez Estévez, M. Comedias sueltas del "Institut del Teatre" en Barcelona.
  A.R. Williamsen, 238:May89–301
Vázquez Rial, H. Historia del Triste. La Libertad de Italia. Territorios vigilados.
  J.C. Akers, 532(RCF):Spring89–259
Veatch, H.B. Human Rights.
  G. Nakhnikian, 449:Mar89–108
Veatch, R.M. Death, Dying, and the Biological Revolution. (rev)
  D.H. Jones, 543:Dec89–426
Vecsey, C. Imagine Ourselves Richly.
  B. Swann, 292(JAF):Oct–Dec89–508
Vedlitz, A. Conservative Mythology and Public Policy in America.
  M.F., 185:Apr90–705
Veeder, W. Mary Shelley & Frankenstein.*
  K. Weil, 147:Vol6No3–91
Veeder, W. & S.M. Griffin see Jamon, H.
Veeder, W. & G Hirsch, eds. Dr. Jekyll and Mr. Hyde: After One Hundred Years.*
  J. Wilt, 301(JEGP):Oct89–550
Veenker, W., ed. Dialectologia Uralica.
  I. Futaky, 260(IF):Band94–371
de la Vega, G.L.L. – see under Lasso de la Vega, G.L.
de Vega Carpio, L. El anzuelo de Fenisa. (D.M. Gitlitz, trans)
  F.A. de Armas, 552(REH):Oct89–127
de Vega Carpio, L. El castigo sin venganza. (L. García Lorenzo, ed)
  M. Levisi, 345(KRQ):Feb89–125
de Vega Carpio, L. La niñez del Padro Roxas. (D.L. Bastianutti, ed)
  M. McGaha, 240(HR):Autumn89–514
de Vega Carpio, L. La noche de San Juan. (A.K. Stoll, ed)
  R.L. Fiore, 304(JHP):Winter89–164
de Vega Carpio, L. San Diego de Alcalá. (T.E. Case, ed)
  C.B. Kirby, 304(JHP):Winter90–194
Vega García-Luengos, G. Problemas de un dramaturgo del Siglo de Oro.
  P. Bolaños Donoso, 240(HR):Winter89–99
Vegas, M. Mulva II.
  R. Ludwig, 229:Band61Heft8–754
Veintemilla, J.M.R. – see under Ruiz Veintemilla, J.M.
Veit-Wild, F. & E. Schade, eds. Dambudzo Marechera, 1952–1987.
  D. Riemenschneider, 538(RAL):Fall89–513
Veith, W. & W. Putschke. Kleiner Deutscher Sprachatlas. (Vol 1, Pt 2)
  H. Löffler, 685(ZDL):2/1989–202
Velcheva, B. Proto-Slavic and Old Bulgarian Sound Changes. (E.A. Scatton, ed & trans)
  T. Henninger, 575(SEER):Oct89–600
  C. Wukasch, 574(SEEJ):Fall89–462
Vélez de Guevara, L. El diablo cojuelo. (A.R. Fernández & I. Arellano, eds)
  A.E. Wiltrout, 304(JHP):Winter90–193

Vélez de Guevara, L. Inés Reigned in Death.
　A.L. Mackenzie, 86(BHS):Oct89-381
Velinská, E., comp. IX. mezinárodní sjezd
　slavistů, Kyjiv 1983 (6.-14.9.).
　　D. Short, 575(SEER):Jan89-164
Vella, H.C.R. Repeats and Symmetrical Clus-
　ters of Metrical Patterns in the First Four
　Feet in Latin Silver Age Epic Poetry.
　　V.J.C. Hunink, 394:Vol42fasc1/2-265
Velleius. Vellei Paterculi Historiarum ad M.
　Vinicium consulem libri duo. (W.S. Watt,
　ed)
　　J. Hellegouarc'h, 229:Band61Heft7-627
　　A.J. Woodman, 123:Vol39No2-235
Vellusig, R.H. Dramatik im Zeitalter der Wis-
　senschaft.
　　S. Giles, 402(MLR):Oct90-1029
Veltkamp, I. Marcel Proust.
　　L. Keller, 535(RHL):Mar-Apr89-321
　　N. Segal, 208(FS):Apr89-228
Veltruský, J.F. A Sacred Farce from Medieval
　Bohemia: Mastičkář.*
　　T. Eekman, 104(CASS):Spring-Winter88-
　　521
Vendler, H., ed. The Harvard Book of Con-
　temporary American Poetry.* (British title:
　The Faber Book of Contemporary American
　Poetry.)
　　R. McDowell, 249(HudR):Winter89-605
Vendler, H. The Music of What Happens.*
　　S. Burris, 659(ConL):Summer90-240
　　R. Labrie, 102(CanL):Autumn-Winter89-
　　143
　　B.M., 494:Fall89-648
　　J. Pilling, 677(YES):Vol20-351
Venesoen, C. Le Complexe maternel dans le
　théâtre de Racine.
　　J. Dubu, 535(RHL):Sep-Oct89-932
Vennemann, T. Neuere Entwicklungen in der
　Phonologie.
　　R. Harnisch, 685(ZDL):2/1989-190
Vennemann, T., ed. The New Sound of Indo-
　European.
　　O.J.L. Szemerényi, 159:Vol6No2-237.
Vennemann, T. Preference Laws for Syllable
　Structure and the Explanation of Sound
　Change.*
　　R.D. Woodard, 24:Fall89-524
Ventola, E. The Structure of Social Interac-
　tion.*
　　M. Stubbs, 355(LSoc):Mar89-133
Venturi, F. Settecento riformatore. (Vol 5)
　　F. Arato, 228(GSLI):Vol166fasc534-300
Venzlaff, H. Der Islamische Rosenkranz.
　　K. Reinhart, 318(JAOS):Jul-Sep88-491
Véquaud, Y. - see Lorca, F.G.
Vera, D., ed. La società del Basso Impero.
　　E. Pack, 229:Band61Heft6-529
"Verband des Personals Offentlicher Dienste."
　　E. Hobsbawm, 358:Jun90-10
Verbeek, T. - see Descartes, R. & M. Schoock
Verbrugge, M.H. Able-Bodied Womanhood.
　　658:Spring89-111
Vercillo, L. Nuovo corso, l'Etrusco sillabico.
　(Vol 3: L'epigrafe della stele di Perugia).
　　G. Radke, 229:Band61Heft8-739
Vercruysse, J. & others - see de Voltaire,
　F.M.A.
Verdenius, W.J. Commentaries on Pindar.*
　(Vol 1)
　　S. Instone, 303(JoHS):Vol109-213
Verdeyden, P. - see Porete, M.

Verdi, G. Carteggio Verdi-Ricordi 1880-1881.
　(P. Petrobelli, M. Di Grigorio Casati & C.M.
　Mossa, eds)
　　J. Budden, 410(M&L):Nov89-563
　　P. Weiss, 451:Spring90-268
Verdi, G. Verdi's "Otello" and "Simon Bocca-
　negra" in Letters and Documents.* (H.
　Busch, ed & trans)
　　W. Dean, 415:Aug89-475
Verdié, M., ed. L'Etat de la France et de ses
　habitants. (1989 ed)
　　A.J.M. Prévos, 207(FR):Apr90-915
Verdino-Süllwold, C.M. We Need a Hero!
　　C.J. Thomas, 465:Spring90-187
Verdu, A. Early Buddhist Philosophy in the
　Light of the Four Noble Truths.
　　M. Tatz, 318(JAOS):Jan-Mar88-179
Verene, D.P. Hegel's Recollection.*
　　C-A. Scheier, 53(AGP):Band71Heft1-102
Verene, D.P., ed. Vico and Joyce.*
　　J-M. Rabaté, 125:Fall88-91
Vergil. The Aeneid.* (C.H. Sisson, trans)
　　W. Allen, 577(SHR):Spring89-185
Vergil. Dryden's "Aeneid." (R. Sowerby, ed)
　　T.R. Steiner, 566:Spring90-212
Vergil. Georgics. (R.A.B. Mynors, ed)
　　R. Jenkyns, 617(TLS):23-29Nov90-1268
Vergo, P., ed. The New Museology.*
　　J. Spalding, 324:Mar90-300
Verhoeven, W.M. D.H. Lawrence's Duality
　Concept.
　　M.J. Flay, 179(ES):Apr89-188
Verjat, A. - see Gonzalez Salvador, A.
Verluyten, S.P., ed. La phonologie du schwa
　français.
　　D.G. Churma, 350:Dec90-888
Vermeer, E.B. Economic Development in Pro-
　vincial China.
　　M.F. Martin, 293(JASt):Nov89-847
Vermes, G. István Tisza.
　　I.D. Armour, 575(SEER):Jan89-144
Vermes, G. & J. Boutet, eds. France, pays
　multilingue.
　　J. Lindenfeld, 355(LSoc):Sep89-451
Vermes, G., F. Millar & M. Goodman - see
　Schürer, E.
Vernay, P., ed. Richeut.
　　A.J. Holden, 402(MLR):Oct90-945
Verner, A.M. The Crisis of Russian Autoc-
　racy.
　　J. Keep, 617(TLS):30Nov-6Dec90-1281
Vernet, A., ed. Histoire des bibliothèques
　françaises. (Vol 1)
　　R. McKitterick, 617(TLS):15-21Jun90-
　　650
Vernier, R. Yves Bonnefoy ou les mots comme
　le ciel.
　　M. Bishop, 207(FR):Apr90-878
Vernière, P. Lumières ou clair-obscur?
　　G. Bremner, 208(FS):Apr89-215
Vernon, J. Money and Fiction.*
　　K. Sutherland, 148:Winter86-105
Vernon, T. Fat Man in Argentina.
　　D. Murphy, 617(TLS):2-8Nov90-1188
Vernon, V.V. Daughters of the Moon.*
　　Noguchi Takehiko, 285(JapQ):Jan-
　　Mar89-99
　　M.S. Viswanathan, 293(JASt):Feb89-183
"Paolo Veronese: Disegni e Dipinti."
　　H. Coutts, 380:Autumn89-229
von Verschuer, C. Le commerce extérieur du
　Japon.
　　B. Bernier, 293(JASt):Nov89-882

Versluis, A. The Egyptian Mysteries.
  J.G. Griffiths, 123:Vol39No2-402
Versluys, K. The Poet in the City.*
  S.E. Larsen, 462(OL):Vol44No3-278
  S.A.S., 295(JML):Fall88/Winter89-259
Versteeg, J., ed. Georges Bataille.
  S. Hand, 208(FS):Apr89-232
Vesaas, T. Selected Poems.
  E. Rokkan, 562(Scan):Nov89-219
Vesce, T.E., ed & trans. Medieval Triptych.
  H.R. Runte, 207(FR):Feb90-542
Veseth, M. Mountains of Debt.
  G. Daugherty, 441:28Oct90-22
Vestdijk, S. The Garden Where the Brass
    Band Played.
  L. Graeber, 441:14Jan90-30
Vester, K-E., ed. Gabriele Münter.
  A. Fant, 341:Vol58No1-41
Vettese, R. The Rich Noise and Other Poems.
  J. Hendry, 571(ScLJ):Winter89-63
Vettius Valens. Vettius Valens Antiochenus,
    "Anthologiarum" libri novem. (D. Pingree,
    ed)
  D.R. Dicks, 123:Vol39No1-23
Veyne, P. Bread and Circuses.
  F. Millar, 617(TLS):23-29Mar90-329
Veyne, P. Did the Greeks Believe in Their
    Myths?*
  D.L. Burgess, 478(P&L):Apr89-184
  R.M. Capobianco, 258:Sep89-360
Veyne, P., ed. A History of Private Life.*
    (Vol 1)
  J.C. Traupman, 124:Mar-Apr90-302
Veyne, P. Roman Erotic Elegy.
  M. Wyke, 313:Vol79-165
  639(VQR):Summer89-101
Veyrin-Forrer, J. La lettre et le texte.
  M. Brisebois, 470:Vol27-133
Vezhinskii, K. (K. Wierzyński). Izbrannoe.
  I. Nagurski, 497(PolR):Vol34No1-80
Viagas, R., D. Lee & T. Walsh. On the Line.
  J. Gerard, 441:22Apr90-22
Viani, E. - see Fortis, A.
de Viau, T. Oeuvres complètes.* (Vol 1) (G.
    Saba, ed)
  J-P. Chauveau, 535(RHL):Jul-Aug89-707
de Viau, T. Oeuvres complètes.* (Vol 4) (G.
    Saba, ed)
  J-P. Chauveau, 535(RHL):Jul-Aug89-707
  S. Warman, 208(FS):Jul89-324
Vicens, J. The False Years.
  J. Polk, 441:27May90-16
Vicinus, M. & B. Nergaard - see Nightingale,
    F.
Vickers, B., ed. Arbeit, Musse, Meditation.*
  L.S., 382(MAE):1989/1-135
Vickers, B., ed. English Science, Bacon to
    Newton.*
  M. Grossman, 242:Vol10No2-250
Vickers, B. In Defence of Rhetoric.*
  D. Bialostosky, 128(CE):Mar89-325
  E.P.J. Corbett, 480(P&R):Vol22No4-294
  T.W. Crusius, 126(CCC):May89-231
  A. Quinn, 544:Summer89-291
  M. Trousdale, 402(MLR):Oct90-915
  S. Usher, 123:Vol39No1-41
Vickers, B. Returning to Shakespeare.
  A. Kirsch, 617(TLS):20-26Apr90-421
Vickers, B. & N.S. Struever. Rhetoric and the
    Pursuit of Truth.
  F. Deconinck-Brossard, 83:Spring89-113
Vickers, J.M. Chance and Structure.
  J. Largeault, 542:Oct-Dec89-658

Vico, G. On the Most Ancient Wisdom of the
    Italians Unearthed from the Origins of the
    Latin Language Including the Disputation
    with the "Giornale de' letterati d'Italia."
    (L.M. Palmer, trans)
  L.V.R., 568(SCN):Fall-Winter89-70
Victorio, J., with J-C. Payen - see Boyer, R.
    & others
Vidal, D. Miracles et convulsions jansénistes
    au XVIIIe siècle.
  H. Guénot, 531:Jan-Mar89-156
Vidal, G. At Home.
  639(VQR):Spring89-68
Vidal, G. Hollywood.*
  L. Auchincloss, 453(NYRB):29Mar90-20
  J. Conarroe, 441:21Jan90-1
Vidal Alcover, J. - see D'Olesa, F.
Vidler, A. Claude-Nicolas Ledoux.
  M. Filler, 441:2Dec90-22
Viegnes, M. L'Esthétique de la nouvelle
    française au vingtième siècle.
  W. Thompson, 207(FR):Mar90-720
Viegnes, M. La Milieu et l'individu dans la
    trilogie de Joris-Karl Huysmans.
  R.B. Antosh, 446(NCFS):Spring-
    Summer90-544
Vielberg, M. Pflichten, Werte, Ideale.
  C. Gill, 313:Vol79-265
  R.H. Martin, 123:Vol39No1-37
"Vienne 1900, Naissance du siècle. Mythe et
    réalités."
  F. Claudon, 549(RLC):Jul-Sep89-423
Viera, D.J. Medieval Catalan Literature:
    Prose and Drama.*
  P.J. Boehne, 238:Sep89-539
  J. Dagenais, 240(HR):Summer89-361
Viereck, W. & W-D. Bald, eds. English in
    Contact with Other Languages.*
  H. Ulherr, 38:Band107Heft3/4-478
"Vierge du Soleil/Frille des Lumières."
  J.A. Dainard, 166:Jul90-350
Vieth, D.M., ed. John Wilmot, Earl of Roches-
    ter.
  J.V. Guerinot, 568(SCN):Fall-Winter89-
    44
"Vietnam: 'Renovation' (Doi Moi), The Law and
    Human Rights in the 1990s."
  J. Mirsky, 453(NYRB):16Aug90-29
Vietor-Engländer, D. Faust in der DDR.
  W. Stellmacher, 654(WB):1/1989-154
Vietta, S. Literarische Phantasie.
  M.K. Kremer, 406:Fall89-386
"Viga-Glums Saga with the Tales of Ögmund
    Bash and Thorvald Chatterbox."* (J.
    McKinnell, trans)
  P.A. Jorgensen, 301(JEGP):Apr89-272
  H. O'Donoghue, 541(RES):Feb89-107
  J. Simpson, 203:Vol100No2-256
Vigal, J.B. - see under Barella Vigal, J.
Vigée-Le Brun, E. The Memoirs of Elisabeth
    Vigée-Le Brun.* (S. Evans, trans) Memoirs
    of Madame Vigée Lebrun. (L. Strachey,
    trans)
  R. Dorment, 453(NYRB):15Feb90-23
Vigorita, T.S. - see under Spagnuolo Vigorita,
    T.
Vijayan, O.V. The Saga of Dharmapuri. After
    the Hanging and Other Stories.
  D. Selbourne, 617(TLS):7-13Dec90-1326
Vijfvinkel, E. Das Donaueschinger Passions-
    spiel im Luzerner Osterspiel.
  J.E. Tailby, 680(ZDP):Band108Heft1-125

Vilde, B. Journal et lettres de prisons (1941–1942).
F.G., 98:Mar89–197
Vilensky, S.S., ed. Dodnes tiagoteet. (Vol 1)
J. Keep, 617(TLS):5–11Oct90–1056
Villa, B.L. Unauthorized Action.
H. Strachan, 617(TLS):27Apr–3May90–439
Villanueva, T. Crónica de mis años peores.
M. Pérez-Erdélyi, 36:Summer89–118
de Villaumbrales, P.H. – see under Hernández de Villaumbrales, P.
Villegas, J. Ideología y discurso crítico sobre el teatro de España y América Latina.
R. Perales, 352(LATR):Spring90–169
Villemaire, Y. Quartz and Mica.
S. Scobie, 376:Mar89–129
de Villena, E. The Text and Concordance of Escroial Manuscript f.iv.1: Arte cisoria. (J. O'Neill, ed)
B. Taylor, 304(JHP):Winter89–154
Villey, M. Questions de saint Thomas sur le droit et la politique.
J. Parain-Vial, 192(EP):Jan–Mar89–120
Villey, P. – see de Montaigne, M.E.
Villiers, A. L'acteur comique.
M. Autrand, 535(RHL):Jul–Aug89–757
P. Somville, 542:Oct–Dec89–640
de Villiers, M. White Tribe Dreaming.
D. Papineau, 617(TLS):4–10May90–482
Villoldo, A. & E. Jendresen. The Four Winds.
B. Shore, 441:9Sep90–37
Villon, F. Das Kleine und das Grosse Testament. (F–R. Hausmann, ed & trans)
W. Pöckl, 547(RF):Band101Heft2/3–327
Viñar, M. & M. Exil et Torture.
J–M. Gabaude, 542:Oct–Dec89–632
Vinaver, C. Anthology of Hassidic Music. (E. Schleifer, ed)
J. Frigyesi, 187:Spring/Summer89–360
Vince, R.W. Ancient and Medieval Theatre. Renaissance Theatre. Neoclassical Theatre.
M. Carlson, 612(ThS):Nov88–223
Vincent, A. Theories of the State.*
G.D.R., 185:Jan90–451
Vincent, D. The Eternity of Being.*
E. Shookman, 564:Nov89–353
Vincent, D. Literacy and Popular Culture.
P. Thompson, 617(TLS):16–22Mar90–294
Vincent, J. Disraeli.
P. Smith, 617(TLS):29Jun–5Jul90–693
Vincent, M. Donneau de Visé et le Mercure Galant.
M–O. Sweetser, 475:Vol16No30–358
Vincent, M–C. Le Ravin du monde.
J. Taylor, 532(RCF):Summer89–245
Vine, B. Gallowglass.
P. Craig, 617(TLS):6–12Apr90–375
M. Stasio, 441:10Jun90–18
Viner, A. The Emerging Power of Japanese Money.
Kobayashi Kaoru, 285(JapQ):Apr–Jun89–214
Vinogradov, V.V. Gogol and the Natural School.
L. Trott, 575(SEER):Jan89–118
Viola, L. The Best Sons of the Fatherland
N.B. Weissman, 550(RusR):Jan89–104
Viola, P. Il trono vuoto.
P. Higonnet, 617(TLS):28Sep–4Oct90–1028

Viperano, G.A. On Poetry.
L.V.R., 568(SCN):Spring–Summer89–32
Vipperman, C.J. William Lowndes and the Transition of Southern Politics, 1782–1822.
639(VQR):Autumn89–126
Viré, G. Informatique et classement des manuscrits.
W. Hübner, 229:Band61Heft7–587
Viret, P. L'Interim fait par dialogues. (G.R. Mermier, ed)
J. Beck, 201:Vol15–350
Virgil – see under Vergil
Virgilio, B. Epigrafia e storiografia, studi di storia antica. (Vol 1)
A.G. Woodhead, 123:Vol39No2–425
Virgo, S. Selakhi.*
D. Brydon, 102(CanL):Summer89–161
Viroli, M. Jean-Jacques Rousseau and the "Well-Ordered Society."*
J.H.M., 185:Apr90–705
Virtue, N. In the Country of Salvation.
F. Baveystock, 617(TLS):25–31May90–547
Viscido, L. Studi sulle "Variae" di Cassiodoro.
J.J. O'Donnell, 589:Jan89–235
Vision, G. Modern Anti-Realism and Manufactured Truth.*
M. Luntley, 393(Mind):Oct89–639
A. Millar, 518:Oct89–224
Visser, L.E. & C.L. Voorhoeve. Sahu–Indonesian–English Dictionary and Sahu Grammar Sketch.*
B. Comrie, 361:Nov89–245
Visser, M. Much Depends on Dinner.*
K. Jeffery, 617(TLS):27Jul–2Aug90–809
Vita-Finzi, P. Edith Wharton and the Art of Fiction.
H. Lee, 617(TLS):25–31May90–547
Vital, D. The Future of the Jews.
M. Himmelfarb, 441:30Sep90–36
R.S. Wistrich, 617(TLS):23–29Nov90–1261
Vitale-Brovarone, A., ed. Il Codice Varia 124 della Biblioteca Reale di Torino miniato da Cristoforo De Predis (Milano, 1476).
E.S. Welch, 90:Sep89–650
Vitz, R.C. The Queen and the Arts.
T. Wortham, 445(NCF):Dec89–425
Viudas Camarasa, A. Dialectología hispánica y geografía lingüística en los estudios locales (1920–1984).
J. Rini, 240(HR):Autumn89–498
Vivante, A. The Tales of Arturo Vivante. (M. Kinzie, ed)
B. Fields, 441:23Dec90–12
Vives, J.M. – see under Mas i Vives, J.
Vives, J.M. – see under Mutgé Vives, J.
Viviani, R. Teatro. (Vol 1) (G.D. Bonino, A. Lezza & P. Scialò, eds)
G. Poole, 276:Winter89–480
Vizenor, G. Crossbloods.
R. Carlson, 441:23Sep90–52
Vizinczey, S. Truth and Lies in Literature. (C. Sinclair-Stevenson, ed)
S. Purcell, 478(P&L):Oct89–385
Vlach, J.M. Plain Painters.
D. Tatham, 658:Winter89–287
Vladislav, J. – see Havel, V.
Vlassic, K. Children of Byzantium.
A. Munton, 102(CanL):Summer89–150
Vlček, T. Praha 1900.
R.B. Pynsent, 575(SEER):Oct89–616

Vlieghe, H. Corpus Rubenianum Ludwig Bur-
chard. (Pt 19, Vol 2)
M. Russell, 39:Apr89–293
C. White, 380:Winter89–372
Vodoff, V. Naissance de la Chrétienté Russe.
S.A. Zenkovsky, 550(RusR):Jan89–81
Vogan, S. Blueprints.
B.F. Williamson, 441:16Sep90–22
de Vogel, C.J. Rethinking Plato and Platon-
ism.
W. Beierwaltes, 229:Band61Heft1–23
Vogel, E.F. One Step Ahead in China.*
J. Mirsky, 617(TLS):2–8Mar90–220
Vogel, K. Kant und die Paradoxien der Viel-
heit. (2nd ed)
R.M., 342:Band80Heft4–497
Vogel, S., with R. & N. Nooter. The Art of
Collecting African Art.
P.S. Parker, 2(AfrA):Nov88–92
Vogel, U. Balzac als Briefschreiber.
R. Klein, 547(RF):Band101Heft1–125
Vogelaar, C. Netherlandish Fifteenth and
Sixteenth-Century Paintings in the
National Gallery of Ireland.*
J.O. Hand, 90:Jan89–39
Vogt, H. Johann Sebastian Bach's Chamber
Music.*
M. Boyd, 415:Dec89–745
Vogt, K.D. Vision and Revision.
C. Bedwell, 395(MFS):Winter89–829
de Vogüé, A. Community and Abbot in the
Rule of St. Benedict.
O.B. Bouchard, 589:Apr89–510
Voigt, E.B. The Lotus Flowers.*
R. Jackson, 502(PrS):Fall89–117
Voigt, E.M., ed. Lexikon des frühgriechischen
Epos. (Pt 11)
W.J. Verdenius, 394:Vol42fasc3/4–516
Voinovich, V. The Fur Hat.*
J. Bayley, 453(NYRB):15Mar90–26
D. Ugrešić, 617(TLS):12–18Oct90–1088
Voinovich, V. Moscow 2042.
D. Fanger, 473(PR):Vol56No3–499
P. Lewis, 565:Winter88/89–77
Volek, E. Metaestructuralismo.*
L. Block de Behar, 567:Vol74No1/2–157
Volk, P. All It Takes.
G. Krist, 441:11Feb90–17
Vollenweider, S. Neuplatonische und christ-
liche Theologie bei Synesios von Kyrene.
M. Erler, 229:Band61Heft2–104
Vollhaber, T. Das Nichts.
J.W. Jones, 221(GQ):Spring89–246
Vollhardt, F. Hermann Brochs geschichtliche
Stellung.
G. Brude-Firnau, 222(GR):Spring89–85
Vollmann, W.T. The Ice-Shirt.
D. Sacks, 441:14Oct90–13
Vollmann, W.T. The Rainbow Stories.*
S. Moore, 532(RCF):Summer89–258
Vološinov, V.N. Marxism and the Philosophy
of Language.*
D.H., 355(LSoc):Mar89–148
Volpe, T.M. & B. Cathers. Treasures of the
American Arts and Crafts Movement, 1890–
1920.
C. Zusy, 658:Winter89–294
Volpi, F. & J. Nida-Rümelin, eds. Lexikon der
philosophischen Werke.
R. Schaeffler, 489(PJGG):Band96Heft2–
443
Volta, O. Satie Seen Through His Letters.
R. Shattuck, 453(NYRB):15Mar90–32

de Voltaire, F.M.A. Complete Works of Vol-
taire/Oeuvres complètes de Voltaire. (Vol
8) (D.J. Fletcher, E. Jacobs & N. Masson,
eds)
T.E.D. Braun, 402(MLR):Oct90–957
de Voltaire, F.M.A. The Complete Works of
Voltaire/Oeuvres complètes de Voltaire.*
(Vol 33) (J. Vercruysse & others, eds)
M-H. Cotoni, 535(RHL):Jul–Aug89–718
de Voltaire, F.M.A. The Complete Works of
Voltaire/Oeuvres complètes de Voltaire.*
(Vol 62) (R. Mortier, J. Marchand & J. Ren-
wick, eds)
M-H. Cotoni, 535(RHL):Jul–Aug89–717
de Voltaire, F.M.A. Correspondance. (Vol 12)
(T. Besterman, ed)
J.H. Brumfitt, 208(FS):Apr89–212
Vonnegut, K. Bluebeard.* Galapagos.
P. Lewis, 565:Winter88/89–77
Vonnegut, K. Hocus Pocus.
P-L. Adams, 61:Oct90–137
J. McInerney, 441:9Sep90–12
D. Montrose, 617(TLS):26Oct–1Nov90–
1146
Vorderstemann, J. – see von La Roche, S.
Vorobiov, A. & L. Solgalow, eds. The Russian
Language.
I. Thompson, 574(SEEJ):Fall89–479
Voss, L. Literarische Präfiguration dargest-
ellter Wirklichkeit bei Fontane.*
W. Paulsen, 222(GR):Spring89–80
Voss, R.F. A Life of William Inge.
J.H. Maguire, 649(WAL):Nov89–286
G. Weales, 441:5Aug90–19
Vovelle, M., ed. L'Etat de la France pendant
la Révolution (1789–1799).
A.J.M. Prévos, 207(FR):Apr90–915
"Vox diccionario escolar de la lengua espa-
ñola/Vox School Dictionary of the Spanish
Language."
W.W. Moseley, 399(MLJ):Spring89–104
Voznesenskaya, J., ed. Letters of Love.
V. Rounding, 617(TLS):16–22Feb90–176
Voznesenskaya, J. The Star Chernobyl.
P. Lewis, 565:Winter88/89–77
Voznesensky, A. An Arrow in the Wall.*
(W.J. Smith & F.D. Reeve, eds)
J. Saunders, 565:Autumn89–77
Vranich, S.B. – see de Arguijo, J.
de Vries, W.A. Hegel's Theory of Mental
Activity.
M. George, 518:Jul89–142
639(VQR):Summer89–104
Vrubel', I.N. & V.F. Mulenkova, comps. A.S.
Puškin v russkoj i sovetskoj illjustracii.
S.S. Hoisington, 574(SEEJ):Fall89–449
Vumson. Zo History.
S.M. Bekker, 293(JASt):Aug89–689
Vygotsky, L. Thought and Language. (A.
Kozulin, ed)
W. Frawley, 710:Sep89–331

Waage, F.O., ed. Teaching Environmental
Literature.
A. Carlson, 289:Fall89–119
de Waal, A. Famine That Kills.
R. Gray, 617(TLS):9–15Feb90–141
de Waal, F. Chimpanzee Politics.
S. Rose, 617(TLS):23Feb–1Mar90–204
Wachs, E. Crime-Victim Stories.
S.A. Grider, 440:Winter–Spring89–149

Wachs, M. Die poetische Verwirklichung von Charles Nodiers Konzept des "fantastique vraisemblable."
  R. Killick, 402(MLR):Apr90-449
Wachtel, M. Die Darstellung von Vertrauens-würdigkeit in Wahlwerbespots.
  C. Schäffner, 682(ZPSK):Band42Heft5-690
Wachterhauser, B.R., ed. Hermeneutics and Modern Philosophy.
  G.W. Erickson, 580(SCR):Fall89-127
Wack, M.F. Lovesickness in the Middle Ages.
  L. Roper, 617(TLS):7-13Dec90-1328
Wade, D. & J. Picardie. Music Man.
  R. Christgau, 441:12Aug90-11
Wade, R. Village Republics.
  R.J. Herring, 293(JASt):Nov89-920
Wadlington, W. Reading Faulknerian Trage-dy.*
  J.E. Bassett, 401(MLQ):Dec87-396
  C.S. Brown, 569(SR):Fall89-556
  O.B. Emerson, 27(AL):Mar89-124
Waelti-Walters, J. Feminist Novelists of the Belle Epoque.
  A. Duchêne, 617(TLS):12-18Oct90-1107
van der Waerden, B.L. Die Astronomie der Griechen.
  W. Hübner, 229:Band61Heft6-494
Wagener, H., ed. Absurda Comica.
  E.A. Metzger, 133:Band22Heft3/4-317
Wagenknecht, E. Nathaniel Hawthorne.
  J.L. Idol, 594:Fall89-332
  M.B. Moore, 27(AL):Dec89-691
Wagenschein, M. Die Sprache zwischen Natur und Naturwissenschaft.
  A. Greule, 685(ZDL):2/1989-195
Wagner, C. La première traduction italienne de "La Celestina" par Alphonso Hordóñez, Rome, 1506.
  J. Montero, 86(BHS):Oct89-375
Wagner, G. Geltung und normativer Zwang.
  A. Pickel, 488:Sep89-404
Wagner, G. The Wings of Madness.
  P. Keegan, 617(TLS):15-21Jun90-654
Wagner, G. Zur Semantik der kopulativen Verben des Englischen.
  D. Nehls, 257(IRAL):Aug89-261
Wagner, H. Ästhetik der Tragödie von Aris-toteles bis Lessing.*
  M.W. Roche, 221(GQ):Winter89-96
Wagner, K. & G. Wechsung. Computational Complexity.
  P.V. Boas, 316:Jun89-622
Wagner, L.W., ed. Sylvia Plath: The Critical Heritage.
  M. Dickie, 402(MLR):Apr90-430
Wagner, O. Modern Architecture.
  J.S.C., 324:Apr90-378
  K. Frampton, 46:Jul89-12
  C. Pucci, 45:Sep89-55
Wagner, O. Sketches, Projects and Executed Buildings by Otto Wagner.
  P.V., 90:Feb89-161
Wagner, R. Ausreiseantrag. Exit. Begrüs-sungsgeld.
  M. Hofmann, 617(TLS):10-16Aug90-842
Wagner, R. Selected Letters of Richard Wag-ner.* (S. Spencer & B. Millington, eds & trans)
  C.S. Brown, 569(SR):Spring89-278
  R. Hollinrake, 410(M&L):Aug89-415
Wagner-Martin, L.W. Sylvia Plath.*
  617(TLS):29Jun-5Jul90-708

Wain, J. Comedies.
  J. Melmoth, 617(TLS):7-13Dec90-1325
Wainscott, R.H. Staging O'Neill: The Experi-mental Years, 1920-1934.
  N. Berlin, 130:Spring89-95
  J. Veitch, 432(NEQ):Dec89-601
Wainwright, C., ed. George Bullock: Cabinet Maker.
  I. Gow, 90:May89-363
Wainwright, G. The Henge Monuments.
  R. Mercer, 617(TLS):22-28Jun90-665
Wainwright, J.A. Flight of the Falcon.
  J. Donlan, 102(CanL):Winter88-116
Wainwright, M. Miracle Cure.
  B. Dixon, 617(TLS):22-28Jun90-664
Waith, E.M. Patterns and Perspectives in English Renaissance Drama.*
  A.F. Kinney, 250(HLQ):Autumn89-509
Waithe, M.E., ed. A History of Women Philos-ophers.* (Vol 1)
  R.M. Dancy, 254:Spring89-160
  M.A. Warren, 254:Spring89-155
Wakefield, R. Robert Frost and the Opposing Lights of the Hour.
  R.J. Calhoun, 580(SCR):Fall90-191
Wakefield, T. The Variety Artistes.
  P. Payne, 441:29Apr90-33
Wakeman, R. Tenants of the House.
  I. McMillan, 493:Winter89/90-65
Wakoski, D. Emerald Ice.
  B. Baines, 649(WAL):Nov89-267
Walbank, F.W. & others, eds. The Cambridge Ancient History. (2nd ed) (Vol 7, Pt 2)
  N. Purcell, 617(TLS):6-12Jul90-736
Walberg, G. Tradition and Innovation.
  P. Muhly, 124:Nov-Dec89-138
Walch, G. Australia Felix or Harlequin Laughing Jackass and the Magic Bat. (V. Kelly, ed)
  K. Stewart, 71(ALS):May89-122
Walcott, D. The Arkansas Testament.*
  J. Burt, 473(PR):Vol56No4-668
Walcott, D. Omeros.
  M. Lefkowitz, 441:7Oct90-1
  S. O'Brien, 617(TLS):14-20Sep90-977
Wald, A.M. The New York Intellectuals.*
  S.P., 295(JML):Fall88/Winter89-180
Walden, G. The Shoeblack and the Sover-eign.*
  639(VQR):Summer89-95
Walder, D. Ted Hughes.
  A. Haberer, 189(EA):Jul-Sep89-356
Waldinger, R., ed. Approaches to Teaching Voltaire's "Candide."*
  M. Therrien, 207(FR):Feb90-545
Waldman, G.F. Luis Rafael Sánchez.
  A. González, 352(LATR):Spring90-178
Waldrep, T., ed. Writers on Writing. (Vol 2)
  I. Hashimoto, 126(CCC):May89-245
Waldron, A. Close Connections.*
  J.E. Brown, 580(SCR):Fall90-158
  D.E. Stanford, 569(SR):Fall89-572
Waldron, J. The Law.
  A.W.B. Simpson, 617(TLS):14-20Dec90-1344
Waldrop, K. Hegel's Family.
  I. Malin, 532(RCF):Fall89-225
Waldstein, E. Bettine von Arnim and the Pol-itics of Romantic Conversation.
  M.K. Flavell, 402(M&L):Apr90-519
  H.M.K. Riley, 133:Band22Heft3/4-340
  S. Zantop, 221(GQ):Spring89-276

Walicki, A. Legal Philosophies of Russian
Liberalism.
D. Bakhurst, 518:Apr89-115
P.R. Roosevelt, 550(RusR):Jan89-90
W.G. Wagner, 575(SEER):Apr89-313
Walker, A. Franz Liszt. (Vol 1)
J. Rosenblatt, 309:Vol9No4-300
Walker, A. Franz Liszt.* (Vol 2)
J.R. Ronsheim, 42(AR):Fall89-494
Walker, A.R. The Toda of South India.*
M.B. Emeneau, 318(JAOS):Oct-Dec88-605
Walker, C.B.F. Cuneiform.
E.L. Greenstein, 215(GL):Vol29No1-61
Walker, F.A. Catholic Education and Politics
in Ontario. (Vol 3)
D. Swainson, 529(QQ):Spring89-14
Walker, G. John Skelton and the Politics of
the 1520s.
V. Gillespie, 402(MLR):Jan90-139
Walker, I.M., ed. Edgar Allen Poe: The Criti-
cal Heritage.*
B.F. Fisher 4th, 392:Spring89-215
Walker, J. Rivera: "La vorágine."
G. Martin, 402(MLR):Apr90-486
Walker, J.M., ed. Milton and the Idea of
Woman.*
A. Ferry, 301(JEGP):Jul89-420
D. McColley, 70:Jul89-110
Walker, K. - see Lord Rochester
Walker, M. German National Socialism and the
Quest for Nuclear Power: 1939-1949.
T. Powers, 61:May90-126
Walker, N. & Z. Dresner, eds. Redressing the
Balance.
J. Berman, 659(ConL):Summer90-251
Walker, N.A. A Very Serious Thing.*
L. Wagner-Martin, 27(AL):May89-279
Walker, P.W.L. Holy City, Holy Places?
W.H.C. Frend, 617(TLS):26Oct-1Nov90-
1157
Walker, S. In Defense of American Liberties.
W.L. O'Neill, 441:14Jan90-13
Walker, S.A. British Sporting Art in the
Twentieth Century.
O. Beckett, 324:Dec89-70
Walker, W. The Southern Harmony and Musi-
cal Companion.* (G.C. Wilcox, ed)
D.W. Steel, 187:Spring/Summer89-343
"Walking After Midnight."
M.K. Blakely, 441:29Apr90-29
Wall, C.A., ed. Changing Our Own Words.
E.J. Sundquist, 441:25Feb90-11
Wall, J.F. Alfred I. du Pont.
J.M. Burns, 441:15Apr90-10
Wall, K. The Callisto Myth from Ovid to
Atwood.
C.D. Hlus, 627(UTQ):Fall89-111
Wall, R. - see Behan, B.
Wall, S. Trollope and Character.
G. Butte, 637(VS):Winter90-347
P. Swinden, 447(N&Q):Dec89-527
Wallace, A. Desire.
C. See, 441:26Aug90-24
Wallace, B. The Stubborn Particulars of
Grace.
J. Lynes, 102(CanL):Autumn-Winter89-
212
Wallace, D.F. Girl with Curious Hair.*
S. Moore, 532(RCF):Summer89-258
Wallace, J.D. Moral Relevance and Moral Con-
flict.
K. Pahel, 185:Oct89-177
[continued]

[continuing]
W. Sinnott-Armstrong, 518:Jul89-183
639(VQR):Winter89-31
Wallace, K.Y., ed. "La Estorie de Seint Aed-
ward le Rei."
D. Robertson, 545(RPh):Feb90-478
Wallace, P., ed. Region and Nation in India.
U. Phadnis, 293(JASt):Feb89-211
Wallace, R.K. Emily Brontë and Beethoven.*
M.H. Frank, 301(JEGP):Jan89-116
D.M. Hertz, 678(YCGL):No36-195
Wallace, S. War and the Image of Germany.*
R.A. Rempel, 556:Winter89/90-174
Wallace, W.A. Galileo and His Sources.
R. Ariew & D. Jesseph, 53(AGP):
Band71Heft1-89
Wallace-Crabbe, C. I'm Deadly Serious.*
M. Kinzie, 491:Jun89-151
W. Tonetto, 581:Dec89-660
Wallace-Hadrill, A., ed. Patronage in Ancient
Society.
M. Beard, 617(TLS):19-25Jan90-71
Wallach, J. & J. Arafat.
A. Hertzberg, 453(NYRB):25Oct90-41
R. Wright, 441:25Nov90-9
Waller, A.L. Feud.
M.M. Dunlap, 585(SoQ):Summer89-124
639(VQR):Winter89-7
Waller, G. English Poetry of the Sixteenth
Century.*
E.C. Caldwell, 604:Winter89-10
Waller, G.A., ed. American Horrors.
K. Newman, 707:Winter88/89-68
Wallingford, K. Robert Lowell's Language of
the Self.*
R.A. Sharp, 27(AL):Dec89-724
Wallis, A.D. Wheel Estate.
W. Rybczynski, 453(NYRB):20Dec90-24
Wallis, D., ed. OYO: An Ohio River Anthology.
(Vol 2)
42(AR):Winter89-111
Wallis, P.J. & R.V. Eighteenth Century Med-
ics.
R. Porter, 173(ECS):Winter89/90-229
Walls, R.E., ed. Bibliography of Washington
State Folklore and Folklife.
A. Mattina, 650(WF):Jan89-77
Walrond-Skinner, S. & D. Watson, eds. Ethi-
cal Issues in Family Therapy.
A. Maclean, 291:Vol6No1-117
Walser, G., ed. Die einsiedler Inschriften-
sammlung und der Pilgerführer durch Rom.
J. Curran, 313:Vol79-263
T.F.X. Noble, 589:Jul89-776
Walser, G. Römische Inschrift-Kunst.
B.M. Levick, 229:Band61Heft6-565
Walser, M. Über Deutschland reden.
P. Graves, 617(TLS):15-21Jun90-631
Walser, R. "Masquerade" and Other Stories.
(S. Bernofsky, ed & trans)
L. Hafrey, 441:3Jun90-26
Walsh, B., with G. Dickey. Building a Cham-
pion.
A. Barra, 441:7Oct90-18
Walsh, J.E. Into My Own.*
E.J. Ingebretsen, 27(AL):Dec89-704
Walsh, M. - see Smart, C.
Walsh, P.G. & M.J. Kennedy - see William of
Newburgh
Walsh, S. The Music of Stravinsky.*
B. Northcott, 415:Feb89-83
A. Pople, 410(M&L):Nov89-575

Walter, B. The Jury Summation as Speech Genre.*
  P.M. Tiersma, 603:Vol13No2-527
Walter, E.V. Placeways.*
  S.D. Goldhill, 123:Vol39No2-399
Walter, J. & W. Schofield, eds. Famine, Disease, and the Social Order in Early Modern History.
  R. Porter, 617(TLS):5-11Jan90-21
Walter, M. "Hugenotten"-Studien.
  J.H. Roberts, 410(M&L):Aug89-409
Walter, N. Blasphemy.
  D. Pannick, 617(TLS):4-10May90-471
Walters, K.S. The Sane Society Ideal in Modern Utopianism.
  A. Mineau, 103:May90-209
Walters, L. & T.J. Kahn, eds. Bibliography of Bioethics. (Vol 13)
  M.L., 185:Oct89-226
Walther, W. Tausendundeine Nacht.
  U. Marzolph, 196:Band30Heft1/2-180
Walton, C. & P.J. Johnson, eds. Hobbes's Science of Natural Justice.
  A.P. Martinich, 319:Jul90-451
Walton, D.N. Informal Logic.
  L. Groarke, 103:Jul90-294
Walton, J.M. Living Greek Theatre.
  M. Anderson, 610:Summer89-186
  R. Jones, 615(TJ):Mar89-121
Walton, S. William Walton.*
  M. Hurd, 410(M&L):Feb89-133
  A.F.L.T., 412:May89-145
Walvoord, B.E. Three Steps to Revising Your Writing for Style, Grammar, Punctuation, and Spelling.
  P. Arrington & F. Farmer, 126(CCC):Dec89-486
Walz, J. Annotated Bibliography for Developing Oral Proficiency in Second and Foreign Languages.
  H.J. Siskin, 207(FR):Mar90-734
Walzer, M. The Company of Critics.*
  C. Larmore, 185:Jan90-436
Wambaugh, J. The Golden Orange.
  K. Friedman, 441:6May90-7
Wandor, M. Look Back in Gender.*
  A.H. Kritzer, 397(MD):Mar89-169
Wandycz, P.S. The Twilight of the French Eastern Alliances 1926-36.
  A.K. Shelton, 497(PolR):Vol34No3-257
Wang Anyi. Baotown.*
  N. Tisdall, 364:Oct/Nov89-141
Wang Dang. Tang yulin jiaozheng. (Zhou Xunchu, ed)
  W.H.N., 116:Dec89-169
Wang, H. Beyond Analytic Philosophy.*
  M.D. Resnik, 316:Dec89-1484
Wang, H. Reflections on Kurt Gödel.*
  J.L. Bell, 479(PhQ):Jan89-115
  H.T. Hodes, 316:Sep89-1095
  S.G. Shanker, 103:Apr90-166
Wang, H-P. & L.S. Chang. The Philosophical Foundations of Han Fei's Political Theory.
  S. Young, 485(PE&W):Jan89-83
Wang, I.K. Rural Development Studies.
  H. Hahm, 293(JASt):Nov89-895
Wang Meng. Bolshevik Salute.
  M.L. Wagner, 441:18Mar90-13
Wanley, H. Letters of Humfrey Wanley, Palaeographer, Anglo-Saxonist, Librarian, 1672-1726.* (P.L. Heyworth, ed)
  D. McKitterick, 78(BC):Autumn89-301

Wanner, D. The Development of Romance Clitic Pronouns.*
  S.N. Dworkin, 215(GL):Vol29No3-217
  F. Martineau, 361:Sep89-83
Wapnewski, P., ed. Mittelalter-Rezeption.*
  S. Samples, 221(GQ):Fall89-521
Wapshott, N. The Man Between.
  E.S. Turner, 617(TLS):16-22Nov90-1229
Ward, A. A Nation Alone.
  P. Smith, 617(TLS):5-11Jan90-6
Ward, B. Miracles and the Medieval Mind.
  90:Aug89-568
Ward, C. The Child in the City. (new ed)
  A. Coleman, 617(TLS):11-17May90-505
Ward, C.A. Moscow and Leningrad. (Vol 1)
  M. Winokur, 574(SEEJ):Winter89-616
Ward, C.M. Mae West.
  R. Merlock, 580(SCR):Fall89-145
Ward, G.C., R. Burns & K. Burns. The Civil War.
  D.H. Bain, 441:9Sep90-26
Ward, G.W., ed. The American Illustrated Book in the Nineteenth Century.
  D. McKitterick, 78(BC):Summer89-262
Ward, G.W.R. American Case Furniture in the Mabel Brady Garvan and Other Collections at Yale University.
  L. Taylor, 658:Winter89-267
Ward, R. Baccio Bandinelli 1493-1560.*
  C.M. Goguel, 90:Oct89-712
Ward, R. Finding Australia.
  T.W. Tanner, 529(QQ):Spring89-167
Ward, W.S. A Literary History of Kentucky.
  W.J. Sowder, 27(AL):Dec89-728
  T. Wortham, 445(NCF):Dec89-425
Wardhaugh, R. Languages in Competition.*
  B. Brown, 350:Mar90-167
Wardwell, A. African Sculpture from the University Museum, University of Pennsylvania.
  M. Anderson, 2(AfrA):Nov88-22
Ware, R. & K. Nielsen, eds. Analyzing Marxism.
  T. Smith, 103:Aug90-334
Warhol, A. A Coloring Book.
  H. Ketcham, 441:2Dec90-44
Warhol, A. The Andy Warhol Diaries.* (P. Hackett, ed)
  P. Rose, 676(YR):Autumn89-21
Warland, B. serpent (w)rite.*
  D.E. Smyth, 648(WCR):Vol23No2-70
Warminski, A. Readings in Interpretation.
  R. Flores, 577(SHR):Summer89-272
  R. Nägele, 221(GQ):Fall89-512
Warnant, L. Dictionnaire de la prononciation française dans sa norme actuelle.
  P. Léon, 207(FR):May90-1081
Warner, E. Virginia Woolf: "The Waves."*
  P.R. Broughton, 677(YES):Vol20-327
Warner, F. & J. Barbour — see Liebling, A.J.
Warner, M., ed. The Bible as Rhetoric.
  B. Horne, 617(TLS):6-12Jul90-737
Warner, P. Passchendaele.
  639(VQR):Spring89-45
Warner, W.B. Chance and the Text of Experience.*
  J.A. Bryant, Jr., 569(SR):Summer89-445
Warner-Vieyra, M. Femmes échouées.
  F. Pfaff, 95(CLAJ):Jun90-454
Warnicke, R.M. The Rise and Fall of Anne Boleyn.*
  C.S.L. Davies, 617(TLS):12-18Jan90-42

Warnke, F.J. John Donne.
  A.B. Coiro, 551(RenQ):Autumn89-585
Warnke, G. Gadamer.*
  D. Dutton, 478(P&L):Oct89-428
Warnock, M. A Common Policy for Education.*
  D. Gervais, 97(CQ):Vol18No3-314
Warnock, M. Memory.
  R.W. Beardsmore, 89(BJA):Summer89-261
  G. Strickland, 97(CQ):Vol17No4-386
Warnock, M. Universities.*
  J.F.C. Kingman, 324:Feb90-220
Warren, B. Classifying Adjectives.
  E. Leitzke, 38:Band107Heft3/4-463
Warren, C. T.S. Eliot on Shakespeare.*
  L.A. Cellucci, 295(JML):Fall88/Winter89-
  321
Warren, D. The Wednesday Flower Man.
  R. Marken, 647:Fall89-77
Warren, J.F. At the Edge of Southeast Asian
  History.
  A.W. McCoy, 293(JASt):Aug89-690
Warren, L. Family Fiction. (N.G. Anderson,
  ed)
  R. Abbott, 585(SoQ):Spring90-123
Warren, L. L'Amant gris.
  J.P. Gilroy, 102(CanL):Spring89-187
Warren, M. Nietzsche and Political Thought.*
  P. Franco, 185:Apr90-682
  R. Nicholls, 103:Mar90-123
  G.J. Stack, 543:Sep89-184
Warren, M. - see Shakespeare, W.
Warren, R.P. Portrait of a Father.*
  K. Quinlan, 392:Spring89-107
Warren, R.P. - see Melville, H.
Warren, W.L. The Governance of Norman and
  Angevin England, 1086-1272.
  S.E. Christelow, 589:Oct89-1049
Warrick, P.S. Mind in Motion.*
  J. Ford, 295(JML):Fall88/Winter89-313
Wartelle, A. - see Justin Martyr
Wartman, W. Playing Through.
  M. Cart, 441:20May90-31
Waser, E. Die Entlebucher Namenlandschaft.
  W.F.H. Nicolaisen, 424:Sep89-189
Washabaugh, W. Five Fingers for Survival.
  S.A. Hall, 355(LSoc):Sep89-453
Washburn, D.K. & D.W. Crowe. Symmetries of
  Culture.
  M. Frame, 2(AfrA):Aug89-82
Washburn, M. The Ego and the Dynamic
  Ground.
  H. Coward, 485(PE&W):Oct89-505
Washington, P. Fraud.
  L. Sage, 617(TLS):18-24May90-523
Wason, R.W. Viennese Harmonic Theory from
  Albrechtsberger to Schenker and Schoen-
  berg.
  S.E. Hefling, 308:Spring89-214
Wasserstein, D. The Rise and Fall of the Par-
  ty Kings.
  M.G. Morony, 318(JAOS):Jul-Sep88-445
"Die Wasserversorgung antiker Städte."
  P. Leveau, 229:Band61Heft1-55
Wasson, J.M., ed. Records of Early English
  Drama: Devon.*
  S. Carpenter, 541(RES):Feb89-109
Wasson, R.G. & others. Persephone's Quest.
  E. Kearns, 123:Vol39No2-400
Waswo, R. Language and Meaning in the Re-
  naissance.*
  D. Quint, 551(RenQ):Autumn89-534
  S.G. Wong, 301(JEGP):Apr89-226

Waszek, N. The Scottish Enlightenment and
  Hegel's Account of "Civil Society."
  M. Kuehn, 103:Aug90-336
Waszink, J.H. & J.C.M. van Winden - see Ter-
  tullian
Wat, A. Lucifer Unemployed.
  J. Bayley, 453(NYRB):19Jul90-23
  P.S. Gelbard, 441:25Mar90-23
  G. Hyde, 617(TLS):23-29Nov90-1272
Wat, A. My Century.
  E. Hauser, 390:Oct89-56
  T. Martin, 42(AR):Spring89-245
Wat, A. With the Skin.
  E. Hirsch, 442(NY):16Jul90-79
Watanabe, T. & J. Iwata. The Love of the
  Samurai.
  I. Buruma, 617(TLS):20-26Apr90-413
Waterfield, R., ed & trans. The Theology of
  Arithmetic.
  I. Bulmer-Thomas, 123:Vol39No2-266
  J.A. Novak, 103:Jan90-25
Waterhouse, K. Bimbo.
  A. Hislop, 617(TLS):23-29Mar90-328
Waterman, P.P. A Tale-Type Index of Aus-
  tralian Aboriginal Oral Narratives.
  M.C. Ross, 292(JAF):Jul-Sep89-377
Waters, G.R. Three Elegies of Ch'u.*
  C. Hartman, 116:Jul88-167
Waters, H.A. Théâtre Noir.
  H. Wylie, 538(RAL):Fall89-549
Waters, L. - see de Man, P.
Waters, M. The Burden Lifters.
  W. Harmon, 472:Vol16No1-136
Waters, M. The Garden in Victorian Litera-
  ture.
  G.B. Tennyson, 445(NCF):Jun89-118
Waterson, N. Prosodic Phonology.
  A. Spencer, 361:Dec89-330
Waterson, R. The Living House.
  M. Filler, 441:2Dec90-26
Watkin, D. & T. Mellinghoff. German Archi-
  tecture and the Classical Ideal, 1740-
  1840.*
  R. Carter, 576:Jun89-189
Watkins, A. A Slight Case of Libel.
  J. Campbell, 617(TLS):29Jun-5Jul90-688
Watkins, J. Moscow Despatches. (D. Beeby &
  W. Kaplan, eds)
  R.L. Busch, 102(CanL):Spring89-145
Watkins, P. In the Blue Light of African
  Dreams.
  C. Gaiser, 441:23Dec90-7
  M. Illis, 617(TLS):10-16Aug90-855
  442(NY):8Oct90-117
Watkins, P. Night over Day over Night.
  N. Jones, 364:Jun/Jul89-144
Watkins, R.J. High Crimes and Misdemeanors.
  R. Brownstein, 441:13May90-27
Watkins, T.H. Righteous Pilgrim.
  N. Lichtenstein, 441:9Dec90-12
Watson, A. Failures of the Legal Imagination.
  M.M. Arkin, 31(ASch):Autumn89-604
Watson, A. Roman Slave Law.*
  J. Linderski, 124:Nov-Dec89-138
Watson, A.G., ed. Medieval Libraries of Great
  Britain. (Supp to 2nd ed)
  R. Kottje, 72:Band226Heft1-232
Watson, C. Somebody Killed the Messenger.
  639(VQR):Summer89-92
Watson, D.L. Lion in the Lobby.
  J.A. Moss, 441:15Jul90-20

Watson, E.A. A Study of Selected English
Critical Terms from 1650 to 1800.
G. O'Sullivan, 566:Spring89-197
Watson, G. The Smeatonians.
J. Harrison, 324:Apr90-374
Watson, I. God's World.
G. Jonas, 441:8Jul90-22
Watson, J.G. William Faulkner: Letters and
Fictions.*
C.S. Brown, 569(SR):Fall89-556
W.R., 295(JML):Fall88/Winter89-327
Watson, J.L. & E.S. Rawski, eds. Death Ritual
in Late Imperial and Modern China.
S. Harrell, 293(JASt):May89-379
Watson, J.R., ed. Everyman's Book of Victori-
an Verse.*
P. Davis, 97(CQ):Vol18No1-73
S. Lavabre, 189(EA):Jul-Sep89-349
Watson, O. Persian Lustre Ware.*
R. Hillenbrand, 59:Mar89-109
Watson, P.J., with W.B. Horowitz, eds. Neo-
Sumerian Texts from Drehem.
D.I. Owen, 318(JAOS):Jan-Mar88-111
Watson, R.A. The Breakdown of Cartesian
Metaphysics.
J. Cottingham, 319:Apr90-296
Watson, R.A. - see Sebba, G.
Watson, R.N. Ben Jonson's Parodic Strategy.*
R.S. Ide, 141:Fall89-479
W.D. Kay, 301(JEGP):Jul89-407
G. Parfitt, 677(YES):Vol20-256
Watson, R.N. Shakespeare and the Hazards of
Ambition.*
J.A. Bryant, Jr., 569(SR):Summer89-445
Watson, T.J., Jr. & P. Petre. Father Son & Co.
G. Williams, 441:3Jun90-12
Watt, D.E.R. - see Bower, W.
Watt, I. "Nostromo."
J.H. Stape, 177(ELT):Vol32No3-332
Watt, W.S. - see Velleius
Watten, B. Total Syntax.
T.R. Austin, 599:Spring90-137
Watts, C. "Hamlet."
M. Neill, 402(MLR):Jul90-692
Watts, J. Black Writers from South Africa.
S. Watson, 617(TLS):18-24May90-533
Watts, N. Billy Bayswater.
M. Casserley, 617(TLS):27Jul-2Aug90-
804
Waugh, L.R. & M. Halle - see Jakobson, R.
Waugh, P. Feminist Fictions.
M. Hite, 454:Spring90-324
Waugh, S.L. The Lordship of England.
L.M. Matheson, 377:Mar89-61
Waymack, M.H. & G.A. Taler. Medical Ethics
and the Elderly.
I.R.L., 185:Oct89-227
Wayman, T. In a Small House on the Outskirts
of Heaven.
S. Scobie, 376:Dec89-128
Wayment, H. The Stained Glass of the Church
of St. Mary, Fairford.
M. Michael, 90:Nov89-781
Wcislo, F.W. Reforming Rural Russia.
J. Keep, 617(TLS):30Nov-6Dec90-1281
Weale, A., ed. Cost and Choice in Health
Care.
J. Harris, 291:Vol6No2-240
Wearing, J.P., ed. Bernard Shaw.* (Vol 1)
C.A. Berst, 177(ELT):Vol32No1-71
B.F. Dukore, 610:Autumn89-302
Weatherby, W.J. James Baldwin.*
C. Hitchens, 617(TLS):8-14Jun90-609

Weatherby, W.J. Salman Rushdie.
E. Mortimer, 441:22Jul90-3
Weatherill, L. Consumer Behavior & Material
Culture in Britain 1660-1760.
J.P. Alston, 568(SCN):Fall-Winter89-56
Weaver, C. The Thirteenth Enigma?
R. Anderson, 415:Dec89-747
Weaver, L.T., with P. Nuttgens. Lawrence
Weaver 1876-1930.
J.S. Curl, 324:Dec89-69
Weaver, M., ed. The Art of Photography,
1839-1989.
639(VQR):Autumn89-139
Weaver, R.M. The Southern Essays of Richard
M. Weaver. (G.M. Curtis 3d & J.J. Thomp-
son, Jr., ed)
W. Allen, 577(SHR):Spring89-185
Webb, B. Edmund Blunden.
F. Tuohy, 617(TLS):30Nov-6Dec90-1279
Webb, S. & B. Indian Diary.* (N.G. Jayal, ed)
J. Cox, 293(JASt):Nov89-921
Webby, E. & L. Wevers, eds. Happy Endings.
Goodbye to Romance.
F. Adcock, 617(TLS):2-8Feb90-123
Weber, A. Teresa of Avila and the Rhetoric of
Femininity.
C.P. Thompson, 617(TLS):14-20Sep90-
983
Weber, D. Heimito von Doderer.*
M. Bachem, 221(GQ):Summer89-423
Weber, D. Rhetoric and History in Revolu-
tionary New England.*
W. Breitenbach, 656(WMQ):Jan89-192
M.P. Kramer, 27(AL):Dec89-688
Weber, F.J. Fragmente der Vorsokratiker.
D.W. Graham, 123:Vol39No2-250
Weber, H. Vingt ans après.
A.J.M. Prévos, 207(FR):Mar90-758
Weber, H. & R. Zuber, eds. Linguistik Paris-
ette.
B.J. Koekkoek, 221(GQ):Fall89-514
Weber, H.M. The Restoration Rake-Hero.*
A. Kaufman, 301(JEGP):Jan89-97
E.L. Steeves, 403(MLS):Summer89-81
Weber, M. Die römische Agrargeschichte in
ihrer Bedeutung für das Staats- und Priv-
atrecht, 1891. (J. Deininger, ed)
A. Winterling, 229:Band61Heft5-401
Webster, G., ed. Fortress into City.
L. Keppie, 123:Vol39No2-320
Webster, J. William Temple's "Analysis" of Sir
Philip Sidney's "Apology for Poetry."
L. Černy, 38:Band107Heft1/2-216
Webster, P. Pétain's Crime.
T. Judt, 617(TLS):28Sep-4Oct90-1018
Webster, R. A Brief History of Blasphemy.
J. Bell, 617(TLS):12-18Oct90-1100
Webster, W. Not a Man to Match Her.
R. Clare, 617(TLS):8-14Jun90-602
Weckler, C. Impressions of Giverny.
J. Flam, 453(NYRB):17May90-9
Weddige, H. Einführung in die germanistische
Mediävistik.
U. Küsters, 72:Band226Heft1-114
Wedekind, F. Diary of an Erotic Life. (G.
Hay, ed)
J. Simon, 441:18Nov90-13
Weerman, F. The V2 Conspiracy.
J. Hoeksema, 350:Jun90-363
de Weever, J. Chaucer Name Dictionary.
K.J. Harty, 573(SSF):Spring89-205

Wegeler, F. & F. Ries. Remembering Beetho-
ven.*
   B. Cooper, 410(M&L):Feb89-106
Wegera, K-P., ed. Zur Entstehung der neu-
hochdeutschen Schriftsprache.*
   N.R. Wolf, 133:Band22Heft1-94
Wegera, K-P. Grammatik des Frühneuhoch-
deutschen. (Vol 3)
   E. Bauer, 685(ZDL):1/1989-98
Wehgartner, I. Ein Grabbild des Achilleus-
malers.
   A. Johnston, 303(JoHS):Vol109-266
Wehr, D.S. Jung & Feminism.*
   E.C.R., 295(JML):Fall88/Winter89-189
Weidner, A. Die russischen Übersetzungsä-
quivalente der deutschen Modalverben.
   T. Henninger, 575(SEER):Jan89-114
Weidner, H.D. - see Newman, J.H.
Weier, H-I. - see Stappers, L.
Weier, W. Phänomene und Bilder des Mensch-
seins.*
   H. Beck, 489(PJGG):Band96Heft1-218
Weiger, J.G. In the Margins of Cervantes.
   J.A. Parr, 551(RenQ):Winter89-877
   C. Swietlicki, 238:Dec89-957
   639(VQR):Spring89-48
Weiger, J.G. The Substance of Cervantes.*
   T. Hanrahan, 345(KRQ):Feb89-118
Weigl, B. Song of Napalm.
   R. Schultz, 249(HudR):Spring89-156
Weigle, M., ed. The Two Guadalupes.
   E. Gonzales-Berry, 36:Spring89-122
   U. Diator, 292(JAF):Apr-Jun89-239
Weil, E. La philosophie de Pietro Pomponazzi.
   B. Pinchard, 192(EP):Jul-Dec89-562
Weil, N. La plastique archaïque de Thasos.
(Vol 1)
   A. Moustaka, 229:Band61Heft3-231
Weil, S. Oeuvres complètes. (Vol 2) (S.
Fraisse, ed)
   P. McCarthy, 617(TLS):13-19Jul90 747
Weil, S.W. & I. McGill, eds. Making Sense of
Experiential Learning.
   T. Burgess, 324:Jan90-142
Weiler, A.G., R. Stupperich & C.S.M. Rademaker
- see Erasmus
Weiler, K. Women Teaching for Change.
   M.G. Lewis, 529(QQ):Spring89-117
Weimann, R. Shakespeare and the Popular
Tradition in the Theater. (R. Schwartz, ed)
   D. Ellis, 97(CQ):Vol18No1-86
Weimer, J.M. - see Woolson, C.F.
Weinberg, G. The Taboo Scarf.
   A.K. Offit, 441:18Nov90-18
Weinberger, C.W. Fighting for Peace.
   S. Blumenthal, 441:20May90-15
   L. Freedman, 617(TLS):25-31May90-546
Weinberger, E. & others - see Paz, O.
Weinberger, J. Science, Faith, and Politics.
   C. Walton, 319:Apr90-289
Weinbrot, H.D. Eighteenth-Century Satire.
   R.D. Spector, 402(MLR):Oct90-921
Weindling, P. Health, Race and German Poli-
tics between National Unification and Naz-
ism 1870-1945.
   M. Burleigh, 617(TLS):1-7Jun90-592
Weiner, A.B. & J. Schneider, eds. Cloth and
Human Experience.*
   B. Nevill, 617(TLS):30Mar-5Apr90-352
   139:Dec89/Jan90-24
Weiner, D.R. Models of Nature.
   J.H. Bater, 550(RusR):Oct89-426

Weiner, J. The Next One Hundred Years.
   R. Kanigel, 441:4Mar90-3
Weiner, M. The Origins of the Korean Commu-
nity in Japan, 1910-1923.
   R. Bowen, 407(MN):Autumn89-367
Weiner, M.A. Arthur Schnitzler and the Crisis
of Musical Culture.*
   P.F. Dvorak, 221(GQ):Summer89-397
   J.F. Fetzer, 406:Spring89-133
Weiner, R. Le Barbier.
   Z. Vašíček, 98:Oct89-777
Weiner, T. Blank Check.
   L.J. Korb, 441:16Sep90-28
Weingarten, R. Shadow Shadow.
   R. Jackson, 502(PrS):Fall89-117
Weingartner, P. & L. Schmetterer, eds. Gödel
Remembered.
   J.W. Dawson, Jr., 316:Mar89-282
Weinman, I. Virgil's Ghost.
   M. Stasio, 441:21Jan90-35
Weinreb, R.P. - see d'Epinay, L.
Weinsheimer, J.C. Gadamer's Hermeneutics.*
   M. Salvatori, 128(CE):Feb89-201
   L.K. Schmidt, 131(CL):Spring89-186
   R.R. Sullivan, 488:Mar89-131
Weinstein, A. The Fiction of Relationship.
   P.J. Rabinowitz, 454:Spring90-314
Weinstein, J. - see Schneider, L.
Weinstein, L. The Subversive Tradition in
French Literature. (Vol 1)
   D.W Smith, 166:Apr90-273
Weintraub, S. - see Shaw, G.B.
Weintraub, S. - see "Shaw: The Annual of
Bernard Shaw Studies"
Weir, D.A. The Origins of the Federal Theol-
ogy in Sixteenth-Century Reformation
Thought.
   A. Hamilton, 617(TLS):9-15Nov90-1212
Weisbuch, R. Atlantic Double-Cross.*
   R. Gray, 402(MLR):Apr90-420
Weisenburger, S. A "Gravity's Rainbow" Com-
panion.*
   B. Duyfhuizen, 454:Fall89-76
   M. Hite, 395(MFS):Summer89-305
Weiser, D.K. Mind in Character.
   P. Happé, 447(N&Q):Dec89-502
Weishaupt, J. Die Märchenbrüder.
   D. Haase, 406:Spring89-127
Weisinger, K.D. The Classical Facade.
   C. Gallant, 661(WC):Autumn89-216
   G. Maertz, 173(ECS):Fall89-73
   J. Pizer, 221(GQ):Winter89-118
Weiss, G. - see ibn Daud, A.
Weiss, H.F. Funde und Studien zu Heinrich
von Kleist.
   K. Müller-Salget, 680(ZDP):Band108
   Heft2-289
Weiss, N.J. Whitney M. Young, Jr., and the
Struggle for Civil Rights.
   D. Camper, 441:11Feb90-19
Weiss, R.S. Staying the Course.
   M.S. Kimmel, 441:9Sep90-28
Weiss, S.A. - see Shaw, G.B.
Weiss, T. From Princeton One Autumn After-
noon.*
   D. McDuff, 565:Spring89-76
Weiss, W. Der anglo-amerikanische Universi-
tätsroman.
   R. Borgmeier, 224(GRM):Band39Heft4-484
Weiss, W., H.E. Wiegand & M. Reis, eds. Kon-
troversen, alte und neue. (Vol 3)
   F. Patocka, 685(ZDL):3/1989-339

Weissbort, D., ed. Translating Poetry.
  D.J. Enright, 617(TLS):12–18Jan90–40
Weissenberger, M. Die Dokimasiereden des
  Lysias (orr. 16, 25, 26, 31).
  S. Usher, 123:Vol39No1–19
Weisskopf-Joelson, E. Father, Have I Kept My
  Promise?
  639(VQR):Winter89–18
Weissman, D. Hypothesis and the Spiral of
  Reflection.
  M. Sacks, 617(TLS):13–19Jul90–758
Weissman, S.M. His Brother's Keeper.
  L.E. Nesbitt, 441:11Feb90–19
Weissmann, G. The Doctor with Two Heads.
  G. Hochman, 441:15Jul90–18
  442(NY):4Jun90–104
Weissweiler, E., with S. Ludwig – see Schu-
  mann, C. & R.
Weitzmann, K. & H.L. Kessler. The Cotton
  Genesis.*
  O. Demus, 229:Band61Heft6–571
Weixlmann, J. & H.A. Baker, Jr., eds. Studies
  in Black American Literature. (Vol 3)
  E.L. Steeves, 395(MFS):Summer89–310
Welch, C. Linguistic Responsibility.*
  L. Forguson, 627(UTQ):Fall89–221
  C.G. Prado, 154:Vol28No4–667
Welch, J. The Indian Lawyer.
  E. Hoagland, 441:25Nov90–7
Welch, L. Word-House of a Grandchild.*
  J. Kuropatwa, 102(CanL):Spring89–161
Weldon, F. The Cloning of Joanna May.*
  R. Houston, 441:25Mar90–7
Weldon, F. Darcy's Utopia.
  S. Mackay, 617(TLS):21–27Sep90–998
Weldon, F. The Heart of the Country.
  639(VQR):Summer89–92
Welfield, J. An Empire in Eclipse.
  B. Stronach, 293(JASt):Nov89–884
Wellbery, D.E. – see von Goethe, J.W.
Welle, J.P. The Poetry of Andrea Zanzotto.
  V. Hand, 402(MLR):Jul90–757
Weller, F. Kleine Schriften. (W. Rau, ed)
  J.W. de Jong, 259(IIJ):Jan89–51
Wellington, M. The Art of Voltaire's Theater.
  J. Yashinsky, 210(FrF):May89–234
Wells, C., ed. Perspectives in Vernacular
  Architecture.* (Vol 2)
  T. Carter, 576:Jun89–202
Wells, C.J. German.*
  K-P. Wegera, 680(ZDP):Band108Heft1–144
Wells, G.A. & D.R. Oppenheimer – see Engle-
  field, R.
Wells, H.G. The Definitive Time Machine.*
  (H.M. Geduld, ed)
  P. Parrinder, 677(YES):Vol20–319
Wells, J. Ambion Hill.
  E. Bartlett, 493:Spring89–64
Wells, N. Just Bounce/Wilderness.*
  S. O'Brien, 364:Feb/Mar90–111
Wells, S., ed. The Cambridge Companion to
  Shakespeare Studies.*
  G. Schmitz, 156(ShJW):Jahrbuch1989–332
Wells, S. Shakespeare: An Illustrated Dictio-
  nary.
  G. Schmitz, 156(ShJW):Jahrbuch1989–332
Wells, S. – see "Shakespeare Survey"
Wells, S. & G. Taylor – see Shakespeare, W.
Wells, S. & G. Taylor, with others. William
  Shakespeare, A Textual Companion.*
  C.B. Evans, 301(JEGP):Jul89–401
[continued]

[continuing]
  H.W. Gabler, 156(ShJW):Jahrbuch1989–
  344
  E.A.J. Honigmann, 447(N&Q):Mar89–95
  D. Mehl, 677(YES):Vol20–248
  B. Vickers, 541(RES):Aug89–402
Wells, W. Conversing with the Light.
  D. Sampson, 249(HudR):Autumn89–512
Welsch, W. Aisthesis.
  H. Schmitz, 489(PJGG):Band96Heft2–394
Welsch, W. Unsere postmoderne Moderne.
  (2nd ed)
  I. Hoesterey, 221(GQ):Fall89–505
Welsch, W., ed. Wege aus der Moderne.
  I. Hoesterey, 221(GQ):Fall89–505
Welsh, A. From Copyright to Copperfield.*
  A. Fleishman, 301(JEGP):Jan89–119
  S. Monod, 189(EA):Apr–Jun89–219
  G. Smith, 677(YES):Vol20–303
Welskopf, E.C., ed. Soziale Typenbegriffe im
  alten Griechenland und ihr Fortleben in
  den Sprachen der Welt.
  F. Gschnitzer, 260(IF):Band94–354
Weltens, B., K. De Bot & T. Van Els, eds.
  Language Attrition in Progress.
  N.C. Dorian, 350:Sep90–657
  J.H. Hill, 355(LSoc):Dec89–594
  C.R. Pons, 710:Jun89–217
Welty, E. Photographs.
  C. East, 598(SoR):Spring90–449
  S. MacNeille, 441:22Apr90–24
Welzig, W., ed. Katalog gedruckter deutsch-
  sprachiger katholischer Predigtsammlun-
  gen.* (Vol 1)
  R. Wittmann, 224(GRM):Band39Heft2–241
Welzig, W., ed. Katalog gedruckter deutsch-
  sprachiger katholischer Predigtsammlun-
  gen.* (Vol 2)
  C. Daxelmüller, 196:Band30Heft3/4–358
  R. Wittmann, 224(GRM):Band39Heft2–241
Welzig, W. & others – see Schnitzler, A.
Wendelius, L. Pengar, brott och andeväsen.
  J. Lutz, 563(SS):Winter89–112
Wenders, W. Emotion Pictures.
  M. Wood, 617(TLS):12–18Jan90–33
Wenders, W. & P. Handke. Der Himmel über
  Berlin.
  P. Babin, 98:Oct89–747
Wenham, L.P. & others. St. Mary Bishophill
  Junior and St. Mary Castlegate.
  L. Karlsson, 341:Vol58No4–172
Wenk, E., Jr. Tradeoffs.
  H.M.S., 185:Jan90–462
Wenke, J. Mailer's America.*
  P.R.J., 295(JML):Fall88/Winter89–378
Wentling, J.W. & L. Bookout, eds. Density By
  Design.
  M. Zimmerman, 47:Apr89–51
Wentzlaff-Eggebert, H., ed. Ramón de Valle-
  Inclán (1866–1936).
  J.M. García de la Torre, 547(RF):Band
  101Heft2/3–376
  K. Schoell, 52:Band24Heft3–325
Wenz, P.S. Environmental Justice.
  J.B. Callicott, 185:Oct89–197
Wenzel, H.V., ed. Simone de Beauvoir.*
  M. Rosello, 345(KRQ):May89–239
  K. Woodward, 188(ECr):Winter89–104
Wenzel, S. Preachers, Poets, and the Early
  English Lyric.*
  S. Manning, 131(CL):Fall89–394
  T. Stemmler, 72:Band226Heft1–233

Wenzel, W. Studien zu sorbischen Personen-
  namen. (Pt 1)
    G. Stone, 575(SEER):Jan89-109
Weöres, S. Eternal Moment.* (M. Vajda, ed)
    S. Friebert, 199:Spring89-60
    D. O'Driscoll, 493:Summer89-47
Werckmeister, O.K. The Making of Paul Klee's
  Career, 1914-1920.
    P. Vergo, 617(TLS):12-18Jan90-38
Werewere-Liking. Statues Colons.
    C.B. Steiner, 2(AfrA):Nov88-95
Werewere-Liking & M-J. Hourantier. Specta-
  cles rituels.
    R. Bobia, 538(RAL):Summer89-291
Werfel, F. Cella.
    C. Innes, 441:14Jan90-30
Werlen, I. Gebrauch und Bedeutung der Mod-
  alverben in alemannischen Dialekten.
    H. Tatzreiter, 685(ZDL):3/1989-374
Werlen, I., ed. Probleme der schweizerischen
  Dialektologie.
    H. Tatzreiter, 685(ZDL):3/1989-371
Werner, B.C. Blake's Vision of the Poetry of
  Milton.*
    G. Campbell, 83:Autumn89-225
    J.M.Q. Davies, 481(PQ):Spring89-280
    M.L. Johnson, 301(JEGP):Jul89-429
Werner, C. Adrienne Rich.
    G.R. Hughes, 27(AL):May89-321
Werner, C.H. "Dubliners."
    J.R. Frakes, 670(SSF):Winter89-102
Werner, G. De grymma skuggorna.
    L. Thompson, 562(Scan):May89-161
Werner, J. Darstellung als Kritik, Hegels
  Frage nach den Anfang der Wissenschaft.
    P-P. Druet, 258:Mar89-106
Werner, S. Socratic Satire.*
    C. Lafargue, 530:Apr89-166
    R. Mortier, 547(RF):Band101Heft1-124
Wernher der Gartenaere. Helmbrecht. (U.
  Ocelbach, ed, L B Parshall, trans)
    L. Frisch, 589:Jan89-236
Wertheim, S. & P. Sorrentino - see Crane, S.
Werthelmer, J., ed. Ästhetik der Gewalt,
    R. Galle, 52:Band24Heft1-78
Wortheimer, J. Unwelcome Strangers.
    M. Lamberti, 104(CASS):Spring89-94
Wertsch, J.V., ed. Culture, Communication,
  and Cognition.*
    W. Frawley, 710:Mar89-97
Wertsch, J.V. Vygotsky and the Social For-
  mation of Mind.*
    M. Salvatori, 128(CE):Feb89-201
Weschler, L. A Miracle, a Universe.
    I. Fonseca, 617(TLS):28Sep-4Oct90-1027
    S. Schlesinger, 441:15Apr90-10
Weski, E. & H. Frosien-Leinz, comps. Das
  Antiquarium der Münchner Residenz.
    D. & P. Diemer, 683:Band52Heft4-567
Wesley, M. A Sensible Life.
    E. Barry, 617(TLS):16-22Mar90-293
    E. Pall, 441:29Jul90-10
Wessely, O., ed. Bruckner Symposion.
    W. Kirsch, 417:Apr-Jun89-173
West, J.L.W. 3d. American Authors and the
  Literary Marketplace since 1900.
    M.T. Gilmore, 432(NEQ):Dec89-612
    J.R. McElrath, Jr., 40(AEB):Vol3No1-33
West, J.O., ed. Mexican-American Folklore.
    R. Sanchez, 649(WAL):Nov89-274
West, M. Lazarus.
    H. Knight, 441:15Apr90-14

West, M.L. Crazy Ladies.
    K. Ramsland, 441:21Oct90-24
West, M.L. Introduction to Greek Metre.
    J. Irigoin, 555:Vol62Fasc2-318
West, M.L. - see Euripides
West, M.L. - see Hesiod
West, N. Molehunt.*
    639(VQR):Autumn89-132
West, N. The Sigint Secrets.
    639(VQR):Spring89-62
West, P. Lord Byron's Doctor.*
    S. Moore, 532(RCF):Fall89-215
West, P. Sheer Fiction.*
    P.T.S., 295(JML):Fall88/Winter89-253
West, P. & F.A.M.A. von Geusau, eds. The
  Pacific Rim and the Western World.
    T. Ozawa, 293(JASt):May89-338
Westbrook, P.D. Literary History of New Eng-
  land.
    T. Wortham, 445(NCF):Dec89-426
Westenholz, A. The Power of Aries.*
    M.T. Murray, 295(JML):Fall88/Winter89-
      313
Westergaard, M.R. Definite NP Anaphora.*
    E. König, 38:Band107Heft1/2-116
Westerink, L.G. - see Damascius
Westerink, L.G. - see Photius
Westerkamp, M.J. Triumph of the Laity.
    J.H. Smylie, 656(WMQ):Apr89-386
Westermann, J. Exit Wounds.
    M. Stasio, 441:18Feb90-23
Westermann, K. Joseph Roth, Journalist.
    R. Kunster, 100:Band22Heft1-81
Westerweel, B. Patterns and Patterning.
    D. Higgins, 568(SCN):Spring-Summer89-
      11
Westfall, W. Two Worlds.
    G. Patterson, 529(QQ):Winter89-965
Westlake, D.E. Drowned Hopes.
    K. Dunn, 441:8Apr90-14
Westney, D.E. Imitation and Innovation.*
    L.L. Johnson, 293(JASt):Feb90-184
Westphal, J. Colour.*
    P. Engel, 542:Oct-Dec89-625
    C.L. Hardin, 393(Mind):Jan89-146
    P. Lewis, 521:Apr89-182
    S. Makin, 400.Apr89-271
Westphalen, T. & others, eds. Erich-Maria-
  Remarque-Bibliographie.*
    C.R. Owen, 221(GQ):Fall89-538
    M. Travers, 402(MLR):Oct90-1031
Wetherbee, W. Chaucer and the Poets.
    C.J. Watkin, 148:Winter86-96
Wetherell, W.D. Chekhov's Sister.
    J.T. Hospital, 441:25Mar90-12
    442(NY):18Jun90-95
Wetherill, P.M. - see Ernaux, A.
Wetherill, P.M. - see Flaubert, G.
Wettberg, G. Das Amerika-Bild und seine
  negativen Konstanten in der deutschen
  Nachkriegsliteratur.
    P. Ensberg, 221(GQ):Summer89-433
Wetzel, H.H. Rimbauds Dichtung.
    S. Guers, 446(NCFS):Fall-Winter89/90-
      265
    A. Guyaux, 535(RHL):Jan-Feb89-144
Wetzel, M. Dialektik als Ontologie auf der
  Basis selbstreflexiver Erkenntniskritik.
    W. Schmied-Kowarzik, 489(PJGG):
      Band96Heft1-181
Wevill, D. Figure of Eight.
    R. Labrie, 102(CanL):Autumn-Winter89-
      143

Wexler, P. Explorations in Judeo-Slavic Linguistics.
N.G. Jacobs, 159:Vol6No2-291
Wexler, P. Three Heirs to a Judeo-Latin Legacy.
P-F. Moreau, 531:Jul-Dec89-508
Weyer, H. & J.C. Aschoff. Tsaparang.
H. Eimer, 259(IIJ):Jan89-52
Weyergans, F. Je suis écrivain.
R. Buss, 617(TLS):5-11Jan90-18
Whalen, T. Philip Larkin and English Poetry.*
C. Wiseman, 49:Jan89-104
Whaling, F. Christian Theology and World Religions.
J.D. May, 235:Winter88-77
Whalley, G. The Collected Poems of George Whalley.* (G. Johnston, ed)
J. Baxter, 150(DR):Winter88/89-496
D. McCarthy, 168(ECW):Spring89-78
Whalley, J.I. & T.R. Chester. A History of Children's Book Illustration.*
J. Barr, 354:Sep89-285
517(PBSA):Sep89-408
Wharton, A.J. Art of Empire.*
J. Lowden, 90:Jun89-425
Wharton, E. The Letters of Edith Wharton. (R.W.B. & N. Lewis, eds)
E. Ammons, 432(NEQ):Sep89-441
W.W. Fairey, 639(VQR):Summer89-530
C.J. Singley, 27(AL):Oct89-461
42(AR):Winter89-112
Whatmore, D.E. H. Rider Haggard.*
B. Lake, 78(BC):Summer89-265
Wheare, J. Virginia Woolf.
S. Ferebee, 395(MFS):Winter89-802
Wheatley, P. The Collected Works of Phillis Wheatley.* (J.C. Shields, ed)
P. Edwards, 538(RAL):Summer89-309
Wheatley, P. A Hinge of Spring.*
P.M. St. Pierre, 102(CanL):Spring89-210
Wheatley, P. The Poems of Phillis Wheatley. (J.D. Mason, Jr., ed)
Q. Prettyman, 357:Spring90-68
Wheeler, D., ed. Domestick Privacies.*
D.R. Anderson, 568(SCN):Fall-Winter89-38
C.H. Kullman, 580(SCR):Spring90-176
Wheeler, E. & J. Trainer. The Yachting Cookbook.
R. Flaste, 441:10Jun90-12
Wheeler, R.P. - see Barber, C.L.
Wheeler, T., comp. "The Merchant of Venice."
L. Engle, 570(SQ):Summer89-244
Wheen, F. Tom Driberg.
R. Foster, 617(TLS):11-17May90-487
Whelan, F. Order and Artifice in Hume's Political Philosophy.
I.M. Fowlie, 479(PhQ):Jan89-124
Whelan, G. Playing with Shadows.*
M. Hallissy, 573(SSF):Summer89-356
M. Kuznets, 455:Jun89-69
Whelan, P.T. D.H. Lawrence.
R.M. Burwell, 177(ELT):Vol32No1-117
C. Davidson, 456(NDQ):Winter89-216
Whelan, R. Drawing the Line.
R. Sherrod, 441:6May90-24
442(NY):7May90-109
Whinney, M. Sculpture in Britain 1530-1830. (rev by J. Physick)
J. Kenworthy-Browne, 39:Oct89-287
Whitaker, J.S. How Can Africa Survive?
639(VQR):Winter89-23

Whitaker, T.R. Tom Stoppard.
B. Crow, 610:Spring89-103
Whitby, M. The Emperor Maurice and his Historian.*
M. Angold, 123:Vol39No2-296
White, A.R. Methods of Metaphysics.*
B. Carr, 518:Jan89-38
White, A.R. Rights.
T. Regan, 449:Mar89-112
White, B. Hard Bargains.
B.D. Palmer, 529(QQ):Spring89-199
White, C. Peter Paul Rubens.*
F. Baudouin, 90:Aug89-564
White, C. Russia and America.
A. McAuley, 575(SEER):Apr89-299
White, D.A. The Turning Wheel.*
R. Donington, 415:May89-283
B. Millington, 410(M&L):Aug89-417
White, E.C., ed. The Black Women's Health Book.
L. Villarosa, 441:5Aug90-19
White, E.C. Kaironomia.
A. Calder, 478(P&L):Oct89-408
White, G., ed. Developmental States in East Asia.
K.S. Kim, 293(JASt):Feb89-123
White, G.D. The Audio Dictionary.
D. Vaughan, 415:Jun89-351
White, H. The Content of the Form.*
T. Engebretsen, 577(SHR):Fall89-377
T. Furniss, 506(PSt):May89-105
J. Tambling, 401(MLQ):Jun88-192
White, H. Nature and Salvation in "Piers Plowman."
W. Scase, 447(N&Q):Sep89-366
White, J. The Birth and Rebirth of Pictorial Space. (3rd ed)
H.B.J. Maginnis, 54:Mar89-137
White, J. & A. Wildavsky. The Deficit and the Public Interest.
N.J. Ornstein, 441:3Jun90-14
White, J.B. Heracles' Bow.
V. Kahn, 153:Summer89-21
White, J.J. Literary Futurism.
P. Hainsworth, 617(TLS):13-19Jul90-748
White, K.D. Greek and Roman Technology.
G.W. Houston, 121(CJ):Oct-Nov89-63
White, L.M. Building God's House in the Roman World.
W.H.C. Frend, 617(TLS):26Oct-1Nov90-1157
White, L.T. 3d. Policies of Chaos.
A.G. Walder, 293(JASt):Nov89-848
White, M. The Japanese Educational Challenge.*
J.J. Tobin, 293(JASt):Feb89-186
White, M. Philosophy, "The Federalist," and the Constitution.*
W. Niegorski, 543:Mar90-654
C. Walton, 319:Jul90-456
White, M.I. The Japanese Overseas.
T.C. Bestor, 293(JASt):May89-406
White, M.J. Agency and Integrality.*
M.H. Bernstein, 449:Jun89-391
D. Frede, 41:Spring89-126
White, M.J. & M. Tsvetaeva. Starry Sky to Starry Sky.
J. Meek, 456(NDQ):Winter89-227
White, P. Three Uneasy Pieces.
P. Lewis, 565:Autumn89-72
White, R.H. Tribal Assets.
P-L. Adams, 61:Nov90-172

White, R.L., ed. Sherwood Anderson: Early
Writings.
   K.J. Williams, 40(AEB):Vol3No2-74
White, R.S. Let Wonder Seem Familiar.
   B. Thorne, 539:Vol13No4-412
White, S. The Bolshevik Poster.
   639(VQR):Spring89-68
White, S. The Origins of Detente.
   M. Light, 575(SEER):Jan89-156
White, S., J. Gardner & G. Schöpflin. Commu-
nist Political Sytems.
   H. Stokes, 575(SEER):Jul89-495
White, S. & A. Pravda, eds. Ideology and
Soviet Politics.
   J. Harris, 550(RusR):Jul89-338
White, S., A. Pravda & S. Gitelman, eds.
Developments in Soviet Politics.
   O. Figes, 617(TLS):5-11Oct90-1056
Whiteford, A.H. Southwestern Indian Baskets.
   J.M. Adovasio, 292(JAF):Oct-Dec89-507
Whitehead, B. The Girl With Red Suspenders.
   P. Craig, 617(TLS):16-22Mar90-298
Whitehead, J. Maugham.
   J. Dobrinsky, 189(EA):Oct-Dec89-498
   P. Miles, 447(N&Q):Mar89-124
Whiteley, P.J. Knowledge and Experimental
Realism in Conrad, Lawrence and Woolf.*
   E. Delavenay, 189(EA):Jan-Mar89-106
   I.V., 295(JML):Fall88/Winter89-215
Whitenido, A. & M. Issacharoff, eds. On Re-
ferring in Literature.*
   C. Prendergast, 208(FS):Apr89-238
Whitfield, A. Le Je(u) illocutoiré.*
   N. Bishop, 529(QQ):Spring89-172
   P.S. Noble, 402(MLR):Jan90-203
   D.L. Parris, 208(FS):Jul89-362
   D.W. Russell, 102(CanL):Autumn-
   Winter89-247
Whitfield, S.J. American Space Jewish Time.
   639(VQR):Spring89-62
Whitley, M.S. Spanish/English Contrasts.
   M.M. Azevedo, 545(RPh):Feb90-468
Whitman, J. Allegory.*
   N.L. Harvey, 125:Winter89-100
   J. Marenbon, 72:Band226Heft1-134
   J. Norton Smith, 541(RES):Nov89-602
   R.A. Peck, 149(CLS):Vol26No2-172
   W.G. Thalmann, 478(P&L):Apr89-205
Whitman, R. The Testing of Hanna Senesh.*
   R. Mitchell, 502(PrS):Fall89-129
Whitman, W. The Essential Whitman. (G.
Kinnell, ed)
   P. Mariani, 434:Spring90-313
Whitman, W. Foglie d'Erba. (B. Tedeschini
Lalli, ed)
   R. Asselineau, 646(WWR):Summer89-37
Whitman, W. Vlati trave/Respondez! (H.
Demirović, ed & trans)
   A. Golden & M. Bolta, 646(WWR):
   Summer89-36
Whitney, C. Francis Bacon and Modernity.*
   J. Agassi, 488:Jun89-219
Whitney, D.C. The American Presidents. (rev
by R.V. Whitney)
   S. Neal, 441:13May90-14
Whitney, G. A Choice of Emblemes.
   O. Reynolds, 617(TLS):15-21Jun90-651
Whitney, P.A. The Singing Stones.
   S. Paulos, 441:27May90-15
Whittaker, C.R., ed. Pastoral Economies in
Classical Antiquity.
   J.G. Keenan, 24:Winter89-668
                               [continued]

[continuing]
   R. Osborne, 123:Vol39No1-95
   S. Spurr, 313:Vol79-175
Whittaker, R. Doris Lessing.
   N. Iyer, 395(MFS):Winter89-822
Whittall, J. Troubles in Paradise.
   D. O'Rourke, 102(CanL):Spring89-206
Whittemore, R. Pure Lives.*
   G. Clingham, 77:Spring89-156
   M. New, 566:Autumn89-74
   F.C. Robinson, 569(SR):Spring89-304
Whitton, D. Stage Directors in Modern
France.*
   K. Gore, 208(FS):Apr89-234
Whitworth, J., ed. The Faber Book of Blue
Verse.
   G. Foden, 617(TLS):19-25Oct90-1133
Whitworth, J. Tennis and Sex and Death.*
   G. Ewart, 493:Winter89/90-64
Whyte, W.H. City.*
   D. Gantenbein, 45:Jul89-67
Wiatr, J.J. The Soldier and the Nation.
   P. Wandycz, 497(PolR):Vol34No2-175
Wichmann, T. Heinrich von Kleist.
   S.R. Huff, 406:Winter89-498
   K. Müller-Salget, 680(ZDP):Band108
   Heft2-289
Wichmann, Y. Wotjakischer Wortschatz. (T.E.
Uotila & M. Korhonen, comps)
   L. Campbell, 350:Sep90-642
Wick, D.L. A Conspiracy of Well-Intentioned
Men.
   N. Hampson, 83:Spring89-80
Wicke, J. Advertising Fictions.
   E. Langland, 158:Jun89-71
Wicke, P. Rockmusik.
   B. Tänzer, 654(WB):9/1989-1578
Wickes, G. - see Miller, H.
Wickham, G. The Medieval Theatre. (3rd ed)
   D. Wiles, 611(TN):Vol43No3-138
Wicks, B. No Time to Wave Goodbye.
   L.E. Beattie, 441:28Jan90-23
Widdess, R., ed. Musica Asiatica 5.
   B. Yung, 293(JASt):Nov89-813
Widdicombe, R.T. Edward Bellamy.
   K.M. Roemer, 561(SFS):Jul89-238
Wideman, J.E. Philadelphia Fire
   R.L. Bray, 441:30Sep90-7
Widick, B.J. Detroit. (rev)
   J. Barnard, 385(MQR):Spring90-288
Wiebe, D. Going to the Mountain.
   B.K. Horvath, 532(RCF):Summer89-246
Wiebe, R. Playing Dead.
   W.J. Keith, 627(UTQ):Winter89/90-361
Wieck, F. Piano and Song (Didactic and
Polemical). (H. Pleasants, ed & trans)
   R. Anderson, 415:Jul89-412
   J.W. Finson, 410(M&L):Nov89-553
Wieck, R., with others. Time Sanctified.
(British title: The Book of Hours in Medi-
eval Life and Society.)
   J.J.G. Alexander, 90:Oct89-709
   J. Backhouse, 39:Dec89-428
   K. Gould, 517(PBSA):Jun89-233
Wiedemann, T. Adults and Children in the
Roman Empire.
   L. Ascher, 124:Jul-Aug90-544
   M. Beard, 617(TLS):19-25Jan90-71
   J. Griffin, 453(NYRB):25Oct90-20
Wiedemeier, K. La Religion de Bernardin de
Saint-Pierre.
   J-M. Racault, 535(RHL):Nov-Dec89-1060

Wiedmann, A. Romantic Art Theories.
  H. Nabbe, 564:Sep89-266
Wiegersma, N. Vietnam.
  J.H. Esterline, 293(JASt):Aug89-691
Wiegmann, H., ed. Die ästhetische Leiden-
  schaft.
  M. Wade, 221(GQ):Winter89-103
Wieland, J. The Ensphering Mind.
  F. Jussawalla, 538(RAL):Fall89-529
  B. King, 49:Apr89-84
Wien, F. Rebuilding the Economic Base of
  Indian Communities.
  E.J. Peters, 529(QQ):Spring89-204
Wiener, J.H., ed. Papers for the Millions.
  V. Berridge, 637(VS):Spring90-534
Wier, D. The Book of Knowledge.*
  W. Harmon, 472:Vol16No1-136
Wierenga, E.R. The Nature of God.
  P.L. Quinn, 543:Dec89-428
Wierlacher, A., ed. Das Fremde und das
  Eigene.
  U. Scheck, 564:Nov89-339
Wierlacher, A., ed. Perspektiven und Ver-
  fahren interkultureller Germanistik.
  U. Scheck, 564:Nov89-339
Wierlacher, A. Vom Essen in der deutschen
  Literatur.
  K.J. Campbell, 406:Fall89-381
  J. Kolb, 221(GQ):Winter89-101
Wierzyński, K. — see under Vezhinskii, K.
Wiesand, A. Kunst ohne Grenzen?
  E. Hexelschneider, 654(WB):8/1989-1400
Wiese, W. Johannes Klinckerfuss, Ein Würt-
  tembergischer Ebenist (1770-1831).
  S. Jervis, 90:Oct89-719
Wiesel, E. From the Kingdom of Memory.
  N. Stiller, 441:8Jul90-14
Wiesel, E. Twilight.*
  639(VQR):Winter89-25
Wiesel, E. & J. O'Connor. A Journey of Faith.
  N. Stiller, 441:8Jul90-14
Wiesel, E. & P-M. de Saint-Cheron. Evil and
  Exile.
  N. Stiller, 441:8Jul90-14
Wiesenfarth, J. Gothic Manners and the Clas-
  sic English Novel.
  R. Kiely, 445(NCF):Mar90-554
  E. Langland, 594:Fall89-352
  P.E. Ray, 177(ELT):Vol32No4-524
  D. Richter, 402(MLR):Jul90-698
Wiesenthal, S. Justice Not Vengeance.
  R. Sanders, 441:13May90-7
Wiesinger, P. Die Flexionsmorphologie des
  Verbums im Bairischen.
  L. Zehetner, 685(ZDL):3/1989-365
Wiget, A. Simon Oritz.
  D. Heaberlin, 649(WAL):Feb90-374
Wiggershaus, R. Theodor W. Adorno.
  J. Früchtl, 687:Jan-Mar89-199
Wiggins, D. Needs, Values, Truth.*
  D. Carrier, 89(BJA):Autumn89-370
  J.J.C. Smart, 185:Apr90-628
Wiggins, M. John Dollar.*
  639(VQR):Autumn89-129
Wiggins, P.D. Figures in Ariosto's Tapestry.*
  A. Reynolds, 345(KRQ):Feb89-122
Wigglesworth, M. The Poems of Michael Wig-
  glesworth. (R.A. Bosco, ed)
  R.S. Daly, 165(EAL):Vol25No3-321
Wigmore, R., ed & trans. Schubert: the Com-
  plete Song Texts.
  J. Reed, 410(M&L):May89-263
  M. Whittall, 415:Feb89-88

Wihl, G. & D. Williams, eds. Literature and
  Ethics.
  R.E.H., 185:Oct89-209
  T. Siebers, 478(P&L):Apr89-212
Wihtol, R. The Asian Development Bank and
  Rural Development.
  B. Koppel, 293(JASt):Aug89-582
Wijaya, P. — see under Putu Wijaya
Wijzenbroek, A. De kunst van het begrijpen.
  E. Jongeneel, 204(FdL):Mar89-73
Wilbur, R. New and Collected Poems.*
  B. Howard, 491:May89-99
  D. O'Driscoll, 493:Winter89/90-38
  W. Scammell, 364:Dec89/Jan90-96
  M. Waters, 456(NDQ):Summer89-261
Wilcher, R. — see Marvell, A.
Wilcocks, R., ed. Critical Essays on Jean-
  Paul Sartre.
  J.T. Booker, 207(FR):Feb90-556
Wilcox, D.J. The Measure of Times Past.*
  M. Kerkhoff, 160:Jan89-206
  S.L. Macey, 551(RenQ):Winter89-841
Wilcox, E.J., ed. Robert Frost. (2nd ed)
  R.J. Calhoun, 580(SCR):Fall90-191
Wilcox, E.W., ed. Buckeye Cookery and Prac-
  tical Housekeeping.
  T.C. Humphrey, 650(WF):Jul89-264
Wilcox, G.C. — see Walker, W.
Wilcox, J. Sort of Rich.*
  W. Brandmark, 617(TLS):27Apr-3May90-
  456
Wilcox, J.C. Self and Image in Juan Ramón
  Jiménez.*
  A. Carreño, 240(HR):Spring89-255
  C.A. Holdsworth, 238:Dec89-962
  R.B. Kline, 552(REH):Jan89-137
  H.T. Young, 593:Spring89-78
Wilcox, T. Alphonse Legros, 1837-1911.
  K. McConkey, 90:Nov89-790
Wilczek, F. & B. Devine. Longing for the Har-
  monies.*
  I.S. Towner, 529(QQ):Autumn89-772
Wild, C. & P. Carey, eds. Born in Fire.
  H.A.J. Klooster, 293(JASt):Aug89-693
Wild, F. Patterns of Poetry in Zimbabwe.
  D. Riemenschneider, 538(RAL):Summer89-
  299
de Wild, H. Tradition und Neubeginn.
  R. Krebs, 549(RLC):Jan-Mar89-125
  E. Moore, 221(GQ):Winter89-106
Wild, P. John Nichols.
  D. Heaberlin, 649(WAL):Feb90-374
Wild, P. John C. Van Dyke.
  C. White, 649(WAL):Aug89-163
Wild, R. Die Vernunft der Väter.
  R.E. Lorbe, 406:Fall89-390
Wilde, A. Middle Grounds.*
  J. Clayton, 454:Winter90-221
  R.M. Davis, 223:Summer89-203
  S. Gregory, 659(ConL):Spring90-104
  B.M., 494:Fall89-644
  W.L. Stull, 478(P&L):Oct89-419
Wilde, O. La Graveco de la Fideligo. (W.
  Auld, trans)
  M. Boulton, 447(N&Q):Jun89-224
Wilde, O. Oscar Wilde's Oxford Notebooks.*
  (P.E. Smith 2d & M.S. Helfand, eds)
  M.P. Gillespie, 594:Winter89-466
  D. Lawler, 637(VS):Spring90-532
  R.K. Miller, 395(MFS):Winter89-790
Wilde, W.H. Courage a Grace.
  C. Munro, 71(ALS):May89-138

Wilder, L.I. & R.W. Lane. A Little House Sampler. (W.T. Anderson, ed)
  A. Romines, 649(WAL):May89-72
Wilders, J. New Prefaces to Shakespeare.
  J. Rees, 447(N&Q):Sep89-379
Wilding, M. Dragons Teeth.*
  C.C. Brown, 677(YES):Vol20-263
  T.N. Corns, 506(PSt):May89-97
  J. Holstun, 568(SCN):Spring-Summer89-1
  R. Lejosne, 189(EA):Jul-Sep89-339
  J. Morrill, 541(RES):Aug89-444
  A. Patterson, 301(JEGP):Oct89-537
  M.A. Radzinowicz, 405(MP):Nov89-174
  J.G. Turner, 551(RenQ):Autumn89-594
  D. Womersley, 447(N&Q):Mar89-107
Wildman, A.K. The End of the Russian Imperial Army.
  J. Bushnell, 550(RusR):Apr89-182
Wiles, D. Shakespeare's Clown.*
  D. Ellis, 97(CQ):Vol18No1-86
  R. Knowles, 677(YES):Vol20-251
  J.W. Saunders, 541(RES):Aug89-416
  K. Smidt, 179(ES):Apr89-179
Wiley, R.J. Tchaikovsky's Ballets.*
  M. Mazo, 317:Spring89-194
Wilford, J.N. Mars Beckons.
  M. Bartusiak, 441:15Jul90-1
Wilhelm, J.J. - see Sordello
Wilhelmi, B., ed. Dialektlexikographie.
  P. Seidensticker, 685(ZDL):2/1989-223
Wilkes, K.V. Real People.*
  D. Freedman, 518:Jul89-177
  U. Maddil, 479(PH"Q) 0r 100 b1b
  P. Trotignon, 542:Oct-Dec89-632
Wilkie, A.J. & J-P. Ressayre. Modèles non standard en arithmétique et théorie des ensembles.
  P. Clote, 316:Mar89-284
Wilkie, K. The Van Gogh File.
  A.S. Byatt, 617(TLS):29Jun-5Jul90-683
Wilkins, J. & M. Macleod. Sophocles: "Antigone" and "Oedipus the King."
  V. Bers, 124:Nov-Dec89-117
  A.D. Fitton Brown, 123:Vol39No1-132
Wilkinson, C.K. Nīshāpūr.
  R. Hillenbrand, 463:Spring89-44
Wilkinson, J., J. Hill & W.F. Ryan, eds. Jerusalem Pilgrimage, 1099-1185.
  J. Folda, 589:Oct89-1051
Wilkinson, M. Hemingway and Turgenev.
  R.L. Chapple, 104(CASS):Spring-Winter88-433
Wilkinson, W. Mother, May You Never See the Sights I Have Seen.
  D.H. Bain, 441:13May90-25
  442(NY):23Jul90-88
Will, E., with M. Schmid. Exploration archéologique de Délos faite par l'école française d'Athènes: Le sanctuaire de la déesse syrienne.
  H. Lauter, 229:Band61Heft7-645
Will, F. Thresholds & Testimonies.
  A. Riach, 478(P&L):Oct89-402
Will, F.L. Beyond Deduction.*
  E.J. Lowe, 483:Jul89-424
Will, G.F. Men at Work.
  S.J. Gould, 453(NYRB):11Oct90-3
  B.G. Harrison, 441:1Apr90-1
Will, G.F. Suddenly.
  C. Horner, 441:23Dec90-5
Willard, D. Logic and the Objectivity of Knowledge.*
  D. Münch, 323:May89-173

Willcock, M.M. Plautus, "Pseudolus."
  N.V. Dunbar, 123:Vol39No1-24
  F. Muecke, 313:Vol79-185
  L.P. Wencis, 124:Nov-Dec89-126
Wille, K. Die Versur.
  H-P. Benöhr, 229:Band61Heft1-40
Willett, J. The Theatre of the Weimar Republic.*
  J. Fuegi, 162(TDR):Winter89-28
  M. Silberman, 615(TJ):Dec89-569
Willett, J. - see Brecht, B.
Willett, T.C. A Heritage at Risk.
  S.J. Harris, 529(QQ):Summer89-483
Willey, G.R. New World Archaeology and Culture History.
  W. Bray, 617(TLS):2-8Nov90-1187
Willi, U. & T. Ebneter. Deutsch am Heinzenberg, in Thusis und in Cazis.
  W.G. Moulton, 685(ZDL):2/1989-252
William of Auvergne. The Trinity, or The First Principle. (R.J. Teske & F.C. Wade, trans)
  J.V. Brown, 103:Jul90-297
  L.J. Elders, 543:Jun90-887
William of Auxerre. Magister Guillelmus Altissiodorensis "Summa aurea." (Introduction) (J. Ribaillier, ed)
  G.J. Etzkorn, 589:Oct89-961
William of Newburgh. The History of English Affairs. (Bk 1) (P.G. Walsh & M.J. Kennedy, eds & trans)
  K. Bate, 123:Vol39No2-366
Williams, A. Portrait of Liszt.
  J. Warrack, 617(TLS):0 0Aug00-017
Williams, A. Welcome to the NHL.
  M. van Dijk, 108:Spring89-85
Williams, A.S. The Rich Man and the Diseased Poor in Early Victorian Literature.*
  N. Bradbury, 541(RES):Aug89-425
  F.S. Schwarzbach, 158:Mar89-22
  G. Smith, 677(YES):Vol20-213
Williams, C. Christina Stead.
  L. Sage, 617(TLS):26Jan-1Feb90-85
Williams, C.H., ed. Language in Geographic Context.
  W.G. Moulton, 361:Dec89-333
  S.R. Schecter, 399(MLJ):Autumn89-380
Williams, C.J.F. What Is Identity?
  D.S. Oderberg, 617(TLS):30Nov-6Dec90-1297
Williams, C.K. Collected Poems 1963-85.
  M. Donaghy, 493:Spring89-44
Williams, C.K. Flesh and Blood.*
  M. Donaghy, 493:Spring89-44
  S. Santos, 472:Vol16No1-115
Williams, C.K. Poems 1963-1983.*
  J.D. McClatchy, 491:Apr89-29
  S. Santos, 472:Vol16No1-115
Williams, D. "The Canterbury Tales."*
  N.F. Blake, 179(ES):Feb89-81
  H. Cooper, 541(RES):Feb89-114
  M.E. McAlpine, 589:Jan89-237
Williams, D., with B. Hunter. Quarterblack.
  P. Bashe, 441:7Oct90-18
Williams, D. & B. Plaschke. No More Mr. Nice Guy.
  A. Barra, 441:16Sep90-23
Williams, D.A. "The Hidden Life at Its Source."*
  S. Haig, 210(FrF):May89-239
  R. Huss, 402(MLR):Oct90-972

Williams, F.G. & S. Pachá, eds. Carlos Drummond de Andrade and his Generation.
S.J. Albuquerque, 238:Mar89-152
Williams, G. & A. Frost, eds. Terra Australis to Australia.
F.B. Smith, 617(TLS):9-15Mar90-261
Williams, G. & J. Ramsden. Ruling Britannia.
M. Pugh, 617(TLS):3-9Aug90-827
Williams, G.S. & L. Tatlock, eds. Literatur und Kosmos.
J. Hardin, 133:Band22Heft2-152
Williams, H. Concepts of Ideology.
K.R.M., 185:Apr90-694
Williams, H. Falling for a Dolphin.
H. Lomas, 364:Jun/Jul89-95
G. Maxwell, 493:Autumn89-47
Williams, H. Selected Poems.*
P. Gross, 493:Autumn89-65
S. O'Brien, 364:Jun/Jul89-91
Williams, H. Self-Portrait with a Slide.
L. Norfolk, 617(TLS):13-19Jul90-761
Williams, H.A. - see under Arabena Williams, H.
Williams, J. Escapes.
R.R. Cooper, 441:21Jan90-9
Williams, J. Lady of No Man's Land.
M. Hall, 649(WAL):Aug89-194
Williams, J. Perception and Expression in the Novels of Charlotte Brontë.
I. Ferris, 627(UTQ):Fall89-129
Williams, J., ed. Tambimuttu.*
C. de Beaurepaire, 364:Feb/Mar90-135
Williams, J.M. Style. (3rd ed)
P. Arrington & F. Farmer, 126(CCC):Dec89-486
Williams, J.R. Biomedical Ethics in Canada.
D. Pullman, 154:Vol28No2-335
Williams, J.R. Goethe's "Faust."
D.C. Riechel, 221(GQ):Winter89-115
Williams, J.R. Jules Michelet.*
N. Rinsler, 208(FS):Jan89-95
Williams, K.J. A Storyteller and a City.
H.H. Campbell, 27(AL):May89-302
R.J. Reising, 395(MFS):Summer89-275
Williams, L. Aspectos sociolingüísticos del habla de la ciudad de Valladolid.
E. Martinell Gifre, 548:Jul-Dec89-483
Williams, L. Hard Core.
K. Ellis, 441:16Sep90-31
Williams, M., ed. The Caxton Press Anthology.
C. Doyle, 49:Jul89-87
Williams, M. Patterns of Poetry.*
A.W., 70:Oct89-158
Williams, M. Six Women Novelists.
T. Cosslett, 447(N&Q):Dec89-551
L.L. Doan, 395(MFS):Summer89-395
Williams, M.H. A Strange Way of Killing.
M. Smith, 677(YES):Vol20-305
Williams, M.J.S. A World of Words.*
J.A.L. Lemay, 445(NCF):Sep89-246
Williams, N. The Wimbledon Poisoner.
P. Craig, 617(TLS):9-15Mar90-257
Williams, P. An Introduction to Leopardi's "Canti."
M. Caesar, 278(IS):Vol43-171
Williams, P., ed. The Joe Williams Baseball Reader.
R.B. Heilman, 569(SR):Summer89-475
Williams, P. & B. Owen. The Organ.
A. Bond, 415:Mar89-181

Williams, P. & D. Wallace. Unit 731.
Tsuneishi Keiichi, 285(JapQ):Jul-Sep89-335
Williams, P.T. Robert Hayden.
S.A.S., 295(JML):Fall88/Winter89-345
Williams, R. Arius.
B.H. Warmington, 313:Vol79-256
Williams, R. The Correspondence of Roger Williams. (G.W. La Fantasie & others, eds)
C.G. Pestana, 165(EAL):Vol25No1-83
C. Post, 432(NEQ):Sep89-436
G. Selement, 656(WMQ):Oct89-804
Williams, R. Culture and Society.
617(TLS):19-25Oct90-1137
Williams, R. Notes on the Underground.
P-L. Adams, 61:Feb90-107
E. Toynton, 441:25Feb90-30
Williams, R. The People of the Black Mountains. (Vol 2)
T. Hawkes, 617(TLS):19-25Oct90-1131
Williams, R. A Protestant Legacy.
P. Willmott, 617(TLS):26Oct-1Nov90-1148
Williams, R.D. "The Aeneid."*
H.V. Bender, 124:Sep-Oct89-71
G. D'Anna, 229:Band61Heft7-626
A. Smith, 235:Winter88-66
Williams, R.V. & R. Douglas - see under Vaughan Williams, R. & R. Douglas
Williams, S. Hong Kong Bank.
J. Winter, 46:Aug89-12
Williams, S. Shakespeare on the German Stage. (Vol 1)
R. Ashton, 617(TLS):3-9Aug90-818
Williams, T. The Cocaine Kids.*
M. Gossop, 617(TLS):4-10May90-478
Williams, T. Five O'Clock Angel. (M. St. Just, ed)
E. White, 441:27May90-1
D. Windham, 453(NYRB):19Jul90-12
442(NY):18Jun90-96
Williams, T.T. & J. Telford. Coyote's Canyon.
M. Pettis, 649(WAL):Nov89-271
Williams, V. Ida Kar Photographer 1907-1974.
T. Pepper, 324:Feb90-224
Williams, W.E. & D.E. Wilson - see Emerson, R.W.
Williams, W.P. - see Higginson, F.H.
Williams-Krapp, W. Die deutschen und niederländischen Legendare des Mittelalters.*
K-E. Geith, 680(ZDP):Band108Heft3-428
H. Lomnitzer, 684(ZDA):Band118Heft3-133
Williamson, A. The Muse of Distance.*
M. Boruch, 29(APR):Mar/Apr89-41
Williamson, D., ed. Debrett's Distinguished People of Today.
G. Wheatcroft, 617(TLS):7-13Sep90-941
Williamson, D. Running Out.
M.E. Turner, 102(CanL):Autumn-Winter89-253
Williamson, K. - see Smart, C.
Williamson, M.L. The Patriarchy of Shakespeare's Comedies.*
H. Castrop, 156(ShJW):Jahrbuch1989-360
Williamson, P., ed. The Thyssen-Bornemisza Collection: Medieval Sculpture and Works of Art.*
H.R. Loyn, 39:Sep89-214
Williamson, P., with P. Evelyn. Northern Gothic Sculpture, 1200-1450.
H.R. Loyn, 39:Sep89-214

Williamson, R.B. – see Klein, J.
Willink, C.W. – see Euripides
Willis, S. Marguerite Duras.*
    D.B., 295(JML):Fall88/Winter89–317
    M. Borgomano, 535(RHL):Nov–Dec89–1083
    C.J. Murphy, 210(FrF):Jan89–114
Willoughby, J. Capitalist Imperialism, Crisis
and the State.
    G.H.H., 185:Oct89–212
Wills, G. Under God.
    H. Brogan, 441:28Oct90–1
Wills, K.J., ed. The Pulitzer Prize, 1988.
    639(VQR):Summer89–96
Wilmerding, J., ed. Paintings by Fitz Hugh
Lane.
    D. Anderson, 432(NEQ):Sep89–464
    A. Wilton, 90:Jun89–432
Wilmshurst, R. – see Montgomery, L.M.
Wilner, E. Sarah's Choice.
    639(VQR):Autumn89–136
Wilson, A. The Magical Quest.
    A.J. Kennedy, 402(MLR):Oct90–897
Wilson, A. & N. Bachkatov. Living With Glas-
nost.*
    J. Riordan, 576(SEER):Oct89–667
Wilson, A.N. A Bottle in the Smoke.
    A. Arensberg, 441:26Aug90–9
    A. Ross, 617(TLS):31Aug–6Sep90–916
    442(NY):8Oct90–117
Wilson, A.N. Eminent Victorians.*
    M. Rosenthal, 441:5Aug90–11
Wilson, A.N. Incline Our Hearts.*
    W.H. Pritchard, 249(HudR):Autumn89–484
Wilson, A.N. C.S. Lewis.
    J.M. Cameron, 453(NYRB):12Apr90–3
    P. Fitzgerald, 441:18Feb90–11
    D. Nokes, 617(TLS):16–22Feb90–161
    442(NY):28May90–110
Wilson, A.N. Penfriends from Porlock.*
    639(VQR):Autumn89–122
Wilson, A.N. Tolstoy.*
    J. Frank, 249(HudR):Winter89–652
    42(AR):Winter89–111
Wilson, A.N. – see Newman, J.H.
Wilson, B. Gaudi Afternoon.
    M. Stasio, 441:25Nov90–22
Wilson, B. – see Sandel, C.
Wilson, B., A. Hurwitz & M. Wilson. Teaching
Drawing from Art.
    S. Hagaman, 709:Spring90–189
Wilson, B.R. The Social Dimensions of Sectar-
ianism.
    E. Barker, 617(TLS):28Sep–4Oct90–1017
Wilson, C. Blueglass.
    M. Illis, 617(TLS):27Jul–2Aug90–804
Wilson, C. The Gothic Cathedral.
    J.H. Harvey, 617(TLS):22–28Jun90–671
Wilson, C. Leibniz' Metaphysics.
    N. Jolley, 617(TLS):27Apr–3May90–454
    R. McRae, 103:Dec90–508
Wilson, C. Written in Blood.
    I. Sinclair, 617(TLS):6–12Apr90–371
Wilson, C.R. & W. Ferris, with others, eds.
Encyclopedia of Southern Culture.*
    T. Wortham, 446(NCF):Dec89–424
Wilson, D. The Circumnavigators.
    J.S. Cummins, 617(TLS):6–12Apr90–381
Wilson, D. Gilbert Murray OM 1866–1957.*
    M. Davies, 447(N&Q):Mar89–123
    W.J. Ziobro, 124:Nov–Dec89–136
Wilson, D.A. Paine and Cobbett.
    M. Durey, 656(WMQ):Jul89–623

Wilson, D.M. The British Museum.*
    J. Spalding, 324:Mar90–300
Wilson, E. Adorned in Dreams.
    R. Berman, 289:Fall89–113
Wilson, E. Ethel Wilson: Stories, Essays, Let-
ters.* (D. Stouck, ed)
    M. Doyle, 102(CanL):Summer89–141
    K. McCourt, 376:Sep89–126
    529(QQ):Spring89–213
Wilson, F. Laws and Other Worlds.
    R.M. Martin, 154:Vol28No2–321
Wilson, F. What it Feels Like to Be a Build-
ing.
    M. Salvadori, 47:Mar89–54
Wilson, G. The Great Sex Divide.
    L. Hudson, 617(TLS):9–15Mar90–243
Wilson, G. The Intentionality of Human
Action.
    G.W. Barnes, 103:May90–212
Wilson, G. Narration in Light.
    J. Levinson, 290(JAAC):Summer89–290
Wilson, J. Lawrence of Arabia.
    N. Nicolson, 441:10Jun90–42
    M. Ruthven, 617(TLS):15–21Jun90–635
Wilson, J. On the Boundaries of Conversa-
tion.
    B. Johnstone, 350:Mar90–212
Wilson, J. Specimens of the British Critics.
    J. Freehafer, 566:Autumn89–75
Wilson, J.C. The Loutra Hotel.
    R. Calder, 571(ScLJ):Spring89–57
Wilson, J.F. Ferranti and the British Electri-
cal Industry 1864–1930.
    C. Freeman, 637(VS):Winter90–355
Wilson, J.F. Tearing Down the Color Bar.
    D. Pinckney, 453(NYRB):22Nov90–29
Wilson, J.M. Charles Hamilton Sorley.*
    J. Stallworthy, 541(RES):Aug89–436
Wilson, J.M. Virginia Woolf.
    639(VQR):Autumn89–126
Wilson, J.M. – see Sorley, C.H.
Wilson, J.Q. Bureaucracy.
    B.A. Radin, 441:11Feb90–22
Wilson, K.M., ed. Hrotsvit of Gandersheim.
    A. Classen, 564:May89–167
Wilson, K.M., ed. Women Writers of the
Renaissance and Reformation.*
    C. Clark, 208(FS):Jan89–82
Wilson, K.M. & F.J. Warnke, eds. Women Writ-
ers of the Seventeenth Century.
    I. Maclean, 617(TLS):1–7Jun90–587
    H. Vendler, 453(NYRB):31May90–19
Wilson, M. Line of Fall.
    M.A. Rockland, 441:25Feb90–9
Wilson, M. & P. Romanowski. Supreme Faith.
    A.M. Samuels, 441:4Nov90–25
Wilson, M.K. The Marginal World of Oe Kenza-
buro.*
    M.C. Brownstein, 318(JAOS):Jan–Mar88–
147
Wilson, R., Jr. Terrible Kisses.*
    K. Bucknell, 617(TLS):9–15Feb90–148
Wilson, R.C. Ancient Republicanism.
    R.K. Sherk, 124:Jul–Aug90–544
Wilson, R.C. The Divide.
    G. Jonas, 441:11Feb90–29
Wilson, R.J. Figures of Speech.
    M.T. Gilmore, 432(NEQ):Dec89–612
Wilson, T. Ulster.
    C.C. O'Brien, 453(NYRB):19Jul90–33
Wilson, W. Loose Jam.
    J.A. Cincotti, 441:25Mar90–22

Wilson, W.H. The City Beautiful Movement.
  T.S. Hines, 617(TLS):10-16Aug90-856
Wilton, A. The Turner Collection in the Clore
  Gallery.
  A. Staley, 90:Nov89-777
Wilton, A. Turner in His Time.*
  A. Staley, 90:Nov89-777
Wilton, A. Turner Watercolours in the Clore
  Gallery.
  A. Staley, 90:Nov89-777
Wiltrout, A.E. A Patron and a Playwright in
  Renaissance Spain.
  L. Fothergill-Payne, 402(MLR):Jul90-761
  K.C. Gregg, 593:Fall89-220
  A.M. Pasero, 238:Dec89-955
Wiltshire, S.F. Public and Private in Vergil's
  "Aeneid."
  W.S. Anderson, 124:Jul-Aug90-545
  R.J. Clark, 487:Winter89-378
Wimmer, D. Irish Wine.*
  42(AR):Summer89-375
Wimsatt, J.I., W.W. Kibler & R.A. Baltzer – see
  de Machaut, G.
Win, D. International Careers.
  J.M. Recker, 399(MLJ):Autumn89-348
Winans, C. Malcolm Forbes.
  H. Goodman, 441:28Oct90-23
Winch, P. Trying to Make Sense.*
  P. Francken, 185:Oct89-201
  J. Haldane, 518:Apr89-73
Winchell, M.R. Joan Didion. (rev) John
  Gregory Dunne.
  D. Fine, 580(SCR):Fall89-139
Winchester, A.J.L. Landscape and Society in
  Medieval Cumbria.
  J. Campbell, 447(N&Q):Dec89-487
Winchester, I. & K. Blackwell, eds. Antino-
  mies & Paradoxes.
  H. Hochberg, 103:Apr90-168
Winckler, M. La Vacation.
  J-P.H. Tétart, 450(NRF):Jul-Aug89-193
Wind, B. Velázquez's Bodegones.
  E.H., 90:Feb89-162
Wind, C. Myths.
  L. Manning, 526:Summer89-105
Wind, E. Art et anarchie.
  P. Somville, 542:Oct-Dec89-640
Windfuhr, M. – see Heine, H.
Wineapple, B. Genet.
  K. Gibbons, 441:7Jan90-25
Winegardner, M. Prophet of the Sandlots.
  D. Cole, 441:1Apr90-18
  442(NY):19Mar90-109
Winegarten, R. Simone de Beauvoir.
  R.D. Cottrell, 210(FrF):Sep89-366
  E. Fallaize, 402(MLR):Jul90-748
  M. Whitford, 208(FS):Jul89-359
Winfield, R.D. The Just Economy.
  J.T.K., 185:Oct89-205
Winfield, R.D. Reason and Justice.
  D.M., 185:Jul90-910
Wing, B.H., ed. Listening, Reading, and Writ-
  ing.
  J.K. Swaffar, 399(MLJ):Winter89-492
Wing, D. Short-Title Catalogue of Books
  Printed in England, Scotland, Ireland,
  Wales, and British America and of English
  Books Printed in Other Countries 1641-
  1700.* (2nd ed) (Vol 3) (J.J. Morrison & C.
  Nelson, with others, eds)
  T. Hofmann, 354:Dec89-383

Wing, N. The Limits of Narrative.*
  R. Runyon, 478(P&L):Oct89-409
  E. Smyth, 535(RHL):Mar-Apr89-316
Wingard, K. Socialité, sexualité et les im-
  passes de l'Histoire.
  M. Hecquet, 535(RHL):Jul-Aug89-729
Wingate, A. The Eye of Anna.
  M. Stasio, 441:4Feb90-26
Wingerson, L. Mapping Our Genes.
  P. Klass, 441:2Sep90-19
Wingfield, R.D. A Touch of Frost.
  P. Craig, 617(TLS):9-15Mar90-257
Wingrove, D. Chung Kuo. (Bk 1)
  G. Jonas, 441:4Mar90-30
Wink, A. Land and Sovereignty in India.
  B.G. Gokhale, 318(JAOS):Jul-Sep88-499
Winkler, J.J. Auctor & Actor.
  M.E. Blanchard, 131(CL):Fall89-392
  M-K. Gamel, 122:Jan89-76
Winkler, J.J. The Constraints of Desire.
  J. Griffin, 453(NYRB):29Mar90-6
  M. Nussbaum, 617(TLS):1-7Jun90-571
Winkler, J.J. & F.I. Zeitlin, eds. Nothing To
  Do With Dionysos?
  O. Taplin, 617(TLS):13-19Jul90-759
Winkler, K.P. Berkeley.
  A.R. White, 518:Oct89-213
Winkler, L. Kulturelle Erneuerung und ge-
  sellschaftlicher Auftrag.
  J. Rosellini, 406:Spring89-107
Winks, R.W. & J.R. Rush, eds. Asia in Western
  Fiction.
  P. Conn, 617(TLS):12-18Oct90-1096
Winn, J.A. John Dryden and his World.*
  J.M. Aden, 569(SR):Winter89-ii
  B.S. Hammond, 83:Autumn89-232
  G. McFadden, 141:Winter89-109
  J. Mezciems, 541(RES):Nov89-564
  E. Miner, 301(JEGP):Apr89-240
  M.E. Novak, 566:Autumn89-49
  D. Oakleaf, 529(QQ):Summer89-502
  A. Poyet, 189(EA):Jul-Sep89-340
  C. Winton, 577(SHR):Summer89-274
  D. Wykes, 447(N&Q):Jun89-242
Winner, A. Culture and Irony.*
  T.K. Bender, 301(JEGP):Oct89-549
  B.G. Caraher, 637(VS):Spring90-527
Winner, E. Invented Worlds.
  D. Pariser, 709:Fall89-58
Winner, E. The Point of Words.*
  D. Bogdan, 289:Fall89-114
Winnifrith, T. & E. Chitham. Charlotte and
  Emily Brontë.
  B. Wilks, 82:Vol19No8-375
Winnifrith, T.J. The Vlachs.*
  P.S. Allen, 121(CJ):Oct-Nov89-81
  D. Deletant, 575(SEER):Oct89-632
Winograd, T. & F. Flores. Understanding
  Computers and Cognition.
  J. Schopman, 679:Band20Heft1-156
Winslow, R.E. 3d. "Wealth and Honour."
  D.F. Long, 432(NEQ):Dec89-631
Winspur, S. Saint-John Perse and the Imagi-
  nary Reader.
  A. Berrie, 208(FS):Oct89-487
  N. Bracher, 210(FrF):Sep89-358
  R. Little, 402(MLR):Jul90-743
Winstone, H.V.F. Woolley of Ur.
  S. Piggott, 617(TLS):27Apr-3May90-453
de Winter, P.M. European Decorative Arts
  1400-1600.
  S.S.J., 90:Aug89-568
Winters, M.E. – see Renart, J.

Winterson, J. Sexing the Cherry.*
  M. Gorra, 441:29Apr90-24
  442(NY):21May90-95
Winton, T. A Minimum of Two.
  J. Klinkowitz, 455:Mar89-69
  R. Orodenker, 573(SSF):Summer88-322
Wirmark, M. Kampen med döden.
  M. Robinson, 562(Scan):Nov89-207
Wisdom, J.O. Challengability in Modern Sci-
  ence.*
  A. Lugg, 488:Sep89-379
Wise, S.R. Lifeline of the Confederacy.
  V.J. Laas, 389(MQ):Autumn89-140
Wiseman, A. Memoirs of a Book Molesting
  Childhood and Other Essays.
  G. Deer, 102(CanL):Spring89-150
Wiseman, C. Postcards Home.*
  J. Bell, 526:Spring89-89
Wiseman, T.P. Roman Studies.*
  M. Corbier, 555:Vol62Fasc2-384
Wisenthal, J.L. Shaw's Sense of History.
  A.P. Barr, 637(VS):Winter90-356
  J.A. Bertolini, 177(ELT):Vol32No3-358
  F.D. Crawford, 402(MLR):Apr90-424
  N. Grene, 447(N&Q):Jun89-256
  H.J. Holdèr, 627(UTQ):Fall89-131
Wisse, R.R. A Little Love in Big Manhattan.*
  K. Hellerstein, 508:Sep89-267
  J. Lowie, 390·Jan89-38
  F. Malfi, 287:Jul-Aug89-30
"Wissenschaftliche Zeitschrift der Pädagog-
  ischen Hochschule 'Dr. Theodor Neubauer'
  Erfurt/Mühlhausen."
  H. Ehrhardt, 682(ZPSK):Band42Heft4-550
Wisskirchen, H. Zeitgeschichte im Roman.*
  D.W. Adolphs, 133:Band22Heft1-72
  H. Lehnert, 301(JEGP):Jan89-80
  R. Symington, 564:Feb89-71
Wistrand, E. Felicitas Imperatoria.
  A. Keaveney, 123:Vol39No1-154
  J-P. Martin, 229:Band61Heft3-248
Wistrich, E. After 1992.*
  P. Goodhart, 324:Jan90-140
Wistrich, R.S. The Jews of Vienna in the Age
  of Franz Joseph.*
  L. Botstein, 441:14Jan90-13
  R. Morgan, 617(TLS):9-15Mar90-263
Wither, G. A Collection of Emblemes.
  O. Reynolds, 617(TLS):15-21Jun90-651
Witoszek, N. The Theatre of Recollection.
  G.T. Kapolka, 497(PolR):Vol34No4-377
Witschew, D. Bulgarische Prosa.
  T. Henninger, 402(MLR):Apr90-543
Witte, E. & H.B. Beardsmore, eds. The Inter-
  disciplinary Study of Urban Bilingualism in
  Brussels.*
  R.E. Baecher, 710:Mar89-116
Witte, M.M. Elias und Henoch als Exempel,
  typologische Figuren und apokalyptische
  Zeugen.
  W. Röcke, 196:Band30Heft1/2-181
Witte, S. The Memoirs of Count Witte. (S.
  Harcave, ed & trans)
  J. Keep, 617(TLS):30Nov-6Dec90-1281
Wittgenstein, L. Le Cahier Bleu et le Cahier
  Brun. Cours de 1930-32.
  C. Chauviré, 98:Apr89-282
Wittgenstein, L. Diari segreti. (F. Funto, ed)
  C. Chauviré, 98:Nov89-834
Wittgenstein, L. Lectures on Philosophical
  Psychology 1946-47. (P.T. Geach, ed)
  J.F.M. Hunter, 103:Aug90-339

Witting, A. I for Isobel.
  C. Fein, 441:16Sep90-35
  442(NY):23Jul90-88
Wittkowski, W., ed. Verlorene Klassik?*
  J.F. Hyde, Jr., 406:Winter89-476
Wittreich, J. Feminist Milton.
  J. Leonard, 184(EIC):Jan89-72
  D. McColley, 70:Jul89-110
  D. McColley, 551(RenQ):Autumn89-589
  J.G. Turner, 141:Spring89-193
Wittreich, J. "Image of that Horror."
  J.A. Bryant, Jr., 569(SR):Summer89-445
Wittstock, U. Über die Fähigkeit zu trauern.
  J. Rosellini, 406:Spring89-107
Wivel, H. Snedronningen - en bog om Selma
  Lagerlöfs kaerlighed.
  A.H. Lervik, 172(Edda):1989/2-180
Wittstruck, W. Der dichterische Namenge-
  brauch in der deutschen Lyrik des Spätmit-
  telalters.
  C. Petzschn, 72:Band226Heft1-118
Wlaschek, R.M. Zur Geschichte der Juden in
  Nordostböhmen unter besonderer Berück-
  sichtigung des südlichen Riesengebirgsvor-
  landes.
  R. Muhs, 575(SEER):Jan89-141
Wlassics, T. Nel mondo dei Malavoglia.
  E. Hatzantonis, 276:Summer89-248
Wodak, R. Language Behavior in Therapy
  Groups.
  D. Hymes, 355(LSoc)·Mar89-136
Wodak, R. & P. van de Craen, eds. Neurotic
  and Psychotic Language Behaviour.
  J. Fine, 710:Mar89-96
Wodehouse, P.G. Yours, Plum. (F. Donaldson,
  ed)
  C. Hitchens, 617(TLS):7-13Sep90-939
Wodin, N. Einmal lebt ich.
  P. Graves, 617(TLS):12-18Jan90-41
Woehrlin, W.F., ed & trans. Out of the Depths
  (De Profundis).
  C. Read, 575(SEER):Apr89-282
Woesler, W. - see "Editio"
Wohlfart, G. Der Punkt.
  J. Früchtl, 489(PJGG):Band96Heft1-214
  B. Recki, 687:Jul-Sep89-567
Wohmann, G. Kassensturz
  P. Graves, 617(TLS):12-18Jan90-41
Wöhrle, G. - see Fracastoro, G.
Woiwode, L. Born Brothers.
  K.C. Mason, 649(WAL):May89-64
  42(AR):Winter89-115
Wojcik, M.R. La Villa dei papiri ad Ercolano.
  R. Neudecker, 229:Band61Heft1-59
Wokeck, M.S. & others - see Penn, W.
Woledge, B. Commentaire sur "Yvain" ("Le
  Chevalier au Lion") de Chrétien de Troyes.
  (Vol 1)
  M-L. Chênerie, 356(LR):Aug89-210
  M.A. Freeman, 589:Jan89-239
Woleński, J. Filozoficzna szkoła lwowsko-
  warszawska.
  J. Bednarz, Jr., 316:Dec89-1487
Wolf, C. Accident/A Day's News.*
  G. Krist, 249(HudR):Winter89-661
  P. Lewis, 565:Autumn89-72
Wolf, C. Die Dimension des Autors.*
  A. Stephan, 222(GR):Spring89-96
Wolf, C. The Fourth Dimension.
  I. Buruma, 453(NYRB):20Dec90-34
  P. Lewis, 565:Autumn89-72
Wolf, C. Im Dialog.
  P. Graves, 617(TLS):15-21Jun90-631

Wolf, C. Patterns of Childhood. The Quest
for Christa T. No Place on Earth. Cassan-
dra.
  I. Buruma, 453(NYRB):20Dec90-34
Wolf, C. Was bleibt.
  I. Buruma, 453(NYRB):20Dec90-34
  P. Graves, 617(TLS):24-30Aug90-890
Wolf, E. 2d. The Book Culture of a Colonial
American City.
  N. Barker, 78(BC):Winter89-557
  C. Winton, 656(WMQ):Jul89-609
Wolf, E. 2d, ed. Legacies of Genius.
  N. Barker, 78(BC):Winter89-557
Wolf, F.A. Prolegomena to Homer (1795).* (A.
Grafton, G.W. Most & J.E.G. Zetzel, eds &
trans)
  D. Arnould, 555:Vol62Fasc1-135
Wolf, K.B. Christian Martyrs in Muslim Spain.
  T.F. Glick, 589:Apr89-512
Wolf, M. Die Troika.
  K. Kändler, 654(WB):9/1989-1531
Wolf, M.E. Eros under Glass.*
  E. Wilson, 208(FS):Jul89-347
Wolf, N. The Beauty Myth.
  R. Davenport-Hines, 617(TLS):12-
18Oct90-1097
Wolfart, H.C. - see Beardy, L.
Wolfe, G. Castleview.
  G. Jonas, 441:13May90-35
Wolfe, K.W. & P.J. - see Naudé, G.
Wolfe, M.R. Kingsport, Tennessee.*
  D.L. Ames, 658:Summer/Autumn89-204
Wolfe, R.J. Marbled Paper.
  G. Mackie, 324:Oct90-797
Wolfenstein, A. Werke. (Vols 1-4) (G. Holz &
H. Haarmann, eds)
  W. Paulsen, 133:Band22Heft3/4-365
Wolfersdorf, P., ed. Westfälische Sagen.
  H. Fischer, 196:Band30Heft1/2-185
Wolff, C. Gesammelte Werke, Materialien und
Dokumente. (Section 3, Vol 11) (J. École &
others, eds)
  S. Carboncini, 706:Band21Heft2-214
Wolff, G., ed. The Best American Essays
1989.
  R.G. O'Meally, 441:14Jan90-37
Wolff, G. The Final Club.
  E. Allen, 441:16Sep90-14
442(NY):1Oct90-110
Wolff, L. Postcards from the End of the
World.
  E. Showalter, 617(TLS):13-19Apr90-401
Wolford, C.L. Stephen Crane.
  W. Carse, 649(WAL):Feb90-383
Wolfram, H. Die Geburt Mitteleuropas.
  C.R. Bowlus, 589:Jan89-241
Wolfram, H. History of the Goths.* (rev)
  K.F. Drew, 377:Mar89-58
  P.J. Heather, 313:Vol79-256
  639(VQR):Spring89-44
Wolfson, N. & J. Manes, eds. Language of
Inequality.*
  P. Pupier, 320(CJL):Jun89-205
Wolfson, S.J. The Questioning Presence.*
  A. Bewell, 677(YES):Vol20-292
  M. Jones, 529(QQ):Spring89-146
  T.M. Kelley, 591(SIR):Winter89-643
Wolfzettel, F. Ce désir de vagabondage cos-
mopolite.*
  H. Harder, 547(RF):Band101Heft4-479
Wolgast, E. The Grammar of Justice.
  S. Lovibond, 185:Oct89-183

von Wolkenstein, O. - see under Oswald von
Wolkenstein
Wollaston, N. Tilting at Don Quixote.
  X. Fielding, 617(TLS):12-18Oct90-1108
Wollheim, R. Painting as an Art.*
  G. Currie, 63:Sep89-371
  J. Margolis, 290(JAAC):Summer89-281
  M. Mothersill, 518:Apr89-122
  S.R., 185:Jan90-452
  617(TLS):23Feb-1Mar90-204
Wollstonecraft, M. The Works of Mary Woll-
stonecraft. (J. Todd & M. Butler, eds) A.
Wollstonecraft Anthology. (J. Todd, ed)
  D. Bromwich, 617(TLS):19-25Jan90-51
Wolters, G. Mach I, Mach II, Einstein und die
Relativitatstheorie.
  J.T. Blackmore, 488:Jun89-235
Wolters, O.W. Two Essays on Dai-Viet in the
Fourteenth Century.
  K.W. Taylor, 293(JASt):Nov89-943
Womack, J.P., D.T. Jones & D. Roos. The
Machine That Changed the World.
  D. Graulich, 441:28Oct90-22
Womack, P. Improvement and Romance.
  R. Mitchison, 617(TLS):9-15Feb90-150
Womack, P. Ben Jonson.*
  L. Manley, 677(YES):Vol20-255
Womack, S. Murphy's Fault.
  M. Stasio, 441:4Mar90-35
"Women in German Yearbook, 4." (M. Burkhard
& J. Clausen, eds)
  M.K. Flavell, 402(MLR):Apr90-519
  P.H. Stanley, 221(GQ):Spring89-245
Womersley, D. The Transformation of "The
Decline and Fall of the Roman Empire."*
  J.B. Bullen, 402(MLR):Jul90-696
  J.G.A. Pocock, 173(ECS):Spring90-318
  639(VQR):Summer89-81
Wong, J.Y. The Origins of an Heroic Image.
  G. Chan, 244(HJAS):Jun89-229
Wood, A., ed. The Times Guide to the Euro-
pean Parliament 1989.
  D. Leonard, 617(TLS):5-11Jan90-8
Wood, A.W., ed. Self and Nature in Kant's
Philosophy.
  C.A. Van Kirk, 342:Band80Heft3-362
Wood, C. Paradise Lost.
  D. Cherry, 59:Sep89-374
Wood, C.T. Joan of Arc and Richard III.
  M. Keen, 453(NYRB):22Nov90-37
Wood, D. Constant: "Adolphe."*
  N. Addinall, 402(MLR):Jan90-190
  P. Delbouille, 535(RHL):Jul-Aug89-725
  B. Rigby, 242:Vol10No6-735
  M. Spencer, 210(FrF):Jan89-102
Wood, D. The Deconstruction of Time.
  P. Oppenheimer, 363(LitR):Spring90-388
Wood, D. & R. Bernasconi, eds. Derrida and
"Différance."
  M.K., 185:Jan90-453
Wood, E.M. Peasant-Citizen and Slave.*
  S. Meikle, 123:Vol39No2-278
  S.D. Olson, 124:Nov-Dec89-132
Wood, F. A Companion to China.*
  T. Swick, 441:10Jun90-49
Wood, G.C. - see Foote, H.
Wood, M. Alla Ricerca della Guerra di Troia.
  D. Arnould, 555:Vol62Fasc2-332
Wood, M. America in the Movies or "Santa
Maria, It Had Slipped My Mind."
  P. O'Connor, 617(TLS):27Jul-2Aug90-801

Wood, N. Cicero's Social and Political Thought.
  R.J. Rabel, 319:Jul90-441
  A.M. Ward, 124:Nov-Dec89-137
Wood, N. Swift.*
  D.W. Lindsay, 506(PSt):May87-109
Wood, R.C. The Comedy of Redemption.
  E. Brown-Guillory, 27(AL):Dec89-711
  F. Crews, 453(NYRB):26Apr90-49
  J. Dewey, 395(MFS):Winter89-776
Woodbridge, H.C. & D.S. Zubatsky, comps. Pablo Neruda.
  D.G. Anderson, 238:May89-308
Woodbridge, K. Princely Gardens.
  A.T. Friedman, 576:Mar89-89
Woodcock, G. The Century That Made Us.
  L. McDonald, 150(DR):Spring89-140
Woodcock, G. Northern Spring.*
  L. Monkman, 168(ECW):Fall89-151
Woodfield, I. The Early History of the Viol.
  M. Remnant, 410(M&L):Feb89-82
Woodfield, M. R.H. Hutton.*
  R.D. Fulton, 635(VPR):Spring89-40
Woodfield, M. - see Murry, J.M.
Woodfield, R. - see Gombrich, E.H.
Woodhead, A. The Protestants Plea for a Socinian.
  R. Smolinski, 568(SCN):Spring-Summer89-16
Woodhouse, C.M. George Gemistos Plethon.*
  R. Browning, 303(JoHS):Vol109-277
Woodhouse, H.F. Language and Style in a Renaissance Epic.
  K.W. Hempfer, 224(GRM):Band39Heft3-350
Woodhouse, R. Celebration.
  R. Jackson, 611(TN):Vol43No1-32
Woodman, A.J. Rhetoric in Classical Historiography.*
  T.J. Luce, 487:Summer89-174
  Z.M. Packman, 124:Nov-Dec89-136
Woodress, J. Willa Cather.*
  P.J. Casagrande, 594:Summer89-229
  M. Pers, 597(SN):Vol61No1-120
  M.A. Peterman, 106:Fall89-211
Woods, G. Articulate Flesh.
  R. Bentman, 295(JML):Fall88/Winter89-259
  A. Golding, 27(AL):Mar89-143
  C.M. Jackson-Houlston, 447(N&Q):Jun89-284
  J. Meyers, 301(JEGP):Jan89-126
Woods, M. - see "Oxford Studies in Ancient Philosophy"
Woods, R.D., comp. Mexican Autobiography/La autobiografía mexicana, An Annotated Bibliography/Una bibliografía razonada.
  Bruce-Novoa, 238:Sep89-557
Woodson, T. & others - see Hawthorne, N.
Woodward, A. Living in the Eternal.*
  D.M. MacDonald, 619:Spring89-214
  H.J.S., 185:Oct89-215
Woodward, C.V. The Future of the Past.*
  D.B. Davis, 453(NYRB):17May90-30
Woodward, G. The Unwriter and Other Poems.
  C. Hurford, 617(TLS):21-27Dec90-1383
Woodward, K. & M.M. Schwartz, eds. Memory and Desire.
  S.B., 295(JML):Fall88/Winter89-238
Woodward, K.L. Making Saints.
  P. Hebblethwaite, 441:4Nov90-9

Woolf, L. Letters of Leonard Woolf.* (F. Spotts, ed)
  N. Annan, 453(NYRB):29Mar90-28
  P. Clarke, 617(TLS):2-8Mar90-211
  442(NY):8Jan90-100
Woolf, R. Art and Doctrine. (H. O'Donoghue, ed)
  J. Frankis, 541(RES):Aug89-399
Woolf, V. The Essays of Virginia Woolf.* (Vol 1) (A. McNeillie, ed)
  S. Rudikoff, 473(PR):Vol56No3-489
Woolf, V. The Essays of Virginia Woolf.* (Vol 2) (A. McNeillie, ed)
  S. Ferebee, 395(MFS):Winter89-802
  S. Rudikoff, 473(PR):Vol56No3-489
Woolf, V. A Moment's Liberty. (A.O. Bell, ed) Congenial Spirits. (J.T. Banks, ed)
  L. Duguid, 617(TLS):20-26Jul90-770
Woolf, V. A Passionate Apprentice. (M.A. Leaska, ed)
  S. Raitt, 617(TLS):14-20Dec90-1346
Woolford, J. Browning the Revisionary.
  T.J. Collins, 445(NCF):Mar90-560
Woolhouse, R.S. The Empiricists.
  T.M. Lennon, 103:Apr90-172
  A.E. Pitson, 518:Jul89-141
Woollen, G. Balzac: "Le Curé de Tours."
  I. Pickup, 402(MLR):Oct90-971
Woolley, J.D. Swift's Later Poems.
  E.L. Steeves, 566:Spring90-207
Woolmer, J.H. A Checklist of the Hogarth Press 1917-1946.
  C. Franklin, 78(BC):Summer89-259
Woolmer, J.H. The Poetry Bookshop, 1912-1935.
  R. Fifoot, 354:Sep89-288
  C. Franklin, 78(BC):Summer89-259
  D. Laing, 470:Vol27-137
Woolson, C.F. Women Artists, Women Exiles.* (J.M. Weimer, ed)
  K.E. Kier, 357:Spring90-70
Wooten, C.W. - see Hermogenes
Wootton, D., ed. Divine Right and Democracy.
  R. Lejosne, 189(EA):Apr-Jun89-213
Wordsworth, W. The Essential Wordsworth. (S. Heaney, ed)
  P. Mariani, 434:Spring90-310
Wordsworth, W., ed. Jacquelin du Pré. (2nd ed)
  R. Anderson, 415:Oct89-610
Wordsworth, W. Wordsworth's Poems of 1807.* (A.R. Jones, ed)
  W.J.B. Owen, 541(RES):Feb89-130
Wormald, F. Collected Writings. (Vol 1) (J.J.G. Alexander, T.J. Brown & J. Gibbs, eds)
  C. Nordenfalk, 341:Vol58No2-89
Wormald, F. Collected Writings.* (Vol 2) (J.J.G. Alexander, T.J. Brown & J. Gibbs, eds)
  H.R. Loyn, 39:Sep89-214
  M.M., 90:Aug89-567
  C. Nordenfalk, 341:Vol58No2-89
Wormald, J. Mary Queen of Scots. (D. Starkey, ed)
  A.H. Williamson, 551(RenQ):Summer89-320
Wormald, M. Stills and Reflections.
  C. Hurford, 617(TLS):21-27Dec90-1383
  D. Kennedy, 493:Summer89-54
Woronoff, J. Politics the Japanese Way.*
  S.K. Johnson, 293(JASt):May89-407

Worrall, N. Modernism to Realism on the
Soviet Stage.
G. McVay, 511:Jul89-46
Wörrle, M. Stadt und Fest im kaiserzeitlichen
Kleinasien.
N.P. Milner, 123:Vol39No2-355
"Wörterbuch der mittelhochdeutschen Urkun-
densprache." (Pts 1 & 2) (B. Kirschstein &
others, eds)
F.G. Banta, 301(JEGP):Jan89-62
C.V.J. Russ, 402(MLR):Apr90-488
Worth, V. Practising Translation in Renais-
sance France.
D.J. Shaw, 402(MLR):Oct90-950
Worthen, J. - see Lawrence, D.H.
Wortzel, L.W., ed. China's Military Modern-
ization.
W. Frieman, 293(JASt):Feb89-152
Wouters, L. & A. Bosquet, eds. La Poésie
francophone de Belgique, 1885-1900. (Vol
1)
C.F. Coates, 207(FR):Mar90-750
Wouters, L. & A. Bosquet, eds. La poésie
francophone de Belgique 1885-1900. (Vol
2)
C.F. Coates, 207(FR):Mar90-750
P. Gorceix, 535(RHL):Mar-Apr89-318
Woysch-Méautis, D. La représentation des
animaux et des êtres fabuleux sur les mon-
uments funéraires grecs de l'époque archa-
ïque à la fin du IVe siècle av. J-C.
U. Vedder, 229:Band61Heft2-152
Wozencraft, K. Rush.
C. Hiaasen, 441:15Apr90-5
Wren, C.S. The End of the Line.
D. Schorr, 441:5Aug90-8
Wright, A. Fictional Discourse and Historical
Space.*
K.L. Cope, 594:Spring89-112
I.V., 295(JML):Fall88/Winter89-253
Wright, A.F. Studies in Chinese Buddhism.
(R.M. Somers, ed)
T.H. Barrett, 617(TLS):21-27Dec90-1380
Wright, C. John Masefield.
517(PBSA):Jun89-250
Wright, C. Realism, Meaning and Truth.*
Q. Cassam, 518:Jan89-10
P. Smith, 521:Jan89-70
Wright, C. Zone Journals.*
L. Gregerson, 491:Dec89-229
E. Pankey, 271:Spring-Summer89-175
N. Van Winckel, 434:Spring90-308
Wright, C.D. Further Adventures with You.
P. Booth, 219(GaR):Spring89-161
Wright, D. Elegies.
C. Hurford, 617(TLS):21-27Dec90-1383
Wright, D. - see Chaucer, G.
Wright, E. The Poetry of Protest under Fran-
co.*
G. Barrow, 86(BHS):Apr89-189
Wright, E. Postmodern Brecht.
S. Giles, 402(MLR):Apr90-527
P.D. Murphy, 590:Dec89-122
Wright, E. A Question of Murder.
639(VQR):Spring89-58
Wright, E. A Sensitive Case.
P. Craig, 617(TLS):16-22Mar90-298
Wright, F. Entry in an Unknown Hand.
W. Harmon, 472:Vol16No1-136
Wright, G.T. Shakespeare's Metrical Art.*
A. Graham-White, 615(TJ):Dec89-572
P. Levi, 447(N&Q):Sep89-387
[continued]

[continuing]
J.T. Styan, 191(ELN):Mar90-78
M. Tarlinskaja, 599:Spring90-142
Wright, J. Above the River.
J.D. McClatchy, 441:17Jun90-22
Wright, J. After the Image.
M.T. Lane, 198:Winter89-115
Wright, J. Elaine's Book.
639(VQR):Summer89-98
Wright, J. The Last Frame.
S. Krulwich, 441:14Oct90-48
Wright, J. Reflections of a Public Man.
N. Lemann, 453(NYRB):17May90-18
Wright, J. Selected Poems of Jay Wright.*
(R.B. Stepto, ed)
M. Fabre, 189(EA):Oct-Dec89-497
Wright, K. Poems 1974-1983.*
J. Whitworth, 493:Spring89-42
Wright, K. Short Afternoons.
B. Morrison, 617(TLS):5-11Jan90-19
Wright, L.R. A Chill Rain in January.
M. Stasio, 441:8Apr90-26
Wright, M.G.H. A Berlioz Bibliography.
R.P. Locke, 309:Vol9No1-65
Wright, R., ed & trans. Spanish Ballads.*
D. Hook 86(BHS):Jul89-274
Wright, R. Three Scientists and Their Gods.
42(AR):Winter89-108
Wright, R.G. The Social Christian Novel.
J.J. Murphy, 27(AL):Dec89-702
Wright, S. M31.*
G. Krist, 249(HudR):Spring89-129
Wright, S. Peter Taylor.
J.R. Kelly, 517(PBSA):Sep89-408
Wright, S.K. The Vengeance of Our Lord.
D.A. Wells, 402(MLR):Jul90-676
Wright, T.R. Hardy and the Erotic.*
C.E. May, 637(VS):Summer90-670
Wright, T.R. Theology and Literature.
A. Bordeaux, 189(EA):Oct-Dec89-441
Wright, W.J. Capitalism, the State, and the
Lutheran Reformation.
L.P. Wandel, 551(RenQ):Winter89-846
Wright, W.M. & J.F. Power - see de Sales, F. &
J. de Chantal
Wrobel, A., ed. Pseudo-Science and Society
in Nineteenth-Century America.
K. Hawkins, 658(Summer/Autumn89-190
Wtulich, J. - see Kula, W., N. Assorodobraj-
Kula & M. Kula
Wu Guang. Huang-Lao zhi xue tong lun.
R.P. Peerenboom, 485(PE&W):Jan89-100
Wu Hung. The Wu Liang Shrine.
J. Rawson, 617(TLS):18-24May90-530
Wu, Y. Chinese Philosophical Terms.
C. Hansen, 485(PE&W):Apr89-203
Wubnig, J. - see Martin, G.
Wurfel, D. Filipino Politics.
A.W. McCoy, 293(JASt):Aug89-694
Würffel, S.B. Der produktive Widerspruch.*
H. Spencer, 564:Nov89-360
Wurst, K.A. Familiale Liebe ist die "wahre
Gewalt."
D. Jonnes, 133:Band22Heft3/4-324
F.J. Lamport, 402(MLR):Apr90-505
Würzner, H., ed. Österreichische Exilliteratur
in den Niederlanden 1934-1940.
H. Famira, 564:May89-182
L.J. King, 406:Spring89-116
Wuthnow, R. Meaning and Moral Order.
J. Johnson, 185:Jul90-895

Wyatt, D. The Fall into Eden.*
    R.F. Gleckner, 27(AL):Oct89-508
    J.R. Leo, 403(MLS):Summer89-91
Wyatt, T. The Essential Wyatt. (W.S. Merwin, ed)
    P. Mariani, 434:Spring90-313
Wyatt, W., ed. The Way We Lived Then.*
    D. Durrant, 364:Dec89/Jan90-134
Wycherley, W. The Plain Dealer. (S. Trussler, ed)
    P. Holland, 611(TN):Vol43No2-84
Wyckoff, W. The Developer's Frontier.
    A. Taylor, 656(WMQ):Jul89-621
Wyclif, J. Johannis Wyclif "Summa Insolubilium."* (P.V. Spade & G.A. Wilson, eds)
    G-H. Allard, 154:Vol28No3-510
Wylie, I. Young Coleridge and the Philosophers of Nature.
    K. Everest, 661(WC):Autumn89-176
Wylie, J. The Faroe Islands.*
    R.F. Tomasson, 563(SS):Spring/Summer89-268
Wyman, B., with R. Coleman. Stone Alone.
    J. Maslin, 441:18Nov90-12
Wymelenberg, S. Science and Babies.
    J.D. Schwartz, 441:19Aug90-19
Wynar, B. - see "American Reference Books Annual"
van den Wyngaerde, A. Spanish Cities of the Golden Age. (R.L. Kagan, ed)
    D.J.R. Bruckner, 441:11Feb90-13
Wynn, A. Notes of a Non-Conspirator.
    J. Rubenstein, 550(RusR):Jul89-340
Wynn, W. Keeper of the Keys.
    M.E. Hussey, 42(AR):Winter89-101
Wyrick, D.B. Jonathan Swift and the Vested Word.*
    D. Oakleaf, 166:Jan90-165
    W.B. Piper, 191(ELN):Jun90-76
    F.N. Smith, 566:Autumn89-57
    T. Woodman, 402(MLR):Jul90-695
Wyrwa, T. L'Idée européenne dans la Résistance à travers la Presse clandestine en France et en Pologne, 1939-1945.
    H. Brugmans, 242:Vol10No2-231
Wyschogrod, E. Spirit in Ashes.*
    R.E. Lauder, 438:Winter89-118
Wysc, L. Seconds.
    A. Solomon, 441:17Jun90-16
Wysling, H. - see Mann, T.
Wysling, H., with W. Pfister - see Mann, T. & J. Ponten
Wyver, J. The Moving Image.
    P. Kemp, 707:Autumn89-285

Xavier, F. Correspondance 1535-1552. (H. Didier, ed & trans)
    P.E.H. Hair, 86(BHS):Oct89-377
Xiaoxuan, B. - see under Bian Xiaoxuan
Xrakovskij, V.S. & A.P. Volodin. Semantika i tipologija imperativa.*
    G.H. Toops, 574(SEEJ):Summer89-321
Xuancong, F. - see under Fu Xuancong
Xue Tao. Brocade River Poems.* (J. Larsen, ed & trans)
    P.W. Kroll, 318(JAOS):Oct-Dec88-621
Xueqin, C. & Gao E. - see under Cao Xueqin & Gao E.
Xueqin, L. - see under Li Xueqin
Xunchu, Z. - see under Zhou Xunchu

"Xunzi: A Translation and Study of the Complete Works."* (Vol 1) (J. Knoblock, ed & trans)
    K-L. Shun, 293(JASt):May89-364

Ya Ding. The Earth Sings.
    S. Salisbury, 441:27May90-16
Yaari, M. Ironie paradoxale et ironie poétique.
    C.S. Brosman, 210(FrF):Sep89-361
Yablonskaya, M.N. Women Artists of Russia's New Age 1900-1935. (A. Parton, ed)
    J. Milner, 617(TLS):31Aug-6Sep90-919
    S.F. Starr, 441:22Jul90-13
Yager, J.A. Transforming Agriculture in Taiwan.
    P.H. Tai, 293(JASt):Aug89-606
Yaguello, M. Catalogue des idées reçues sur la langue.
    J-M. Klinkenberg, 209(FM):Oct89-265
Yah, L.C. & others - see under Lim Chong Yah & others
Yahil, L. The Holocaust.
    R. Sanders, 441:4Nov90-7
Yalden, J. Principles of Course Design for Language Teaching.*
    S.B. Ross, 399(MLJ):Spring89-82
Yalom, M. Maternity, Mortality, and the Literature of Madness.*
    H. Murray, 102(CanL):Winter88-143
Yamaguchi Jirō. Okura kanryō shihai no shūen.
    G.D. Allinson, 293(JASt):May89-624
Yamamoto, C. Mantrayana in Japan.
    J.H. Sanford, 407(NM):Autumn89-383
Yamasaki, T. Shingon. (R. & C. Petersen, eds & trans)
    J.H. Sanford, 407(MN):Autumn89-383
Yampolsky, P. Lokananta.
    H. Susilo, 187:Spring/Summer89-358
Yan Jiaqi & Gao Gao. Zhongguo "wenge" shinian shi.
    M. Schoenhals, 293(JASt):Aug89-563
Vanarella, E.J. & L. Sigelman, eds. Political Mythology and Popular Fiction.
    J. Cohn, 27(AL):Mar89-150
Yang, L. The City Gardener's Handbook.
    A. Lovejoy, 441:10Jun90-13
Yanghwe, C.T. - see under Chao Tzang Yanghwe
"Yankee Drover."
    S. McMurry, 658:Summer/Autumn89-189
Yanovsky, V.S. Elysian Fields.
    R. Bowie, 295(JML):Fall88/Winter89-204
    J.M. Kopper, 104(CASS):Spring-Winter88-510
Yao, T-C. & S. McGinnis. Let's Play Games in Chinese.
    W.K. Sergent, Jr., 399(MLJ):Winter89-495
Yarshater, E. - see "Encyclopaedia Iranica"
Yastrzemski, C. & G. Eskenazi. Yaz.
    J. Chace, 441:1Apr90-15
Yasuo, Y. - see under Yuasa Yasuo
Yates, D.A. & J.B. Dalbor. Imaginación y Fantasía. (5th ed)
    E. Echevarria, 399(MLJ):Winter89-534
Yates, F. Giordano Bruno et la tradition hermétique.
    S. Filippini, 450(NRF):Jun89-109

Yates, F.A. The French Academies of the Sixteenth Century.
  B. Guthmüller, 547(RF):Band101Heft2/3–330
Yates, J.M. Torque. (Vol 1)
  A. Weiss, 102(CanL):Autumn–Winter89–259
Yates, R.D.S. Washing Silk.
  S. Van Zoeren, 116:Jul88–184
Yeager, G.M., comp. Bolivia.
  E. Echevarría, 263(RIB):Vol39No2–215
"The Yearbook of Langland Studies." (Vol 1)
  (J.A. Alford & M.T. Tavormina, eds)
  P. Martin, 402(MLR):Jul90–684
  D. Mehl, 72:Band226Heft1–168
  D. Pearsall, 589:Jul89–646
  A.V.C. Schmidt, 382(MAE):1989/2–325
"The Yearbook of Langland Studies." (Vol 2)
  (J.A. Alford & M.T. Tavormina, eds)
  P. Martin, 402(MLR):Jul90–684
  D. Mehl, 72:Band226Heft1–168
"Yearbook of Morphology." (1988) (G. Booij & J. van Marle, eds)
  M. Hammond, 350:Mar90–152
Yearling, E.M. – see Shirley, J.
Yeats, W.B. The Collected Works of W.B. Yeats. (Vol 1) (R.J. Finneran, ed)
  H. Kenner, 441:27May90–10
Yeats, W.B. The Collected Works of W.B. Yeats. (Vol 6) (W.H. O'Donnell, ed)
  H. Kenner, 441:27May90–10
Yeats, W.B. The Collected Works of W.B. Yeats. (Vol 7) (G. Bornstein & H. Witemeyer, eds)
  H. Kenner, 441:27May90–10
Yeats, W.B. Fairy Tales of Ireland. (N. Philip, ed)
  J. Westwood, 617(TLS):30Mar–5Apr90–355
Yeats, W.B. Yeats's Poems. (A.N. Jeffares, ed) The Poems. (D. Albright, ed) Collected Poems. (A. Martin, ed)
  J. McGann, 617(TLS):11–17May90–493
"Yeats Annual No. 5." (W. Gould, ed)
  A. Robinson, 541(RES):Nov89–585
"Yeats Annual No. 6."* (W. Gould, ed)
  A. Bradley, 637(VS):Spring90–537
Yehoshua, A.B. Five Seasons.*
  A. Balaban, 390:May89–48
  B. Zelechow, 390:Dec89–44
Yellin, J.F. Women and Sisters.
  K. Sánchez–Eppler, 357:Fall90–56
Yellin, J.F. – see Jacobs, H.A.
Yellin, V.F. Chadwick.
  W. Mellers, 617(TLS):26Oct–1Nov90–1154
Yeltsin, B. Against the Grain.
  A. Nove, 617(TLS):4–10May90–466
  D. Remnick, 453(NYRB):17May90–3
  P. Taubman, 441:25Mar90–3
Yenser, S. The Consuming Myth.
  B.M., 494:Fall89–648
  R.D. Sell, 541(RES):Aug89–441
  L.M. Steinman, 301(JEGP):Apr89–269
  H.H. Thomas, 295(JML):Fall88/Winter89–382
Yeomans, D. Bartók for Piano.
  D.C., 412:Feb89–72
  D. Fanning, 415:Jun89–350
Yergin, D. The Prize.
  L.H. Gelb, 441:9Dec90–1
Yevtushenko, Y. Early Poems.
  M. Horovitz, 493:Autumn89–56

Yglesias, J. Tristan and the Hispanics.*
  42(AR):Spring89–249
Yglesias, R. The Murderer Next Door.
  F.J. Prial, 441:14Oct90–46
Yi, K. – see under Khin Yi
Yllö, K. & M. Bograd, eds. Feminist Perspectives on Wife Abuse.
  D.H., 185:Oct89–219
Ynduráin, F. & D. – see Foz, B.
Yngve, V.H. Linguistics as a Science.
  L. Barsalou, 355(LSoc):Jun89–287
  P.H. Salus, 567:Vol73No1/2–145
Yoke, C.B., ed. Phoenix from the Ashes.
  W.W. Wagar, 561(SFS):Mar89–109
Yokoyama, T. Japan in the Victorian Mind.*
  D. Richardson, 637(VS):Winter90–349
Yolton, J.W. & J.S. – see Locke, J.
York, A. Agapanthus.*
  R. Anderson, 102(CanL):Autumn–Winter89–178
  L. McKinney, 526:Summer89–99
York, L.M. "The Other Side of Dailiness."
  T.E. Tausky, 627(UTQ):Fall89–161
York, R.A. The Poem as Utterance.*
  E. Brunazzi, 149(CLS):Vol26No2–183
"The York Gospels." (N. Barker, ed)
  M.P. Brown, 78(BC):Winter89–551
Yorke, M. The Spirit of the Place.*
  A. Summerfield, 39:Aug89–139
Yorke, M. Keith Vaughan.
  F. Spalding, 617(TLS):30Nov–6Dec90–1293
Young, A. The Credit Book Two/Book Three.
  G.M. McCarthy, 272(IUR):Spring89–175
Young, A. Tudor and Jacobean Tournaments.*
  D.M. Bergeron, 551(RenQ):Summer89–322
Young, A. & T. Fulwiler, eds. Writing Across the Disciplines.
  S. Watson, 580(SCR):Fall89–133
Young, B.A. The Rattigan Version.
  R.F. Gross, 615(TJ):May89–263
Young, C.W. – see Bariolla, O.
Young, D. Troubled Mirror.
  T.R. Whitaker, 677(YES):Vol20–317
Young, D. – see Holub, M.
Young, D.C. The Olympic Myth of Greek Amateur Athletics.
  M.B. Poliakoff, 24:Spring89–166
Young, E. Catalogue of Spanish Paintings in the Bowes Museum.
  R. Mulcahy, 39:Dec89–432
Young, E. Night Thoughts. (S. Cornford, ed)
  D. Wu, 617(TLS):9–15Feb90–150
Young, H. The Iron Lady.*
  P. Jenkins, 453(NYRB):12Apr90–30
  J. Newhouse, 442(NY):12Feb90–95
Young, J.R. The Beckett Actor.
  R.C. Lamont, 397(MD):Sep89–462
  K. Worth, 611(TN):Vol43No2–88
  W.B. Worthen, 615(TJ):Dec89–561
Young, K.G. Taleworlds and Storyrealms.
  E. O'Reilly, 292(JAF):Oct–Dec89–497
Young, L.B. Sowing the Wind.
  T. Bay, 441:16Dec90–19
Young, P. All I Ever Needed Was a Beautiful Room.*
  C.L. Beran, 168(ECW):Fall89–98
  J.K. Gardiner, 102(CanL):Summer89–172
Young, T.D., ed. Modern American Fiction.
  J.W. Tuttleton, 395(MFS):Winter89–743
Young, T.D. & E. Sarcone – see Lytle, A. & A. Tate

Young-Bruehl, E. Anna Freud.*
   P. Roazen, 639(VQR):Autumn89-749
Young-Bruehl, E. - see Freud, S.
Younge, G. Art of the South African Town-
ships.
   C.B. Pike, 2(AfrA):Aug89-83
Yourcenar, M. Quoi? L'Éternité.
   J. Blot, 450(NRF):Jun89-99
   J. Taylor, 617(TLS):2-8Feb90-108
Yourcenar, M. En pèlerin et en étranger.
   J. Taylor, 617(TLS):2-8Feb90-108
Yovel, Y., ed. Nietzsche as Affirmative
Thinker.
   A.P. Fell, 529(QQ):Spring89-66
Yovel, Y. Spinoza and Other Heretics.
   E. Curley, 617(TLS):17-23Aug90-880
   S. Feldman, 441:18Mar90-26
   S. Hampshire, 453(NYRB):17May90-40
   Z. Janowski, 543:Jun90-888
Yu, C-S. & R. Guisso, eds. Shamanism.
   C. Choi, 293(JASt):Feb89-192
Yu Haocheng, ed. Shinian qiyuan lu.
   M. Schoenhals, 293(JASt):Aug89-563
Yu, L. - see under Li Yu
Yu, P. The Reading of Imagery in the Chinese
Poetic Tradition.*
   A. Bailey, 529(QQ):Spring89-143
Yuan Shishuo. Pu Songling shiji zhushu xin-
kao.
   J.T. Zeitlin, 293(JASt):Aug89-608
Yuasa Yasuo. The Body.* (T.P. Kasulis, ed)
   D.A. Dilworth, 407(MN):Winter89-517
   D. Nagarajan, 529(QQ):Spring89-197
Yue Daiyun. Intellectuals in Chinese Fiction.
   J.C. Kinkley, 116:Dec89-154
Yue Daiyun & C. Wakeman. To the Storm.
   R.E. Hegel, 116:Jul88-197
Yule, A. Enigma.
   A. Barker, 707:Winter88/89-66
Yunsheng, Z. - see under Zhang Yunsheng
Yurieff, Z., ed. Transactions of the Associa-
tion of Russian-American Scholars in the
U.S.A. (Vol 17)
   J. Zeldin, 104(CASS):Spring-Winter88-
530

Zabatsky, D. Latin American Literary
Authors.
   P.N. Klingenberg, 552(REH):Oct89-140
Zabel, H., ed. Fremdwortorthographie.
   S. Clausing, 133:Band22Heft3/4-385
   G. Starke, 682(ZPSK):Band42Heft5-691
Zac, S. Spinoza en Allemagne.
   D. Bourel, 531:Jul-Dec89-547
Zadworna-Fjellestad, D. "Alice's Adventures
in Wonderland" and "Gravity's Rainbow."
   L.O. Sauerberg, 462(OL):Vol44No1-93
Zafris, N. The People I Know.
   G. Johnson, 441:27May90-9
Zagajewski, A. Solidarity, Solitude.
   442(NY):24Dec90-100
Zagona, H.G. Flaubert's "Roman Philoso-
phique" and the Voltairian Heritage.*
   D.T. Wight, 546(RR):Jan89-152
Zagona, K. Verb Phrase Syntax.
   M-L. Rivero, 239:Fall89-301
Zahar, E. Einstein's Revolution.
   N. Shanks, 103:Jan90-42
Zajaczkowski, H. Tchaikovsky's Musical
Style.
   D. Brown, 410(M&L):Nov89-566

Żak, A. Vom reinen Denken zur Sprachver-
nunft.
   X. Tilliette, 489(PJGG):Band96Heft2-435
Zaki, H.M. Phoenix Renewed.
   T. Moylan, 561(SFS):Jul89-228
Zaleski, C. Otherworld Journeys.
   M.M. Gatch, 589:Oct89-1053
   B.M., 494:Winter89-853
Zaluska-Strömberg, A., ed & trans. Edda
poetycka.
   Z. Ciesielski, 562(Scan):Nov89-193
Zamora, L.P. Writing the Apocalypse.
   J. Dewey, 395(MFS):Winter89-776
Zamora, M. Language, Authority and Indige-
nous History in the "Comentarios reales de
los Incas."
   J.S. Cummins, 402(MLR):Apr90-485
   L.A. Daniel, 238:Sep89-553
   S. MacCormack, 400(MLN):Mar89-506
Zamora Munné, J.C. & J.M. Guitart. Dialectol-
ogía hispanoamericana.
   J.M. Lipski, 239:Fall89-271
   E.J. Morel, 263(RIB):Vol39No2-216
Zamyatin, E. A Godforsaken Hole.
   E.K. Beaujour, 574(SEEJ):Winter89-631
Zaner, R.M., ed. Death.
   R. Geis, 543:Mar90-656
   G.G. Griener, 103:Aug90-341
Zangrilli, F. Bonaviri e il tempo.
   M.R. Vitti-Alexander, 276:Summer89-250
Zanker, G. Realism in Alexandrian Poetry.*
   J. Clack, 124:Mar-Apr90-371
Zanker, P. The Power of Images in the Age of
Augustus. (German title: Augustus und die
Macht der Bilder.)
   G. Alföldy, 229:Band61Heft5-407
   R.F. Thomas, 124:Jul-Aug90-546
   A. Wallace-Hadrill, 313:Vol79-157
Zannini Quirini, B. Nephelokokkygia.
   A.H. Sommerstein, 123:Vol39No2-383
   B. Zimmermann, 229:Band61Heft4-350
Zantop, S. Zeitbilder.
   W. Krömer, 547(RF):Band101Heft2/3-373
de Zapata, C.C. - see under Correas de Zapa-
ta, C.
Zapf, H. Hermann Zapf and His Design Philos-
ophy.*
   517(PBSA):Jun89-244
"Zapiski russkoj akademičeskoj gruppy v sša."
(Vol 18)
   C. Popkin, 104(CASS):Spring-Winter88-
469
Zappella, G. Le marche dei tipografi e degli
editori italiani del Cinquecento.
   D.E. Rhodes, 354:Mar89-65
Zarka, Y-C. La Décision Métaphysique de
Hobbes.
   Y. Thierry, 242:Vol10No5-602
Zaslavskaya, T. The Second Socialist Revo-
lution.
   A. Nove, 617(TLS):4-10May90-466
Zaslaw, N., ed. The Classical Era.
   D. Fallows, 617(TLS):20-26Jul90-778
Zaslaw, N. Mozart's Symphonies.
   W. Dean, 617(TLS):7-13Dec90-1331
Zaslow, J. Tell Me All About It.
   B. Raskin, 441:4Feb90-16
Zavala, I.M. Lecturas y lectores del discurso
narrativo dieciochesco.
   P. Deacon, 402(MLR):Jul90-765
   I.L. McClelland, 86(BHS):Jul89-285
   G. Paolini, 238:Mar89-144

Zavalloni, M., ed. L'Emergence d'une culture au féminin.
    J-A. Elder, 102(CanL):Autumn-Winter89-159
Zebouni, S.A., ed. Actes de Baton Rouge, 1985.*
    D. Lopez, 535(RHL):Jul-Aug89-714
Zeeman, P. The Later Poetry of Osip Mandelstam.*
    D. Rayfield, 402(MLR):Apr90-540
Zehbe, J. - see Kant, I.
Zeitlin, I.M. Ancient Judaism.
    C. Schäfer-Lichtenberger, 318(JAOS):Jan-Mar88-160
Zeitlin, M. & R.E. Ratcliff. Landlords and Capitalists.
    J. Nef, 529(QQ):Winter89-991
Zelinsky, W. Nation into State.
    T. Wortham, 445(NCF):Dec89-420
Zeller, S. Inventing Canada.
    C. Kent, 637(VS):Autumn89-200
Zellerbach, M. Rittenhouse Square.
    J. Cohen, 441:18Mar90-20
Zender, K.F. The Crossing of the Ways.
    A. Bleikasten, 395(MFS):Winter89-748
    S. Pinsker, 219(GaR):Winter89-795
    C.N. Slaughter, 27(AL):Dec89-708
Zenowich, C. Economies of the Heart.
    C. Bloom, 441:11Mar90-18
Zeri, F. La Collezione Federico Mason Perkins.
    J. Pope-Hennessy, 39:Apr89-290
von Zesen, P. Philipp von Zesen: Sämtliche Werke.* (Vol 15) (F. van Ingen, ed)
    E.A. Philippson, 301(JEGP):Oct89-583
Zhadova, L.A., ed. Tatlin.*
    D.D. Boles, 505:Apr89-121
    B. Fer, 59:Sep89-382
    C. Lodder, 90:Sep89-646
Zhang Yunsheng. Maojiawan jishi.
    M. Schoenhals, 293(JASt):Aug89-563
Zhitkov, B. Chto ya videl (What I Saw). (R.L. Leed & L. Paperno, eds)
    R.F. Druien, 399(MLJ):Spring89-97
    R.E. Flynn, 574(SEEJ):Fall89-477
Zhong Kan. Kang Sheng pingzhuan.
    M. Schoenhals, 293(JASt):Aug89-563
"Zhongguo chuantong wenhua zai jiantao."
    J. Thoraval, 98:Aug-Sep89-558
"Zhōngguó dà bǎikē quánshū: Yǔyán wénzi."
    M.S. Erbaugh, 350:Sep90-580
"Zhongguo Wenhua (yanjiu jikan)."
    J. Thoraval, 98:Aug-Sep89-558
Zhongshu, Q. - see under Qian Zhongshu
Zhou Ming, ed. Lishi zai zheli chensi.
    M. Schoenhals, 293(JASt):Aug89-563
Zhou Xunchu - see Wang Dang
Zhuravleva, N.I. Antisovetizm burzhuaznoi demografii.
    A. Jones, 550(RusR):Jul89-339
Ziegeler, H-J. Erzählen im Spätmittelalter.*
    H. Kugler, 684(ZDA):Band118Heft4-166
    H. Ragotzky, 680(ZDP):Band108Heft1-111
Ziegler, G. - see Karamsin, N.
Ziegler, H. John Barth.
    E.B. Safer, 677(YES):Vol20-347
Ziegler, H., ed. Facing Texts.*
    D. Kramer, 573(SSF):Fall88-482
    J. Raab, 268(IFR):Summer89-132
Ziegler, H.F. Nazi Germany's New Aristocracy.
    R. Overy, 617(TLS):29Jun-5Jul90-699

Ziegler, P. King Edward VIII.
    R. Davenport-Hines, 617(TLS):28Sep-4Oct90-1021
Ziff, P. Antiaesthetics.
    B.C. Adam, 438:Autumn89-516
Zifonun, G., ed. Vor-Sätze zu einer neuen deutschen Grammatik.
    P. Suchsland, 682(ZPSK):Band42Heft2-255
Zigas, V. Laughing Death.
    S. Lindenbaum, 441:1Jul90-12
Zilliacus, K. Skärgårdsnamn.
    A.M. Carlberger, 350:Dec90-889
Zim, R. English Metrical Psalms.*
    M.G. Brennan, 447(N&Q):Sep89-377
    J. Daalder, 541(RES):Nov89-549
    P. le Huray, 410(M&L):Feb89-83
    G.J. Siertsema, 250(HLQ):Autumn89-517
Zima, P.V. Roman und Ideologie.*
    C. Becker, 224(GRM):Band39Heft3-350
    S. Dowden, 221(GQ):Summer89-414
    R. Galle, 52:Band24Heft3-329
    J. Leeker, 547(RF):Band101Heft1-101
Zimansky, P.E. Ecology and Empire.
    M.N. van Loon, 318(JAOS):Jan-Mar88-163
Zimmer, J. Joseph Heintz der Ältere.
    K. Andrews, 90:Jun89-427
Zimmer, P. Family Reunion.*
    G. Kuzma, 152(UDQ):Summer89-109
Zimmer, W. Répertoire du théâtre camerounais.*
    M.E. Mudimbe-Boyi, 207(FR):Feb90-541
Zimmerman, D.W. - see Lamb, M.W.
Zimmerman, L. Intricate and Simple Things.
    A. Dunn, 27(AL):Oct89-494
Zimmerman, M.E. Heidegger's Confrontation with Modernity.
    D.E. Cooper, 617(TLS):23-29Nov90-1269
Zimmerman, W. Open Borders, Nonalignment, and the Political Evolution of Yugoslavia.
    M. Wheeler, 575(SEER):Apr89-323
Zimmermann, F.W. - see al-Fārābī
Zimmermann, V. Rezeption und Rolle der Heilkunde in landessprachigen handschriftlichen Komendien des Spätmittelalters.
    B.D. Haage, 680(ZDP):Band108Heft3-452
Zimunya, M., P. Porter & K. Anyidoho, eds. The Fate of Vultures.
    G. Foden, 617(TLS):18-24May90-533
Zinguer, I. - see Béroalde De Verville
Zink, G. Phonétique historique du français.*
    M. Kilani-Schoch, 209(FM):Oct89-255
Zink, M. & X. Ravier, eds. Réception et identification du conte depuis le Moyen Age.
    C. Lecouteux, 196(ZFSL):2-187
Ziolkowski, J. - see Nigel of Canterbury
Ziolkowski, T. German Romanticism and its Institutions.
    T.J. Reed, 617(TLS):20-26Jul90-783
Zion, S. Markers.
    D. Freeman, 441:20May90-14
Zipes, J. The Brothers Grimm.
    L. Bluhm, 196:Band30Heft3/4-359
    J. Schmidt, 268(IFR):Winter90-72
Zipes, J. Don't Bet on the Prince.*
    G. Boyes, 203:Vol100No1-121
Zipes, J., ed. Victorian Fairy Tales.*
    L.J. Bird, 635(VPR):Summer89-76
Zipes, J. - see Grimm, J. & W.
Zirker, M.R. - see Fielding, H.

Zitzelsberger, O.J., ed. Konráðs Saga Keisa-
rasonar.
  D. Slay, 562(Scan):May89-81
Zivie, C.M., with Y. Hamed. Le temple de Deir
Chelouit III.
  R.S. Bianchi, 318(JAOS):Jan-Mar88-149
Zohar, D., with I.N. Marshall. The Quantum
Self.
  D. Papineau, 617(TLS):23Feb-1Mar90-
  193
Zohary, D. & M. Hopf. Domestication of Plants
in the Old World.
  A.G. Morton, 123:Vol39No1-160
Zola, E. Carnets d'enquêtes.*
  B. Lane, 207(FR):Oct89-213
Zola, E. Correspondance. (Vol 6) (B.H. Bak-
ker, ed)
  D. Baguley, 446(NCFS):Fall-Winter89/90-
  281
  C. Bertrand-Jennings, 207(FR):May90-
  1068
  C.A. Burns, 402(MLR):Jan90-196
  M.G. Lerner, 356(LR):Feb-May89-120
Zola, E. La Curée.* (J. Noiray, ed)
  R. Godwin-Jones, 207(FR):Dec89-379
Zola, E. Un Homme à Vendre. (J.B. Sanders,
ed)
  R.J. Cummings, 446(NCFS):Spring-
  Summer90-547
"Aleksandr Žolkovskij i Jurij Ščegolev."
  J.P. Mozur, 104(CASS):Spring-Winter88-
  482
Zongji, T. & others - see under Tan Zongji &
others
Zotz, T., general ed. Die deutschen Königs-
pfalzen. (Vol 1, Pts 1-3; Vol 2, Pts 1 & 2)
  S. Bonde, 589:Apr89-513
Zsuffa, J. Béla Balázs.
  D.J. Wenden, 575(SEER):Apr89-291
  D.J. Youngblood, 574(SEEJ):Summer89-
  314
Ztkind, Z. Simmetričeskie kompozicii u Puš-
kina.
  A. Kodjak, 104(CASS):Spring-Winter88-
  465
Zuber, R. - see Perrault, C.
Zubizarreta, M.L. Levels of Representation in
the Lexicon and in the Syntax.
  L. Haegeman, 297(JL):Sep89-484
Zuccotti, S. The Italians and the Holocaust.*
  E.M. Schächter, 278(IS):Vol44-186
Zufferey, F. Recherches linguistiques sur les
chansonniers provençaux.*
  J.H. Marshall, 382(MAE):1989/1-175
Zukofsky, L. Collected Fiction.
  A. Whitehouse, 441:9Sep90-45
Žukov, V.P., M.I. Sidorenko & V.T. Škljarov.
Slovar' frazeologičeskix sinonimov russkogo
jazyka. (V.P. Žukova, ed)
  S. Lubensky, 574(SEEJ):Summer89-325
Žukova, V.P. - see Žukov, V.P., M.I. Sidorenko
& V.T. Škljarov
Zukowsky, J., ed. Chicago Architecture,
1872-1922.*
  T.J. Garvey, 658:Spring89-94
  F. Toker, 576:Mar89-91
Zumthor, P. La Fête des fous.
  E.A. Heinemann, 102(CanL):Autumn-
  Winter89-196
Zumwalt, R.L. American Folklore Scholarship.
  W.F. Nicolaisen, 440:Winter-Spring89-
  142

Zurbrugg, N. Beckett and Proust.
  J. Fletcher, 402(MLR):Oct90-976
  A. King, 395(MFS):Winter89-812
  R. Lydenberg, 532(RCF):Spring89-253
Zurbuchen, M.S. The Language of Balinese
Shadow Theater.
  N.J. Smith-Hefner, 293(JASt):May89-445
Zurier, R. Art for the Masses.
  M.H. Bogart, 658:Spring89-86
Zuriff, G.E. Behaviorism.
  R.J. Nelson, 606:Aug89-305
Zurli, L., ed. Aegritudo Perdicae.
  G. Brugnoli, 229:Band61Heft3-203
Zürrer, P. Deutscher Dialekt in mehrsprach-
iger Gemeinschaft.
  G. Lerchner, 682(ZPSK):Band42Heft4-532
Zusne, L. Eponyms in Psychology.
  E.D. Lawson, 424:Jun89-187
Zviguilsky, A. - see Flaubert, G. & I. Turge-
nev
Zweig, D. Agrarian Radicals in China, 1968-
1981.
  639(VQR):Autumn89-134
Zweig, J. Emotional Reactions.
  G. Gessert, 448:Vol27No2-121
Zweite, A. & A. Hoberg. The Blue Rider in the
Lenbachhaus, Munich.
  S. West, 617(TLS):16-22Mar90-291
Zwerdling, A. Virginia Woolf and the Real
World.*
  J. Marcus, 620(TSWL):Spring89-101
  K. Mezei, 677(YES):Vol20-325
Zwicky, J. Wittgenstein Elegies.*
  J. Harris, 168(ECW):Spring90-66
Zwierlein, O. Kritischer Kommentar zu den
Tragödien Senecas.*
  J. Delz, 229:Band61Heft6-501
  J.G. Fitch, 122:Jul89-236
Zwierlein, O. Prolegomena zu einer kritischen
Ausgabe der Tragödien Senecas.*
  J. Delz, 229:Band61Heft6-501
Zwierlein, O. - see Seneca
Žygas, E.V. & P. Voorheis, eds. Folklorica.
  B. Krader, 187:Spring/Summer89-332
Zynda, S. Sexualität bei Klaus Mann.
  W.G. Cunliffe, 564:Feb89-78
Zysk, K.G. Religious Healing in the Veda.
  G. Wujillla, 259(IIJ):Apr89-161
  F. Zimmermann, 318(JAOS):Jul-Sep88-
  502

WITHDRAWAL